Steps in Analyzing a Transaction

STEP 1. Decide which accounts are involved.

STEP 2. Classify the accounts involved (asset, liability, owner's equity, revenue, expense).

STEP 3. Decide if the accounts are increased or decreased.

STEP 4. Write the transaction as a debit to one account (or accounts) and a credit to another account (or accounts).

STEP 5. Check to see if the equation is in balance after the transaction has been recorded.

Journalizing and Posting

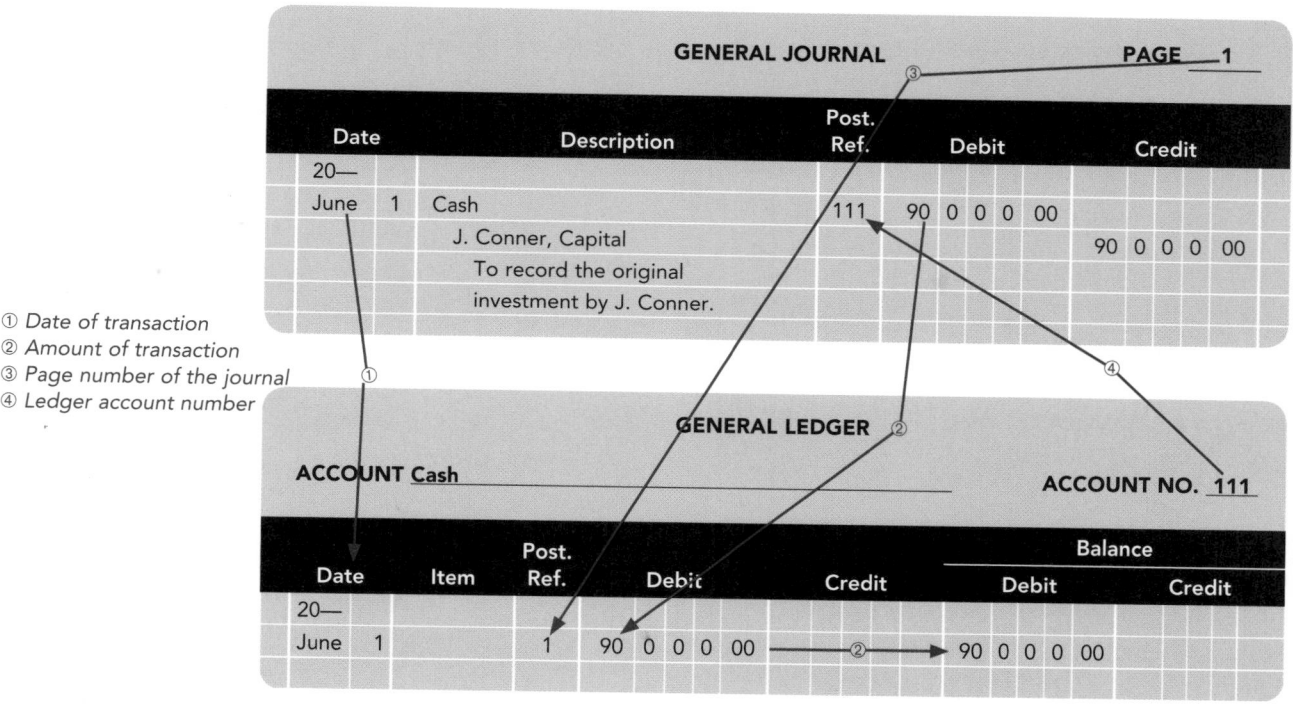

① Date of transaction
② Amount of transaction
③ Page number of the journal
④ Ledger account number

The Work Sheet

Account Name	Trial Balance		Adjustments		Adjusted Trial Balance		Income Statement		Balance Sheet	
	Debit	Credit	Debit	Credit	Debit	Credit	Debit	Credit	Debit	Credit
	Assets				Assets				Assets	
		Liabilities				Liabilities				Liabilities
		Capital				Capital				Capital
	Drawing				Drawing				Drawing	
		Revenue				Revenue		Revenue		
	Expenses				Expenses		Expenses			

MAKE IT YOURS!

Create a quality College Accounting text tailored to your course — simply, quickly, and affordably.

CONSIDER THESE COURSE-ENHANCING OPTIONS:

- Build a College Accounting textbook with the content and chapter progression that *precisely* matches your course syllabus.
- Let us bind-in your syllabus, course notes, study guides, and working papers to create a convenient "all-in-one" solution for your students.

- Prepare your students for the *real world* of accounting by including general ledger software and guides from QuickBooks Pro®, Peachtree®, and Klooster & Allen.
- Peruse our extensive Cover Gallery or create a personalized cover that reflects the uniqueness of your course.

---

1 Get started!
Visit www.cengage.com/custom/makeityours/McQuaig.

2 Select the chapters from McQuaig/Bille/Nobles' *College Accounting, 10e*
ISBN-13: 978-1-4390-3775-1

3 Enhance your students' mastery of accounting concepts with valuable study tools. MAKE IT YOURS by including **Practice Sets** to simulate real-world accounting using general ledger software. Reinforce concepts covered in your textbook by binding in **Study Guides** and **Working Papers**:

Trey's Fast Cleaning Service Practice Set, featuring Peachtree® GL software with data files
ISBN-13: 978-0-538-75322-7

Coolspring Furniture Practice Set, featuring Peachtree® GL software with data files
ISBN-13: 978-0-538-75074-5

Working Papers with Study Guide, Chapters 1-12
ISBN-13: 978-0-538-75285-5

Working Papers with Study Guide, Chapters 13-24
ISBN-13: 978-0-538-75228-2

4 Prepare your students for their careers by including your choice of full-functioning general ledger software from **QuickBooks Pro®**, **Peachtree®**, or **Klooster & Allen**. Each software is packaged with a concise text that teaches your students how technology will help them to create and use accounting information.

Klooster & Allen's *Integrated Accounting for Windows®, 7e*
Includes Klooster & Allen General Ledger software
ISBN-13: 978-0-538-74797-4

Owen's *Using Peachtree® Complete 2010 for Accounting*
Includes Peachtree® Complete 2010 (Sage Complete Accounting Educational Version)
ISBN-13: 978-0-538-47427-6

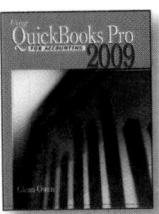

Owen's *Using QuickBooks Pro® 2009 for Accounting*
Includes Trial Version of QuickBooks Accounting Pro 2009
ISBN-13: 978-0-324-66404-1

5 Add your unique content!
Bind-in your syllabus, course notes, or career-readiness content.

College Accounting

10e
1–24

College Accounting

10e
1–24

Douglas J. McQuaig
Wenatchee Valley College, Emeritus

Patricia A. Bille
Highline Community College

Tracie L. Nobles, CPA
Austin Community College

Judy McQuaig Courshon, CPA
Contributing Editor

SOUTH-WESTERN
CENGAGE Learning

Australia • Brazil • Japan • Korea • Mexico • Singapore • Spain • United Kingdom • United States

SOUTH-WESTERN
CENGAGE Learning™

College Accounting, 10th Edition, Chapters 1–24

**Douglas J. McQuaig, Patricia A. Bille,
Tracie L. Nobles, Judy McQuaig Courshon, CPA**

Vice President of Editorial, Business: Jack W. Calhoun

Editor-in-Chief: Rob Dewey

Executive Editor: Sharon Oblinger

Developmental Editor: Leslie Kauffman, LEAP
Publishing Services, Inc.

Editorial Assistant: Julie Warwick

Associate Marketing Manager: Laura-Aurora Stopa

Marketing Coordinator: Heather Mooney

Senior Content Project Manager: Tim Bailey

Media Development Director: Rick Lindgren

Media Editor: Bryan England

Senior Frontlist Buyer, Manufacturing: Doug Wilke

Production Service: LEAP Publishing Services, Inc.

Compositor: Knowledgeworks Global Limited

Senior Art Director: Stacy Jenkins Shirley

Cover and Internal Designer: Craig Ramsdell

Cover Image: Alamy

Rights Acquisition Account Manager-Image:
Deanna Ettinger

Photo Researcher: Raquel Sousa, Pre-PressPMG

For product information and technology assistance, contact us at **Cengage Learning Customer & Sales Support, 1-800-354-9706**

For permission to use material from this text or product, submit all requests online at **www.cengage.com/permissions**

Further permissions questions can be emailed to **permissionrequest@cengage.com**

ExamView® is a registered trademark of eInstruction Corp. Windows is a registered trademark of the Microsoft Corporation used herein under license. Excel® spreadsheet software is a registered trademark of Microsoft Corporation. Peachtree® and the Peachtree logo are registered trademarks of Sage Software, Inc. in the United States and other countries.

Cengage Learning WebTutor™ is a trademark of Cengage Learning.

Library of Congress Control Number: 2010922976
ISBN-13: 978-1-4390-3775-1
ISBN-10: 1-4390-3775-2

South-Western Cengage Learning
5191 Natorp Boulevard
Mason, OH 45040
USA

Cengage Learning products are represented in Canada by Nelson Education, Ltd.

For your course and learning solutions, visit **www.cengage.com**
Purchase any of our products at your local college store or at our preferred online store **www.CengageBrain.com**

Printed in the United States of America
1 2 3 4 5 6 7 13 12 11 10

This book is dedicated to the founding author,
Douglas J. McQuaig.

Doug started this project in 1972 so he could give his students the best foundation to develop their accounting skills. He loved to teach and wanted his students to succeed and create new opportunities for themselves. Doug is an inspiration to us all, and his vision to have the best possible book for students to learn basic accounting skills continues to this day.

Brief Contents

Contents

About the Authors

PATRICIA A. BILLE received her Associates of Arts from Olympic College and her Bachelor of Arts and Master of Education from the University of Washington. She has completed the first year of her doctorate at Capella University in distance learning design. Her accounting experience includes Norris Grain and Phelps Dodge Copper in Chicago as well as nonprofit organizations and small business accounting. Pat teaches accounting at Highline Community College, formerly in the classroom and now solely online. She developed and directed the Business Division's satellite-campus learning center. She coordinated the Accounting Department's cooperative education program and was instrumental in developing and implementing computer labs for the Business Division. Pat had the honor of representing the Accounting Department in South Africa and Namibia as part of Highline's long-time relationship with African educators in these countries. She has been persistent in supporting instructional development as well as serving on tenure review and peer review committees, helping to secure and grow an effective and dedicated diverse faculty. She has been a long-time member of Northwest Accounting Educators and has educational affiliations with the American Accounting Association and the Washington Society of CPAs. These affiliations have allowed her to attend and speak at a

variety of state, regional, and national conferences and workshops, sharing her love of teaching and enthusiasm for accounting education. She has authored and co-authored two College Accounting textbooks as well as videos, practice sets, and a variety of accounting ancillaries. Pat and her husband Bruce enjoy traveling and spending time with their two beagles and their two young grandchildren.

TRACIE L. NOBLES, CPA, received her bachelor's and master's degrees in accounting from Texas A&M University. She has served as Department Chair of the Accounting, Business, Computer Information Systems, and Marketing/Management Department at Aims Community College, Greely, Colorado, and is currently an Associate Professor of Accounting at Austin Community College, Austin, Texas. Tracie has consulted on numerous other accounting and computerized accounting books. She has public accounting experience with Deloitte Tax LLP and Sample & Bailey, CPAs. She is a recipient of Aims Community College Excellence in Teaching Award and the NISOD Excellence Award. Tracie is a member of the Teachers of Accounting at Two-Year Colleges, the American Accounting Association, the American Institute of Certified Public Accountants, and the Texas Community College Teachers Association. She is currently serving on the board of directors

and as webmaster of Teachers of Accounting at Two-Year Colleges, as member of the American Institute of Certified Public Accountants Pre-certification Education Executive Committee, and as Two-Year College Section Vice-Chair for the American Accounting Association. In addition, she is the current Accounting Section Co-chair for the Texas Community Colleges Teachers Association. In her spare time, Tracie enjoys camping and fishing with her husband, Trey, and spending time with her family and friends.

JUDY MCQUAIG COURSHON, CPA, MT, graduated from Western Washington University with a B.A. in Business Administration and Computer Science and then earned her Master of Taxation degree from the University of Denver. She has been practicing public accounting for the past 34 years with Deloitte Touche LLP, PricewaterhouseCoopers, and a local firm she founded in 1985. She is currently president and founder of Wellspring Group P.S., CPAs, which is an independent accounting firm that provides personalized financial management, consulting, and tax services to individuals and their families. Judy consulted on various editions of this book, most significantly on the ninth and tenth editions. She has taught accounting and uses these accounting skills every day in her accounting profession. Judy is a member of the American Society of CPAs and the Washington Society of CPAs and serves on numerous charitable gift planning and private foundation boards. Judy's interests outside the office include spending time with her family, participating in sports, and enjoying time at Chelan, Washington.

Best Wishes To You and Your Students,
Sharon Oblinger and the South-Western/Cengage
Accounting Team

Preface

College Accounting is a course for the times. The practical concepts and skills students take away from the College Accounting course have the power to launch new careers and bright futures. Students of College Accounting have many different goals: to train for accounting careers; to develop skills that lend themselves to technical, managerial, and executive positions; or to go on and earn Accounting or Business degrees. *College Accounting, 10e* was written with the singular purpose of helping students reach these goals. And because achieving goals in today's fast-paced, competitive job market requires more than just basic accounting skills, *College Accounting, 10e* takes the study of accounting to the next level. The authors emphasize the importance of student experience with current accounting technology, business ethics, and correlate problem solving and communication skills to improve student marketability and post-classroom success. *College Accounting, 10e* is revised for optimum currency and relevance to today's modern business.

CONNECTING THE CLASSROOM TO THE REAL WORLD

To emphasize the significance of the College Accounting course as a launching pad to rewarding careers and continued college success, *College Accounting, 10e* has added new features designed to grab students' interest and relate their coursework to a real-world context.

Why It Matters

These chapter-opening vignettes introduce the concepts covered in the chapter in the context of a real-world small business.

SOLID ROCK GYM, Phoenix, Arizona

Individuals and groups of all ages come to Solid Rock Gym for fun and fitness. Part of the appeal of Solid Rock Gym, whose services include several types of indoor rock-climbing experiences, is around-the-clock access with its all-day-and-night passes. Services include individual and group instruction, team development, fitness programs, and bouldering (climbing close to the bottom—no rope or hardware), top-roping (climbing while protected by a rope running through anchors above the intended route), or lead climbing (climbing while protected by a rope clipped to anchors as the climber ascends a route).

In Chapter 1, we learned that a company such as Solid Rock Gym would have a chart of accounts with many different kinds of accounts. Can you imagine the kinds of accounts that Solid Rock Gym might have? In this chapter, you will learn that the chart of accounts can be used as the starting point for recording transactions with T accounts and debits and credits.

Accounting in Your Future

This feature focuses on various real careers that your students could have. It emphasizes that solid accounting skills are necessary for employment in these types of jobs.

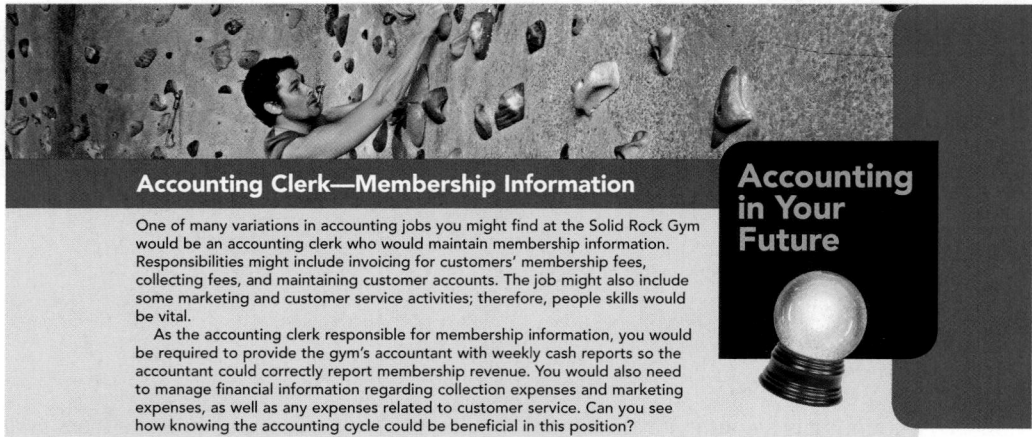

Accounting Clerk—Membership Information

One of many variations in accounting jobs you might find at the Solid Rock Gym would be an accounting clerk who would maintain membership information. Responsibilities might include invoicing for customers' membership fees, collecting fees, and maintaining customer accounts. The job might also include some marketing and customer service activities; therefore, people skills would be vital.

As the accounting clerk responsible for membership information, you would be required to provide the gym's accountant with weekly cash reports so the accountant could correctly report membership revenue. You would also need to manage financial information regarding collection expenses and marketing expenses, as well as any expenses related to customer service. Can you see how knowing the accounting cycle could be beneficial in this position?

Accounting in Your Future

You Make the Call

These boxed features encourage critical thinking and problem solving by placing the student into a realistic accounting dilemma. Each scenario is followed by a detailed, clearly explained solution.

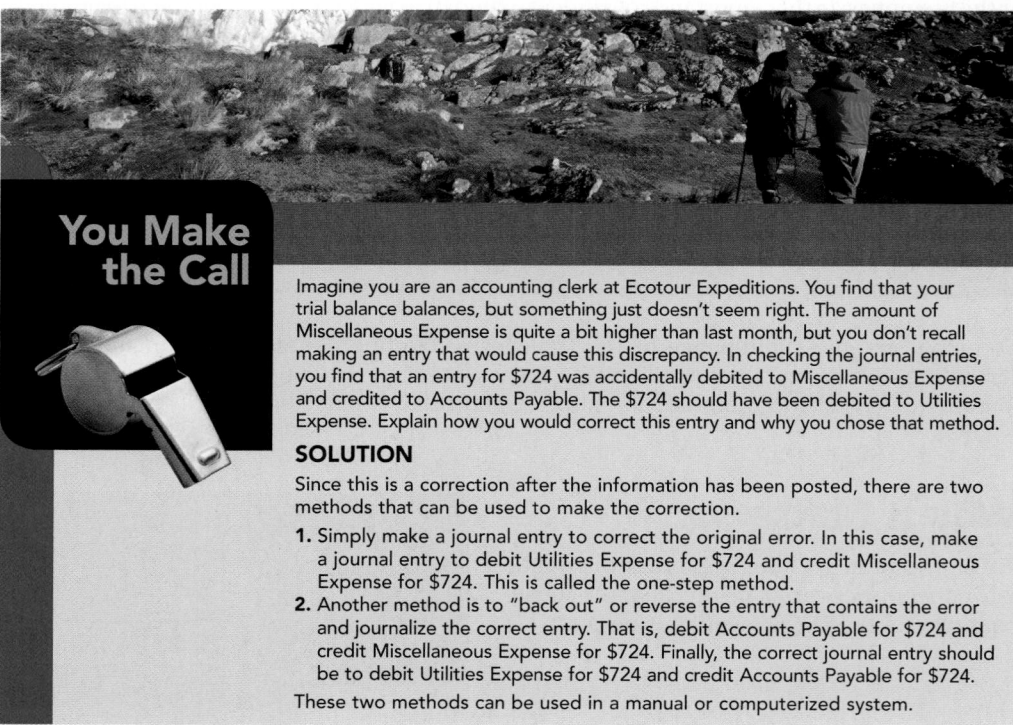

You Make the Call

Imagine you are an accounting clerk at Ecotour Expeditions. You find that your trial balance balances, but something just doesn't seem right. The amount of Miscellaneous Expense is quite a bit higher than last month, but you don't recall making an entry that would cause this discrepancy. In checking the journal entries, you find that an entry for $724 was accidentally debited to Miscellaneous Expense and credited to Accounts Payable. The $724 should have been debited to Utilities Expense. Explain how you would correct this entry and why you chose that method.

SOLUTION

Since this is a correction after the information has been posted, there are two methods that can be used to make the correction.

1. Simply make a journal entry to correct the original error. In this case, make a journal entry to debit Utilities Expense for $724 and credit Miscellaneous Expense for $724. This is called the one-step method.
2. Another method is to "back out" or reverse the entry that contains the error and journalize the correct entry. That is, debit Accounts Payable for $724 and credit Miscellaneous Expense for $724. Finally, the correct journal entry should be to debit Utilities Expense for $724 and credit Accounts Payable for $724.

These two methods can be used in a manual or computerized system.

Small Business Success

Students will find this motivating feature in several chapters throughout the text. Here, the authors emphasize how accounting knowledge and best practices ensure the success of a small business in a competitive environment.

Choosing an Accounting Software Package

SMALL BUSINESS SUCCESS

Choosing an accounting software package is an important decision for small businesses. There are two popular software packages designed for small businesses: Peachtree and QuickBooks™. When picking an accounting software package, it's important to consider the needs of the business such as:

- How many individuals will use the software?
- What tools are available?
- Can the software handle inventory?
- Is it easy to use?
- What is the cost of the program?

Both of the accounting software packages listed here will handle most basic small business accounting transactions. Each software program includes general ledger, subsidiary ledgers, and financial statements and also the ability to export data into Excel® or Word®. Most of the differences among the packages relate to appearance and how to enter transactions. For example, QuickBooks uses different "centers" such as vendors, customers, employees, company, and banking. Peachtree uses navigation bars that are located across the top of the screen.

Almost all local colleges offer courses that can teach you how to use either of these accounting software programs. It is highly recommended that all small business owners and accounting majors take at least one course in how to use accounting software, as the knowledge of accounting software is a skill needed for success in the business world.

PROVEN PEDAGOGY

College Accounting, 10e is built on the solid pedagogical foundation created by Douglas McQuaig and appreciated by instructors and students through nine editions. The careful pacing of new topics, consistent review, and thorough and meaningful assignments create the well-balanced presentation that has launched thousands of accounting students into successful careers.

- **Learning Objectives** appear at the beginning of each chapter to help students focus on key learning outcomes. They are then highlighted in the margin alongside the related text discussion. A learning objective number serves as a reference to the objectives in the chapter review, exercises, and problems.

- **Key Terms** appear in blue and are defined in the text and repeated in the glossary at the end of each chapter. In addition, page numbers are included for each glossary term, making it easy for students to refer to a term in the chapter. This consistent emphasis on accounting terminology as the language of business is found throughout the text.

- **Remember** margin notes provide learning hints or summaries, often alerting students to common procedural pitfalls to help them complete their work successfully.

- **FYI** margin notes provide practical tips or information about accounting and business.

- **Color-Coding of Documents and Reports** continues in the tenth edition of *College Accounting*. This tried and true visual system helps students recognize and remember key points. This use of color also helps students understand the flow of accounting data by clearly identifying the different documents and reports used in the accounting cycle. Students begin to visualize how accountants transform data into useful information.

  - Source documents, such as invoices, bank statements, tax forms, and other material that originates with outside sources, are shown in yellow, salmon, and beige.

  - Journals, ledgers, trial balances, work sheets, and other forms and schedules used as part of the internal accounting process are shown in green.

  - Financial statements, including balances sheets, income statements, statements of owner's equity, and statements of cash flows, are shown in blue.

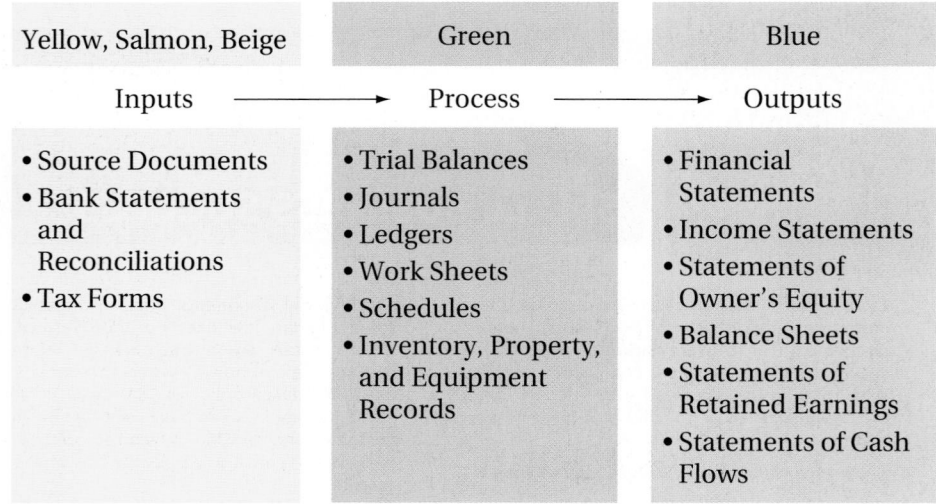

Yellow, Salmon, Beige	Green	Blue
Inputs →	Process →	Outputs
• Source Documents • Bank Statements and Reconciliations • Tax Forms	• Trial Balances • Journals • Ledgers • Work Sheets • Schedules • Inventory, Property, and Equipment Records	• Financial Statements • Income Statements • Statements of Owner's Equity • Balance Sheets • Statements of Retained Earnings • Statements of Cash Flows

THOROUGHLY REVISED CHAPTERS

College Accounting, 10e has been thoroughly revised for clarity and relevance. Here is a list of the important revisions we have made in this edition based on customer feedback and reviews:

- **Introduction to Accounting** Added discussion of the SEC, IASB, and IFRS in the section on Accounting Standards. Updated the Accounting and Technology section to discuss the need for accounting and computer skills. Expanded the Career Opportunities in Accounting section to include forensic accounting and internal auditors, as well as a new figure showing salary ranges for various accounting positions.

- **Chapter 6: Bank Accounts and Cash Funds** Increased the coverage of internal control of cash.

- **Chapter 7: Employee Earnings and Deductions** Added more discussion and examples of independent contractors in the section on Employer/Employee Relationships. Added discussion of pre-tax deductions in the section on Deductions from Total Earnings. Updated all examples, figures, and end-of-chapter materials for 2009 tax rates.

- **Chapter 8: Employer Taxes, Payments, and Reports** Updated the discussion on electronic tax deposits and the depositing of FUTA taxes. Updated all figures to show 2009 tax forms; updated discussion of those forms accordingly. Added a new section on Payroll Fraud.

- **Chapter 9: Sales and Purchases** Divided this chapter into two main parts: recording sales and purchases transactions in the general journal, and recording sales and purchases transactions in special journals.

- **Chapter 10: Cash Receipts and Cash Payments** Divided this chapter into two main parts: recording cash receipts and cash payments transactions in the general journal, and recording cash receipts and cash payments transactions in special journals. Added a new section on recording cash receipts and cash payments using a computerized accounting system.

- **Chapter 17: Property and Equipment and Intangible Assets** Expanded the coverage of the different types of property and equipment. Introduced a new step method for recording disposals and sales. Updated the coverage of how exchanges are reported in accordance to GAAP. Added a new section on Intangible Assets.

- **Chapter 20: Corporate Taxes, Retained Earnings, and Dividends** Updated the calculation of corporate income taxes to match current law. Added an illustration of journal entries for corporate tax payments and simplified this discussion. Removed the coverage of corporate work sheets. Added a section on calculating cash dividends on cumulative preferred stock.

- **Chapter 22: The Statement of Cash Flows—Indirect Method** Moved the discussion of the indirect method of the statement of cash flows into the body of the chapter, and moved the direct method to an appendix. Significantly expanded and revised the discussion of the indirect method.

- **Chapter 24: Manufacturing Accounting** Completed the income statement introduced at the beginning of the chapter so students can see the complete income statement. Added a new section on flow of costs through inventory and cost of goods sold. Added a new section and example of a balance sheet for a manufacturing firm.

ROBUST END-OF-CHAPTER ACTIVITIES

Chapter Review

Each chapter ends with a comprehensive Chapter Review that includes:

- **Learning Objectives** are repeated for reinforcement of key chapter points and include a brief summary of the critical concepts covered in the chapter.

- **Practice Exercises** provide short exercises keyed to the learning objectives, with solutions provided, for aid in student comprehension and study.

- **Before a Test Check** review quizzes give students the opportunity to test their knowledge on concepts covered in the previous two–three chapters.

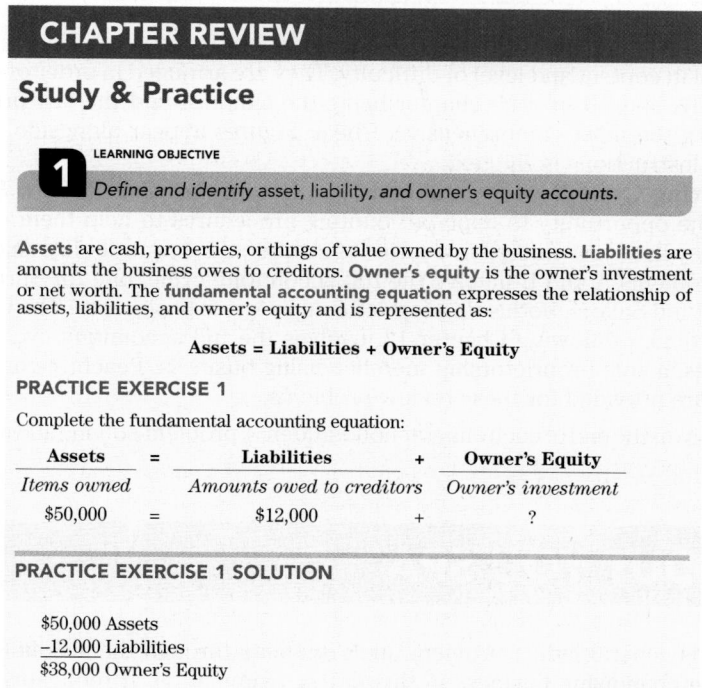

Glossary

Key terms with definitions are provided in an alphabetical glossary at the end of each chapter. Page references are provided for easy student reference.

Chapter Assignments

A variety of study and homework assignments are provided at the end of each chapter and include:

- **Discussion Questions** are found at the end of each chapter and can be used for class discussion or for individual practice.

- **Exercises** are provided in each chapter to help students learn to apply new concepts. Each exercise includes margin references to the appropriate learning objective and Chapter Review practice exercise.

- **Problems** are found in every chapter. For those problems designed for Excel, students have access to Excel templates on the student website. The General Ledger problems can be completed on any general ledger software you package with your students' textbook: Klooster & Allen, QuickBooks, or Peachtree. Each problem is designated with an Excel or GL icon to direct students to the correct application.

1,2,3

PROBLEM 3-3B Following is the chart of accounts of Vance Rehab Clinic.

Assets
111 Cash
113 Accounts Receivable
117 Prepaid Insurance
124 Equipment

Liabilities
221 Accounts Payable

Owner's Equity
311 J. Vance, Capital
312 J. Vance, Drawing

Revenue
411 Professional Fees

Expenses
511 Salary Expense
512 Rent Expense
513 Laboratory Expense
514 Utilities Expense
515 Supplies Expense

Each chapter contains a minimum of four A and four B problems. The A and B problems are parallel in content and level of difficulty. They are arranged in order of difficulty, with Problems 1A and 1B in each chapter being the simplest and the last problem in each series being the most comprehensive. Check Figures appear alongside every A and B problem's instructions in the text.

Accounting Cycle Review Problems and **Comprehensive Review Problems** give students the opportunity to apply accounting procedures to help them understand the process they have just studied in a series of chapters (1–5) and (6–12). Accounting Cycle Review Problems A and B involve the full accounting cycle, one for Surf's Up! and the other for Wind Sailors, both sole proprietorship service businesses. The Comprehensive Review Problem following Chapter 12 involves the full accounting cycle for Fabulous Furnishings, a sole proprietorship merchandising business. Peachtree and QuickBooks data files are provided for these review problems.

- **Activities** at the end of each chapter hone students' problem-solving and communication skills.

ALL ABOUT YOU SPA

This continuous general ledger problem takes students through the accounting cycles of a service and merchandising business in this day spa simulation. It replicates the continuity and follow-through of real accounting operations, putting students in the "driver's seat" of a small business.

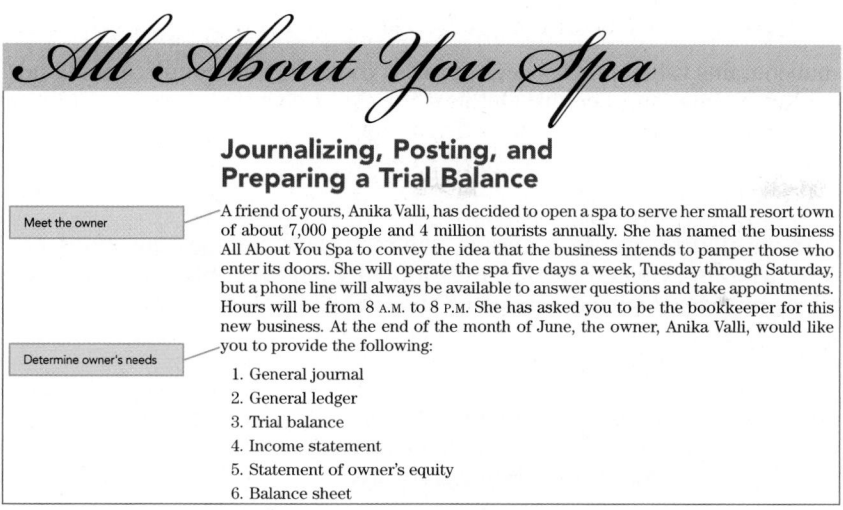

CUSTOMIZABLE CHAPTER AND TECHNOLOGY COVERAGE

Individual teaching styles may call for unique approaches to College Accounting curricula. Through Cengage Learning's *Make It Yours* program, you can—simply, quickly, and affordably—create a quality College Accounting text that is tailored to your course.

Consider some of the following customization options:

- Build a College Accounting textbook with the content and chapter progression that *precisely* matches your course syllabus.

- Let us bind-in your syllabus, course notes, study guides, and working papers to create a convenient "all-in-one" solution for your students.

- Prepare your students for the *real world* of accounting by including practice sets or general ledger software and guides from Peachtree, QuickBooks Pro, and Klooster & Allen.

- Peruse our extensive Cover Gallery or create a personalized cover that reflects the uniqueness of your course.

Get Started!

Visit www.cengage.com/custom/makeityours/McQuaig to make your selections and provide details on anything else you would like to include.

INSTRUCTOR SUPPLEMENTS

McQuaig/Bille/Nobles' *College Accounting, 10e* provides you with the robust and flexible teaching supplements you need to launch your course efficiently and successfully semester after semester.

CengageNOW™ for *College Accounting, 10e*

CengageNOW offers you a flexible course management system that allows you to assign, grade, and assess your students' progress quickly and easily. End-of-chapter materials are available online, and your students can test their mastery of new concepts through pre- and post-tests. Students engage with multimedia study tools via personalized study plans that target the areas on which they need to focus. CengageNOW also allows you to identify course content as it relates to ACBSP, AICPA, and AACSB accreditation standards. Ideal for both your traditional lecture-based courses and distance learning, CengageNOW is compatible with both WebCT® and Blackboard®. For more information on CengageNOW, please visit www.cengage.com/tlc.

Instructor's Resource Manual with Solutions

This manual contains valuable resources to assist you with your course. You'll find Teaching Objectives, Key Points, and Lecture Outlines for every chapter as well as solutions for all questions, exercises, problems, and activities in the text.

Test Bank

Revised and verified to ensure accuracy, the test bank includes questions now clearly identified by Learning Objectives, level of difficulty, and AACSB standards to allow you greater guidance in developing assessments and evaluating student progress.

Instructor's Resource CD

This powerful tool contains the content from the instructor's resource manual as well as PowerPoint® lecture slides, solutions manual, solutions to Excel template problems, achievement tests, and ExamView® testing software.

Instructor Companion Site
www.cengage.com/accounting/mcquaig

The companion site contains online versions of the instructor's resource manual, solutions manual, PowerPoint® lecture slides, Excel template solutions, and teaching transparency masters.

STUDENT SUPPLEMENTS THAT LAUNCH SUCCESSFUL STUDENTS

Preparing your students for the real world means giving them the confidence to tackle a variety of accounting challenges. Including Working Papers with Study Guides, Practice Sets, and General Ledger Software with your students' course materials will give them the practical skills and employability they deserve.

Working Papers with Study Guide, Chapters 1–12

Working Papers with Study Guide, Chapters 13-24

The Working Papers with Study Guides are provided together in one convenient resource. The Study Guide portion reinforces learning with chapter outlines that are linked to chapter learning objectives. The Working Papers are tailored to the text's end-of-chapter assignments.

New General Ledger Practice Sets

Give your students hands-on practice tackling accounting challenges with our practice sets. These realistic simulations include a CD with both Klooster & Allen and Peachtree software along with the data files needed to complete the practice sets.

- **Trey's Fast Cleaning Service Practice Set** Put your students to work in this dynamic sole-proprietorship simulation. This practice set will thoroughly review the Accounting Cycle and accounting for cash. (Chapters 1–6)

- **Coolspring Furniture Practice Set** This practice set features a sole-proprietorship merchandising business that can be completed using the general journal alone or with special journals. This more advanced practice set also covers the topic of payroll. (Chapters 1–12)

General Ledger Software

Launching your students to the next level requires preparing them to use real-world software and applications. Real general ledger software is available for your course and will provide your students with current job skills.

- **Quickbooks Pro, 2009 and Peachtree, 2009** Clear step-by-step instructions and a continuing problem provide students with hands-on experience completing the accounting cycle with QuickBooks Pro 2009 and Peachtree 2009.
- **Klooster & Allen Integrated Accounting for Windows, 7e** Designed to duplicate the look, feel, and capabilities of commercial software packages, Klooster & Allen General Ledger Software is a best-selling, educational, general ledger package that introduces students to the world of computerized accounting. With an interface that is user-friendly, Klooster & Allen General Ledger Software ensures your students will adapt quickly to computerized accounting systems used in business today.

CengageNOW™ for *College Accounting, 10e*

CengageNOW allows students to test their mastery of new concepts through pre- and post-tests. Students engage with multimedia study tools via personalized study plans that target the areas on which they need to focus. Ideal for both traditional lecture-based courses and distance learning, CengageNOW is compatible with both WebCT® and Blackboard®. For more information on CengageNOW and how it will enhance your students' mastery of accounting, please visit www.cengage.com/tlc

Acknowledgments

We sincerely thank the editorial staff of South-Western/Cengage Learning for their continuous support. During the writing of the tenth edition, we consulted many users of the text throughout the country. Their constructive suggestions are reflected in the changes that we have made. Unfortunately, space does not permit mention of all those who have contributed to this volume. Those reviewers and advisors who have contributed to *College Accounting, 10e* through their reviews, focus group attendance, class testing, market feedback, and accuracy checking are as follows:

Ellen Benowitz, *Mercer County Community College*

Daniel Biddlecom, *Erie Community College—North Campus*

Jane C. Bloom, *Palm Beach Community College*

Anna Marie Boulware, *St. Charles Community College*

Gary R. Bower, *Community College of Rhode Island*

Leonor Cabrera, *Canada College*

Dan Carroll, *Miami University—Hamilton Campus*

Susan S. Davis, *Green River Community College*

Larry Dragosavac, *Edison Community College*

Charles D. Edwards, *Miami University—Hamilton Campus*

James Ellis, *Central Oregon Community College*

Steven Ernest, *Baton Rouge Community College*

John Fasler, *Centralia College*

Janice Feingold, *Moorpark College*

Irena Gallio, *Western Nevada College*

Marina Grau, *Houston Community College*

Toni R. Hartley, *Laurel Business Institute*

Scott Hays, *Central Oregon Community College*

Lora Hines, *John A. Logan College*

Patricia H. Holmes, *Des Moines Area Community College—Ankeny Campus*

James Hurst, *National College—Lexington*

Linda Jaeger, *Southeast Community College*

Jennifer Mack, *Eastern Oklahoma State College*

Josephine Mathias, *Mercer County Community College*

Ken Newton, *Cleveland State Community College*

Jon Nitschke, *Montana State University*

Rafael Pulmano, *College of Micronesia—FSM*

Aaron L. Reeves Jr., *St. Louis Community College at Forest Park*

Tom Schaffer, *Spencerian College*

Carolyn M. Seefer, *Diablo Valley College*

Ercan Sinmaz, *Houston Community College*

Linda L. Stevens, *Alamance Community College*

Leslie Thompson, *Hutchinson Community College*

Ski R. VanderLaan, *Delta College*

Richard O. Vogel, *Forrest Junior College*

Linda Whitten, *Skyline College*

As always, we would like to thank our families for their understanding and cooperation. Without their support, this text would never have been written. Pat Bille would like to express continued gratitude to Bruce Bille, Tracy Bille-Newkirk, and James Newkirk, CPA, for their encouragement and assistance; and to the memory of Ryan Bille and Wesley and Adeline Harris for their courage and inspiration. Tracie Nobles would like to thank her husband, Trey, for his love, support, and understanding. She would also like to express gratitude to the world's best cheerleaders: her parents, Kipp and Sylvia Miller; her sister, Michelle Miller; and a great friend, Wendy Wilson. Judy Courshon would like to thank her father, Doug McQuaig, for giving her the opportunity to be a part of this project. Also, for technical support, she would like to thank her brother, John McQuaig, CPA, CMC; her sister, Laurie McQuaig; and William Courshon and Caitlin Courshon for their writing and editing skills.

Douglas J. McQuaig
Patricia A. Bille
Tracie L. Nobles
Judy M. Courshon

College Accounting

10e
1–24

Introduction to Accounting

WHERE'S YOUR FUTURE?

WHY IT MATTERS

In this book, you hold one of the keys to your future—knowledge of accounting and business! Throughout the pages of this text, you'll be introduced to individuals, just like yourself, who dreamed about working in, operating, or even owning a business. You will read about businesses such as a small cupcake business that has grown to international fame, an exotic catering business that brings food to far-reaching destinations, and an indoor rock-climbing business that caters to all ages. With all of these companies, one important skill stands out—the need to know and understand accounting!

So where's your future? It is in learning accounting, and this book is designed to help you succeed. As you go through this book, you will learn keys to understanding accounting, business success, and why the study of accounting matters. So let's get started working toward your future!

LEARNING OBJECTIVES

After you have completed this introduction to accounting, you will be able to do the following:

1 *Define accounting.*

2 *Explain the importance of accounting information.*

3 *Describe the various career opportunities in accounting.*

4 *Define ethics.*

ACCOUNTING LANGUAGE

Accountant *(p. 3)*

Accounting *(p. 2)*

Economic unit *(p. 3)*

Ethics *(p. 8)*

Financial Accounting Standards Board (FASB) *(p. 3)*

Generally accepted accounting principles (GAAP) *(p. 3)*

International Accounting Standards Board (IASB) *(p. 3)*

International Financial Reporting Standards (IFRS) *(p. 3)*

Paraprofessional accountants *(p. 6)*

Sarbanes-Oxley Act *(p. 8)*

Securities and Exchange Commission (SEC) *(p. 3)*

Transaction *(p. 2)*

Accounting is often called the language of business because, when confronted with events of a business nature, all people in society—owners, managers, creditors, employees, attorneys, engineers, and so forth—must use accounting terms and concepts to describe these events. Examples of accounting terms are *net, gross, yield, valuation, accrued, deferred*—the list could go on and on. So it is logical that anyone entering the business world should know enough of its "language" to communicate with others and to understand their communications.

As you acquire knowledge of accounting, you will gain an understanding of the way businesses operate and the reasoning involved in making business decisions. Even if you are not involved directly in accounting activities, you will certainly need to be sufficiently acquainted with the "language" to be able to understand the meaning of accounting information, how it is compiled, how it can be used, and its limitations.

You may be surprised to find that you are already familiar with many accounting terms. Recalling your personal business activities and relating them to your study of accounting will be very helpful to you. For example, when you purchased this textbook, you exchanged cash or a promise to pay cash for the book. As you will see, this exchange is an accounting event. You are going to recognize many activities and terms as you begin your study of accounting.

DEFINITION OF ACCOUNTING

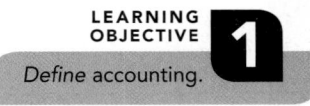
LEARNING OBJECTIVE **1**
Define accounting.

Accounting is the process of analyzing, classifying, recording, summarizing, and interpreting business transactions in financial or monetary terms. A business **transaction** is an event that has a direct effect on the operation of an economic unit, is expressed in terms of money, and is recorded. Examples of business transactions are buying or selling goods, renting a building, paying employees, and buying insurance.

The primary purpose of accounting is to provide the financial information needed for the efficient operation of an economic unit. The term **economic unit** includes not only business enterprises but also not-for-profit entities, such as government bodies, churches and synagogues, clubs, and public charities. Business enterprises or organizations may be called firms or companies.

Another important purpose of accounting is to provide useful information for decision making in the business enterprise. Similar to decisions that you have to make in your daily life, accounting helps businesses make decisions. For example, knowing whether or not there is enough cash to purchase new equipment or whether or not the business is making a profit requires knowledge of accounting.

All business entities require some type of accounting records. An **accountant** is a person who keeps the financial history of the transactions of an economic unit in written or computerized form.

Accounting Standards

Because it is important that all those who receive accounting reports be able to interpret them, a set of rules or guidelines for the accounting process has been developed. These guidelines or rules are known as **generally accepted accounting principles (GAAP)** and are developed by the **Financial Accounting Standards Board (FASB)**.

The FASB was created by the **Securities and Exchange Commission (SEC)** in 1973. The SEC is the agency responsible for regulating public companies that are traded on a U.S. stock exchange. The SEC relies on the FASB to create accounting standards. However, the ultimate responsibility for setting and enforcing accounting standards for public companies lies with the SEC.

With the globalization of the world economy, an international standard-setting board, the **International Accounting Standards Board (IASB)**, has been created to provide guidelines or rules on international accounting standards known as **International Financial Reporting Standards (IFRS)**. The IASB and FASB are currently working to combine GAAP and IFRS into one set of standards.

Bookkeeping and Accounting

There are distinctions between bookkeeping and accounting. The two processes are closely related, but there is no universally accepted line of separation. Generally, bookkeeping involves the systematic recording of business transactions in financial terms. Accounting functions at a higher level. An accountant sets up the system that a bookkeeper uses to record business transactions. An accountant may supervise the work of the bookkeeper and prepare financial statements and tax reports. Although the bookkeeper's work is more routine, it is hard to draw a line where the bookkeeper's work ends and the accountant's begins.

IMPORTANCE OF ACCOUNTING INFORMATION

Anyone who aspires to a position of leadership in business or government needs knowledge of accounting. A study of accounting gives a person the necessary background and also gives him or her an understanding of the scope, functions, and policies of an organization. A person may not be doing the accounting work, but he or she will be continually dealing with accounting forms, language, and reports.

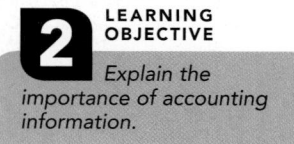

2 LEARNING OBJECTIVE

Explain the importance of accounting information.

Users of Accounting Information

There are many users of accounting information, as outlined below.

Owners

Owners have invested their money or goods in a business organization. They desire information regarding the company's earnings, its prospects for future earnings, and its ability to pay its debts.

Managers

Managers and supervisors have to prepare financial reports, understand accounting data contained in reports and budgets, and express future plans in financial terms. People who have management jobs must know how accounting information is developed in order to evaluate performance in meeting goals.

Creditors

Creditors lend money or extend credit to the company for the purchase of goods and services. The company's creditors include suppliers, banks, and other lending institutions, such as loan companies. Creditors are interested in the firm's ability to pay its debts.

Government Agencies

Taxing authorities verify information submitted by companies concerning a variety of taxes, such as income taxes, sales taxes, and employment taxes. Public utilities, such as electric and gas companies, must provide financial information to regulatory agencies.

Accounting and Technology

Before the invention of computers, all business transactions were recorded by hand. Now computers perform routine recordkeeping operations and prepare financial reports. Computers are used today in all types of businesses, both large and small. All accounting positions now require that workers use computers, have knowledge of word processing and spreadsheet software, and possess an understanding of accounting software such as QuickBooks® or Peachtree®.

Even though virtually all businesses now use computers to do their accounting, the nature of accounting is the same. The computer is a powerful tool of the accountant. However, as a tool, the computer is only as useful as the ability of and understanding of accounting by the operator. The operator must be skilled to key the correct information into the computer program; otherwise, as the saying goes, "garbage in, garbage out."

CAREER OPPORTUNITIES IN ACCOUNTING

LEARNING OBJECTIVE 3

Describe the various career opportunities in accounting.

There are a number of career opportunities in accounting in every industry. To find job opportunities in accounting, all you need to do is browse Internet job sites or read the newspapers' classified advertisements. Although the jobs listed in these ads require varying amounts of education and experience, many of them are for positions as accounting and auditing clerks, general bookkeepers, or accountants. The Bureau of Labor Statistics *Occupational Outlook Handbook* estimates that employment is expected to grow faster than average for accountants, bookkeepers, clerks, and auditors. The number of accounting-related jobs is expected to grow by 12 percent between 2006 and 2016. The requirements and duties of these positions are discussed next. Figure 1 provides a listing of the average salaries for some of these various positions.

TITLE	SALARY RANGE
ACCOUNTING CLERK	$27,250–$36,000
– Accounts receivable/Accounts payable clerk	$29,750–$39,250[a]
	$29,250–$38,000[b]
	$27,250–$35,500[c]
– Inventory clerk	$29,250–$36,500[a]
	$27,750–$35,250[b]
– Payroll clerk	$30,500–$39,000[a]
	$29,750–$38,250[b]
	$27,750–$34,750[c]
BOOKKEEPER	$31,750–$40,750
PARAPROFESSIONAL ACCOUNTANT	$37,000–$51,000
ACCOUNTANT	
– Chief financial officer	$94,250–$384,000
– Controller	$66,000–$167,750
– Financial analyst (entry level)	$39,500–$49,500[a]
	$38,000–$45,500[b]
	$35,000–$42,750[c]
– Forensic accountant	$58,500–$92,750
– General accountant (entry level)	$38,000–$46,250[a]
	$35,750–$43,000[b]
	$33,500–$40,000[c]
– Internal auditor (entry level)	$43,250–$52,750[a]
	$41,500–$51,500[b]

[a]Large companies
[b]Midsize companies
[c]Small companies

Source: Robert Half International, *2009 Salary Guide—Accounting & Finance*, © 2009 Robert Half International.

FIGURE 1

Salary ranges for various accounting positions

Accounting Clerk/Technician

An accounting clerk/technician performs routine recording of financial information. The duties of accounting clerks vary with the size of the company. In small businesses, accounting clerks handle most of the recordkeeping functions. In large companies, clerks specialize in one part of the accounting system, such as payroll, accounts receivable, accounts payable, cash, inventory, or purchases. The minimum requirement for most accounting clerk positions is usually one term or semester of an accounting course. Experience in a related job and working in an office environment is also recommended, as is knowledge of word processing and spreadsheet software. Accounting clerks/technicians should also be detail-oriented and have good communication skills.

Auditing Clerk

Auditing clerks are an organization's financial recordkeepers. An auditing clerk's primary responsibility involves verifying transactions and records posted by other employees. Other responsibilities include maintaining and updating individual or groups of accounting records, checking documents to ensure they are mathematically correct, and correcting or noting errors for accountants or other workers to adjust. Most auditing clerks are required to have a high school degree at a minimum, while an associate's degree in business or accounting is required for some positions. Knowledge of word processing and spreadsheet software and experience in a related job are also recommended.

General Bookkeeper

Many small- and medium-sized companies employ one person to oversee their bookkeeping operations. This person is called a general or full-charge bookkeeper. The general bookkeeper supervises the work of accounting clerks. Requirements for this job vary with the size of the company and the complexity of the accounting system. The minimum requirement for most general bookkeeper jobs is one or two years of accounting education as well as experience as an accounting clerk. Many companies require a certificate in business or accounting and experience working with computers and accounting software.

Paraprofessional Accountant

To bridge a gap between the general bookkeeper and the professional accountant, many firms are hiring **paraprofessional accountants**. They are able to manage the duties of the general bookkeeper as well as many of the duties of a professional accountant under that accountant's supervision. Qualifications generally include a two-year degree in accounting and knowledge of accounting software, as well as appropriate prior experience.

Certifications Available

Several organizations offer certification for accounting and auditing clerks, bookkeepers, and paraprofessional accountants. The Certified Bookkeeper (CB) designation is awarded by the American Institute of Professional Bookkeepers (www.aipb.org) and certifies that an individual has the knowledge needed to carry out bookkeeping functions. For certification, candidates must have at least two years of bookkeeping experience, pass an examination, and adhere to a code of ethics. The Accreditation Council for Accountancy and Taxation (www.acatcredentials .org) offers an Accredited Business Accountant® (ABA) certification designed for individuals who work with small- to medium-sized businesses in the areas of financial accounting, tax, and ethics. For accreditation, candidates must pass a one-day, seven-hour exam.

Accountant

The term *accountant* describes a fairly broad range of jobs. The accountant may design and manage the entire accounting system for a business. The accountant may also prepare the financial statements and tax returns and perform audits. Many accountants enter the field with a four-year college degree in accounting; however, it is not unusual for accountants to start at entry-level positions and work their way up to management positions. Although accountants are employed in every kind of economic unit, they are classified into one of four categories: public accounting, managerial or private accounting, government and not-for-profit accounting, and internal auditing. We'll briefly look at these categories.

Public Accounting

Most public accountants are Certified Public Accountants (CPAs). To become a CPA, a person must have a bachelor's degree, complete 150 hours of college coursework (in most states), pass a rigorous examination, and complete a work-experience requirement. CPAs design accounting systems, prepare tax returns, provide financial advice about business operations, and audit financial statements. Many CPAs work for a public accounting firm such as Deloitte LLP or own their own small business. CPAs can also be employed by corporations in the private sector in finance positions such as chief financial officers (CFOs), controllers, or financial analysts.

A relatively new and upcoming career opportunity in public accounting is forensic accounting. Forensic accountants specialize in investigating business crimes such as fraud, embezzlement, and money laundering. Accountants in this area of

CHUCK SAVAGE/SURF/CORBIS

Accountants are employed in every kind of economic unit. Many start in entry-level positions and work their way up to management.

specialty require knowledge of accounting, law, and finance and work closely with law enforcement personnel. Individuals wishing to specialize in forensic accounting can apply for a Certified Fraud Examiner (CFE) certificate (www.acfe.com). Requirements for a CFE certificate include a minimum of a bachelor's degree and two years of professional experience in a field either directly or indirectly related to the detection or deterrence of fraud.

If you are interested in finding out more about becoming a CPA or other public accounting jobs, the American Institute of Certified Public Accountants (www .aicpa.org) has an excellent Web site that describes accounting degrees and job opportunities called Start Here, Go Places (www.startheregoplaces.com). The site includes study information, simulation games, scholarship and internship listings, profiles of successful CPAs, and career opportunities.

Managerial or Private Accounting

Most people who are accountants are employed by private business organizations. These accountants (not necessarily CPAs) manage the accounting system, prepare budgets, determine costs of products, and provide financial information for managers and owners. Accountants have many opportunities to advance into top management positions. The Certified Management Accountant (CMA) exam (www.imanet.org) has become an important partner to the CPA credentials.

Government and Not-for-Profit Accounting

Not-for-profit accounting is used for government agencies, hospitals, churches and synagogues, and schools. Accountants for these organizations prepare budgets and maintain records of revenues and expenses. Local, state, and federal government bodies employ vast numbers of people in accounting positions. For example, a top federal government employer in the area of accounting is the Internal Revenue Service (IRS).

Internal Auditing

Due to recent accounting regulations, the demand for internal auditors has increased. Internal auditors verify the effectiveness of an organization's accounting system and controls. They examine and ensure that the company's financial information is accurate and protected. Internal auditors also ensure that organizations are following government regulations and corporate policies.

ETHICS

LEARNING OBJECTIVE 4
Define ethics.

Ethics is a philosophy or code or system of morality—that is, how we conduct ourselves from day to day in a variety of situations requiring a decision, usually of a right or wrong nature. Ethics, as it relates to accounting, is the way accountants and other keepers of financial information conduct the business of accounting according to laws of the state and their own personal code or system of morality.

There are many books and textbooks available on ethics, as well as classes on the subject. All organizations provide a code of ethical conduct for their members. With mounting evidence of questionable ethics in business reported in print and portrayed through the visual media, it is apparent that understanding and learning about ethics is an important part of accounting.

Related to ethics, a recent change to the accounting profession is the **Sarbanes-Oxley Act**, commonly referred to as SOX. SOX was created as a response to various large-scale corporate accounting frauds such as Enron and WorldCom. The Sarbanes-Oxley Act established a wide range of new rules related to the audit environment and internal controls.

CHAPTER REVIEW

Study & Practice

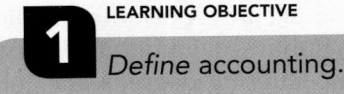

LEARNING OBJECTIVE
1 *Define accounting.*

Accounting is the process of analyzing, classifying, recording, summarizing, and interpreting business **transactions** in financial or monetary terms. It is also an information system and the language of business.

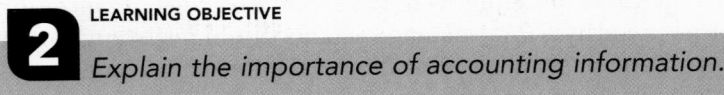

LEARNING OBJECTIVE
2 *Explain the importance of accounting information.*

A study of accounting gives a person the necessary background to understand the scope, functions, and policies of an organization.

3 LEARNING OBJECTIVE

Describe the various career opportunities in accounting.

Accounting and auditing clerks, bookkeepers, **paraprofessional accountants**, and **accountants** will find employment opportunities in several areas—in the public sector, the private sector, or not-for-profit organizations.

4 LEARNING OBJECTIVE

Define ethics.

Ethics is a code of morality—that is, how we respond to a variety of situations on a daily basis that require a decision, usually of a right or wrong nature. Ethics, as it relates to accounting, is the way accountants and other keepers of financial information conduct themselves according to laws of the state and their own personal code or system of morality.

Glossary

Accountant A person who keeps the financial history of the transactions of an economic unit in written form. *(p. 3)*

Accounting The process of analyzing, classifying, recording, summarizing, and interpreting business transactions in financial or monetary terms. *(p. 2)*

Economic unit Includes both business enterprises and not-for-profit entities. *(p. 3)*

Ethics A philosophy or code or system of morality—that is, how we conduct ourselves from day to day in a variety of situations requiring a decision, usually of a right or wrong nature. *(p. 8)*

Financial Accounting Standards Board (FASB) The organization created in 1973 by the SEC that creates GAAP. *(p. 3)*

Generally accepted accounting principles (GAAP) The rules or guidelines used for carrying out the accounting process. *(p. 3)*

International Accounting Standards Board (IASB) The international organization that provides standards or rules for international financial reporting. *(p. 3)*

International Financial Reporting Standards (IFRS) The rules or guidelines that guide international financial reporting. *(p. 3)*

Paraprofessional accountants Persons who are qualified in accounting to assume the duties of a general bookkeeper as well as some of those of a professional accountant under that accountant's supervision. *(p. 6)*

Sarbanes-Oxley Act A U.S. federal law enacted as a response to a number of major corporate and accounting scandals that establishes a wide range of rules related to the audit environment and internal controls. *(p. 8)*

Securities and Exchange Commission (SEC) The agency responsible for regulating public companies traded on a U.S. stock exchange. *(p. 3)*

Transaction An event directly affecting an economic entity that can be expressed in terms of money and that must be recorded in the accounting records. *(p. 2)*

CHAPTER REVIEW

1 Asset, Liability, Owner's Equity, Revenue, and Expense Accounts

WHY IT MATTERS

EXTREME EVENTS CATERING, Memphis, Tennessee

Extreme Events Catering goes way beyond the day-to-day events of delivering food to a customer. Extreme Events Catering caters to clientele who prefer either food with unusual tastes or unusual dining locations.

While Extreme Events Catering is unusual in its mission, it must still account for changes in assets, liabilities, owner's equity, revenues, and expenses. Each financial change in business requires an entry in the company's accounting records.

Extreme Events Catering, like other businesses, has assets— for example, equipment, serving pieces, and vehicles. To buy these assets, the company either paid cash or created a liability by promising to pay for them later. The company also has expenses such as wages and rent. These are some of the costs of doing business as the company earns revenue or income by preparing and serving delicious dishes to special diners in unusual venues.

LEARNING OBJECTIVES

After you have completed this chapter, you will be able to do the following:

1 *Define and identify asset, liability, and owner's equity accounts.*

2 *Record a group of business transactions, in column form, involving changes in assets, liabilities, and owner's equity.*

3 *Define and identify revenue and expense accounts.*

4 *Record a group of business transactions, in column form, involving all five elements of the fundamental accounting equation.*

ACCOUNTING LANGUAGE

Accounts *(p. 14)*

Accounts Payable *(p. 15)*

Accounts Receivable *(p. 23)*

Assets *(p. 11)*

Business entity *(p. 11)*

Capital *(p. 11)*

Chart of accounts *(p. 19)*

Creditor *(p. 12)*

Double-entry accounting *(p. 17)*

Equity *(p. 11)*

Expenses *(p. 18)*

Fair market value *(p. 16)*

Fundamental accounting equation *(p. 12)*

Liabilities *(p. 12)*

Owner's equity *(p. 11)*

Revenues *(p. 18)*

Separate entity concept *(p. 14)*

Sole proprietorship *(p. 14)*

Withdrawal *(p. 26)*

As we stated in the Introduction, accounting is the process of analyzing, classifying, recording, summarizing, and interpreting business transactions. We now introduce the analyzing, classifying, and recording steps in the accounting process.

ASSETS, LIABILITIES, AND OWNER'S EQUITY

The Fundamental Accounting Equation

Assets are properties or things of value, such as cash, equipment, copyrights, buildings, and land, owned and controlled by an economic unit or business entity. By the term **business entity**, we mean that the business is an economic unit in itself, and the assets or properties of the business are completely separate from the owner's personal assets. However, the owner has a claim on the assets of the business and generally has a responsibility for its debts. **The owner's right, claim, or financial interest is expressed by the word equity in the business.** Another term that could be used is **capital**. Whenever you see the term **owner's equity**, it means the owner's right to or investment in the business.

1 **LEARNING OBJECTIVE** *Define and identify asset, liability, and owner's equity accounts.*

FYI Other terms for equity are *investment, net worth,* or *proprietorship.*

Assets	=	Owner's Equity
Properties or things of value owned by the business		Owner's *right* to or investment in the business

Suppose the total value of the assets is $80,000 and the business entity does not owe any amount against the assets. Then,

Assets	=	Owner's Equity
$80,000	=	$80,000

Or suppose the assets consist of a truck that costs $35,000. The owner has invested $12,000 for the truck, and the business entity has borrowed the remainder from the bank, which is a **creditor** (one to whom money is owed). This business transaction or event can be shown as follows:

Assets	=	Liabilities	+	Owner's Equity
Items owned		Amounts owed to creditors		Owner's investment
$35,000	=	$23,000	+	$12,000

We have now introduced a new classification, **liabilities**, which represent debts. They are the amounts that the business entity owes its creditors. The debts may originate because the business bought goods or services on credit, borrowed money, or otherwise created an obligation to pay. The creditors' claims to the assets have priority over the claims of the owner.

An equation expressing the relationship of assets, liabilities, and owner's equity is called the **fundamental accounting equation**:

$$\text{Assets} = \text{Liabilities} + \text{Owner's Equity}$$

We'll deal with this equation constantly from now on. If we know two parts of this equation, we can determine the third. Let's look at some examples.

Determine Assets

Millie Adair has $17,000 invested in her travel agency, and the agency owes creditors $5,000; that is, the agency has liabilities of $5,000. Then,

Assets	=	Liabilities	+	Owner's Equity
?	=	$5,000	+	$17,000

We can find the amount of the business's assets by adding the liabilities and the owner's equity:

```
$ 5,000 Liabilities
+17,000 Owner's Equity
$22,000 Assets
```

The completed equation now reads

Assets	=	Liabilities	+	Owner's Equity
$22,000	=	$5,000	+	$17,000

Determine Owner's Equity

Larry Roland owns a car repair shop. His business has assets of $40,000, and it owes creditors $16,000; that is, it has liabilities of $16,000. Then,

Assets	=	Liabilities	+	Owner's Equity
$40,000	=	$16,000	+	?

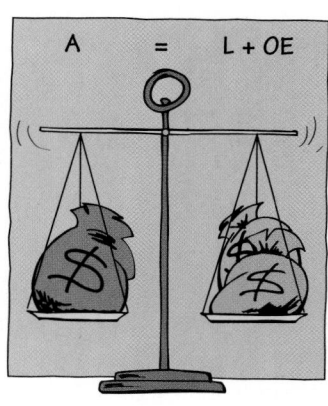

Like a balancing scale, the equation stays in balance by making equal or offsetting increases and decreases to one side or both sides.

We find the owner's equity by subtracting the liabilities from the assets:

$40,000 Assets
−16,000 Liabilities
$24,000 Owner's Equity

The completed equation now reads

Assets	=	Liabilities	+	Owner's Equity
$40,000	=	$16,000	+	$24,000

Determine Liabilities

Theo Viero's insurance agency has assets of $86,000; his investment (his equity) amounts to $46,000. Then,

Assets	=	Liabilities	+	Owner's Equity
$86,000	=	?	+	$46,000

To find the firm's total liabilities, we subtract the equity from the assets:

$86,000 Assets
−46,000 Owner's Equity
$40,000 Liabilities

The completed equation reads

Assets	=	Liabilities	+	Owner's Equity
$86,000	=	$40,000	+	$46,000

Recording Business Transactions

As you know, business transactions are events that have a direct effect on the operations of an economic unit or enterprise and are expressed in terms of money. Each business transaction must be recorded in the accounting records. As business transactions are recorded, the amounts listed under the headings Assets, Liabilities, and Owner's Equity change. However, **the total of one side of the fundamental**

2 LEARNING OBJECTIVE

Record a group of business transactions, in column form, involving changes in assets, liabilities, and owner's equity.

accounting equation must always equal the total of the other side. The categories under these three main headings are called **accounts**.

Let's look at a group of business transactions. These transactions are typical of those seen in a service or professional type of business. In these transactions, let's assume that J. Conner establishes her own business and calls it Conner's Whitewater Adventures. Conner's Whitewater Adventures is a **sole proprietorship**, or a one-owner business.

Transaction (a). **Conner deposited $90,000 in a bank account in the name of the business.** Conner deposits $90,000 cash in a separate bank account in the name of Conner's Whitewater Adventures. This separate bank account will help Conner keep her business investment separate from her personal funds. This is an example of the **separate entity concept**, according to which a business is treated as a separate economic or accounting entity. (See Figure 1.) The business is independent or stands by itself; it is separate from its owners, creditors, and customers.

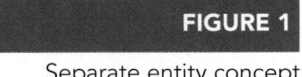

FIGURE 1

Separate entity concept

The separate entity concept means that a business is separated from its owners, creditors, and customers. In other words, the assets, liabilities, and capital of a business entity are maintained separately from the individuals who may own it, be owed, or owe it.

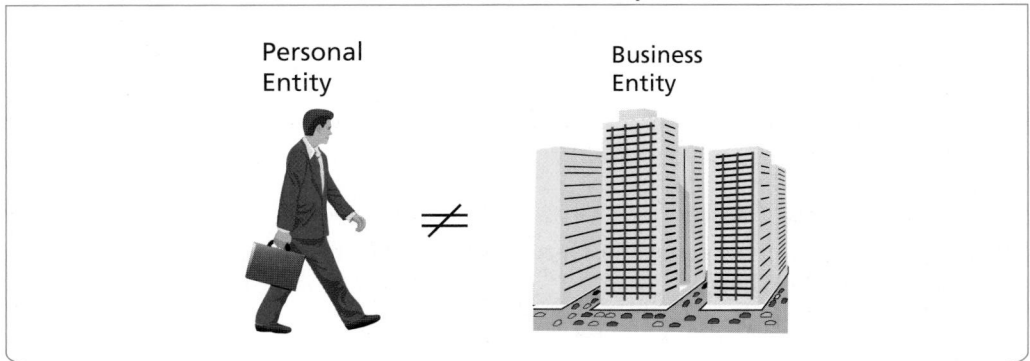

Personal Entity   ≠   Business Entity

The Cash account consists of bank deposits and money on hand. The business now has $90,000 more in cash than before, and Conner's investment has also increased by $90,000. The account denoted by the owner's name followed by the word *Capital* records the amount of the owner's investment, or equity, in the business. The effect of this transaction on the fundamental accounting equation is as follows:

	Assets	**=**	**Liabilities**	**+**	**Owner's Equity**
	Items owned		*Amounts owed to creditors*		*Owner's investment*
	Cash	=			J. Conner, Capital
(a)	+90,000	=			+90,000

Besides cash, an investment may be in the form of goods, such as equipment. The word *Capital* used under Owner's Equity therefore does not always mean that cash was invested.

Transaction (b). **Company bought equipment, paying cash, $38,000.** Conner's first task is to get her company ready for business; to do that, she needs the proper equipment. Accordingly, Conner buys equipment costing $38,000 and pays cash. **It is important to note at this point that Conner does not invest any new money. She simply exchanges part of the business's cash for equipment.** Because equipment is a new type of property for the firm, a new account, Equipment, is created. Equipment is included under Assets. As a result of this transaction, the accounting equation changes:

	Assets	=	Liabilities	+	Owner's Equity
	Items owned		Amounts owed to creditors		Owner's investment
	Cash + Equipment =				J. Conner, Capital
Initial Investment	90,000		=		90,000
(b)	–38,000 + 38,000				
New balances	52,000 + 38,000	=			90,000
	90,000				90,000

Transaction (c). **Company bought equipment on account from Signal Products, $4,320.** Conner's Whitewater Adventures buys equipment costing $4,320 on credit from Signal Products.

The Equipment account shows an increase because the business owns $4,320 more in equipment. The term "on credit" means that Conner's Whitewater Adventures does not pay cash for the equipment but instead will owe the money to Signal Products to be paid in the future. This causes an increase in liabilities because the business now owes $4,320. The liability account **Accounts Payable** is used for short-term liabilities or charge accounts, usually due within 30 days. Because Conner's Whitewater Adventures owes money to Signal Products, Signal Products is called a creditor of Conner's Whitewater Adventures. (The company to which money is owed is called a creditor.) There is now a total of $94,320 on each side of the equals sign.

	Assets	=	Liabilities	+	Owner's Equity
	Items owned		Amounts owed to creditors		Owner's investment
	Cash + Equipment =		Accounts Payable	+	J. Conner, Capital
Previous balances	52,000 + 38,000	=			90,000
(c)	+4,320		+4,320		
New balances	52,000 + 42,320	=	4,320	+	90,000
	94,320			94,320	

Observe that the recording of each transaction must yield an equation that is in balance. For example, transaction (b) resulted in a minus $38,000 and a plus $38,000 *on the same side,* with nothing recorded on the other side, and transaction (c) resulted in a $4,320 increase to both sides of the equation. It does not matter whether you change one side or both sides. **The important point is that whenever a transaction is properly recorded, the accounting equation remains in balance.**

Transaction (d). **Company paid Signal Products, a creditor, on account, $2,000.** Conner's Whitewater Adventures pays $2,000 to Signal Products, to be applied against the firm's liability of $4,320.

With this payment, cash is being reduced. At the same time, the firm *owes* less than before, so the transaction should be recorded as a reduction in liabilities.

	Assets			=	Liabilities	+	Owner's Equity
		Items owned			*Amounts owed to creditors*		*Owner's investment*
	Cash	+	Equipment	=	Accounts Payable	+	J. Conner, Capital
Previous balances	52,000	+	42,320	=	4,320	+	90,000
(d)	–2,000				–2,000		
New balances	50,000	+	42,320	=	2,320	+	90,000
		92,320				92,320	

Transaction (e). **Owner invested equipment in the business.** Conner invested her own computer equipment, having a **fair market value** of $5,200 in Conner's Whitewater Adventures. **Fair market value is the present worth of an asset.** It is the amount that would be received if the asset were sold on the open market. Additional investments may be in the form of equipment, cash, tools, or real estate.

	Assets			=	Liabilities	+	Owner's Equity
		Items owned			*Amounts owed to creditors*		*Owner's investment*
	Cash	+	Equipment	=	Accounts Payable	+	J. Conner, Capital
Previous balances	50,000	+	42,320	=	2,320	+	90,000
(e)			+5,200				+5,200
New balances	50,000	+	47,520	=	2,320	+	95,200
		97,520				97,520	

Accounting, as we said before, is the process of analyzing, classifying, recording, summarizing, and interpreting business transactions in terms of money. Look at the transactions thus far for Conner's Whitewater Adventures and see if you understand that we have gone through certain steps (in the form of questions). Let's illustrate these steps using transaction (e), owner invested equipment in the business.

STEP 1. What accounts are involved? Equipment and J. Conner, Capital are involved.

STEP 2. What are the classifications of the accounts involved? Equipment is an asset, and J. Conner, Capital is an owner's equity account.

STEP 3. Are the accounts increased or decreased? Equipment is increased because Conner's Whitewater Adventures has more equipment than before. J. Conner, Capital is increased because Conner has a greater investment than before.

STEP 4. Is the equation in balance after the transaction has been recorded? Yes.

We will stress this step-by-step process throughout the text. This example serves as an introduction to **double-entry accounting**. The "double" entry method is demonstrated by the fact that each transaction must be recorded in at least two accounts, keeping the accounting equation in balance.

Summary of Transactions

Let's summarize the business transactions of Conner's Whitewater Adventures in column form, identifying each transaction by a letter of the alphabet. To test your understanding of the recording procedure, describe the nature of the transactions that have taken place.

	Assets		=	Liabilities	+	Owner's Equity
	Items owned			Amounts owed to creditors		Owner's investment
	Cash	+ Equipment	=	Accounts Payable	+	J. Conner, Capital
Transaction (a)	+90,000					+90,000
Transaction (b)	−38,000	+38,000				
Balance	52,000 +	38,000	=			90,000
Transaction (c)		+4,320		+4,320		
Balance	52,000 +	42,320	=	4,320	+	90,000
Transaction (d)	−2,000			−2,000		
Balance	50,000 +	42,320	=	2,320	+	90,000
Transaction (e)		+5,200				+5,200
Balance	50,000 +	47,520	=	2,320	+	95,200
	97,520			97,520		

The following observations apply to all types of business transactions:

1. Every transaction is recorded as an increase and/or decrease in two or more accounts.

2. One side of the equation is always equal to the other side of the equation.

In this chapter we are using a column arrangement as a practical device to show how transactions are recorded. This arrangement is useful for showing increases and decreases in various accounts as a result of the transactions. We also show new balances after recording each transaction.

Accounting in Your Future

Accounting Clerk

You may wonder why taking an accounting class is important to you. One possible career for students who study accounting is as an entry-level accounting clerk for a company like Extreme Events Catering. As an accounting clerk, you would be the financial recordkeeper for the business. Your responsibilities would include maintaining accounting records, such as those that you are learning about in this chapter. You could also be responsible for preparing financial statements, making bank deposits, and handling payroll.

Many businesses require that an accounting clerk have a high school diploma and some accounting coursework. An associate's degree in accounting is highly recommended. Minimum requirements would be a knowledge of basic accounting terminology, concepts, and processes, using either a manual accounting system or an automated accounting system such as a general ledger accounting software package. Skills related to Microsoft® Word®, Excel®, and Outlook® would also be helpful.* You would need to be able to work with others in the accounting department and be very attentive to detail and accuracy. Accounting clerks, sometimes called bookkeepers, can be certified as certified bookkeepers by the American Institute of Professional Bookkeepers (www.aipb.org).

The U.S. Department of Labor's Bureau of Labor Statistics (www.bls.gov) provides information about this field regarding job locations and pay scales.

*Microsoft, Encarta, MSN, and Windows are either registered trademarks or trademarks of Microsoft Corporation in the United States and/or other countries.

REVENUE AND EXPENSE ACCOUNTS

LEARNING OBJECTIVE 3

Define and identify revenue and expense accounts.

Revenues are the amounts earned by a business. Examples of revenues are fees earned for performing services, income from selling merchandise, rent income for the use of property, and interest income for lending money. Revenues may be in the form of cash or credit card receipts. Revenues may also result from credit sales to charge customers, in which case cash will be received at a later time.

Expenses are the costs that relate to earning revenue (or the costs of doing business). Examples of expenses are wages expense for labor performed, rent expense for the use of property, interest expense for the use of money, and advertising expense for the use of various media (for example, newspapers, radio, direct mail, and the Internet). Another example is supplies expense to include supplies used in the completion of a task performed by a service business, such as cleaning fluids used by a carpet cleaning company. Expenses may be paid in cash when incurred or at a later time. Expenses to be paid at a later time involve Accounts Payable.

Revenues and expenses directly affect owner's equity. **If a business earns revenue, an increase in owner's equity occurs. When a business incurs expenses, owner's equity decreases.** For the present, think of it this way: If the company makes money, the owner's equity is increased. If the company has to pay out money for the costs of doing business, then the owner's equity is decreased. Revenues and expenses fall under the umbrella of owner's equity: Revenue increases owner's equity; expenses decrease owner's equity. (See Figure 2.)

| FIGURE 2 | These temporary accounts fall under the umbrella of owner's equity, In Chapter 5, we will learn how temporary accounts are closed into the Capital account to determine net income or net loss as well as the increase or decrease to Capital. |

The umbrella of owner's equity

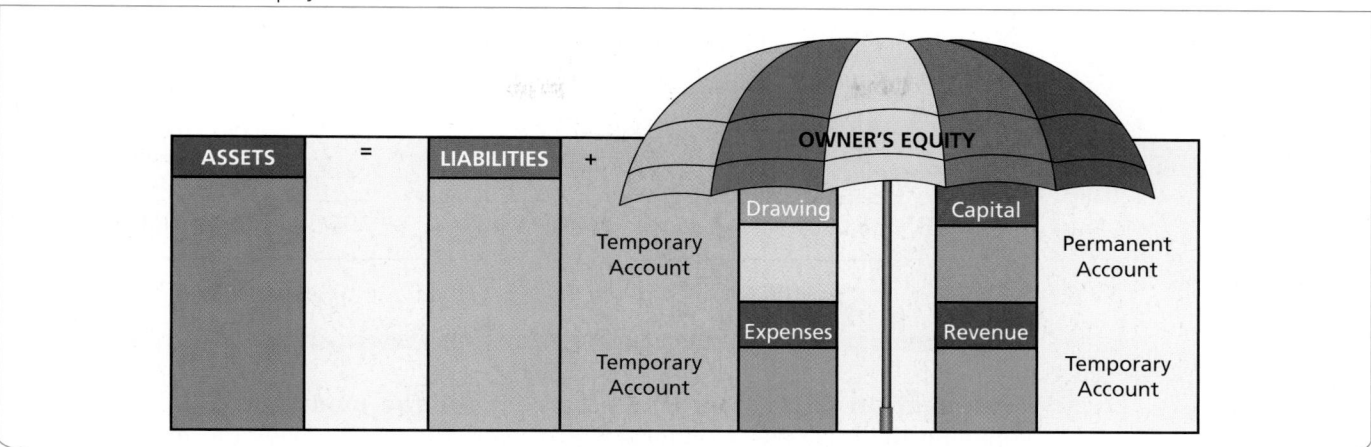

Chart of Accounts

The **chart of accounts** is the official list of accounts *tailor-made* for the business. All the company's transactions must be recorded using the official account titles.

We now present the chart of accounts for Conner's Whitewater Adventures. Some of the accounts are new to you, but they will be explained as we move along. When numbering account titles, the 100s are used for assets, the 200s are used for liabilities, the 300s are used for owner's equity accounts, the 400s are used for revenue accounts, and the 500s are used for expense accounts. You will encounter longer account numbers, but the first digit will usually be the same for any service business. In any case, use the exact account titles listed in the company's chart of accounts. Any changes must be approved by management.

CHART OF ACCOUNTS

Assets
111 Cash
113 Accounts Receivable
117 Prepaid Insurance
124 Equipment

Liabilities
221 Accounts Payable

Owner's Equity
311 J. Conner, Capital
312 J. Conner, Drawing

Revenue (increase in Owner's Equity)
411 Income from Tours

Expenses (decrease in Owner's Equity)
511 Wages Expense
512 Rent Expense
513 Supplies Expense
514 Advertising Expense
515 Utilities Expense

FYI

When setting up and maintaining the chart of accounts on a computer, you may find that you must reserve the 500 accounts for cost accounts (used in a merchandising business). You may need to number expenses as 600s. Read the setup instructions in your software package.

Recording Business Transactions

Soon after the opening of Conner's Whitewater Adventures the first customers arrive, beginning a flow of revenue for the business. Let's examine more transactions of Conner's Whitewater Adventures for the first month of operations.

Transaction (f). **Company sold whitewater rafting tours for cash, $8,000.** Conner's Whitewater Adventures receives cash revenue of $8,000 in return for whitewater rafting tours performed for customers over two weeks. In other words, the company earns $8,000 for services performed for cash customers. Revenue has the effect of increasing owner's equity, but because the company wants to know how much revenue is earned, we set up a special column for revenue. The revenue account for Conner's Whitewater Adventures is called Income from Tours. The accounting equation is affected as follows (PB stands for previous balance, and NB stands for new balance).

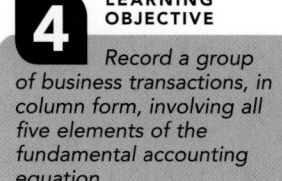

4 **LEARNING OBJECTIVE**

Record a group of business transactions, in column form, involving all five elements of the fundamental accounting equation.

	Assets		=	Liabilities	+		Owner's Equity		
	Cash	+ Equipment	=	Accounts Payable	+	J. Conner, Capital	+	Revenue	
PB	50,000	+ 47,520	=	2,320	+	95,200			
(f)	+8,000							+8,000 (Income from Tours)	
NB	58,000	+ 47,520	=	2,320	+	95,200	+	8,000	
	105,520					105,520			

Transaction (g).   Company paid rent for the month, $1,250. Shortly after opening the business, Conner's Whitewater Adventures pays the month's rent of $1,250. Rent is payment for the privilege of occupying a building.

It seems logical that, if revenue is added to owner's equity, then expenses (the opposite of revenue) must be subtracted from owner's equity. To be consistent, a separate column is set up for expenses.

We want to have a running total of the amount of expenses to be subtracted from owner's equity. To keep up this running total, as each new expense is incurred (or happens), it must be added to the previous total.

	Assets		=	Liabilities	+		Owner's Equity		
	Cash	+ Equip.	=	Accounts Payable	+	J. Conner, Capital	+ Revenue	– Expenses	
PB	58,000	+ 47,520	=	2,320	+	95,200	+ 8,000		
(g)	–1,250							+1,250 (Rent Expense)	
NB	56,750	+ 47,520	=	2,320	+	95,200	+ 8,000	– 1,250	
	104,270					104,270			

Because the time period represented by the rent payment is one month or less, we record the $1,250 as an expense. If the payment covered a period longer than one month, we would record the amount under an asset called Prepaid Rent.

Let's review the mental process for formulating the entry by asking:

STEP 1. What are the accounts involved? In this transaction, they are Cash and Rent Expense.

STEP 2. What are the classifications of the accounts involved? Cash is an asset, and Rent Expense is an expense and part of owner's equity.

STEP 3. Are the accounts increased or decreased? Cash is decreased because after the payment we have less cash than we had before. Rent Expense is increased. Thus there is a $1,250 reduction in total owner's equity.

STEP 4. Is the equation in balance after the transaction has been recorded?
Yes.

Transaction (h). Company bought supplies on credit, $675. Conner's Whitewater Adventures buys office supplies costing $675 on credit from Fineman Company. Computer paper, ink cartridges, invoice pads, pens and pencils, folders, filing cabinets, and 10-key calculators are considered to be supplies to be used up by Conner's Whitewater Adventures for clients and are recorded as an expense. For a service business, for tax purposes (IRS Notice 2001-76), supplies may be originally recorded as an expense rather than being added to an inventory account.

	Assets		= Liabilities +		Owner's Equity		
	Cash	+ Equip. =	Accounts Payable	+	J. Conner, Capital	+ Revenue	− Expenses
PB	56,750	+ 47,520 =	2,320	+	95,200	+ 8,000	− 1,250
(h)			+675				+675 (Supplies Expense)
NB	56,750	+ 47,520 =	2,995	+	95,200	+ 8,000	− 1,925
	104,270				104,270		

Transaction (i). Company paid for insurance, $1,875. Conner's Whitewater Adventures paid $1,875 for a three-month liability insurance policy. At the time of payment, the company has not used up the insurance; thus, it is not yet an expense. As the insurance expires (is used), it will become an expense. **However, because it is paid in advance for a period longer than one month, it has value and is therefore recorded as Prepaid Insurance, an asset.**

	Assets			= Liabilities +		Owner's Equity		
	Cash	+ Equip. +	Ppd. Ins. =	Accounts Payable	+	J. Conner, Capital	+ Revenue	− Expenses
PB	56,750	+ 47,520	=	2,995	+	95,200	+ 8,000	− 1,925
(i)	−1,875		+1,875					
NB	54,875	+ 47,520 +	1,875 =	2,995	+	95,200	+ 8,000	− 1,925
	104,270					104,270		

At the end of the year or accounting period, an adjustment will have to be made to take out the expired portion (that is, coverage for the months that have been used up) and record it as an expense. We discuss this adjustment in a later chapter.

Observe that each time a transaction is recorded, the total amount on one side of the equation **remains equal** to the total amount on the other side. As proof of this equality, look at the following computation:

Cash	$ 54,875	Accounts Payable	$ 2,995
Equipment	47,520	J. Conner, Capital	95,200
Prepaid Insurance	1,875	Revenue	8,000
		Expenses	−1,925
	$104,270		$104,270

Steps in Analyzing Transactions

Now that we have recorded transactions in all five classifications of accounts, let's pause to go through the steps we have followed:

STEP 1. Read the transaction to understand what is happening and how it affects the business. For example, the business has more revenue, or has more expenses, or has more cash, or owes less to creditors. Identify the accounts involved. Look for Cash first; you will quickly recognize if cash is coming in or going out.

STEP 2. Decide on the classifications of the accounts involved. For example, Equipment is something the business owns, and it's an asset; Accounts Payable is an amount the business owes, and it's a liability; Rent is an expense.

STEP 3. Decide whether the accounts are increased or decreased.

STEP 4. After recording the transaction, make sure the accounting equation is in balance.

Tools to Success—The U.S. Small Business Administration

SMALL BUSINESS SUCCESS

Throughout the pages of this text, you will occasionally find a feature labeled Small Business Success. This feature is designed to provide insight into accounting issues surrounding small businesses. Some of you will probably own a small business when you graduate; maybe you are thinking of starting your own small bookkeeping firm. Or many of you will work in small businesses such as a local or regional accounting firm. These features contain information that is useful to small and large businesses and will be helpful if you are thinking about owning your own business.

The U.S. Small Business Administration Web site (www.sba.gov) is a great place to find information about managing, accounting for, and running a small business. Take a moment to go to the Web site and review the tools that are available to small

businesses. Click on the Tools link, and you will find different series that deal with management, finances, and crime prevention.

You can also find audio and video podcasts on the Web site that provide information about business success. If you are interested in hearing about other successful small businesses, you can find a series on small business features. The series discusses various small businesses that have used the tools provided by the Small Business Administration and have grown to be successful and profitable entities.

Keep an eye out for the Small Business Success feature! It will add some insight into how businesses use the accounting information that you are learning in this course.

Transaction (j). **Company received a bill for an expense, $620.** Conner's Whitewater Adventures receives a bill from *The Times* for newspaper advertising, $620. **Conner's Whitewater Adventures has simply received the bill for advertising; it has not paid any cash.** Previously, we described an expense as money to be paid for the cost of doing business. An expense of $620 has now been incurred (or has taken place), and it should be recorded as an increase in expenses (Advertising Expense). Also, since the company owes $620 more than before and intends to pay at a later time, this amount should be recorded as an increase in Accounts Payable. Notice Cash is not used because the bill has not been paid.

	Assets			= Liabilities +		Owner's Equity		
	Cash	+ Equip. +	Ppd. Ins. =	Accounts Payable +	J. Conner, Capital	+ Revenue –	Expenses	
PB	54,875	+ 47,520 +	1,875 =	2,995 +	95,200	+ 8,000 –	1,925	
(j)				+620			+620 (Advertising Expense)	
NB	54,875	+ 47,520 +	1,875 =	3,615 +	95,200	+ 8,000 –	2,545	
		104,270				104,270		

Transaction (k). **Company sold services on account, $6,750.** Conner's Whitewater Adventures signs a contract with Crystal River Lodge to provide rafting adventures for guests. Conner's Whitewater Adventures provides 27 one-day rafting tours and bills Crystal River Lodge for $6,750.

A company uses the **Accounts Receivable** account to record the amounts due from (legal claims against) charge customers. Since Conner's Whitewater Adventures' claim against Crystal River Lodge of $6,750 is promised to be paid, it is recorded in Accounts Receivable. Revenue is earned or recognized when the service is performed, even though the $6,750 has not been received in cash. We count the $6,750 as an increase in revenue and an increase in Accounts Receivable. Keep in mind that Accounts Receivable is an asset; or something that is owned. Conner's Whitewater Adventures owns a claim of $6,750 against Crystal River Lodge.

	Assets				= Liabilities +		Owner's Equity		
	Cash +	Equip. +	Ppd. Ins. +	Accts. Rec. =	Accounts Payable +	J. Conner, Capital	+ Revenue –	Expenses	
PB	54,875 +	47,520 +	1,875	=	3,615 +	95,200	+ 8,000 –	2,545	
(k)				+6,750			+6,750 (Income from Tours)		
NB	54,875 +	47,520 +	1,875 +	6,750 =	3,615 +	95,200	+ 14,750 –	2,545	
		111,020				111,020			

When Crystal River Lodge pays the $6,750 bill in cash, Conner's Whitewater Adventures will record this transaction as an increase in Cash and a decrease in Accounts Receivable. At that time, Conner's Whitewater Adventures will *not* have to make an entry for the revenue, because the revenue was earned and recorded when the service was performed.

Transaction (l). **Company paid creditor on account.** Conner's Whitewater Adventures pays $1,500 to Signal Products, its creditor (the party to whom it owes money), as partial payment on account.

	Assets					= Liabilities +		Owner's Equity		
	Cash	+ Equip.	+ Ppd. Ins.	+ Accts. Rec.	=	Accounts Payable	+	J. Conner, Capital	+ Revenue	– Expenses
PB	54,875	+ 47,520	+ 1,875	+ 6,750	=	3,615	+	95,200	+ 14,750	– 2,545
(l)	–1,500					–1,500				
NB	53,375	+ 47,520	+ 1,875	+ 6,750	=	2,115	+	95,200	+ 14,750	– 2,545

109,520   109,520

Transaction (m). **Company paid an expense in cash, $225.** Conner's Whitewater Adventures receives a bill from Solar Power, Inc. for $225. Because the bill was not previously recorded as a liability and is to be paid immediately, we record the amount directly as an expense.

	Assets					= Liabilities +		Owner's Equity		
	Cash	+ Equip.	+ Ppd. Ins.	+ Accts. Rec.	=	Accounts Payable	+	J. Conner, Capital	+ Revenue	– Expenses
PB	53,375	+ 47,520	+ 1,875	+ 6,750	=	2,115	+	95,200	+ 14,750	– 2,545
(m)	–225									+225 (Utilities Expense)
NB	53,150	+ 47,520	+ 1,875	+ 6,750	=	2,115	+	95,200	+ 14,750	– 2,770

109,295   109,295

Transaction (n). **Company paid creditor on account, $620.** Conner's Whitewater Adventures pays $620 to *The Times* for advertising. **Recall that this bill had previously been recorded as a liability in transaction (j).**

	Assets					= Liabilities +		Owner's Equity		
	Cash	+ Equip.	+ Ppd. Ins.	+ Accts. Rec.	=	Accounts Payable	+	J. Conner, Capital	+ Revenue	– Expenses
PB	53,150	+ 47,520	+ 1,875	+ 6,750	=	2,115	+	95,200	+ 14,750	– 2,770
(n)	–620					–620				
NB	52,530	+ 47,520	+ 1,875	+ 6,750	=	1,495	+	95,200	+ 14,750	– 2,770

108,675   108,675

Transaction (o). **Company paid an expense in cash, $2,360.** Conner's Whitewater Adventures pays wages of a part-time employee, $2,360.

Summary of transactions (f) through (s) **FIGURE 3**

	Assets				=	Liabilities +		Owner's Equity			
	Cash +	Equip. +	Ppd. Ins. +	Accts. Rec.	=	Accounts Payable +	J. Conner, Capital	− J. Conner, Drawing	+ Revenue	− Expenses
Bal.	50,000 +	47,520			=	2,320 +	95,200			
(f)	**+8,000**								**+8,000** (Income from Tours)	
Bal.	58,000 +	47,520			=	2,320 +	95,200		+ 8,000	
(g)	**−1,250**									**+1,250** (Rent Exp.)
Bal.	56,750 +	47,520			=	2,320 +	95,200		+ 8,000 −	1,250
(h)						**+675**				**+675** (Sup. Exp.)
Bal.	56,750 +	47,520			=	2,995 +	95,200		+ 8,000 −	1,925
(i)	**−1,875**		**+1,875**							
Bal.	54,875 +	47,520 +	1,875		=	2,995 +	95,200		+ 8,000 −	1,925
(j)						**+620**				**+620** (Adv. Exp.)
Bal.	54,875 +	47,520 +	1,875		=	3,615 +	95,200		+ 8,000 −	2,545
(k)				**+6,750**					**+6,750** (Income from Tours)	
Bal.	54,875 +	47,520 +	1,875 +	6,750	=	3,615 +	95,200		+ 14,750 −	2,545
(l)	**−1,500**					**−1,500**				
Bal.	53,375 +	47,520 +	1,875 +	6,750	=	2,115 +	95,200		+ 14,750 −	2,545
(m)	**−225**									**+225** (Util. Exp.)
Bal.	53,150 +	47,520 +	1,875 +	6,750	=	2,115 +	95,200		+ 14,750 −	2,770
(n)	**−620**					**−620**				
Bal.	52,530 +	47,520 +	1,875 +	6,750	=	1,495 +	95,200		+ 14,750 −	2,770
(o)	**−2,360**									**+2,360** (Wages Exp.)
Bal.	50,170 +	47,520 +	1,875 +	6,750	=	1,495 +	95,200		+ 14,750 −	5,130
(p)	**−1,850**	**+3,780**				**+1,930**				
Bal.	48,320 +	51,300 +	1,875 +	6,750	=	3,425 +	95,200		+ 14,750 −	5,130
(q)	**+2,500**			**−2,500**						
Bal.	50,820 +	51,300 +	1,875 +	4,250	=	3,425 +	95,200		+ 14,750 −	5,130
(r)	**+8,570**								**+8,570** (Income from Tours)	
Bal.	59,390 +	51,300 +	1,875 +	4,250	=	3,425 +	95,200		+ 23,320 −	5,130
(s)	**−3,500**							**+3,500**		
Bal.	55,890 +	51,300 +	1,875 +	4,250	=	3,425 +	95,200 −	3,500	+ 23,320 −	5,130

Left Side of Equals Sign:

Cash	$ 55,890
Equipment	51,300
Prepaid Insurance	1,875
Accounts Receivable	4,250
	$113,315

Right Side of Equals Sign:

Accounts Payable	$ 3,425
J. Conner, Capital	95,200
J. Conner, Drawing	−3,500
Revenue	23,320
Expenses	−5,130
	$113,315

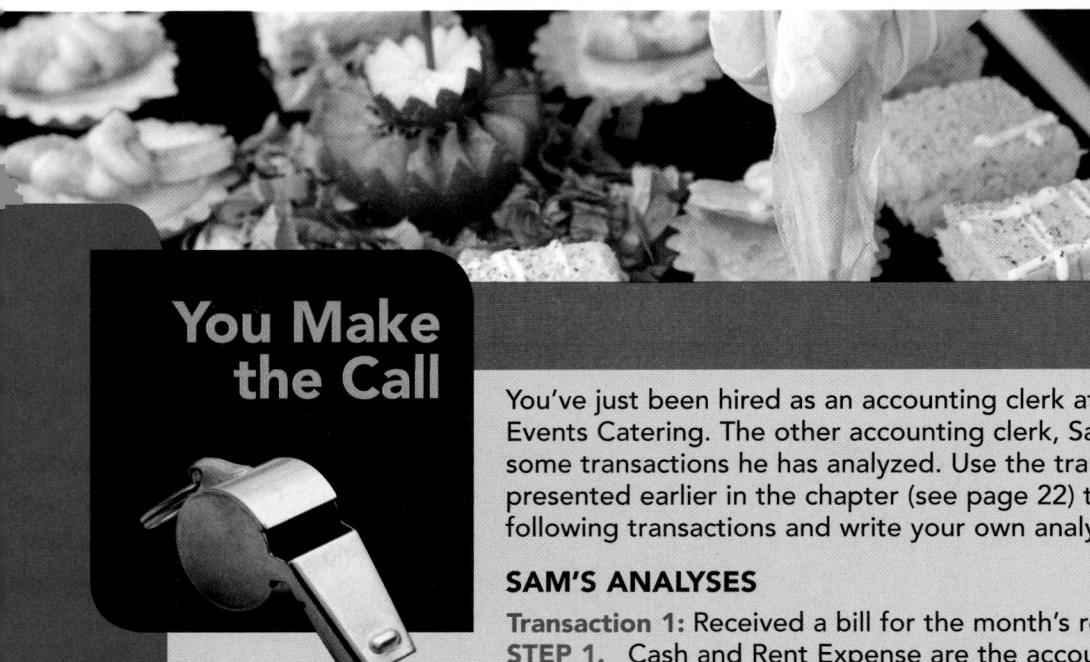

You Make the Call

You've just been hired as an accounting clerk at a business similar to Extreme Events Catering. The other accounting clerk, Sam, has asked you to check some transactions he has analyzed. Use the transaction-analysis steps presented earlier in the chapter (see page 22) to determine the accuracy of the following transactions and write your own analysis.

SAM'S ANALYSES

Transaction 1: Received a bill for the month's rent, $1,000.
STEP 1. Cash and Rent Expense are the accounts involved.
STEP 2. Cash is an asset, and Rent Expense is an expense.
STEP 3. Equipment is decreased, and Rent Expense is decreased.

Transaction 2: Bought equipment on account for $1,800.
STEP 1. Equipment and Accounts Receivable are the accounts involved.
STEP 2. Equipment is an asset, and Accounts Receivable is an asset.
STEP 3. Equipment is decreased, and Accounts Receivable is increased.

SOLUTION

Sam's analyses for both transactions are incorrect.

Transaction 1:
STEP 1. Accounts Payable and Rent Expense are the accounts involved.
STEP 2. The bill was received but not paid, therefore creating a liability. Cash is not involved because the business has not paid the monthly rent. Accounts Payable is a liability, and Rent Expense is an expense.
STEP 3. Accounts Payable is increased, and Rent Expense is increased. Remember, the bill was only received, not paid; therefore no cash is involved. Rent Expense increases, but its ultimate effect is a subtraction in the fundamental accounting equation.

Transaction 2:
STEP 1. Equipment and Accounts Payable are the accounts involved.
STEP 2. Accounts Payable is involved because the business owes money to the seller. Accounts Payable is the account used to manage short-term liabilities. Accounts Receivable is the account used to keep track of what customers owe us.
Equipment is an asset, and Accounts Payable is a liability.
STEP 3. Equipment is increased, and Accounts Payable is increased.

CHAPTER REVIEW

Study & Practice

LEARNING OBJECTIVE

1 *Define and identify* asset, liability, *and* owner's equity *accounts.*

Assets are cash, properties, or things of value owned by the business. **Liabilities** are amounts the business owes to creditors. **Owner's equity** is the owner's investment or net worth. The **fundamental accounting equation** expresses the relationship of assets, liabilities, and owner's equity and is represented as:

$$\text{Assets} = \text{Liabilities} + \text{Owner's Equity}$$

PRACTICE EXERCISE 1

Complete the fundamental accounting equation:

Assets	=	Liabilities	+	Owner's Equity
Items owned		*Amounts owed to creditors*		*Owner's investment*
$50,000	=	$12,000	+	?

PRACTICE EXERCISE 1 SOLUTION

$50,000 Assets
−12,000 Liabilities
$38,000 Owner's Equity

LEARNING OBJECTIVE

2 *Record a group of business transactions, in column form, involving changes in assets, liabilities, and owner's equity.*

The accounting equation is stated as assets equals liabilities plus owner's equity. Under the appropriate classification, a separate column is set up for each **account**. Transactions are recorded by listing amounts as either additions to or deductions from the various accounts. The equation must always remain in balance.

PRACTICE EXERCISE 2

Write the corresponding amounts for each transaction where you see question marks. Compute the balance to be sure the equation is in balance before proceeding to the next transaction.

	Assets		=	Liabilities	+	Owner's Equity
	Items owned			*Amounts owed to creditors*		*Owner's investment*
	Cash	+ Equipment =		Accounts Payable	+	J. Lawson, Capital
						?
Transaction (a)	+90,000					
Transaction (b)	?	+53,000				
Balance	? +	?	=			?
Transaction (c)		?		+9,000		
Balance	? +	?	=	?	+	?
Transaction (d)	?			−4,000		
Balance	? +	?	=	?	+	?
Transaction (e)		?				+5,200
Balance	? +	?	=	?	+	?
	?				?	

PRACTICE EXERCISE 2 SOLUTION

	Assets		=	Liabilities	+	Owner's Equity
	Items owned			*Amounts owed to creditors*		*Owner's investment*
	Cash	+ Equipment =		Accounts Payable	+	J. Lawson, Capital
Transaction (a)	+90,000					+90,000
Transaction (b)	−53,000	+53,000				
Balance	37,000 +	53,000	=			90,000
Transaction (c)		+9,000		+9,000		
Balance	37,000 +	62,000	=	9,000	+	90,000
Transaction (d)	−4,000			−4,000		
Balance	33,000 +	62,000	=	5,000	+	90,000
Transaction (e)		+5,200				+5,200
Balance	33,000 +	67,200	=	5,000	+	95,200
	100,200				100,200	

---

3 LEARNING OBJECTIVE

Define and identify revenue and expense accounts.

Revenues consist of amounts earned by a business, such as fees earned for performing services, income from selling merchandise, rent income for the use of property, or interest earned for lending money. **Expenses** are the costs of earning revenue—that is, of doing business—such as wages expense, rent expense, interest expense, and advertising expense.

PRACTICE EXERCISE 3

Identify the revenue and expense accounts from the following list of accounts. If the account is a revenue account, write R. If the account is an expense account, write E. If it is neither, leave blank.

___ Accounts Payable   ___ Service Income
___ Rent Expense   ___ Utilities Expense
___ J. Martin, Drawing   ___ Professional Fees Earned
___ Wages Expense   ___ Accounts Receivable

PRACTICE EXERCISE 3 SOLUTION

___ Accounts Payable   _R_ Service Income
_E_ Rent Expense   _E_ Utilities Expense
___ J. Martin, Drawing   _R_ Professional Fees Earned
_E_ Wages Expense   ___ Accounts Receivable

4 **LEARNING OBJECTIVE**

Record a group of business transactions, in column form, involving all five elements of the fundamental accounting equation.

The accounting equation has been expanded and should appear as follows:

Assets = Liabilities + Owner's Equity (Capital) – Drawing + Revenue – Expenses

Accounts are classified and listed under each heading. Transactions are recorded by listing amounts as either additions to or deductions from the various accounts. The equation must always remain in balance.

PRACTICE EXERCISE 4

Record the following transactions in the grid provided below:

Transaction (a).   Company bought equipment for $8,000 on account.
Transaction (b).   Company sold services on account for $6,200.
Transaction (c).   Customer paid $3,000 on account.
Transaction (d).   Company owner invested personal computer system in the business, fair market value, $3,400 (Equipment).

Assets			=	Liabilities	+	Owner's Equity				
Cash +	Equipment +	Accounts Receivable	=	Accounts Payable	+	Capital –	Drawing +	Revenue –	Expenses	
(a)										
(b)										
(c)										
(d)										

PRACTICE EXERCISE 4 SOLUTION

	Assets			=	Liabilities +		Owner's Equity			
	Cash +	Equipment +	Accounts Receivable	=	Accounts Payable	+	Capital	– Drawing +	Revenue	– Expenses
(a)		+8,000			+8,000					
(b)			+6,200						+6,200	
(c)	+3,000		–3,000							
(d)		+3,400					+3,400			
Bal.	3,000 +	11,400 +	3,200	=	8,000	+	3,400		+ 6,200	

17,600

17,600

Glossary

Accounts The categories under the Assets, Liabilities, and Owner's Equity headings. (p. 14)

Accounts Payable A liability account used for short-term liabilities or charge accounts, usually due within 30 days. (p. 15)

Accounts Receivable An account used to record the amounts owed by (legal claims against) charge customers. (p. 23)

Assets Cash, properties, and other things of value owned by an economic unit or business entity. (p. 11)

Business entity A business enterprise, separate and distinct from the persons who supply the assets it uses. (p. 11)

Capital The owner's investment, or equity, in an enterprise. (p. 11)

Chart of accounts The official list of account titles to be used to record the transactions of a business. (p. 19)

Creditor One to whom money is owed. (p. 12)

Double-entry accounting The system by which each business transaction is recorded in at least two accounts and the accounting equation is kept in balance. (p. 17)

Equity The value of a right or claim to or financial interest in an asset or group of assets. (p. 11)

Expenses The costs that relate to earning revenue (the costs of doing business); examples are wages, rent, interest, and advertising. They may be paid in cash immediately or at a future time (Accounts Payable). (p. 18)

Fair market value The present worth of an asset or the amount that would be received if the asset were sold to an outsider on the open market. (p. 16)

Fundamental accounting equation (Assets = Liabilities + Owner's Equity) An equation expressing the relationship of assets, liabilities, and owner's equity. (p. 12)

Liabilities Debts or amounts owed to creditors. (p. 12)

Owner's equity The owner's right to or investment in the business. (p. 11)

Revenues The amounts a business earns; examples are fees earned for performing services, sales of merchandise, rent income, and interest income. They may be in the form of cash, credit card receipts, or accounts receivable (charge accounts). (p. 18)

Separate entity concept The concept by which a business is treated as a separate economic or accounting entity. The business stands by itself, separate from its owners, creditors, and customers. (p. 14)

Sole proprietorship A one-owner business. (p. 14)

Withdrawal The taking of cash or other assets out of a business by the owner for his or her own use. (This is also referred to as drawing.) A withdrawal is treated as a temporary decrease in owner's equity. (p. 26)

CHAPTER ASSIGNMENTS

Discussion Questions

1. Define *assets*, *liabilities*, *owner's equity*, *revenues*, and *expenses*.
2. Explain the separate entity concept.
3. How do Accounts Payable and Accounts Receivable differ?
4. Describe two ways to increase owner's equity and two ways to decrease owner's equity.
5. What is the effect on the fundamental accounting equation if supplies are purchased on account? How will the fundamental accounting equation change if supplies are purchased with cash? Explain how this purchase will or will not change the owner's equity.
6. When an owner withdraws cash or goods from the business, why is this considered an increase to the Drawing account and not an increase to the Wages Expense account?
7. Define *chart of accounts*, and identify the categories of accounts.
8. What account titles would you suggest for the chart of accounts for a city touring company owned by W. Sanders? List the accounts by account category and include an appropriate account number for each.

Exercises

EXERCISE 1-1 Complete the following equations:

LO 1

PRACTICE EXERCISE 1

a. Assets of $22,000 = Liabilities of $7,200 + Owner's Equity of $_____
b. Assets of $_____ – Liabilities of $18,000 = Owner's Equity of $22,000
c. Assets of $27,000 – Owner's Equity of $15,000 = Liabilities of $_____

EXERCISE 1-2 Determine the following amounts:

LO 1

PRACTICE EXERCISE 1

a. The amount of the liabilities of a business that has $60,800 in assets and in which the owner has $34,500 equity.
b. The equity of the owner of a tour bus that cost $57,000 who owes $21,800 on an installment loan payable to the bank.
c. The amount of the assets of a business that has $11,780 in liabilities and in which the owner has $28,500 equity.

EXERCISE 1-3 Dr. L. M. Patton is an ophthalmologist. As of December 31, Dr. Patton owned the following property that related to his professional practice, Patton Eye Clinic:

LO 1

PRACTICE EXERCISE 1

Cash, $2,995
Professional Equipment, $63,000
Office Equipment, $8,450

On the same date, he owed the following business creditors:

Munez Supply Company, $3,816
Martin Equipment Sales, $3,728

Compute the following amounts in the accounting equation:

Assets $_____ = Liabilities $_____ + Owner's Equity $_____

1,3 LO

PRACTICE EXERCISES 1,3

EXERCISE 1-4 Describe a business transaction that will do the following:

a. Increase an asset and increase a liability
b. Decrease an asset and decrease a liability
c. Decrease an asset and increase an expense
d. Increase an asset and increase owner's equity
e. Increase an asset and decrease an asset
f. Increase an asset and increase revenue

2 LO

PRACTICE EXERCISE 2

EXERCISE 1-5 Describe a transaction that resulted in each of the following entries affecting the accounting equation.

		Assets			=	Liabilities	+	Owner's Equity
	Cash	+ Office Equipment +	Professional Equipment	=		Accounts Payable	+	B. Lake, Capital
(a)	+18,200							+18,200
(b)	−1,375		+1,375					
Bal.	16,825	+	1,375	=				18,200
(c)		+640				+640		
Bal.	16,825 +	640	+ 1,375	=		640	+	18,200
(d)	−2,200		+7,000			+4,800		
Bal.	14,625 +	640	+ 8,375	=		5,440	+	18,200
(e)	−1,000					−1,000		
Bal.	13,625 +	640	+ 8,375	=		4,440	+	18,200

1,3 LO

PRACTICE EXERCISES 1,3

EXERCISE 1-6 Label each of the following accounts as an asset (A), liability (L), owner's equity (OE), revenue (R), or expense (E):

a. Office Supplies Expense
b. Professional Fees
c. Prepaid Insurance
d. R. Baker, Drawing
e. Accounts Payable
f. Service Income
g. R. Baker, Capital
h. Rent Expense
i. Accounts Receivable
j. Wages Expense

4 LO

PRACTICE EXERCISES 2,4

EXERCISE 1-7 Describe a transaction that resulted in the following changes in accounts:

a. Rent Expense is increased by $1,050, and Cash is decreased by $1,050.
b. Advertising Expense is increased by $835, and Accounts Payable is increased by $835.
c. Accounts Receivable is increased by $372, and Service Income is increased by $372.
d. Cash is decreased by $410, and C. Tryon, Drawing, is increased by $410.
e. Equipment is increased by $1,850, Cash is decreased by $850, and Accounts Payable is increased by $1,000.
f. Cash is increased by $1,650, and Accounts Receivable is decreased by $1,650.

EXERCISE 1-8 Describe the transactions that are recorded in the following equation.

	Assets			= Liabilities +		Owner's Equity				
Cash	+	Accounts Receivable	+ Equipment =	Accounts Payable	+	J. Onyx, Capital	− J. Onyx, Drawing	+ Revenue	−	Expenses
(a) +25,000			+4,500			+29,500				
(b) −1,250										+1,250 (Rent Expense)
Bal. 23,750			+ 4,500 =			29,500			−	1,250
(c)		+2,000						+2,000 (Income from Services)		
Bal. 23,750	+	2,000	+ 4,500 =			29,500		+ 2,000	−	1,250
(d) −3,700			+16,000	+12,300						
Bal. 20,050	+	2,000	+ 20,500 =	12,300	+	29,500		+ 2,000	−	1,250
(e) −2,500							+2,500			
Bal. 17,550	+	2,000	+ 20,500 =	12,300	+	29,500	− 2,500	+ 2,000	−	1,250

40,050   40,050

Problem Set A

For additional help, see the demonstration problem at the beginning of each chapter in your Working Papers.

PROBLEM 1-1A On June 1 of this year, J. Larkin, Optometrist, established the Larkin Eye Clinic. The clinic's account names are presented below. Transactions completed during the month follow.

	Assets		= Liabilities	+	Owner's Equity			
Cash	+	Office Equipment	= Accounts Payable	+	Capital − Drawing	+ Revenue	− Expenses	

a. Larkin deposited $25,000 in a bank account in the name of the business.
b. Paid the office rent for the month, $950, Ck. No. 1001 (Rent Expense).
c. Bought supplies for cash, $357, Ck. No. 1002 (Supplies Expense).
d. Bought office equipment on account from NYC Office Equipment Store, $8,956.
e. Bought a computer from Warden's Office Outfitters, $1,636, paying $750 in cash and placing the balance on account, Ck. No. 1003.
f. Sold professional services for cash, $3,482 (Professional Fees).
g. Paid on account to Warden's Office Outfitters, a creditor, $900, Ck. No. 1004.
h. Received and paid the bill for utilities, $382, Ck. No. 1005 (Utilities Expense).
i. Paid the salary of the assistant, $1,050, Ck. No. 1006 (Salary Expense).
j. Sold professional services for cash, $3,295 (Professional Fees).
k. Larkin withdrew cash for personal use, $1,250, Ck. No. 1007 (J. Larkin, Drawing).

Required

1. In the equation, write the owner's name above the terms *Capital* and *Drawing*.
2. Record the transactions and the balance after each transaction. Identify the account affected when the transaction involves revenues or expenses.
3. Write the account totals from the left side of the equals sign and add them. Write the account totals from the right side of the equals sign and add them. If the two totals are not equal, first check the addition and subtraction. If you still cannot find the error, reanalyze each transaction.

1,2,3,4 **LO**

PROBLEM 1-2A On July 1 of this year, R. Green established the Green Rehab Clinic. The organization's account headings are presented below. Transactions completed during the month of July follow.

Assets			= Liabilities +	Owner's Equity			
	Office	Professional	Accounts	———,	———,		
Cash +	Equipment +	Equipment =	Payable	+ Capital	– Drawing	+ Revenue	– Expenses

a. Green deposited $30,000 in a bank account in the name of the business.
b. Paid the office rent for the month, $1,800, Ck. No. 2001 (Rent Expense).
c. Bought supplies for cash, $362, Ck. No. 2002 (Supplies Expense).
d. Bought professional equipment on account from Rehab Equipment Company, $18,000 (Professional Equipment).
e. Bought office equipment from Hi-Tech Computers, $2,890, paying $890 in cash and placing the balance on account, Ck. No. 2003.
f. Sold professional services for cash, $4,600 (Professional Fees).
g. Paid on account to Rehab Equipment Company, a creditor, $700, Ck. No. 2004.
h. Received and paid the bill for utilities, $367, Ck. No. 2005 (Utilities Expense).
i. Paid the salary of the assistant, $1,150, Ck. No. 2006 (Salary Expense).
j. Sold professional services for cash, $3,868 (Professional Fees).
k. Green withdrew cash for personal use, $1,800, Ck. No. 2007 (R. Green, Drawing).

Required

1. In the equation, write the owner's name above the terms *Capital* and *Drawing*.
2. Record the transactions and the balance after each transaction. Identify the account affected when the transaction involves revenues or expenses.
3. Write the account totals from the left side of the equals sign and add them. Write the account totals from the right side of the equals sign and add them. If the two totals are not equal, first check the addition and subtraction. If you still cannot find the error, reanalyze each transaction.

1,2,3,4 **LO**

PROBLEM 1-3A S. Davis, a graphic artist, opened a studio for her professional practice on August 1. The account headings are presented below. Transactions completed during the month follow.

Assets				= Liabilities +	Owner's Equity			
	Prepaid	Office	Photo	Accounts	———,	———,		
Cash +	Insurance +	Equipment +	Equipment =	Payable	+ Capital	– Drawing	+ Revenue	+ Expenses

a. Davis deposited $20,000 in a bank account in the name of the business.
b. Bought office equipment on account from Starkey Equipment Company, $4,120.
c. Davis invested her personal photographic equipment, $5,370. (Increase the account Photo Equipment and increase the account S. Davis, Capital.)

d. Paid the rent for the month, $1,500, Ck. No. 1000 (Rent Expense).
e. Bought supplies for cash, $215, Ck. No. 1001 (Supplies Expense).
f. Bought insurance for two years, $1,840, Ck. No. 1002.
g. Sold graphic services for cash, $3,616 (Professional Fees).
h. Paid the salary of the part-time assistant, $982, Ck. No. 1003 (Salary Expense).
i. Received and paid the bill for telephone service, $134, Ck. No. 1004 (Telephone Expense).
j. Paid cash for minor repairs to graphics equipment, $185, Ck. No. 1005 (Repair Expense).
k. Sold graphic services for cash, $3,693 (Professional Fees).
l. Paid on account to Starkey Equipment Company, a creditor, $650, Ck. No. 1006.
m. Davis withdrew cash for personal use, $1,800, Ck. No. 1007 (S. Davis, Drawing).

Required

1. In the equation, write the owner's name above the terms *Capital* and *Drawing*.
2. Record the transactions and the balance after each transaction. Identify the account affected when the transaction involves revenues or expenses.
3. Write the account totals from the left side of the equals sign and add them. Write the account totals from the right side of the equals sign and add them. If the two totals are not equal, first check the addition and subtraction. If you still cannot find the error, reanalyze each transaction.

Check Figure
Right side of equals sign total, $31,333

PROBLEM 1-4A On March 1 of this year, B. Gervais established Gervais Catering Service. The account headings are presented below. Transactions completed during the month follow.

 LO 1,2,3,4

	Assets				=	Liabilities +		Owner's Equity			
Cash +	Accounts Receivable +	Prepaid Insurance +	Truck +	Equipment =		Accounts Payable	+ Capital –	Drawing +	Revenue –	Expenses

a. Gervais deposited $25,000 in a bank account in the name of the business.
b. Bought a truck from Kelly Motors for $26,329, paying $8,000 in cash and placing the balance on account, Ck. No. 500.
c. Bought catering equipment on account from Luigi's Equipment, $3,795.
d. Paid the rent for the month, $1,255, Ck. No. 501 (Rent Expense).
e. Bought insurance for the truck for one year, $400, Ck. No. 502.
f. Sold catering services for cash for the first half of the month, $3,012 (Catering Income).
g. Bought supplies for cash, $185, Ck. No. 503 (Supplies Expense).
h. Sold catering services on account, $4,307 (Catering Income).
i. Received and paid the heating bill, $248, Ck. No. 504 (Utilities Expense).
j. Received a bill from GC Gas and Lube for gas and oil for the truck, $128 (Gas and Oil Expense).
k. Sold catering services for cash for the remainder of the month, $2,649 (Catering Income).
l. Gervais withdrew cash for personal use, $1,550, Ck. No. 505 (B. Gervais, Drawing).
m. Paid the salary of the assistant, $1,150, Ck. No. 506 (Salary Expense).

Required

1. In the equation, write the owner's name above the terms *Capital* and *Drawing*.
2. Record the transactions and the balance after each transaction. Identify the account affected when the transaction involves revenues or expenses.
3. Write the account totals from the left side of the equals sign and add them. Write the account totals from the right side of the equals sign and add them. If the two totals are not equal, first check the addition and subtraction. If you still cannot find the error, reanalyze each transaction.

Check Figure
Cash, $17,873

Problem Set B

For additional help, see the demonstration problem at the beginning of each chapter in your Working Papers.

1,2,3,4 **LO**

PROBLEM 1-1B In July of this year, M. Wallace established a business called Wallace Realty. The account headings are presented below. Transactions completed during the month follow.

Assets		= Liabilities +	Owner's Equity				
	Office	Accounts					
Cash +	Equipment =	Payable	+ Capital −	Drawing +	Revenue −	Expenses	

a. Wallace deposited $24,000 in a bank account in the name of the business.
b. Paid the office rent for the current month, $650, Ck. No. 1000 (Rent Expense).
c. Bought office supplies for cash, $375, Ck. No. 1001 (Supplies Expense).
d. Bought office equipment on account from Dellos Computers, $6,300.
e. Received a bill from the *City Crier* for advertising, $455 (Advertising Expense).
f. Sold services for cash, $3,944 (Service Income).
g. Paid on account to Dellos Computers, a creditor, $1,500, Ck. No. 1002.
h. Received and paid the bill for utilities, $340, Ck. No. 1003 (Utilities Expense).
i. Paid on account to the *City Crier*, a creditor, $455, Ck. No. 1004.
j. Paid truck expenses, $435, Ck. No. 1005 (Truck Maintenance Expense).
k. Wallace withdrew cash for personal use, $1,500, Ck. No. 1006 (M. Wallace, Drawing).

Check Figure
Left side of equals sign total, $28,989

Required

1. In the equation, write the owner's name above the terms *Capital* and *Drawing*.
2. Record the transactions and the balance after each transaction. Identify the account affected when the transaction involves revenues or expenses.
3. Write the account totals from the left side of the equals sign and add them. Write the account totals from the right side of the equals sign and add them. If the two totals are not equal, first check the addition and subtraction. If you still cannot find the error, reanalyze each transaction.

1,2,3,4 **LO**

PROBLEM 1-2B In March, K. Haas, M.D., established the Haas Sports Injury Clinic. The clinic's account headings are presented below. Transactions completed during the month of March follow.

Assets		= Liabilities +	Owner's Equity				
	Office	Accounts					
Cash +	Equipment =	Payable	+ Capital −	Drawing +	Revenue −	Expenses	

a. Haas deposited $48,000 in a bank account in the name of the business.
b. Paid the rent for the month, $2,200, Ck. No. 1000 (Rent Expense).
c. Bought supplies for cash from Medco Co., $2,138.
d. Bought professional equipment on account from Med-Tech Company, $18,000.
e. Bought office equipment on account from Equipment Depot, $1,955.
f. Sold professional services for cash, $8,960 (Professional Fees).
g. Paid on account to Med-Tech Company, a creditor, $3,000, Ck. No. 1001.
h. Received and paid the bill for utilities, $472, Ck. No. 1002 (Utilities Expense).
i. Paid the salary of the assistant, $1,738, Ck. No. 1003 (Salary Expense).
j. Sold professional services for cash, $10,196 (Professional Fees).
k. Haas withdrew cash for personal use, $3,500, Ck. No. 1004 (K. Haas, Drawing).

Required

1. In the equation, write the owner's name above the terms *Capital* and *Drawing*.
2. Record the transactions and the balance after each transaction. Identify the account affected when the transaction involves revenue, expenses, or a withdrawal.
3. Write the account totals from the left side of the equals sign and add them. Write the account totals from the right side of the equals sign and add them. If the two totals are not equal, first check the addition and subtraction. If you still cannot find the error, reanalyze each transaction.

PROBLEM 1-3B P. Schwartz, Attorney at Law, opened his office on October 1. The account headings are presented below. Transactions completed during the month follow.

		Assets			= Liabilities +			Owner's Equity		
	Prepaid	Office			Accounts					
Cash +	Insurance +	Equipment +	Library	=	Payable	+ Capital –	Drawing +	Revenue –	Expenses	

a. Schwartz deposited $25,000 in a bank account in the name of the business.
b. Bought office equipment on account from QuipCo, $9,670.
c. Schwartz invested his personal law library, which cost $2,800. (Increase the account Library and increase the account P. Schwartz, Capital.)
d. Paid the office rent for the month, $1,700, Ck. No. 2000 (Rent Expense).
e. Bought office supplies for cash, $418, Ck. No. 2001 (Supplies Expense).
f. Bought insurance for two years, $944, Ck. No. 2002.
g. Sold legal services for cash, $8,518 (Professional Fees).
h. Paid the salary of the part-time receptionist, $1,820, Ck. No. 2003 (Salary Expense).
i. Received and paid the telephone bill, $388, Ck. No. 2004 (Telephone Expense).
j. Received and paid the bill for utilities, $368, Ck. No. 2005 (Utilities Expense).
k. Sold legal services for cash, $9,260 (Professional Fees).
l. Paid on account to QuipCo, a creditor, $2,670, Ck. No. 2006.
m. Schwartz withdrew cash for personal use, $2,500, Ck. No. 2007 (P. Schwartz, Drawing).

Required

1. In the equation, write the owner's name above the terms *Capital* and *Drawing*.
2. Record the transactions and the balance after each transaction. Identify the account affected when the transaction involves revenues or expenses.
3. Write the account totals from the left side of the equals sign and add them. Write the account totals from the right side of the equals sign and add them. If the two totals are not equal, first check the addition and subtraction. If you still cannot find the error, reanalyze each transaction.

PROBLEM 1-4B In March, T. Carter established Carter Delivery Service. The account headings are presented below. Transactions completed during the month of March follow.

		Assets				= Liabilities +			Owner's Equity		
	Accounts	Prepaid				Accounts					
Cash +	Receivable +	Insurance +	Truck +	Equipment	=	Payable	+ Capital –	Drawing +	Revenue –	Expenses	

a. Carter deposited $25,000 in a bank account in the name of the business.
b. Bought a used business from Degroot Motors for $15,140, paying $5,140 in cash and placing the remainder on account.

   c.   Bought equipment on account from Flemming Company, $3,450.
   d.   Paid the rent for the month, $1,000, Ck. No. 3001 (Rent Expense).
   e.   Sold services for cash for the first half of the month, $6,927 (Service Income).
   f.   Bought supplies for cash, $301, Ck. No. 3002 (Supplies Expense).
   g.   Bought insurance for the truck for the year, $1,200, Ck. No. 3003.
   h.   Received and paid the bill for utilities, $349, Ck. No. 3004 (Utilities Expense).
   i.   Received a bill for gas and oil for the truck, $218 (Gas and Oil Expense).
   j.   Sold services on account, $3,603 (Service Income).
   k.   Sold services for cash for the remainder of the month, $4,612 (Service Income).
   l.   Paid wages to the employees, $3,958, Ck. Nos. 3005–3007 (Wages Expense).
   m.   Carter withdrew cash for personal use, $1,250, Ck. No. 3008 (T. Carter, Drawing).

Check Figure
Cash, $23,341

Required

1. In the equation, write the owner's name above the terms *Capital* and *Drawing*.
2. Record the transactions and the balance after each transaction. Identify the account affected when the transaction involves revenues or expenses.
3. Write the account totals from the left side of the equals sign and add them. Write the account totals from the right side of the equals sign and add them. If the two totals are not equal, first check the addition and subtraction. If you still cannot find the error, reanalyze each transaction.

ACTIVITIES

CONSIDER AND COMMUNICATE

A friend of yours wants to start her own pet sitting business. She already has a business license that is required in her city. She has had a personal checking account for years. You have told her that she also needs to open a separate account for her business needs, but she does not understand why she needs to have two separate accounts. Explain to her why she should have a business account separate from her personal account. Use some of the language of business you have learned in your text's Introduction and in this chapter.

CRITICAL THINKING

Please read the following memorandum and follow the instructions set forth.

MEMORANDUM

TO: Your Name   DATE: July 31, 20—
FROM: J. Perrault, Supervisor   SUBJECT: Calculations for Richter Co.

Please provide the following ASAP (as soon as possible).

1. The balance of cash in Richter Company's checkbook shows $13,364. I need to know if this ties to or matches the Cash account balance. I do know that total assets amount to $43,560, Office Equipment amounts to $3,896, and other noncash assets are Professional Equipment, $24,375 and Prepaid Insurance, $1,925.
2. D. Richter, the owner, wants to know the amount of his owner's equity. I pulled the outstanding bills, which amount to $7,942.
3. Please put the information in a memo addressed to me.
4. Thank you for your prompt response.

T Accounts, Debits and Credits, Trial Balance, and Financial Statements

2

SOLID ROCK GYM, Phoenix, Arizona

Individuals and groups of all ages come to Solid Rock Gym for fun and fitness. Part of the appeal of Solid Rock Gym, whose services include several types of indoor rock-climbing experiences, is around-the-clock access with its all-day-and-night passes. Services include individual and group instruction, team development, fitness programs, and bouldering (climbing close to the bottom—no rope or hardware), top-roping (climbing while protected by a rope running through anchors above the intended route), or lead climbing (climbing while protected by a rope clipped to anchors as the climber ascends a route).

In Chapter 1, we learned that a company such as Solid Rock Gym would have a chart of accounts with many different kinds of accounts. Can you imagine the kinds of accounts that Solid Rock Gym might have? In this chapter, you will learn that the chart of accounts can be used as the starting point for recording transactions with T accounts and debits and credits.

WHY IT MATTERS

LEARNING OBJECTIVES

After you have completed this chapter, you will be able to do the following:

1 Determine balances of T accounts having entries recorded on both sides of the accounts.

2 Present the fundamental accounting equation using the T account form, and label the plus and minus sides.

3 Present the fundamental accounting equation using the T account form, and label the debit and credit sides.

4 Record directly in T accounts a group of business transactions involving changes in asset, liability, owner's equity, revenue, and expense accounts for a service business.

5 Prepare a trial balance.

6 Prepare (a) an income statement, (b) a statement of owner's equity, and (c) a balance sheet.

7 Recognize the effect of transpositions and slides on account balances.

ACCOUNTING LANGUAGE

Balance sheet (p. 58)
Compound entry (p. 53)
Credit (p. 45)
Debit (p. 45)
Financial position (p. 58)
Financial statement (p. 56)
Footings (p. 44)
Income statement (p. 56)
Net income (p. 56)

Net loss (p. 56)
Normal balance (p. 44)
Report form (p. 58)
Slide (p. 60)
Statement of owner's equity (p. 58)
T account form (p. 43)
Transposition (p. 60)
Trial balance (p. 55)

In the previous chapter, we introduced the fundamental accounting equation as *Assets = Liabilities + Owner's Equity*. We also discussed the recording of transactions involving two other classifications of accounts: *Revenue* and *Expenses*. With the addition of Revenue and Expenses, the fundamental accounting equation was brought up to its full size of five account classifications: Assets, Liabilities, Owner's Equity, Revenue, and Expenses. There are only five classifications in accounting; so, whether you are dealing with a small, one-owner business or a large corporation, there will be these five major classifications of accounts only.

In this chapter, we will record the same transactions from Chapter 1 (see pages 14–27) in T account form and prove the equality of both sides of the fundamental accounting equation using a trial balance, which is discussed later in this chapter.

THE T ACCOUNT FORM

In Chapter 1, we recorded business transactions in a column arrangement. For example, the Cash account column in the books of Conner's Whitewater Adventures is as follows:

Cash Account Column

Transaction	(a)	90,000
Transaction	(b)	–38,000
Balance		52,000
Transaction	(d)	–2,000
Balance		50,000
Transaction	(f)	+8,000
Balance		58,000
Transaction	(g)	–1,250
Balance		56,750
Transaction	(i)	–1,875
Balance		54,875
Transaction	(l)	–1,500
Balance		53,375
Transaction	(m)	–225
Balance		53,150
Transaction	(n)	–620
Balance		52,530
Transaction	(o)	–2,360
Balance		50,170
Transaction	(p)	–1,850
Balance		48,320
Transaction	(q)	+2,500
Balance		50,820
Transaction	(r)	+8,570
Balance		59,390
Transaction	(s)	–3,500
		55,890

Cash

	+		–
(a)	90,000	(b)	38,000
(f)	8,000	(d)	2,000
(q)	2,500	(g)	1,250
(r)	8,570	(i)	1,875
		(l)	1,500
	109,070	(m)	225
		(n)	620
		(o)	2,360
		(p)	1,850
		(s)	3,500
Footings			
Balance → 55,890			53,180

As an introduction to the recording of transactions, the column arrangement had the following advantages:

1. In the process of analyzing the transaction, you

   a. Recognized the need to determine which accounts are involved.

   b. Determined the classification of the accounts involved.

   c. Decided whether the transaction resulted in an increase or a decrease in each of these accounts.

2. You further realized that, after each transaction was recorded, the two sides of the fundamental accounting equation were in balance. In other words, the total of one side of the accounting equation equaled the total of the other side.

Now, instead of recording transactions in a column for each account, we will use a **T account form** for each account, as shown in the Cash T account above. *The T account form has the advantage of providing two sides for each account; one side is used to record increases in the account, and the other side is used to record decreases.*

After we record a group of transactions in a T account, we add both sides and record the totals in small, pencil-written figures called **footings**. Next, we subtract one footing from the other to determine the balance of the account. For the Cash account, shown previously, the balance is $55,890 ($109,070 − $53,180).

We now record the balance on the side of the account having the larger footing, which, with a few minor exceptions, is the plus (+) side. The plus side of a T account is the side that represents the **normal balance** of that account. The normal balance may, however, fall on either the left or the right side of an account, depending on the type of account.

LEARNING OBJECTIVE **1**

Determine balances of T accounts having entries recorded on both sides of the accounts.

How to Determine Balances of T Accounts

STEP 1. Add each side separately and record the totals (called footing).

STEP 2. Subtract the large footing number from the small footing number.

STEP 3. Record the balance on the large footing side.

To review, we presented the T account for Cash. Cash is classified as an asset, and all assets look like the following T account:

Assets

+	−
Left	Right

However, **not all classifications of accounts have the increase side on the left.**

Recall that we placed revenue and expenses under the umbrella of owner's equity. Revenue increases owner's equity, and expenses decrease owner's equity. The T accounts for this situation are as follows:

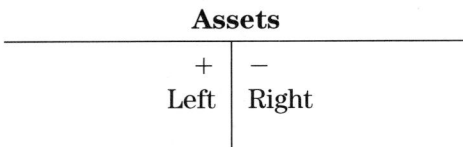

Owner's Equity

−	+
Left	Right
↓	↓
Expenses	**Revenue**

Expenses cause a decrease in owner's equity

Expenses

+	−
Left	Right

Revenues cause an increase in owner's equity

Revenue

−	+
Left	Right

Increases in owner's equity are recorded on the right side of the account. Because revenue increases owner's equity, additions to revenue are also recorded on the right side.

Decreases in owner's equity are recorded on the left side of the account. Because expenses decrease owner's equity, additions to expenses are also recorded on the left side.

Using the five classifications of accounts, the fundamental accounting equation looks like this:

Assets = Liabilities + **Owner's Equity**

Capital − Drawing + Revenue − Expenses

Because revenue and expenses appear separately on the income statement, we will stretch out the equation to include them as separate headings, as shown here:

Assets = Liabilities + Owner's Equity + Revenue − Expenses

We can now restate the equation with the T account forms and plus and minus signs for each account classification:

Assets	=	Liabilities	+	Owner's Equity	+	Revenue	–	Expenses
+ | –		– | +		– | +		– | +		+ | –
Left | Right		Left | Right		Left | Right		Left | Right		Left | Right

Before we go on, let us point out the increase, or plus, side of each account classification. You can recognize these in the accounting equation using T accounts.

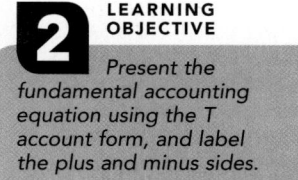

2 LEARNING OBJECTIVE

Present the fundamental accounting equation using the T account form, and label the plus and minus sides.

Assets　　　　　　The *left* side is the *increase* side.
Liabilities　　　　The *right* side is the *increase* side.
Owner's Equity　The *right* side is the *increase* side.
Revenue　　　　The *right* side is the *increase* side.
Expenses　　　　The *left* side is the *increase* side.

Because revenue is an addition to owner's equity, the placement of the plus and minus signs is the same as for owner's equity. On the other hand, because expenses are treated as deductions from owner's equity, the placement of the plus and minus signs is reversed. We will use this form of the fundamental accounting equation throughout the remainder of the text.

Your accounting background up to this point has taught you to analyze business transactions to determine which accounts are involved and to recognize that each amount should be recorded as either an increase or a decrease in these accounts. Now the recording process becomes a simple matter of knowing which side of the T accounts should be used to record increases and which should be used to record decreases. **Generally, you will not be using the minus side of the revenue and expense accounts, since transactions involving revenue and expense accounts usually result in increases in these accounts.** An exception to this statement is where errors have been made and require correction. Let's now add the last element to the T account before we record the familiar Conner's Whitewater Adventures transactions.

THE T ACCOUNT FORM WITH DEBITS AND CREDITS

The left side of a T account is called the **debit** side; the right side is called the **credit** side. The T accounts representing the accounting equation now contain both the signs and the words *Debit* and *Credit*. There are only five classifications of accounts. These classifications are contained in the fundamental accounting equation:

3 LEARNING OBJECTIVE

Present the fundamental accounting equation using the T account form, and label the debit and credit sides.

Assets	=	Liabilities	+	Owner's Equity	+	Revenue	–	Expenses
+ | –		– | +		– | +		– | +		+ | –
Debit | Credit		Debit | Credit		Debit | Credit		Debit | Credit		Debit | Credit

Before we begin recording transactions, notice the new T account following the Capital account, Drawing. Recall that the Capital account is increased when amounts are invested and decreased when amounts are taken out.

Capital

–	+
Debit	Credit
	Amounts invested

Drawing

+ Debit Amounts withdrawn	− Credit

We reserve the minus or debit side of the Capital account for permanent withdrawals, those made when the owner decides to reduce the size of the business permanently or when a net loss forces such a reduction. This concept is best illustrated by showing the Drawing T account under the umbrella of the Capital T account.

Capital

− Debit	+ Credit

Drawing

+ Debit	− Credit

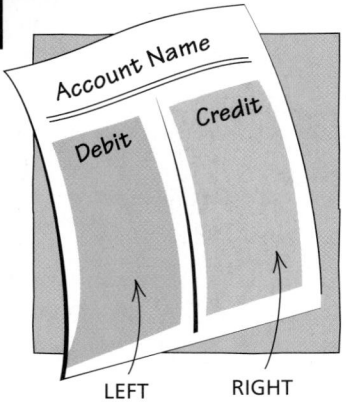

Debit is always the left side of the account, and credit is always the right side of the account. The + or −, however, changes with the type of account.

The following table summarizes debits and credits and how they are affected by increases and decreases. **The critical rule to remember is that the amount placed on the debit side of one or more accounts MUST equal the amount placed on the credit side of another account or accounts.**

Debits Signify		Credits Signify	
Increases in	Assets Drawing Expenses	Decreases in	Assets Drawing Expenses
Decreases in	Liabilities Capital Revenue	Increases in	Liabilities Capital Revenue

RECORDING BUSINESS TRANSACTIONS IN T ACCOUNTS

LEARNING OBJECTIVE 4

Record directly in T accounts a group of business transactions involving changes in asset, liability, owner's equity, revenue, and expense accounts for a service business.

Our task now is to learn how to record business transactions in the T account form. First, let's review the steps in analyzing a business transaction.

STEP 1. Decide which accounts are involved.

STEP 2. Classify the accounts involved (asset, liability, owner's equity, revenue, expense).

STEP 3. Decide if the accounts involved are increased or decreased.

STEP 4. Write the transaction as a debit to one account (or accounts) and a credit to another account (or accounts).

STEP 5. Check to see if the equation is in balance after the transaction has been recorded.

For example, let's analyze the first transaction of the Conner's Whitewater Adventures transactions using this five-step process. To formulate the entry, you must be able to visualize the fundamental accounting equation in the form of T accounts. With that in mind, the first transaction is as follows:

In transaction (a), Conner deposited $90,000 in a bank account in the name of the business. This transaction results in an increase to Cash with a debit and an increase in the Capital account with a credit.

STEP 1. Decide which accounts are involved. The two accounts involved are Cash and J. Conner, Capital.

STEP 2. Classify the accounts involved (asset, liability, owner's equity, revenue, expense). Cash is an asset and J. Conner, Capital, is an owner's equity account.

STEP 3. Decide if the accounts involved are increased or decreased. Cash is being deposited in the bank account, an increase to Cash. The owner has invested that cash in the business and has increased J. Conner, Capital.

STEP 4. Write the transaction as a debit to one account (or accounts) and a credit to another account (or accounts). Since Cash is an asset and Cash is increased, Cash is debited. We now need an offsetting credit. J. Conner, Capital, is an owner's equity account and is increased. J. Conner, Capital, is credited.

STEP 5. Check to see if the equation is in balance. There is at least one account debited and at least one account credited, *and* the total amount(s) debited equals the total amount(s) credited. You now have a debit equal to a credit, a $90,000 debit to Cash and a $90,000 credit to J. Conner, Capital.

© CREATAS/PHOTOLIBRARY

Stores such as this bike shop classify revenue accounts for each activity—sales, repairs, and rentals. They also classify expense accounts separately.

The resulting transaction in T account form follows:

Assets	=	Liabilities	+	Owner's Equity	+	Revenue	−	Expenses
+ | −		− | +		− | +		− | +		+ | −
Debit | Credit		Debit | Credit		Debit | Credit		Debit | Credit		Debit | Credit

Cash

+	−
Debit	Credit
(a) 90,000	

J. Conner, Capital

−	+
Debit	Credit
	(a) 90,000

In transaction (b), Conner's Whitewater Adventures bought equipment, paying cash, $38,000. This transaction results in an increase to Equipment with a debit and a decrease to Cash with a credit.

Assets	=	Liabilities	+	Owner's Equity	+	Revenue	−	Expenses
+ | −		− | +		− | +		− | +		+ | −
Debit | Credit		Debit | Credit		Debit | Credit		Debit | Credit		Debit | Credit

Cash

+	−
Debit	Credit
	(b) 38,000

Equipment

+	−
Debit	Credit
(b) 38,000	

> When we describe the transactions of the business, notice that we say "Conner's Whitewater Adventure's paid or bought" and "J. Conner paid or bought." We do so because the business is treated as a separate economic entity—independent and separate from its owner.

Remember

In transaction (c), Conner's Whitewater Adventures bought equipment on account from Signal Products, $4,320. This transaction results in an increase to Equipment with a debit and an increase to Accounts Payable with a credit and is shown in T account form as follows:

Assets	=	Liabilities	+	Owner's Equity	+	Revenue	–	Expenses
+ –		– +		– +		– +		+ –
Debit Credit		Debit Credit		Debit Credit		Debit Credit		Debit Credit

Equipment	Accounts Payable
+ –	– +
Debit Credit	Debit Credit
(c) 4,320	(c) 4,320

In transaction (d), Conner's Whitewater Adventures paid Signal Products, a creditor, $2,000. This transaction results in a decrease to Cash with a credit and a decrease to Accounts Payable with a debit.

Assets	=	Liabilities	+	Owner's Equity	+	Revenue	–	Expenses
+ –		– +		– +		– +		+ –
Debit Credit		Debit Credit		Debit Credit		Debit Credit		Debit Credit

Cash	Accounts Payable
+ –	– +
Debit Credit	Debit Credit
(d) 2,000	(d) 2,000

In transaction (e), J. Conner invests her personal computer, with a fair market value of $5,200, in the business.

Assets	=	Liabilities	+	Owner's Equity	+	Revenue	–	Expenses
+ –		– +		– +		– +		+ –
Debit Credit		Debit Credit		Debit Credit		Debit Credit		Debit Credit

Equipment	J. Conner, Capital
+ –	– +
Debit Credit	Debit Credit
(e) 5,200	(e) 5,200

Here is a restatement of the accounts after recording transactions (a) through (e). To test your understanding of the process, trace through the recording of each transaction and describe what happened in the transaction. Footings or subtotals (remember, always write the footings smaller than the entries and in pencil) are required to compute the balances of the accounts. The balances are written in the accounts on the side with the larger total.

Assets	=	Liabilities	+	Owner's Equity	+	Revenue	−	Expenses
+ −		− +		− +		− +		+ −
Debit Credit		Debit Credit		Debit Credit		Debit Credit		Debit Credit

Cash

+	−
Debit	Credit
(a) 90,000	(b) 38,000
	(d) 2,000
	40,000
Bal. 50,000	

Accounts Receivable

+	−
Debit	Credit

Prepaid Insurance

+	−
Debit	Credit

Equipment

+	−
Debit	Credit
(b) 38,000	
(c) 4,320	
(e) 5,200	
Bal. 47,520	

Accounts Payable

−	+
Debit	Credit
(d) 2,000	(c) 4,320
	Bal. 2,320

J. Conner, Capital

−	+
Debit	Credit
	(a) 90,000
	(e) 5,200
	Bal. 95,200

J. Conner, Drawing

+	−
Debit	Credit

Income from Tours

−	+
Debit	Credit

Wages Expense

+	−
Debit	Credit

Rent Expense

+	−
Debit	Credit

Supplies Expense

+	−
Debit	Credit

Advertising Expense

+	−
Debit	Credit

Utilities Expense

+	−
Debit	Credit

Let's pause to see if the debits are equal to the credits by listing the balances of the accounts:

Account Name	Accounts with Normal Balances on the Left or Debit Side: Assets Drawing Expenses	Accounts with Normal Balances on the Right or Credit Side: Liabilities Capital Revenue
Cash	$50,000	
Equipment	47,520	
Accounts Payable		$ 2,320
J. Conner, Capital		95,200
	$97,520	$97,520

Remember

The normal balance of an account classification is on the plus side.

FYI

The T account is not only a learning tool; it will serve you well as a problem-solving device when you need to analyze a transaction, whether recording it manually or on a computer.

In transaction (f), Conner's Whitewater Adventures sold rafting tours for cash, $8,000. This transaction results in an increase to Cash with a debit and an increase to Income from Tours with a credit.

Assets	=	Liabilities	+	Owner's Equity	+	Revenue	–	Expenses
+ –		– +		– +		– +		+ –
Debit Credit		Debit Credit		Debit Credit		Debit Credit		Debit Credit

Cash

+	–
Debit	Credit
(f) 8,000	

Income from Tours

–	+
Debit	Credit
	(f) 8,000

In transaction (g), Conner's Whitewater Adventures paid rent for the month, $1,250. This transaction results in an increase to Rent Expense with a debit and a decrease to Cash with a credit.

Assets	=	Liabilities	+	Owner's Equity	+	Revenue	–	Expenses
+ –		– +		– +		– +		+ –
Debit Credit		Debit Credit		Debit Credit		Debit Credit		Debit Credit

Cash

+	–
Debit	Credit
	(g) 1,250

Rent Expense

+	–
Debit	Credit
(g) 1,250	

In transaction (h), Conner's Whitewater Adventures bought computer paper, ink cartridges, invoice pads, pens and pencils, folders, filing cabinets, and 10-key calculators on account. These items are considered to be supplies to be used up by Conner's Whitewater Adventures and are recorded as an expense for $675 on account from Fineman Company. This transaction results in an increase to Supplies Expense with a debit and an increase to Accounts Payable with a credit.

Assets	=	Liabilities	+	Owner's Equity	+	Revenue	–	Expenses
+ –		– +		– +		– +		+ –
Debit Credit		Debit Credit		Debit Credit		Debit Credit		Debit Credit

Accounts Payable

–	+
Debit	Credit
	(h) 675

Supplies Expense

+	–
Debit	Credit
(h) 675	

In transaction (i), Conner's Whitewater Adventures bought a three-month liability insurance policy, $1,875. This transaction results in an increase to Prepaid Insurance with a debit and a decrease to Cash with a credit.

Assets	=	Liabilities	+	Owner's Equity	+	Revenue	–	Expenses
+ –		– +		– +		– +		+ –
Debit Credit		Debit Credit		Debit Credit		Debit Credit		Debit Credit

Cash

+	–
Debit	Credit
	(i) 1,875

Prepaid Insurance

+	–
Debit	Credit
(i) 1,875	

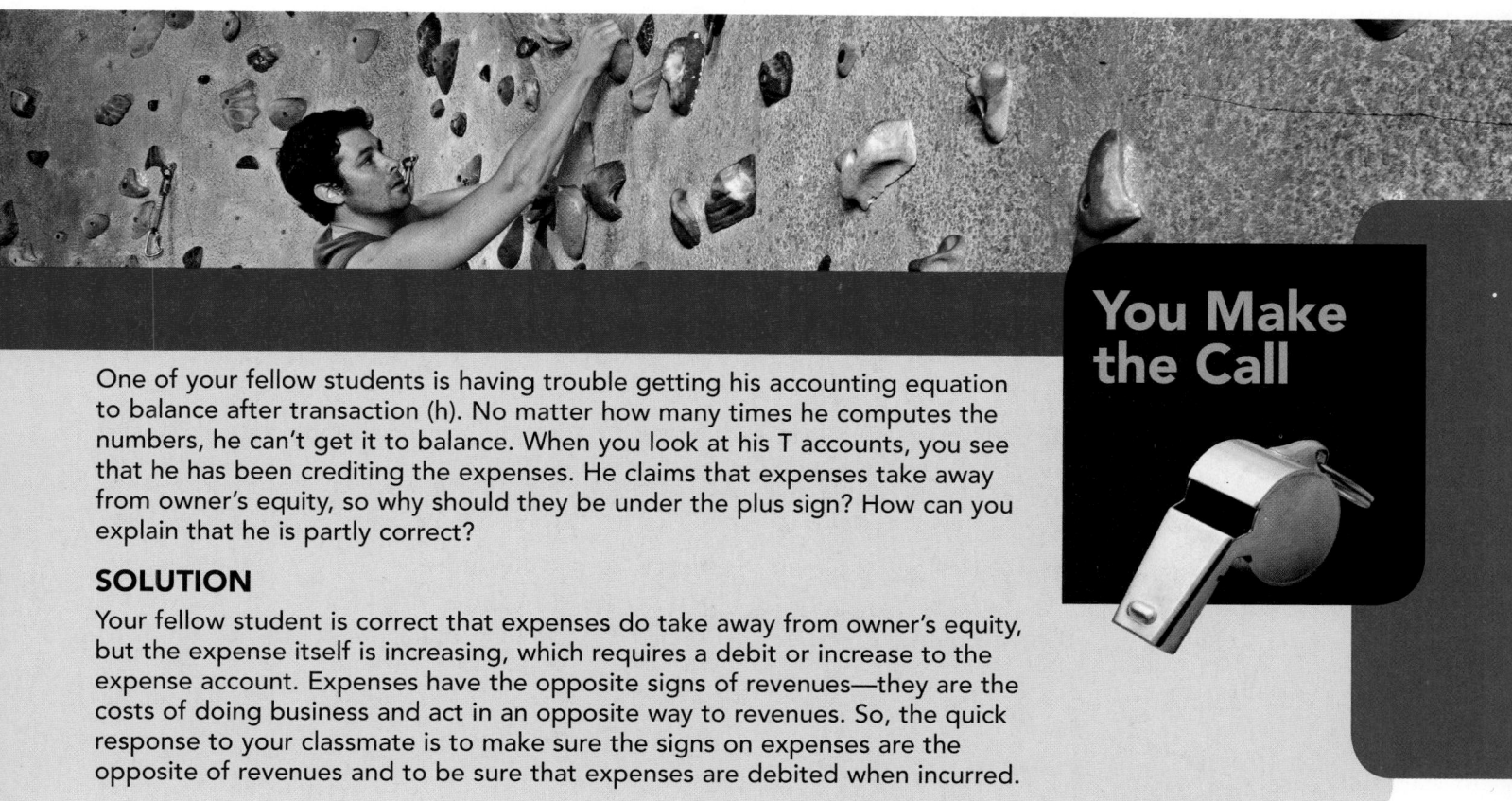

You Make the Call

One of your fellow students is having trouble getting his accounting equation to balance after transaction (h). No matter how many times he computes the numbers, he can't get it to balance. When you look at his T accounts, you see that he has been crediting the expenses. He claims that expenses take away from owner's equity, so why should they be under the plus sign? How can you explain that he is partly correct?

SOLUTION

Your fellow student is correct that expenses do take away from owner's equity, but the expense itself is increasing, which requires a debit or increase to the expense account. Expenses have the opposite signs of revenues—they are the costs of doing business and act in an opposite way to revenues. So, the quick response to your classmate is to make sure the signs on expenses are the opposite of revenues and to be sure that expenses are debited when incurred.

In transaction (j), Conner's Whitewater Adventures received a bill for newspaper advertising from *The Times*, $620. This results in an increase to Advertising Expense with a debit and an increase to Accounts Payable with a credit.

Assets		=	Liabilities		+	Owner's Equity		+	Revenue		–	Expenses	
+	–		–	+		–	+		–	+		+	–
Debit	Credit		Debit	Credit		Debit	Credit		Debit	Credit		Debit	Credit

Accounts Payable

–	+
Debit	Credit
	(j) 620

Advertising Expense

+	–
Debit	Credit
(j) 620	

In transaction (k), Conner's Whitewater Adventures signs a contract with Crystal River Lodge to provide rafting adventures for guests. Conner's Whitewater Adventures provides 27 one-day rafting tours and bills Crystal River Lodge for $6,750. This results in an increase to Accounts Receivable with a debit and an increase to Income from Tours with a credit.

Assets		=	Liabilities		+	Owner's Equity		+	Revenue		–	Expenses	
+	–		–	+		–	+		–	+		+	–
Debit	Credit		Debit	Credit		Debit	Credit		Debit	Credit		Debit	Credit

Accounts Receivable

+	–
Debit	Credit
(k) 6,750	

Income from Tours

–	+
Debit	Credit
	(k) 6,750

In transaction (l), Conner's Whitewater Adventures pays on account to Signal Products, $1,500. This transaction results in a decrease to Accounts Payable with a debit and a decrease to Cash with a credit.

Assets	=	Liabilities	+	Owner's Equity	+	Revenue	–	Expenses
+ | –		– | +		– | +		– | +		+ | –
Debit | Credit		Debit | Credit		Debit | Credit		Debit | Credit		Debit | Credit

Cash	Accounts Payable
+ | –	– | +
Debit | Credit	Debit | Credit
(1) 1,500	(1) 1,500

In transaction (m), Conner's Whitewater Adventures received and paid Solar Power, Inc. for the electric bill, $225. The result of this transaction is an increase to Utilities Expense with a debit and a decrease to Cash with a credit.

Assets	=	Liabilities	+	Owner's Equity	+	Revenue	–	Expenses
+ | –		– | +		– | +		– | +		+ | –
Debit | Credit		Debit | Credit		Debit | Credit		Debit | Credit		Debit | Credit

Cash	Utilities Expense
+ | –	+ | –
Debit | Credit	Debit | Credit
(m) 225	(m) 225

In transaction (n), Conner's Whitewater Adventures paid on account to *The Times*, $620. This transaction results in a decrease to Accounts Payable with a debit and a decrease to Cash with a credit. **Recall that this bill had previously been recorded as a liability in transaction (j).**

Assets	=	Liabilities	+	Owner's Equity	+	Revenue	–	Expenses
+ | –		– | +		– | +		– | +		+ | –
Debit | Credit		Debit | Credit		Debit | Credit		Debit | Credit		Debit | Credit

Cash	Accounts Payable
+ | –	– | +
Debit | Credit	Debit | Credit
(n) 620	(n) 620

In transaction (o), Conner's Whitewater Adventures paid the wages of a part-time employee, $2,360. This transaction results in an increase to Wages Expense with a debit and a decrease to Cash with a credit.

Assets	=	Liabilities	+	Owner's Equity	+	Revenue	–	Expenses
+ | –		– | +		– | +		– | +		+ | –
Debit | Credit		Debit | Credit		Debit | Credit		Debit | Credit		Debit | Credit

Cash	Wages Expense
+ | –	+ | –
Debit | Credit	Debit | Credit
(o) 2,360	(o) 2,360

In transaction (p), Conner's Whitewater Adventures bought additional equipment from Signal Products, $3,780, paying $1,850 in cash and placing the balance on account. This transaction results in an increase to Equipment with a debit, an increase to Accounts Payable with a credit, and a decrease to Cash with a credit. This is called a **compound entry**; that is, more than one debit or more than one credit is recorded.

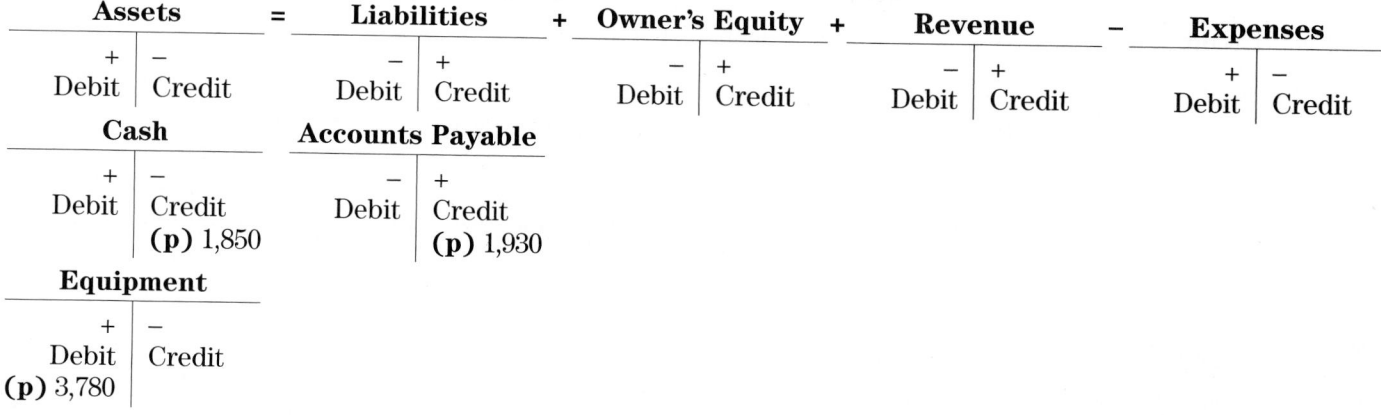

In transaction (q), Conner's Whitewater Adventures received $2,500 cash from Crystal River Lodge to apply against the amount billed in transaction (k). This transaction results in an increase to Cash with a debit and a decrease to Accounts Receivable with a credit.

Assets	=	Liabilities	+	Owner's Equity	+	Revenue	−	Expenses
+ −		− +		− +		− +		+ −
Debit Credit		Debit Credit		Debit Credit		Debit Credit		Debit Credit

Cash

+	−
Debit	Credit
(q) 2,500	

Accounts Receivable

+	−
Debit	Credit
	(q) 2,500

In transaction (r), Conner's Whitewater Adventures sold tours for cash, $8,570. This transaction results in an increase to Cash with a debit and an increase to Income from Tours with a credit.

Assets	=	Liabilities	+	Owner's Equity	+	Revenue	−	Expenses
+ −		− +		− +		− +		+ −
Debit Credit		Debit Credit		Debit Credit		Debit Credit		Debit Credit

Cash

+	−
Debit	Credit
(r) 8,570	

Income from Tours

−	+
Debit	Credit
	(r) 8,570

In transaction (s), J. Conner withdrew cash for her personal use, $3,500. This transaction increases J. Conner, Drawing with a debit and decreases Cash with a credit.

Assets	=	Liabilities	+	Owner's Equity	+	Revenue	−	Expenses
+ | −		− | +		− | +		− | +		+ | −
Debit | Credit		Debit | Credit		Debit | Credit		Debit | Credit		Debit | Credit

Cash

+	−
Debit	Credit
	(s) 3,500

J. Conner, Drawing

+	−
Debit	Credit
(s) 3,500	

The Drawing account is used to record any withdrawals by the owner from the business for his or her living expenses. The owner hopes that the withdrawals will be offset by net income which will cause the Capital account to be increased. If, instead, the withdrawals are more than net income, the Capital account will be decreased.

Summary of Transactions

The following T accounts provide a summary of all transactions for Conner's Whitewater Adventures. Footings are shown in color. You will notice that the balance of each account is normally on the plus side. Note that, in recording expenses, you normally place the entries only on the plus, or debit, side. Also, in recording revenue, you normally place the entries only on the plus, or credit, side.

Assets	=	Liabilities	+	Owner's Equity	+	Revenue	−	Expenses
+ | −		− | +		− | +		− | +		+ | −
Debit | Credit		Debit | Credit		Debit | Credit		Debit | Credit		Debit | Credit

Cash

+		−	
(a)	90,000	(b)	38,000
(f)	8,000	(d)	2,000
(q)	2,500	(g)	1,250
(r)	8,570	(i)	1,875
	109,070	(l)	1,500
		(m)	225
		(n)	620
		(o)	2,360
		(p)	1,850
		(s)	3,500
			53,180
Bal. 55,890			

Accounts Receivable

+		−	
(k)	6,750	(q)	2,500
Bal. 4,250			

Prepaid Insurance

+		−	
(i)	1,875		

Equipment

+		−	
(b)	38,000		
(c)	4,320		
(e)	5,200		
(p)	3,780		
Bal. 51,300			

Accounts Payable

−		+	
(d)	2,000	(c)	4,320
(l)	1,500	(h)	675
(n)	620	(j)	620
	4,120	(p)	1,930
			7,545
		Bal. 3,425	

J. Conner, Capital

−		+	
		(a)	90,000
		(e)	5,200
		Bal. 95,200	

J. Conner, Drawing

+		−	
(s)	3,500		

Income from Tours

−		+	
		(f)	8,000
		(k)	6,750
		(r)	8,570
		Bal. 23,320	

Wages Expense

+		−	
(o)	2,360		

Rent Expense

+		−	
(g)	1,250		

Supplies Expense

+		−	
(h)	675		

Advertising Expense

+		−	
(j)	620		

Utilities Expense

+		−	
(m)	225		

FIGURE 1	A memory tool that helps some students to memorize debits and credits in T accounts is the
Accounting memory tool	equation A + D + E = L + C + R. All accounts on the left side of the equation have normal debit balances and all accounts on the right side have normal credit balances. You can make up a memorable sentence or use this one—All Drippy Eels Love Cucumbers and Radishes. Picture an eel dripping with water devouring cucumbers and radishes.

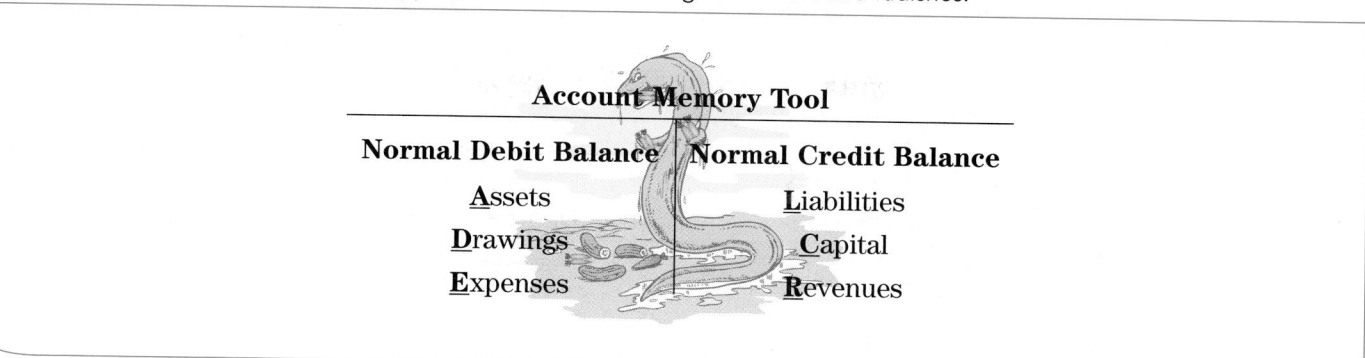

Account Memory Tool

Normal Debit Balance	Normal Credit Balance
Assets	Liabilities
Drawings	Capital
Expenses	Revenues

THE TRIAL BALANCE

After recording the transactions in the T accounts, you can now prepare a trial balance by simply recording the balances of the T accounts in two columns. The **trial balance** is a listing of account balances in two columns—one labeled Debit and one labeled Credit—to prove that the total of all the debit balances equals the total of all the credit balances. A trial balance is not considered a financial statement; it is, as the name implies, a trial run by the accountant to prove that the total of the debit balances equals the total of the credit balances. This is evidence of the equality of the two sides of the fundamental accounting equation. The accountant must prove that the accounts are in balance before preparing the company's financial statements.

In preparing a trial balance, shown in Figure 2, record the accounts with balances in the same order as they are listed in the chart of accounts.

- Assets
- Liabilities
- Owner's Equity
- Revenue
- Expenses

5 LEARNING OBJECTIVE

Prepare a trial balance.

Conner's Whitewater Adventures
Trial Balance
June 30, 20—

Column headings identify information in each column

Account Name	Debit	Credit
Cash	55,890	
Accounts Receivable	4,250	
Prepaid Insurance	1,875	
Equipment	51,300	
Accounts Payable		3,425
J. Conner, Capital		95,200
J. Conner, Drawing	3,500	
Income from Tours		23,320
Wages Expense	2,360	
Rent Expense	1,250	
Supplies Expense	675	
Advertising Expense	620	
Utilities Expense	225	
	121,945	121,945

Accounts listed in order of the chart of accounts

Single underline beneath figures to be added

Double underline beneath column totals

FIGURE 2

Trial balance

Dollar signs not used on a trial balance

The normal balance of each account is on its plus side. Remember that when there is more than one entry in an account, we record the totals in footings and subtract one footing from the other to determine the balance. **Record this balance on the side of the account with the larger footing.** (Here we record the Drawing account balance in the debit column because it has a debit balance. We do not deduct Drawing from the Capital account when we prepare the trial balance.) The following table indicates where each of the account balances would normally be shown in a trial balance.

	TRIAL BALANCE	
Account Titles	**Left or Debit Balances**	**Right or Credit Balances**
Assets	Assets	
Liabilities		Liabilities
Capital		Capital
Drawing	Drawing	
Revenue		Revenue
Expenses	Expenses	
Totals	X,XXX	X,XXX

MAJOR FINANCIAL STATEMENTS

Earlier we listed summarizing as one of the five basic tasks of the accounting process. To accomplish this task, accountants use financial statements. A **financial statement** is a report prepared by accountants to summarize the financial affairs of a business for managers and others, both inside and outside the business.

Note that the headings of all financial statements require three lines:

1. Name of the company (or owner, if there is no company name)
2. Title of the financial statement
3. Period of time covered by the financial statement, or its date

Also, note that dollar signs are placed at the head of each column and with each total. Single lines are used to show that the figures above are being added or subtracted. Lines should be drawn across the entire column. A double line is drawn under the final total in a column.

The financial statements are all interconnected. The income statement must be prepared first, followed by the statement of owner's equity, and then the balance sheet.

The Income Statement

LEARNING OBJECTIVE 6a

Prepare an income statement.

The **income statement** shows total revenue minus total expenses, which yields the net income or net loss. The income statement reports the results of business transactions involving revenue and expense accounts—in other words, how the business has performed—over a period of time, usually a month or a year. When total revenue exceeds total expenses over the period, the result is **net income**, or profit. If the total revenue is less than the total expenses, the result is a **net loss**.

The income statement in Figure 3 shows the results of the first month of operations for Conner's Whitewater Adventures.

For convenience, the individual expense amounts are recorded in the first amount column. Thus, the total expenses ($5,130) may be subtracted directly from the total revenue ($23,320).

Where to locate a business expansion is an important business decision. The decision to expand a business—as well as other operating decisions—is made from financial statements such as an income statement.

© JUPITERIMAGES

The income statement covers a period of time, whereas the balance sheet has only one date: the end of the financial period. On the income statement, the revenue for June, less the expenses for June, shows the results of operations—a net income of $18,190. To the accountant, the term *net income* means "clear" income, or profit after all expenses have been deducted. Expenses are usually listed in the same order as in the chart of accounts. Revenue and expense amounts are taken directly from the trial balance. If total expenses were greater than the revenue, then a net loss would be recorded.

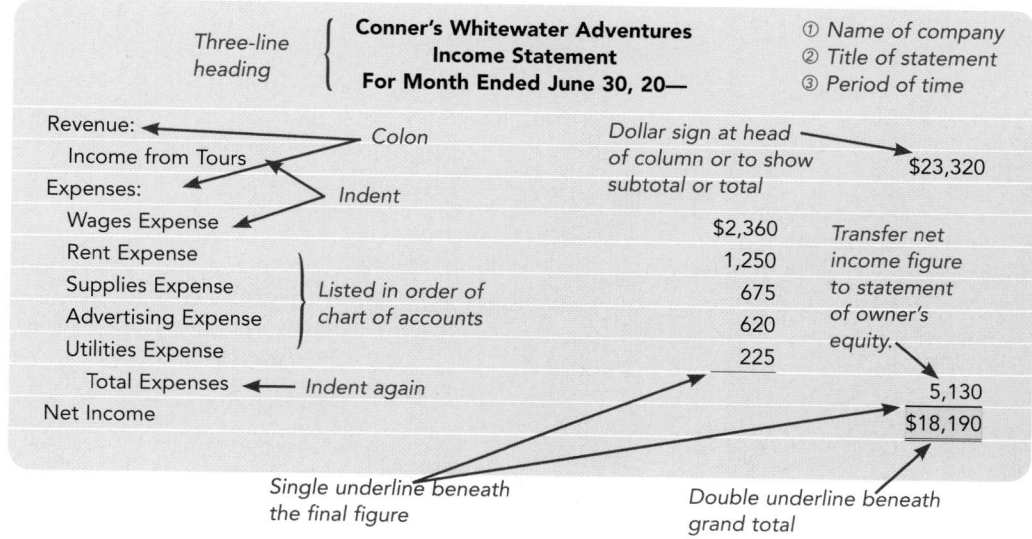

FIGURE 3

Income statement

The Statement of Owner's Equity

Remember

The income statement is prepared first, so that the net income can be recorded on the statement of owner's equity. The statement of owner's equity is prepared second, so that the ending amount of capital can be recorded on the balance sheet, which is prepared last. Here's another memory tool for recalling the order of statement preparation: <u>I</u>zzy <u>S</u>wung <u>O</u>ff <u>E</u>very <u>B</u>ranch (<u>I</u>ncome, <u>S</u>tatement of <u>O</u>wner's <u>E</u>quity, <u>B</u>alance Sheet).

In the previous chapter, we said that revenue and expenses are connected with owner's equity through the financial statements. Now let's demonstrate this by a statement of owner's equity, shown in Figure 4, which the accountant prepares after he or she has determined the net income or net loss on the income statement.

The **statement of owner's equity** shows how—and why—the owner's equity, or Capital account, has changed over a stated period of time (in this case, the month of June). Notice the third line in the heading of Figure 4. It shows that the statement of owner's equity covers the same period of time as the income statement.

Now look at the body of the statement. The first line shows the zero balance in the Capital account at the beginning of the month. The beginning balance is zero because this is a new business. All new businesses will start with a zero beginning balance in the Capital account. An investment of $95,200 was made by J. Conner: total investment, $95,200. Two items have affected owner's equity during the month: A net income of $18,190 was earned, and the owner withdrew $3,500. To perform the calculations, move to the left-hand column and add the total investments and the net income ($95,200 + $18,190 = $113,390). Then subtract the withdrawals from the subtotal ($113,390 – $3,500 = $109,890). The difference ($109,890) represents an increase in capital. This difference is placed in the right-hand column to be added directly to the beginning capital. The final figure is the ending amount in the owner's Capital account.

The Balance Sheet

After preparing the statement of owner's equity, we prepare a balance sheet. The **balance sheet** shows the **financial position**, or the condition of a business's assets offset by claims against them *as of one particular date*. It summarizes the balances of the asset, liability, and owner's equity accounts on a given date (usually the end of a month or year). The balance sheet is, thus, like a snapshot—a picture of the financial condition of the business at that particular date.

The ending capital balance on the balance sheet is taken from the statement of owner's equity. Note that the accounts appear in the same order as in the chart of accounts.

In the **report form** of the balance sheet, the elements in the accounting equation are presented one on top of the other. A balance sheet prepared on June 30 for Conner's Whitewater Adventures in report form would look like Figure 5.

FIGURE 4

Statement of owner's equity

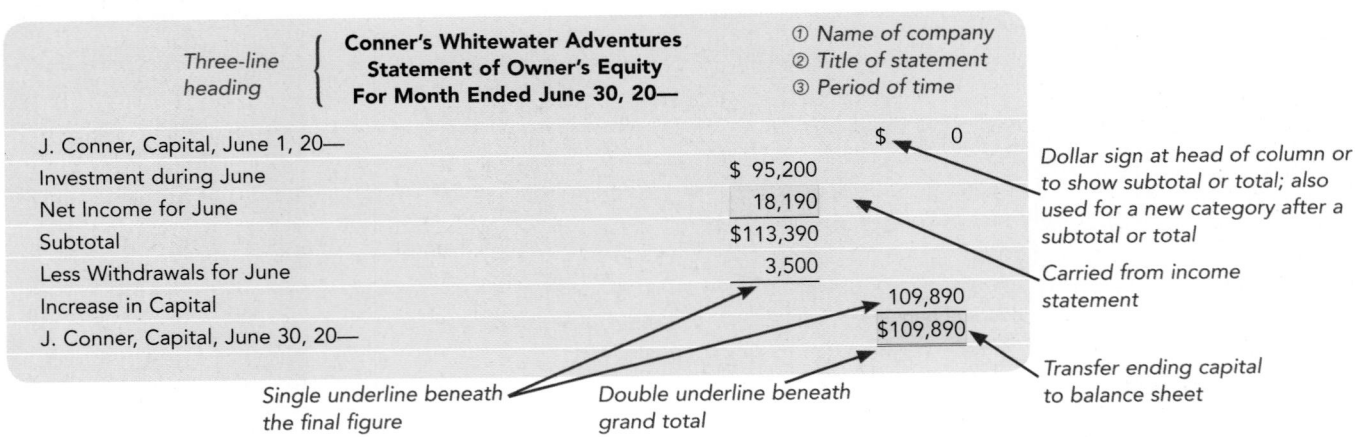

FIGURE 5

Balance sheet

Conner's Whitewater Adventures
Balance Sheet
June 30, 20—

Assets		
Cash	$55,890	
Accounts Receivable	4,250	
Prepaid Insurance	1,875	
Equipment	51,300	
Total Assets		$113,315
Liabilities		
Accounts Payable		$ 3,425
Owner's Equity		
J. Conner, Capital		109,890
Total Liabilities and Owner's Equity		$ 113,315

Carried from
statement of
owner's equity

ERRORS EXPOSED BY THE TRIAL BALANCE

If the debit and credit columns in a trial balance are not equal, then it is evident that we have made an error. Possible mistakes include the following:

- Making errors in arithmetic, such as errors in adding the trial balance columns or in finding the balances of the accounts.

- Recording only half an entry, such as a debit without a corresponding credit, or vice versa.

- Recording both halves of the entry on the same side, such as two debits rather than a debit and a credit.

- Recording one or more amounts incorrectly.

Accounting Clerk—Membership Information

Accounting in Your Future

One of many variations in accounting jobs you might find at the Solid Rock Gym would be an accounting clerk who would maintain membership information. Responsibilities might include invoicing for customers' membership fees, collecting fees, and maintaining customer accounts. The job might also include some marketing and customer service activities; therefore, people skills would be vital.

As the accounting clerk responsible for membership information, you would be required to provide the gym's accountant with weekly cash reports so the accountant could correctly report membership revenue. You would also need to manage financial information regarding collection expenses and marketing expenses, as well as any expenses related to customer service. Can you see how knowing the accounting cycle could be beneficial in this position?

Procedure for Locating Errors

Suppose that you are in a business situation where you have recorded transactions for a month in the account books, and the accounts do not balance. To save yourself time, you need to have a definite procedure for tracking down the errors. The best method is to do everything in reverse, as follows:

- Look at the pattern of balances to see if a normal balance was placed in the wrong column on the trial balance.
- Re-add the trial balance columns.
- Check the transferring of the figures from the accounts to the trial balance.
- Verify the footings and balances of the accounts.

As an added precaution, form the habit of verifying all addition and subtraction as you go along. You can thus correct many mistakes *before* the time comes to prepare a trial balance.

When the trial balance totals do not balance, the difference might indicate that you forgot to record half of an entry in the accounts. For example, if the difference in the trial balance totals is $20, you may have recorded $20 on the debit side of one account without recording $20 on the credit side of another account.

Another possibility is to divide the difference by 2; this may provide a clue that you accidentally recorded half an entry twice. For example, if the difference in the trial balance is $600, you may have recorded $300 on the debit side of one account and an additional $300 on the debit side of another account. Look for a transaction that involved $300 and then see if you have recorded both a debit and a credit. By knowing which transactions to check, you can save a lot of time.

Transpositions and Slides

LEARNING OBJECTIVE 7

Recognize the effect of transpositions and slides on account balances.

If the difference is evenly divisible by 9, the discrepancy may be either a transposition or a slide. A **transposition** means that the digits have been transposed, or switched around, when the numbers were copied from one place to another. For example, one transposition of digits in 916 can be written as 619:

Correct Number	Number Copied	Difference	Difference Divided by 9
916	619	297	297 ÷ 9 = 33

A **slide** is an error in placing the decimal point; in other words, a slide in the decimal point. For example, $27,000 could be inadvertently written as $2,700:

Correct Number	Number Copied	Difference	Difference Divided by 9
27,000	2,700	24,300	24,300 ÷ 9 = 2,700

Or the error may be a combination of a transposition and a slide, as when $450 is written as $54:

Correct Number	Number Copied	Difference	Difference Divided by 9
450	54	396	396 ÷ 9 = 44

Again, the difference is evenly divisible by 9 (with no remainder).

CHAPTER REVIEW

Study & Practice

1 LEARNING OBJECTIVE

Determine balances of T accounts having entries recorded on both sides of the accounts.

To determine balances of T accounts, add the amounts listed on each side of the T account. The totals are called **footings**. To get the account balance, subtract the total of the smaller side from the total of the larger side. Record the account balance on the larger side.

PRACTICE EXERCISE 1

Using the T accounts presented below, determine the balances.

Cash		
+	–	
Debit	Credit	
(a) 90,000	**(b)** 38,000	
	(f) 1,200	

Accounts Payable		
–	+	
Debit	Credit	
(d) 1,500	**(c)** 4,500	

J. Jay, Capital		
–	+	
Debit	Credit	
	(a) 90,000	
	(e) 5,000	

Equipment		
+	–	
Debit		
(b) 38,000	**(d)** 1,500	
(c) 4,500		
(e) 5,000		

J. Jay, Drawing		
+	–	
Debit	Credit	
(f) 1,200		

PRACTICE EXERCISE 1 SOLUTION

Cash		
+	–	
Debit	Credit	
(a) 90,000	**(b)** 38,000	
	(f) 1,200	
	39,200	
Bal. 50,800		

Accounts Payable		
–	+	
Debit	Credit	
(d) 1,500	**(c)** 4,500	
	Bal. 3,000	

J. Jay, Capital		
–	+	
Debit	Credit	
	(a) 90,000	
	(e) 5,000	
	Bal. 95,000	

Equipment		
+	–	
Debit		
(b) 38,000	**(d)** 1,500	
(c) 4,500		
(e) 5,000		
47,500		
Bal. 46,000		

J. Jay, Drawing		
+	–	
Debit	Credit	
(f) 1,200		

LEARNING OBJECTIVE

2 *Present the fundamental accounting equation using the T account form, and label the plus and minus sides.*

The fundamental accounting equation can be restated in **T account form** using plus and minus sides. The following table summarizes the rules:

Assets	The *left* side is the *increase* side.
Liabilities	The *right* side is the *increase* side.
Owner's Equity	The *right* side is the *increase* side.
Revenue	The *right* side is the *increase* side.
Expenses	The *left* side is the *increase* side.

PRACTICE EXERCISE 2

Using the fundamental accounting equation in T account form, label each side with plus and minus.

PRACTICE EXERCISE 2 SOLUTION

Assets	=	**Liabilities**	+	**Owner's Equity**	+	**Revenue**	–	**Expenses**
+ | –		– | +		– | +		– | +		+ | –
Left | Right		Left | Right		Left | Right		Left | Right		Left | Right

LEARNING OBJECTIVE

3 *Present the fundamental accounting equation using the T account form, and label the debit and credit sides.*

Each account category in the fundamental accounting equation has a debit and credit. The left side of a T account, regardless of the account category, is called the **debit** side. The right side is called the **credit** side. A debit or credit could signify either an increase or a decrease—it depends on the account category. The following table summarizes these rules:

Debits Signify		**Credits Signify**	
Increases in	Assets / Drawing / Expenses	Decreases in	Assets / Drawing / Expenses
Decreases in	Liabilities / Capital / Revenue	Increases in	Liabilities / Capital / Revenue

PRACTICE EXERCISE 3

Using the fundamental accounting equation in T account form, label each side as debit and credit.

PRACTICE EXERCISE 3 SOLUTION

Assets	=	Liabilities	+	Owner's Equity	+	Revenue	−	Expenses
+ −		− +		− +		− +		+ −
Left Right		Left Right		Left Right		Left Right		Left Right
Debit Credit		Debit Credit		Debit Credit		Debit Credit		Debit Credit

4 **LEARNING OBJECTIVE**

Record directly in T accounts a group of business transactions involving changes in asset, liability, owner's equity, revenue, and expense accounts for a service business.

Transactions can be recorded directly into the T accounts. When analyzing a business transaction, follow these steps:

STEP 1. Decide which accounts are involved.

STEP 2. Classify the accounts involved (asset, liability, owner's equity, revenue, expense).

STEP 3. Decide if the accounts involved are increased or decreased.

STEP 4. Write the transaction as a debit to one account (or accounts) and a credit to another account (or accounts).

STEP 5. Check to see if the equation is in balance after the transaction has been recorded.

PRACTICE EXERCISE 4

Record the following transactions directly into the appropriate T accounts.

a. J. Molson deposited $90,000 in the name of the business.

b. Bought equipment for cash, $38,000.

c. Bought equipment on account, $4,320.

d. Paid $2,000 on account.

e. J. Molson invested his personal equipment, valued at $5,200, in the business.

f. J. Molson withdrew $1,200 from the business for personal use.

PRACTICE EXERCISE 4 SOLUTION

Assets	=	Liabilities	+	Owner's Equity	+	Revenue	−	Expenses
+ −		− +		− +		− +		+ −
Debit Credit		Debit Credit		Debit Credit		Debit Credit		Debit Credit

Cash

+	−
Debit	Credit
(a) 90,000	(b) 38,000
	(d) 2,000
	(f) 1,200
	41,200
Bal. 48,800	

Equipment

+	−
Debit	Credit
(b) 38,000	
(c) 4,320	
(e) 5,200	
Bal. 47,520	

Accounts Payable

−	+
Debit	Credit
(d) 2,000	(c) 4,320
	Bal. 2,320

J. Molson, Capital

−	+
Debit	Credit
	(a) 90,000
	(e) 5,200
	Bal. 95,200

J. Molson, Drawing

+	−
Debit	Credit
(f) 1,200	

5 Prepare a trial balance.

A **trial balance** is a list of all account balances in two columns—one labeled Debit and one labeled Credit. The trial balance shows that both sides of the accounting equation are equal. The heading consists of the company name, the title of the form (trial balance), and the date.

PRACTICE EXERCISE 5

Using the following account balances, prepare a trial balance for Collins's Backpack Adventures as of July 31, 20—.

Accounts Receivable	4,150	J. Collins, Capital	95,400
Equipment	51,500	Income from Treks	23,220
Cash	55,990	Accounts Payable	3,325
Prepaid Insurance	1,675	J. Collins, Drawing	3,400
Wages Expense	2,460	Rent Expense	1,350
Supplies Expense	575	Advertising Expense	520
Utilities Expense	325		

PRACTICE EXERCISE 5 SOLUTION

Collins's Backpack Adventures Trial Balance July 31, 20—		
Account Name	**Debit**	**Credit**
Cash	55,990	
Accounts Receivable	4,150	
Prepaid Insurance	1,675	
Equipment	51,500	
Accounts Payable		3,325
J. Collins, Capital		95,400
J. Collins, Drawing	3,400	
Income from Treks		23,220
Wages Expense	2,460	
Rent Expense	1,350	
Supplies Expense	575	
Advertising Expense	520	
Utilities Expense	325	
	121,945	121,945

6 Prepare (a) an income statement, (b) a statement of owner's equity, and (c) a balance sheet.

(a) An **income statement** shows the results of operations of a business for a period of time. It includes revenue and expense accounts and reports either a **net income** or a **net loss**. (b) A **statement of owner's equity** shows the activity in the owner's equity, or Capital account, for a period of time. It includes the balance in the Capital account at the beginning of the period plus any additional investments and any increase or decrease in capital as the result of a net income (or a net loss) minus any withdrawals. (c) A **balance sheet** shows the financial condition of a business at a particular date in time. It summarizes the balances of the asset, liability, and owner's equity accounts on a given date.

PRACTICE EXERCISE 6

Use the trial balance in Practice Exercise 5 to prepare (a) an income statement, (b) a statement of owner's equity, and (c) a balance sheet. Assume Collins's Backpack Adventures started business on July 1, 20—.

PRACTICE EXERCISE 6 SOLUTION

(a)

	Collins's Backpack Adventures Income Statement For Month Ended July 31, 20—	
Revenue:		
Income from Treks		$23,220
Expenses:		
Wages Expense	$2,460	
Rent Expense	1,350	
Supplies Expense	575	
Advertising Expense	520	
Utilities Expense	325	
Total Expenses		5,230
Net Income		$17,990

(b)

	Collins's Backpack Adventures Statement of Owner's Equity For Month Ended July 31, 20—	
J. Collins, Capital, July 1, 20—		$ 0
Investments during July	$ 95,400	
Net Income for July	17,990	
Subtotal	$113,390	
Less Withdrawals for July	3,400	
Increase in Capital		109,990
J. Collins, Capital, July 31, 20—		$109,990

(c)

	Collins's Backpack Adventures Balance Sheet July 31, 20—	
Assets		
Cash	$55,990	
Accounts Receivable	4,150	
Prepaid Insurance	1,675	
Equipment	51,500	
Total Assets		$ 113,315
Liabilities		
Accounts Payable		$ 3,325
Owner's Equity		
J. Collins, Capital		109,990
Total Liabilities and Owner's Equity		$ 113,315

LEARNING OBJECTIVE

7
Recognize the effect of transpositions and slides on account balances.

Transpositions and slides account for many trial balance errors. The clue is whether the difference in account balances or trial balance totals is evenly divisible by 9.

a. A **transposition** occurs when digits are switched around, such as 541 written as 415.

b. A **slide** is an error in placing the decimal point; in other words, a *slide* in the decimal point. For example, $35,000 could be inadvertently written as $3,500.

c. An error in a trial balance may be a combination of a transposition and a slide, as when $230 is written as $32.

PRACTICE EXERCISE 7

Identify the following errors as transpositions or slides, and indicate the amount of the difference and whether it is divisible by 9.

a. The amount of supplies bought totaled $341, but it was written as $431.

b. Equipment was purchased for $3,500, but it was written as $35,000.

c. An error was made in the trial balance because $35 was written as $530.

PRACTICE EXERCISE 7 SOLUTION

a. Transposition: The difference is $90 and can be evenly divided by 9.

Correct Number	Number Copied	Difference	Difference Divided by 9
$341	$431	$90	$90 ÷ 9 = $10

b. Slide: The difference is $31,500 and can be evenly divided by 9.

Correct Number	Number Copied	Difference	Difference Divided by 9
$3,500	$35,000	$31,500	$31,500 ÷ 9 = $3,500

c.   Transposition and slide: The difference is $495 and can be evenly divided by 9.

Correct Number	Number Copied	Difference	Difference Divided by 9
$35	$530	$495	$495 ÷ 9 = $55

Glossary

Balance sheet A financial statement showing the financial position of an organization on a given date, such as June 30 or December 31. The balance sheet lists the balances in the asset, liability, and owner's equity accounts. (p. 58)

Compound entry A transaction that requires more than one debit or more than one credit to be recorded. (p. 53)

Credit The right side of a T account; to credit is to record an amount on the right side of a T account. Credits represent increases in liability, capital, or revenue accounts and decreases in asset, drawing, or expense accounts. (p. 45)

Debit The left side of a T account; to debit is to record an amount on the left side of a T account. Debits represent increases in asset, drawing, or expense accounts and decreases in liability, capital, or revenue accounts. (p. 45)

Financial position The resources or assets owned by an organization at a point in time, offset by the claims against those resources and owner's equity; shown on a balance sheet. (p. 58)

Financial statement A report prepared by accountants that summarizes the financial affairs of a business. (p. 56)

Footings The totals of each side of a T account, recorded in small, pencil-written figures. (p. 44)

Income statement A financial statement showing the results of business transactions involving revenue and expense accounts over a period of time. (p. 56)

Net income The result when total revenue exceeds total expenses over a period of time. (p. 56)

Net loss The result when total expenses exceed total revenue over a period of time. (p. 56)

Normal balance The plus side of a T account. (p. 44)

Report form The form of the balance sheet in which assets are placed at the top and liabilities and owner's equity are placed below. (p. 58)

Slide An error in placing the decimal point in a number. (p. 60)

Statement of owner's equity A financial statement showing the activity in the owner's equity, or Capital account, over the financial period. (p. 58)

T account form A form of account shaped like the letter T in which increases and decreases in the account may be recorded. One side of the T is for entries on the debit or left side. The other side of the T is for entries on the credit or right side. (p. 43)

Transposition An error that involves interchanging, or switching around, digits during the recording of a number. (p. 60)

Trial balance A list of all account balances to prove that the total of all the debit balances equals the total of all the credit balances. (p. 55)

CHAPTER ASSIGNMENTS

Discussion Questions

1. Explain how a trial balance and a balance sheet differ.
2. Explain why the term *debit* doesn't always mean "increase" and why the term *credit* doesn't always mean "decrease."
3. What are footings in accounting?
4. How are the three financial statements shown in this chapter connected?
5. What is a compound entry?
6. List two reasons why the debits and credits in the trial balance might not balance.
7. Give an example of a slide and an example of a transposition. Explain how you might decide whether an error is a slide or a transposition.
8. What do we mean when we say that revenue and expense accounts are under the "umbrella" of owner's equity?

Exercises

2,3

PRACTICE EXERCISES 2,3

EXERCISE 2-1 On a sheet of paper, draw the fundamental accounting equation with T accounts under each of the five account classifications, with plus and minus signs and debit and credit on the appropriate sides of each account. Under each of the five classifications, draw T accounts, again with the correct plus and minus signs and debit and credit, for each of the following accounts of Barlow Engine Repair.

Cash
Accounts Receivable
Equipment
Accounts Payable
D. Barlow, Capital
D. Barlow, Drawing

Income from Repairs
Wages Expense
Rent Expense
Supplies Expense
Utilities Expense
Miscellaneous Expense

2,3

PRACTICE EXERCISES 2,3

EXERCISE 2-2 List the classification of each of the following accounts as A (asset), L (liability), OE (owner's equity), R (revenue), or E (expense). Write Debit or Credit to indicate the increase side, the decrease side, and the normal balance side.

Account	Classification	Increase Side	Decrease Side	Normal Balance Side
0. Cash	A	Debit	Credit	Debit
1. Wages Expense				
2. Equipment				
3. L. Cross, Capital				
4. Service Revenue				
5. L. Cross, Drawing				
6. Accounts Receivable				
7. Rent Expense				
8. Fees Earned				
9. Accounts Payable				

2,3,4

PRACTICE EXERCISE 4

EXERCISE 2-3 R. Dalberg operates Dalberg's Tours. The company has the following chart of accounts:

Assets
Cash
Accounts Receivable
Prepaid Insurance
Display Equipment
Van
Office Equipment

Liabilities
Accounts Payable

Owner's Equity
R. Dalberg, Capital
R. Dalberg, Drawing

Revenue
Income from Tours

Expenses
Wages Expense
Gas Expense
Supplies Expense
Advertising Expense
Utilities Expense

Using the chart of accounts, record the following transactions in pairs of T accounts. Give the T account to be debited first and the account to be credited to the right. Show debit and credit and plus and minus signs. (Example: Received and paid the bill for the month's rent, $480.)

Rent Expense			Cash		
+	−		+	−	
Debit	Credit		Debit	Credit	
480				480	

a. Received and paid the electric bill, $175.
b. Bought supplies on account, $135.
c. Paid for insurance for one year, $580.
d. Made a payment on account to a creditor, $65.
e. Received and paid the telephone bill, $186.
f. Sold services on account, $1,375.
g. Received and paid the gasoline bill for the van, $130.
h. Received cash on account from customers, $1,458.
i. Dalberg withdrew cash for personal use, $700.

EXERCISE 2-4 During the first month of operation, Lorens's Expeditions recorded the following transactions. Describe what has happened in each of the transactions (a) through (k).

PRACTICE EXERCISE 4

Cash			Accounts Payable		D. L. Lorens, Capital		Income from Tours		Rent Expense	
(a) 3,200	(b)	525	(d) 280			(a) 3,200	(h) 615		(b) 525	
(k) 1,125	(c)	98	(g) 1,000			(f) 3,510	(k) 1,125			
	(e)	75							**Supplies Expense**	
	(g)	1,050			**D. L. Lorens, Drawing**				(d) 280	
	(i)	92								
	(j)	345			(j) 345				**Advertising Expense**	
									(c) 98	

Accounts Receivable	
(h) 615	

Utilities Expense

(i) 92

Equipment	
(f) 3,510	
(g) 2,050	

Miscellaneous Expense

(e) 75

EXERCISE 2-5 Business Services, owned by T. Morris, hired a new bookkeeper who is not entirely familiar with the process of preparing a trial balance. All the accounts

PRACTICE EXERCISE 5

CHAPTER ASSIGNMENTS

have normal balances. Find the errors, and prepare a corrected trial balance for December 31 of this year.

Business Services
Trial Balance
December 31, 20—

Account Name	Debit	Credit
Accounts Receivable		7,700
Cash	3,200	
Accounts Payable		8,700
Equipment	26,000	
T. Morris, Capital		24,800
T. Morris, Drawing		1,900
Prepaid Insurance		1,300
Income from Services		33,000
Wages Expense	17,500	
Rent Expense		3,700
Supplies Expense	1,800	
Utilities Expense	3,400	
	51,900	81,100

5,6

PRACTICE EXERCISES 5,6

EXERCISE 2-6 During the first month of operations, Landish Modeling Agency recorded transactions in T account form. Foot and balance the accounts; then prepare a trial balance, an income statement, a statement of owner's equity, and a balance sheet dated March 31, 20—.

Cash

(a)	8,200	(b)	350
(c)	8,400	(d)	1,600
(i)	7,580	(f)	175
		(g)	3,400
		(h)	2,200

Accounts Receivable

(e)	2,600

Office Furniture

(b)	350

Office Equipment

(k)	2,800

Accounts Payable

		(k)	2,800
		(j)	82

R. Landish, Capital

		(a)	8,200

R. Landish, Drawing

(h)	2,200

Modeling Fees

		(c)	8,400
		(e)	2,600
		(i)	7,580

Salary Expense

(g)	3,400

Rent Expense

(d)	1,600

Supplies Expense

(j)	82

Utilities Expense

(f)	175

7

PRACTICE EXERCISE 7

EXERCISE 2-7 The following errors were made in journalizing transactions. In each case, calculate the amount of the error and indicate whether the debit or the credit column of the trial balance will be understated or overstated.

	Amount of Difference	Debit or Credit Column of Trial Balance Understated or Overstated
0. Example: A $149 debit to Accounts Receivable was not recorded.	$149	Debit column understated
a. A $42 debit to Supplies Expense was recorded as $420.		
b. A $155 debit to Accounts Receivable was recorded twice.		
c. A $179 debit to Prepaid Insurance was not recorded.		
d. A $65 credit to Cash was not recorded.		
e. A $190 debit to Equipment was recorded twice.		
f. A $57 debit to Utilities Expense was recorded as $75.		

EXERCISE 2-8 Would the following errors cause the trial balance to have equal or unequal totals? As a result of the errors, which accounts are overstated (by how much) or understated (by how much)?

PRACTICE EXERCISE 7

a. A purchase of office equipment for $380 was recorded as a debit to Office Equipment for $38 and a credit to Cash for $38.
b. A payment of $280 to a creditor was debited to Accounts Receivable and credited to Cash for $280 each.
c. A purchase of supplies for $245 was recorded as a debit to Equipment for $245 and a credit to Cash for $245.
d. A payment of $76 to a creditor was recorded as a debit to Accounts Payable for $76 and a credit to Cash for $67.

Problem Set A

For additional help, see the demonstration problem at the beginning of each chapter in your Working Papers.

PROBLEM 2-1A During December of this year, G. Elden established Ginny's Gym. The following asset, liability, and owner's equity accounts are included in the chart of accounts:

Cash
Exercise Equipment
Store Equipment
Office Equipment
Accounts Payable
G. Elden, Capital
Income from Services
Supplies Expense

During December, the following transactions occurred:

a. Elden deposited $35,000 in a bank account in the name of the business.
b. Bought exercise equipment for cash, $8,150, Ck. No. 1001.
c. Bought supplies on account from Hazel Company, $105.
d. Bought a display rack (Store Equipment) on account from Cyber Core, $790.
e. Bought office equipment on account from Office Aids, $185.
f. Elden invested her exercise equipment with a fair market value of $1,200 in the business.
g. Made a payment to Cyber Core, a creditor, $200, Ck. No. 1002.
h. Sold services for the month of December for cash, $800.

Required

1. Write the account classifications (Assets, Liabilities, Owner's Equity, Revenue, Expense) in the fundamental accounting equation, as well as the plus and minus signs and Debit and Credit.
2. Write the account names on the T accounts under the classifications, place the plus and minus signs for each T account, and label the debit and credit sides of the T accounts.
3. Record the amounts in the proper positions in the T accounts. Write the letter next to each entry to identify the transaction.
4. Foot and balance the accounts.

PROBLEM 2-2A B. Kelso established Computer Wizards during November of this year. The accountant prepared the following chart of accounts:

Assets	**Revenue**
Cash	Income from Services
Computer Software	
Office Equipment	**Expenses**
Neon Sign	Wages Expense
	Rent Expense
Liabilities	Supplies Expense
Accounts Payable	Advertising Expense
	Utilities Expense
Owner's Equity	Miscellaneous Expense
B. Kelso, Capital	
B. Kelso, Drawing	

The following transactions occurred during the month:

a. Kelso deposited $45,000 in a bank account in the name of the business.
b. Paid the rent for the current month, $1,800, Ck. No. 2001.
c. Bought office desks and filing cabinets for cash, $790, Ck. No. 2002.
d. Bought a computer and printer (Office Equipment) from Cyber Center for use in the business, $2,700, paying $1,700 in cash and placing the balance on account, Ck. No. 2003.
e. Bought a neon sign on account from Signage Co., $1,350.
f. Kelso invested her personal computer software with a fair market value of $600 in the business.
g. Received a bill from *Country News* for newspaper advertising, $365.
h. Sold services for cash, $1,245.
i. Received and paid the electric bill, $345, Ck. No. 2004.
j. Paid on account to *Country News*, a creditor, $285, Ck. No. 2005.
k. Sold services for cash, $1,450.
l. Paid wages to an employee, $925, Ck. No. 2006.
m. Received and paid the bill for the city business license, $75, Ck. No. 2007 (Miscellaneous Expense).
n. Kelso withdrew cash for personal use, $850, Ck. No. 2008.
o. Bought printer paper and letterhead stationery on account from Office Aids, $115.

Required

1. Record the owner's name in the Capital and Drawing T accounts.
2. Correctly place the plus and minus signs for each T account, and label the debit and credit sides of the accounts.
3. Record the transactions in T accounts. Write the letter of each entry to identify the transaction.
4. Foot the T accounts and show the balances.
5. Prepare a trial balance, with a three-line heading, dated November 30, 20—.

PROBLEM 2-3A R. Morgis, a speech therapist, opened a clinic in the name of Morgis Clinic. Her accountant prepared the following chart of accounts:  **LO** 1,2,3,4,5,6

Assets
Cash
Accounts Receivable
Office Equipment
Office Furniture

Liabilities
Accounts Payable

Owner's Equity
R. Morgis, Capital
R. Morgis, Drawing

Revenue
Professional Fees

Expenses
Salary Expense
Rent Expense
Utilities Expense
Miscellaneous Expense

The following transactions occurred during June of this year:

a. Morgis deposited $40,000 in a bank account in the name of the business.
b. Bought waiting room chairs and tables (Office Furniture) on account, $1,330.
c. Bought a fax/copier/scanner combination (Office Equipment) from Max's Equipment for $595, paying $200 in cash and placing the balance on account, Ck. No. 1001.
d. Bought an intercom system (Office Equipment) on account from Regan Office Supply, $375.
e. Received and paid the telephone bill, $155, Ck. No. 1002.
f. Sold professional services on account, $1,484.
g. Received and paid the electric bill, $190, Ck. No. 1003.
h. Received and paid the bill for the state speech therapy convention, $450, Ck. No. 1004 (Miscellaneous Expense).
i. Sold professional services for cash, $2,575.
j. Paid on account to Regan Office Supply, a creditor, $300, Ck. No. 1005.
k. Paid the rent for the current month, $940, Ck. No. 1006.
l. Paid salary of the receptionist, $880, Ck. No. 1007.
m. R. Morgis withdrew cash for personal use, $800, Ck. No. 1008.
n. Received $885 on account from patients who were previously billed.

Required
1. Record the owner's name in the Capital and Drawing T accounts.
2. Correctly place the plus and minus signs for each T account, and label the debit and credit sides of the accounts.
3. Record the transactions in the T accounts. Write the letter of each entry to identify the transaction.
4. Foot the T accounts and show the balances.
5. Prepare a trial balance as of June 30, 20—.
6. Prepare an income statement for June 30, 20—.
7. Prepare a statement of owner's equity for June 30, 20—.
8. Prepare a balance sheet as of June 30, 20—.

Check Figure
Net Income, $1,444

PROBLEM 2-4A On May 1, B. Bangle opened Self-Wash Laundry. His accountant listed the following chart of accounts: **LO** 1,2,4,5,6

Cash
Prepaid Insurance
Equipment
Furniture and Fixtures
Accounts Payable
B. Bangle, Capital
B. Bangle, Drawing

Laundry Revenue
Wages Expense
Rent Expense
Supplies Expense
Utilities Expense
Miscellaneous Expense

The following transactions were completed during May:

a. Bangle deposited $35,000 in a bank account in the name of the business.
b. Bought chairs and tables (Furniture and Fixtures) paying cash, $1,870, Ck. No. 1000.
c. Bought supplies on account from Barnes Supply Company, $225.
d. Paid the rent for the current month, $875, Ck. No. 1001.
e. Bought washing machines and dryers from Lara Equipment Company, $12,500, paying $3,600 in cash and placing the balance on account, Ck. No. 1002.
f. Sold services for cash for the first half of the month, $1,925.
g. Bought insurance for one year, $1,560, Ck. No. 1003.
h. Paid on account to Lara Equipment Company, a creditor, $1,800, Ck. No. 1004.
i. Received and paid electric bill, $285, Ck. No. 1005.
j. Sold services for cash for the second half of the month, $1,835.
k. Paid wages to an employee, $940, Ck. No. 1006.
l. Bangle withdrew cash for his personal use, $800, Ck. No. 1007.
m. Paid on account to Barnes Supply Company, a creditor, $225, Ck. No. 1008.
n. Received and paid bill from the county for sidewalk repair assessment, $280, Ck. No. 1009 (Miscellaneous Expense).

Check Figure
Trial balance total, $45,860

Required

1. Record the owner's name in the Capital and Drawing T accounts.
2. Correctly place the plus and minus signs for each T account, and label the debit and credit sides of the accounts.
3. Record the transactions in the T accounts. Write the letter of each entry to identify the transaction.
4. Foot the T accounts and show the balances.
5. Prepare a trial balance as of May 31, 20—.
6. Prepare an income statement for May 31, 20—.
7. Prepare a statement of owner's equity for May 31, 20—.
8. Prepare a balance sheet as of May 31, 20—.

Problem Set B

For additional help, see the demonstration problem at the beginning of each chapter in your Working Papers.

1,2,3,4 **LO**

PROBLEM 2-1B During February of this year, R. Willard established Willard Shoe Hospital. The following asset, liability, and owner's equity accounts are included in the chart of accounts:

Cash
Shop Equipment
Store Equipment
Office Equipment
Accounts Payable
R. Willard, Capital
Income from Services
Supplies Expense

The following transactions occurred during the month of February:

a. Willard deposited $25,000 cash in a bank account in the name of the business.
b. Bought shop equipment for cash, $1,525, Ck. No. 1000.
c. Bought supplies on account from Milland Company, $325.
d. Bought store shelving on account from Inger Hardware, $750.
e. Bought office equipment from Shara's Office Supply, $625, paying $225 in cash and placing the balance on account, Ck. No. 1001.
f. Paid on account to Inger Hardware, a creditor, $750, Ck. No. 1002
g. Willard invested his personal leather working tools with a fair market value of $800 in the business.
h. Sold services for the month of February for cash, $250.

Required

1. Write the account classifications (Assets, Liabilities, Owner's Equity, Revenue, Expense) in the fundamental accounting equation, as well as the plus and minus signs and Debit and Credit.

2. Write the account names on the T accounts under the classifications, place the plus and minus signs for each T account, and label the debit and credit sides of the T accounts.

3. Record the amounts in the proper positions in the T accounts. Write the letter next to each entry to identify the transaction.

4. Foot and balance the accounts.

PROBLEM 2-2B J. Carrie established Carrie Photo Tours during June of this year. The accountant prepared the following chart of accounts:

LO 1,2,3,4,5

Assets
Cash
Computer Software
Office Equipment
Neon Sign

Liabilities
Accounts Payable

Owner's Equity
J. Carrie, Capital
J. Carrie, Drawing

Revenue
Income from Services

Expenses
Wages Expense
Rent Expense
Supplies Expense
Advertising Expense
Utilities Expense
Miscellaneous Expense

The following transactions occurred during the month of June:

a. Carrie deposited $30,000 cash in a bank account in the name of the business.
b. Bought office equipment for cash, $1,850, Ck. No. 1001.
c. Bought computer software from Morey's Computer Center, $640, paying $350 in cash and placing the balance on account, Ck. No. 1002.
d. Paid current month's rent, $950, Ck. No. 1003 (Rent Expense).
e. Sold services for cash, $1,575 (Income from Services).
f. Bought a neon sign from The Sign Company, $1,335, paying $435 in cash and placing the balance on account, Ck. No. 1004.
g. Received bill from *The Gossiper* for advertising, $445 (Advertising Expense).
h. Bought supplies on account from City Supply, $460.
i. Received and paid the electric bill, $380, Ck. No. 1005.
j. Paid on account to *The Gossiper*, a creditor, $245, Ck. No. 1006.
k. Sold services for cash, $3,474.
l. Paid wages to an employee, $930, Ck. No. 1007.
m. Carrie invested his personal computer (Office Equipment) with a fair market value of $1,000 in the business.
n. Carrie withdrew cash for personal use, $800, Ck. No. 1008.
o. Received and paid the bill for city business license, $75, Ck. No. 1009 (Miscellaneous Expense).

Required

1. Record the owner's name in the Capital and Drawing T accounts.
2. Correctly place the plus and minus signs for each T account, and label the debit and credit sides of the accounts.
3. Record the transactions in the T accounts. Write the letter of each entry to identify the transaction.
4. Foot the T accounts and show the balances.
5. Prepare a trial balance, with a three-line heading, dated June 30, 20—.

1,2,3,4,5,6 LO

PROBLEM 2-3B D. Julia, a physical therapist, opened Julia's Clinic. His accountant provided the following chart of accounts:

Assets
Cash
Accounts Receivable
Office Equipment
Office Furniture

Liabilities
Accounts Payable

Owner's Equity
D. Julia, Capital
D. Julia, Drawing

Revenue
Professional Fees

Expenses
Salary Expense
Rent Expense
Utilities Expense
Miscellaneous Expense

The following transactions occurred during July of this year:

a. Julia deposited $35,000 in a bank account in the name of the business.
b. Bought filing cabinets (Office Equipment) on account from Muller Office Supply, $560.
c. Paid cash for chairs and carpeting (Office Furniture) for the waiting room, $835, Ck. No. 1000.
d. Bought a photocopier from Rob's Office Equipment, $650, paying $250 in cash and placing the balance on account, Ck. No. 1001.
e. Received and paid the telephone bill, which included installation charges, $185, Ck. No. 1002.
f. Sold professional services on account, $2,255.
g. Received and paid the bill for the state physical therapy convention, $445, Ck. No. 1003 (Miscellaneous Expense).
h. Received and paid the electric bill, $335, Ck. No. 1004.
i. Received cash on account from credit customers, $1,940.
j. Paid on account to Muller Office Supply, a creditor, $250, Ck. No. 1005.
k. Paid the office rent for the current month, $1,245, Ck. No. 1006.
l. Sold professional services for cash, $1,950.
m. Paid the salary of the receptionist, $960, Ck. No. 1007.
n. Julia withdrew cash for personal use, $1,200, Ck. No. 1008.

Check Figure
Net Income, $1,035

Required

1. Record the owner's name in the Capital and Drawing T accounts.
2. Correctly place the plus and minus signs for each T account, and label the debit and credit sides of the accounts.
3. Record the transactions in the T accounts. Write the letter of each entry to identify the transaction.
4. Foot the T accounts and show the balances.
5. Prepare a trial balance as of July 31, 20—.
6. Prepare an income statement for July 31, 20—.
7. Prepare a statement of owner's equity for July 31, 20—.
8. Prepare a balance sheet as of July 31, 20—.

1,2,4,5,6 LO

PROBLEM 2-4B On July 1, K. Resser opened Resser's Quick Clean. Resser's accountant listed the following chart of accounts:

Cash
Prepaid Insurance
Equipment
Furniture and Fixtures
Accounts Payable
K. Resser, Capital
K. Resser, Drawing

Laundry Revenue
Wages Expense
Rent Expense
Supplies Expense
Utilities Expense
Miscellaneous Expense

The following transactions were completed during July:

a. Resser deposited $25,000 in a bank account in the name of the business.
b. Bought tables and chairs (Furniture and Fixtures) for cash, $725, Ck. No. 1200.
c. Paid the rent for the current month, $1,750, Ck. No. 1201.
d. Bought washers and dryers from Ferber Equipment, $15,700, paying $4,000 in cash and placing the balance on account, Ck. No. 1202.
e. Bought supplies on account from Wiggins's Distributors, $535.
f. Sold services for cash, $1,742.
g. Bought insurance for one year, $1,375, Ck. No. 1203.
h. Paid on account to Ferber Equipment, a creditor, $700, Ck. No. 1204.
i. Received and paid the electric bill, $438, Ck. No. 1205.
j. Paid on account to Wiggins's Distributors, a creditor, $315, Ck. No. 1206.
k. Sold services to customers for cash for the second half of the month, $1,820.
l. Received and paid the bill for the business license, $75, Ck. No. 1207 (Miscellaneous Expense).
m. Paid wages to an employee, $1,200, Ck. No. 1208.
n. Resser withdrew cash for personal use, $700, Ck. No. 1209.

Required

Check Figure
Net Loss, $(436)

1. Record the owner's name in the Capital and Drawing T accounts.
2. Correctly place the plus and minus signs for each T account, and label the debit and credit sides of the accounts.
3. Record the transactions in the T accounts. Write the letter of each entry to identify the transaction.
4. Foot the T accounts and show the balances.
5. Prepare a trial balance as of July 31, 20—.
6. Prepare an income statement for July 31, 20—.
7. Prepare a statement of owner's equity for July 31, 20—.
8. Prepare a balance sheet as of July 31, 20—.

ACTIVITIES

CONSIDER AND COMMUNICATE

A fellow accounting student has difficulty understanding how the fundamental accounting equation stays in balance when a compound entry with one debit and two credits is recorded. Consider, for example, that a business bought equipment for $7,000, paid $3,000 in cash, and placed the remainder on account.

This means that there are two credits and one debit—one debit and one credit on the left side of the equation and the other credit on the right side of the equation. Explain to your fellow student how the equation stays in balance.

WHAT'S WRONG WITH THIS PICTURE?

A new bookkeeper can't find the errors that are causing the company's month-end trial balance to be out of balance. The bookkeeper is too shy to ask for help at the office, so she takes the financial records home and asks her uncle, a retired bookkeeper, to help her locate the errors. Even with the help of her uncle, she is still out of balance and is now too embarrassed to return to the office and ask for help. What is wrong with this practice, if anything?

3

The General Journal and the General Ledger

WHY IT MATTERS

ECOTOUR EXPEDITIONS, INC., Jamestown, Rhode Island

You probably have never imagined the possibility of being an accountant who could have a direct impact on improving global ecosystems. Accountants who work for Ecotour Expeditions, Inc., might manage accounting details for guest air travel and accommodations, tour guide compensation, expedition revenue, and a variety of other expenses. Not only would you need to know debits and credits within the accounting cycle, but you would have to become familiar with many countries and their languages and currencies. Supplies Expense might include reusable water bottles and malaria nets. Prepaid Insurance might include trip insurance for cancellations or delays due to weather or other problems.

In this chapter, you will journalize and post transactions and prepare a trial balance to see if debits equal credits. You'll need these skills to understand how to record accounting transactions similar to those you might find if you worked for Ecotour Expeditions, Inc.

LEARNING OBJECTIVES

After you have completed this chapter, you will be able to do the following:

1 Record a group of transactions pertaining to a service business in a two-column general journal.

2 Post entries from a two-column general journal to general ledger accounts.

3 Prepare a trial balance from the ledger accounts.

4 Correct entries using the manual ruling method.

5 Correct entries using the manual or computerized correcting entry method.

ACCOUNTING LANGUAGE

Account numbers *(p. 88)*

Cost principle *(p. 83)*

Cross-reference *(p. 89)*

General ledger *(p. 88)*

Journal *(p. 79)*

Journalizing *(p. 80)*

Ledger account *(p. 88)*

Posting *(p. 88)*

Source documents *(p. 80)*

Two-column general journal *(p. 80)*

In Chapter 2, we learned how to use T accounts as a tool for practicing debits and credits. We also used the trial balance as a means of making sure the debits equal the credits. In this chapter, we will further formalize our accounting procedures by presenting the general journal and the posting procedure.

Recall that *recording* is a step in the definition of accounting. Here we introduce the journal as the official record of business transactions. We have recorded business transactions as debits and credits to T accounts because, in the process of formulating debits and credits for business transactions, it's easier to visualize these debits and credits as the plus and minus sides of the T accounts involved. **Formulating the appropriate transaction debits and credits is the most important element in the accounting process.** It represents the very basic foundation of accounting, and all the structure represented by financial statements and other reports is entirely dependent upon it. After determining the debits and credits, the accountant records the transactions in a journal and a ledger.

The initial steps in the accounting process are:

STEP 1. Record business transactions in a journal.

STEP 2. Post entries to accounts in the ledger.

STEP 3. Prepare a trial balance.

In this chapter, we present the general journal and the posting procedure.

THE GENERAL JOURNAL

We have seen that an accountant must keep a record of each transaction. In Chapter 2, we recorded the transactions directly in T accounts; however, only part of the transaction would be listed in each T account. A **journal** is a book in which business transactions are recorded as they happen. In the journal, both the debits and the

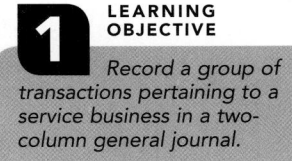

1 LEARNING OBJECTIVE

Record a group of transactions pertaining to a service business in a two-column general journal.

credits of the entire transaction are recorded in one place. Actually, the journal is a diary for the business, in which you record in day-by-day or chronological order all the events involving financial affairs. A journal is called a *book of original entry.* In other words, a transaction is always recorded first in the journal. The process of recording a business transaction in the journal is called **journalizing**. The information about transactions comes from business papers, such as checks, invoices, receipts, letters, and memos. These **source documents** furnish proof (objective evidence) that a transaction has taken place, and they should be identified in the journal entry whenever possible. The basic form of journal is the **two-column general journal**. The term *two-column* refers to the two columns used for debit and credit amounts.

As an example of journalizing business transactions, let's use the transactions for Conner's Whitewater Adventures. The pages of the journal are numbered in consecutive order. This is the first page, so we write a 1 in the space for the page number. Also, we must write the date of each transaction. Let's begin with the first entry.

Transaction (a). **June 1: J. Conner deposited $90,000 in a bank account in the name of Conner's Whitewater Adventures.** First, we will show the complete journal entry.

	GENERAL JOURNAL			PAGE 1
Date	**Description**	**Post. Ref.**	**Debit**	**Credit**
20—				
June 1	Cash		90 0 0 0 00	
	J. Conner, Capital			90 0 0 0 00
	To record the original			
	investment by J. Conner.			

The same elements will be found whether handwriting the entries or journalizing them in an accounting software package. To explain the entry, we break it down line by line. At the top of the page, we record the page number where indicated. On the first line, we record the year in the left part of the Date column. On the second line, we record the month in the left part of the Date column and the day of the month in the right part of the Date column. We don't have to repeat the year and month until we start a new page, or until the year or month changes. (Because our illustrations are separated, however, the month may be repeated to eliminate confusion.)

	GENERAL JOURNAL	Page number	PAGE 1
Date	**Description**	**Post. Ref.**	**Debit**	**Credit**
20—	Date			
June 1				

Decide which accounts should be debited and credited. We do this by analyzing the transactions as we did in Chapter 2.

STEP 1. Decide which accounts are involved.

STEP 2. Classify the accounts involved (asset, liability, owner's equity, revenue, expense).

STEP 3. Decide if the accounts involved are increased or decreased.

STEP 4. Write the transactions as a debit to one account (or accounts) and a credit to another account (or accounts).

STEP 5. Check to see if the equation is in balance.

Cash is involved in our example. Cash is an asset because it falls within the definition of "things owned." Cash is increased, and the increase side of Cash is the left or debit side. So we debit Cash $90,000.

J. Conner, Capital, is involved. J. Conner, Capital, is an owner's equity account because it represents the owner's investment. J. Conner, Capital, is increased, and the increase side of Capital is the right or credit side. So we credit J. Conner, Capital, $90,000. Let's show these entries by referring to our reliable fundamental accounting equation with the accompanying T accounts:

Assets		=	Liabilities		+	Owner's Equity		+	Revenue		−	Expenses	
+	−		−	+		−	+		−	+		+	−
Debit	Credit		Debit	Credit		Debit	Credit		Debit	Credit		Debit	Credit

Cash			J. Conner, Capital	
+	−		−	+
90,000				90,000

You perform this process mentally. If the transaction is more complicated, draw the T accounts on paper. Using T accounts is the accountant's way of drawing a picture of the transaction. You must get into the T account habit; it will be a great help to you in the future.

Always record the debit part of the entry first. Enter the account title—in this case, Cash—in the Description column. Record the amount—$90,000—in the Debit amount column.

GENERAL JOURNAL   PAGE 1

Account title   *Debit amount*

Date	Description	Post. Ref.	Debit	Credit
20—				
June 1	Cash		90 0 0 0 00	

Next, record the credit part of the entry. Enter the account title—in this case, J. Conner, Capital—on the line below the debit in the Description column, indented about one-half inch. On the same line, enter the amount—$90,000—in the Credit column.

GENERAL JOURNAL   PAGE ___1___

Date		Description	Post. Ref.	Debit	Credit
20—					
June	1	Cash		90 0 0 0 00	
		J. Conner, Capital			90 0 0 0 00

Indent the account title that is credited

FYI

In accounting software, there is also space for a brief explanation.

You should now write a brief explanation, in which you should refer to source documents, giving such information as check numbers, receipt numbers, or invoice numbers. You may also list names of charge customers or creditors, or terms of payment. Enter the explanation below the credit entry, indented an additional one-half inch.

GENERAL JOURNAL   PAGE ___1___

Date		Description	Post. Ref.	Debit	Credit
20—					
June	1	Cash		90 0 0 0 00	
		J. Conner, Capital			90 0 0 0 00
		To record the original			
		investment by J. Conner.			

Indent again for the explanation

Remember

As in a trial balance, there are no dollar signs in journal entries.

For an entry in the general journal to be complete, it must contain (1) the date, (2) a debit entry, (3) a credit entry, and (4) an explanation. To anyone thoroughly familiar with the accounts, the explanation may seem quite obvious. Nevertheless, record the explanation as a required, integral part of the entry. To make the journal entries easier to read, leave one blank line between each transaction in your homework.

Transaction (b).   June 2: Conner's Whitewater Adventures bought equipment, paying cash, $38,000. Decide which accounts are involved. Next, determine which of the five possible classifications each part of the transaction applies to. Visualize the plus and minus signs for each classification. Decide whether the accounts are increased or decreased. When you use T accounts to analyze the transaction, the results are as follows:

Equipment		Cash	
+	−	+	−
Debit	Credit	Debit	Credit
38,000			38,000

Now journalize this analysis below the first transaction. Record the day of the month in the Date column. Remember, you do not have to record the month and year again until the month or year changes or you use a new journal page.

GENERAL JOURNAL PAGE 1

Date		Description	Post. Ref.	Debit	Credit
20—					
June	1	Cash		90 0 0 0 00	
		J. Conner, Capital			90 0 0 0 00
		To record the original			
		investment by J. Conner.			
	2	Equipment		38 0 0 0 00	
		Cash			38 0 0 0 00
		Bought equipment for cash.			

Skip a line between entries in homework

Transaction (c).   June 3: Conner's Whitewater Adventures bought equipment on account from Signal Products, $4,320. Again, start with the T accounts.

Equipment			Accounts Payable	
+	–		–	+
Debit	Credit		Debit	Credit
4,320				4,320

After skipping a line in the journal, record the day of the month and then the entry. In journalizing a transaction involving Accounts Payable, always state the name of the creditor in the explanation. Similarly, in journalizing a transaction involving Accounts Receivable, always state the name of the customer who charged the amount in the explanation.

GENERAL JOURNAL PAGE 1

Date		Description	Post. Ref.	Debit	Credit
	3	Equipment		4 3 2 0 00	
		Accounts Payable			4 3 2 0 00
		Bought equipment on account			
		from Signal Products.			

When a business buys an asset, the asset should be recorded at the actual cost (the agreed amount of a transaction). This is called the **cost principle**. For example, suppose that the $4,320 that Conner's Whitewater Adventures paid for the equipment from Signal Products was a bargain price, as Signal Products had been asking $7,500 for the equipment. Conner's Whitewater Adventures *should record the cost of the equipment as the actual amount paid in the transaction that occurred*, which is $4,320. This is true even though the fair market value may indeed be $7,500.

Transaction (d).   June 4: Conner's Whitewater Adventures paid Signal Products, a creditor, on account, $2,000. Picture the T accounts like this:

Cash			Accounts Payable	
+	–		–	+
Debit	Credit		Debit	Credit
	2,000		2,000	

Remember

In trying to figure out how a transaction should be recorded, first decide on the accounts involved. Then classify the accounts as A, L, OE, R, or E. Next, ask yourself whether the accounts are increased or decreased, and think of the related accounts with their plus and minus sides. Now the debits and credits of the transaction will fall into place.

Accounting in Your Future

ACCOUNTING SKILLS

If you decide to work in the field of accounting in a business like Ecotour Expeditions, Inc., there are a number of skills that you need to bring to the position. Of course, you will need to be able to write well, compute accurately, and speak at least one language fluently—those skills are assumed capabilities for nearly any job. But, if you are in the accounting department at Ecotour Expeditions, Inc., you will be expected to be skilled at analyzing transactions, debiting and crediting accounts accurately as you journalize and post those transactions. You may also be required to prepare a trial balance and perhaps financial statements. While your work will be primarily on the computer using a general ledger software package, you still need to understand what goes on behind the screen. This is especially important when totals don't balance or some other error needs to be uncovered and corrected. That is why the first three chapters presented in this textbook are particularly critical to the building of your accounting skills.

Remember

Get in the T account habit. Picture the T accounts in your mind, or draw T accounts on paper with their plus and minus signs. The T account habit is a must.

In this case, we see that cash is decreasing, so we record it on the minus side. We now have a credit to Cash and have completed half of the entry. Next, we recognize that Accounts Payable is involved. We ask ourselves, "Do we owe more or less as a result of this transaction?" The answer is "less," so we record it on the minus, or debit, side of the account.

GENERAL JOURNAL   PAGE ___1___

Date	Description	Post. Ref.	Debit	Credit
4	Accounts Payable		2 0 0 0 00	
	Cash			2 0 0 0 00
	Paid Signal Products on account.			

Now let's list the transactions for June for Conner's Whitewater Adventures with the date of each transaction. The journal entries are illustrated in Figures 1, 2, and 3.

June   1   J. Conner invests $90,000 cash in her new business.

       2   Buys equipment costing $38,000, paying cash.

June 3 Buys equipment costing $4,320 on credit from Signal Products.

4 Pays $2,000 to Signal Products to be applied against the firm's liability of $4,320.

4 J. Conner invests her personal equipment valued at $5,200 in her new business.

7 Receives cash revenue, $8,000.

8 Pays rent for the month, $1,250.

10 Buys supplies on account from Fineman Company, $675.

	GENERAL JOURNAL			PAGE 1	
Date	**Description**	**Post. Ref.**	**Debit**	**Credit**	
20—					
June 1	Cash		90 0 0 0 00		
	J. Conner, Capital			90 0 0 0 00	
	To record the original				
	investment by J. Conner.				
2	Equipment		38 0 0 0 00		
	Cash			38 0 0 0 00	
	Bought equipment for cash.				
3	Equipment		4 3 2 0 00		
	Accounts Payable			4 3 2 0 00	
	Bought equipment on account				
	from Signal Products.				
4	Accounts Payable		2 0 0 0 00		
	Cash			2 0 0 0 00	
	Paid Signal Products on				
	account.				
4	Equipment		5 2 0 0 00		
	J. Conner, Capital			5 2 0 0 00	
	To record the investment				
	by J. Conner in Conner's				
	Whitewater Adventures.				
7	Cash		8 0 0 0 00		
	Income from Tours			8 0 0 0 00	
	Cash revenue.				
8	Rent Expense		1 2 5 0 00		
	Cash			1 2 5 0 00	
	For month ended June 30.				
10	Supplies Expense		6 7 5 00		
	Accounts Payable			6 7 5 00	
	Bought supplies on account				
	from Fineman Company.				

FIGURE 1

Journal entries for Conner's Whitewater Adventures, June 1–10

Remember

You must enter the year and the month at the top of every page in the journal.

Remember

Six types of information must be entered in the general journal for each transaction: the date, the title of the account to be debited, the amount of the debit, the title of the account to be credited, the amount of the credit, and the explanation.

Date	Description	Post. Ref.	Debit	Credit
20—	**GENERAL JOURNAL** PAGE 2			
June 10	Prepaid Insurance		1 8 7 5 00	
	Cash			1 8 7 5 00
	Premium for three-month			
	liability insurance policy.			
14	Advertising Expense		6 2 0 00	
	Accounts Payable			6 2 0 00
	Received bill from			
	advertising with *The Times*.			
15	Accounts Receivable		6 7 5 0 00	
	Income from Tours			6 7 5 0 00
	Billed Crystal River Lodge			
	for services performed.			
15	Accounts Payable		1 5 0 0 00	
	Cash			1 5 0 0 00
	Paid Signal Products on			
	account.			
18	Utilities Expense		2 2 5 00	
	Cash			2 2 5 00
	Paid Solar Power, Inc., for			
	utilities bill.			
20	Accounts Payable		6 2 0 00	
	Cash			6 2 0 00
	Paid *The Times* in full.			
24	Wages Expense		2 3 6 0 00	
	Cash			2 3 6 0 00
	Paid wages of part-time			
	employee.			

June 10 Pays for three-month liability insurance policy, $1,875.

14 Receives bill for newspaper advertising from *The Times*, $620.

15 Conner's Whitewater Adventures signs a contract with Crystal River Lodge to provide rafting adventures for guests. Conner's Whitewater Adventures provides 27 one-day rafting tours and bills Crystal River Lodge for $6,750.

15 Pays $1,500 to Signal Products as a partial payment on account.

18 Receives and pays bill for utilities from Solar Power, Inc., $225.

20 Pays *The Times* for advertising, $620 in full. (This bill has been previously recorded.)

24 Pays wages of part-time employee, $2,360.

26 Buys additional equipment costing $3,780 from Signal Products, paying $1,850 down with the remaining $1,930 on account.

GENERAL JOURNAL PAGE 3

Date		Description	Post. Ref.	Debit	Credit
20—					
June	26	Equipment		3 7 8 0 00	
		Cash			1 8 5 0 00
		Accounts Payable			1 9 3 0 00
		Bought equipment on account			
		from Signal Products.			
	30	Cash		2 5 0 0 00	
		Accounts Receivable			2 5 0 0 00
		Received from Crystal River Lodge			
		to apply on account.			
	30	Cash		8 5 7 0 00	
		Income from Tours			8 5 7 0 00
		Cash revenue.			
	30	J. Conner, Drawing		3 5 0 0 00	
		Cash			3 5 0 0 00
		Withdrawal for personal use.			

FIGURE 3

Journal entries for Conner's Whitewater Adventures, June 26–30

> Every business transaction requires at least one debit and at least one credit. In a general journal, the debit part of the entry is recorded first. The credit part of the entry is recorded next, followed by a brief explanation of the transaction.

Remember

June 30 Receives $2,500 from Crystal River Lodge to apply on amount previously billed.

30 Receives cash revenue, $8,570.

30 J. Conner withdraws cash for personal use, $3,500.

POSTING TO THE GENERAL LEDGER

You can see that the journal is the *book of original entry.* Each transaction must first be recorded in the journal in full. However, it is difficult to determine the balance

The journal is like a diary of the business's financial changes written in chronological or date order.

= DIARY

Diary of the business

The ledger is like sorted laundry—grouped information about each account is summarized in one place.

$$A = L + OE + R - E$$

of any one account, such as Cash, from the general journal entries. So the **ledger account** has been devised to give us a complete record of the transactions recorded in each individual account. The **general ledger** contains all the accounts. It may be a loose-leaf binder so that you can add or remove pages or printouts from your accounting software program. The process of transferring information from the journal to the ledger accounts is called **posting**.

The Chart of Accounts

The accounts in the ledger are arranged according to the chart of accounts, which **is the official list of the ledger accounts in which transactions of a business are recorded.** Assets are listed first, liabilities second, owner's equity third, revenue fourth, and expenses fifth. The chart of accounts for Conner's Whitewater Adventures is as follows:

CHART OF ACCOUNTS

Assets (100–199)
111 Cash
113 Accounts Receivable
117 Prepaid Insurance
124 Equipment

Liabilities (200–299)
221 Accounts Payable

Owner's Equity (300–399)
311 J. Conner, Capital
312 J. Conner, Drawing

Revenue (400–499)
411 Income from Tours

Expenses (500–599)
511 Wages Expense
512 Rent Expense
513 Supplies Expense
514 Advertising Expense
515 Utilities Expense

Notice that the arrangement of the chart of accounts consists of the balance sheet accounts followed by the income statement accounts. The numbers preceding the account titles are the **account numbers**. The digits in the account numbers also indicate account *classifications*. For most companies, assets start with 1, liabilities with 2, owner's equity with 3, revenue with 4, and expenses with 5. The second and third digits indicate the positions of the individual accounts within their respective classifications.

While charts of accounts vary from business to business, the beginning numbers for assets, liabilities, owner's equity, revenues, and expenses are standard for a service business. Some account numbers are much longer than three digits.

For merchandising businesses selling goods (versus services), expenses will start with a 6 because accounts starting with a 5 are reserved for accounts related to the cost of the goods being sold.

Most accounting programs, such as QuickBooks and Peachtree, include a standard chart of accounts set up for many different types of businesses.

The Ledger Account Form (Running Balance Format)

We have been looking at accounts in the simple T account form primarily because T accounts illustrate situations so well. The debit and credit sides are specifically labeled, making the T account form a good way to picture account activity. However, determining the balance of an account using the T account form is difficult. You must add both columns and subtract the smaller total from the larger. To overcome this disadvantage, accountants generally use the four-column account form with Balance columns in the general ledger. Let's look at the Cash account of Conner's Whitewater Adventures in four-column form (Figure 4) compared with the T account form. *Leave the Post. Ref. column blank for now.*

GENERAL LEDGER

ACCOUNT Cash   ACCOUNT NO. 111

Date	Item	Post. Ref.	Debit	Credit	Balance Debit	Balance Credit
20—						
June 1			90 0 0 0 00		90 0 0 0 00	
2				38 0 0 0 00	52 0 0 0 00	
4				2 0 0 0 00	50 0 0 0 00	
7			8 0 0 0 00		58 0 0 0 00	
8				1 2 5 0 00	56 7 5 0 00	
10				1 8 7 5 00	54 8 7 5 00	
15				1 5 0 0 00	53 3 7 5 00	
18				2 2 5 00	53 1 5 0 00	
20				6 2 0 00	52 5 3 0 00	
24				2 3 6 0 00	50 1 7 0 00	
26				1 8 5 0 00	48 3 2 0 00	
30			2 5 0 0 00		50 8 2 0 00	
30			8 5 7 0 00		59 3 9 0 00	
30				3 5 0 0 00	55 8 9 0 00	

⎣_____ Transaction amount _____⎦ ⎣_____ Running balance _____⎦

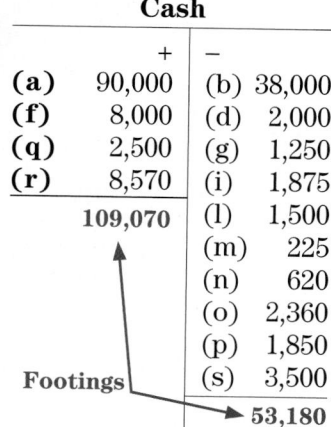

Cash

+	−
(a) 90,000	(b) 38,000
(f) 8,000	(d) 2,000
(q) 2,500	(g) 1,250
(r) 8,570	(i) 1,875
109,070	(l) 1,500
	(m) 225
	(n) 620
	(o) 2,360
	(p) 1,850
Footings	(s) 3,500
	53,180

Balance → 55,890

Note the calculation of the running balance. In the abbreviated form, it looks like this:

GENERAL LEDGER

ACCOUNT Cash   ACCOUNT NO. 111

Date	Item	Post. Ref.	Debit	Credit	Balance Debit	Balance Credit
20—						
June 1			90 0 0 0 00		90 0 0 0 00	
2				38 0 0 0 00	52 0 0 0 00	
4				2 0 0 0 00	50 0 0 0 00	

90,000
− 38,000
52,000
− 2,000
50,000

> To analyze transactions, accountants use T accounts to draw pictures of the transactions. As transactions become more complicated, this is a "must."

Remember

The Posting Process

In the posting process, you must transfer the following information from the journal to the ledger accounts: the *date of the transaction*, the *debit and credit amounts*, and the *page number* of the journal. Post each account separately, using the following steps. Post the debit part of the entry first.

STEP 1. Write the date of the transaction in the account's Date column.

STEP 2. Write the amount of the transaction in the Debit or Credit column, and enter the new balance in the Balance columns under Debit or Credit.

STEP 3. Write the page number of the journal in the Post. Ref. column of the ledger account. (This is a **cross-reference**; it tells where the amount came from.)

STEP 4. Record the ledger account number in the Post. Ref. column of the journal. (This is also a cross-reference; it tells where the amount was posted.)

Entering the account number in the Post. Ref. column of the journal should be the last step. It acts as a verification of the three preceding steps.

2 LEARNING OBJECTIVE

Post entries from a two-column general journal to general ledger accounts.

FIGURE 5

Posting from the general journal to the general ledger—debit entry (Transaction 1)

① Date of transaction
② Amount of transaction
③ Page number of the journal
④ Ledger account number

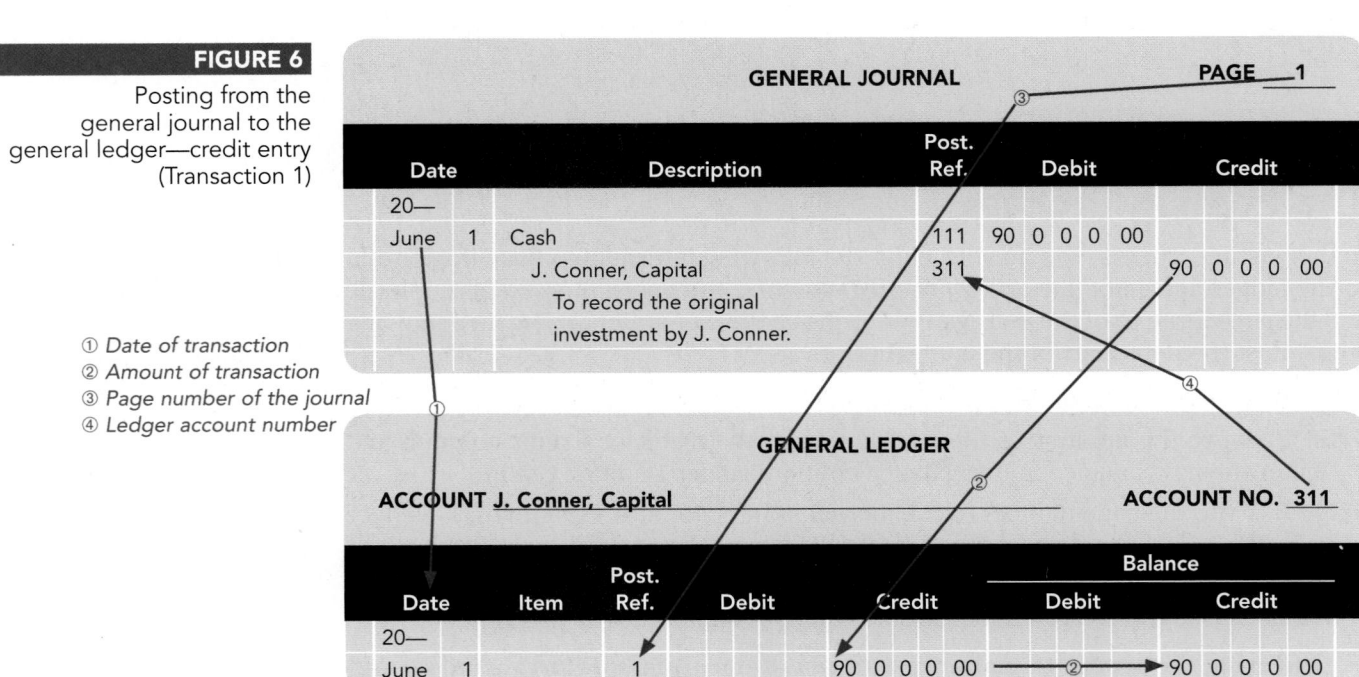

The first transaction for Conner's Whitewater Adventures is illustrated in Figure 5. Let's look first at the debit part of the entry.

Next we post the credit part of the entry, as shown in Figure 6.

The accountant normally uses the Item column only at the end of a financial period. The words that may appear in this column are *balance*, *closing*, *adjusting*, and *reversing*. We will explain the use of these terms later.

Incidentally, some accountants use running balance-type ledger account forms that have only one balance column. However, we have used the two-balance-column arrangement to show clearly the appropriate balance of an account. For example, in Figure 5, Cash has a $90,000 balance recorded in the Debit column (normal balance). In Figure 6, J. Conner, Capital, has a $90,000 balance recorded in the Credit column (normal balance).

FIGURE 6

Posting from the general journal to the general ledger—credit entry (Transaction 1)

① Date of transaction
② Amount of transaction
③ Page number of the journal
④ Ledger account number

In the recording of the second transaction, shown in Figure 7, see if you can identify in order the four steps in the posting process.

GENERAL JOURNAL   PAGE 1

Date	Description	Post. Ref.	Debit	Credit
2	Equipment	124	38 0 0 0 00	
	Cash	111		38 0 0 0 00
	Bought equipment for cash.			

GENERAL LEDGER

ACCOUNT Cash   **ACCOUNT NO. 111**

Date	Item	Post. Ref.	Debit	Credit	Balance Debit	Balance Credit
20—						
June 1		1	90 0 0 0 00		90 0 0 0 00	
2		1		38 0 0 0 00	52 0 0 0 00	

ACCOUNT Equipment   **ACCOUNT NO. 124**

Date	Item	Post. Ref.	Debit	Credit	Balance Debit	Balance Credit
20—						
June 2		1	38 0 0 0 00		38 0 0 0 00	

FIGURE 7
Posting from the general journal to the general ledger (Transaction 2)

Remember

Do not record account numbers in the Post. Ref. column of the journal until the amounts have been posted to the ledger accounts as either debits or credits. When posting with accounting software, the amounts from each transaction are automatically posted to the appropriate general ledger accounts.

Remember

Posting is simply transferring or copying exactly the same date and the debits and credits listed in the journal entry from the journal to the ledger.

Now let's look at the journal entries for the first month of operation for Conner's Whitewater Adventures. As you can see in Figure 8, the Post. Ref. column has been filled in, because the posting has been completed.

If the temporary balance of an account happens to be zero, insert long dashes through both the Debit Balance and the Credit Balance columns. We'll use another business, the Becker Company, in this example. Its Accounts Receivable ledger account follows. Notice that the zero balance on October 29 is represented by long dashes in the Debit and Credit columns.

GENERAL LEDGER

ACCOUNT Accounts Receivable   **ACCOUNT NO. 113**

Date	Item	Post. Ref.	Debit	Credit	Balance Debit	Balance Credit
20—						
Oct. 7		96	1 5 0 00		1 5 0 00	
19		97	2 4 8 00		3 9 8 00	
21		97		1 5 0 00	2 4 8 00	
29		98		2 4 8 00	———	———
31		98	1 8 2 00		1 8 2 00	

FIGURE 8

Journal entries for Conner's Whitewater Adventures (first month of operation)

			GENERAL JOURNAL			PAGE	1	
Date		Description	Post. Ref.	Debit		Credit		
20—								
June	1	Cash	111	90 0 0 0 00				
		J. Conner, Capital	311			90 0 0 0 00		
		To record the original						
		investment by J. Conner.						
	2	Equipment	124	38 0 0 0 00				
		Cash	111			38 0 0 0 00		
		Bought equipment for cash.						
	3	Equipment	124	4 3 2 0 00				
		Accounts Payable	221			4 3 2 0 00		
		Bought equipment on						
		account from Signal						
		Products.						
	4	Accounts Payable	221	2 0 0 0 00				
		Cash	111			2 0 0 0 00		
		Paid Signal Products on						
		account.						
	4	Equipment	124	5 2 0 0 00				
		J. Conner, Capital	311			5 2 0 0 00		
		To record the investment						
		by J. Conner in Conner's						
		Whitewater Adventures.						
	7	Cash	111	8 0 0 0 00				
		Income from Tours	411			8 0 0 0 00		
		Cash revenue.						
	8	Rent Expense	512	1 2 5 0 00				
		Cash	111			1 2 5 0 00		
		For month ended June 30.						
	10	Supplies Expense	513	6 7 5 00				
		Accounts Payable	221			6 7 5 00		
		Bought supplies on account						
		from Fineman Company.						

			GENERAL JOURNAL			PAGE	2	
Date		Description	Post. Ref.	Debit		Credit		
20—								
June	10	Prepaid Insurance	117	1 8 7 5 00				
		Cash	111			1 8 7 5 00		
		Premium for three-month						
		liability insurance policy.						
	14	Advertising Expense	514	6 2 0 00				
		Accounts Payable	221			6 2 0 00		
		Received bill from						
		advertising with *The Times*.						

FIGURE 8

(Concluded)

Date	Description	Post. Ref.	Debit	Credit
15	Accounts Receivable	113	6 7 5 0 00	
	Income from Tours	411		6 7 5 0 00
	Billed Crystal River Lodge			
	for services performed.			
15	Accounts Payable	221	1 5 0 0 00	
	Cash	111		1 5 0 0 00
	Paid Signal Products on			
	account.			
18	Utilities Expense	515	2 2 5 00	
	Cash	111		2 2 5 00
	Paid Solar Power, Inc.,			
	for utilities bill.			
20	Accounts Payable	221	6 2 0 00	
	Cash	111		6 2 0 00
	Paid *The Times* in full.			
24	Wages Expense	511	2 3 6 0 00	
	Cash	111		2 3 6 0 00
	Paid wages of part-time			
	employee.			

		GENERAL JOURNAL		**PAGE** 3	

Date		Description	Post. Ref.	Debit	Credit
20—					
June	26	Equipment	124	3 7 8 0 00	
		Cash	111		1 8 5 0 00
		Accounts Payable	221		1 9 3 0 00
		Bought equipment on			
		account from Signal			
		Products.			
	30	Cash	111	2 5 0 0 00	
		Accounts Receivable	113		2 5 0 0 00
		Received from Crystal			
		River Lodge to apply on			
		account.			
	30	Cash	111	8 5 7 0 00	
		Income from Tours	411		8 5 7 0 00
		Cash revenue.			
	30	J. Conner, Drawing	312	3 5 0 0 00	
		Cash	111		3 5 0 0 00
		Withdrawal for personal use.			

Although Figure 8 contains a written version of the journal entries, journal entries prepared in computerized accounting programs are very similar. Computerized accounting programs still require you to record the journal entries as we have demonstrated, including the journal explanations. The ledger accounts and entries for Conner's Whitewater Adventures are shown in Figure 9.

FIGURE 9

General ledger for Conner's Whitewater Adventures (first month of operation)

GENERAL LEDGER

ACCOUNT Cash   **ACCOUNT NO. 111**

Date	Item	Post. Ref.	Debit	Credit	Balance Debit	Balance Credit
20—						
June 1		1	90 0 0 0 00		90 0 0 0 00	
2		1		38 0 0 0 00	52 0 0 0 00	
4		1		2 0 0 0 00	50 0 0 0 00	
7		1	8 0 0 0 00		58 0 0 0 00	
8		1		1 2 5 0 00	56 7 5 0 00	
10		2		1 8 7 5 00	54 8 7 5 00	
15		2		1 5 0 0 00	53 3 7 5 00	
18		2		2 2 5 00	53 1 5 0 00	
20		2		6 2 0 00	52 5 3 0 00	
24		2		2 3 6 0 00	50 1 7 0 00	
26		3		1 8 5 0 00	48 3 2 0 00	
30		3	2 5 0 0 00		50 8 2 0 00	
30		3	8 5 7 0 00		59 3 9 0 00	
30		3		3 5 0 0 00	55 8 9 0 00	

ACCOUNT Accounts Receivable   **ACCOUNT NO. 113**

Date	Item	Post. Ref.	Debit	Credit	Balance Debit	Balance Credit
20—						
June 15		2	6 7 5 0 00		6 7 5 0 00	
30		3		2 5 0 0 00	4 2 5 0 00	

ACCOUNT Prepaid Insurance   **ACCOUNT NO. 117**

Date	Item	Post. Ref.	Debit	Credit	Balance Debit	Balance Credit
20—						
June 10		2	1 8 7 5 00		1 8 7 5 00	

ACCOUNT Equipment   **ACCOUNT NO. 124**

Date	Item	Post. Ref.	Debit	Credit	Balance Debit	Balance Credit
20—						
June 2		1	38 0 0 0 00		38 0 0 0 00	
3		1	4 3 2 0 00		42 3 2 0 00	
4		1	5 2 0 0 00		47 5 2 0 00	
26		3	3 7 8 0 00		51 3 0 0 00	

ACCOUNT Accounts Payable   **ACCOUNT NO.** 221

Date	Item	Post. Ref.	Debit	Credit	Balance Debit	Balance Credit
20—						
June 3		1		4 3 2 0 00		4 3 2 0 00
4		1	2 0 0 0 00			2 3 2 0 00
10		1		6 7 5 00		2 9 9 5 00
14		2		6 2 0 00		3 6 1 5 00
15		2	1 5 0 0 00			2 1 1 5 00
20		2	6 2 0 00			1 4 9 5 00
26		3		1 9 3 0 00		3 4 2 5 00

ACCOUNT J. Conner, Capital   **ACCOUNT NO.** 311

Date	Item	Post. Ref.	Debit	Credit	Balance Debit	Balance Credit
20—						
June 1		1		90 0 0 0 00		90 0 0 0 00
4		1		5 2 0 0 00		95 2 0 0 00

ACCOUNT J. Conner, Drawing   **ACCOUNT NO.** 312

Date	Item	Post. Ref.	Debit	Credit	Balance Debit	Balance Credit
20—						
June 30		3	3 5 0 0 00		3 5 0 0 00	

ACCOUNT Income from Tours   **ACCOUNT NO.** 411

Date	Item	Post. Ref.	Debit	Credit	Balance Debit	Balance Credit
20—						
June 7		1		8 0 0 0 00		8 0 0 0 00
15		2		6 7 5 0 00		14 7 5 0 00
30		3		8 5 7 0 00		23 3 2 0 00

ACCOUNT Wages Expense   **ACCOUNT NO.** 511

Date	Item	Post. Ref.	Debit	Credit	Balance Debit	Balance Credit
20—						
June 24		2	2 3 6 0 00		2 3 6 0 00	

FIGURE 9
(Continued)

ACCOUNT __Rent Expense__   ACCOUNT NO. __512__

Date	Item	Post. Ref.	Debit	Credit	Balance Debit	Balance Credit
20—						
June 8		1	1 2 5 0 00		1 2 5 0 00	

ACCOUNT __Supplies Expense__   ACCOUNT NO. __513__

Date	Item	Post. Ref.	Debit	Credit	Balance Debit	Balance Credit
20—						
June 10		1	6 7 5 00		6 7 5 00	

ACCOUNT __Advertising Expense__   ACCOUNT NO. __514__

Date	Item	Post. Ref.	Debit	Credit	Balance Debit	Balance Credit
20—						
June 14		2	6 2 0 00		6 2 0 00	

ACCOUNT __Utilities Expense__   ACCOUNT NO. __515__

Date	Item	Post. Ref.	Debit	Credit	Balance Debit	Balance Credit
20—						
June 18		2	2 2 5 00		2 2 5 00	

Preparation of the Trial Balance

LEARNING OBJECTIVE 3

Prepare a trial balance from the ledger accounts.

The trial balance is simply a list of the ledger accounts that have balances. A trial balance is presented in Figure 10.

Remember that the trial balance proves only that the total ledger debit balances equal the total ledger credit balances. Even when the debit and credit balances are equal, other types of errors may slip through—for example,

1. Posting the correct debit or credit amounts to the incorrect account.
2. Neglecting to journalize or post an entire transaction.

Conner's Whitewater Adventures Trial Balance June 30, 20—		
Account Name	**Debit**	**Credit**
Cash	55,890	
Accounts Receivable	4,250	
Prepaid Insurance	1,875	
Equipment	51,300	
Accounts Payable		3,425
J. Conner, Capital		95,200
J. Conner, Drawing	3,500	
Income from Tours		23,320
Wages Expense	2,360	
Rent Expense	1,250	
Supplies Expense	675	
Advertising Expense	620	
Utilities Expense	225	
	121,945	121,945

FIGURE 10

Trial balance for Conner's Whitewater Adventures

Steps in the Accounting Process

So far, you have learned the first three steps in the accounting process.

STEP 1. Record the transactions of a business in a journal (book of original entry or the day-by-day record of the transactions of a firm). An entry should be based on some source document or evidence that a transaction has occurred, such as an invoice, a receipt, or a check.

STEP 2. Post entries to the accounts in the ledger. Transfer the amounts from the journal to the Debit or Credit columns of the specified accounts in the ledger. Use a cross-reference system. Accounts are organized in the ledger according to the account numbers assigned to them in the chart of accounts.

STEP 3. Prepare a trial balance. Record the balances of the ledger accounts in the appropriate column, Debit or Credit, of the trial balance form. Prove that the total of the debit balances equals the total of the credit balances.

Source Document

A source document can be an invoice, a receipt, a check, or so forth. We now add an important detail in the recording of a journal entry. This detail consists of listing the related source document number, which is used as a reference for the proof of a transaction. Figure 11 is an example of a source document followed by the journal entry (Figure 12) and ledger accounts (Figure 13). Note how the explanation differs from the one we showed earlier.

Using the source document, the journal entry is recorded in the journal (Figure 12). Note how the explanation includes important information from the source document.

The journal entry is then posted to the ledger (Figure 13).

FIGURE 11
Source document

INVOICE

FINEMAN COMPANY   No. 4-962

220 East Ames Street, Denver CO 80012
Sold By: 203 Date: 6/10/20—
Name: Conner's Whitewater Adventures
Address: 1701 East Delaware Street
           Colorado Springs, CO 80902
Terms: Net 30 days

Quantity	Description	Unit Price		Amount	
10 bx	Invoice forms	12	00	120	00
5 bx	Ink cartridges	32	00	160	00
3 bx	8 x 11 copy paper	20	00	60	00
2	File cabinets, 2-drawer	32	00	64	00
4 bx	3-tab folders	12	00	48	00
3	10-key electric calculators	24	00	72	00
5 bx	12-count black ink pens	12	00	60	00
5 bx	10-count mechanical pencils	10	00	50	00
	SUBTOTAL			634	00
	SALES TAX			41	00
	SHIPPING—free			0	00
	TOTAL			675	00

FIGURE 12
Journal entry related to
source document

GENERAL JOURNAL   PAGE 1

Date		Description	Post. Ref.	Debit	Credit
June	10	Supplies Expense	513	6 7 5 00	
		Accounts Payable	221		6 7 5 00
		Bought supplies on account			
		from Fineman Company,			
		Invoice No. 4-962.			

FIGURE 13
Ledger posting

ACCOUNT Accounts Payable   **ACCOUNT NO.** 221

Date		Item	Post. Ref.	Debit	Credit	Balance Debit	Balance Credit
20—							
June	3		1		4 3 2 0 00		4 3 2 0 00
	4		1	2 0 0 0 00			2 3 2 0 00
	10		1		6 7 5 00		2 9 9 5 00

Previous postings

ACCOUNT Supplies Expense   **ACCOUNT NO.** 513

Date		Item	Post. Ref.	Debit	Credit	Balance Debit	Balance Credit
20—							
June	10		1	6 7 5 00		6 7 5 00	

SMALL BUSINESS SUCCESS

Paperwork—Why It's Worth Keeping Track Of!

As you analyze transactions for a business, you may have noticed that each transaction must be evidenced by a source document. Source documents, or the paperwork for transactions, is very important to all businesses. This is because all accounting transactions are developed from source documents. So what are some examples of source documents? Bills from vendors, checks from customers, deposit slips, credit card receipts, bank statements, and customer invoices are all example of source documents.

Many times businesses will use an accounting software program to create source documents that can be printed for the businesses' or customers' records. Source documents should include the name and address of the business, as well as the date, amount, and description of the transaction. The documents should also include any customer information. The detail provided on the source documents will help the accountant record the transactions.

Source documents are also needed to substantiate the transactions should the business be audited. Internal and external auditors will review the paperwork when determining if the transactions recorded by the business are accurate. The Internal Revenue Service (IRS) will also require the business to provide proof of transactions for income and deductions shown on the entity's tax return.

Is it necessary for the business to keep source documents forever? Well, that depends on what the source document is and who you talk to! Many accountants agree on the following guidelines:

Source Document	Time Period
Support for your tax return	3 years
Related to assets purchased, such as a business vehicle or computer	Keep until you sell or dispose
Documents such as accounts receivable or accounts payable ledgers, bank statements, canceled checks, and invoices	7 years
Items such as loan documents, tax returns, and financial statements	Indefinitely

Source documents are an important part of the accounting cycle. Take a moment to make sure that you are comfortable with the information provided on the documents and also that you are familiar with the most common documents used in accounting, such as invoices, deposit slips, receipts, and bills from vendors. As you go through the chapters of the textbook, you will be introduced to many types of source documents. Be sure to review them—there is important information included on these documents!

CORRECTION OF ERRORS—MANUAL AND COMPUTERIZED

Errors are occasionally made in recording journal entries and posting to the ledger accounts whether recording them manually or on a computer. Never erase them, because it might look as if you were trying to hide something. The method for correcting errors depends on how and when the errors were made. There are two manual methods for correcting errors; they are

1. The ruling method.
2. The correcting entry method.

Manual Ruling Method

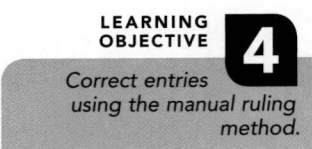

You can use the manual ruling method to correct an error in the journal before posting or to correct an error in the ledger after an entry has been posted.

Manually Correcting Errors Before Posting Has Taken Place

When an error has been made in recording an account title in a journal entry, draw a line through the incorrect account title in the journal entry, and write the correct account title immediately above it. Include your initials with the correction. For example, an entry to record payment of $1,500 rent was incorrectly debited to Salary Expense.

	GENERAL JOURNAL				PAGE 1
Date	Description	Post. Ref.	Debit	Credit	
20—	*Rent Expense*				
Mar. 1	~~Salary Expense~~ *DJM*		1 5 0 0 00		
	Cash			1 5 0 0 00	
	Paid rent for the month.				

When an error has been made in recording an amount, draw a line through the incorrect amount in the journal entry, and write the correct amount immediately above it. For example, an entry for a $120 payment for office supplies was recorded as $210. Include your initials with the correction.

	GENERAL JOURNAL				PAGE 1
Date	Description	Post. Ref.	Debit	Credit	
20—			*DJM* 1 2 0 00		
Apr. 6	Supplies Expense		~~2 1 0~~ 00	*DJM* 1 2 0 00	
	Cash			~~2 1 0~~ 00	
	Bought office supplies.				

Manually Correcting Errors After Posting Has Taken Place

When an entry was journalized correctly but one of the amounts was posted incorrectly, correct the error by drawing a single line through the amount and recording the correct amount above it. For example, an entry to record cash received for professional fees was correctly journalized as $400. However, it was posted as a debit to Cash for $400 and a credit to Professional Fees for $4,000. In the Professional Fees account, draw a line through $4,000 and insert $400 either above or next to the incorrect amount. Change the running balance of the account and initial the corrections.

ACCOUNT Professional Fees					ACCOUNT NO. 411	
		Post.			Balance	
Date	Item	Ref.	Debit	Credit	Debit	Credit
				DJM 4 0 0 00		*DJM* 25 6 0 0 00
6		94		~~4 0 0 0~~ 00		~~29 2 0 0~~ 00

Correcting Entry Method—Manual or Computerized

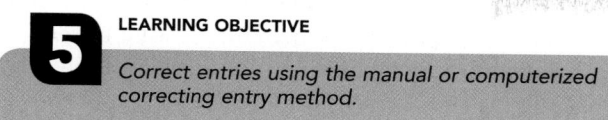

5 LEARNING OBJECTIVE

Correct entries using the manual or computerized correcting entry method.

You should use the correcting entry method when incorrectly journalized amounts have been posted. There are two correcting entry methods; they are

1. *One-step method.* Simply make one entry that undoes the error and provides the correct account.

2. *Two-step method.* The first step reverses the error made by the original entry. The second step includes the correct entry.

The correcting entry should *always* include an explanation. For example, on January 9, a $620 payment for advertising was incorrectly journalized and posted as a debit to Miscellaneous Expense for $620 and a credit to Cash for $620. The error was discovered and corrected on January 27 as follows using the one-step method:

Whether you are preparing accounting records manually or on computer, accuracy is of primary importance. Rapid and accurate ten-key calculator and computer keyboard skills are a must for the accountant or bookkeeper.

	GENERAL JOURNAL			PAGE 1
Date	**Description**	**Post. Ref.**	**Debit**	**Credit**
20—				
Jan. 27	Advertising Expense		6 2 0 00	
	Miscellaneous Expense			6 2 0 00
	To correct error of			
	January 9 in which a			
	payment for Advertising			
	Expense was debited to			
	Miscellaneous Expense.			

Following the two-step method, if the original entry was recorded as a debit to Miscellaneous Expense and a credit to Cash, then reverse this entry by debiting Cash and crediting Miscellaneous Expense, and then record the correct entry.

	GENERAL JOURNAL			PAGE 1
Date	**Description**	**Post. Ref.**	**Debit**	**Credit**
20—				
Jan. 27	Cash		6 2 0 00	
	Miscellaneous Expense			6 2 0 00
	To reverse out an			
	incorrect entry recorded			
	January 9.			
27	Advertising Expense		6 2 0 00	
	Cash			6 2 0 00
	To correct error of			
	January 9 in which a			
	payment for Advertising			
	Expense was debited to			
	Miscellaneous Expense.			

Correcting Errors on the Computer

Again, never delete an error; most commercial accounting programs will not allow deletion because if you could delete an entry, it would destroy the audit trail that tracks the life of each transaction. The procedure (as previously discussed) is to make a correcting entry with a brief and appropriate explanation followed by posting.

After the correcting entry has been journalized, the accounts are posted as for any other entry. After posting, the account balances should be correct.

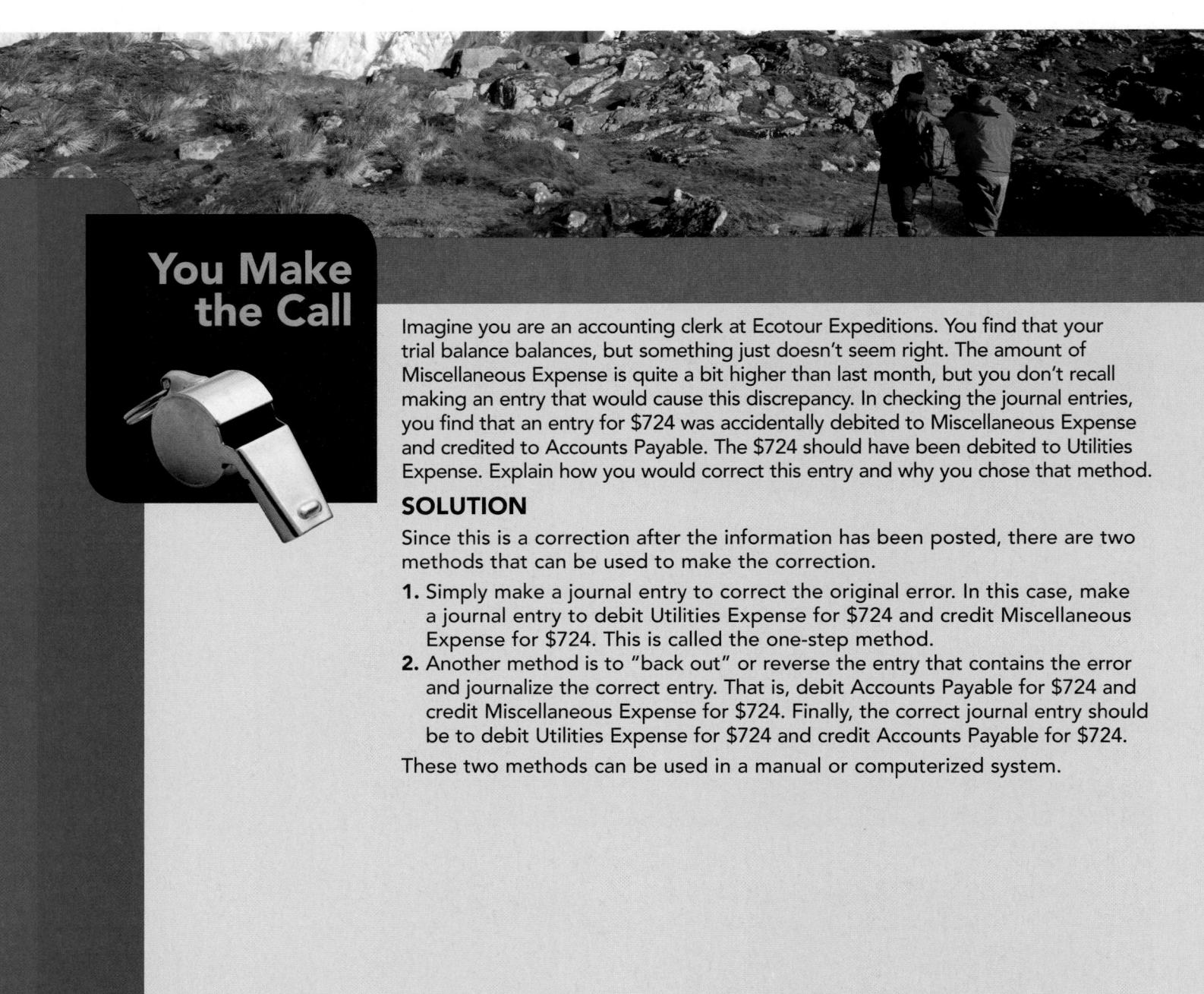

You Make the Call

Imagine you are an accounting clerk at Ecotour Expeditions. You find that your trial balance balances, but something just doesn't seem right. The amount of Miscellaneous Expense is quite a bit higher than last month, but you don't recall making an entry that would cause this discrepancy. In checking the journal entries, you find that an entry for $724 was accidentally debited to Miscellaneous Expense and credited to Accounts Payable. The $724 should have been debited to Utilities Expense. Explain how you would correct this entry and why you chose that method.

SOLUTION

Since this is a correction after the information has been posted, there are two methods that can be used to make the correction.

1. Simply make a journal entry to correct the original error. In this case, make a journal entry to debit Utilities Expense for $724 and credit Miscellaneous Expense for $724. This is called the one-step method.
2. Another method is to "back out" or reverse the entry that contains the error and journalize the correct entry. That is, debit Accounts Payable for $724 and credit Miscellaneous Expense for $724. Finally, the correct journal entry should be to debit Utilities Expense for $724 and credit Accounts Payable for $724.

These two methods can be used in a manual or computerized system.

CHAPTER REVIEW

Study & Practice

1 LEARNING OBJECTIVE
Record a group of transactions pertaining to a service business in a two-column general journal.

Based on **source documents**, the transactions are analyzed to determine the accounts involved and whether the accounts are debited or credited. For each transaction, total debits must equal total credits. The **journal** is a book of original entry in which a day-by-day record of business transactions is maintained. The parts of a journal entry consist of the transaction date, the title of the account(s) debited, the title of the account(s) credited, the amounts recorded in the Debit and Credit columns, and an explanation.

PRACTICE EXERCISE 1

Journalize the following transactions for the month of June:

June   1   J. Jonah deposited $35,000 in the bank in the name of the business (Jonah Company).

      2   The business purchased $8,000 in equipment, paying $2,000 in cash and placing the remainder on account.

      4   The business purchased supplies for cash, $250.

   10   The business received cash revenue, $3,250.

   20   The business paid the monthly rent, $1,800.

   24   J. Jonah withdrew $500 for personal use.

PRACTICE EXERCISE 1 SOLUTION

GENERAL JOURNAL												PAGE 1				
Date	Description	Post. Ref.	Debit						Credit					
20—														
June 1	Cash		35	0	0	0	00							
	J. Jonah, Capital								35	0	0	0	00
	Jonah invested cash.												
2	Equipment		8	0	0	0	00						
	Cash								2	0	0	0	00
	Accounts Payable								6	0	0	0	00
	Purchased equipment.												
4	Supplies Expense			2	5	0	00						
	Cash									2	5	0	00
	Purchased supplies.												
10	Cash		3	2	5	0	00						
	Income from Services								3	2	5	0	00
	Cash revenue.												
20	Rent Expense		1	8	0	0	00						
	Cash								1	8	0	0	00
	Paid the monthly rent.												
24	J. Jonah, Drawing			5	0	0	00						
	Cash									5	0	0	00
	Withdrawal for personal use.												

2 LEARNING OBJECTIVE

Post entries from a two-column general journal to general ledger accounts.

The **general ledger** is a book that contains all the accounts, arranged according to the chart of accounts. **Posting** is the process of transferring information from the journal to the **ledger accounts**. The posting process consists of four steps:

STEP 1. Write the date of the transaction in the account's Date column.

STEP 2. Write the amount of the transaction in the Debit or Credit column, and enter the new balance in the Balance columns under Debit or Credit.

STEP 3. Write the page number of the journal in the Post. Ref. column of the ledger account.

STEP 4. Record the ledger account number in the Post. Ref. column of the journal.

PRACTICE EXERCISE 2

Post the journal entries from Practice Exercise 1 to the following general ledger accounts:

Assets
111 Cash
124 Equipment

Liabilities
221 Accounts Payable

Owner's Equity
311 J. Jonah, Capital
312 J. Jonah, Drawing

Revenue
411 Income from Services

Expenses
512 Rent Expense
513 Supplies Expense

PRACTICE EXERCISE 2 SOLUTION

GENERAL LEDGER

ACCOUNT Cash　　　　ACCOUNT NO. 111

Date		Item	Post. Ref.	Debit	Credit	Balance Debit	Balance Credit
20—							
June	1		1	35 0 0 0 00		35 0 0 0 00	
	2		1		2 0 0 0 00	33 0 0 0 00	
	4		1		2 5 0 00	32 7 5 0 00	
	10		1	3 2 5 0 00		36 0 0 0 00	
	20		1		1 8 0 0 00	34 2 0 0 00	
	24		1		5 0 0 00	33 7 0 0 00	

ACCOUNT Equipment　　　　ACCOUNT NO. 124

Date		Item	Post. Ref.	Debit	Credit	Balance Debit	Balance Credit
20—							
June	2		1	8 0 0 0 00		8 0 0 0 00	

ACCOUNT Accounts Payable   **ACCOUNT NO.** 221

Date	Item	Post. Ref.	Debit	Credit	Balance Debit	Balance Credit
20—						
June 2		1		6 0 0 0 00		6 0 0 0 00

ACCOUNT J. Jonah, Capital   **ACCOUNT NO.** 311

Date	Item	Post. Ref.	Debit	Credit	Balance Debit	Balance Credit
20—						
June 1		1		35 0 0 0 00		35 0 0 0 00

ACCOUNT J. Jonah, Drawing   **ACCOUNT NO.** 312

Date	Item	Post. Ref.	Debit	Credit	Balance Debit	Balance Credit
20—						
June 24		1	5 0 0 00		5 0 0 00	

ACCOUNT Income from Services   **ACCOUNT NO.** 411

Date	Item	Post. Ref.	Debit	Credit	Balance Debit	Balance Credit
20—						
June 10		1		3 2 5 0 00		3 2 5 0 00

ACCOUNT Rent Expense   **ACCOUNT NO.** 512

Date	Item	Post. Ref.	Debit	Credit	Balance Debit	Balance Credit
20—						
June 20		1	1 8 0 0 00		1 8 0 0 00	

ACCOUNT Supplies Expense   **ACCOUNT NO.** 513

Date	Item	Post. Ref.	Debit	Credit	Balance Debit	Balance Credit
20—						
June 4		1	2 5 0 00		2 5 0 00	

LEARNING OBJECTIVE

Prepare a trial balance from the ledger accounts.

The trial balance consists of a listing of account balances in two columns, one labeled Debit and one labeled Credit. The balances come from the ledger accounts.

PRACTICE EXERCISE 3

Prepare a trial balance from the ledger accounts in Practice Exercise 2.

PRACTICE EXERCISE 3 SOLUTION

Jonah Company
Trial Balance
June 30, 20—

Account Name	Debit	Credit
Cash	33,700	
Equipment	8,000	
Accounts Payable		6,000
J. Jonah, Capital		35,000
J. Jonah, Drawing	500	
Income from Services		3,250
Rent Expense	1,800	
Supplies Expense	250	
	44,250	44,250

LEARNING OBJECTIVE

Correct entries using the manual ruling method.

The manual ruling method can be used if an error is discovered before or after an entry has been posted. Draw a line through the incorrect account title or amount, and write the correct account title or amount immediately above. Include your initials with the correction.

PRACTICE EXERCISE 4

Show the manual correction for the following error: On March 1, an entry to record a payment of $950 rent was incorrectly debited to Wages Expense.

PRACTICE EXERCISE 4 SOLUTION

GENERAL JOURNAL   **PAGE** 1

Date	Description	Post. Ref.	Debit	Credit
20—	*Rent Expense*			
Mar. 1	~~Wages Expense~~ *DJM*		9 5 0 00	
	Cash			9 5 0 00
	Paid rent for the month.			

5 LEARNING OBJECTIVE

Correct entries using the manual or computerized correcting entry method.

This method is used if an error is discovered after an incorrectly journalized entry has been posted. If the error consists of the wrong account(s), an entry is made to cancel out or reverse the incorrect account(s) and insert the correct account(s). The correcting entry should *always* include an explanation.

PRACTICE EXERCISE 5

On July 9, a $380 payment for Supplies Expense was incorrectly journalized and posted as a debit to Utilities Expense for $380 and a credit to Cash for $380. Provide the correcting entry, following the one-step method.

PRACTICE EXERCISE 5 SOLUTION

GENERAL JOURNAL PAGE 1

Date		Description	Post. Ref.	Debit	Credit
20—					
July	9	Supplies Expense		3 8 0 00	
		Utilities Expense			3 8 0 00
		To correct error of July 9			
		in which a payment for			
		Supplies Expense was			
		debited to Utilities Expense.			

Before a Test Check: Chapters 1–3

PART I: MULTIPLE-CHOICE QUESTIONS

____ **1.** Which of the following is not considered an account?
a. Cash
b. Prepaid Insurance
c. Equipment
d. Assets
e. Accounts Receivable

____ **2.** In which of the following transactions would an expense be recorded?
a. Received a bill for advertising.
b. Paid on an account payable for the utility bill.
c. Received and paid a bill for repairs.
d. All of these should be recorded as an expense.
e. Only a and c should be recorded as an expense.

____ **3.** The ending capital balance appears on which of the following statements?
a. Statement of owner's equity
b. Balance sheet
c. Income statement
d. Statement of owner's equity and balance sheet
e. Statement of owner's equity and income statement

____ **4.** On a statement of owner's equity, if beginning capital is $42,000 and there are an additional investment of $5,000, a net loss of $9,000, and owner withdrawals of $15,000, the ending capital amount would be

    a. $70,000.

    b. $23,000.

    c. $40,000.

    d. $54,000.

    e. none of these.

____ **5.** If a $26 cash purchase of supplies is recorded as a $62 debit to Supplies Expense and a $62 credit to Cash, the result will be that

    a. the trial balance will be in balance.

    b. the Supplies Expense account will be overstated.

    c. the Cash account will be understated.

    d. Supplies Expense will be overstated and Cash will be understated.

    e. all of these will be true.

____ **6.** A person who wanted to know the balance of an account would look in

    a. the ledger.

    b. the chart of accounts.

    c. the journal.

    d. the source documents.

    e. none of these.

PART II: THE ACCOUNTING CYCLE

Journalizing, Posting, Trial Balance, and Financial Statements

The accounts and their balances, as of December 1 of this year, for Antec Services are as follows:

111 Cash	$18,900	411 Service Income	$39,600
113 Accounts Receivable	6,300		
116 Prepaid Insurance	1,230	511 Wages Expense	10,450
124 Equipment	31,200	512 Utilities Expense	2,760
		513 Rent Expense	12,620
221 Accounts Payable	6,340	514 Supplies Expense	870
311 J. Dunn, Capital	49,590		
312 J. Dunn, Drawing	11,200		

Check Figure

Net Income, $21,153

Required

1. Journalize the following December transactions in general journal form on journal page 31.

Dec.   1   Sold services for cash, $9,500.

       4   Received and paid the bill for the rent for December, $1,000, Ck. No. 2331.

     11   Received $1,750 on account from customers, Cash Receipt Nos. 1430–1438.

     19   Sold services on account, $2,075, Sales Inv. No. 2591.

     22   Received and paid the bill for utilities, $255, Ck. No. 2332.

     23   Bought supplies on account from Office Works, $292, Inv. No. 2606.

     31   Paid the wages for the month, $1,775, Ck. No. 2333.

     31   Dunn withdrew $1,500 for personal use, Ck. No. 2334.

2. Label T accounts with the above account names.

3. Correctly place the plus and minus signs under all T accounts, and label the debit and credit sides of each T account.

4. Post the entries to the T accounts by date, and foot and balance the accounts.

5. Prepare a trial balance as of December 31.
6. Prepare an income statement for the year ended December 31.
7. Prepare a statement of owner's equity for the year ended December 31.
8. Prepare a balance sheet as of December 31.

ANSWERS: PART I

1. d;   **2.** e;   **3.** d;   **4.** b;   **5.** e;   **6.** a

ANSWERS: PART II

1.

GENERAL JOURNAL								PAGE 31	
Date		**Description**	**Post. Ref.**		**Debit**			**Credit**	
20—									
Dec.	1	Cash	111	9	5 0 0	00			
		Service Income	411				9	5 0 0	00
		Sold services for cash.							
	4	Rent Expense	513	1	0 0 0	00			
		Cash	111				1	0 0 0	00
		Ck. No. 2331.							
	11	Cash	111	1	7 5 0	00			
		Accounts Receivable	113				1	7 5 0	00
		Cash on account from customers,							
		Cash Receipt Nos. 1430–1438.							
	19	Accounts Receivable	113	2	0 7 5	00			
		Service Income	411				2	0 7 5	00
		Sales Inv. No. 2591.							
	22	Utilities Expense	512		2 5 5	00			
		Cash	111					2 5 5	00
		Ck. No. 2332.							
	23	Supplies Expense	514		2 9 2	00			
		Accounts Payable	221					2 9 2	00
		Office Works, Inv. No. 2606.							
	31	Wages Expense	511	1	7 7 5	00			
		Cash	111				1	7 7 5	00
		Paid month's wages, Ck. No. 2333.							
	31	J. Dunn, Drawing	312	1	5 0 0	00			
		Cash	111				1	5 0 0	00
		Ck. No. 2334.							

2, 3, and 4.

Assets = **Liabilities** + **Owner's Equity** + **Revenue** − **Expenses**

Assets

	+ Debit	− Credit

Cash 111

	+ Debit		− Credit
Bal.	18,900	12/4	1,000
12/1	9,500	12/22	255
12/11	1,750	12/31	1,775
	30,150	12/31	1,500
			4,530
Bal.	25,620		

Accounts Receivable 113

	+ Debit		− Credit
Bal.	6,300	12/11	1,750
12/19	2,075		
	8,375		
Bal.	6,625		

Prepaid Insurance 116

	+ Debit	− Credit
Bal.	1,230	

Equipment 124

	+ Debit	− Credit
Bal.	31,200	

Liabilities

− Debit	+ Credit

Accounts Payable 221

− Debit		+ Credit
	Bal.	6,340
	12/23	292
	Bal.	6,632

Owner's Equity

− Debit	+ Credit

J. Dunn, Capital 311

− Debit		+ Credit
	Bal.	49,590

J. Dunn, Drawing 312

	+ Debit	− Credit
Bal.	11,200	
12/31	1,500	
Bal.	12,700	

Revenue

− Debit	+ Credit

Service Income 411

− Debit		+ Credit
	Bal.	39,600
	12/1	9,500
	12/19	2,075
	Bal.	51,175

Expenses

+ Debit	− Credit

Wages Expense 511

	+ Debit	− Credit
Bal.	10,450	
12/31	1,775	
Bal.	12,225	

Utilities Expense 512

	+ Debit	− Credit
Bal.	2,760	
12/22	255	
Bal.	3,015	

Rent Expense 513

	+ Debit	− Credit
Bal.	12,620	
12/4	1,000	
Bal.	13,620	

Supplies Expense 514

	+ Debit	− Credit
Bal.	870	
12/23	292	
Bal.	1,162	

5.

Antec Services
Trial Balance
December 31, 20—

Account Name	Debit	Credit
Cash	25,620	
Accounts Receivable	6,625	
Prepaid Insurance	1,230	
Equipment	31,200	
Accounts Payable		6,632
J. Dunn, Capital		49,590
J. Dunn, Drawing	12,700	
Service Income		51,175
Wages Expense	12,225	
Utilities Expense	3,015	
Rent Expense	13,620	
Supplies Expense	1,162	
	107,397	107,397

6.

Antec Services
Income Statement
For Year Ended December 31, 20—

Revenue:		
Service Income		$51,175
Expenses:		
Wages Expense	$12,225	
Utilities Expense	3,015	
Rent Expense	13,620	
Supplies Expense	1,162	
Total Expenses		30,022
Net Income		$21,153

7.

Antec Services
Statement of Owner's Equity
For Year Ended December 31, 20—

J. Dunn, Capital, January 1, 20—		$49,590
Investments during Year	$ 0	
Net Income for Year	21,153	
Subtotal	$21,153	
Less Withdrawals for Year	12,700	
Increase in Capital		8,453
J. Dunn, Capital, December 31, 20—		$58,043

8.

Antec Services Balance Sheet December 31, 20—		
Assets		
Cash	$25,620	
Accounts Receivable	6,625	
Prepaid Insurance	1,230	
Equipment	31,200	
Total Assets		$64,675
Liabilities		
Accounts Payable		$ 6,632
Owner's Equity		
J. Dunn, Capital		58,043
Total Liabilities and Owner's Equity		$64,675

Glossary

Account numbers The numbers assigned to accounts according to the chart of accounts. *(p. 88)*

Cost principle The principle that a purchased asset should be recorded at its actual cost. *(p. 83)*

Cross-reference The ledger account number in the Post. Ref. column of the journal and the journal page number in the Post. Ref. column of the ledger account. *(p. 89)*

General ledger A book or file containing the activity (by accounts), either manual or computerized, of a business. *(p. 88)*

Journal The book in which a person makes the original record of a business transaction; commonly referred to as a *book of original entry. (p. 79)*

Journalizing The process of recording a business transaction in a journal. *(p. 80)*

Ledger account A complete record of the transactions recorded in an individual account. *(p. 88)*

Posting The process of transferring figures from the journal to the ledger accounts. *(p. 88)*

Source documents Business papers, such as checks, invoices, receipts, letters, and memos, that furnish proof that a transaction has taken place. *(p. 80)*

Two-column general journal A general journal in which there are two amount columns, one used for debit amounts and one used for credit amounts. *(p. 80)*

CHAPTER ASSIGNMENTS

Discussion Questions

1. Why is the journal called a book of original entry?

2. How does the journal differ from the ledger?

3. What is the purpose of providing a ledger account for each account?

4. List by account classification the order of the accounts in the general ledger.

5. Arrange the following steps in the posting process in correct order:

   a. Write the ledger account number in the Post. Ref. column of the journal.

   b. Write the amount of the transaction.

   c. Write the date of the transaction.

   d. Write the page number of the journal in the Post. Ref. column of the ledger account.

6. What does cross-referencing mean in the posting process?

7. Why is a source document important?

8. What is the first number for each of the following accounts in a chart of accounts listed by account number?
   a. Professional Fees
   b. Utilities Expense
   c. J. R. Watson, Capital
   d. Accounts Receivable
   e. Accounts Payable

Exercises

EXERCISE 3-1 In the following two-column journal, the capital letters represent where parts of a journal entry appear. Write the numbers 1 through 8 on a piece of paper. After each number, match the capital letter where these items appear with the number of the item.

PRACTICE EXERCISE 1

GENERAL JOURNAL   **PAGE** 1

Date	Description	Post. Ref.	Debit	Credit
G				
H	I J	O M		
	K	P		N
	L			

1. Year
2. Month
3. Explanation
4. Title of account debited
5. Ledger account number of account credited
6. Amount of debit
7. Day of the month
8. Title of account credited

EXERCISE 3-2 Decor Services completed the following transactions. Journalize the transactions in general journal form, including brief explanations.

PRACTICE EXERCISE 1

Oct. 7   Received cash on account from Ron Hoyt, a customer, Inv. No. 312, $790.
    15   Paid on account to Modern Ideas, a creditor, $275, Ck. No. 2242.
    20   B. Bunge, the owner, withdrew cash for personal use, $780, Ck. No. 2243.
    23   Bought store supplies for $92 and office supplies for $83 on account from Wegner Office Supply, Inv. No. 1040.
    29   B. Bunge, the owner, invested $4,500 cash and $2,500 of her personal equipment.

EXERCISE 3-3 Montoya Tutoring Service completed the following transactions. Journalize the transactions in general journal form, including brief explanations.

PRACTICE EXERCISE 1

Mar. 1   Bought equipment for $5,798 from Teaching Suppliers, paying $3,798 in cash and placing the balance on account, Ck. No. 3230.
    10   Paid the wages for the first week of March, $1,536, Ck. No. 3231.
    15   Sold services for cash to Mason District, $1,481, Sales Inv. 121.
    26   Sold services on account to Tempe School, $1,400, Sales Inv. 122.
    31   Paid on account to Teaching Suppliers, $725, Ck. No. 3232.

2 LO

PRACTICE EXERCISE 2

EXERCISE 3-4 The following May journal entries all involved cash.

Increases to Cash—Debits		Decreases to Cash—Credits	
5/1	8,500	5/3	840
5/9	1,748	5/8	952
5/16	4,600	5/12	2,100
5/23	890	5/25	3,842
5/30	5,900		

Post the amounts to the ledger account for Cash, Account No. 111. Assume that all transactions appeared on page 6 of the general journal.

2 LO

PRACTICE EXERCISE 2

EXERCISE 3-5 Arrange the following steps in the posting process in correct order:

a. The amount of the balance of the ledger account is recorded in the Debit Balance or Credit Balance column.

b. The amount of the transaction is recorded in the Debit or Credit column of the ledger account.

c. The ledger account number is recorded in the Post. Ref. column of the journal.

d. The date of the transaction is recorded in the Date column of the ledger account.

e. The page number of the journal is recorded in the Post. Ref. column of the ledger account.

3 LO

PRACTICE EXERCISE 3

EXERCISE 3-6 The bookkeeper for Nevado Company has prepared the following trial balance.

Nevado Company
Trial Balance
June 30, 20—

Account Name	Debit	Credit
Cash		2,500
Accounts Receivable	8,300	
Prepaid Insurance	650	
Equipment	15,300	
Accounts Payable		2,700
M. Nevado, Capital		12,500
M. Nevado, Drawing	4,890	
Professional Fees		17,540
Supplies Expense	600	
Rent Expense	500	
Miscellaneous Expense	1,800	
	32,040	35,240

The bookkeeper has asked for your help. In examining the company's journal and ledger, you discover the following errors. Use this information to construct a corrected trial balance.

a. The debits to the Cash account total $8,000, and the credits total $3,300.

b. A $500 payment to a creditor was entered in the journal correctly but was not posted to the Accounts Payable account.

c. The first two numbers in the balance of the Accounts Receivable account were transposed in copying the balance from the ledger to the trial balance.

d. The $1,500 amount withdrawn by the owner for personal use was debited to Miscellaneous Expense by mistake—it was correctly credited to Cash.

EXERCISE 3-7 Determine the effect of the following errors on a company's total revenue, total expenses, and net income. Indicate the effect by writing O for "Overstated (too much)"; U for "Understated (too little)"; or NA for "Not Affected."

LO 4,5

PRACTICES EXERCISES 4,5

Transactions	Total Revenue	Total Expenses	Net Income
Example: A check for $325 was written to pay on account. The accountant debited Rent Expense for $325 and credited Cash for $325.	NA	O	U
a. $420 was received on account from customers. The accountant debited Cash for $420 and credited Professional Fees for $420.			
b. The owner withdrew $1,200 for personal use. The accountant debited Wages Expense for $1,200 and credited Cash for $1,200.			
c. A check was written for $1,250 to pay the rent. The accountant debited Rent Expense for $1,520 and credited Cash for $1,520.			
d. $1,800 was received on account from customers. The accountant debited Cash for $1,800 and credited the Capital account for $1,800.			
e. A check was written for $225 to pay the phone bill received and recorded earlier in the month. The accountant debited Phone Expense for $225 and credited Cash for $225.			

EXERCISE 3-8 Journalize correcting entries for each of the following errors and include a brief explanation.

LO 4,5

PRACTICE EXERCISES 4,5

a. A cash purchase of office equipment for $680 was journalized as a cash purchase of store equipment for $680. (Use the ruling method; assume the entry has not been posted.)

b. An entry for a $180 payment for office supplies was journalized as $810. (Use the ruling method; assume the entry has not been posted.)

c. A $620 payment for repairs was journalized and posted as a debit to Equipment instead of a debit to Repair Expense. (Use the correcting entry method to journalize the correction.)

d. A $750 bill for vehicle insurance was received and immediately paid. It was journalized and posted as $660. (Use the correcting entry method to journalize the correction.)

Problem Set A

For additional help, see the demonstration problem at the beginning of each chapter in your Working Papers.

PROBLEM 3-1A The chart of accounts of the Barnes School is shown here, followed by the transactions that took place during October of this year:

Assets
111 Cash
113 Accounts Receivable
115 Prepaid Insurance
124 Equipment
127 Furniture

Liabilities
221 Accounts Payable

Owner's Equity
311 R. Barnes, Capital
312 R. Barnes, Drawing

Revenue
411 Tuition Income

Expenses
511 Salary Expense
512 Rent Expense
513 Gas and Oil Expense
514 Advertising Expense
515 Repair Expense
516 Telephone Expense
517 Utilities Expense
529 Miscellaneous Expense

Oct. 1 Bought liability insurance for one year, $1,850, Ck. No. 1527.
      3 Received a bill for advertising from *Business Summary*, $415.
      4 Paid the rent for the current month, $1,870, Ck. No. 1528.
      7 Received a bill for equipment repair from Fix-It Service, $318, Inv. No. 436.
     10 Received and deposited tuition from students, $6,375.
     11 Received and paid the telephone bill, $312, Ck. No. 1529.
     15 Bought desks and chairs from The Oak Center, $1,980, paying $980 in cash and placing the balance on account, Ck. No. 1530.
     18 Paid on account to *Business Summary*, a creditor, $415, Ck. No. 1531.
     21 R. Barnes withdrew $1,000 for personal use, Ck. No. 1532.
     24 Received a bill for gas and oil from Wagner Oil Company, $225, Inv. No. 682.
     25 Received and deposited tuition from students, $6,380.
     27 Paid the salary of the part-time office assistant, $1,150, Ck. No. 1533.
     28 Bought a photocopier on account from Gorst Office Machines, $1,950, Inv. No. 417.
     29 Received $950 tuition from a student who had charged the tuition on account last month.
     30 Received and paid the bill for utilities, $623, Ck. No. 1534.
     31 Paid for flower arrangements for front office, $87, Ck. No. 1535.
     31 R. Barnes invested his personal computer and printer, with a fair market value of $1,549, in the business.

Check Figure
Equipment increased by $3,499 in October

Required
Record these transactions in the general journal, including a brief explanation for each entry. Number the journal pages 31 and 32.

PROBLEM 3-2A The journal entries for August, Carley's Car Care's second month of business, have been journalized in the general journal in your Working Papers. The balances of the accounts as of July 31 have been recorded in the general ledger in your Working Papers. Notice the word *Balance* in the Item column, the check mark in the Post. Ref. column, and that the amount is in the Balance column only. This indicates a balance brought forward from a prior page or month.

Required

Check Figure
Net Income, $10,534

1. Write the owner's name, M. Carley, in the Capital and Drawing accounts.
2. Post the general journal entries to the general ledger accounts.
3. Prepare a trial balance as of August 31, 20—.
4. Prepare an income statement for the two months ended August 31, 20—.
5. Prepare a statement of owner's equity for the two months ended August 31, 20—.
6. Prepare a balance sheet as of August 31, 20—.

PROBLEM 3-3A Following is the chart of accounts of the C. Lucern Clinic.

LO 1,2,3

Assets
111 Cash
113 Accounts Receivable
117 Prepaid Insurance
124 Equipment

Liabilities
221 Accounts Payable

Owner's Equity
311 C. Lucern, Capital
312 C. Lucern, Drawing

Revenue
411 Professional Fees

Expenses
511 Salary Expense
512 Rent Expense
513 Laboratory Expense
514 Utilities Expense
515 Supplies Expense

Dr. Lucern completed the following transactions during July:

July 1 Bought laboratory equipment on account from Laser Surgical Supply Company, $3,660, paying $1,660 in cash and placing the remainder on account, Ck. No. 1730.
     3 Paid the office rent for the current month, $1,300, Ck. No. 1731.
     5 Received cash on account from patients, $360.
     6 Bought supplies on account from McRae Supply Company, $315, Inv. No. 3455.
     7 Received and paid the bill for laboratory services, $1,380, Ck. No. 1732.
     8 Bought insurance for one year, $2,650, Ck. No. 1733.
   12 Performed medical services for patients on account, $5,886.
   15 Performed medical services for patients for cash, $4,793.
   16 The equipment purchased on July 1 was found to be broken. Dr. Lucern returned the damaged part and received a reduction in his bill, $518, Inv. No. 3162, Credit Memo No. 141. (Credit Equipment.)
   18 Paid the salary of the part-time nurse, $2,100, Ck. No. 1734.
   24 Received and paid the telephone bill for the month, $624, Ck. No. 1735.
   28 Performed medical services for patients on account, $7,381.
   29 Dr. Lucern withdrew cash for his personal use, $2,000, Ck. No. 1736.

Required

Check Figure
Trial balance total, $62,679

1. Journalize the transactions for July in the general journal, beginning on page 21.
2. Write the name of the owner next to the Capital and Drawing accounts in the general ledger. The balances of the accounts as of June 30 have been recorded in the general ledger in your Working Papers. Notice the word *Balance* in the Item column, the check mark in the Post. Ref. column, and that the amount is in the Balance column only. This indicates a balance brought forward from a prior page or month.
3. Post the entries to the general ledger accounts.
4. Prepare a trial balance.

1,2,3 LO

PROBLEM 3-4A Lara's Landscaping Service has the following chart of accounts:

Assets
111 Cash
113 Accounts Receivable
117 Prepaid Insurance
124 Equipment

Liabilities
221 Accounts Payable

Owner's Equity
311 J. Lara, Capital
312 J. Lara, Drawing

Revenue
411 Landscaping Income

Expenses
511 Salary Expense
512 Rent Expense
513 Gas and Oil Expense
514 Utilities Expense
515 Supplies Expense

The following transactions were completed by Lara's Landscaping Service:

Mar. 1 Lara deposited $35,000 in a bank account in the name of the business.
4 Lara invested his personal landscaping equipment, with a fair market value of $1,325, in the business.
6 Bought a used trailer on account from Tow Sales, $915, Inv. No. 314.
7 Paid the rent for the current month, $950, Ck. No. 1000.
9 Bought a used backhoe from Digger's Equipment, $5,300, paying $3,000 in cash and placing the balance on account, Inv. 4166, Ck. No. 1001.
10 Bought liability insurance for one year, $1,800, Ck. No. 1002.
13 Sold landscaping services on account to Fredkey's, $3,895, Inv. No. 100.
14 Bought supplies on account from Office Requip, $380, Inv. No. 5172.
15 Sold landscaping services on account to C. Endel, $2,832, Inv. No. 101.
17 Received and paid the bill from Commercial Services for gas and oil for the equipment, $180, Ck. No. 1003.
19 Sold landscaping services for cash to Riston Company, $1,864, Inv. No. 102.
22 Paid on account to Tow Sales, a creditor, $500, Inv. No. 314, Ck. No. 1004.
24 Received on account from Fredkey's, a customer, $800, Inv. No. 100.
28 Sold landscaping services on account to Stevens, Inc., $1,830, Inv. No. 103.
29 Received and paid the telephone bill, $260, Ck. No. 1005.
30 Paid the salary of the employee, $1,850, Ck. No. 1006.
31 Lara withdrew cash for his personal use, $1,500, Ck. No. 1007.

Check Figure
Trial balance total, $49,841

Required
1. Journalize the transactions in the general journal, beginning on page 1. Write a brief explanation for each entry.
2. Write the name of the owner on the Capital and Drawing accounts.
3. Post the journal entries to the general ledger accounts.
4. Prepare a trial balance dated March 31, 20—.

Problem Set B

For additional help, see the demonstration problem at the beginning of each chapter in your Working Papers.

1 LO

PROBLEM 3-1B The chart of accounts of Ethan Academy is shown here, followed by the transactions that took place during December of this year:

Assets
111 Cash
113 Accounts Receivable
115 Prepaid Insurance
124 Equipment
127 Furniture

Liabilities
221 Accounts Payable

Owner's Equity
311 R. Ethan, Capital
312 R. Ethan, Drawing

Revenue
411 Tuition Income

Expenses
511 Salary Expense
512 Rent Expense
513 Gas and Oil Expense
514 Advertising Expense
515 Repair Expense
516 Telephone Expense
517 Utilities Expense
518 Supplies Expense
529 Miscellaneous Expense

Dec. 1 Bought liability insurance for one year, $2,260, Ck. No. 1627.
11 Received a bill for advertising from the *City News*, $415, Statement No. 4267.
12 Paid the rent for the current month, $1,850, Ck. No. 1628.
13 Received a bill for equipment repair from Electronic Services, $345, Inv. No. 547.
16 Received and deposited tuition from students, $5,850.
17 Received and paid the telephone bill, $305, Ck. No. 1629.
18 Bought desks and chairs from School Furniture, $1,625, paying $625 in cash and placing the balance on account, Ck. No. 1630.
20 Paid on account to the *City News*, a creditor, $415, Statement No. 4267, Ck. No. 1631.
21 R. Ethan withdrew $1,000 for personal use, Ck. No. 1632.
26 Received a bill for gas and oil from Discount Oil Company, $210, Inv. No. 591.
27 Received and deposited tuition from students, $6,045.
31 Paid the salary of the office assistant, $1,375, Ck. No. 1633.
31 Bought a fax machine on account from EquipCo, $118, Inv. No. 529.
31 Received $1,150 tuition from a student who had charged the tuition on account last month.
31 Received and paid the bill for utilities, $470, Ck. No. 1634.
31 R. Ethan invested her personal computer and printer, with a fair market value of $1,150, in the business.
31 Bought supplies, $295, Ck. No. 1635.

Required
Record these transactions in the general journal, including a brief explanation for each entry. Number the journal pages 31 and 32.

Check Figure
Equipment increased by $1,268 in December

PROBLEM 3-2B The journal entries for May, Kiddy Day Care's second month of business, have been journalized in the general journal in your Working Papers. The balances of the accounts as of April 30 have been recorded in the general ledger in your Working Papers. Notice the word *Balance* in the Item column, the check mark in the Post. Ref. column, and that the amount is in the Balance column only. This indicates a balance brought forward from a prior page or month.

Required

1. Write the owner's name, R. Ramirez, in the Capital and Drawing accounts.
2. Post the general journal entries to the general ledger accounts.
3. Prepare a trial balance as of May 31, 20—.
4. Prepare an income statement for the two months ended May 31, 20—.
5. Prepare a statement of owner's equity for the two months ended May 31, 20—.
6. Prepare a balance sheet as of May 31, 20—.

Check Figure
Net Income, $11,726

1,2,3 **LO**

GL

PROBLEM 3-3B Following is the chart of accounts of Vance Rehab Clinic.

Assets
111 Cash
113 Accounts Receivable
117 Prepaid Insurance
124 Equipment

Liabilities
221 Accounts Payable

Owner's Equity
311 J. Vance, Capital
312 J. Vance, Drawing

Revenue
411 Professional Fees

Expenses
511 Salary Expense
512 Rent Expense
513 Laboratory Expense
514 Utilities Expense
515 Supplies Expense

Vance completed the following transactions during July:

July 1 Bought laboratory equipment on account from Sage Surgical Supply Company, $6,520, paying $1,520 in cash and placing the remainder on account, Inv. No. 2071, Ck. No. 1930.
3 Paid the office rent for the current month, $1,550, Ck. No. 1931.
5 Received cash on account from patients, $3,045.
6 Bought supplies on account from Allround Supply, $320, Inv. No. 3455.
9 Received and paid the bill for laboratory services, $1,484, Ck. No. 1932.
10 Bought insurance for one year, $2,600, Ck. No. 1933.
12 Performed rehab services for patients on account, $5,185.
14 Performed rehab services for patients for cash, $5,050.
18 Part of the equipment purchased on July 1 was found to be broken. Vance returned the damaged part and received a reduction in her bill, $410, Inv. No. 2071, Credit Memo No. 218. (Credit Equipment.)
20 Paid the salary of the part-time nurse, $2,200, Ck. No. 1934.
22 Received and paid the telephone bill for the month, $380, Ck. No. 1935.
24 Performed rehab services for patients on account, $4,235.
30 Vance withdrew cash for her personal use, $2,000, Ck. No. 1936.

Check Figure
Trial balance total, $46,028

Required
1. Journalize the transactions for July in the general journal, beginning on page 21.
2. Write the name of the owner next to the Capital and Drawing accounts in the general ledger. The balances of the accounts as of June 30 have been recorded in the general ledger in your Working Papers. Notice the word *Balance* in the Item column, the check mark in the Post. Ref. column, and that the amount is in the Balance column only. This indicates a balance brought forward from a prior page or month.
3. Post the entries to the general ledger accounts.
4. Prepare a trial balance.

1,2,3 **LO**

PROBLEM 3-4B Leander's Landscaping Service maintains the following chart of accounts.

Assets
111 Cash
113 Accounts Receivable
117 Prepaid Insurance
124 Equipment

Liabilities
221 Accounts Payable

Owner's Equity
311 O. Leander, Capital
312 O. Leander, Drawing

Revenue
411 Landscaping Income

Expenses
511 Salary Expense
512 Rent Expense
513 Gas and Oil Expense
514 Utilities Expense
515 Supplies Expense

The following transactions were completed by Leander:

Apr. 1 Leander deposited $30,000 in a bank account in the name of the business.
4 Leander invested his personal landscaping equipment, with a fair market value of $1,750, in the business.
6 Bought a used trailer on account from Used Mart, $1,450, Inv. No. 415.
7 Paid the rent for the current month, $925, Ck. No. 100.
9 Bought a used bulldozer from Dray's Equipment, $5,100, paying $2,100 in cash and placing the balance on account, Inv. No. 3255, Ck. No. 101.
10 Bought liability insurance for one year, $2,800, Ck. No. 102.
13 Sold landscaping services on account to Fulton Homes, $4,595, Inv. No. 100.
14 Bought supplies on account from Perry's Supply, $427, Inv. No. 4281.
15 Sold landscaping services on account to D. D. Mau Inc., $3,997, Inv. No. 101.
17 Received and paid the bill from Pumpers for gas and oil for the equipment, $227, Ck. No. 103.
19 Sold landscaping services for cash to Cliff's House, $1,437, Inv. No. 102.
22 Paid on account to Used Mart, a creditor, $450, Inv. No. 415, Ck. No. 104.
24 Received on account from Fulton Homes, a customer, $800, Inv. No. 100.
28 Sold landscaping services on account to H. Ron, $1,785, Inv. No. 103.
29 Received and paid the telephone bill, $321, Ck. No. 105.
30 Paid the salary of the employee, $1,836, Ck. No. 106.
30 Leander withdrew cash for his personal use, $1,500, Ck. No. 107.

Required

1. Journalize the transactions in the general journal, beginning on page 1. Write a brief explanation for each entry.
2. Write the name of the owner on the Capital and Drawing accounts.
3. Post the journal entries to the general ledger accounts.
4. Prepare a trial balance dated April 30, 20—.

Check Figure
Trial balance total, $47,991

ACTIVITIES

CONSIDER AND COMMUNICATE

You are the new bookkeeper in a small business. The bookkeeper whose job you are taking is training you on the business's manual system. As he journalizes, he writes the account number in the Post. Ref. column because he thinks it's easier. Then, when he posts, he won't have to be bothered writing the account numbers. How would you explain why he should *not* write the account number in the Post. Ref. column immediately and should instead enter the account number after he has posted the amount to the ledger?

CRITICAL THINKING

You work as an accounting clerk. You have received the following information supplied by a client, S. Winston, from the client's bank statement, the client's tax returns, and a variety of other July documents. The client wants you to prepare an income statement, a statement of owner's equity, and a balance sheet for the month of July for Winston Company.

Income from Services	$ 9,570	Utilities Expense	$ 388
Beginning Capital	50,000	Drawing	2,500
Cash	24,940	Supplies Expense	635
Truck	?	Equipment	16,148
Accounts Payable	?	Total Liabilities and Owner's	
Rent Expense	1,200	Equity	56,838
Wages Expense	4,200		

All About You Spa

Journalizing, Posting, and Preparing a Trial Balance

Meet the owner

A friend of yours, Anika Valli, has decided to open a spa to serve her small resort town of about 7,000 people and 4 million tourists annually. She has named the business All About You Spa to convey the idea that the business intends to pamper those who enter its doors. She will operate the spa five days a week, Tuesday through Saturday, but a phone line will always be available to answer questions and take appointments. Hours will be from 8 A.M. to 8 P.M. She has asked you to be the bookkeeper for this new business. At the end of the month of June, the owner, Anika Valli, would like you to provide the following:

Determine owner's needs

1. General journal
2. General ledger
3. Trial balance
4. Income statement
5. Statement of owner's equity
6. Balance sheet

Gather information and make assessment

She has kept a checkbook and a file folder with summary evidence of June's spa activity: a check register, a summary report of charges by customers for services provided, all receipts that were issued, and a summary of charges made by All About You Spa. Most of the income from services is received in cash and as charges to credit cards. No checks are accepted, except from approved clients (primarily conference planners and other organizations that book packages as prizes for attendees or gifts for employees, speakers, or other people they want to thank with a spa service or package of services). Anika deposits cash receipts on the 7th, 14th, 21st, and last day of each month.

The first page in the file folder contains the following chart of accounts.

CHART OF ACCOUNTS FOR ALL ABOUT YOU SPA

Assets
111 Cash
113 Accounts Receivable
117 Prepaid Insurance
124 Spa Equipment
128 Office Equipment

Liabilities
211 Accounts Payable

Owner's Equity
311 A. Valli, Capital
312 A. Valli, Drawing

Revenue
411 Income from Services

Expenses
511 Wages Expense
512 Rent Expense
513 Office Supplies Expense
514 Spa Supplies Expense
515 Laundry Expense
516 Advertising Expense
517 Utilities Expense
530 Miscellaneous Expense

Clipped to the front of the file folder is a brochure listing the services of All About You Spa. Part of the brochure is shown on the following page.

1. Install and open Klooster and Allen's General Ledger Software, Version 7.0.
2. Click on the **Open** toolbar button, and select the file entitled **All_About_You_Spa_Ch03.IA7**.
3. Enter your name when prompted and click **OK**.
4. You will be asked if you want to open on-screen instructions and check figures. If you select "No" at this time, you may pull the information up at any time by clicking on the **Info.** toolbar button.

WHERE TO START
Open the data file and save it under a new name that identifies it as containing your work.

All About You Spa Services

Massages

Type	Time	Description	Price
Deep-Tissue Destresser	90 min.	Vigorous, prescriptive	$90.00
Herbal Body Sea Wrap	90 min.	Gentle, cleansing	$90.00
Aromatherapy Healing Experience	90 min.	Gentle, relaxing	$90.00
Healing Stones Experience	90 min.	Healing, relaxing	$90.00
Post-Workout Massage	90 min.	Invigorating, prescriptive	$90.00
Exfoliating Ginger and Sea Salt Scrub	90 min.	Cleansing, invigorating	$90.00
Custom Massage	60 min.	Highlights problem areas	$60.00

Other Spa Experiences

Type	Time	Description	Price
Reflexology Points Experience	60 min.	Problem areas, relaxing	$60.00
Reiki Healing Experience	60 min.	Full body, relaxing	$60.00
All About You Women's Facial	60 min.	Relaxing, individualized	$60.00
All About You Men's Facial	60 min.	Relaxing, individualized	$60.00
All About You Pedicure	60 min.	Beautifying, relaxing	$60.00
Day of Beauty	Full day or Half day	Let us help you select a memorable combination of services.	
Body Analysis and Consultation	60 min.	Informative, prescriptive	$60.00
All About You Makeup Consultation	60 min.	Beautifying, individualized	$60.00

Packages and Gift Certificates

Type	Time	Description	Price
Package of three 90-minute services	270 min.	Mix and match to your needs.	$250.00
Package of two 90-minute services	180 min.	Select your favorite duo.	$160.00
Package of three 60-minute services	180 min.	Mix and match to your needs.	$160.00
Package of two 60-minute services	120 min.	Select your favorite duo.	$110.00
Gift certificates available at any price		Reward employees, friends, or relatives.	

5. Click on the **Save As** toolbar button. When the Save As window appears, select the folder in which you wish to save your data files (if not already selected). In the File Name box, key **All_About_You_Spa_Ch03_Your_Name.IA7** (for example, All_About_You_Spa_Ch03_John_Doe.IA7) to identify the file containing your work. Click on the **Save** button.

6. Key the journal entries for June. The chart of accounts for All About You Spa has already been set up in the data file, but there are no beginning balances since this is a new business. Click on the *Journal* toolbar button and key the journal entries for the month of June in the General Journal, following these steps:

WHAT TO DO FIRST
Enter June's transactions from documents and/or input forms.

a. Key the date of each transaction in the Date column.

b. Enter check numbers and invoice numbers, as appropriate, in the Refer. column (this is optional).

c. In the Account column, key the account number, key the account name (must be exact), or select from the Chart of Accounts list (click on the *Chart of Accounts* button that is activated when the Account field is selected) of the account to be debited.

d. Tab to the Debit column and enter the amount to be debited (omit commas).

e. Tab to the next line and enter the account to be credited in the Account column.

f. Tab to the Credit column and enter the amount to be credited.

g. When you have entered all debit and credit parts of an entry, click on the *Post* button (or press Enter on your keypad).

The basis of your entries will be the following documents:

Checkbook Entries
(Deposits made and checks written)

Check No.	Date	Explanation	√	Deposits	Check Amount
	6/1	Invested cash in business.		15,000.00	
1011	6/3	Bought 6-month liability insurance policy.			960.00
1012	6/3	Bought spa equipment for $4,235.00, putting $2,000.00 cash down.			2,000.00
1013	6/3	Paid June rent.			1,650.00
1014	6/5	Bought office supplies.			248.00
1015	6/5	Purchased flowers and balloons for grand opening (Misc. Exp.).			112.00
1016	6/7	Paid first week's wages.			1,847.50
	6/7	Deposited first week's cash revenue.		2,630.00	
1017	6/11	Paid on account payable for spa equipment (June 3).			873.00
	6/14	Deposited second week's cash revenue.		3,703.00	
1018	6/14	Paid second week's wages.			1,847.50
1019	6/18	Paid on account payable for spa equipment (June 3).			1,200.00
	6/21	Deposited third week's cash revenue.		4,758.00	
1020	6/21	Paid third week's wages.			1,847.50
1021	6/25	Paid on account payable for spa equipment (June 3).			73.00
1022	6/28	Paid fourth week's wages.			1,847.50
1023	6/28	Paid month's laundry bill.			84.00
	6/30	Deposited end of month's cash revenue.		5,992.00	
1024	6/30	A. Valli withdrew $1,850 for personal use.			1,850.00
1025	6/30	Paid June telephone bill.			225.00
1026	6/30	Paid June power and water bill.			248.00

Other documents that also require journal entries:

Receipt: 6/1
A. Valli, owner of All About
You Spa, invested her
personal spa equipment
valued at $3,158.00.

June Accounts Payable Charges Summary Report

6/3 Bought spa supplies on account from
Spa Supplies, Inv. No. 804
$492.00

6/5 Bought office equipment on account from
Office Equipment, Inv. No. 3415
$318.00

6/5 Bought advertising pamphlets on account
from Adco, Inv. No. 512
$397.00

6/5 Bought office equipment on account from
Office Equipment, Co. Inv. No. 3445
$832.00

6/5 Bought office supplies on account from
Office Staples, Inv. No. 522
$120.00

June Sales to Customers on Account Summary Report

6/7	$325.00
6/14	$486.00
6/21	$344.00
6/30	$109.00

7. Display the journal entries. Click on the **Reports** toolbar button. Click on **Journals** and **General Journal** to choose a report to display. Click on **Include All Journal Entries** and the **OK** button to display a General Journal report. To print the report, click on the **Print** button.

8. Review your entries and make corrections to them, if necessary. In the General Journal window, click on the entry to be corrected, key the correction(s), and click on the **Post** button (or press Enter). If you need to add an additional line to an entry, select the entry and then click on the **Insert** button. If you wish to delete an entry, select any portion of it, and click on the **Delete** button. If an entry was omitted, key it on the next available lines. The software will automatically put the entry in its proper date order when you post.

9. Display the Trial Balance report. Click on the **Reports** toolbar button. Click on **Ledger Reports** and **Trial Balance** to choose a report to display. Be sure the Run Date is set to June 30. Click **OK** to display the report. To print the report, click on the **Print** button at the bottom of the report window.

10. Display the income statement. Click on the **Reports** toolbar button. Click on **Financial Statements** and select **Income Statement** to choose the report to display. To print the report, click on the **Print** button.

11. Display the statement of owner's equity. Click on the **Reports** toolbar button. Click on **Financial Statements** and select **Statement of Owner's Equity** to choose the report to display. To print the report, click on the **Print** button.

WHAT TO DO AT THE END OF THE MONTH
Month-end wrap-up.

Check Figures

9. Trial balance total, $38,753
10. Net income, $7,381
11. A. Valli, Capital, ending balance, $23,689
12. Total assets, $25,937

12. Display the balance sheet. Click on the **Reports** toolbar button. Click on **Financial Statements** and select **Balance Sheet** to choose the report to display. To print the report, click on the **Print** button.

13. Click on the **Save** toolbar button to save your data file.

14. Click on the **Check** toolbar button to check your solution against the answer key. If there are errors, go back to Steps 7 and 8.

Note: The trial balance and financial statements are unadjusted. In the next chapter, you will learn that certain accounts need to be adjusted. These adjustments will change some of the figures in these reports.

Adjusting Entries and the Work Sheet

4

WHY IT MATTERS

RIDE THE DUCKS OF SEATTLE, Seattle, Washington

Ride the Ducks of Seattle seems an unlikely name for a thriving business—but, it actually is! The year-round Seattle tour company employs vehicles that can be doing a road tour one minute and plying the waters of Elliott Bay the next. One of Ride the Ducks' employees is a bookkeeper who also serves as a reservationist, tour vehicle cleaner, and computer specialist. In addition to recording and posting journal entries each month, he makes adjusting entries for such accounts as insurance, wages, and depreciation of the Ducks (tour bus/tour boat) at the end of each fiscal period. The method used to depreciate such an asset would most likely require the advice of a professional, such as a CPA (Certified Public Accountant). So, the next time you see a Duck, remember that it cannot operate without the skills of a bookkeeper/accountant.

LEARNING OBJECTIVES

After you have completed this chapter, you will be able to do the following:

1 Define *fiscal period* and *fiscal year.*

2 List the classifications of the accounts that occupy each column of a ten-column work sheet.

3 Complete a work sheet for a service enterprise, involving adjustments for expired insurance, depreciation, and accrued wages.

4 Prepare an income statement, a statement of owner's equity, and a balance sheet for a service business directly from the work sheet.

5 Journalize and post the adjusting entries.

6 Prepare (a) an income statement involving more than one revenue account and a net loss, (b) a statement of owner's equity with an additional investment and either a net income or a net loss, (c) a balance sheet for a business having more than one accumulated depreciation account, and (d) a balance sheet containing the statement of owner's equity information.

ACCOUNTING LANGUAGE

Accounting cycle (p. 129)

Accrual (p. 136)

Accrued wages (p. 136)

Adjusting entries (p. 145)

Adjustments (p. 131)

Book value (carrying value) (p. 134)

Contra account (p. 134)

Depreciation (p. 133)

Fiscal period (p. 128)

Fiscal year (p. 128)

Matching principle (p. 147)

Mixed accounts (p. 138)

Straight-line depreciation (p. 133)

Work sheet (p. 129)

Remember

*Accounting steps:
Analyzing: Which accounts are involved?
Classifying: assets, liabilities, owner's equity, revenue, and expenses
Recording: journalizing
Summarizing: financial statements
Interpreting: drawing conclusions*

As part of the *summarizing* step in the definition of accounting, we now introduce the work sheet and the financial statements. Now that you are familiar with the classifying and recording phases of accounting for a service business, let's look at the remaining steps in the accounting process.

FISCAL PERIOD

LEARNING OBJECTIVE **1**

Define fiscal period and fiscal year.

A **fiscal period** is any period of time covering a complete accounting cycle. A **fiscal year** is a fiscal period consisting of twelve consecutive months. It does not have to coincide with the calendar year. If a business has seasonal peaks, it is a good idea to complete the accounting operations at the end of the most active season. At that time, management wants to know the results of the year and where the business stands financially. The fiscal year of a resort that operates during the summer may be from October 1 of one year to September 30 of the next year. The government has a fiscal year from October 1 of one year to September 30 of the following year. Department stores often use a fiscal period from February 1 of one year to January 31 of the next year.

THE ACCOUNTING CYCLE

The **accounting cycle** represents the sequence of steps in the accounting process completed during the fiscal period. Figure 1 shows how we introduce these steps on a chapter-by-chapter basis. This outline brings you up to date on what we have accomplished so far and how each chapter fits into the steps in the accounting cycle.

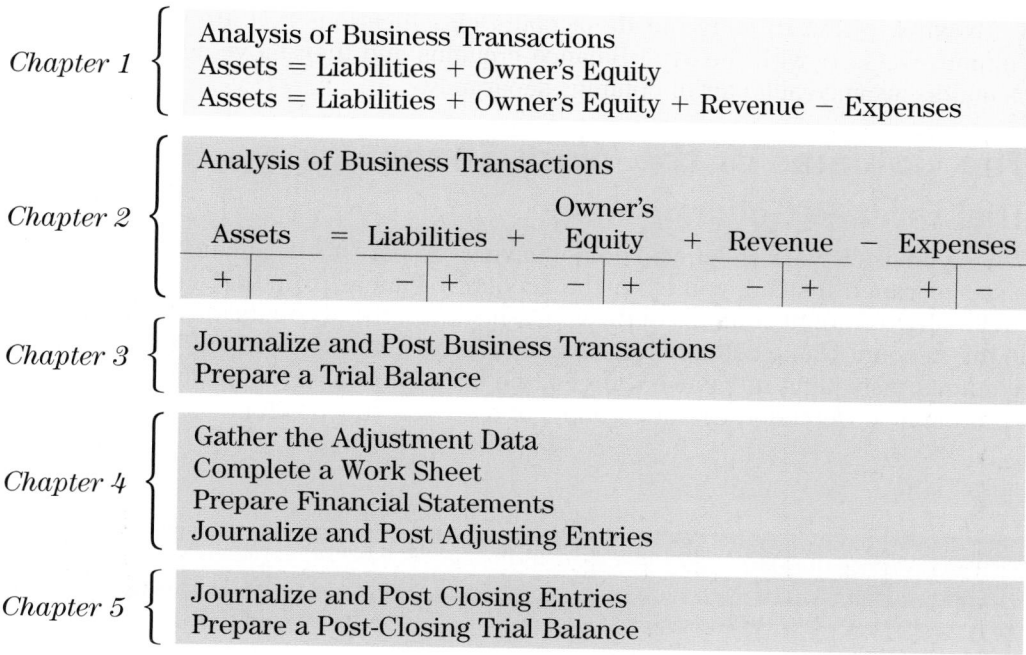

FIGURE 1

The accounting cycle by chapter

Chapter 1 — Analysis of Business Transactions / Assets = Liabilities + Owner's Equity / Assets = Liabilities + Owner's Equity + Revenue − Expenses

Chapter 2 — Analysis of Business Transactions

Assets	=	Liabilities	+	Owner's Equity	+	Revenue	−	Expenses
+ −		− +		− +		− +		+ −

Chapter 3 — Journalize and Post Business Transactions / Prepare a Trial Balance

Chapter 4 — Gather the Adjustment Data / Complete a Work Sheet / Prepare Financial Statements / Journalize and Post Adjusting Entries

Chapter 5 — Journalize and Post Closing Entries / Prepare a Post-Closing Trial Balance

THE WORK SHEET

The **work sheet** is a working paper used by accountants to record necessary adjustments and provide up-to-date account balances needed to prepare the financial statements. **The work sheet is a tool that accountants use to help in preparing the financial statements.** As a tool, the work sheet serves as a central place for bringing together the information needed to record the adjustments. With up-to-date account balances, the accountant can then prepare the financial statements.

First, we present the work sheet form so that you can see the big picture. Next, we describe and show examples of adjustments. Finally, we show how the adjustments are entered on the work sheet and how the work sheet is completed.

We will use a ten-column work sheet—so called because two amount columns are provided for each of the work sheet's five major sections. Work sheets are most often prepared by using a spreadsheet program such as Microsoft Excel®. We will explain the function of each of these sections, again basing our discussion on the accounting activities of Conner's Whitewater Adventures. But first we need to fill in the heading, which consists of three lines: (1) the name of the company, (2) the title of the working paper, and (3) the period of time covered.

FYI

The use of computerized accounting software can eliminate the preparation of the work sheet, which can be prepared manually or electronically. It does not, however, eliminate the journalizing and posting of the adjusting entries.

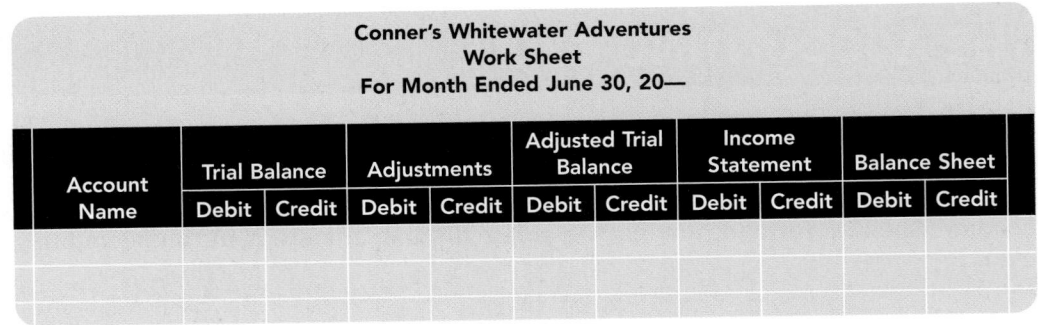

	Conner's Whitewater Adventures Work Sheet For Month Ended June 30, 20—									
Account Name	**Trial Balance**		**Adjustments**		**Adjusted Trial Balance**		**Income Statement**		**Balance Sheet**	
	Debit	Credit	Debit	Credit	Debit	Credit	Debit	Credit	Debit	Credit

Next, we want to point out the account classifications that are placed in each column. We start with the Trial Balance columns and then move across the work sheet, discussing each pair of columns separately.

The Columns of the Work Sheet

Trial Balance Columns

LEARNING OBJECTIVE 2

List the classifications of the accounts that occupy each column of a ten-column work sheet.

When you use a work sheet, you do not have to prepare a trial balance on a separate sheet of paper. Instead, you enter the account balances from the general ledger in the first two amount columns of the work sheet. List the accounts that have balances in the Account Name column in the same order in which they appear in the chart of accounts. Assuming **normal balances,** the account classifications are listed in the Trial Balance Debit and Credit columns of the work sheet as follows:

Account Name	Trial Balance		Adjustments		Adjusted Trial Balance		Income Statement		Balance Sheet	
	Debit	Credit	Debit	Credit	Debit	Credit	Debit	Credit	Debit	Credit
	Assets				Assets					
		Liabilities				Liabilities				
		Capital				Capital				
	Drawing				Drawing					
		Revenue				Revenue				
	Expenses				Expenses					

As we move along in this chapter, we will discuss the adjustments. The Adjusted Trial Balance columns contain the same account classifications as the Trial Balance columns. **The Adjusted Trial Balance columns are merely extensions of the Trial Balance columns, plus or minus any adjustment amounts.** If an adjustment is required, the amounts are carried from the Trial Balance columns through the Adjustments columns and into the Adjusted Trial Balance columns.

Income Statement Columns

An income statement contains the revenues minus the expenses. Revenue accounts have credit balances, so they are recorded in the Income Statement Credit column. Expense accounts have debit balances, so they are recorded in the Income Statement Debit column.

Remember

You have already prepared a trial balance. Record the normal balances in the Trial Balance Debit or Credit column. The normal balance is the + side of any account.

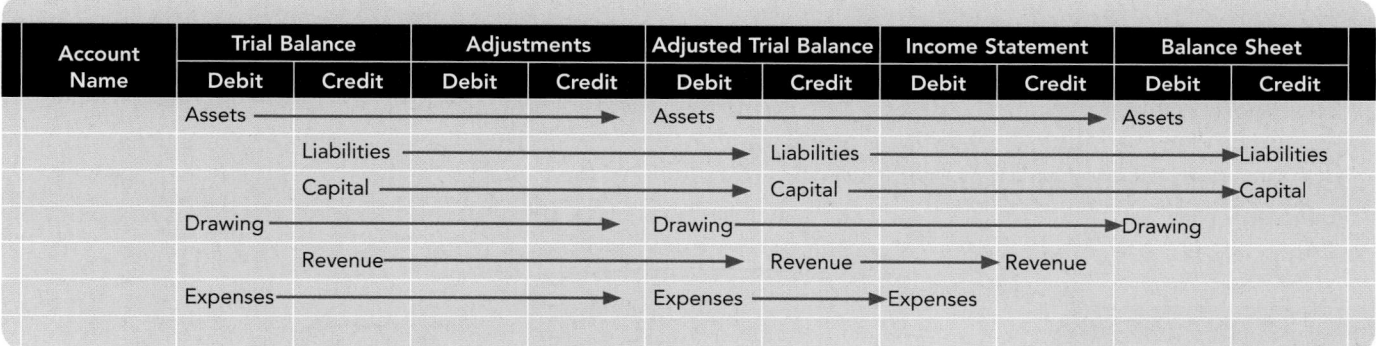

Balance Sheet Columns

As you recall, the balance sheet is a statement showing assets, liabilities, and owner's equity. Asset accounts have debit balances, so they are recorded in the Balance Sheet Debit column. Liability accounts have credit balances, so they are recorded in the Balance Sheet Credit column. The Capital account has a credit balance, so it is recorded in the Balance Sheet Credit column. Because the Drawing account is a deduction from Capital, it has a debit balance and is recorded in the Balance Sheet Debit column (the opposite column from that in which Capital is recorded).

Account Name	Trial Balance		Adjustments		Adjusted Trial Balance		Income Statement		Balance Sheet	
	Debit	Credit	Debit	Credit	Debit	Credit	Debit	Credit	Debit	Credit
	Assets				Assets				Assets	
		Liabilities				Liabilities				Liabilities
		Capital				Capital				Capital
	Drawing				Drawing				Drawing	
		Revenue				Revenue	Revenue			
	Expenses				Expenses		Expenses			

ADJUSTMENTS

Adjustments are a way of updating the ledger accounts. They may be considered *internal transactions*. They have not been recorded in the accounts up to this time because no outside party has been involved. Adjustments are determined after the trial balance has been prepared. Adjustments fine-tune the accounts to present a more accurate concept of the accounts.

Only a few accounts are adjusted. To describe the reasons for making adjustments, let's return to Conner's Whitewater Adventures. First, we select the accounts that require adjustments. Next, we show the adjustments recorded in T accounts so you can see the effect on the accounts. **However, bear in mind that the adjustments are first recorded on the work sheet when using a manual accounting system.** When using general ledger software, adjustments are recorded in the general journal. The adjustments are made at the end of the company's accounting period—in the case of Conner's Whitewater Adventures, June 30.

3 **LEARNING OBJECTIVE**

Complete a work sheet for a service enterprise, involving adjustments for expired insurance, depreciation, and accrued wages.

Choosing an Accounting Software Package

SMALL BUSINESS SUCCESS

Choosing an accounting software package is an important decision for small businesses. There are two popular software packages designed for small businesses: Peachtree and QuickBooks™. When picking an accounting software package, it's important to consider the needs of the business such as:

- How many individuals will use the software?
- What tools are available?
- Can the software handle inventory?
- Is it easy to use?
- What is the cost of the program?

Both of the accounting software packages listed here will handle most basic small business accounting transactions. Each software program includes general ledger, subsidiary ledgers, and financial statements and also the ability to export data into Excel® or Word®. Most of the differences among the packages relate to appearance and how to enter transactions. For example, QuickBooks uses different "centers" such as vendors, customers, employees, company, and banking. Peachtree uses navigation bars that are located across the top of the screen.

Almost all local colleges offer courses that can teach you how to use either of these accounting software programs. It is highly recommended that all small business owners and accounting majors take at least one course in how to use accounting software, as the knowledge of accounting software is a skill needed for success in the business world.

Remember

When using a manual accounting system, adjustments are recorded on the work sheet first. They will be journalized and posted later in the accounting cycle. When using a general ledger software package, adjustments are entered directly into the general journal.

The Financial Picture Before Adjustments   The Financial Picture After Adjustments

Without adjustments, the financial statements would be out of focus.

Prepaid Insurance

The $1,875 balance in Prepaid Insurance represents the premium paid in advance for a three-month liability insurance policy. One month of the three months of premium has now expired, which amounts to $625.

$$\$1,875 \text{ premium} \div 3 \text{ months} = \$625 \text{ per month}$$

In the adjustment, Conner's Whitewater Adventures deducts the expired or used portion from Prepaid Insurance and adds it to Insurance Expense.

	Prepaid Insurance			Insurance Expense		
	+	−			+	−
(Old) Balance	1,875	Adjusting 625		Adjusting	625	
(New) Balance	1,250					

The new balance of Prepaid Insurance, $1,250 ($1,875 − $625), represents the cost of insurance that remains paid in advance and should therefore appear in the Balance Sheet Debit column. The $625 amount in Insurance Expense represents the cost of insurance that has expired and should therefore appear in the Income Statement Debit column.

> **Remember**
>
> For the adjustment of insurance, you are given the amount used (expired). So, in the adjusting entry, take the amount used directly out of Prepaid Insurance and put it into Insurance Expense.

Depreciation of Equipment

We have recorded durable items, such as appliances and fixtures, under Equipment because they will last longer than one year. The benefits of these assets will eventually be used up (the assets will either wear out or become obsolete). Therefore, we should systematically spread out the cost of these assets over their useful lives. That is, we allocate the cost of the equipment as an expense *over its estimated useful life* and call this **depreciation** because such equipment loses its usefulness. A part of this depreciation expense is allotted to each fiscal period. In the case of Conner's Whitewater Adventures, the Equipment account has a balance of $51,300. Suppose we estimate that the equipment will have a useful life of seven years, with a trade-in (salvage) value of $8,292 at the end of that time. Using **straight-line depreciation**, we can allocate the cost of an asset, less any trade-in value, evenly over the useful life of the asset. Depreciation for one month is figured like this:

STEP 1. Subtract the trade-in (salvage) value from the cost to get the full depreciation.

$$\$51,300 − \$8,292 = \$43,008 \text{ full depreciation}$$

STEP 2. Divide the full depreciation by the number of years in the asset's useful life to get the depreciation for one year.

$$\$43,008 \text{ full depreciation} ÷ 7 \text{ years} = \$6,144 \text{ per year}$$

STEP 3. Divide the depreciation for one year by 12 to get the depreciation for one month.

$$\$6,144 \text{ per year} ÷ 12 \text{ months} = \$512 \text{ per month}$$

When depreciation is recorded, we do not subtract it directly from the asset account. In asset accounts, such as Equipment or Building, we must keep the original cost recorded in the account. Consequently, the amount of depreciation has to be recorded in another account; that account is Accumulated Depreciation. If you were to incorrectly record depreciation by crediting the asset account, the balance of your asset account will eventually reach zero, which is not correct. You still have the equipment and need to maintain the original cost in the account; therefore, the credit should be to the contra asset account, Accumulated Depreciation.

Always record the adjusting entry for depreciation as a debit to Depreciation Expense (an income statement item) and a credit to Accumulated Depreciation (a balance sheet item), which increases both accounts. The adjustment in T account form would appear as follows:

> **FYI**
>
> There are several methods of depreciation for assets. Straight-line depreciation is shown here—equal amounts of estimated loss of usefulness are taken each year. There are also accelerated methods that assign larger amounts to expense in the early years of the life of an asset.

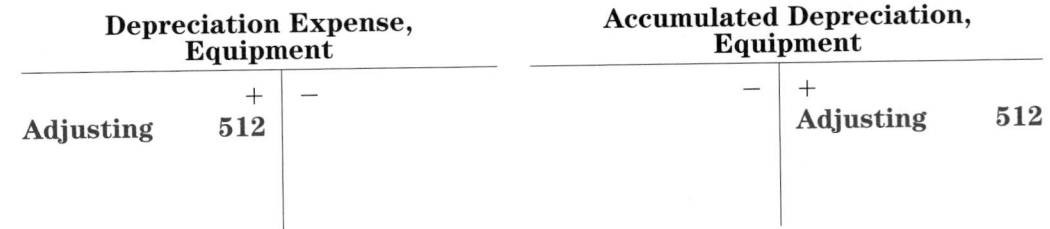

Accumulated Depreciation, Equipment, is contrary to, or a deduction from, Equipment, so we call it a **contra account**. To show the accounts under their proper headings, let's look at the fundamental accounting equation. Brackets indicate that Accumulated Depreciation, Equipment, is a deduction from the Equipment account. Note that the plus and minus signs are opposite.

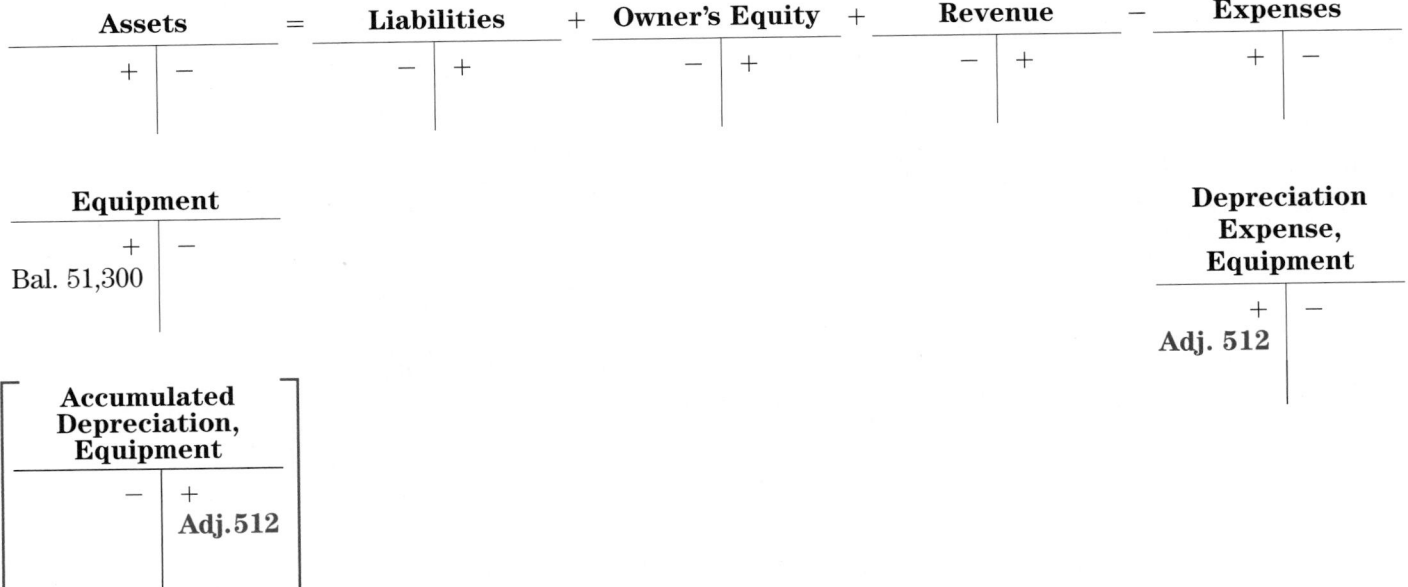

FYI

If we had a Building account, the adjusting entry would be a debit to Depreciation Expense, Building, and a credit to Accumulated Depreciation, Building. Building and Accumulated Depreciation, Building, would be listed separately on the balance sheet.

If we had a Land account, it would have no adjusting entry. Land supposedly lasts forever, so it is not depreciated.

On the work sheet, Equipment (an asset) appears in the Balance Sheet Debit column. Accumulated Depreciation (a deduction from an asset) appears in the opposite column, which is the Balance Sheet Credit column.

Accumulated Depreciation, Equipment, as the title implies, is the total depreciation that the company has taken since the original purchase of the asset. Rather than crediting the Equipment account, Conner's Whitewater Adventures keeps track of the total depreciation taken since it first acquired the asset in a separate account. The maximum depreciation it could take would be the cost of the equipment, $51,300, less the trade-in value of $8,292. So, for the first year, Accumulated Depreciation, Equipment, will increase at the rate of $512 per month, assuming that no additional equipment has been purchased. For example, at the end of the second month, Accumulated Depreciation, Equipment, will amount to $1,024 ($512 + $512).

On the balance sheet, the balance of Accumulated Depreciation is deducted from the balance of the related asset account as illustrated on the following partial balance sheet for Conner's Whitewater Adventures. The net amount shown, $50,788, is referred to as the book value of the asset. Thus, **book value** (or **carrying value**) is the cost of an asset minus its accumulated depreciation ($51,300 − $512).

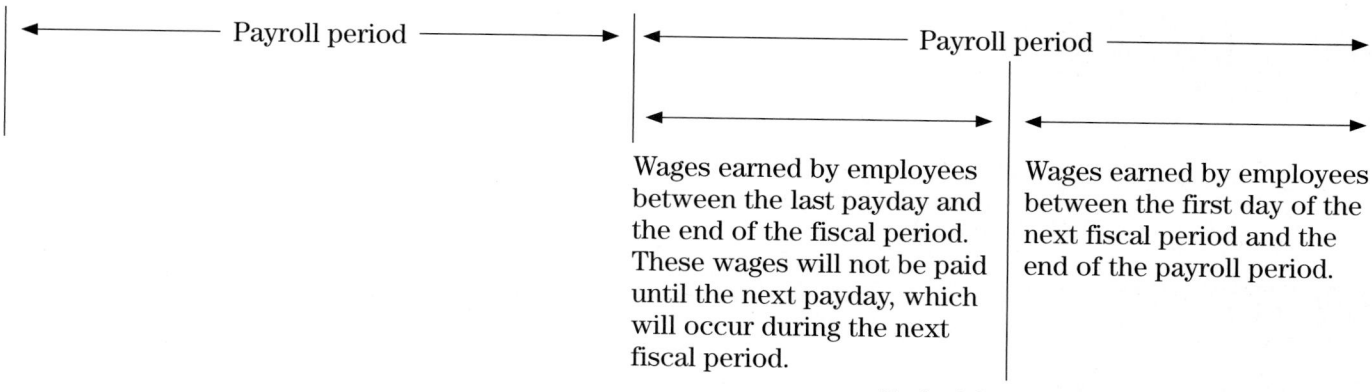

Conner's Whitewater Adventures Partial Balance Sheet June 30, 20—		
Assets		
Equipment	$51,300	
Less Accumulated Depreciation	512	$50,788

Wages Expense

The end of the fiscal period and the end of the employees' payroll period rarely fall on the same day. A diagram of the situation looks like this:

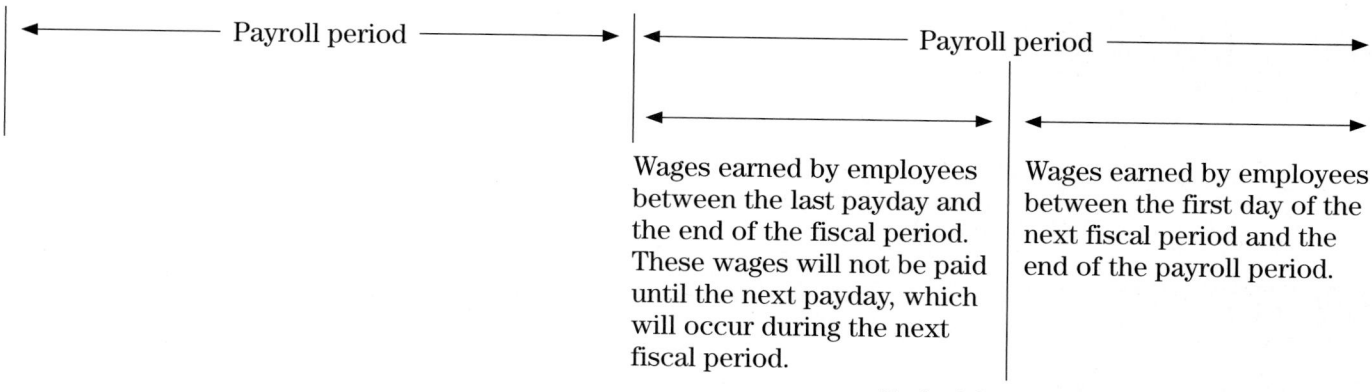

Since the last day of the fiscal period falls in the middle of the payroll period, we have to split up the wages earned in that payroll period between the fiscal period just ended and the next fiscal period. We will use another company for this example.

Assume that Brown Company pays its employees $400 per day and that payday falls on Friday. The employees work a five-day week. When employees pick up their paychecks on Friday, the amount of the checks includes their wages for that day and for the preceding four days. Suppose that the last day of the fiscal period falls on Wednesday, December 31. The following diagram illustrates this situation.

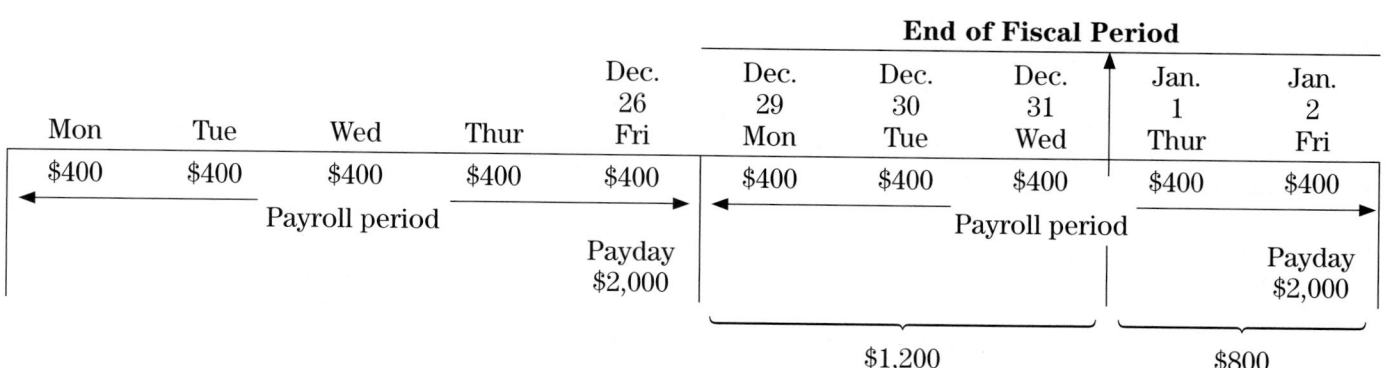

December						
S	M	T	W	R	F	S
	1	2	3	4	⑤	6
7	8	9	10	11	⑫	13
14	15	16	17	18	⑲	20
21	22	23	24	25	㉖	27
28	29	30	31			

– *Paydays*

To have the Wages Expense account show an accurate balance for the fiscal period, you need to add $1,200 for the cost of labor between the last payday, December 26, and the end of the year, December 31 ($400 for December 29; $400 for December 30; $400 for December 31). Because the $1,200 will not be paid at this time but is owed to the employees as of December 31, you also need to add $1,200 to Wages Payable, a liability account, because the company owes this amount to employees.

Wages Expense				Wages Payable	
	+	−		−	+
(Old) Balance	104,000			Adj.	1,200
Adj.	**1,200**				
(New) Balance	105,200				

Returning to our illustration of Conner's Whitewater Adventures, the amount of wages that has been paid so far for the month of June is $2,360. However, the last payday was June 24. Between June 24 and the end of the month, Conner's Whitewater Adventures has determined that it owes an additional $472 in wages to its employees.

Accountants refer to this extra amount that has not been recorded at the end of the month as **accrued wages**. In accounting terms, **accrual** means recognition of an expense or a revenue that has been incurred (expense) or earned (revenue) but has not yet been recorded.

Wages Expense				Wages Payable	
	+	−		−	+
(Old) Balance	2,360			Adj.	472
Adj.	**472**				
(New) Balance	2,832				

Placement of Accounts on the Work Sheet

We have to enter the adjustments on the work sheet, but before doing so, let's briefly discuss the Drawing and Accumulated Depreciation accounts, as well as net income, and their effect on the work sheet.

Capital and Drawing Account Balances

The Drawing account is a contra account (contrary to Capital). In the statement of owner's equity, Drawing is deducted from Capital. To show one account as a deduction from another, the plus and minus signs are switched around. The T accounts look like this:

J. Conner, Capital			J. Conner, Drawing	
−	+		+	−
Debit	Credit		Debit	Credit
	Balance		Balance	

The normal balance for the Capital account is recorded in the Credit columns of the Trial Balance, the Adjusted Trial Balance, and the Balance Sheet sections. The normal balance for the Drawing account is recorded in the Debit columns of the Trial Balance, the Adjusted Trial Balance, and the Balance Sheet sections.

Equipment and Accumulated Depreciation, Equipment, Account Balances

The Accumulated Depreciation, Equipment, account is a contra account (contrary to Equipment). On the balance sheet, Accumulated Depreciation, Equipment, is deducted from Equipment. The T accounts look like this:

Equipment		Accumulated Depreciation, Equipment	
+	−	−	+
Debit Balance	Credit	Debit	Credit Balance

The normal balance for the Equipment account is recorded in the Debit columns of the Trial Balance, the Adjusted Trial Balance, and the Balance Sheet sections. The normal balance for the Accumulated Depreciation, Equipment, account is recorded in the Credit columns of the Trial Balance, the Adjusted Trial Balance, and the Balance Sheet sections.

Net Income

Net income (or net loss) is the difference between revenue and expenses. It is used to balance the Income Statement columns; since revenue is normally larger than expenses, the balancing amount must be added to the expense side. Net income (or net loss) is also used to balance the Balance Sheet columns. On the statement of owner's equity, you add net income to the owner's beginning Capital balance. Since the Capital balance is located in the Balance Sheet Credit column, net income must also be added to that side. The following diagram shows these relationships.

Account Name	Trial Balance		Adjustments		Adjusted Trial Balance		Income Statement		Balance Sheet	
	Debit	Credit	Debit	Credit	Debit	Credit	Debit	Credit	Debit	Credit
	A + Draw. + E	Accum. Depr. + L + Cap. + R			A + Draw. + E	Accum. Depr. + L + Cap. + R	E	R	A + Draw.	Accum. Depr. + L + Cap.
Net Income							NI			NI

On the other hand, if expenses are larger than revenue, the result is a net loss. You must add net loss to the revenue side to balance the Income Statement columns. Also, because a net loss is deducted from the owner's beginning Capital balance, you must include net loss in the debit side of the Balance Sheet columns, thereby balancing these columns. To show this, let's look at the Income Statement and Balance Sheet columns diagrammed here.

Account Name	Income Statement		Balance Sheet	
	Debit	Credit	Debit	Credit
			A + Draw.	Accum. Depr. + L + Cap.
	E			
		R		
Net Loss		NL	NL	

Mixed Accounts

At this point, take special notice of the fact that each **adjusting entry contains an income statement account (revenue or expense) and a balance sheet account (asset, contra asset, or liability).** Accountants refer to these accounts as **mixed accounts**—accounts with balances that are partly income statement amounts and partly balance sheet amounts. The income statement and balance sheet accounts involved are separate accounts having a part of their name in common, like Prepaid Insurance and Insurance Expense. Prepaid Insurance is recorded as $1,875 in the Trial Balance columns but is apportioned as $625 in Insurance Expense in the Income Statement columns and $1,250 in Prepaid Insurance in the Balance Sheet columns. In other words, portions of these trial balance amounts are recorded in each section.

In the previous examples, we used T accounts to explain how to handle adjustments. T accounts help organize any type of accounting entry into debits and credits. But now it is time to record the adjustments on the work sheet. To help you remember which classifications of accounts appear in each column of the work sheet, we will label the columns with letters specifying each classification of accounts; for example, A for assets, L for liabilities, etc., as shown in Figure 2.

Steps in the Completion of the Work Sheet

A completed work sheet is shown in Figure 3. Before we complete the work sheet, let's list the recommended steps to follow.

STEP 1. Complete the Trial Balance columns, total, and rule (single underline before double underlining totals).

STEP 2. Complete the Adjustments columns, total, and rule.

STEP 3. Complete the Adjusted Trial Balance columns, total, and rule.

STEP 4. Record balances in the Income Statement and Balance Sheet columns and total each column.

STEP 5. Record net income or net loss in the Income Statement columns by subtracting the smaller side from the larger side and adding the difference to the smaller side, total, and rule.

STEP 6. Record net income or net loss in the Balance Sheet columns by subtracting the smaller side from the larger side and adding the difference to the smaller side (the amount should be the same as the difference between the Income Statement column totals—if not, there is an error), total, and rule.

The steps assume the work sheet is prepared manually. The work sheet can also be prepared using a computer spreadsheet program, such as Microsoft Excel®. Whether the work sheet is prepared manually or on a computer, the columns must be completed, totaled, and ruled. An Excel version of the work sheet is shown in Figure 4 on page 142.

FIGURE 2	Partial work sheet for Conner's Whitewater Adventures

Conner's Whitewater Adventures
Work Sheet
For Month Ended June 30, 20—

Account Name	Trial Balance Debit A + Draw. + E	Trial Balance Credit Accum. Depr. + L + Cap. + R	Adjustments Debit	Adjustments Credit
Cash	55 8 9 0 00			
Accounts Receivable	4 2 5 0 00			
Prepaid Insurance	1 8 7 5 00			(a) 6 2 5 00
Equipment	51 3 0 0 00			
Accounts Payable		3 4 2 5 00		
J. Conner, Capital		95 2 0 0 00		
J. Conner, Drawing	3 5 0 0 00			
Income from Tours		23 3 2 0 00		
Wages Expense	2 3 6 0 00		(c) 4 7 2 00	
Rent Expense	1 2 5 0 00			
Supplies Expense	6 7 5 00			
Advertising Expense	6 2 0 00			
Utilities Expense	2 2 5 00			
	121 9 4 5 00	121 9 4 5 00		
Insurance Expense			(a) 6 2 5 00	
Depreciation Expense, Equipment			(b) 5 1 2 00	
Accumulated Depreciation, Equipment				(b) 5 1 2 00
Wages Payable				(c) 4 7 2 00
			1 6 0 9 00	1 6 0 9 00

Step 1: Trial Balance Columns

Note that the trial balance in Figure 2 is the same trial balance presented earlier for Conner's Whitewater Adventures. You will be able to follow the completion of the entire work sheet for Conner's Whitewater Adventures in Figure 3.

Step 2: Adjustments Columns

When we enter the adjustments, we identify them as (a), (b), (c), to indicate the relationships between the debit and credit sides and the sequence of the individual adjusting entries (see Figures 2 and 3).

Note that Insurance Expense; Depreciation Expense, Equipment; Accumulated Depreciation, Equipment; and Wages Payable did not appear in the trial balance because there were no balances in the accounts at that time. We wrote them below the Trial Balance totals to complete the work sheet.

Here is a brief review of the adjustments:

a. To record the $625 cost of insurance expired during June.

b. To record $512 depreciation for the month of June.

c. To record $472 of accrued wages owed at the end of June.

Now let's look at the work sheet shown in Figure 5 on pages 144 and 145. To reinforce the idea of adjusting entries, see the brief explanation of each adjustment at the right of the work sheet. Again, the completed work sheet is shown in Figure 3.

> **Remember**
>
> The Trial Balance columns are exactly the same as they are listed in the Trial Balance presented in Chapter 3.

FIGURE 3

Work sheet with steps of completion explained for Conner's Whitewater Adventures

Conner's Whitewater Adventures
Work Sheet
For Month Ended June 30, 20—

Account Name	Trial Balance Debit (A + Draw. + E)	Trial Balance Credit (Accum. Depr. + L + Cap. + R)	Adjustments Debit	Adjustments Credit
Cash	55 8 9 0 00			
Accounts Receivable	4 2 5 0 00			
Prepaid Insurance	1 8 7 5 00			(a) 6 2 5 00
Equipment	51 3 0 0 00			
Accounts Payable		3 4 2 5 00		
J. Conner, Capital		95 2 0 0 00		
J. Conner, Drawing	3 5 0 0 00			
Income from Tours		23 3 2 0 00		
Wages Expense	2 3 6 0 00		(c) 4 7 2 00	
Rent Expense	1 2 5 0 00			
Supplies Expense	6 7 5 00			
Advertising Expense	6 2 0 00			
Utilities Expense	2 2 5 00			
	121 9 4 5 00	121 9 4 5 00		
Insurance Expense			(a) 6 2 5 00	
Depr. Expense, Equipment		Step 1	(b) 5 1 2 00	
Accum. Depr., Equipment				(b) 5 1 2 00
Wages Payable				(c) 4 7 2 00
			1 6 0 9 00	1 6 0 9 00
Net Income				
			Step 2	

(a) Insurance expired, $625
(b) Depr. of equip., $512
(c) Accrued wages, $472

Step 1
In the Account Name column, list the accounts that have balances. Enter the account balances in the Trial Balance columns. Total and rule the columns.

Step 2
Enter the adjustments, labeling each adjustment as (a), (b), (c), and so on. Total and rule the columns.

	Adjusted Trial Balance		Income Statement		Balance Sheet	
	Debit	Credit	Debit	Credit	Debit	Credit
	A + Draw. + E	Accum. Depr. + L + Cap. + R	E	R	A + Draw.	Accum. Depr. + L + Cap.
	55 8 9 0 00				55 8 9 0 00	
	4 2 5 0 00				4 2 5 0 00	
	1 2 5 0 00				1 2 5 0 00	
	51 3 0 0 00				51 3 0 0 00	
		3 4 2 5 00				3 4 2 5 00
		95 2 0 0 00				95 2 0 0 00
	3 5 0 0 00				3 5 0 0 00	
		23 3 2 0 00		23 3 2 0 00		
	2 8 3 2 00		2 8 3 2 00			
	1 2 5 0 00		1 2 5 0 00			
	6 7 5 00		6 7 5 00			
	6 2 0 00		6 2 0 00			
	2 2 5 00		2 2 5 00			
	6 2 5 00		6 2 5 00			
	5 1 2 00		5 1 2 00			
		5 1 2 00				5 1 2 00
		4 7 2 00				4 7 2 00
	122 9 2 9 00	122 9 2 9 00	6 7 3 9 00	23 3 2 0 00	116 1 9 0 00	99 6 0 9 00
			16 5 8 1 00			16 5 8 1 00
	Step 3		23 3 2 0 00	23 3 2 0 00	116 1 9 0 00	116 1 9 0 00
			Steps 4, 5, 6			

Step 3
Carry amounts across from the Trial Balance columns plus or minus any amounts appearing in the Adjustments columns. Total and rule the columns.

Step 4
From the top of the Adjusted Trial Balance columns, go down line by line carrying each amount over to the Income Statement or Balance Sheet columns. Total the columns.

Step 5
Write Net Income or Net Loss in the Account Name column and the amount in the appropriate Income Statement column. Total and rule the columns.

Step 6
Enter the net income or loss amount in the appropriate Balance Sheet column. Total, balance, and rule the columns.

FIGURE 4   Work sheet for Conner's Whitewater Adventures—Excel version

Conner's Whitewater Adventures
Work Sheet
For Month Ended June 30, 20—

ACCOUNT NAME	TRIAL BALANCE DEBIT	TRIAL BALANCE CREDIT	ADJUSTMENTS DEBIT	ADJUSTMENTS CREDIT	ADJUSTED TRIAL BALANCE DEBIT	ADJUSTED TRIAL BALANCE CREDIT	INCOME STATEMENT DEBIT	INCOME STATEMENT CREDIT	BALANCE SHEET DEBIT	BALANCE SHEET CREDIT
	$A + Draw. + E$	$+ L + Cap. + R$ (Accum. Depr.)			$A + Draw. + E$	$+ L + Cap. + R$ (Accum. Depr.)	E	R	$A + Draw.$	$+ L + Cap.$ (Accum. Depr.)
Cash	55,890.00				55,890.00				55,890.00	
Accounts Receivable	4,250.00				4,250.00				4,250.00	
Prepaid Insurance	1,875.00			(a) 625.00	1,250.00				1,250.00	
Equipment	51,300.00				51,300.00				51,300.00	
Accounts Payable		3,425.00				3,425.00				3,425.00
J. Conner, Capital		95,200.00				95,200.00				95,200.00
J. Conner, Drawing	3,500.00				3,500.00				3,500.00	
Income from Tours		23,320.00				23,320.00		23,320.00		
Wages Expense	2,360.00		(c) 472.00		2,832.00		2,832.00			
Rent Expense	1,250.00				1,250.00		1,250.00			
Supplies Expense	675.00				675.00		675.00			
Advertising Expense	620.00				620.00		620.00			
Utilities Expense	225.00				225.00		225.00			
	121,945.00	121,945.00								
Insurance Expense			(a) 625.00		625.00		625.00			
Depr. Exp., Equip.			(b) 512.00		512.00		512.00			
Accum. Depr., Equip.				(b) 512.00		512.00				512.00
Wages Payable				(c) 472.00		472.00				472.00
			1,609.00	1,609.00	122,929.00	122,929.00	6,739.00	23,320.00	116,190.00	99,609.00
Net Income							16,581.00			16,581.00
							23,320.00	23,320.00	116,190.00	116,190.00

Sheet1   Sheet2   Sheet3

In this chapter, the business is in its first accounting period; therefore, Accumulated Depreciation, Equipment had no balance until the end of the fiscal period adjustments, which meant it was not in the trial balance prior to adjustments. After the first fiscal period, Accumulated Depreciation will always have a balance until the related asset is sold or disposed of and will be listed in the Trial Balance columns immediately below the appropriate asset.

Again, we emphasize that the work sheet is strictly a tool used to gather all the up-to-date information needed to prepare the financial statements. **The adjustments are always recorded in the work sheet first.**

Step 3: Adjusted Trial Balance Columns

Once the Adjustments columns are totaled and ruled, extend each Trial Balance amount, plus or minus any adjustment from the Adjustments columns, to the Adjusted Trial Balance columns as shown in Figure 3.

Step 4: Income Statement and Balance Sheet Columns

Extend the balances in the Adjusted Trial Balance columns to either the Income Statement or the Balance Sheet columns (see Figure 3).

Step 5: Net Income or Net Loss—Income Statement Columns

Total each of the two Income Statement columns. Subtract the smaller side from the larger side, write the difference under the smaller Income Statement column total, and total and rule as shown in Figure 3.

If there is a net income, the credit side of the Income Statement columns will be larger than the debit side—more revenue than expenses. In this case, write Net Income in the Account Name column on the same line as the difference you calculated. If there is a net loss, the debit side of the Income Statement columns will be larger than the credit side—more expenses than revenue. In this case, write Net Loss in the Account Name column on the same line as the difference you calculated.

Step 6: Net Income or Net Loss—Balance Sheet Columns

Total the two Balance Sheet columns. Subtract the smaller side from the larger side, write the difference under the smaller Balance Sheet column total (the amount should equal the difference between the Income Statement column totals—if not, there is an error), and total and rule as shown in Figure 3.

Finding Errors in the Income Statement and Balance Sheet Columns

As you have seen, the amount of the net income or net loss must be recorded in both an Income Statement column and a Balance Sheet column. Suppose that, after the net income is added to the Balance Sheet Credit column, the Balance Sheet columns are not equal. To find the error, follow this procedure:

STEP 1. Check to see that the amount of the net income or loss is recorded in the correct columns. For example, net income is placed in the Income Statement Debit column and the Balance Sheet Credit column.

STEP 2. Verify the addition of all the columns.

STEP 3. Look to see if the appropriate amounts have been recorded in the Income Statement and Balance Sheet columns. For example, asset amounts should be listed in the Balance Sheet Debit column, expense amounts should be listed in the Income Statement Debit column, and so forth.

STEP 4. Verify, by adding or subtracting across each line, that the amounts carried over from the Trial Balance columns through the Adjustments columns into the Adjusted Trial Balance columns are correct.

Remember

After the first fiscal period, Accumulated Depreciation will have a balance, so it will be listed immediately below the asset being depreciated (which in this example is Equipment). Consequently, Accumulated Depreciation will not appear at the bottom of next month's work sheet.

Remember

Insurance is adjusted by adding the amount expired to Insurance Expense while deducting the same amount from Prepaid Insurance.

Depreciation is added to both Depreciation Expense and Accumulated Depreciation.

Accrued wages are added to both Wages Expense and Wages Payable.

FIGURE 5

Work sheet with explanations of adjustments for Conner's Whitewater Adventures

Conner's Whitewater Adventures
Work Sheet
For Month Ended June 30, 20—

Account Name	Trial Balance Debit A + Draw. + E	Trial Balance Credit Accum. Depr. + L + Cap. + R	Adjustments Debit	Adjustments Credit
Cash	55 8 9 0 00			
Accounts Receivable	4 2 5 0 00			
Prepaid Insurance	1 8 7 5 00			(a) 6 2 5 00
Equipment	51 3 0 0 00			
Accounts Payable		3 4 2 5 00		
J. Conner, Capital		95 2 0 0 00		
J. Conner, Drawing	3 5 0 0 00			
Income from Tours		23 3 2 0 00		
Wages Expense	2 3 6 0 00		(c) 4 7 2 00	
Rent Expense	1 2 5 0 00			
Supplies Expense	6 7 5 00			
Advertising Expense	6 2 0 00			
Utilities Expense	2 2 5 00			
	121 9 4 5 00	121 9 4 5 00		
Insurance Expense		Step 1	(a) 6 2 5 00	
Depr. Expense, Equipment			(b) 5 1 2 00	
Accum. Depr., Equipment				(b) 5 1 2 00
Wages Payable				(c) 4 7 2 00
			1 6 0 9 00	1 6 0 9 00
				Step 2

(a) Insurance expired, $625
(b) Depr. of equip., $512
(c) Accrued wages, $472

STEP 5. Verify that the correct amounts of the revenue and expense accounts are transferred to the Income Statement columns.

STEP 6. Verify that the correct amounts of assets, liabilities, and owner's equity accounts are transferred to the Balance Sheet columns.

Generally, one of these steps will expose the error.

Completion of the Financial Statements

LEARNING OBJECTIVE 4

Prepare an income statement, a statement of owner's equity, and a balance sheet for a service business directly from the work sheet.

As we stated, the purpose of the work sheet is to help the accountant prepare the financial statements. Since we have completed the work sheet for Conner's Whitewater Adventures, we can now prepare the income statement, the statement of owner's equity, and the balance sheet by taking the figures directly from the work sheet. These statements are shown in Figure 6 on page 146.

Note that you record Accumulated Depreciation, Equipment, in the asset section of the balance sheet as a direct deduction from Equipment. As we have said, accountants refer to this as a contra account because it is contrary to its companion asset account. The difference, $50,788, is called the book value or carrying value because it represents the cost of the asset after Accumulated Depreciation has been deducted.

Adjusted Trial Balance		
Debit	**Credit**	
	Accum. Depr. +	
A + Draw. + E	L + Cap. + R	
55 8 9 0 00		No adjustment, so carry over amount directly
4 2 5 0 00		
1 2 5 0 00		Adjustment involved, subtract $625.00 (expired) from $1,875.00
51 3 0 0 00		No adjustment, so carry over amount directly
	3 4 2 5 00	
	95 2 0 0 00	
3 5 0 0 00		
	23 3 2 0 00	
2 8 3 2 00		Adjustment involved, add $472.00 (accrued) to $2,360.00
1 2 5 0 00		No adjustment, so carry over amount directly
6 7 5 00		
6 2 0 00		
2 2 5 00		
		This line is blank because of the trial balance total
6 2 5 00		Adjustment involved, carry $625.00 over to the same column
5 1 2 00		Adjustment involved, carry $512.00 over to the same column
	5 1 2 00	Adjustment involved, carry $512.00 over to the same column
	4 7 2 00	Adjustment involved, carry $472.00 over to the same column
122 9 2 9 00	122 9 2 9 00	

Step 3

When preparing the statement of owner's equity, always remember to check the beginning balance of Capital against the balance shown in the Capital account in the general ledger. An additional investment may have been made during the fiscal period, and you need to record any such additional investment in the statement of owner's equity.

JOURNALIZING ADJUSTING ENTRIES

To change the balance of a ledger account, you need a journal entry as evidence of the change. So far, we have been listing adjustments only in the Adjustments columns of the work sheet. The work sheet is not a journal, so we must journalize **adjusting entries** to update the ledger accounts. **Take the information for these entries directly from the Adjustments columns of the work sheet, debiting and crediting exactly the same accounts and amounts in the journal entries.**

In the Description column of the general journal, write "Adjusting Entries" before you begin making these entries. This eliminates the need to write an explanation for each entry. The adjusting entries for Conner's Whitewater Adventures are shown in Figure 7 on page 147.

LEARNING OBJECTIVE 5

Journalize and post the adjusting entries.

FIGURE 6

Financial statements for Conner's Whitewater Adventures

Remember

The columns shown on the financial statements do not represent Debit or Credit. Each column simply shows account balances. Amounts in these columns are either added or subtracted.

Remember

Ruling columns correctly is very important. There should be a single rule below a column to be added or subtracted and double rules below the totals.

Conner's Whitewater Adventures
Income Statement
For Month Ended June 30, 20—

Revenue:		
Income from Tours		$23,320
Expenses:		
Wages Expense	$2,832	
Rent Expense	1,250	
Supplies Expense	675	
Advertising Expense	620	
Utilities Expense	225	
Insurance Expense	625	
Depreciation Expense, Equipment	512	
Total Expenses		6,739
Net Income		$16,581

Conner's Whitewater Adventures
Statement of Owner's Equity
For Month Ended June 30, 20—

J. Conner, Capital, June 1, 20—		$ 0
Investment during June	$ 95,200	
Net Income for June	16,581	
Subtotal	$111,781	
Less Withdrawals for June	3,500	
Increase in Capital		108,281
J. Conner, Capital, June 30, 20—		$108,281

Conner's Whitewater Adventures
Balance Sheet
June 30, 20—

Assets		
Cash		$ 55,890
Accounts Receivable		4,250
Prepaid Insurance		1,250
Equipment	$51,300	
Less Accumulated Depreciation	512	50,788
Total Assets		$112,178
Liabilities		
Accounts Payable	$ 3,425	
Wages Payable	472	
Total Liabilities		$ 3,897
Owner's Equity		
J. Conner, Capital		108,281
Total Liabilities and Owner's Equity		$112,178

GENERAL JOURNAL   PAGE 4

Date		Description	Post. Ref.	Debit	Credit
20—		Adjusting Entries			
June	30	Insurance Expense	516	6 2 5 00	
		Prepaid Insurance	117		6 2 5 00
	30	Depr. Expense, Equipment	517	5 1 2 00	
		Accum. Depr., Equipment	125		5 1 2 00
	30	Wages Expense	511	4 7 2 00	
		Wages Payable	222		4 7 2 00

FIGURE 7

Adjusting entries for Conner's Whitewater Adventures

> **Remember**
>
> Each adjusting entry consists of an income statement account and a balance sheet account.

When you post the adjusting entries to the ledger accounts, write the abbreviation "Adj." in the Item column of the ledger account. The adjusting entry for Prepaid Insurance is posted as follows:

ACCOUNT Prepaid Insurance   ACCOUNT NO. 117

Date		Item	Post. Ref.	Debit	Credit	Balance Debit	Balance Credit
20—							
June	10		2	1 8 7 5 00		1 8 7 5 00	
	30	Adj.	4		6 2 5 00	1 2 5 0 00	

ACCOUNT Insurance Expense   ACCOUNT NO. 516

Date		Item	Post. Ref.	Debit	Credit	Balance Debit	Balance Credit
20—							
June	30	Adj.	4		6 2 5 00		6 2 5 00

In the adjusted accounts for Conner's Whitewater Adventures, notice that the intent is to make sure that the expenses recorded match up or compare with the revenues for the same period of time. In other words, for the month of June, we record all the revenues for June and all the expenses for June. Thus the revenues and expenses for the same time period are matched. This is called the **matching principle**.

> **FYI**
>
> Many businesses produce monthly financial statements. Adjustments must be made every time a financial statement is produced.

Accounting Treatment for the Cost of Supplies

In Chapter 1, when Conner's Whitewater Adventures bought supplies, the amount paid was recorded as an expense. Generally, most service businesses expense supplies when they buy them. An alternative to expensing supplies is to record the cost as an asset (debit to Supplies, credit to Cash). At the end of the accounting period, an inventory is taken to determine the amount of supplies used in operations. The debit would be to Supplies Expense for the amount of supplies used during the accounting period, and the credit would be to Supplies (an asset account). The ending balance in Supplies (asset account) would be the supplies on hand at the end of the accounting period.

You Make the Call

Imagine that you have just been hired as an accounting clerk for Ride the Ducks of Seattle. Part of your job is to prepare adjusting entries prior to producing the financial statements. You have spent the week familiarizing yourself with the accounting system. You find the following preliminary adjusting notes left by the prior accounting clerk.

(a) Ride the Ducks of Seattle pays weekly salaries of $606.65 for a five-day workweek. The end of the accounting period is on a Thursday. The amount of wages per day was computed to be $121.33.

(b) The depreciation for the Ducks using the straight-line method is $33,392.86 per year and $2,782.74 per month. (The Ducks cost $275,000, with an estimated useful life of 7 years and a trade-in value of $41,250 at the end of that time.)

(c) The balance of the Prepaid Insurance account is $2,480, which covers one year. The amount of the adjusting entry for Insurance Expense for this one-month period is $206.67.

As the new accounting clerk, it is your job to review these figures for accuracy and then record the appropriate adjusting entries in the general journal.

SOLUTION

(a) $606.65 ÷ 5 = $121.33
     $121.33 × 4 days = $485.32 adjustment amount
(b) 1. $275,000 − $41,250 = $233,750 full depreciation
     2. $233,750 full depreciation ÷ 7 years = $33,392.86 per year
     3. $33,392.86 per year ÷ 12 months = $2,782.74 per month
(c) $2,480 per year ÷ 12 months = $206.67 per month

GENERAL JOURNAL   **PAGE   6**

Date		Description	Post. Ref.	Debit	Credit
		Adjusting Entries			
	(a)	Wages Expense		4 8 5 32	
		Wages Payable			4 8 5 32
	(b)	Depreciation Expense, Equipment		2 7 8 2 74	
		Accumulated Depreciation, Equipment			2 7 8 2 74
	(c)	Insurance Expense		2 0 6 67	
		Prepaid Insurance			2 0 6 67

If supplies are a major cost to a business and expensing the supplies when they are purchased would distort the income statement, then recording the cost as an asset and adjusting accordingly would be the preferable method of accounting for supplies. **We will continue expensing supplies in this text when they are purchased.**

Income Statement Involving More than One Revenue Account and a Net Loss

When an organization has more than one distinct source of revenue, a separate revenue account is set up for each source. See, for example, the income statement of Harris Miniature Golf presented in Figure 8. Also note that expenses are greater than revenues, resulting in a net loss.

6a LEARNING OBJECTIVE

Prepare an income statement involving more than one revenue account and a net loss.

FIGURE 8

Income statement for Harris Miniature Golf

Harris Miniature Golf Income Statement For Month Ended September 30, 20—		
Revenue:		
Admissions Fees	$2,624	
Concession Fees	1,512	
Total Revenue		$ 4,136
Expenses:		
Wages Expense	$3,123	
Advertising Expense	1,317	
Rent Expense	1,900	
Miscellaneous Expense	128	
Total Expenses		6,468
Net Loss		$(2,332)

Statement of Owner's Equity with an Additional Investment and a Net Income

Any additional investment by the owner during the period covered by the financial statements should be shown on the statement of owner's equity, since such a statement should show everything that has affected the Capital account from the *beginning* until the *end* of the period covered by the financial statements. For example, in Figure 9, assume that the following information is true for L. A. Grand Company, which has a net income:

6b LEARNING OBJECTIVE

Prepare a statement of owner's equity with an additional investment and either a net income or a net loss.

Balance of L. A. Grand, Capital, on April 1	$86,000
Additional investment by L. A. Grand on April 12	8,000
Net income for the month (from income statement)	6,200
Total withdrawals for the month	4,000

The additional investment may be in the form of cash. Or the investment may be in the form of other assets, such as tools, equipment, and similar items. In the case of investments of assets other than cash, the assets should be recorded at their fair market value. Fair market value is the present worth of an asset, or the amount that would be received if the asset were sold to an outsider on the open market. Fair market value may differ greatly from the amount the owner originally paid for the asset.

L. A. Grand Company Statement of Owner's Equity For Month Ended April 30, 20—		
L. A. Grand, Capital, April 1, 20—		$86,000
Investment during April	$ 8,000	
Net Income for April	6,200	
Subtotal	$14,200	
Less Withdrawals for April	4,000	
Increase in Capital		10,200
L. A. Grand, Capital, April 30, 20—		$96,200

FYI

The information normally shown on the statement of owner's equity is sometimes included as part of the owner's equity section of the balance sheet in computerized general ledger systems.

Statement of Owner's Equity with an Additional Investment and a Net Loss

Assume the following for J. D. Ross Company, which has a net loss:

J. D. Ross, Capital, on Oct. 1	$75,000
Additional investment by J. D. Ross on Oct. 25	10,000
Net loss for the month (from income statement)	1,500
Total withdrawals for the month	5,100

The statement of owner's equity in Figure 10 shows this information.

J. D. Ross Company Statement of Owner's Equity For Month Ended October 31, 20—		
J. D. Ross, Capital, October 1, 20—		$75,000
Investment during October	$10,000	
Net Loss for October	1,500	
Subtotal	$ 8,500	
Less Withdrawals for October	5,100	
Increase in Capital		3,400
J. D. Ross, Capital, October 31, 20—		$78,400

Businesses with More than One Depreciation Expense Account and More than One Accumulated Depreciation Account

LEARNING OBJECTIVE 6c

Prepare a balance sheet for a business having more than one accumulated depreciation account.

Figures 11 and 12 show the income statement and the balance sheet for Molen Veterinary Clinic. In Figure 12, note that the company has two assets subject to depreciation: Building and Equipment. In the financial statements, Depreciation Expense and Accumulated Depreciation must be listed for each asset.

Balance Sheet with Statement of Owner's Equity Included

LEARNING OBJECTIVE 6d

Prepare a balance sheet containing the statement of owner's equity information.

The information normally shown in the statement of owner's equity is sometimes included as part of the owner's equity section of the balance sheet, as shown in Figure 13.

FIGURE 11

Income statement for Molen Veterinary Clinic

Molen Veterinary Clinic
Income Statement
For Month Ended December 31, 20—

Revenue:		
Professional Fees	$332,300	
Boarding Fees	65,270	
Total Revenue		$397,570
Expenses:		
Salary Expense	$250,000	
Depreciation Expense, Building	19,450	
Depreciation Expense, Equipment	11,500	
Supplies Expense	11,380	
Insurance Expense	2,240	
Miscellaneous Expense	4,420	
Total Expenses		298,990
Net Income		$ 98,580

FIGURE 12

Balance sheet for Molen Veterinary Clinic

Molen Veterinary Clinic
Balance Sheet
December 31, 20—

Assets		
Cash		$ 21,320
Land		15,200
Building	$349,100	
Less Accumulated Depreciation	112,200	236,900
Equipment	$124,800	
Less Accumulated Depreciation	87,600	37,200
Total Assets		$310,620
Liabilities		
Accounts Payable		$ 7,400
Owner's Equity		
R. N. Molen, Capital		303,220
Total Liabilities and Owner's Equity		$310,620

FIGURE 13

Balance sheet for Conner's Whitewater Adventures

Conner's Whitewater Adventures
Balance Sheet
June 30, 20—

Assets		
Cash		$ 55,890
Accounts Receivable		4,250
Prepaid Insurance		1,250
Equipment	$ 51,300	
Less Accumulated Depreciation	512	50,788
Total Assets		$112,178
Liabilities		
Accounts Payable	$ 3,425	
Wages Payable	472	
Total Liabilities		$ 3,897
Owner's Equity		
J. Conner, Capital, June 1, 20—		$ 0
Investment during June	$ 95,200	
Net Income for June	16,581	
Subtotal	$111,781	
Less Withdrawals for June	3,500	
Increase in Capital		108,281
J. Conner, Capital, June 30, 20—		$108,281
Total Liabilities and Owner's Equity		$112,178

FYI

Computerized accounting programs frequently do not produce a separate statement of owner's equity.

CHAPTER REVIEW

Study & Practice

 LEARNING OBJECTIVE

1 *Define* fiscal period *and* fiscal year.

A **fiscal period** is any period of time covering a complete accounting cycle. A **fiscal year** consists of twelve consecutive months.

PRACTICE EXERCISE 1

Which of the following would be considered a fiscal year?

(a) July 1, 20— to June 30, 20—
(b) October 1, 20— to August 31, 20—
(c) April 1, 20— to January 31, 20—
(d) January 1, 20— to December 31, 20—

PRACTICE EXERCISE 1 SOLUTION

(a) and (d)

2 **LEARNING OBJECTIVE**
List the classifications of the accounts that occupy each column of a ten-column work sheet.

Trial Balance Debit	Assets + Drawing + Expenses
Trial Balance Credit	Accum. Depr. + Liabilities + Capital + Revenue
Adjusted Trial Balance Debit	Assets + Drawing + Expenses
Adjusted Trial Balance Credit	Accum. Depr. + Liabilities + Capital + Revenue
Income Statement Debit	Expenses
Income Statement Credit	Revenue
Balance Sheet Debit	Assets + Drawing
Balance Sheet Credit	Accum. Depr. + Liabilities + Capital

PRACTICE EXERCISE 2

Using a ten-column work sheet, list the classifications of accounts that are found in each column, with the exception of the Adjustments columns (Trial Balance, Adjusted Trial Balance, Income Statement, and Balance Sheet).

PRACTICE EXERCISE 2 SOLUTION

Account Name	Trial Balance		Adjustments		Adjusted Trial Balance		Income Statement		Balance Sheet	
	Debit	Credit	Debit	Credit	Debit	Credit	Debit	Credit	Debit	Credit
	Assets	Accum. Depr.			Assets	Accum. Depr.			Assets	Accum. Depr.
	Drawing	Liabilities			Drawing	Liabilities			Drawing	Liabilities
	Expenses	Capital			Expenses	Capital	Expenses			Capital
		Revenue				Revenue		Revenue		

3 LEARNING OBJECTIVE

Complete a work sheet for a service enterprise, involving adjustments for expired insurance, depreciation, and accrued wages.

Adjustment for expired insurance: debit Insurance Expense and credit Prepaid Insurance.

Adjustment for **depreciation**: debit Depreciation Expense and credit Accumulated Depreciation.

Adjustment for accrued wages: debit Wages Expense and credit Wages Payable.

PRACTICE EXERCISE 3

Complete the work sheet on page 154 for Fun and Games for the month of September.

Adjustment information:

(a) Insurance expired during September, $175
(b) Depreciation of equipment for the month of September, $540
(c) Accrued wages owed at the end of September, $260

PRACTICE EXERCISE 3 SOLUTION

See the completed work sheet on page 155.

4 LEARNING OBJECTIVE

Prepare an income statement, a statement of owner's equity, and a balance sheet for a service business directly from the work sheet.

Prepare the income statement directly from the amounts listed in the Income Statement Debit and Credit columns. The net income should equal the net income previously determined on the **work sheet**. For the statement of owner's equity, use the amount of the beginning capital listed in the Balance Sheet Credit column after checking the general ledger for any additional investment(s), the amount of the net income from the Balance Sheet Credit column, and the amount of Drawing from the Balance Sheet Debit column. Prepare the balance sheet directly from the amounts listed in the Balance Sheet Debit and Credit columns (except Drawing and Capital).

Fun and Games
Work Sheet
For Month Ended September 30, 20—

Account Name	Trial Balance Debit	Trial Balance Credit	Adjustments Debit	Adjustments Credit	Adjusted Trial Balance Debit	Adjusted Trial Balance Credit	Income Statement Debit	Income Statement Credit	Balance Sheet Debit	Balance Sheet Credit
Cash	24 9 0 0 00									
Accounts Receivable	5 7 5 0 00									
Prepaid Insurance	2 1 0 0 00									
Equipment	36 0 0 0 00									
Accum. Depr., Equip.		5 4 0 00								
Accounts Payable		3 9 8 5 00								
J. Jay, Capital		54 0 7 5 00								
J. Jay, Drawing	5 0 0 0 00									
Income from Services		21 0 0 0 00								
Wages Expense	2 6 7 0 00									
Rent Expense	1 9 5 0 00									
Supplies Expense	5 0 0 00									
Advertising Expense	4 5 0 00									
Utilities Expense	2 8 0 00									
	79 6 0 0 00	79 6 0 0 00								
Insurance Expense										
Depr. Exp., Equip.										
Wages Payable										
Net Income										

Fun and Games
Work Sheet
For Month Ended September 30, 20—

Account Name	Trial Balance Debit	Trial Balance Credit	Adjustments Debit	Adjustments Credit	Adjusted Trial Balance Debit	Adjusted Trial Balance Credit	Income Statement Debit	Income Statement Credit	Balance Sheet Debit	Balance Sheet Credit
Cash	24 9 0 0 00				24 9 0 0 00				24 9 0 0 00	
Accounts Receivable	5 7 5 0 00				5 7 5 0 00				5 7 5 0 00	
Prepaid Insurance	2 1 0 0 00			(a) 1 7 5 00	1 9 2 5 00				1 9 2 5 00	
Equipment	36 0 0 0 00				36 0 0 0 00				36 0 0 0 00	
Accum. Depr., Equip.		5 4 0 00		(b) 5 4 0 00		1 0 8 0 00				1 0 8 0 00
Accounts Payable		3 9 8 5 00				3 9 8 5 00				3 9 8 5 00
J. Jay, Capital		54 0 7 5 00				54 0 7 5 00				54 0 7 5 00
J. Jay, Drawing	5 0 0 0 00				5 0 0 0 00				5 0 0 0 00	
Income from Services		21 0 0 0 00				21 0 0 0 00		21 0 0 0 00		
Wages Expense	2 6 7 0 00		(c) 2 6 0 00		2 9 3 0 00		2 9 3 0 00			
Rent Expense	1 9 5 0 00				1 9 5 0 00		1 9 5 0 00			
Supplies Expense	5 0 0 00				5 0 0 00		5 0 0 00			
Advertising Expense	4 5 0 00				4 5 0 00		4 5 0 00			
Utilities Expense	2 8 0 00				2 8 0 00		2 8 0 00			
	79 6 0 0 00	79 6 0 0 00								
Insurance Expense			(a) 1 7 5 00		1 7 5 00		1 7 5 00			
Depr. Exp., Equip.			(b) 5 4 0 00		5 4 0 00		5 4 0 00			
Wages Payable				(c) 2 6 0 00		2 6 0 00				2 6 0 00
			9 7 5 00	9 7 5 00	80 4 0 0 00	80 4 0 0 00	6 8 2 5 00	21 0 0 0 00	73 5 7 5 00	59 4 0 0 00
Net Income							14 1 7 5 00			14 1 7 5 00
							21 0 0 0 00	21 0 0 0 00	73 5 7 5 00	73 5 7 5 00

PRACTICE EXERCISE 4

Prepare an income statement, a statement of owner's equity, and a balance sheet for Fun and Games using the information from Practice Exercise 3.

PRACTICE EXERCISE 4 SOLUTION

Fun and Games
Income Statement
For Month Ended September 30, 20—

Revenue:		
Income from Services		$21,000
Expenses:		
Wages Expense	$2,930	
Rent Expense	1,950	
Supplies Expense	500	
Advertising Expense	450	
Utilities Expense	280	
Insurance Expense	175	
Depreciation Expense, Equipment	540	
Total Expenses		6,825
Net Income		$14,175

Fun and Games
Statement of Owner's Equity
For Month Ended September 30, 20—

J. Jay, Capital, September 1, 20—		$54,075
Investment during September	$ 0	
Net Income for September	14,175	
Subtotal	$14,175	
Less Withdrawals for September	5,000	
Increase in Capital		9,175
J. Jay, Capital, September 30, 20—		$63,250

Fun and Games
Balance Sheet
September 30, 20—

Assets		
Cash		$24,900
Accounts Receivable		5,750
Prepaid Insurance		1,925
Equipment	$36,000	
Less Accumulated Depreciation	1,080	34,920
Total Assets		$67,495
Liabilities		
Accounts Payable	$ 3,985	
Wages Payable	260	
Total Liabilities		$ 4,245
Owner's Equity		
J. Jay, Capital		63,250
Total Liabilities and Owner's Equity		$67,495

LEARNING OBJECTIVE

5

Journalize and post the adjusting entries.

Adjustments are a way of updating the ledger accounts. They are determined after the trial balance has been prepared. To change the balance of the ledger accounts, **adjusting entries** are needed in the general journal as evidence of the changes. The information for these entries are taken directly from the Adjustments columns of the work sheet, debiting and crediting exactly the same accounts and amounts in the journal entries. Therefore, each adjusting entry consists of an income statement account and a balance sheet account. When the adjusting entries are posted to the ledger accounts, the abbreviation "Adj." is written in the Item column of the ledger account.

PRACTICE EXERCISE 5

Journalize and post the adjusting entries for Fun and Games from Practice Exercise 3.

PRACTICE EXERCISE 5 SOLUTION

GENERAL JOURNAL   **PAGE   4**

Date		Description	Post. Ref.	Debit	Credit
20—		Adjusting Entries			
Sept.	30	Insurance Expense	516	1 7 5 00	
		Prepaid Insurance	117		1 7 5 00
	30	Depr. Expense, Equipment	517	5 4 0 00	
		Accum. Depr., Equipment	125		5 4 0 00
	30	Wages Expense	511	2 6 0 00	
		Wages Payable	222		2 6 0 00

ACCOUNT Prepaid Insurance   **ACCOUNT NO. 117**

Date		Item	Post. Ref.	Debit	Credit	Balance Debit	Balance Credit
20—							
Sept.	15		2	2 1 0 0 00		2 1 0 0 00	
	30	Adj.	4		1 7 5 00	1 9 2 5 00	

ACCOUNT Accumulated Depreciation, Equipment   **ACCOUNT NO. 125**

Date		Item	Post. Ref.	Debit	Credit	Balance Debit	Balance Credit
20—							
		Bal.	2		5 4 0 00		5 4 0 00
Sept.	30	Adj.	4		5 4 0 00		1 0 8 0 00

ACCOUNT __Wages Payable__   ACCOUNT NO. __222__

Date	Item	Post. Ref.	Debit	Credit	Balance Debit	Balance Credit
20—						
Sept. 30	Adj.	4		2 6 0 00		2 6 0 00

ACCOUNT __Wages Expense__   ACCOUNT NO. __511__

Date	Item	Post. Ref.	Debit	Credit	Balance Debit	Balance Credit
20—						
Sept. 15		2	2 6 7 0 00		2 6 7 0 00	
30	Adj.	4	2 6 0 00		2 9 3 0 00	

ACCOUNT __Insurance Expense__   ACCOUNT NO. __516__

Date	Item	Post. Ref.	Debit	Credit	Balance Debit	Balance Credit
20—						
Sept. 30	Adj.	4	1 7 5 00		1 7 5 00	

ACCOUNT __Depreciation Expense, Equipment__   ACCOUNT NO. __517__

Date	Item	Post. Ref.	Debit	Credit	Balance Debit	Balance Credit
20—						
Sept. 30	Adj.	4	5 4 0 00		5 4 0 00	

6 LEARNING OBJECTIVE

Prepare (a) an income statement involving more than one revenue account and a net loss, (b) a statement of owner's equity with an additional investment and either a net income or a net loss, (c) a balance sheet for a business having more than one accumulated depreciation account, and (d) a balance sheet containing the statement of owner's equity information.

(a) An income statement containing more than one revenue account requires an additional line for each type of revenue, followed by a total amount of revenue.

(b) A statement of owner's equity involving an additional investment requires a line for each additional investment beneath the beginning capital amount, followed by a total amount of investment.

(c) Businesses that have more than one type of asset that is subject to depreciation must show a separate account for each on the balance sheet.

(d) A balance sheet sometimes contains in the owner's equity section the information normally placed in a separate statement of owner's equity. The section would contain the beginning capital, plus the amount of net income (or minus the net loss), minus total withdrawals. The result is the same amount that would be calculated in a separate statement of owner's equity—the ending capital.

PRACTICE EXERCISE 6a

Using the following information, prepare an income statement for the month of September for The Swim Shack.

Depreciation Expense, Equipment	$ 525
Income from Concessions	4,000
Income from Services	1,500
Insurance Expense	200
Rent Expense	1,950
Utilities Expense	890
Wages Expense	3,580

PRACTICE EXERCISE 6a SOLUTION

The Swim Shack
Income Statement
For Month Ended September 30, 20—

Revenue:		
Income from Concessions	$4,000	
Income from Services	1,500	
Total Revenue		$ 5,500
Expenses:		
Wages Expense	$3,580	
Rent Expense	1,950	
Utilities Expense	890	
Insurance Expense	200	
Depreciation Expense, Equipment	525	
Total Expenses		7,145
Net Loss		$(1,645)

PRACTICE EXERCISE 6b

Using the following information, prepare a statement of owner's equity for the month of July for Stanley's Computers and Electronics.

P. Stanley, Capital, on July 1	$205,077
Additional investment by P. Stanley on July 21	15,500
Net loss for the month (from income statement)	1,850
Total withdrawals for the month	3,500

PRACTICE EXERCISE 6b SOLUTION

Stanley's Computers and Electronics
Statement of Owner's Equity
For Month Ended July 31, 20—

P. Stanley, Capital, July 1, 20—		$205,077
Investment during July	$15,500	
Net Loss for July	1,850	
Subtotal	$13,650	
Less Withdrawals for July	3,500	
Increase in Capital		10,150
P. Stanley, Capital, July 31, 20—		$215,227

PRACTICE EXERCISE 6c

Using the following information, prepare a year-end balance sheet for Moreland Clinic as of December 31.

Accounts Payable	$ 7,380
Accumulated Depreciation, Building	112,200
Accumulated Depreciation, Equipment	87,600
Building	339,100
Cash	31,520
Equipment	114,800
Land	25,000
W. Moreland, Capital	303,240

PRACTICE EXERCISE 6c SOLUTION

Moreland Clinic
Balance Sheet
December 31, 20—

Assets		
Cash		$ 31,520
Land		25,000
Building	$339,100	
Less Accumulated Depreciation	112,200	226,900
Equipment	$114,800	
Less Accumulated Depreciation	87,600	27,200
Total Assets		$310,620
Liabilities		
Accounts Payable		$ 7,380
Owner's Equity		
W. Moreland, Capital		303,240
Total Liabilities and Owner's Equity		$310,620

PRACTICE EXERCISE 6d

Complete a balance sheet at the end of July for Stanley's Computers and Electronics by (a) using the following information for the Assets and Liabilities sections, and (b) including the information from the statement of owner's equity you created in Practice Exercise 6b for the Owner's Equity section.

Accounts Payable	$ 4,030
Accounts Receivable	4,725
Accumulated Depreciation, Building	1,420
Accumulated Depreciation, Equipment	600
Building	119,700
Cash	47,270
Equipment	48,500
Prepaid Insurance	1,500
Wages Payable	418

PRACTICE EXERCISE 6d SOLUTION

Stanley's Computers and Electronics
Balance Sheet
July 31, 20—

Assets

Cash			$ 47,270
Accounts Receivable			4,725
Prepaid Insurance			1,500
Building		$119,700	
Less Accumulated Depreciation		1,420	118,280
Equipment		$ 48,500	
Less Accumulated Depreciation		600	47,900
Total Assets			$219,675

Liabilities

Accounts Payable		$ 4,030	
Wages Payable		418	
Total Liabilities			$ 4,448

Owner's Equity

P. Stanley, Capital, July 1, 20—			$205,077
Investment during July		$ 15,500	
Net Loss for July		1,850	
Subtotal		$ 13,650	
Less Withdrawals for July		3,500	
Increase in Capital			10,150
P. Stanley, Capital, July 31, 20—			$215,227
Total Liabilities and Owner's Equity			$219,675

Glossary

Accounting cycle The sequence of steps in the accounting process completed during the fiscal period. (p. 129)

Accrual Recognition of an expense or a revenue that has been incurred or earned but has not yet been recorded. (p. 136)

Accrued wages Unpaid wages owed to employees for the time between the end of the last pay period and the end of the fiscal period. (p. 136)

Adjusting entries Entries that bring the books up to date at the end of the fiscal period. (p. 145)

Adjustments Internal transactions that bring ledger accounts up to date, as a planned part of the accounting procedure. They are first recorded in the Adjustments columns of the work sheet when using a manual accounting system. (p. 131)

Book value or carrying value The cost of an asset minus the accumulated depreciation. (p. 134)

Contra account An account that is contrary to, or a deduction from, another account; for example, Accumulated Depreciation, Equipment is listed as a deduction from Equipment. (p. 134)

Depreciation An expense based on the expectation that an asset will gradually decline in usefulness due to time, wear and tear, or obsolescence; the

cost of the asset is therefore spread out over its estimated useful life. A part of depreciation expense is apportioned to each fiscal period. (p. 133)

Fiscal period Any period of time covering a complete accounting cycle, generally consisting of twelve consecutive months. (p. 128)

Fiscal year A fiscal period consisting of twelve consecutive months. (p. 128)

Matching principle The principle that the revenue for one time period is matched up with the related expenses for the same time period. (p. 147)

Mixed accounts Certain accounts that appear on the trial balance with balances that are partly income statement amounts and partly balance sheet amounts—for example, Prepaid Insurance and Insurance Expense. (p. 138)

Straight-line depreciation A means of calculating depreciation in which the cost of an asset, less any trade-in value, is allocated evenly over the useful life of the asset. (p. 133)

Work sheet A working paper used by accountants to record necessary adjustments and provide up-to-date account balances needed to prepare the financial statements. (p. 129)

CHAPTER ASSIGNMENTS

Discussion Questions

1. What is the purpose of a work sheet in a manual system?
2. What is the purpose of adjusting entries?
3. What is a mixed account? A contra account? Give an example of each.
4. In which column of the work sheet—Income Statement (IS) or Balance Sheet (BS)—would the adjusted balances of the following accounts appear?

Account	IS or BS?	Account	IS or BS?
a. Prepaid Insurance		e. Accumulated Depreciation, Equipment	
b. Wages Expense		f. J. Karl, Drawing	
c. Wages Payable		g. Insurance Expense	
d. Income from Services		h. Depreciation Expense, Equipment	

5. Why is it necessary to make an adjustment if wages for work performed for the pay period Monday through Friday are paid on Friday and the accounting period ends on a Wednesday?
6. Define depreciation as it relates to a van you bought for your business.
7. Define an internal transaction and provide an example.
8. Why is it necessary to journalize and post adjusting entries?

Exercises

2

PRACTICE EXERCISE 2

EXERCISE 4-1 List the following classifications of accounts in all the columns in which they appear on the work sheet, with the exception of the Adjustments columns. (Example: Assets.)

Assets   Capital
Accumulated Depreciation   Drawing
   (with previous balance)   Revenue
Liabilities   Expenses

Write Net Income in the appropriate columns.

Account Name	Trial Balance		Adjustments		Adjusted Trial Balance		Income Statement		Balance Sheet	
	Debit	Credit	Debit	Credit	Debit	Credit	Debit	Credit	Debit	Credit
Assets					Assets				Assets	
Net Income										

EXERCISE 4-2 Classify each of the accounts listed below as assets (A), liabilities (L), owner's equity (OE), revenue (R), or expenses (E). Indicate the normal debit or credit balance of each account. Indicate whether each account will appear in the Income Statement columns (IS) or the Balance Sheet columns (BS) of the work sheet. Item 0 is given as an example.

 **LO** 2

PRACTICE EXERCISE 2

Account	Classification	Normal Balance	IS or BS Columns
0. Example: Wages Expense	E	Debit	IS
a. Prepaid Insurance			
b. Accounts Payable			
c. Wages Payable			
d. T. Bristol, Capital			
e. Accumulated Depreciation, Building			
f. T. Bristol, Drawing			
g. Rental Income			
h. Equipment			
i. Depreciation Expense, Equipment			
j. Supplies Expense			

EXERCISE 4-3 Place a check mark next to any account(s) requiring adjustment. Explain why those accounts must be adjusted.

 **LO** 3

✓	Account Name (in trial balance order)	Reason for Adjusting This Account
	a. Cash	
	b. Prepaid Insurance	
	c. Equipment	
	d. Accumulated Depreciation, Equipment	
	e. Wages Payable	
	f. R. Wesley, Capital	
	g. R. Wesley, Drawing	
	h. Wages Expense	

EXERCISE 4-4 A partial work sheet for Marge's Place is on page 164. Prepare the following adjustments on this work sheet for the month ended June 30, 20—.

 **LO** 3

PRACTICE EXERCISE 3

a. Expired or used-up insurance, $450.

b. Depreciation expense on equipment, $750 (remember to credit the Accumulated Depreciation account for equipment, not Equipment).

c. Wages accrued or earned since the last payday, $380 (owed and to be paid on the next payday).

Marge's Place
Work Sheet
For Month Ended June 30, 20—

Account Name	Trial Balance Debit	Trial Balance Credit	Adjustments Debit	Adjustments Credit
Cash	4 6 2 0 00			
Prepaid Insurance	1 8 0 0 00			
Equipment	4 8 8 0 00			
Accumulated Depreciation, Equipment		1 3 5 0 00		
Accounts Payable		2 5 3 9 00		
M. Benson, Capital		4 5 4 4 00		
M. Benson, Drawing	2 0 0 0 00			
Income from Services		6 9 3 7 00		
Rent Expense	1 0 8 6 00			
Supplies Expense	2 5 6 00			
Wages Expense	6 6 0 00			
Miscellaneous Expense	6 8 00			
	15 3 7 0 00	15 3 7 0 00		

3 LO

PRACTICE EXERCISE 3

EXERCISE 4-5 Complete the work sheet for Ramey Company, dated December 31, 20—, through the adjusted trial balance using the following adjustment information:

a. Expired or used-up insurance, $460.

b. Depreciation expense on equipment, $870 (remember to credit the Accumulated Depreciation account for equipment, not Equipment).

c. Wages accrued or earned since the last payday, $120 (owed and to be paid on the next payday).

Ramey Company
Work Sheet
For Year Ended December 31, 20—

Account Name	Trial Balance Debit	Trial Balance Credit	Adjustments Debit	Adjustments Credit	Adjusted Trial Balance Debit	Adjusted Trial Balance Credit
Cash	5 6 2 0 00					
Prepaid Insurance	1 2 0 0 00					
Equipment	4 6 7 8 00					
Accumulated Depr., Equip.		1 5 5 6 00				
Accounts Payable		1 8 7 5 00				
S. Ramey, Capital		6 0 2 6 00				
S. Ramey, Drawing	1 7 0 0 00					
Service Fees		5 8 3 6 00				
Rent Expense	9 6 5 00					
Supplies Expense	2 6 7 00					
Wages Expense	7 6 5 00					
Miscellaneous Expense	9 8 00					
	15 2 9 3 00	15 2 9 3 00				

EXERCISE 4-6 Journalize the three adjusting entries from the partial work sheet below for Brady Company for the month ended May 31. (*Hint:* Use what you know about opening new accounts for adjusting entries.)

 **LO 5**

PRACTICE EXERCISE 5

Brady Company
Work Sheet
For Month Ended May 31, 20—

Account Name	Income Statement Debit	Income Statement Credit	Balance Sheet Debit	Balance Sheet Credit
Cash			5 7 3 1 00	
Prepaid Insurance			8 4 1 00	
Equipment			4 8 3 2 00	
Accumulated Depreciation, Equipment				1 7 2 0 00
Accounts Payable				1 0 8 5 00
S. Brady, Capital				6 8 0 0 00
S. Brady, Drawing			2 1 5 0 00	
Professional Fees		9 6 7 3 00		
Salary Expense	3 7 8 7 00			
Rent Expense	1 2 0 0 00			
Supplies Expense	2 8 4 00			
Miscellaneous Expense	1 3 4 00			
Insurance Expense	2 8 5 00			
Depreciation Expense, Equipment	3 6 4 00			
Salaries Payable				3 3 0 00
	6 0 5 4 00	9 6 7 3 00	13 5 5 4 00	9 9 3 5 00
Net Income	3 6 1 9 00			3 6 1 9 00
	9 6 7 3 00	9 6 7 3 00	13 5 5 4 00	13 5 5 4 00

EXERCISE 4-7 Journalize the adjustments for Newkirk Company as of August 31.

 **LO 5**

PRACTICE EXERCISE 5

Newkirk Company
Work Sheet
For Month Ended August 31, 20—

Account Name	Trial Balance Debit	Trial Balance Credit	Adjustments Debit	Adjustments Credit
Cash	3 8 7 1 00			
Prepaid Insurance	3 9 7 3 00			(a) 3 6 5 00
Equipment	3 6 7 8 00			
Accumulated Depreciation, Equipment		6 4 5 00		(b) 2 0 6 00
Accounts Payable		1 8 4 3 00		
J. Newkirk, Capital		10 7 5 2 00		
J. Newkirk, Drawing	3 0 0 0 00			
Service Fees		5 6 8 3 00		
Rent Expense	1 7 9 5 00			
Supplies Expense	6 6 3 00			
Wages Expense	1 8 6 5 00		(c) 2 6 8 00	
Miscellaneous Expense	7 8 00			
	18 9 2 3 00	18 9 2 3 00		
Insurance Expense			(a) 3 6 5 00	
Depreciation Expense, Equipment			(b) 2 0 6 00	
Wages Payable				(c) 2 6 8 00
			8 3 9 00	8 3 9 00

 5 **LO**

EXERCISE 4-8 Journalize the following adjusting entries that were included on the work sheet for the month ended December 31. Assume the financial statements have been prepared.

Dec. 31   Salaries for three days are unpaid at December 31, $2,700. Salaries are $4,500 for a five-day week.

31   Insurance was bought on September 1 for $3,600 for 12 months' coverage. Four months' coverage has expired, $1,200.

31   Depreciation for the month on equipment, $50, based on an asset costing $3,200 with a trade-in value of $200 and an estimated life of 5 years.

Problem Set A

For additional help, see the demonstration problem at the beginning of each chapter in your Working Papers.

 3 **LO**

PROBLEM 4-1A The trial balance of Morgan's Insurance Agency as of September 30, after the firm has completed its first month of operations, is as follows:

Morgan's Insurance Company Trial Balance September 30, 20—		
Account Name	**Debit**	**Credit**
Cash	3,337	
Accounts Receivable	1,428	
Prepaid Insurance	775	
Office Equipment	5,146	
Accounts Payable		1,367
S. Morgan, Capital		9,528
S. Morgan, Drawing	1,000	
Commissions Earned		2,843
Rent Expense	885	
Supplies Expense	487	
Travel Expense	388	
Utilities Expense	227	
Miscellaneous Expense	65	
	13,738	13,738

Check Figure
Net Loss, $259

Required

1. Record the amounts in the Trial Balance columns of the work sheet.
2. Complete the work sheet by making the following adjustments and lettering each adjustment:
   a. Expired or used-up insurance, $300.
   b. Depreciation expense on office equipment, $750.

 4,5 **LO**

PROBLEM 4-2A The completed work sheet for Chelsey Decorators for the month of March is in your Working Papers.

Check Figure
Total Assets, $14,471

Required

1. Prepare an income statement.
2. Prepare a statement of owner's equity. Assume no additional investments were made in March.
3. Prepare a balance sheet.
4. Journalize the adjusting entries.

PROBLEM 4-3A The trial balance of Clayton Cleaners for the month ended September 30 is as follows:

LO 3,5

Clayton Cleaners Trial Balance September 30, 20—		
Account Name	Debit	Credit
Cash	2,589	
Prepaid Insurance	1,136	
Equipment	21,752	
Accumulated Depreciation, Equipment		14,357
Accounts Payable		2,647
K. Clayton, Capital		28,169
K. Clayton, Drawing	21,359	
Income from Services		40,850
Wages Expense	23,983	
Rent Expense	11,673	
Utilities Expense	1,254	
Supplies Expense	652	
Telephone Expense	1,144	
Miscellaneous Expense	481	
	86,023	86,023

Data for the adjustments are as follows:

a. Expired or used-up insurance, $800.
b. Depreciation expense on equipment, $2,700.
c. Wages accrued or earned since the last payday, $585 (owed and to be paid on the next payday).

Required

1. Complete a work sheet.
2. Journalize the adjusting entries.

Check Figure
Net Loss, $2,422

PROBLEM 4-4A The trial balance for Game Time on July 31 is as follows:

LO 3,4,5,6

GL

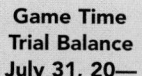

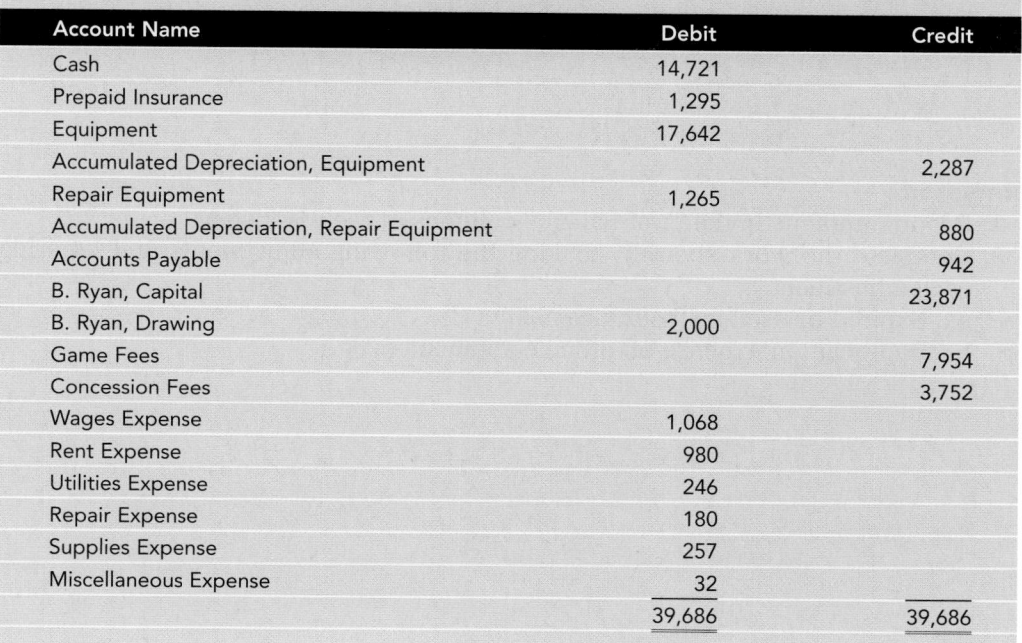

Game Time Trial Balance July 31, 20—		
Account Name	Debit	Credit
Cash	14,721	
Prepaid Insurance	1,295	
Equipment	17,642	
Accumulated Depreciation, Equipment		2,287
Repair Equipment	1,265	
Accumulated Depreciation, Repair Equipment		880
Accounts Payable		942
B. Ryan, Capital		23,871
B. Ryan, Drawing	2,000	
Game Fees		7,954
Concession Fees		3,752
Wages Expense	1,068	
Rent Expense	980	
Utilities Expense	246	
Repair Expense	180	
Supplies Expense	257	
Miscellaneous Expense	32	
	39,686	39,686

Data for month-end adjustments are as follows:

a. Expired or used-up insurance, $480.
b. Depreciation expense on equipment, $850.
c. Depreciation expense on repair equipment, $120.
d. Wages accrued or earned since the last payday, $525 (owed and to be paid on the next payday).

Check Figure
Net Income, $6,968

Required
1. Complete a work sheet for the month.
2. Prepare an income statement, a statement of owner's equity, and a balance sheet. Assume that no additional investments were made during July.
3. Journalize the adjusting entries.

Problem Set B

For additional help, see the demonstration problem at the beginning of each chapter in your Working Papers.

 3 LO

PROBLEM 4-1B The trial balance for Mason's Insurance Agency as of August 31, after the firm has completed its first month of operations, is as follows:

Mason's Insurance Company Trial Balance August 31, 20—		
Account Name	Debit	Credit
Cash	3,527	
Accounts Receivable	1,219	
Prepaid Insurance	1,362	
Office Equipment	3,939	
Accounts Payable		2,071
C. Mason, Capital		9,020
C. Mason, Drawing	1,900	
Commissions Earned		3,520
Rent Expense	1,695	
Supplies Expense	492	
Travel Expense	225	
Utilities Expense	198	
Miscellaneous Expense	54	
	14,611	14,611

Check Figure
Net Loss, $304

Required
1. Record amounts in the Trial Balance columns of the work sheet.
2. Complete the work sheet by making the following adjustments and lettering each adjustment:
   a. Expired or used-up insurance, $260.
   b. Depreciation expense on office equipment, $900.

PROBLEM 4-2B The completed work sheet for Juarez Design for the month of March is in your Working Papers.

 **LO** 4,5

Required
1. Prepare an income statement.
2. Prepare a statement of owner's equity. Assume that no additional investments were made in March.
3. Prepare a balance sheet.
4. Journalize the adjusting entries.

Check Figure
Total Assets, $21,817

PROBLEM 4-3B The trial balance of The New Decors for the month ended September 30 is as follows:

 **LO** 3,5

	The New Decors Trial Balance September 30, 20—	
Account Name	**Debit**	**Credit**
Cash	4,378	
Prepaid Insurance	1,345	
Equipment	30,978	
Accumulated Depreciation, Equipment		15,235
Accounts Payable		3,751
R. Becker, Capital		44,208
R. Becker, Drawing	20,445	
Income from Services		44,791
Wages Expense	29,761	
Rent Expense	15,932	
Supplies Expense	1,864	
Utilities Expense	1,573	
Telephone Expense	1,271	
Miscellaneous Expense	438	
	107,985	107,985

Data for the adjustments are as follows:

a. Expired or used-up insurance, $425.
b. Depreciation expense on equipment, $2,750.
c. Wages accrued or earned since the last payday, $475 (owed and to be paid on the next payday).

Required
1. Complete a work sheet.
2. Journalize the adjusting entries.

Check Figure
Net Loss, $9,698

3,4,5,6 **LO**

PROBLEM 4-4B The trial balance for Harris Pitch and Putt on June 30 is as follows:

Harris Pitch and Putt Trial Balance June 30, 20—		
Account Name	Debit	Credit
Cash	5,532	
Prepaid Insurance	1,284	
Equipment	21,687	
Accumulated Depreciation, Equipment		1,478
Repair Equipment	5,289	
Accumulated Depreciation, Repair Equipment		1,285
Accounts Payable		860
W. Harris, Capital		23,110
W. Harris, Drawing	2,565	
Golf Fees		11,487
Concession Fees		3,763
Wages Expense	3,163	
Rent Expense	1,350	
Utilities Expense	457	
Repair Expense	171	
Supplies Expense	246	
Miscellaneous Expense	239	
	41,983	41,983

Data for month-end adjustments are as follows:

a. Expired or used-up insurance, $380.
b. Depreciation expense on equipment, $1,950.
c. Depreciation expense on repair equipment, $1,650.
d. Wages accrued or earned since the last payday, $585 (owed and to be paid on the next payday).

Check Figure
Net Income, $5,059

Required

1. Complete a work sheet for the month.
2. Prepare an income statement, a statement of owner's equity, and a balance sheet. Assume that no additional investments were made during June.
3. Journalize the adjusting entries.

ACTIVITIES

CONSIDER AND COMMUNICATE

You are the bookkeeper for a small but thriving business. You have asked the owner for the information you need in order to make adjusting entries for depreciation, insurance, and wages. He says he's really busy, and what you've done so far is "close enough." Explain the need for adjusting entries and how they can affect his balance sheet and the "bottom line" on the income statement.

A QUESTION OF ETHICS

Your client is preparing financial statements to show the bank. You know that he has incurred a refrigeration repair expense during the month, but you see no such expense on the books. When you question the client, he tells you that he has not paid the $1,255 bill yet. Your client is on the accrual basis of accounting. He does not want the refrigeration repair expense on the books as of the end of the month because he wants his profits to look good for the bank. Is your client behaving ethically by suggesting that the refrigeration repair expense should not be booked until the $1,255 is paid? Are you behaving ethically if you go along with the client's request? What principle is involved here?

CRITICAL THINKING

Your supervisor just finished a work sheet for the month of June, but all the columns except the following were destroyed by a spilled latte. You have been asked to journalize the adjusting entries using the surviving partial work sheet.

Account Name	Income Statement Debit	Income Statement Credit	Balance Sheet Debit	Balance Sheet Credit
Cash			8 4 7 6 00	
Accounts Receivable			1 4 8 6 00	
Equipment			12 3 6 7 00	
Accumulated Depreciation, Equipment				3 6 1 0 00
Accounts Payable				2 8 1 3 00
G. Kramer, Capital				11 7 0 7 00
G. Kramer, Drawing			1 1 0 0 00	
Income from Services		11 2 1 6 00		
Rent Expense	1 4 0 0 00			
Supplies Expense	1 1 1 0 00			
Wages Expense	2 4 6 7 00			
Insurance Expense	2 1 0 00			
Depreciation Expense, Equipment	7 5 0 00			
Wages Payable				6 2 0 00
	5 9 3 7 00	11 2 1 6 00	24 0 2 9 00	18 7 5 0 00
Net Income	5 2 7 9 00			5 2 7 9 00
	11 2 1 6 00	11 2 1 6 00	24 0 2 9 00	24 0 2 9 00

All About You Spa

Adjustments

Although you printed the trial balance and financial statements to get an idea of how All About You Spa is doing, some accounts are not accurate. You need to make adjusting entries to provide a clearer picture of how the spa is doing.

| Month-end adjusting entries |

HOW TO COMPUTE THE ADJUSTMENTS

Compute the adjustment amounts for the month of June, using the following information:

Adjustment (a):   Liability insurance for six months was purchased during the first days of the month. That protection for one month has been used or expended (Insurance Expense), and the asset (Prepaid Insurance) is not worth what the balance sheet says. Therefore, since All About You Spa paid $960 for a six-month policy and one month of the coverage has been used, $160 of that policy is no longer an asset and represents an expense to the company. How was the figure $160 computed?

Adjustments (b) and (c):   Spa equipment and office equipment have depreciated. That means that they have been in use for a month and have, for accounting purposes, lost some usefulness. This is an estimate, of course, which allows us to expense the depreciation and, in effect, lowers the book value (value on the books) of both types of equipment.

(b):   The owner, Anika Valli, invested spa equipment totaling $7,393 in the business ($3,158 of her own spa equipment, plus $4,235 of new spa equipment purchased). The spa equipment will be depreciated using the straight-line method. The spa equipment is estimated to have a trade-in or salvage value of $3,500 and is expected to last five years. Therefore, the spa equipment is estimated to have depreciated $64.88 for the month of June. How was the figure $64.88 computed? Remember, you want to compute the depreciation for one month, not one year.

(c):   Anika Valli purchased office equipment totaling $1,150. The office equipment will be depreciated using the straight-line method. The office equipment is estimated to have a salvage (trade-in) value of $550 and is expected to last five years. Therefore, the office equipment is estimated to have depreciated $10 for the month of June. How was the figure $10 computed? Remember, you want to compute the depreciation for one month, not one year.

Adjustment (d):   All About You Spa owes one day of wages to its employees. The month's total wages paid in June amounted to $7,390. The employees worked 21 days, but were paid for only 20 days because the payday for the last day worked is in the next pay period. Therefore, the spa owes them one day's pay ($369.50), which also needs to be expensed. How was the figure $369.50 computed?

WHAT TO DO WITH THE ADJUSTMENT AMOUNTS

Follow these steps to enter the adjusting entries in your general ledger software.
1. If you are completing a work sheet (separately on paper or spreadsheet software), enter the adjusting entries and complete the work sheet by extending totals to the Adjusted Trial Balance columns and those totals to either the Income Statement or Balance Sheet columns. Total and compute the adjusted net income or net loss.

2. Open the file entitled **All_About_You_Spa_Ch04.IA7**. Enter your name when prompted and click **OK**. Select "Yes" or "No" as desired when asked if you want to open on-screen instructions and check figures.

3. Click on the **Save As** toolbar button. When the Save As window appears, select the folder in which you wish to save your data files (if not already selected). In the File Name box, key **All_About_You_Ch04_Your_Name.IA7** (for example, All_About_You_Spa_Ch04_John_Doe.IA7) to identify the file containing your work. Click on the **Save** button.

4. You need to add six new accounts to the Chart of Accounts. Click on the **Accts.** toolbar button. On the next available line, key "125" in the Account column and "Accum. Depr., Spa Equip." in the Account Title column. (Note that abbreviation is necessary because there is a limited number of characters allowed per account title.) Click on the **Add Account** button. The new account will be inserted in account number order in the Chart of Accounts. Follow the same procedure for the remaining five accounts to be entered:

   129 Accum. Depr., Office Eq.
   212 Wages Payable
   518 Insurance Expense
   519 Depr. Exp., Spa Equip.
   520 Depr. Exp., Office Eq.

   If you make a mistake and need to go back and change an account title, click on the title, key the change, and click on the **Change** button (The Add Account button becomes activated as a Change button when an existing account is selected). If you enter a wrong account number, the account will need to be deleted and re-entered. Select the account and click on the **Delete** button (but note that an account with an existing balance may not be deleted).

5. Click on the **Journal** toolbar button and key the adjusting journal entries in the General Journal. Follow these steps for each entry:
   (a) Key the date, June 30, in the Date column.
   (b) Enter a reference of "Adj.Ent." in the Refer. column (this is required for generating the Adjusting Journal Entries report later).
   (c) Enter the debit and credit parts of the entry as you learned to do in Chapter 3.

6. Display the adjusting journal entries. Click on the **Reports** toolbar button. Click on **Journals** and **General Journal** to choose a report to display. Click on **Customize Journal Report**. In the Reference drop-down list, choose "Adj. Ent." and then click the **OK** button to display the Adjusting Journal Entries report. To print the report, click on the **Print** button.

7. Review your entries and make corrections to them, if necessary. In the General Journal window, click on the entry to correct, key the correction(s), and click on the **Post** button (or press **Enter**).

8. Display the Trial Balance report. Click on the **Reports** toolbar button. Click on **Ledger Reports** and select **Trial Balance** to choose the report to display. Be sure the run date is set to June 30. To print the report, click on the **Print** button at the bottom of the report window.

9. Display the income statement. Click on the **Reports** toolbar button. Click on **Financial Statements** and select **Income Statement** to choose the report to display. To print the report, click on the **Print** button.

10. Display the statement of owner's equity. Click on the **Reports** toolbar button. Click on **Financial Statements** and select **Statement of Owner's Equity** to choose the report to display. To print the report, click on the **Print** button.

11. Display the balance sheet. Click on the **Reports** toolbar button. Click on **Financial Statements** and select **Balance Sheet** to choose the report to display. To print the report, click on the **Print** button.

12. Compare the statements before adjustments (that you generated for All About You Spa in Chapter 3) with the statements after adjustments. What do you find?

Check Figures
8. Adjusted trial balance total, $39,197.38
9. Net income, $6,776.62
10. A. Valli, Capital, ending balance, $23,084.62
11. Total assets, $25,702.12

5 Closing Entries and the Post-Closing Trial Balance

WHY IT MATTERS

REAL GAP EXPERIENCE, Tunbridge Wells, Kent (UK)

Rather than going directly to college, some students take time off to travel abroad, learn new skills, or volunteer. This period is known as a "gap year." Real Gap Experience provides hundreds of gap year traveling opportunities in over 45 countries around the world. The company offers everything from volunteering to build houses in Guatemala to a paid teaching job in China to a year-long, around-the-world trip.

What does this have to do with accounting, and why is it important? Every company needs to keep a record of its financial activities so that financial statements can be presented and used for decision making. Real Gap Experience's accounting records are most likely computerized, but the company's employees will still make adjustments if they are using the accrual basis of accounting. They will also need to prepare the accounting records for the next year of business. This process is known as the closing process, which you will learn about in this chapter.

LEARNING OBJECTIVES

After you have completed this chapter, you will be able to do the following:

1 List the steps in the accounting cycle.

2 Journalize and post closing entries for a service enterprise.

3 Prepare a post-closing trial balance.

4 Define the following methods of accounting: cash basis and accrual basis.

5 Prepare interim statements.

ACCOUNTING LANGUAGE

Accrual basis of accounting *(p. 187)*
Cash basis of accounting *(p. 187)*
Closing entries *(p. 178)*
Income Summary account *(p. 179)*
Interim statements *(p. 187)*

Nominal (temporary-equity) accounts *(p. 184)*
Post-closing trial balance *(p. 186)*
Real (permanent) accounts *(p. 184)*

1 LEARNING OBJECTIVE
List the steps in the accounting cycle.

Let's review the steps in the accounting cycle for an entire fiscal period. Remember that a fiscal period is generally twelve consecutive months, but it can also consist of other time frames like three months or six months.

STEP 1. Analyze source documents and record business transactions in a journal.

STEP 2. Post journal entries to the accounts in the ledger.

STEP 3. Prepare a trial balance.

STEP 4. Gather adjustment data and record the adjusting entries on a work sheet.

STEP 5. Complete the work sheet.

STEP 6. Prepare financial statements from the data on the work sheet.

STEP 7. Journalize and post the adjusting entries from the data on the work sheet.

STEP 8. Journalize and post the closing entries.

STEP 9. Prepare a post-closing trial balance.

This chapter explains the procedure for completing the final steps: journalizing and posting the closing entries and preparing the post-closing trial balance.

Adjusting entries, closing entries, and a post-closing trial balance are prepared at the end of a fiscal period. The number of months in a fiscal period varies. To introduce you to these final steps in the accounting cycle, we assume here that the fiscal period for Conner's Whitewater Adventures is one month. We make this assumption so that we can thoroughly cover the material and give you a chance to practice its application. The entire accounting cycle is outlined in Figure 1.

CLOSING ENTRIES

To help you understand the reason for the closing entries, let's take a look at a version of the fundamental accounting equation:

$$\text{Assets} = \text{Liabilities} + \text{Capital} + \text{Revenue} - \text{Expenses} - \text{Drawing}$$

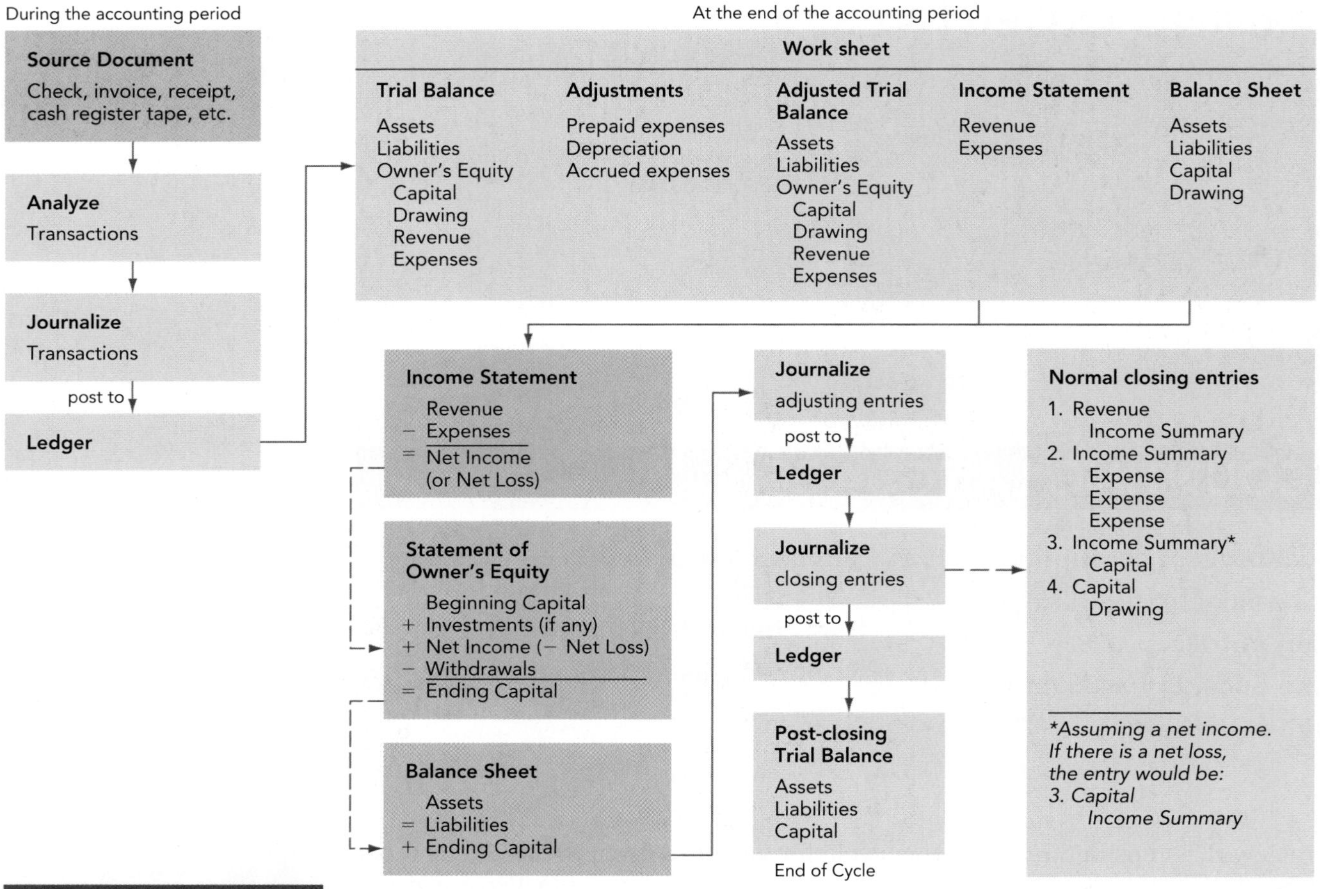

During the accounting period

Source Document

Check, invoice, receipt, cash register tape, etc.

↓

Analyze

Transactions

↓

Journalize

Transactions

post to ↓

Ledger

At the end of the accounting period

Work sheet

Trial Balance	Adjustments	Adjusted Trial Balance	Income Statement	Balance Sheet
Assets	Prepaid expenses	Assets	Revenue	Assets
Liabilities	Depreciation	Liabilities	Expenses	Liabilities
Owner's Equity	Accrued expenses	Owner's Equity		Capital
Capital		Capital		Drawing
Drawing		Drawing		
Revenue		Revenue		
Expenses		Expenses		

Income Statement

  Revenue
− Expenses
= Net Income
  (or Net Loss)

Statement of Owner's Equity

  Beginning Capital
+ Investments (if any)
+ Net Income (− Net Loss)
− Withdrawals
= Ending Capital

Balance Sheet

  Assets
= Liabilities
+ Ending Capital

Journalize

adjusting entries

post to ↓

Ledger

↓

Journalize

closing entries

post to ↓

Ledger

↓

Post-closing Trial Balance

Assets
Liabilities
Capital

End of Cycle

Normal closing entries

1. Revenue
    Income Summary
2. Income Summary
    Expense
    Expense
    Expense
3. Income Summary*
    Capital
4. Capital
    Drawing

_____

*Assuming a net income. If there is a net loss, the entry would be:
3. Capital
    Income Summary

FIGURE 1

The accounting cycle

We know that the income statement, as stated in the third line of its heading, covers a period of time. The income statement consists of revenue minus expenses for this period of time only. So, when the next fiscal period begins, we should start with zero balances. We start over again each period.

Purpose of Closing Entries

This year's revenue and expenses...

BEFORE CLOSING

AFTER CLOSING

Closing entries empty or zero out temporary owner's equity accounts and prepare the accounts for the new accounting period—much like when you empty the information from your tax folders one year so that the folders can be filled with the new year's revenue and expense receipts.

This brings us to the *purpose* of the **closing entries**, which is to close (or zero) the temporary-equity or nominal accounts (revenue, expense, and Drawing accounts). We do this because their balances apply to only one fiscal period. Closing entries are made after the last adjusting entry and after the financial statements have been prepared. With the coming of the next fiscal period, we want to start from zero, recording revenue and expenses for the new fiscal period. The closing entries also update the owner's Capital account.

Accountants also refer to closing the accounts as *clearing the accounts*. For income tax purposes, this is certainly understandable. No one wants to pay income tax more than once on the same income, and the Internal Revenue Service doesn't allow you to count an expense more than once. So now we have this:

$$\text{Assets} = \text{Liabilities} + \text{Capital} + \overset{\text{(closed)}}{\cancel{\text{Revenue}}} - \overset{\text{(closed)}}{\cancel{\text{Expenses}}} - \overset{\text{(closed)}}{\cancel{\text{Drawing}}}$$

The assets, liabilities, and owner's Capital accounts remain open. The balance sheet gives the present balances of these accounts. The accountant carries the asset, liability, and Capital account balances over to the next fiscal period.

Procedure for Closing

The procedure for closing is simply to balance off the account; in other words, to make the balance *equal to zero*. This meets our objective, which is to start from zero in the next fiscal period. Let's illustrate this first with T accounts. Suppose an account to be closed has a debit balance of $870. To make the balance equal to zero, we *credit* the account for $870.

Debit		Credit	
Balance	870	Closing	870

Now suppose an account to be closed has a credit balance of $1,400. To make the balance equal to zero, we *debit* the account for $1,400.

Debit		Credit	
Closing	1,400	Balance	1,400

Remember, every entry must have at least one debit and one credit. So, to record the other half of the closing entry, we bring into existence the **Income Summary account**. The Income Summary account does not have plus and minus signs, just debit and credit.

There are four steps in the closing procedure:

STEP 1. Close the revenue account(s) into Income Summary.

STEP 2. Close the expense accounts into Income Summary.

STEP 3. Close the Income Summary account into the Capital account, transferring the net income or net loss to the Capital account.

STEP 4. Close the Drawing account into the Capital account.

To illustrate, we return to Conner's Whitewater Adventures. For the purpose of the illustration, assume that Conner's Whitewater Adventures' fiscal period consists of one month. We have the following T account balances in the revenue and expense accounts after the adjustments have been posted.

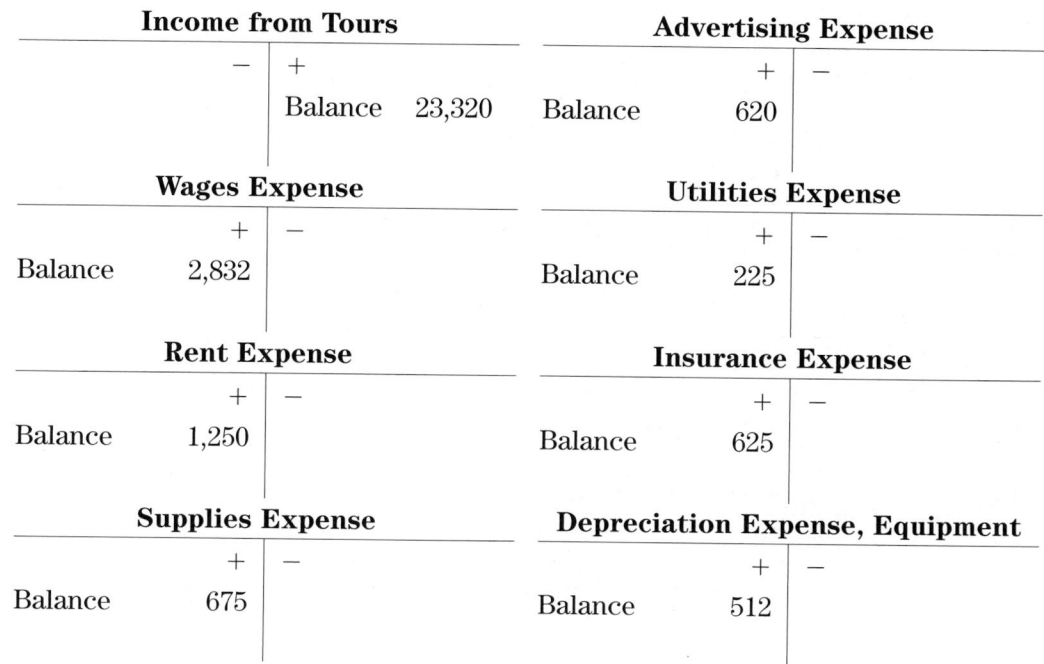

Income from Tours		
−	+	
	Balance	23,320

Advertising Expense		
+	−	
Balance 620		

Wages Expense		
+	−	
Balance	2,832	

Utilities Expense		
+	−	
Balance 225		

Rent Expense		
+	−	
Balance	1,250	

Insurance Expense		
+	−	
Balance 625		

Supplies Expense		
+	−	
Balance	675	

Depreciation Expense, Equipment		
+	−	
Balance 512		

STEP 1. Close the revenue account(s) into Income Summary.

In order to make the balance of Income from Tours equal to zero, we *balance it off,* or debit it, in the amount of $23,320. Because we need an offsetting credit, we credit Income Summary for the same amount. Notice that there are no signs in Income Summary, only Debit and Credit like the other accounts.

Income from Tours			Income Summary	
−	+			
Closing **23,320**	Balance 23,320			(Revenue) **23,320**

The balance of Income from Tours is transferred to Income Summary.

STEP 2. Close the expense accounts into Income Summary.

To make the balances of the expense accounts equal to zero, we need to balance them off, or credit them. Again the T accounts are useful for formulating this journal entry.

Wages Expense			Income Summary	
+	−			
Balance 2,832	Closing **2,832**		(Expenses) **6,739**	(Revenue) 23,320

Rent Expense	
+	−
Balance 1,250	Closing **1,250**

Supplies Expense	
+	−
Balance 675	Closing **675**

Advertising Expense	
+	−
Balance 620	Closing **620**

Utilities Expense	
+	−
Balance 225	Closing **225**

Insurance Expense	
+	−
Balance 625	Closing **625**

Depreciation Expense, Equipment	
+	−
Balance 512	Closing **512**

STEP 3. Close the Income Summary account into the Capital account, transferring the net income or loss to the Capital account.

Recall that we created Income Summary so that we could have a debit and a credit in each closing entry. Now that it has done its job, we close it out. We use the same procedure as before, in that we make the balance equal to zero, or balance off the account. We transfer, or close, the balance of the Income Summary account into the Capital account, as shown in the T accounts and in Figure 2.

Income Summary			J. Conner, Capital	
			−	+
(Expenses) 6,739	(Revenue) 23,320		Balance 95,200	
Closing **16,581**			(Net Inc.) **16,581**	

GENERAL JOURNAL   **PAGE** 4

	Date	Description	Post. Ref.	Debit	Credit
		Closing Entries			
Step 1	30	Income from Tours		23 3 2 0 00	
		Income Summary			23 3 2 0 00
	30	Income Summary		6 7 3 9 00	
		Wages Expense			2 8 3 2 00
		Rent Expense			1 2 5 0 00
		Supplies Expense			6 7 5 00
Step 2		Advertising Expense			6 2 0 00
		Utilities Expense			2 2 5 00
		Insurance Expense			6 2 5 00
		Depreciation Expense, Equipment			5 1 2 00
Step 3	30	Income Summary		16 5 8 1 00	
		J. Conner, Capital			16 5 8 1 00

FIGURE 2

Closing entries for Conner's Whitewater Adventures

Income Summary is always closed into the Capital account by the amount of the net income (revenue minus expenses) or the net loss. Comparing net income or net loss on the work sheet with the closing entry for Income Summary can serve as a checkpoint or verification for you.

Net income is added (credited) to the Capital account because, as shown in the statement of owner's equity, net income is treated as an addition. Net loss, on the other hand, is subtracted from (debited to) the Capital account, because net loss is treated as a deduction in the statement of owner's equity. Here's how to close Income Summary for J. Doe Company (net loss of $600):

Income Summary			J. Doe, Capital	
			−	+
(Expenses) 3,000	(Revenue) **2,400**	(Net Loss) **600**	Balance 42,000	
	Closing **600**			

The entry to close Income Summary into J. Doe's Capital account would look like the following.

| | | | | | | | GENERAL JOURNAL | | | | | | | | | | | | PAGE | 3 | |
Date		Description		Post. Ref.			Debit						Credit			
		Closing Entries														
31	J. Doe, Capital					6	0	0	00							
	Income Summary										6	0	0	00		

STEP 4. Close the Drawing account into the Capital account.

Let's return to the example of Conner's Whitewater Adventures. The Drawing account applies to only one fiscal period, so it too must be closed. Drawing is not an expense because it did not help the business generate revenue. **And because Drawing is not an expense, it cannot affect net income or net loss.** It appears in the statement of owner's equity as a deduction from the Capital account, so it is closed directly into the Capital account. We balance off the Drawing account, or make its balance equal to zero. The balance of Drawing is transferred to the Capital account.

J. Conner, Drawing		J. Conner, Capital	
+	−	−	+
Balance 3,500	Closing 3,500	(Drawing) 3,500	Balance 95,200
			(Net Inc.) 16,581

The journal entries in the closing procedure are shown in Figure 3.

FIGURE 3

Closing entries for Conner's Whitewater Adventures

FYI

As a memory tool for the sequence of steps in the closing procedure, use the letters of the closing elements, **REID:** Revenue, Expenses, Income Summary, Drawing.

| | | | | GENERAL JOURNAL | | | | | | | | | | PAGE | 4 | | |
	Date		Description		Post. Ref.			Debit						Credit			
			Closing Entries														
Step 1	30	Income from Tours			411	23	3	2	0	00							
		Income Summary			313							23	3	2	0	00	
	30	Income Summary			313	6	7	3	9	00							
		Wages Expense			511							2	8	3	2	00	
		Rent Expense			512							1	2	5	0	00	
		Supplies Expense			513								6	7	5	00	
Step 2		Advertising Expense			514								6	2	0	00	
		Utilities Expense			515								2	2	5	00	
		Insurance Expense			516								6	2	5	00	
		Depreciation Expense, Equipment			517								5	1	2	00	
Step 3	30	Income Summary			313	16	5	8	1	00							
		J. Conner, Capital			311							16	5	8	1	00	
Step 4	30	J. Conner, Capital			311	3	5	0	0	00							
		J. Aconner, Drawing			312							3	5	0	0	00	

These closing entries show that Conner's Whitewater Adventures has net income of $16,581, the owner has withdrawn $3,500 for personal expenses, and $13,081 ($16,581 − $3,500) has been retained in the business, thereby increasing capital.

Making closing entries using accounting software is frequently an instantaneous procedure. Be sure that all financial statements required have been printed and saved prior to closing, since the closing procedure causes zero balances in the temporary owner's equity accounts. The operator selects the command/function to close the accounting period, and the revenue and expense accounts are automatically closed. The Drawing account may need to be closed with a journal entry. The net income (or loss) is sent to the Capital account. The bad news is that any errors made prior to closing are included. Always make a backup copy of your file prior to closing in case you have made a mistake and need to backtrack to correct an error.

Closing Entries Taken Directly from the Work Sheet

You can gather the information for the closing entries either directly from the ledger accounts or from the work sheet. Since the Income Statement columns of the work sheet consist entirely of revenues and expenses, you can pick up the figures for three of the four closing entries from these columns. Figure 4 shows a partial work sheet for Conner's Whitewater Adventures.

You may plan the closing entries by balancing off all the figures that appear in the Income Statement columns. For example, in the Income Statement Credit column, there is a credit for $23,320 (Income from Tours), so we debit that account for $23,320 and credit Income Summary for $23,320.

FIGURE 4

Partial work sheet for Conner's Whitewater Adventures

Account Name	Trial Balance Debit	Trial Balance Credit	Adjustments Debit	Adjustments Credit	Income Statement Debit	Income Statement Credit
Cash	55 8 9 0 00					
Accounts Receivable	4 2 5 0 00					
Prepaid Insurance	1 8 7 5 00			(a) 6 2 5 00		
Equipment	51 3 0 0 00					
Accounts Payable		3 4 2 5 00				
J. Conner, Capital		95 2 0 0 00				
J. Conner, Drawing	3 5 0 0 00					
Income from Tours		23 3 2 0 00				23 3 2 0 00
Wages Expense	2 3 6 0 00		(c) 4 7 2 00		2 8 3 2 00	
Rent Expense	1 2 5 0 00				1 2 5 0 00	
Supplies Expense	6 7 5 00				6 7 5 00	
Advertising Expense	6 2 0 00				6 2 0 00	
Utilities Expense	2 2 5 00				2 2 5 00	
	121 9 4 5 00	121 9 4 5 00				
Insurance Expense			(a) 6 2 5 00		6 2 5	
Depr. Exp., Equip.			(b) 5 1 2 00		5 1 2 00	
Accum. Depr., Equip.				(b) 5 1 2 00		
Wages Payable				(c) 4 7 2 00		
			1 6 0 9 00	1 6 0 9 00	6 7 3 9 00	23 3 2 0 00
Net Income					16 5 8 1 00	
					23 3 2 0 00	23 3 2 0 00

There are debits for $2,832, $1,250, $675, $620, $225, $625, and $512 (expense accounts). So now we *credit* these accounts for the same amounts, and we debit Income Summary for their total ($6,739).

Next, we close Income Summary into Capital, using the net income figure already shown on the work sheet in Figure 4.

We do, of course, have to get the last closing entry from the Balance Sheet columns to close Drawing.

Incidentally, accountants call the accounts that are to be closed (such as revenue, expenses, Income Summary, and Drawing) **nominal (temporary-equity) accounts**. These accounts are temporary in that their balances apply to only one fiscal period. The *equity* aspect pertains because these accounts all come under the umbrella of owner's equity.

On the other hand, accountants call the accounts that remain open (such as assets, liabilities, and Capital) **real (permanent) accounts**. These accounts have balances that will be carried over to the next fiscal period. They are *permanent* because as long as the company exists, there will be balances in these accounts.

> **Remember**
>
> The temporary-equity accounts (revenue, expenses, and Drawing) are closed out because they apply to only one fiscal period.

Posting the Closing Entries

In the Item column of the ledger account, we write the word *Closing*. To show that the balance of an account is zero, we draw a line through both the Debit Balance and the Credit Balance columns.

After we have posted the closing entries, the Capital, Drawing, Income Summary, revenue, and expense accounts of Conner's Whitewater Adventures appear as follows:

GENERAL LEDGER

ACCOUNT J. Conner, Capital   **ACCOUNT NO. 311**

Date		Item	Post. Ref.	Debit	Credit	Balance Debit	Balance Credit
20—							
June	1		1		90 0 0 0 00		90 0 0 0 00
	4		1		5 2 0 0 00		95 2 0 0 00
	30	Closing	4		16 5 8 1 00		111 7 8 1 00
	30	Closing	4	3 5 0 0 00			108 2 8 1 00

ACCOUNT J. Conner, Drawing   **ACCOUNT NO. 312**

Date		Item	Post. Ref.	Debit	Credit	Balance Debit	Balance Credit
20—							
June	30		3	3 5 0 0 00		3 5 0 0 00	
	30	Closing	4		3 5 0 0 00	————	————

ACCOUNT Income Summary   **ACCOUNT NO. 313**

Date		Item	Post. Ref.	Debit	Credit	Balance Debit	Balance Credit
20—							
June	30	Closing	4		23 3 2 0 00		23 3 2 0 00
	30	Closing	4	6 7 3 9 00			16 5 8 1 00
	30	Closing	4	16 5 8 1 00		————	————

ACCOUNT Income from Tours   **ACCOUNT NO.** 411

Date		Item	Post. Ref.	Debit	Credit	Balance	
						Debit	Credit
20—							
June	7		1		8 0 0 0 00		8 0 0 0 00
	15		2		6 7 5 0 00		14 7 5 0 00
	30		3		8 5 7 0 00		23 3 2 0 00
	30	Closing	4	23 3 2 0 00			

ACCOUNT Wages Expense   **ACCOUNT NO.** 511

Date		Item	Post. Ref.	Debit	Credit	Balance	
						Debit	Credit
20—							
June	24		2	2 3 6 0 00		2 3 6 0 00	
	30	Adj.	4	4 7 2 00		2 8 3 2 00	
	30	Closing	4		2 8 3 2 00		

ACCOUNT Rent Expense   **ACCOUNT NO.** 512

Date		Item	Post. Ref.	Debit	Credit	Balance	
						Debit	Credit
20—							
June	8		1	1 2 5 0 00		1 2 5 0 00	
	30	Closing	4		1 2 5 0 00		

ACCOUNT Supplies Expense   **ACCOUNT NO.** 513

Date		Item	Post. Ref.	Debit	Credit	Balance	
						Debit	Credit
20—							
June	10		1	6 7 5 00		6 7 5 00	
	30	Closing	4		6 7 5 00		

ACCOUNT Advertising Expense   **ACCOUNT NO.** 514

Date		Item	Post. Ref.	Debit	Credit	Balance	
						Debit	Credit
20—							
June	14		2	6 2 0 00		6 2 0 00	
	30	Closing	4		6 2 0 00		

ACCOUNT Utilities Expense   **ACCOUNT NO. 515**

Date		Item	Post. Ref.	Debit	Credit	Balance Debit	Balance Credit
20—							
June	18		2	2 2 5 00		2 2 5 00	
	30	Closing	4		2 2 5 00	——	——

ACCOUNT Insurance Expense   **ACCOUNT NO. 516**

Date		Item	Post. Ref.	Debit	Credit	Balance Debit	Balance Credit
20—							
June	30	Adj.	4	6 2 5 00		6 2 5 00	
	30	Closing	4		6 2 5 00	——	——

ACCOUNT Depreciation Expense, Equipment   **ACCOUNT NO. 517**

Date		Item	Post. Ref.	Debit	Credit	Balance Debit	Balance Credit
20—							
June	30	Adj.	4	5 1 2 00		5 1 2 00	
	30	Closing	4		5 1 2 00	——	——

THE POST-CLOSING TRIAL BALANCE

LEARNING OBJECTIVE 3

Prepare a post-closing trial balance.

After posting the closing entries and before going on to the next fiscal period, verify the balances of the accounts that remain open. To do so, prepare a **post-closing trial balance**, using the final balance figures from the ledger accounts. The purpose of the post-closing trial balance is to make sure that the debit balances equal the credit balances.

  Note that the accounts listed in the post-closing trial balance (assets, liabilities, and Capital) are the *real* or *permanent accounts* (see Figure 5). The accountant carries forward the balances of the permanent accounts from one fiscal period to another.

FIGURE 5

Post-closing trial balance for Conner's Whitewater Adventures

Conner's Whitewater Adventures
Post-Closing Trial Balance
June 30, 20—

Account Name	Debit	Credit
Cash	55,890	
Accounts Receivable	4,250	
Prepaid Insurance	1,250	
Equipment	51,300	
Accumulated Depreciation, Equipment		512
Accounts Payable		3,425
Wages Payable		472
J. Conner, Capital		108,281
	112,690	112,690

Contrast this to the handling of *nominal* or *temporary-equity accounts* (revenue, expenses, Income Summary, and Drawing), which are closed at the end of each fiscal period.

If the total debits and total credits of the post-closing trial balance are not equal, here's a recommended procedure for tracking down the error.

1. Re-add the trial balance columns.
2. Check to see that the figures were correctly transferred from the ledger accounts to the post-closing trial balance.
3. Verify the posting of the adjusting entries and the recording of the new balances.
4. Make sure that the closing entries have been posted and that all revenue, expense, Income Summary, and Drawing accounts have zero balances.

THE BASES OF ACCOUNTING: CASH AND ACCRUAL

The basis of accounting that a company chooses has a direct effect on the company's net income and the company's income tax. The business must use the same basis of accounting from year to year, and the basis of accounting must clearly reflect the net income of the business.

Under the **cash basis of accounting**, revenue is recorded when it is received in cash, and generally expenses are recorded when they are paid in cash. If the expenditures have an economic life of more than one year (for example, equipment purchases and insurance), then the cost of these items must be prorated or spread out over their useful lives. Many small businesses' and individuals' personal income taxes are recorded on the cash basis.

Under the **accrual basis of accounting**, revenue is recorded when it is earned, and expenses are recorded when they are incurred (when they occur or the bill is received). For example, in the sale of goods, revenue is counted by the seller when the buyer accepts delivery of the goods. Expenses are recorded by the seller of the goods when the costs are incurred. This is called the matching principle, since revenue in one fiscal period is matched up with expenses incurred in the same period. If your business produces, purchases, or sells merchandise, the business must keep an inventory and use the accrual method for sales and purchases of merchandise.

Most businesses will use the same method of accounting for their financial statements and income tax reporting. According to the Internal Revenue Service, businesses with average annual gross receipts of $5 million or less may be allowed to use the cash method rather than the accrual method, which is more complicated and time consuming. However, there are some important exceptions to this general rule. A business may also use a combination of cash and accrual bases of accounting, called the *hybrid method*. Selecting a basis of accounting can often be complicated and confusing. IRS Publication 538, Accounting Periods and Methods, provides information that makes this decision less confusing. Publication 538 is available on the IRS Web site at www.irs.gov.

4 LEARNING OBJECTIVE

Define the following methods of accounting: cash basis and accrual basis.

INTERIM STATEMENTS

The owner of a business understandably does not want to wait until the end of the twelve-month fiscal period to determine whether the company is making a profit or a loss. Instead, most owners want financial statements at the end of each month. Financial statements prepared during the fiscal year, for periods of less than twelve months, are called **interim statements**. (They are given this name because they are

5 LEARNING OBJECTIVE

Prepare interim statements.

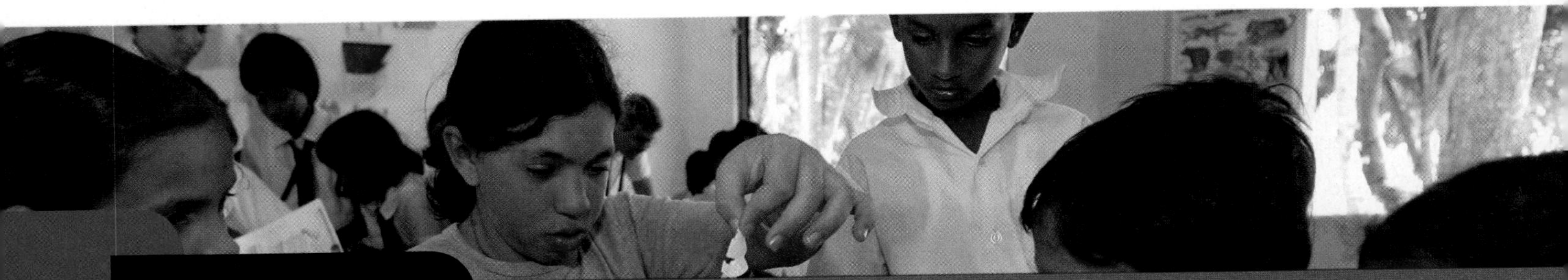

You Make the Call

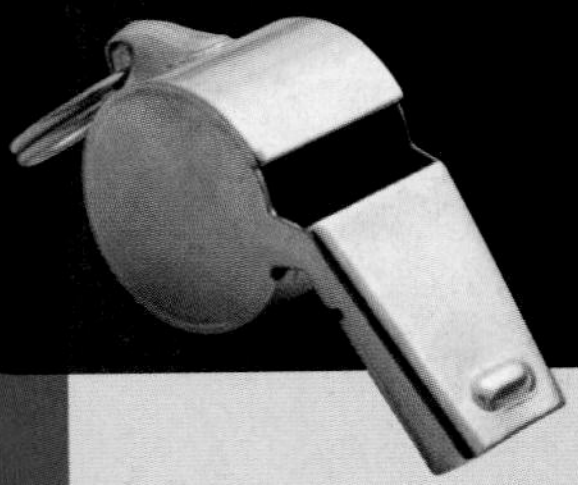

Using the information you know about the cash basis versus the accrual basis, review the four types of businesses listed below. First, consider the type of accounting transactions the following businesses might make. Second, suggest whether the cash basis or the accrual basis would be a logical fit for the business.

1. An investment advisory firm owned by outside investors with $12 million in annual gross receipts
2. A crane sales company with $1 million in annual gross receipts
3. A travel agency with $2 million in annual gross receipts
4. A tractor sales company with $6 million in annual gross receipts

SOLUTION

The travel agency would probably be on the cash basis because it has less than $5 million in annual gross receipts. However, the investment advisory firm would likely be on the accrual basis because its annual gross receipts exceed $5 million. The crane sales company and the tractor sales company would also use the accrual basis since both companies have inventory.

prepared within the fiscal period.) For example, a business may prepare the income statement, the statement of owner's equity, and the balance sheet *monthly*. These statements provide up-to-date information about the results and status of operations. For example, a company might have the following interim statements:

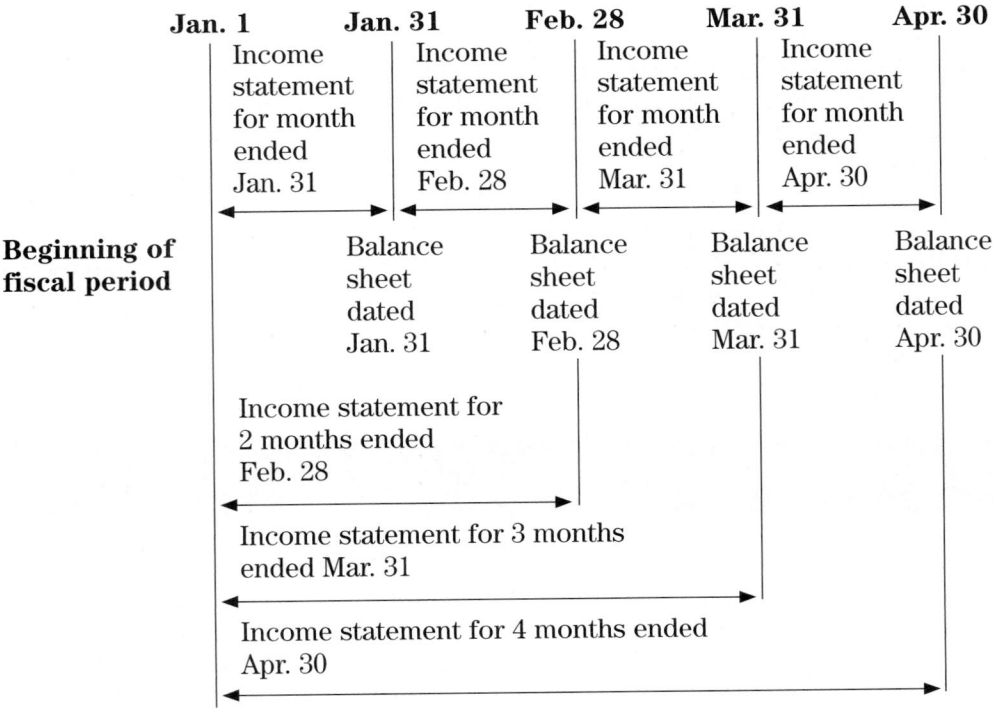

SMALL BUSINESS SUCCESS

Do I Need an Accountant?

If you are not taking this class because you want to be an accountant or bookkeeper, you might be taking this class because you plan on owning and operating a small business. Many new small business owners take on the responsibilities of being the accountant for their business. However, at some point your business will begin to grow, and you might need to consider hiring an accountant to manage your accounting books so that your time is free to run the business.

An accountant can help you in many areas of your small business, such as:

• What should my business structure be—sole proprietorship, partnership, S corporation, or corporation?

• What software should I use for my accounting?
• How do I handle the payroll for employees?
• What are my requirements for filing taxes?
• What expenses are deductible for tax purposes?
• How do I prepare financial statements when applying for a loan?

So, how do you find an accountant? The best way is by referrals. Ask other businesses in your industry for references or visit your local Certified Public Accounting Society Web site (www.aicpa.org/yellow/ypascpa.htm) for more recommendations.

In this case, the accountant would prepare a work sheet at the end of each month. Next, based on these work sheets, he or she would prepare the financial statements. However, the remaining steps—journalizing the adjusting and closing entries and preparing the post-closing trial balance—would be performed only at the end of the year.

CHAPTER REVIEW

Study & Practice

LEARNING OBJECTIVE

1 *List the steps in the accounting cycle.*

STEP 1. Analyze source documents and record business transactions in a journal.
STEP 2. Post journal entries to the accounts in the ledger.
STEP 3. Prepare a trial balance.
STEP 4. Gather adjustment data and record the adjusting entries on a work sheet.
STEP 5. Complete the work sheet.
STEP 6. Prepare financial statements from the data on the work sheet.
STEP 7. Journalize and post the adjusting entries from the data on the work sheet.
STEP 8. Journalize and post the **closing entries**.
STEP 9. Prepare a post-closing trial balance.

PRACTICE EXERCISE 1

Match the steps of the accounting cycle to their corresponding number.

_____ **1.** Step 1
_____ **2.** Step 2
_____ **3.** Step 3
_____ **4.** Step 4
_____ **5.** Step 5
_____ **6.** Step 6
_____ **7.** Step 7
_____ **8.** Step 8
_____ **9.** Step 9

a. Journalize and post the closing entries.
b. Prepare a trial balance.
c. Analyze source documents and record business transactions in a journal.
d. Prepare a post-closing trial balance.
e. Prepare financial statements from the data on the work sheet.
f. Post journal entries to the accounts in the ledger.
g. Complete the work sheet.
h. Journalize and post the adjusting entries from the data on the work sheet.
i. Gather adjustment data and record the adjusting entries on a work sheet.

PRACTICE EXERCISE 1 SOLUTION

1. c;   **2.** f;   **3.** b;   **4.** i;   **5.** g;   **6.** e;   **7.** h;   **8.** a;   **9.** d

LEARNING OBJECTIVE

2 *Journalize and post closing entries for a service enterprise.*

The four steps in the closing procedure are as follows:

STEP 1. Close the revenue account(s) into Income Summary.
STEP 2. Close the expense accounts into Income Summary.
STEP 3. Close the **Income Summary account** into the Capital account, transferring the net income or net loss to the Capital account.
STEP 4. Close the Drawing account into the Capital account.

PRACTICE EXERCISE 2

The following is a work sheet for the month of June for Larson Floral:

Larson Floral
Work Sheet
For the Month Ended June 30, 20—

Account Name	Trial Balance Debit	Trial Balance Credit	Adjustments Debit	Adjustments Credit	Adjusted Trial Balance Debit	Adjusted Trial Balance Credit	Income Statement Debit	Income Statement Credit	Balance Sheet Debit	Balance Sheet Credit
Cash	14 9 3 5 00				14 9 3 5 00				14 9 3 5 00	
Accounts Receivable	5 0 0 00				5 0 0 00				5 0 0 00	
Prepaid Insurance	3 5 0 00			(a) 3 0 00	3 2 0 00				3 2 0 00	
Delivery Van	28 2 7 5 00				28 2 7 5 00				28 2 7 5 00	
Accum. Depr., Delivery Van		5 1 0 00		(b) 3 0 0 00		8 1 0 00				8 1 0 00
Accounts Payable		7 5 0 00				7 5 0 00				7 5 0 00
E. Larson, Capital		37 4 3 5 00				37 4 3 5 00				37 4 3 5 00
E. Larson, Drawing	1 5 0 0 00				1 5 0 0 00				1 5 0 0 00	
Income from Services		12 1 7 0 00				12 1 7 0 00		12 1 7 0 00		
Wages Expense	3 3 0 0 00		(c) 3 0 0 00		3 6 0 0 00		3 6 0 0 00			
Rent Expense	7 7 5 00				7 7 5 00		7 7 5 00			
Supplies Expense	7 1 0 00				7 1 0 00		7 1 0 00			
Advertising Expense	2 7 0 00				2 7 0 00		2 7 0 00			
Utilities Expense	2 5 0 00				2 5 0 00		2 5 0 00			
	50 8 6 5 00	50 8 6 5 00								
Insurance Expense			(a) 3 0 00		3 0 00		3 0 00			
Depr. Exp., Delivery Van			(b) 3 0 0 00		3 0 0 00		3 0 0 00			
Wages Payable				(c) 3 0 0 00		3 0 0 00				3 0 0 00
			6 3 0 00	6 3 0 00	51 4 6 5 00	51 4 6 5 00	5 9 3 5 00	12 1 7 0 00	45 5 3 0 00	39 2 9 5 00
Net Income							6 2 3 5 00			6 2 3 5 00
							12 1 7 0 00	12 1 7 0 00	45 5 3 0 00	45 5 3 0 00

Using information from the work sheet and assuming the fiscal period is the month of June, journalize the four closing entries for Larson Floral.

PRACTICE EXERCISE 2 SOLUTION

			GENERAL JOURNAL										PAGE	4		
Date			Description	Post. Ref.		Debit						Credit				
20—			Closing Entries													
June	30	Income from Services			12	1	7	0	00							
			Income Summary							12	1	7	0	00		
	30	Income Summary			5	9	3	5	00							
		Wages Expense								3	6	0	0	00		
		Rent Expense									7	7	5	00		
		Supplies Expense									7	1	0	00		
		Advertising Expense									2	7	0	00		
		Utilities Expense									2	5	0	00		
		Insurance Expense										3	0	00		
		Depreciation Expense, Delivery Van										3	0	0	00	
	30	Income Summary			6	2	3	5	00							
		E. Larson, Capital								6	2	3	5	00		
	30	E. Larson, Capital			1	5	0	0	00							
		E. Larson, Drawing								1	5	0	0	00		

LEARNING OBJECTIVE 3

Prepare a post-closing trial balance.

A **post-closing trial balance** consists of the final balances of the accounts remaining open. It is the final proof that the debit balances equal the credit balances before the posting for the new fiscal period begins.

PRACTICE EXERCISE 3

Using the information from the work sheet in Practice Exercise 2, prepare a post-closing trial balance for Larson Floral.

PRACTICE EXERCISE 3 SOLUTION

Larson Floral
Post-Closing Trial Balance
June 30, 20—

Account Name	Debit	Credit
Cash	14,935	
Accounts Receivable	500	
Prepaid Insurance	320	
Delivery Van	28,275	
Accumulated Depreciation, Delivery Van		810
Accounts Payable		750
Wages Payable		300
E. Larson, Capital		42,170
	44,030	44,030

LEARNING OBJECTIVE

4 *Define the following methods of accounting: cash basis and accrual basis.*

Under the **cash basis of accounting**, revenue is recorded when it is received in cash, and expenses are generally recorded when they are paid in cash. Under the **accrual basis of accounting**, revenue is recorded when earned, even if cash is received at a later date, and expenses are recorded when incurred, even if cash is to be paid at a later date.

PRACTICE EXERCISE 4

Considering the following events, determine which month the revenue or expenses would be recorded using the accounting method specified.

a. Crane Company uses the *accrual basis of accounting*. Crane prepays cash in June for insurance that covers the following month, July, only.

b. Loggins & Rogers Tax Services uses the *cash basis of accounting*. Loggins & Rogers receives cash from customers in January for services to be performed in March.

c. Red Tractor Supplies Company uses the *accrual basis of accounting*. Red Tractor Supplies makes a sale to a customer in September but does not expect payment until November.

d. Norton Company uses the *cash basis of accounting*. Norton prepays cash in February for insurance that covers the following month, March, only.

PRACTICE EXERCISE 4 SOLUTION

a. July
b. January
c. September
d. February

LEARNING OBJECTIVE

5 *Prepare interim statements.*

Interim statements consist of year-to-date income statements, statements of owner's equity, and balance sheets as of various dates during the fiscal period.

PRACTICE EXERCISE 5

Assume that Larson Floral's fiscal period does not end on June 30 but rather December 31. Using the information from the work sheet from Practice Exercise 2, complete an interim balance sheet for the month of June for Larson Floral.

PRACTICE EXERCISE 5 SOLUTION

Larson Floral
Balance Sheet
June 30, 20—

Assets		
Cash		$14,935
Accounts Receivable		500
Prepaid Insurance		320
Delivery Van	$28,275	
Less Accumulated Depreciation	810	27,465
Total Assets		$43,220
Liabilities		
Accounts Payable	$ 750	
Wages Payable	300	
Total Liabilities		$ 1,050
Owner's Equity		
E. Larson, Capital		42,170
Total Liabilities and Owner's Equity		$43,220

Before a Test Check: Chapters 4–5

PART I: MULTIPLE-CHOICE QUESTIONS

____ **1.** The net income appears on all of the following statements except
a. the statement of owner's equity.
b. the balance sheet.
c. the income statement.
d. all of these.
e. none of these.

____ **2.** Which of the following entries records the withdrawal of cash for personal use by Dolan, the owner of a business firm?
a. Debit Cash and credit Drawing.
b. Debit Salary Expense and credit Cash.
c. Debit Cash and credit Salary Expense.
d. Debit Drawing and credit Cash.
e. None of these.

____ **3.** Which of the following errors, considered individually, would cause the trial balance totals to be unequal?
a. A payment of $52 for supplies was posted as a debit of $52 to Supplies Expense and a credit of $25 to Cash.
b. A payment of $625 to a creditor was posted as a debit of $625 to Accounts Payable and a debit of $625 to Cash.
c. Cash received from customers on account was posted as a debit of $380 to Cash and a credit of $38 to Accounts Receivable.
d. All of these.
e. None of these.

____ **4.** The balance in the Prepaid Insurance account before adjustment at the end of the year is $600. This represents six months' insurance paid on November 1. No adjusting entry was made on November 30. The adjusting entry required on December 31 is

    a. debit Insurance Expense, $200; credit Prepaid Insurance, $200.
    b. debit Prepaid Insurance, $100; credit Insurance Expense, $100.
    c. debit Prepaid Insurance, $600; credit Insurance Expense, $600.
    d. debit Insurance Expense, $600; credit Prepaid Insurance, $600.
    e. none of these.

____ **5.** If an accountant fails to make an adjusting entry to record expired insurance at the end of a fiscal period, the omission will cause
    a. total expenses to be understated.
    b. total revenue to be understated.
    c. total assets to be understated.
    d. all of these.
    e. none of these.

____ **6.** Farmer Company bought equipment on January 2 of this year for $9,000. At the time of purchase, the equipment was estimated to have a useful life of eight years and a trade-in value of $1,000 at the end of eight years. Using the straight-line method, the amount of depreciation for the first year is
    a. $900.
    b. $1,000.
    c. $800.
    d. $950.
    e. none of these.

____ **7.** If expenses are greater than revenue, the Income Summary account will be closed by a debit to
    a. Cash and a credit to Income Summary.
    b. Income Summary and a credit to Cash.
    c. Capital and a credit to Income Summary.
    d. Income Summary and a credit to Capital.
    e. none of these.

____ **8.** In preparing closing entries, it is helpful to refer to which of the following columns of the work sheet first?
    a. The Balance Sheet columns
    b. The Adjusted Trial Balance columns
    c. The Income Statement columns
    d. Both the Adjusted Trial Balance and the Income Statement columns
    e. None of these

PART II: PRACTICAL APPLICATION

On December 31, the ledger accounts of Kristopher's Upholstery Shop have the following balances after all adjusting entries have been posted.

Cash	$ 1,200
Equipment	15,400
Accumulated Depreciation, Equipment	1,100
Accounts Payable	300
K. Payton, Capital	16,500
K. Payton, Drawing	16,400
Income Summary	
Income from Services	35,900
Wages Expense	11,500
Rent Expense	2,400
Supplies Expense	4,100
Utilities Expense	1,000
Depreciation Expense, Equipment	500
Miscellaneous Expense	900

Required

Journalize the four closing entries in the proper order.

PART III: MATCHING QUESTIONS

_____ **1.** Creditor
_____ **2.** Business entity
_____ **3.** Fundamental accounting equation
_____ **4.** Income statement
_____ **5.** Owner's equity
_____ **6.** Accounts Receivable
_____ **7.** Net loss
_____ **8.** Ledger
_____ **9.** Credit
_____ **10.** Compound entry
_____ **11.** Trial balance
_____ **12.** Journalizing
_____ **13.** Posting
_____ **14.** Cross-reference
_____ **15.** Journal
_____ **16.** Work sheet
_____ **17.** Book value
_____ **18.** Depreciation
_____ **19.** Accounting cycle
_____ **20.** Fiscal year
_____ **21.** Contra account
_____ **22.** Mixed accounts
_____ **23.** Temporary-equity accounts
_____ **24.** Real accounts
_____ **25.** Debit

a. The book of original entry
b. One to whom money is owed
c. Accounts that are partly income statement and partly balance sheet accounts
d. Assets – Liabilities
e. A listing of the ending balances of all ledger accounts that proves the equality of total debits and total credits
f. The process of recording transactions in a journal
g. The left side of a T account
h. A business enterprise, separate and distinct from the person who owns its assets
i. The process of transferring accounts and amounts from the journal to the ledger
j. An account that is deducted from another account
k. Amounts owed by charge customers
l. Balance sheet accounts
m. Assets = Liabilities + Owner's Equity
n. A bookkeeping device for referring from journal to ledger or ledger to journal
o. The right side of a T account
p. Allocation of the cost of a plant asset over its estimated life
q. Financial statement that shows the net results of operations
r. Accounts that belong to only one fiscal period and are closed out at the end of each fiscal period
s. A transaction that has two or more debits and/or credits
t. Paper or spreadsheet used to record adjustments and provide balances to prepare financial statements
u. Excess of total expenses over total revenues
v. A period of twelve consecutive months
w. A book containing all the accounts of a business
x. The cost of an asset minus its accumulated depreciation
y. Steps in the accounting process, completed during the fiscal period

ANSWERS: PART I

1. b;   **2.** d;   **3.** d;   **4.** a;   **5.** a;   **6.** b;   **7.** c;   **8.** c

ANSWERS: PART II

		GENERAL JOURNAL					PAGE 4	
Date		**Description**	**Post. Ref.**	**Debit**			**Credit**	
20—		Closing Entries						
Dec.	31	Income from Services		35 9 0 0 00				
		Income Summary					35 9 0 0 00	
	31	Income Summary		20 4 0 0 00				
		Wages Expense					11 5 0 0 00	
		Rent Expense					2 4 0 0 00	
		Supplies Expense					4 1 0 0 00	
		Utilities Expense					1 0 0 0 00	
		Depreciation Expense, Equipment					5 0 0 00	
		Miscellaneous Expense					9 0 0 00	
	31	Income Summary		15 5 0 0 00				
		K. Payton, Capital					15 5 0 0 00	
	31	K. Payton, Capital		16 4 0 0 00				
		K. Payton, Drawing					16 4 0 0 00	

ANSWERS: PART III

1. b; **2.** h; **3.** m; **4.** q; **5.** d; **6.** k; **7.** u; **8.** w; **9.** o; **10.** s; **11.** e;
12. f; **13.** i; **14.** n; **15.** a; **16.** t; **17.** x; **18.** p; **19.** y; **20.** v; **21.** j;
22. c; **23.** r; **24.** l; **25.** g

Glossary

Accrual basis of accounting An accounting method under which revenue is recorded when it is earned, regardless of when it is received, and expenses are recorded when they are incurred, regardless of when they are paid. (p. 187)

Cash basis of accounting An accounting method under which revenue is recorded only when it is received in cash. Most expenses are recorded only when they are paid in cash. (p. 187)

Closing entries Entries made at the end of a fiscal period to close off the revenue, expense, and Drawing accounts—that is, to make the balances of the temporary-equity accounts equal to zero. Closing is also called *clearing the accounts*. (p. 178)

Income Summary account An account brought into existence in order to have a debit and credit in each closing entry. The revenue and expense account balances are transferred to this account to allow calculations of net income or net loss. (p. 179)

Interim statements Financial statements prepared during the fiscal year, covering a period of time of less than twelve months. (p. 187)

Nominal (temporary-equity) accounts Accounts that apply to only one fiscal period and that are to be closed at the end of that fiscal period, such as revenue, expense, Income Summary, and Drawing accounts. This category may also be described as all accounts except assets, liabilities, and the Capital account. (p. 184)

Post-closing trial balance The listing of the final balances of the real accounts at the end of the fiscal period. (p. 186)

Real (permanent) accounts The accounts that remain open (assets, liabilities, and the Capital account in owner's equity) and that have balances that will be carried over to the next fiscal period. (p. 184)

CHAPTER ASSIGNMENTS

Discussion Questions

1. Number in order the following steps in the accounting cycle.
   a. Prepare a trial balance.
   b. Post journal entries to the accounts in the ledger.
   c. Journalize and post the adjusting entries from the data on the work sheet.
   d. Analyze source documents and record business transactions in a journal.
   e. Prepare financial statements from the data on the work sheet.
   f. Gather adjustment data and record the adjusting entries on a work sheet.
   g. Journalize and post the closing entries.
   h. Prepare a post-closing trial balance.
   i. Complete the work sheet.
2. List the steps in the closing procedure in the correct order.
3. What is the purpose of closing entries? Consider the consequence of forgetting to make closing entries.
4. What happens if you do not print, save, and back up your financial statements before the closing entries occur?
5. What are real accounts? What are nominal accounts? Give examples of each.
6. What is the purpose of the Income Summary account, and how does it relate to the revenue and expense accounts?
7. What is the purpose of the post-closing trial balance? What is the difference between a trial balance and a post-closing trial balance?
8. Write the third closing entry to transfer the net income or net loss to the P. Hernandez, Capital account, assuming the following:
   a. A net income of $3,842 during the first quarter (Jan.–Mar.)
   b. A net loss of $1,781 during the second quarter (Apr.–Jun.)

Exercises

2  LO

PRACTICE EXERCISE 2

EXERCISE 5-1 Classify the following accounts as real (permanent) or nominal (temporary), and indicate with an X whether the account is closed. Also, indicate the financial statement in which each account will appear. The Building account is given as an example.

Account Title	Real	Nominal	Closed Yes	Closed No	Income Statement	Balance Sheet
0. Example: Building	X			X		X
a. Prepaid Insurance						
b. Accounts Payable						
c. Wages Payable						
d. Services Revenue						
e. Rent Expense						
f. Supplies Expense						
g. Accum. Depr., Equipment						

EXERCISE 5-2 Number the closing entries as steps 1 through 4. Journalize the following closing entries.

LO 2

PRACTICE EXERCISE 2

Assets	=	Liabilities	+	Owner's Equity	+	Revenue	−	Expenses
Dr. | Cr.		Dr. | Cr.		Dr. | Cr.		Dr. | Cr.		Dr. | Cr.
+ | −		− | +		− | +		− | +		+ | −

Cash

Bal. 8,500	

Wages Payable

	(a) 210

J. Cortez, Capital

	605	Bal. 24,000
	400	
		Bal. 22,995

Professional Fees

3,850	Bal. 3,850

Wages Expense

Bal. 2,900	
(a) 210	
Bal. 3,110	3,110

Prepaid Insurance

Bal. 990	(c) 460
Bal. 530	

J. Cortez, Drawing

Bal. 400	400

Insurance Expense

(c) 460	460

Equipment

Bal. 18,125	

Income Summary

4,455	3,850
	605

Depr. Expense, Equipment

(b) 750	750

Accum. Depr., Equipment

	Bal. 3,200
	(b) 750
	Bal. 3,950

Misc. Expense

Bal. 135	135

EXERCISE 5-3 As of December 31, the end of the current year, the ledger of Harris Company contained the following account balances after adjustment. All accounts have normal balances. Journalize the closing entries.

PRACTICE EXERCISE 2

Cash	$ 8,440	C. Harris, Drawing	$1,498
Equipment	11,586	Professional Fees	7,075
Accumulated Depreciation, Equipment	2,587	Wages Expense	1,268
		Rent Expense	1,090
Accounts Payable	1,674	Depreciation Expense, Equipment	1,143
Wages Payable	658		
C. Harris, Capital	13,376	Miscellaneous Expense	345

EXERCISE 5-4 The Income Statement columns of the work sheet of Dunn Company for the fiscal year ended June 30 follow. During the year, K. Dunn withdrew $4,000. Journalize the closing entries.

PRACTICE EXERCISE 2

Account Name	Income Statement									
	Debit					Credit				
Service Revenue							6	7	9 7	00
Rental Revenue							3	5	7 6	00
Rent Expense		2	8	0 0	00					
Wages Expense		1	8	5 4	00					
Utilities Expense			4	6 5	00					
Miscellaneous Expense				5 9	00					
		5	1	7 8	00		10	3	7 3	00
Net Income		5	1	9 5	00					
		10	3	7 3	00		10	3	7 3	00

2 **LO**

PRACTICE EXERCISE 2

EXERCISE 5-5 The Income Statement columns of the work sheet of Cederblom Company for the fiscal year ended December 31 follow. During the year, S. Cederblom withdrew $17,000. Journalize the closing entries.

Account Name	Income Statement									
	Debit					Credit				
Service Revenue							41	7	4 0	00
Rental Revenue							22	0	0 0	00
Wages Expense		48	5	2 0	00					
Utilities Expense		7	1	3 0	00					
Miscellaneous Expense		2	2	0 0	00					
		57	8	5 0	00		63	7	4 0	00
Net Income		5	8	9 0	00					
		63	7	4 0	00		63	7	4 0	00

2 **LO**

PRACTICE EXERCISE 2

EXERCISE 5-6 After all revenue and expenses have been closed at the end of the fiscal period ended December 31, Income Summary has a debit of $45,550 and a credit of $36,520. On the same date, D. Mau, Drawing, has a debit balance of $12,000, and D. Mau, Capital, had a beginning credit balance of $63,410.

a. Journalize the entries to close the remaining temporary accounts.
b. What is the new balance of D. Mau, Capital, after closing the remaining temporary accounts? Show your calculations.

5 **LO**

PRACTICE EXERCISE 5

EXERCISE 5-7 Indicate with an X whether each of the following would appear on the income statement, statement of owner's equity, or balance sheet. An item may appear on more than one statement. The first item is provided as an example.

Item	Income Statement	Statement of Owner's Equity	Balance Sheet
0. Example: The total liabilities of the business at the end of the year.			X
a. The amount of the owner's Capital balance at the end of the year.			
b. The amount of depreciation expense on equipment during the year.			
c. The amount of the company's net income for the year.			
d. The book value of the equipment.			
e. Total insurance expired during the year.			
f. Total accounts receivable at the end of the year.			
g. Total withdrawals by the owner.			
h. The cost of utilities used during the year.			
i. The amount of the owner's Capital balance at the beginning of the year.			

EXERCISE 5-8 Prepare a statement of owner's equity for The Lindal Clinic for the year ended December 31. P. Lindal's capital amount on January 1 was $124,000, and there was an additional investment of $7,000 on May 12 and withdrawals of $31,500 for the year. Net income for the year was $20,418.

PRACTICE EXERCISE 5

Problem Set A

For additional help, see the demonstration problem at the beginning of each chapter in your Working Papers.

PROBLEM 5-1A After the accountant posted the adjusting entries for B. Lyon, Designer, the work sheet contained the following account balances on May 31:

Account Name	Adjusted Trial Balance Debit A + Draw. + E	Adjusted Trial Balance Credit Accum. Deprec. + L + C + R
Cash	2 3 1 8 00	
Accounts Receivable	1 4 0 8 00	
Prepaid Insurance	9 8 7 00	
Office Equipment	5 7 9 0 00	
Accumulated Depreciation, Office Equipment		1 3 7 2 00
Accounts Payable		8 8 0 00
B. Lyon, Capital		7 5 2 0 00
B. Lyon, Drawing	1 5 5 0 00	
Commissions Earned		4 6 7 9 00
Rent Expense	9 9 5 00	
Supplies Expense	5 7 5 00	
Depreciation Expense, Office Equipment	4 6 2 00	
Utilities Expense	2 6 9 00	
Miscellaneous Expense	9 7 00	
	14 4 5 1 00	14 4 5 1 00

Check Figure
Net Income, $2,281

Required
1. Write the owner's name on the Capital and Drawing T accounts found in the Working Papers.
2. Record the account balances in the T accounts for owner's equity, revenue, and expenses.
3. Journalize the closing entries with the four steps in correct order. Number the closing entries 1 through 4.
4. Post the closing entries to the T accounts right after you journalize each one to see the effect of the closing entries. Number the closing entries 1 through 4.

PROBLEM 5-2A The partial work sheet for Ho Consulting for the month of May follows.

Account Name	Income Statement Debit E	Income Statement Credit R	Balance Sheet Debit A + Draw.	Balance Sheet Credit Accum. Depr. + L + C
Cash			5 9 1 9 00	
Prepaid Insurance			1 1 2 3 00	
Equipment			5 7 3 1 00	
Accumulated Depreciation, Equipment				1 4 4 4 00
Accounts Payable				1 8 4 1 00
G. Ho, Capital				4 3 0 2 00
G. Ho, Drawing			2 4 0 0 00	
Consulting Revenue		13 0 6 0 00		
Rent Expense	2 2 0 0 00			
Wages Expense	1 8 2 8 00			
Supplies Expense	4 2 2 00			
Miscellaneous Expense	2 3 0 00			
Insurance Expense	3 2 5 00			
Depreciation Expense, Equipment	8 3 5 00			
Wages Payable				3 6 6 00
	5 8 4 0 00	13 0 6 0 00	15 1 7 3 00	7 9 5 3 00
Net Income	7 2 2 0 00			7 2 2 0 00
	13 0 6 0 00	13 0 6 0 00	15 1 7 3 00	15 1 7 3 00

Check Figure
Debit to Income Summary, second entry, $5,840

Required
1. Write the owner's name on the Capital and Drawing T accounts found in the Working Papers.
2. Record the account balances in the T accounts for owner's equity, revenue, and expenses.
3. Journalize the closing entries with the four steps in correct order. Number the closing entries 1 through 4.
4. Post the closing entries to the T accounts right after you journalize each one to see the effect of the closing entries. Number the closing entries 1 through 4.

PROBLEM 5-3A The completed work sheet for Valerie Insurance Agency as of December 31 is presented in your Working Papers, along with the general ledger as of December 31 before adjustments.

Required

Check Figure
Post-closing trial balance total, $9,930

1. Write the name of the owner, M. Valerie, in the Capital and Drawing accounts.
2. Write the balances from the unadjusted trial balance in the general ledger.
3. Journalize and post the adjusting entries.
4. Journalize and post the closing entries in the correct order.
5. Prepare a post-closing trial balance.

PROBLEM 5-4A The account balances of Bryan Company as of June 30, the end of the current fiscal year, are as follows:

Account Name	Trial Balance Debit	Trial Balance Credit
Cash	5 4 9 1 00	
Accounts Receivable	6 2 4 00	
Prepaid Insurance	1 2 8 0 00	
Equipment	6 4 9 7 00	
Accumulated Depreciation, Equipment		2 6 7 2 00
Van	10 9 8 9 00	
Accumulated Depreciation, Van		4 3 6 8 00
Accounts Payable		1 0 3 6 00
B. Bryan, Capital		18 5 8 3 00
B. Bryan, Drawing	18 0 0 0 00	
Fees Earned		38 4 1 7 00
Salary Expense	18 6 0 0 00	
Advertising Expense	1 8 8 7 00	
Supplies Expense	3 9 7 00	
Van Operating Expense	4 6 2 00	
Utilities Expense	6 8 5 00	
Miscellaneous Expense	1 6 4 00	
	65 0 7 6 00	65 0 7 6 00

Required

Check Figure
Net Income, $13,327

1. Complete the work sheet. Data for the adjustments are as follows:
   a. Expired or used up insurance, $495
   b. Depreciation expense on equipment, $670.
   c. Depreciation expense on the van, $1,190.
   d. Salary accrued (earned) since the last payday, $540 (owed and to be paid on the next payday).
2. Prepare an income statement.
3. Prepare a statement of owner's equity; assume there was an additional investment of $2,000 on June 10.
4. Prepare a balance sheet.
5. Journalize the adjusting entries.
6. Journalize the closing entries with the four steps in the correct sequence.

Problem Set B

For additional help, see the demonstration problem at the beginning of each chapter in your Working Papers.

PROBLEM 5-1B After the accountant posted the adjusting entries for M. Wally, Designer, the work sheet contained the following account balances on May 31:

Account Name	Adjusted Trial Balance			
	Debit		Credit	
	A + Draw. + E		Accum. Deprec. +L+C+R	
Cash	2 4 2 9 00			
Accounts Receivable	8 8 6 00			
Prepaid Insurance	1 4 6 0 00			
Office Equipment	4 6 7 2 00			
Accumulated Depreciation, Office Equipment			1 1 7 0 00	
Accounts Payable			9 4 3 00	
M. Wally, Capital			6 2 2 1 00	
M. Wally, Drawing	1 6 0 0 00			
Commissions Earned			4 9 9 7 00	
Rent Expense	9 9 0 00			
Supplies Expense	4 8 0 00			
Depreciation Expense, Office Equipment	4 2 0 00			
Utilities Expense	2 8 6 00			
Miscellaneous Expense	1 0 8 00			
	13 3 3 1 00		13 3 3 1 00	

Check Figure
Net Income, $2,713

Required

1. Write the owner's name on the Capital and Drawing T accounts found in the Working Papers.
2. Record the account balances in the T accounts for owner's equity, revenue, and expenses.
3. Journalize the closing entries with the four steps in correct order. Number the closing entries 1 through 4.
4. Post the closing entries to the T accounts right after you journalize each one to see the effect of the closing entries. Number the closing entries 1 through 4.

2 **PROBLEM 5-2B** The partial work sheet for Emil Consulting for the month of June is as follows.

Account Name	Income Statement				Balance Sheet			
	Debit		Credit		Debit		Credit	
	E		R		A + Draw.		Accum. Depr. +L+C	
Cash					6 1 0 4 00			
Prepaid Insurance					1 3 4 4 00			
Equipment					6 7 5 1 00			
Accumulated Depreciation, Equipment							4 2 1 2 00	
Accounts Payable							1 3 5 6 00	
W. Emil, Capital							5 3 6 7 00	
W. Emil, Drawing					1 7 0 0 00			
Consulting Fees			9 5 4 6 00					
Rent Expense	1 8 0 0 00							
Wages Expense	1 5 3 3 00							
Miscellaneous Expense	1 6 8 00							
Supplies Expense	3 6 5 00							
Insurance Expense	3 6 4 00							
Depreciation Expense, Equipment	7 0 0 00							
Wages Payable							3 4 8 00	
	4 9 3 0 00		9 5 4 6 00		15 8 9 9 00		11 2 8 3 00	
Net Income	4 6 1 6 00						4 6 1 6 00	
	9 5 4 6 00		9 5 4 6 00		15 8 9 9 00		15 8 9 9 00	

Required

1. Write the owner's name on the Capital and Drawing T accounts found in the Working Papers.
2. Record the account balances in the T accounts for owner's equity, revenue, and expenses.
3. Journalize the closing entries with the four steps in correct order. Number the closing entries 1 through 4.
4. Post the closing entries to the T accounts right after you journalize each one to see the effect of the closing entries. Number closing entries 1 through 4.

Check Figure
Debit to Income Summary, second entry, $4,930

PROBLEM 5-3B The completed work sheet for Oliver Tour Company as of December 31 is presented in your Working Papers, along with the general ledger as of December 31 before adjustments.

 LO 1,2,3

Required

1. Write the name of the owner, S. Oliver, in the Capital and Drawing accounts.
2. Write the balances from the unadjusted trial balance in the general ledger.
3. Journalize and post the adjusting entries.
4. Journalize and post the closing entries in the correct order.
5. Prepare a post-closing trial balance.

Check Figure
Post-closing trial balance total, $8,869

PROBLEM 5-4B The account balances of Miss Beverly's Tutoring Service as of June 30, the end of the current fiscal year, are as follows.

 LO 1,2,3

 GL

Account Name	Trial Balance	
	Debit	Credit
Cash	6 4 9 1 00	
Accounts Receivable	6 2 4 00	
Prepaid Insurance	1 2 8 0 00	
Equipment	5 4 9 7 00	
Accumulated Depreciation, Equipment		2 4 7 2 00
Van	13 6 7 4 00	
Accumulated Depreciation, Van		4 1 6 8 00
Accounts Payable		1 4 3 6 00
B. Morrow, Capital		14 8 4 8 00
B. Morrow, Drawing	18 0 0 0 00	
Fees Earned		43 6 8 0 00
Salary Expense	16 0 0 0 00	
Advertising Expense	2 2 0 0 00	
Van Operating Expense	7 0 5 00	
Supplies Expense	5 2 7 00	
Utilities Expense	1 2 4 8 00	
Miscellaneous Expense	3 5 8 00	
	66 6 0 4 00	66 6 0 4 00

Required

1. Complete the work sheet. Data for the adjustments are as follows:
   a. Expired or used up insurance, $470.
   b. Depreciation expense on equipment, $948.
   c. Depreciation expense on the van, $1,490.
   d. Salary accrued (earned) since the last payday, $574 (owed and to be paid on the next payday).

Check Figure
Net income, $19,160

2. Prepare an income statement.

3. Prepare a statement of owner's equity; assume there was an additional investment of $3,000 on June 10.

4. Prepare a balance sheet.

5. Journalize the adjusting entries.

6. Journalize the closing entries with the four steps in the proper sequence.

Accounting Cycle Review Problem A

This problem is designed to enable you to apply the knowledge you have acquired in the preceding chapters. In accounting, the ultimate test is being able to handle data in real-life situations. This problem will give you valuable experience.

CHART OF ACCOUNTS

Assets
111 Cash
112 Accounts Receivable
114 Prepaid Insurance
121 Land
122 Building
123 Accumulated Depreciation, Building
124 Pool/Slide Facility
125 Accumulated Depreciation, Pool/Slide Facility
126 Pool Furniture
127 Accumulated Depreciation, Pool Furniture

Liabilities
221 Accounts Payable
222 Wages Payable
223 Mortgage Payable

Owner's Equity
311 L. Lacy, Capital
312 L. Lacy, Drawing
313 Income Summary

Revenue
411 Income from Services
412 Income from Concessions

Expenses
511 Pool Maintenance Expense
512 Wages Expense
513 Advertising Expense
514 Utilities Expense
515 Interest Expense
517 Insurance Expense
518 Depreciation Expense, Building
519 Depreciation Expense, Pool/Slide Facility
520 Depreciation Expense, Pool Furniture
522 Miscellaneous Expense

You are to record transactions in a two-column general journal. Assume that the fiscal period is one month. You will then be able to complete all the steps in the accounting cycle.

When you are analyzing the transactions, think them through by visualizing the T accounts or by writing them down on scratch paper. For unfamiliar types of transactions, specific instructions for recording them are included. However, reason them out for yourself as well. Check off each transaction as it is recorded.

July   1   Lacy deposited $150,000 in a bank account for the purpose of buying Surf's Up! The business is a recreation area offering three large waterslides (called "tubes"), one children's slide, an inner tube run, and a looping extreme slide.

2   Bought Surf's Up! in its entirety for a total price of $540,800. The assets include pool furniture, $3,800; the pool/slide facility (includes filter system, pools, pump, and slides), $148,800; building, $96,200; and land, $292,000. Paid $120,000 down and signed a mortgage note for the remainder. (Debit the assets, and credit Cash and Mortgage Payable.)

2   Received and paid the bill for a one-year premium for insurance, $12,240.

2   Bought 125 inner tubes from Worn Tires for $1,225, paying $500 down, with the remainder due in 20 days. (Debit Pool/Slide Facility.)

3   Signed a contract with a video game company to lease space for video games and to provide a food concession. The rental income agreed upon is 10 percent of the revenues generated from the machines and food, with the estimated monthly rental income paid in advance. Received cash payment for July, $250. (Debit Cash and credit Concessions Income.)

July 5 Received bills totaling $1,320 for the grand opening/Fourth of July party. The bill from Party Rentals for the promotional handouts, balloons, decorations, and prizes was $620, and the newspaper advertising bills from the *City Star* were $700. (These expenses should all be considered advertising expense.)

6 Signed a one-year contract for the pool maintenance with All-Around Maintenance and paid the maintenance fee for July of $800.

6 Paid cash for employee picnic food and beverages, $128. (Debit Miscellaneous Expense.)

7 Received $12,086 in cash as income for the use of the facilities.

9 Bought parts for the filter system on account from Arlen's Pool Supply, $646. (Debit Pool Maintenance Expense.)

14 Received $10,445 in cash as income for the use of the facilities.

15 Paid wages to employees for the period ended July 14, $8,460.

16 Paid cash as partial payment on account for promotional expenses recorded on July 5, $1,150.

16 Lacy withdrew cash for personal use, $2,500.

17 Bought additional pool furniture from Pool Suppliers for $2,100; payment due in 30 days.

18 Paid cash to seamstress for alterations and repairs to the character costumes, $248. (Debit Miscellaneous Expense.)

21 Received $10,330 in cash as income for the use of the facilities.

21 Paid cash to Worn Tires as partial payment on account, $600.

23 Received a $225 reduction of our account from Pool Suppliers for lawn chairs received in damaged condition.

25 Received and paid telephone bill, $292.

29 Paid wages for the period July 15 through 28 of $8,227.

31 Received $11,870 in cash as income for the use of the facilities.

31 Paid cash to Arlen's Pool Supply to apply on account, $360.

31 Received and paid water bill, $684.

31 Paid cash as an installment payment on the mortgage, $3,890. Of this amount, $1,910 represents a reduction in the principal, and the remainder is interest. (Debit Mortgage Payable, debit Interest Expense, and credit Cash.)

31 Received and paid electric bill, $824.

31 Bought additional inner tubes from Worn Tires for $480, paying $100 down, with the remainder due in 30 days.

31 Lacy withdrew cash for personal use, $2,200.

31 Sales for the video and food concessions amounted to $4,840, and 10 percent of $4,840 equals $484. Since you have already recorded $250 as concessions income, record the additional $234 revenue due from the concessionaire (cash was not received).

Required

1. Journalize the transactions, starting on page 1 of the general journal.
2. Post the transactions to the ledger accounts.
3. Prepare a trial balance in the first two columns of the work sheet.

Check Figures
Trial balance total, $616,941; net income, $18,391; post-closing trial balance total, $587,612

4. Complete the work sheet. Data for the adjustments are as follows:
   a. Insurance expired during the month, $1,020.
   b. Depreciation of building for the month, $480.
   c. Depreciation of pool/slide facility for the month, $675.
   d. Depreciation of pool furniture for the month, $120.
   e. Wages accrued at July 31, $920.

5. Prepare the income statement.

6. Prepare the statement of owner's equity.

7. Prepare the balance sheet.

8. Journalize adjusting entries.

9. Post adjusting entries to the ledger accounts.

10. Journalize closing entries.

11. Post closing entries to the ledger accounts.

12. Prepare a post-closing trial balance.

Accounting Cycle Review Problem B

This problem is designed to enable you to apply the knowledge you have acquired in the preceding chapters. In accounting, the ultimate test is being able to handle data in real-life situations. This problem will give you valuable experience.

CHART OF ACCOUNTS

Assets
111 Cash
112 Accounts Receivable
114 Prepaid Insurance
121 Land
125 Pool Structure
126 Accumulated Depreciation, Pool Structure
127 Fan System
128 Accumulated Depreciation, Fan System
129 Sailboats
130 Accumulated Depreciation, Sailboats

Liabilities
221 Accounts Payable
222 Wages Payable
223 Mortgage Payable

Owner's Equity
311 R. Arden, Capital
312 R. Arden, Drawing
313 Income Summary

Revenue
411 Income from Services
412 Income from Concessions

Expenses
511 Sailboat Rental Expense
512 Wages Expense
513 Advertising Expense
514 Utilities Expense
515 Interest Expense
516 Insurance Expense
517 Depreciation Expense, Pool Structure
518 Depreciation Expense, Fan System
519 Depreciation Expense, Sailboats
522 Miscellaneous Expense

You are to record transactions in a two-column general journal. Assume that the fiscal period is one month. You will then be able to complete all the steps in the accounting cycle.

When you are analyzing the transactions, think them through by visualizing the T accounts or by writing them down on scratch paper. For unfamiliar types of transactions, specific instructions for recording them are included. However, reason them out for yourself as well. Check off each transaction as it is recorded.

June   1   Arden deposited $85,000 in a bank account for the purpose of buying Wind Sailors, a business offering the use of small sailboats to the public at a large indoor pool with a fan system that provides wind.

       2   Bought Wind Sailors in its entirety for a total price of $216,100. The assets include sailboats, $25,800; fan system, $13,300; pool structure, $140,000; and land, $37,000. Paid $60,000 down, and signed a mortgage note for the remainder. (Debit each asset and credit Cash and Mortgage Payable.)

       3   Received and paid bill for newspaper advertising, $350.

June 3 Received and paid bill for a one-year premium for insurance, $12,000.

  3 Bought additional boats from Larkin Manufacturing Co. for $7,200, paying $3,200 down, with the remainder due in 30 days.

  3 Signed a contract with a vending machine service to lease space for vending machines. The rental income agreed upon is 10 percent of the sales generated from the machines, with the estimated total rental income payable in advance. Received estimated cash payment for June, $150. (Debit Cash and credit Concessions Income.)

  3 Received bill from Quick Printing for promotional handouts, $460 (Advertising Expense).

  3 Signed a contract for leasing sailboats from K. Erdmon Boat Co. and paid rental fee for June, $700.

  5 Paid cash for miscellaneous expenses, $96.

  8 Received $2,855 in cash as income for the use of the boats.

  9 Bought an addition for the fan system on account from Stark Pool Supply, $745.

  15 Paid wages to employees for the period ended June 14, $3,900.

  16 Paid on account for promotional handouts already recorded on June 3, $460.

  16 Arden withdrew cash for personal use, $1,200.

  16 Bought additional sails from Canvas Products, Inc., $850; payment due in 30 days. (Debit Sailboats.)

  16 Received $4,850 in cash as income for the use of the boats.

  19 Paid cash for miscellaneous expenses, $40.

  20 Paid cash to Larkin Manufacturing Co. as part payment on account, $1,300.

  22 Received $8,260 in cash for the use of the boats (Income from Services).

  23 Received a reduction in the outstanding bill from Larkin Manufacturing Co. for a boat received in damaged condition, $380. (Debit Accounts Payable, credit Sailboats.)

  24 Received and paid telephone bill, $284.

  29 Paid wages for period June 15 through 28, $4,973.

  30 Paid cash to Stark Pool Supply to apply on account, $475.

  30 Received and paid electric bill, $345.

  30 Paid cash as an installment payment on the mortgage, $1,848. Of this amount, $497 represents a reduction in the principal, and the remainder is interest. (Debit Mortgage Payable, debit Interest Expense, and credit Cash.)

  30 Received and paid water bill, $590.

  30 Bought additional boats from Ranger and Son for $5,320, paying $1,550 down, with the remainder due in 30 days.

  30 Arden withdrew cash for personal use, $1,500.

  30 Received $5,902 in cash as income for the use of the boats.

  30 Sales from vending machines for the month amounted to $1,780. Ten percent of $1,780 equals $178. Since you have already recorded $150 as concessions income, list the additional $28 revenue earned from the vending machine operator. (Cash was not received.)

Required

1. Journalize the transactions, starting on page 1 of the general journal.
2. Post the transactions to the ledger accounts.
3. Prepare a trial balance in the first two columns of the work sheet.
4. Complete the work sheet. Data for the adjustments are as follows:
   a. Insurance expired during the month, $1,000.
   b. Depreciation of pool structure for the month, $715.
   c. Depreciation of fan system for the month, $260.
   d. Depreciation of sailboats for the month, $900.
   e. Wages accrued at June 30, $790.
5. Prepare the income statement.
6. Prepare the statement of owner's equity.
7. Prepare the balance sheet.
8. Journalize adjusting entries.
9. Post adjusting entries to the ledger accounts.
10. Journalize closing entries.
11. Post closing entries to the ledger accounts.
12. Prepare a post-closing trial balance.

ACTIVITIES

CONSIDER AND COMMUNICATE

Your uncle owns a small sole proprietorship. He does his own bookkeeping, although he didn't finish the chapter on closing entries before he opened his business. He mentions to you that closing entries look like they take a long time. He wonders why he should bother to do them, because all he really looks at is the checkbook anyway. What would you say to convince him that closing entries are necessary?

CRITICAL THINKING

Following is the post-closing trial balance submitted to you by the bookkeeper. Assume that the debit total ($41,048) is correct.

a. Analyze the work and prepare a response to what you have reviewed.
b. Journalize the closing entries.
c. What is the net income or net loss?
d. Is there an increase or a decrease in Capital?
e. What would be the ending amount of Capital?
f. What is the new balance of the post-closing trial balance?

Tafoya Consulting Company
Post-Closing Trial Balance
December 31, 20—

Account Name	Debit	Credit
Cash	3,412	
Accounts Receivable	1,693	
Prepaid Insurance	2,147	
Accounts Payable		
C. Tafoya, Capital		13,818
C. Tafoya, Drawing	6,360	
Consulting Fees		25,603
Wages Expense	11,994	
Rent Expense	9,600	
Advertising Expense	2,582	
Supplies Expense	914	
Insurance Expense	1,610	
Miscellaneous Expense	736	
	41,048	41,048

A QUESTION OF ETHICS

You are preparing a post-closing trial balance for the company where you work, but it doesn't balance. You are tired, and besides, you don't think they pay you for this kind of hassle and extra time. You decide to increase the balance of an asset account to make the totals balance. Discuss this action and whether it is ethical or illegal.

WHAT'S WRONG WITH THIS PICTURE?

The bookkeeper has completed a work sheet and has journalized and posted the closing entries, but he forgot to journalize and post the adjusting entries from the work sheet. What are the effects of these actions and omissions? How would these actions and omissions affect the accounting records and the resulting financial statements?

All About You Spa

Closing Entries

What to do *before* you perform the closing entries:

1. Open the file entitled ***All_About_You_Spa_Ch05.IA7***. Enter your name when prompted and click ***OK***. Select "Yes" or "No" as desired when asked if you want to open on-screen instructions and check figures.

2. Click on the ***Save As*** toolbar button. When the Save As window appears, select the folder in which you wish to save your data files (if not already selected). In the File Name box, key ***All_About_You_Ch05_Your_Name.IA7*** (for example, All_About_You_Spa_Ch05_John_Doe.IA7) to identify the file containing your work. Click on the ***Save*** button.

3. If you did not print out and keep the adjusted trial balance and financial statements you generated for Chapter 4, generate and print them out now. Click on the ***Reports*** toolbar button, then click on ***Ledger Reports*** and select ***Trial Balance*** to generate the Trial Balance report. Click on the ***Reports*** toolbar button, then in turn click on ***Income Statement, Statement of Owner's Equity,*** and ***Balance Sheet*** to generate each of these financial statements. To print these reports, click on the ***Print*** button at the bottom of the report window.

4. You will need a new account, Income Summary, to complete the closing process. This account has been added as Account No. 313.

What to do to *close* (or zero out) the temporary owner's equity accounts (revenue(s), expenses, Income Summary, and Drawing), a process that transfers the net income into or deducts the net loss and the withdrawals from the Capital account. In addition, the closing process prepares the records for the new fiscal period:

5. Generate closing entries. Select ***Generate Closing Journal Entries*** from the ***Options*** menu. When the dialog box appears, click ***Yes*** to confirm that you wish the computer to generate the closing journal entries. The entries will display in a preview window. Click on the ***Post*** button to post the closing journal entries to the general journal.

6. Display the closing journal entries. Click on the ***Reports*** toolbar button. Click on ***Journals*** and ***General Journal*** to choose the report to display. Click on ***Customize Journal Report***. In the Reference drop-down list, choose "Clo.Ent." and then click the ***OK*** button to display the Closing Journal Entries report. To print the report, click on the ***Print*** button.

Check Figures

6. Closing Journal Entries report total, $38,544

7. Post closing trial balance total, $25,777

8. Net income from post-closing income statement, $0

What to do *after* the closing entries:

7. Display and print a post-closing trial balance. Post means "after," so you are printing a trial balance after closing. Click on the ***Reports*** toolbar button. Click on ***Ledger Reports*** and ***Trial Balance*** to choose the report to display. To print the report, click on the ***Print*** button at the bottom of the report window.

8. Display and print financial statements. Click on the ***Reports*** toolbar button, then in turn click on ***Income Statement, Statement of Owner's Equity,*** and ***Balance Sheet*** to generate each of these financial statements. To print these reports, click on the ***Print*** button at the bottom of the report window.

9. Compare the pre- and post-closing trial balance and financial statements. Notice that the post-closing trial balance is shorter and excludes the Drawing, revenue, and expense accounts, which now have zero balances after the closing process.

Likewise, the Drawing, revenue, and expense accounts no longer appear in any of the financial statements. Indeed, an income statement generated after closing will show no data whatsoever. The income statement accounts are ready to begin accumulating data for the next accounting period.

10. If you have not already done so, click on the **Save** toolbar button to save your data file.

11. Click on the **Check** toolbar button to check your solution against the answer key.

PART 2

6 Bank Accounts and Cash Funds

WHY IT MATTERS

FEELEY & DRISCOLL, Boston, Massachusetts

Based in Boston, Massachusetts, Feeley & Driscoll is a full-service consulting and forensic accounting firm. Its services range from determining contract damages to fraud examination. Its forensic accountants are experts at finding even the cleverest trails of fraudulent financial data and then providing the hard numbers needed to prove a case of fraud. The forensic accountants look beyond the numbers to analyze and reveal all relevant aspects of the situation.

Feeley & Driscoll has extensive experience in information technology for consulting audits and assessments. It also delivers complete data analysis of electronic business records and files, including e-mails, financial spreadsheets, hard drives, tape backups, and more.

In this chapter, you will learn about the importance of managing bank accounts and cash funds, which is key to a company's internal control and its avoidance of fraudulent financial practices.

LEARNING OBJECTIVES

After you have completed this chapter, you will be able to do the following:

1 Describe the procedure for depositing checks.

2 Reconcile a bank statement.

3 Record the required journal entries from the bank reconciliation.

4 Record journal entries to establish and reimburse a Petty Cash Fund.

5 Complete petty cash vouchers and petty cash payments records.

6 Record the journal entries to establish a Change Fund.

7 Record journal entries for transactions involving Cash Short and Over.

ACCOUNTING LANGUAGE

ABA number (p. 215)

ATMs (automated teller machines) (p. 217)

Bank reconciliation (p. 222)

Bank statement (p. 219)

Blank endorsement (p. 218)

Canceled checks (p. 221)

Cash funds (p. 214)

Change Fund (p. 233)

Collections (p. 222)

Denominations (p. 231)

Deposit in transit (p. 222)

Deposit slips (p. 215)

Drawer (p. 218)

Electronic Funds Transfer (EFT) (p. 217)

Endorsement (p. 217)

Errors (p. 223)

Interest income (p. 222)

Internal control (p. 213)

Ledger balance of cash (p. 222)

MICR (p. 216)

NSF (not sufficient funds) check (p. 222)

Outstanding checks (p. 222)

Payee (p. 218)

Petty Cash Fund (p. 230)

Petty cash payments record (p. 232)

Petty cash voucher (p. 231)

Promissory note (p. 224)

Qualified endorsement (p. 218)

Restrictive endorsement (p. 218)

Service charge (p. 222)

Signature card (p. 215)

A very important aspect of any financial accounting system, either for an individual or for a business enterprise, is the accurate and efficient management of assets. The handling of assets in a manner that will prevent employees from stealing cash funds is known as **internal control**. Internal control is the system of policies and procedures that is designed to:

1. Protect assets against fraud and waste
2. Provide for accurate accounting data
3. Promote efficient operation
4. Encourage adherence to management policies

When we talk about cash, we mean currency, coins, checks, money orders, traveler's checks, and bank drafts or bank cashier's checks. Personal checks are accepted conditionally—that is, based on the condition that they are valid. In other words, we consider checks to be good until they are otherwise proven not to be good.

Managing cash is an important aspect of business. All embezzlement starts with an employee(s) failing to follow internal control procedures. Following are some simple internal control guidelines for better management of cash receipts and payments:

Cash receipts

- Maintain separation between cash handling and cash recording.
- Designate someone other than the bookkeeper to open mail.
- Make a record of cash received.
- Endorse checks immediately upon receipt with the stamp, "For Deposit Only."
- Deposit cash daily.
- Journalize cash receipts as soon as possible, preferably by someone different than the person who first received the cash.
- Post cash receipts to the Accounts Receivable account as soon as possible.

Cash payments

- Make sure that all cash payments are made by check (with the exception of petty cash).
- Make certain that all checks are prenumbered.
- Keep check supplies under lock.
- Assign someone different than the signer of the checks to prepare the checks.
- Appoint someone other than the person preparing checks to prepare the bank reconciliations.
- Keep petty cash under lock with access limited to one person other than the bookkeeper.

When cash register drawers are involved, additional security is involved. Cashiers must have their register drawer totals verified by a designated employee, manager, or owner when their shifts end. Later, we will see how the bank deposit amount is determined considering the cash in the till at the start of business.

Internal control of cash is a critical activity in any business. Divide the cash activities among several people to deter mishandling.

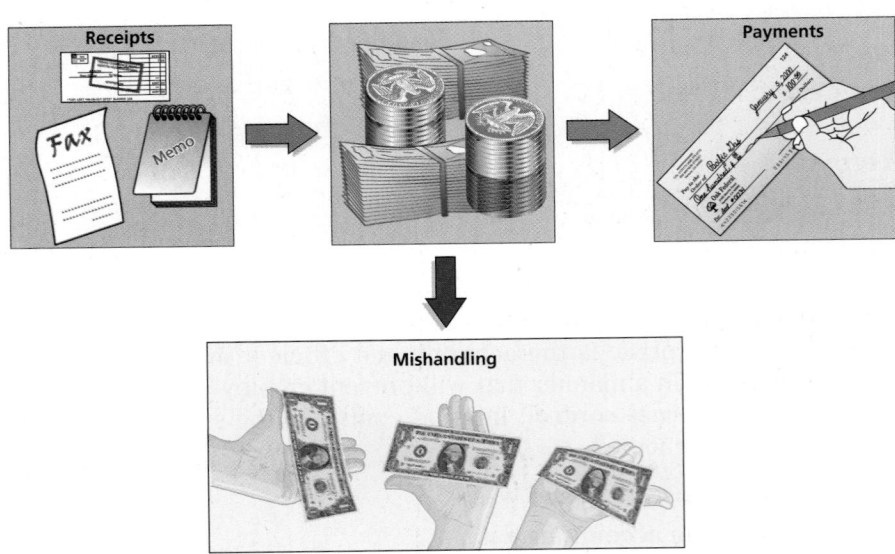

In this chapter, besides discussing bank accounts, we are going to talk about **cash funds**—Petty Cash Funds and Change Funds—which are separately held reserves of cash set aside for specific purposes.

SMALL BUSINESS SUCCESS

What Is Fraud?

Fraud is defined as an intentional misrepresentation of the truth. In its most recent 2008 Report to the Nation, the Association of Certified Fraud Examiners (ACFE) estimated that "small businesses are especially vulnerable to occupational fraud. The median loss suffered by organizations with fewer than 100 employees was $200,000." The ACFE is an organization that provides anti-fraud training and education (www.acfe.com).

A common type of fraud that occurs in small businesses involves theft of assets by employees.

Theft of assets involves stealing of cash, supplies, inventory, and so forth. Employees will go to such extent as to create fake employees who receive payroll and falsify invoices for payment.

The ACFE suggests several strategies to prevent fraud in small business, such as promoting honesty in the workplace and removing the opportunity to commit fraud by maintaining internal controls on accounting records. In addition, companies should be especially careful when hiring employees and always conduct background checks.

USING A CHECKING ACCOUNT

Although you may be familiar with the process of opening a checking account, making deposits, and writing checks, let's review these and other procedures associated with opening and maintaining a business checking account. We will discuss signature cards, deposit slips, automated teller machines, Electronic Funds Transfer, night deposits, and endorsements.

Signature Card

When Melinda B. Roland founded Roland's Delivery Services, she opened a checking account in the name of the business. When she opened the account, she filled out a **signature card** for the bank's files. Because Roland gave her assistant Sheila R. Bayes the right to sign checks too, the assistant also signed the card. The signature card gives the bank a copy of the official signatures of any persons authorized to sign checks. The bank can use it to verify the signatures on any checks of Roland's Delivery Services presented for payment. This card helps the bank detect forgeries. Each banking entity has its own signature card. Figure 1 shows a typical signature card.

FYI

As a means of preventing employee theft, many companies require more than one signature on checks over a certain dollar amount.

Deposit Slips

The bank provides printed **deposit slips** on which customers record the amount of coins and currency they are depositing and list each individual check being deposited. A typical deposit slip is shown in Figure 2.

Each check should be listed according to its American Bankers Association (ABA) transit number. The **ABA number** is the small series of numbers located in the upper right corner of a check. The first part of the number indicates the city or state in which the bank is located and the specific bank on which the check is drawn. The second part of the number indicates the Federal Reserve District in

1 LEARNING OBJECTIVE

Describe the procedure for depositing checks.

FIGURE 1
Signature card for Roland's Delivery Services

Title **Roland's Delivery Services**

Account number 5008-3007

In consideration of the acceptance by COMPASS BANK of my/our account of the type indicated below, I/we agree to be bound by such rules and regulations and/or such schedules of interest, fees and charges applicable to such account as may now or hereafter be adopted by and in effect at said Bank, and also by the provisions printed hereon. It is understood that the acceptance by said Bank of my/our account is subject to the receipt by said Bank of satisfactory credit information.

(1) Sign Here *Melinda B. Roland*

(2) Sign Here *Sheila R. Bayes*

Address	City	State	Zip
951 Bay Road	San Diego	California	92109

☑ CHECKING ☐ MULTIPLE MATURITY ☐ CASH MANAGER
☐ SAVINGS ☐ GUARANTEED INTEREST (Multiple Maturity) ☐ SAFE DEPOSIT ☐ OTHER ____________

IF THIS IS A JOINT ACCOUNT, BOTH OWNERS MUST SIGN ABOVE

Each of the signers guarantees the genuineness of the signature of the other. Each signer also agrees with the other and the Bank that deposits now or hereafter made to this account may be withdrawn in whole or part by either or survivor, and that each may endorse for deposit to this account any instrument payable to the order of either or both. Provisions respecting this agreement shall be modified only upon receipt by the Bank of written notice, signed by both.

FIGURE 2
Deposit slip for Roland's Delivery Services

DEPOSIT TICKET

Roland's Delivery Services
951 Bay Road
San Diego, CA 92109

DATE *April 3* 20 —

COMPASS BANK
485 Mission Avenue
San Diego, California 92104

CURRENCY		118	00
COIN		15	35
CHECKS — LIST SINGLY	90-310	115	20
	90-164	38	33
	90-837	155	46
	90-111	110	80
	90-722	75	00
TOTAL		628	14

BE SURE EACH ITEM IS PROPERLY ENDORSED

⑆122290310⑆5008 3007⑈

ITEMS CREDITED SUBJECT TO VERIFICATION AND DEPOSIT AGREEMENT OF THIS BANK.

which the check is cleared and the routing number used by the Federal Reserve Bank. For example,

$$\frac{90\text{-}310}{1222}$$

FYI The 12 in the last part of the ABA number represents the Twelfth Federal Reserve District, and the 22 represents the routing number used by the Federal Reserve Bank.

The 90 identifies the city or state, and the 310 indicates the specific bank within that area (see Figures 3 and 5).

For a business account, the depositor fills out the deposit slip in duplicate, giving the original to the bank teller and keeping the copy. (This procedure may vary from bank to bank.)

The bank prints the amount of each deposited check on the lower right side of the check in a distinctive script called **MICR**, which stands for *magnetic ink character recognition*. The routing number (as well as the depositor's number) used by the Federal Reserve Bank was printed on the lower left side of the blank check before it was sent to the account holder. The electronic equipment used to process the checks is able to rapidly read the script identifying the bank on which the check is drawn and the amount of the check.

A federal law called The Check Clearing for the 21st Century Act (or Check 21 Act) enacted in 2004 allows banks that receive a check from a depositor to create a two-sided digital version of the original check, called a *substitute* check. This substitute check eliminates the need to handle a paper check through the banking system. One of the several effects of the Check 21 Act is that consumers will no longer be able to require a bank to return to them their original cancelled checks with their monthly statement. Another side effect of the law is that it is now legal for anyone to use a computer scanner to capture images of checks and deposit them electronically, a process known as *remote deposit*. The Federal Reserve's Web site (www.federalreserve.gov/pubs/check21/consumer_guide.htm) provides more information about the Check 21 Act.

Automated Teller Machines

Deposits, withdrawals, and transfers can be made at all hours at banks with **ATMs (automated teller machines)**. Each depositor uses a plastic card that contains a code number and has a personal identification number (PIN). The amount to be deposited, withdrawn, or transferred is keyed in by the depositor. To make a deposit, the customer inserts an envelope containing cash and/or checks and, if required, a copy of the deposit slip into the ATM. To make a withdrawal, the customer requests an amount, the ATM dispenses it, and the customer removes the cash. In addition to deposits and withdrawals, a customer may transfer amounts from one account to another (for example, from savings to checking) as well as check the balance of their accounts.

Electronic Funds Transfer

A transfer of funds initiated through an electronic terminal, such as a telephone, computer, or magnetic tape, is an **Electronic Funds Transfer (EFT)**. There is no paper document, such as a check or deposit slip, starting the transaction. The monthly bank statement will list the EFT deposits and payments. Examples of EFTs include an ATM transaction, a wire transfer in or out of an account, electronic bill paying, and payments to the IRS for income and payroll taxes.

Night Deposits

Most banks provide night depositories so that businesses and individuals can make deposits after regular hours. These are secured chutes into which a business's representative can insert a bag of cash and checks, knowing that the day's receipts will be safe until the bank opens in the morning.

Endorsements

The bank does not accept for deposit a check made out to a business until someone from the business has endorsed the check by signature or by stamp. The endorsement should appear on the back of the left end of a check, as it does in Figure 3. The **endorsement** (1) transfers title to the money and (2) authorizes the payment of

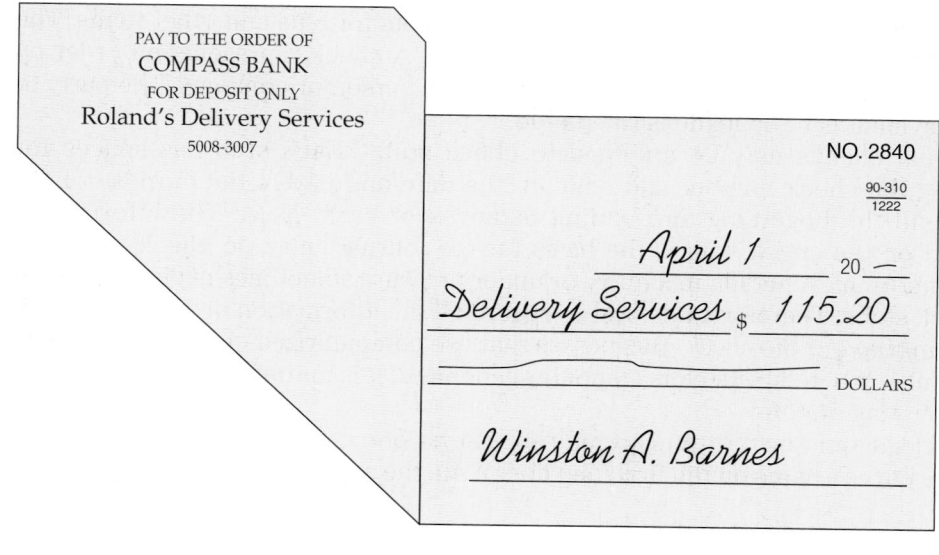

FIGURE 3

Endorsement for Roland's Delivery Services

Restrictive Endorsement
(with rubber stamp)

Blank Endorsement

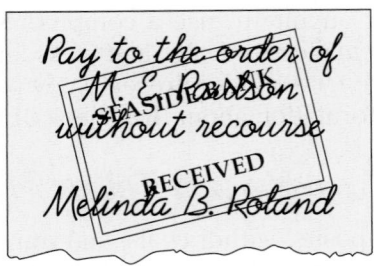

Qualified Endorsement

FIGURE 4

Types of endorsements

the check. In other words, if the check is not good (does not have sufficient funds), then the bank, in order to protect itself, will deduct the amount of the check from the depositor's account.

Restrictive Endorsement

All checks made payable to Roland's Delivery Services are endorsed by stamping on the back of the checks "Pay to the Order of Compass Bank, For Deposit Only, Roland's Delivery Services." This is called a **restrictive endorsement** (see Figure 4) because it restricts or limits any further transfer of the check. This endorsement also forces the deposit of the check, because the endorsement is not valid for any other purpose.

Blank Endorsement

When the party to whom a check is made payable (the payee) endorses the check by signing only her or his name on the back of the check, this is known as a **blank endorsement** (Figure 4). With a blank endorsement, there are no restrictions attached.

Qualified Endorsement

A third type of endorsement is a **qualified endorsement** (see Figure 4), which generally includes the phrase "Pay to the order of," followed by the name of the person to whom the check is being transferred, and then followed by the phrase "without recourse." Such an endorsement frees the endorser from future liability in case the drawer of the check does not have sufficient funds to cover the check.

WRITING CHECKS

Most people generally use a check to make payments for bills and other items. The party who writes the check is called the **drawer**. A check represents an order by the drawer, directing the bank to pay a designated person or company. The party to whom payment is to be made is the **payee**.

Manual checks may be attached to check stubs. Each stub has spaces for recording the check number and amount, the date and payee, the purpose of the check, and the beginning and ending balances of cash. *Note:* The information recorded on the check stub is the basis for the journal entry, so check stubs are vitally important. A person in a hurry or under pressure sometimes neglects to fill in the check stubs. Therefore, it is best to record all the information on the check stub *before making out the check*. Businesses that use computerized checks do not need check stubs. When the check is computer generated, it is automatically entered into the accounting system.

Checks should be written carefully so that no one can successfully alter them. Write the payee's name on the first long line. Write the amount of the check in figures

FIGURE 5

Manual check with accompanying stub for Roland's Delivery Services

close to the dollar sign, then write the amount in words at the extreme left of the line provided for this information. Write cents as a fraction of 100. For example, write $727.50 as "Seven hundred twenty-seven and 50/100," or $89.00 as "Eighty-nine and 00/100." Legally, if there is a discrepancy between the amount in figures and the written amount, the written amount prevails. However, generally, the bank gets in touch with the drawer and asks what the correct amount should be.

Finally, the drawer's signature on the face of the check should match that on the signature card on file at the drawer's bank.

Figure 5 is a manual check, with the accompanying stub, drawn on the account of Roland's Delivery Services. A description of the script appears in Figure 6.

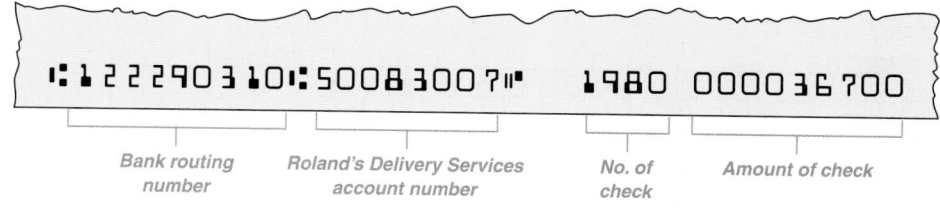

| Bank routing number | Roland's Delivery Services account number | No. of check | Amount of check |

FIGURE 6

Description of the script from Ck. No. 1980 in Figure 5

BANK STATEMENTS

The bank prepares the **bank statement**, which is created from the bank's viewpoint. Keep in mind that, to the bank, a customer's account is a liability and, therefore, has a credit balance. Once a month, the bank sends each of its customers the following information with the bank statement:

- The balance at the beginning of the month
- Additions in the form of deposits and credit memos
- Deductions in the form of checks and debit memos
- Electronic transactions
- The final balance at the end of the month

A bank statement for Roland's Delivery Services is shown in Figure 7. The following legend of symbols is listed on the bottom of the statement:

CM (credit memo) Increases in or credits to the account, such as notes or accounts left with the bank for collection and interest income earned.

COMPASS BANK
485 Mission Avenue
San Diego, CA 92104

STATEMENT OF ACCOUNT	**Roland's Delivery Services** **951 Bay Road** **San Diego, CA 92109**	ACCOUNT NUMBER **5008-3007** STATEMENT DATE September 30, 20— – October 31, 20— TAX ID NUMBER **83-5249862**

	SUMMARY		
		Balance Last Statement	$10,403.57
		Amount of Checks and Debits	$37,947.06
		Number of Checks	69
		Amount of Deposits and Credits	$44,793.10
		Number of Deposits	21
		Balance This Statement	$17,249.61

CHECKS/ OTHER DEBITS	CHECKS	CHECK NUMBER	DATE POSTED	AMOUNT	CHECK NUMBER	DATE POSTED	AMOUNT
		1952	10-01	55.00	1988	10-17	65.22
		1953	10-01	210.40	1989	10-17	465.30
		1954	10-01	440.00	1990	10-18	560.00
		1955	10-02	146.80	1991	10-19	114.57
		1956	10-02	186.25	1992	10-19	24.90
		1957	10-02	651.75	1993	10-19	135.36
		1958	10-03	742.20	1994	10-20	118.36
		1984	10-14	564.55	2018	10-30	120.75
		1985	10-15	617.00	2019	10-30	843.54
		1986	10-16	60.64	2020	10-31	743.20
		1987	10-16	481.85	2021	10-31	123.92

OTHER DEBITS	DESCRIPTION	DATE POSTED	AMOUNT
	DM NSF check from B. R. Rumson	10-15	283.00
	DM Automated Teller Trans. 092349 customer M3272348 at terminal 30962—cash	10-16	100.00
	DM Service charge	10-31	19.50

DEPOSITS/ OTHER CREDITS	DEPOSITS	DATE POSTED	AMOUNT	DATE POSTED	AMOUNT
		10-01	832.00	10-17	973.22
		10-02	1,567.20	10-18	836.79
		10-03	451.63	10-21	438.49
		10-04	790.46	10-22	1,217.25
		10-07	1,048.15	10-23	814.15
		10-08	1,399.00	10-26	377.82
		10-14	872.25	10-28	559.47
		10-15	760.42	10-29	713.14
		10-16	636.34	10-30	854.32

OTHER CREDITS	DESCRIPTION	DATE POSTED	AMOUNT
	CM Note collected, principal $1,000, interest $10	10-29	1,010.00

PLEASE EXAMINE THIS STATEMENT CAREFULLY. REPORT ANY POSSIBLE ERRORS WITHIN 10 DAYS.

CODE SYMBOLS

CM Credit Memo
DM Debit Memo

OD Overdraft
EC Error Correction

FIGURE 7 Bank statement for Roland's Delivery Services

DM (debit memo) Decreases in or debits to the account, such as NSF checks (discussed later in this chapter) and service charges. Service charges are based on the number of items processed and the average account balance. Special charges may also be levied against the account for collections and other services performed, including check printing.

OD (overdraft) The withdrawal of more than the cash balance in the account, resulting in a negative balance.

EC (error correction) Corrections of errors made by the bank, such as encoding mistakes.

The bank statement is a valuable aid to efficiency and accuracy because it provides a double record of the Cash account. If a business entity deposits all cash receipts in the bank and makes all payments by check, then the bank is keeping an independent record of the business's cash. You might think that the two balances—the business's and the bank's—should be equal, but this is unlikely. Some transactions may have been recorded in the business's account before being entered in the bank's records. In addition, there are unavoidable delays (by either the business or the bank) in recording transactions. Ordinarily, there is a delay of one or more days between the date on which a check is written and the date when it is presented to the bank for payment. Also, banks may not record deposits until the following business day. During this time lag, deposits made or checks written are recorded in the business's check register, but they are not yet listed on the bank statement.

The bank mails statements to its depositors each month either physically or via the Internet. The **canceled checks** (checks that have been paid or cleared by the bank) are listed on the bank statement. They are called *canceled checks* because they are canceled by a stamp on the back, indicating that they have been paid. Debit or credit memos are generally described on the bank statement.

> **Remember**
>
> Debit memos represent deductions from and credit memos represent additions to a bank account.

Recording Deposits or Withdrawals

Each business entity keeps its accounts from its *own* point of view. As far as the bank is concerned, each customer's deposits are liabilities, in that the bank owes the customer the amount of the deposits. Using T accounts, it looks like this:

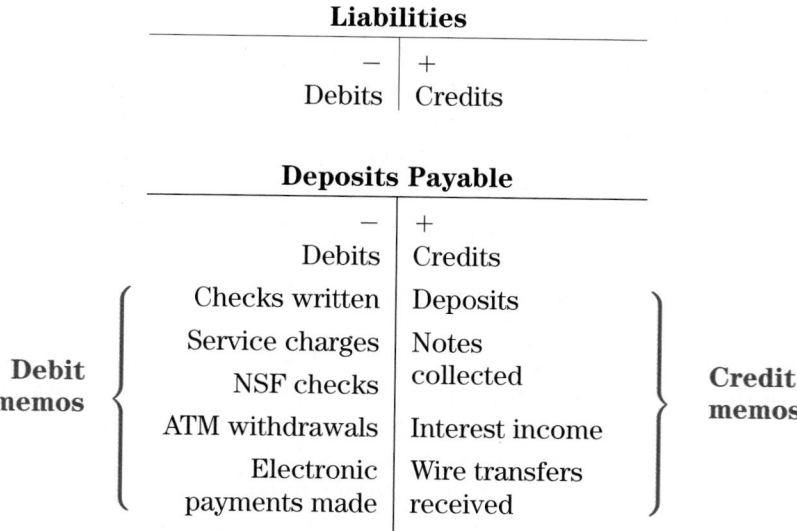

Liabilities

−	+
Debits	Credits

Deposits Payable

−	+
Debits	Credits

Debit memos: Checks written, Service charges, NSF checks, ATM withdrawals, Electronic payments made

Credit memos: Deposits, Notes collected, Interest income, Wire transfers received

When the bank receives a cash deposit from a customer, the bank credits Deposits Payable, because it owes more to its customer. When the bank cashes a check (pays out) for a customer, the bank debits Deposits Payable, because it owes less to its customer.

The customer, on the other hand, uses the account titled Cash, or Cash in Bank, or simply the name of the bank. Deposits are recorded as debits and withdrawals are recorded as credits in the account. On a bank reconciliation, the balance of the account is listed as the **ledger balance of cash** before reconciliation with the bank statement.

Need for Reconciling Bank Balance and Ledger Balance

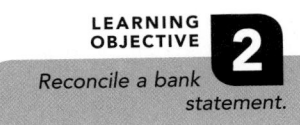

LEARNING OBJECTIVE 2

Reconcile a bank statement.

Since the bank statement balance and the ledger balance of cash are not always equal, a business prepares a **bank reconciliation** to uncover the reasons for the difference between the two balances and to correct any errors that may have been made by either the bank or the business. This makes it possible to arrive at the same balance in each account, which is called the *adjusted balance*, or *true balance*, of the Cash account.

Because identity theft and white-collar crimes are potential problems for a business, another purpose of the bank reconciliation is to make sure all of the amounts paid out from the account are proper disbursements for the business. As stated earlier, it is a mark of good internal control to have the bank reconciliation prepared by someone other than the check signer (if someone other than the business owner is signing checks). The person performing the bank reconciliation will be making sure (a) the dollar amount of each check has not been altered, (b) all of the charges, checks, and electronic transfers belong to the company, and (c) deposits are made in a timely way.

There are a variety of reasons for differences between the bank statement balance and the customer's cash balance. Here are some of the more common ones:

Deposit in transit A deposit made after the bank statement was issued. The depositor has already added the amount to the Cash account in his or her books, but the deposit has not been recorded by the bank (this is also called a *late deposit*).

Outstanding checks Checks that have been written by the company but not yet received for payment by the time the bank sends out its statement. The company employee, when preparing the checks, deducted the amounts from the Cash account in the company's books, which explains the difference.

Collections Money collected by the bank for the customer. When the bank acts as a collection point for its customers by accepting payments on their behalf, it adds the proceeds to the customer's bank account and sends a credit memorandum to notify the customer of the transaction or includes it on the next bank statement.

Interest income Interest earned for keeping cash in the bank account. Some checking accounts are interest bearing or earning. The depositor will not learn how much interest the bank has credited to the bank account until the bank statement is received.

NSF (not sufficient funds) check A deposited check that the bank cannot process because the check writer's account does not contain enough money. When a bank customer deposits a check, it is recorded as cash on the customer's books. Occasionally, however, a check is not paid (bounces). When the bank notifies the customer of this, the customer must make a deduction from the Cash account. Simultaneously, the depositor records an increase in accounts receivable because the client's debt to the depositor remains unpaid. An NSF check may also be called a *dishonored check*.

Service charge A bank charge for services rendered: For handling checks, for collecting money, for receiving payment of notes turned over to it by the customer for collection, for check printing, and for other such services. The bank immediately deducts the fee from the balance of the bank account and identifies the charges on the bank statement.

Errors Mistakes made by the customer or the bank. In spite of internal controls and systems designed to double-check to prevent errors, sometimes either the customer or the bank makes a mistake. Often these errors do not become evident until the bank reconciliation is performed.

Steps in Reconciling the Bank Statement

Follow these steps to reconcile a bank statement:

STEP 1. Canceled checks

a. Compare the amount of each canceled check with the bank statement and note any differences. The amount of the machine-readable characters should appear at the lower right-hand corner of the check, which should match the amount written on the check and the bank statements.

b. In the checkbook beside the check number, list the date of the bank statement. In some cases, a bank may not pay a check until one or two months after it was written. If a question arises as to whether or not you have paid a particular bill, you can look at the checkbook. Then you can refer directly to the bank statement to pick up the accompanying canceled check as proof of payment.

STEP 2. Deposits

a. Compare the deposits in transit (not recorded by the bank at the time of the statement) listed on last month's bank reconciliation with the deposits shown on the bank statement. All of last month's deposits in transit should be listed on this month's bank statement. If they are not, notify the bank immediately.

b. Compare the remaining deposits listed on this month's bank statement with deposits written in the company's accounting records. Consider any deposits not shown on the bank statement as deposits in transit.

STEP 3. Outstanding checks

a. Arrange the canceled checks in order by check number.

b. Look over the list of outstanding checks left over from last month's bank reconciliation, and note the checks that have now been returned or cleared.

c. For each canceled check, compare the amount recorded in MICR numbers at the lower right-hand corner of the check with the amount recorded in the checkbook. Next, compare the canceled check with the numerical listing in the statement. Use a check mark (✓) to indicate that the check has been paid and that the amount is correct. Any payments that have not been marked off, including the outstanding checks from last month's bank reconciliation, are the present outstanding checks.

d. Review the endorsements on the backs of the checks to verify that money has been sent to the correct payee.

STEP 4. Bank memoranda Trace the credit memos and debit memos to the journal. If the memos have not been recorded, make separate entries for them.

For businesses that have computerized check registers, the bank reconciliation can also be done on the computer. The procedures are similar as there is still the need to compare canceled checks, compare deposits, identify outstanding checks and deposits, and record adjustments.

Examples of Bank Reconciliations

Let's go through the reconciliation process for two businesses, W. Carson Company and Roland's Delivery Services.

W. Carson Company

The bank statement of W. Carson Company indicates a balance of $6,446 as of March 31. The balance of the Cash account in Carson's ledger as of that date is $4,650. Carson's accountant has taken the following steps:

STEP 1. Verified that canceled checks were recorded correctly on the bank statement.

STEP 2. Noted that the deposit made on March 31 was not recorded on the bank statement, $2,174.

STEP 3. Noted outstanding checks: no. 920, $1,695; no. 975, $325; no. 976, $1,279.

STEP 4. Noted credit memo: Note collected by the bank from T. Landon, $700, not recorded in the journal. Noted debit memo: Collection charge and service charge not recorded in the journal, $29.

The note received from T. Landon is called a promissory note. A **promissory note** is a written promise to pay a definite amount at a definite future time. Let's assume that W. Carson Company received the 60-day non-interest-bearing note from T. Landon for services performed. In recording the transaction, Carson's accountant debited Notes Receivable and credited Income from Services. (The account Notes Receivable is similar to Accounts Receivable. However, Accounts Receivable is reserved for customer charge accounts, with payments usually due in 30 days.) Next, W. Carson Company turned the note over to its bank for collection.

The bank will use a credit memo form to notify W. Carson Company that the note has been collected and that the company's bank account has been increased by the amount of the note. Based on the credit memo, Carson's accountant will make a journal entry debiting Cash and crediting Notes Receivable.

Think of the bank reconciliation in terms of the following:

1. Bring the bank statement balance up to date by recording the activities or transactions that we knew about but the bank did not know about when it prepared the statement (deposits in transit and outstanding checks as shown in our checkbook, for example).

2. Bring the balance of the Cash account up to date by recording the activities of transactions that the bank knew about but we did not know about until we received the statement (bank fees, NSF checks, notes collected, checks cleared, interest income, debit memos and credit memos as shown on the bank statement, for example).

Figure 8 shows W. Carson Company's bank reconciliation. The items in the reconciliation that require journal entries are shown in color.

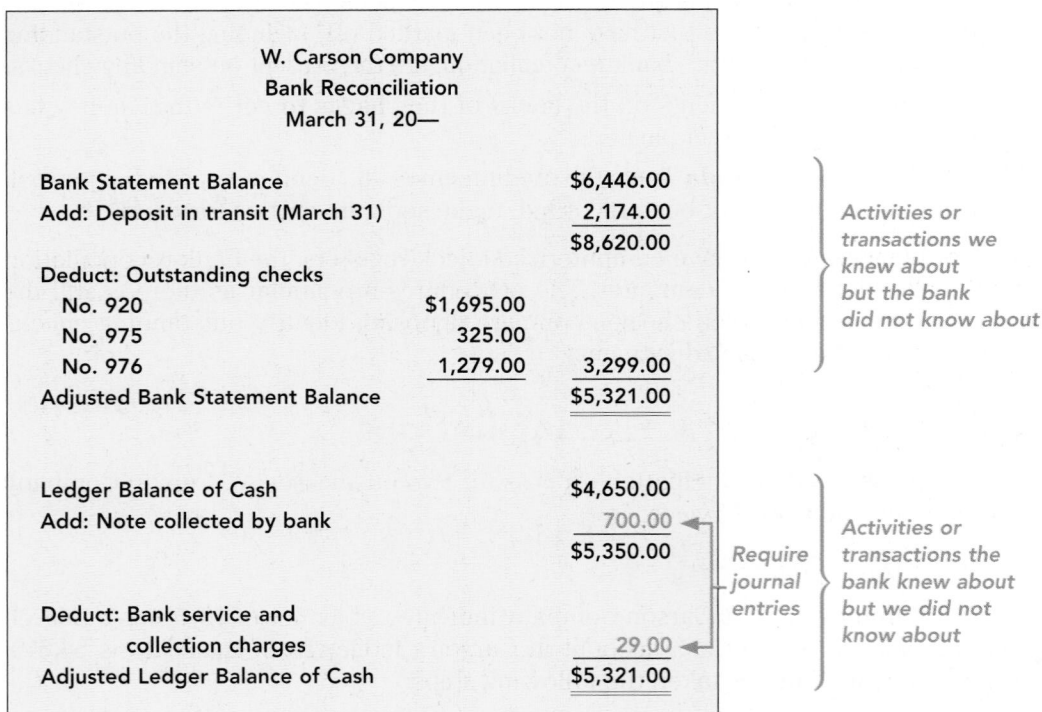

FIGURE 8

Bank reconciliation for W. Carson Company

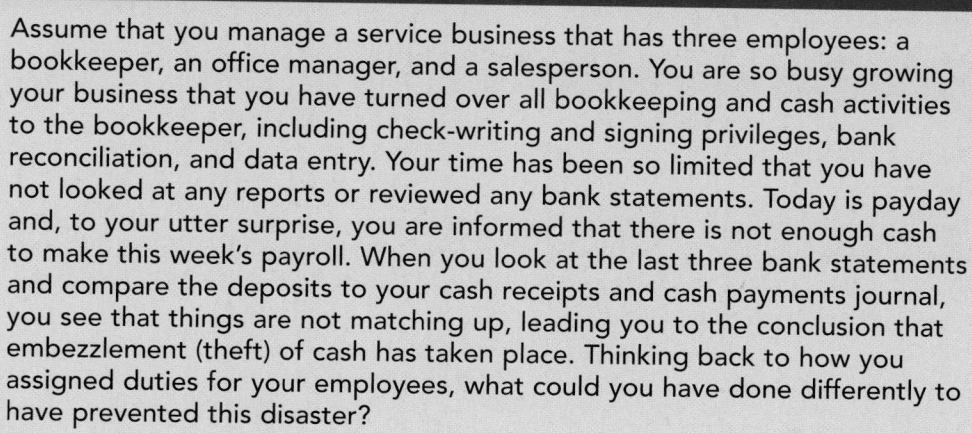

You Make the Call

Assume that you manage a service business that has three employees: a bookkeeper, an office manager, and a salesperson. You are so busy growing your business that you have turned over all bookkeeping and cash activities to the bookkeeper, including check-writing and signing privileges, bank reconciliation, and data entry. Your time has been so limited that you have not looked at any reports or reviewed any bank statements. Today is payday and, to your utter surprise, you are informed that there is not enough cash to make this week's payroll. When you look at the last three bank statements and compare the deposits to your cash receipts and cash payments journal, you see that things are not matching up, leading you to the conclusion that embezzlement (theft) of cash has taken place. Thinking back to how you assigned duties for your employees, what could you have done differently to have prevented this disaster?

SOLUTION

There should have been a better segregation of duties to prevent this occurrence. First of all, the bookkeeper should never have been assigned all cash activities, especially check-writing and signing privileges. Checks should have been written and signed by you or the office manager only. The checks should also be mailed by you and no other employee in the business. The office manager should have the responsibility of opening and endorsing each check by stamping on the back of the check "For Deposit Only." This restricts or limits any further transfer of the check and also forces the deposit of the check, because the endorsement is not valid for any other purpose. The bank reconciliation should also be done by the office manager rather than the bookkeeper, with the completed statements reviewed by you. The bookkeeper's primary responsibilities should be to make journal entries for cash received for the general ledger as well as for the Accounts Receivable and Accounts Payable accounts.

Note that the journal entries are based on the items used to adjust the ledger balance of Cash. These items represent the transactions that the bank has knowledge of but the business does not. According to the bank reconciliation, the true balance of Cash is $5,321, which is the balance we wish to show on the business's books. We can't change the balance of an account unless we first make a journal entry and then post the entry to the accounts involved. **Consequently, we have to make journal entries for items in the Ledger Balance of Cash section of the bank reconciliation.** The additions are debited to the Cash account, and the deductions are credited to the Cash account. W. Carson Company records the entries in its general journal:

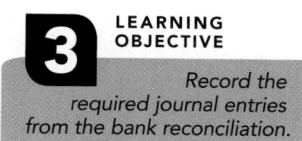

3 **LEARNING OBJECTIVE**

Record the required journal entries from the bank reconciliation.

GENERAL JOURNAL				PAGE _____

Date	Description	Post. Ref.	Debit	Credit
20—				
Mar. 31	Cash		7 0 0 00	
	Notes Receivable			7 0 0 00
	Non-interest-bearing note			
	signed by T. Landon was			
	collected by the bank.			
31	Miscellaneous Expense		2 9 00	
	Cash			2 9 00
	Service charge and collection			
	charge levied by bank.			

Here bank service and collection charges are recorded in Miscellaneous Expense because the amounts are relatively small. Some accountants may use a separate expense account, such as Bank Charge Expense. After the entries have been posted, the T account for Cash looks like this:

Cash

Balance	4,650	Mar. 31	29
Mar. 31	700		
Bal.	**5,321**		

Note that the balance in the T account is now equal to both the adjusted bank statement balance and the adjusted ledger balance of cash.

Form of Bank Reconciliation

Now that you have seen an example of a bank reconciliation, let's look at the standard form of a bank reconciliation for an imaginary company.

Bank Statement Balance (last figure on the statement)		$4,000
Add:		
Deposits in transit (deposits made after the bank statement was issued and already added to the ledger balance of Cash)	$300	
Bank errors (that understate balance)	20	320
		$4,320
Deduct:		
Outstanding checks and transfers (they have already been deducted from the Cash account)	$960	
Bank errors (that overstate balance)	40	1,000
Adjusted Bank Statement Balance (the true balance of Cash)		$3,320

Ledger Balance of Cash (the latest balance of the Cash account if it has been posted up to date; otherwise take the beginning balance of Cash, plus cash receipts, minus cash payments)		$2,850
Add:		
Credit memos (additions by the bank not recorded in the Cash account, such as collections of notes)	$500	
Book errors (that understate balance)	40	540
		$3,390
Deduct:		
Debit memos (deductions by the bank not recorded in the Cash account, such as service charges or collection charges and NSF checks)	$ 20	
Book errors (that overstate balance)	50	70
Adjusted Ledger Balance of Cash (the true balance of Cash)		$3,320

Roland's Delivery Services

The bank statement of Roland's Delivery Services shows a final balance of $17,249.61 as of October 31 (see Figure 7). The present balance of the Cash account in the ledger, after Roland's Delivery Services' accountant has posted from the journal, is $16,296.11. The accountant took the following steps:

STEP 1. Verified that canceled checks were recorded correctly on the bank statement.

STEP 2. Discovered that a deposit of $1,012 made on October 31 was not recorded on the bank statement.

STEP 3. Noted outstanding checks: no. 1951, $687; no. 2022, $185; no. 2023, $367; no. 2024, $110.

STEP 4. Noted that a credit memo for a note collected by the bank from Lawson and Richards, $1,000 principal plus $10 interest, was not recorded in the journal. Found that check no. 2002 for $745, payable to Sanders, Inc., on account, was recorded in the journal as $754. (The correct amount is $745.) Noted that a debit memo for a collection charge and service charge of $19.50 was not recorded in the journal. Noted that a debit memo for an NSF check for $283 from B. R. Rumson was not recorded. Noted that a $100 personal withdrawal by Melinda B. Roland, the owner, using an ATM, was not recorded.

> **Remember**
>
> When you are reconciling a bank statement, always double-check for any outstanding checks or deposits from previous statements that have been carried forward. Also double-check for any bank service charges.

Look at Figure 9 to see how each step relates to the bank reconciliation.

The accountant makes journal entries for the items indicated in Figure 9 to change the balance of the Cash account from its present balance of $16,296.11 to the true balance of $16,912.61. Again, those items that require journal entries are highlighted in Figure 9 and shown in Figure 10.

Interest Income is classified as a revenue account. It represents the amount received on the promissory note that is over and above the face value of the note.

As for the NSF check, upon being notified by the bank, Roland's Delivery Services calls its customer (B. R. Rumson). Rumson can now take steps to cover the check. Review Roland's Delivery Services' transaction with B. R. Rumson. In return for services provided, Roland's Delivery Services received Rumson's check for $283. At that time, Roland's Delivery Services' accountant recorded the transaction as a debit to Cash for $283 and a credit to Income from Services for $283. Then the bank, through its debit memorandum, notified Roland's Delivery Services about Rumson's NSF check. To avoid overdrawing its own bank account, Roland's Delivery Services makes an entry crediting Cash (to correct its earlier debit to Cash) and debiting Accounts Receivable (to put the amount into Accounts Receivable). Since B. R. Rumson owes the money, it is logical to add the amount to Accounts Receivable.

FIGURE 9

Bank reconciliation for
Roland's Delivery Services

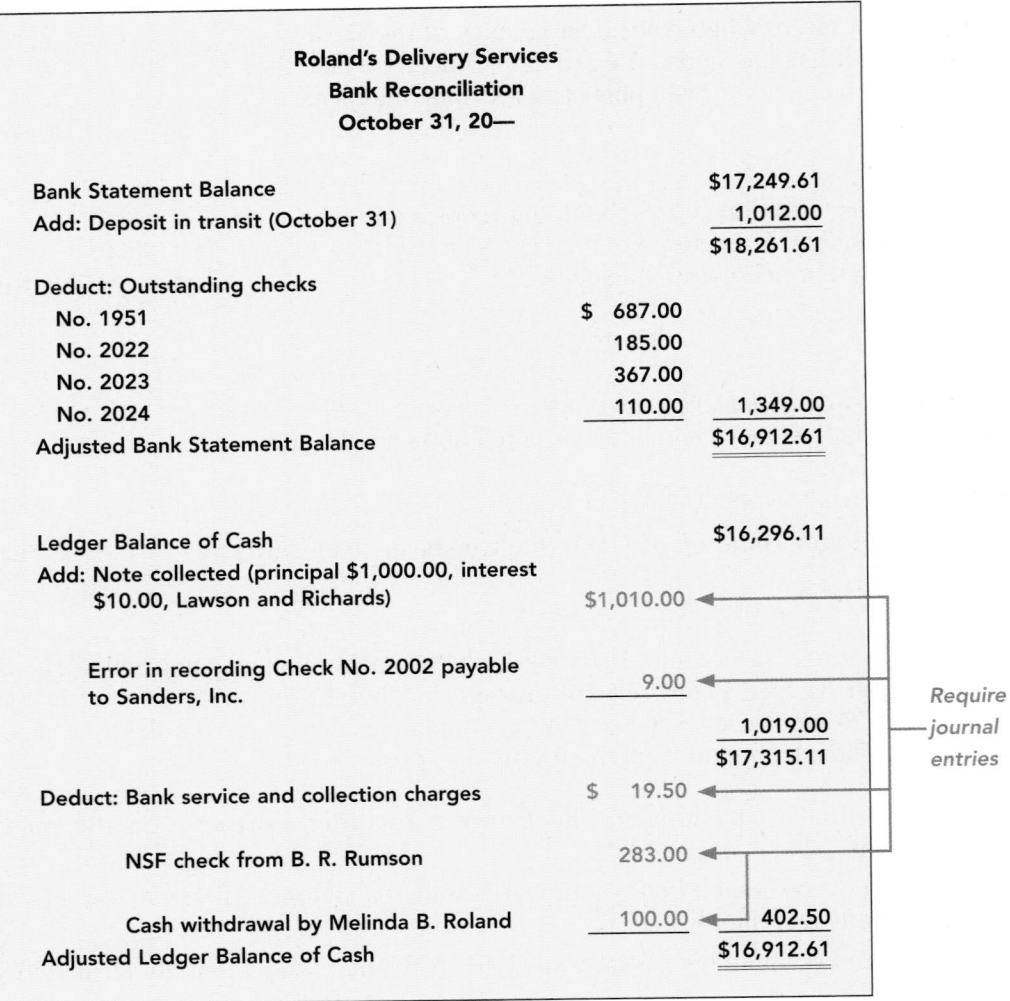

Roland's Delivery Services
Bank Reconciliation
October 31, 20—

Bank Statement Balance		$17,249.61
Add: Deposit in transit (October 31)		1,012.00
		$18,261.61
Deduct: Outstanding checks		
No. 1951	$ 687.00	
No. 2022	185.00	
No. 2023	367.00	
No. 2024	110.00	1,349.00
Adjusted Bank Statement Balance		$16,912.61
Ledger Balance of Cash		$16,296.11
Add: Note collected (principal $1,000.00, interest $10.00, Lawson and Richards)	$1,010.00 ←	
Error in recording Check No. 2002 payable to Sanders, Inc.	9.00 ←	
		1,019.00
		$17,315.11
Deduct: Bank service and collection charges	$ 19.50 ←	
NSF check from B. R. Rumson	283.00 ←	
Cash withdrawal by Melinda B. Roland	100.00 ←	402.50
Adjusted Ledger Balance of Cash		$16,912.61

Require journal entries

FIGURE 10

Journal entries for Roland's
Delivery Services

GENERAL JOURNAL   PAGE _____

Date		Description	Post. Ref.	Debit	Credit
20—					
Oct.	31	Cash		1 0 1 0 00	
		Notes Receivable			1 0 0 0 00
		Interest Income			1 0 00
		Bank collected note signed			
		by Lawson and Richards.			
	31	Cash		9 00	
		Accounts Payable			9 00
		Error in recording Ck. No.			
		2002 payable to Sanders, Inc.			
	31	Miscellaneous Expense		1 9 50	
		Cash			1 9 50
		Bank service charge and			
		collection charge.			
	31	Accounts Receivable		2 8 3 00	
		Cash			2 8 3 00
		NSF check received from			
		B. R. Rumson.			
	31	M. B. Roland, Drawing		1 0 0 00	
		Cash			1 0 0 00
		Withdrawal for personal use.			

THIS FORM IS PROVIDED TO HELP YOU BALANCE
YOUR BANK STATEMENT

CHECKS OUTSTANDING—NOT
CHARGED TO ACCOUNT

NO. 1951	$ 687	00
2022	185	00
2023	367	00
2024	110	00
TOTAL	$ 1,349	00

BEFORE YOU START

PLEASE BE SURE YOU HAVE ENTERED IN YOUR CHECKBOOK ALL AUTOMATIC
TRANSACTIONS SHOWN ON THE FRONT OF YOUR STATEMENT.

YOU SHOULD HAVE ADDED IF
ANY OCCURRED:
1. Loan advances.
2. Credit memos.
3. Other automatic deposits.

YOU SHOULD HAVE SUBTRACTED
IF ANY OCCURRED:
1. Automatic loan payments.
2. Automatic savings transfers.
3. Service charges.
4. Debit memos.
5. Other automatic deductions and
   payments.

BANK BALANCE SHOWN ON THIS STATEMENT	$ 17,249.61
ADD DEPOSITS NOT SHOWN ON THIS STATEMENT (IF ANY)	$ 1,012.00
TOTAL	$ 18,261.61
SUBTRACT CHECKS OUTSTANDING	$ 1,349.00
BALANCE	$ 16,912.61

SHOULD AGREE WITH YOUR CHECKBOOK
BALANCE AFTER DEDUCTING SERVICE CHARGE
(IF ANY) SHOWN ON THIS STATEMENT.

Please examine immediately and report if incorrect. If no reply
is received within 10 days, the account will be considered correct.

FIGURE 11

Bank form for Roland's
Delivery Services

A bank reconciliation form is ordinarily printed on the back of the bank statement. The adjusted balance of the ledger balance of cash has already been determined. Consequently, the bank form is provided only for calculating the adjusted bank statement balance of the bank reconciliation. The bank form for Roland's Delivery Services is shown in Figure 11 above.

THE PETTY CASH FUND

Day after day, businesses are confronted with transactions requiring small immediate payments, such as paying for delivery charges, birthday cards, or pizza for after-hours workers. If the business had to make all payments by check, the time consumed would be frustrating and the whole process would be unduly expensive. For many businesses, the cost of writing each check is more than $10; this includes the cost

Accounting in Your Future

Forensic Accountant

If the super detective Sherlock Holmes was around today and needed to investigate corporate financial crimes, he would need to rely on not only his detective skills but also his accounting knowledge. The combination of accounting and detective skills is what makes accountants such good investigators in today's financial world. Many public accountants specialize in forensic accounting—investigating and interpreting white-collar crimes such as securities fraud and embezzlement, bankruptcies and contract disputes, as well as other complex and possibly criminal financial transactions such as money laundering. Forensic accountants combine their knowledge of accounting and finance with law and investigative techniques to determine whether an activity is illegal. Many forensic accountants work closely with law enforcement personnel and lawyers during investigations and often appear as expert witnesses during trials.

Increased focus on and numbers of financial crimes such as embezzlement, bribery, and securities fraud will increase the demand for forensic accountants. Computer technology has made these crimes easier to commit, and they are on the rise. At the same time, the development of new computer software and electronic surveillance technology has made tracking down financial criminals easier, thus increasing the ease and likelihood of discovery. As success rates of investigations grow, demand for forensic accountants will increase. In 2009, *U.S. News & World Report* listed forensic accounting as one of the eight most secure career tracks in America, while *SmartMoney* Magazine counted forensic accounting as one of its "ten hottest jobs" with salary amounts in six figures.

The Association of Certified Fraud Examiners offers the Certified Fraud Examiner (CFE) designation for forensic or public accountants involved in fraud prevention, detection, deterrence, and investigation. To obtain the designation, individuals must have a bachelor's degree, two years of relevant experience, pass a four-part exam, and abide by a code of ethics. Therefore, if you take the additional steps of securing your CPA status as well as education leading to you becoming a CFE, you can feed your taste for detective work while still enjoying your life as an accountant!

of an employee's time for writing and reconciling the check. Suppose you buy five stamps from an employee for $2.20, and you want to reimburse her. To write a check would not be practical. It only makes sense to pay in cash, using the **Petty Cash Fund**. *Petty* means "small," so the business sets a maximum amount that can be paid immediately out of petty cash. Payments that exceed this maximum must be processed by regular check through the journal.

Establishing the Petty Cash Fund

LEARNING OBJECTIVE 4

Record journal entries to establish and reimburse a Petty Cash Fund.

After the business has set the maximum amount of a payment from petty cash, the next step is to estimate how much cash will be needed during a given period of time, such as a month. It is also important to consider the element of security when keeping cash in the office. If the risk is great, the amount kept in the fund should be small. Roland's Delivery Services decides to establish a Petty Cash Fund of $100 and put it under the control of the assistant. Accordingly, Roland's Delivery Services' accountant writes a check, cashes it at the bank, and records this transaction in the journal as follows:

		GENERAL JOURNAL			PAGE _____	
Date		Description	Post. Ref.	Debit	Credit	
20—						
Sept.	1	Petty Cash Fund		1 0 0 00		
		Cash			1 0 0 00	
		Established a Petty Cash Fund,				
		Ck. No. 1880.				

T accounts for the entry look like this:

Petty Cash Fund		Cash	
+	−	+	−
100			100

Because the Petty Cash Fund is an asset account, it is listed on the balance sheet immediately below Cash.

Once the fund has been created, it is not debited again unless the original amount is not large enough to handle the necessary transactions. In that case, the accountant has to increase the Petty Cash Fund—perhaps from $100 to $200. **But, if no change is made in the size of the fund, Petty Cash Fund is debited only once.**

The check is written to the assistant, "Sheila R. Bayes, Petty Cash Fund." She converts it into convenient **denominations**, which are varieties of coins and currency, such as quarters and dimes and $1 and $5 bills. Then the assistant puts the money in a locked drawer and will not pay anything larger than $20 (or whatever is the agreed-upon amount) out of petty cash.

Payments from the Petty Cash Fund

The assistant is designated as the only person who can make payments from the Petty Cash Fund. In case of her illness, another employee should be named as stand-in. A **petty cash voucher** must be used to account for every payment from the fund. The voucher constitutes a receipt signed by the person who authorized the payment and by the person who received payment as well as the purpose of the payment. Thus, even for small payments of $20 or less, there would have to be collusion between the payee and the assistant for any theft to occur. Figure 12 shows an example of a petty cash voucher.

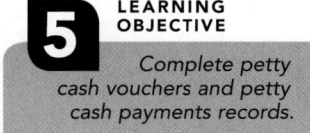

Remember

If no change is made in the size of the fund, the Petty Cash Fund account is debited only once, and this happens when the fund is first established.

5 LEARNING OBJECTIVE

Complete petty cash vouchers and petty cash payments records.

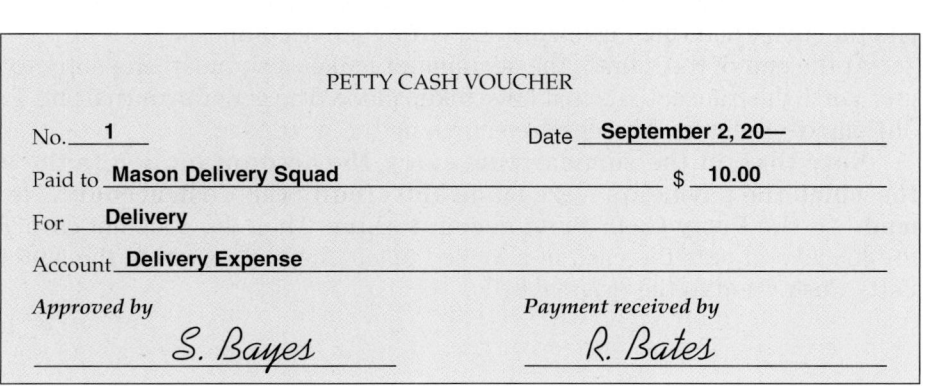

FIGURE 12

Petty cash voucher

PETTY CASH VOUCHER

No. __1__   Date __September 2, 20—__

Paid to __Mason Delivery Squad__ $ __10.00__

For __Delivery__

Account __Delivery Expense__

Approved by   *Payment received by*

___S. Bayes___   ___R. Bates___

Petty Cash Payments Record

Some businesses prefer to have a written record on one sheet of paper, so they keep a **petty cash payments record**. In a petty cash payments record, petty cash vouchers and the accounts that are to be charged are listed as well as the purpose of the expenditure. Special columns for frequent types of expenditures are included in the Distribution of Payments section. The petty cash payments record is not a journal.

Roland's Delivery Services made the following payments from its Petty Cash Fund during September:

Sept.   2   Paid $10 for flowers for the front counter to Mason Delivery Squad, voucher no. 1.

3   Bought pencils and pens, $8.59, voucher no. 2.

5   Bought local newspapers for article related to Roland's Delivery Services, $2.50, voucher no. 3.

7   Paid postage on incoming packages, $3.70, voucher no. 4.

10   Melinda B. Roland, the owner, withdrew $10 for personal use, voucher no. 5.

14   Reimbursed employee for stamps, $2.20, voucher no. 6.

21   Bought stick-on tabs, $4.10, voucher no. 7.

22   Paid $14 for gift for retiring employee, voucher no. 8.

26   Paid for mailing packages, $3.60, voucher no. 9.

27   Paid $9 for Girl Scout cookies, voucher no. 10.

29   Bought memo pads, $4.40, voucher no. 11.

29   Paid for making duplicate keys, $8.20, voucher no. 12.

30   Paid $8 to have parking area swept, voucher no. 13.

30   Paid for trash removal, $5, voucher no. 14.

Figure 13 on pages 234 and 235 shows how these payments are recorded.

Reimbursement of the Petty Cash Fund

To bring the fund back up to the original amount when it is nearly exhausted (for instance, at the end of the month), the accountant reimburses the fund for expenditures made. Consequently, the Petty Cash Fund may be considered a revolving fund. If the amount initially put in the Petty Cash Fund is $100 and at the end of the month only $6.71 is left, the accountant puts $93.29 in the fund as a reimbursement, thereby bringing the fund back up to $100 to start the new month.

Bear in mind that the petty cash payments record is only a supplementary record for gathering information. A less formal way of compiling the information concerning petty cash payments might consist of collecting one month's petty cash vouchers, then sorting them by accounts, such as Office Supplies Expense, Delivery Expense, and the like. Then run a calculator tape for each account.

At the end of the month, the accountant makes a summarizing entry to officially journalize the transactions that have taken place. The general journal and T accounts of Roland's Delivery Services are shown on the next page.

Note that, in the summarizing entry, the accountant debits the accounts for which the payments were made and credits the Cash account. No entry is made to the Petty Cash Fund account alone. Then the assistant cashes a check for $93.29 and puts the cash in a locked place, thereby restoring the amount in the Petty Cash Fund to the original $100.

		GENERAL JOURNAL			PAGE _____	
Date		Description	Post. Ref.	Debit	Credit	
20—						
Sept.	30	Office Supplies Expense		1 7 09		
		Maintenance Expense		2 1 20		
		Miscellaneous Expense		4 5 00		
		M. B. Roland, Drawing		1 0 00		
		Cash			9 3 29	
		Reimbursed the Petty Cash				
		Fund, Ck. No. 1950.				

Cash		M. B. Roland, Drawing	
+	−	+	−
	93.29	10.00	

Office Supplies Expense		Maintenance Expense		Miscellaneous Expense	
+	−	+	−	+	−
17.09		21.20		45.00	

THE CHANGE FUND

Anyone who has tried to pay for a small item with a $20 bill knows that any business that carries out numerous cash transactions needs a **Change Fund**.

Establishing the Change Fund

Before setting up a Change Fund, you have to decide two things: (1) how much money needs to be in the fund, and (2) what denominations of bills and coins are needed. Like the Petty Cash Fund, **the Change Fund is debited only once: when it is established.** It is left at the initial figure unless the person in charge decides to make it larger. The Change Fund account, like the Petty Cash Fund account, is an asset. It is recorded in the balance sheet immediately below Cash. If the Petty Cash Fund account is larger than the Change Fund account, it precedes the Change Fund.

The owner of Roland's Delivery Services, Melinda B. Roland, decides to establish a Change Fund; she decides this at the same time she sets up the company's Petty Cash Fund. The entries for the two transactions look like this:

6 LEARNING OBJECTIVE

Record the journal entries to establish a Change Fund.

FIGURE 13

Petty cash payments record for Roland's Delivery Services

Petty Cash Payments Record
Month of September 20—

Date	Vou. No.	Explanation	Payments	Office Supplies Expense	
Sept. 1		Establish fund, Ck. No. 1880, $100			
2	1	Mason Delivery Squad	1 0 00		
3	2	Pencils and pens	8 59	8 59	
5	3	Local newspapers	2 50		
7	4	Postage on incoming packages	3 70		
10	5	Melinda B. Roland	1 0 00		
14	6	Reimburse employee for stamps	2 20		
21	7	Stick-on tabs	4 10	4 10	
22	8	Gift for retiring employee	1 4 00		
26	9	Postage for mailings	3 60		
27	10	Girl Scout cookies	9 00		
29	11	Memo pads	4 40	4 40	
29	12	Making duplicate keys	8 20		
30	13	Sweeping of parking area	8 00		
30	14	Trash removal	5 00		
30		Totals	9 3 29	1 7 09	
		Balance in Fund	$ 6.71		
		Reimburse fund, Ck. No. 1950	93.29		
		Total	$100.00		

GENERAL JOURNAL   **PAGE** _____

Date	Description	Post. Ref.	Debit	Credit
20—				
Sept. 1	Petty Cash Fund		1 0 0 00	
	Cash			1 0 0 00
	Established a Petty Cash Fund,			
	Ck. No. 1880.			
1	Change Fund		1 5 0 00	
	Cash			1 5 0 00
	Established a Change Fund,			
	Ck. No. 1881.			

The T accounts for establishing the Change Fund are as follows:

Change Fund		Cash	
+	−	+	−
150			150

Roland cashes a check for $150 and gets the money in several denominations. She is now prepared to make change for any normal business transactions.

Depositing Cash

At the end of each business day, Roland's Delivery Services' accountant deposits the cash taken in during the day but holds back the amount of the Change Fund, being

Distribution of Payments				
Maintenance Expense	Miscellaneous Expense	Other Accounts		
		Account	Amount	
	1 0 00			
	2 50			
	3 70			
		M. B. Roland, Drawing	1 0 00	
	2 20			
	1 4 00			
	3 60			
	9 00			
8 20				
8 00				
5 00				
2 1 20	4 5 00		1 0 00	

sure that it is in convenient denominations. Let's say that on September 1, Roland's Delivery Services had $1,575 on hand at the end of the day.

$1,575   Total cash count

– 150   Change Fund

$1,425   New cash deposit

The day's receipts are journalized as follows:

	GENERAL JOURNAL			PAGE _____
Date	Description	Post. Ref.	Debit	Credit
20—				
Sept. 1	Cash		1 4 2 5 00	
	Income from Services			1 4 2 5 00
	To record revenue earned			
	during the day.			

The T accounts look like this:

Cash			Income from Services	
+	–		–	+
1,425				1,425

The amount of the cash deposit is the total cash count less the amount of the Change Fund. This should be equal to the income earned.

On September 9, the cash count is $1,672. So the accountant deposits $1,522 ($1,672 – $150). Roland's Delivery Services' accountant makes the following entry to record the day's receipts:

	GENERAL JOURNAL				PAGE _____
Date	Description	Post. Ref.	Debit	Credit	
20—					
Sept. 9	Cash		1 5 2 2 00		
	Income from Services			1 5 2 2 00	
	To record revenue earned				
	during the day.				

Some businesses label the Cash account *Cash in Bank* and label the Change Fund *Cash on Hand*.

CASH SHORT AND OVER

There is an inherent danger in making change: Human beings make mistakes, especially when there are many customers to be waited on or when the business is temporarily short-handed. Because mistakes do happen, accounting records must be set up to cope with the situation. One reason that a business uses a cash register is to detect mistakes in handling cash. **If, after removing the Change Fund, the day's receipts are less than the register reading, then a cash shortage exists. Conversely, when the day's receipts are greater than the register reading, a cash overage exists.** Both shortages and overages are recorded in the same account, which is called Cash Short and Over. Shortages are considered an expense of operating a business, and therefore shortages are recorded on the debit side of the account. Overages are treated as another form of revenue, and therefore overages are recorded on the credit side of the account.

Let's say that on September 14, Roland's Delivery Services is faced with the following situation:

Cash Register Tape	Cash Count	Amount of the Change Fund
$1,515	$1,663	$150

After deducting the $150 in the Change Fund, Roland will deposit $1,513 ($1,663 – $150). Note that this amount is $2 less than the amount indicated by the cash register tape ($1,515 – $1,513); therefore, a $2 cash shortage exists. The following T accounts show how the accountant entered this transaction into the books:

Cash		Income from Services		Cash Short and Over
+	–	–	+	
1,513			1,515	2

FYI

The Cash Short and Over account may also be used to handle shortages and overages in the Petty Cash Fund.

FYI

Like the Income Summary account, which has no normal balance, the Cash Short and Over account has no signs.

The next day, September 15, the pendulum happens to swing in the other direction:

Cash Register Tape	Cash Count	Amount of the Change Fund
$1,578	$1,732	$150

The amount to be deposited is $1,582 ($1,732 – $150). This figure is $4 greater than the $1,578 in income from services indicated by the cash register tape. Thus, there is a $4 cash overage ($1,582 – $1,578). The analysis of this transaction is shown in the following T accounts:

Cash		Income from Services		Cash Short and Over
+	–	–	+	
1,582			1,578	4

Roland's Delivery Services' revenue for September 14 and 15 is recorded in the general journal as follows:

	GENERAL JOURNAL			PAGE _____
Date	Description	Post. Ref.	Debit	Credit
20—				
Sept. 14	Cash		1 5 1 3 00	
	Cash Short and Over		2 00	
	Income from Services			1 5 1 5 00
	To record revenue earned for the day			
	involving a cash shortage of $2.00.			
15	Cash		1 5 8 2 00	
	Income from Services			1 5 7 8 00
	Cash Short and Over			4 00
	To record revenue earned for the day			
	involving a cash overage of $4.00.			

As far as errors are concerned, one would think that shortages would be offset by overages. However, customers receiving change are more likely to report shortages than overages. **Consequently, the business usually experiences a greater number of shortages.** A business may set a tolerance level for the cashiers. If the shortages consistently exceed the level of tolerance, either fraud is being committed or somebody is making entirely too many careless mistakes.

Now let's summarize our discussion of the Cash Short and Over account by drawing the following conclusions from the illustration:

1. At the close of the business day, the business deposits the difference between the amount in the cash drawer and the amount in the Change Fund.

2. The business records the amount shown on the cash register tape as its income from services.

3. If the amount of the cash deposit disagrees with the record of receipts, Cash Short and Over makes up the difference. In the first situation just described, there was a shortage of $2, and so there was a debit to Cash Short and Over. In the second situation, there was an overage of $4, and so there was a credit to

Cash Short and Over. It is apparent that, as a result of these transactions, the account looks like this:

Cash Short and Over

Shortage	2	Overage	4

Throughout any fiscal period, the accountant must continually record shortages and overages in the Cash Short and Over account. Let's say that Roland's Delivery Services' final balance is $18 on the debit side. Roland's Delivery Services winds up with a net shortage of $18.

At the end of the fiscal period, **if the account has a debit balance or net shortage, the accountant classifies it as an expense and credits Cash Short and Over and debits Miscellaneous Expense, so that the amount is put in the income statement under Miscellaneous Expense.** The T account would look like this:

Cash Short and Over

Shortage	2	Overage	4
	4		1
	3		1
	7		2
	5		1
	2		2
	3		1
	4		
Bal.	**18**		

Conversely, **if the account has a credit balance or net overage, the accountant classifies it as a revenue account and debits Cash Short and Over and credits Miscellaneous Income, so that the amount is put in the income statement under Miscellaneous Income.** This is an exception to the policy of recording accounts under their exact account title in financial statements. Rather than attaching plus and minus signs to the Cash Short and Over account immediately, we wait until we find out its final balance, then make a journal entry to send the balance to the correct account classification.

CHAPTER REVIEW

Study & Practice

LEARNING OBJECTIVE

Describe the procedure for depositing checks.

The procedure for depositing checks consists of first endorsing each check and then completing a **deposit slip**. On the deposit slip, record the date, the amount of currency to be deposited, the amount and **ABA number** of each check, and the total amount to be deposited. The checks to be deposited should accompany the deposit slip.

PRACTICE EXERCISE 1

What are the three types of endorsements and how are they different from each other?

PRACTICE EXERCISE 1 SOLUTION

1. *Restrictive endorsement* – An endorsement, such as "Pay to the order of (name of bank), for deposit only," that restricts or limits any further negotiation of a check. It forces the check's deposit, because the endorsement is not valid for any other purpose.
2. *Blank endorsement* – An endorsement in which the holder (payee) of a check simply signs his or her name on the back of the check. There are no restrictions attached.
3. *Qualified endorsement* – An endorsement in which the holder (payee) of a check avoids future liability, in case the drawer of the check does not have sufficient funds to cover the check, by adding the words "Pay to the order of" and "without recourse" to the endorsement on the back of the check.

LEARNING OBJECTIVE

2 *Reconcile a bank statement.*

The standard form for a **bank reconciliation** is as follows:

Bank Statement Balance

Add:
Deposits in transit
Bank errors that understate the **bank statement** balance

Deduct:
Outstanding checks or electronic transfers
Bank errors that overstate the bank statement balance

Adjusted Bank Statement Balance
Ledger Balance of Cash

Add:
Notes collected
Interest income earned
Checkbook errors that understate the ledger balance of cash
Bank credit memos

Deduct:
Bank service charges
Checkbook errors that overstate the ledger balance of cash
NSF checks
Bank debit memos

Adjusted Ledger Balance of Cash

PRACTICE EXERCISE 2

The bank statement of M. C. Johnson Company indicates a balance of $7,428 as of July 31. The balance of the Cash account in Johnson's ledger as of that date is $6,872. Johnson's accountant has taken the following steps:

STEP 1. Verified that canceled checks were recorded correctly on the bank statement.

STEP 2. Noted that the deposit made on July 31 was not recorded on the bank statement, $2,071.

STEP 3. Noted outstanding checks: no. 1066, $1,075; no. 1099, $462; no. 1100, $605.

STEP 4. Noted credit memo: Note collected by the bank from L. Stewart, $500, not recorded in the journal. Noted debit memo: Collection charge and service charge not recorded in the journal, $15.

Based on the information above, prepare a bank reconciliation for M. C. Johnson Company.

PRACTICE EXERCISE 2 SOLUTION

M. C. Johnson Company
Bank Reconciliation
July 31, 20—

Bank Statement Balance		$7,428.00
Add: Deposit in transit (July 31)		2,071.00
		$9,499.00
Deduct: Outstanding checks		
No. 1066	$1,075.00	
No. 1099	462.00	
No. 1100	605.00	2,142.00
Adjusted Bank Statement Balance		$7,357.00
Ledger Balance of Cash		$6,872.00
Add: Note collected by bank		500.00
		$7,372.00
Deduct: Bank service and collection charges		15.00
Adjusted Ledger Balance of Cash		$7,357.00

LEARNING OBJECTIVE

3

Record the required journal entries from the bank reconciliation.

Journal entries for the Ledger Balance of Cash section are required. The entry for notes and interest collected is a debit to Cash and credits to Notes Receivable and Interest Income. The entry for a bank service charge is a debit to Miscellaneous Expense and a credit to Cash. The entry for an NSF check is a debit to Accounts Receivable and a credit to Cash.

PRACTICE EXERCISE 3

Prepare the necessary journal entries from the bank reconciliation in Practice Exercise 2 for M. C. Johnson Company.

PRACTICE EXERCISE 3 SOLUTION

		GENERAL JOURNAL			PAGE _____
Date		Description	Post. Ref.	Debit	Credit
20—					
July	31	Cash		5 0 0 00	
		Notes Receivable			5 0 0 00
		Non-interest-bearing note			
		signed by L. Stewart was			
		collected by the bank.			
	31	Miscellaneous Expense		1 5 00	
		Cash			1 5 00
		Service charge and collection			
		charge levied by bank.			

4 LEARNING OBJECTIVE

Record journal entries to establish and reimburse a Petty Cash Fund.

The entry to establish a **Petty Cash Fund** is a debit to Petty Cash Fund and a credit to Cash. The entry to reimburse the Petty Cash Fund consists of debits to the items for which payments from the Petty Cash Fund were made and one credit to Cash for the total payments.

PRACTICE EXERCISE 4

A Petty Cash Fund of $100 was established on October 1. At the end of the month, the following accounts were charged for expenditures from the Petty Cash Fund: Office Supplies Expense, $13.75; Delivery Expense, $15.00; Miscellaneous Expense, $36.00; B. Thomas, Drawing, $25.00. Record the journal entries for the establishment and reimbursement of the Petty Cash Fund.

PRACTICE EXERCISE 4 SOLUTION

		GENERAL JOURNAL			PAGE _____
Date		Description	Post. Ref.	Debit	Credit
20—					
Oct.	1	Petty Cash Fund		1 0 0 00	
		Cash			1 0 0 00
		Established a Petty Cash Fund.			
	31	Office Supplies Expense		1 3 75	
		Delivery Expense		1 5 00	
		Miscellaneous Expense		3 6 00	
		B. Thomas, Drawing		2 5 00	
		Cash			8 9 75
		Reimbursed the Petty Cash Fund.			

5 LEARNING OBJECTIVE

Complete petty cash vouchers and petty cash payments records.

A **petty cash voucher** is made out for each payment from the Petty Cash Fund. In the **petty cash payments record**, each voucher is listed and a notation is made concerning the accounts involved; also, an explanation of why the money was paid out is recorded. The petty cash payments record is used as a source of information for making the journal entry to reimburse the Petty Cash Fund.

PRACTICE EXERCISE 5

Answer True (T) or False (F) for the following statements:

_____ 1. A petty cash voucher must be used to account for every payment from the Petty Cash Fund.

_____ 2. A petty cash voucher constitutes a receipt signed by the person who authorized the payment and by the person who received payment.

_____ 3. The petty cash payments record is a type of journal.

_____ 4. The petty cash payments record is used as a basis for compiling information for the journal entry to reimburse the Petty Cash Fund.

PRACTICE EXERCISE 5 SOLUTION

1. T
2. T
3. F
4. T

6 LEARNING OBJECTIVE

Record the journal entries to establish a Change Fund.

The entry to establish the **Change Fund** is a debit to Change Fund and a credit to Cash.

PRACTICE EXERCISE 6

Journalize the entry to establish a Change Fund amounting to $150 on July 1.

PRACTICE EXERCISE 6 SOLUTION

			GENERAL JOURNAL		PAGE _____	
Date		Description	Post. Ref.	Debit	Credit	
20—						
July	1	Change Fund		1 5 0 00		
		Cash			1 5 0 00	
		Established a Change Fund.				

LEARNING OBJECTIVE

7 *Record journal entries for transactions involving Cash Short and Over.*

The Cash Short and Over account provides a way to keep a record of errors in making change. A debit balance in Cash Short and Over denotes a shortage, which is listed as Miscellaneous Expense; the entry is a debit to Miscellaneous Expense and a credit to Cash Short and Over. A credit balance in Cash Short and Over denotes an overage, which becomes Miscellaneous Income; the entry is a debit to Cash Short and Over and a credit to Miscellaneous Income.

PRACTICE EXERCISE 7

Journalize the entries to account for two bank deposits on June 29 and June 30. The amount of the Change Fund is $100.

a. On June 29, the cash register tape showed $950.86 in income from sales. The amount in the cash drawer was $1,051.86.
b. On June 30, the cash register tape showed $1,327.44 in income from sales. The amount in the cash drawer was $1,426.12.

PRACTICE EXERCISE 7 SOLUTION

	GENERAL JOURNAL				PAGE _____	
Date	Description	Post. Ref.	Debit		Credit	
20—						
June 29	Cash		9 5 1	86		
	Income from Sales				9 5 0	86
	Cash Short and Over				1	00
	To record revenue earned for the					
	day involving a cash overage					
	of $1.00.					
30	Cash		1 3 2 6	12		
	Cash Short and Over		1	32		
	Income from Sales				1 3 2 7	44
	To record revenue earned for the					
	day involving a cash shortage					
	of $1.32.					

Glossary

ABA number The number assigned by the American Bankers Association to a given bank. The first part of the number denotes the city or state in which the bank is located and the specific bank on which the check is drawn. The second part of the number indicates the Federal Reserve District in which the check is cleared and the routing number used by the Federal Reserve Bank. (p. 215)

ATMs (automated teller machines) Machines that enable depositors to make deposits, withdrawals, and transfers using a coded plastic card. (p. 217)

Bank reconciliation A process by which an accountant determines whether and why there is a difference between the balance shown on the bank statement and the balance of the Cash account in the business's general ledger. The object is to determine the adjusted (or true) balance of the Cash account. (p. 222)

Bank statement A periodic statement that a bank sends to the drawer/depositor of a checking account listing deposits received and checks paid by the bank, debit and credit memos, electronic transactions, and beginning and ending balances. (p. 219)

Blank endorsement An endorsement in which the holder (payee) of a check simply signs her or his name on the back of the check. There are no restrictions attached. (p. 218)

Canceled checks Checks issued by the depositor that have been paid (cleared) by the bank and listed on the bank statement. They are called canceled checks because they are canceled by a stamp or perforation, indicating that they have been paid. (p. 221)

Cash funds Separately held reserves of cash set aside for specific purposes. (p. 214)

Change Fund A cash fund used by a business to make change for customers who pay cash for goods or services. (p. 233)

Collections Payments collected by the bank and added to the customer's bank account in the form of a credit memorandum. (p. 222)

Denominations Varieties of coins and currency, such as quarters, dimes, and nickels and $1 and $5 bills and so on. (p. 231)

Deposit in transit A deposit not recorded on the bank statement because the deposit was made between the time of the bank's closing date for compiling items for its statement and the time the statement is received by the depositor; also known as a *late deposit*. (p. 222)

Deposit slips Printed forms provided by a bank on which customers can list all items being deposited; also known as *deposit tickets*. (p. 215)

Drawer The party who writes the check. (p. 218)

Electronic Funds Transfer (EFT) A transfer of funds initiated through an electronic terminal, such as a telephone, computer, or magnetic tape. (p. 217)

Endorsement The process by which the payee transfers ownership of the check to a bank or another party. A check must be endorsed when deposited in a bank, because the bank must have legal title to it in order to collect payment from the drawer of the check (the person or firm who wrote the check). In case the check cannot be collected, the endorser guarantees all subsequent holders (*exception:* an endorsement "without recourse"). (p. 217)

Errors Mistakes made by the customer or bank. (p. 223)

Interest income The amount earned from lending money to another person or business. (p. 222)

Internal control Plans and procedures built into the accounting system with the following objectives: (1) to protect assets against fraud and waste, (2) to provide accurate accounting data, (3) to promote efficient operation, and (4) to encourage adherence to management policies. (p. 213)

Ledger balance of cash The balance of the Cash account in the general ledger before it is reconciled with the bank statement. (p. 222)

MICR Magnetic ink character recognition; the characters the bank uses to print the number of the depositor's account and the bank's number at the bottom of checks and deposit slips. The bank also prints the amount of the check in MICR when the check is deposited. A number written in these characters can be read by electronic equipment used by banks in clearing checks. (p. 216)

NSF (not sufficient funds) check Check drawn against an account in which there are *not sufficient funds* and returned by the payee's bank to the drawer's bank because of nonpayment; also known as a *dishonored check*. (p. 222)

Outstanding checks Checks that have been written by the drawer and deducted on his or her records but have not reached the bank for payment and are not deducted from the bank balance by the time the bank issues its statement. (p. 222)

Payee The person to whom a check is payable. (p. 218)

Petty Cash Fund A cash fund used to make small, immediate cash payments. (p. 230)

Petty cash payments record A record indicating the amount of each petty cash voucher, the accounts to which it should be charged, and the purpose of the expenditure. (p. 232)

Petty cash voucher A form stating who requested cash from the Petty Cash Fund, signed by (1) the person in charge of the fund and (2) the person who received the cash, and indicating the purpose of the petty cash payment. (p. 231)

Promissory note A written promise to pay a definite sum at a definite future time. (p. 224)

Qualified endorsement An endorsement in which the holder (payee) of a check avoids future liability, in case the drawer of the check does not have sufficient funds to cover the check, by adding the words "Pay to the order of" and "without recourse" to the endorsement on the back of the check. (p. 218)

Restrictive endorsement An endorsement, such as "Pay to the order of (name of bank), for deposit only," that restricts or limits any further negotiation of a check. It forces the check's deposit, because the endorsement is not valid for any other purpose. (p. 218)

Service charge The fee the bank charges for handling checks, collections, and other items. It is in the form of a debit memorandum. (p. 222)

Signature card The form a depositor signs to give the bank a copy of the official signatures of any persons authorized to sign checks. The bank can use it to verify the depositors' signatures on checks. (p. 215)

CHAPTER ASSIGNMENTS

Discussion Questions

1. Why does a bank keep a signature card on file for your account(s)?

2. What is the purpose of endorsing a check?

3. Why is there generally a difference between the balance in the Cash account on the company's books and the balance on the bank statement?

4. Indicate whether the following items in a bank reconciliation should be (1) added to the Cash account balance, (2) deducted from the Cash account balance, (3) added to the bank statement balance, or (4) deducted from the bank statement balance.

   a. NSF check

   b. Deposit in transit

   c. Outstanding check

   d. Bank error charging the business's account with another company's check

   e. Bank service charge

5. Why is it necessary to make general journal entries for the ledger balance side of the bank reconciliation?

6. a. Why would a business use a Petty Cash Fund?

   b. Describe the entry needed to establish a $50 Petty Cash Fund and an entry to reimburse the fund.

7. a. What does a debit balance in Cash Short and Over mean?

   b. Where does a debit balance in Cash Short and Over appear in the financial statements?

   c. What does a credit balance in Cash Short and Over mean?

   d. Where does a credit balance in Cash Short and Over appear in the financial statements?

Exercises

EXERCISE 6-1 Fill in the missing amounts for the following bank reconciliation:

PRACTICE EXERCISE 2

Bank Reconciliation		
March 31, 20—		
Bank Statement Balance		$3,764.00
Add: Deposit in transit		(a)
		$4,031.00
Deduct: Outstanding checks		
No. 211	$212.00	
No. 225	(b)	
No. 228	318.00	850.00
Adjusted Bank Statement Balance		(c)
Ledger Balance of Cash		$2,837.00
Add: Note collected by bank		430.00
		(d)
Deduct: Bank service and collection charges	(e)	
NSF check from customer	74.00	86.00
Adjusted Ledger Balance of Cash		(f)

EXERCISE 6-2 The Ledger Balance of Cash section of the bank reconciliation for Lasha Company for July 31 follows.

PRACTICE EXERCISE 3

Ledger Balance of Cash		$6,360.00
Add: Note collected (principal $700.00, interest		
$17.50, signed by D. Dansky)	$717.50	
Error in recording Ck. No. 2225 payable to		
Denton Company (recorded check for		
$12 too much)	12.00	729.50
		$7,089.50
Deduct: NSF check from J. Kenyon	$ 95.00	
Bank service and collection charges	29.00	124.00
Adjusted Ledger Balance of Cash		$6,965.50

Journalize the entries required to bring the general ledger up to date as of July of this year.

EXERCISE 6-3 When the bank statement is received on December 3, it shows a balance, before reconciliation, of $3,600 as of November 30. After reconciliation, the adjusted balance is $2,500. If there was one deposit in transit amounting to $1,500, what was the total of the outstanding checks, assuming that there were no other adjustments to be made to the bank statement?

PRACTICE EXERCISE 2

EXERCISE 6-4 Place a check mark in the column that indicates the location of each item that would be found on a bank reconciliation. Assume that the checks written by the company are written correctly.

PRACTICE EXERCISE 2

Item	Add to Bank Statement Balance	Subtract from Bank Statement Balance	Add to Ledger Balance of Cash	Subtract from Ledger Balance of Cash
a. A check-printing charge				
b. An outstanding check				
c. A deposit for $197 listed incorrectly on the bank statement as $179				
d. A collection charge the bank made for a note it collected for its depositor				
e. A check written for $41.73 and recorded incorrectly in the checkbook as $41.37				
f. A deposit in transit				
g. An NSF check received from a customer				
h. A check written for $82.40 and recorded incorrectly in the checkbook as $820.40				

EXERCISE 6-5 Hosung Company's Cash account shows a balance of $801.65 as of August 31 of this year. The balance on the bank statement on that date is $1,383. Checks for $260.50, $425.10, and $331 are outstanding. The bank statement shows a check issued by another depositor for $237.25 (in other words, the bank made an error and charged Hosung Company for a check written by another company). The bank statement also shows an NSF check for $180 received from one of Hosung's customers. Service charges for the month were $18. What is the adjusted ledger balance of cash as of August 31?

PRACTICE EXERCISE 2

EXERCISE 6-6 Record entries in general journal form to record the following:
a. Established a Petty Cash Fund, $100. Issued Ck. No. 857.
b. Reimbursed the Petty Cash Fund for expenditures of $98: Store Supplies Expense, $38; Office Supplies Expense, $21; Miscellaneous Expense, $39. Issued Ck. No. 889.
c. Increased the amount of the fund by an additional $50. Issued Ck. No. 891.
d. Reimbursed the Petty Cash Fund for expenditures of $96.58: Store Supplies Expense, $41.68; Delivery Expense, $35; Miscellaneous Expense, $19.90. Issued Ck. No. 936.

PRACTICE EXERCISE 4

EXERCISE 6-7 At the end of the day, the cash register tape lists $881.40 as total income from services. Cash on hand consists of $18.25 in coins, $433.60 in currency, $100 in traveler's checks, and $427 in customers' checks. The amount of the Change Fund is $100. In general journal form, record the entry to record the day's cash revenue.

PRACTICE EXERCISE 7

EXERCISE 6-8
a. Describe the entries that have been posted to the following accounts after the Change Fund was established.

PRACTICE EXERCISES 6,7

Change Fund		Sales		Cash	
200		Jan. 3 1,520		Jan. 3 1,522	
		4 1,421		4 1,418	
		6 1,665		6 1,664	

Cash Short and Over		
Jan. 4 3	Jan. 3	2
6 1		

b. How will the balance of Cash Short and Over be reported on the income statement?

Problem Set A

For additional help, see the demonstration problem at the beginning of each chapter in your Working Papers.

PROBLEM 6-1A Arthur's Men's Shop deposits all receipts in the bank each evening and makes all payments by check. On November 30 its ledger balance of cash is

$2,375.05. The bank statement balance of cash as of November 30 is $2,784.77. Use the following information to reconcile the bank statement:

a. The reconciliation for October, the previous month, showed three checks outstanding on October 31: no. 1417 for $95, no. 1420 for $125.87, and no. 1422 for $136. Checks no. 1417 and 1422 were returned with the November bank statement; however, check no. 1420 was not returned.

b. Checks no. 1500 for $155, no. 1517 for $132, no. 1518 for $218, and no. 1519 for $128.85 were written during November and have not been returned by the bank.

c. A deposit of $945 was placed in the night depository on November 30 and did not appear on the bank statement.

d. The canceled checks were compared with the entries in the checkbook, and it was observed that check no. 1487, for $89, was written correctly, payable to M. A. Golden, the owner, for personal use, but was recorded in the checkbook as $98.

e. Included in the bank statement was a bank debit memo for service charges, $29.

f. A bank credit memo was also enclosed for the collection of a note signed by C. G. Tolson, $615, including $600 principal and $15 interest.

Check Figure
Adjusted ledger balance of cash, $2,970.05

Required

1. Prepare a bank reconciliation as of November 30, assuming that the debit and credit memos have not been recorded.

2. Record the necessary entries in general journal form.

PROBLEM 6-2A On May 1 of this year, Ellsworth and Company established a Petty Cash Fund. The following petty cash transactions took place during the month:

May 1 Cashed check no. 956 for $150 to establish a Petty Cash Fund, and put the $150 in a locked drawer in the office.

3 Bought postage stamps, $8.80, voucher no. 1 (Miscellaneous Expense).

4 Issued voucher no. 2 for taxi fare, $12 (Miscellaneous Expense).

6 Issued voucher no. 3 for delivery charges on outgoing parts, $15.

9 B. Ellsworth, the owner, withdrew $25 for personal use, voucher no. 4.

13 Paid $8.29 for postage, voucher no. 5 (Miscellaneous Expense).

19 Bought pens for office, $6, voucher no. 6.

23 Paid $3.59 for a box of staples, voucher no. 7.

28 Paid $15 for window cleaning service, voucher no. 8 (Miscellaneous Expense).

29 Paid $2 for pencils for office, voucher no. 9.

31 Issued for cash check no. 1098 for $95.68 to reimburse Petty Cash Fund.

Check Figure
Office Supplies Expense, $11.59

Required

1. Journalize the entry establishing the Petty Cash Fund in the general journal.

2. Record the disbursements of petty cash in the petty cash payments record.

3. Journalize the summarizing entry to reimburse the Petty Cash Fund.

PROBLEM 6-3A Ellie Harrod, owner of Harrod's Dry Cleaners, makes bank deposits in the night depository at the close of each business day. The following information for the last four days of July is available.

	July			
	28	29	30	31
Cash register tape	$895.20	$ 977.40	$884.50	$1,027.25
Cash count	993.50	1,075.80	986.60	1,124.40

Required

In general journal form, record the cash deposit for each day, assuming that there is a $100 Change Fund.

Check Figure
Cash Short and Over, July 31, $2.85 cash shortage

PROBLEM 6-4A On August 31, Baginski and Company receives its bank statement (shown below). The company deposits its receipts in the bank and makes all payments by check. The debit memo for $95 is for an NSF check written by L. Pitts. Check no. 925 for $47, payable to Jardin Company (a creditor), was recorded in the checkbook and journal as $74.

The ledger balance of cash as of August 31 is $1,563. Outstanding checks as of August 31 are: no. 928, $150; no. 929, $292. The accountant notes that the deposit of August 31 for $599 did not appear on the bank statement.

LO 2,3
GL

Required

1. Prepare a bank reconciliation as of August 31, assuming that the debit memos have not been recorded.
2. Record the necessary journal entries.
3. Complete the bank form to determine the adjusted balance of cash.

Check Figure
Adjusted ledger balance of cash, $1,480

PEABODY NATIONAL BANK

STATEMENT OF ACCOUNT	Baginski and Company 416 Seneca Avenue Kansas City, Missouri 64102	ACCOUNT NO. 152-655-217 STATEMENT DATE August 1–31, 20—

SUMMARY	
Balance Last Statement	$961.00
Amount of Checks and Debits	$2,289.00
Number of Checks	11
Amount of Deposits and Credits	$2,651.00
Number of Deposits	7
Balance This Statement	$1,323.00

CHECKS/ OTHER DEBITS	CHECKS	CHECK NUMBER	DATE POSTED	AMOUNT	CHECK NUMBER	DATE POSTED	AMOUNT
		917	8-04	172.00	923	8-09	621.00
		918	8-04	76.00	924	8-17	37.00
		919	8-05	146.00	925	8-17	47.00
		920	8-07	206.00	926	8-23	454.00
		921	8-07	139.00	927	8-28	94.00
		922	8-07	200.00			

OTHER DEBITS	DESCRIPTION	DATE POSTED	AMOUNT
	DM NSF check	8-31	95.00
	DM Service charge	8-31	15.00

DEPOSITS/ OTHER CREDITS	DEPOSITS	DATE POSTED	AMOUNT	DATE POSTED	AMOUNT
		8-02	326.00	8-18	419.00
		8-05	412.00	8-24	398.00
		8-09	437.00	8-28	291.00
		8-14	368.00		

PLEASE EXAMINE THIS STATEMENT CAREFULLY. REPORT ANY POSSIBLE ERRORS WITHIN 10 DAYS.

CODE SYMBOLS

CM Credit Memo   DM Debit Memo   OD Overdraft   EC Error Correction

Problem Set B

For additional help, see the demonstration problem at the beginning of each chapter in your Working Papers.

2,3

PROBLEM 6-1B Merkle Company deposits all receipts in the bank each evening and makes all payments by check. On November 30 its ledger balance of cash is $3,219.72. The bank statement balance of cash as of November 30 is $3,490.72. You are given the following information with which to reconcile the bank statement:

a. A deposit of $525.30 was placed in the night depository on November 30 and did not appear on the bank statement.
b. The reconciliation for October, the previous month, showed three checks outstanding on October 31: no. 728 for $80.20, no. 731 for $129, and no. 732 for $145.34. Checks no. 728 and 731 were returned with the November bank statement; however, check no. 732 was not returned.
c. Checks no. 743 for $42, no. 744 for $16.20, no. 745 for $119, and no. 746 for $35.26 were written during November but were not returned by the bank.
d. A $150 personal withdrawal by C. R. Merkle, the owner, using an ATM, was not recorded.
e. Included in the bank statement was a bank debit memo for service charges, $19.
f. A bank credit memo was also enclosed for the collection of a note signed by O. L. Leland, $607.50, including $600 principal and $7.50 interest

Check Figure
Adjusted ledger balance of cash, $3,658.22

Required
1. Prepare a bank reconciliation as of November 30, assuming that the debit and credit memos have not been recorded.
2. Record the necessary entries in general journal form.

4,5 **LO**

PROBLEM 6-2B On March 1 of this year, Stowe Company established a Petty Cash Fund, and the following petty cash transactions took place during the month:

Mar. 1 Cashed check no. 314 for $100 to establish a Petty Cash Fund, and put the $100 in a locked drawer in the office.

4 Issued voucher no. 1 for taxi fare, $7.60 (Miscellaneous Expense).

7 Issued voucher no. 2 for memo pads, $6.50 (Office Supplies Expense).

9 Paid $21.50 for an advertisement in a college basketball program, voucher no. 3.

16 Bought postage stamps, $8.80, voucher no. 4 (Miscellaneous Expense).

20 Paid $10 to have snow removed from office front sidewalk, voucher no. 5 (Miscellaneous Expense).

25 Issued voucher no. 6 for delivery charge, $12.

28 R. C. Stowe, the owner, withdrew $20 for personal use, voucher no. 7.

29 Paid $4.20 for postage, voucher no. 8 (Miscellaneous Expense).

30 Paid $5.90 for delivery charge, voucher no. 9.

31 Issued for cash check no. 372 for $96.50 to reimburse Petty Cash Fund.

Check Figure
Office Supplies Expense, $6.50

Required
1. Journalize the entry establishing the Petty Cash Fund in the general journal.
2. Record the disbursements of petty cash in the petty cash payments record.
3. Journalize the summarizing entry to reimburse the Petty Cash Fund.

PROBLEM 6-3B Roberta Felino, owner of Roberta's Beauty Salon, makes bank deposits in the night depository at the close of each business day. The following information for the first four days of April is available.

	April			
	1	**2**	**3**	**4**
Cash register tape	$386.75	$582.65	$586.65	$623.25
Cash count	485.50	685.75	685.75	726.15

Required

In general journal form, record the cash deposit for each day, assuming that there is a $100 Change Fund.

Check Figure
Cash Short and Over, April 3, $0.90 cash shortage

PROBLEM 6-4B On August 2, Northern Motel receives its bank statement (shown below). The company deposits its receipts in the bank and makes all payments by check. The debit memo for $37 is for an NSF check written by T. R. Royce. Check no.

STANTON NATIONAL BANK							
STATEMENT OF ACCOUNT	**Northern Motel** 423 E. Long Avenue Rockford, IL 61104				ACCOUNT NO. 750-135-772 STATEMENT DATE July 1–31, 20—		

	SUMMARY	Balance Last Statement	$1,153.80
		Amount of Checks and Debits	$2,105.91
		Number of Checks	14
		Amount of Deposits and Credits	$2,528.17
		Number of Deposits	7
		Balance This Statement	$1,576.06

CHECKS/ OTHER DEBITS	CHECKS	CHECK NUMBER	DATE POSTED	AMOUNT	CHECK NUMBER	DATE POSTED	AMOUNT
		1617	7-03	75.50	1624	7-08	120.00
		1618	7-03	164.00	1625	7-09	429.60
		1619	7-03	124.20	1626	7-12	37.40
		1620	7-05	137.20	1627	7-14	38.49
		1621	7-06	236.25	1628	7-22	182.71
		1622	7-06	159.89	1629	7-25	96.87
		1623	7-08	244.50	1630	7-26	19.20

	OTHER DEBITS	DESCRIPTION		DATE POSTED	AMOUNT
		DM NSF check		7-22	37.00
		DM Service charge		7-31	23.00

DEPOSITS/ OTHER CREDITS	DEPOSITS	DATE POSTED	AMOUNT	DATE POSTED	AMOUNT
		7-03	491.50	7-15	291.76
		7-06	415.72	7-18	142.90
		7-09	439.16	7-28	368.93
		7-11	378.20		

PLEASE EXAMINE THIS STATEMENT CAREFULLY. REPORT ANY POSSIBLE ERRORS WITHIN 10 DAYS.

CODE SYMBOLS

CM Credit Memo   DM Debit Memo   OD Overdraft   EC Error Correction

Check Figure
Adjusted ledger balance of cash,
$1,831.30

1617 for $75.50, payable to Mitchel Company (a creditor), was incorrectly recorded in the checkbook and journal as $57.50.

The ledger balance of Cash as of July 31 is $1,909.30. Outstanding checks as of July 31 are: no. 1631, $118.20; no. 1632, $78.20; no. 1633, $178.36. The accountant notes that the July 31 deposit of $630 did not appear on the bank statement.

Required
1. Prepare a bank reconciliation as of July 31, assuming that the debit memos have not been recorded.
2. Record the necessary journal entries.
3. Complete the bank form to determine the adjusted balance of cash.

ACTIVITIES

CONSIDER AND COMMUNICATE

As the new bookkeeper at a small business, you find the Petty Cash Fund is accessed by several people, usually without anyone leaving any written explanation of what the money was used for. The amount of cash does not match the recorded amount of the fund. Explain how the Petty Cash Fund operation can be made more efficient in order to maintain an accurate accounting of how the money is used.

WHAT'S WRONG WITH THIS PICTURE?

You work as a cashier in a service business. Some days you are short of cash at the end of the day, and some days you have more cash than the cash register tape says was earned. You are embarrassed when your cash is short and don't want the owner to know, so you use your own money to make up the difference. On days when you are over, you keep the difference to help pay back what you paid to cover your shortages. What do you think of this practice and why?

Employee Earnings and Deductions

7

WHY IT MATTERS

RECREATIONAL EQUIPMENT INC. (REI), Sumner, Washington

Attracting and retaining the best employees are crucial to operating a business. Employees will join a company based upon opportunities for advancement, training, and company culture as well as the salary and benefits provided.

One business that is often listed in *Fortune* magazine's "100 Best Companies to Work For" is Recreational Equipment Inc. (REI). REI is committed to inspire, educate, and outfit its customers for a lifetime of outdoor adventure. REI offers competitive salaries as well as benefits, including paid sabbaticals, an onsite fitness center, health-care coverage, telecommuting, and a compressed workweek.

The accounting department at REI is responsible for determining salaries or wages and benefits for employees, calculating payroll deductions for taxes and other expenses, and ensuring that company payrolls are processed in a timely and accurate manner. In this chapter, you will learn how companies like REI complete the payroll records for their employees.

LEARNING OBJECTIVES

After you have completed this chapter, you will be able to do the following:

1 Understand the role of income tax laws that affect payroll deductions and contributions.

2 Calculate total earnings based on an hourly, salary, piece-rate, or commission basis.

3 Determine deductions from gross pay, such as federal income tax withheld, Social Security tax, and Medicare tax, to calculate net pay.

4 Complete a payroll register.

5 Journalize the payroll entry from a payroll register.

6 Maintain employees' individual earnings records.

ACCOUNTING LANGUAGE

Calendar year *(p. 263)*

Current Tax Payment Act *(p. 256)*

Employee *(p. 255)*

Employee's individual earnings record *(p. 270)*

Employee's Withholding Allowance Certificate (Form W-4) *(p. 260)*

Exemption *(p. 260)*

Fair Labor Standards Act *(p. 255)*

FICA taxes *(p. 261)*

Gross pay *(p. 254)*

Independent contractor *(p. 255)*

Medicare taxes *(p. 263)*

Net pay *(p. 254)*

Payroll bank account *(p. 269)*

Payroll register *(p. 264)*

Pre-tax deductions *(p. 259)*

Social Security Act of 1935 *(p. 256)*

Social Security taxes *(p. 263)*

Taxable earnings *(p. 260)*

Wage-bracket tax tables *(p. 261)*

Withholding allowance *(p. 260)*

Workers' compensation laws *(p. 257)*

Until now, we have been recording employees' earnings as a debit to Salary or Wages Expense and a credit to Cash, but we have really been talking only about **gross pay**—the total amount of an employee's pay before deductions. We have not mentioned the various deductions that we all know are taken out of our gross pay before we get to the **net pay**, or take-home pay. In this chapter, we will talk about types of deductions and how to enter them in the payroll records, and about journal entries to record the payroll and pay the employees.

OBJECTIVES OF PAYROLL RECORDS AND ACCOUNTING

There are two primary reasons to maintain accurate payroll records. First, we must collect the data necessary to compute the compensation for each employee for each payroll period.

Second, we must provide the information needed to complete the various government reports—federal and state—required of all employers. All business enterprises, both large and small, are required by law to withhold certain amounts from employees' pay for taxes, to make payments to government agencies by specific deadlines, and to submit reports on official forms. Because governments impose penalties if the requirements are not met, employers are vitally concerned with payroll accounting.

The employer is required to keep records of the following information:

1. **Personal data on employee** Name, address, Social Security number, date of birth
2. **Data on wage payments** Dates and amounts of payments, and payroll periods
3. **Amount of taxable wages paid** Dates and amount earned year to date for the calendar year involved
4. **Amount of tax withheld from each employee's earnings by pay period**

Many companies use software, such as Excel or Quickbooks, or outside payroll services, such as ADP or Paychex, to assist with their payroll accounting.

EMPLOYER/EMPLOYEE RELATIONSHIPS

Payroll accounting is concerned with employees and their compensation, withholdings, records, reports, and taxes. There is an important distinction between an employee and an independent contractor. An **employee** is one who is under the direction and control of the employer, such as a salesperson, administrative assistant, vice president, controller, and so on. An **independent contractor** is engaged for a definite job or service and may choose his or her own means of doing the work. Payments made to independent contractors are in the form of fees or charges. Independent contractors submit bills or invoices for the work they do. The payment is not subject to any withholding or payroll taxes by the person or firm paying that invoice. Such taxes are the responsibility of the independent contractor. Businesses are required to give an independent contractor an IRS Form 1099-MISC for the year if the fees paid exceed $600. If the worker is classified as an independent contractor and should be an employee, the IRS will impose substantial penalties on the employer. The IRS has published guidelines to determine the classification of workers. For more information, go to www.irs.gov.

FYI

Examples of independent contractors include a plumber, a lawyer, or a CPA that offers his or her services to the public.

LAWS AFFECTING EMPLOYEES' PAY DEDUCTIONS

Both federal and state laws require the employer to act as a collecting agent and deduct specified amounts from employees' gross earnings. The employer sends the withholdings to the appropriate government agencies, along with reports substantiating the figures. Let's look at some of the more important laws that pertain to employees' pay.

1 LEARNING OBJECTIVE

Understand the role of income tax laws that affect payroll deductions and contributions.

Fair Labor Standards Act

The **Fair Labor Standards Act** of 1938 is referred to as "the Act" or "FLSA." The Act provides for minimum standards for both wages and overtime. Included in the Act are also provisions related to child labor and equal pay for equal work. In addition, the Act exempts specified employees or groups of employees from the application of certain of its provisions. Details of the Act may be read at www.opm.gov.

Federal Income Tax Withholding

The **Current Tax Payment Act**, passed in 1943, requires employers not only to withhold the tax and then pay it to the U.S. Treasury but also to keep records of the names and addresses of persons employed, their earnings and withholdings, and the amounts and dates of payment. The employer has to submit reports to the Internal Revenue Service on a quarterly basis (Form 941) and to the employee on an annual basis (W-2 form). We will discuss these reports and the related deposits in Chapter 8.

FICA Taxes (Employees' Share)

The **Social Security Act of 1935** began as an attempt to provide retired workers with benefits based upon their work history. Several amendments have added benefits for spouses and minor children of retired workers, disability insurance, increasing the age when benefits may be collected, Medicare, and supplemental security income.

Currently, FICA consists of Social Security and Medicare. At the writing of this text, employees contribute 6.2 percent (0.062) on the first $106,800 earned in a calendar year for Social Security. Employees contribute 1.45 percent (0.0145) on all earnings in a calendar year with no limit for Medicare. Throughout this chapter, we will use these percentages and earnings limitations for our calculations.

LAWS AFFECTING EMPLOYER'S PAYROLL TAX CONTRIBUTIONS (PAYROLL TAX EXPENSE)

Certain payroll taxes, based on the total wages paid to employees, are levied on the employer. Let's look at some of the more important laws that pertain to the pay of employees.

FICA Taxes (Employer's Share)

The employer has to match the amount of FICA taxes withheld from the employees' wages, and the employer's share is recorded under Payroll Tax Expense. Every three months the employer has to submit reports to the U.S. Treasury, recording the information on Form 941, the same form that is used to report the income tax withheld. The employer's payment to the Internal Revenue Service consists of (1) the employee's share of the FICA taxes, (2) the employer's matching portion of the FICA taxes, and (3) the employee's income tax withheld. We will talk about this in detail in Chapter 8.

State Unemployment Taxes (SUTA)

Each state is responsible for paying its own unemployment compensation benefits. The revenue provided by state unemployment taxes is used exclusively for this purpose. However, there is considerable variation among the states concerning the tax rates and the amount of taxable income. **This tax is paid by employers only.** Most states, under a State Unemployment Tax Act, charge their employers a percentage of the first $7,000 based on the taxable income stipulated in the Federal Unemployment Tax Act. In this text, we will use 5.4 percent (0.054) of the first $7,000. States require employers to file reports on a quarterly, or three-month, basis. Included in these reports are a listing of employees' names, Social Security numbers, amounts of wages paid to each employee, and computations of unemployment taxes.

Federal Unemployment Tax Act (FUTA)

The purpose of the Federal Unemployment Tax Act is to provide financial support for the maintenance of government-run employment offices throughout the country. **FUTA taxes are paid by employers only**. Generally this includes all employers except nonprofit schools and charities.

The federal unemployment tax is based on the total earnings of each employee during the calendar year. For the examples and problems in this text, we will use the current federal unemployment tax rate of 0.8 percent (0.008) of the first $7,000 of earnings of each employee during the calendar year. Reports to the federal government (Form 940) must be submitted annually. We will discuss these reports in Chapter 8.

Workers' Compensation Laws

Workers' compensation laws protect employees and their dependents against losses due to death or injury incurred on the job. Most states require employers either to contribute to a state compensation insurance fund or to buy similar insurance from a private insurance company. The employer ordinarily pays the cost of the insurance premiums. The premium rates vary according to the degree of danger inherent in each job category and the employer's number of accidents. The employer has to keep records of job descriptions and classifications as well as claims of insured persons.

The following table presents a summary of the various payroll taxes and who is responsible for each.

Employee Pays	Employer Pays
Federal income tax withholding (based on income tax rates)	FICA taxes
FICA taxes	– Social Security (6.2% of earnings up to $106,800.)
– Social Security (6.2% of earnings up to $106,800)	– Medicare (1.45% of all earnings)
– Medicare (1.45% of all earnings)	Federal and state unemployment taxes
	Workers' compensation

HOW EMPLOYEES GET PAID

Employees may be paid salaries or wages, depending on the type of work and the period of time covered. Money paid to a person for managerial or administrative services is usually called a salary, and the time period covered is generally a month or a year. Money paid for either skilled or unskilled labor is usually called wages, and the time period covered is hours or weeks. Wages may also be paid on a piece-work basis (or per-unit basis, such as number of boxes of strawberries picked). A company may also supplement an employee's salary or wage by other benefits such as commissions, bonuses, cost-of-living adjustments, and profit-sharing plans. As a rule, employees are paid by check or by direct deposit to their bank account. However, their compensation may also include amounts for items such as personal use of company automobiles, athletic club dues, or holiday gift cards. When the compensation is in these forms, you must determine the fair value of the property or service given in payment for an employee's labor. See Publication 15-B, Employer's Tax Guide to Fringe Benefits, located on the IRS's Web site at www.irs.gov, for more information on what fringe benefits are taxable and how to value them.

Calculating Total Earnings

When compensation is based on the amount of time worked, the accountant must have a record of the number of hours worked by each employee. When there are only a few employees, this can be accomplished by means of a time book. When there are many employees, time clocks or other electronic time-keeping systems are used.

Employees may be paid weekly, biweekly, semimonthly, or monthly. Biweekly is every two weeks. Semimonthly is twice a month.

Wages

Consider Mark Anderson, who works for Green Sales Company. His regular rate of pay is $22.95 per hour. The company pays time-and-a-half for hours worked in excess of 40 per week. In addition, it pays him double time for any work he does on Sundays and holidays. Anderson has a ½-hour lunch break during an 8½-hour day. He is not paid for the lunch break nor is he paid for minutes before 8:00 A.M. or after 4:30 P.M. unless hours of overtime are authorized in advance. His time card for the week is shown in Figure 1.

Anderson's gross wages can be computed by one of two methods. The first method works like this:

40 hours at straight time	40 × $22.95 per hour =	$ 918.00
2 hours overtime on Thursday	2 × $34.43 per hour =	68.86
($22.95 × 1.5 = $34.43)		
1 hour overtime on Friday	1 × $34.43 per hour =	34.43
3 hours overtime on Saturday	3 × $34.43 per hour =	103.29
Total hours and gross wages	46	$1,124.58

The second method of calculating gross wages is often used when it is necessary to identify or track overtime premium.

46 hours at straight time	46 × $22.95 per hour =	$1,055.70
Overtime premium:		
6 hours overtime ($22.95 × 0.5 = $11.48)	6 × $11.48 per hour =	68.88
Total hours and gross wages	52	$1,124.58

Salaries

Employees who are paid a regular salary may also be entitled to extra pay for overtime. It is necessary to figure out their regular hourly rate of pay before you can determine their overtime rate. Consider Madeline Huan, who receives a salary of $4,350 per month. She is entitled to overtime pay for all hours worked in excess of 40 during a week at time-and-a-half her regular hourly rate. This past week she worked 44 hours, so we calculate her gross pay as follows:

$4,350 per month × 12 months	= $52,200 per year
$52,200 per year ÷ 52 weeks	= $1,003.85 per week
$1,003.85 per week ÷ 40 hours	= $25.10 per regular hour
$25.10 per regular hour × 1.5	= $37.65 per overtime hour

Earnings for 44 hours:		
40 hours at straight time (as calculated above)	=	$1,003.85
4 hours overtime	(4 × $37.65) =	150.60
Total gross earnings		$1,154.45

A shortcut to determine the hourly rate is to divide the annual salary by 2,080 (the standard work hours in a year). In this case, the calculation would be ($4,350 × 12) ÷ 2,080 = $25.10.

TIME CARD

Name Anderson, Mark

Week ended Oct. 7, 20—

Day	In	Out	In	Out	Hours Worked	
					Regular	Overtime
Mon	7 57	12 00	12 20	4 32	8	
Tue	7 56	12 06	12 36	4 37	8	
Wed	7 57	12 02	12 31	4 31	8	
Thu	8 00	12 11	12 40	6 32	8	2
Fri	8 00	12 03	12 33	5 33	8	1
Sat	7 59	11 02				3
Sun						

FIGURE 1

Time card for Mark Anderson

Piece-Rate

Workers under the piece-rate system are paid at the rate of so much per unit of production. For example, John Joseph, a strawberry picker, is paid $3 for each box of strawberries picked. If he picks 24 boxes during the day, his total earnings are $24 \times \$3 = \$72$.

Commissions

Some salespersons are paid on a purely commission basis. However, a more common arrangement is a salary plus a commission or bonus. Assume that Lora Brown receives an annual salary of $44,000. Her employer agrees to pay her a 5 percent commission on all sales during the year in excess of $200,000. Her sales for the year total $445,000. Her commission is $12,250 [($445,000 − $200,000) × 0.05]. Therefore, her total earnings are $56,250 ($44,000 + $12,250).

DEDUCTIONS FROM TOTAL EARNINGS

Anyone who has ever earned a paycheck has encountered some of the many types of deductions. Total earnings minus deductions equal net pay. The most common deductions are for

1. Federal income tax withholding
2. State income tax withholding
3. FICA taxes (Social Security and Medicare), employee's share
4. Union dues
5. Medical insurance premiums and medical expenses under a flexible spending plan
6. Contributions to a charitable organization, such as United Way
7. Repayment of personal loans from the company
8. Savings through the company 401(k) plan
9. Dependent care expenses under a flexible spending plan (subject to a $5,000 limit)

Medical insurance premiums, medical expenses, and dependent care expenses under a flexible spending plan and 401(k) deductions are usually **pre-tax deductions**. If a deduction is pre-tax, the employee does not have to pay income tax on the amount withheld for federal income tax and sometimes FICA taxes. For example, if Lynn

LEARNING OBJECTIVE 3

Determine deductions from gross pay, such as federal income tax withheld, Social Security tax, and Medicare tax, to calculate net pay.

Workers paid by the piece-rate system are paid according to how much they produce. Here, the number of boxes of strawberries picked determines the worker's total compensation.

Langseth has a weekly salary of $4,000 and the company deducts $200 for medical premiums paid for Lynn's dependents, her payroll subject to income tax is $3,800, not $4,000. If Lynn also contributes $100 to charity, her payroll subject to income tax is still $3,800 as the charitable deduction is not a pre-tax deduction.

Employees' Federal Income Tax Withholding

Employers are required not only to withhold employees' taxes and then pay them to the U.S. Treasury but also to keep records of the names and addresses of persons employed, their **taxable earnings** (the earnings subject to tax) and withholdings, and the amounts and dates of payment.

FYI

Federal tax rates change frequently, but the procedure stays the same. We will use the tax table given in this chapter for all computations.

The amount of federal income tax withheld from an employee's earnings depends on the amount of his or her total earnings, marital status, and number of withholding allowances claimed. A **withholding allowance** is an amount of an individual's earnings that is exempt from income taxes (nontaxable). An employee is entitled to one personal allowance for the taxpayer, one for his or her spouse, and one for each dependent. An **exemption** is an amount of an employee's annual earnings not subject to income tax. Each employee has to fill out an **Employee's Withholding Allowance Certificate (Form W-4)**, shown in Figure 2. The employer retains this form as authorization to withhold money for the employee's federal income tax.

Publication 15 (Circular E), Employer's Tax Guide, and Publication 15-T

Publication 15 (Circular E) contains the rules for depositing federal income, Social Security, and Medicare taxes, while Publication 15-T contains the withholding tables for these taxes. They are regularly updated to reflect changes in tax laws and withholding rates. Publication 15 also describes filing requirements for official

Form **W-4**	**Employee's Withholding Allowance Certificate**	OMB No. 1545-0074
Department of the Treasury Internal Revenue Service	▶ **Whether you are entitled to claim a certain number of allowances or exemption from withholding is subject to review by the IRS. Your employer may be required to send a copy of this form to the IRS.**	20**XX**

1 Type or print your first name and middle initial. **Mark E.**	Last name **Anderson**	2 Your social security number **543 24 1680**

Home address (number and street or rural route) **1104 Rosewood Street**	3 ☐ Single ☒ Married ☐ Married, but withhold at higher Single rate. **Note.** If married, but legally separated, or spouse is a nonresident alien, check the "Single" box.
City or town, state, and ZIP code **Bangor, Maine 04401**	4 If your last name differs from that shown on your social security card, check here. You must call 1-800-772-1213 for a new card. ▶ ☐

5 Total number of allowances you are claiming (from line **H** above **or** from the applicable worksheet on page 2) . . . . **5** | **1**

6 Additional amount, if any, you want withheld from each paycheck . . . . **6** $

7 I claim exemption from withholding for 20XX, and I certify that I meet **both** of the following conditions for exemption.
 • Last year I had a right to a refund of **all** federal income tax withheld because I had **no** tax liability **and**
 • This year I expect a refund of **all** federal income tax withheld because I expect to have **no** tax liability.
 If you meet both conditions, write "Exempt" here . . . . ▶ | **7**

Under penalties of perjury, I declare that I have examined this certificate and to the best of my knowledge and belief, it is true, correct, and complete.

Employee's signature (Form is not valid unless you sign it.) ▶ *Mark E. Anderson*   Date ▶ *January 2, 20XX*

8 Employer's name and address (Employer: Complete lines 8 and 10 only if sending to the IRS.)	9 Office code (optional)	10 Employer identification number (EIN)

For Privacy Act and Paperwork Reduction Act Notice, see page 2.   Cat. No. 10220Q   Form **W-4** (20XX)

FIGURE 2

Employee's Withholding Allowance Certificate (Form W-4) for Mark Anderson

employer reports. Both Publication 15 (Circular E) and Publication 15-T are provided free of charge by the Internal Revenue Service and are available on the Internet at www.irs.gov. Accountants responsible for preparation of payroll registers and forms should be familiar with the contents of these publications.

The **wage-bracket tax tables** cover monthly, semimonthly, biweekly, weekly, and daily payroll periods. The tables are also subdivided on the basis of marital status. To determine the federal income tax withheld, perform the following steps:

STEP 1. Locate the wage bracket in the first two columns of the table.

STEP 2. Find the column for the number of allowances claimed and read down this column until you get to the appropriate wage-bracket line.

A portion of the weekly federal income tax withholding table for married persons is reproduced in Figure 3 on pages 262–263.

Assume that Mark Anderson, who claims one allowance as of the October 7 payroll, has gross wages of $1,124.58 for the week. As $1,124.58 falls in the $1,120–$1,130 bracket, you can see from the table that $104 should be withheld.

Note the headings of the bracket columns: "At least" and "But less than." A strict interpretation of the $1,120–$1,130 bracket really means $1,120–$1,129.99. Therefore, if Anderson's salary were $1,130, it would fall into the $1,130–$1,140 bracket.

Employees' State Income Tax Withholding

Many states that levy state income taxes also furnish employers with withholding tables. Other states use a fixed percentage of the federal income tax withholding as the amount to be withheld for state taxes. In our illustration, we assume that the amount of each employee's state income tax deduction is 20 percent (0.20) of that employee's federal income tax deduction.

Employees' FICA Taxes Withholding (Social Security and Medicare)

The Federal Insurance Contributions Act provides for retirement pensions after a worker reaches age 62, disability benefits for any worker who becomes disabled (and for her or his dependents), and a health insurance program after age 65 (Medicare). Both the employee and the employer must pay **FICA taxes**, which are commonly

MARRIED Persons—WEEKLY Payroll Period
(For Wages Paid Through December 2009)

If the wages are—		And the number of withholding allowances claimed is—										
At least	But less than	0	1	2	3	4	5	6	7	8	9	10
		The amount of income tax to be withheld is—										
$0	$310	$0	$0	$0	$0	$0	$0	$0	$0	$0	$0	$0
310	320	1	0	0	0	0	0	0	0	0	0	0
320	330	2	0	0	0	0	0	0	0	0	0	0
330	340	3	0	0	0	0	0	0	0	0	0	0
340	350	4	0	0	0	0	0	0	0	0	0	0
350	360	5	0	0	0	0	0	0	0	0	0	0
360	370	6	0	0	0	0	0	0	0	0	0	0
370	380	7	0	0	0	0	0	0	0	0	0	0
380	390	8	1	0	0	0	0	0	0	0	0	0
390	400	9	2	0	0	0	0	0	0	0	0	0
400	410	10	3	0	0	0	0	0	0	0	0	0
410	420	11	4	0	0	0	0	0	0	0	0	0
420	430	12	5	0	0	0	0	0	0	0	0	0
430	440	13	6	0	0	0	0	0	0	0	0	0
440	450	14	7	0	0	0	0	0	0	0	0	0
450	460	15	8	1	0	0	0	0	0	0	0	0
460	470	16	9	2	0	0	0	0	0	0	0	0
470	480	17	10	3	0	0	0	0	0	0	0	0
480	490	19	11	4	0	0	0	0	0	0	0	0
490	500	20	12	5	0	0	0	0	0	0	0	0
500	510	22	13	6	0	0	0	0	0	0	0	0
510	520	23	14	7	0	0	0	0	0	0	0	0
520	530	25	15	8	1	0	0	0	0	0	0	0
530	540	26	16	9	2	0	0	0	0	0	0	0
540	550	28	17	10	3	0	0	0	0	0	0	0
550	560	29	19	11	4	0	0	0	0	0	0	0
560	570	31	20	12	5	0	0	0	0	0	0	0
570	580	32	22	13	6	0	0	0	0	0	0	0
580	590	34	23	14	7	0	0	0	0	0	0	0
590	600	35	25	15	8	1	0	0	0	0	0	0
600	610	37	26	16	9	2	0	0	0	0	0	0
610	620	38	28	17	10	3	0	0	0	0	0	0
620	630	40	29	19	11	4	0	0	0	0	0	0
630	640	41	31	20	12	5	0	0	0	0	0	0
640	650	43	32	22	13	6	0	0	0	0	0	0
650	660	44	34	23	14	7	0	0	0	0	0	0
660	670	46	35	25	15	8	1	0	0	0	0	0
670	680	47	37	26	16	9	2	0	0	0	0	0
680	690	49	38	28	17	10	3	0	0	0	0	0
690	700	50	40	29	19	11	4	0	0	0	0	0
700	710	52	41	31	20	12	5	0	0	0	0	0
710	720	53	43	32	22	13	6	0	0	0	0	0
720	730	55	44	34	23	14	7	0	0	0	0	0
730	740	56	46	35	25	15	8	1	0	0	0	0
740	750	58	47	37	26	16	9	2	0	0	0	0
750	760	59	49	38	28	17	10	3	0	0	0	0
760	770	61	50	40	29	19	11	4	0	0	0	0
770	780	62	52	41	31	20	12	5	0	0	0	0
780	790	64	53	43	32	22	13	6	0	0	0	0
790	800	65	55	44	34	23	14	7	0	0	0	0
800	810	67	56	46	35	25	15	8	1	0	0	0
810	820	68	58	47	37	26	16	9	2	0	0	0
820	830	70	59	49	38	28	17	10	3	0	0	0
830	840	71	61	50	40	29	19	11	4	0	0	0
840	850	73	62	52	41	31	20	12	5	0	0	0
850	860	74	64	53	43	32	22	13	6	0	0	0
860	870	76	65	55	44	34	23	14	7	0	0	0
870	880	77	67	56	46	35	25	15	8	1	0	0
880	890	79	68	58	47	37	26	16	9	2	0	0
890	900	80	70	59	49	38	28	17	10	3	0	0
900	910	82	71	61	50	40	29	19	11	4	0	0
910	920	83	73	62	52	41	31	20	12	5	0	0
920	930	85	74	64	53	43	32	22	13	6	0	0
930	940	86	76	65	55	44	34	23	14	7	0	0
940	950	88	77	67	56	46	35	25	15	8	1	0
950	960	89	79	68	58	47	37	26	16	9	2	0
960	970	91	80	70	59	49	38	28	17	10	3	0
970	980	92	82	71	61	50	40	29	19	11	4	0
980	990	94	83	73	62	52	41	31	20	12	5	0
990	1,000	95	85	74	64	53	43	32	22	13	6	0
1,000	1,010	97	86	76	65	55	44	34	23	14	7	0
1,010	1,020	98	88	77	67	56	46	35	25	15	8	1
1,020	1,030	100	89	79	68	58	47	37	26	16	9	2
1,030	1,040	101	91	80	70	59	49	38	28	17	10	3
1,040	1,050	103	92	82	71	61	50	40	29	19	11	4

FIGURE 3   2009 federal income tax withholding table for married persons (weekly payroll period)

MARRIED Persons—WEEKLY Payroll Period
(For Wages Paid Through December 2009)

If the wages are—		And the number of withholding allowances claimed is—										
At least	But less than	0	1	2	3	4	5	6	7	8	9	10
		The amount of income tax to be withheld is—										
$1,050	$1,060	$104	$94	$83	$73	$62	$52	$41	$31	$20	$12	$5
1,060	1,070	106	95	85	74	64	53	43	32	22	13	6
1,070	1,080	107	97	86	76	65	55	44	34	23	14	7
1,080	1,090	109	98	88	77	67	56	46	35	25	15	8
1,090	1,100	110	100	89	79	68	58	47	37	26	16	9
1,100	1,110	112	101	91	80	70	59	49	38	28	17	10
1,110	1,120	113	103	92	82	71	61	50	40	29	19	11
1,120	1,130	115	104	94	83	73	62	52	41	31	20	12
1,130	1,140	116	106	95	85	74	64	53	43	32	22	13
1,140	1,150	118	107	97	86	76	65	55	44	34	23	14
1,150	1,160	119	109	98	88	77	67	56	46	35	25	15
1,160	1,170	121	110	100	89	79	68	58	47	37	26	16
1,170	1,180	122	112	101	91	80	70	59	49	38	28	17
1,180	1,190	124	113	103	92	82	71	61	50	40	29	19
1,190	1,200	125	115	104	94	83	73	62	52	41	31	20
1,200	1,210	127	116	106	95	85	74	64	53	43	32	22
1,210	1,220	128	118	107	97	86	76	65	55	44	34	23
1,220	1,230	130	119	109	98	88	77	67	56	46	35	25
1,230	1,240	131	121	110	100	89	79	68	58	47	37	26
1,240	1,250	133	122	112	101	91	80	70	59	49	38	28
1,250	1,260	134	124	113	103	92	82	71	61	50	40	29
1,260	1,270	136	125	115	104	94	83	73	62	52	41	31
1,270	1,280	137	127	116	106	95	85	74	64	53	43	32
1,280	1,290	139	128	118	107	97	86	76	65	55	44	34
1,290	1,300	140	130	119	109	98	88	77	67	56	46	35
1,300	1,310	142	131	121	110	100	89	79	68	58	47	37
1,310	1,320	143	133	122	112	101	91	80	70	59	49	38
1,320	1,330	145	134	124	113	103	92	82	71	61	50	40
1,330	1,340	146	136	125	115	104	94	83	73	62	52	41
1,340	1,350	148	137	127	116	106	95	85	74	64	53	43
1,350	1,360	149	139	128	118	107	97	86	76	65	55	44
1,360	1,370	151	140	130	119	109	98	88	77	67	56	46
1,370	1,380	152	142	131	121	110	100	89	79	68	58	47
1,380	1,390	154	143	133	122	112	101	91	80	70	59	49
1,390	1,400	155	145	134	124	113	103	92	82	71	61	50

$1,400 and over   Use Table 1(b) for a **MARRIED person** on page 5. Also see the instructions on page 3.

FIGURE 3
(Concluded)

referred to as **Social Security taxes** and **Medicare taxes**. The employer withholds FICA taxes from employees' wages and pays them to the U.S. Treasury.

FICA tax rates apply to the gross earnings of an employee during the **calendar year** (January 1 through December 31). After an employee has paid Social Security tax on the maximum taxable earnings, the employer stops deducting Social Security tax until the next calendar year begins. Congress has frequently changed the schedule of rates and taxable incomes.

In this text, we assume a Social Security rate of 6.2 percent (0.062) of the first $106,800 for each employee and a Medicare rate of 1.45 percent (0.0145) of all earnings for each employee. Both tax rates apply to earnings during the calendar year. (Tables for Social Security and Medicare tax withholdings are available in the Internal Revenue Service Publication 15-T.)

Let's return to Mark Anderson, who had gross wages of $1,124.58 for the week ending October 7. Suppose that his total accumulated gross wages earned this year prior to this payroll period are $44,960. Anderson's total gross wages including this payroll period were $46,084.58 ($44,960 + $1,124.58). Since the Social Security tax applies to the first $106,800 and the Medicare tax applies to all earnings, Anderson's earnings are subject to both taxes. For Anderson's Social Security tax, multiply $1,124.58 by 6.2 percent ($1,124.58 × 0.062 = $69.72). For Anderson's Medicare tax, multiply $1,124.58 by 1.45 percent ($1,124.58 × 0.0145 = $16.31).

Here's another example. At the beginning of the pay period, Grace Wallace had cumulative earnings of $103,900, which is $2,900 less than $106,800. During this pay period, she earned $3,010.35, which is greater than $2,900. Thus, she must pay Social Security tax of $179.80 ($2,900 × 0.062) on $2,900. However, because

FYI

At one time, Social Security and Medicare were not separated for tax computation and there was a limit on Medicare taxable earnings. Now ALL earnings are taxable for Medicare.

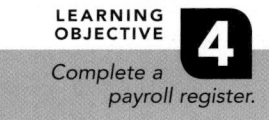

Accounting in Your Future

Payroll Department

The payroll department is an important part of the accounting and finance functions at companies such as REI. Payroll personnel are responsible for ensuring that all company employees receive compensation and benefits critical to maintaining a productive and motivated workforce. The payroll department at REI works closely with the Information Technology, Human Resources, and other departments to ensure that the company's payroll is accurate, up-to-date, and serving the company's current business objectives. For these reasons, it is important to understand how payroll is determined, whether you are directly responsible for processing payroll or you are employed in any other business department.

the Medicare tax applies to all earnings, she is not exempt from any Medicare tax. Her Medicare tax is $43.65 ($3,010.35 × 0.0145). Since Grace's cumulative earnings after this pay period are now over $106,800, any remaining pay will not be subject to Social Security tax.

PAYROLL REGISTER

LEARNING OBJECTIVE 4

Complete a payroll register.

The **payroll register** is a manual or computerized schedule prepared for each payroll period listing the earnings, deductions, and net pay for each employee. In Figure 4 (shown on pages 266–267) we see a payroll register using Excel. It shows the data for each employee on a separate line. This would be suitable for a firm, like Green Sales Company, that has a small number of employees.

First, we'll show the entire payroll register; then, we'll break it down and explain it column by column. The number at the foot of each column refers to the related text description.

The payroll period shown in Figure 4 covers October 1 through October 7. The first part consists of employees' names, hours worked, beginning cumulative earnings, and taxable earnings.

(1) **Total Hours**—Taken from employees' time records (manual or computerized).

(2) **Beginning Cumulative Earnings**—The amount each employee has earned between January 1 and September 30 (the last day of the previous payroll period). It is taken from each employee's individual earnings record. (See Figure 7, pages 270–271.)

(3) **Regular Earnings**—Earnings for hours worked up to and including 40. In other words, the first 40 hours multiplied by each employee's regular hourly rate.

(4) **Overtime Earnings**—Hours in excess of 40 (relative to a 40-hour week) worked by each employee, multiplied by that employee's overtime rate.

(5) Total Earnings—Regular earnings plus overtime earnings.

(6) Ending Cumulative Earnings—Beginning Cumulative Earnings plus Total Earnings.

(7) Taxable Earnings—The amount of earnings subject to taxation, **not the tax itself.** We will use these columns later to figure the amount of each tax. In other words, **Taxable Earnings is the base on which to figure the tax. Taxable Earnings multiplied by the tax rate equals the amount of the tax.**

(7A) Unemployment Taxable Earnings—In our illustration, we are using a maximum of $7,000 for unemployment tax liability on the employer for each employee. This column represents the previously untaxed portion remaining of the $7,000 for the individual employees. **Unemployment tax is paid only by the employer in most states. An unemployment tax may be paid both to the state and to the federal government.** Actually, states may use different maximum earnings and different rates than does the federal government. However, many states use $7,000, which at the time of this writing is the amount used by the federal government. There are three possibilities for Unemployment Taxable Earnings, as follows:

a. **Employee's cumulative earnings including this pay period have not reached $7,000.** When an employee's cumulative earnings so far during the calendar year (since January 1) are less than $7,000, we record the total earnings for the payroll period in the Unemployment Taxable Earnings column. For example, Anna Bodell's cumulative earnings before this week were $5,987. Bodell's cumulative earnings after this week are $6,731.20 ($5,987 + $744.20). Because Bodell's cumulative earnings are still less than $7,000 (after the current check of $744.20), her entire $744.20 in wages earned during this pay period is listed in the Unemployment Taxable Earnings column.

b. **Employee's cumulative earnings were less than $7,000 before this week and are more than $7,000 after this week.** Look at the line for David Dorn and notice that his cumulative earnings before this week were $6,786. Dorn's new cumulative earnings (ending) are $7,702 ($6,786 + $916), putting him over the $7,000 maximum. Therefore, to bring Dorn up to the $7,000 limit, $214 ($7,000 − $6,786) of his earnings for the week are taxable. After this week, none of Dorn's earnings for the remainder of this calendar year will be taxable for unemployment.

c. **Employee's cumulative earnings before this week were more than $7,000.** After an employee's earnings top $7,000 during the calendar year, record a zero or a dash in the Unemployment Taxable Earnings column to indicate that the column has not been forgotten or overlooked. For example, Mark Anderson's total earnings before the payroll period ended October 7 (beginning) were $44,960 (as shown in his individual earnings record in Figure 7 on pages 270–271). Since he had previously earned more than $7,000 this year, we record a zero in the Unemployment Taxable Earnings column.

(7B) Social Security Taxable Earnings—The first $106,800 for each employee. We assume a Social Security tax rate of 6.2 percent of the first $106,800 paid to each employee during the calendar year.

a. **Employee's cumulative earnings including this pay period have not reached $106,800.** When an employee's cumulative earnings so far during the year are less than $106,800, we record the total earnings for the payroll period in the Social Security Taxable Earnings column. For example, Anna Bodell's cumulative earnings so far this year amount to $6,731.20. Because Bodell's total earnings are less than $106,800, the entire $744.20 of wages earned during this pay period is listed in the Social Security Taxable Earnings column. Note that this is true of all the employees except Grace Wallace.

Remember

Taxable earnings are the base on which to figure the tax, not the tax itself.

Remember

Unemployment taxable earnings are used for calculating the amount of the unemployment tax, which is paid by the employer only.

FYI

Social Security and Medicare taxes are recorded separately in the payroll register because there is no limit on Medicare as there is on Social Security.

	A	B	C	D	E	F	G	H	
1					EARNINGS				
2			BEGINNING				ENDING		
3		TOTAL	CUMULATIVE				CUMULATIVE		
4	NAME	HOURS	EARNINGS	REGULAR	OVERTIME	TOTAL	EARNINGS	UNEMPLOYMENT	
5	Anderson, Mark	46	44,960.00	918.00	206.58	1,124.58	46,084.58	0.00	
6	Bodell, Anna	45	5,987.00	626.20	118.00	744.20	6,731.20	744.20	
7	Dorn, David	49	6,786.00	686.00	230.00	916.00	7,702.00	214.00	
8	Fields, Sarah	40	38,462.00	1,084.50	0.00	1,084.50	39,546.50	0.00	
9	Graham, Jason	40	68,600.00	1,798.45	0.00	1,798.45	70,398.45	0.00	
10	Lee, Jeremy	40	68,500.00	1,895.58	0.00	1,895.58	70,395.58	0.00	
11	Mankowitz, Hanna	55	37,850.00	1,264.30	580.00	1,844.30	39,694.30	0.00	
12	Olsen, Barbara	40	45,820.00	1,487.20	0.00	1,487.20	47,307.20	0.00	
13	Parker, William	44	46,430.00	1,581.58	194.70	1,776.28	48,206.28	0.00	
14	Raman, Soma	45	54,867.00	1,674.16	275.00	1,949.16	56,816.16	0.00	
15	Tabor, Annette	40	42,740.00	1,168.83	0.00	1,168.83	43,908.83	0.00	
16	Wallace, Grace	40	103,900.00	3,010.35	0.00	3,010.35	106,910.35	0.00	
17			564,902.00	17,195.15	1,604.28	18,799.43	583,701.43	958.20	
18		(1)	(2)	(3)	(4)	(5)	(6)	(7A)	
19									

17,195.15 + 1,604.28 = 18,799.43

564,902.00 + 18,799.43 = 583,701.43

FIGURE 4

Payroll register for Green Sales Company

b. **Employee's cumulative earnings were less than $106,800 before this week and are more than $106,800 after this week.** The line for Grace Wallace shows her cumulative earnings before the payroll period ended October 7 were $103,900. However, the cumulative earnings including those of this payroll period total $106,910.35, which is greater than the $106,800 limit. That means only $2,900 ($106,800 − $103,900) of her current pay period earnings is recorded in the Social Security Taxable Earnings column. After an employee's earnings top $106,800 during the calendar year, record a zero or dash to indicate that the column has not been forgotten or overlooked. (Use the same procedure as for the Unemployment Taxable Earnings column.)

(7C) **Medicare Taxable Earnings**—All earnings for this period. We have assumed a Medicare tax rate of 1.45 percent (0.0145) on all earnings that are paid to each employee during the calendar year. Therefore, all earnings for this period are taxable and are recorded in the Medicare Taxable Earnings column.

(8) **Deductions**—Amounts taken away (withheld) from total earnings.

(8A) **Federal Income Tax Deductions**—The amount of the federal income tax deduction for each employee can be located directly on the wage-bracket tables or calculated on a percentage basis. We assumed the employees are married and have one withholding allowance.

(8B) **State Income Tax Deductions**—States that impose income taxes also provide wage-bracket tables. The state tax deduction for each employee can be located directly in the appropriate table. As stated previously, we are assuming a rate of 20 percent of the federal income tax.

(8C) **Social Security Tax Deductions**—For each employee's Social Security tax deduction, we first go to the Social Security Taxable Earnings column and note the amount subject to tax. Next, we multiply the Social Security taxable earnings by 6.2 percent (0.062). For example, Bodell's taxable earnings are $744.20, and her Social Security tax deduction is $46.14 ($744.20 × 0.062).

(8D) **Medicare Tax Deductions**—For each employee's Medicare tax deduction, we go to the Medicare Taxable Earnings column and note the amount subject to tax. Next, we multiply the Medicare taxable earnings by 1.45 percent. For example, Bodell's taxable earnings are $744.20, and her Medicare tax deduction is $10.79 ($744.20 × 0.0145).

Remember

Taxable earnings multiplied by the tax rate equals the tax.

GREEN SALES COMPANY
PAYROLL REGISTER FOR WEEK ENDED   October 7, 20—

	I	J	K	L	M	N	O	P	Q
	(7) TAXABLE EARNINGS		(8) DEDUCTIONS						
	SOCIAL SECURITY	MEDICARE	FEDERAL INCOME TAX	STATE INCOME TAX	SOCIAL SECURITY TAX	MEDICARE TAX		OTHER DEDUCTIONS	TOTAL
	1,124.58	1,124.58	104.00	20.80	69.72	16.31		0.00	210.83
	744.20	744.20	47.00	9.40	46.14	10.79	UW	35.00	148.33
	916.00	916.00	73.00	14.60	56.79	13.28	UW	25.00	182.67
	1,084.50	1,084.50	98.00	19.60	67.24	15.73	UW	10.00	210.57
	1,798.45	1,798.45	232.77	46.55	111.50	26.08		0.00	416.90
	1,895.58	1,895.58	257.05	51.41	117.53	27.49	AR	20.00	473.48
	1,844.30	1,844.30	244.23	48.85	114.35	26.74		0.00	434.17
	1,487.20	1,487.20	158.75	31.75	92.21	21.56		0.00	304.27
	1,776.28	1,776.28	227.22	45.44	110.13	25.76		0.00	408.55
	1,949.16	1,949.16	270.44	54.09	120.85	28.26	AR	30.00	503.64
	1,168.83	1,168.83	110.00	22.00	72.47	16.95	UW	25.00	246.42
	2,900.00	3,010.35	555.78	111.16	179.80	43.65	UW	100.00	990.39
	18,689.08	18,799.43	2,378.24	475.65	1,158.73	272.60		245.00	4,530.22
	(7B)	(7C)	(8A)	(8B)	(8C)	(8D)		(8E)	(8F)

2,378.24 + 475.65 + 1,158.73 + 272.60 + 245.00 = 4,530.22

PAGE   56

FIGURE 4
(Concluded)

	R	S	T	U
	(9) PAYMENTS		(10) EXPENSE ACCOUNT DEBITED	
	NET AMOUNT	CK. NO.	SALES WAGES EXPENSE	OFFICE WAGES EXPENSE
	913.75	832	1,124.58	
	595.87	833	744.20	
	733.33	834	916.00	
	873.93	835		1,084.50
	1,381.55	836	1,798.45	
	1,422.10	837		1,895.58
	1,410.13	838	1,844.30	
	1,182.93	839		1,487.20
	1,367.73	840	1,776.28	
	1,445.52	841	1,949.16	
	922.41	842	1,168.83	
	2,019.96	843		3,010.35
	14,269.21		11,321.80	7,477.63
	(9A)	(9B)	(10A)	(10B)

4,530.22 + 14,269.21
= 18,799.43

11,321.80 + 7,477.63 = 18,799.43

(8E) Other Deductions—Employees' voluntary withholdings. In our illustration, UW represents the United Way, and AR stands for Accounts Receivable (employee pays off a loan with the company). For example, Jeremy Lee paid $20 on his loan with the company.

(8F) Total Deductions—The combined total of each employee's deductions for taxes and other. For example, Bodell's total deduction is $148.33 ($47.00 + $9.40 + $46.14 + $10.79 + $35.00).

(9) Payments—The amount of each employee's payroll check (net pay or take-home pay).

(9A) Net Amount—Each employee's Total Earnings minus Total Deductions. For example, Bodell's net amount is $595.87 ($744.20 − $148.33).

(9B) Ck. No.—The number of each employee's payroll check.

(10) **Expense Account Debited**—Columns used for distributing each amount into the appropriate wages expense account. Green Sales Company uses Sales Wages Expense and Office Wages Expense. The sum of these two columns equals the total earnings.

(10A) **Sales Wages Expense**—Amounts earned by employees involved in sales activities.

(10B) **Office Wages Expense**—Amounts earned by employees involved in office activities.

THE PAYROLL ENTRY

LEARNING OBJECTIVE 5

Journalize the payroll entry from a payroll register.

Because the payroll register summarizes the payroll data for the period, it is used as the basis for recording the payroll in the ledger accounts. Since the payroll register does not have the status of a journal, a journal entry is necessary. Figure 5 shows the entry in general journal form.

Note that the accountant records the total cost to the company for services of employees as debits to the Wages Expense accounts.

Also note that the total Social Security tax deductions ($1,158.73) and the total Medicare tax deductions ($272.60) are combined to become FICA Taxes Payable of $1,431.33 ($1,158.73 + $272.60). The two tax deductions are combined into the one liability account because they are paid together at the same time. Social Security and Medicare taxes are recorded separately in the payroll register because they must be listed separately on each employee's W-2 form (Wage and Tax Statement).

Remember

The totals from the payroll register are the amounts used in the payroll entry.

Social Security (6.2%, limited to $106,800) + Medicare (1.45%, unlimited) = FICA Taxes Payable

FIGURE 5

Payroll journal entry for Green Sales Company

To pay the employees from the company's regular checking account, the accountant now makes the journal entry shown at the top of the next page.

Date		Description	Post. Ref.	Debit	Credit	
20—						
Oct.	7	Sales Wages Expense		11 3 2 1 80		
		Office Wages Expense		7 4 7 7 63		
		Employees' Federal Income				
		Tax Payable			2 3 7 8 24	
		FICA Taxes Payable			1 4 3 1 33	$1,158.73 + $272.60
		Employees' State Income Tax				
		Payable			4 7 5 65	
		Employees' United Way Payable			1 9 5 00	
		Accounts Receivable			5 0 00	
		Wages Payable			14 2 6 9 21	
		Payroll register for the week				
		ended October 7, 20—.				

GENERAL JOURNAL   PAGE 31

			Debit	Credit
Oct.	8	Wages Payable	14 2 6 9 21	
		Cash—M. Anderson		9 1 3 75
		Cash—A. Bodell		5 9 5 87
		Cash—D. Dorn		7 3 3 33
		Cash—S. Fields		8 7 3 93
		Cash—J. Graham		1 3 8 1 55
		Cash—J. Lee		1 4 2 2 10
		Cash—H. Mankowitz		1 4 1 0 13
		Cash—B. Olson		1 1 8 2 93
		Cash—W. Parker		1 3 6 7 73
		Cash—S. Raman		1 4 4 5 52
		Cash—A. Tabor		9 2 2 41
		Cash—G. Wallace		2 0 1 9 96

> **Remember**
>
> The amount shown as Wages Payable is the employees' take-home pay.

FIGURE 5

(Concluded)

Special Payroll Bank Account—An Alternative

A firm with a large number of employees would probably open a special **payroll bank account** with its bank. One check drawn on the regular bank account is made payable to the special payroll account for the amount of the total net pay for a payroll period. All payroll checks for the period are then written on the special payroll account. To record this, the accountant makes the following journal entry. In this book, assume the entry to debit Cash—Payroll Bank Account and to credit Cash has already been made.

> **FYI**
>
> A company with a small number of employees would probably use its regular bank account to issue a check to each employee.

	GENERAL JOURNAL				PAGE 31	

Date		Description	Post. Ref.	Debit	Credit
Oct.	8	Wages Payable		14 2 6 9 21	
		Cash—Payroll Bank Account			14 2 6 9 21
		Paid wages for week ended			
		October 7.			

Paycheck

All the data needed to make out a payroll check are available in the payroll register. Mark Anderson's paycheck is shown in Figure 6.

EMPLOYEE	TOTAL HOURS	O.T. HOURS	REG. PAY	O.T. PREM. PAY	GROSS PAY	FED INC. TAX	STATE INC. TAX	SOCIAL SECURITY TAX	MEDICARE TAX	OTHER	TOTAL DED.	NET PAY
Mark Anderson	46	6	918.00	206.58	1,124.58	104.00	20.80	69.72	16.31	—	210.83	913.75

Payroll Account
Green Sales Company
610 First Avenue
Bangor, Maine 04401

CENTRAL NATIONAL BANK

98-461
252

October 8 20 — No. 832

PAY TO THE ORDER OF *Mark Anderson* $ *913.75*

Nine hundred thirteen and 75/100 DOLLARS

Eileen Green

⑆252⑈046⑈

> **FYI**
>
> With the use of the special payroll bank account, if employees delay cashing their paychecks, then the checks do not have to be listed on the bank reconciliation of the firm's regular bank account. Balances of Employees' United Way Payable and other employee deductions are paid out of the firm's regular bank account.

FIGURE 6

Paycheck for Mark Anderson

EMPLOYEE'S INDIVIDUAL EARNINGS RECORD

NAME   Mark E. Anderson

ADDRESS   1104 Rosewood Street

MALE   Bangor, Maine 04401

MALE   _____X_____   FEMALE _____

MARRIED   _____X_____   SINGLE _____

PHONE NO. 207-555-2256   DATE OF BIRTH   9/17/72

EMPLOYEE NO.   55

SOC. SEC. NO.   543-24-1680

PAY RATE $22.95

EQUIVALENT HOURLY RATE $22.95

DATE TERMINATED   _____

CLASSIFICATION FOR WORKERS' COMPENSATION INSURANCE   Sales floor

	A	B	C	D	E	F	G	H	I	J	
1			HOURS WORKED		EARNINGS				DEDUCTIONS		
2	PERIOD	DATE						ENDING	FEDERAL	STATE	
3			REGULAR	OVERTIME	REGULAR	OVERTIME	TOTAL	CUMULATIVE	INCOME	INCOME	
4	ENDED	PAID						EARNINGS	TAX	TAX	
5	9/2	9/3	40	8	918.00	275.44	1,193.44	40,771.55	115.00	23.00	
6	9/9	9/10	40	2	918.00	68.86	986.86	41,758.41	83.00	16.60	
7	9/16	9/17	40	2	918.00	68.86	986.86	42,745.27	83.00	16.60	
8	9/23	9/24	40	5	918.00	172.15	1,090.15	43,835.42	100.00	20.00	
9	9/30	10/1	40	6	918.00	206.58	1,124.58	44,960.00	104.00	20.80	
10	10/7	10/8	40	6	918.00	206.58	1,124.58	46,084.58	104.00	20.80	
11											

FIGURE 7

Employee's individual earnings record for Mark Anderson

Employees' Individual Earnings Records

LEARNING OBJECTIVE 6

Maintain employees' individual earnings records.

To comply with government regulations, a firm has to keep current data on each employee's accumulated earnings, deductions, and net pay. The information contained in the payroll register is recorded each payday in each **employee's individual earnings record**. Figure 7 shows a portion of the earnings record for Mark Anderson.

CHAPTER REVIEW

Study & Practice

1 LEARNING OBJECTIVE

Understand the role of income tax laws that affect payroll deductions and contributions.

Employees and employers involved in the computation and paying of employees for their work must understand the laws, know the percentages and limits involved, and when and to whom to submit the funds deducted from employees and contributed by employees. The federal income tax withholding tables are provided by the IRS in Publication 15-T. FICA payroll taxes are currently 6.2 percent (0.062) on the first $106,800 of wages for Social Security and 1.45 percent (0.0145) on all wages for Medicare.

DATE EMPLOYED   2/1/--

NO. OF EXEMPTIONS   1

PER HOUR   X   PER DAY

PER WEEK   PER MONTH

	K	L	M	N	O	P	Q
	DEDUCTIONS					PAID	
	SOCIAL SECURITY TAX	MEDICARE TAX	OTHER			NET AMOUNT	CK. NO.
			CODE	AMOUNT	TOTAL		
	73.99	17.30	UW	5.00	234.29	959.15	771
	61.19	14.31	UW	0.00	175.10	811.76	783
	61.19	14.31	UW	5.00	180.10	806.76	795
	67.59	15.81	UW	0.00	203.40	886.75	807
	69.72	16.31	UW	5.00	215.83	908.75	819
	69.72	16.31	UW	0.00	210.83	913.75	832

FIGURE 7
(Concluded)

PRACTICE EXERCISE 1

Sally Quinn earns an annual salary of $150,000. How much does she pay in FICA payroll taxes this year?

PRACTICE EXERCISE 1 SOLUTION

Social Security taxes (limited to first $106,800)	$106,800 \times 0.062 = $6,621.60
Medicare taxes	$150,000 \times 0.0145 = \underline{2,175.00}
Total FICA taxes	$\underline{\underline{\$8,796.60}}$

2   **LEARNING OBJECTIVE**

Calculate total earnings based on an hourly, salary, piece-rate, or commission basis.

Earnings calculated on an *hourly basis* equal the hourly rate multiplied by the number of hours worked. If an employee is paid on a *salary basis* and is entitled to extra pay for overtime, the overtime rate is the annual salary divided by 52 (weeks) divided by 40 (normal hours per week). Earnings calculated on a *piece-rate basis* equals the total number of products produced multiplied by the rate per unit of product. Earnings calculated on a *commission basis* equal the total number of units sold or the price of units sold multiplied by the commission rate.

PRACTICE EXERCISE 2

Soma Raman worked 45 hours for the week ended November 7. His hourly rate is $41.85. Determine his gross wages if he is paid time-and-a-half for all overtime hours.

PRACTICE EXERCISE 2 SOLUTION

40 hours at straight time	$40 \times $41.85 per hour =$	$1,674.00
5 hours overtime ($41.85 \times 1.5 = $62.78)	$5 \times $62.78 per hour =$	313.90
Total hours and gross wages	45	$1,987.90

CHAPTER REVIEW

3 **LEARNING OBJECTIVE**

Determine deductions from gross pay, such as federal income tax withheld, Social Security tax, and Medicare tax, to calculate net pay.

Starting with **gross pay**, an employee's pay is reduced for federal and state income tax withholding, **FICA taxes** (**Social Security** and **Medicare taxes**), and other items such as retirement savings through a 401(k) plan, medical reimbursement plans, etc., to arrive at **net pay**.

PRACTICE EXERCISE 3

Using Figure 3 on pages 262–263, calculate the federal income tax withholding for an employee who is married, paid weekly, and whose wages are $1,360 with one withholding allowance. Then calculate the Social Security tax and Medicare tax for the employee, assuming the employee has cumulative earnings of less than $106,800 for the calendar year to date.

PRACTICE EXERCISE 3 SOLUTION

According to Figure 3, $140 should be withheld for an employee who is married, paid weekly, and whose wages are $1,360 with one withholding allowance. Social Security and Medicare taxes would be computed as follows:

$1,360 × 0.062 = $84.32 Social Security tax
$1,360 × 0.0145 = $19.72 Medicare tax

 4 **LEARNING OBJECTIVE**

Complete a payroll register.

To complete the **payroll register**, list the employees' names, hours worked, and beginning cumulative earnings. Add the total earnings to the beginning cumulative earnings to get ending cumulative earnings. The Unemployment Taxable Earnings column is used for the first $7,000 of each employee's earnings for FUTA and SUTA. The Social Security Taxable Earnings column is used for the first $106,800 paid to each employee during the **calendar year**. The Medicare Taxable Earnings column is used for all earnings. Under the Deductions columns, list the federal and state income taxes withheld, the Social Security taxes withheld, the Medicare taxes withheld, and other deductions. The Social Security tax deduction equals the Social Security **taxable earnings** multiplied by an assumed rate of 6.2 percent. The Medicare tax deduction equals the Medicare taxable earnings multiplied by an assumed rate of 1.45 percent. The Net Amount column equals Total Earnings minus Total Deductions.

PRACTICE EXERCISE 4

Complete the payroll register on the following page. The employees are paid time-and-a-half for overtime.

	A	B	C	D	E	F	G	H
1					EARNINGS			
2			BEGINNING				ENDING	
3		TOTAL	CUMULATIVE				CUMULATIVE	
4	NAME	HOURS	EARNINGS	REGULAR	OVERTIME	TOTAL	EARNINGS	UNEMPLOYMENT
5	Abbott, Jack	40	55,820.00	1,487.20				0.00
6	Monohan, William	44	56,430.00	1,581.60				0.00
7	Romar, Sue	45	58,967.00	1,674.16				0.00
8	Williams, Emma	40	140,000.00	3,010.35				0.00
9			311,217.00	7,753.31				0.00
10								

SMITH COMPANY

PAYROLL REGISTER FOR WEEK ENDED   December 8, 20—

	I	J	K	L	M	N	O	P	Q
	TAXABLE EARNINGS		DEDUCTIONS					PAYMENTS	
	SOCIAL SECURITY	MEDICARE	FEDERAL INCOME TAX	STATE INCOME TAX	SOCIAL SECURITY TAX	MEDICARE TAX	TOTAL	NET AMOUNT	CK. NO.
			158.75	31.75					1520
			237.86	47.57					1521
			280.17	56.03					1522
			555.78	111.16					1523
			1,232.56	246.51					

PRACTICE EXERCISE 4 SOLUTION

	A	B	C	D	E	F	G	H
1					EARNINGS			
2			BEGINNING				ENDING	
3		TOTAL	CUMULATIVE				CUMULATIVE	
4	NAME	HOURS	EARNINGS	REGULAR	OVERTIME	TOTAL	EARNINGS	UNEMPLOYMENT
5	Abbott, Jack	40	55,820.00	1,487.20	0.00	1,487.20	57,307.20	0.00
6	Monohan, William	44	56,430.00	1,581.60	237.24	1,818.84	58,248.84	0.00
7	Romar, Sue	45	58,967.00	1,674.16	313.90	1,988.06	60,955.06	0.00
8	Williams, Emma	40	140,000.00	3,010.35	0.00	3,010.35	143,010.35	0.00
9			311,217.00	7,753.31	551.14	8,304.45	319,521.45	0.00
10								

SMITH COMPANY

PAYROLL REGISTER FOR WEEK ENDED   December 8, 20—

	I	J	K	L	M	N	O	P	Q
	TAXABLE EARNINGS		DEDUCTIONS					PAYMENTS	
	SOCIAL SECURITY	MEDICARE	FEDERAL INCOME TAX	STATE INCOME TAX	SOCIAL SECURITY TAX	MEDICARE TAX	TOTAL	NET AMOUNT	CK. NO.
	1,487.20	1,487.20	158.75	31.75	92.21	21.56	304.27	1,182.93	1520
	1,818.84	1,818.84	237.86	47.57	112.77	26.37	424.57	1,394.27	1521
	1,988.06	1,988.06	280.17	56.03	123.26	28.83	488.29	1,499.77	1522
	0.00	3,010.35	555.78	111.16	0.00	43.65	710.59	2,299.76	1523
	5,294.10	8,304.45	1,232.56	246.51	328.24	120.41	1,927.72	6,376.73	

LEARNING OBJECTIVE

Journalize the payroll entry from a payroll register.

Totals are taken directly from the payroll register. Refer to the general journal illustrations on pages 268 and 269 for an example of the first payroll entry and examples of two ways to journalize the payment of the payroll—one from the company's regular checking account and one from a special **payroll bank account**.

PRACTICE EXERCISE 5

Based on the payroll register created in Practice Exercise 4, prepare the journal entry to record the payroll for the week of December 8, 20—.

PRACTICE EXERCISE 5 SOLUTION

	GENERAL JOURNAL				PAGE 31	
Date	Description	Post. Ref.	Debit		Credit	
20—						
Dec. 8	Wages Expense		8 3 0 4 45			
	Employees' Federal Income					
	Tax Payable				1 2 3 2 56	
	FICA Taxes Payable				4 4 8 65	→ $328.24 + $120.41
	Employees' State Income Tax					
	Payable				2 4 6 51	
	Wages Payable				6 3 7 6 73	
	Payroll register for the					
	week ended December 8, 20—.					

LEARNING OBJECTIVE

Maintain employees' individual earnings records.

In the **employees' individual earnings records**, list the personal data for each employee. Based on the information contained in the payroll register, record the earnings and deductions for each payroll period.

PRACTICE EXERCISE 6

Update the following employee's individual earnings record for William Monohan for the December 8 payroll from the payroll register in Practice Exercise 4.

EMPLOYEE'S INDIVIDUAL EARNINGS RECORD

NAME   William Monohan

ADDRESS   17058 SE 97th Court

     Miami, Florida 33158

MALE   X   FEMALE _____

MARRIED   X   SINGLE _____

PHONE NO.   305-999-9001   DATE OF BIRTH   6/17/73

EMPLOYEE NO.   592

SOC. SEC. NO.   544-64-8240

PAY RATE $39.54

OVERTIME PAY   1½x

DATE EMPLOYED   2/1/—

NO. OF EXEMPTIONS   1

PER HOUR   X   PER DAY _____ PER WEEK _____ PER MONTH _____

	A	B	C	D	E	F	G	H	I	J
1			HOURS WORKED		EARNINGS				DEDUCTIONS	
2								ENDING CUMULATIVE EARNINGS	FEDERAL INCOME TAX	STATE INCOME TAX
3	PERIOD ENDED	DATE PAID	REGULAR	OVERTIME	REGULAR	OVERTIME	TOTAL			
4										
5	11/17	11/18	40	8	1,581.60	474.48	2,056.08	53,029.56	297.17	59.43
6	11/24	11/25	40	2	1,581.60	118.62	1,700.22	54,729.78	208.21	41.64
7	12/1	12/2	40	2	1,581.60	118.62	1,700.22	56,430.00	208.21	41.64
8										
9										

	K	L	M	N	O
		DEDUCTIONS		PAYMENTS	
	SOCIAL SECURITY TAX	MEDICARE TAX	TOTAL	NET AMOUNT	CK. NO.
	127.48	29.81		1,542.19	920
	105.41	24.65	513.89	1,320.31	1120
	105.41	24.65	379.91	1,320.31	1325
			379.91		

PRACTICE EXERCISE 6 SOLUTION

EMPLOYEE'S INDIVIDUAL EARNINGS RECORD

NAME   William Monohan

ADDRESS   17058 SE 97th Court

     Miami, Florida 33158

MALE   X   FEMALE _____

MARRIED   X   SINGLE _____

PHONE NO.   305-999-9001   DATE OF BIRTH   6/17/73

EMPLOYEE NO.   592

SOC. SEC. NO.   544-64-8240

PAY RATE $39.54

OVERTIME PAY   1½x

DATE EMPLOYED   2/1/—

NO. OF EXEMPTIONS   1

PER HOUR   X   PER DAY _____ PER WEEK _____ PER MONTH _____

	A	B	C	D	E	F	G	H	I	J
1			HOURS WORKED		EARNINGS				DEDUCTIONS	
2								ENDING CUMULATIVE EARNINGS	FEDERAL INCOME TAX	STATE INCOME TAX
3	PERIOD ENDED	DATE PAID	REGULAR	OVERTIME	REGULAR	OVERTIME	TOTAL			
4										
5	11/17	11/18	40	8	1,581.60	474.48	2,056.08	53,029.56	297.17	59.43
6	11/24	11/25	40	2	1,581.60	118.62	1,700.22	54,729.78	208.21	41.64
7	12/1	12/2	40	2	1,581.60	118.62	1,700.22	56,430.00	208.21	41.64
8	12/8	12/9	40	4	1,581.60	237.24	1,818.84	58,248.84	237.86	47.57
9										

	K	L	M	N	O
		DEDUCTIONS		PAYMENTS	
	SOCIAL SECURITY TAX	MEDICARE TAX	TOTAL	NET AMOUNT	CK. NO.
	127.48	29.81	513.89	1,542.19	920
	105.41	24.65	379.91	1,320.31	1120
	105.41	24.65	379.91	1,320.31	1325
	112.77	26.37	424.57	1,394.27	1521

Glossary

Calendar year A twelve-month period beginning on January 1 and ending on December 31 of the same year. *(p. 263)*

Current Tax Payment Act (Income Tax Withholding) An act to require employers to withhold and pay to the U.S. Treasury employee funds. *(p. 256)*

Employee One who works for compensation under the direction and control of the employer. *(p. 255)*

Employee's individual earnings record A supplementary record for each employee showing personal payroll data and yearly cumulative earnings, deductions, and net pay. *(p. 270)*

Employee's Withholding Allowance Certificate (Form W-4) A form that specifies the number of allowances claimed by each employee and gives the employer the authority to withhold money for an employee's federal income taxes. *(p. 260)*

Exemption An amount of an employee's annual earnings not subject to income tax for the taxpayer, taxpayer's spouse, and dependents *(usually children)*. *(p. 260)*

Fair Labor Standards Act The act of 1938 that provides for minimum standards for wages and overtime, including provisions related to child labor and equal pay for equal work. *(p. 255)*

FICA taxes Social Security taxes plus Medicare taxes, paid by both employee and employer under the provisions of the Federal Insurance Contributions Act. The proceeds are used to pay old-age and disability pensions and to fund the Medicare program. *(p. 261)*

Gross pay The total amount of an employee's pay before any deductions. *(p. 254)*

Independent contractor Someone who is engaged for a definite job or service, and who may choose his or her own means of doing the work. This person is not an employee of the firm for which the service is provided. *(p. 255)*

Medicare taxes Federal government taxes levied on employees and employers; proceeds are used for medical insurance for eligible people age 65 or over. *(p. 263)*

Net pay Gross pay minus deductions. Also called *take-home pay*. *(p. 254)*

Payroll bank account A special checking account used to pay a company's employees. *(p. 269)*

Payroll register A manual or computerized schedule prepared for each payroll period listing the earnings, deductions, and net pay for each employee. *(p. 264)*

Pre-tax deductions Employee deductions that are not subject to income tax. The deductions include medical insurance premiums and medical and dependent care expenses under a flexible spending plan. *(p. 259)*

Social Security Act of 1935 An act to provide for worker retirement funding through deductions from their wages and matching amounts from the employers. *(p. 256)*

Social Security taxes Federal government taxes levied on employees and employers; proceeds are used for old-age pensions and disability benefits. *(p. 263)*

Taxable earnings The amount of an employee's earnings subject to a tax. *(p. 260)*

Wage-bracket tax tables A chart providing the amounts to be deducted for income taxes based on amount of earnings, marital status, and number of allowances claimed. *(p. 261)*

Withholding allowance An amount of an employee's annual earnings not subject to income tax. *(p. 260)*

Workers' compensation laws Laws that protect employees and dependents against losses due to death or injury incurred on the job. *(p. 257)*

CHAPTER ASSIGNMENTS

Discussion Questions

1. Why must employers maintain employees' individual earnings records?
2. What information is included in an employee's individual earnings record?
3. What is the purpose of the payroll register?
4. Explain the difference between gross earnings and net earnings for a payroll period.
5. Describe how a special payroll bank account is useful in paying the wages and salaries of employees.
6. List three required deductions and four voluntary deductions from an employee's total earnings.

7. What is the difference between an employee and an independent contractor? List two examples of an independent contractor.

8. What information is needed to use the wage-bracket withholding table and where is it found?

Exercises

EXERCISE 7-1 Determine the gross pay for each employee listed below.

LO 1,2

a. Gary Dale is paid time-and-a-half for all hours over 40. He worked 44 hours during the week. His regular pay rate is $21.60 per hour.

PRACTICE EXERCISES 1,2

b. Moira Nole worked 50 hours during the week. She is entitled to time-and-a-half for all hours in excess of 40 per week. Her regular pay rate is $25.00 per hour.

c. Lora Mikel is paid a commission of 8 percent of her sales, which amounted to $20,885.

d. Margo Best's yearly salary is $81,600. During the week, Best worked 43 hours, and she is entitled to time-and-a-half for all hours over 40.

EXERCISE 7-2 Lisa Meilo works for Pacific Company, which pays its employees time-and-a-half for all hours worked in excess of 40 per week. Meilo's pay rate is $37.00 per hour. Her wages are subject to federal income tax, a Social Security tax deduction at the rate of 6.2 percent, and a Medicare tax deduction at the rate of 1.45 percent. She is married and claims three allowances. Meilo has an unpaid half-hour lunch break during an 8½-hour day. In the most recent pay period, she worked 50 hours. Meilo's beginning cumulative earnings are $73,654.

LO 1,2,3

PRACTICE EXERCISES 1,2,3

Complete the following.

a. _____ hours at straight time × $_____ per hour $ _____

b. _____ hours overtime × $_____ per hour

c. Total gross pay $ _____

d. Federal income tax withholding $256.81

e. Social Security tax withholding at 6.2 percent

f. Medicare tax withholding at 1.45 percent   _____

g. Total withholding

h. Net pay $ _____

EXERCISE 7-3 Using the income tax withholding table in Figure 3, pages 262–263, for each employee of Miller Company, determine the net pay for the week ended January 21. Assume a Social Security tax of 6.2 percent and a Medicare tax of 1.45 percent. All employees have cumulative earnings, including this pay period, of less than $106,800. Assume all employees are married.

LO 1,2,3,4

PRACTICE EXERCISES 1,2,3,4

Employee	Allowances	Total Earnings	Federal Income Tax Withheld	Social Security Tax Withheld	Medicare Tax Withheld	Union Dues Withheld	United Way Contribution	Net Pay
a. Aston, F. B.	1	$ 900.00	$	$	$	$ 25.00	$ 35.00	$
b. Dwyer, S. J.	2	920.00				25.00	35.00	
c. Flynn, K. A.	3	1,110.00				25.00	40.00	
d. Harden, J. L.	0	1,025.00				25.00	40.00	
e. Nguyen, H.	2	925.00				25.00	35.00	
Totals		$4,880.00	$	$	$	$125.00	$185.00	$

	A	B	C	D	E	F	G	H
1				EARNINGS			TAXABLE EARNINGS	
2		BEGINNING				ENDING		SOCIAL
3		CUMULATIVE				CUMULATIVE		SECURITY
4	NAME	EARNINGS	REGULAR	OVERTIME	TOTAL	EARNINGS	UNEMPLOYMENT	
9		245,754.00	6,724.00	1,220.00	7,494.00	253,248.00	2,456.00	7,944.00
10								
11								

FIGURE 8

Payroll register for
Benton, Inc.

1,4 LO

PRACTICE EXERCISES 1,4

EXERCISE 7-4 For the week ended September 7, the totals of the payroll register for Benton, Inc., are presented in Figure 8. The regular and overtime earnings are correct. List six errors that exist. None of the employees have earned more than $106,800, so all earnings are subject to Social Security and Medicare taxes. Assume that amounts for federal income tax, union dues, and charity are correct.

1,4 LO

PRACTICE EXERCISES 1,4

EXERCISE 7-5 For tax purposes, assume that the maximum taxable earnings are $106,800 for Social Security and $7,000 for the unemployment tax, and that all earnings are taxable for Medicare. For the payroll register for the month of November for Shelby, Inc., determine the taxable earnings for each employee.

	A	B	C	D	E	F	G
1						TAXABLE EARNINGS	
2		BEGINNING		ENDING			
3		CUMULATIVE		CUMULATIVE			
4	NAME	EARNINGS	TOTAL EARNINGS	EARNINGS	UNEMPLOYMENT	SOCIAL SECURITY	MEDICARE
5	Axton, C.	106,000.00	7,691.00	113,691.00			
6	Edgar, E.	145,465.00	10,900.00	156,365.00			
7	Gorman, L.	36,879.00	3,064.00	39,943.00			
8	Jolson, R.	24,634.00	2,325.00	26,959.00			
9	Nixel, P.	6,850.00	2,463.00	9,313.00			
10							

1,4,5 LO

PRACTICE EXERCISES 1,4,5

EXERCISE 7-6 On January 21, the column totals of the payroll register for Great Products Company showed that its sales employees had earned $14,960, its trucking employees had earned $10,692, and its office employees had earned $8,670. Social Security taxes were withheld at an assumed rate of 6.2 percent, and Medicare taxes were withheld at an assumed rate of 1.45 percent. Other deductions consisted of federal income tax, $3,975; and union dues, $560. Determine the amount of Social Security and Medicare taxes withheld, and record the general journal entry for the payroll, crediting Salaries Payable for the net pay. All earnings were taxable.

1,2,3 LO

PRACTICE EXERCISES 1,2,3

EXERCISE 7-7 Precision Labs has two employees. The following information was taken from its individual earnings records for the month of September. Determine the missing amounts, assuming that the Social Security tax is 6.2 percent and the

	I	J	K	L	M	N	O	P	Q	R
				DEDUCTIONS				PAYMENTS		
	MEDICARE	FEDERAL INCOME TAX	SOCIAL SECURITY TAX	MEDICARE TAX	UNION DUES	CHARITY	TOTAL	NET AMOUNT	CK. NO.	WAGES EXPENSE DEBIT
	7,944.00	949.00	429.53	115.19	193.00	292.00	2,083.00	5,456.00		7,494.00

FIGURE 8
(Concluded)

Medicare tax is 1.45 percent. All earnings are subject to Social Security and Medicare taxes. Round amounts to the nearest penny.

	Brown	Ringness	Total
Regular earnings	$3,500.00	$?	$?
Overtime earnings	?	120.00	
Total earnings	$3,646.00	$?	$?
Federal income tax withheld	$ 268.07	$?	$?
State income tax withheld	?	26.37	?
Social Security tax withheld	226.05	169.76	?
Medicare tax withheld	52.87	39.70	?
Charity withheld	35.00	97.00	?
Total deductions	$ 635.60	$ 464.70	$?
Net pay	$?	$ 2,273.30	$?

EXERCISE 7-8 Assume that the employees in Exercise 7-7 are paid from the company's regular bank account (check numbers 981 and 982). Prepare the entry to record and pay the payroll in general journal form, dated September 30.

LO 5

PRACTICE EXERCISE 5

Problem Set A

For additional help, see the demonstration problem at the beginning of each chapter in your Working Papers.

PROBLEM 7-1A Jennifer Ross, an employee of Hampton Company, worked 44 hours during the week of February 9 through 15. Her rate of pay is $30.00 per hour, and she receives time-and-a-half for work in excess of 40 hours per week. She is married and claims two allowances on her W-4 form. Her wages are subject to the following deductions:

LO 1,2,3

a. Federal income tax (use the table in Figure 3, pages 262–263).
b. Social Security tax at 6.2 percent.
c. Medicare tax at 1.45 percent.
d. Union dues, $30.00.
e. Repay employee loan, $32.00.

Required
Compute Ross's regular pay, overtime pay, gross pay, and net pay.

Check Figure
Net pay, $1,079.43

1,2,3,4,5   **PROBLEM 7-2A** Highridge Homes has the following payroll information for the week ended February 21:

Name	Earnings at End of Previous Week	Daily Time							Pay Rate	Federal Income Tax
		S	M	T	W	T	F	S		
Arthur, P.	7,800.00	8	8	8	8	8			45.00	233.15
Bills, D.	2,060.00			8	8	8	8	8	12.50	13.00
Carney, W.	2,085.00	8	8	8			8	8	12.95	14.00
Dorn, J.	748.00				8	8			22.00	0.00
Edgar, L.	2,687.00	8	8	8			8	8	15.00	26.00
Fitzwilson, G.	4,150.00	8	8		8	8	8	8	23.00	115.00

Taxable earnings for Social Security are based on the first $106,800. Taxable earnings for Medicare are based on all earnings. Taxable earnings for federal and state unemployment are based on the first $7,000. Employees are paid time-and-a-half for work in excess of 40 hours per week.

Check Figure
Net amount, $4,184.96

Required

1. Complete the payroll register. The Social Security tax rate is 6.2 percent, and the Medicare tax rate is 1.45 percent. Begin payroll checks with No. 2080.
2. Prepare a general journal entry to record the payroll. The firm's general ledger contains a Wages Expense account and a Wages Payable account.
3. Assuming that the firm has transferred funds from its regular bank account to its special payroll bank account, and that this entry has been made, prepare a general journal entry to record the payment of wages.

1,2,3,4,5  **PROBLEM 7-3A** Alpine Company pays its employees time-and-a-half for hours worked in excess of 40 per week. The information available from time cards and employees' individual earnings records for the pay period ended October 14 is shown in the following chart.

Name	Earnings at End of Previous Week	Daily Time						Pay Rate	Income Tax Allowances
		M	T	W	T	F	S		
Bardin, J.	43,627.00	8	8	8	8	8	2	21.30	2
Caris, A.	44,340.00	8	8	8	8	8	8	21.60	1
Drew, W.	43,845.00	8	10	10	8	8	0	21.50	1
Garen, S.	105,900.00	8	8	8	8	8	0	49.00	3
North, O.	43,875.00	8	8	8	8	8	5	21.40	3
Ovid, N.	40,150.00	8	8	8	8	8	0	21.50	1
Ross, J.	6,430.00	8	8	8	8	8	4	20.50	1
Springer, O.	44,175.00	8	8	8	8	8	3	21.25	2

Taxable earnings for Social Security are based on the first $106,800. Taxable earnings for Medicare are based on all earnings. Taxable earnings for federal and state unemployment are based on the first $7,000.

Required

1. Complete the payroll register, using the wage-bracket income tax withholding table in Figure 3 (pages 262–263). The Social Security tax rate is 6.2 percent, and the Medicare tax rate is 1.45 percent. Assume that all employees are married. Garen's federal income tax is $238.06. In the payroll register, begin payroll checks with No. 3945.
2. Prepare a general journal entry to record the payroll. The firm's general ledger contains a Wages Expense account and a Wages Payable account.
3. Assuming that the firm has transferred funds from its regular bank account to its special payroll bank account, and that this entry has been made, prepare a general journal entry to record the payment of wages.

PROBLEM 7-4A The information for Titan Company, shown in the following chart, is available from Titan's time records and the employees' individual earnings records for the pay period ended December 22.

LO 1,3,4,5

Name	Hours Worked	Earnings at End of Previous Week	Total Earnings	Class.	Federal Income Tax	Other Deductions	
Albee, C.	44	63,340.00	1,650.00	Sales	195.65	UW	25.00
Don, V.	40	136,410.00	2,841.00	Sales	508.37	AR	95.00
Fine, J.	40	76,860.00	1,507.00	Sales	161.72	UW	25.00
Ginny, N.	46	33,590.00	660.00	Office	35.00	UW	35.00
Johnson, J.	47	56,980.00	1,117.00	Office	103.00	UW	25.00
Lund, D.	43	104,900.00	2,100.00	Sales	308.15	UW	20.00
Maya, R.	42	66,860.00	1,310.00	Sales	133.00	AR	70.00
Nord, P.	41	36,750.00	720.00	Sales	44.00	UW	20.00
Oscar, T.	43	93,480.00	1,832.00	Sales	241.15	UW	25.00
Troy, B.	40	47,250.00	930.00	Sales	76.00	UW	20.00

Taxable earnings for Social Security are based on the first $106,800. Taxable earnings for Medicare are based on all earnings. Taxable earnings for federal and state unemployment are based on the first $7,000. The company does not pay for overtime hours.

Required

1. Complete the payroll register, using a Social Security tax rate of 6.2 percent and a Medicare tax rate of 1.45 percent. Concerning Other Deductions, AR refers to Accounts Receivable and UW refers to United Way. Begin payroll checks in the payroll register with No. 2914.
2. Prepare the general journal entry to record the payroll. The firm's general ledger contains a Salary Expense account and a Salaries Payable account.
3. Prepare the general journal entry to pay the payroll. Assume that funds for this payroll have been transferred to Cash—Payroll Bank Account and that this entry has been made.

Problem Set B

For additional help, see the demonstration problem at the beginning of each chapter in your Working Papers.

1,2,3

PROBLEM 7-1B Erin Chang, an employee of Solutions Company, worked 48 hours during the week of October 11 through 17. Her rate of pay is $17.50 per hour, and she receives time-and-a-half for all work in excess of 40 hours per week. Chang is married and claims two allowances on her W-4 form. Her wages are subject to the following deductions:

a. Federal income tax (use the table in Figure 3, pages 262–263).
b. Social Security tax at 6.2 percent.
c. Medicare tax at 1.45 percent.
d. Union dues, $32.00.
e. Repay employee loan, $44.75.

Check Figure
Net pay, $701.63

Required

Compute Chang's regular pay, overtime pay, gross pay, and net pay.

1,2,3,4,5

PROBLEM 7-2B Harvest Company has the following payroll information for the pay period ended April 14:

Name	Earnings at End of Previous Week	M	T	W	T	F	S	Pay Rate	Federal Income Tax
		Daily Time							
Grant, L.	7,536.00	8	8	8	8	8	0	18.00	44.00
Hamn, R.	6,496.00	8	8	8	8	8	0	18.10	44.00
Lisk, J.	6,798.00	0	8	8	8	8	8	17.80	43.00
Myre, G.	9,589.00	8	8	8	0	8	8	19.25	52.00
Segel, T.	6,585.00	8	8	8	8	8	6	17.95	67.00
Torgel, I.	7,501.00	0	8	8	8	8	8	18.70	47.00

Taxable earnings for Social Security are based on the first $106,800. Taxable earnings for Medicare are based on all earnings. Taxable earnings for federal and state unemployment are based on the first $7,000. Employees are paid time-and-a-half for work in excess of 40 hours per week.

Check Figure
Net amount, $3,908.23

Required

1. Complete the payroll register. The Social Security tax rate is 6.2 percent, and the Medicare tax rate is 1.45 percent. Begin payroll checks with No. 2944.
2. Prepare a general journal entry to record the payroll. The firm's general ledger contains a Wages Expense account and a Wages Payable account.
3. Assuming that the firm has transferred funds from its regular bank account to its special payroll bank account, and that this entry has been made, prepare a journal entry to record the payment of wages.

1,2,3,4,5 **LO**

PROBLEM 7-3B Williams Company pays its employees time-and-a-half for hours worked in excess of 40 per week. The information available from time records and employees' individual earnings records for the pay period ended September 21 is shown in the following chart.

| Name | Earnings at End of Previous Week | Daily Time | | | | | | Pay Rate | Income Tax Allowances |
		M	T	W	T	F	S		
Bolt, D.	6,745.00	8	8	8	10	8	0	25.00	1
Dore, C.	136,240.00	8	8	8	8	8	0	49.50	2
Gayle, A.	32,730.00	8	10	8	8	8	0	24.50	2
Hale, R.	105,900.00	8	8	8	8	8	4	40.00	3
Jilly, B.	35,154.00	8	8	8	8	8	0	49.50	0
Karn, S.	29,938.00	8	8	9	8	8	0	20.50	2
Ober, N.	6,795.00	8	8	8	9	9	4	21.00	1
Wong, J.	27,252.00	8	8	10	8	8	0	20.00	2

Taxable earnings for Social Security are based on the first $106,800. Taxable earnings for Medicare are based on all earnings. Taxable earnings for federal and state unemployment are based on the first $7,000.

Required

Check Figure
Net amount, $8,891.78

1. Complete the payroll register, using the wage-bracket income tax withholding table in Figure 3 (pages 262–263). The Social Security tax rate is 6.2 percent, and the Medicare tax rate is 1.45 percent. Assume that all employees are married. The federal income tax deduction is $260.61 for Dore, $208.06 for Hale, and $295.70 for Jilly. In the payroll register, begin payroll checks with No. 1863.
2. Prepare a general journal entry to record the payroll. The firm's general ledger contains a Wages Expense account and a Wages Payable account.
3. Assuming that the firm has transferred funds from its regular bank account to its special payroll bank account, and that this entry has been made, prepare a general journal entry to record the payment of wages.

 1,3,4,5

PROBLEM 7-4B The information for Best Sports Company, shown in the following chart, is available from Best Sports' time records and employees' individual earnings records for the pay period ended December 29.

Name	Hours Worked	Earnings at End of Previous Week	Total Earnings	Class.	Federal Income Tax	Other Deductions	
Chang, C.	40	33,900.00	680.00	Sales	38.00	AR	80.00
Dugan, T.	42	38,270.00	2,841.00	Sales	508.37	UW	20.00
Fancher, K.	40	37,680.00	725.00	Sales	44.00	UW	25.00
Gannon, T.	40	33,245.00	660.00	Office	35.00		——
Jones, L.	40	37,789.00	750.00	Office	49.00	UW	25.00
Lange, M.	40	106,200.00	2,100.00	Office	308.15	UW	35.00
Milton, D.	40	37,684.00	1,310.00	Sales	133.00	UW	20.00
Naylor, B.	40	37,499.00	720.00	Sales	44.00		——
Orton, A.	44	94,338.00	1,780.00	Sales	228.15	AR	70.00
Tiosha, J.	42	48,120.00	1,065.00	Sales	95.00	UW	25.00

Taxable earnings for Social Security are based on the first $106,800. Taxable earnings for Medicare are based on all earnings. Taxable earnings for federal and state unemployment are based on the first $7,000. The company does not pay for overtime hours.

Required

1. Complete the payroll register, using a Social Security tax rate of 6.2 percent and a Medicare tax rate of 1.45 percent. Concerning Other Deductions, AR refers to Accounts Receivable and UW refers to United Way. Begin payroll checks in the payroll register with No. 2914.
2. Prepare the general journal entry to record the payroll. The firm's general ledger contains a Salary Expense account and a Salaries Payable account.
3. Prepare the general journal entry to pay the payroll. Assume that funds for this payroll have been transferred to Cash—Payroll Bank Account and that this entry has been made.

ACTIVITIES

CONSIDER AND COMMUNICATE

Southern Company pays its employees weekly by issuing checks on its regular bank account. The owner thinks it would be too much trouble to have a second checking account. Explain to the owner why this might be worth the additional effort.

A QUESTION OF ETHICS

An employee who is married and has three children submits a W-4 form to his employer. He checks the box that says "Single" and writes zero in the "Deductions Claimed" box. Is this action ethical, unethical, or illegal? Explain your reasoning.

Employer Taxes, Payments, and Reports

8

TRUGREEN, Memphis, Tennessee; PAWTUCKET RED SOX, Pawtucket, Rhode Island; HOCK IT TO ME, Albuquerque, New Mexico

WHY IT MATTERS

TruGreen is the world's largest lawn and landscape company, employing over 10,000 employees and serving more than 3.4 million customers through its 270 locations.

The Pawtucket Red Sox is a minor league baseball affiliate of the Boston Red Sox. The team's current roster consists of 24 active players, along with the team's manager, coaches, and mascots.

Hock It To Me is a privately owned pawn shop. The company has annual revenue of less than $500,000 and employs a staff of 1 to 4 people.

Even though each of these businesses has a unique payroll due to different amounts of salaries or wages, benefits, and withholdings, each business needs to accurately calculate the amount of payroll for each employee, determine the amount of payroll taxes for which the employer is liable, make the payroll tax deposits as required, and file the appropriate payroll tax returns on a timely basis.

LEARNING OBJECTIVES

After you have completed this chapter, you will be able to do the following:

1 Calculate the amount of payroll tax expense and journalize the entry.

2 Journalize the entry for the deposit of employees' federal income taxes withheld and FICA taxes (both employees' withheld and employer's matching share) and prepare the deposit coupon.

3 Journalize the entries for the payment of employer's state and federal unemployment taxes.

4 Journalize the entry for the deposit of employees' state income taxes withheld.

5 Complete Employer's Quarterly Federal Tax Return, Form 941.

6 Prepare W-2 and W-3 forms and Form 940.

7 Calculate the premium for workers' compensation insurance, and prepare the entry for payment in advance.

8 Determine the amount of the end-of-the-year adjustments for (a) workers' compensation insurance and (b) accrued salaries and wages, and record the adjustments.

ACCOUNTING LANGUAGE

Employer Identification Number (EIN) (p. 286)

Federal unemployment tax (FUTA) (p. 289)

Form 940 (p. 300)

Form 941 (p. 295)

Form W-2 (p. 298)

Form W-3 (p. 299)

Payroll Tax Expense (p. 286)

Quarter (p. 291)

State unemployment tax (SUTA) (p. 289)

Workers' compensation insurance (p. 304)

We have talked about how to compute and record such payroll data as gross pay, employees' income tax withheld, employees' FICA taxes withheld, and various deductions requested by employees. Now we will learn how to record the transactions to pay these withholding liabilities and the taxes levied on the employer.

EMPLOYER IDENTIFICATION NUMBER

Everyone must have a Social Security number or an Individual Taxpayer Identification Number (ITIN), a vital part of federal income tax returns. An employer's counterpart to the Social Security number is the **Employer Identification Number (EIN)** assigned by the Internal Revenue Service. Employers of one or more persons are required to have such a number, and it must be listed on all reports and payments of employees' federal income tax withholding and FICA taxes.

EMPLOYER'S PAYROLL TAXES

An employer's payroll taxes are based on the gross wages paid to employees. Payroll taxes—like property taxes—are an expense of doing business. Green Sales Company records these taxes in the **Payroll Tax Expense** account and debits the account for

The skyrocketing costs of Medicare have caused Congress and the president to try to make sweeping reforms. The issues are far-reaching. Medicare affects a large percentage of the population, who fear their benefits may be reduced.

the company's portion of FICA taxes and for state and federal unemployment taxes. In T account form, Payroll Tax Expense for Green Sales Company would look like the following example.

Payroll Tax Expense

+	−
FICA taxes (employer's matching portion) State unemployment tax Federal unemployment tax	Closed at the end of the year along with all other expense accounts

As you can see, **FICA taxes (employer's share of Social Security and Medicare taxes), state unemployment tax, and federal unemployment tax are included under the Payroll Tax Expense heading.** In most states, the unemployment taxes are levied on the employer only.

Employer's Matching Portion of FICA Taxes

FICA taxes (the combined Social Security and Medicare taxes) are imposed equally on both employer and employee. The employer's share is determined by multiplying the employer's tax rates (assumed to be 6.2 percent (0.062) for Social Security and 1.45 percent (0.0145) for Medicare) by the taxable earnings (assumed to be a

	A	B		F	G	H	I	J
							(7) TAXABLE EARNINGS	
		TOTAL			ENDING CUMULATIVE		SOCIAL	
	NAME	HOURS		TOTAL	EARNINGS	UNEMPLOYMENT	SECURITY	MEDICARE
5	Anderson, Mark	46		1,124.58	46,084.58	0.00	1,124.58	1,124.58
6	Bodell, Anna	45		744.20	6,731.20	744.20	744.20	744.20
7	Dorn, David	49		916.00	7,702.00	214.00	916.00	916.00
8	Fields, Sarah	40		1,084.50	39,546.50	0.00	1,084.50	1,084.50
9	Graham, Jason	40		1,798.45	70,398.45	0.00	1,798.45	1,798.45
10	Lee, Jeremy	40		1,895.58	70,395.58	0.00	1,895.58	1,895.58
11	Mankowitz, Hanna	55		1,844.30	39,694.30	0.00	1,844.30	1,844.30
12	Olsen, Barbara	40		1,487.20	47,307.20	0.00	1,487.20	1,487.20
13	Parker, William	44		1,776.28	48,206.28	0.00	1,776.28	1,776.28
14	Raman, Soma	45		1,949.16	56,816.16	0.00	1,949.16	1,949.16
15	Tabor, Annette	40		1,168.83	43,908.83	0.00	1,168.83	1,168.83
16	Wallace, Grace	40		3,010.35	106,910.35	0.00	2,900.00	3,010.35
17				18,799.43	583,701.43	958.20	18,689.08	18,799.43
18		(1)		(5)	(6)	(7A)	(7B)	(7C)

Amount of employees' earnings for the period that has not, as yet, been taxed as part of the $7,000 maximum liability

Amount of employees' earnings that are less than $106,800 per employee for the year

Amount of all employees' earnings

Employer's state unemployment tax
$958.20 × 0.054 = **$51.74**

Employer's Social Security tax
$18,689.08 × 0.062 = **$1,158.72**

Employer's Medicare tax
$18,799.43 × 0.0145 = **$272.59**

Employer's federal unemployment tax
$958.20 × 0.008 = **$7.67**

Combined Employer's FICA taxes
(Social Security $1,158.72 + Medicare $272.59) = **$1,431.31**

maximum of $106,800 for Social Security and all earnings for Medicare). The same tax rates apply to both the employer and the employees.

The accountant obtains the Social Security and Medicare taxable earnings amounts from the payroll register. Figure 1 shows the Taxable Earnings columns taken from the payroll register for Green Sales Company as prepared in the previous chapter for the week ended October 7.

Before we look at the journal entry to record the employer's share of FICA taxes, let's look at the entry in T account form.

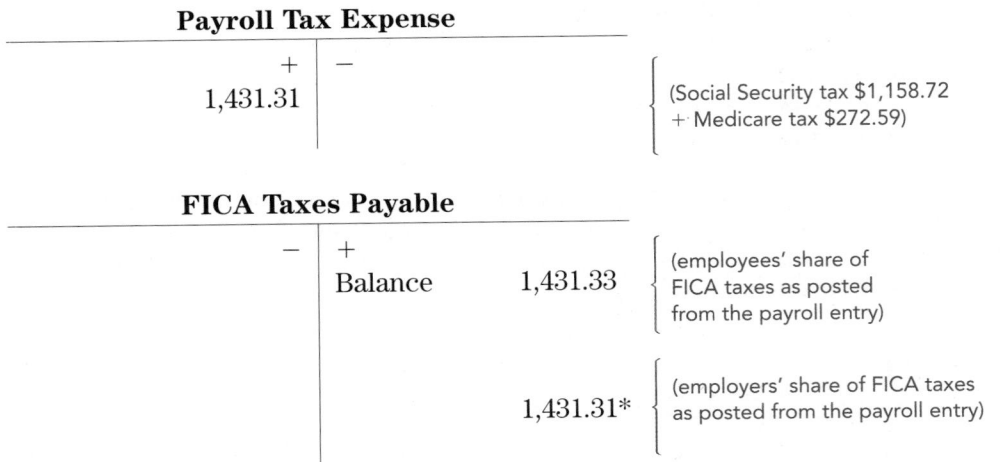

Payroll Tax Expense

+	−
1,431.31	

(Social Security tax $1,158.72 + Medicare tax $272.59)

FICA Taxes Payable

−	+
	Balance 1,431.33

(employees' share of FICA taxes as posted from the payroll entry)

1,431.31* (employers' share of FICA taxes as posted from the payroll entry)

*$0.02 difference due to rounding.

Note particularly that the FICA Taxes Payable account is often used for both the tax liability of the employer and the amounts withheld from the employees. This is logical because both FICA taxes are paid at the same time and to the same place. There may be a slight difference (such as seen above) between the employer's and the employees' share of FICA taxes because of the rounding process. For the employees' share, the accountant uses the total of the employees' Social Security and Medicare tax deductions. For the employer's share, the accountant multiplies the total taxable earnings (Social Security and Medicare) by the tax rates.

Employer's State Unemployment Tax

The proceeds of the **state unemployment tax (SUTA)**, which is levied only on the employer in most states, are used to pay subsistence benefits to unemployed workers. The rate of the state unemployment tax varies considerably among the states. Assume that Green Sales Company is subject to a rate of 5.4 percent (0.054) of the first $7,000 of each employee's earnings (the same base amount as for the federal unemployment tax). As shown in the portion of the payroll register illustrated in Figure 1, $958.20 of earnings are subject to the state unemployment tax. Accordingly, by T accounts, the state unemployment tax based on taxable earnings is as follows:

Payroll Tax Expense	State Unemployment Tax Payable
+ −	− +
(958.20 × 0.054) 51.74	(958.20 × 0.054) 51.74

Employer's Federal Unemployment Tax

The **federal unemployment tax (FUTA)** is paid only by the employer. Congress may from time to time change the rate. Let's assume a rate of 0.8 percent (0.008) of the first $7,000 earned by each employee during the calendar year. For the weekly payroll period for Green Sales Company, the tax liability is $7.67 ($958.20 of unemployment taxable earnings, taken from the payroll register, multiplied by 0.008, the tax rate). The T account is as follows:

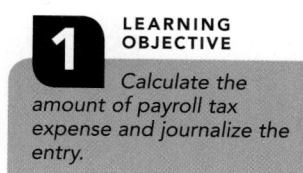

1 LEARNING OBJECTIVE

Calculate the amount of payroll tax expense and journalize the entry.

Payroll Tax Expense	Federal Unemployment Tax Payable
+ −	− +
(958.20 × 0.008) 7.67	(958.20 × 0.008) 7.67

To make things clearer, figures for the employer's three payroll taxes have been presented separately. Now let's combine all of this information into one entry, which follows the regular payroll entry. Green Sales Company pays its employees weekly, so it also makes its Payroll Tax Expense entry weekly.

Date	Description	Post. Ref.	Debit	Credit
Oct. 7	Payroll Tax Expense		1 4 9 0 72	
	FICA Taxes Payable			1 4 3 1 31
	State Unemployment Tax Payable			5 1 74
	Federal Unemployment Tax Payable			7 67
	To record employer's share of FICA			
	taxes and employer's state and			
	federal unemployment taxes.			

JOURNAL ENTRIES FOR RECORDING PAYROLL

At this point, let's restate in general journal form the entries that have already been recorded. The sequence of steps for recording the payroll entries is:

STEP 1. Record the payroll for the present period in the payroll register.

STEP 2. Based on the payroll register, record the payroll entry in the journal.

STEP 3. Based on the Taxable Earnings columns of the payroll register, record Payroll Tax Expense in the journal.

STEP 4. Record a journal entry to pay the employees.

Once the payroll for the present period is recorded in the payroll register (see Chapter 7), the entry to record the payroll, which was also presented in Chapter 7, is journalized.

Date		Description	Post. Ref.	Debit	Credit
20—					
Oct.	7	Sales Wages Expense		11 3 2 1 80	
		Office Wages Expense		7 4 7 7 63	
		Employees' Federal Income Tax Payable			2 3 7 8 24
		FICA Taxes Payable			1 4 3 1 33
		Employees' State Income Tax Payable			4 7 5 65
		Employees' United Way Payable			1 9 5 00
		Accounts Receivable			5 0 00
		Wages Payable			14 2 6 9 21
		Payroll register for the week ended			
		October 7, 20—.			

Next, the entry to record the employer's payroll taxes is journalized.

Date		Description	Post. Ref.	Debit	Credit
Oct.	7	Payroll Tax Expense		1 4 9 0 72	
		FICA Taxes Payable			1 4 3 1 31
		State Unemployment Tax Payable			5 1 74
		Federal Unemployment Tax Payable			7 67
		To record employer's share of FICA			
		taxes and employer's state and			
		federal unemployment taxes.			

Finally, the entry to pay the employees is journalized. Green Sales Company issues one check payable to a payroll bank account. To pay its employees, it will draw separate payroll checks on this payroll account. (The entry to transfer cash to the payroll bank account is not shown here.)

Date		Description	Post. Ref.	Debit	Credit
Oct.	8	Wages Payable		14 2 6 9 21	
		Cash—Payroll Bank Account			14 2 6 9 21
		Paid wages for week			
		ended October 7, 20—.			

As stated previously, in the first payroll entry, small employers will credit Cash directly instead of Wages Payable. These employers issue separate checks out of their regular bank accounts for each employee.

Next, we describe the entries for paying withholdings for employees' federal income tax and FICA taxes and the employer's matching share of FICA taxes. We also show the entries for paying the federal and state unemployment taxes and the withholdings for employees' state income taxes.

PAYMENTS OF FICA TAXES AND EMPLOYEES' FEDERAL INCOME TAX WITHHOLDING

After paying employees, the employer must make payments in the form of federal tax deposits. A deposit includes the combined total of three items:

1. Employees' federal income taxes withheld
2. Employees' FICA taxes (Social Security and Medicare) withheld
3. Employer's share of FICA taxes (Social Security and Medicare)

The timing for when the deposits are required to be made depends on the amount of payroll.

Deposits are made with a coupon to an authorized financial institution or electronically using the Electronic Federal Tax Payment System (EFTPS). The IRS requires some companies to make their deposits electronically because they have met certain criteria. Specifically, if total deposits during a calendar year exceed $200,000, the business is required to use EFTPS in the second succeeding calendar year. Once the business is required to use EFTPS, it will continue to be required to make its deposits electronically in subsequent years, even if its annual deposits fall below $200,000. See IRS Publication 15 (Circular E), Employer's Tax Guide, for more information on deposit requirements at www.irs.gov.

Employers submit a return, Form 941, every **quarter** (three consecutive months). The due dates for filing this return are as follows:

Quarter	Ending Date of Quarter	Due Date for Forms 941/941e
January–February–March	March 31	April 30
April–May–June	June 30	July 31
July–August–September	September 30	October 31
October–November–December	December 31	January 31

2 LEARNING OBJECTIVE

Journalize the entry for the deposit of employees' federal income taxes withheld and FICA taxes (both employees' withheld and employer's matching share) and prepare the deposit coupon.

FYI

There are substantial penalties applied for late deposits of federal taxes.

FYI

We will show a Form 941 later in this chapter.

Federal Tax Deposit Coupon

Let's go back to Green Sales Company, where tax payments were up to date. From the payroll of October 7, the following federal taxes are owed:

Employees' federal income taxes withheld	$2,378.24
Employees' FICA taxes withheld ($1,158.73 + $272.60)	1,431.33
Employer's share of FICA taxes	1,431.31
Total federal undeposited taxes	$5,240.88

We continue on for the next payroll period, ended October 14. Assuming the payroll information for the week is the same as it was for the week ended October 7, the two periods would be:

	Oct. 7	Oct. 14	Total
Employees' federal income taxes withheld	$2,378.24	$2,378.24	$ 4,756.48
Employees' FICA taxes withheld	1,431.33	1,431.33	2,862.66
Employer's share of FICA taxes	1,431.31	1,431.31	2,862.62
Total federal undeposited taxes	$5,240.88	$5,240.88	$10,481.76

Green Sales Company, which deposits taxes semiweekly, receives a federal tax deposit card (printed with the company's name and employer identification number) from the Internal Revenue Service (Figure 2).

The accountant records the amount of the deposit, the employer identification number (unless preprinted), the type of tax, the tax period, and the name and address of the company. The entry in general journal form to record the deposit of two weeks' taxes looks like the following.

Date		Description	Post. Ref.	Debit	Credit
20—					
Oct.	15	Employees' Federal Income Tax Payable		4 7 5 6 48	
		FICA Taxes Payable ($2,862.66 + $2,862.62)		5 7 2 5 28	
		Cash			10 4 8 1 76
		Issued check for federal tax deposit, Central National Bank.			

FIGURE 2

Federal Tax Deposit Coupon (Form 8109-B) for Green Sales Company

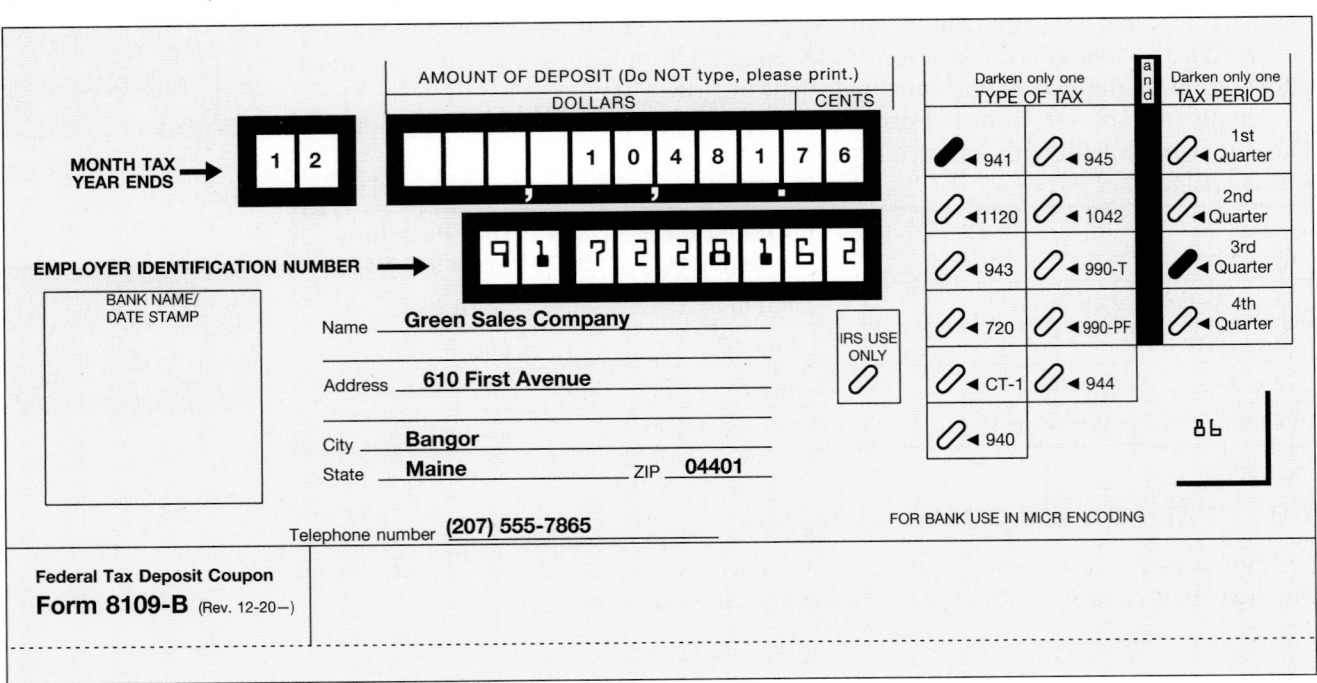

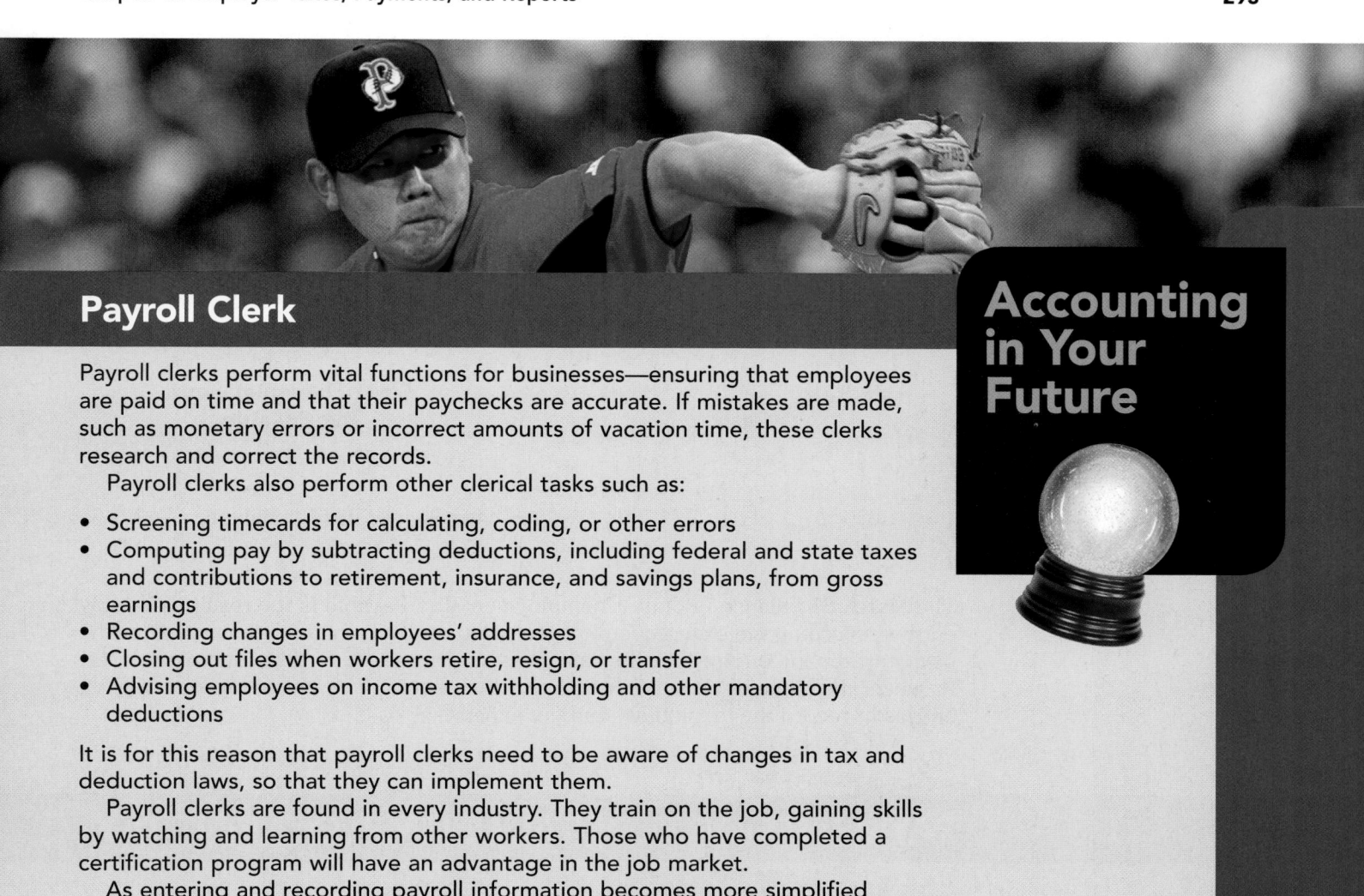

Payroll Clerk

Payroll clerks perform vital functions for businesses—ensuring that employees are paid on time and that their paychecks are accurate. If mistakes are made, such as monetary errors or incorrect amounts of vacation time, these clerks research and correct the records.

Payroll clerks also perform other clerical tasks such as:

- Screening timecards for calculating, coding, or other errors
- Computing pay by subtracting deductions, including federal and state taxes and contributions to retirement, insurance, and savings plans, from gross earnings
- Recording changes in employees' addresses
- Closing out files when workers retire, resign, or transfer
- Advising employees on income tax withholding and other mandatory deductions

It is for this reason that payroll clerks need to be aware of changes in tax and deduction laws, so that they can implement them.

Payroll clerks are found in every industry. They train on the job, gaining skills by watching and learning from other workers. Those who have completed a certification program will have an advantage in the job market.

As entering and recording payroll information becomes more simplified due to the increasing use of computers, the job itself is becoming more varied and complex. For example, companies now offer a greater variety of pension, 401(k), and other investment plans to their employees. These developments will contribute to job growth for payroll clerks in the years to come.

PAYMENTS OF STATE UNEMPLOYMENT INSURANCE

As we stated before, states differ with regard to both the rate and the taxable base for unemployment insurance. In our example, we assume that the state tax is 5.4 percent (0.054) of the first $7,000 paid to each employee during the calendar year. **The state tax is usually paid quarterly and is due by the end of the month following the end of the quarter (the same as the due dates for Form 941).** Here is the entry in general journal form made by Green Sales Company for the first quarter (covering the months of January, February, and March). We assume that $70,325 was taxable for the quarter. The amount of the tax is $3,797.55 ($70,325 × 0.054).

3 LEARNING OBJECTIVE

Journalize the entries for the payment of employer's state and federal unemployment taxes.

Date	Description	Post. Ref.	Debit	Credit
20—				
Apr. 30	State Unemployment Tax Payable		3 7 9 7 55	
	Cash			3 7 9 7 55
	Issued check for payment of			
	state unemployment tax.			

The T accounts are as follows:

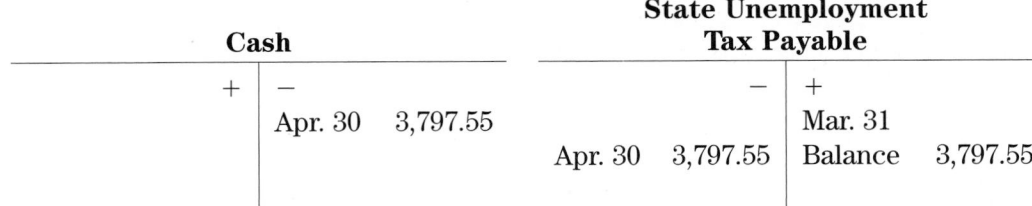

	Cash		State Unemployment Tax Payable
+	−	−	+
	Apr. 30 3,797.55		Mar. 31
		Apr. 30 3,797.55	Balance 3,797.55

The March 31 balance in State Unemployment Tax Payable is the result of weekly entries recording the state unemployment portion of payroll tax expense. After the payment is made on April 30, the balance is shown as zero for illustrative purposes. However, throughout the month of April, the company would be making weekly entries to record the tax liability and tax expense.

PAYMENTS OF FEDERAL UNEMPLOYMENT TAX

The FUTA tax is calculated quarterly, during the month following the end of each calendar quarter. **If the accumulated tax liability is greater than $500, the tax is deposited in a financial institution, accompanied by a preprinted federal tax deposit card** like that used to deposit employees' federal income tax withholding and FICA taxes. The deposit may also be made electronically. The due date for this deposit is the last day of the month following the end of the quarter, the same as the due dates for the Employer's Quarterly Federal Tax Return and for state unemployment taxes.

Here is the entry in general journal form made by Green Sales Company for the first quarter. In our example, since the FUTA and state unemployment taxable earnings are the same (the first $7,000 for each employee), we assume that $70,325 was taxable for the quarter. The amount of the tax is $562.60 ($70,325 × 0.008).

Date	Description	Post. Ref.	Debit	Credit
20—				
Apr. 30	Federal Unemployment Tax Payable		5 6 2 60	
	Cash			5 6 2 60
	Issued check for payment of			
	federal unemployment tax.			

The T accounts are as follows:

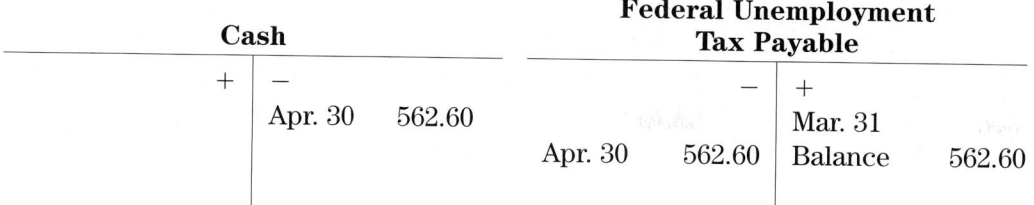

Cash			Federal Unemployment Tax Payable		
+	−			−	+
	Apr. 30 562.60		Apr. 30 562.60		Mar. 31 Balance 562.60

The balance in Federal Unemployment Tax Payable is the result of weekly entries recording the federal unemployment portion of payroll tax expense.

DEPOSITS OF EMPLOYEES' STATE INCOME TAX WITHHOLDING

Assume that the withholdings for employees' state income taxes are deposited on a quarterly basis, payable at the same time as state unemployment tax. Also, as of March 31, the credit balance of Employees' State Income Tax Payable is $1,674.10. The entry in general journal form to record the payment for the first quarter takes the following form.

LEARNING OBJECTIVE 4
Journalize the entry for the deposit of employees' state income taxes withheld.

Date		Description	Post. Ref.	Debit	Credit
20—					
Apr.	30	Employees' State Income Tax Payable		1 6 7 4 10	
		Cash			1 6 7 4 10
		Issued check for state income			
		tax deposit.			

The T accounts are as follows:

Cash			Employees' State Income Tax Payable		
+	−			−	+
	Apr. 30 1,674.10		Apr. 30 1,674.10		Mar. 31 Balance 1,674.10

EMPLOYER'S QUARTERLY FEDERAL TAX RETURN (FORM 941)

If you are an employer, you must file a quarterly **Form 941**, Employer's Quarterly Federal Tax Return. The purpose of Form 941 is to report the tax liability for withholdings of employees' federal income tax and FICA taxes, and also the employer's share of FICA taxes. Total tax deposits made are also listed. As the title implies, the time period is three months. Remember that the due dates for

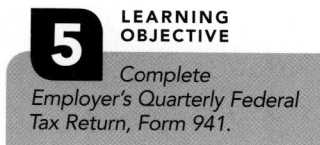

LEARNING OBJECTIVE 5
Complete Employer's Quarterly Federal Tax Return, Form 941.

the calendar year are: first quarter, April 30; second quarter, July 31; third quarter, October 31; fourth quarter, January 31.

A completed Form 941 for Green Sales Company is shown in Figure 3. There are five parts to this form. Figure 3 shows the information for Green Sales Company for Parts 1 and 2. Part 3 is used when you close your business and stop paying wages—this will also stop the IRS from automatically sending 941 forms. Part 4 is for you to give the IRS permission—or not—to speak with your third-party designee (employee, paid tax preparer for example). Part 5 is the signature, title, and date block for the paid preparer and/or employer. You can get instructions and can complete the form online at www.irs.gov, if you wish.

The top of the form contains basic information about the employer. Once an employer has secured an identification number and has filed the first return, the Internal Revenue Service automatically sends forms directly to the employer. These subsequent forms will have the employer's name, address, and identification number filled in.

Now let's look at completed Parts 1 and 2 of an Employer's Quarterly Federal Tax Return (Form 941) starting with its heading.

FIGURE 3

Employer's Quarterly Federal Tax Return (Form 941) for Green Sales Company

Form **941 for 20—: Employer's QUARTERLY Federal Tax Return** 950109
(Rev. April 20—) Department of the Treasury — Internal Revenue Service OMB No. 1545-0029

(EIN) Employer identification number: 9 1 – 7 2 2 8 1 6 2

Name (not your trade name):

Trade name (if any): Green Sales Company

Address: 610 First Avenue (Number, Street, Suite or room number)

Bangor (City) ME (State) 04401 (ZIP code)

Report for this Quarter of 20— (Check one.)
- ☐ 1: January, February, March
- ☐ 2: April, May, June
- ☐ 3: July, August, September
- ☑ 4: October, November, December

Read the separate instructions before you complete Form 941. Type or print within the boxes.

Part 1: Answer these questions for this quarter.

1	Number of employees who received wages, tips, or other compensation for the pay period including: *Mar. 12* (Quarter 1), *June 12* (Quarter 2), *Sept. 12* (Quarter 3), *Dec. 12* (Quarter 4)		1	12
2	Wages, tips, and other compensation		2	197,622.00
3	Income tax withheld from wages, tips, and other compensation		3	35,572.00
4	If no wages, tips, and other compensation are subject to social security or Medicare tax			☐ Check and go to line 6.
5	Taxable social security and Medicare wages and tips:			

	Column 1		Column 2
5a Taxable social security wages	177,621.00	× .124 =	22,025.00
5b Taxable social security tips	0.00	× .124 =	0.00
5c Taxable Medicare wages & tips	197,622.00	× .029 =	5,731.04

5d	Total social security and Medicare taxes (*Column 2*, lines 5a + 5b + 5c = line 5d)		5d	27,756.04
6	Total taxes before adjustments (lines 3 + 5d = line 6)		6	63,328.04
7	CURRENT QUARTER'S ADJUSTMENTS, for example, a fractions of cents adjustment. See the instructions.			
7a	Current quarter's fractions of cents	0.00		
7b	Current quarter's sick pay	0.00		
7c	Current quarter's adjustments for tips and group-term life insurance	0.00		
7d	TOTAL ADJUSTMENTS. Combine all amounts on lines 7a through 7c		7d	0.00
8	Total taxes after adjustments. Combine lines 6 and 7d		8	63,328.04
9	Advance earned income credit (EIC) payments made to employees		9	0.00
10	Total taxes after adjustment for advance EIC (line 8 – line 9 = line 10)		10	63,328.04
11	Total deposits for this quarter, including overpayment applied from a prior quarter and overpayment applied from Form 941-X or Form 944-X	63,328.04		
12a	COBRA premium assistance payments (see instructions)	0.00		
12b	Number of individuals provided COBRA premium assistance reported on line 12a			
13	Add lines 11 and 12a		13	63,328.04
14	Balance due. If line 10 is more than line 13, write the difference here. For information on how to pay, see the instructions.		14	0.00
15	Overpayment. If line 13 is more than line 10, write the difference here	.		Check one ☐ Apply to next return. ☐ Send a refund.

▶ You **MUST** complete both pages of Form 941 and **SIGN** it.

Next ➔

Part 2: Tell us about your deposit schedule and tax liability for this quarter.

If you are unsure about whether you are a monthly schedule depositor or a semiweekly schedule depositor, see *Pub. 15 (Circular E)*, section 11.

16 M E   Write the state abbreviation for the state where you made your deposits OR write "MU" if you made your deposits in *multiple* states.

17 Check one: ☐ Line 10 is less than $2,500. Go to Part 3.

☐ You were a monthly schedule depositor for the entire quarter. Enter your tax liability for each month. Then go to Part 3.

Tax liability: Month 1 [   ] .

Month 2 [   ] .

Month 3 [   ] .

Total liability for quarter [   ] .   Total must equal line 10.

☑ You were a semiweekly schedule depositor for any part of this quarter. Complete *Schedule B (Form 941): Report of Tax Liability for Semiweekly Schedule Depositors*, and attach it to Form 941.

FIGURE 3

(Concluded)

Questions Listed on Form 941 (Figure 3)

Tax forms can be somewhat intimidating. The best approach to completing a tax form is to have accurate and complete records, read and complete the form line by line, and don't look ahead. Green Sales Company's fourth quarter form, shown in Figure 3, has been completed as follows. Note that the employees at Green Sales Company earn only wages. Had they also earned tips or other compensation, such as bonuses, those would have been included in the form.

Part 1:

1. **Line 1** indicates the number of employees (12) who received wages.
2. **Line 2** shows the total of those wages for the quarter ($197,622.00).
3. **Line 3** shows the total income tax withheld from wages for the quarter ($35,572.00).
4. **Line 4** is not checked because all wages during the quarter are subject to Medicare tax.
5. **Lines 5a–d** provide information that indicates how the total of the Social Security and Medicare taxes ($22,025.00 + $5,731.04 = $27,756.04) is calculated. Note that the multipliers represent the combined FICA employee and employer contributions (for Social Security, $0.062 \times 2 = 0.124$; for Medicare, $0.0145 \times 2 = 0.029$).
6. **Line 6** ($63,328.04) is the total of the income taxes withheld (line 3) and the Social Security and Medicare taxes (line 5d), before adjustments.
7. **Lines 7a–d** indicate any tax adjustments that may be needed. Green Sales Company did not have any of those for the quarter. Note that these adjustments may be for fractions of cents due to rounding (line 7a) or corrections of errors in earlier filings of Form 941 (lines 7b and 7c).
8. **Line 8** shows the total taxes after adjustments (line 6 plus line 7d = $63,328.04).
9. **Line 9** discloses any payments of advanced earned income credit (EIC), a refundable federal income tax credit for low-income working individuals and families, that may have been made to employees. Green Sales Company did not have any this quarter.
10. **Line 10** is the total of lines 8 and 9 ($63,328.04).
11. **Line 11** shows the total deposits ($63,328.04) made by Green Sales Company for this quarter and includes any overpayments from prior quarters. As indicated, the company has made deposits equaling the total due for this quarter.
12. **Lines 12a and 12b** disclose any premium assistance payments of COBRA for eligible individuals and the number of individuals who were provided COBRA premium assistance. COBRA provides certain former employees, retirees, spouses, former spouses, and dependent children the right to temporary continuation of health coverage at group rates if their previous coverage is lost due to specific events such as a reduction in the number of hours of employment or a voluntary or

involuntary termination of employment for reasons other than gross misconduct. Green Sales Company did not have any COBRA payments this quarter.

13. **Line 13** is the total of lines 11 and 12a ($63,328.04).

14. **Lines 14** (underpayment) and 15 (overpayment), which indicate the difference between lines 10 and 13, show that the company's balance for the quarter is zero.

Part 2:

15. **Line 16** shows ME, the abbreviation for Maine, the state in which the deposits were made.

16. **Line 17** shows a checkmark in the third box because Green Sales Company was a semiweekly scheduled depositor for this quarter.

As stated earlier, the remaining parts of the 941 form require stating whether your business is closing, permission to allow third-party inquiries, signatures and titles of the preparer, and the date Form 941 is submitted. For thorough instructions to assist you in filling out any IRS form, go to www.irs.gov and enter the form or descriptive words into the search box.

Wage Withholding Statements for Employees (Form W-2)

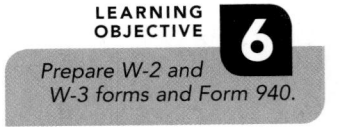

LEARNING OBJECTIVE 6

Prepare W-2 and W-3 forms and Form 940.

After the end of a year (December 31) and by the following January 31, the employer must furnish for each employee a Wage and Tax Statement, known as **Form W-2.** This form contains information about the employee's earnings and tax deductions for the year. The source of the information used to complete Form W-2 is the employee's individual earnings record. The amounts used to complete Mark Anderson's W-2 form (in Figure 4) represent the amounts taken from his earnings record at the end of the calendar year, December 31.

FIGURE 4

Wage and Tax Statement (Form W-2) for Mark Anderson

Box 9 shows the total paid to the employee as advance earned income credit (EIC) payments. Box 13 is used for miscellaneous items, such as statutory employees

a Employee's social security number **543-24-1680**		
22222	OMB No. 1545-0008	Safe, accurate, FAST! Use IRS *e~file* Visit the IRS website at www.irs.gov/efile

b Employer identification number (EIN) **91-7228162**	1 Wages, tips, other compensation **58,404.58**	2 Federal income tax withheld **10,920.00**
c Employer's name, address, and ZIP code **Green Sales Company** **610 First Avenue** **Bangor, Maine 04401**	3 Social security wages **58,404.58**	4 Social security tax withheld **3,621.08**
	5 Medicare wages and tips **58,404.58**	6 Medicare tax withheld **846.87**
	7 Social security tips **0**	8 Allocated tips
d Control number	9 Advance EIC payment **0**	10 Dependent care benefits **0**
e Employee's first name and initial Last name Suff.	11 Nonqualified plans **0**	12a See instructions for box 12
Mark E. Anderson **1104 Rosewood Street** **Bangor, Maine 04401**	13 Statutory employee ☐ Retirement plan ☐ Third-party sick pay ☐	12b
	14 Other	12c
		12d
f Employee's address and ZIP code		

15 State	Employer's state ID number	16 State wages, tips, etc.	17 State income tax	18 Local wages, tips, etc.	19 Local income tax	20 Locality name
ME	**464-729**	**58,404.58**	**2,184.00**	**0**	**0**	**0**

Form **W-2** Wage and Tax Statement   **20—**   Department of the Treasury—Internal Revenue Service

Copy B—To Be Filed With Employee's FEDERAL Tax Return.
This information is being furnished to the Internal Revenue Service.

(i.e., workers who are independent contractors under the common-law rules but are treated by statute as employees, such as full-time life insurance sales agents and traveling salespersons), 401(k) plan contributions, or sick pay that is not included in income because the employee contributed to the sick pay plan. Box 14 may include the value of noncash fringe benefits, such as providing a vehicle for the employee.

At least four copies of the W-2 form are required for each employee:

Copy A—Employer sends to the Social Security Administration.

Copy B—Employer gives to employee to be attached to the employee's individual federal income tax return.

Copy C—Employer gives to employee to be kept for his or her personal records.

Copy D—Employer keeps this copy as a record of payments made.

If state and local income taxes are withheld, the employer prepares additional copies to be sent to the appropriate tax agency.

FYI

A copy is also sent (if applicable) to the state and/or local tax department, and a copy is given to the employee to attach to the state/local tax return.

Employer's Annual Federal Income Tax Reports (Form W-3)

Accompanying Copy A of the employees' W-2 forms, Green Sales Company sends **Form W-3**, Transmittal of Wage and Tax Statements, to the Social Security Administration. This form is due on February 28, following the end of the calendar year.

For all employees, Form W-3 shows the total wages and tips, total federal income tax withheld, total Social Security and Medicare taxable wages, total Social Security and Medicare taxes withheld, and other information. These amounts must be the same as the grand totals of the W-2 forms and the four quarterly 941 forms for the year. Green Sales Company's completed Form W-3 is presented in Figure 5.

FIGURE 5

Transmittal of Wage and Tax Statements (Form W-3) for Green Sales Company

DO NOT STAPLE

a Control number: 33333	For Official Use Only ▶ OMB No. 1545-0008

b Kind of Payer	941 [X] Military ☐ 943 ☐ 944 ☐ CT-1 ☐ Hshld. emp. ☐ Medicare govt. emp. ☐ Third-party sick pay ☐	1 Wages, tips, other compensation **861,530.00**	2 Federal income tax withheld **155,075.00**

3 Social security wages **775,358.00**	4 Social security tax withheld **48,072.20**

c Total number of Forms W-2 **12**	d Establishment number – – – – – –	5 Medicare wages and tips **861,530.00**	6 Medicare tax withheld **12,492.19**

e Employer identification number (EIN) **64-7228162**	7 Social security tips **0**	8 Allocated tips **0**

f Employer's name **Green Sales Company** **610 First Avenue** **Bangor, Maine 04401**	9 Advance EIC payments **0**	10 Dependent care benefits **0**

	11 Nonqualified plans **0**	12 Deferred compensation **0**

	13 For third-party sick pay use only

	14 Income tax withheld by payer of third-party sick pay **0**

g Employer's address and ZIP code	

h Other EIN used this year **0**	

15 State **ME** Employer's state ID number **464-729**	16 State wages, tips, etc. **861,530.00**	17 State income tax **31,015.00**

	18 Local wages, tips, etc.	19 Local income tax

Contact person **Eileen Green**	Telephone number **(207) 555-7865**	For Official Use Only

Email address **egreen@emailme.net**	Fax number **(207) 555-1477**	

Under penalties of perjury, I declare that I have examined this return and accompanying documents, and, to the best of my knowledge and belief, they are true, correct, and complete.

Signature ▶ *Eileen Green*   Title ▶ *Owner*   Date ▶ 2/27/20–

Form **W-3** Transmittal of Wage and Tax Statements   20—   Department of the Treasury Internal Revenue Service

Some boxes deserve an explanation. Box d, establishment number, may be used for a company that has separate establishments, with each establishment filing W-2 and W-3 forms separately. Box 9 is used for recording the amount of advance earned income credits shown on W-2 forms for qualified employees. Box h is used by a company that had more than one employer identification number (EIN) during the year.

To sum up thus far: The employer must submit the following at the end of the calendar year: Employer's Quarterly Federal Tax Return, Form 941, for the fourth quarter by January 31; Wage and Tax Statements, Form W-2, for all employees by January 31; Transmittal of Wage and Tax Statements, Form W-3, by February 28.

REPORTS AND PAYMENTS OF FEDERAL UNEMPLOYMENT TAX

Remember

If the accumulated FUTA tax liability at the end of a quarter is greater than $500, a deposit must be made.

As we stated previously, generally all employers are subject to the Federal Unemployment Tax Act. These employers must submit an Employer's Annual Federal Unemployment (FUTA) Tax Return, Form 940, no later than January 31 following the close of the calendar year. This deadline may be extended until February 10 if the employer has made deposits paying the FUTA tax liability in full. **Form 940** shows total wages paid to employees, total wages subject to federal unemployment tax, and other information.

Using Green Sales Company as our example, federal unemployment taxable earnings by quarter are as follows:

Federal Unemployment Tax	1st Quarter	2nd Quarter	3rd Quarter	4th Quarter	Cumulative Total
Taxable earnings	$70,325	$9,485	$10,316	$3,520	$93,646
Tax rate	× 0.008	× 0.008	× 0.008	× 0.008	× 0.008
Tax liability	$562.60	$75.88	$ 82.53	$28.16	$749.17

We now repeat the journal entry for the first quarter, in which $562.60 was deposited on April 30.

Date		Description	Post. Ref.	Debit	Credit
20—					
Apr.	30	Federal Unemployment Tax Payable		5 6 2 60	
		Cash			5 6 2 60
		Issued check for deposit of			
		federal unemployment tax.			

During the second and third quarters, many employees' total earnings passed the $7,000 limit of taxable earnings, and the firm's tax liability was reduced accordingly. Because Green Sales Company's total accumulated liability of $158.41 ($75.88 + $82.53) was less than $500, deposits covering those quarters were not made.

By the end of the fourth quarter, each of the twelve employees' earnings passed the $7,000 mark. The total accumulated liability for the second, third, and fourth quarters is $186.57 ($75.88 + $82.53 + $28.16). This amount will be paid by January 31, accompanied by the completed Employer's Annual Federal Unemployment (FUTA) Tax Return, Form 940.

The T account for Federal Unemployment Tax Payable follows. The credits to the account were part of the entries to record the federal unemployment tax portion of Payroll Tax Expense for each payroll period.

Federal Unemployment Tax Payable

	−	+	
Apr. 30 deposit	562.60	1st quarter (liability)	562.60
		2nd quarter (liability)	75.88
		3rd quarter (liability)	82.53
Jan. 31 deposit	186.57	4th quarter (liability)	28.16

Employer's Annual Federal Unemployment (FUTA) Tax Return (Form 940)

Figure 6 shows a completed Form 940 for Green Sales Company. This form has seven parts. (Bear in mind that all forms change from time to time. Go to www.irs.gov for updates.)

Part 1:

1. **Line 1a** indicates the abbreviation for the state in which the business was required to pay taxes, while **line 1b** is for multi-state employers.

2. **Line 2** is for businesses that paid wages in a state that is subject to credit reduction. A credit reduction state is one that has not repaid money it borrowed from the federal government to pay unemployment benefits. Let's assume the U.S. Department of Labor announced that there are no credit reduction states for the current tax year, so Green Sales Company skips this line.

Part 2:

3. **Line 3** lists the total wages paid during the calendar year ($861,530.00).

4. **Line 4** lists the amount of wages exempt from FUTA tax—this includes such items as agricultural labor, family employment, and the value of meals and lodging. It is assumed that Green Sales Company had no such wages. If it had, the appropriate box or boxes on lines 4a–e would need to be checked to show the types of payments exempt from FUTA tax.

5. **Line 5** shows the exempt wages paid ($767,884.00)—wages paid to each employee over and above $7,000 for the calendar year.

6. **Line 6** is the total exempt payments ($767,884.00).

7. **Line 7** shows the total taxable FUTA wages ($93,646.00), which is computed by subtracting the total amount of exempt payments (line 6) from the total wages paid (line 3).

8. **Line 8** indicates the total amount of FUTA tax due before adjustments ($93,646.00 × 0.008 = $749.17).

Part 3:

9. **Lines 9 and 10** are to be completed if all or some of the FUTA wages paid were excluded from state unemployment tax. These lines do not apply to Green Sales Company, so they are left blank.

10. **Line 11** is also left blank due to the fact that the U.S. Department of Labor announced that there are no credit reduction states for the current tax year.

FIGURE 6   Employer's Annual Federal Unemployment (FUTA) Tax Return (Form 940) for Green Sales Company

---

Form **940 for 20—:**   **Employer's Annual Federal Unemployment (FUTA) Tax Return**

Department of the Treasury — Internal Revenue Service

850108

OMB No. 1545-0028

(EIN) Employer identification number: 9 1 – 7 2 2 8 1 6 2

Name (not your trade name):

Trade name (if any): **Green Sales Company**

Address: 610 First Avenue
Number   Street   Suite or room number

Bangor   ME   04401
City   State   ZIP code

Type of Return (Check all that apply.)

- [ ] a. Amended
- [ ] b. Successor employer
- [ ] c. No payments to employees in 20--
- [ ] d. Final: Business closed or stopped paying wages

Read the separate instructions before you fill out this form. Please type or print within the boxes.

Part 1: Tell us about your return. If any line does NOT apply, leave it blank.

1   If you were required to pay your state unemployment tax in ...

   1a One state only, write the state abbreviation . . .   1a   **ME**

   - OR -

   1b More than one state (You are a multi-state employer) . . . . . . 1b [ ]   Check here. Fill out Schedule A.

          Skip line 2 for 20-- and go to line 3.

2   If you paid wages in a state that is subject to CREDIT REDUCTION . . . . 2 [ ]   Check here. Fill out Schedule A (Form 940), Part 2.

Part 2: Determine your FUTA tax before adjustments for 20--. If any line does NOT apply, leave it blank.

3   Total payments to all employees   3   **861,530 . 00**

4   Payments exempt from FUTA tax   4   **0 . 00**

   Check all that apply: 4a [ ] Fringe benefits   4c [ ] Retirement/Pension   4e [ ] Other

                  4b [ ] Group-term life insurance   4d [ ] Dependent care

5   Total of payments made to each employee in excess of $7,000   5   **767,884 . 00**

6   **Subtotal** (line 4 + line 5 = line 6)   6   **767,884 . 00**

7   **Total taxable FUTA wages** (line 3 – line 6 = line 7)   7   **93,646 . 00**

8   **FUTA tax before adjustments** (line 7 × .008 = line 8)   8   **749 . 17**

Part 3: Determine your adjustments. If any line does NOT apply, leave it blank.

9   If ALL of the taxable FUTA wages you paid were excluded from state unemployment tax, multiply line 7 by .054 (line 7 × .054 = line 9). Then go to line 12   9   **0 . 00**

10   If SOME of the taxable FUTA wages you paid were excluded from state unemployment tax, OR you paid ANY state unemployment tax late (after the due date for filing Form 940), fill out the worksheet in the instructions. Enter the amount from line 7 of the worksheet onto line 10 .   10   **0 . 00**

         Skip line 11 for 20-- and go to line 12.

11   If credit reduction applies, enter the amount from line 3 of Schedule A (Form 940)   11   **.**

Part 4: Determine your FUTA tax and balance due or overpayment for 20--. If any line does NOT apply, leave it blank.

12   **Total FUTA tax after adjustments** (lines 8 + 9 + 10 + 11 = line 12)   12   **749 . 17**

13   **FUTA tax deposited for the year,** including any payment applied from a prior year   . . .   13   **562 . 60**

14   **Balance due** (If line 12 is more than line 13, enter the difference on line 14.)

   • If line 14 is more than $500, you must deposit your tax.

   • If line 14 is $500 or less, you may pay with this return. For more information on how to pay, see the separate instructions   14   **186 . 57**

15   **Overpayment** (If line 13 is more than line 12, enter the difference on line 15 and check a box below.)   . . .   15   **.**

   Check one: [ ] Apply to next return.   [ ] Send a refund.

▶ You **MUST** fill out both pages of this form and **SIGN** it.

Next ➡

For Privacy Act and Paperwork Reduction Act Notice, see the back of Form 940-V, Payment Voucher.   Cat. No. 11234O   Form **940** (20--)

Part 5: Report your FUTA tax liability by quarter only if line 12 is more than $500. If not, go to Part 6.

16   Report the amount of your FUTA tax liability for each quarter; do NOT enter the amount you deposited. If you had no liability for a quarter, leave the line blank.

16a   1st quarter (January 1 – March 31) . . . .   16a | 562.60

16b   2nd quarter (April 1 – June 30) . . . .   16b | 75.88

16c   3rd quarter (July 1 – September 30) . . . .   16c | 82.53

16d   4th quarter (October 1 – December 31) . . . . . . 16d | 28.16

17   Total tax liability for the year (lines 16a + 16b + 16c + 16d = line 17) **17** | 749.17 | Total must equal line 12.

Part 6: May we speak with your third-party designee?

Do you want to allow an employee, a paid tax preparer, or another person to discuss this return with the IRS? See the instructions for details.

☐ **Yes.**   Designee's name and phone number   ( )   –

Select a 5-digit Personal Identification Number (PIN) to use when talking to IRS ☐ ☐ ☐ ☐ ☐

☑ **No.**

Part 7: Sign here. You MUST fill out both pages of this form and SIGN it.

Under penalties of perjury, I declare that I have examined this return, including accompanying schedules and statements, and to the best of my knowledge and belief, it is true, correct, and complete, and that no part of any payment made to a state unemployment fund claimed as a credit was, or is to be, deducted from the payments made to employees. Declaration of preparer (other than taxpayer) is based on all information of which preparer has any knowledge.

X Sign your name here   *Eileen Green*

Print your name here   **Eileen Green**

Print your title here   **Owner**

Date   1 / 31 / 20—

Best daytime phone   (207) 555 – 7865

FIGURE 6
(Concluded)

Part 4:

11. **Line 12** indicates the amount of total FUTA tax after adjustments ($749.17), which is the sum of line 8 + lines 9–11.

12. **Line 13** shows the amount of total FUTA tax that was deposited for the year ($562.60).

13. **Line 14** is the difference between line 12 and line 13 ($749.17 – $562.60 = $186.57). This represents the balance due.

14. **Line 15** is completed if FUTA tax deposited for the year (line 13) is more than the total FUTA tax after adjustments (line 12). This indicates an overpayment.

Part 5:

15. **Lines 16a–d** ask for the amount of FUTA tax liability for each quarter.

16. **Line 17** discloses the total tax liability for the calendar year ($749.17). It should equal the amount given on line 12 and the total of lines 16a–d.

The remaining parts of the 940 form require whether or not you grant permission for third-party inquiries, signature and title of the preparer, and the date Form 940 is submitted.

WORKERS' COMPENSATION INSURANCE

LEARNING OBJECTIVE 7

Calculate the premium for workers' compensation insurance, and prepare the entry for payment in advance.

Most states require employers to provide **workers' compensation insurance** or industrial accident insurance for employees killed or injured on the job, either through plans administered by the state or through private insurance companies authorized by the state. The employer usually has to pay all the premiums. The premium rate varies with the amount of risk the job entails and the company's claims history. For example, handling molten steel ingots is much more dangerous than typing reports. Thus, it is important that employees be identified properly in terms of the insurance premium classifications. The rates as percentages of the payroll may be 0.15 percent for office work, 0.5 percent for sales work, and 3.5 percent for industrial labor in heavy manufacturing. These same rates may be expressed as $0.15 per $100 of the salaries or wages for office work, $0.50 per $100 for sales work, and $3.50 per $100 for industrial labor.

Generally, the employer pays a premium in advance, based on the estimated payroll for the year. After the year ends, the employer knows the exact amount of the payroll and can calculate the exact premium. At that time, depending on the difference between the estimated and exact premiums, the employer either pays an additional premium or gets a credit for having made an overpayment.

At Green Sales Company, there are two work classifications: office work and sales work. At the beginning of the year, the firm's accountant computed the estimated annual premium as follows:

Classification	Estimated Payroll	Rate per Hundred (Percent)	Estimated Premium
Office work	$182,000	0.15	($182,000 ÷ 100) × 0.15 = $ 273.00
Sales work	660,000	0.50	($660,000 ÷ 100) × 0.50 = 3,300.00
			Total estimated premium $ 3,573.00

As shown by T accounts, the accountant made the following entry.

Prepaid Insurance, Workers' Compensation		Cash	
+	−	+	−
Jan. 10 3,573.00			Jan. 10 3,573.00

Then, at the end of the calendar year, the accountant calculated the exact premium:

Classification	Actual Payroll	Rate per Hundred (Percent)	Exact Premium
Office work	$188,990	0.15	($188,990 ÷ 100) × 0.15 = $ 283.49
Sales work	672,540	0.50	($672,540 ÷ 100) × 0.50 = 3,362.70
			Total estimated premium $3,646.19

Therefore, the amount of the unpaid premium is

$3,646.19	Total exact premium
3,573.00	Less total estimated premium paid
$ 73.19	Additional premium owed

Now the accountant makes an adjusting entry, similar to the adjusting entry for expired insurance. This entry appears on the work sheet. The accountant then makes an additional adjusting entry for the extra premium owed. By T accounts, the entries are as follows:

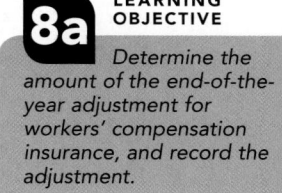

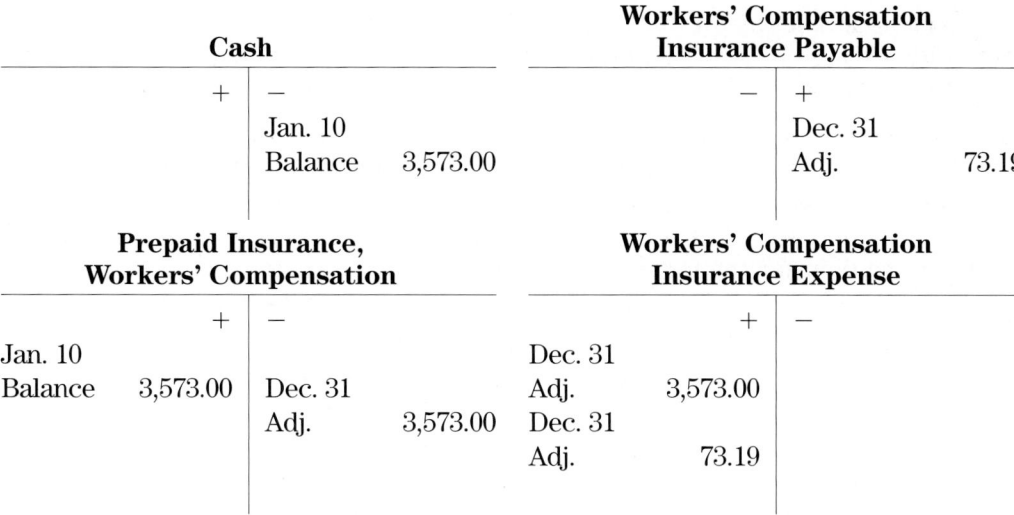

Green Sales Company will pay $73.19, the amount of unpaid premium, in January, together with the estimated premium for the next year.

ADJUSTING FOR ACCRUED SALARIES AND WAGES

Assume that $2,400 of wages accrue for the time between the last payday and the end of the year. An adjusting entry is necessary.

Date	Description	Post. Ref.	Debit	Credit
20—	Adjusting Entry			
Dec. 31	Wages Expense		2 4 0 0 00	
	Wages Payable			2 4 0 0 00

For the accrual adjustment, gross salary and wages are recorded, not the net salary and wages. When the accrued salary and wages are paid, the amounts withheld for federal and state taxes, FICA taxes, and other deductions are then recorded.

Adjusting Entry for Accrual of Payroll Taxes

As you have seen, the following taxes come under the umbrella of the Payroll Tax Expense account: the employer's share of the FICA taxes, the state unemployment tax, and the federal unemployment tax. The employer becomes liable for these taxes only when the employees are actually paid, rather than at the time the liability to the employees is incurred. So there is no adjusting entry for Payroll Tax Expense until the wages are actually paid.

TAX CALENDAR

Now let's put it all together. To keep up with the task of paying and reporting the various taxes, the accountant compiles a chronological list of the due dates. We are including only the payroll taxes here, but any kind of taxes, such as sales taxes and property taxes, should also be listed. When you think about the penalties for nonpayment of taxes by the due dates, this chronological list seems to be well worth the effort. We assume for this purpose the employer is a monthly depositor for the federal tax deposit.

Jan. 10 Pay estimated annual premium for workers' compensation insurance. (This is an approximate date, as it varies among the states.)

15 Make federal tax deposit for employees' income tax withholding, employees' FICA taxes withheld, and employer's FICA taxes for wages paid during the month of December.

31 Complete Employer's Quarterly Federal Tax Return, Form 941, for the fourth quarter.

31 Issue Copies B and C of Wage and Tax Statement, Form W-2, to employees.

31 Pay state unemployment tax liability for the previous quarter, and submit state return, employer's tax report.

31 Pay any remaining federal unemployment tax liability for the previous year, and submit Form 940, Employer's Annual Federal Unemployment (FUTA) Tax Return.

31 Make state deposit for employees' state income tax withholding and submit any required state payroll reports. (Timing and required reports may differ from state to state.)

Feb. 15 Make federal tax deposit for employees' income tax withholding, employees' FICA taxes withholding, and employer's FICA taxes for wages paid during the month of January.

28 Complete Transmittal of Wage and Tax Statements, Form W-3, and attach Copy A of W-2 forms for employees.

Mar. 15 Make federal tax deposit for employees' income tax withholding, employees' FICA taxes withholding, and employer's FICA taxes for wages paid during the month of February.

Apr. 15 Make federal tax deposit for employees' income tax withholding, employees' FICA taxes withholding, and employer's FICA taxes for wages paid during the month of March.

30 Pay state unemployment tax liability for the previous quarter and submit state return, employer's tax report.

30 Complete Employer's Quarterly Federal Tax Return, Form 941, for the first quarter.

30 Make federal tax deposit for federal unemployment tax liability if it exceeds $500.

30 Make state deposit for employees' state income tax withholding.

PAYROLL FRAUD

Payroll fraud can be a huge problem for a business in terms of both monies lost and time and frustration dealing with the problem. Payroll fraud can be categorized into three general areas:

1. *Ghost employee fraud*—Someone is recorded in the payroll system who does not work for the business.
2. *False wage claim fraud*—Extra hours or other relevant factors are added to wage information to increase the amount of pay.
3. *False expense reimbursement fraud*—Improper claims are made for the reimbursement of business expenses.

Internal controls should be in place to prevent and detect payroll fraud. Some of those controls would include the following:

1. Require mandatory vacations for those with payroll responsibilities, with other employees performing this function in their absence.
2. Use cash payments or checks minimally and increase the use of direct deposit of payroll checks.
3. Have employees physically sign and show proper identification to receive their paychecks.
4. Conduct periodic unannounced audits to ensure, for example, that all employees on the payroll actually work for the company.
5. Cross-reference the payroll roster for duplicate addresses or Social Security numbers.
6. Conduct a thorough pre-employment reference check for all payroll personnel.
7. Compare payroll expense per the payroll register to the actual amounts paid. Also, compare amounts to payroll deposits made.
8. Outsource payroll administration.

CHAPTER REVIEW

Study & Practice

LEARNING OBJECTIVE

Calculate the amount of payroll tax expense and journalize the entry.

Payroll tax expense consists of the employer's matching portion of FICA taxes, plus the **state unemployment tax (SUTA)**, plus the **federal unemployment tax (FUTA)**. *FICA taxes* consist of Social Security and Medicare taxes. *Social Security tax* equals total Social Security taxable earnings multiplied by 0.062 (6.2 percent assumed rate) on the taxable earnings. For this text, the maximum taxable is assumed to be $106,800. Total *Medicare tax* equals Medicare taxable earnings multiplied by 0.0145 (1.45 percent assumed rate). There is no maximum limit for Medicare— all earnings are taxable. *State unemployment tax* equals unemployment taxable earnings multiplied by 0.054 (5.4 percent assumed rate). *Federal unemployment tax* equals unemployment taxable earnings multiplied by 0.008 (0.8 percent assumed rate). Refer to the related journal entry on page 289.

PRACTICE EXERCISE 1

Quality Roofing has the following payroll information for the week ended May 31:

Total payroll	$56,000
Taxable earnings subject to Social Security	45,000
Taxable earnings subject to unemployment tax	2,000

Using the tax rates given above, prepare the journal entry to record the employer's payroll tax liability.

PRACTICE EXERCISE 1 SOLUTION

Date	Description	Post. Ref.	Debit	Credit
20—				
May 31	Payroll Tax Expense		3 7 2 6 00	
	FICA Taxes Payable			3 6 0 2 00
	State Unemployment Tax Payable			1 0 8 00
	Federal Unemployment Tax Payable			1 6 00
	To record employer's share of FICA			
	taxes and employer's state and			
	federal unemployment taxes.			

Computations:

FICA taxes payable:

Social Security	$45,000 × 0.062 =	$2,790.00
Medicare	$56,000 × 0.0145 =	812.00
Total		$3,602.00

State unemployment tax payable: $2,000 × 0.054 = $ 108.00
Federal unemployment tax payable: $2,000 × 0.008 = $ 16.00

2 **LEARNING OBJECTIVE**

Journalize the entry for the deposit of employees' federal income taxes withheld and FICA taxes (both employees' withheld and employer's matching share) and prepare the deposit coupon.

Refer to this journal entry on page 292.

PRACTICE EXERCISE 2

For the week ended May 31, Quality Roofing withheld the following taxes from its employees:

Federal income taxes withheld	$12,000
FICA taxes withheld	3,602

Prepare the journal entry to record the tax deposit to People's Bank. Include both the employees' and the employer's share of FICA taxes.

PRACTICE EXERCISE 2 SOLUTION

Date		Description	Post. Ref.	Debit	Credit
20—					
May	31	Employees' Federal Income Tax			
		Payable		12 0 0 0 00	
		FICA Taxes Payable*		7 2 0 4 00	
		Cash			19 2 0 4 00
		Issued check for federal tax			
		deposit, People's Bank.			

*FICA taxes payable include the employees' share of $3,602 plus the employer's share of $3,602, for a total of $7,204.

3 **LEARNING OBJECTIVE**

Journalize the entries for the payment of employer's state and federal unemployment taxes.

State unemployment tax is paid on a quarterly basis. Payment is due by the end of the next month following the end of the calendar **quarter**. Refer to this journal entry on the top of page 294.

If the amount of the accumulated federal unemployment tax liability exceeds $500 at the end of any quarter, the tax is due by the end of the next month following the end of the quarter. If the federal unemployment tax payable is less than $500 at the end of the year, it is due by January 31 of the next year. Refer to this journal entry on the bottom of page 294.

PRACTICE EXERCISE 3

Assume Best Computers had $90,325 taxable earnings for the first quarter (covering the months of January, February, and March). Assuming that the state tax is 5.4 percent (0.054) and the federal tax is 0.8 percent (0.008) of the first $7,000 paid to each employee during the calendar year, journalize the entries for the payment of Best Computers' state and federal unemployment taxes. Assume that no employee has surpassed the $7,000 limit.

PRACTICE EXERCISE 3 SOLUTION

Date		Description	Post. Ref.	Debit	Credit
20—					
Apr.	30	State Unemployment Tax Payable		4 8 7 7 55	
		Cash			4 8 7 7 55
		Issued check for payment of			
		state unemployment tax.			
	30	Federal Unemployment Tax Payable		7 2 2 60	
		Cash			7 2 2 60
		Issued check for payment of			
		federal unemployment tax.			

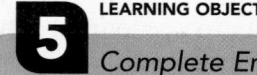

LEARNING OBJECTIVE

4

Journalize the entry for the deposit of employees' state income taxes withheld.

Employees' state income taxes withheld are paid on a quarterly basis or as required by the state. Payment may be due by the end of the next month following the end of the calendar quarter. Refer to this journal entry on page 295.

PRACTICE EXERCISE 4

For the quarter ended June 30, Quality Roofing has a credit balance of $28,000 for Employee's State Income Tax Payable. Assuming the withholdings are deposited on a quarterly basis, prepare the journal entry to record the payment.

PRACTICE EXERCISE 4 SOLUTION

Date		Description	Post. Ref.	Debit	Credit
20—					
July	31	Employees' State Income Tax			
		Payable		28 0 0 0 00	
		Cash			28 0 0 0 00
		Issued check for state income			
		tax deposit.			

LEARNING OBJECTIVE

5

Complete Employer's Quarterly Federal Tax Return, Form 941.

Form 941 is illustrated on page 296.

PRACTICE EXERCISE 5

Based on the Form 941 shown on page 296, what is the difference between Green Sales Company's taxable Social Security wages and taxable Medicare wages? How are the rates for each determined?

PRACTICE EXERCISE 5 SOLUTION

For taxable Medicare wages all wages are taxable, so the amount in Column 1 of $197,622 is the same amount as on line 2, Wages, tips and other compensation. For taxable Social Security wages of $177,621, only the first $106,800 of wages is taxable, so in this case some of the employees of Green Sales Company exceeded this limit. The rates of 0.124 and 0.029 represent both the employer's and employees' share of these taxes:

Social Security   6.2% + 6.2%   = 12.4% or 0.124
Medicare   1.45% + 1.45% = 2.9% or 0.029

LEARNING OBJECTIVE

6

Prepare W-2 and W-3 forms and Form 940.

Form W-2 (Wage and Tax Statement) is illustrated on page 298. **Form W-3** (Transmittal of Wage and Tax Statements) is illustrated on page 299. **Form 940** (Employer's Annual Federal Unemployment (FUTA) Tax Return) is illustrated on pages 302 and 303.

PRACTICE EXERCISE 6

What do Form W-2, Form W-3, and Form 940 have in common?

PRACTICE EXERCISE 6 SOLUTION

Form W-2, Form W-3, and Form 940 all report the name, address, and Employer Identification Number of the company. (See Figures 4, 5, and 6 on pages 298, 299, and 302–303, respectively.) The total wages should be the same in Box 1 on Form W-3 and on Line 3 on Form 940. All three forms report state information, in this case for the State of Maine.

LEARNING OBJECTIVE

7 *Calculate the premium for workers' compensation insurance, and prepare the entry for payment in advance.*

Rates for **workers' compensation insurance** vary depending on the degree of physical risk involved in different occupations. The amount of the premium equals the predicted annual payroll multiplied by the premium rate. The entry is a debit to Prepaid Insurance, Workers' Compensation, and a credit to Cash.

PRACTICE EXERCISE 7

On January 15, Quality Roofing estimated the following payroll for the year:

Classification	Predicted Payroll	Rate (Percent)
Clerical/office work	$150,000	0.11
Project estimators	200,000	0.15
Roofer construction	670,000	2.20

Calculate the estimated premium and prepare the journal entry to record payment.

PRACTICE EXERCISE 7 SOLUTION

Classification	Predicted Payroll	Rate per Hundred (Percent)	Estimated Premium	
Clerical/office work	$150,000	0.11	($150,000 ÷ 100) × 0.11 = $	165.00
Project estimators	200,000	0.15	($200,000 ÷ 100) × 0.15 =	300.00
Roofer construction	670,000	2.20	($670,000 ÷ 100) × 2.20 =	14,740.00
			Total estimated premium	$15,205.00

Date	Description	Post. Ref.	Debit	Credit
20—				
Jan. 15	Prepaid Insurance, Workers' Compensation		15 2 0 5 00	
	Cash			15 2 0 5 00
	To record payment of estimated workers' compensation premium for 20—.			

LEARNING OBJECTIVE

8

Determine the amount of the end-of-the-year adjustments for (a) workers' compensation insurance and (b) accrued salaries and wages, and record the adjustments.

When the total annual payroll is known, the exact cost of workers' compensation insurance can be determined by multiplying the total payroll by the premium rate. Two adjusting entries are required. The first adjusting entry records the expired insurance as a debit to Workers' Compensation Insurance Expense and a credit to Prepaid Insurance, Workers' Compensation. The second adjusting entry records the difference between the estimated and the actual premiums. If the actual premium is greater than the premium that was paid in advance, the entry is a debit to Workers' Compensation Insurance Expense and a credit to Workers' Compensation Insurance Payable. The adjustment for accrued salaries and wages accounts for the additional amount of salaries or wages paid in the next payroll that are incurred in the current fiscal period—a debit to Wages (or Salary) Expense. The credit to Wages (or Salaries) Payable accounts for the additional amount of liability incurred in the current period that will be paid with the next payroll that occurs in the following fiscal period.

PRACTICE EXERCISE 8

a. At the end of the year, Quality Roofing had the following payroll:

Classification	Actual Payroll	Rate (Percent)
Clerical/office work	$189,000	0.11
Project estimators	195,000	0.15
Roofer construction	695,000	2.20

Determine the amount of the end-of-the-year adjustment for workers' compensation insurance and prepare the journal entries to record the year-end adjustments for the insurance expired and for the additional premium.

b. Assume that Quality Roofing had $2,000 of salaries accrue for the time between the last payday and the end of the year. Record the adjusting entry for the accrued salaries.

PRACTICE EXERCISE 8 SOLUTION

a.

Classification	Actual Payroll	Rate per Hundred (Percent)	Exact Premium
Clerical/office work	$189,000	0.11	($189,000 ÷ 100) × 0.11 = $ 207.90
Project estimators	195,000	0.15	($195,000 ÷ 100) × 0.15 = 292.50
Roofer construction	695,000	2.20	($695,000 ÷ 100) × 2.20 = 15,290.00
			Total exact premium $15,790.40

The amount of the unpaid premium is

$15,790.40	Total exact premium
15,205.00	Less total estimated premium paid (from PE 7)
$ 585.40	Additional premium owed

Date		Description	Post. Ref.	Debit	Credit
20—		Adjusting Entries			
Dec.	31	Workers' Compensation Insurance			
		Expense		15 2 0 5 00	
		Prepaid Insurance, Workers'			
		Compensation			15 2 0 5 00
	31	Workers' Compensation Insurance			
		Expense		5 8 5 40	
		Workers' Compensation			
		Insurance Payable			5 8 5 40

b.

Date		Description	Post. Ref.	Debit	Credit
20—		Adjusting Entry			
Dec.	31	Salary Expense		2 0 0 0 00	
		Salaries Payable			2 0 0 0 00

Before a Test Check: Chapters 6–8

PART I: COMPLETION

1. Checks issued by the depositor that have been paid or have cleared the bank are called _____ checks.
2. A deposit that is not recorded on the bank statement because it was made after the bank's closing date for preparation of bank statements is called a(n) _____.
3. The process by which the payee transfers ownership of the check to a bank or other party is called a(n) _____.
4. The person to whom a check is payable is called the _____.
5. A cash fund used to make small immediate cash payments is called a(n) _____.

PART II: APPLICATION

1. Cheryl Chang's salary is $3,550 per month. If she works more than 40 hours in one week, she is entitled to overtime pay at the rate of 1½ times her regular hourly rate. During the current week, she worked 45 hours. Calculate her gross pay.
2. On June 30, the column totals of Expert Training's payroll register showed that its training employees had earned $18,000 and its office employees had earned $6,000. Social Security taxes were withheld at 6.2 percent, and Medicare taxes were withheld at 1.45 percent. All earnings are taxable. Other deductions consisted of federal income tax, $3,600, and charitable contributions to the United Way, $500. Determine the amount of Social Security and Medicare taxes that should be withheld. Record the general journal entry to record the payroll, crediting Salaries Payable for the net pay.

3. Roxy Company's payroll for the week ended December 31 is as follows:

Gross earnings of employees	$155,000
Social Security taxable earnings	143,000
Medicare taxable earnings	155,000
Federal unemployment taxable earnings	22,000
State unemployment taxable earnings	22,000

Assume that the payroll is subject to Security tax of 6.2 percent (0.062), Medicare tax of 1.45 percent (0.0145), federal unemployment tax of 0.8 percent (0.008), and state unemployment tax of 5.4 percent (0.054). Write the entry in general journal form to record the employer's payroll tax expense.

PART III: TRUE/FALSE

T F **1.** There is no limit on the amount of taxable earnings for Medicare.

T F **2.** When journalizing the entry to reimburse the Petty Cash Fund, include a credit to Petty Cash Fund.

T F **3.** When journalizing the entry to account for a customer's NSF check, debit Accounts Payable.

T F **4.** An employee's net pay is the result of subtracting his or her deductions from gross pay.

T F **5.** The gross pay for an employee who works 45 hours, earns $8.50 per hour, and receives time and a half for hours worked over 40 hours is $402.75.

ANSWERS: PART I

1. canceled;   **2.** deposit in transit or late deposit;   **3.** endorsement;   **4.** payee;   **5.** petty cash fund

ANSWERS: PART II

1.

$3,550 per month × 12 months = $42,600 per year

$42,600 per year ÷ 52 weeks   = $819.23 per week (rounded)

$819.23 per week ÷ 40 hours   = $20.48 per regular hour (rounded)

$20.48 per regular hour × 1.5   = $30.72 per overtime hour

Earnings for 45 hours:

40 hours at straight time	(40 × $20.48) =	$819.20
5 hours overtime	(5 × $30.72) =	153.60
Total gross earnings		$972.80

2.

		GENERAL JOURNAL			PAGE _____	
Date		Description	Post. Ref.	Debit	Credit	
20—						
June	30	Training Salary Expense		18 0 0 0 00		
		Office Salary Expense		6 0 0 0 00		
		Employees' Federal Income Tax				
		Payable			3 6 0 0 00	
		FICA Taxes Payable				
		($24,000 × 0.062) + ($24,000 × 0.0145)			1 8 3 6 00	
		Employees' United Way Payable			5 0 0 00	
		Salaries Payable			18 0 6 4 00	
		Payroll register for the week ended,				
		June 30, 20—.				

3.

		Description	Post. Ref.	Debit	Credit	
Date						
20—						
Dec.	31	Payroll Tax Expense		12 4 7 7 50		
		FICA Taxes Payable ($143,000 ×				
		0.062) + ($155,000 × 0.0145)			11 1 1 3 50	
		State Unemployment Tax Payable				
		($22,000 × 0.054)			1 1 8 8 00	
		Federal Unemployment Tax Payable				
		($22,000 × 0.008)			1 7 6 00	
		To record employer's share of FICA				
		taxes and employer's state and				
		federal unemployment taxes.				

ANSWERS: PART III

1. T;   **2.** F;   **3.** F;   **4.** T;   **5.** F

Glossary

Employer Identification Number (EIN) The number assigned to each employer by the Internal Revenue Service for use in the submission of reports and payments for FICA taxes and federal income tax withheld. (p. 286)

Federal unemployment tax (FUTA) A tax levied only on the employer, equal to 0.8 percent of the first $7,000 of total earnings paid to each employee during the calendar year. This tax is used to administer the funds. (p. 289)

Form 940 An annual report filed by employers showing total wages paid to employees, total wages subject to federal unemployment tax, total federal unemployment tax, and other information. Also called the *Employer's Annual Federal Unemployment (FUTA) Tax Return.* (p. 300)

Form 941 A quarterly report showing the tax liability for withholdings of employees' federal income tax and FICA taxes and the employer's share of FICA taxes. Total tax deposits made in the quarter are also listed on this Employer's Quarterly Federal Tax Return. *(p. 295)*

Form W-2 A form containing information about employee earnings and tax deductions for the year. Also called *Wage and Tax Statement. (p. 298)*

Form W-3 An annual report sent to the Social Security Administration listing the total wages and tips, total federal income tax withheld, total Social Security and Medicare taxable wages, total Social Security and Medicare tax withheld, and other information for all employees of a firm. Also called the *Transmittal of Wage and Tax Statements. (p. 299)*

Payroll Tax Expense A general expense account used for recording the employer's matching portion of the FICA taxes, the federal unemployment tax, and the state unemployment tax. *(p. 286)*

Quarter Three consecutive months, also referred to as a *calendar quarter. (p. 291)*

State unemployment tax (SUTA) A tax levied only on the employer in most states. Rates differ among the various states; however, they are generally 5.4 percent or higher of the first $7,000 of total earnings paid to each employee during the calendar year. The proceeds are used to pay subsistence benefits to unemployed workers. *(p. 289)*

Workers' compensation insurance This insurance, primarily paid for by the employer, provides benefits for employees injured or killed on the job. The rates vary according to the degree of risk inherent in the job. The plans may be sponsored by states or by private firms. The employer generally pays the premium in advance at the beginning of the year, based on the estimated payroll. The rates are adjusted after the exact payroll is known. *(p. 304)*

CHAPTER ASSIGNMENTS

Discussion Questions

1. What taxes are employers accounting for that increase the debit to Payroll Tax Expense?
2. Describe the journal entry to
   a. record the payroll.
   b. record the employer's payroll tax contributions.
   c. pay the payroll.
3. Explain the deposit requirement for federal unemployment tax.
4. What is the purpose of Form 941? How often is it prepared, and what are the due dates?
5. How many copies are made of a Form W-2, and who uses the copies of the W-2 form?
6. What is the purpose of Form 940? How often is it prepared, and what is the due date?
7. Generally, what is the time schedule for payment of workers' compensation insurance premiums?
8. Explain the advantage of establishing a tax calendar.

Exercises

EXERCISE 8-1 Signature Company's partial payroll register for the week ended January 7 is as follows.

PRACTICE EXERCISE 1

Name	Beginning Cumulative Earnings	Total Earnings	Ending Cumulative Earnings	Taxable Earnings		
				Unemployment	Social Security	Medicare
Barney, R. S.	———	1 9 3 2 00	1 9 3 2 00	1 9 3 2 00	1 9 3 2 00	1 9 3 2 00
Fisk, M. C.	———	5 6 7 00	5 6 7 00	5 6 7 00	5 6 7 00	5 6 7 00
Hayes, W. O.	———	4 8 3 00	4 8 3 00	4 8 3 00	4 8 3 00	4 8 3 00
Lee, L. B.	———	6 7 9 00	6 7 9 00	6 7 9 00	6 7 9 00	6 7 9 00
Parks, S. J.	———	5 7 8 00	5 7 8 00	5 7 8 00	5 7 8 00	5 7 8 00
Tempy, E. B.	———	5 4 6 00	5 4 6 00	5 4 6 00	5 4 6 00	5 4 6 00
		4 7 8 5 00	4 7 8 5 00	4 7 8 5 00	4 7 8 5 00	4 7 8 5 00

Assume that the payroll is subject to a Social Security tax of 6.2 percent of the first $106,800 and a Medicare tax of 1.45 percent on all earnings. Also assume that the federal unemployment tax is 0.8 percent of the first $7,000, and the state unemployment tax is 5.4 percent of the first $7,000. Give the entry in general journal form to record the payroll tax expense.

EXERCISE 8-2 On January 14, at the end of the second week of the year, the totals of Castle Company's payroll register showed that its store employees' wages amounted to $33,482 and its warehouse wages amounted to $13,560. Withholdings consisted of federal income taxes, $5,110; Social Security taxes at the rate of 6.2 percent of the first $106,800 and no employee has reached the limit; Medicare taxes at the rate of 1.45 percent on all earnings; charitable contributions withheld, $845.

PRACTICE EXERCISE 1

a. Calculate the amount of Social Security and Medicare taxes to be withheld, and write the general journal entry to record the payroll.
b. Write the general journal entry to record the employer's payroll taxes, assuming that the federal unemployment tax is 0.8 percent of the first $7,000, that the state unemployment tax is 5.4 percent of the same base, and that no employee has surpassed the $7,000 limit.

EXERCISE 8-3 Go Systems had the following payroll data for wages for the week ended February 5. The state income tax is assumed to be 20% of the federal income tax.

PRACTICE EXERCISE 1

Total Earnings	Ending Cumulative Earnings	Taxable Earnings			Deductions			
		Unemployment	Social Security	Medicare	Federal Income Tax	State Income Tax	Social Security Tax	Medicare Tax
6 7 7 0 00	27 8 5 0 00	6 7 7 0 00	6 7 7 0 00	6 7 7 0 00	1 0 1 5 00	2 0 3 00	4 1 9 74	9 8 17

a. Write the general journal entry to record the payroll.
b. Write the general journal entry to record the employer's payroll taxes. Assume rates of 0.8 percent for federal unemployment tax and 5.4 percent for state unemployment tax based on the first $7,000 for each employee and that no employee has earned more than $7,000.

CHAPTER ASSIGNMENTS

EXERCISE 8-4 The information on earnings and deductions for the pay period ended December 14 from King Company's payroll records is as follows.

Name	Gross Pay	Beginning Cumulative Earnings
Burgess, J. L.	$ 410	$ 6,750
Clayton, M. E.	785	40,200
Drugden, T. F.	860	38,500
Lui, L. W.	990	39,700
Sparks, C. R.	4,094	104,000
Stevers, D. H.	850	6,810

For each employee, the Social Security tax is 6.2 percent of the first $106,800 and the Medicare tax is 1.45 percent on all earnings. The federal unemployment tax is 0.8 percent of the first $7,000 of earnings of each employee. The state unemployment tax is 5.4 percent of the same base. Determine the total taxable earnings for unemployment, Social Security, and Medicare. Prepare a general journal entry to record the employer's payroll taxes.

EXERCISE 8-5 Selected columns of Lion Company's payroll register for the month of January are as follows. The employees' FICA taxes are matched by the employer.

Payment Date	Employees' Federal Income Tax	Employees' Social Security Tax	Employees' Medicare Tax
Jan. 7	1,192.00	475.00	112.25
14	1,135.00	518.14	122.31
21	1,245.00	572.62	124.24
28	1,452.00	561.27	143.26

Lion Company deposits taxes monthly. In general journal form, record the entry for the February 15 payment of FICA and federal income taxes for employees and employer.

EXERCISE 8-6 On September 30, Cody Company's selected account balances are as follows:

Employees' Federal Income Tax Payable	$4,738.00
FICA Taxes Payable (employer and employee)	5,208.92
State Unemployment Tax Payable	2,500.00 } (Some employees have
Federal Unemployment Tax Payable	570.00 } reached the limit.)

In general journal form, prepare the entries to record the following:

Oct. 15   Payment of liabilities for FICA taxes and the federal income tax.

   31   Payment of liability for state unemployment tax.

   31   Payment of liability for federal unemployment tax.

EXERCISE 8-7 On September 30, Hilltop Company's selected payroll accounts are as follows:

 LO 2,3

PRACTICE EXERCISES 2,3

FICA Taxes Payable				State Unemployment Tax Payable		
−	+			−	+	
	Sept. 30	2,314.84			Sept. 30	1,183.40
	Sept. 30	2,314.84				

Federal Unemployment Tax Payable				Employees' Federal Income Tax Payable		
−	+			−	+	
	Sept. 30	575.32			Sept. 30	3,210.85

Prepare general journal entries to record the following:

Oct. 15 Payment of federal tax deposit of FICA taxes and the federal income tax.

    31 Payment of state unemployment tax.

    31 Payment of federal unemployment tax.

EXERCISE 8-8 Great Manufacturing Company received and paid a premium notice on January 2 for workers' compensation insurance stating the rates for the new year. Estimated employees' earnings for the year are as follows:

 LO 7,8

PRACTICE EXERCISES 7,8

Classification	Estimated Wages and Salaries	Rate per Hundred (Percent)	Estimated Premium
Office clerical	$ 92,000	0.11	$ 101.20
Warehouse work	29,000	0.92	266.80
Manufacturing	264,000	2.20	5,808.00
			$6,176.00

At the end of the year, the exact figures for the payroll are as follows:

Classification	Actual Wages and Salaries	Rate per Hundred (Percent)	Exact Premium
Office clerical	$ 93,000	0.11	$ 102.30
Warehouse work	30,000	0.92	276.00
Manufacturing	267,000	2.20	5,874.00
			$6,252.30

a. Record the entry in general journal form for the payment on January 2 of the estimated premium.

b. Record the adjusting entries on December 31 for the insurance expired and for the additional premium.

Problem Set A

For additional help, see the demonstration problem at the beginning of each chapter in your Working Papers.

1

PROBLEM 8-1A Mooney Labs had the following payroll for the week ended February 28:

Salaries		Deductions	
Technicians' salaries	$6,955.00	Federal income tax withheld	$1,145.00
Office salaries	2,260.00	Social Security tax withheld	571.33
Total	$9,215.00	Medicare tax withheld	133.62
		Charity withheld	165.00
		Total	$2,014.95

Assumed tax rates are as follows:

a. FICA: Social Security, 6.2 percent (0.062) on the first $106,800 for each employee, and Medicare, 1.45 percent (0.0145) on all earnings for each employee.
b. State unemployment tax, 5.4 percent (0.054) on the first $7,000 for each employee.
c. Federal unemployment tax, 0.8 percent (0.008) on the first $7,000 for each employee.

Check Figure
Payroll Tax Expense, $1,045.33

Required

Record the following entries in general journal form:

1. The payroll entry as of February 28.
2. The entry to record the employer's payroll taxes as of February 28, assuming that the total payroll is subject to the FICA taxes (combined Social Security and Medicare) and that $5,490 is subject to unemployment taxes.
3. The payment to the employees on March 2. (Assume that the company has transferred cash to Cash—Payroll Bank Account for this payroll.)

1

PROBLEM 8-2A Complete Accounting Services has the following payroll information for the week ended December 7. State income tax is computed as 20 percent of federal income tax.

	A	B	C	D	E
1				DEDUCTIONS	
2		BEGINNING			
3		CUMULATIVE		FEDERAL	STATE
4	NAME	EARNINGS	TOTAL EARNINGS	INCOME TAX	INCOME TAX
5	Denato, T.	6,820.00	480.00	11.00	2.20
6	Herrera, M.	6,840.00	470.00	10.00	2.00
7	Joyner, J.	36,320.00	740.00	47.00	9.40
8	King, L.	26,200.00	540.00	17.00	3.40
9	Wilson, M.	104,360.00	2,720.00	474.49	94.90
10	Yee, N.	28,426.00	605.00	26.00	5.20

Assumed tax rates are as follows:

a. FICA: Social Security, 6.2 percent (0.062) on the first $106,800 for each employee, and Medicare, 1.45 percent (0.0145) on all earnings for each employee.

b. State unemployment tax, 5.4 percent (0.054) on the first $7,000 for each employee.

c. Federal unemployment tax, 0.8 percent (0.008) on the first $7,000 for each employee.

Required

1. Complete the payroll register. Payroll checks begin with Ck. No. 5714 in the payroll register.

2. Prepare a general journal entry to record the payroll as of December 7. The company's general ledger contains a Salary Expense account and a Salaries Payable account.

3. Prepare a general journal entry to record the payroll taxes as of December 7.

4. Journalize the entry to pay the payroll on December 9. (Assume that the company has transferred cash to the Cash—Payroll Bank Account for this payroll.)

Check Figure
Payroll Tax Expense, $428.68

PROBLEM 8-3A For the third quarter of the year, Johnson Company, 415 Circle Avenue, Chicago, Illinois 60652, received Form 941 from the Internal Revenue Service. The identification number of Johnson Company is 91-4213171. Its payroll for the quarter ended September 30 is as follows.

	A	B	C	D	E	F	G
1			TAXABLE EARNINGS		DEDUCTIONS		
2							
3		TOTAL	SOCIAL		FEDERAL	SOCIAL	MEDICARE
4	NAME	EARNINGS	SECURITY	MEDICARE	INCOME TAX	SECURITY TAX	TAX
5	Brown, D. D.	16,629.00	16,629.00	16,629.00	2,494.00	1,031.00	241.12
6	Carey, L. R.	18,528.00	18,528.00	18,528.00	2,780.00	1,148.74	268.66
7	Domzalski, T. P.	14,665.00	14,665.00	14,665.00	2,100.00	909.23	212.64
8	Grisson, R. O.	13,721.00	13,721.00	13,721.00	2,058.00	850.70	198.95
9	Tyler, J. L.	17,406.00	17,406.00	17,406.00	2,510.00	1,079.17	252.39
10	Valdez, K. R.	15,287.00	15,287.00	15,287.00	2,295.00	947.79	221.66
11		96,236.00	96,236.00	96,236.00	14,237.00	5,966.63	1,395.42

The company has had six employees throughout the year. Assume that the Social Security tax is 6.2 percent of the first $106,800, and that the Medicare tax is 1.45 percent of all earnings. The employer matches the employees' FICA (Social Security and Medicare) taxes. There are no taxable tips, adjustments, backup withholding, or earned income credits. Johnson Company has submitted the following federal tax deposits and written the accompanying checks:

On August 15 for the July Payroll		On September 15 for the August Payroll		On October 15 for the September Payroll	
Employees' income tax withheld	$4,370.00	Employees' income tax withheld	$5,122.00	Employees' income tax withheld	$ 4,745.00
Employees' Social Security and Medicare tax withheld	2,259.76	Employees' Social Security and Medicare tax withheld	2,326.28	Employees' Social Security and Medicare tax withheld	2,776.01
Employer's Social Security and Medicare tax contributed	2,259.76	Employer's Social Security and Medicare tax contributed	2,326.28	Employer's Social Security and Medicare tax contributed	2,776.01
	$8,889.52		$9,774.56		$10,297.02

Required

Complete Part 1 of Form 941 for the third quarter for Johnson Company.

Check Figure
Total taxes, $28,961.10

1,2,3

PROBLEM 8-4A Lynden Company has the following balances in its general ledger as of June 1 of this year:

a. FICA Taxes Payable (liability for May), $1,719.40 (employee and employer).
b. Employees' Federal Income Tax Payable (liability for May), $995.00.
c. Federal Unemployment Tax Payable (liability for April and May), $380.00.
d. State Unemployment Tax Payable (liability for April and May), $1,205.75.

The company completed the following transactions involving the payroll during June and July:

June 13 Issued check for $2,714.40 payable to Security Bank, for the monthly deposit of May FICA taxes and employees' federal income tax withheld.

30 Recorded the payroll entry in the general journal from the payroll register for June. The payroll register has the following column totals:

Sales salaries	$11,490.00	
Office salaries	5,147.00	
Total earnings		$16,637.00
Employees' federal income tax deductions	$ 1,725.00	
Employees' Social Security tax deductions	1,031.49	
Employees' Medicare tax deductions	241.24	
Total deductions		2,997.73
Net pay		$13,639.27

30 Recorded payroll taxes. Employer matches the employees' FICA taxes. State unemployment tax is 5.4 percent, and federal unemployment tax is 0.8 percent. At this time, all employees' earnings are taxable for FICA and unemployment taxes.

30 Issued check for $13,639.27 from Cash—Payroll Bank Account to pay salaries for the month.

July 14 Issued check for $4,270.46, payable to Security Bank, for the monthly deposit of June FICA taxes (employee and employer matching) and employees' federal income tax withheld.

31 Issued check for $2,104.15, payable to the State Tax Commission, for state unemployment tax for April, May, and June. The check was accompanied by the quarterly tax return.

31 Issued check for $513.10, payable to Security Bank, for the deposit of federal unemployment tax for the months of April, May, and June.

Check Figure
Payroll Tax Expense, $2,304.23

Required
Record the transactions in the general journal, pages 77–78.

Problem Set B

For additional help, see the demonstration problem at the beginning of each chapter in your Working Papers.

PROBLEM 8-1B Kovarik Company had the following payroll for the week ended March 21:

Salaries		Deductions	
Sales salaries	$7,620.00	Federal income tax withheld	$1,094.00
Office salaries	1,790.00	Social Security tax withheld	583.42
Total	$9,410.00	Medicare tax withheld	136.45
		Charity withheld	153.00
		Total	$1,966.87

Assumed tax rates are as follows:

a. FICA: Social Security, 6.2 percent (0.062) on the first $106,800 for each employee, and Medicare, 1.45 percent (0.0145) on all earnings for each employee.
b. State unemployment tax, 5.4 percent (0.054) on the first $7,000 for each employee.
c. Federal unemployment tax, 0.8 percent (0.008) on the first $7,000 for each employee.

Required

Record the following entries in general journal form:

Check Figure
Payroll Tax Expense, $1,027.70

1. The payroll entry as of March 21.
2. The entry to record the employer's payroll taxes as of March 21, assuming that the total payroll is subject to the FICA taxes (combined Social Security and Medicare) and that $4,965 is subject to unemployment taxes.
3. The payment of the employees on March 23. (Assume that the company has transferred cash to Cash—Payroll Bank Account for this payroll.)

PROBLEM 8-2B Kay's Agency has the following payroll information for the week ended December 14. State income tax is computed as 20 percent of federal income tax.

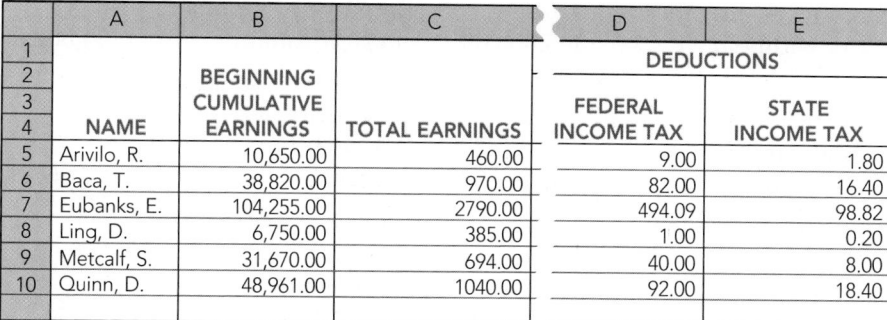

	A	B	C	D	E
1				DEDUCTIONS	
2		BEGINNING			
3		CUMULATIVE		FEDERAL	STATE
4	NAME	EARNINGS	TOTAL EARNINGS	INCOME TAX	INCOME TAX
5	Arivilo, R.	10,650.00	460.00	9.00	1.80
6	Baca, T.	38,820.00	970.00	82.00	16.40
7	Eubanks, E.	104,255.00	2790.00	494.09	98.82
8	Ling, D.	6,750.00	385.00	1.00	0.20
9	Metcalf, S.	31,670.00	694.00	40.00	8.00
10	Quinn, D.	48,961.00	1040.00	92.00	18.40

Assumed tax rates are as follows:

a. FICA: Social Security, 6.2 percent (0.062) on the first $106,800 for each employee, and Medicare, 1.45 percent (0.0145) on all earnings for each employee.
b. State unemployment tax, 5.4 percent (0.054) on the first $7,000 for each employee.

c. Federal unemployment tax, 0.8 percent (0.008) on the first $7,000 for each employee.

Required

1. Complete the payroll register. Payroll checks begin with Ck. No. 5923 in the payroll register.
2. Prepare a general journal entry to record the payroll as of December 14. The company's general ledger contains a Salary Expense account and a Salaries Payable account.
3. Prepare a general journal entry to record the payroll taxes as of December 14.
4. Journalize the entry to pay the payroll on December 16. (Assume that the company has transferred cash to the Cash—Payroll Bank Account for this payroll.)

5  **PROBLEM 8-3B** For the third quarter of the year, Barney Construction, 715 Red Rock Boulevard, San Francisco, California 94121, received Form 941 from the District Office of the Internal Revenue Service. The identification number for Barney Construction is 91-7382476. Its payroll for the quarter ended September 30 is as follows.

	A	B		D		E	F	G
1				TAXABLE EARNINGS			DEDUCTIONS	
2								
3		TOTAL		SOCIAL		FEDERAL	SOCIAL	MEDICARE
4	NAME	EARNINGS		SECURITY	MEDICARE	INCOME TAX	SECURITY TAX	TAX
5	Britton, D. L.	13,387.00		13,387.00	13,387.00	2,010.00	829.99	194.11
6	Finn, J. A.	16,753.00		16,753.00	16,753.00	2,510.00	1,038.69	242.92
7	Harrell, N. E.	17,780.00		17,780.00	17,780.00	2,767.00	1,102.36	257.81
8	Kelly, T. L.	16,243.00		16,243.00	16,243.00	2,430.00	1,007.07	235.52
9	Morton, S. M.	14,215.00		14,215.00	14,215.00	2,130.00	881.33	206.12
10	Rieck, A. J.	20,264.00		20,264.00	20,264.00	3,040.00	1,256.37	293.83
11		98,642.00		98,642.00	98,642.00	14,887.00	6,115.81	1,430.31

The company has had six employees throughout the year. Assume that the Social Security tax is 6.2 percent of the first $106,800, and that the Medicare tax is 1.45 percent of all earnings. The employer matches the employees' FICA (Social Security and Medicare) taxes. There are no taxable tips, adjustments, backup withholding, or earned income credits. Barney Construction has submitted the following federal tax deposits and written the accompanying checks:

On August 15 for the July Payroll		On September 15 for the August Payroll		On October 15 for the September Payroll	
Employees' income tax withheld	$ 5,226.00	Employees' income tax withheld	$ 5,059.00	Employees' income tax withheld	$4,602.00
Employees' Social Security and Medicare tax withheld	2,597.21	Employees' Social Security and Medicare tax withheld	2,591.58	Employees' Social Security and Medicare tax withheld	2,357.33
Employer's Social Security and Medicare tax contributed	2,597.21	Employer's Social Security and Medicare tax contributed	2,591.58	Employer's Social Security and Medicare tax contributed	2,357.32
	$10,420.42		$10,242.16		$9,316.65

Required

Complete Part 1 of Form 941 for the third quarter for Barney Construction.

PROBLEM 8-4B Grande Company has the following balances in its general ledger as of March 1 of this year:

a. FICA Taxes Payable (liability for February), $9,180.00 (employee and employer).
b. Employees' Federal Income Tax Payable (liability for February), $9,000.00.
c. State Unemployment Tax Payable (liability for January and February), $3,442.50.
d. Federal Unemployment Tax Payable (liability for January and February), $510.00.

The company completed the following transactions involving the payroll during March and April:

Mar. 12 Issued check for $18,180.00 payable to Coast Bank, for the monthly deposit of February FICA taxes and employees' federal income tax withheld.

31 Recorded the payroll entry in the general journal from the payroll register for March. The payroll register had the following column totals:

Sales salaries	$47,654.00	
Office salaries	11,982.00	
Total earnings		$59,636.00
Employees' federal income tax deductions	$ 8,945.40	
Employees' Social Security tax deductions	3,697.43	
Employees' Medicare tax deductions	864.72	
Total deductions		13,507.55
Net pay		$46,128.45

31 Recorded payroll taxes. Employer matches the employees' FICA taxes. State unemployment tax is 5.4 percent. Federal unemployment tax is 0.8 percent. At this time, all employees' earnings are taxable for FICA and $1,000 of the earnings are taxable for unemployment taxes.

31 Issued check for $46,128.45 from Cash—Payroll Bank Account to pay salaries for the month.

Apr. 14 Issued check for $18,069.70, payable to Coast Bank, for the monthly deposit of March FICA taxes (employee and employer matching) and employees' federal income tax withheld.

30 Issued check for $3,496.50, payable to State Department of Revenue, for state unemployment tax for January, February, and March. The check was accompanied by the quarterly tax return.

30 Issued check for $518.00, payable to Coast Bank, for the deposit of federal unemployment tax for the months of January, February, and March.

Required
Record the transactions in the general journal, pages 77–78.

Check Figure
Payroll Tax Expense, $4,624.15

ACTIVITIES

A QUESTION OF ETHICS

Between the end of one month and the fifteenth day of the next month, the balance in the employer's business bank account has been getting smaller and smaller. An employee prepares the next payroll and correctly computes the necessary withholding taxes. The employer is supposed to pay accumulated employment taxes on the fifteenth of the next month. Payday is the last day of the month. However, the employer has used the funds withheld from employees to pay some of the business's bills. He hopes that enough of the customers who owe him money will pay their outstanding debts. If his assumption is true, the checking account will have enough in it to pay the federal deposit on the fifteenth of the month. Is the employer acting ethically? After all, he says he intends to have enough money in the account for the deposit.

Sales and Purchases

9

JAX MERCANTILE, Fort Collins, Colorado

Jax Mercantile Co. has been Northern Colorado's premier outdoor gear source for over 50 years. Jax sells men's, women's, and children's clothing for any outdoor activity. You can also find camping and fishing gear, mountaineering tools, and hunting items. If you're not the outdoor type, Jax still has plenty of items for you, such as specialty kitchenware and household decorative items. Jax also carries a full line of optics and photography products, agricultural and automotive accessories, animal care products, and lawn and garden accessories.

Jax has succeeded in stocking a large inventory that meets customers' outdoor and indoor gear needs. When Jax purchases inventory for resale, it must have a way of recording these purchases. Jax also must have a way to record the sales of goods to customers and be able to handle returns and discounts. We will learn in this chapter how to record the sales and purchases of inventory for merchandising stores like Jax.

WHY IT MATTERS

LEARNING OBJECTIVES

After you have completed this chapter, you will be able to do the following:

1 Describe the specific accounts used by a merchandising firm.

2 Journalize sales transactions in a general journal, and post to the accounts receivable ledger and general ledger.

3 Prepare a schedule of accounts receivable.

4 Journalize sales returns and allowances, including credit memorandums and returns, in a general journal, and post to the accounts receivable ledger and general ledger.

5 Journalize sales transactions and returns involving sales tax.

6 Journalize purchase transactions in a general journal, and post to the accounts payable ledger and general ledger.

7 Prepare a schedule of accounts payable.

8 Journalize transactions involving purchases returns and allowances in a general journal, and post to the accounts payable ledger and general ledger.

9 Describe the procedures for handling freight charges on merchandise and other goods.

10 Journalize transactions in a sales journal, and post to the accounts receivable ledger and general ledger.

11 Journalize transactions in a three-column purchases journal, and post to the accounts payable ledger and general ledger.

ACCOUNTING LANGUAGE

Accounts payable ledger (p. 342)

Accounts receivable ledger (p. 333)

Controlling account (p. 334)

Credit memorandum (p. 335)

FOB destination (p. 346)

FOB shipping point (p. 346)

Freight In account (p. 329)

Invoices (p. 330)

Merchandise inventory (p. 329)

Merchandising businesses (p. 329)

Periodic inventory system (p. 329)

Perpetual inventory system (p. 329)

Purchase order (p. 339)

Purchase requisition (p. 339)

Purchases account (p. 329)

Purchases Discounts account (p. 329)

Purchases journal (p. 351)

Purchases Returns and Allowances account (p. 329)

Retail business (p. 329)

Sales account (p. 329)

Sales Discounts account (p. 329)

Sales journal (p. 348)

Sales Returns and Allowances account (p. 329)

Sales Tax Payable account (p. 329)

Special journals (p. 348)

Subsidiary ledger (p. 334)

Summarizing entry (p. 349)

Wholesale business (p. 329)

In the previous chapters, we discussed companies that specialized in providing a service, such as Conner's Whitewater Adventures. Now, we will turn our focus to companies that buy and sell goods. These types of companies are known as **merchandising businesses**. A merchandising business can be a wholesale or a retail business. A **wholesale business**, which is sometimes called a "middleman" or a "distributor," buys goods from manufacturers and sells them to retailers. A **retail business** sells goods directly to consumers ("the public").

This chapter is divided into two parts. In part one, we discuss how to record sales and purchases transactions directly into the general journal. In part two, we explain the use of special journals in recording sales and purchases transactions. Before we begin analyzing transactions, let's take a moment to review the specific accounts for merchandising firms.

SPECIFIC ACCOUNTS FOR MERCHANDISING FIRMS

Merchandise inventory consists of a stock of goods that a company buys and intends to resell at a profit. Merchandise should be differentiated from other assets, such as furniture and equipment, that are acquired for use in the business and are not for resale.

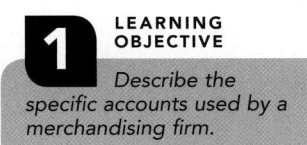

LEARNING OBJECTIVE

1

Describe the specific accounts used by a merchandising firm.

Merchandise inventory can be recorded using either the periodic inventory system or the perpetual inventory system. The **periodic inventory system** requires that companies periodically take a physical count of merchandise on hand and then attach a value to it. Under the **perpetual inventory system,** companies keep continuous records of inventories by recording all transactions, so that at any given time they know what they should have on hand and the current cost of each item. In this chapter, we will assume that the company will record merchandise inventory using the periodic inventory system. We will demonstrate how to record the journal entries for merchandise inventory under the perpetual inventory system in the appendix to this chapter.

When merchandising firms record sales of merchandise, they use the **Sales account**.

The **Sales Returns and Allowances account** is a contra account that is used to record the physical return of merchandise by customers or a reduction in a bill because merchandise was damaged. Remember that a contra account is an account that is contrary to, or a deduction from, another account. Therefore, Sales Returns and Allowances is treated as a deduction from Sales.

The **Sales Tax Payable account** is used to record a tax levied by a state or city government on the retail sale of goods and services. The tax is paid by the consumer but collected by the retailer.

The **Purchases account** is used strictly to record the cost of merchandise bought for resale. The Purchases account is considered an expense because the accountant closes it along with the expense accounts at the end of the fiscal period. (This is explained more fully in Chapter 12.)

The **Purchases Returns and Allowances account** is a contra account that is used to record the company's returns of merchandise it had purchased from suppliers or reductions in bills because of damaged merchandise. It is treated as a deduction from Purchases.

The **Sales Discounts account** and **Purchases Discounts account** are also contra accounts that are used to record cash discounts granted for prompt payments, in accordance with the credit terms.

The **Freight In account** is used to record the transportation charges on incoming merchandise intended for resale. Debits to this account increase the cost of purchases.

Following is the fundamental accounting equation with the T accounts for merchandising businesses.

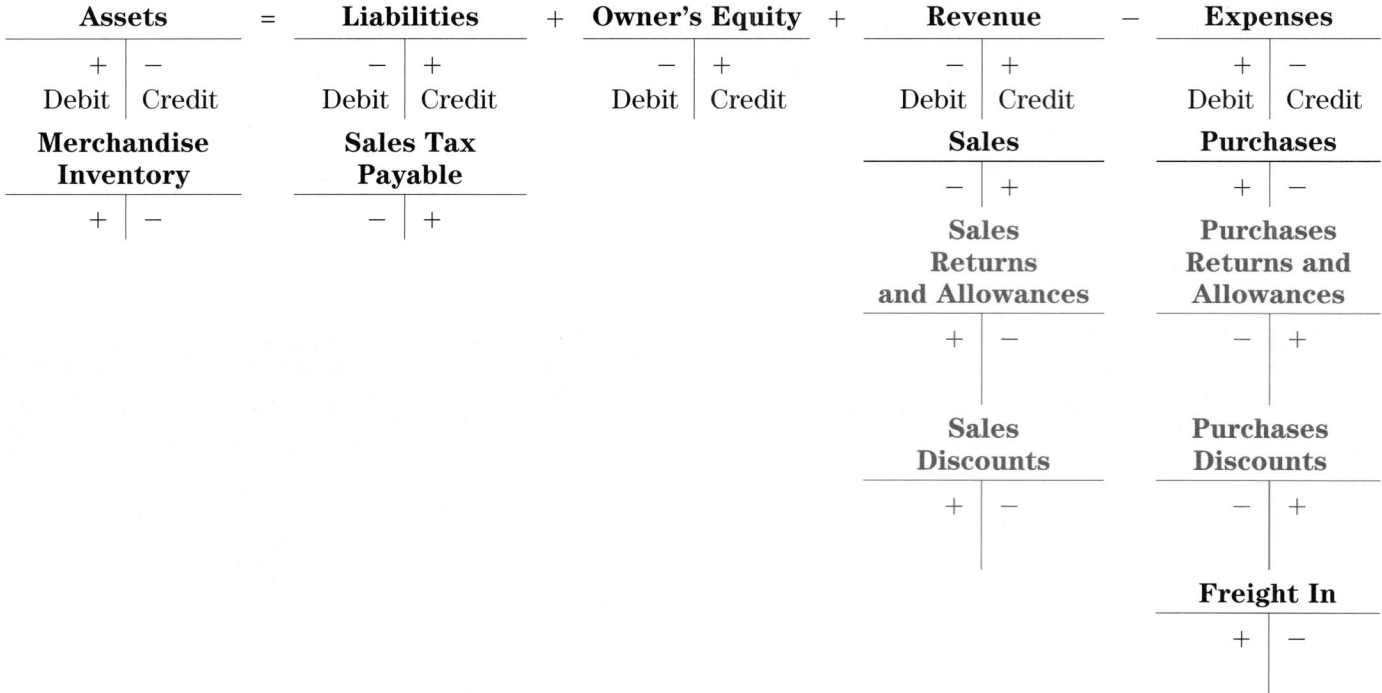

Notice that the T accounts for returns and allowances and for discounts (all contra accounts) are shown in red to emphasize that we are treating them as deductions from the related accounts placed above them. We list these accounts as deductions because they appear as deductions in the financial statements. Their relationship is similar to that between the Drawing account and the Capital account; remember that we deduct Drawing from Capital in the statement of owner's equity. These same types of accounts pertain to both retail and wholesale businesses.

PART ONE—RECORDING TRANSACTIONS INTO GENERAL JOURNAL

Source Documents Related to Sales

In a retail business, a salesperson usually prepares a sales ticket in either duplicate or triplicate for a sale on account. One copy goes to the customer and another to the accounting department, where it serves as the basis for an entry in the general journal (or the sales journal if the company is using special journals). A third copy may be used as a record of sales—to compute sales commissions or control inventory, for example.

In a wholesale business, the company usually receives a written order directly from a customer or through a salesperson who obtained the order from the customer. The credit department approves the order, and then sends it to the billing department, where the sales invoice is prepared.

Invoices are prepared in multiple copies. Figure 1 shows one possible distribution of sales invoice copies to various parties. The sales invoice for Whitewater Raft Supply's sale of merchandise to Mesa River Raft Company is shown in Figure 2.

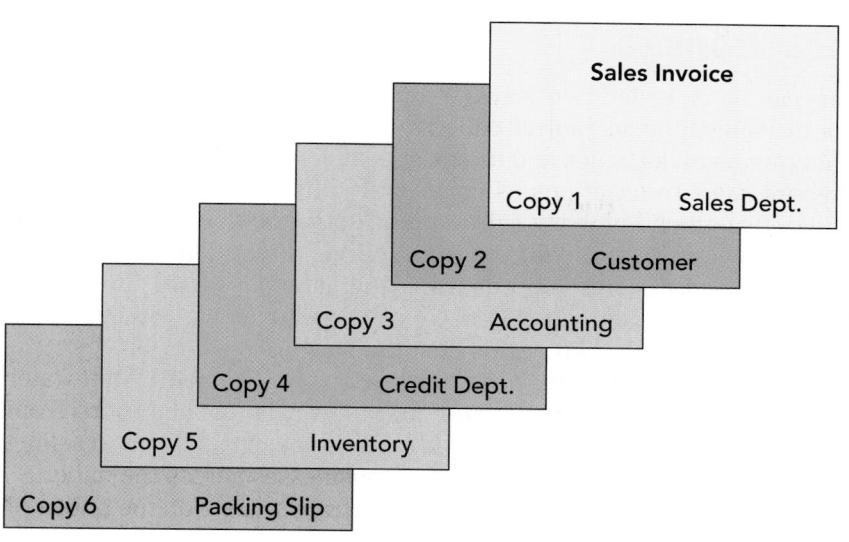

The sales invoice is a source document and as such is evidence that serves as the basis for recording a transaction.

Remember

FIGURE 2

Sales invoice

Whitewater Raft Supply

Whitewater Raft Supply
1400 Front Street
Seattle, WA 98101
419-555-6123

Invoice

DATE	INVOICE #
08/01/20—	9384
TERMS	**DUE DATE**
2/10, n/30	08/31/20—

BILL TO

Mesa River Raft Company
5120 Gilman Avenue
Portland, OR 97202
503-555-6123

AMOUNT DUE	ENCLOSED
$1,933.50	

- - - - - - - - - - - - - - - ✂ Please detach top portion and return with your payment. ✂ - - - - - - - - - - - - - -

Activity	Description	Quantity	Rate	Discount	Amount
15' Self Bailing Outfitter Raft #22B652		1	1,599.00		1,599.00
8" Outfitter Blades #37B411		2	63.00		126.00
Boat Bags #42B782		3	69.50		208.50
			Total Discount:	$0.00	
				Subtotal:	*$1,933.50*
				Sales Tax:	*$0.00*
				Total:	*$1,933.50*
				Payments:	*$0.00*
				Balance Due:	*$1,933.50*
				TOTAL	$1,933.50

Sales Transactions

Sales transactions can be recorded two ways—either by recording directly into the general journal or by using a special journal called the sales journal. If a company has numerous transactions involving sales and uses a special journal, then the company would want to record sales transactions using special journals. If a company does not have as many transactions involving sales and/or does not want to use special journals, the company would then record the transactions directly into the general journal. We will introduce sales transactions using the general journal first. Then, because of the importance of understanding accounting systems, we will introduce the use of the sales journal in part two of this chapter.

In the previous chapters, we examined the transactions for Conner's Whitewater Adventures. Conner purchases the whitewater rafts she uses on her tours from Whitewater Raft Supply. Whitewater Raft Supply is a wholesaler specializing in selling rafts, kayaks, oars, paddles, and other accessories to businesses across the nation.

We will introduce recording sales by looking at five transactions on the books of Whitewater Raft Supply for the month of August.

Aug. 1 Sold merchandise on account to Mesa River Raft Company, invoice no. 9384, $1,933.50.

8 Sold merchandise on account to Green River Rafts, invoice no. 9385, $1,116.

14 Sold merchandise on account to Marty's Fly Fishing Adventures, invoice no. 9386, $1,594.

19 Sold merchandise on account to Hi-Flying Adventures, Inc., invoice no. 9387, $552.30.

25 Sold merchandise on account to Hi-Flying Adventures, Inc., invoice no. 9388, $1,674.

Whitewater Raft Supply will record the transactions into the general journal as follows:

	GENERAL JOURNAL			**PAGE 26**
Date	Description	Post. Ref.	Debit	Credit
20—				
Aug. 1	Accounts Receivable, Mesa River			
	Raft Company		1 9 3 3 50	
	Sales			1 9 3 3 50
	Sold merchandise to Mesa			
	River Raft Company,			
	invoice no. 9384.			
8	Accounts Receivable, Green River			
	Rafts		1 1 1 6 00	
	Sales			1 1 1 6 00
	Sold merchandise to Green			
	River Rafts, invoice no. 9385.			
14	Accounts Receivable, Marty's Fly			
	Fishing Adventures		1 5 9 4 00	
	Sales			1 5 9 4 00
	Sold merchandise to Marty's			
	Fly Fishing Adventures,			
	invoice no. 9386.			

19	Accounts Receivable, Hi-Flying Adventures, Inc.		5 5 2 30							
	Sales						5 5 2 30			
	Sold merchandise to Hi-Flying Adventures, Inc., invoice no. 9387.									
25	Accounts Receivable, Hi-Flying Adventures, Inc.		1 6 7 4 00							
	Sales						1 6 7 4 00			
	Sold merchandise to Hi-Flying Adventures, Inc., invoice no. 9388.									

Whitewater Raft Supply's accountant records a debit to Accounts Receivable to record the amount each customer owes the company and a credit to Sales for each transaction. The Sales account is credited because it is a revenue account that is used for recording sales of merchandise.

Here's how the accounts appear in the fundamental accounting equation:

Assets		=	Liabilities		+	Owner's Equity		+	Revenue		−	Expenses	
+	−		−	+		−	+		−	+		+	−
Debit	Credit		Debit	Credit		Debit	Credit		Debit	Credit		Debit	Credit

Accounts Receivable									Sales	
+	−								−	+
1,933.50										1,933.50
1,116.00										1,116.00
1,594.00										1,594.00
552.30										552.30
1,674.00										1,674.00

Remember that the transactions are recorded assuming that Whitewater Raft Supply records merchandise inventory using the periodic inventory method. If Whitewater Raft Supply instead used the perpetual inventory method, an additional journal entry would be required. This additional journal entry will be discussed in the appendix to this chapter.

The Accounts Receivable Ledger

In the sales transactions for Whitewater Raft Supply, we recorded the receivable directly into the Accounts Receivable account. In order to know how much each credit customer owes a business, the firm also maintains an **accounts receivable ledger**. This ledger is a separate record containing a list of the credit customers with their respective balances, listed in either alphabetical order or by account number. It is important to maintain an accounts receivable ledger so that the company will know at any point in time the amount owed by the customer, if the amount is past due, and any payments made on the account. All computerized accounting systems post sales on account into an accounts receivable ledger. Figure 3 is an example of the accounts receivable ledger using a computerized accounting program, and Figure 4 is an example of a manual accounts receivable ledger. Note that either method includes much of the same information.

> **Remember**
>
> The balance of the Accounts Receivable controlling account at the end of the month must equal the total of the balances of the credit customer accounts in the accounts receivable ledger.

FIGURE 3

Accounts receivable ledger (computerized)

Whitewater Raft Supply
Customer Balance Detail
All Dates

Date	Type	Num	Due Date	Amount	Open Balance	Balance
Hi-Flying Adventures, Inc.						
08/19/20—	Invoice	9387	09/18/20—	552.30	552.30	552.30
08/25/20—	Invoice	9388	09/24/20—	1,674.00	1,674.00	2,226.30
Total for Hi-Flying Adventures, Inc.				**$2,226.30**	**$2,226.30**	
TOTAL				$2,226.30	$2,226.30	

FIGURE 4

Accounts receivable ledger (manual)

ACCOUNTS RECEIVABLE LEDGER

NAME   Hi-Flying Adventures, Inc.

ADDRESS 3631 Crooked Tree Road

Seattle, WA 98101

Date		Item	Post. Ref.	Debit	Credit	Balance
20—						
Aug.	19		J26	5 5 2 30		5 5 2 30
	25		J26	1 6 7 4 00		2 2 2 6 30

Even though an accounts receivable ledger is maintained, the Accounts Receivable account in the general ledger should still be maintained. When all the postings are up to date, the balance of this account should equal the total of all the credit customers' individual account balances. The Accounts Receivable *account* in the general ledger is called a **controlling account**. The accounts receivable *ledger*, containing the accounts of all the credit customers, is really a special type of ledger, called a **subsidiary ledger**.

3 LEARNING OBJECTIVE

Prepare a schedule of accounts receivable.

Schedule of Accounts Receivable

From the information contained in the accounts receivable subsidiary ledger, the accountant can prepare a schedule of accounts receivable, like the one shown in Figure 5 listing each credit customer's account balance.

FIGURE 5

Schedule of accounts receivable

Whitewater Raft Supply
Schedule of Accounts Receivable
August 31, 20—

Green River Rafts	$1,116.00
Hi-Flying Adventures, Inc.	2,226.30
Marty's Fly Fishing Adventures	1,594.00
Mesa River Raft Company	1,933.50
Total Accounts Receivable	$6,869.80

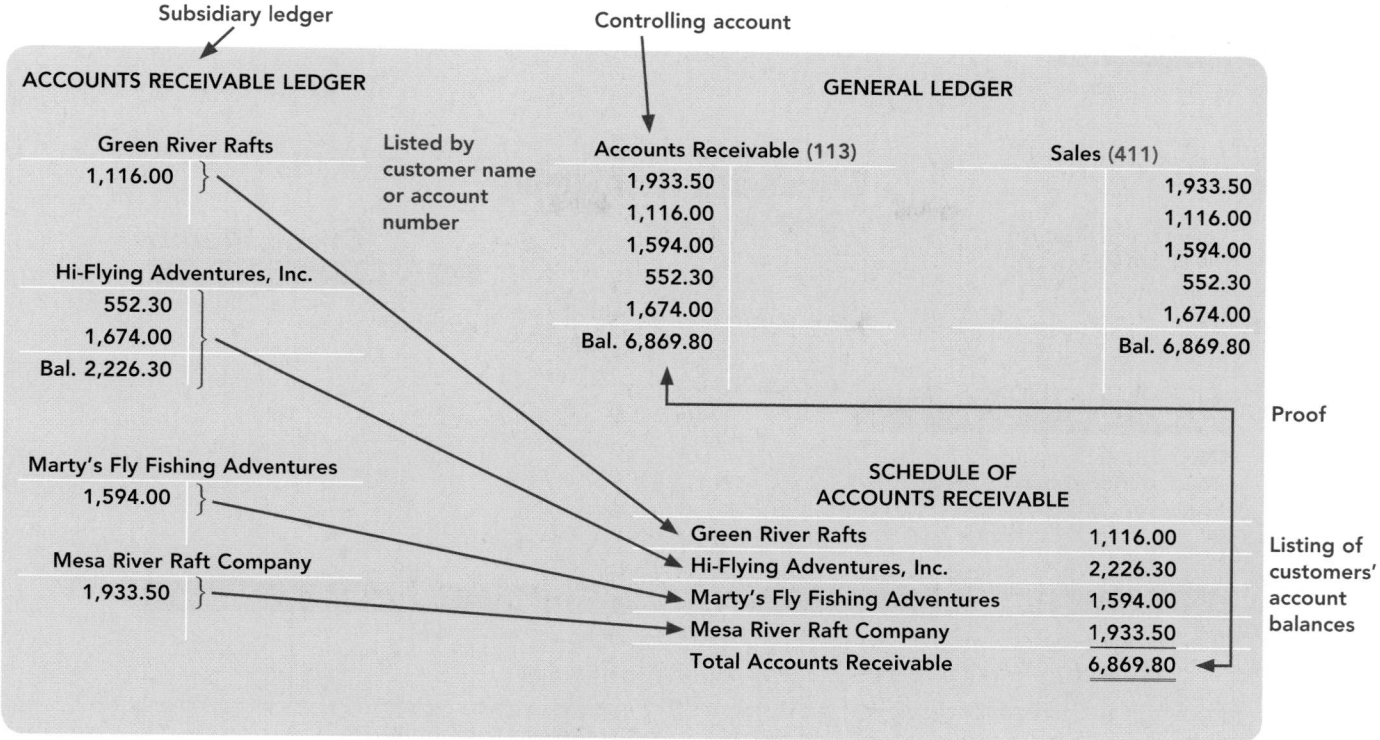

FIGURE 6

Interrelationship of the accounts receivable ledger, general ledger, and schedule of accounts receivable

Figure 6 diagrams the interrelationships of the subsidiary ledger, general ledger, and schedule of accounts receivable for Whitewater Raft Supply for the month of August. Notice that each entry is posted to Accounts Receivable and Sales in the general ledger. Also, the amount owed by the customer is posted to the subsidiary accounts receivable ledger to maintain a running balance of the amount each customer owes. If performing the posting manually, the accountant should post the individual amounts to the accounts receivable ledger every day, so that this ledger will have up-to-date information. Finally, since we assume that there were no previous balances in the customers' accounts, the Accounts Receivable controlling account in the general ledger will have the same balance, $6,869.80, as the schedule of accounts receivable.

In the simplified illustration in Figure 6, it just so happens that, since no payments were received from credit customers, the total of the Sales account equals the balance of Accounts Receivable. However, if $1,200 had been received from credit customers, both the balance of the Accounts Receivable controlling account and the total of the schedule of accounts receivable would be $5,669.80 ($6,869.80 − $1,200.00). The total of the Sales account would still be $6,869.80. Also, if some sales were cash only transactions, this would cause a difference between total Sales and the balance of Accounts Receivable.

Sales Returns and Allowances

The Sales Returns and Allowances account handles two types of transactions related to merchandise that has previously been sold. A *return* is a physical return of the goods. An *allowance* is a reduction from the original price because the goods were defective or damaged. It may not be economically worthwhile to have customers return the goods; each situation is a special case. To avoid writing a formal business letter each time to inform customers of their account adjustments, businesses use a special form called a **credit memorandum**. A credit memorandum (Figure 7) is a written statement indicating a seller's willingness to reduce the amount of a buyer's debt.

The Sales Returns and Allowances account is a contra account that is deducted from Sales. Using an account separate from Sales provides a better record of the total returns and allowances. Accountants deduct Sales Returns and Allowances from Sales on the income statement to determine net sales.

4 LEARNING OBJECTIVE

Journalize sales returns and allowances, including credit memorandums and returns, in a general journal, and post to the accounts receivable ledger and general ledger.

FIGURE 7

Credit memorandum

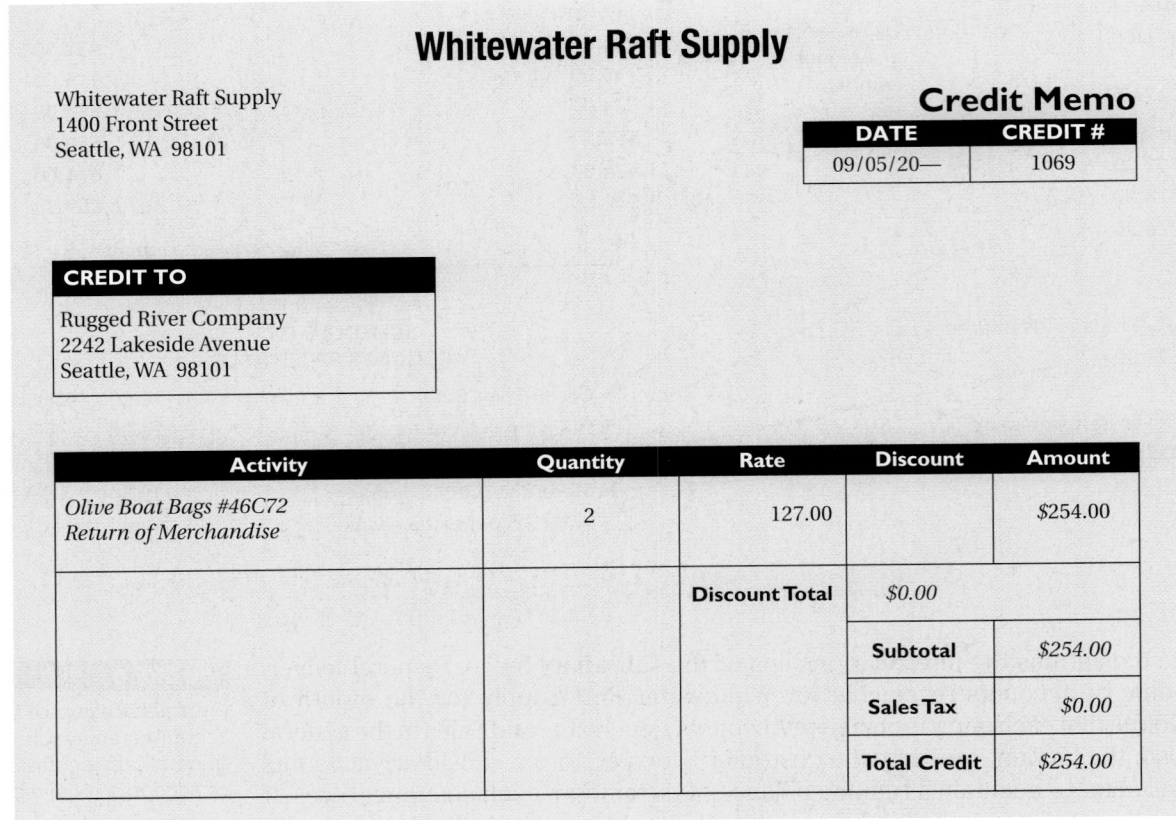

Using T accounts, here's an example of a return. The original sale is shown first, followed by the issuance of a credit memorandum.

Transaction (a). On September 1, Whitewater Raft Supply sold merchandise on account to Rugged River Company, $3,614, and recorded the sale in the general journal.

Transaction (b). On September 5, Rugged River Company returned $254 worth of the merchandise. Whitewater Raft Supply issued credit memorandum no. 1069 (see Figure 7).

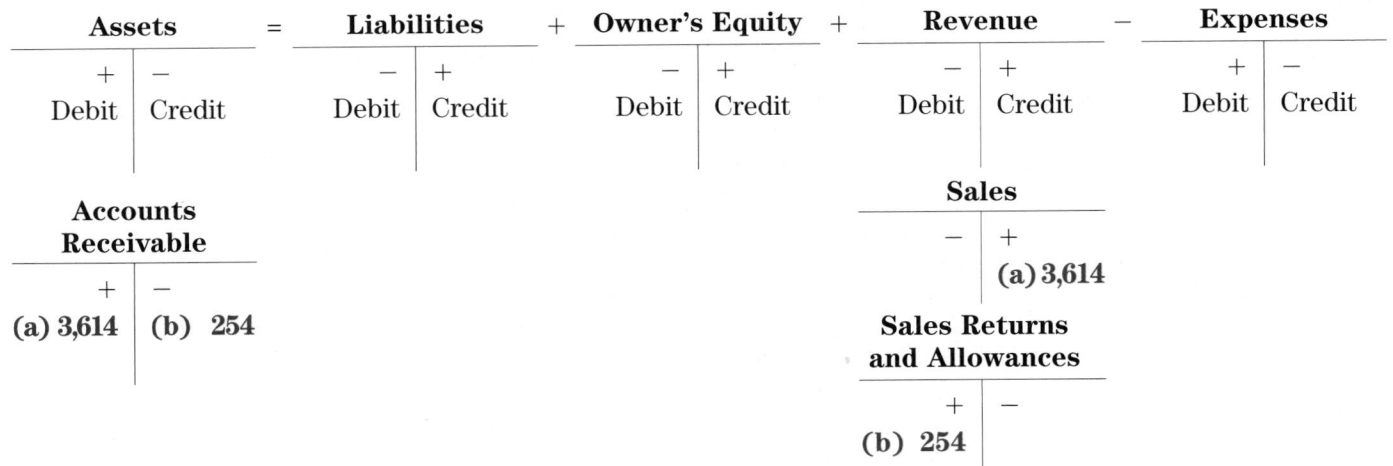

Whitewater Raft Supply's accountant debits Sales Returns and Allowances to increase it; then, the accountant credits Accounts Receivable to decrease it because the credit customer, Rugged River Company, owes less than before. If Whitewater Raft Supply was recording sales transactions using the perpetual system of inventory method, the accountant would be required to record another journal entry. This will be discussed in the appendix to this chapter.

The general journal entry serves as the posting source for crediting the Accounts Receivable controlling account in the general ledger. It also serves as the posting source for updating the accounts receivable ledger and therefore includes the name of the credit customer. If the balance of the Accounts Receivable controlling account is to equal the total of the individual account balances in the accounts receivable ledger, one must post to *both* the Accounts Receivable account in the general ledger *and* the account of Rugged River Company in the accounts receivable ledger.

If the accountant was using a computerized accounting system, the software would automatically post the credit memorandum to the Accounts Receivable controlling account and Rugged River Company's account in the accounts receivable ledger when the credit has been applied. In a manual system, to take care of this double posting, the accountant draws a slanted line in the Post. Ref. column. When the amount has been posted as a credit to the general ledger account, the accountant writes the account number of Accounts Receivable in the left part of the Post. Ref. column. After the credit has been posted to Rugged River Company's account in the subsidiary ledger, the accountant puts a check mark in the right portion of the Post. Ref. column. Sales Returns and Allowances is posted in the usual manner. The following entries in the general journal, general ledger, and accounts receivable ledger are shown after posting of the transaction is complete.

FYI

A company must manage its return policy carefully. Customers often take advantage of return privileges, creating significant handling costs for the merchant.

GENERAL JOURNAL — PAGE 27

Date	Description	Post. Ref.	Debit	Credit
20—				
Sept. 5	Sales Returns and Allowances	412	2 5 4 00	
	Accounts Receivable, Rugged	113 ✓		
	River Company			2 5 4 00
	Issued credit memo no. 1069.			

GENERAL LEDGER

ACCOUNT Sales Returns and Allowances   **ACCOUNT NO.** 412

Date	Item	Post. Ref.	Debit	Credit	Balance Debit	Balance Credit
20—						
Sept. 5		J27	2 5 4 00		2 5 4 00	

ACCOUNTS RECEIVABLE LEDGER

NAME Rugged River Company
ADDRESS 2242 Lakeside Avenue
Seattle, WA 98101

Date	Item	Post. Ref.	Debit	Credit	Balance
20—					
Sept. 1		J26	3 6 1 4 00		3 6 1 4 00
5		J27		2 5 4 00	3 3 6 0 00

Sales Transactions Involving Sales Tax

Most states and some cities levy a sales tax on retail sales of goods and services. The retailer collects the sales tax from customers and later pays it to the tax authorities.

When goods or services are sold on credit, the sales tax is charged to the customer and recorded at the time of the sale. It is necessary to compute and include the amount of the sales tax for each transaction. The customer owes the amount of the sale plus the applicable sales tax.

Assume that David Fly Fishing Outfitters, a retail store, had the following transaction that includes sales tax computed on the amount of the sale of merchandise:

Jan. 3 Sold merchandise on account to R. Martinez, invoice no. 101, $153.50 plus sales tax of $12.28.

The transaction would be recorded in T accounts and in the general journal as follows:

Assets	=	Liabilities	+	Owner's Equity	+	Revenue	−	Expenses
+ −		− +		− +		− +		+ −
Debit Credit		Debit Credit		Debit Credit		Debit Credit		Debit Credit

Accounts Receivable	Sales Tax Payable		Sales
+ −	− +		− +
165.78	12.28		153.50

GENERAL JOURNAL PAGE 5

Date	Description	Post. Ref.	Debit	Credit
20—				
Jan. 3	Accounts Receivable, R. Martinez		1 6 5 78	
	Sales			1 5 3 50
	Sales Tax Payable			1 2 28
	Sold merchandise to			
	R. Martinez, invoice no. 101.			

At the end of the first quarter, the accountant for David Fly Fishing Outfitters determines that the total sales tax payable for the quarter is $124.50. When the sales tax is paid to the state, the accountant debits Sales Tax Payable and credits Cash for the total amount due.

GENERAL JOURNAL PAGE 8

Date	Description	Post. Ref.	Debit	Credit
20—				
Apr. 20	Sales Tax Payable		1 2 4 50	
	Cash			1 2 4 50
	Paid sales tax due for first			
	quarter.			

Sales Returns Involving Sales Tax

If a customer who returns merchandise to a retail store was originally charged a sales tax, the amount of the sale and the sales tax must be returned to the customer. Review the following two transactions for David Fly Fishing Outfitters.

Transaction (a). On May 1, David Fly Fishing Outfitters sold merchandise on account to B. Hill, $1,550, plus $124 sales tax.

Transaction (b). On May 5, B. Hill returned the merchandise and David Fly Fishing Outfitters issued credit memorandum no. 1152.

Following is the general journal entry required for this type of return:

	GENERAL JOURNAL			PAGE 5	
Date	Description	Post. Ref.	Debit	Credit	
20—					
May 5	Sales Returns and Allowances		1 5 5 0 00		
	Sales Tax Payable		1 2 4 00		
	Accounts Receivable, B. Hill			1 6 7 4 00	
	Issued credit memo no. 1152.				

Notice that David Fly Fishing Outfitters credited B. Hill's account for the amount of the sale ($1,550) and the amount of the sales tax payable ($124).

Source Documents Related to Purchases

In a small retail store, the owner may do the buying. In large retail and wholesale businesses, department heads or division managers do the buying, after which the Purchasing Department goes into action: It places purchase orders, follows up on the orders, and sees that deliveries are made to the right departments. The Purchasing Department also acts as a source of information on current prices, price trends, quality of goods, prospective suppliers, and reliability of suppliers.

The Purchasing Department normally requires that any requests to buy merchandise be in writing, in the form of a **purchase requisition**. After the purchase requisition is approved, the Purchasing Department sends a purchase order to the supplier. A **purchase order** is the company's written offer to buy certain goods. The accountant does not make any entry at this point because the supplier has not yet indicated acceptance of the order. A purchase order has at least four copies. The original goes to the supplier; copies go to the Purchasing Department (as proof of what was ordered), the department that issued the requisition (telling it that the goods it wanted have been ordered), the Accounting Department, and a blind copy (with quantities omitted) goes to Receiving.

To continue with the accounts of Whitewater Raft Supply, the Boat Accessories Department submits a purchase requisition to the Purchasing Department, as shown in Figure 8.

The Purchasing Department completes the rest of the purchase requisition and then sends out the purchase order shown in Figure 9.

The seller then sends an invoice to the buyer as shown in Figure 10. This invoice should arrive in advance of the goods (or at least *with* the goods). Notice the line *Terms*. *Terms* means the terms of payment. For example, 2/10, n/30 means that if the buyer pays the amount due within 10 days, the buyer will receive a 2 percent discount; otherwise, the entire amount is due in 30 days.

Pataponia, Inc. (the seller) prepaid the freight cost and added the $85.50 to the bill, listing it separately. This is similar to buying something by mail order or online. Freight In is discussed in more detail later in the chapter.

FIGURE 8
Purchase requisition

NO. C–726

Whitewater Raft Supply
1400 Front Street
Seattle, WA 98101

PURCHASE REQUISITION

| DEPARTMENT | *Boat Accessories* | DATE OF REQUEST | *July 2, 20—* |
| ADVISE ON DELIVERY | *C. Fenwick* | DATE REQUIRED | *Aug. 5, 20—* |

QUANTITY	DESCRIPTION
12	*Rio Frio Personal Flotation Device (PFD) #772R*

| APPROVED BY | *D. M. Bruce* | REQUESTED BY | *J. C. Garcia* |

FOR PURCHASING DEPT. USE ONLY

PURCHASE ORDER NO. *7918*	ISSUED TO: *Pataponia, Inc.*
DATE *July 5, 20—*	*1614 Olivera Street*
	San Francisco, CA 94129

FIGURE 9
Purchase order

Whitewater Raft Supply
1400 Front Street
Seattle, WA 98101

PURCHASE ORDER

TO: *Pataponia, Inc.*
1614 Olivera Street
San Francisco, CA 94129

DATE: *July 5, 20—*
ORDER NO.: *7918*
SHIPPED BY:
TERMS: *2/10, n/30*

QUANTITY	DESCRIPTION	UNIT PRICE	TOTAL
12	*Rio Frio Personal Flotation Device (PFD) #772R*	142 50	1,710 00
	Total		1,710 00

D. M. Bruce

FIGURE 10
Purchase invoice

Pataponia, Inc.
No. 2706
1614 Olivera Street
San Francisco, CA 94129

INVOICE

SOLD TO *Whitewater Raft Supply*
1400 Front Street
Seattle, WA 98101

DATE: *July 31, 20—*
CUSTOMER'S P.O. NO.: *7918*
SHIPPED BY: *Western Freight Line*
TERMS: *2/10, n/30*

YOUR ORDER NO.	SALESPERSON	TERMS
7918	*C.L.*	*2/10, n/30*

DATE SHIPPED	SHIPPED BY	FOB
July 31, 20—	*Western Freight Line*	*San Francisco*

QUANTITY	DESCRIPTION	UNIT PRICE	TOTAL
12	*Rio Frio Personal Flotation Device (PFD) #772R*	142 50	1,710 00
	Freight		85 50
	Total		1,795 50

Purchase Transactions

Now that we have reviewed the source documents for purchase transactions, let's move on to recording purchase transactions. Purchase transactions can be recorded in two ways—either by recording directly into the general journal or by using a special journal called the purchases journal. As with sales transactions, a company determines which method to use when recording purchase transactions based upon the occurrence of the transaction and the type of journals that are used in the company.

LEARNING OBJECTIVE **6**

Journalize purchase transactions in a general journal, and post to the accounts payable ledger and general ledger.

We will introduce purchase transactions using the general journal first. Then, we will discuss how to record the transactions into the purchases journal in part two of this chapter. As a reminder all transactions are recorded assuming a periodic inventory method. The perpetual inventory method will be demonstrated in the appendix to this chapter.

Let's look at four purchase transactions on the books of Whitewater Raft Supply for the month of August. Some of these transactions include the cost of delivering the merchandise, called Freight In, which will be discussed later in the chapter.

Aug. 2 Bought merchandise on account from Pataponia, Inc., invoice no. 2706, $1,710; terms 2/10, n/30; dated July 31; FOB San Francisco, freight prepaid and added to the invoice, $85.50 (total $1,795.50).

10 Bought merchandise on account from Langseth and Son, invoice no. 982, $2,772; terms net 30 days; dated August 8; FOB Cleveland, freight prepaid and added to the invoice, $157 (total $2,929).

17 Bought merchandise on account from Dana Manufacturing Company, invoice no. 10611, $564; terms 2/10, n/30; dated August 15; FOB Los Angeles.

26 Bought merchandise on account from Pataponia, Inc., invoice no. 2801, $2,503.70; terms 2/10, n/30; dated August 24; FOB San Francisco, freight prepaid and added to the invoice, $102.30 (total $2,606).

Whitewater Raft Supply will record the transactions into the general journal as follows:

	GENERAL JOURNAL			PAGE 26
Date	Description	Post. Ref.	Debit	Credit
20—				
Aug. 2	Purchases		1 7 1 0 00	
	Freight In		8 5 50	
	Accounts Payable, Pataponia, Inc.			1 7 9 5 50
	Purchased merchandise from			
	Pataponia, Inc., invoice no.			
	2706, invoice dated 7/31,			
	terms 2/10, n/30.			
10	Purchases		2 7 7 2 00	
	Freight In		1 5 7 00	
	Accounts Payable, Langseth			
	and Son			2 9 2 9 00
	Purchased merchandise from			
	Langseth and Son, invoice			
	no. 982, invoice dated 8/8,			
	terms n/30.			

(continued)

Aug.	17	Purchases	5 6 4 00	
		Accounts Payable, Dana		
		Manufacturing Company		5 6 4 00
		Purchased merchandise from		
		Dana Manufacturing Company,		
		invoice no. 10611, invoice dated		
		8/15, terms 2/10, n/30.		
	26	Purchases	2 5 0 3 70	
		Freight In	1 0 2 30	
		Accounts Payable, Pataponia, Inc.		2 6 0 6 00
		Purchased merchandise from		
		Pataponia, Inc., invoice no.		
		2801, invoice dated 8/24,		
		terms 2/10, n/30.		

Whitewater Raft Supply's accountant records a debit to the Purchases account to record the cost of merchandise bought for resale. Remember that the Purchases account is similar to an expense account and, therefore, has a normal debit balance. Freight In (if applied) is also debited to record the increase to the cost of purchases for the transportation charges on incoming merchandise. The corresponding credit is to the Accounts Payable account. Note that the transactions are recorded on the day the merchandise is received.

Here's how the accounts appear in the fundamental accounting equation:

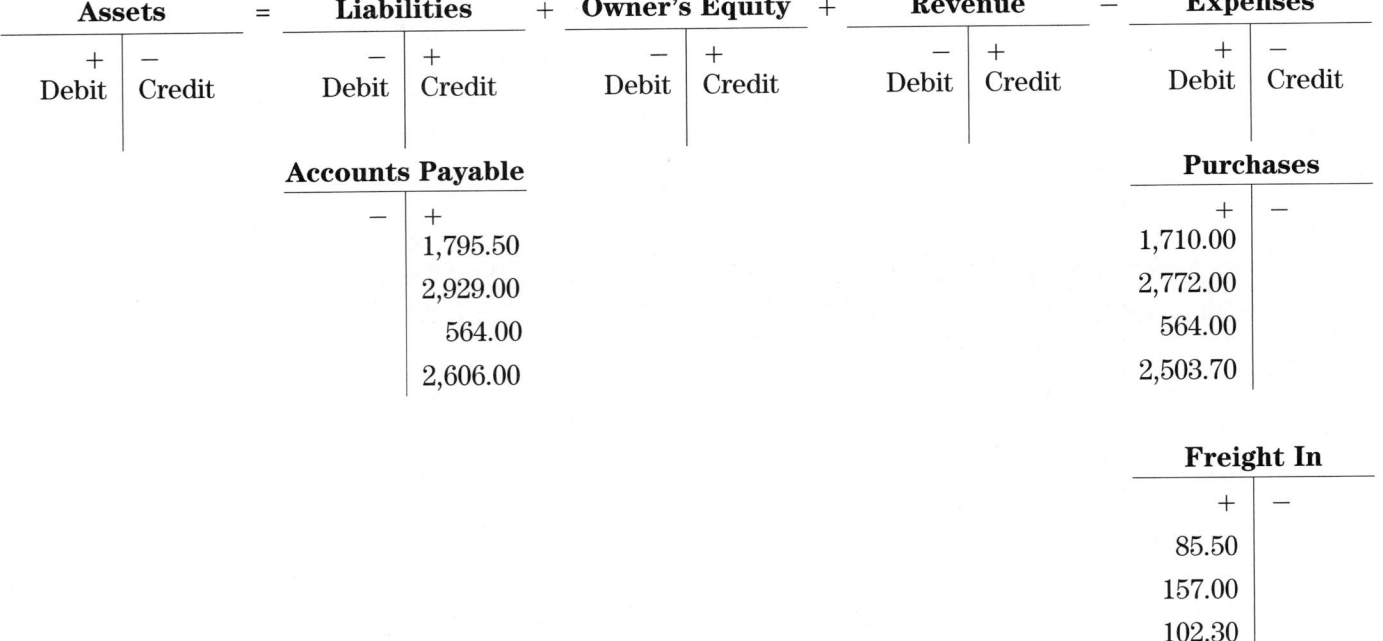

Assets	=	**Liabilities**	+	**Owner's Equity**	+	**Revenue**	–	**Expenses**
+ | –		– | +		– | +		– | +		+ | –
Debit | Credit		Debit | Credit		Debit | Credit		Debit | Credit		Debit | Credit

Accounts Payable

–	+
	1,795.50
	2,929.00
	564.00
	2,606.00

Purchases

+	–
1,710.00	
2,772.00	
564.00	
2,503.70	

Freight In

+	–
85.50	
157.00	
102.30	

The Accounts Payable Ledger

Previously, we called the Accounts Receivable account in the general ledger a **controlling** account, and we saw that the accounts receivable ledger consists of an individual account for each credit customer.

Accounts Payable is a parallel case; it, too, is a controlling account in the general ledger. **The accounts payable ledger is a subsidiary ledger, and it consists of individual accounts for all the creditors listed in either alphabetical or**

numerical order. In a computerized accounting system, when the purchase is recorded, the software automatically posts to the appropriate accounts payable ledger. If posting manually, posting to the accounts payable ledger is usually done daily. Figure 11 is an example of the accounts payable ledger using a computerized system, while Figure 12 is an example of the manual version of the accounts payable ledger.

Even though an accounts payable ledger is maintained, the Accounts Payable account in the general ledger should still be maintained. When all the postings are up to date, the balance of this account should equal the total of all the creditors' individual account balances.

> **Remember**
>
> Increases in Accounts Payable are recorded in the Credit column. Decreases in Accounts Payable are recorded in the Debit column.

Whitewater Raft Supply
Vendor Balance Detail
All Dates

Date	Type	Num	Due Date	Amount	Balance
Pataponia, Inc.					
08/02/20—	Bill	2706	09/01/20—	1,795.50	1,795.50
08/26/20—	Bill	2801	09/25/20—	2,606.00	4,401.50
Total for Pataponia, Inc.				$4,401.50	
TOTAL				$4,401.50	

FIGURE 11

Accounts payable ledger (computerized)

ACCOUNTS PAYABLE LEDGER

NAME   Pataponia, Inc.
ADDRESS 1614 Olivera Street
         San Francisco, CA 94129

Date		Item	Post. Ref.	Debit	Credit	Balance
20—						
Aug.	2		J26		1 7 9 5 50	1 7 9 5 50
	26		J26		2 6 0 6 00	4 4 0 1 50

FIGURE 12

Accounts payable ledger (manual)

Schedule of Accounts Payable

Assuming there were no previous balances in the creditors' accounts and that no other transactions for Whitewater Raft Supply involved Accounts Payable, the schedule of accounts payable would appear as shown in Figure 13. Note that the schedule of accounts payable lists each creditor's account balance and that it equals the Accounts Payable account shown in the general ledger (Figure 14).

7 LEARNING OBJECTIVE

Prepare a schedule of accounts payable.

Purchases Returns and Allowances

As its title implies, the Purchases Returns and Allowances account handles either a return of merchandise previously purchased or an allowance made for merchandise that arrived in damaged condition. In both cases, there is a reduction in the amount owed to the supplier. The buyer sends a letter or printed form to the supplier, who acknowledges the reduction by sending a credit memorandum. The buyer should wait for notice of the agreed deduction before making an entry.

8 LEARNING OBJECTIVE

Journalize transactions involving purchases returns and allowances in a general journal, and post to the accounts payable ledger and general ledger.

FIGURE 13

Schedule of accounts payable

Whitewater Raft Supply
Schedule of Accounts Payable
August 31, 20—

Dana Manufacturing Company	$ 564.00
Langseth and Son	2,929.00
Pataponia, Inc.	4,401.50
Total Accounts Payable	$7,894.50

FIGURE 14

Accounts Payable controlling account

GENERAL LEDGER

ACCOUNT **Accounts Payable**   ACCOUNT NO.   212

Date		Item	Post. Ref.	Debit	Credit	Balance Debit	Balance Credit
20—							
Aug.	2		J26		1 7 9 5 50		1 7 9 5 50
	10		J26		2 9 2 9 00		4 7 2 4 50
	17		J26		5 6 4 00		5 2 8 8 50
	26		J26		2 6 0 6 00		7 8 9 4 50

The Purchases Returns and Allowances account is a contra account to Purchases and is considered to be a deduction from Purchases. Using a separate account provides a better record of the total returns and allowances. Purchases Returns and Allowances is deducted from the Purchases account on the income statement. (We'll talk about this point later.) For now, let's look at an example consisting of a return on the books of Whitewater Raft Supply.

Transaction (a). On September 2, bought merchandise on account from Dana Manufacturing Company, $830.

Transaction (b). On September 8, received credit memorandum no. 1629 from Dana Manufacturing Company for $270.

First, here is how the transactions appear in the fundamental accounting equation:

Assets	=	Liabilities	+	Owner's Equity	+	Revenue	−	Expenses
+ | −		− | +		− | +		− | +		+ | −
Debit | Credit		Debit | Credit		Debit | Credit		Debit | Credit		Debit | Credit

Accounts Payable

−	+
(b) 270	(a) 830

Purchases

+	−
(a) 830	

Purchases Returns and Allowances

−	+
	(b) 270

In the general journal, transaction (a) was journalized as a debit to Purchases and a credit to Accounts Payable. Transaction (b) is journalized as follows:

GENERAL JOURNAL   PAGE   27

Date	Description	Post. Ref.	Debit	Credit
20—				
Sept. 8	Accounts Payable, Dana	212 ✓		
	Manufacturing Company		2 7 0 00	
	Purchases Returns and			
	Allowances	512		2 7 0 00
	Credit memo no. 1629 for			
	return of merchandise.			

Purchases Returns and Allowances is credited because Whitewater Raft Supply has more returns and allowances than before. Accounts Payable is debited because Whitewater Raft Supply owes less than before.

The accountant must post the amount to both the Accounts Payable controlling account and the individual creditor's account in the accounts payable ledger. The account numbers in the Post. Ref. column indicate postings to the accounts in the general ledger, and the check marks indicate postings to the accounts in the accounts payable ledger.

GENERAL LEDGER

ACCOUNT <u>Accounts Payable</u>   ACCOUNT NO.   212

Date	Item	Post. Ref.	Debit	Credit	Balance Debit	Balance Credit
20—						
Sept. 1	Balance	✓				7 8 9 4 50
2		J27		8 3 0 00		8 7 2 4 50
8		J27	2 7 0 00			8 4 5 4 50

ACCOUNT <u>Purchases Returns and Allowances</u>   ACCOUNT NO.   512

Date	Item	Post. Ref.	Debit	Credit	Balance Debit	Balance Credit
20—						
Sept. 1	Balance	✓				1 6 4 0 00
8		J27		2 7 0 00		1 9 1 0 00

ACCOUNTS PAYABLE LEDGER

NAME   <u>Dana Manufacturing Company</u>
ADDRESS   <u>254 Calle Mancha</u>
<u>Los Angeles, CA 90025</u>

Date	Item	Post. Ref.	Debit	Credit	Balance
20—					
Sept. 1	Balance	✓			5 6 4 00
2		J27		8 3 0 00	1 3 9 4 00
8		J27	2 7 0 00		1 1 2 4 00

Freight Charges on Incoming Merchandise

Companies use the Freight In account to keep a record of all separately charged delivery costs on incoming merchandise.

Freight costs are expressed as FOB (free on board) destination or shipping point. **(Destination is the buyer's location; shipping point is the seller's location.)** In both cases, the supplier loads the goods free on board the carrier. Beyond that point, there must be an understanding as to who is responsible for paying the freight charges. **If the seller assumes the entire cost of transportation, without any reimbursement from the buyer, the terms are FOB destination.** In this case, title or ownership changes hands when the buyer receives the goods. **If the buyer is responsible for paying the freight cost, the shipping terms are called FOB shipping point.** In this case, title or ownership changes hands when goods are transferred to a common carrier (freight company).

Briefly, when goods are shipped FOB destination, the freight charges are not stated, and the seller simply pays the amount of the freight. Suppose Whitewater Raft Supply, which is in Seattle, buys merchandise from a supplier in Chicago with shipping terms of FOB Seattle listed on the invoice. The total of the invoice is $1,740, and there is no separate listing of freight charges. In other words, the seller has included the transportation costs in the price.

When goods are shipped FOB shipping point, with the buyer responsible for paying the freight charges, transportation costs may be handled in two ways:

1. The buyer may pay the freight charges directly to the transportation company. For example, an automobile dealer in Houston buys cars FOB Detroit. In this case, the automobile dealer makes one check payable to the manufacturer and another check payable to the carrier for the freight charges. (FOB Detroit is the same as FOB shipping point.)

2. The transportation or shipping costs may be listed separately on the invoice. For example, suppose a person orders a computer from a company online. The company has prepaid (paid in advance) the freight charges as a favor or convenience for the buyer. However, the freight charges are listed on the bill or invoice, and the buyer is responsible for reimbursing the company for the freight charges. Similarly, when a business buys merchandise, the amount of the freight charges may be prepaid by the seller and listed separately on the invoice.

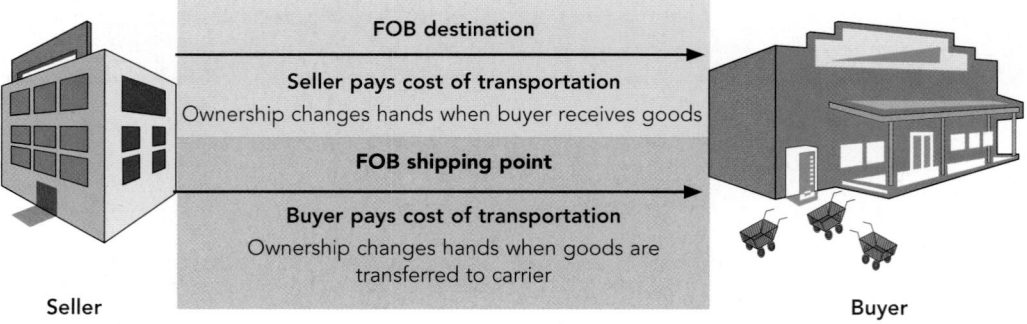

Look again at the invoice from Pataponia, Inc., on page 340. Note that the freight cost is listed separately, and the terms are FOB shipping point (San Francisco). Pataponia paid the transportation cost; Whitewater Raft Supply must reimburse Pataponia for this cost.

The transaction for the purchase from Pataponia, Inc., was recorded as follows:

Date		Description	Post. Ref.	Debit	Credit
20—					
Aug.	2	Purchases		1 7 1 0 00	
		Freight In		8 5 50	
		Accounts Payable, Pataponia, Inc.			1 7 9 5 50
		Purchased merchandise from			
		Pataponia, Inc., invoice no.			
		2706, invoice dated 7/31,			
		terms 2/10, n/30.			

GENERAL JOURNAL — PAGE 26

Notice that the transportation cost is recorded separately as a debit to the Freight In account for $85.50. Also notice that because this purchase was FOB shipping point, the buyer (Whitewater Raft Supply) must reimburse the seller for the transportation costs by paying the total invoice cost of $1,795.50.

When the buyer pays for the cost of freight, the buyer records the cost as Freight In. Freight In is included in the cost of purchases and is reported on the income statement. If the seller pays for the cost of freight, the seller records the cost as Delivery Expense or Freight Out. Delivery Expense is recorded as a selling expense on the income statement.

Transportation Charges on the Buying of Goods and Services Other than Merchandise

Any freight charges incurred when buying any other assets, such as supplies or equipment, should be debited to the respective asset accounts. The Freight In account is used only to record the incoming transportation charges on merchandise intended for resale. For example, assume that Whitewater Raft Supply bought display cases on account from Carter Cabinet Shop, at a cost of $2,700 plus freight charges of $290. The seller of the display cases prepaid the transportation costs for Whitewater Raft Supply and then added the $290 to the invoice price of the cases. Let's visualize this with T accounts.

Store Equipment			Accounts Payable	
+	−		−	+
2,990				2,990

Notice that Whitewater Raft Supply did not use the Freight In account to record the transportation costs. Instead, the company recorded the transportation costs directly into the Store Equipment account.

Internal Control of Purchases

Purchases is one of the areas in which internal control is essential. Efficiency and security require most companies to work out careful procedures for buying and paying for goods. This is understandable, as large sums of money are usually involved. The control aspect generally involves the following measures:

1. Purchases are made only after proper authorization is given. Purchase requisitions and purchase orders are all prenumbered, so that each form can be accounted for.

2. The receiving department carefully checks all goods upon receipt for count, damages, and description. Later, the report of the receiving department is verified against the purchase order and the purchase invoice.

3. The person who authorizes the payment is neither the person doing the ordering nor the person actually writing the check. Payment is authorized only after verifying the purchase invoice data against the receiving report and purchase order.

4. The person who actually writes the check has not been involved in any of the foregoing purchasing procedures.

PART TWO—RECORDING TRANSACTIONS INTO SALES JOURNAL AND PURCHASES JOURNAL

Special Journals

We have demonstrated sales and purchases by recording the transactions directly into the general journal. Companies can, however, also record sales and purchases into a special journal. **Special journals** are books of original entry used to simplify the recording process. One or more of these journals may be used in a manual accounting system, or they may be used in certain computerized systems designed to facilitate specialized types of repetitive transactions. The four most commonly used special journals are:

Sales journal (S) Used to record sales of merchandise sold on account *only*. For example, if Whitewater Raft Supply sells a kayak to a customer, on account, Whitewater Raft Supply could use this journal to record that sale. However, if the customer paid cash for the kayak, the sale would not be recorded in this journal. Also, if Whitewater Raft Supply sells some of its old computer equipment, on account, this journal would not be used because the equipment was not part of the business's merchandise sales.

Purchases journal (P) Used to record purchases of merchandise purchased on account for resale *only*. For example, this journal could be used by Whitewater Raft Supply for its purchase, on account, of whitewater rafts to resell to customers. However, this journal would not be used by Whitewater Raft Supply when buying a copy machine or supplies for the office, even though purchased on account, because those goods are not intended for resale to customers.

Cash receipts journal (CR) Used to record all transactions that include a debit to Cash, such as cash sales, checks received, or interest earned on a checking account.

Cash payments journal (CP) Used to record all transactions that include a credit to Cash, such as payments by check or bank service charges.

In part two of this chapter, we will demonstrate how Whitewater Raft Supply records sales and purchases transactions using the sales journal and purchases journal. In the next chapter, we will discuss the cash receipts journal and cash payments journal.

The Sales Journal

LEARNING OBJECTIVE 10

Journalize transactions in a sales journal, and post to the accounts receivable ledger and general ledger.

The **sales journal** records sales of merchandise **on account only.** This specialized type of transaction calls for debits to Accounts Receivable and credits to Sales.

Recall the sales transactions introduced for Whitewater Raft Supply for the month of August:

Aug.   1   Sold merchandise on account to Mesa River Raft Company, invoice no. 9384, $1,933.50.

Aug. 8 Sold merchandise on account to Green River Rafts, invoice no. 9385, $1,116.

14 Sold merchandise on account to Marty's Fly Fishing Adventures, invoice no. 9386, $1,594.

19 Sold merchandise on account to Hi-Flying Adventures, Inc., invoice no. 9387, $552.30.

25 Sold merchandise on account to Hi-Flying Adventures, Inc., invoice no. 9388, $1,674.

Let's assume that Whitewater Raft Supply uses the sales journal *instead of* the general journal to record the five transactions. The accountant will record each transaction into the sales journal only.

The sales journal is a book of original entry. Do not duplicate the transaction in the general journal.

Remember

			SALES JOURNAL			PAGE 38		
Date		Inv. No.	Customer's Name	Post. Ref.	Accounts Receivable Dr. Sales Cr.			
20—								
Aug.	1	9384	Mesa River Raft Company		1 9 3 3	50
	8	9385	Green River Rafts		1 1 1 6	00
	14	9386	Marty's Fly Fishing Adventures		1 5 9 4	00
	19	9387	Hi-Flying Adventures, Inc.		5 5 2	30
	25	9388	Hi-Flying Adventures, Inc.		1 6 7 4	00

Because *one* column is headed Accounts Receivable Dr./Sales Cr., each transaction requires only a single line. Repetition is avoided, and all entries for sales of merchandise on account are found in one place. Listing the invoice number makes it easier to check the details of a particular sale at a later date.

As with the general journal, the amount of each sale should be posted daily to the account of each credit customer in the accounts receivable ledger. After you post an amount from the sales journal to a credit customer's account in the accounts receivable ledger, put a check mark in the Post. Ref. column of the sales journal.

Posting from the Sales Journal

Using the sales journal also saves time and space in posting to the ledger accounts. Because every entry is a debit to Accounts Receivable and a credit to Sales, you can make a single posting to these accounts for the amount of the total as of the last day of the month. This entry is called a **summarizing entry** because it summarizes one month's transactions. Since Whitewater Raft Supply had no other sales transactions after August 25, the amounts in the Accounts Receivable Dr./Sales Cr. Column from the sales journal above are added up and totaled. The total ($6,869.80) is then posted to the Accounts Receivable and Sales accounts in the general ledger. In the Post. Ref. columns of the ledger accounts, the letter S designates the sales journal.

			GENERAL LEDGER					
ACCOUNT Accounts Receivable						ACCOUNT NO. 113		
Date	Item	Post. Ref.	Debit	Credit	Balance			
					Debit		Credit	
20—								
Aug. 31		S38	6 8 6 9 80		6 8 6 9 80			

The purpose of posting reference numbers is to tell where in the ledger an amount was posted or the journal from which it came.

Remember

Remember

The T accounts look like this:

Accounts Receivable	
+	−
6,869.80	

Sales	
−	+
	6,869.80

GENERAL LEDGER

ACCOUNT Sales   ACCOUNT NO. 411

Date	Item	Post. Ref.	Debit	Credit	Balance Debit	Balance Credit
20—						
Aug. 31		S38		6 8 6 9 80		6 8 6 9 80

After posting the total of the sales journal to the Accounts Receivable account in the general ledger, write the account number of Accounts Receivable at the left below the total of the sales journal. Repeat the process of posting for the total of the sales journal to the Sales account in the general ledger, placing the account number of Sales at the right below the total of the sales journal. **Don't record these account numbers until you have completed the postings.** Figure 15 shows the completed sales journal for Whitewater Raft Supply for the month of August. Notice that the ruling consists of a single line under the amount column and double lines extended through the Date, Post. Ref., and amount columns. The last day of the month is recorded on the same line as the total.

FIGURE 15
Sales journal

SALES JOURNAL   PAGE 38

Date	Inv. No.	Customer's Name	Post. Ref.	Accounts Receivable Dr. Sales Cr.
20—				
Aug. 1	9384	Mesa River Raft Company	✓	1 9 3 3 50
8	9385	Green River Rafts	✓	1 1 1 6 00
14	9386	Marty's Fly Fishing Adventures	✓	1 5 9 4 00
19	9387	Hi-Flying Adventures, Inc.	✓	5 5 2 30
25	9388	Hi-Flying Adventures, Inc.	✓	1 6 7 4 00
31		Total		6 8 6 9 80
				(113) (411)

Sales Journal with Sales Tax Payable

When recording sales transactions that involve sales tax, the sales journal will need to include three columns: Accounts Receivable Debit, Sales Tax Payable Credit, and Sales Credit.

Recall the transaction given for David Fly Fishing Outfitters earlier in the chapter:

Jan.   3 Sold merchandise on account to R. Martinez, invoice no. 101, $153.50 plus sales tax of $12.28.

As shown below, David Fly Fishing Outfitters would record the transaction in the sales journal as follows:

Remember

The sales journal is used to record only the sales of merchandise (goods) on account.

SALES JOURNAL   PAGE 3

Date	Inv. No.	Customer's Name	Post. Ref.	Accounts Receivable Debit	Sales Tax Payable Credit	Sales Credit
20—						
Jan. 3	101	R. Martinez		1 6 5 78	1 2 28	1 5 3 50

At the end of the month, the accountant for David Fly Fishing Outfitters would total the columns and post them as a debit to Accounts Receivable, a credit to Sales Tax Payable, and a credit to Sales. However, with a journal that has more than one column, you should use the column totals to prove that the total debits equal the total credits before posting to the general ledger accounts. After posting, the respective account numbers are recorded in parentheses below the totals.

Purchases Journal (Three-Column)

Following are the purchase transactions for Whitewater Raft Supply for the month of August. We will use these transactions to demonstrate the purchases journal.

11 LEARNING OBJECTIVE
Journalize transactions in a three-column purchases journal, and post to the accounts payable ledger and general ledger.

Aug. 2 Bought merchandise on account from Pataponia, Inc., invoice no. 2706, $1,710; terms 2/10, n/30; dated July 31; FOB San Francisco, freight prepaid and added to the invoice, $85.50 (total $1,795.50).

10 Bought merchandise on account from Langseth and Son, invoice no. 982, $2,772; terms net 30 days; dated August 8; FOB Cleveland, freight prepaid and added to the invoice, $157 (total $2,929).

17 Bought merchandise on account from Dana Manufacturing Company, invoice no. 10611, $564; terms 2/10, n/30; dated August 15; FOB Los Angeles.

26 Bought merchandise on account from Pataponia, Inc., invoice no. 2801, $2,503.70; terms 2/10, n/30; dated August 24; FOB San Francisco, freight prepaid and added to the invoice, $102.30 (total $2,606).

As shown below, Whitewater Raft Supply's accountant will record each transaction into the **purchases journal**. Notice that by including a separate column for each account, Whitewater Raft Supply can record a typical purchase of merchandise on account on one line.

PURCHASES JOURNAL								PAGE 29	
Date	Supplier's Name	Inv. No.	Inv. Date	Terms	Post. Ref.	Accounts Payable Credit	Freight In Debit	Purchases Debit	
20—									
Aug. 2	Pataponia, Inc.	2706	7/31	2/10, n/30		1 7 9 5 50	8 5 50	1 7 1 0 00	
10	Langseth and Son	982	8/8	n/30		2 9 2 9 00	1 5 7 00	2 7 7 2 00	
17	Dana Manufacturing Co.	10611	8/15	2/10, n/30		5 6 4 00		5 6 4 00	
26	Pataponia, Inc.	2801	8/24	2/10, n/30		2 6 0 6 00	1 0 2 30	2 5 0 3 70	

Posting from the Purchases Journal to the General Ledger

If using a manual system, the accountant posts the totals of each column into the appropriate general ledger accounts. Figure 16 shows the journal entries in the purchases journal for Whitewater Raft Supply for all transactions involving the purchase of merchandise on account for August and the related ledger accounts for the same time period. In the Post. Ref. column of the ledger accounts, P designates the purchases journal. After posting the column totals for the month to the ledger accounts, the accountant goes back to the purchases journal and puts a check mark (✓) in the Post. Ref column and records the account numbers in parentheses directly below the total.

FIGURE 16

Purchases journal and general ledger accounts

								PURCHASES JOURNAL									**PAGE 29**	

Date	Supplier's Name	Inv. No.	Inv. Date	Terms	Post. Ref.	Accounts Payable Credit				Freight In Debit				Purchases Debit			
20—																	
Aug. 2	Pataponia, Inc.	2706	7/31	2/10, n/30	✓	1	7	9	5 50		8	5	50	1	7	1	0 00
10	Langseth and Son	982	8/8	n/30	✓	2	9	2	9 00	1	5	7	00	2	7	7	2 00
17	Dana Manufacturing Co.	10611	8/15	2/10, n/30	✓		5	6	4 00						5	6	4 00
26	Pataponia, Inc.	2801	8/24	2/10, n/30	✓	2	6	0	6 00	1	0	2	30	2	5	0	3 70
31	Totals					7	8	9	4 50	3	4	4	80	7	5	4	9 70
						(2	1	2)		(5	1	4)		(5	1	1)	

GENERAL LEDGER

ACCOUNT **Accounts Payable**　　　　　　　　　　　　　ACCOUNT NO. **212**

Date	Item	Post. Ref.	Debit	Credit	Balance Debit	Balance Credit
20—						
Aug. 31		P29		7 8 9 4 50		7 8 9 4 50

ACCOUNT **Purchases**　　　　　　　　　　　　　　　　ACCOUNT NO. **511**

Date	Item	Post. Ref.	Debit	Credit	Balance Debit	Balance Credit
20—						
Aug. 31		P29	7 5 4 9 70		7 5 4 9 70	

ACCOUNT **Freight In**　　　　　　　　　　　　　　　　ACCOUNT NO. **514**

Date	Item	Post. Ref.	Debit	Credit	Balance Debit	Balance Credit
20—						
Aug. 31		P29	3 4 4 80		3 4 4 80	

CHAPTER REVIEW

Study & Practice

LEARNING OBJECTIVE 1

Describe the specific accounts used by a merchandising firm.

The **Merchandise Inventory** account is an asset account representing the cost of goods bought for resale.

The **Sales account** is a revenue account representing the total sales of merchandise.

The **Sales Returns and Allowances account** is a deduction from the Sales account, representing amounts allowed for returns of merchandise and damaged goods.

The **Sales Tax Payable account** is a liability account representing amounts owed to state or city governments.

The **Sales Discounts account** is a deduction from the Sales account, representing amounts deducted for prompt payments.

The **Purchases account** is a cost (expense) account representing the costs of goods bought for resale.

The **Purchases Returns and Allowances account** is a deduction from the Purchases account, representing amounts granted by suppliers for the return of merchandise or damaged goods.

The **Purchases Discounts account** is a deduction from the Purchases account, representing amounts suppliers allow for prompt payments.

The **Freight In account** is a cost (expense) representing the transportation charges on incoming merchandise.

LEARNING OBJECTIVE 2

Journalize sales transactions in a general journal, and post to the accounts receivable ledger and general ledger.

Sales transactions are recorded in the general journal by debiting Accounts Receivable and crediting Sales. The entry is posted to the Accounts Receivable and Sales accounts in the general ledger. The entries are also posted daily to the **accounts receivable ledger**.

PRACTICE EXERCISE 1

Record the following transaction for Rodgers Refrigerator Supply in general journal form.

Aug. 23 Sold merchandise on account to Robbins Hardware Store, invoice no. 3209, $1,340.

PRACTICE EXERCISE 1 SOLUTION

GENERAL JOURNAL				PAGE _____
Date	Description	Post. Ref.	Debit	Credit
20—				
Aug. 23	Accounts Receivable, Robbins			
	Hardware Store		1 3 4 0 00	
	Sales			1 3 4 0 00
	Sold merchandise to Robbins			
	Hardware Store, invoice			
	no. 3209.			

3 LEARNING OBJECTIVE

Prepare a schedule of accounts receivable.

The schedule of accounts receivable consists of a listing of the individual account balances of the credit customers taken from the accounts receivable ledger.

PRACTICE EXERCISE 2

Fill in the missing amounts in the accounts receivable subsidiary ledgers for Willis Spas and Pools. Then, using the information from the ledgers, prepare a schedule of accounts receivable.

ACCOUNTS RECEIVABLE LEDGER

NAME   J. Hersch
ADDRESS   3540 Key Avenue
Lampasas, TX 76550

Date	Item	Post. Ref.	Debit	Credit	Balance
20—					
May 2		J26	7 8 1 40		7 8 1 40
8		J26	1 7 8 0 00		(a)
22		J26		1 2 0 5 00	(b)

NAME   M. Hill
ADDRESS   220 Lawrence Avenue
Copperas Cove, TX 76522

Date	Item	Post. Ref.	Debit	Credit	Balance
20—					
May 15		J26	4 8 1 40		4 8 1 40
18		J26		2 0 4 80	(c)

NAME R. D. Moen
ADDRESS 416 Fifth Avenue
Dallas, TX 75204

Date		Item	Post. Ref.	Debit	Credit	Balance
20—						
May	31		J26	3 1 2 60		3 1 2 60

PRACTICE EXERCISE 2 SOLUTION

(a) $2,561.40
(b) $1,356.40
(c) $276.60

Willis Spas and Pools
Schedule of Accounts Receivable
May 31, 20—

J. Hersch	$1,356.40
M. Hill	276.60
R. D. Moen	312.60
Total Accounts Receivable	$1,945.60

LEARNING OBJECTIVE

4 Journalize sales returns and allowances, including credit memorandums and returns, in a general journal, and post to the accounts receivable ledger and general ledger.

When a customer returns merchandise, or when his or her bill is reduced owing to an allowance for defective or damaged merchandise, the Sales Returns and Allowances account is debited and the Accounts Receivable account is credited. The entry is recorded in the general journal and posted to both the general ledger and the accounts receivable ledger.

PRACTICE EXERCISE 3

Refer to the transaction in Practice Exercise 1. Assume that on September 1, Robbins Hardware Store returned $81 of the merchandise. Rodgers Refrigerator Supply issued credit memo no. 114. Record the journal entry for the return.

PRACTICE EXERCISE 3 SOLUTION

GENERAL JOURNAL   **PAGE** _____

Date		Description	Post. Ref.	Debit	Credit
20—					
Sept.	1	Sales Returns and Allowances		8 1 00	
		Accounts Receivable, Robbins			
		Hardware Store			8 1 00
		Issued credit memo no. 114.			

5 LEARNING OBJECTIVE

Journalize sales transactions and returns involving sales tax.

Sales tax is collected from customers by the retailer and then later paid to the appropriate tax authorities. When goods are sold, the sales tax is charged to the customer and recorded at the time of sale. The entry involves recording a debit to Accounts Receivable or Cash and credits to Sales and Sales Tax Payable.

PRACTICE EXERCISE 4

Record the following transaction for Powers Company in general journal form.

July   14   Sold merchandise on account to C. Heald, invoice no. D446, $560 plus $44.80 sales tax.

PRACTICE EXERCISE 4 SOLUTION

GENERAL JOURNAL   PAGE _____

Date		Description	Post. Ref.	Debit	Credit
20—					
July	14	Accounts Receivable, C. Heald		6 0 4 80	
		Sales			5 6 0 00
		Sales Tax Payable			4 4 80
		Sold merchandise to C. Heald,			
		invoice no. D446.			

6 LEARNING OBJECTIVE

Journalize purchase transactions in a general journal, and post to the accounts payable ledger and general ledger.

Purchase transactions are recorded in the general journal by debiting the Purchases account and crediting Accounts Payable. If the company pays for freight, the company will also record a debit to Freight In. The purchase transactions are posted to the general ledger as a debit to Purchases, a debit to Freight In, and a credit to Accounts Payable. Each transaction must also be posted daily to the **accounts payable ledger**.

PRACTICE EXERCISE 5

Record the following transaction for Byrne Corporation in general journal form:

Apr.   14   Bought merchandise on account from Jabari, Inc., invoice no. C3009, $1,125; terms net 30 days; dated April 12; FOB shipping point, freight prepaid and added to the invoice, $72.50 (total $1,197.50).

PRACTICE EXERCISE 5 SOLUTION

	GENERAL JOURNAL			PAGE _____
Date	Description	Post. Ref.	Debit	Credit
20—				
Apr. 14	Purchases		1 1 2 5 00	
	Freight In		7 2 50	
	Accounts Payable, Jabari, Inc.			1 1 9 7 50
	Purchased merchandise from			
	Jabari, Inc., invoice no. C3009,			
	invoice dated 4/12, terms n/30.			

7 **LEARNING OBJECTIVE**

Prepare a schedule of accounts payable.

A schedule of accounts payable, listing the balance of each individual creditor's account, is prepared from the accounts payable ledger.

PRACTICE EXERCISE 6

Fill in the missing amounts in the accounts payable subsidiary ledgers for Updike Train Supply. Then, using the information from the ledgers, prepare a schedule of accounts payable.

ACCOUNTS PAYABLE LEDGER

NAME J. Fletcher and Sons

ADDRESS 326 Fairway Drive

Richmond, CA 94805

Date	Item	Post. Ref.	Debit	Credit	Balance
20—					
June 1		J73		1 7 5 1 55	1 7 5 1 55
14		J73	1 5 7 6 15		(a)

NAME Rocky and Schlink

ADDRESS 542 Roselle Blvd.

Oakland, CA 94601

Date	Item	Post. Ref.	Debit	Credit	Balance
20—					
June 13		J73		2 1 8 00	2 1 8 00

NAME   Tan Supplies
ADDRESS 120 Fish Road
         Berkeley, CA 94720

Date		Item	Post. Ref.	Debit	Credit	Balance
20—						
June	5		J73		2 7 1 0 00	2 7 1 0 00
	23		J73		1 7 4 0 25	(b)
	29		J73	1 5 0 0 00		(c)

PRACTICE EXERCISE 6 SOLUTION

(a) $175.40

(b) $4,450.25

(c) $2,950.25

Updike Train Supply
Schedule of Accounts Payable
June 30, 20—

J. Fletcher and Sons	$ 175.40
Rocky and Schlink	218.00
Tan Supplies	2,950.25
Total Accounts Payable	$3,343.65

8 LEARNING OBJECTIVE

Journalize transactions involving purchases returns and allowances in a general journal, and post to the accounts payable ledger and general ledger.

When a credit memo is received for the return of merchandise or as an allowance for damaged goods, the buyer credits Purchase Returns and Allowances. If the merchandise was bought on account, the buyer debits Accounts Payable. The entry is recorded in the general journal and posted to both the general ledger and the accounts receivable ledger.

PRACTICE EXERCISE 7

Refer to the transaction in Practice Exercise 5. Assume that on April 24, Byrne Corporation received credit memo no. 117 from Jabari, Inc., for merchandise returned, $127. Record the transaction for the purchase return.

PRACTICE EXERCISE 7 SOLUTION

	GENERAL JOURNAL			PAGE _____	
Date	Description	Post. Ref.	Debit	Credit	
20—					
Apr. 24	Accounts Payable, Jabari, Inc.		1 2 7 00		
	Purchases Returns and				
	Allowances			1 2 7 00	
	Credit memo no. 117 for				
	return of merchandise.				

9 **LEARNING OBJECTIVE**

Describe the procedures for handling freight charges on merchandise and other goods.

The Freight In account is debited for the cost of transportation charges on incoming merchandise intended for resale. Freight costs that apply to non-merchandise assets purchased are added to the asset account that applies.

PRACTICE EXERCISE 8

a. Who pays the freight when the terms of sale are FOB shipping point?
b. Who pays the freight when the terms of the sale are FOB destination?

PRACTICE EXERCISE 8 SOLUTION

a. Buyer
b. Seller

10 **LEARNING OBJECTIVE**

Journalize transactions in a sales journal, and post to the accounts receivable ledger and general ledger.

The **sales journal** is used to record only sales of merchandise on account. The entries are posted daily to the accounts receivable ledger. At the end of the month, the total is posted to the general ledger as a debit to the Accounts Receivable controlling account and a credit to the Sales account.

PRACTICE EXERCISE 9

Record the following sales of merchandise on account on page 25 of the sales journal and then post to the general ledger. (The company uses the same account numbers as Whitewater Raft Supply.)

Apr. 1 Sold merchandise on account to West Company, invoice no. 1054, $1,378.95.

15 Sold merchandise on account to Ruiz Company, invoice no. 1055, $578.15.

PRACTICE EXERCISE 9 SOLUTION

SALES JOURNAL					PAGE 25

Date	Inv. No.	Customer's Name	Post. Ref.	Accounts Receivable Dr. Sales Cr.
20—				
Apr. 1	1054	West Company		1 3 7 8 95
15	1055	Ruiz Company		5 7 8 15
30		Total		1 9 5 7 10
				(113) (411)

GENERAL LEDGER

ACCOUNT __Accounts Receivable__   ACCOUNT NO. 113

Date	Item	Post. Ref.	Debit	Credit	Balance Debit	Credit
20—						
Apr. 30		S25	1 9 5 7 10		1 9 5 7 10	

ACCOUNT __Sales__   ACCOUNT NO. 411

Date	Item	Post. Ref.	Debit	Credit	Balance Debit	Credit
20—						
Apr. 30		S25		1 9 5 7 10		1 9 5 7 10

11 LEARNING OBJECTIVE

Journalize transactions in a three-column purchases journal, and post to the accounts payable ledger and general ledger.

The three-column **purchases journal** handles the purchase of merchandise on account and freight charges that are prepaid by the seller and included in the invoice total. Amounts in the Accounts Payable credit column are posted daily to the accounts payable ledger. At the end of the month, the totals are posted to the general ledger as a debit to Purchases, a debit to Freight In, and a credit to Accounts Payable.

PRACTICE EXERCISE 10

Record the following purchases of merchandise on account on page 52 of the purchases journal and then post to the general ledger. (The company uses the same account numbers as Whitewater Raft Supply.)

Jan.   4   Bought merchandise on account from Switzer Corporation, invoice no. A459, $578; terms net 60 days; dated January 2; FOB destination.

24   Bought merchandise on account from Stevens Company, invoice no. 48512, $799.80; terms 2/10, n/30; dated January 22; FOB shipping point, freight prepaid and added to the invoice, $50 (total $849.80).

PRACTICE EXERCISE 10 SOLUTION

PURCHASES JOURNAL — PAGE 52

Date		Supplier's Name	Inv. No.	Inv. Date	Terms	Post. Ref.	Accounts Payable Credit	Freight In Debit	Purchases Debit
20—									
Jan.	4	Switzer Corporation	A459	1/2	n/60		5 7 8 00		5 7 8 00
	24	Stevens Company	48512	1/22	2/10, n/30		8 4 9 80	5 0 00	7 9 9 80
	31	Totals					1 4 2 7 80	5 0 00	1 3 7 7 80
							(2 1 2)	(5 1 4)	(5 1 1)

GENERAL LEDGER

ACCOUNT **Accounts Payable**   ACCOUNT NO. 212

Date		Item	Post. Ref.	Debit	Credit	Balance Debit	Balance Credit
20—							
Jan.	31		P52		1 4 2 7 80		1 4 2 7 80

ACCOUNT **Purchases**   ACCOUNT NO. 511

Date		Item	Post. Ref.	Debit	Credit	Balance Debit	Balance Credit
20—							
Jan.	31		P52	1 3 7 7 80		1 3 7 7 80	

ACCOUNT **Freight In**   ACCOUNT NO. 514

Date		Item	Post. Ref.	Debit	Credit	Balance Debit	Balance Credit
20—							
Jan.	31		P52	5 0 00		5 0 00	

Glossary

Accounts payable ledger A subsidiary ledger that lists the individual accounts of creditors in either alphabetical or numerical order with their respective balances. (p. 342)

Accounts receivable ledger A subsidiary ledger that lists the individual accounts of credit customers in either alphabetical or numerical order, with their respective transactions and balances. (p. 333)

Controlling account An account in the general ledger that summarizes the balances of a subsidiary ledger. (p. 334)

Credit memorandum A written statement indicating a seller's willingness to reduce the amount of a buyer's debt. The seller records the amount of the credit memorandum in the Sales Returns and Allowances account. (p. 335)

FOB destination Shipping terms under which the seller pays the freight charges and includes them in the selling price. Title or ownership changes hands when the buyer receives the goods. (p. 346)

FOB shipping point Shipping terms under which the buyer pays the freight charges between the point of shipment and the destination. Payment may be made directly to the carrier upon receiving the goods or to the supplier if the supplier prepaid the freight charges on behalf of the buyer. Title or ownership changes hands when goods are transferred to the freight company. (p. 346)

Freight In account The account used to record transportation charges on incoming merchandise intended for resale. (p. 329)

Invoices Business forms prepared by the seller that list the items shipped, their cost, the terms of the sale, and the mode of shipment. They may also state the freight charges. The buyer considers them purchase invoices; the seller considers them sales invoices. (p. 330)

Merchandise inventory Goods (an asset account) that a company buys and intends to resell at a profit. (p. 329)

Merchandising businesses Businesses that buy and sell goods. (p. 329)

Periodic inventory system A method of recording inventory that requires the company to determine the amount of goods on hand by periodically taking a physical count and then attaching a value to it. (p. 329)

Perpetual inventory system A method of recording inventory that provides the firm with a running balance of inventory. (p. 329)

Purchase order A written order from the buyer of goods to the supplier, listing the items wanted and the terms of the transaction. (p. 339)

Purchase requisition A form used to request that the Purchasing Department buy something. This form is intended for internal use within a company. (p. 339)

Purchases account An account for recording the cost of merchandise acquired for resale. (p. 329)

Purchases Discounts account An account that records cash discounts granted by suppliers in return for prompt payment; it is treated as a deduction from Purchases. (p. 329)

Purchases journal A special journal used to record only the buying of goods on account. It may be used to record the purchase of merchandise only. (p. 351)

Purchases Returns and Allowances account An account that records a company's return of merchandise it has purchased or a reduction in the bill because of damaged merchandise; it is treated as a deduction from Purchases. (p. 329)

Retail business A business that sells goods directly to consumers. (p. 329)

Sales account A revenue account for recording the sale of merchandise. (p. 329)

Sales Discounts account An account that records a deduction from the original price, granted by the seller to the buyer for the prompt payment of an invoice. (p. 329)

Sales journal A special journal for recording only the sale of merchandise on account. (p. 348)

Sales Returns and Allowances account The account a seller uses to record the physical return of merchandise by customers or a reduction in a bill because merchandise was damaged. Sales Returns and Allowances is treated as a deduction from Sales. This account is usually evidenced by a credit memorandum issued by the seller. (p. 329)

Sales Tax Payable account An account used to record a tax levied by a state or city government on the retail sale of goods and services. The tax is paid by the consumer but collected by the retailer. (p. 329)

Special journals Books of original entry in which specialized types of repetitive transactions are recorded. (p. 348)

Subsidiary ledger A group of accounts representing individual subdivisions showing the debits and credits of a controlling account. (p. 334)

Summarizing entry An entry made to post the column totals of a special journal to the appropriate accounts in the general ledger. (p. 349)

Wholesale business A business that buys goods from manufacturers and sells those goods (normally in large quantities) to retailers for resale. (p. 329)

CHAPTER ASSIGNMENTS

Discussion Questions

1. What is the difference between a wholesale business and a retail business?
2. For each of the following accounts, identify if the normal balance is a debit or credit. Also, specify if the account is a contra account.
   a. Sales Returns and Allowances
   b. Merchandise Inventory
   c. Sales

    d. Freight In
    e. Purchases Returns and Allowances
    f. Sales Tax Payable
    g. Sales Discounts
    h. Purchases
    i. Purchases Discounts

3. What is the purpose of a:
    a. Schedule of accounts receivable?
    b. Schedule of accounts payable?

4. Why is an accounts receivable ledger or an accounts payable ledger necessary for a business with large numbers of credit customers or large numbers of vendors/suppliers?

5. Why is it a good practice to post daily to the accounts receivable or accounts payable ledgers?

6. With regard to goods sold and purchased, explain how sales returns and allowances and purchases returns and allowances are different from each other.

7. Explain the meaning and importance of the shipping terms FOB destination and FOB shipping point. Who has title to the goods once they have been shipped?

8. Describe the four procedures that most companies follow to maintain internal control of purchases of merchandise.

9. Describe the posting procedures to the general ledger and the rules for totaling and ruling the:
    a. Sales journal.
    b. Purchases journal.

10. Describe the procedure for posting:
    a. From the sales journal to the accounts receivable ledger.
    b. From the purchases journal to the accounts payable ledger.

Exercises

EXERCISE 9-1 Record the following transactions in general journal form.

a. Sold merchandise on account to G. Frank, invoice no. 1230, $1,233.50.
b. Sold merchandise on account to Gregory Productions, invoice no. 1231, $950.00.
c. Gregory Productions returned $615.75 worth of the merchandise. Issued credit memo no. 93.

LO 2,4

PRACTICE EXERCISES 1,3

EXERCISE 9-2 Post the following entry to the general ledger and subsidiary ledger.

LO 2,4

PRACTICE EXERCISES 1,3

GENERAL JOURNAL				PAGE 52
Date	Description	Post. Ref.	Debit	Credit
20—				
June 16	Sales Returns and Allowances		2 4 1 27	
	Accounts Receivable, F. E. Dixon			2 4 1 27
	Issued credit memo no. 131.			

GENERAL LEDGER

ACCOUNT <u>Accounts Receivable</u>   ACCOUNT NO. <u>113</u>

Date	Item	Post. Ref.	Debit	Credit	Balance Debit	Balance Credit
20—						
June 1	Balance	✓			6 5 1 1 19	

ACCOUNT <u>Sales Returns and Allowances</u>   ACCOUNT NO. <u>412</u>

Date	Item	Post. Ref.	Debit	Credit	Balance Debit	Balance Credit
20—						
June 1	Balance	✓			3 1 4 60	

ACCOUNTS RECEIVABLE LEDGER

NAME   <u>F. E. Dixon</u>
ADDRESS <u>416 Fifth Avenue</u>
           <u>Dallas, TX 75204</u>

Date	Item	Post. Ref.	Debit	Credit	Balance
20—					
May 31		J51	3 1 2 60		3 1 2 60

---

 5 LO

EXERCISE 9-3 Describe the transactions recorded in the following T accounts.

PRACTICE EXERCISE 4

Accounts Receivable	
(a) 967.50	(b) 53.70

Sales	
	(a) 900.00

Sales Tax Payable	
(b) 3.75	(a) 67.50

Sales Returns and Allowances	
(b) 49.95	

---

5 LO

EXERCISE 9-4 Record the following transactions in general journal form.

PRACTICE EXERCISE 4

a. Sold merchandise on account to A. Bauer, $680 plus $54.40 sales tax (invoice no. D446).

b. Bauer returned $105.50 of the merchandise. Issued credit memo no. 114 for $113.94 ($105.50 for the amount of the sale plus $8.44 for the amount of the sales tax).

EXERCISE 9-5 Describe the transactions recorded in the following T accounts.

PRACTICE EXERCISES 5,7

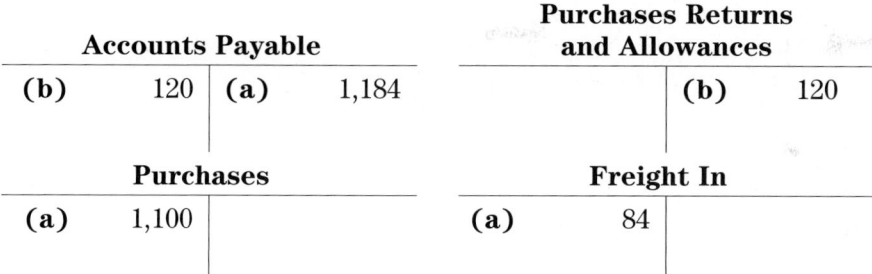

Accounts Payable		Purchases Returns and Allowances	
(b) 120	**(a)** 1,184		**(b)** 120

Purchases		Freight In	
(a) 1,100		**(a)** 84	

EXERCISE 9-6 Journalize the following transactions in general journal form.

a. Bought merchandise on account from Brewer, Inc., invoice no. B2997, $914; terms net 30 days; FOB destination.
b. Received credit memo no. 96 from Brewer, Inc., for merchandise returned, $238.

PRACTICE EXERCISES 5,7

EXERCISE 9-7 Post the following entry to the general ledger and the subsidiary ledger.

PRACTICE EXERCISES 5,7

GENERAL JOURNAL   **PAGE** 92

Date	Description	Post. Ref.	Debit	Credit
20—				
July 14	Accounts Payable, Jensen and Silva		1 9 2 30	
	Purchases Returns and			
	Allowances			1 9 2 30
	Credit memo no. 942 for			
	return of merchandise.			

GENERAL LEDGER

ACCOUNT Accounts Payable   **ACCOUNT NO.** 212

Date	Item	Post. Ref.	Debit	Credit	Balance Debit	Balance Credit
20—						
July 1	Balance	✓				2 7 6 1 24

ACCOUNT Purchases Returns and Allowances   **ACCOUNT NO.** 512

Date	Item	Post. Ref.	Debit	Credit	Balance Debit	Balance Credit
20—						
July 1	Balance	✓				2 3 0 16

ACCOUNTS PAYABLE LEDGER

NAME   Jensen and Silva

ADDRESS 542 Roselle Blvd.

Chicago, IL 60141

Date		Item	Post. Ref.	Debit	Credit	Balance
20—						
June	13		J92		2 1 8 00	2 1 8 00

2,4,6,8 LO

PRACTICE EXERCISES 1,3,5,7

EXERCISE 9-8 Record the following transactions in general journal form for Ford Education Outfitters and Romero Textbooks, Inc.

a. Ford Educational Outfitters bought merchandise on account from Romero Textbooks, Inc., invoice no. 10594, $1,875.34; terms net 30 days; FOB destination. Romero Textbooks, Inc., paid $93.80 for shipping.

b. Ford Education Outfitters received credit memo no. 513A from Romero Textbooks, Inc., for merchandise returned, $135.78.

4,8 LO

PRACTICE EXERCISES 3,7

EXERCISE 9-9 Using the following source document (credit memo issued by Chang Electronics), record the transaction in general journal form on the books of Chang Electronics, then on the books of The Merchandise Market.

Chang Electronics
4160 Broad Street
Chicago, Illinois 60627

CREDIT MEMORANDUM   No.   **121**

DATE: **November 6, 20—**

CREDIT TO:
   The Merchandise Market
   2241 Sullivan Street
   Chicago, Illinois   60632

Your account has been credited for:

      1 CPU tower $725.50

10 LO

PRACTICE EXERCISE 9

EXERCISE 9-10 Toby Company had the following sales transactions for the month of March:

Mar. 6 Sold merchandise on account to Osbourne, Inc., invoice no. 1128, $563.17.

      14 Sold merchandise on account to Ortiz Company, invoice no. 1129, $823.50.

      20 Sold merchandise on account to Bailey Corporation, invoice no. 1130, $2,350.98.

      24 Sold merchandise on account to Shannon Corporation, invoice no. 1131, $1,547.07.

Assume that Toby Company had beginning balances on March 1 of $3,569.80 (Sales 411) and $2,450.39 (Accounts Receivable 113). Record the sales of merchandise on account in the sales journal (page 24) and then post to the general ledger.

EXERCISE 9-11 Williams Corporation had the following purchases for the month of May:

LO 11

PRACTICE EXERCISE 10

May 3 Bought ten lawn rakes from Owens Company, invoice no. J34Y9, $250.25; terms net 15 days; dated May 1; FOB shipping point, freight prepaid and added to the invoice, $15 (total $265.25).

11 Bought one weedeater from Lionel's Lawn & Landscaping, invoice no. R7740, $219.72; terms 2/10, n/30; dated May 9; FOB shipping point, freight prepaid and added to the invoice, $35 (total $254.72).

15 Bought five bags of fertilizer from Wright's Farm Supplies, invoice no. 478, $210.97; terms net 30 days; dated May 13; FOB destination.

25 Bought one lawnmower from Gutierrez Corporation, invoice no. 2458, $425.39; terms net 30 days; dated May 22; FOB destination.

Assume that Williams Corporation had beginning balances on May 1 of $3,492.29 (Accounts Payable 212), $4,239.49 (Purchases 511), and $234.89 (Freight In 514). Record the purchases of merchandise on account in the purchases journal (page 13) and then post to the general ledger.

EXERCISE 9-12 Kelley Company has completed October's sales and purchases journals (see below and on the following page). Your job is to:

LO 3,7,10,11

PRACTICE EXERCISES 2,6,9,10

a. Total and post the journals to T accounts for the general ledger and the accounts receivable and accounts payable ledgers.
b. Complete a schedule of accounts receivable for October 31, 20—.
c. Complete a schedule of accounts payable for October 31, 20—.
d. Compare the balances of the schedules with their respective general ledger accounts. If they are not the same, find and correct the error(s).

SALES JOURNAL   **PAGE   18**

Date		Inv. No.	Customer's Name	Post. Ref.	Accounts Receivable Dr. Sales Cr.			
20—								
Oct.	3	414	Anderson Company		4	4 3	24	
	4	415	R. T. Holcomb		1 4	2 6	90	
	7	416	Gray and Malo		1 6	4 7	00	
	11	417	Mercer Mobil		3 1	1 2	16	
	16	418	J. L. Anthony		2 1	3 0	00	
	22	419	C. A. Goldschmidt		1 9	4 4	05	
	31	420	F. A. Baumann		2 7	9 1	00	
	31		Total					
					(	) (	)	

| | | | | | PURCHASES JOURNAL | | | | | | | | PAGE 10 | |

PURCHASES JOURNAL　　　　PAGE __10__

Date	Supplier's Name	Inv. No.	Inv. Date	Terms	Post. Ref.	Accounts Payable Credit	Freight In Debit	Purchases Debit
20—								
Oct. 2	Colter, Inc.	2706	7/31	2/10, n/30		7 5 9 00	4 9 00	7 1 0 00
3	Thomas and Son	982	8/2	n/30		8 2 9 00	5 7 00	7 7 2 00
5	Archer Manufacturing Co.	10611	8/3	2/10, n/30		5 6 4 00		5 6 4 00
9	Spence Products Co.	B643	8/6	1/10, n/30		1 6 5 00	1 0 00	1 5 5 00
18	L. C. Walter	46812	8/17	n/60		2 2 8 00		2 2 8 00
25	Delaney and Cox	1024	8/23	2/10, n/30		3 7 6 00	1 4 00	3 6 2 00
26	Colter, Inc.	2801	8/25	2/10, n/30		4 0 6 00	2 2 00	3 8 4 00
31	Totals							
						( )	( )	( )

Problem Set A

For additional help, see the demonstration problem at the beginning of each chapter in your Working Papers.

2,3,4,5 **LO**

PROBLEM 9-1A Bell Florists sells flowers on a retail basis. Most of the sales are for cash; however, a few steady customers have credit accounts. Bell's sales staff fills out a sales slip for each sale. There is a state retail sales tax of 5 percent, which is collected by the retailer and submitted to the state. The following represent Bell Florists' charge sales for March:

Mar. 4 Sold potted plant on account to C. Morales, sales slip no. 242, $27, plus sales tax of $1.35, total $28.35.

6 Sold floral arrangement on account to R. Dixon, sales slip no. 267, $54, plus sales tax of $2.70, total $56.70.

12 Sold corsage on account to B. Cox, sales slip no. 279, $16, plus sales tax of $0.80, total $16.80.

16 Sold wreath on account to All-Star Legion, sales slip no. 296, $104, plus sales tax of $5.20, total $109.20.

18 Sold floral arrangements on account to Tucker Funeral Home, sales slip no. 314, $260, plus sales tax of $13, total $273.00.

21 Tucker Funeral Home complained about a wrinkled ribbon on the floral arrangement. Bell Florists allowed a $30 credit, plus the sales tax of $1.50, credit memo no. 27.

23 Sold flower arrangements on account to Price Savings and Loan Association for their fifth anniversary, sales slip no. 337, $180, plus sales tax of $9, total $189.

24 Allowed Price Savings and Loan Association credit, $25, plus sales tax of $1.25, because of a few withered blossoms in floral arrangements, credit memo no. 28.

Check Figure
Schedule of Accounts Receivable total, $726.52

Required

1. Record these transactions in the general journal (pages 57 and 58).
2. Post the amounts from the general journal to the general ledger and accounts receivable ledger; Accounts Receivable 113, Sales Tax Payable 214, Sales 411, Sales Returns and Allowances 412.
3. Prepare a schedule of accounts receivable and compare its total with the balance of the Accounts Receivable controlling account.

PROBLEM 9-2A Berry's Pet Store records purchase transactions in the general journal. The company is located in Boston, Massachusetts. In addition to a general ledger, Berry's Pet Store also uses an accounts payable ledger. Transactions for April related to the purchase of merchandise are as follows:

LO 6,7,8

Apr. 2 Bought ten Carefree Pet Bedding bags from Blackburn Company, $399.90, invoice no. 4R48, dated April 1; terms net 30 days; FOB destination.

5 Bought seven Marine Betta Kits from Herrera Company, $83.93, invoice no. 4851, dated April 3; terms 2/10, n/30; FOB shipping point, freight prepaid and added to the invoice, $15 (total $98.93).

6 Bought fifteen Two Door Deluxe Kennels from Barrett, Inc., $719.85, invoice no. 1845R, dated April 5; terms 1/10, n/30; FOB destination.

8 Bought five Dome Top Bird Cages from Faulkner Company, $1,849.95, invoice no. 1485, dated April 7; terms 2/10, n/30; FOB shipping point, freight prepaid and added to the invoice, $76 (total $1,925.95).

13 Received credit memo no. 415 from Faulkner Company for merchandise returned, $589.13.

23 Bought three Five Tiered Cat Trees from Rhodes Manufacturing, $1,107, invoice no. 246J, dated April 21; terms net 60 days; FOB destination.

27 Bought thirty Glitter Collection Leashes from Solomon Products Company, $299.70, invoice no. 2675, dated April 25; terms net 30 days; FOB destination.

30 Received credit memo no. 861 from Solomon Products Company for merchandise returned, $76.25.

Required

1. Open the following accounts in the accounts payable ledger and record the April 1 balances, if any, as given: Barrett, Inc., $185.25; Blackburn Company, $254.64; Faulkner Company, $485.12; Herrera Company; Rhodes Manufacturing, $452.31; Solomon Products Company, $1,785.23. For the accounts having balances, write "Balance" in the Item column and place a check mark in the Post. Ref. column.
2. Record the April 1 balances in the general ledger as given: Accounts Payable 212 controlling account, $3,162.55; Purchases 511, $559.06; Purchases Returns and Allowances 512, $123.50; Freight In 514, $15.20. Write "Balance" in the Item column and place a check mark in the Post. Ref. column.
3. Record the transactions in the general journal beginning on page 115.
4. Post to the general ledger and the accounts payable ledger.
5. Prepare a schedule of accounts payable, and compare the balance of the Accounts Payable controlling account with the total of the schedule of accounts payable.

Check Figure
Accounts Payable account balance, $7,048.50 credit

PROBLEM 9-3A Shirley's Beauty Store records sales and purchase transactions in the general journal. In addition to a general ledger, Shirley's Beauty Store also uses an accounts receivable ledger and an accounts payable ledger. Transactions for January related to the sales and purchase of merchandise are as follows:

LO 2,3,4,5,6,7,8

Jan. 3 Bought thirty Mango Bath and Shower Gels from Madden, Inc., $660.00, invoice no. 3487, dated January 1; terms 2/10, n/30; FOB shipping point, freight prepaid and added to the invoice, $125.43 (total $785.43).

4 Bought ten Beauty Candle Travel Sets from Calhoun Candles, Inc., $420.00, invoice no. 4513, dated January 1; terms net 45; FOB destination.

12 Sold four Mango Bath and Shower Gels on account to R. Kielman, sales slip no. 1456, $120, plus sales tax of $9.60, total $129.60.

Jan. 13 Received credit memo no. 8715 from Calhoun Candles, Inc., for merchandise returned, $84.

21 Bought five Winter Skin Essentials Kits from Whitney and Waters, $197.50, invoice no. A875, dated January 18; terms 2/15, n/45; FOB destination.

25 Sold three Winter Skin Essentials on account to A. Benner, sales slip no. 1457, $135.75, plus sales tax of $10.86, total $146.61.

27 Issued credit memo no. 33 to A. Benner for merchandise returned, $45.25 plus $3.62 sales tax, total $48.87.

Check Figure
Schedule of Accounts Payable total, $2,297.56

Required

1. Open the following accounts in the accounts receivable ledger and record the balances as of January 1: A. Benner, $45.77; R. Kielman, $175.39. Write "Balance" in the Item column and place a check mark in the Post. Ref. column.
2. Open the following accounts in the accounts payable ledger and record the balances as of January 1: Calhoun Candles, Inc., $355.23; Madden, Inc., $573.15; Whitney and Waters, $50.25. Write "Balance" in the Item column and place a check mark in the Post. Ref. column.
3. Record the January 1 balances in the general ledger as given: Accounts Receivable 113 controlling account, $221.16; Accounts Payable 212 controlling account, $978.63; Sales Tax Payable 214, $128.45. Write "Balance" in the Item column and place a check mark in the Post. Ref. column.
4. Record the transactions in the general journal beginning on page 25.
5. Post the entries to the general journal and accounts receivable ledger or accounts payable ledger, as appropriate.
6. Prepare a schedule of accounts receivable.
7. Prepare a schedule of accounts payable.
8. Compare the totals of the schedules with the balances of the controlling accounts.

2,3,4,10 **PROBLEM 9-4A** Gomez Company sells electrical supplies on a wholesale basis. The following transactions took place during April of this year:

Apr. 1 Sold merchandise on account to Myers Company, invoice no. 761, $570.40.

5 Sold merchandise on account to L. R. Foster Company, invoice no. 762, $486.10.

6 Issued credit memo no. 50 to Myers Company for merchandise returned, $40.70.

10 Sold merchandise on account to Diaz Hardware, invoice no. 763, $293.35.

14 Sold merchandise on account to Brooks and Bennett, invoice no. 764, $640.16.

17 Sold merchandise on account to Powell and Reyes, invoice no. 765, $582.12.

21 Issued credit memo no. 51 to Brooks and Bennett for merchandise returned, $68.44.

24 Sold merchandise on account to Ortiz Company, invoice no. 766, $652.87.

26 Sold merchandise on account to Diaz Hardware, invoice no. 767, $832.19.

30 Issued credit memo no. 52 to Diaz Hardware for damage to merchandise, $98.50.

Check Figure
Accounts Receivable account balance, $5,018.97 debit

Required

1. Record these sales of merchandise on account in the sales journal (page 39). Record the sales returns and allowances in the general journal (page 74).

2. Immediately after recording each transaction, post to the accounts receivable ledger.

3. Post the amounts from the general journal daily. Post the sales journal amount as a total at the end of the month; Accounts Receivable 113, Sales 411, Sales Returns and Allowances 412.

4. Prepare a schedule of accounts receivable. Compare the balance of the Accounts Receivable controlling account with the total of the schedule of accounts receivable.

PROBLEM 9-5A Patterson Appliance uses a three-column purchases journal. The company is located in Fresno, California. In addition to a general ledger, Patterson Appliance also uses an accounts payable ledger. Transactions for January related to the purchase of merchandise are as follows:

LO 7,11

Jan. 2 Bought eighty 12-inch, 3-speed Brighton Oscillating Fans from Snyder and Jordan, $1,890, invoice no. 268J, dated January 2; terms net 60 days; FOB Fresno.

4 Bought ten 35-pint-capacity Crystal Humidifiers from Simpson Company, $2,300, invoice no. 39426, dated January 2; terms 2/10, n/30; FOB Durango, freight prepaid and added to the invoice, $90 (total $2,390).

7 Bought ten 16-inch Axel Window Fans from Tran, Inc., $360, invoice no. 452AD, dated January 6; terms 1/10, n/30; FOB Fresno.

10 Bought twenty-four 4-blade Tiempo Ceiling Fans, Model 2760, from Ukele Company, $3,550, invoice no. D7742, dated January 7; terms 2/10, n/30; FOB Sacramento, freight prepaid and added to the invoice, $84 (total $3,634).

14 Bought four Charger Electric Hedge Trimmers from Fernandez Products Company, $186, invoice no. 2542, dated January 13; terms net 30 days; FOB Fresno.

22 Bought forty Lindon Electric Bug Killers from Snyder and Jordan, $2,265, invoice no. 392J, dated January 22; terms net 60 days; FOB Fresno.

28 Bought ten Charger Electric Blowers from Fernandez Products Company, $830, invoice no. 2691, dated January 27; terms net 30 days; FOB Fresno.

30 Bought ten Kole Powered Attic Ventilators from Porter Company, $446, invoice no. 664CC, dated January 27; terms 2/10, n/30; FOB Seattle, freight prepaid and added to the invoice, $48 (total $494).

Required

1. Open the following accounts in the accounts payable ledger and record the January 1 balances, if any, as given: Fernandez Products Company; Porter Company, $163.17; Simpson Company, $167.19; Snyder and Jordan; Tran, Inc., $228.70; Ukele Company. For the accounts having balances, write "Balance" in the Item column and place a check mark in the Post. Ref. column.

2. Record the balance of $559.06 in the Accounts Payable 212 controlling account as of January 1. Write "Balance" in the Item column and place a check mark in the Post. Ref. column.

3. Record the transactions in the purchases journal beginning on page 81.

4. Post to the accounts payable ledger daily.

5. Post to the general ledger at the end of the month.

6. Prepare a schedule of accounts payable, and compare the balance of the Accounts Payable controlling account with the total of the schedule of accounts payable.

Check Figure
Accounts Payable account balance, $12,608.06 credit

2,3,4,6,7,8,10,11

PROBLEM 9-6A The following transactions relate to Reynolds Company during April of this year. Terms of sale are 2/10, n/30. The company is located in Atlanta.

Apr. 2 Sold merchandise on account to Shaw Company, invoice no. 1126, $1,746.

4 Bought merchandise on account from Payne Company, invoice no. 16521, $800; terms 1/10, n/30; dated April 2; FOB Atlanta.

9 Sold merchandise on account to Peterson and Black, invoice no. 1127, $860.

12 Bought merchandise on account from Vix Company, invoice no. L8552, $2,482; terms 2/10, n/30; dated April 11; FOB Rome, freight prepaid and added to the invoice, $49 (total $2,531).

15 Received credit memo no. 79 for merchandise returned to Knight and Company, for $120.

17 Sold merchandise on account to C. N. Hunt, invoice no. 1128, $1,015.

19 Issued credit memo no. 34 to Peterson and Black for merchandise returned, $86.

26 Bought merchandise on account from M. R. Palmer, Inc., invoice no. 7447, $1,482; terms 2/10, n/30; dated April 23; FOB Macon, freight prepaid and added to the invoice, $45 (total $1,527).

29 Bought office supplies on account from Thornton Stationery Company, invoice no. S336, $152; terms net 30 days; dated April 29.

30 Sold merchandise on account to Sampson and McDonald, invoice no. 1129, $2,601.

30 Issued credit memo no. 35 to Sampson and McDonald for merchandise returned, $153.

Check Figure

Accounts Payable account balance, $5,268 credit

Required

1. Open the following accounts in the accounts receivable ledger and record the balances as of April 1: C. N. Hunt; Peterson and Black, $426; Sampson and McDonald, $974; Shaw Company. For the accounts having balances, write "Balance" in the Item column and place a check mark in the Post. Ref. column.

2. Open the following accounts in the accounts payable ledger and record the balances as of April 1: Knight and Company, $262; M. R. Palmer, Inc., $116; Payne Company; Thornton Stationery Company; Vix Company. For the accounts having balances, write "Balance" in the Item column and place a check mark in the Post. Ref. column.

3. Record the transactions in the sales (page 24), purchases (page 18), or general journal (page 68), as appropriate.

4. Post the entries to the accounts receivable ledger daily.

5. Post the entries to the accounts payable ledger daily.

6. Post the entries in the general journal immediately after you make each journal entry.

7. Post the totals from the special journals at the end of the month.

8. Prepare a schedule of accounts receivable.

9. Prepare a schedule of accounts payable.

10. Compare the totals of the schedules with the balances of the controlling accounts.

Problem Set B

For additional help, see the demonstration problem at the beginning of each chapter in your Working Papers.

PROBLEM 9-1B Abbott Florists sells flowers on a retail basis. Most of the sales are for cash; however, a few steady customers have credit accounts. Abbott's sales staff fills out a sales slip for each sale. There is a state retail tax of 5 percent, which is collected by the retailer and submitted to the state. Abbott Florists' charge sales for March are as follows:

 **LO** 2,3,4,5

Mar. 4 Sold floral arrangement on account to R. Duarte, sales slip no. 236, $45, plus sales tax of $2.25, total $47.25.

7 Sold potted plant on account to C. Meadows, sales slip no. 272, $61, plus sales tax of $3.05, total $64.05.

12 Sold wreath on account to Anthony Realty, sales slip no. 294, $63, plus sales tax of $3.15, total $66.15.

17 Sold floral arrangements on account to Travis Dress Shop, sales slip no. 299, $170, plus sales tax of $8.50, total $178.50.

20 Travis Dress Shop returned a flower spray, complaining that there were dead blooms. Abbott Florists allowed a credit of $36, plus the sales tax of $1.80, credit memo no. 27.

21 Sold flower arrangements on account to Porter Computers for their anniversary, sales slip no. 310, $236, plus sales tax of $11.80, total $247.80.

22 Allowed Porter Computers credit, $25, plus sales tax of $1.25, because of withered blossoms in floral arrangements, credit memo no. 28.

27 Sold corsage on account to B. Crosby, sales slip no. 332, $30, plus sales tax of $1.50, total $31.50.

Required
1. Record these transactions in the general journal (pages 57 and 58).
2. Post the amounts from the general journal to the general ledger and accounts receivable ledger; Accounts Receivable 113, Sales Tax Payable 214, Sales 411, Sales Returns and Allowances 412.
3. Prepare a schedule of accounts receivable and compare its total with the balance of the Accounts Receivable controlling account.

Check Figure
Schedule of Accounts Receivable total, $682.42

PROBLEM 9-2B Lowery's Pet Depot records purchase transactions in the general journal. The company is located in Cleveland, Ohio. In addition to a general ledger, Lowery's Pet Depot also uses an accounts payable ledger. Transactions for October related to the purchase of merchandise are as follows:

 **LO** 6,7,8

Oct. 3 Bought twelve Automatic Fish Feeders from Barrera Company, $959.88, invoice no. 5493, dated October 2; terms net 30 days; FOB shipping point, freight prepaid and added to the invoice, $79.45 (total $1,039.33).

4 Bought two 18 × 18 Terrarium Stands from Hickman Company, $259.98, invoice no. 2JYX, dated October 2; terms 2/10, n/30; FOB destination.

7 Bought four Chinchilla Bath Houses from Baldwin, Inc., $67.96, invoice no. 4183, dated October 6; terms 1/10, n/30; FOB destination.

Oct. 10 Received credit memo no. 123 from Baldwin, Inc., for merchandise returned, $13.94.

14 Bought twenty Zoo Slider Hoods from Douglas, Inc., $2,599.80, invoice no. X431, dated October 12; terms 2/10, n/30; FOB shipping point, freight prepaid and added to the invoice, $140.50 (total $2,740.30).

15 Bought four Hanging Bird Baths from Krause, Inc., $71.96, invoice no. A499, dated October 11; terms net 60 days; FOB destination.

24 Bought eight Automatic Cat Litter Boxes from Villa Manufacturing, $2,399.92, invoice no. 4429, dated October 21; terms net 30 days; FOB destination.

27 Received credit memo no. 452 from Villa Manufacturing for merchandise returned, $346.78.

Check Figure

Accounts Payable account balance, $8,372.74 credit

Required

1. Open the following accounts in the accounts payable ledger and record the October 1 balances, if any, as given: Baldwin, Inc., $46.57; Barrera Company, $743.15; Douglas, Inc., $615.20; Hickman Company; Krause, Inc., $23.45; Villa Manufacturing, $725.64. For the accounts having balances, write "Balance" in the Item column and place a check mark in the Post. Ref. column.
2. Record the October 1 balances in the general ledger as given: Accounts Payable 212 controlling account, $2,154.01; Purchases 511, $2,485.12; Purchases Returns and Allowances 512, $287.52; Freight In 514, $48.57. Write "Balance" in the Item column and place a check mark in the Post. Ref. column.
3. Record the transactions in the general journal beginning on page 95.
4. Post to the general ledger and the accounts payable ledger.
5. Prepare a schedule of accounts payable, and compare the balance of the Accounts Payable controlling account with the total of the schedule of accounts payable.

2,3,4,5,6,7,8 **LO**

PROBLEM 9-3B May's Beauty Store records sales and purchase transactions in the general journal. In addition to a general ledger, May's Beauty Store also uses an accounts receivable ledger and an accounts payable ledger. Transactions for January related to the sales and purchase of merchandise are as follows:

Jan. 2 Bought nine Matte Nail Color Kits from Mejia, Inc., $450, invoice no. 4521, dated January 1; terms 2/10, n/30; FOB shipping point, freight prepaid and added to the invoice, $87.50 (total $537.50).

5 Bought thirty Perfume Cocktail Rings from Braun, Inc., $1,200, invoice no. 37A, dated January 3; terms 2/10, n/30; FOB destination.

8 Sold two Matte Nail Color Kits on account to J. Herbert, sales slip no. 113, $110, plus sales tax of $8.80, total $118.80.

11 Received credit memo no. 455 from Braun, Inc., for merchandise returned, $315.25.

18 Bought fifteen Eye Palettes from Vargas, Inc., $660, invoice no. 910, dated January 14; terms net 30; FOB destination.

23 Sold four Eye Palettes on account to T. Cantrell, sales slip no. 114, $200, plus sales tax of $16, total $216.

26 Issued credit memo no. 12 to T. Cantrell for merchandise returned, $50 plus $4 sales tax, total $54.

Check Figure

Schedule of Accounts Payable balance, $2,776

Required

1. Open the following accounts in the accounts receivable ledger and record the balances as of January 1: T. Cantrell, $86.99; J. Hebert, $63.47. Write "Balance" in the Item column and place a check mark in the Post. Ref. column.
2. Open the following accounts in the accounts payable ledger and record the balances as of January 1: Braun, Inc., $513.20; Mejia, Inc., $113.40; Vargas, Inc.,

$67.15. Write "Balance" in the Item column and place a check mark in the Post. Ref. column.

3. Record the January 1 balances in the general ledger as given: Accounts Receivable 113 controlling account, $150.46; Accounts Payable 212 controlling account, $693.75; Sales Tax Payable 214, $237.89. Write "Balance" in the Item column and place a check mark in the Post. Ref. column.

4. Record the transactions in the general journal beginning on page 17.

5. Post the entries to the general journal and accounts receivable ledger or accounts payable ledger, as appropriate.

6. Prepare a schedule of accounts receivable.

7. Prepare a schedule of accounts payable.

8. Compare the totals of the schedules with the balances of the controlling accounts.

PROBLEM 9-4B R. J. Hinton Company sells electrical supplies on a wholesale basis. The following transactions took place during April of this year.

Apr. 3 Sold merchandise on account to Maxwell Company, invoice no. 822, $652.80.

7 Sold merchandise on account to B. A. Fitzpatrick Company, invoice no. 823, $462.15.

8 Sold merchandise on account to Durham Hardware, invoice no. 824, $205.60.

13 Issued credit memo no. 61 to B. A. Fitzpatrick Company for merchandise returned, $136.50.

15 Sold merchandise on account to Briggs and Campos, invoice no. 825, $831.47.

21 Sold merchandise on account to Pena and Carr, invoice no. 826, $590.34.

24 Issued credit memo no. 62 to Briggs and Campos for merchandise returned, $80.45.

26 Sold merchandise on account to O'Neill Company, invoice no. 827, $569.90.

28 Issued credit memo no. 63 to Durham Hardware for damage to merchandise, $52.48.

30 Sold merchandise on account to Durham Hardware, invoice no. 828, $735.50.

Required

1. Record these sales of merchandise on account in the sales journal (page 39). Record the sales returns and allowances in the general journal (page 74).

2. Immediately after recording each transaction, post to the accounts receivable ledger.

3. Post the amounts from the general journal daily. Post the sales journal amount as a total at the end of the month; Accounts Receivable 113, Sales 411, Sales Returns and Allowances 412.

4. Prepare a schedule of accounts receivable. Compare the balance of the Accounts Receivable controlling account with the total of the schedule of accounts receivable.

Check Figure
Accounts Receivable account balance, $4,947.75 debit

7,11  **LO**

PROBLEM 9-5B West Bicycle Shop uses a three-column purchases journal. The company is located in Topeka, Kansas. In addition to a general ledger, the company also uses an accounts payable ledger. Transactions for January related to the purchase of merchandise are as follows:

Jan.   4   Bought fifty 10-speed bicycles from Nielsen Company, $4,775, invoice no. 26145, dated January 3; terms net 60 days; FOB Topeka.

7   Bought tires from Barton Tire Company, $792, invoice no. 9763, dated January 5; terms 2/10, n/30; FOB Topeka.

8   Bought bicycle lights and reflectors from Gross Products Company, $384, invoice no. 17317, dated January 6; terms net 30 days; FOB Topeka.

11   Bought hand brakes from Bray, Inc., $470, invoice no. 291GE, dated January 9; terms 1/10, n/30; FOB Kansas City, freight prepaid and added to the invoice, $36 (total $506).

19   Bought handle grips from Gross Products Company, $96.50, invoice no. 17520, dated January 17; terms net 30 days; FOB Topeka.

24   Bought thirty 5-speed bicycles from Nielsen Company, $1,487, invoice no. 26942, dated January 23; terms net 60 days; FOB Topeka.

29   Bought knapsacks from Davila Manufacturing Company, $304.80, invoice no. 762AC, dated January 26; terms 2/10, n/30; FOB Topeka.

31   Bought locks from Lamb Safety Net, $415.47, invoice no. 27712, dated January 26; terms 2/10, n/30; FOB Dodge City, freight prepaid and added to the invoice, $22 (total $437.47).

Check Figure
Accounts Payable account
balance, $9,205.85 credit

Required

1. Open the following accounts in the accounts payable ledger and record the January 1 balances, if any, as given: Barton Tire Company, $156; Bray, Inc.; Davila Manufacturing Company, $82.88; Gross Products Company; Lamb Safety Net, $184.20; Nielsen Company. For the accounts having balances, write "Balance" in the Item column and place a check mark in the Post. Ref. column.
2. Record the balance of $423.08 in the Accounts Payable 212 controlling account as of January 1. Write "Balance" in the Item column and place a check mark in the Post. Ref. column.
3. Record the transactions in the purchases journal beginning with page 81.
4. Post to the accounts payable ledger daily.
5. Post to the general ledger at the end of the month.
6. Prepare a schedule of accounts payable, and compare the balance of the Accounts Payable controlling account with the total of the schedule of accounts payable.

4,6,7,8,10,11 **LO**

PROBLEM 9-6B The following transactions relate to Kaufman Metal Products during April of this year. Terms of sale are 2/10, n/30. The company is located in Los Angeles.

Apr.   1   Sold merchandise on account to Hubbard Hardware, invoice no. 5522, $607.40.

4   Bought merchandise on account from Roth Manufacturing Company, invoice no. C1142, $556; terms 1/10, n/30; dated April 2; FOB San Diego, freight prepaid and added to the invoice, $34 (total $590).

9   Sold merchandise on account to Booth Stores, invoice no. 5523, $1,025.30.

Apr. 11 Bought merchandise on account from Baird Products Company, invoice no. 8990, $1,756.80; terms 2/10, n/30; dated April 11; FOB San Francisco, freight prepaid and added to the invoice, $75 (total $1,831.80).

16 Sold merchandise on account J. A. Acevedo, invoice no. 5524, $921.56.

19 Issued credit memo no. 32 to Booth Stores for merchandise returned, $86.

24 Bought merchandise on account from Atkins Manufacturing Company, invoice no. P1981, $1,432.80; terms 2/10, n/30; dated April 22; FOB Santa Rosa, freight prepaid and added to the invoice, $76 (total $1,508.80).

27 Bought office supplies on account from Carson and Dyer, invoice no. E621A, $84.40; terms net 30 days; dated April 25.

28 Sold merchandise on account to Grimes Specialty Company, invoice no. 5525, $3,598.70.

29 Issued credit memo no. 33 to J. A. Acevedo for allowance on damaged merchandise, $80.

30 Received credit memo no. 79 for merchandise returned to Barajas, Inc., for $115.20.

Required

1. Open the following accounts in the accounts receivable ledger and record the balances as of April 1: J. A. Acevedo; Booth Stores, $352.50; Grimes Specialty Company, $225.50; Hubbard Hardware, $822. For the accounts having balances, write "Balance" in the Item column and place a check mark in the Post. Ref. column.
2. Open the following accounts in the accounts payable ledger and record the balances as of April 1: Atkins Manufacturing Company; Baird Products Company, $122.46; Barajas, Inc., $255.54; Carson and Dyer; Roth Manufacturing Company. For the accounts having balances, write "Balance" in the Item column and place a check mark in the Post Ref. column.
3. Record the transactions in the sales (page 24), purchases (page 18), or general journal (page 68), as appropriate.
4. Post the entries to the accounts receivable ledger daily.
5. Post the entries to the accounts payable ledger daily.
6. Post the entries in the general journal immediately after you make each journal entry.
7. Post the totals from the special journals at the end of the month.
8. Prepare a schedule of accounts receivable.
9. Prepare a schedule of accounts payable.
10. Compare the totals of the schedules with the balances of the controlling accounts.

Check Figure
Accounts Payable account balance, $4,277.80 credit

ACTIVITIES

CONSIDER AND COMMUNICATE

You are the bookkeeper at a small merchandising firm. You are comparing the income statements from the last three years. You notice that the Purchases Returns and Allowances account (as a percentage of net sales) has been increasing at an alarming rate. If you were a manager, who would you speak to in the organization to help you understand why so much merchandise is being returned? What types of questions would you ask?

CRITICAL THINKING

TO: Accounting Clerk   SUBJECT: Errors in trial balance

FROM: Senior Accountant   DATE: April 1, 20—

Following is a trial balance prepared just before you were hired. There are two accounts missing, and the amount for Sales is off. Here are a few facts to consider. Our business is in a state that collects sales tax. I ran some totals, and we collected $1,800 in sales tax. Customers returned $900 in goods, which would reduce the above sales tax by $70. Our books need to reflect these events. The former accounting clerk said she did record everything—somewhere. She said she may have credited the $1,800 sales tax to Sales and not to Sales Tax Payable. Plus, she looked confused when Sales Returns and Allowances was mentioned. She asked, "Why not just debit Sales?" Please determine the two missing accounts and correct the accounts that are off.

Pierce Retail Outlet
Trial Balance
March 31, 20—

Account Name	Debit	Credit
Cash	8,940	
Accounts Receivable	480	
Store Equipment	9,460	
Accounts Payable		958
D. Pierce, Capital		11,959
D. Pierce, Drawing	4,480	
Sales		18,000
Rent Expense	2,400	
Wages Expense	4,864	
Supplies Expense	175	
Miscellaneous Expense	118	
	30,917	30,917

1. Think about where these amounts might have been put, think about what accounts are missing, and use T accounts to solve the problems.
2. Prepare a corrected trial balance.

All About You Spa

Sales and Purchases

Ms. Valli of All About You Spa has decided to expand her business by adding two lines of merchandise—a selection of products used in the salon for the body, the feet, and the face, as well as logo mugs, T-shirts, and baseball caps that can provide advertising benefits. She believes she will be able to increase her profits significantly. She has provided paper copies and computer files that report her revenues, operating expenses, and other accounting activity that occurred in June.

The first thing you want to do is to look at the post-closing trial balance as of June 30, 20— shown below. As you look at the post-closing trial balance for the spa, answer the question, "Why is the trial balance so short?"

> Why is the trial balance so short?

All About You Spa
Post-Closing Trial Balance
June 30, 20—

Account Name	Debit	Credit
Cash	15,170.00	
Accounts Receivable	1,264.00	
Prepaid Insurance	800.00	
Spa Equipment	7,393.00	
Accumulated Depreciation, Spa Equipment		64.88
Office Equipment	1,150.00	
Accumulated Depreciation, Office Equipment		10.00
Accounts Payable		2,248.00
Wages Payable		369.50
A. Valli, Capital		23,084.62
	25,777.00	25,777.00

If you answered "There are no revenue, expense, or Drawing accounts," you are correct. But why are there no revenue, expense, or Drawing accounts? What happened to them?*

Directions for July Journal Entries

1. Open the file entitled **All_About_You_Spa_Ch09.IA7**. Enter your name when prompted and click **OK**. Select "Yes" or "No" as desired when asked if you want to open on-screen instructions and check figures. As a reminder, these instructions may be opened at any time by clicking on the **Info.** toolbar button.

> What do I do next?

2. Click on the **Save As** toolbar button. When the Save As window appears, select the folder in which you wish to save your data files (if not already selected). In the File Name box, key **All_About_You_Ch09_Your_Name.IA7** (for example,

*Answer: There are no temporary owner's equity accounts (revenue, expense, or Drawing accounts) because they were closed; their balances were made zero to prepare the books for the next fiscal period. The only accounts remaining open (having a balance) are the real accounts—assets, liabilities, and owner's capital.

All_About_You_Spa_Ch09_John_Doe.IA7) to identify the file containing your work. Click on the *Save* button.

3. Make the following reversing entry, dated July 1, in the general journal. (The purpose of this entry is to reverse or undo the adjusting entry you made in Chapter 4. Reversing entries are explained in Chapter 12.)

Wages Payable			Wages Expense	
−	+		+	−
369.50				369.50

So that you can complete the journal entries for the month of July, Ms. Valli has also left the information you will need and directions on how to proceed.

4. Note that with the expansion of the business into merchandising, new accounts have been added to the chart of accounts. For example, an additional revenue account, Merchandise Sales, is needed. Since All About You Spa now needs a Purchases account, the chart of accounts needs to be modified as follows: All expense accounts need to be in the 600–699 range; for example, Wages Expense changes from 511 to 611. The 500–599 range is now used for the purchase-related accounts; for example, Purchases 511 and Freight In 515. Your new chart of accounts appears as follows.

CHART OF ACCOUNTS FOR ALL ABOUT YOU SPA

Assets
111 Cash
113 Accounts Receivable
117 Prepaid Insurance
124 Spa Equipment
125 Accum. Depr., Spa Equip.
128 Office Equipment
129 Accum. Depr., Office Eq.

Liabilities
211 Accounts Payable
212 Wages Payable
215 Sales Tax Payable

Owner's Equity
311 A. Valli, Capital
312 A. Valli, Drawing
313 Income Summary

Revenue
411 Income from Services
412 Merchandise Sales

Purchases
511 Purchases
515 Freight In

Expenses
611 Wages Expense
612 Rent Expense
613 Office Supplies Expense
614 Spa Supplies Expense
615 Laundry Expense
616 Advertising Expense
617 Utilities Expense
618 Insurance Expense
619 Depr. Expense, Spa Equip.
620 Depr. Expense, Office Eq.
630 Miscellaneous Expense

5. Note also that since you will be making purchases on account and sales on account, subsidiary ledgers will be needed to track what is due from individual customers and owed to individual vendors. A listing of customers and vendors with current balances are as follows.

ACCOUNTS RECEIVABLE LEDGER		ACCOUNTS PAYABLE LEDGER	
About Face Spa	$ 0.00	Adco, Inc.	$ 397.00
Jill Anson	325.00	Giftco	0.00
Chaco's	0.00	Golden Spa Supplies	492.00
Holmes Condos	0.00	Logo Products	0.00
Tory Ligman	344.00	Office Staples	120.00
Los Obrigados Lodge	0.00	Spa Equipment, Inc.	89.00
Mini Spa	0.00	Spa Goods	0.00
Jack Morgan	486.00	Spa Magic	0.00
Pleasant Spa	0.00	Superior Equipment	1,150.00
Judy Wilcox	109.00		

6. Click on the *Journals* toolbar button and key the journal entries for July. Use the information in the checkbook register and the transactions listings on the

following pages as the basis of your entries. Follow option a or b below, as directed by your instructor.

a. Key all transactions into the general journal, as you learned to do in previous chapters.

b. Key all transactions into the general journal, except sales on account and purchases on account transactions.

(1) For a sale on account, click on the **Journals** toolbar button and then the **Sales** tab. Enter the total amount of merchandise sold in the Merch. Sales Cr. column. Enter the amount of sales tax in the Sales Tax Pay. Cr. column. The software will automatically calculate the total and enter it into the Accounts Rec. Dr. column. Select a customer from the Customer drop-down list. Then click on the **Post** button (or press Enter).

(2) For a purchase on account, click on the **Journals** toolbar button and then the **Purchases** tab. Enter the total amount of merchandise purchased in the Purchases Dr. column. Enter the amount of freight charges in the Freight In Dr. column. The software will automatically calculate the total and enter it into the Accounts Pay. Cr. column. Select a vendor from the Vendor drop-down list. Then click on the **Post** button (or press Enter).

> Remember to journalize a transaction in only one journal—either the sales journal or the purchases journal or the general journal.

7. Generate journal reports. Click on the **Reports** toolbar button. Click on **Journals** and **General Journal** to choose the report to display. Accept the **Include All Journal Entries** option and then click the **OK** button to display the General Journal report. To print the report, click on the **Print** button. If following option 6b above, also generate a Sales Journal report and a Purchases Journal report in the same manner by clicking on those options in the Report Selection window. Review the journal entries and make corrections as necessary.

8. Display a trial balance. Click on the **Reports** toolbar button. Click on **Ledger Reports** and **Trial Balance** to choose the report to display. To print the report, click on the **Print** button at the bottom of the report window.

9. Display a schedule of accounts receivable. Click on the **Reports** toolbar button. Click on **Ledger Reports** and **Schedule of Accounts Receivable** to choose the report to display. To print the report, click on the **Print** button at the bottom of the report window.

10. Display a schedule of accounts payable. Click on the **Reports** toolbar button. Click on **Ledger Reports** and **Schedule of Accounts Payable** to choose the report to display. To print the report, click on the **Print** button at the bottom of the report window.

11. Click on the **Save** toolbar button to save your data file.

12. Click on the **Check** toolbar button to check your solution against the answer key.

Check Figures
8. Trial balance total, July 31, $95,383.05
9. Schedule of accounts receivable total, July 31, $4,568.79
10. Schedule of accounts payable total, July 31, $20,720.00

Checkbook Register

Check No.	Date	Explanation	✓	Deposits	Check Amount
	7/1	Owner invested cash in business.		25,000.00	
1027	7/3	Bought additional spa equipment from Spa Equipment, Inc., for $8,235.00, paying $2,000.00 cash down, invoice no. 2731, dated 7/3; terms 2/10, n/60.			2,000.00
1028	7/3	Paid July's rent.			1,650.00

Check No.	Date	Explanation	✓	Deposits	Check Amount
1029	7/3	Paid on account to Spa Equipment, Inc., invoice no. 2013, dated June 3 (no discount). Paid in full.			89.00
1030	7/5	Paid on account to Golden Spa Supplies, invoice no. 804, dated June 3 (no discount). Paid in full.			492.00
1031	7/5	Paid on account to Office Staples, invoice no. 522, dated June 5 (no discount). Paid in full.			120.00
1032	7/5	Paid Celebrate, Inc., for flowers and balloons for lobby (Miscellaneous Expense).			98.00
1033	7/5	Paid on account to Adco, Inc., invoice no. 512, dated June 5 (no discount). Paid in full.			397.00
1034	7/5	Paid week's wages. *Note:* Payroll taxes related to wages will be ignored here for purposes of simplification.			1,845.50
	7/7	Deposited first week's cash sales: merchandise, $1,410.00; services, $3,110.00; sales tax collected, $361.60. (Use the new accounts Merchandise Sales 412 and Sales Tax Payable 215.)		4,881.60	
	7/7	Deposited check from Jill Anson, invoice no. 10, dated June 7 (balance due in August, $175.00).		150.00	
1035	7/12	Paid week's wages.			1,845.50
	7/14	Deposited check from Jack Morgan, invoice no. 11, dated June 14 (balance due in August, $286.00).		200.00	
	7/14	Deposited second week's cash sales: merchandise, $1,220.00; services, $2,630.00; sales tax collected, $308.00.		4,158.00	
1036	7/18	Paid on account to Superior Equipment, invoice no. 3140, dated June 5 (no discount). Paid in full.			1,150.00
1037	7/19	Paid week's wages.			1,840.50
	7/21	Deposited check from Tory Ligman, invoice no. 12, dated June 21 (balance due in August, $164.00).		180.00	
	7/21	Deposited third week's cash sales: merchandise, $1,940.00; services, $2,920.00; sales tax collected, $388.80.		5,248.80	
1038	7/25	Bought new nail cart for cash (debit Spa Equipment).			173.00
1039	7/26	Paid week's wages.			1,842.00

Check No.	Date	Explanation	✓	Deposits	Check Amount
1040	7/28	Paid month's laundry bill.			84.00
	7/28	Deposited check from Judy Wilcox, invoice no. 13, dated June 28 (paid in full).		109.00	
	7/31	Deposited end of month's cash sales: merchandise, $1,930.00; services, $4,062.00; sales tax collected, $479.36.		6,471.36	
1041	7/31	Owner withdrew cash for personal use.			2,500.00
1042	7/31	Paid July telephone bill.			225.00
1043	7/31	Paid July power and water bill.			248.00

Purchases Invoices for Merchandise Bought on Account During July

All About You Spa will pay all freight costs associated with purchases of merchandise to the supplier. Use the new accounts Purchases 511 and Freight In 515.

Date of Purchase	Transaction Information	Amount
July 1	Bought aromatherapy products from Spa Goods; invoice no. 312, dated 7/1; terms 2/10, n/60.	$5,300.00 plus $145.00 freight
1	Bought logo merchandise from Logo Products; invoice no. 1579, dated 7/1; terms 2/10, n/60.	$3,692.00 plus $104.00 freight
2	Bought bath and beauty products from Spa Magic; invoice no. 5033, dated 7/2; terms 2/10, n/30.	$2,623.00 plus $98.00 freight
5	Bought logo merchandise from Giftco; invoice no. 316, dated 7/5; terms 2/10, n/60.	$1,253.00 plus $56.00 freight

Sales Invoices for Gift Certificates Sold on Account During July

All About You Spa is responsible for collecting and paying the sales tax on merchandise that it sells. The sales tax rate where All About You Spa does business is 8 percent of each sale; for example, $325.00 × 0.08 = $26.00.

Date of Sale	Transaction Information	Sales Amount (Before Tax)
July 2	Los Obrigados Lodge, invoice no. 14.	$ 325.00
4	Chaco's, invoice no. 15.	481.50
5	Pleasant Spa, invoice no. 16.	1,815.95
10	Holmes Condos, invoice no. 17.	340.25
10	Mini Spa, invoice no. 18.	206.00
12	About Face Spa, invoice no. 19.	482.95

Note: All gift certificates were redeemed for merchandise by the end of the month.

CONTINUING CASE

Other July Transactions

There were five other transactions in July. None involved cash.

Date	Transaction Information	Amount
July 1	Bought spa supplies on account from Golden Spa Supplies, invoice no. 1836, dated 7/1; terms n/45.	$ 490.00
5	Bought office equipment on account from Superior Equipment, invoice no. 3608, dated 7/5; terms 2/10, n/60.	420.00
5	Bought self-help books for the waiting room on account (Miscellaneous Expense) from Office Staples, invoice no. 1417, dated 7/5; terms n/30.	186.00
5	Bought office supplies on account from Office Staples, invoice no. 1418, dated 7/5; terms n/30.	118.00
31	Owner invested additional personal spa equipment (treadmill and bicycle) valued at $1,800.00.	1,800.00

Sales and Purchases— Perpetual Method

LEARNING OBJECTIVES

After you have completed this chapter, you will be able to do the following:

1 *Journalize sales transactions, including sales returns and allowances, in the general journal using the perpetual inventory system.*

2 *Journalize purchase transactions, including purchases returns and allowances, in the general journal using the perpetual inventory system.*

In Chapter 9, we discussed how to record sales and purchases transactions in the general journal using the periodic inventory system. The periodic inventory system requires that companies periodically take a physical count of inventory at the end of the period to determine the amount of inventory on hand.

The perpetual inventory system, on the other hand, keeps continuous records of inventories by recording all transactions, so that at any given time the companies knows the current amount of inventory. Under the perpetual inventory system, sales and purchases are recorded differently than the periodic inventory system.

SALES TRANSACTIONS

Let's review the first two transactions on the books of Whitewater Raft Supply for the month of August:

Aug. 1 Sold merchandise on account to Mesa River Raft Company, invoice no. 9384, $1,933.50. *Cost of inventory sold is $1,643.48.*

8 Sold merchandise on account to Green River Rafts, invoice no. 9385, $1,116. *Cost of inventory sold is $948.60.*

Note the new information provided in italics. This information concerning the cost of the inventory sold is needed when sales transactions are recorded using the perpetual inventory system.

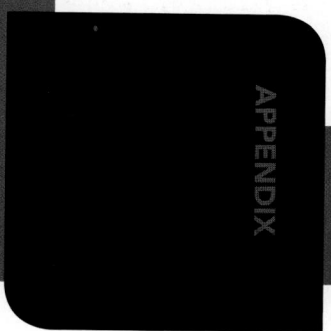

LEARNING OBJECTIVE

Journalize sales transactions, including sales returns and allowances, in the general journal using the perpetual inventory system.

Whitewater Raft Supply's accountant would record the transactions in the general journal as follows:

GENERAL JOURNAL				PAGE 26
Date	Description	Post. Ref.	Debit	Credit
20—				
Aug. 1	Accounts Receivable, Mesa River Raft Company		1 9 3 3 50	
	Sales			1 9 3 3 50
	Sold merchandise to Mesa River Raft Company, invoice no. 9384.			
	Cost of Goods Sold		1 6 4 3 48	
	Merchandise Inventory			1 6 4 3 48
	Cost of merchandise sold to Mesa River Raft Company, invoice no. 9384.			
8	Accounts Receivable, Green River Rafts		1 1 1 6 00	
	Sales			1 1 1 6 00
	Sold merchandise to Green River Rafts, invoice no. 9385.			
	Cost of Goods Sold		9 4 8 60	
	Merchandise Inventory			9 4 8 60
	Cost of merchandise sold to Green River Rafts, invoice no. 9385.			

The sales portion of the transaction is recorded the same under either method. Whitewater Raft Supply's accountant records a debit to Accounts Receivable to record the amount each customer owes the company and a credit to Sales for each transaction. However, using the perpetual inventory system, the accountant must also record a debit to Cost of Goods Sold for the cost of the inventory sold and a credit to Merchandise Inventory. Cost of Goods Sold represents the cost of the inventory sold and is an expense account that is reported on the income statement. Cost of Goods Sold must increase and is therefore debited. The Merchandise Inventory account must decrease by the cost of the inventory sold, and so the accountant records a credit to Merchandise Inventory.

By recording sales transactions in this manner, the company can easily calculate the gross profit, or the profit on the sale of the inventory, by subtracting Cost of Goods Sold from Sales. Whitewater Raft Supply's gross profit is $290.02 ($1,933.50 – $1,643.48) on the August 1 sale.

SALES RETURNS AND ALLOWANCES

Sales returns and allowances must also be recorded differently under the perpetual inventory system. Let's look at Whitewater Raft Supply's return on September 5, with the original sale described first.

Transaction (a). On September 1, Whitewater Raft Supply sold merchandise on account to Rugged River Company, $3,614, and recorded the sale in the general journal. *Cost of inventory sold is $3,071.50.*

Transaction (b). On September 5, Rugged River Company returned $254 worth of the merchandise *having a cost of $215.90.* Whitewater Raft Supply issued credit memorandum no. 1069.

Again, note the additional information provided describing the cost of the inventory sold and returned. This information is necessary to record the transactions using the perpetual inventory system.

Whitewater Raft Supply's accountant would record the return on September 5 as follows:

	GENERAL JOURNAL				PAGE 27	
Date	Description	Post. Ref.	Debit		Credit	
20—						
Sept. 5	Sales Returns and Allowances		2 5 4 00			
	Accounts Receivable, Rugged					
	River Company				2 5 4 00	
	Issued credit memo no. 1069.					
	Merchandise Inventory		2 1 5 90			
	Cost of Goods Sold				2 1 5 90	
	Cost of merchandise returned,					
	credit memo no. 1069.					

The first part of the journal entry is the same as when using the periodic inventory system. The accountant debits Sales Returns and Allowances and credits Accounts Receivable to decrease it because the customer owes less than before. However, since Whitewater Raft Supply is using the perpetual inventory system, the company must also record the effect of this return on merchandise inventory by debiting Merchandise Inventory to increase it for the returned items and crediting Cost of Goods Sold to decrease the expense.

PURCHASE TRANSACTIONS

As we learned in Chapter 9, when using the periodic inventory system, the accountant uses the Purchases and Freight In (if applied) accounts to record transactions involving purchases. Under the perpetual inventory system, all transactions related to the purchase of inventory are recorded in the Merchandise Inventory account. The accountant never uses the Purchases and Freight In accounts when recording purchase transactions under the perpetual inventory system because *all* costs of merchandise inventory (including freight) are included in the Merchandise Inventory account.

2 LEARNING OBJECTIVE

Journalize purchase transactions, including purchases returns and allowances, in the general journal using the perpetual inventory system.

Let's look at two purchase transactions on the books of Whitewater Raft Supply for the month of August.

Aug. 2 Bought merchandise on account from Pataponia, Inc., invoice no. 2706, $1,710; terms 2/10, n/30; dated July 31; FOB San Francisco, freight prepaid and added to the invoice, $85.50 (total $1,795.50).

10 Bought merchandise on account from Langseth and Son, invoice no. 982, $2,772; terms net 30 days; dated August 8; FOB Cleveland, freight prepaid and added to the invoice, $157 (total $2,929).

Whitewater Raft Supply's accountant will record the transactions in the general journal as follows:

		GENERAL JOURNAL			PAGE 26	
Date		Description	Post. Ref.	Debit	Credit	
20—						
Aug.	2	Merchandise Inventory		1 7 9 5 50		
		Accounts Payable, Pataponia, Inc.			1 7 9 5 50	
		Purchased merchandise from				
		Pataponia, Inc., invoice no.				
		2706, invoice dated 7/31,				
		terms 2/10, n/30.				
	10	Merchandise Inventory		2 9 2 9 00		
		Accounts Payable, Langseth				
		and Son			2 9 2 9 00	
		Purchased merchandise from				
		Langseth and Son, invoice				
		no. 982, invoice dated 8/8,				
		terms n/30.				

Note that Whitewater Raft Supply records a debit to the Merchandise Inventory account (not Purchases and Freight In) to record the cost of merchandise, including freight, bought for resale.

PURCHASES RETURNS AND ALLOWANCES

Under the perpetual inventory system, purchases returns and allowances transactions are recorded directly into the Merchandise Inventory account. The Purchases Returns and Allowances account that is used to record returns and allowances under the periodic inventory system is not used.

Let's look at a return on September 8 for Whitewater Raft Supply, with the original purchase described first.

Transaction (a).   On September 2, bought merchandise on account from Dana Manufacturing Company, $830.

Transaction (b).   On September 8, received credit memorandum no. 1629 from Dana Manufacturing Company for $270.

Under the perpetual inventory system, the accountant would record the return on September 8 as follows:

		GENERAL JOURNAL			PAGE 27	
Date		Description	Post. Ref.	Debit	Credit	
20—						
Sept.	8	Accounts Payable, Dana				
		Manufacturing Company		2 7 0 00		
		Merchandise Inventory			2 7 0 00	
		Credit memo no. 1629 for				
		return of merchandise.				

Whitewater Raft Supply's accountant debits the creditor's Accounts Payable account to decrease it and credits Merchandise Inventory (not Purchases Returns and Allowances) to decrease it. Recording the credit to the Merchandise Inventory account automatically decreases it for the cost of the inventory returned.

PERIODIC INVENTORY SYSTEM VS. PERPETUAL INVENTORY SYSTEM

Chart of Accounts

Following is an abbreviated version of the chart of accounts for both the periodic and perpetual inventory systems. Note that in the periodic inventory system, the company would use accounts such as Purchases, Purchases Returns and Allowances, and Freight In that are not used in the perpetual inventory system.

PERIODIC INVENTORY SYSTEM	PERPETUAL INVENTORY SYSTEM
Revenue (400–499)	**Revenue (400–499)**
411 Sales	411 Sales
412 Sales Returns and Allowances	412 Sales Returns and Allowances
Cost of Goods Sold (500–599)	**Cost of Goods Sold (500–599)**
511 Purchases	511 Cost of Goods Sold
512 Purchases Returns and Allowances	
514 Freight In	

Journal Entries

Now that we have reviewed the main differences between the periodic and perpetual inventory systems, let's take a moment to reflect on those differences. Figure A shows a comparison of the transactions that we have learned for both inventory systems. Make sure that you are familiar with each system and also how they differ.

FIGURE A   Comparison of journal entries for periodic and perpetual inventory systems

Comparison: Periodic Versus Perpetual Inventory Systems		
Transaction	**Periodic Inventory System**	**Perpetual Inventory System**

Sold merchandise to customer on account, $1,933.50, having a cost of $1,643.48.	Accounts Receivable, Mesa River Raft Company 1,933.50
	    Sales 1,933.50
		Accounts Receivable, Mesa River Raft Company 1,933.50
		    Sales 1,933.50
		
		Cost of Goods Sold 1,643.48
		    Merchandise Inventory 1,643.48

Customer returned merchandise, $254, having a cost of $215.90.	Sales Returns and Allowances 254.00
	    Accounts Receivable, Rugged River Company 254.00
		Sales Returns and Allowances 254.00
		    Accounts Receivable, Rugged River Company 254.00
		
		Merchandise Inventory 215.90
		    Cost of Goods Sold 215.90

Purchased merchandise from supplier on account, $1,710, with prepaid freight of $85.50.	Purchases 1,710.00
	Freight In 85.50
	    Accounts Payable, Pataponia, Inc. 1,795.50
		Merchandise Inventory 1,795.50
		    Accounts Payable, Pataponia, Inc. 1,795.50

Returned merchandise to supplier, $270.	Accounts Payable, Dana Manufacturing Company 270.00
	    Purchases Returns and Allowances 270.00
		Accounts Payable, Dana Manufacturing Company 270.00
		    Merchandise Inventory 270.00

Problems

1,2 **LO**

PROBLEM 9A-1 The following transactions relate to Hawkins, Inc., an office store wholesaler, during June of this year. Terms of sale are 2/10, n/30. The company is located in Los Angeles, California.

June   1   Sold merchandise on account to Hendrix Office Store, invoice no. 1001, $451.20. The cost of the merchandise was $397.06.

        3   Bought merchandise on account from Krueger, Inc., invoice no. 845A, $485.15; terms 1/10, n/30; dated June 1; FOB San Diego, freight prepaid and added to the invoice, $15 (total $500.15).

     10   Sold merchandise on account to Ballard Stores, invoice no. 1002, $2,483.65. The cost of the merchandise was $2,235.29.

     13   Bought merchandise on account from Kennedy, Inc., invoice no. 4833, $2,450.13; terms 2/10, n/30; dated June 11; FOB San Francisco, freight prepaid and added to the invoice, $123 (total $2,573.13).

     18   Sold merchandise on account to Lawson Office Store, invoice no. 1003, $754.99. The cost of the merchandise was $671.94.

     20   Issued credit memo no. 33 to Lawson Office Store for merchandise returned, $103.25. The cost of the merchandise was $91.89.

     25   Bought merchandise on account from Villarreal, Inc., invoice no. 4R32, $1,552.30; terms net 30; dated June 18; FOB Santa Rosa, freight prepaid and added to the invoice, $84 (total $1,636.30).

     30   Received credit memo no. 44 for merchandise returned to Villarreal, Inc., for $224.50.

Check Figure

Net Merchandise Inventory, $1,272.68 debit

Required

Record the transactions in the general journal (pages 25 and 26) using the perpetual inventory system.

1,2 **LO**

PROBLEM 9A-2 The following transactions relate to Khan, Inc., a sporting goods wholesaler, during November of this year. Terms of sale are 2/10, n/30. The company is located in Denver, Colorado.

Nov.   3   Sold merchandise on account to Spence Tennis Shop, invoice no. 5420, $2,482.51. The cost of the merchandise was $1,961.18.

      5   Issued credit memo no. 38 to Spence Tennis Shop for merchandise returned, $287.45. The cost of the merchandise was $227.09.

      7   Bought merchandise on account from Maldonado Manufacturing, Inc., invoice no. 1548, $3,854.16; terms n/45; dated November 4; FOB Memphis, freight prepaid and added to the invoice, $135 (total $3,989.16).

      9   Bought merchandise on account from Lozano, Inc., invoice no. 8755, $426.65; terms 1/15, n/30; dated November 5; FOB New York City, freight prepaid and added to the invoice, $67 (total $493.65).

     12   Received credit memo no. 542 to Lozano, Inc., for merchandise returned, $102.20.

     17   Sold merchandise on account to Jack's Golfing Shop, invoice no. 5421, $486.35. The cost of the merchandise was $432.85.

Nov. 23 Sold merchandise on account to Yates Sporting Goods, invoice no. 5422, $2,465.99. The cost of the merchandise was $1,972.79.

28 Bought merchandise on account from Fields, Inc., invoice no. 4599, $441.29; terms 2/10, n/30; dated November 25; FOB Austin, freight prepaid and added to the invoice, $102 (total $543.29).

Required

Record the transactions in the general journal (pages 84 and 85) using the perpetual inventory system.

Check Figure
Total Gross Sales, $5,434.85 credit

10 Cash Receipts and Cash Payments

WHY IT MATTERS

BOOKSHOP SANTA CRUZ, Santa Cruz, California

If you're ever in Santa Cruz, California, take a few hours and step inside Bookshop Santa Cruz. Inside the doors you'll find books "that entertain, help solve problems, or, occasionally, change a life."

Since opening in 1966, Bookshop Santa Cruz has been a vital member of the Bay Area. It takes immense pride in being an independent bookseller, a rare commodity in today's world of large corporate booksellers such as Barnes & Noble and Borders.

The bookstore has several buyers who are responsible for spotting reading trends, reordering current books, and purchasing the newest and hottest books on the market. Each time a buyer makes a purchase and every time Bookshop Santa Cruz sells one of its books, a transaction must be recorded. In Chapter 9, we discussed how to record the purchase and sale of inventory. In this chapter, we will look at how a store, such as Bookshop Santa Cruz, records the receipt of cash from sales and the payment of cash for purchases.

LEARNING OBJECTIVES

After you have completed this chapter, you will be able to do the following:

1 Determine cash discounts according to credit terms.

2 Journalize sales transactions in a general journal involving cash receipts from credit customers who are entitled to deduct the cash discount.

3 Journalize purchase transactions in a general journal involving cash payments when entitled to deduct the cash discount.

4 Journalize transactions involving trade discounts.

5 Journalize transactions for a merchandising business in a cash receipts journal and post from a cash receipts journal to a general ledger and an accounts receivable ledger.

6 Journalize transactions for a merchandising business in a cash payments journal and post from a cash payments journal to a general ledger and an accounts payable ledger.

ACCOUNTING LANGUAGE

Cash discount (p. 393)

Cash payments journal (p. 410)

Cash receipts journal (p. 405)

Credit period (p. 393)

Notes Payable (p. 408)

Promissory note (p. 408)

Trade discounts (p. 402)

In the previous chapter, we discussed sales and purchases on account. Now we will learn how a company records cash receipts and cash payments for those transactions. We will begin by reviewing discounts and terms available to purchasers and sellers and then discuss recording the cash associated with merchandising transactions.

CREDIT TERMS

When we discussed sales and purchases of merchandise in Chapter 9, we noted that each sale or purchase was associated with a *term*. The seller always stipulates the *terms*: How much credit can a customer be allowed? And, how much time should the customer be given to pay the full amount? The **credit period** is the time the seller allows the buyer before full payment has to be made. Retailers generally allow 25 to 30 days for payment.

Wholesalers and manufacturers often specify a **cash discount** in their credit terms. A cash discount is an amount that a customer can deduct if a bill is paid within a specified time. The discount is based on the *total amount of the invoice after any returns and allowances and freight charges billed on the invoice have been deducted*. Naturally, this discount acts as an incentive for credit customers to pay their bills promptly.

Let's say that a wholesaler offers customers credit terms of 2/10, n/30. These terms mean that the customer gets a 2 percent discount if the bill is paid within 10 days after the invoice date. The discount period begins the day after the invoice date. If the bill is not paid within the 10 days, the entire amount is due within 30 days after the invoice date. Other types of cash discounts that may be used are the following:

- **1/15, n/60** The seller offers a 1 percent discount if the bill is paid within 15 days after the invoice date, and the whole bill must be paid within 60 days after the invoice date.

1 **LEARNING OBJECTIVE**

Determine cash discounts according to credit terms.

- **2/10, EOM, n/60** The seller offers a 2 percent discount if the bill is paid within 10 days after the end of the month, and the whole bill must be paid within 60 days after the last day of the month.

A wholesaler or manufacturer that offers a cash discount adopts a single cash discount as a credit policy and makes this available to all its customers. The seller considers cash discounts as sales discounts; the buyer, on the other hand, considers cash discounts as purchases discounts.

PART ONE—RECORDING TRANSACTIONS INTO THE GENERAL JOURNAL

Occasionally, sales or purchases of merchandise will involve discounts. In this section, we will discuss discounts and how they are recorded in the general journal.

Sales Discounts

LEARNING OBJECTIVE 2

Journalize sales transactions in a general journal involving cash receipts from credit customers who are entitled to deduct the cash discount.

First we will concentrate on the sales discount. *The Sales Discounts account, like Sales Returns and Allowances, is a contra revenue account and is therefore deducted from Sales.*

To illustrate, we return to Whitewater Raft Supply. We will record the following transactions in the general journal and T accounts.

Transaction (a).   On August 1, Whitewater Raft Supply sold merchandise on account to Mesa River Raft Company, invoice no. 9384, $1,933.50; terms 2/10, n/30. (Take a moment to review the source document on page 331 in Chapter 9 and identify the terms on the invoice.)

Transaction (b).   On August 10, received check from Mesa River Raft Company for $1,894.83 in payment of invoice no. 9384, less cash discount ($1,933.50 × 0.02 = $38.67; $1,933.50 − $38.67 = $1,894.83).

			GENERAL JOURNAL				PAGE 26
Date		Description	Post. Ref.	Debit		Credit	
20—							
Aug.	1	Accounts Receivable, Mesa River					
		Raft Company		1 9 3 3 50			
		Sales				1 9 3 3 50	
		Sold merchandise to Mesa River Raft					
		Company, invoice no. 9384.					
	10	Cash		1 8 9 4 83			
		Sales Discounts		3 8 67			
		Accounts Receivable, Mesa River Raft					
		Company				1 9 3 3 50	
		Collected cash on account,					
		invoice no. 9384.					

Remember

When journalizing a cash receipt involving a sales discount, be sure to credit Accounts Receivable for the total amount of the sales transaction.

To record the receipt of payment on August 10 from the customer, the accountant records a debit to Cash for the amount of cash received. The amount of discount granted is recorded as a debit to Sales Discounts. The Accounts Receivable account is credited so that the customer's account will decrease. Notice that the accountant records a credit to Accounts Receivable, Mesa River Raft Company for the total invoice amount, $1,933.50. This is important because if the receivable was credited for only the cash received, the customer's account would still show a balance owed.

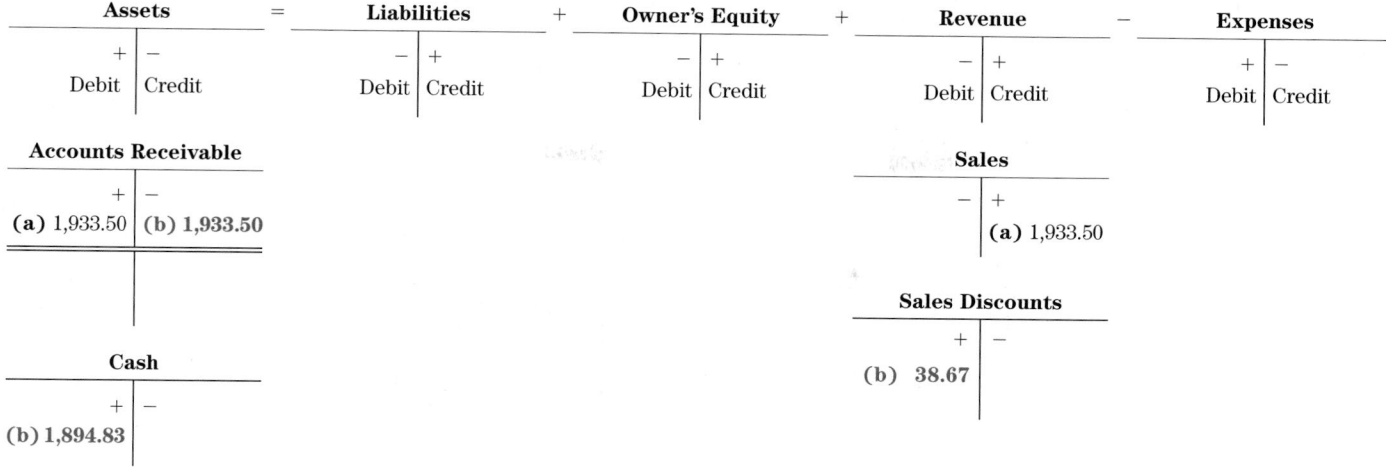

When a company receives a return of merchandise sold, the sales discount is calculated by excluding the amount of the returned items. Let's take a look at this example. The journal and T accounts for the following transactions are shown below and on the next page.

Transaction (a). On September 1, Whitewater Raft Supply sold merchandise on account to Rugged River Company, invoice no. 9391; $3,614, terms 2/10, n/30; and recorded the sale in the general journal.

Transaction (b). On September 5, Rugged River Company returned $254 worth of the merchandise. Whitewater Raft Supply issued credit memorandum no. 1069 and recorded the transaction. *Notice that after the return there is a balance in Accounts Receivable of $3,360, the amount of the original invoice less the return ($3,614 − $254).*

Transaction (c). On September 8, received check from Rugged River Company for $3,292.80 in payment of invoice no. 9391, less return and cash discount [($3,614 − $254) × 0.02 = $67.20; ($3,614 − $254) − $67.20 = $3,292.80].

GENERAL JOURNAL — PAGE 27

Date	Description	Post. Ref.	Debit	Credit
20—				
Sept. 1	Accounts Receivable, Rugged River Company		3 6 1 4 00	
	Sales			3 6 1 4 00
	Sold merchandise to Rugged River Company, invoice no. 9391.			
5	Sales Returns and Allowances		2 5 4 00	
	Accounts Receivable, Rugged River Company			2 5 4 00
	Issued credit memo no. 1069.			
8	Cash		3 2 9 2 80	
	Sales Discounts		6 7 20	
	Accounts Receivable, Rugged River Company			3 3 6 0 00
	Collected cash on account, invoice no. 9391.			

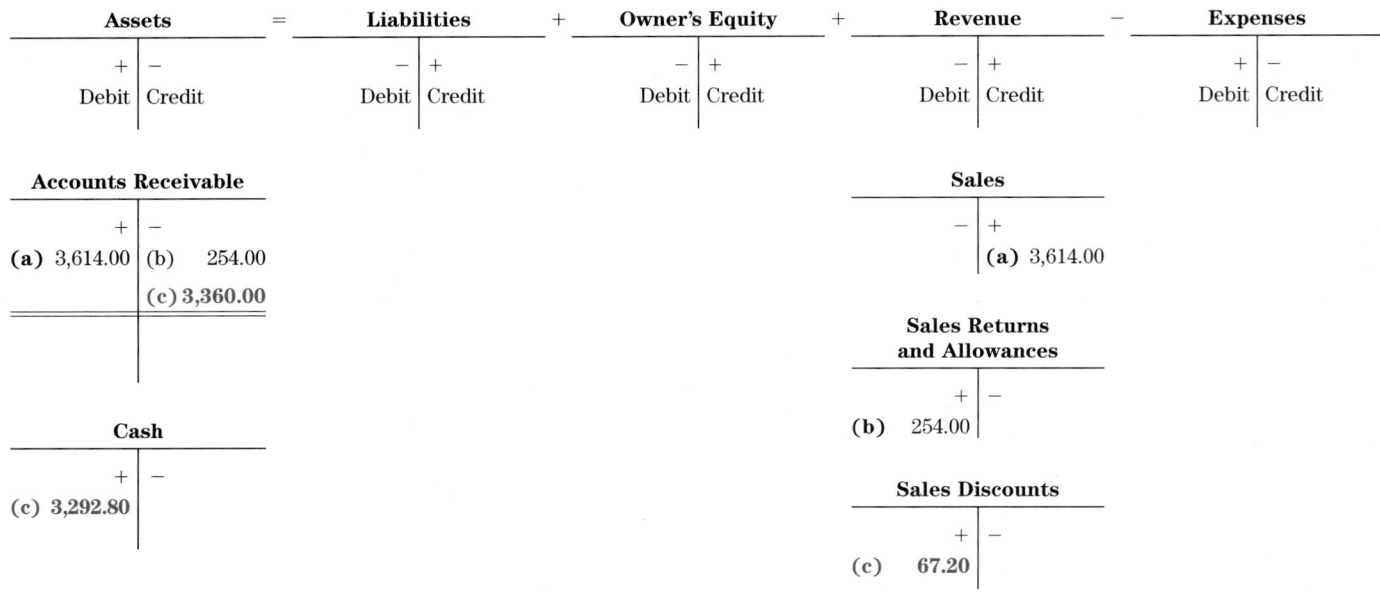

Notice that when the accountant records the receipt of cash, the discount is calculated less the sales return. This is because the company would grant a discount only on the remaining amount owed, not for the full sale amount.

No Sales Discounts Involved

When a transaction does not involve a sales discount or the discount has expired, the seller will record the receipt of payment on account by debiting Cash and crediting Accounts Receivable. Assume that Blue Merchandise Company recorded the following transactions:

Transaction (a). On April 1, Blue Merchandise Company sold merchandise on account to Yellow Company, invoice no. 1294, $9,450; terms 2/10, n/30; and recorded the sale in the general journal.

Transaction (b). On April 26, received check from Yellow Company for $9,450 in payment of invoice no. 1294.

Blue Merchandise Company's accountant would record the transactions in the general journal as:

	GENERAL JOURNAL				PAGE 65
Date	Description	Post. Ref.	Debit		Credit
20—					
Apr. 1	Accounts Receivable, Yellow Company		9 4 5 0 00		
	Sales				9 4 5 0 00
	Sold merchandise to Yellow Company, invoice no. 1294.				
26	Cash		9 4 5 0 00		
	Accounts Receivable, Yellow Company				9 4 5 0 00
	Collected cash on account, invoice no. 1294.				

Notice that since Yellow Company did not make payment within 10 days, the discount was not applied to the invoice amount. Yellow Company paid the invoice in full.

Posting to the General Ledger and Subsidiary Ledger

To post cash receipts of sales, post each entry to Cash and any other accounts involved in the general ledger. Also, post the amounts paid by customers to the subsidiary accounts receivable ledger to maintain a running balance of the amount each customer owes.

Posting to the General Ledger and Subsidiary Ledger—A Computerized Approach

Most computer accounting software allows businesses to post cash receipts for sales and apply discounts. In Figure 1, the cash receipt of $1,894.83 in payment of invoice no. 9384 is being recorded into the accounting software.

Notice that this software system allows the accountant to apply a discount. Look in the lower right corner to see the discount application button. In Figure 2, the accountant is recording the discount into the system.

After the discount has been applied, the invoice is now showing as paid (Figure 3) and the balance due is $0.00. Using a computerized accounting system is an excellent way for businesses to keep track of cash receipts and discounts. Most computerized accounting software can also handle returns and allowances of merchandise that has been sold.

Sales Returns and Allowances and Sales Discounts on an Income Statement

In the fundamental accounting equation, to be consistent with the income statement, we placed Sales Returns and Allowances and Sales Discounts under Sales with the plus and minus signs reversed. Both accounts are contra accounts, so we subtract their totals from Sales on the income statement. The Revenue from Sales section of the annual income statement of Whitewater Raft Supply is shown in Figure 4.

FIGURE 1

Recording a cash receipt using accounting software

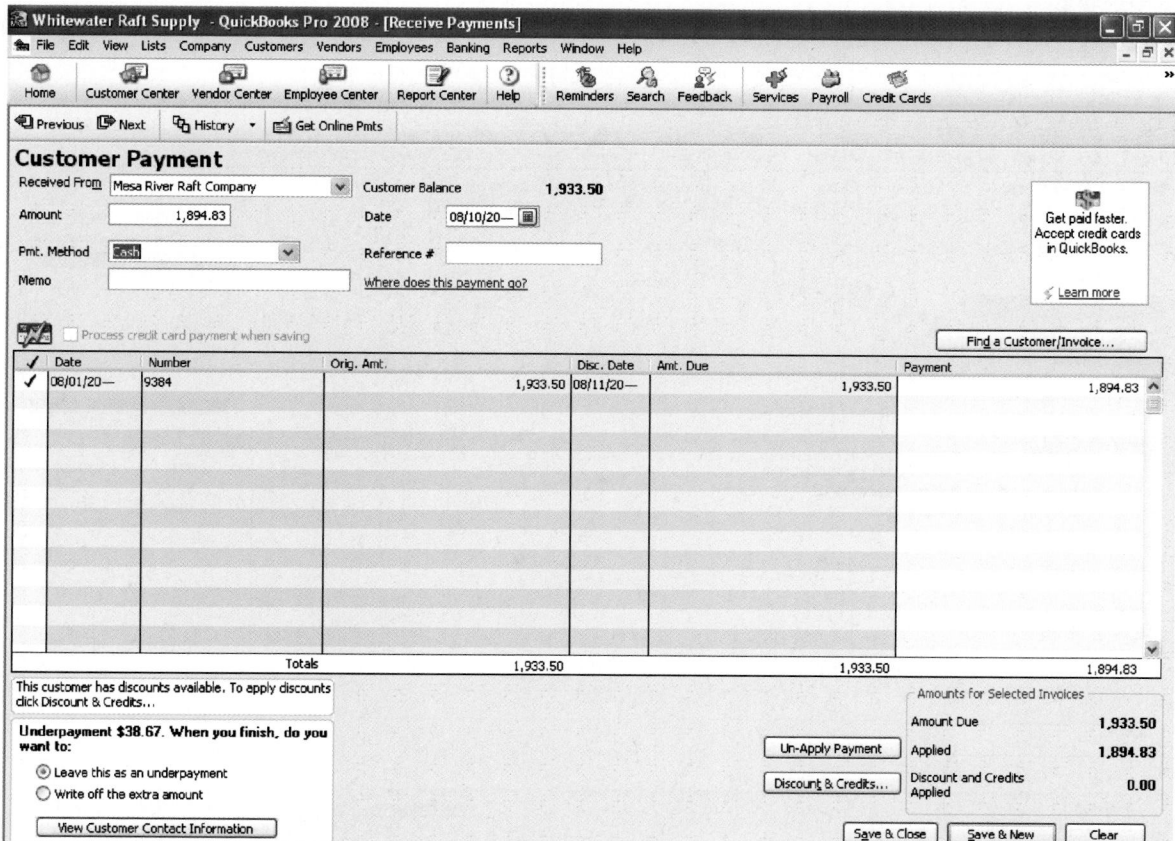

FIGURE 2

Recording a cash discount
using accounting software

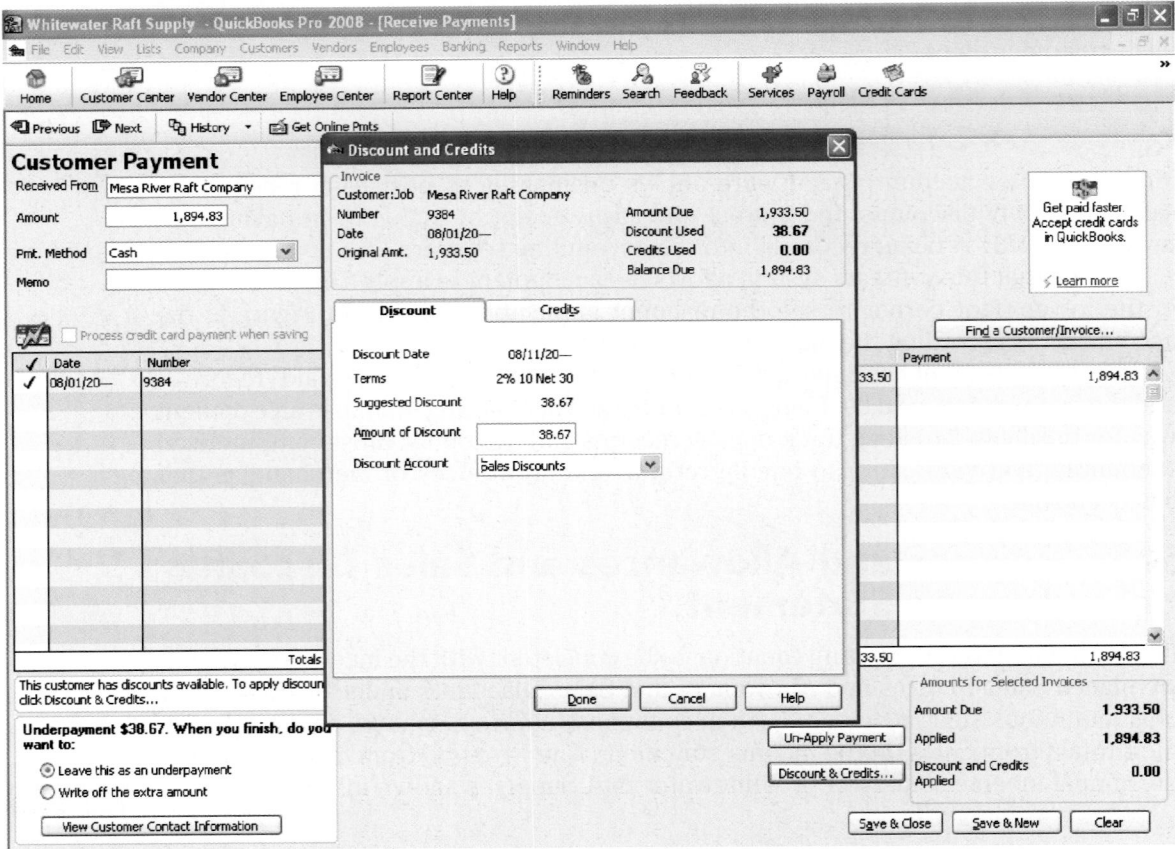

FIGURE 3

Paid invoice

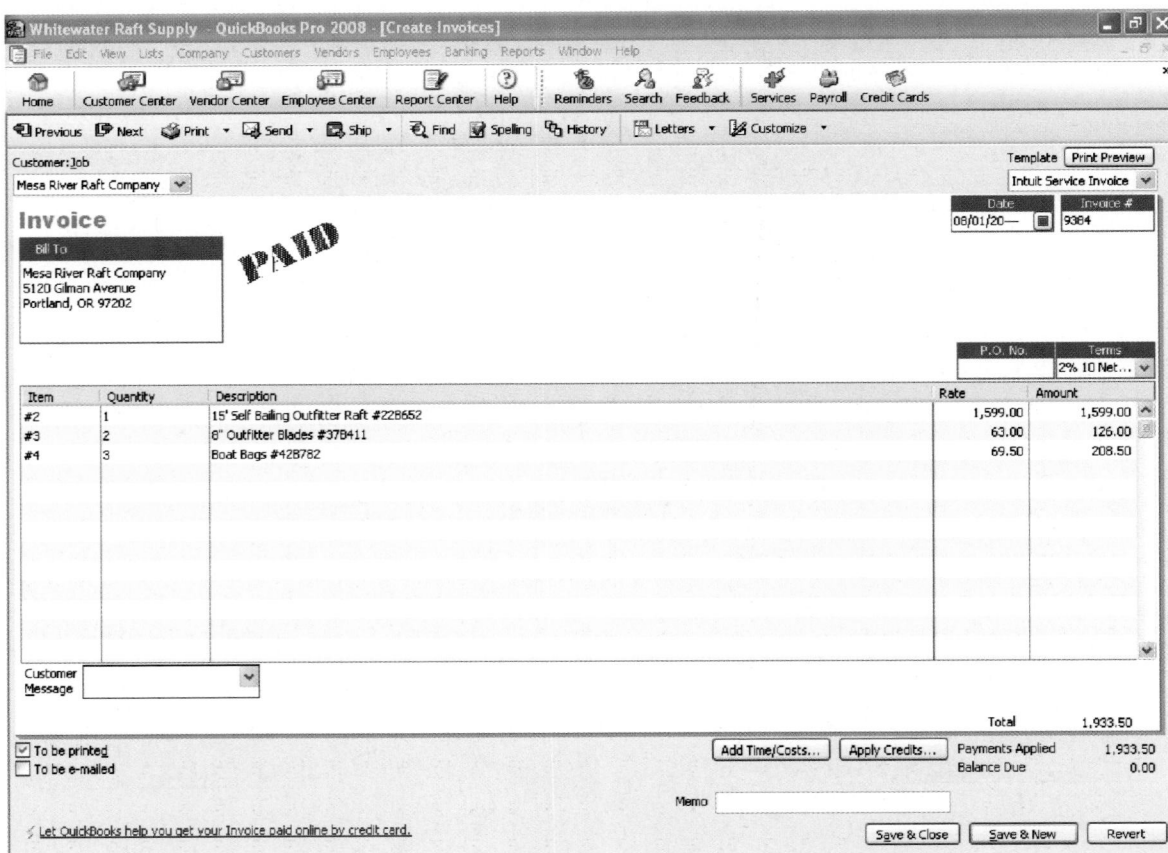

Whitewater Raft Supply
Income Statement
For the Year Ended December 31, 20—

Revenue from Sales:		
Sales		$257,180
Less: Sales Returns and Allowances	$ 940	
Sales Discounts	1,980	2,920
Net Sales		$254,260

FIGURE 4
Revenue from sales section of income statement

Purchase Discounts

Recall that a cash discount is the amount that the buyer may deduct from the bill; this acts as an incentive to get the buyer to pay the bill promptly. The buyer considers the cash discount to be a purchases discount, because it relates to the buyer's purchase of merchandise. *The Purchases Discounts account, like Purchases Returns and Allowances, is a contra account and is treated as a deduction from Purchases on the buyer's income statement.*

Let's return to Whitewater Raft Supply and assume that the following transactions take place.

LEARNING OBJECTIVE 3
Journalize purchase transactions in a general journal involving cash payments when entitled to deduct the cash discount.

Transaction (a). On August 2, Whitewater Raft Supply bought merchandise on account from Pataponia, Inc., invoice no. 2706, $1,710; terms 2/10, n/30; dated July 31; FOB San Francisco, freight prepaid and added to the invoice, $85.50 (total $1,795.50).

Transaction (b). On August 8, issued Ck. No. 2076 to Pataponia, Inc., in payment of invoice no. 2706, less cash discount of $34.20, $1,761.30 ($1,795.50 − $34.20).

Notice that when calculating the discount, the discount applies only to the amount billed for the merchandise ($1,710 × 0.02 = $34.20). **You do not include the freight cost when determining the discount**.

The cash discount does not apply to freight charges billed separately on an invoice.

Remember

	GENERAL JOURNAL			PAGE 26	
Date	Description	Post. Ref.	Debit	Credit	
20—					
Aug. 2	Purchases		1 7 1 0 00		
	Freight In		8 5 50		
	Accounts Payable, Pataponia, Inc.			1 7 9 5 50	
	Purchased merchandise from				
	Pataponia, Inc., invoice no. 2706,				
	invoice dated 7/31, terms				
	2/10, n/30.				
8	Accounts Payable, Pataponia, Inc.		1 7 9 5 50		
	Cash			1 7 6 1 30	
	Purchases Discounts			3 4 20	
	Paid Pataponia, Inc., for				
	invoice no. 2706, Ck. No. 2076.				

To record the payment to Pataponia, Inc., the accountant records a debit to Accounts Payable and a credit to Cash for the amount of cash paid. The amount of discount received is recorded as a credit to Purchases Discounts. Notice that the accountant records a debit to Accounts Payable, Pataponia, Inc., for the total invoice amount, $1,795.50. This is important because if the payable was debited for only the cash paid, the account would still show a balance due.

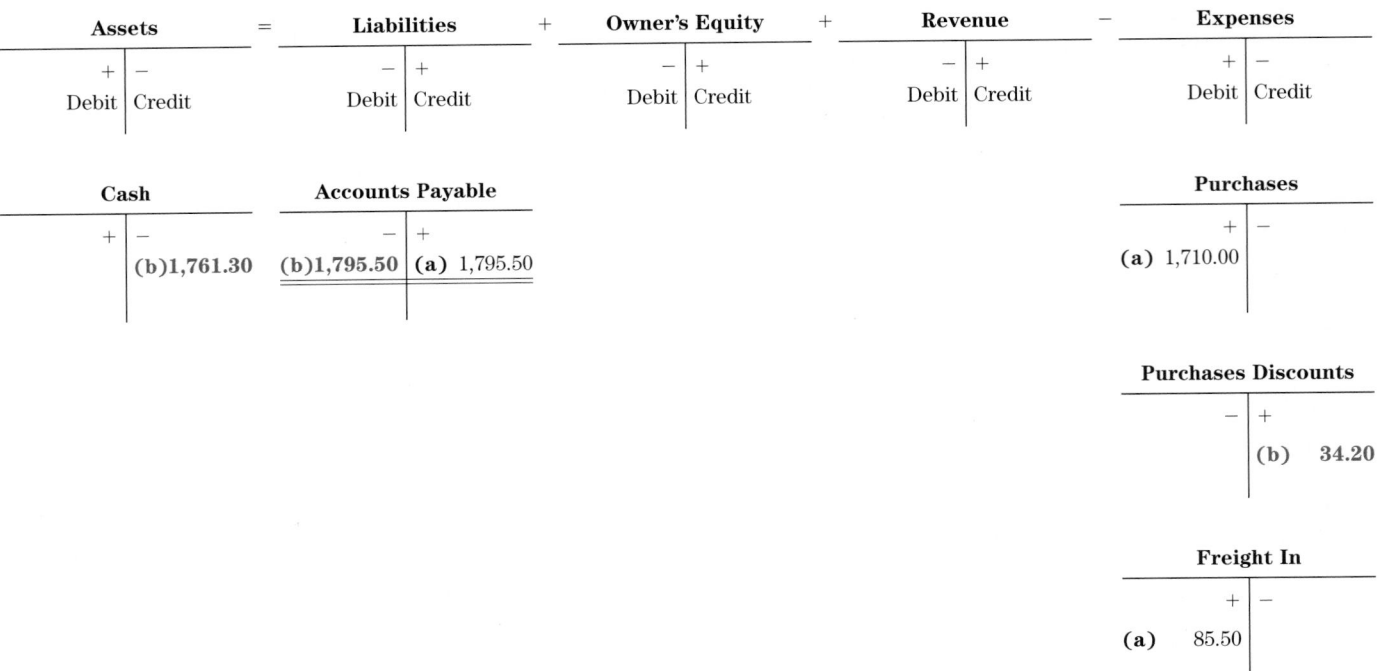

Similar to sales returns, purchase returns and allowances are also not included when calculating the discount. Remember to always leave out any prepaid freight and returns and allowances when determining the amount of the discount.

No Purchase Discounts Involved

When a transaction does not involve a purchase discount or the discount has expired, the buyer will record the payment by debiting Accounts Payable and crediting Cash. Assume that Blue Merchandise Company recorded the following transactions:

Transaction (a). On November 1, Blue Merchandise Company bought merchandise on account from Grey, Inc., invoice no. 3901, $4,600; terms 2/10, n/30; dated October 31.

Transaction (b). On November 28, issued Ck. No. 1151 to Grey, Inc., in payment of invoice no. 3901, $4,600.

Blue Merchandise Company's accountant would record the transactions in the general journal as:

GENERAL JOURNAL				PAGE 81	
Date	Description	Post. Ref.	Debit		Credit
20—					
Nov. 1	Purchases		4 6 0 0 00		
	Accounts Payable, Grey, Inc.				4 6 0 0 00
	Purchased merchandise from				
	Grey, Inc., invoice no. 3901,				
	invoice dated 10/31, terms				
	2/10, n/30.				
28	Accounts Payable, Grey, Inc.		4 6 0 0 00		
	Cash				4 6 0 0 00
	Paid Grey, Inc., for invoice				
	no. 3901, Ck. No. 1151.				

Notice that since Blue Merchandise Company did not make payment within 10 days, the discount was not applied to the invoice amount. Blue Merchandise Company paid the invoice in full.

Posting to the General Ledger and Subsidiary Ledger

To post cash payments of purchases, post each entry to Cash, Accounts Payable, and any other accounts involved in the general ledger. Also, post the amounts owed to vendors to the subsidiary accounts payable ledger to maintain a running balance of the amount owed to each vendor.

Posting to the General Ledger and Subsidiary Ledger—A Computerized Approach

Businesses can use a computerized accounting program to enter cash payments to vendors. Cash payments are applied to vendor invoices that are created by the accountant in the software program. In Figure 5, the accountant is beginning to record the payment of the invoice by selecting the correct invoice due.

After the accountant has selected the bill on which to make payment, the accountant can then apply any discount granted and process the payment. Figure 6 shows the bill payment check screen that shows payment has been applied to the invoice.

Purchases Returns and Allowances, Purchases Discounts, and Freight In on an Income Statement

In the fundamental accounting equation, to be consistent with the income statement, we placed Purchases Returns and Allowances and Purchases Discounts under Purchases with the plus and minus signs reversed. Both accounts are contra accounts, so we subtract their totals from Purchases on the income statement. Since Freight In increases the cost of purchases, it must be added. A portion of the Cost of Goods Sold section of the annual income statement of Whitewater Raft Supply, as well as the Revenue from Sales section (taken from Figure 4 on page 399), is shown in Figure 7.

FIGURE 5

Recording a cash payment using accounting software

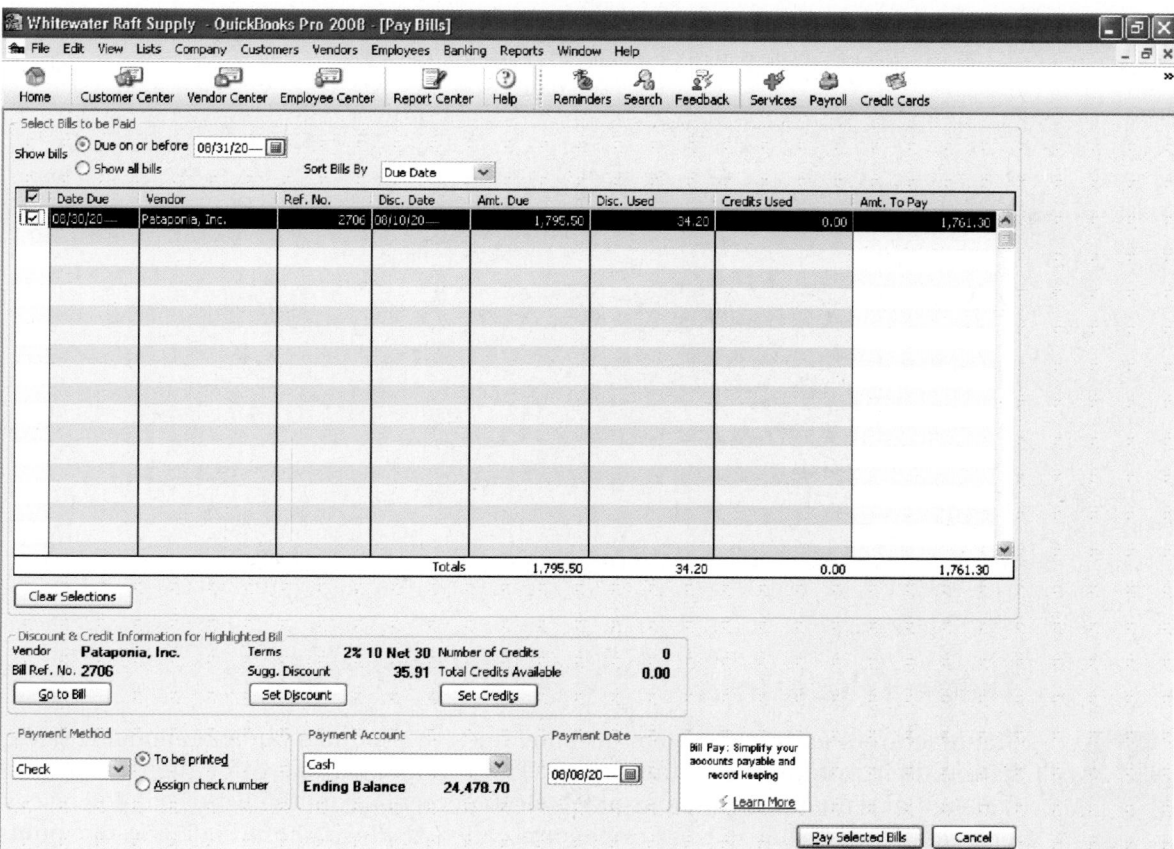

FIGURE 6

Bill payment

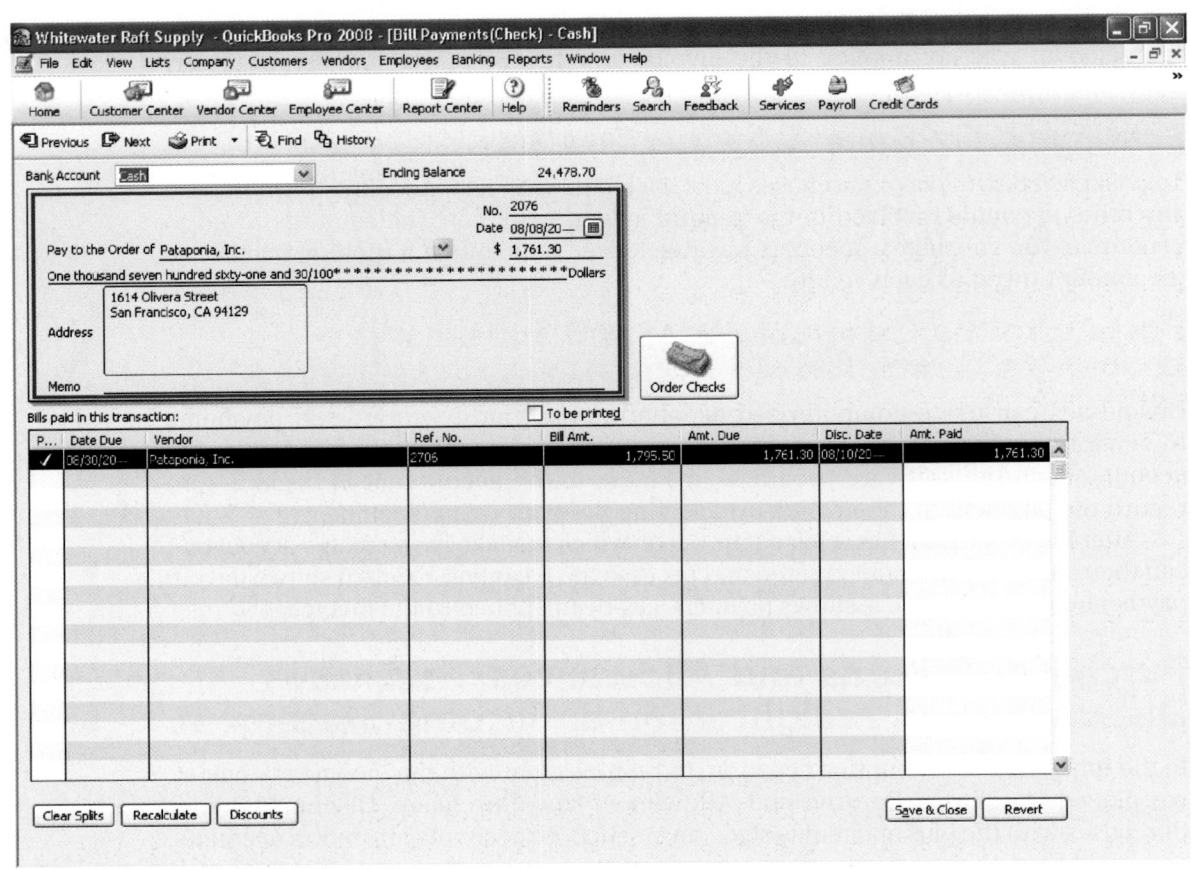

FIGURE 7

Partial income statement for
Whitewater Raft Supply

Whitewater Raft Supply
Income Statement
For the Year Ended December 31, 20—

Revenue from Sales:			
Sales		$257,180	
Less: Sales Returns and Allowances	$ 940		
Sales Discounts	1,980	2,920	
Net Sales			$254,260
Cost of Goods Sold:			
Merchandise Inventory, January 1, 20—		$ 67,000	
Purchases	$87,840		
Less: Purchases Returns and Allowances	$ 932		
Purchases Discounts	1,348	2,280	
Net Purchases		$85,560	
Add Freight In		2,360	
Delivered Cost of Purchases		87,920	
Cost of Goods Available for Sale		$154,920	

Trade Discounts

LEARNING
OBJECTIVE **4**

*Journalize
transactions involving
trade discounts.*

Manufacturers and wholesalers of many lines of products publish annual catalogs listing their products at retail prices. These organizations offer their customers substantial reductions (often as much as 40 percent) from the list or catalog prices. The reductions from the list prices are called **trade discounts**. Trade discounts are not journalized. Remember, firms grant cash discounts for prompt payment of invoices. Trade discounts are *not related* to cash payments. Manufacturers and wholesalers use trade discounts to avoid the high cost of reprinting catalogs when selling prices change. To change prices, the manufacturer or wholesaler simply issues a sheet or online posting that shows a new list of trade discounts to be applied to the catalog prices. Trade discounts can also be used to differentiate between classes of customers. For example, a manufacturer may use one schedule of trade discounts for wholesalers and another schedule for retailers.

Firms may quote trade discounts as a single percentage. *Example:* A distributor of furnaces grants a single discount of 40 percent off the listed catalog price of $8,000. In this case, the selling price is calculated as follows:

List or catalog price	$8,000
Less trade discount of 40% ($8,000 × 0.40)	3,200
Selling price	$4,800

Neither the seller nor the buyer records trade discounts in the accounts; they enter only the selling price. Using T accounts, the furnace distributor records the sale like this:

Accounts Receivable		Sales	
+	−	−	+
4,800			4,800

The buyer records the purchase as follows:

Purchases		Accounts Payable	
+	−	−	+
4,800			4,800

Firms may also quote trade discounts as a chain, or series, of percentages. For example, a distributor of automobile parts grants discounts of 30 percent, 10 percent, and 10 percent off the listed catalog price of $900. In this case, the selling price is calculated as follows:

List or catalog price	$900.00
Less first trade discount of 30% ($900 × 0.30)	270.00
Remainder after first discount	$630.00
Less second trade discount of 10% ($630 × 0.10)	63.00
Remainder after second discount	$567.00
Less third discount of 10% ($567 × 0.10)	56.70
Selling price	$510.30

Using T accounts, the automobile parts distributor records the sale as follows:

Accounts Receivable		Sales	
+	−	−	+
510.30			510.30

The buyer records the purchase as follows:

Purchases		Accounts Payable	
+	−	−	+
510.30			510.30

In the situation involving a chain of discounts, the additional discounts are granted for large-volume transactions, either in dollar amount or in size of shipment, such as carload lots.

Cash discounts could also apply in situations involving trade discounts. *Example:* Suppose that the credit terms of the preceding sale include a cash discount of 2/10, n/30, and that the buyer pays the invoice within 10 days. The seller applies the cash discount to the selling price. The seller records the transaction as shown in the following T accounts:

Cash	Sales Discounts	Accounts Receivable
+ | −	+ | −	+ | −
500.09 |	10.21 |	| 510.30

The buyer records the transaction as follows:

Cash	Purchases Discounts	Accounts Payable
+ | −	+ | −	+ | −
| 500.09	| 10.21	510.30 |

Remember

To the seller, a cash discount is a sales discount, and to the purchaser, a cash discount is a purchases discount.

A Review of Purchases and Sales Transactions

Now that we have covered all of the transactions involving purchases and sales, let's take a moment to review. Remember that each transaction affects a purchaser and a seller. In Figure 8, we show how each transaction would be recorded by a purchaser (Able Company) and a seller (Baker Company).

FIGURE 8

Transactions for two companies' purchases and sales

Purchaser's Books—Able Company			Seller's Books—Baker Company		
Bought merchandise from Baker Company, $500; terms 2/10, n/30.			Sold merchandise to Able Company, $500; terms 2/10, n/30.		
Purchases	500		Accounts Receivable	500	
Accounts Payable		500	Sales		500
Received credit memo from Baker Company for return of merchandise, $100.			Issued credit memo to Able Company for return of merchandise, $100.		
Accounts Payable	100		Sales Returns and		
Purchases Returns and			Allowances	100	
Allowances		100	Accounts Receivable		100
Paid Baker Company within the discount period, $392 ($500 − $100 = $400; $400 × .02 = $8; $400 − $8 = $392).			Received cash from Able Company within the discount period, $392.		
Accounts Payable	400		Cash	392	
Cash		392	Sales Discounts	8	
Purchases Discounts		8	Accounts Receivable		400

PART TWO—RECORDING TRANSACTIONS INTO THE CASH RECEIPTS JOURNAL AND CASH PAYMENTS JOURNAL

In Chapter 9, we saw that using a sales journal and a purchases journal enables an accountant to carry out the journalizing and posting processes much more efficiently. These special journals make it possible to post column totals rather than individual figures. They also make the division of labor more efficient because the journalizing functions can be delegated to different persons. The *cash receipts journal* and the *cash payments journal* further extend these advantages.

The Cash Receipts Journal

The **cash receipts journal** contains all transactions in which cash is received, or increased. When a cash receipts journal is used, all transactions in which cash is debited *must* be recorded in it. It may be used for a service as well as a merchandising business. Let's list some typical transactions of a merchandising business, Whitewater Raft Supply, that result in an increase in cash. To get a better picture of the transactions, let's first record them in T accounts and then in the general journal.

5 **LEARNING OBJECTIVE**

Journalize transactions for a merchandising business in a cash receipts journal and post from a cash receipts journal to a general ledger and an accounts receivable ledger.

Oct. 1 **Sold merchandise on account to Green River Rafts, invoice no. 10050, $3,500; terms 2/10, n/30.**

Accounts Receivable			Sales	
+	−		−	+
3,500				3,500

Oct. 4 **Sold merchandise, $500, and the customer used a credit card.**

The bank issuing the card bills the customer directly each month. The business, on the other hand, deposits the bank credit card receipts every day. The bank *deducts a discount* and credits the firm's account with cash. We will assume that the discount is 4 percent. The firm therefore records the amount of the discount under Credit Card Expense: $500.00 \times 0.04 = \$20.00$ credit card expense; $500.00 - \$20.00 = \$480.00$.

Cash		Credit Card Expense		Sales	
+	−	+	−	−	+
480		20			500

As an alternative, many businesses postpone recording the amount of bank credit card expense until they actually receive notification from their bank on their bank statement. For example, total credit card sales for a restaurant for a time period amount to $10,600 plus 8 percent sales tax. The entry is as follows:

Cash		Sales Tax Payable		Sales	
+	−	−	+	−	+
11,448			848		10,600

The restaurant's next bank statement includes a debit memorandum for credit card charges of $457.92, using an assumed 4 percent discount rate ($11,448 \times 0.04$). The business handles this in a similar manner to a check service charge:

Credit Card Expense		Cash	
+	−	+	−
457.92			457.92

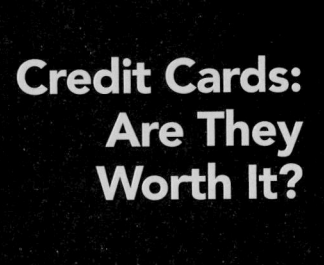

Credit Cards: Are They Worth It?

SMALL BUSINESS SUCCESS

Accepting credit cards for sales of merchandise or services has become a natural part of business for most companies. However, some small businesses still don't accept credit cards and rely only on cash sales. The decision to accept credit cards comes at a cost to the business, in the form of a fee. The bank that processes your credit card sales will charge your company a fee for any credit card sales. The amount of the fee will vary, based on the bank that you are using and the amount of transactions your company processes. In addition to banks, there are specific companies, often called merchant service companies, that offer credit card processing services.

Why would a company choose to accept credit cards in the form of payment? There are many reasons. One is that it will possibly increase sales by allowing customers more flexibility in payment methods. Also, the bank or processing

company assumes all risk associated with non-paying customers. Unlike uncollectible accounts receivables, the company will always get paid when a transaction involves a credit card sale.

How does a company begin accepting credit cards? The first step is to apply for merchant status. Applying for merchant status is similar to applying for a loan. Your company must fill out an application and have its financial records reviewed. Once merchant status is approved for your company, you will be able to accept most common credit cards. The bank or merchant services company that you partner with will transfer the cash proceeds, less the fee, for each credit card sale to your bank account. The transaction fee or service charge usually ranges from 1.5 to 5 percent of the sale. In addition, there may be monthly or other fees associated with credit card transactions.

Oct. 5   Collected cash on account from L. R. Ray, a charge customer, $416.

Cash			Accounts Receivable	
+	−		+	−
416				416

Oct. 7   The owner, D. M. Bruce, invested cash in the business, $9,000.

Cash			D. M. Bruce, Capital	
+	−		−	+
9,000				9,000

Oct. 8   Sold equipment for cash at cost, $500.

Cash			Equipment	
+	−		+	−
500				500

Oct. 10   Received check from Green River Rafts for $3,430 in payment of invoice no. 10050, less cash discount ($3,500 × 0.02 = $70; $3,500 − $70 = $3,430).

Cash		Sales Discounts		Accounts Receivable	
+	−	+	−	+	−
3,430		70			3,500

Oct 15. **Cash sales for first half of the month, $2,460.**

Cash			Sales	
+	−		−	+
2,460				2,460

The same transactions are shown in general journal form as follows:

GENERAL JOURNAL   PAGE 29

Date	Description	Post. Ref.	Debit	Credit
20—				
Oct. 1	Accounts Receivable, Green River Rafts		3 5 0 0 00	
	Sales			3 5 0 0 00
	Sold merchandise to Green			
	River Rafts, invoice no. 10050.			
4	Cash		4 8 0 00	
	Credit Card Expense		2 0 00	
	Sales			5 0 0 00
	Sold merchandise involving a credit			
	card.			
5	Cash		4 1 6 00	
	Accounts Receivable, L. R. Ray			4 1 6 00
	Collected cash on account.			
7	Cash		9 0 0 0 00	
	D. M. Bruce, Capital			9 0 0 0 00
	Owner invested cash.			
8	Cash		5 0 0 00	
	Equipment			5 0 0 00
	Sold equipment at cost.			
10	Cash		3 4 3 0 00	
	Sales Discounts		7 0 00	
	Accounts Receivable, Green River Rafts			3 5 0 0 00
	Received a check in payment of			
	invoice no. 10050, less cash			
	discount.			
15	Cash		2 4 6 0 00	
	Sales			2 4 6 0 00
	Cash sales for the first half			
	of the month.			

Now let's analyze these seven transactions: The transaction on October 1 does not involve cash; therefore, it would not be recorded in the cash receipts journal. Instead, this transaction would be recorded in either the general journal or the sales journal. The transactions occurring on October 4, 5, 10, and 15 would occur frequently; the transactions on October 7 and 8 would occur less frequently. When designing a cash receipts journal, it is logical to include a Cash Debit column because all the transactions involve an increase in cash. If a business regularly collects cash from credit customers, there should be an Accounts Receivable Credit column and Sales Discounts Debit column. If a firm often sells merchandise for cash and collects a sales tax, there should be a Sales Credit column and a Sales Tax Payable Credit column. If the business accepts credit cards and wants to record the amount of the discount at the time of each transaction, there should be a Credit Card Expense Debit column for the amount deducted by the bank.

However, the credit to D. M. Bruce, Capital, and the credit to Equipment do not occur very often, so it would not be practical to set up special columns for these credits. They can be handled adequately by an Other Accounts Credit column, which can be used for credits to all accounts that have no special column.

The accountant would record these transactions in a cash receipts journal (see Figure 9). Notice that there are columns for each of the most common cash transactions. The accountant would record each transaction directly into the cash receipts journal by placing each amount into the appropriate column.

FIGURE 9

Cash receipts journal

CASH RECEIPTS JOURNAL   PAGE 41

Date	Account Credited	Post. Ref.	Cash Debit	Credit Card Expense Debit	Sales Discounts Debit	Accounts Receivable Credit	Sales Credit	Other Accounts Credit
20—								
Oct. 4	————		4 8 0 00	2 0 00			5 0 0 00	
5	L. R. Ray		4 1 6 00			4 1 6 00		
7	D.M. Bruce,							
	Capital		9 0 0 0 00					9 0 0 0 00
8	Equipment		5 0 0 00					5 0 0 00
10	Green							
	River Rafts		3 4 3 0 00		7 0 00	3 5 0 0 00		
15	————		2 4 6 0 00				2 4 6 0 00	

Posting from the Cash Receipts Journal

Here are some other transactions made during the month that involve increases in cash.

Oct.   16   Received check from Floyd Mercantile for $1,366.12 in payment of invoice no. 10052, less cash discount ($1,394.00 − $27.88 = $1,366.12).

     17   Borrowed $9,000 from the bank, receiving cash and giving the bank a promissory note.

     21   Received check from Hartman Guides for $3,696.80 in payment of invoice no. 10055, less cash discount ($3,772.24 − $75.44 = $3,696.80).

     30   Received check from Bowers River Co. for $1,710.00 in payment of invoice no. 10054. (This is longer than the 10-day period, so the cash discount is not allowed.)

     31   Cash sales for second half of the month, $2,620.

In the transaction of October 17, in which $9,000 was borrowed from the bank, the bank was given a **promissory note** (a written promise to pay a specified amount at a specified time) as evidence of the debt. The account **Notes Payable**, instead of Accounts Payable, is used to represent the amount owed on the promissory note. The Accounts Payable account is reserved for charge accounts with creditors, which are normally paid on a 30-day basis.

Let's assume that all the month's transactions involving debits to Cash have now been recorded in the cash receipts journal. The cash receipts journal (see Figure 10) and the T accounts following it illustrate the postings to the general ledger and the accounts receivable ledger.

Individual amounts in the Accounts Receivable Credit column of the cash receipts journal are usually posted daily to the accounts receivable ledger. Individual amounts in the Other Accounts Credit column are usually posted daily.

At the end of the month, we can post the special column totals in the cash receipts journal to the general ledger accounts. These columns include Cash Debit, Credit Card Expense Debit, Sales Discounts Debit, Accounts Receivable Credit, and Sales Credit.

FIGURE 10

Posting from the cash receipts
journal to the general ledger
and accounts receivable ledger

CASH RECEIPTS JOURNAL

PAGE 41

Date	Account Credited	Post. Ref.	Cash Debit	Credit Card Expense Debit	Sales Discounts Debit	Accounts Receivable Credit	Sales Credit	Other Accounts Credit
20—								
Oct. 4	—————	—	4 8 0 00	2 0 00			5 0 0 00	
5	L. R. Ray	✓	4 1 6 00			4 1 6 00		
7	D. M. Bruce, Capital	311	9 0 0 0 00					9 0 0 0 00
8	Equipment	124	5 0 0 00					5 0 0 00
10	Green River Rafts	✓	3 4 3 0 00		7 0 00	3 5 0 0 00		
15	—————	—	2 4 6 0 00				2 4 6 0 00	
16	Floyd Mercantile	✓	1 3 6 6 12		2 7 88	1 3 9 4 00		
17	Notes Payable	211	9 0 0 0 00					9 0 0 0 00
21	Hartman Guides	✓	3 6 9 6 80		7 5 44	3 7 7 2 24		
30	Bowers River Co.	✓	1 7 1 0 00			1 7 1 0 00		
31	—————	—	2 6 2 0 00				2 6 2 0 00	
31	Total		34 6 7 8 92	2 0 00	1 7 3 32	10 7 9 2 24	5 5 8 0 00	18 5 0 0 00
			(1 1 1)	(6 1 5)	(4 1 3)	(1 1 3)	(4 1 1)	(X)

Accounts Receivable Ledger

General Ledger

Bowers River Co.

	+		−	
Beg. Bal.	2,500.00	Oct. 30	1,710.00	
End. Bal.	790.00			

Floyd Mercantile

	+		−	
Beg. Bal.	1,394.00	Oct. 16	1,394.00	

Green River Rafts

	+		−	
Beg. Bal.	5,000.00	Oct. 10	3,500.00	
End Bal.	1,500.00			

Hartman Guides

	+		−	
Beg. Bal.	3,772.24	Oct. 21	3,772.24	

L. R. Ray

	+		−	
Beg. Bal.	416.00	Oct. 5	416.00	

Cash 111

	+		−
Oct. 31	34,678.92		

Accounts Receivable 113

	+		−
		Oct. 31	10,792.24

Equipment 124

	+		−
		Oct. 8	500.00

Notes Payable 211

	−		+
		Oct. 17	9,000.00

D. M. Bruce, Capital 311

	−		+
		Oct. 7	9,000.00

Sales 411

	−		+
Oct. 31	5,580.00		

Sales Discounts 413

	+		−
Oct. 31	173.32		

Credit Card Expense 615

	+		−
Oct. 31	20.00		

In the Post. Ref. column, the check marks (✓) indicate that the amounts in the Accounts Receivable Credit column have been posted to the individual credit customers' accounts as credits. The account numbers show that the amounts in the Other Accounts Credit column have been posted separately to the accounts described in the Account Credited column. An (X) goes under the total of the Other Accounts Credit column; it means "do not post—the figures have already been posted separately." This column is totaled to make it easier to prove that the debits equal the credits.

Debit Totals		Credit Totals	
Cash	$34,678.92	Accounts Receivable	$10,792.24
Credit Card Expense	20.00	Sales	5,580.00
Sales Discounts	173.32	Other Accounts	18,500.00
	$34,872.24		$34,872.24

Advantages of a Cash Receipts Journal

The advantages of using a cash receipts journal include:

1. Transactions generally can be recorded on one line.
2. All transactions involving debits to Cash are recorded in one place.
3. It eliminates much repetition in posting when there are numerous transactions involving Cash debits. The Cash Debit side can be posted as one total.
4. Special columns can be used for specialized transactions and posted as one total.

The Cash Payments Journal

LEARNING OBJECTIVE 6

Journalize transactions for a merchandising business in a cash payments journal and post from a cash payments journal to a general ledger and an accounts payable ledger.

The **cash payments journal**, as the name implies, is a special journal used to record all transactions in which cash goes out, or decreases. When the cash payments journal is used, all transactions in which cash is credited *must* be recorded in it. This journal may be used for either a service or a merchandising business.

To get acquainted with the cash payments journal, let's list some typical transactions of a merchandising business that result in a decrease in cash. To illustrate, we record the following transactions in T accounts:

Oct.   2   **Bought merchandise on account from Pataponia, Inc., invoice no. 2746, $2,500; terms 2/10, n/30; dated September 30; FOB San Francisco, freight prepaid and added to the invoice, $100.25 (total $2,600.25).**

Accounts Payable		Purchases		Freight In	
−	+	+	−	+	−
	2,600.25	2,500.00		100.25	

Oct.   8   **Issued Ck. No. 2226 to Pataponia, Inc., in payment of invoice no. 2730, less cash discount of $50.00, $2,550.25 ($2,600.25 − $50.00).** (Notice that the discount applies only to the amount billed for the merchandise (2 percent of $2,500).

Cash		Accounts Payable		Purchases Discounts	
+	−	−	+	−	+
	2,550.25	2,600.25			50.00

Oct. 10 Paid cash for liability insurance, Ck. No. 2227 $4,890.

Prepaid Insurance		Cash	
+	−	+	−
4,890			4,890

Oct. 12 Paid wages for two weeks, Ck. No. 2228, $6,220 (previously recorded in the payroll entry).

Wages Payable		Cash	
−	+	+	−
6,220			6,220

Oct. 14 Paid rent for the month, Ck. No. 2229, $2,950.

Rent Expense		Cash	
+	−	+	−
2,950			2,950

The same transactions are now shown in general journal form as follows:

				GENERAL JOURNAL					PAGE 29	
Date			**Description**	**Post. Ref.**	**Debit**		**Credit**			
20—										
Oct.	2	Purchases			2 5 0 0 00					
		Freight In			1 0 0 25					
		Accounts Payable, Pataponia, Inc.					2 6 0 0 25			
		Purchased merchandise								
		from Pataponia, Inc., invoice								
		no. 2746, invoice dated 9/30,								
		terms 2/10, n/30.								
	8	Accounts Payable, Pataponia, Inc.			2 6 0 0 25					
		Cash					2 5 5 0 25			
		Purchases Discounts					5 0 00			
		Paid on account, Ck. No. 2226.								
	10	Prepaid Insurance			4 8 9 0 00					
		Cash					4 8 9 0 00			
		Paid liability insurance,								
		Ck. No. 2227.								
	12	Wages Payable			6 2 2 0 00					
		Cash					6 2 2 0 00			
		Paid wages for two weeks,								
		Ck. No. 2228.								
	14	Rent Expense			2 9 5 0 00					
		Cash					2 9 5 0 00			
		Paid rent for month, Ck. No. 2229.								

Now let's analyze these five transactions. The transaction on October 2 does not involve cash; therefore, it would not be recorded in the cash payments journal. Instead, this transaction would be recorded in either the general journal or the purchases journal. The transaction on October 8 would occur frequently, as payments to creditors are made several times a month. Of the other transactions, the debit to Wages Payable might occur twice a month, the debit to Rent Expense once a month, and the debit to Prepaid Insurance only occasionally.

It is logical to include a Cash Credit column in a cash payments journal because all transactions recorded in this journal involve a decrease in cash. Since payments to creditors are made often, there should also be an Accounts Payable Debit column and a Purchases Discounts Credit column. You can set up any other column that is used often enough to warrant it. Otherwise, an Other Accounts Debit column takes care of all the other transactions.

Now let's record these same transactions in a cash payments journal and include a column titled Ck. No. (see Figure 11). If you think for a moment, you will see that this is consistent with good management of cash. All expenditures except Petty Cash expenditures should be paid for by check.

FIGURE 11

Cash payments journal

CASH PAYMENTS JOURNAL   PAGE 62

Date	Ck. No.	Account Debited	Post. Ref.	Other Accounts Debit	Accounts Payable Debit	Purchases Discounts Credit	Cash Credit
20—							
Oct. 8	2226	Pataponia, Inc.			2 6 0 0 25	5 0 00	2 5 5 0 25
10	2227	Prepaid Insurance		4 8 9 0 00			4 8 9 0 00
12	2228	Wages Payable		6 2 2 0 00			6 2 2 0 00
14	2229	Rent Expense		2 9 5 0 00			2 9 5 0 00

Here are some other transactions of Whitewater Raft Supply involving decreases in cash during October. Note that credit terms vary among the different creditors.

Oct.   15   Issued Ck. No. 2230 to Gibbs Company in payment of invoice no. 10611 ($564), less return ($270); less cash discount, terms 2/10, n/30; $288.12 ($564 − $270 = $294; $294.00 × 0.02 = $5.88; $294.00 − $5.88 = $288.12).

     16   Issued Ck. No. 2231 to Gardner Products Company in payment of invoice no. B643 ($1,245), less return ($315); less cash discount, terms 1/10, n/30; $921.60 [$1,245 − $315 = $930; freight charges totaled $90 ($930 − $90 = $840); $840.00 × 0.01 = $8.40; $930.00 − $8.40 = $921.60].

     17   Bought merchandise for cash, Ck. No. 2232, payable to Jones and Son, $200.

     19   Received bill and issued Ck. No. 2233 to Monroe Express for freight charges on merchandise purchased earlier from Gibbs Company, $60.

     23   Voided Ck. No. 2234.

     25   Paid wages for two-week period, Ck. No. 2235, $1,750 (previously recorded in the payroll entry).

     27   Paid F. P. Franz for merchandise returned on a cash sale, Ck. No. 2236, $51.

     27   Issued Ck. No. 2237 to Langseth and Son in payment of invoice no. 902, $1,180; terms net 30 days.

The transaction of October 19 paying the freight bill to Monroe Express increases the Freight In account, as the transportation charges are for merchandise purchased.

You should list all checks in consecutive order, even those checks that must be voided. In this way, *every* check is accounted for, which is necessary for internal control.

These transactions are recorded in the cash payments journal illustrated in Figure 12. Notice that an (X) is placed under the Other Accounts column. That means "do not post—the figures have already been posted separately."

The posting process for the cash payments journal is similar to the posting process for the cash receipts journal. Individual amounts in the Accounts Payable Debit column are usually posted daily to the subsidiary ledger. After posting, put a check mark (✓) in the Post. Ref. column. Individual amounts in the Other Accounts Debit column are usually posted daily to the general ledger. Post these figures individually, then place the account number in the Post. Ref. column. Totals of the Cash Credit column, Purchases Discounts Credit column, and Accounts Payable Debit column are posted to the general ledger accounts at the end of the month. Write the appropriate general ledger account number in parentheses below the column totals. Put an (X) below the total of the Other Accounts Debit column to indicate that the total amount is not posted.

At the end of the month, after totaling the columns, check the accuracy of the footings by proving that the sum of the debit totals equals the sum of the credit totals. Since you have posted the individual amounts in the Other Accounts Debit column to the general ledger, the only posting that remains is the credit to the Cash account for $21,060.97, the credit to Purchases Discounts account for $64.28 and the debit to the Accounts Payable (controlling) account for $5,004.25.

> The (X) below the total of the Other Accounts Debit column means "do not post total."

Remember

Debit Totals		Credit Totals	
Accounts Payable	$ 5,004.25	Cash	$21,060.97
Other Accounts	16,121.00	Purchases Discounts	64.28
	$21,125.25		$21,125.25

FIGURE 12

Cash payments journal

					Post. Ref.	Other Accounts Debit	Accounts Payable Debit	Purchases Discounts Credit	Cash Credit
Date		**Ck. No.**	**Account Debited**						
20—									
Oct.	8	2226	Pataponia, Inc.		✓		2 6 0 0 25	5 0 00	2 5 5 0 25
	10	2227	Prepaid Insurance		116	4 8 9 0 00			4 8 9 0 00
	12	2228	Wages Payable		213	6 2 2 0 00			6 2 2 0 00
	14	2229	Rent Expense		612	2 9 5 0 00			2 9 5 0 00
	15	2230	Gibbs Company		✓		2 9 4 00	5 88	2 8 8 12
	16	2231	Gardner Products Company		✓		9 3 0 00	8 40	9 2 1 60
	17	2232	Purchases		511	2 0 0 00			2 0 0 00
	19	2233	Freight In		514	6 0 00			6 0 00
	23	2234	Void		—				
	25	2235	Wages Payable		213	1 7 5 0 00			1 7 5 0 00
	27	2236	Sales Returns and Allowances		412	5 1 00			5 1 00
	27	2237	Langseth and Son		✓		1 1 8 0 00		1 1 8 0 00
	31		Totals			16 1 2 1 00	5 0 0 4 25	6 4 28	21 0 6 0 97
						(X)	(2 1 2)	(5 1 3)	(1 1 1)

CASH PAYMENTS JOURNAL — PAGE 62

Advantages of a Cash Payments Journal

The advantages of the cash payments journal are similar to the advantages of the cash receipts journal:

1. Transactions generally can be recorded on one line.
2. All transactions involving credits to Cash are recorded in one place.
3. For numerous transactions involving Cash credits, the Cash Credit side can be posted as one total.
4. Special columns can be used for specialized transactions and posted as one total.

COMPARISON OF THE FIVE TYPES OF JOURNALS

We have now looked at four special journals and the general journal. It is important for a business to select and use the journals that provide the most efficient accounting system possible. Figure 13 summarizes the applications of the journals we have discussed and the correct procedures for using them.

FIGURE 13

Using special journals

Types of Transactions

Sale of merchandise on account	Purchase of merchandise on account	Receipt of cash	Payment of cash	All other

Evidenced by Source Documents

Sales invoice	Purchase invoice	Credit card receipts Cash Checks Electronic funds transfers	Check stub Electronic funds transfers	Miscellaneous

Types of Journals

Sales journal	Purchases journal	Cash receipts journal	Cash payments journal	General journal

Posting to Ledger Accounts

Individual amounts posted daily to the accounts receivable ledger and the total posted monthly to the general ledger.	Individual amounts posted daily to the accounts payable ledger and the totals of the special columns posted monthly to the general ledger.	Individual amounts in the Accounts Receivable Credit column posted daily to the accounts receivable ledger. Individual amounts in the Other Accounts columns posted daily to the general ledger. Totals of special columns posted monthly to the general ledger.	Individual amounts in the Accounts Payable Debit column posted daily to the accounts payable ledger. Individual amounts in the Other Accounts columns posted daily to the general ledger. Totals of special columns posted monthly to the general ledger.	Entries posted daily to the subsidiary ledgers and the general ledger.

Recommended Order of Posting to the Subsidiary Ledgers and the General Ledger

To avoid errors and negative balances in accounts, post from the special journals in this order:

1. Sales journal
2. Purchases journal
3. Cash receipts journal
4. Cash payments journal

CHAPTER REVIEW

Study & Practice

LEARNING OBJECTIVE

Determine cash discounts according to credit terms.

The amount of the discount is determined by multiplying the invoice total (excluding freight charges and any returns and allowances) by the **cash discount** rate.

PRACTICE EXERCISE 1

For the following purchases of merchandise, determine the amount of cash to be paid:

Purchase	Invoice Date	Credit Terms	FOB	Amount of Purchase	Freight Charges	Total Invoice Amount	Returns and Allowances	Date Paid
a.	June 12	1/10, n/30	Destination	$700	—	$ 700	$100	June 21
b.	June 14	2/10, n/30	Shipping point	940	$60	1,000	—	June 20
c.	June 18	n/30	Shipping point	820	40	860	30	July 17

PRACTICE EXERCISE 1 SOLUTION

a. $594   ($700 − $100) − ($600 × 0.01) = $600 − $6 = $594
b. $981.20   ($940 + $60) − ($940 × 0.02) = $1,000 − $18.80 = $981.20
c. $830   ($820 + $40) − $30 = $830

2 **LEARNING OBJECTIVE**

Journalize sales transactions in a general journal involving cash receipts from credit customers who are entitled to deduct the cash discount.

When recording a cash receipt from a customer within the discount period, the business records a debit to Cash for the amount received, a debit to Sales Discounts for the amount of the discount, and a credit to Accounts Receivable for the full amount of the invoice less any returns and allowances.

PRACTICE EXERCISE 2

Record the following sales transactions in general journal form on the books of Fry Company (the seller).

a. Sold merchandise on account to Lee Company, invoice no. 8765, $1,500; terms 2/10, n/30.

b. Issued credit memo no. 967 to Lee Company for damaged merchandise, $100.

c. Lee Company paid the account in full within the discount period.

PRACTICE EXERCISE 2 SOLUTION

	GENERAL JOURNAL				PAGE _____
Date	Description	Post. Ref.	Debit	Credit	
	a. Accounts Receivable, Lee Company		1 5 0 0 00		
	Sales			1 5 0 0 00	
	Sold merchandise to Lee				
	Company, invoice no. 8765.				
	b. Sales Returns and Allowances		1 0 0 00		
	Accounts Receivable, Lee Company			1 0 0 00	
	Issued credit memo no. 967.				
	c. Cash		1 3 7 2 00		
	Sales Discounts		2 8 00		
	Accounts Receivable, Lee Company			1 4 0 0 00	
	Received payment in full.				

LEARNING OBJECTIVE

3 *Journalize purchase transactions in a general journal involving cash payments when entitled to deduct the cash discount.*

When recording a payment to a vendor within the discount period, the business records a debit to Accounts Payable for the full amount of the invoice less any returns and allowances, a credit to Purchase Discounts for the amount of the discount, and a credit to Cash for the amount paid.

PRACTICE EXERCISE 3

Record the following purchase transactions in general journal form on the books of Lee Company (the buyer).

a. Purchased merchandise on account from Fry Company, invoice no. 8765, $1,500; terms 2/10, n/30.

b. Received credit memo no. 967 from Fry Company for damaged merchandise, $100.

c. Paid Fry Company in full within the discount period.

PRACTICE EXERCISE 3 SOLUTION

| | | | | | GENERAL JOURNAL | | | | | PAGE _____ | | |

GENERAL JOURNAL   **PAGE** _____

Date	Description	Post. Ref.	Debit	Credit
	a. Purchases		1 5 0 0 00	
	Accounts Payable, Fry Company			1 5 0 0 00
	Purchased merchandise from			
	Fry Company, invoice no. 8765.			
	b. Accounts Payable, Fry Company		1 0 0 00	
	Purchases Returns and Allowances			1 0 0 00
	Received credit memo no. 967.			
	c. Accounts Payable, Fry Company		1 4 0 0 00	
	Purchases Discounts			
	(($1,500 − $100) × .02)			2 8 00
	Cash			1 3 7 2 00
	Paid invoice no. 8675 in full.			

LEARNING OBJECTIVE

4 *Journalize transactions involving trade discounts.*

In transactions involving **trade discounts**, the trade discounts are deducted from the list prices to arrive at the selling prices. Both sellers and buyers record the transactions at the selling prices.

PRACTICE EXERCISE 4

Record the following transaction involving a trade discount.

Feb. 2 Bought merchandise on account from Coffee Company, $3,500, received a 40% trade discount, invoice no. 234C, dated Jan. 31; terms 2/10, n/EOM.

PRACTICE EXERCISE 4 SOLUTION

GENERAL JOURNAL   **PAGE** _____

Date	Description	Post. Ref.	Debit	Credit
20—				
Feb. 2	Purchases		2 1 0 0 00	
	Accounts Payable, Coffee Company			2 1 0 0 00
	Purchased merchandise from			
	Coffee Company, invoice no. 234C.			
	($3,500 − ($3,500 × .40))			

LEARNING OBJECTIVE

5 *Journalize transactions for a merchandising business in a cash receipts journal and post from a cash receipts journal to a general ledger and an accounts receivable ledger.*

A transaction for a merchandising business can be recorded on one line in a **cash receipts journal.** The cash receipts journal usually contains the following columns: Date, Account Credited, Post. Ref., Cash Debit, Credit Card Expense Debit, Sales Discounts Debit, Accounts Receivable Credit, Sales Credit, Sales Tax Payable Credit, and Other Accounts Credit.

The accountant posts daily from the Accounts Receivable Credit column to the individual credit customers' accounts in the accounts receivable ledger. After posting, the accountant puts a check mark (✓) in the Post. Ref. column. The accountant also posts the amounts in the Other Accounts Credit column daily and records the account numbers in the Post. Ref. column. The special columns are posted as totals at the end of the month. The accountant then writes the account numbers in parentheses under the totals. An (X) below the total of the Other Accounts Credit column shows that amounts are posted individually and the total is not posted.

PRACTICE EXERCISE 5

Indicate the appropriate columns in which each of the following transactions would be recorded in the cash receipts journal.

Transaction	Cash Debit	Credit Card Expense Debit	Sales Discounts Debit	Accounts Receivable Credit	Sales Credit	Other Accounts Credit
a. Collected cash on account from a charge customer.						
b. Received check from a charge customer in payment of an invoice within the discount period.						
c. Borrowed money from the bank, receiving cash and giving the bank a promissory note.						
d. Received check from a charge customer in payment of an invoice past the discount period.						
e. Recorded cash sales for the month.						

PRACTICE EXERCISE 5 SOLUTION

Transaction	Cash Debit	Credit Card Expense Debit	Sales Discounts Debit	Accounts Receivable Credit	Sales Credit	Other Accounts Credit
a. Collected cash on account from a charge customer.	✓			✓		
b. Received check from a charge customer in payment of an invoice within the discount period.	✓		✓	✓		
c. Borrowed money from the bank, receiving cash and giving the bank a promissory note.	✓					✓
d. Received check from a charge customer in payment of an invoice past the discount period.	✓			✓		
e. Recorded cash sales for the month.	✓				✓	

6 **LEARNING OBJECTIVE**

Journalize transactions for a merchandising business in a cash payments journal and post from a cash payments journal to a general ledger and an accounts payable ledger.

A cash payment by a merchandising business that includes a purchase discount can be recorded on one line in a **cash payments journal**. The cash payments journal usually contains the following columns: Date, Ck. No., Account Debited, Post. Ref., Other Accounts Debit, Accounts Payable Debit, Purchases Discounts Credit, and Cash Credit.

The accountant posts daily from the Accounts Payable Debit column to the individual suppliers' accounts in the accounts payable ledger. After posting, the accountant puts a check mark (✓) in the Post. Ref. column. The accountant also posts the amounts in the Other Accounts Debit column daily and records the account numbers in the Post. Ref. column. The special columns are posted as totals at the end of the month. The accountant then writes the account numbers in parentheses under the totals. An (X) below the total of the Other Accounts Debit column shows that amounts are posted individually and the total is not posted.

PRACTICE EXERCISE 6

Indicate the appropriate columns in which each of the following transactions would be recorded in the cash payments journal.

Transaction	Other Accounts Debit	Accounts Payable Debit	Purchases Discounts Credit	Cash Credit
a. Issued check to vendor in payment of an invoice within the discount period.				
b. Paid customer for merchandise returned on a cash sale.				
c. Paid wages for two weeks.				
d. Issued check to vendor in payment of an invoice past the discount period.				
e. Paid rent for the month.				

PRACTICE EXERCISE 6 SOLUTION

Transaction	Other Accounts Debit	Accounts Payable Debit	Purchases Discounts Credit	Cash Credit
a. Issued check to vendor in payment of an invoice within the discount period.		✓	✓	✓
b. Paid customer for merchandise returned on a cash sale.	✓			✓
c. Paid wages for two weeks.	✓			✓
d. Issued check to vendor in payment of an invoice past the discount period.		✓		✓
e. Paid rent for the month.	✓			✓

Before a Test Check: Chapters 9–10

PART I: COMPLETION

Complete each of the following statements by writing the appropriate word(s) in the spaces provided.

1. The normal balance of the Purchases Discounts account is on the _____ side.

2. Entries in the Accounts Payable Debit column of a cash payments journal are posted daily to the _____.

3. A(n) _____ is the amount a customer may deduct for paying a bill within a specified period of time.

4. The form sent to the supplier of merchandise is called a(n) _____.

5. The _____ account is used to record the buying of merchandise only.

6. If the freight charges are FOB shipping point, the _____ pays the transportation charges.

7. The time the seller allows the buyer before full payment has to be made is the _____.

8. Increases in Sales Returns and Allowances are recorded on the _____ side.

9. The sales journal is used to record all _____.

10. The schedule of accounts receivable lists the balances of all the _____ accounts at the end of the month.

PART II: MATCHING

For each numbered item, choose the appropriate journal, and write the identifying letter.

_____	1. Paid freight bill on merchandise purchased.	S Sales journal
_____	2. Bought office equipment on account.	P Purchases journal (3 columns)
_____	3. Received a credit memo for merchandise returned.	CR Cash receipts journal CP Cash payments journal J General journal
_____	4. Bought office equipment for cash.	
_____	5. Sold merchandise on account.	
_____	6. Journalized the closing entries.	
_____	7. Paid state sales tax to the state revenue department.	
_____	8. Bought merchandise on account.	
_____	9. Sold merchandise for cash.	
_____	10. Bought merchandise for cash.	

PART III: TRUE/FALSE

For each statement circle T if it is True or circle F if it is False.

T   F   **1.** The Purchases Discounts account is classified as a revenue account.

T   F   **2.** The normal balance of the Sales Discounts account is on the debit side.

T   F   **3.** Check marks in the Posting Reference column of the sales journal indicate that the amounts are not to be posted.

T   F   **4.** The purchases journal is used for the buying of merchandise for cash and on account.

T   F   **5.** On the income statement, Freight In is subtracted from Purchases.

ANSWERS: PART I

1. credit;   **2.** accounts payable ledger;   **3.** cash discount;   **4.** purchase order;   **5.** Purchases;   **6.** buyer;   **7.** credit period;   **8.** debit;   **9.** sales of merchandise on account;   **10.** credit customers

ANSWERS: PART II

1. CP;   **2.** J;   **3.** J;   **4.** CP;   **5.** S;   **6.** J;   **7.** CP;   **8.** P;   **9.** CR;   **10.** CP

ANSWERS: PART III

1. F;   **2.** T;   **3.** F;   **4.** F;   **5.** F

Glossary

Cash discount The amount a customer can deduct for paying a bill within a specified period of time; used to encourage prompt payment. Not all sellers offer cash discounts. *(p. 393)*

Cash payments journal A special journal used to record all transactions involving cash payments or decreases. *(p. 410)*

Cash receipts journal A special journal used to record all transactions involving cash receipts or increases. *(p. 405)*

Credit period The time the seller allows the buyer before full payment on a charge sale has to be made. *(p. 393)*

Notes Payable The account containing the balance of promissory notes. *(p. 408)*

Promissory note A written promise to pay a specified amount at a specified time. *(p. 408)*

Trade discounts Substantial discounts from the list or catalog prices of goods, granted by the seller; not recorded by the buyer or the seller. *(p. 402)*

CHAPTER ASSIGNMENTS

Discussion Questions

1. What are the normal balances of (a) Purchases? (b) Sales Discounts? (c) Purchases Returns and Allowances? (d) Sales? (e) Purchases Discounts? (f) Sales Returns and Allowances?
2. What does an X under the total of a special journal's Other Accounts column signify?
3. Explain the following credit terms: (a) n/30; (b) 2/10, n/60; (c) 1/15, EOM, n/30.
4. In a cash receipts journal, both the Accounts Receivable Credit column and the Cash Debit column were mistakenly underadded by $700. How will this error be discovered?
5. If a cash payments journal is supposed to save writing, why are there so many entries in the Other Accounts Debit column?
6. Describe the posting procedure for a cash payments journal with an Other Accounts Debit column and several special columns, including an Accounts Payable Debit column.
7. An electronics business purchased speakers for resale. The total of the invoice is $2,580, and it is subject to trade discounts of 15 percent, 10 percent, and 5 percent. Compute the amount the dealer will pay for the speakers.
8. What is the difference between a cash discount and a trade discount?

Exercises

EXERCISE 10-1 For the following purchases of merchandise, determine the amount of cash to be paid:

LO 1,3

PRACTICE EXERCISES 1,3

Purchase	Invoice Date	Credit Terms	FOB	Amount of Purchase	Freight Charges	Total Invoice Amount	Returns and Allowances	Date Paid
a.	June 1	2/10, n/30	Destination	$550	—	$ 550	—	June 30
b.	June 12	1/10, n/30	Destination	700	—	700	$100	June 21
c.	June 14	2/10, n/30	Shipping point	940	$60	1,000	—	June 23
d.	June 21	n/30	Shipping point	830	70	900	130	July 20
e.	June 24	1/10, n/30	Shipping point	760	50	810	90	July 3

2  **EXERCISE 10-2** Describe the transactions recorded in the following T accounts:

PRACTICE EXERCISE 2

Cash		Accounts Receivable		Sales

Cash

(c) 5,042.10

Accounts Receivable

(a)   5,320 | (b)   175
          (c)   5,145

Sales

(a)   5,320

Sales Returns and Allowances

(b)   175

Sales Discounts

(c)   102.90

3 **LO** **EXERCISE 10-3** Describe the transactions recorded in the following T accounts:

PRACTICE EXERCISE 3

Cash

(c)   1,176

Accounts Payable

(b)   150 | (a)   1,350
(c)   1,200

Purchases

(a)   1,350

Purchases Returns and Allowances

(b)   150

Purchases Discounts

(c)   24

2,3 **LO** **EXERCISE 10-4** Record the following transactions in general journal form:

PRACTICE EXERCISES 2,3

May   4   Sold merchandise on account to Singh, Inc., $640; terms 2/10, n/30.

10   Bought merchandise on account from Mack Company, $750; terms 1/10, n/60; FOB shipping point.

11   Paid Gaines Freight Lines for freight charges on merchandise purchased from Mack Company, $22.

13   Received full payment from Singh, Inc.

14   Received a credit memo from Mack Company for defective merchandise returned, $104.

19   Paid Mack Company in full within the discount period.

28   Bought merchandise on account from Baldwin Company, $900; terms 2/10, n/30; freight prepaid and added to the invoice, $47 (total $947).

EXERCISE 10-5 Record the following transactions in general journal form, first on the books of the seller (Fuentes Company) and then on the books of the buyer (Lowe Company).

 LO 2,3

PRACTICE EXERCISES 2,3

Fuentes Company

a. Sold merchandise on account to Lowe Company, $1,500; terms 2/10, n/30.
b. Issued a credit memo to Lowe Company for damaged merchandise, $100.
c. Lowe Company paid the account in full within the discount period.

Lowe Company

a. Purchased merchandise on account from Fuentes Company, $1,500; terms 2/10, n/30.
b. Received a credit memo from Fuentes Company for damaged merchandise, $100.
c. Paid Fuentes Company in full within the discount period.

EXERCISE 10-6 Record general journal entries to correct the errors described below. Assume that the incorrect entries were posted in the same period in which the errors occurred.

 LO 2,3,4

PRACTICE EXERCISES 2,3,4

a. A freight cost of $57 incurred on equipment purchased for use in the business was debited to Freight In.
b. The issuance of a credit memo to Marks Company for $126 for merchandise returned was recorded as a debit to Purchases Returns and Allowances and a credit to Accounts Receivable, Marks Company.
c. A cash sale of $92 to M. A. Manning was recorded as a sale on account.
d. A purchase of merchandise from Avila Company in the amount of $1,000 with a 30 percent trade discount was recorded as a debit to Purchases and a credit to Accounts Payable of $1,000 each.

EXERCISE 10-7 Label the blanks in the column heads as either debit or credit.

 LO 5

PRACTICE EXERCISE 5

				CASH RECEIPTS JOURNAL				PAGE _____
Date	Account Credited	Post. Ref.	Cash _____	Sales Discounts _____	Accounts Receivable _____	Sales _____	Other Accounts _____	

EXERCISE 10-8 Describe the transaction recorded.

 LO 5

PRACTICE EXERCISE 5

Cash	Sales Tax Payable	Sales	Credit Card Expense
322.56	16.00	320.00	13.44

EXERCISE 10-9 Label the blanks in the column heads as either debit or credit.

 LO 6

PRACTICE EXERCISE 6

				CASH PAYMENTS JOURNAL			PAGE _____
Date	Ck. No.	Account Debited	Post. Ref.	Other Accounts _____	Accounts Payable _____	Purchases Discounts _____	Cash _____

CHAPTER ASSIGNMENTS

5,6 LO

EXERCISE 10-10 Indicate the journal in which each of the following transactions should be recorded. Assume a three-column purchases journal.

Transaction	S	P	CR	CP	J
a. Paid a creditor on account.					
b. Bought merchandise on account.					
c. Sold merchandise for cash.					
d. Adjusted for insurance expired.					
e. Received payment on account from a charge customer.					
f. Received a credit memo for merchandise returned.					
g. Bought equipment on credit.					
h. Sold merchandise on account.					
i. Recorded a customer's NSF check.					
j. Invested personal noncash assets in the business.					
k. Withdrew cash for personal use.					

Problem Set A

For additional help, see the demonstration problem at the beginning of each chapter in your Working Papers.

1,2,3 LO

PROBLEM 10-1A The following transactions were completed by Hammond Auto Supply during January, which is the first month of this fiscal year. Terms of sale are 2/10, n/30.

Jan. 2 Issued Ck. No. 6981 for monthly rent, $775.

2 J. Hammond, the owner, invested an additional $3,500 in the business.

4 Bought merchandise on account from Valencia and Company, invoice no. A691, $2,930; terms 2/10, n/30; dated January 2.

4 Received check from Vega Appliance for $980 in payment of $1,000 invoice less discount.

4 Sold merchandise on account to L. Paul, invoice no. 6483, $850.

6 Received check from Petty, Inc., $637, in payment of $650 invoice less discount.

7 Issued Ck. No. 6982, $588, to Fischer and Son, in payment of invoice no. C1272 for $600 less discount.

7 Bought supplies on account from Doyle Office Supply, invoice no. 1906B, $108; terms net 30 days.

7 Sold merchandise on account to Ellison and Clay, invoice no. 6484, $787.

9 Issued credit memo no. 43 to L. Paul, $54, for merchandise returned.

11 Cash sales for January 1 through January 10, $4,863.20.

11 Issued Ck. No. 6983, $2,871.40, to Valencia and Company, in payment of $2,930 invoice less discount.

14 Sold merchandise on account to Vega Appliance, invoice no. 6485, $2,050.

Feb.   28   Voided Ck. No. 4321.

28   Paid wages recorded previously for second half of February, $641; Ck. No. 4322.

Required

1. Journalize the transactions for February in the cash payments journal.
2. Total and rule the journal.
3. Prove the equality of the debit and credit totals.

Check Figure
Total Cash Credit, $6,233.90

PROBLEM 10-4A Refer to the information for Problem 10-1A on pages 424–425.

LO 1,2,3,5,6

Required

1. Record the transactions for January, using a sales journal, page 73; a purchases journal, page 56; a cash receipts journal, page 38; a cash payments journal, page 45; and a general journal, page 100.

Check Figure
Schedule of Accounts Receivable total, $5,468.00

111 Cash	411 Sales
113 Accounts Receivable	412 Sales Returns and Allowances
114 Merchandise Inventory	413 Sales Discounts
116 Prepaid Insurance	
121 Equipment	511 Purchases
	512 Purchases Returns and Allowances
212 Accounts Payable	513 Purchases Discounts
215 Salaries Payable	514 Freight In
216 Employees' Federal Income	
Tax Payable	621 Salary Expense
217 FICA Taxes Payable	622 Payroll Tax Expense
218 State Unemployment	625 Supplies Expense
Tax Payable	627 Rent Expense
219 Federal Unemployment	631 Miscellaneous Expense
Tax Payable	
311 J. Hammond, Capital	
312 J. Hammond, Drawing	

2. Post daily all entries involving customer accounts to the accounts receivable ledger.
3. Post daily all entries involving creditor accounts to the accounts payable ledger.
4. Post daily those entries involving the Other Accounts columns and the general journal to the general ledger. Write the owner's name in the Capital and Drawing accounts.
5. Add the columns of the special journals, and prove the equality of debit and credit totals on scratch paper.
6. Post the appropriate totals of the special journals to the general ledger.
7. Prepare a trial balance.
8. Prepare a schedule of accounts receivable and a schedule of accounts payable. Do the totals equal the balances of the related controlling accounts?

Problem Set B

For additional help, see the demonstration problem at the beginning of each chapter in your Working Papers.

1,2,3

PROBLEM 10-1B The following transactions were completed by Yang Restaurant Equipment during January, the first month of this fiscal year. Terms of sale are 2/10, n/30.

Jan. 2 Issued Ck. No. 6981 for monthly rent, $850.

2 L. Yang, the owner, invested an additional $4,500 in the business.

4 Bought merchandise on account from Valentine and Company, invoice no. A694, $2,830; terms 2/10, n/30; dated January 2.

4 Received check from Velez Appliance for $980 in payment of invoice for $1,000 less discount.

4 Sold merchandise on account to L. Parrish, invoice no. 6483, $755.

6 Received check from Peck, Inc., $637, in payment of $650 invoice less discount.

7 Issued Ck. No. 6982, $588, to Frost and Son, in payment of invoice no. C127 for $600 less discount.

7 Bought supplies on account from Dudley Office Supply, invoice no. 190B, $93.54; terms net 30 days.

7 Sold merchandise on account to Ewing and Charles, invoice no. 6484, $1,115.

9 Issued credit memo no. 43 to L. Parrish, $47, for merchandise returned.

11 Cash sales for January 1 through January 10, $4,454.87.

11 Issued Ck. No. 6983, $2,773.40, to Valentine and Company, in payment of $2,830 invoice less discount.

14 Sold merchandise on account to Velez Appliance, invoice no. 6485, $2,100.

14 Received check from L. Parrish, $693.84, in payment of $755 invoice, less return of $47 and less discount.

19 Bought merchandise on account from Crawford Products, invoice no. 7281, $3,700; terms 2/10, n/60; dated January 16; FOB shipping point, freight prepaid and added to invoice, $142 (total $3,842).

21 Issued Ck. No. 6984, $245, to A. Bautista for miscellaneous expenses not recorded previously.

21 Cash sales for January 11 through January 20, $3,689.

23 Received credit memo no. 163, $87, from Crawford Products for merchandise returned.

29 Sold merchandise on account to Bradford Supply, invoice no. 6486, $1,697.20.

29 Issued Ck. No. 6985 to Western Freight, $64, for freight charges on merchandise purchased January 4.

31 Cash sales for January 21 through January 31, $3,862.

31 Issued Ck. No. 6986, $65, to M. Pineda for miscellaneous expenses not recorded previously.

Jan. 31 Recorded payroll entry from the payroll register: total salaries, $5,900; employees' federal income tax withheld, $795; FICA taxes withheld, $451.35.

31 Recorded the payroll taxes: FICA taxes, $451.35; state unemployment tax, $265.50; federal unemployment tax, $47.20.

31 Issued Ck. No. 6987, $4,653.65, for salaries for the month.

31 L. Yang, the owner, withdrew $1,000 for personal use, Ck. No. 6988.

Required

Check Figure
Trial balance totals, $63,187.61

1. Record the transactions for January, using a general journal, page 1. The chart of accounts is as follows:

111 Cash	311 L. Yang, Capital
113 Accounts Receivable	312 L. Yang, Drawing
114 Merchandise Inventory	
116 Prepaid Insurance	411 Sales
121 Equipment	412 Sales Returns and Allowances
	413 Sales Discounts
212 Accounts Payable	
215 Salaries Payable	511 Purchases
216 Employees' Federal Income	512 Purchases Returns and Allowances
Tax Payable	513 Purchases Discounts
217 FICA Taxes Payable	514 Freight In
218 State Unemployment	
Tax Payable	621 Salary Expense
219 Federal Unemployment	622 Payroll Tax Expense
Tax Payable	625 Supplies Expense
	627 Rent Expense
	631 Miscellaneous Expense

2. Post daily all entries involving customer accounts to the accounts receivable ledger.
3. Post daily all entries involving creditor accounts to the accounts payable ledger.
4. Post daily the general journal entries to the general ledger. Write the owner's name in the Capital and Drawing accounts.
5. Prepare a trial balance.
6. Prepare a schedule of accounts receivable and a schedule of accounts payable. Do the totals equal the balances of the related controlling accounts?

LO 1,5

PROBLEM 10-2B C. R. McIntyre Company sells candy wholesale, primarily to vending machine operators. Terms of sales on account are 2/10, n/30, FOB shipping point. The following transactions involving cash receipts and sales of merchandise took place in May of this year:

May 2 Received $411.60 cash from N. Rojas in payment of April 23 invoice of $420, less cash discount.

5 Received $2,085 cash in payment of $2,000 note receivable and interest of $85.

8 Sold merchandise on account to G. Soto, invoice no. 862, $830.

9 Received $11,838.40 cash from D. Maddox in payment of April 30 invoice of $12,080, less cash discount.

May 15 Received cash from G. Soto in payment of invoice no. 862, less cash discount.

16 Cash sales for first half of May, $3,259.

19 Received $296 cash from R. O. Higgins in payment of April 14 invoice, no discount.

22 Sold merchandise on account to N. T. Jennings, invoice no. 863 $753.

25 Received $239 cash refund for return of defective equipment bought in April for cash.

28 Sold merchandise on account to M. E. Mueller, invoice no. 864 $964.

31 Cash sales for second half of May, $4,728.

Check Figure
Total Cash Debit, $23,670.40

Required

1. Journalize the transactions for May in the cash receipts journal and the sales journal.
2. Total and rule the journals.
3. Prove the equality of debit and credit totals.

1,6  **LO**

PROBLEM 10-3B Jacobs Company had the following transactions that occurred during February of this year:

Feb. 1 Issued Ck. No. 4311, $637, to Barker Company for invoice no. 3113E, recorded previously for $650, less cash discount of $13.

2 Issued Ck. No. 4312 to Bonilla Express Company for freight charges, $48, for merchandise purchased.

4 Issued Ck. No. 4313 to Dillon Realty for monthly rent, $560.

9 Received and paid bill for advertising in *The Nickel News*, $84, Ck. No. 4314.

10 Issued Ck. No. 4315, $990, to Dorsey Company for invoice no. D642, recorded previously for $1,000, less 1 percent cash discount.

15 Paid wages recorded previously for first half of month, $1,678; Ck. No. 4316.

19 R. Jacobs, the owner, withdrew $900 for personal use; Ck. No. 4317.

25 Issued Ck. No. 4318 to First National Bank for payment on bank loan, $896, consisting of $800 on principal and $96 interest.

27 Issued Ck. No. 4319, $430, to Long Company for invoice no. 6317, recorded previously (no discount).

28 Voided Ck. No. 4320.

28 Paid wages recorded previously for second half of month, $1,648; Ck. No. 4321.

28 Received and paid telephone bill, $86; Ck. No. 4322, payable to Southwestern Telephone Company.

Check Figure
Total Cash Credit, $7,957

Required

1. Journalize the transactions for February in the cash payments journal.
2. Total and rule the journal.
3. Prove the equality of the debit and credit totals.

PROBLEM 10-4B Refer to the information for Problem 10-1B on pages 428−429.

LO 1,2,3,5,6

GL

Check Figure
Schedule of Accounts Receivable
total, $4,912.20

Required

1. Record the transactions for January, using a sales journal, page 91; a purchases journal, page 74; a cash receipts journal, page 56; a cash payments journal, page 63; and a general journal, page 119.

111 Cash	311 L. Yang, Capital
113 Accounts Receivable	312 L. Yang, Drawing
114 Merchandise Inventory	
116 Prepaid Insurance	411 Sales
121 Equipment	412 Sales Returns and Allowances
	413 Sales Discounts
212 Accounts Payable	
215 Salaries Payable	511 Purchases
216 Employees' Federal Income	512 Purchases Returns and Allowances
Tax Payable	513 Purchases Discounts
217 FICA Taxes Payable	514 Freight In
218 State Unemployment	
Tax Payable	621 Salary Expense
219 Federal Unemployment	622 Payroll Tax Expense
Tax Payable	625 Supplies Expense
	627 Rent Expense
	631 Miscellaneous Expense

2. Post daily all entries involving customer accounts to the accounts receivable ledger.
3. Post daily all entries involving creditor accounts to the accounts payable ledger.
4. Post daily those entries involving the Other Accounts columns and the general journal to the general ledger. Write the owner's name in the Capital and Drawing accounts.
5. Add the columns of the special journals, and prove the equality of debit and credit totals on scratch paper.
6. Post the appropriate totals of the special journals to the general ledger.
7. Prepare a trial balance.
8. Prepare a schedule of accounts receivable and a schedule of accounts payable. Do the totals equal the balances of the related controlling accounts?

ACTIVITIES

CONSIDER AND COMMUNICATE

You are the manager of the Accounts Receivable Department for a merchandising business. Your billing clerk sent a bill for $2 to a customer who had charged $100 in goods (including sales tax) with terms 2/10, n/30. The customer has called and indicated his displeasure; he can't understand an error like this, since he paid on time. Explain to your billing clerk why Accounts Receivable is credited for $100 and not $98. How was permission given to send less than the full amount?

WHAT'S WRONG WITH THIS PICTURE?

Suppose we collected cash from a charge customer, and our debit was to Cash and the credit to Sales. How and when would this error be discovered?

CRITICAL THINKING

You work for Gregory Plumbing Supply. You are responsible for training a new accounting clerk. He has the following questions for you to answer about this invoice:

Gregory Plumbing Supply   No. 320

14 Indiana Avenue
Chicago, Illinois 60612

INVOICE

SOLD TO: C. P. Lund Company
5210 Gilman Avenue
San Diego, CA 92102

DATE: August 1, 20—
CUSTOMER'S P.O. NO.: 5384
SHIPPED BY: Faster Freight
TERMS: 2/10, n/30
SALESPERSON: H. T.

QUANTITY	DESCRIPTION	UNIT PRICE		TOTAL	
6	Olin single-control tub shower faucet #44B652	51	50	309	00
6	Olin dual-control washerless lavatory faucet #59B641	22	20	133	20
12	Olin massage shower head, antique brass #37B411	11	56	138	72
	Subtotal			580	92
	Freight			63	80
	Total			644	72

---

1. Who is the buyer?
2. Who is paying the freight?
3. What is the customer's order number?
4. What percentage of the goods bought is the cost of the freight?
5. What are the credit terms and what do they mean?
6. How much will the buyer actually have to pay if the money is received within 10 days?
7. What is the dollar amount of the discount?
8. Who receives the discount?
9. What is the due date for payment to get the discount?
10. Why would a seller give a buyer a discount?

All About You Spa

Cash Receipts and Cash Payments

All About You Spa decided to expand into merchandising. Because of instances where goods received or sold may prove less than satisfactory, new accounts for purchases returns and allowances and sales returns and allowances need to be added to the chart of accounts. Although not applicable to this period, sales discounts may be granted to customers in the future and purchases discounts may be taken based on terms from vendors in the future, so accounts for these are being added as well. A revised chart of accounts for All About You Spa is as follows:

CHART OF ACCOUNTS FOR ALL ABOUT YOU SPA

Assets
111 Cash
113 Accounts Receivable
117 Prepaid Insurance
124 Spa Equipment
125 Accum. Depr., Spa Equip.
128 Office Equipment
129 Accum. Depr., Office Eq.

Liabilities
211 Accounts Payable
212 Wages Payable
215 Sales Tax Payable

Owner's Equity
311 A. Valli, Capital
312 A. Valli, Drawing
313 Income Summary

Revenue
411 Income from Services
412 Merchandise Sales
413 Sales Discounts
414 Sales Returns & Allow.

Purchases
511 Purchases
512 Purchases Discounts
513 Purch. Ret. & Allow.
515 Freight In

Expenses
611 Wages Expense
612 Rent Expense
613 Office Supplies Expense
614 Spa Supplies Expense
615 Laundry Expense
616 Advertising Expense
617 Utilities Expense
618 Insurance Expense
619 Depr. Expense, Spa Equip.
620 Depr. Expense, Office Eq.
630 Miscellaneous Expense

Ms. Valli has provided the trial balance as of July 31, schedules of accounts receivable and payable, as well as transactions for the month of August to be entered into the system.

Directions for August Journal Entries

1. Open the file entitled **All_About_You_Spa_Ch10.IA7**. Enter your name when prompted and click **OK**. Select "Yes" or "No" as desired when asked if you want to open on-screen instructions and check figures. As a reminder, these instructions may be opened at any time by clicking on the **Info.** toolbar button.

All About You Spa
Trial Balance
July 31, 20—

Account Name	Debit	Credit
Cash	44,969.26	
Accounts Receivable	4,568.79	
Prepaid Insurance	800.00	
Spa Equipment	17,601.00	
Accumulated Depreciation, Spa Equipment		64.88
Office Equipment	1,570.00	
Accumulated Depreciation, Office Equipment		10.00
Accounts Payable		20,720.00
Sales Tax Payable		1,829.90
A. Valli, Capital		49,884.62
A. Valli, Drawing	2,500.00	
Income from Services		12,722.00
Merchandise Sales		10,151.65
Purchases	12,868.00	
Freight In	403.00	
Wages Expense	7,004.00	
Rent Expense	1,650.00	
Office Supplies Expense	118.00	
Spa Supplies Expense	490.00	
Laundry Expense	84.00	
Utilities Expense	473.00	
Miscellaneous Expense	284.00	
	95,383.05	95,383.05

All About You Spa
Schedule of Accounts Receivable
July 31, 20—

About Face Spa	$ 521.59
Jill Anson	175.00
Chaco's	520.02
Holmes Condos	367.47
Tory Ligman	164.00
Los Obrigados Lodge	351.00
Mini Spa	222.48
Jack Morgan	286.00
Pleasant Spa	1,961.23
Total Accounts Receivable	$4,568.79

All About You Spa
Schedule of Accounts Payable
July 31, 20—

Giftco	$ 1,309.00
Golden Spa Supplies	490.00
Logo Products	3,796.00
Office Staples	304.00
Spa Equipment, Inc.	6,235.00
Spa Goods	5,445.00
Spa Magic	2,721.00
Superior Equipment	420.00
Total Accounts Payable	$20,720.00

2. Click on the **Save As** toolbar button. When the Save As window appears, select the folder in which you wish to save your data files (if not already selected). In the File Name box, key **All_About_You_Spa_Ch10_Your_Name.IA7** (for example, All_About_You_Spa_Ch10_John_Doe.IA7) to identify the file containing your work. Click on the **Save** button.

3. Click on the **Journals** toolbar button and key the journal entries for August. Use the information in the checkbook register and the transactions listings on the following pages as the basis of your entries. Follow option a or b below, as directed by your instructor.

   a. Key all August transactions into the General Journal.

   b. Key August transactions into special journals and the General Journal. Key sales on account and purchases on account transactions as you learned to do in Chapter 9. Key credit memo transactions into the General Journal. Key cash receipts and cash payments transactions as follows:

      (1) For a cash receipt, click on the **Journals** toolbar button and then the **Cash Receipts** tab.

      For a receipt of a payment on account, enter the amount of the payment in the Accounts Rec. Cr. column. The debit to Cash will automatically be entered for you by the software. Tab to the Customer column and select from the drop-down list. Then click on the **Post** button (or press Enter).

      For weekly cash sales, enter the amount received for services in the Services Inc., Cr. column, enter the amount received for merchandise in the Merch. Sales Cr. column, and enter the amount of sales tax in the Sales Tax Pay. Cr. column. The debit to Cash will automatically be calculated and entered for you by the software. Then click on the **Post** button (or press Enter).

      (2) For a cash payment, click on the **Journals** toolbar button and then the **Cash Payments** tab.

      For a payment on account, enter the check number in the Refer. column (abbreviate as "Ck.1044" for fit). Enter the amount of the payment in the Accounts Pay. Dr. column. The credit to Cash will automatically be entered for you in the Cash Cr. column. Tab to the Customer column and select from the drop-down list. Then click on the **Post** button (or press Enter).

      For all other payments, enter the check number in the Refer. column. Enter the account number of the account to be debited in the Acct. No. column (or select from the Chart of Accounts while the Acct. No. column has the focus). Enter the amount to be debited in the Debit column. The credit to Cash will automatically be entered for you in the Cash Cr. column. Then click on the **Post** button (or press Enter).

4. Generate journal reports. Click on the **Reports** toolbar button. Click on **Journals** and **General Journal** to choose the report to display. Accept the **Include All Journal Entries** option and then click the **OK** button to display the General Journal report. To print the report, click on the **Print** button. If following option 2b above, also generate a Sales Journal report, a Purchases Journal report, a Cash Payments Journal report, and a Cash Receipts Journal report in the same manner by clicking on those options in Report Selection window. Review the journal entries and make corrections as necessary.

5. Display a trial balance. Click on the **Reports** toolbar button. Click on **Ledger Reports** and **Trial Balance** to choose the report to display. To print the report, click on the **Print** button at the bottom of the report window.

6. Display a schedule of accounts receivable. Click on the **Reports** toolbar button. Click on **Ledger Reports** and **Schedule of Accounts Receivable** to choose the report to display. To print the report, click on the **Print** button at the bottom of the report window.

7. Display a schedule of accounts payable. Click on the **Reports** toolbar button. Click on **Ledger Reports** and **Schedule of Accounts Payable** to choose the report to display. To print the report, click on the **Print** button at the bottom of the report window.

8. Click on the **Save** toolbar button to save your data file.

9. Click on the **Check** toolbar button to check your solution against the answer key.

Check Figures
5. Trial balance total, August 31, $120,364.27
6. Schedule of accounts receivable total, August 31, $7,196.63
7. Schedule of accounts payable total, August 31, $20,393.00

Checkbook Register

Check No.	Date	Explanation	✓	Deposits	Check Amount
1044	8/1	Paid August's rent.			1,650.00
	8/1	Deposited Chaco's payment received on account, invoice no. 15.		400.00	
	8/1	Deposited Mini Spa's payment received on account, invoice no. 18. Paid in full.		222.48	
1045	8/1	Paid accumulated sales tax payable to State Revenue Dept.			1,829.90
1046	8/2	Paid advertising expense for August photo ad.			455.00
1047	8/2	Paid week's wages.			1,845.50
1048	8/2	Paid Spa Magic for invoice no. 5033, dated June 2. Paid in full.			2,721.00
1049	8/3	Bought silk flower arrangement for the salon (Miscellaneous Expense).			87.90
	8/3	Deposited Tory Ligman's payment received on account. Paid in full.		164.00	
1050	8/4	Bought spa supplies—5 cases of bottled water for clients (debit Spa Supplies Expense).			45.00
	8/4	Deposited Jill Anson's payment received on account.		87.50	
1051	8/5	Bought a digital camera for confidential before-and-after pictures (debit Spa Equipment).			482.00
1052	8/5	Paid Office Staples for invoice 1417, dated July 5. Paid in full.			186.00
1053	8/5	Paid on account to Giftco, invoice no. 316, dated July 5.			709.00
	8/6	Deposited Pleasant Spa's payment received on account, invoice no. 16.		997.42	
1054	8/6	Paid Golden Spa Supplies for invoice no. 1836, dated July 1. Paid in full.			490.00
	8/7	Deposited first week's cash sales: merchandise $1,630.00; services $3,350.00; sales tax collected $398.40.		5,378.40	

Check No.	Date	Explanation	✓	Deposits	Check Amount
	8/8	Deposited Los Obrigados Lodge's payment received on account, invoice no. 14.		200.00	
	8/9	Deposited Holmes Condo's payment received on account, invoice no. 17.		200.00	
1055	8/9	Paid week's wages.			1,850.00
	8/14	Deposited second week's cash sales: merchandise $1,330.00; services $2,340.00; sales tax collected $293.60.		3,963.60	
	8/15	Deposited About Face Spa's payment received on account, invoice no. 19.		265.00	
1056	8/16	Paid week's wages.			1,853.00
1057	8/18	Paid Superior Equipment for invoice no. 3608, dated July 5. Paid in full.			420.00
	8/19	Deposited Jack Morgan's payment received on account. Paid in full.		286.00	
	8/21	Deposited third week's cash sales: merchandise $2,220.00; services $2,810.00; sales tax collected $402.40.		5,432.40	
1058	8/22	Paid on account to Logo Products, invoice no. 1579, dated July 1.			2,500.00
1059	8/23	Paid on account to Spa Goods, invoice no. 312, dated July 1.			2,000.00
1060	8/23	Paid week's wages.			1,847.50
1061	8/28	Paid month's laundry bill.			95.00
1062	8/28	Owner withdrew cash for personal use.			2,500.00
1063	8/30	Paid week's wages.			1,850.00
	8/31	Deposited end of month's cash sales: merchandise $2,030.00; services $4,176.00; $496.48 sales tax.		6,702.48	
1064	8/31	Paid August telephone bill.			235.00
1065	8/31	Paid on account to Spa Equipment, Inc., invoice no. 2731, dated July 3.			3,000.00
1066	8/31	Paid August power and water bill.			255.00

Purchases Invoices for Merchandise Bought on Account During August

All About You Spa will pay all freight costs associated with purchases of merchandise to the supplier.

Date of Purchase	Transaction Information	Amount
Aug. 1	Bought logo merchandise from Giftco; invoice no. 416, dated 8/1; terms 2/10, n/30.	$4,100.00 plus $180.00 freight
1	Bought bath and beauty products from Spa Magic; invoice no. 5235, dated 8/1; terms 2/10, n/30.	$3,562.00 plus $155.00 freight
2	Bought logo merchandise from Logo Products; invoice no. 1680, dated 8/2; terms 2/10, n/30.	$2,451.00 plus $144.00 freight
5	Bought spa accessories from Spa Goods; invoice no. 387, dated 8/5; terms 2/10, n/30.	$1,120.00 plus $110.00 freight

Sales Invoices for Gift Certificates Sold on Account During August

All About You Spa is responsible for collecting and paying the sales tax on merchandise that it sells. The sales tax rate where All About You Spa does business is 8 percent of each sale; for example, $650.00 \times 0.08 = \$52.00$.

Date of Sale	Transaction Information	Sales Amount (Before Tax)
Aug. 1	About Face Spa, invoice no. 20.	$ 650.00
5	Chaco's, invoice no. 21.	395.00
8	Holmes Condos, invoice no. 22.	1,294.00
9	Pleasant Spa, invoice no. 23.	1,560.00
11	Los Obrigados Lodge, invoice no. 24.	356.00
14	Mini Spa, invoice no. 25.	873.00

Note: All gift certificates were redeemed for merchandise by the end of the month.

Other August Transactions

There were two other transactions in August. Neither involved cash.

Date	Transaction Information	Amount
Aug. 9	Issued credit memorandum no. 1 to About Face Spa for an allowance for damaged goods. (Debit the new account Sales Returns and Allowances 414.)	$ 88.00
29	Received a credit memorandum for damaged spa accessories from Spa Magic. (Credit the new account Purchases Returns and Allowances 513.)	123.00

The Voucher System of Accounting

LEARNING OBJECTIVES

After you have completed this chapter, you will be able to do the following:

1 Prepare vouchers.

2 Record vouchers in a voucher register.

3 Record payment of vouchers in a check register.

4 Record transactions involving canceling or altering an original voucher.

ACCOUNTING LANGUAGE

Voucher (p. 439)

Voucher register (p. 443)

The voucher system is a means of achieving internal control and enabling the owner or manager to maintain contact with day-to-day transactions. This system promotes the delegation of duties and responsibilities.

OBJECTIVE OF THE VOUCHER SYSTEM

The objective of the voucher system is to control the incurrence of all liabilities and the payment of all expenditures—in other words, to control the purchase of (1) merchandise or materials, (2) other assets, and (3) services. The voucher system is suitable for companies of varying sizes that require a clear separation of duties. The voucher system has the following components: vouchers, voucher register, check register, unpaid voucher file, paid voucher file, and general journal.

VOUCHERS

A **voucher** is a document that serves as proof of a transaction and, from a business point of view, also serves as a full description of the transaction. **When a business is using the voucher system, a voucher must be filled out for every invoice**

439

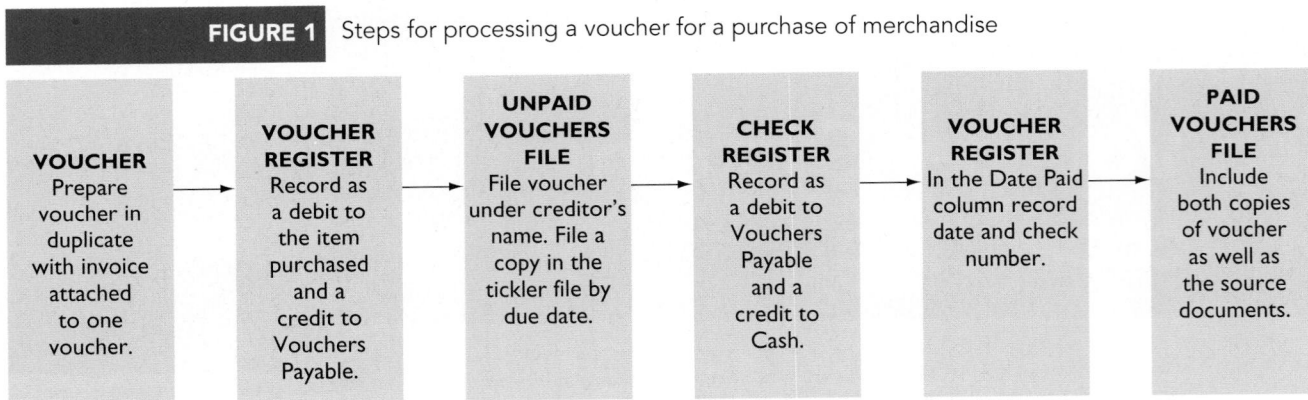

FIGURE 1   Steps for processing a voucher for a purchase of merchandise

or bill received, whether it is to be paid immediately or in the future. The invoice or bill is usually stapled to the voucher.

Characteristics of Vouchers

Just as the form of invoices varies from one company to another, so too the form of vouchers varies from one company to another. However, the following characteristics are usually present.

- Vouchers are numbered consecutively.
- The name and address of the payee or creditor appear on the voucher.
- The amount and credit terms of the invoice appear on the voucher.
- Vouchers state due dates so that firms can take advantage of possible cash discounts.
- For internal control, vouchers require signatures approving payment.
- Vouchers record payment: date paid and check number.

A completed voucher, with the invoice or bill stapled to it, describes an entire transaction as well as the procedure for processing the voucher. First, so that you can see the big picture, Figure 1 presents the steps involved in processing a voucher for a purchase of merchandise.

Preparation and Approval of Vouchers

LEARNING OBJECTIVE

1

Prepare vouchers.

To cite a familiar example, let's assume that Whitewater Raft Supply has now achieved such a volume of business that it is using a voucher system. Let's also assume that Whitewater Raft Supply has received from its supplier, Pataponia, Inc., the invoice shown here.

Pataponia, Inc.		No. 3101

1614 Olivera Street
San Francisco, CA 94129

INVOICE

SOLD TO: Whitewater Raft Supply
1400 Front Street
Seattle, WA 98101

DATE: December 1, 20—
CUSTOMER'S P.O. NO.: 9103
SHIPPED BY: Western Freight Line
TERMS: 2/10, n/30

YOUR ORDER NO.	SALESPERSON	TERMS
9103	C.L.	2/10, n/30

DATE SHIPPED	SHIPPED BY	FOB
December 1, 20—	Western Freight Line	San Francisco

QUANTITY	DESCRIPTION	UNIT PRICE	TOTAL
12	Reinforced Whitewater Spray Skirt #6020	118	95	1,427	40
	Freight			42	82
	Total			1,470	22

Whitewater Raft Supply's accountant, using the invoice as the source of information, fills out the following voucher. The face of the voucher lists the details of the transaction.

WHITEWATER RAFT SUPPLY

No. 118

1400 Front Street
Seattle, WA 98101

VOUCHER

PAY TO: Pataponia, Inc.
1614 Olivera St.
San Francisco, CA 94129

DATE _____ 12/1/20— _____

DATE OF INVOICE	TERMS	DESCRIPTION	AMOUNT	
12/1	2/10, n/30	Invoice No. 3101	1,427	40
		Less discount	28	55
		Freight	42	82
		Net amount payable	1,441	67

APPROVAL	DATES	APPROVED BY
Extensions and footings verified	12/2	M. C. L.
Prices in agreement with purchase order	12/2	S. T.
Credit terms in agreement with purchase order	12/2	S. T.
Quantities in agreement with receiving report	12/2	J. D. S.
Approved for payment	12/7	R. L. R.

ACCOUNT DISTRIBUTION

VOUCHER NO. __118__

ACCOUNT DEBITED	AMOUNT
Purchases	1,427.40
Freight In	42.82
Wages Payable	
Supplies Expense	
Miscellaneous Expense	
Total Vouchers Payable Cr.	1,470.22

DUE DATE: 12/8

PAY TO: Pataponia, Inc.
1614 Olivera Street
San Francisco, CA 94129

SUMMARY OF CHARGES

Amount of invoice	1,470.22
Less cash discount	28.55
Net amount	1,441.67

RECORD OF PAYMENT

Paid by check no.	2815
Date of check	12/8
Amount of check	1,441.67

ACCOUNT DISTRIBUTION by ___R. R. H.___

ENTERED IN VOUCHER REG. by ___M. C. L.___

> **Remember**
>
> Since the check register replaces the cash payments journal and the voucher register replaces the purchases journal, the special-column totals from the voucher register must be posted before those from the check register.

The *due date* represents the last day on which one can take advantage of the cash discount. For example, the invoice of Pataponia, Inc., was dated December 1, with terms of 2/10, n/30. The discount period ends on December 11. Therefore, at the latest, send the check on December 8 to receive the discount.

The Account Distribution section is used to record the account titles and amounts to be debited, the total amount to be credited to Vouchers Payable, and the initials of the person authorized to determine the distribution.

THE VOUCHERS PAYABLE ACCOUNT

When you use a voucher system, you substitute the Vouchers Payable account for Accounts Payable. For example, when a firm buys merchandise on account, the accountant enters it as a debit to Purchases and a credit to Vouchers Payable. Similarly, when a firm buys store equipment on account, the accountant records it as a debit to Store Equipment and a credit to Vouchers Payable. Also, if a company incurs an expense on account, such as Advertising, the entry is a debit to Advertising Expense and a credit to Vouchers Payable.

When a check is issued in payment of a voucher, record the entry in the check register as a debit to Vouchers Payable and a credit to Cash. Again, we emphasize that *all* liabilities are recorded in the Vouchers Payable account.

Date	Vou. No.	Creditor	Payment Date	Ck. No.	Vouchers Payable Credit	Purchases Debit
20—						
Dec. 1	117	Fast-Way Freight	12 1	2808	6 3 00	
1	118	Pataponia, Inc.	12 8	2815	1 4 7 0 22	1 4 2 7 40
3	119	Dell Office Supply	12 3	2809	4 8 72	
5	120	Stable Ins. Company	12 5	2812	1 7 4 00	
9	121	Langseth and Son	12 18	2829	3 2 8 00	3 0 6 00
10	122	Payroll Bank Account	12 10	2818	1 6 9 0 00	
12	123	Southland Journal			1 7 6 00	
12	124	Bradley Construction	12 12	2820	1 1 6 00	
15	125	D. M. Bruce	12 15	2824	5 0 0 00	
15	126	C. A. Waters, Inc.	12 18	Note	4 2 1 00	4 2 1 00
29	149	Dana Mfg. Company			7 1 4 00	7 1 4 00
30	150	Safety National Bank	12 30	2837	1 5 0 7 50	
31		Totals			11 6 7 4 90	5 0 9 5 10
					(2 1 2)	(5 1 1)

	Debits		Credit
Purchases	$ 5,095.10	Vouchers Payable	$11,674.90
Freight In	234.32		
Wages Payable	3,314.00		
Supplies Expense	121.79		
Miscellaneous Expense	83.69		
Other Accounts	2,826.00		
	$11,674.90		

THE VOUCHER REGISTER

2 LEARNING OBJECTIVE

Record vouchers in a voucher register.

The **voucher register** has the status of a journal; it is a book of original entry. All vouchers must be recorded in it, in numerical order. Think of it as a multicolumn purchases journal. The voucher register has only one credit column, Vouchers Payable Credit, but a number of debit columns. Headings for the debit columns are selected on the basis of their frequency of use. In addition to the special columns, the voucher register also has space for recording the voucher number, the name of the creditor, the date of payment, and the check number. The voucher register for Whitewater Raft Supply appears below.

When you first record the voucher, leave the Payment Date and Ck. No. columns blank. After you have recorded the payment in the check register, go back to the voucher register and enter the date of payment and the number of the check.

> A voucher is prepared for every invoice or bill the company receives.

> Remember

Posting from the Voucher Register

The entries in the Other Accounts columns are posted *daily* to the general ledger, just as the Other Accounts columns of the other special journals are posted daily.

VOUCHER REGISTER   PAGE 3

Freight In Debit	Wages Payable Debit	Supplies Expense Debit	Miscellaneous Expense Debit	Other Accounts Debit Account	Post. Ref.	Amount
	63 00					
	42 82					
		48 72				
				Prepaid Insurance	116	1 74 00
22 00						
	1 690 00					
				Advertising Expense	618	1 76 00
				Sales Returns and Allowances	412	1 16 00
				D. M. Bruce, Drawing	312	5 00 00
				Notes Payable	211	1 5 00 00
				Interest Expense	634	7 50
2 34 32	3 3 14 00	1 21 79	83 69			2 8 26 00
(5 1 4)	(2 1 3)	(6 2 2)	(6 1 9)			(X)

The (X) under the column total means "do not post." At the end of the month, total all the columns, and prove the equality of the debit and credit entries by comparing the combined total of the debit columns with the total of the Vouchers Payable Credit column.

THE CHECK REGISTER

3 LEARNING OBJECTIVE

Record payment of vouchers in a check register.

Any company or organization using a voucher system uses both the voucher register and the check register as books of original entry. Now let's look at the procedure for the check register. Since checks are issued only in payment of approved and recorded vouchers, the entry in the check register is always a debit to Vouchers Payable and a credit to Cash. A Vouchers Payable Debit column in the check register offsets the Vouchers Payable Credit column in the voucher register. Recall that after you record the entry in the check register, you enter the date and check number on the appropriate line in the voucher register and on the outside of the voucher in the Record of Payment section.

						Vouchers Payable Debit			Purchases Discounts Credit			Cash Credit		
CHECK REGISTER													**PAGE 11**	
Date		Ck. No.	Payee	Vou. No.										
20—														
Dec.	1	2808	Fast-Way Freight	117		6	3	00				6	3	00
	3	2809	Dell Office Supply	119		4	8	72				4	8	72
	3	2810	Gardner Products Company	114	2	0	6	00	2	06	2	0	3	94
	4	2811	Dana Manufacturing Company	115	5	4	0	00	1 0	80	5	2	9	20
	5	2812	Stable Insurance Company	120	1	7	4	00			1	7	4	00
	6	2813	Void											
	6	2814	Langseth and Son	116	4	6	4	00	9	28	4	5	4	72
	8	2815	Pataponia, Inc.	118	1 4	7	0	22	2 8	55	1 4	4	1	67
	30	2837	Safety National Bank	150	1 5	0	7	50			1 5	0	7	50
	31		Totals		7 2	8	1	20	9 0	09	7 1	9	1	11
					(2	1	2	)	(5 1	3)	(1 1	1	)	

Debit	Credit
$7,281.20	$ 90.09
	7,191.11
	$7,281.20

HANDLING OF UNPAID VOUCHERS

Firms usually prepare vouchers in duplicate. In the system used by Whitewater Raft Supply, the invoice is attached to the original copy of the voucher. Then the voucher is circulated within the company for the necessary signatures. After a voucher is recorded in the voucher register, it is filed under the name of the creditor. (Other companies may prepare only one copy of the voucher and file it only under the date on which it is supposed to be paid.)

At Whitewater Raft Supply, the Unpaid Vouchers file contains all outstanding vouchers or credit memos. This file, organized by names of creditors, now acts as a subsidiary ledger. In fact, at Whitewater Raft Supply, this file substitutes for the accounts payable ledger.

The *second* copy of the voucher goes to the treasurer, who files it chronologically by due date. This tickler file (a file of unpaid vouchers filed by due date) helps the treasurer forecast the amount of cash that will be needed to pay outstanding bills and take advantage of cash discounts.

At the end of the month, the accountant lists all the vouchers payable, taking the information directly from the Unpaid Vouchers file.

> **Remember**
> The Vouchers Payable account is a controlling account, similar to Accounts Payable being a controlling account.

Whitewater Raft Supply Schedule of Vouchers Payable December 31, 20—		
Vou. No.	**Name of Creditor**	**Amount**
123	Southland Journal	$176
149	Dana Manufacturing Company	714
	Total Vouchers Payable	$890

FILING PAID VOUCHERS

Now let's assume that the firm has paid its bill. The payment is recorded in the check register and in the Payment columns of the voucher register. Then the voucher is stapled to the copy in the tickler file, marked paid, and filed in numerical order in a Paid Vouchers file.

SITUATIONS REQUIRING SPECIAL TREATMENT

When a firm is using the voucher system, it inevitably runs into an occasional nonroutine transaction that does not fit into the fixed channels of the voucher system and therefore may require an entry in the general journal. You can consider such treatment as an adjustment to the voucher system.

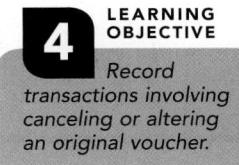

4 LEARNING OBJECTIVE

Record transactions involving canceling or altering an original voucher.

Return of a Purchase Before Original Voucher Has Been Recorded

Normally, if a business with an efficient purchasing department is going to return any merchandise, it returns the merchandise before the vouchers are recorded in the voucher register. The accountant records the deduction right on the invoice and records the invoice in the voucher register for the net amount.

Return of a Purchase After Original Voucher Has Been Recorded

Assume that a business purchased merchandise for $566. The transaction was recorded in the voucher register as a debit to Purchases and a credit to Vouchers Payable. Later, the company returns $26 worth of defective merchandise. The return is recorded in the general journal as a debit to Vouchers Payable and a credit to Purchases Returns and Allowances. A notation "Return" is entered in the Payment column of the voucher register.

Installment Payments Planned at Time of Original Purchase

In a voucher system, invoices not subject to cash discounts are generally paid in full. Sometimes, however, management prefers to pay for an item in installments. When this happens, the company's accountant prepares a separate voucher for each installment and records each of these vouchers in the voucher register. Each voucher's due date corresponds to the date on which that installment is to be paid.

Installment Payments After Original Voucher Has Been Recorded

However, suppose that the buyer records the entire amount of the invoice on one voucher and *later* decides to pay the invoice in installments. The accountant must now cancel the original voucher by means of a general journal entry and issue a new voucher for each installment. A notation listing the new voucher numbers is made in the Payment column of the voucher register.

Correcting an Amount After Original Voucher Has Been Recorded

If an error in the purchase of merchandise is discovered after the voucher has been recorded in the voucher register, the original voucher must be canceled by means of a general journal entry debiting Vouchers Payable and crediting Purchases. Next, a new entry is made in the voucher register for the correct amount, debiting Purchases and crediting Vouchers Payable. A notation listing the new voucher number is made in the Payment column of the voucher register.

Issuing a Note Payable After Original Voucher Has Been Recorded

If a note is issued for the amount of an unpaid invoice after the voucher has been recorded, an entry must be made in the general journal to cancel the original voucher. The entry is a debit to Vouchers Payable and a credit to Notes Payable. A notation, "Note," is made in the Date Paid column of the voucher register. When the note is to be paid, a new voucher is issued for the amount of the principal and interest, debiting Notes Payable and Interest Expense and crediting Vouchers Payable.

Glossary

Voucher A document that serves as proof of a transaction and, from a business point of view, also serves as a full description of the transaction. (p. 439)

Voucher register A book of original entry in which all vouchers are recorded in numerical order. (p. 443)

Problems

2,3 **LO**

PROBLEM 10A-1 Saenz Company uses a voucher system in which it records invoices at the **gross amount**. The following vouchers were issued during February and were unpaid on March 1:

Voucher Number	Company	For	Date of Voucher	Amount
1729	Kipley Company	Merchandise, FOB destination	Feb. 26	$3,436
1732	J. R. Steven	Merchandise, FOB destination	Feb. 28	4,710

The following transactions were completed during March:

Mar. 3 Issued voucher no. 1734 in favor of Larry Company for March rent, $1,220.

3 Issued Ck. No. 1829 in payment of voucher no. 1734, $1,220.

5 Bought merchandise on account from Lorenzo, Inc., $3,890; terms 2/10, n/30; FOB shipping point; freight prepaid and added to the invoice, $72 (total, $3,962). Issued voucher no. 1735.

5 Issued Ck. No. 1830 in payment of voucher no. 1729, $3,401.64 ($3,436 less 1 percent cash discount).

9 Issued voucher no. 1736 in favor of Mario Electric Company for electric bill, $216.

9 Issued Ck. No. 1831 in payment of voucher no. 1736, $216.

9 Issued Ck. No. 1832 in payment of voucher no. 1732, $4,615.80 ($4,710 less 2 percent cash discount).

13 Issued Ck. No. 1833 in payment of voucher no. 1735, less the cash discount, $3,884.20. Recall that the freight portion is not eligible for discount.

16 Bought merchandise on account from McGinnis Manufacturing Company, $6,260; terms 2/10 EOM; FOB destination. Issued voucher no. 1737.

25 Issued voucher no. 1738 for note payable previously recorded in the general journal: principal, $4,000, plus $30 interest. The note is payable to the Keller State Bank.

25 Issued Ck. No. 1834 in payment of voucher no. 1737, $6,134.80 ($6,260 less 2 percent cash discount).

31 Issued voucher no. 1739 for wages payable, $4,985, in favor of the payroll bank account. (Assume that the payroll entry was previously recorded in the general journal.)

31 Paid voucher no. 1739 by issuing Ck. No. 1835, $4,985, payable to Payroll Bank Account.

Required

1. Using the voucher issue date, enter the unpaid invoices in the voucher register (page 65), beginning with voucher no. 1729. Then draw double lines across all columns to separate the vouchers of February from those of March.
2. Record the transactions for March in the voucher register. Also record the appropriate transactions in the check register (page 71).
3. Total and rule the voucher register and the check register.
4. Prove the equality of the debits and credits in the voucher register and the check register.

Check Figure
Voucher Register, Vouchers Payable Credit total, $20,673

PROBLEM 10A-2 Hartman Company, which uses a voucher system, has the following unpaid vouchers on July 1. The firm follows the practice of recording vouchers at the **gross amount**.

Voucher Number	Company	For	Date of Voucher	Amount
4789	Garrison and Son	Store equipment	June 15	$ 4,996
4795	Fenner and Company	Merchandise, FOB destination	June 28	8,571
4797	J. R. Paige Company	Merchandise, FOB destination	June 28	10,710

The company completed the following transactions during July:

July   1   Issued voucher no. 4800 in favor of Mortenson Insurance Company for a premium on a 12-month fire insurance policy, $890.

2   Paid voucher no. 4789 by issuing Ck. No. 8219, $4,996.

2   Issued Ck. No. 8220 in payment of voucher no. 4800, $890.

3   Issued voucher no. 4801 in favor of Quinn Quick Freight for transportation charges on merchandise purchases, $223.

5   Paid voucher no. 4801 by issuing Ck. No. 8221, $223.

7   Issued Ck. No. 8222 in payment of voucher no. 4795, $8,485.29 ($8,571 less 1 percent cash discount).

8   Issued Ck. No. 8223 in payment of voucher no. 4797, $10,602.90 ($10,710 less 1 percent cash discount).

11   Established a petty cash fund of $250. Issued voucher no. 4802.

11   Paid voucher no. 4802 by issuing Ck. No. 8224, $250.

13   Issued voucher no. 4803 in favor of Mohammad Company for merchandise, $14,708; terms 2/10, n/30; FOB shipping point; freight prepaid and added to the invoice, $384 (total, $15,092).

15   Received bill for advertising in the *Weekly Ads*. Issued voucher no. 4804 in the amount of $410.

17   Received a credit memo for $764 from Mohammad Company for merchandise returned to them, credit memo no. 540 (pertaining to voucher no. 4803).

20   Issued voucher no. 4805 in favor of Vinson County for six months' property tax (Prepaid Property Taxes), $2,272.

20   Paid voucher no. 4805 by issuing Ck. No. 8225, $2,272.

21   Issued Ck. No. 8226 in payment of voucher no. 4803, $14,049.12 ($14,708 less $764 return, less cash discount, plus freight).

23   Bought merchandise on account from Summers and Company, $6,039; terms 1/10, n/30; FOB destination. Issued voucher no. 4806.

27   Received a credit memo for $984 from Summers and Company for damaged merchandise, credit memo no. 437 (pertaining to voucher no. 4806).

31   Issued voucher no. 4807 to reimburse petty cash fund. The charges were:

Supplies Expense	$110.43
H. Hartman, Drawing	75.00
Miscellaneous Expense	39.67

31   Issued Ck. No. 8227 in payment of voucher no. 4807, $225.10.

31   Issued voucher no. 4808 for wages payable, $8,448, in favor of the payroll bank account. (Assume that the payroll entry was recorded previously in the general journal.)

31   Paid voucher no. 4808 by issuing Ck. No. 8228, payable to Payroll Bank Account.

Check Figure
Check Register, Cash Credit total
$50,441.41

Required

1. Using the voucher issue date, enter the unpaid invoices in the voucher register (page 75), beginning with voucher no. 4789. Then draw double lines across all columns to separate the vouchers of June from those of July.

2. Enter the transactions for July in the voucher register at the **gross amount**. Also record the appropriate transactions in the check register (page 86) and the general journal (page 41).

3. Total and rule the voucher register and the check register for the transactions recorded during July.

4. Prove the equality of the debits and credits on the voucher register and the check register.

PROBLEM 10A-3 Nathan Systems uses a voucher system in which it records invoices at the **gross amount**. During October, it completed the following transactions:

Oct. 2 Issued voucher no. 2632 in favor of Myers and Horn for the purchase of merchandise with an invoice price of $5,831; terms n/30; FOB shipping point; freight prepaid and added to the invoice, $192 (total, $6,023). Leave an extra line after this entry.

3 Issued vouchers no. 2633 for $1,010, 2634 for $1,010, and 2635 for $1,010. The debt arose because Nathan Systems bought a laptop and printer from Fitzpatrick, Inc., The terms are $1,010 cash on delivery, $1,010 in 30 days, and $1,010 in 60 days. (Use three lines.)

5 Issued Ck. No. 2725 in payment of voucher no. 2633, $1,010.

9 Issued voucher no. 2636 in favor of Cordero Company for the purchase of supplies, $360.50; terms n/30.

12 Issued voucher no. 2637 in favor of Goode Realty for rent for the month, $1,650.

12 Issued Ck. No. 2726 in payment of voucher no. 2637, $1,650.

16 Issued voucher no. 2638 in favor of French Cargo for freight charges on merchandise purchased, $104.

16 Issued voucher no. 2639 in favor of Holley Company for the purchase of merchandise having a list price of $6,512 with a 25 percent trade discount (record voucher for $4,884); terms 2/10, n/30; FOB shipping point. Leave an extra line after this entry.

16 Issued Ck. No. 2727 in payment of voucher no. 2638, $104.00.

16 Canceled voucher no. 2632 because the invoice will be paid in two installments as follows: voucher no. 2640, payable November 1, $3,011.50; voucher no. 2641, payable November 15, $3,011.50. Issued vouchers no. 2640 and 2641.

17 Received a credit memo from Holley Company for merchandise returned, $352, credit memo no. 580, voucher no. 2639.

22 Issued voucher no. 2642 in favor of Pardo Telephone Company for telephone bill, $164.90.

22 Issued Ck. No. 2728 in payment of voucher no. 2642, $164.90.

23 Issued Ck. No. 2729 in payment of voucher no. 2639, $4,441.36. ($4,884 less $352 return, less cash discount.)

31 Issued voucher no. 2643 for wages payable, $4,550, in favor of Payroll Bank Account. (Assume that the payroll entry was recorded previously in the general journal.)

31 Issued Ck. No. 2730 in payment of voucher no. 2643, $4,550.

31 Issued voucher no. 2644 in favor of N. S. Nathan, the owner, for personal withdrawal, $1,400.

31 Issued Ck. No. 2731 in payment of voucher no. 2644, $1,400.

Required

1. Record the transactions for October in the voucher register (page 32), the check register (page 34), and the general journal (page 18).
2. Total and rule the voucher register and the check register.
3. Prove the equality of the debits and credits on the voucher register and the check register.
4. Post the amounts from the registers and the general journal to the Vouchers Payable account, No. 212. Assume no previous balance in the account. (Posting from the voucher register should be marked as VR32. Posting from the check register should be marked as CkR34.)
5. Prepare a schedule of vouchers payable. Compare this total with the balance of the Vouchers Payable account.

Work Sheet and Adjusting Entries

11

BURT'S BEES, Durham, North Carolina

Burt's Bees describes itself as an "Earth Friendly, Natural Personal Care Company" making products for health, beauty, and personal hygiene. The company manufactures over 150 products distributed in nearly 30,000 retail outlets worldwide.

As a merchandising company, Burt's Bees closely follows its inventory. This requires monitoring the receipt, production, purchasing, and planning of inventory. At the end of each time period, Burt's Bees must make necessary adjusting entries in order to prepare its financial statements accurately. Many of the adjustments are entries that you have already learned, such as depreciation, expiration of prepaid expenses, and recording accrued expenses. However, merchandising companies also require adjusting entries related to merchandise inventory. In this chapter, you will learn how companies such as Burt's Bees monitor inventory, prepare a work sheet, and record adjusting entries using either the perpetual or periodic inventory system.

WHY IT MATTERS

LEARNING OBJECTIVES

After you have completed this chapter, you will be able to do the following:

1 Prepare an adjustment for supplies.

2 Prepare an adjustment for unearned revenue.

3 Prepare an adjustment for merchandise inventory under the periodic inventory system.

4 Record the adjustment data in a work sheet (including merchandise inventory, unearned revenue, supplies remaining, expired insurance, depreciation, and accrued wages or salaries).

5 Complete the work sheet.

6 Journalize the adjusting entries for a merchandising business under the periodic inventory system.

7 Prepare and journalize the adjusting entry for merchandise inventory under the perpetual inventory system.

ACCOUNTING LANGUAGE

Inventory shrinkage *(p. 464)*   **Unearned revenue** *(p. 453)*
Physical inventory *(p. 455)*

We have talked about the journals and accounts kept by a merchandising business. Now we take another step toward completing the accounting cycle by presenting the related adjustments and the work sheet. First, let's briefly review the adjusting entries that you have learned so far. To begin, look over the following accounts. Here are the data for the adjustments, along with the related adjusting entries:

Insurance expired, $3,600. (The amount expired is the amount used.)

Prepaid Insurance

	+		−	
Bal.	4,000	Adj.	3,600	
Bal.	**400**			

Insurance Expense

	+	−
Adj.	3,600	

Additional depreciation, $1,800. (Add to both accounts.)

Depreciation Expense, Equipment

	+	−
Adj.	1,800	

Accumulated Depreciation, Equipment

	−	+	
		Bal.	11,000
		Adj.	1,800
		Bal.	**12,800**

Accrued wages (owed but not yet paid), $2,900. (Add to both accounts.)

Wages Expense

	+	−
Bal.	25,000	
Adj.	2,900	
Bal.	**27,900**	

Wages Payable

	−	+	
		Adj.	2,900

In this chapter, we introduce three more adjusting entries:

1. **Supplies.** This adjustment can be used for merchandising and manufacturing businesses.

2. **Unearned revenue.** This adjustment could apply to either a merchandising, manufacturing, or a service business.

3. **Merchandise inventory.** This adjustment is used exclusively for a merchandising business. We will show adjusting entries for both the periodic inventory and perpetual inventory methods.

ADJUSTMENT FOR SUPPLIES

Previously, when we were talking about the buying of supplies for a service business, we debited Supplies Expense and credited Cash or Accounts Payable.

When a merchandising business buys supplies for cash or on credit, the accounting would generally be the same as for a service business. However, if the amount of supplies held at the end of the accounting period is substantial, then an adjustment should be made to capitalize the supplies that were not consumed during the accounting period. The adjustment would be to debit Supplies (an asset account) and credit Supplies Expense. The amount is determined by a physical count of the supplies left over. For a retail business, supplies would consist of everything from paper or plastic bags to paper forms.

As an illustration, let's say that Marlin & Co. has a balance of $12,000 in the Supplies Expense account as a result of buying supplies during the fiscal period. Now, by taking a count of the supplies on hand, it is determined that $9,052 of supplies are left.

To record the amount of the supplies used, Marlin & Co. has to make an adjusting entry. The purpose of an adjusting entry is to bring the books up to date at the end of the accounting period.

Let's look at this in T account form. We need to add to the balance sheet the supplies still on hand at the end of the accounting period (debit Supplies, an asset account) and reduce the amount of supplies expensed during the accounting period (credit Supplies Expense).

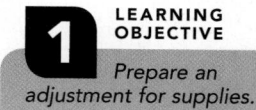

LEARNING OBJECTIVE 1

Prepare an adjustment for supplies.

Remember

For the adjustment of supplies, first find the amount of the adjustment by determining the amount of the supplies that remain. In the adjusting entry, deduct the amount of the remaining supplies from Supplies Expense and add it to the asset account Supplies.

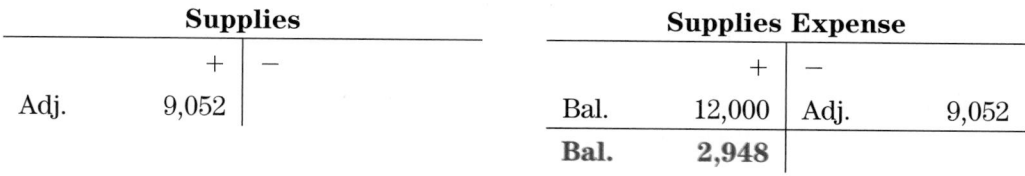

	Supplies				Supplies Expense		
	+	−			+	−	
Adj.	9,052			Bal.	12,000	Adj.	9,052
				Bal.	**2,948**		

ADJUSTMENT FOR UNEARNED REVENUE

Now let's introduce another adjusting entry, **unearned revenue**, which is cash received in advance for goods or services to be delivered or performed later. This entry could pertain to a service business as well as to a merchandising or manufacturing business. Frequently, cash is received in advance for services to be performed in the future. For example, a professional sports team sells tickets in advance, a concert association sells season tickets in advance, a magazine publisher sells subscriptions in advance, and an insurance company receives premiums in advance. If the cash

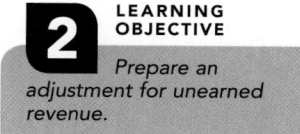

LEARNING OBJECTIVE 2

Prepare an adjustment for unearned revenue.

College students pay in advance to participate in a meal plan. Until all those meals are consumed, this money represents *unearned revenue* for the college or university dining hall services.

© DAVID MENDELSOHN/MASTERFILE

amounts received by each of these organizations will be earned during the present fiscal period, the amounts should be credited to revenue accounts. On the other hand, if the amounts received will *not* be earned during the current fiscal period, the amounts should be credited to unearned revenue accounts. **An unearned revenue account is classified as a liability,** because an organization is liable for (owes) the amount received in advance until it is earned.

To illustrate, assume that on April 1, Ressor Publishing Company receives $73,000 in cash for subscriptions paid in advance and records them originally as debits to Cash and credits to Unearned Subscriptions. At the end of the year, Ressor finds that $32,400 of the subscriptions has been earned. Accordingly, Ressor's accountant makes an adjusting entry, debiting Unearned Subscriptions and crediting Subscriptions Income. In other words, the accountant takes the earned portion out of Unearned Subscriptions and adds it to Subscriptions Income. T accounts show the situation as follows:

	Cash				**Unearned Subscriptions**		
	+	−			−	+	
Apr. 1	73,000			Dec. 31 Adj.	32,400	Apr. 1	73,000
						Bal.	**40,600**

	Subscriptions Income	
	−	+
		Dec. 31 Adj. 32,400

To look at another example, suppose that Trey's Landscape Supply offers a how-to course in landscape maintenance. On November 1, Trey's Landscape Supply receives $2,400 in fees for a three-month course. Because Trey's Landscape Supply's fiscal period ends on December 31, the three months' worth of fees received in advance will not all be earned during this fiscal period. Therefore, Trey's Landscape Supply's accountant records the transaction as a debit to Cash of $2,400 and a credit to Unearned Course Fees of $2,400. Unearned Course Fees is a liability account, because Trey's Landscape Supply must complete the how-to course or refund a portion of the money it collected. **Any account beginning with the word *Unearned* is always a liability.**

On December 31, because two months' worth of course fees have now been earned, Trey's Landscape Supply's accountant makes an adjusting entry to transfer $1,600 (⅔ of $2,400) from Unearned Course Fees to Course Fees Income. T accounts for the entries look like this:

Cash			Unearned Course Fees			
	+	−		−	+	
Nov. 1	2,400		Dec. 31 Adj.	1,600	Nov. 1	2,400
					Bal.	800

Course Fees Income		
−	+	
	Dec. 31 Adj.	1,600

ADJUSTMENT FOR MERCHANDISE INVENTORY USING THE PERIODIC INVENTORY SYSTEM

Under the periodic inventory system, we do not make an entry in the Merchandise Inventory account until an actual **physical inventory** or count of the stock of goods on hand has been taken. Instead, we record the purchase of merchandise as a debit to Purchases for the amount of the cost and the sale of the merchandise as a credit to Sales for the amount of the selling price. Finally, after a physical count of merchandise has been taken, one method of adjusting inventory is to make two adjusting entries to record the dollar amount of the inventory. The first adjusting entry is to remove the beginning inventory. The second entry is to enter the ending inventory.

Consider this example. A firm has a Merchandise Inventory balance of $183,000, which represents the cost of the inventory at the beginning of the fiscal period. At the end of the fiscal period, the firm takes an actual count of the stock on hand and determines the cost of the ending inventory to be $186,000. Naturally, in any business, goods are constantly being bought, sold, and replaced. The cost of the ending inventory is larger than the cost of the beginning inventory because the firm bought more than it sold. When we adjust the Merchandise Inventory account, we place the new figure of $186,000 in the account. This method requires two steps.

STEP 1. Eliminate the amount of the beginning inventory from the Merchandise Inventory account by transferring the amount into Income Summary. (Remove the beginning inventory.)

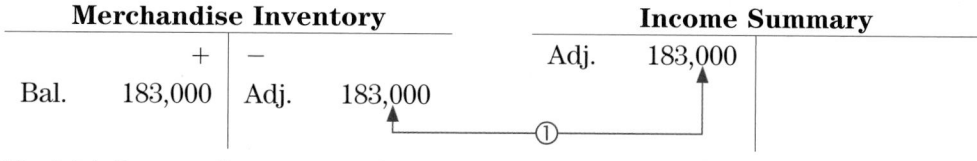

We debit Income Summary and then credit Merchandise Inventory.

3 LEARNING OBJECTIVE

Prepare an adjustment for merchandise inventory under the periodic inventory system.

The Income Summary account is the same Income Summary account that we used to record closing entries for service businesses. Income Summary now has the extra function of being the balancing or offsetting account in the adjustment of Merchandise Inventory.

Remember

STEP 2. Enter the ending or latest physical count of Merchandise Inventory, because you must record on the books the cost of the asset remaining on hand. (Enter the ending inventory.)

Let's repeat the T accounts, showing step 1 and adding step 2.

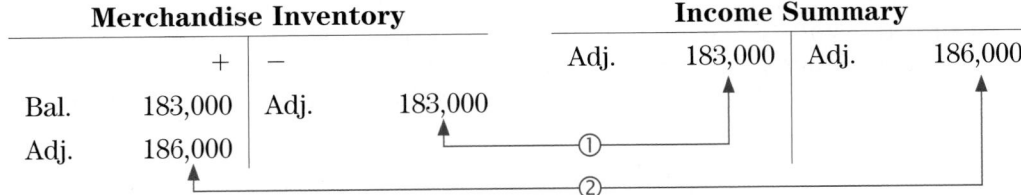

In step 2, we debit Merchandise Inventory (recording the asset on the plus side of the account) and credit Income Summary.

The reason for adjusting the Merchandise Inventory account in these two steps is that both the beginning and the ending amounts appear as distinct figures in the Income Statement columns of a work sheet, and these columns are used as the basis for preparing the income statement.

Whitewater Raft Supply's chart of accounts follows. Notice that Whitewater Raft Supply has an account titled Unearned Course Fees. In addition to selling rafting supplies, Whitewater Raft Supply also provides courses to small business owners on how to start and run a successful rafting company. If the small business owner pays in advance for the course before it is offered, the receipt of cash is recorded as Unearned Course Fees. The account number arrangement will be discussed in Chapter 12.

Assets (100–199)
111 Cash
112 Notes Receivable
113 Accounts Receivable
114 Merchandise Inventory
115 Supplies
116 Prepaid Insurance
121 Land
122 Building
123 Accumulated Depreciation, Building
124 Equipment
125 Accumulated Depreciation, Equipment

Liabilities (200–299)
211 Notes Payable
212 Accounts Payable
213 Wages Payable
217 Unearned Course Fees
221 Mortgage Payable

Owner's Equity (300–399)
311 D. M. Bruce, Capital
312 D. M. Bruce, Drawing
313 Income Summary

Revenue (400–499)
411 Sales
412 Sales Returns and Allowances
413 Sales Discounts
421 Course Fees Income
422 Interest Income

Cost of Goods Sold (500–599)
511 Purchases
512 Purchases Returns and Allowances
513 Purchases Discounts
514 Freight In

Expenses (600–699)
611 Wages Expense
622 Supplies Expense
623 Insurance Expense
624 Depreciation Expense, Building
625 Depreciation Expense, Equipment
626 Property Tax Expense
634 Interest Expense

Before we demonstrate how to record adjustments, let's first look at the trial balance section of Whitewater Raft Supply's work sheet (Figure 1).

FIGURE 1 Trial balance section of Whitewater Raft Supply's work sheet

Whitewater Raft Supply
Work Sheet
For Year Ended December 31, 20—

Account Name	Trial Balance Debit	Trial Balance Credit	Adjustments Debit	Adjustments Credit
Cash	24 1 5 4 00			
Notes Receivable	4 0 0 0 00			
Accounts Receivable	29 5 4 6 00			
Merchandise Inventory	67 0 0 0 00			
Prepaid Insurance	9 6 0 00			
Land	122 1 0 0 00			
Building	129 0 0 0 00			
Accumulated Depreciation, Building		51 0 0 0 00		
Equipment	33 1 0 0 00			
Accumulated Depreciation, Equipment		16 4 0 0 00		
Notes Payable		36 6 0 0 00		
Accounts Payable		3 3 0 0 00		
Unearned Course Fees		1 2 0 0 00		
Mortgage Payable		7 8 0 0 00		
D. M. Bruce, Capital		253 7 7 4 00		
D. M. Bruce, Drawing	77 0 0 0 00			
Sales		257 1 8 0 00		
Sales Returns and Allowances	9 4 0 00			
Sales Discounts	1 9 8 0 00			
Interest Income		2 2 0 00		
Purchases	87 8 4 0 00			
Purchases Returns and Allowances		9 3 2 00		
Purchases Discounts		1 3 4 8 00		
Freight In	2 3 6 0 00			
Wages Expense	45 9 0 0 00			
Supplies Expense	1 5 4 0 00			
Property Tax Expense	1 8 6 0 00			
Interest Expense	4 7 4 00			
	629 7 5 4 00	629 7 5 4 00		

DATA FOR THE ADJUSTMENTS

Listing the adjustment data appears to be a relatively minor task. In a business situation, however, one must take actual physical counts of the inventories and match them up with costs. One must check insurance policies to determine the amount of insurance that has expired. Finally, one must systematically write off, or depreciate, the cost of buildings and equipment.

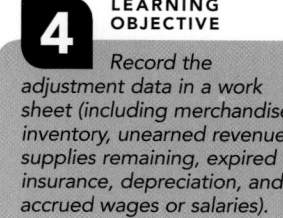

4 LEARNING OBJECTIVE

Record the adjustment data in a work sheet (including merchandise inventory, unearned revenue, supplies remaining, expired insurance, depreciation, and accrued wages or salaries).

Here are the adjustment data for Whitewater Raft Supply. We will show the adjustments recorded in T accounts.

a–b. Ending merchandise inventory, $64,800. The adjustments for inventory are generally placed first.

Merchandise Inventory		
	+	−
Bal.	67,000	**(a)** Adj. 67,000
(b) Adj. 64,800		

Income Summary	
(a) Adj. 67,000	**(b)** Adj. 64,800

c. Course fees earned, $800.

Unearned Course Fees		
	−	+
(c) Adj. 800	Bal.	1,200

Course Fees Income	
−	+
	(c) Adj. 800

d. Ending supplies inventory, $415.

Supplies		
	+	−
(d) Adj. 415		

Supplies Expense		
	+	−
Bal.	1,540	**(d)** Adj. 415

e. Insurance expired, $520.

Prepaid Insurance		
	+	−
Bal.	960	**(e)** Adj. 520

Insurance Expense		
	+	−
(e) Adj. 520		

f. Additional year's depreciation of building, $3,500.

Accumulated Depreciation, Building		
	−	+
		Bal. 51,000
		(f) Adj. 3,500

Depreciation Expense, Building		
	+	−
(f) Adj. 3,500		

g. Additional year's depreciation of equipment, $4,900.

Accumulated Depreciation, Equipment		
	−	+
		Bal. 16,400
		(g) Adj. 4,900

Depreciation Expense, Equipment		
	+	−
(g) Adj. 4,900		

h. Wages owed but not paid to employees at end of year, $1,030.

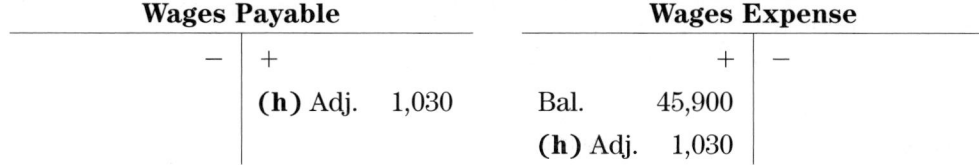

Wages Payable		Wages Expense	
−	+	+	−
	(h) Adj. 1,030	Bal. 45,900	
		(h) Adj. 1,030	

We now record these in the Adjustments columns of the work sheet, using the same letters to identify the adjustments (see Figure 2).

FIGURE 2   Trial balance and adjustments sections of Whitewater Raft Supply's work sheet

Whitewater Raft Supply
Work Sheet
For Year Ended December 31, 20—

Account Name	Trial Balance Debit	Trial Balance Credit	Adjustments Debit	Adjustments Credit
Cash	24 1 5 4 00			
Notes Receivable	4 0 0 0 00			
Accounts Receivable	29 5 4 6 00			
Merchandise Inventory	67 0 0 0 00		(b) 64 8 0 0 00	(a) 67 0 0 0 00
Prepaid Insurance	9 6 0 00			(e) 5 2 0 00
Land	122 1 0 0 00			
Building	129 0 0 0 00			
Accumulated Depreciation, Building		51 0 0 0 00		(f) 3 5 0 0 00
Equipment	33 1 0 0 00			
Accumulated Depreciation, Equipment		16 4 0 0 00		(g) 4 9 0 0 00
Notes Payable		36 6 0 0 00		
Accounts Payable		3 3 0 0 00		
Unearned Course Fees		1 2 0 0 00	(c) 8 0 0 00	
Mortgage Payable		7 8 0 0 00		
D. M. Bruce, Capital		253 7 7 4 00		
D. M. Bruce, Drawing	77 0 0 0 00			
Sales		257 1 8 0 00		
Sales Returns and Allowances	9 4 0 00			
Sales Discounts	1 9 8 0 00			
Interest Income		2 2 0 00		
Purchases	87 8 4 0 00			
Purchases Returns and Allowances		9 3 2 00		
Purchases Discounts		1 3 4 8 00		
Freight In	2 3 6 0 00			
Wages Expense	45 9 0 0 00		(h) 1 0 3 0 00	
Supplies Expense	1 5 4 0 00			(d) 4 1 5 00
Property Tax Expense	1 8 6 0 00			
Interest Expense	4 7 4 00			
	629 7 5 4 00	629 7 5 4 00		
Income Summary			(a) 67 0 0 0 00	(b) 64 8 0 0 00
Course Fees Income				(c) 8 0 0 00
Supplies			(d) 4 1 5 00	
Insurance Expense			(e) 5 2 0 00	
Depreciation Expense, Building			(f) 3 5 0 0 00	
Depreciation Expense, Equipment			(g) 4 9 0 0 00	
Wages Payable				(h) 1 0 3 0 00
			142 9 6 5 00	142 9 6 5 00

COMPLETION OF THE WORK SHEET

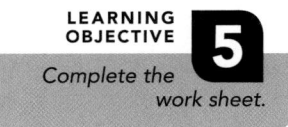

LEARNING OBJECTIVE 5

Complete the work sheet.

Previously, in introducing work sheets, we included the Adjusted Trial Balance columns as a means of verifying that the accounts were in balance after recording the adjusting entries. At this time, to reduce the number of columns in the work sheet, we will eliminate the Adjusted Trial Balance columns. The account balances after the adjusting entries will be carried directly into the Income Statement and Balance Sheet columns.

The completed work sheet looks like Figure 3 below.

FIGURE 3   Completed work sheet for Whitewater Raft Supply

Whitewater Raft Supply
Work Sheet
For Year Ended December 31, 20—

Account Name	Trial Balance Debit	Trial Balance Credit	Adjustments Debit	Adjustments Credit
Cash	24 1 5 4 00			
Notes Receivable	4 0 0 0 00			
Accounts Receivable	29 5 4 6 00			
Merchandise Inventory	67 0 0 0 00		(b) 64 8 0 0 00	(a) 67 0 0 0 00
Prepaid Insurance	9 6 0 00			(e) 5 2 0 00
Land	122 1 0 0 00			
Building	129 0 0 0 00			
Accumulated Depreciation, Building		51 0 0 0 00		(f) 3 5 0 0 00
Equipment	33 1 0 0 00			
Accumulated Depreciation, Equipment		16 4 0 0 00		(g) 4 9 0 0 00
Notes Payable		36 6 0 0 00		
Accounts Payable		3 3 0 0 00		
Unearned Course Fees		1 2 0 0 00	(c) 8 0 0 00	
Mortgage Payable		7 8 0 0 00		
D. M. Bruce, Capital		253 7 7 4 00		
D. M. Bruce, Drawing	77 0 0 0 00			
Sales		257 1 8 0 00		
Sales Returns and Allowances	9 4 0 00			
Sales Discounts	1 9 8 0 00			
Interest Income		2 2 0 00		
Purchases	87 8 4 0 00			
Purchases Returns and Allowances		9 3 2 00		
Purchases Discounts		1 3 4 8 00		
Freight In	2 3 6 0 00			
Wages Expense	45 9 0 0 00		(h) 1 0 3 0 00	
Supplies Expense	1 5 4 0 00			(d) 4 1 5 00
Property Tax Expense	1 8 6 0 00			
Interest Expense	4 7 4 00			
	629 7 5 4 00	629 7 5 4 00		
Income Summary			(a) 67 0 0 0 00	(b) 64 8 0 0 00
Course Fees Income				(c) 8 0 0 00
Supplies			(d) 4 1 5 00	
Insurance Expense			(e) 5 2 0 00	
Depreciation Expense, Building			(f) 3 5 0 0 00	
Depreciation Expense, Equipment			(g) 4 9 0 0 00	
Wages Payable				(h) 1 0 3 0 00
Net Income			142 9 6 5 00	142 9 6 5 00

Observe in particular the way we carry forward the figures for Merchandise Inventory and Income Summary. **Income Summary is the only account in which we don't combine the debit and credit figures. Instead, we carry them into the Income Statement columns in Figure 3 as two distinct figures—move the two figures as a pair to the Income Statement columns.** The reason for moving them as a pair is that both figures are needed for completion of the income statement. The debit amount in Income Summary in the Income Statement Debit column is the *beginning* merchandise inventory. The credit amount in Income Summary in the Income Statement Credit column is the *ending* merchandise inventory. We will talk about this topic in greater detail in Chapter 12 when we formulate the income statement for a merchandising entity.

Income Statement		Balance Sheet	
Debit	Credit	Debit	Credit
		24 1 5 4 00	
		4 0 0 0 00	
		29 5 4 6 00	
		64 8 0 0 00	
		4 4 0 00	
		122 1 0 0 00	
		129 0 0 0 00	
			54 5 0 0 00
		33 1 0 0 00	
			21 3 0 0 00
			36 6 0 0 00
			3 3 0 0 00
			4 0 0 00
			7 8 0 0 00
			253 7 7 4 00
		77 0 0 0 00	
	257 1 8 0 00		
9 4 0 00			
1 9 8 0 00			
	2 2 0 00		
87 8 4 0 00			
	9 3 2 00		
	1 3 4 8 00		
2 3 6 0 00			
46 9 3 0 00			
1 1 2 5 00			
1 8 6 0 00			
4 7 4 00			
67 0 0 0 00	64 8 0 0 00		
	8 0 0 00		
		4 1 5 00	
5 2 0 00			
3 5 0 0 00			
4 9 0 0 00			
			1 0 3 0 00
219 4 2 9 00	325 2 8 0 00	484 5 5 5 00	378 7 0 4 00
105 8 5 1 00			105 8 5 1 00
325 2 8 0 00	325 2 8 0 00	484 5 5 5 00	484 5 5 5 00

Using an electronic spreadsheet, such as Excel, can be an efficient way of preparing a work sheet. When completing a work sheet, complete one stage at a time before moving to the next stage:

STEP 1. Record the trial balance, and make sure that the total of the Debit column equals the total of the Credit column before going to the adjustments.

STEP 2. Record the adjustments in the Adjustments columns, and make sure that the totals are equal before extending the new totals into the Income Statement and Balance Sheet columns.

STEP 3. Complete the Income Statement and Balance Sheet columns by recording the adjusted balance of each account. The accounts and classifications pertaining to a merchandising business using the periodic inventory system appear in these columns:

Income Statement		Balance Sheet	
Debit	**Credit**	**Debit**	**Credit**
Expenses	Revenues	Assets	Accumulated
+	+	+	Depreciation
Sales Returns	Purchases Returns	Drawing	+
and Allowances	and Allowances		Liabilities
+	+		+
Sales Discounts	Purchases		Capital
+	Discounts		
Purchases	+		
+	Income Summary		
Freight In			
+			
Income Summary			

Study the following example of a work sheet, noting especially the way we treat these accounts for a merchandising business using the periodic inventory system:

	Location on Work Sheet			
	Income Statement		Balance Sheet	
Account Name	**Debit**	**Credit**	**Debit**	**Credit**
Merchandise Inventory			64,800.00	
Sales		257,180.00		
Sales Returns and Allowances	940.00			
Sales Discounts	1,980.00			
Purchases	87,840.00			
Purchases Returns and Allowances		932.00		
Purchases Discounts		1,348.00		
Freight In	2,360.00			
Income Summary	67,000.00	64,800.00		

ADJUSTING ENTRIES USING THE PERIODIC INVENTORY SYSTEM

LEARNING OBJECTIVE 6

Journalize the adjusting entries for a merchandising business under the periodic inventory system.

Figure 4 shows the adjusting entries as taken from the Adjustments columns of the work sheet and recorded in the general journal.

GENERAL JOURNAL PAGE **96**

Date		Description	Post. Ref.	Debit	Credit
20—		Adjusting Entries			
Dec.	31	Income Summary		67 0 0 0 00	
(a)		Merchandise Inventory			67 0 0 0 00
(b)	31	Merchandise Inventory		64 8 0 0 00	
		Income Summary			64 8 0 0 00
(c)	31	Unearned Course Fees		8 0 0 00	
		Course Fees Income			8 0 0 00
(d)	31	Supplies		4 1 5 00	
		Supplies Expense			4 1 5 00
(e)	31	Insurance Expense		5 2 0 00	
		Prepaid Insurance			5 2 0 00
(f)	31	Depreciation Expense, Building		3 5 0 0 00	
		Accumulated Depreciation, Building			3 5 0 0 00
(g)	31	Depreciation Expense, Equipment		4 9 0 0 00	
		Accumulated Depreciation, Equipment			4 9 0 0 00
(h)	31	Wages Expense		1 0 3 0 00	
		Wages Payable			1 0 3 0 00

FIGURE 4

Adjusting entries for Whitewater Raft Supply

ADJUSTMENT FOR MERCHANDISE INVENTORY UNDER THE PERPETUAL INVENTORY SYSTEM

Before we demonstrate how to record the adjustment for the perpetual inventory system, let's first look at a portion of the trial balance section of Whitewater Raft Supply's work sheet (Figure 5) assuming they were using the perpetual inventory system.

Under the perpetual inventory system, a business continually maintains a record of each item in stock. **When merchandise is purchased, the Merchandise**

7 **LEARNING OBJECTIVE**

Prepare and journalize the adjusting entry for merchandise inventory under the perpetual inventory system.

	Debit	Credit
Sales		25 7 1 8 0 00
Sales Returns and Allowances	9 4 0 00	
Sales Discounts	1 9 8 0 00	
Interest Income		2 2 0 00
Cost of Goods Sold	90 1 2 0 00	
Wages Expense	46 9 3 0 00	
Supplies Expense	1 1 2 5 00	

FIGURE 5

A portion of the trial balance section of Whitewater Raft Supply's work sheet (perpetual inventory system)

Inventory account (not the Purchases account) is debited for the cost of the merchandise and Accounts Payable or Cash is credited. When merchandise is sold, there are two journal entries. First, debit Accounts Receivable or Cash and credit Sales. Second, the Cost of Goods Sold account is debited for the cost of merchandise and the Merchandise Inventory account is credited for the cost of merchandise.

Many firms use electronic devices to keep track of stock items under the perpetual inventory system. For example, when a sale is made at a supermarket checkout counter, as the bar code on each item is scanned, the price and stock number are recorded. The cash register is connected to a computer that updates the inventory record and records the cost of the item. So the business perpetually (always) knows how much inventory it should have on hand.

However, to verify the inventory record, a physical count should be taken from time to time. The amount shown by the physical count may be less than the computer record as a result of errors, shrinkage, or shoplifting. This difference is called **inventory shrinkage**, and an adjusting entry must be. This entry is a debit to the Cost of Goods Sold account (an expense account) and a credit to the Merchandise Inventory account. The opposite is true if the physical count is more than the computer record; the adjusting entry would then be a debit to Merchandise Inventory and a credit to Cost of Goods Sold.

ADJUSTING ENTRY UNDER THE PERPETUAL INVENTORY SYSTEM

Here are examples of entries under the perpetual inventory system when the physical count does not agree with the computer record of merchandise inventory. Assume a beginning inventory of $75,000.

1. Bought merchandise on account, $50,000.

Merchandise Inventory				Accounts Payable		
	+	−			−	+
Bal.	75,000					(1) 50,000
(1)	50,000					

2. Sold merchandise for $84,000 having a cost of $60,300.

Accounts Receivable				Sales		
	+	−			−	+
(2)	84,000					(2) 84,000

Cost of Goods Sold				Merchandise Inventory		
	+	−			+	−
(2)	60,300			Bal.	75,000	(2) 60,300
				(1)	50,000	
				Bal.	**64,700**	

3a. The adjusting entry for the perpetual inventory system is computed by determining the difference between the computer record and the physical count for ending inventory, $63,200. The recorded balance of the perpetual inventory is $64,700 ($75,000 + $50,000 − $60,300).

The ending inventory of one period becomes the beginning inventory of the next period.

Remember

Cost of Goods Sold		
+	−	
(2) 60,300		
(3) Adj. 1,500		
Bal. 61,800		

Merchandise Inventory		
+	−	
Bal. 75,000	(2) 60,300	
(1) 50,000	(3) Adj. 1,500	
Bal. 63,200		

The difference of $1,500 ($64,700 − $63,200) is the adjustment amount under the perpetual inventory system. The adjusting entry required to record the $1,500 loss is shown in Figure 6.

3b. Suppose, on the other hand, that the physical count of the stock of merchandise ($65,200) were more than the recorded amount ($64,700). The adjusting entry is to debit Merchandise Inventory and credit Cost of Goods Sold (account) for the difference ($65,200 − $64,700 = $500). (See Figure 6.)

Additional adjusting entries would follow, such as those for supplies remaining, insurance expired, accrued wages, and other such expenses.

On the income statement, under the perpetual inventory system, the Cost of Goods Sold account is listed under one line, rather than there being a Cost of Goods Sold section. The following is a comparison of income statements under the periodic and perpetual inventory systems assuming scenario 3a from above.

Periodic

Sales (net)		$84,000
Cost of Goods Sold:		
Merchandise Inventory (beginning)	$ 75,000	
Purchases (net)	50,000	
Cost of Goods Available for Sale	$125,000	
Less Merchandise Inventory (ending)	63,200	
Cost of Goods Sold		61,800
Gross Profit		$22,200

Perpetual

Sales (net)	$84,000
Cost of Goods Sold	61,800
Gross Profit	$22,200

GENERAL JOURNAL					PAGE 96		
Date	Description	Post. Ref.	Debit		Credit		
20—	Adjusting Entries						
3a. Dec. 31	Cost of Goods Sold		1 5 0 0 00				
	Merchandise Inventory				1 5 0 0 00		
3b. 31	Merchandise Inventory		5 0 0 00				
	Cost of Goods Sold				5 0 0 00		

FIGURE 6

Adjusting entry for ending inventory under the perpetual inventory system

You Make the Call

You and a college friend have decided to start a merchandising business that markets "green" products—people- and earth-friendly products for the home or business. You have identified approximately 100 different items from bath soaps to home cleaning products, plant-friendly foods and pesticides, as well as a line of organic canned foods. You have both taken accounting courses and are trying to decide whether to use the periodic or perpetual inventory system. What are the advantages, disadvantages, and implications of each system?

SOLUTION

For simplicity, using the periodic inventory system would be the way to go. It is less complicated than the perpetual inventory system, requires fewer accounting entries, and is less costly than the perpetual inventory system since you would not have to buy computer software and hardware and various electronic devices to keep track of the inventory. However, the perpetual inventory system offers a higher degree of control and is better for management of proper inventory levels since it allows for up-to-the-minute data for your purchasing needs—two advantages that might very well outweigh the disadvantages of using a perpetual inventory system.

CHAPTER REVIEW

Study & Practice

1   LEARNING OBJECTIVE
Prepare an adjustment for supplies.

When supplies are bought during the year, they are recorded by debiting (increasing) Supplies Expense. At the end of the year, an inventory is taken to determine the amount of supplies on hand. If the ending inventory of supplies is significant, then an adjusting entry is made for the amount remaining, debiting Supplies (an asset account) and crediting Supplies Expense.

PRACTICE EXERCISE 1

Assume that Bowie Corporation has a balance of $9,340 in the Supplies Expense account as a result of buying supplies throughout the year. However, after taking a count of the supplies on hand, it is determined that $2,599 of supplies are left. Journalize the year-end adjusting entry for Bowie Corporation.

PRACTICE EXERCISE 1 SOLUTION

		GENERAL JOURNAL			PAGE _____	
Date		Description	Post. Ref.	Debit	Credit	
20—		Adjusting Entries				
Dec.	31	Supplies		2 5 9 9 00		
		Supplies Expense			2 5 9 9 00	

---

2 LEARNING OBJECTIVE

Prepare an adjustment for unearned revenue.

For revenue received in advance, an adjustment is required to separate the portion that has been earned from the portion that is unearned. We assume that the amount of cash received in advance was originally recorded as **unearned revenue**, which is a liability. In the adjusting entry for the amount actually earned, debit the unearned revenue account (Unearned Course Fees) and credit the revenue account (Course Fees Income).

PRACTICE EXERCISE 2

On June 1, Thompson Company receives $148,540 in cash for subscriptions covering two years. At the end of the year, December 31, Thompson finds that $94,302 of the subscriptions have been earned. Record in general journal form (a) the original receipt of cash on June 1 and (b) the year-end adjusting entry for Thompson Company.

PRACTICE EXERCISE 2 SOLUTION

		GENERAL JOURNAL			PAGE _____	
Date		Description	Post. Ref.	Debit	Credit	
20—						
June	1	Cash		148 5 4 0 00		
(a)		Unearned Subscriptions			148 5 4 0 00	
		Adjusting Entries				
Dec.	31	Unearned Subscriptions		94 3 0 2 00		
(b)		Subscriptions Income			94 3 0 2 00	

---

3 LEARNING OBJECTIVE

Prepare an adjustment for merchandise inventory under the periodic inventory system.

The adjustment for merchandise inventory under the periodic inventory system requires two adjusting entries. In the first adjusting entry (to remove the beginning inventory), debit Income Summary and credit Merchandise Inventory. In the second adjusting entry (to enter the ending inventory), debit Merchandise Inventory and credit Income Summary.

PRACTICE EXERCISE 3

Morkin Company's beginning inventory amounted to $264,072. A physical count at the end of the year reveals that the ending inventory amount is $267,322. Record the necessary adjustments in the T accounts.

PRACTICE EXERCISE 3 SOLUTION

Merchandise Inventory			
	+	−	
Bal.	264,072	(a) Adj. 264,072	
(b) Adj.	267,322		

Income Summary	
(a) Adj. 264,072	(b) Adj. 267,322

4 LEARNING OBJECTIVE

Record the adjustment data in a work sheet (including merchandise inventory, unearned revenue, supplies remaining, expired insurance, depreciation, and accrued wages or salaries).

In the Adjustments columns of the work sheet, record the following adjusting entries:

For merchandise inventory: First, debit Income Summary and credit Merchandise Inventory (to remove the beginning inventory); next, debit Merchandise Inventory and credit Income Summary (to enter the ending inventory).

For unearned revenue: Debit the unearned revenue account and credit the revenue account (to record revenue earned).

For supplies remaining: Debit Supplies and credit Supplies Expense.

For expired insurance: Debit Insurance Expense and credit Prepaid Insurance.

For depreciation: Debit Depreciation Expense and credit Accumulated Depreciation.

For accrued wages or salaries: Debit Wages Expense or Salaries Expense and credit Wages Payable or Salaries Payable.

PRACTICE EXERCISE 4

Following are the adjustment data for Majors Company:

a–b. Merchandise inventory, $64,800.

   c. Course fees earned, $1,800.

   d. Supplies inventory, $2,415.

   e. Insurance expired, $1,520.

   f. Depreciation of building, $13,500.

   g. Depreciation of equipment, $5,900.

   h. Wages accrued, $2,030.

Record these data in the Adjustments column of the following work sheet.

Majors Company
Work Sheet
For Year Ended December 31, 20—

Account Name	Trial Balance		Adjustments	
	Debit	Credit	Debit	Credit
Cash	23 0 1 0 00			
Notes Receivable	6 0 0 0 00			
Accounts Receivable	28 5 4 0 00			
Merchandise Inventory	68 0 0 0 00			
Prepaid Insurance	2 1 1 0 00			
Land	120 1 0 0 00			
Building	128 0 0 0 00			
Accumulated Depreciation, Building		50 0 0 0 00		
Equipment	34 1 0 0 00			
Accumulated Depreciation, Equipment		19 6 0 0 00		
Notes Payable		34 6 0 0 00		
Accounts Payable		4 3 0 0 00		
Unearned Course Fees		2 2 0 0 00		
Mortgage Payable		8 8 0 0 00		
R. L. Majors, Capital		252 7 7 4 00		
R. L. Majors, Drawing	65 0 0 0 00			
Sales		253 9 8 0 00		
Sales Returns and Allowances	9 4 0 00			
Sales Discounts	1 8 8 0 00			
Interest Income		1 2 2 0 00		
Purchases	88 8 4 0 00			
Purchases Returns and Allowances		8 3 2 00		
Purchases Discounts		1 4 4 8 00		
Freight In	2 4 6 0 00			
Wages Expense	44 9 0 0 00			
Supplies Expense	12 4 4 0 00			
Property Tax Expense	2 8 6 0 00			
Interest Expense	5 7 4 00			
	629 7 5 4 00	629 7 5 4 00		
Income Summary				
Course Fees Income				
Supplies				
Insurance Expense				
Depreciation Expense, Building				
Depreciation Expense, Equipment				
Wages Payable				

PRACTICE EXERCISE 4 SOLUTION

Majors Company
Work Sheet
For Year Ended December 31, 20—

Account Name	Trial Balance Debit	Trial Balance Credit	Adjustments Debit	Adjustments Credit
Cash	23 0 1 0 00			
Notes Receivable	6 0 0 0 00			
Accounts Receivable	28 5 4 0 00			
Merchandise Inventory	68 0 0 0 00		(b) 64 8 0 0 00	(a) 68 0 0 0 00
Prepaid Insurance	2 1 1 0 00			(e) 1 5 2 0 00
Land	120 1 0 0 00			
Building	128 0 0 0 00			
Accumulated Depreciation, Building		50 0 0 0 00		(f) 13 5 0 0 00
Equipment	34 1 0 0 00			
Accumulated Depreciation, Equipment		19 6 0 0 00		(g) 5 9 0 0 00
Notes Payable		34 6 0 0 00		
Accounts Payable		4 3 0 0 00		
Unearned Course Fees		2 2 0 0 00	(c) 1 8 0 0 00	
Mortgage Payable		8 8 0 0 00		
R. L. Majors, Capital		252 7 7 4 00		
R. L. Majors, Drawing	65 0 0 0 00			
Sales		253 9 8 0 00		
Sales Returns and Allowances	9 4 0 00			
Sales Discounts	1 8 8 0 00			
Interest Income		1 2 2 0 00		
Purchases	88 8 4 0 00			
Purchases Returns and Allowances		8 3 2 00		
Purchases Discounts		1 4 4 8 00		
Freight In	2 4 6 0 00			
Wages Expense	44 9 0 0 00		(h) 2 0 3 0 00	
Supplies Expense	12 4 4 0 00			(d) 2 4 1 5 00
Property Tax Expense	2 8 6 0 00			
Interest Expense	5 7 4 00			
	629 7 5 4 00	629 7 5 4 00		
Income Summary			(a) 68 0 0 0 00	(b) 64 8 0 0 00
Course Fees Income				(c) 1 8 0 0 00
Supplies			(d) 2 4 1 5 00	
Insurance Expense			(e) 1 5 2 0 00	
Depreciation Expense, Building			(f) 13 5 0 0 00	
Depreciation Expense, Equipment			(g) 5 9 0 0 00	
Wages Payable				(h) 2 0 3 0 00
			159 9 6 5 00	159 9 6 5 00

5 **LEARNING OBJECTIVE**

Complete the work sheet.

Carry the Income Summary account from the Adjustments columns into the Income Statement columns as two separate figures. For merchandise inventory, record the amount of the ending inventory in the Balance Sheet Debit column. For unearned revenue, record the unearned revenue account in the Balance Sheet Credit column and the revenue account in the Income Statement Credit column.

PRACTICE EXERCISE 5

Complete the Income Statement and Balance Sheet columns of the work sheet for Majors Company from Practice Exercise 4.

PRACTICE EXERCISE 5 SOLUTION

Majors Company
Work Sheet
For Year Ended December 31, 20—

Account Name	Trial Balance Debit	Trial Balance Credit	Adjustments Debit	Adjustments Credit
Cash	23 0 1 0 00			
Notes Receivable	6 0 0 0 00			
Accounts Receivable	28 5 4 0 00			
Merchandise Inventory	68 0 0 0 00		(b) 64 8 0 0 00	(a) 68 0 0 0 00
Prepaid Insurance	2 1 1 0 00			(e) 1 5 2 0 00
Land	120 1 0 0 00			
Building	128 0 0 0 00			
Accumulated Depreciation, Building		50 0 0 0 00		(f) 13 5 0 0 00
Equipment	34 1 0 0 00			
Accumulated Depreciation, Equipment		19 6 0 0 00		(g) 5 9 0 0 00
Notes Payable		34 6 0 0 00		
Accounts Payable		4 3 0 0 00		
Unearned Course Fees		2 2 0 0 00	(c) 1 8 0 0 00	
Mortgage Payable		8 8 0 0 00		
R. L. Majors, Capital		252 7 7 4 00		
R. L. Majors, Drawing	65 0 0 0 00			
Sales		253 9 8 0 00		
Sales Returns and Allowances	9 4 0 00			
Sales Discounts	1 8 8 0 00			
Interest Income		1 2 2 0 00		
Purchases	88 8 4 0 00			
Purchases Returns and Allowances		8 3 2 00		
Purchases Discounts		1 4 4 8 00		
Freight In	2 4 6 0 00			
Wages Expense	44 9 0 0 00		(h) 2 0 3 0 00	
Supplies Expense	12 4 4 0 00			(d) 2 4 1 5 00
Property Tax Expense	2 8 6 0 00			
Interest Expense	5 7 4 00			
	629 7 5 4 00	629 7 5 4 00		
Income Summary			(a) 68 0 0 0 00	(b) 64 8 0 0 00
Course Fees Income				(c) 1 8 0 0 00
Supplies			(d) 2 4 1 5 00	
Insurance Expense			(e) 1 5 2 0 00	
Depreciation Expense, Building			(f) 13 5 0 0 00	
Depreciation Expense, Equipment			(g) 5 9 0 0 00	
Wages Payable				(h) 2 0 3 0 00
Net Income			159 9 6 5 00	159 9 6 5 00

| Income Statement | | Balance Sheet | |
Debit	Credit	Debit	Credit
		23 0 1 0 00	
		6 0 0 0 00	
		28 5 4 0 00	
		64 8 0 0 00	
		5 9 0 00	
		120 1 0 0 00	
		128 0 0 0 00	
			63 5 0 0 00
		34 1 0 0 00	
			25 5 0 0 00
			34 6 0 0 00
			4 3 0 0 00
			4 0 0 00
			8 8 0 0 00
			252 7 7 4 00
		65 0 0 0 00	
	253 9 8 0 00		
9 4 0 00			
1 8 8 0 00			
	1 2 2 0 00		
88 8 4 0 00			
	8 3 2 00		
	1 4 4 8 00		
2 4 6 0 00			
46 9 3 0 00			
10 0 2 5 00			
2 8 6 0 00			
5 7 4 00			
68 0 0 0 00	64 8 0 0 00		
	1 8 0 0 00		
		2 4 1 5 00	
1 5 2 0 00			
13 5 0 0 00			
5 9 0 0 00			
			2 0 3 0 00
243 4 2 9 00	324 0 8 0 00	472 5 5 5 00	391 9 0 4 00
80 6 5 1 00			80 6 5 1 00
324 0 8 0 00	324 0 8 0 00	472 5 5 5 00	472 5 5 5 00

6 LEARNING OBJECTIVE

Journalize the adjusting entries for a merchandising business under the periodic inventory system.

Take the adjusting entries recorded in the journal directly from the Adjustments columns of the work sheet.

PRACTICE EXERCISE 6

Prepare the year-end adjusting entries from the Adjustments column of Major Company's work sheet from Practice Exercise 4.

PRACTICE EXERCISE 6 SOLUTION

		GENERAL JOURNAL			PAGE ____
Date		Description	Post. Ref.	Debit	Credit
20—		Adjusting Entries			
Dec. 31		Income Summary		68 0 0 0 00	
(a)		Merchandise Inventory			68 0 0 0 00
(b) 31		Merchandise Inventory		64 8 0 0 00	
		Income Summary			64 8 0 0 00
(c) 31		Unearned Course Fees		1 8 0 0 00	
		Course Fees Income			1 8 0 0 00
(d) 31		Supplies		2 4 1 5 00	
		Supplies Expense			2 4 1 5 00
(e) 31		Insurance Expense		1 5 2 0 00	
		Prepaid Insurance			1 5 2 0 00
(f) 31		Depreciation Expense, Building		13 5 0 0 00	
		Accumulated Depreciation, Building			13 5 0 0 00
(g) 31		Depreciation Expense, Equipment		5 9 0 0 00	
		Accumulated Depreciation, Equipment			5 9 0 0 00
(h) 31		Wages Expense		2 0 3 0 00	
		Wages Payable			2 0 3 0 00

7 LEARNING OBJECTIVE

Prepare and journalize the adjusting entry for merchandise inventory under the perpetual inventory system.

Assuming that the amount of the physical count of the stock of merchandise is less than the recorded amount, the adjusting entry is a debit to Cost of Goods Sold and a credit to Merchandise Inventory for the amount of the difference. On the other hand, if the physical count of the stock of merchandise is more than the recorded amount, the adjusting entry is to debit Merchandise Inventory and credit Cost of Goods Sold for the amount of the difference.

PRACTICE EXERCISE 7

Larkin Company employs the perpetual inventory system. Cost of Goods Sold for the year before any adjustment is $553,250. The computer record shows the amount of ending inventory to be $369,583, while the physical count shows ending inventory to be $362,720. Record the adjustment into T accounts and then journalize the adjusting entry.

PRACTICE EXERCISE 7 SOLUTION

Cost of Goods Sold			Merchandise Inventory		
+	−		+	−	
Bal. 553,250		Bal.	369,583	Adj.	6,863*
Adj. 6,863					

*Adjustment = $362,720 − $369,583 = $(6,863)

		GENERAL JOURNAL			PAGE ____

Date		Description	Post. Ref.	Debit	Credit
20—		Adjusting Entries			
Dec.	31	Cost of Goods Sold		6 8 6 3 00	
		Merchandise Inventory			6 8 6 3 00

Glossary

Inventory shrinkage The amount by which inventory diminishes due to theft, misplacement, loss, or mismarking. (p. 464)

Physical inventory An actual count of the stock of goods on hand. (p. 455)

Unearned revenue Cash received in advance for goods or services to be delivered later; considered to be a liability until the revenue is earned. (p. 453)

CHAPTER ASSIGNMENTS

Discussion Questions

1. What is a physical inventory? What does the word *periodic* mean in the term *periodic inventory*?
2. On the Income Summary line of a work sheet, $126,220 appears in the Income Statement Debit column, and $123,300 appears in the Income Statement Credit column. Which figure represents the beginning inventory?
3. Using the perpetual inventory system, what account is debited when a business finds its physical count of inventory is greater than the recorded amount?
4. On a work sheet, where will the amount of the ending merchandise inventory be recorded?

5. Explain what is meant by unearned revenue, and why it is treated as a liability.
6. Why is it necessary to adjust the Merchandise Inventory account under a periodic inventory system?
7. A merchandising company shows $8,842 in the Supplies Expense account on the preadjusted trial balance. After taking inventory of the actual supplies, it still owns $3,638.
   a. Write the adjusting entry.
   b. How much was used or expired?
8. Assume that a college receives $84,000 for one semester's dormitory rent in advance and an entry is made debiting Cash and crediting Unearned Rent. At the end of the year, $68,000 of the rent has been earned. What adjusting entry would be made?

Exercises

 **1 LO**

PRACTICE EXERCISE 1

EXERCISE 11-1 For the following Supplies Expense ledger account, determine the debits and credits for each amount posted to the account and briefly describe each transaction. The entry of December 16 involved the return of defective goods.

ACCOUNT **Supplies Expense**   ACCOUNT NO.   615

Date		Item	Post. Ref.	Debit	Credit	Balance Debit	Balance Credit
20—							
Jan.	1	Balance	✓			7 4 0 00	
Apr.	7		J25	2 9 0 00		1 0 3 0 00	
May	30		J82	4 2 0 00		1 4 5 0 00	
Nov.	19		J104	3 1 5 00		1 7 6 5 00	
Dec.	16		J115		1 8 6 00	1 5 7 9 00	
	18		J127	5 7 1 00		2 1 5 0 00	
	31	Adj.	J141		1 4 7 0 00	6 8 0 00	

 **2 LO**

PRACTICE EXERCISE 2

EXERCISE 11-2 For the university football program's Unearned Season Tickets account, list the debits and credits for each amount posted to the account and briefly describe each transaction.

ACCOUNT **Unearned Season Tickets**   ACCOUNT NO.   214

Date		Item	Post. Ref.	Debit	Credit	Balance Debit	Balance Credit
20—							
Jan.	1	Balance	✓				12 9 0 0 00
Oct.	15		J42		36 7 8 0 00		49 6 8 0 00
Nov.	1		J43		42 6 0 0 00		92 2 8 0 00
Dec.	31	Adj.	J52	43 1 2 5 00			49 1 5 5 00

EXERCISE 11-3 On October 31, the Vermillion Igloos Hockey Club received $800,000 in cash in advance for season tickets for eight home games. The transaction was recorded as a debit to Cash and a credit to Unearned Admissions. By December 31, the end of the fiscal year, the team had played three home games and received an additional $450,000 cash admissions income at the gate.

a. Journalize the adjusting entry as of December 31.
b. List the title of the account and the related balance that will appear on the income statement.
c. List the title of the account and the related balance that will appear on the balance sheet.

PRACTICE EXERCISE 2

EXERCISE 11-4 Basga Company uses the periodic inventory system. Beginning inventory amounted to $241,072. A physical count reveals that the latest inventory amount is $256,339. Record the adjusting entries using T accounts.

PRACTICE EXERCISE 3

EXERCISE 11-5 Indicate the work sheet columns (Income Statement Debit, Income Statement Credit, Balance Sheet Debit, Balance Sheet Credit) in which the balances of the following accounts should appear:

a. F. Dexter, Drawing
b. Advertising Expense
c. Merchandise Inventory (ending)
d. Purchases Discounts
e. Unearned Fees
f. Sales Returns and Allowances
g. Accumulated Depreciation, Building
h. Income Summary
i. Fees Income
j. Prepaid Rent

PRACTICE EXERCISE 5

EXERCISE 11-6 Journalize the required adjusting entries for the year ended December 31 for Morgan Yoga Accessories. Morgan Yoga Accessories uses the periodic inventory system.

a–b. On December 31, a physical count of inventory was taken. The physical count amounted to $19,342. The Merchandise Inventory account shows a balance of $18,368.
c. On June 1 of this year, $1,200 was paid for a one-year insurance policy.
d. On October 1 of this year, $360 was paid for four months of advertising.
e. As of December 31, the balance of the Unearned Membership Fees account is $12,800. Of this amount, $7,800 has now been earned.
f. Equipment purchased on April 1 of this year for $6,500 is expected to have a useful life of five years, with a trade-in value of $1,000. All other equipment has been fully depreciated. The straight-line method is used.
g. As of December 31, two days' wages at $230 per day had accrued.

PRACTICE EXERCISE 6

EXERCISE 11-7 On December 31, the end of the year, the accountant for *Fireside Magazine* was called away suddenly because of an emergency. However, before leaving, the accountant jotted down a few notes pertaining to the adjustments. Journalize the necessary adjusting entries. Assume that *Fireside Magazine* uses the periodic inventory system.

a–b. A physical count of inventory revealed a balance of $199,830. The Merchandise Inventory account shows a balance of $202,839.

PRACTICE EXERCISE 6

c. Subscriptions received in advance amounting to $156,200 were recorded as Unearned Subscriptions. At year end, $103,120 has been earned.
d. Depreciation of equipment for the year is $12,300.
e. The amount of expired insurance for the year is $1,612.
f. The balance of Prepaid Rent is $2,400, representing four months' rent. Three months' rent has now expired.
g. Three days' salaries will be unpaid at the end of the year; total weekly (five days') salaries are $4,000.

7 **LO**

PRACTICE EXERCISE 7

EXERCISE 11-8 On December 31, Marchant Company took a physical count of its merchandise inventory. It operates under the perpetual inventory system. The physical count amounted to $185,294. The Merchandise Inventory account shows a balance of $187,936. Journalize the adjusting entry.

Problem Set A

For additional help, see the demonstration problem at the beginning of each chapter in your Working Papers.

4,5 **LO**

PROBLEM 11-1A The trial balance of Hadden Company as of December 31, the end of its current fiscal year, is as follows:

Hadden Company Trial Balance December 31, 20—		
Account Name	Debit	Credit
Cash	9,246.52	
Merchandise Inventory	63,674.80	
Prepaid Insurance	1,420.00	
Store Equipment	36,230.00	
Accumulated Depreciation, Store Equipment		22,726.00
Accounts Payable		13,196.96
Sales Tax Payable		1,236.98
R. M. Hadden, Capital		56,339.32
R. M. Hadden, Drawing	28,000.00	
Sales		175,864.31
Sales Returns and Allowances	1,573.72	
Purchases	77,300.04	
Purchases Returns and Allowances		1,744.32
Purchases Discounts		1,413.62
Freight In	2,427.00	
Salary Expense	35,458.85	
Rent Expense	14,600.00	
Store Supplies Expense	1,466.34	
Miscellaneous Expense	1,124.24	
	272,521.51	272,521.51

Here are the data for the adjustments:

a–b. Merchandise Inventory at December 31, $64,742.80.
c. Store supplies inventory, $420.20.

d. Insurance expired, $738.
e. Salaries accrued, $684.50.
f. Depreciation of store equipment, $3,620.

Required
Complete the work sheet after entering the account names and balances onto the work sheet.

 **4,5,6**

PROBLEM 11-2A The balances of the ledger accounts of Beldren Home Center as of December 31, the end of its fiscal year, are as follows:

Cash	$ 10,592
Accounts Receivable	43,962
Merchandise Inventory	120,838
Prepaid Insurance	2,628
Store Equipment	35,924
Accumulated Depreciation, Store Equipment	29,420
Office Equipment	10,436
Accumulated Depreciation, Office Equipment	1,720
Notes Payable	5,000
Accounts Payable	29,822
Unearned Rent	3,200
A. P. Beldren, Capital	120,532
A. P. Beldren, Drawing	29,000
Sales	653,000
Sales Returns and Allowances	9,748
Purchases	519,374
Purchases Returns and Allowances	12,440
Purchases Discounts	8,634
Freight In	24,724
Wages Expense	54,200
Supplies Expense	1,570
Interest Expense	772

Data for the adjustments are as follows:

a–b. Merchandise Inventory at December 31, $102,765.
  c. Wages accrued at December 31, $1,834.
  d. Supplies inventory at December 31, $645.
  e. Depreciation of store equipment, $5,782.
  f. Depreciation of office equipment, $1,791.
  g. Insurance expired during the year, $845.
  h. Rent earned, $2,500.

Required
1. Complete the work sheet after entering the account names and balances onto the work sheet.
2. Journalize the adjusting entries on journal page 16.

 **4,5,6**

PROBLEM 11-3A A portion of the work sheet of Sadie's Flowers for the year ended December 31 is as follows:

Account Name	Income Statement Debit	Income Statement Credit	Balance Sheet Debit	Balance Sheet Credit
Cash			9 3 4 0 00	
Merchandise Inventory			76 9 4 0 00	
Prepaid Insurance			2 4 0 00	
Store Equipment			39 2 8 0 00	
Accumulated Depreciation, Store Equipment				26 2 2 0 00
Accounts Payable				14 6 0 0 00
S. R. Rodriguez, Capital				68 9 4 0 00
S. R. Rodriguez, Drawing			27 6 0 0 00	
Sales		173 4 2 0 00		
Sales Returns and Allowances	1 5 2 0 00			
Purchases	82 3 1 2 00			
Purchases Returns and Allowances		9 4 0 00		
Purchases Discounts		1 6 0 0 00		
Freight In	1 9 4 8 00			
Salary Expense	37 5 6 0 00			
Rent Expense	14 8 0 0 00			
Supplies Expense	9 4 4 00			
Income Summary	65 6 8 0 00	76 9 4 0 00		
Depreciation Expense, Store Equipment	4 0 4 0 00			
Insurance Expense	7 6 0 00			
Supplies			2 5 6 00	
Salaries Payable				5 6 0 00
	209 5 6 4 00	252 9 0 0 00	153 6 5 6 00	110 3 2 0 00

Check Figure

Salaries accrued, $560

Required

1. Determine the entries that appeared in the Adjustments columns and present them in general journal form on page 41.
2. Determine the net income for the year.
3. What is the amount of the ending capital?

4,5,7 **LO**

PROBLEM 11-4A Here are the accounts in the ledger of Misha's Jewel Box, with the balances as of December 31, the end of its fiscal year.

Cash	$ 13,242
Accounts Receivable	3,984
Merchandise Inventory	126,540
Prepaid Insurance	2,655
Land	18,000
Building	97,000
Accumulated Depreciation, Building	38,240
Store Equipment	46,170
Accumulated Depreciation, Store Equipment	16,250
Accounts Payable	8,270
Sales Tax Payable	2,371
Mortgage Payable	77,871
M. Beloit, Capital	185,000
M. Beloit, Drawing	48,000
Sales	379,354
Sales Returns and Allowances	3,892
Cost of Goods Sold	279,198
Salary Expense	54,400

Advertising Expense	$ 3,526
Store Supplies Expense	2,484
Utilities Expense	2,538
Property Tax Expense	1,162
Miscellaneous Expense	1,613
Interest Expense	2,952

Here are the data for the adjustments. Assume that Misha's Jewel Box uses the perpetual inventory system.

a. Merchandise Inventory at December 31, $124,630.
b. Insurance expired during the year, $1,294.
c. Depreciation of building, $3,300.
d. Depreciation of store equipment, $6,470.
e. Salaries accrued at December 31, $2,470.
f. Store supplies inventory at December 31, $1,959.

Required

1. Complete the work sheet after entering the account names and balances onto the work sheet.
2. Journalize the adjusting entries on journal page 63.

Check Figure
Net income, $14,104

Problem Set B

For additional help, see the demonstration problem at the beginning of each chapter in your Working Papers.

PROBLEM 11-1B The trial balance of Jillson Company as of December 31, the end of its current fiscal year, is as follows:

Jillson Company
Trial Balance
December 31, 20—

Account Name	Debit	Credit
Cash	18,463.92	
Merchandise Inventory	47,356.00	
Prepaid Insurance	1,660.00	
Store Equipment	26,580.00	
Accumulated Depreciation, Store Equipment		15,320.00
Accounts Payable		25,578.80
Sales Tax Payable		1,243.36
G. L. Jillson, Capital		75,630.00
G. L. Jillson, Drawing	28,440.00	
Sales		92,026.74
Sales Returns and Allowances	1,542.04	
Purchases	43,348.45	
Purchases Returns and Allowances		1,748.09
Purchases Discounts		1,987.90
Freight In	2,775.00	
Salary Expense	25,758.80	
Rent Expense	15,300.00	
Store Supplies Expense	1,321.12	
Miscellaneous Expense	989.56	
	213,534.89	213,534.89

Here are the data for the adjustments.

a–b. Merchandise Inventory at December 31, $54,845.00.
  c. Store supplies inventory, $488.50.
  d. Insurance expired, $680.
  e. Salaries accrued, $692.
  f. Depreciation of store equipment, $3,760.

Check Figure
Net income, $7,573.26

Required

Complete the work sheet after entering the account names and balances onto the work sheet.

 **4,5,6**

PROBLEM 11-2B The balances of the ledger accounts of Pelango Furniture as of December 31, the end of its fiscal year, are as follows:

Cash	$ 12,482
Accounts Receivable	38,962
Merchandise Inventory	118,628
Prepaid Insurance	2,488
Store Equipment	32,824
Accumulated Depreciation, Store Equipment	26,420
Office Equipment	11,236
Accumulated Depreciation, Office Equipment	3,410
Notes Payable	6,000
Accounts Payable	23,420
Unearned Rent	3,150
L. Pelango, Capital	120,532
L. Pelango, Drawing	28,000
Sales	647,090
Sales Returns and Allowances	8,848
Purchases	519,374
Purchases Returns and Allowances	12,440
Purchases Discounts	8,634
Freight In	22,824
Wages Expense	52,800
Supplies Expense	1,850
Interest Expense	780

Data for the adjustments are as follows:

a–b. Merchandise Inventory at December 31, $104,565.
  c. Wages accrued at December 31, $934.
  d. Supplies inventory at December 31, $755.
  e. Depreciation of store equipment, $4,982.
  f. Depreciation of office equipment, $1,531.
  g. Insurance expired during the year, $935.
  h. Rent earned, $2,450.

Check Figure
Net income, $42,448

Required

1. Complete the work sheet after entering the account names and balances onto the work sheet.
2. Journalize the adjusting entries on journal page 16.

 **4,5,6**

PROBLEM 11-3B A portion of the work sheet of Habib Company for the year ended December 31 follows.

Account Name	Income Statement		Balance Sheet	
	Debit	Credit	Debit	Credit
Cash			7 7 3 6 00	
Merchandise Inventory			74 2 9 8 00	
Prepaid Insurance			2 5 0 00	
Store Equipment			37 9 6 0 00	
Accumulated Depreciation, Store Equipment				29 4 4 0 00
Accounts Payable				13 7 6 0 00
O. B. Habib, Capital				75 1 4 2 00
O. B. Habib, Drawing			30 8 0 0 00	
Sales		171 8 1 6 00		
Sales Returns and Allowances	1 4 3 4 00			
Purchases	85 9 3 4 00			
Purchases Returns and Allowances		9 6 4 00		
Purchases Discounts		1 6 3 6 00		
Freight In	2 6 5 8 00			
Salary Expense	37 8 5 2 00			
Rent Expense	14 4 0 0 00			
Supplies Expense	8 8 4 00			
Income Summary	68 2 2 8 00	74 2 9 8 00		
Depreciation Expense, Store Equipment	4 3 6 0 00			
Insurance Expense	5 5 2 00			
Supplies			2 9 8 00	
Salaries Payable				5 8 8 00
	216 3 0 2 00	248 7 1 4 00	151 3 4 2 00	118 9 3 0 00

Required

1. Determine the entries that appeared in the Adjustments columns and present them in general journal form on page 41.

2. Determine the net income for the year.

3. What is the amount of the ending capital?

Check Figure
Salaries accrued, $588

PROBLEM 11-4B The accounts in the ledger of Markey's Mountain Shop, with the balances as of December 31, the end of its fiscal year, are as follows:

Cash	$ 12,840
Accounts Receivable	3,242
Merchandise Inventory	137,757
Prepaid Insurance	2,845
Land	22,000
Building	86,000
Accumulated Depreciation, Building	36,940
Store Equipment	54,952
Accumulated Depreciation, Store Equipment	13,348
Notes Payable	10,500
Accounts Payable	18,540
Sales Tax Payable	5,706
B. Markey, Capital	171,000
B. Markey, Drawing	52,000
Sales	458,905
Sales Returns and Allowances	7,590
Cost of Goods Sold	265,315
Salary Expense	52,973
Advertising Expense	6,288
Utilities Expense	7,355

(Continued)

Store Supplies Expense	$ 1,530
Property Tax Expense	800
Miscellaneous Expense	775
Interest Expense	677

Data for the adjustments are as follows. Assume that Markey's Mountain Shop uses the perpetual inventory system.

a. Merchandise Inventory at December 31, $140,357.
b. Store supplies inventory at December 31, $540.
c. Depreciation of building, $3,400.
d. Depreciation of store equipment, $3,800.
e. Salaries accrued at December 31, $1,250.
f. Insurance expired during the year, $1,480.

Check Figure
Net income, $108,812

Required

1. Complete the work sheet after entering the account names and balances onto the work sheet.
2. Journalize the adjusting entries on journal page 63.

ACTIVITIES

CONSIDER AND COMMUNICATE

You have a friend who is a seamstress specializing in *Star Wars* ensembles. She receives cash well in advance of the required date, often in the fiscal period prior to the date of delivery of the ensemble, not only to enable her to purchase material, but to cover her labor. She always debits Cash and credits Ensemble Income. First, explain to her why this entry violates the matching principle. Second, identify the classification of Unearned Revenue. Third, explain when the Unearned Revenue account is used.

WHAT'S WRONG WITH THIS PICTURE?

What could happen if a business spent the cash it had received in advance for services it promised to perform at a later date?

CRITICAL THINKING

On November 1, an exterior painting company received $5,310 for a paint job that will not be finished for a few months. As of December 31, which is the end of the fiscal period, $2,400 worth of painting will not have been completed. The bookkeeper completed the following entries prior to leaving on vacation:

Cash		Painting Income		Unearned Painting Income	
11/1 5,310		12/31 2,400	11/1 5,310		12/31 2,400

The owner wants to get a bank loan by December 1. The bank requires interim financial statements to be submitted as of December 1. How will the bookkeeper's entries affect the accuracy of the interim balance sheet and income statements? What difference will the bookkeeper's methods make in the December 31 balance sheet and income statement?

A QUESTION OF ETHICS

The owner of a motorcycle shop allows his two sons to take motorcycles home to try them out on different types of surfaces because he believes that they need to be familiar with the products they sell. Sometimes the motorcycles are not returned to the store by the time the physical count of inventory takes place. Respond to this practice.

All About You Spa

Adjusting Entries

Two months (July and August) have passed since Ms. Valli has seen the financial statements for All About You Spa. It is time to begin their preparation. Several accounts need adjusting. These include the accounts you adjusted in Chapter 4 as well as any accounts involved with merchandising.

> What additional accounts need to be adjusted?

Directions for Adjusting Entries

1. If desired, or as instructed, prepare a work sheet on paper or with a spreadsheet program. Then enter the adjustments shown on the work sheet into your software program. Adjustment information is provided on the following pages.

2. Open the file entitled **All_About_You_Spa_Ch11.IA7**. Enter your name when prompted and click **OK**. Select "Yes" or "No" as desired when asked if you want to open on-screen instructions and check figures. As a reminder, these instructions may be opened at any time by clicking on the **Info.** toolbar button.

3. Click on the **Save As** toolbar button. When the Save As window appears, select the folder in which you wish to save your data files (if not already selected). In the File Name box, key **All_About_You_Ch11_Your_Name.IA7** (for example, All_About_You_Spa_Ch11_John_Doe.IA7) to identify the file containing your work. Click on the **Save** button.

4. Click on the **Journals** toolbar button and key the adjusting journal entries in the General Journal. Follow these steps for each entry: (a) Key the date, Aug. 31, in the Date column. (b) Enter a reference of "Adj.Ent." in the Refer. column (this is required for generating the Adjusting Journal Entries report later). (c) Enter the debit and credit parts of the entry as you learned to do in Chapter 3.

5. Display the adjusting journal entries. Click on the **Reports** toolbar button. Click on **Journals** and **General Journal** to choose a report to display. Click on **Customize Journal Report**. In the Reference drop-down list, choose "Adj. Ent." and then click the **OK** button to display the Adjusting Journal Entries report. To print the report, click on the **Print** button.

6. Review your entries and make corrections to them, if necessary. In the General Journal window, click on the entry to correct, key the correction(s), and click on the **Post** button (or press Enter).

7. Display the adjusted Trial Balance report. Click on the **Reports** toolbar button. Click on **Ledger Reports** and **Trial Balance** to choose the report to display. Be sure the run date is set to Aug. 31. To print the report, click on the **Print** button at the bottom of the report window.

8. Click on the **Save** toolbar button to save your data file.

9. Click on the **Check** toolbar button to check your solution against the answer key.

Check Figures
5. Adjusting Entries
   General Journal
   report total, $13,961.43
7. Adjusted trial
   balance total, $133,624.03

Adjusting Entry Information

The pre-adjusted trial balance for August 31 is as follows:

All About You Spa
Trial Balance
August 31, 20—

Account Name	Debit	Credit
Cash	40,361.74	
Accounts Receivable	7,196.63	
Prepaid Insurance	800.00	
Spa Equipment	18,083.00	
Accumulated Depreciation, Spa Equipment		64.88
Office Equipment	1,570.00	
Accumulated Depreciation, Office Equipment		10.00
Accounts Payable		20,393.00
Sales Tax Payable		2,001.12
A. Valli, Capital		49,884.62
A. Valli, Drawing	5,000.00	
Income from Services		25,398.00
Merchandise Sales		22,489.65
Sales Returns and Allowances	88.00	
Purchases	24,101.00	
Purchases Returns and Allowances		123.00
Freight In	992.00	
Wages Expense	16,250.00	
Rent Expense	3,300.00	
Office Supplies Expense	118.00	
Spa Supplies Expense	535.00	
Laundry Expense	179.00	
Advertising Expense	455.00	
Utilities Expense	963.00	
Miscellaneous Expense	371.90	
	120,364.27	120,364.27

Merchandise Inventory Adjustment (a)

A new account, Merchandise Inventory 116, has been added to the Chart of Accounts. The August 31 pre-adjustment balance in that account is zero. But you know that merchandise has been purchased for resale and that you have sold merchandise. In addition, there is possible inventory shrinkage for several reasons: breakage, theft, misplacement, use as samples, etc. A physical count was taken, and the inventory was valued at $13,110. Enter the correct inventory count by debiting Merchandise Inventory and crediting Income Summary.

Supplies Adjustments (b) and (c)

A physical count has been taken of the two supplies accounts. The values of the remaining inventories of supplies are:

Office Supplies	$ 75.00
Spa Supplies	345.00

All About You Spa has been entering all purchases of supplies directly into the expense accounts, but the inventories of supplies remaining should appear as assets. Therefore, two asset accounts have been added to the Chart of Accounts: Spa Supplies 114 and Office Supplies 115. You will need to make two adjusting entries removing (crediting) the above amounts from the expense accounts and debiting the asset accounts.

Prepaid Insurance Adjustment (d)

A review of the insurance records determined that $281.67 in liability insurance coverage had been used during the last two months.

Depreciation Adjustments (e) and (f)

Estimated depreciation amounts for the two equipment accounts are:

Spa Equipment	$129.76
Office Equipment	20.00

Remember to credit the accumulated depreciation (contra asset) accounts, *not* the equipment accounts.

Wages Expense/Wages Payable Adjustment

There is no need for a Wages Expense/Wages Payable adjustment because the end of the fiscal period did not come in the middle of a pay period. (The spa was closed on August 31.)

12

Financial Statements, Closing Entries, and Reversing Entries

WHY IT MATTERS

COSTCO WHOLESALE CORPORATION, Issaquah, Washington

Costco is the largest membership warehouse club chain in the world based on sales volume and is the fifth largest general retailer in the United States. Costco focuses on selling products at low prices, often at very high volume. These goods are usually bulk-packaged and marketed primarily to large families and businesses. Costco became the first company ever to grow from zero to $3 billion in sales in less than six years.

For fiscal year 2008, Costco's sales totaled $70.9 billion, a 12.5 percent increase from 2007, and its net income reached $1.28 billion in 2008, an 18.5 percent increase from 2007. This information, and much more, can be derived from the financial statements that merchandising firms such as Costco must prepare on a regular basis to provide shareholders and other interested parties information about the company's activities and financial performance. These various financial statements and the information contained in them are the focus of this chapter.

LEARNING OBJECTIVES

After you have completed this chapter, you will be able to do the following:

1 Prepare a classified income statement for a merchandising firm.

2 Prepare a classified balance sheet for any type of business.

3 Compute working capital and current ratio.

4 Journalize the closing entries for a merchandising firm.

5 Determine which adjusting entries can be reversed, and journalize the reversing entries.

ACCOUNTING LANGUAGE

Cost of Goods Sold (p. 494)
Current Assets (p. 499)
Current Liabilities (p. 499)
Current ratio (p. 500)
Delivered Cost of Purchases (p. 495)
General Expenses (p. 495)
Gross Profit (p. 492)
Liquidity (p. 499)
Long-Term Liabilities (p. 499)

Net Income or **Net Profit** (p. 492)
Net Purchases (p. 495)
Net Sales (p. 493)
Notes Receivable (current) (p. 499)
Property and Equipment (p. 499)
Reversing entries (p. 505)
Selling Expenses (p. 495)
Temporary-equity accounts (p. 502)
Working capital (p. 500)

In this chapter, we review how to prepare financial statements directly from a work sheet. We also explain the functions of closing entries and reversing entries as means of completing the accounting cycle. Finally, we look at the financial statements in their entirety and explain their various subdivisions.

First, here is the chart of accounts for Whitewater Raft Supply.

PERIODIC INVENTORY CHART OF ACCOUNTS	**PERPETUAL INVENTORY CHART OF ACCOUNTS**
Assets (100–199)	**Assets (100–199)**
111 Cash	111 Cash
112 Notes Receivable	112 Notes Receivable
113 Accounts Receivable	113 Accounts Receivable
114 Merchandise Inventory	114 Merchandise Inventory
115 Supplies	115 Supplies
116 Prepaid Insurance	116 Prepaid Insurance
121 Land	121 Land
122 Building	122 Building
123 Accumulated Depreciation, Building	123 Accumulated Depreciation, Building
124 Equipment	124 Equipment
125 Accumulated Depreciation, Equipment	125 Accumulated Depreciation, Equipment
Liabilities (200–299)	**Liabilities (200–299)**
211 Notes Payable	211 Notes Payable
212 Accounts Payable	212 Accounts Payable

213 Wages Payable
217 Unearned Course Fees
221 Mortgage Payable

Owner's Equity (300–399)
311 D. M. Bruce, Capital
312 D. M. Bruce, Drawing
313 Income Summary

Revenue (400–499)
411 Sales
412 Sales Returns and Allowances
413 Sales Discounts
421 Course Fees Income
422 Interest Income

Cost of Goods Sold (500–599)
511 Purchases
512 Purchases Returns and Allowances
513 Purchases Discounts
514 Freight In

Expenses (600–699)
611 Wages Expense
622 Supplies Expense
623 Insurance Expense
624 Depreciation Expense, Building
625 Depreciation Expense, Equipment
626 Property Tax Expense
634 Interest Expense

213 Wages Payable
217 Unearned Course Fees
221 Mortgage Payable

Owner's Equity (300–399)
311 D. M. Bruce, Capital
312 D. M. Bruce, Drawing
313 Income Summary

Revenue (400–499)
411 Sales
412 Sales Returns and Allowances
413 Sales Discounts
421 Course Fees Income
422 Interest Income

Cost of Goods Sold (500–599)
511 Cost of Goods Sold

Expenses (600–699)
611 Wages Expense
622 Supplies Expense
623 Insurance Expense
624 Depreciation Expense, Building
625 Depreciation Expense, Equipment
626 Property Tax Expense
634 Interest Expense

THE INCOME STATEMENT

LEARNING OBJECTIVE 1

Prepare a classified income statement for a merchandising firm.

As you know, the work sheet is merely a tool used by accountants to prepare the financial statements. In Figure 1, we present the part of the work sheet for Whitewater Raft Supply that includes the Income Statement columns. Of course, **each of the amounts that appear in the Income Statement columns of the work sheet will be used in the income statement**. Notice that the amounts for the beginning and ending merchandise inventory appear separately on the Income Summary line. Recall that you were asked to pick up the two figures and move them—not to take the difference between the two. Figure 2 shows the entire income statement. Take your time to look it over carefully; then we will break it down into its components.

The income statement follows a logical pattern that is much the same for any type of merchandising business. The ability to interpret the income statement and extract parts from it is very useful when gathering information for decision making. To realize the full value of an income statement, however, you need to know the basic format of an income statement. Let's look at the statement section by section.

Net Sales	$254,260
– Cost of Goods Sold	90,120
Gross Profit	$164,140
– Operating Expenses	58,835
Income from Operations	$105,305

FIGURE 1   Partial work sheet for Whitewater Raft Supply

Whitewater Raft Supply
Work Sheet
For Year Ended December 31, 20—

Account Name	Trial Balance Debit	Trial Balance Credit	Adjustments Debit	Adjustments Credit	Income Statement Debit	Income Statement Credit
Cash	24 1 5 4 00					
Notes Receivable	4 0 0 0 00					
Accounts Receivable	29 5 4 6 00					
Merchandise Inventory	67 0 0 0 00		(b) 64 8 0 0 00	(a) 67 0 0 0 00		
Prepaid Insurance	9 6 0 00			(e) 5 2 0 00		
Land	122 1 0 0 00					
Building	129 0 0 0 00					
Accumulated Depr., Building		51 0 0 0 00		(f) 3 5 0 0 00		
Equipment	33 1 0 0 00					
Accumulated Depr., Equipment		16 4 0 0 00		(g) 4 9 0 0 00		
Notes Payable		36 6 0 0 00				
Accounts Payable		3 3 0 0 00				
Unearned Course Fees		1 2 0 0 00	(c) 8 0 0 00			
Mortgage Payable		7 8 0 0 00				
D. M. Bruce, Capital		253 7 7 4 00				
D. M. Bruce, Drawing	77 0 0 0 00					
Sales		257 1 8 0 00				257 1 8 0 00
Sales Returns and Allowances	9 4 0 00				9 4 0 00	
Sales Discounts	1 9 8 0 00				1 9 8 0 00	
Interest Income		2 2 0 00				2 2 0 00
Purchases	87 8 4 0 00				87 8 4 0 00	
Purchases Returns and Allowances		9 3 2 00				9 3 2 00
Purchases Discounts		1 3 4 8 00				1 3 4 8 00
Freight In	2 3 6 0 00				2 3 6 0 00	
Wages Expense	45 9 0 0 00		(h) 1 0 3 0 00		46 9 3 0 00	
Supplies Expense	1 5 4 0 00			(d) 4 1 5 00	1 1 2 5 00	
Property Tax Expense	1 8 6 0 00				1 8 6 0 00	
Interest Expense	4 7 4 00				4 7 4 00	
	629 7 5 4 00	629 7 5 4 00				
Income Summary			(a) 67 0 0 0 00	(b) 64 8 0 0 00	67 0 0 0 00	64 8 0 0 00
Course Fees Income				(c) 8 0 0 00		8 0 0 00
Supplies			(d) 4 1 5 00			
Insurance Expense			(e) 5 2 0 00		5 2 0 00	
Depreciation Expense, Building			(f) 3 5 0 0 00		3 5 0 0 00	
Depreciation Expense, Equipment			(g) 4 9 0 0 00		4 9 0 0 00	
Wages Payable				(h) 1 0 3 0 00		
			142 9 6 5 00	142 9 6 5 00	219 4 2 9 00	325 2 8 0 00
Net Income					105 8 5 1 00	
					325 2 8 0 00	325 2 8 0 00

FIGURE 2

Income statement for
Whitewater Raft Supply

Whitewater Raft Supply
Income Statement
For Year Ended December 31, 20—

Revenue from Sales:			
Sales		$257,180	
Less: Sales Returns and Allowances	$ 940		
Sales Discounts	1,980	2,920	
Net Sales			$254,260
Cost of Goods Sold:			
Merchandise Inventory, January 1, 20—		$ 67,000	
Purchases	$87,840		
Less: Purchases Returns and Allowances	$ 932		
Purchases Discounts	1,348	2,280	
Net Purchases	$85,560		
Add Freight In	2,360		
Delivered Cost of Purchases		87,920	
Cost of Goods Available for Sale		$154,920	
Less Merchandise Inventory, December 31, 20—		64,800	
Cost of Goods Sold			90,120
Gross Profit			$164,140
Operating Expenses:			
Wages Expense		$ 46,930	
Supplies Expense		1,125	
Insurance Expense		520	
Depreciation Expense, Building		3,500	
Depreciation Expense, Equipment		4,900	
Property Tax Expense		1,860	
Total Operating Expenses			58,835
Income from Operations			$105,305
Other Income:			
Course Fees Income		$ 800	
Interest Income		220	
Total Other Income		$ 1,020	
Other Expenses:			
Interest Expense		474	546
Net Income			$105,851

To illustrate the concepts of **gross** and **net**, here is an example of a simple single-sale transaction.

Several years ago, Della Reyes bought an antique table at a second-hand store for $800. She sold the table for $1,850. She advertised it in the daily newspaper at a cost of $73. How much did she make as clear profit?

Sale of Table	$1,850
Less Cost of Table	800
Gross Profit	$1,050
Less Advertising Expense	73
Net Income or Net Profit (gain on the sale)	$ 977

Gross Profit is the profit on the sale of the table before any expenses have been deducted; in this case, it is $1,050. **Net Income,** or **Net Profit,** is the final or clear profit after all expenses have been deducted. In a single-sale situation such as this, we refer to the final outcome as the net profit. But for a business that has many sales and expenses, most accountants prefer the term *net income*. Regardless of which word you use, *net* refers to clear profit—after all expenses have been deducted.

Revenue from Sales

Now let's look at the Revenue from Sales section of the income statement for Whitewater Raft Supply:

Revenue from Sales:		
Sales		$257,180
Less: Sales Returns and Allowances	$ 940	
Sales Discounts	1,980	2,920
Net Sales		$254,260

When we introduced Sales Returns and Allowances and Sales Discounts, we treated them as deductions from Sales. You can see that on the income statement, they are deducted from Sales to give us **Net Sales**. Note that we record these items in the same order in which they appear in the ledger.

Ratio Analysis

An important function of accounting is to provide tools for interpreting the financial statements or the results of operations. One ratio that is frequently used to analyze financial statements is *gross profit percentage*.

Southern Office Furniture will serve as our example (see the comparative income statement below).

Gross Profit Percentage

Southern Office Furniture Comparative Income Statement For Years Ended January 31, 2011, and January 31, 2010				
	2011		**2010**	
	Amount	Percent	Amount	Percent
Revenue from Sales:				
Sales	$533,600	101%	$510,000	102%
Less Sales Returns and Allowances	5,600	1	10,000	2
Net Sales	$528,000	100%	$500,000	100%
Cost of Goods Sold:				
Merchandise Inventory, February 1	$ 46,000	9%	$ 64,000	13%
Delivered Cost of Purchases	290,000	55	230,000	46
Cost of Goods Available for Sale	$336,000	64%	$294,000	59%
Less Merchandise Inventory, January 31	58,000	11	46,000	9
Cost of Goods Sold	$278,000	53%	$248,000	50%
Gross Profit	$250,000	47%	$252,000	50%
Operating Expenses:				
Sales Salary Expense	$ 63,600	12%	$ 58,000	12%
Rent Expense	24,000	5	24,000	5
Advertising Expense	21,400	4	16,000	3
Depreciation Expense, Equipment	20,000	4	18,000	4
Insurance Expense	2,000	—	2,000	—
Store Supplies Expense	1,000	—	1,000	—
Miscellaneous Expense	1,000	—	1,000	—
Total Operating Expenses	$133,000	25%	$120,000	24%
Net Income	$117,000	22%	$132,000	26%

For each year, net sales is the base (100 percent). All other items on the income statement can be expressed as a percentage of net sales for the particular year involved. For example, let's look at the following percentages:

$$\text{Gross Profit \% (2011)} = \frac{\text{Gross Profit for 2011}}{\text{Net Sales for 2011}} = \frac{\$250,000}{\$528,000} = 0.473 = 47\%$$

$$\text{Gross Profit \% (2010)} = \frac{\text{Gross Profit for 2010}}{\text{Net Sales for 2010}} = \frac{\$252,000}{\$500,000} = 0.504 = 50\%$$

$$\text{Sales Salary Expense \% (2011)} = \frac{\text{Sales Salary Expense for 2011}}{\text{Net Sales for 2011}}$$

$$= \frac{\$63,600}{\$528,000} = 0.120 = 12\%$$

$$\text{Sales Salary Expense \% (2010)} = \frac{\text{Sales Salary Expense for 2010}}{\text{Net Sales for 2010}}$$

$$= \frac{\$58,000}{\$500,000} = 0.116 = 12\%$$

Here's how you might interpret a few of the percentages:

2011

- For every $100 in net sales, gross profit amounted to $47.
- For every $100 in net sales, sales salary expense amounted to $12.
- For every $100 in net sales, net income amounted to $22.

2010

- For every $100 in net sales, gross profit amounted to $50.
- For every $100 in net sales, sales salary expense amounted to $12.
- For every $100 in net sales, net income amounted to $26.

The gross profit percentage declined from 50% in 2010 to 47% in 2011 because the Cost of Goods Sold percentage increased from 50% in 2010 to 53% in 2011.

Cost of Goods Sold

The section of the income statement that requires the greatest amount of concentration is the **Cost of Goods Sold** section, where the cost of the goods we sold is computed. Let's repeat it in its entirety:

Cost of Goods Sold:			
Merchandise Inventory, January 1, 20—			$ 67,000
Purchases		$87,840	
Less: Purchases Returns and Allowances	$ 932		
Purchases Discounts	1,348	2,280	
Net Purchases		$85,560	
Add Freight In		2,360	
Delivered Cost of Purchases			87,920
Cost of Goods Available for Sale			$154,920
Less Merchandise Inventory, December 31, 20—			64,800
Cost of Goods Sold			90,120

First, let's look closely at the Purchases section.

Purchases		$87,840
Less: Purchases Returns and Allowances	$ 932	
Purchases Discounts	1,348	2,280
Net Purchases		$85,560
Add Freight In		2,360
Delivered Cost of Purchases		87,920

Note the parallel to the Revenue from Sales section. To arrive at **Net Purchases**, we deduct the sum of Purchases Returns and Allowances and Purchases Discounts from Purchases. To complete the Purchases section we add Freight In to Net Purchases to get **Delivered Cost of Purchases**.

Now let's look at the full Cost of Goods Sold section. You might think of Cost of Goods Sold like this:

Amount we started with (beginning inventory)	$ 67,000
+ Net amount we purchased, including freight charges	87,920
Total amount that could have been sold (available)	$154,920
− Amount left over (ending inventory)	64,800
Cost of the goods that were actually sold	$ 90,120

Here's the Cost of Goods Sold expressed in proper wording.

Merchandise Inventory, January 1, 20—	$ 67,000
+ Delivered Cost of Purchases	87,920
Cost of Goods Available for Sale	$154,920
− Merchandise Inventory, December 31, 20—	64,800
Cost of Goods Sold	$ 90,120

Operating Expenses

Operating expenses, as the name implies, are the regular expenses of doing business. We list the accounts and their respective balances in the order in which they appear in the ledger.

Many firms use subclassifications of operating expenses, such as the following:

1. **Selling Expenses** Any expenses directly connected with the selling activity, such as
   - Sales Salary Expense
   - Sales Commissions Expense
   - Advertising Expense
   - Store Supplies Expense
   - Delivery Expense
   - Depreciation Expense, Store Equipment

2. **General Expenses** Any expenses related to the office or administration, or any expense that cannot be directly connected with a selling activity:
   - Office Salary Expense
   - Property Tax Expense
   - Depreciation Expense, Office Equipment
   - Rent Expense
   - Insurance Expense

FYI

In preparing the income statement, classifying expense accounts as selling expenses or general expenses is a matter of judgment. The only reason we're not using this breakdown here is that we're trying to keep the number of accounts to a basic few.

- Office Supplies Expense
- Miscellaneous General Expense*

Income from Operations

Now let's repeat the skeleton outline:

Net Sales
− Cost of Goods Sold

Gross Profit
− Operating Expenses

Income from Operations

If Operating Expenses are the regular, recurring expenses of doing business, then Income from Operations should be the regular or recurring income from normal business operations. When you compare the results of operations over a number of years, Income from Operations is the figure to use as a basis for comparison.

Other Income and Other Expenses

The Other Income classification, as the name implies, includes any revenue account other than Revenue from Sales. What we are trying to do is to isolate Sales at the top of the income statement as the major revenue account, so that the Gross Profit figure represents the profit made on the sale of merchandise *only*. Additional accounts that may appear under the heading of Other Income are Rent Income (the firm is subletting part of its premises), Interest Income (the firm holds an interest-bearing note or contract), Gain on Disposal of Property and Equipment (the firm makes a profit on the sale of property and equipment), and Miscellaneous Income (the firm has an overage recorded in the Cash Short and Over account).

The classification Other Expenses records various nonoperating expenses, such as Interest Expense or Loss on Disposal of Property and Equipment.

THE STATEMENT OF OWNER'S EQUITY AND THE BALANCE SHEET

Remember

> Net income appears on both the income statement and the statement of owner's equity.

Remember

> The columns on the financial statements *do not* represent debit or credit columns. The columns are for making computations and listing totals.

Figure 3 is a partial work sheet for Whitewater Raft Supply. Here again we find that **every figure in the Balance Sheet columns of the work sheet is used in either the statement of owner's equity or the balance sheet.**

Preparation of the financial statements follows the same order we presented before: first, the income statement; second, the statement of owner's equity; third, the balance sheet. The statement of owner's equity shows why the balance of the Capital account has changed from the beginning of the fiscal period to the end of it. In preparing the statement of owner's equity, always look into the ledger for the owner's Capital account to find any changes, such as additional investments, made during the year.

In Figure 4 we observe the balance of D. M. Bruce, Capital, listed on the work sheet as $253,774. We note from the ledger account a credit of $9,000 representing an additional investment. Therefore, the beginning balance of D. M. Bruce, Capital, was $244,774 ($253,774 − $9,000).

---

*If the Cash Short and Over account has a debit balance (net shortage), the balance is added to and reported as Miscellaneous General Expense. Conversely, if the Cash Short and Over account has a credit balance (net overage), the balance is added to and reported as Miscellaneous Income, which is classified as Other Income.

FIGURE 3   Partial work sheet for Whitewater Raft Supply

Whitewater Raft Supply
Work Sheet
For Year Ended December 31, 20—

Account Name	Trial Balance Debit	Trial Balance Credit	Adjustments Debit	Adjustments Credit	Balance Sheet Debit	Balance Sheet Credit
Cash	24 1 5 4 00				24 1 5 4 00	
Notes Receivable	4 0 0 0 00				4 0 0 0 00	
Accounts Receivable	29 5 4 6 00				29 5 4 6 00	
Merchandise Inven.	67 0 0 0 00		(b) 64 8 0 0 00	(a) 67 0 0 0 00	64 8 0 0 00	
Prepaid Insurance	9 6 0 00			(e) 5 2 0 00	4 4 0 00	
Land	122 1 0 0 00				122 1 0 0 00	
Building	129 0 0 0 00				129 0 0 0 00	
Accum. Depr., Building		51 0 0 0 00		(f) 3 5 0 0 00		54 5 0 0 00
Equipment	33 1 0 0 00				33 1 0 0 00	
Accum. Depr., Equipment		16 4 0 0 00		(g) 4 9 0 0 00		21 3 0 0 00
Notes Payable		36 6 0 0 00				36 6 0 0 00
Accounts Payable		3 3 0 0 00				3 3 0 0 00
Unearn. Course Fees		1 2 0 0 00	(c) 8 0 0 00			4 0 0 00
Mortgage Payable		7 8 0 0 00				7 8 0 0 00
D. M. Bruce, Capital		253 7 7 4 00				253 7 7 4 00
D. M. Bruce, Draw.	77 0 0 0 00				77 0 0 0 00	
Sales		257 1 8 0 00				
Sales Returns and Allowances	9 4 0 00					
Sales Discounts	1 9 8 0 00					
Interest Income		2 2 0 00				
Purchases	87 8 4 0 00					
Purchases Returns and Allowances		9 3 2 00				
Purchases Discounts		1 3 4 8 00				
Freight In	2 3 6 0 00					
Wages Expense	45 9 0 0 00		(h) 1 0 3 0 00			
Supplies Expense	1 5 4 0 00			(d) 4 1 5 00		
Property Tax Expense	1 8 6 0 00					
Interest Expense	4 7 4 00					
	629 7 5 4 00	629 7 5 4 00				
Income Summary			(a) 67 0 0 0 00	(b) 64 8 0 0 00		
Course Fees Income				(c) 8 0 0 00		
Supplies			(d) 4 1 5 00		4 1 5 00	
Insurance Expense			(e) 5 2 0 00			
Depr. Expense, Building			(f) 3 5 0 0 00			
Depr. Expense, Equipment			(g) 4 9 0 0 00			
Wages Payable				(h) 1 0 3 0 00		1 0 3 0 00
			142 9 6 5 00	142 9 6 5 00	484 5 5 5 00	378 7 0 4 00
Net Income						105 8 5 1 00
					484 5 5 5 00	484 5 5 5 00

FIGURE 4

Statement of owner's equity
for Whitewater Raft Supply

Whitewater Raft Supply
Statement of Owner's Equity
For Year Ended December 31, 20—

D. M. Bruce, Capital, January 1, 20—		$244,774
Investment during the Year	$ 9,000	
Net Income for the Year	$105,851	
Subtotal	$114,851	
Less Withdrawals for the Year	77,000	
Increase in Capital		37,851
D. M. Bruce, Capital, December 31, 20—		$282,625

BALANCE SHEET CLASSIFICATIONS

LEARNING OBJECTIVE 2

Prepare a classified balance sheet for any type of business.

Balance sheet classifications are generally uniform for all types of business enterprises. You are strongly urged to take the time to learn the following definitions of the classifications and the order of accounts within them. As you read, refer to Figure 5.

FIGURE 5

Balance sheet for Whitewater Raft Supply

Whitewater Raft Supply
Balance Sheet
December 31, 20—

Assets			
Current Assets:			
Cash		$ 24,154	
Notes Receivable		4,000	
Accounts Receivable		29,546	
Merchandise Inventory		64,800	
Prepaid Insurance		440	
Supplies		415	
Total Current Assets			$123,355
Property and Equipment:			
Land		$122,100	
Building	$129,000		
Less Accumulated Depreciation	54,500	74,500	
Equipment	$ 33,100		
Less Accumulated Depreciation	21,300	11,800	
Total Property and Equipment			208,400
Total Assets			$331,755
Liabilities			
Current Liabilities:			
Notes Payable		$ 36,600	
Mortgage Payable (current portion)		2,000	
Accounts Payable		3,300	
Wages Payable		1,030	
Unearned Course Fees		400	
Total Current Liabilities			$ 43,330
Long-Term Liabilities:			
Mortgage Payable			5,800
Total Liabilities			$ 49,130
Owner's Equity			
D. M. Bruce, Capital			282,625
Total Liabilities and Owner's Equity			$331,755

Current Assets

Current Assets consist of cash and any other assets or resources that are expected to be realized in cash or to be sold or consumed during the normal operating cycle of the business (or one year, if the normal operating cycle is less than twelve months).

Accountants list current assets in the order of their convertibility into cash—in other words, their **liquidity**. (If you have an asset such as a car or a stereo and you sell it quickly and turn it into cash, you are said to be turning it into a *liquid* state.) If the first four accounts shown under Current Assets in Figure 5 are present, they are always recorded in the same order: (1) Cash, (2) Notes Receivable, (3) Accounts Receivable, and (4) Merchandise Inventory.

Notes Receivable (current) are short-term (one year or less) promissory notes (promise-to-pay notes) held by the firm. A note is generally received from a customer as a substitute for a charge account.

Prepaid Insurance and Supplies are considered prepaid items that will be used up or will expire within the following operating cycle or year. Generally, these prepaid items are not converted into cash and that's why they appear at the bottom of the Current Assets section.

Property and Equipment

Property and Equipment are relatively long-lived assets that are held for use in the production or sale of other assets or services; some accountants refer to them as *fixed assets*. The three types of accounts that usually appear in this category are Land, Building, and Equipment (refer to Figure 5). Note that the Building and Equipment accounts are followed by their respective Accumulated Depreciation accounts. We list these assets in order of their length of life, with the longest-lived asset placed first.

Current Liabilities

Current Liabilities are debts that will become due within the normal operating cycle of the business, usually within one year; they normally will be paid, when due, from current assets. List current liabilities in the order of their expected payment. Notes Payable represents the amount owed on promissory notes. Mortgage Payable is the payment one makes to reduce the principal of the mortgage in a given year. Accounts Payable are debts owed to creditors. Wages Payable and any other accrued liabilities, such as Commissions Payable and the current portion of unearned revenue accounts, usually fall at the bottom of the list of current liabilities.

Long-Term Liabilities

Long-Term Liabilities are debts that are payable over a comparatively long period, usually longer than one year. The current portion of notes, contracts, and loans (the amount of principal due within the next year) is shown as a current liability. The remaining amount is shown as a long-term liability. Note that for Whitewater Raft Supply, $2,000 of the Mortgage Payable represents the current portion and is shown as a current liability. The remaining $5,800 is shown as a long-term liability. (Refer to Figure 5.)

Working Capital and Current Ratio

Both the management and the short-term creditors of a firm are vitally interested in two questions:

1. Does the firm have a sufficient amount of capital to operate?

2. Does the firm have the ability to pay its debts?

Two measures used to answer these questions are a firm's working capital and its current ratio; the necessary data are taken from a classified balance sheet.

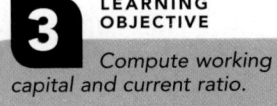

3 LEARNING OBJECTIVE

Compute working capital and current ratio.

© GEORGE ROBINSON/PHOTOLIBRARY

The barn, the tractor, and the land this man is working are all classified as fixed assets in the Property and Equipment section. Only the barn and tractor, however, are subject to depreciation.

Working capital is determined by subtracting current liabilities from current assets; thus,

$$\text{Working Capital} = \text{Current Assets} - \text{Current Liabilities}$$

The normal operating cycle for most firms is less than one year. Because current assets equal cash—or items that can be converted into cash or used up within one year—and current liabilities equal the total amount that the company must pay out within one year, working capital is appropriately named. It is the amount of capital the company has available to use or to work with. The working capital for Whitewater Raft Supply is as follows:

$$\text{Working Capital} = \$123,355 - \$43,330 = \$80,025$$

The **current ratio** is useful in revealing a firm's ability to pay its bills. It is determined by dividing current assets by current liabilities:

$$\text{Current Ratio} = \frac{\text{Current Assets (amount coming in within one year)}}{\text{Current Liabilities (amount going out within one year)}}$$

The current ratio for Whitewater Raft Supply is calculated like this:

$$\text{Current Ratio} = \frac{\$123,355}{\$43,330} = 2.85$$

In the case of Whitewater Raft Supply, $2.85 in current assets is available to pay every dollar currently due on December 31.

You Make the Call

J. J. Marston owns Woodland Toys, a small business selling handmade wooden toys. Sales have been a bit slow, so he has come up with some strategies to increase sales as well as to begin exporting his specialty toys. The problem is that he needs cash to hire assistants and to purchase several woodworking tools to increase production. He has tried to figure out how he can manage the investment. He has no idea how to analyze his financial statements to provide valuable decision-making information. How would you recommend that he use his most recent balance sheet (shown below) and the two formulas discussed in the chapter to help in making the decision to expand his operation?

Woodland Toys
Balance Sheet
December 31, 20—

Assets		
Current Assets:		
Cash	$22,751	
Accounts Receivable	7,692	
Merchandise Inventory	45,018	
Prepaid Insurance	1,265	
Total Current Assets		$76,726
Property and Equipment:		
Shop Equipment	$18,357	
Less Accumulated Depreciation	6,020	
Total Property and Equipment		12,337
Total Assets		$89,063
Liabilities		
Current Liabilities:		
Accounts Payable	$10,340	
Total Current Liabilities		$10,340
Long-Term Liabilities:		
Mortgage Payable		3,500
Total Liabilities		$13,840
Owner's Equity		
J. J. Marston, Capital		75,223
Total Liabilities and Owner's Equity		$89,063

SOLUTION

While there are many more tools for analyzing financial statements than we have introduced, you have learned two formulas in this chapter that can assist your friend in determining his ability to expand his business—working capital and current ratio.

Working capital is the amount of capital the company has available to use or to work with. To compute Woodland Toys' working capital, subtract its current liabilities from its current assets:

$$\text{Working Capital} = \$76,726 - \$10,340 = \$66,386$$

While J. J. Marston does not want to liquidate all his assets, he can see that there is adequate capital to begin planning his business expansion.

A second formula that can help in making the decision to expand is the current ratio. It is useful in revealing a firm's ability to pay its bills. To compute Woodland Toys' current ratio, divide its current assets by its current liabilities.

$$\text{Current Ratio} = \frac{\$76,726}{\$10,340} = 7.42$$

This means that $7.42 in current assets is available to pay every dollar of debt currently due on December 31. The higher the current ratio the better position the company is in to pay short-term debt. A current ratio of 7.42 shows that Woodland Toys is in a very favorable position.

Chart of Accounts

When we introduced the chart of accounts and the account number arrangement, we said that the first digit represents the classification of an account. Since you are now acquainted with classified income statements and balance sheets, we can introduce the second digit. The second digit stands for the subclassification.

Assets	1--	Revenue	4--
Current Assets	11-	Revenue from Sales	41-
Property and Equipment	12-	Other Income	42-
Liabilities	2--	Cost of Goods Sold	5--
Current Liabilities	21-	Purchases	51-
Long-Term Liabilities	22-	Expenses	6--
Owner's Equity	3--	Selling Expenses	61-
Capital	31-	General Expenses	62-
		Other Expenses	63-

Remember

A common organization for the chart of accounts is

Assets	1--
Liabilities	2--
Owner's Equity	3--
Revenue	4--
Cost of Goods Sold	5--
Expenses	6--

The third digit indicates the placement of the account within the subclassification. For example, account number 411 represents Sales, which is the first account listed under Revenue. Account number 512 represents Purchases Returns and Allowances, which is the second account listed under Cost of Goods Sold. Account number 312 represents Drawing, which is the second account listed under Owner's Equity.

CLOSING ENTRIES

LEARNING OBJECTIVE 4

Journalize the closing entries for a merchandising firm.

Now let's look at closing entries for a merchandising business. You follow the same four steps to close or zero out the revenue, expense, and Drawing accounts as you do for a service business.

At the end of a fiscal period, you close the revenue and expense accounts so that you can start the next fiscal period with zero balances. You close the Drawing account because it, too, applies to one fiscal period. Recall that these accounts are called **temporary-equity accounts**, or *nominal accounts*.

Figure 6 shows the isolated Income Statement columns. After you have looked them over, let's look at the four steps of the closing procedure.

FIGURE 6   Partial work sheet for Whitewater Raft Supply

Account Name	Trial Balance Debit	Trial Balance Credit	Income Statement Debit	Income Statement Credit
Cash	24 1 5 4 00			
Notes Receivable	4 0 0 0 00			
Accounts Receivable	29 5 4 6 00			
Merchandise Inventory	67 0 0 0 00			
Prepaid Insurance	9 6 0 00			
Land	122 1 0 0 00			
Building	129 0 0 0 00			
Accumulated Depreciation, Building		51 0 0 0 00		
Equipment	33 1 0 0 00			
Accumulated Depreciation, Equipment		16 4 0 0 00		
Notes Payable		36 6 0 0 00		
Accounts Payable		3 3 0 0 00		
Unearned Course Fees		1 2 0 0 00		
Mortgage Payable		7 8 0 0 00		
D. M. Bruce, Capital		253 7 7 4 00		
D. M. Bruce, Drawing	77 0 0 0 00			
Sales		257 1 8 0 00		257 1 8 0 00
Sales Returns and Allowances	9 4 0 00		9 4 0 00	
Sales Discounts	1 9 8 0 00		1 9 8 0 00	
Interest Income		2 2 0 00		2 2 0 00
Purchases	87 8 4 0 00		87 8 4 0 00	
Purchases Returns and Allowances		9 3 2 00		9 3 2 00
Purchases Discounts		1 3 4 8 00		1 3 4 8 00
Freight In	2 3 6 0 00		2 3 6 0 00	
Wages Expense	45 9 0 0 00		46 9 3 0 00	
Supplies Expense	1 5 4 0 00		1 1 2 5 00	
Property Tax Expense	1 8 6 0 00		1 8 6 0 00	
Interest Expense	4 7 4 00		4 7 4 00	
	629 7 5 4 00	629 7 5 4 00		
Income Summary			67 0 0 0 00	64 8 0 0 00
Course Fees Income				8 0 0 00
Supplies				
Insurance Expense			5 2 0 00	
Depreciation Expense, Building			3 5 0 0 00	
Depreciation Expense, Equipment			4 9 0 0 00	
Wages Payable				
			219 4 2 9 00	325 2 8 0 00
Net Income			105 8 5 1 00	
			325 2 8 0 00	325 2 8 0 00

Four Steps in the Closing Procedure

These four steps should be followed when closing:

STEP 1. Close the revenue accounts and the other accounts that appear on the income statement and have credit balances (all temporary or nominal accounts with credit balances) into Income Summary. **(Debit the figures that are credited in the Income Statement columns of the work sheet, except the figure on the Income Summary line.)** This entry is illustrated for Whitewater Raft Supply as follows:

	GENERAL JOURNAL					PAGE 97	
Date	**Description**	**Post. Ref.**	**Debit**		**Credit**		
20—	Closing Entries					
Dec. 31	Sales		257 1 8 0 00			
	Interest Income		2 2 0 00			
	Purchases Returns and Allowances		9 3 2 00			
	Purchases Discounts		1 3 4 8 00			
	Course Fees Income		8 0 0 00			
	Income Summary				260 4 8 0 00	

STEP 2. Close the expense accounts and the other accounts appearing on the income statement that have debit balances (all temporary or nominal accounts with debit balances) into Income Summary. **(Credit the figures that are debited in the Income Statement columns of the work sheet, except the figure on the Income Summary line.)**

Note that you close Purchases Discounts and Purchases Returns and Allowances in step 1 along with the revenue accounts. Note also that in step 2 you close Sales Discounts and Sales Returns and Allowances along with the expense accounts.

	GENERAL JOURNAL					PAGE 97	
Date	**Description**	**Post. Ref.**	**Debit**		**Credit**		
Dec. 31	Income Summary		152 4 2 9 00			
	Sales Returns and Allowances				9 4 0 00	
	Sales Discounts				1 9 8 0 00	
	Purchases				87 8 4 0 00	
	Freight In				2 3 6 0 00	
	Wages Expense				46 9 3 0 00	
	Supplies Expense				1 1 2 5 00	
	Property Tax Expense				1 8 6 0 00	
	Interest Expense				4 7 4 00	
	Insurance Expense				5 2 0 00	
	Depreciation Expense, Building				3 5 0 0 00	
	Depreciation Expense, Equipment				4 9 0 0 00	

STEP 3. Close the Income Summary account into the Capital account, transferring the net income or loss to the Capital account.

	GENERAL JOURNAL					PAGE 97	
Date	**Description**	**Post. Ref.**	**Debit**		**Credit**		
Dec. 31	Income Summary		105 8 5 1 00			
	D. M. Bruce, Capital				105 8 5 1 00	

Here is what the T accounts look like. Note that the Income Summary account already contains adjusting entries for merchandise inventory.

Income Summary

Adj. (Beginning Merchandise Inventory)	67,000	Adj. (Ending Merchandise Inventory)	64,800
Closing (Expenses and other debit balance accounts)	152,429	Closing (Revenue and other credit balance accounts)	260,480
Closing (Net Income)	105,851		

D. M. Bruce, Capital

−	+
	Bal. 253,774
	Closing 105,851
	(Net Income)

STEP 4. Close the Drawing account into the Capital account.

GENERAL JOURNAL				PAGE 97
Date	Description	Post. Ref.	Debit	Credit
Dec. 31	D. M. Bruce, Capital		77 0 0 0 00	
	D. M. Bruce, Drawing			77 0 0 0 00

Here is what the T accounts would look like:

D. M. Bruce, Drawing

+	−
Bal. 77,000	Closing 77,000

D. M. Bruce, Capital

−	+
Closing 77,000 (Drawing)	Bal. 253,774
	Closing 105,851 (Net Income)
	Bal. 282,625

REVERSING ENTRIES

Reversing entries are general journal entries that are the exact reverse of certain adjusting entries. A reversing entry enables the accountant to record routine transactions in the usual manner, *even though* an adjusting entry affecting one of the accounts involved in the transaction has intervened. We can understand this concept best by looking at an example.

Suppose there is an adjusting entry for accrued wages owed to employees at the end of the fiscal year. Assume that all the employees of Mason Company earn, altogether, $400 per day for a five-day week and that payday occurs every Friday throughout the year. When the employees get their checks at 5:00 P.M. on Friday, the checks include their wages for that day and for the preceding four days. And

5 LEARNING OBJECTIVE

Determine which adjusting entries can be reversed, and journalize the reversing entries.

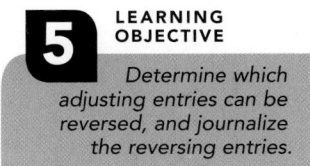

The use of reversing entries is optional.

FYI

assume that, one year, the last day of the fiscal year happens to fall on Wednesday, December 31. A diagram of this situation would look like this:

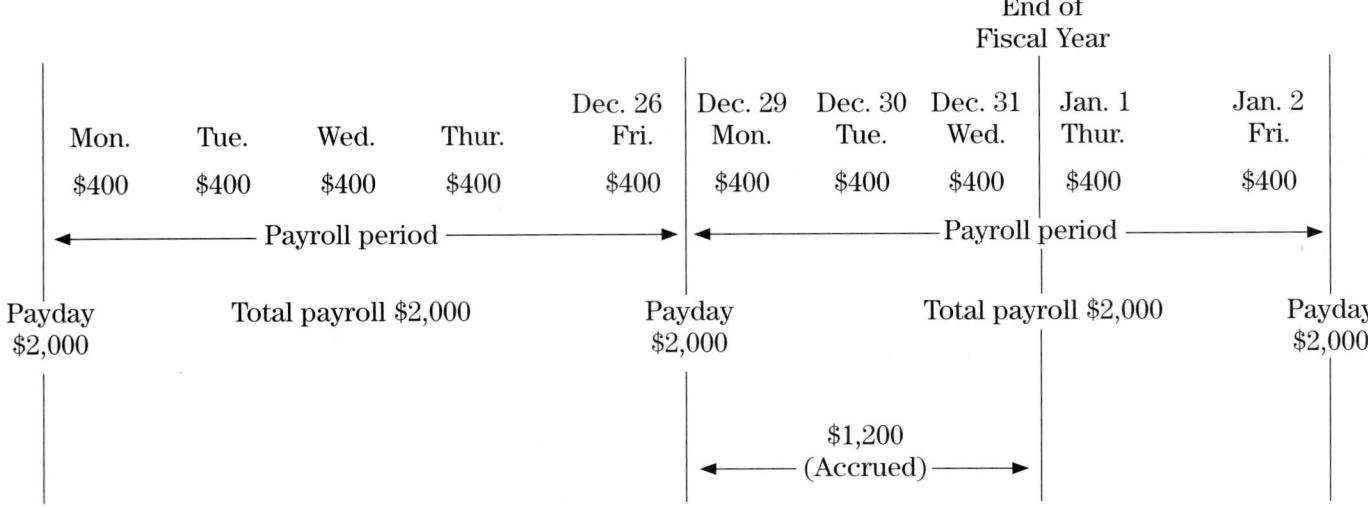

Each Friday during the year, the payroll has been debited to the Wages Expense account and credited to the Cash account. As a result, Wages Expense has a debit balance of $102,000. Here is the adjusting entry in T account form:

Wages Expense

	+	−
Bal.	102,000	
Dec. 31 Adj.	1,200	

Wages Payable

	−	+
Dec. 31 Adj.		1,200

Next, when all the expense accounts are closed, Wages Expense is closed by crediting it for $103,200. However, Wages Payable continues to have a credit balance of $1,200. The $2,000 payroll on January 2 must be split up by debiting Wages Payable $1,200, debiting Wages Expense $800, and crediting Cash $2,000.

The employee who records the payroll not only has to record this particular payroll differently from all other weekly payrolls for the year but also has to refer back to the adjusting entry to determine what portion of the $2,000 is debited to Wages Payable and what portion is debited to Wages Expense. In many companies, however, the employee who records the payroll does not have access to the adjusting entries.

There is a solution to this problem. The need to refer to the earlier entry and divide the debit total between the two accounts is eliminated *if a reversing entry is made on the first day of the following fiscal period*. You make an entry that is the exact reverse of the adjusting entry, as follows:

| | | | | | GENERAL JOURNAL | | | | | | | PAGE | 118 | |

Date		Description	Post. Ref.	Debit	Credit
20—		Reversing Entries			
Jan.	1	Wages Payable		1 2 0 0 00	
		Wages Expense			1 2 0 0 00

Now let's bring the T accounts up to date.

Wages Expense

	+	−		
Bal.	102,000	Dec. 31 Closing	103,200	
Dec. 31 Adjusting	1,200			
Bal.	——	Jan. 1 Reversing	1,200	

Wages Payable

	+	−		
Jan. 1 Reversing	1,200	Dec. 31 Adj.	1,200	

The reversing entry has the effect of transferring the $1,200 liability from Wages Payable to the credit side of Wages Expense. Wages Expense will temporarily have a credit balance until the next payroll is recorded in the routine manner. In our example, this occurs on January 2 as follows:

Wages Expense

	+	−		
Bal.	102,000	Dec. 31 Closing	103,200	
Dec. 31 Adj.	1,200			
Bal.	——			
Jan. 2	2,000	Jan. 1 Reversing	1,200	
Bal.	800			

Wages Payable

	−	+		
Jan. 1 Reversing	1,200	Dec. 31 Adj.	1,200	

Cash

	+	−		
		Jan. 2	2,000	

There is now a *net debit balance* of $800 in Wages Expense, which is the correct amount ($400 for January 1 and $400 for January 2). To see this, look at the following ledger accounts. December 26 was the last payday of one year, and January 2 is the first payday of the next year.

GENERAL LEDGER

ACCOUNT Wages Expense   ACCOUNT NO. 611

Date		Item	Post. Ref.	Debit	Credit	Balance Debit	Balance Credit
20—							
Dec.	26		CP16	2 0 0 0 00		102 0 0 0 00	
	31	Adjusting	J116	1 2 0 0 00		103 2 0 0 00	
	31	Closing	J117		103 2 0 0 00	————	————
20—							
Jan.	1	Reversing	J118		1 2 0 0 00		1 2 0 0 00
	2		CP17	2 0 0 0 00		8 0 0 00	

ACCOUNT Wages Payable   ACCOUNT NO. 213

Date		Item	Post. Ref.	Debit	Credit	Balance Debit	Balance Credit
20—							
Dec.	31	Adjusting	J116		1 2 0 0 00		1 2 0 0 00
20—							
Jan.	1	Reversing	J118	1 2 0 0 00		————	————

The reversing entry for accrued salaries or wages applies to service as well as merchandising companies. You can see that a reversing entry simply switches around an adjusting entry. The question is: Which adjusting entries should be reversed? Here are two handy rules for reversing. **If an adjusting entry is to be reversed, it must meet both of the following qualifications:**

1. **The adjusting entry increases an asset or liability account.**
2. **The asset or liability account did not have a previous balance.**

    With the exception of the first year of operations, Merchandise Inventory and contra accounts—such as Accumulated Depreciation—always have previous balances. Consequently, adjusting entries involving these accounts should never be reversed.

Let's apply these rules to the adjusting entries for Whitewater Raft Supply.

(Do not reverse; Merchandise Inventory is an asset, but it was decreased. Also, it has a previous balance.)

Merchandise Inventory				Income Summary		
+	−		Adj.	67,000	
Bal.	67,000	Adj.	67,000		

(Do not reverse; Merchandise Inventory is an asset, but it has a previous balance.)

Merchandise Inventory				Income Summary		
+	−		Adj.	67,000	Adj.	64,800
Bal.	67,000	Adj.	67,000			
Adj.	64,800					

(Do not reverse; Unearned Course Fees is a liability, but it was decreased. Also, it has a previous balance.)

Course Fees Income		Unearned Course Fees	
−	+	−	+
	Adj.	800	Adj.	800	Bal.	1,200

Supplies		
+	−	
Adj. 415		

Supplies Expense		
+	−	
Bal. 1,540	Adj.	415

(Reverse; Supplies is an asset account. It was increased, and it had no previous balance.)

Insurance Expense		
+	−	
Adj. 520		

Prepaid Insurance		
+	−	
Bal. 960	Adj.	520

(Do not reverse; Prepaid Insurance is an asset account, but it was decreased. Also, it has a previous balance.)

Depreciation Expense, Building		
+	−	
Adj. 3,500		

Accumulated Depreciation, Building		
−	+	
	Bal.	51,000
	Adj.	3,500

(Do not reverse; Accumulated Depreciation is a contra asset, and it always has a previous balance after the first year.)

Depreciation Expense, Equipment		
+	−	
Adj. 4,900		

Accumulated Depreciation, Equipment		
−	+	
	Bal.	16,400
	Adj.	4,900

(Do not reverse; Accumulated Depreciation is a contra asset, and it always has a previous balance after the first year.)

Wages Expense		
+	−	
Bal. 45,900		
Adj. 1,030		

Wages Payable		
−	+	
	Adj.	1,030

(Reverse; Wages Payable is a liability account. It was increased, and it had no previous balance.)

Whenever we introduce additional adjusting entries, we will make it a point to state whether they can be reversed.

> Reversing entries are optional.

Remember

CHAPTER REVIEW

Study & Practice

1 LEARNING OBJECTIVE

Prepare a classified income statement for a merchandising firm.

The outline of the income statement looks like this:

Revenue from Sales
- Gross Sales
- − Sales Returns and Allowances
- − Sales Discounts
- = **Net Sales**

(Continued)

CHAPTER REVIEW

$$
\begin{array}{l}
- \textbf{Cost of Goods Sold} \left\{
\begin{array}{l}
\text{Beginning Merchandise Inventory} \\
+ \textbf{Delivered Cost of Purchases} \left\{
\begin{array}{l}
\text{Gross Purchases} \\
- \text{ Purchases Returns and Allowances} \\
- \text{ Purchases Discounts} \\
+ \text{ Freight In} \\
\hline
= \text{ Delivered Cost of Purchases}
\end{array}
\right. \\
= \text{Cost of Goods Available for Sale} \\
- \text{ Ending Merchandise Inventory} \\
\hline
= \text{Cost of Goods Sold}
\end{array}
\right.
\end{array}
$$

= **Gross Profit**

− **Operating Expenses** { Selling Expenses / General Expenses

= **Income from Operations**

+ **Other Income** { Interest Income / Rent Income / Gain on Disposal of Property and Equipment

− **Other Expenses** { Interest Expense / Loss on Disposal of Property and Equipment

= **Net Income**

PRACTICE EXERCISE 1

Using the following information, prepare the Cost of Goods Sold section of an income statement.

Purchases Discounts	$ 9,000
Merchandise Inventory, December 31	192,000
Purchases	480,000
Merchandise Inventory, January 1	188,000
Purchases Returns and Allowances	16,000
Freight In	27,000

PRACTICE EXERCISE 1 SOLUTION

Cost of Goods Sold:			
Merchandise Inventory, January 1, 20—			$188,000
Purchases		$480,000	
Less: Purchases Returns and Allowances	$16,000		
Purchases Discounts	9,000	25,000	
Net Purchases		$455,000	
Add Freight In		27,000	
Delivered Cost of Purchases			482,000
Cost of Goods Available for Sale			$670,000
Less Merchandise Inventory, December 31, 20—			192,000
Cost of Goods Sold			478,000

 LEARNING OBJECTIVE

Prepare a classified balance sheet for any type of business.

The outline of the balance sheet looks like this:

Assets Current Assets (listed in the order of their convertibility into cash)
1. Cash
2. Notes Receivable
3. Accounts Receivable
4. Merchandise Inventory
5. Prepaid items (Supplies; Prepaid Insurance)

Property and Equipment (listed in the order of their length of life; the asset with the longest life is placed first)
1. Land
2. Buildings
3. Equipment

Liabilities Current Liabilities (listed in the order of their urgency of payment; the most pressing obligation is placed first)
1. Notes Payable
2. Mortgage Payable or Contracts Payable (current portion)
3. Accounts Payable
4. Accrued liabilities (Wages Payable; Commissions Payable)
5. Unearned Revenue

Long-Term Liabilities (Contracts Payable; Mortgage Payable)

Owner's Equity Capital balance at end of the fiscal year

PRACTICE EXERCISE 2

Identify each of the following items relating to sections of a balance sheet as Current Assets (CA), Property and Equipment (PE), Current Liabilities (CL), Long-Term Liabilities (LTL), or Owner's Equity (OE).

a. Land
b. Unearned Course Fees
c. Merchandise Inventory
d. Cash
e. Salaries Payable
f. Accumulated Depreciation, Building
g. Note Payable (current)
h. Note Payable (due in 10 years)
i. F. R. Fred, Capital

PRACTICE EXERCISE 2 SOLUTION

a. Land, PE
b. Unearned Course Fees, CL
c. Merchandise Inventory, CA
d. Cash, CA
e. Salaries Payable, CL
f. Accumulated Depreciation, Building, PE
g. Note Payable (current), CL
h. Note Payable (due in 10 years), LTL
i. F. R. Fred, Capital, OE

3 LEARNING OBJECTIVE
Compute working capital and current ratio.

These two measures help analysts determine whether a firm has enough capital to operate and whether it can pay its debts.

$$\textbf{Working capital} = \text{Current assets} - \text{Current liabilities}$$

$$\textbf{Current ratio} = \frac{\text{Current assets}}{\text{Current liablities}}$$

PRACTICE EXERCISE 3

On December 31, 20—, Laredo Company's balance sheet shows that total current assets equal $450,784, and total current liabilities equal $435,209. Determine the amount of Laredo Company's working capital and current ratio, and explain what these measures mean.

PRACTICE EXERCISE 3 SOLUTION

$$\text{Working capital} = \$450{,}784 - \$435{,}209 = \$15{,}575$$

$$\text{Current ratio} = \frac{\$450{,}784}{\$435{,}209} = 1.04$$

Laredo Company's working capital shows that it has $15,575 to use or to work with; for example, for expansion or other improvements. Its current ratio shows that the company has $1.04 available to pay for every dollar currently due.

 LEARNING OBJECTIVE

4   *Journalize the closing entries for a merchandising firm.*

There are four steps in making closing entries for a merchandising business:

STEP 1. Close the revenue accounts and the other accounts that appear on the income statement and have credit balances (all temporary or nominal accounts with credit balances) into Income Summary.

STEP 2. Close the expense accounts and the other accounts appearing on the income statement that have debit balances (all temporary or nominal accounts with debit balances) into Income Summary.

STEP 3. Close the Income Summary account into the Capital account, transferring the net income or loss to the Capital account.

STEP 4. Close the Drawing account into the Capital account.

PRACTICE EXERCISE 4

From the following partial work sheet for Glasco Company, journalize the closing entries dated December 31:

Account Name	Trial Balance Debit	Trial Balance Credit	Income Statement Debit	Income Statement Credit
O. E. Glasco, Capital		250 8 0 0 00		
O. E. Glasco, Drawing	77 0 0 0 00			
Sales		256 1 5 0 00		256 1 5 0 00
Sales Returns and Allowances	9 6 0 00		9 6 0 00	
Sales Discounts	1 8 6 0 00		1 8 6 0 00	
Interest Income		1 2 3 0 00		1 2 3 0 00
Purchases	87 8 4 0 00		87 8 4 0 00	
Purchases Returns and Allowances		9 2 2 00		9 2 2 00
Purchases Discounts		1 3 4 8 00		1 3 4 8 00
Freight In	2 4 6 0 00		2 4 6 0 00	
Wages Expense	45 9 0 0 00		46 9 3 0 00	
Supplies Expense	1 5 4 0 00		1 1 2 5 00	
Property Tax Expense	1 9 6 0 00		1 9 6 0 00	
Interest Expense	3 7 4 00		3 4 4 00	
	630 6 3 1 00	630 6 3 1 00		
Income Summary			65 7 4 0 00	62 7 0 0 00
Course Fees Income				7 3 0 00
Supplies				
Insurance Expense			5 5 0 00	
Depreciation Expense, Building			5 0 0 0 00	
Depreciation Expense, Equipment			3 4 0 0 00	
Wages Payable				
			218 1 6 9 00	323 0 8 0 00
Net Income			104 9 1 1 00	
			323 0 8 0 00	323 0 8 0 00

PRACTICE EXERCISE 4 SOLUTION

		GENERAL JOURNAL								PAGE _____			
Date		Description	Post. Ref.			Debit					Credit		
20—		Closing Entries											
Dec.	31	Sales		256	1 5 0	00							
		Interest Income		1	2 3 0	00							
		Purchases Returns and Allowances			9 2 2	00							
		Purchases Discounts		1	3 4 8	00							
		Course Fees Income			7 3 0	00							
		Income Summary						260	3 8 0	00			
	31	Income Summary		152	4 2 9	00							
		Sales Returns and Allowances							9 6 0	00			
		Sales Discounts						1	8 6 0	00			
		Purchases						87	8 4 0	00			
		Freight In						2	4 6 0	00			
		Wages Expense						46	9 3 0	00			
		Supplies Expense						1	1 2 5	00			
		Property Tax Expense						1	9 6 0	00			
		Interest Expense							3 4 4	00			
		Insurance Expense							5 5 0	00			
		Depreciation Expense, Building							5 0 0	00			
		Depreciation Expense, Equipment							3 4 0	00			
	31	Income Summary*		104	9 1 1	00							
		O. E. Glasco, Capital						104	9 1 1	00			
		*($62,700 + $260,380) −											
		($65,740 + $152,429)											
	31	O. E. Glasco, Capital		77	0 0 0	00							
		O. E. Glasco, Drawing						77	0 0 0	00			

5 LEARNING OBJECTIVE

Determine which adjusting entries can be reversed, and journalize the reversing entries.

The use of **reversing entries** is optional. Reverse the adjusting entries that increase either asset or liability accounts that do not have previous balances. A contra account like Accumulated Depreciation should not be reversed. Reversing entries are dated as of the first day of the next fiscal period.

PRACTICE EXERCISE 5

From the following T accounts, determine which adjusting entries can be reversed, and journalize the reversing entries.

Merchandise Inventory			
	+	−	
Bal.	68,500	Adj.	68,500

Income Summary			
Adj.	68,500		

Merchandise Inventory			
	+	−	
Bal.	68,500	Adj.	68,500
Adj.	70,320		

Income Summary			
Adj.	68,500	Adj.	70,320

Course Fees Income			
	−	+	
		Adj.	800

Unearned Course Fees			
	−	+	
Adj.	800	Bal.	850

Supplies			
	+	−	
Adj.	735		

Supplies Expense			
	+	−	
Bal.	1,620	Adj.	735

Insurance Expense			
	+	−	
Adj.	1,620		

Prepaid Insurance			
	+	−	
Bal.	2,110	Adj.	1,620

Depreciation Expense, Building			
	+	−	
Adj.	3,200		

Accumulated Depreciation, Building			
	−	+	
		Bal.	46,000
		Adj.	3,200

Depreciation Expense, Equipment			
	+	−	
Adj.	4,300		

Accumulated Depreciation, Equipment			
	−	+	
		Bal.	21,400
		Adj.	4,300

Wages Expense			
	+	−	
Bal.	32,560		
Adj.	2,230		

Wages Payable			
	−	+	
		Adj.	2,230

PRACTICE EXERCISE 5 SOLUTION

			GENERAL JOURNAL				PAGE ____	
Date			Description	Post. Ref.	Debit		Credit	
20—			Reversing Entries					
Jan.	1		Supplies Expense		7 3 5 00			
			Supplies				7 3 5 00	
	1		Wages Payable		2 2 3 0 00			
			Wages Expense				2 2 3 0 00	

Before a Test Check: Chapters 11–12

PART I: COMPLETION

Complete each of the following statements by writing the appropriate word(s) in the spaces provided.

1. An actual count of a stock of goods is called a(n) _____.

2. Under the _____ system, entries to record the purchase of merchandise are recorded in the Merchandise Inventory account.

3. Unearned revenue is classified as a(n) _____.

4. Under the periodic inventory system, the first adjustment is to debit _____ for the amount of the beginning inventory.

5. Under the perpetual inventory system, after recording the sale of the goods, the accountant debits _____ and credits _____.

6. An increase in Rent Expense results in a(n) _____ to net income.

7. Gross Profit is calculated by subtracting _____ from Net Sales.

8. Current Assets minus Current Liabilities equals _____.

9. Gross Profit minus Total Operating Expenses equals _____.

10. Net Purchases plus _____ equals Delivered Cost of Purchases.

PART II: TRUE/FALSE

For each statement, circle T if it is True or circle F if it is false.

T F **1.** The second adjustment for Merchandise Inventory under the periodic inventory system is to debit Cost of Goods Sold and credit Merchandise Inventory.

T F **2.** Unearned Rent Income is classified as a revenue.

T F **3.** The perpetual inventory system requires that each sale of goods has two entries: one to reduce inventory and affix the cost of the goods sold and one to record the sale.

T F **4.** The periodic inventory system requires two adjusting entries: one to remove the old inventory amount and one to enter the latest inventory amount.

T F **5.** The adjustment to unearned revenue allows the correct amount of liability and revenue to be applied to each fiscal period involved.

T F **6.** Freight In is classified in the Operating Expenses section of an income statement.

T F **7.** Under the perpetual inventory system, the cost of goods sold is calculated by subtracting ending inventory from the cost of goods available for sale.

T F **8.** Reversing entries are optional, and only some adjusting entries are reversed.

T F **9.** Delivery Expense is added to Net Purchases to arrive at Delivered Cost of Purchases.

T F **10.** Purchases Returns and Allowances increases Income from Operations.

PART III: APPLICATION

1. Alphonse Company uses the periodic inventory system. Employees have just taken a physical count of its inventory. This ending inventory has been valued at $136,000. The company's accounting records show the Merchandise Inventory account with a debit balance of $132,000. Journalize the entries on December 31 to adjust the records for this situation.

2. Regletto Company uses the perpetual inventory system. Employees have just taken a physical count of its inventory. This ending inventory has been valued at $146,000. The company's accounting records show the Merchandise Inventory account with a debit balance of $148,000. Journalize the entry on December 31 to adjust the records for this situation.

3. On December 1, Wesley Company collected $20,000 for a remodeling job that will be completed on March 31 of the following year. The revenue will be earned evenly over four months. Wesley Company's fiscal period ends December 31. Make the entries to record the collection of the cash and the year-end adjustment to reflect the amount of revenue earned in December.

4. Yorkland Company has total assets of $250,000, of which noncurrent assets amount to $140,000. The company also has total liabilities of $130,000, of which $80,000 are long-term liabilities. Calculate (a) working capital and (b) current ratio.

ANSWERS: PART I

1. physical inventory;   2. perpetual inventory;   3. current liability;   4. Income Summary;   5. Cost of Goods Sold;   Merchandise Inventory;   6. decrease;   7. Cost of Goods Sold;   8. working capital;   9. Income from Operations;   10. Freight In

ANSWERS: PART II

1. F;   2. F;   3. T;   4. T;   5. T;   6. F;   7. F;   8. T;   9. F;   10. T

ANSWERS: PART III

1.

GENERAL JOURNAL   PAGE _____

Date		Description	Post. Ref.	Debit	Credit
20—		Adjusting Entries			
Dec.	31	Income Summary		132 0 0 0 00	
		Merchandise Inventory			132 0 0 0 00
	31	Merchandise Inventory		136 0 0 0 00	
		Income Summary			136 0 0 0 00

2.

GENERAL JOURNAL   PAGE _____

Date		Description	Post. Ref.	Debit	Credit
20—		Adjusting Entries			
Dec.	31	Cost of Goods Sold		2 0 0 0 00	
		Merchandise Inventory			2 0 0 0 00

3.

		GENERAL JOURNAL			PAGE _____	
Date		Description	Post. Ref.	Debit	Credit	
20—						
Dec.	1	Cash		20 0 0 0 00		
		Unearned Revenue			20 0 0 0 00	
		To record collection of cash for a				
		four-month job.				
		Adjusting Entry				
	31	Unearned Revenue		5 0 0 0 00		
		Remodeling Revenue			5 0 0 0 00	
		To record one month's revenue				
		earned.				

4. a. $250,000 total assets – $140,000 noncurrent assets = $110,000 current assets

$130,000 total liabilities – $80,000 long-term liabilities = $50,000 current liabilities

$110,000 current assets – $50,000 current liabilities = $60,000 working capital

b. $\dfrac{\$110,000 \text{ current assets}}{\$50,000 \text{ current liabilities}} = 2.20$ current ratio

Glossary

Cost of Goods Sold A section of the income statement in which the amount of the cost of the goods the business sold is calculated. Terms often used to describe the same thing are *cost of merchandise sold* and *cost of sales.*

Merchandise Inventory (beginning)
+ Delivered Cost of Purchases

Cost of Goods Available for Sale
− Merchandise Inventory (ending)

Cost of Goods Sold   (p. 494)

Current Assets Cash and any other assets or resources that are expected to be realized in cash or to be sold or consumed during the normal operating cycle of the business (or one year, if the normal operating cycle is less than twelve months). (p. 499)

Current Liabilities Debts that will become due within the normal operating cycle of a business, usually within one year, and that are normally paid from current assets. (p. 499)

Current ratio A firm's current assets divided by its current liabilities. Portrays a firm's short-term debt-paying ability. (p. 500)

Delivered Cost of Purchases Net Purchases plus Freight In:

Net Purchases
+ Freight In

Delivered Cost of Purchases (p. 495)

General Expenses Expenses incurred in the administration of a business, including office expenses and any expenses that are not completely classified as Selling Expenses or Other Expenses. (p. 495)

Gross Profit Net Sales minus Cost of Goods Sold, or profit before deducting expenses:

Net Sales
− Cost of Goods Sold

Gross Profit   (p. 492)

Liquidity The ability of an asset to be quickly turned into cash, either by selling it or by putting it up as security for a loan. (p. 499)

Long-Term Liabilities Debts payable over a comparatively long period, usually more than one year. (p. 499)

Net Income or **Net Profit** The final figure on an income statement after all expenses have been deducted from revenues. (p. 492)

Net Purchases Purchases minus Purchases Returns and Allowances and minus Purchases Discounts:

    Purchases
    − Purchases Returns and Allowances
    − Purchases Discounts
    ─────────────────────────
    Net Purchases   *(p. 495)*

Net Sales Sales minus Sales Returns and Allowances and minus Sales Discounts:

    Sales
    − Sales Returns and Allowances
    − Sales Discounts
    ─────────────────────────
    Net Sales   *(p. 493)*

Notes Receivable (current) Written promises to pay the seller/lender the amount due in a period of less than one year. *(p. 499)*

Property and Equipment Long-lived assets that are held for use in the production or sale of other assets or services; also called *fixed assets*. *(p. 499)*

Reversing entries The reverse of certain adjusting entries, recorded as of the first day of the following fiscal period. The use of reversing entries is optional. *(p. 505)*

Selling Expenses Expenses directly connected with the selling activity, such as salaries of sales staff, advertising expenses, and delivery expenses. *(p. 495)*

Temporary-equity accounts Accounts whose balances apply to one fiscal period only, such as revenues, expenses, and the Drawing account. Temporary-equity accounts are also called *nominal accounts*. *(p. 502)*

Working capital A firm's current assets less its current liabilities. The amount of capital a firm has available to use or to work with during a normal operating cycle. *(p. 500)*

CHAPTER ASSIGNMENTS

Discussion Questions

1. What is the order for listing accounts in the Current Assets section of the balance sheet?
2. What is the difference between the cost of goods available for sale and the cost of goods sold?
3. What are the basic classifications found on an income statement for a merchandising business as compared to a service business?
4. On a balance sheet, what is the difference between Current Liabilities and Long-Term Liabilities? Give an example of an account in each classification.
5. On an income statement, what is the difference between income from operations and net income? Which is more useful in comparing the results of operations over a number of years?
6. Explain the calculation of net sales and net purchases.
7. In the closing procedure, what happens to (a) Purchases Discounts, (b) Sales Returns and Allowances, (c) Freight In, (d) Gain on Disposal of Property and Equipment?
8. What are the rules for recognizing whether or not an adjusting entry should be reversed?

Exercises

1    **EXERCISE 12-1** Calculate the missing items in the following:

PRACTICE EXERCISE 1

	Sales	Sales Returns and Allowances	Net Sales	Beginning Merchandise Inventory	Net Purchases	Cost of Goods Available for Sale	Ending Merchandise Inventory	Cost of Goods Sold	Gross Profit
a.	$242,000	$ 6,000	———	$152,000	$170,000	———	$136,000	$186,000	———
b.	304,000	———	$297,000	134,000	———	$404,000	176,000	228,000	———
c.	———	10,000	628,000	———	416,000	486,000	89,000	———	———

EXERCISE 12-2 Using the following information, prepare the Cost of Goods Sold section of an income statement.

PRACTICE EXERCISE 1

Purchases Discounts	$ 8,500
Merchandise Inventory, December 31	189,000
Purchases	476,000
Merchandise Inventory, January 1	185,000
Purchases Returns and Allowances	9,000
Freight In	12,000

EXERCISE 12-3 Identify each of the following items relating to sections of an income statement as Revenue from Sales (S), Cost of Goods Sold (CGS), Selling Expenses (SE), General Expenses (GE), Other Income (OI), or Other Expenses (OE).

PRACTICE EXERCISE 1

a. Advertising Expense
b. Rent Expense
c. Purchases Discounts
d. Sales Returns and Allowances
e. Interest Income
f. Freight In
g. Depreciation Expense, Building
h. Interest Expense
i. Insurance Expense
j. Delivery Expense

EXERCISE 12-4 The Income Statement columns of the June 30 (year-end) work sheet for Bajia Company are shown here. From the information given, prepare an income statement for the company. To save time and space, the expenses have been grouped together into two categories.

PRACTICE EXERCISE 1

	Income Statement	
Account Name	**Debit**	**Credit**
Income Summary	26 0 0 0 00	22 0 0 0 00
Sales		292 9 0 0 00
Sales Returns and Allowances	12 1 0 0 00	
Sales Discounts	6 1 0 0 00	
Purchases	115 0 0 0 00	
Purchases Returns and Allowances		1 1 0 0 00
Purchases Discounts		1 2 0 0 00
Freight In	6 5 0 0 00	
Selling Expenses	57 0 0 0 00	
General Expenses	46 0 0 0 00	
	268 7 0 0 00	317 2 0 0 00
Net Income	48 5 0 0 00	
	317 2 0 0 00	317 2 0 0 00

EXERCISE 12-5 Identify each of the following items relating to sections of a balance sheet as Current Assets (CA), Property and Equipment (PE), Current Liabilities (CL), Long-Term Liabilities (LTL), or Owner's Equity (OE).

PRACTICE EXERCISE 2

a. Accounts Receivable
b. Building
c. Wages Payable
d. Prepaid Property Taxes
e. Mortgage Payable (current)
f. Supplies
g. Mortgage Payable (due in 3 years)
h. Unearned Fees
i. D. Marlor, Capital
j. Notes Payable (due in 3 months)

 3 LO

PRACTICE EXERCISE 3

EXERCISE 12-6 On December 31, 20—, the following selected accounts and amounts appeared on the balance sheet for Delo Company. Determine the amount of the working capital and the current ratio.

Building	$170,000
Prepaid Insurance	1,600
Merchandise Inventory	72,000
Store Equipment	14,000
Unearned Fees	800
Notes Payable (due in 6 months)	5,000
Accumulated Depreciation, Building	72,000
Accounts Payable	23,000
Land	40,000
Cash	19,000
Store Supplies	1,200
Accumulated Depreciation, Store Equipment	6,000
Notes Receivable (due in 4 months)	3,000
Mortgage Payable (current portion)	3,500
Salaries Payable	2,700
D. Delo, Capital	101,500
Mortgage Payable (due in 4 years)	85,000

 **4 LO**

PRACTICE EXERCISE 4

EXERCISE 12-7 From the following T accounts, journalize the closing entries dated December 31 for Baylor Company:

Salary Expense		H. Baylor, Drawing		Purchases Returns and Allowances	
+	−	+	−	−	+
65,000		55,000			8,600

Purchases		Miscellaneous Expense		Rent Expense	
+	−	+	−	+	−
235,600		12,200		22,000	

Sales Returns and Allowances		Freight In		Sales	
+	−	+	−	−	+
7,400		11,200			502,000

Income Summary		H. Baylor, Capital		Purchases Discounts	
87,000	103,000	−	+	−	+
			335,000		4,300

EXERCISE 12-8 From the following information, journalize the last two closing entries, and present a statement of owner's equity for Nishimoto Company:

PRACTICE EXERCISE 4

H. Nishimoto, Capital

−	+	
	Jan. 1 Bal.	450,000
	Apr. 7	18,000

Income Summary

Dec. 31 Adj.	190,000	Dec. 31 Adj.	206,000
Dec. 31 Closing	415,000	Dec. 31 Closing	492,000

H. Nishimoto, Drawing

	+	−
Mar. 1	35,000	
Dec. 9	40,000	

Problem Set A

For additional help, see the demonstration problem at the beginning of each chapter in your Working Papers.

PROBLEM 12-1A A partial work sheet for The Fan Shop is presented here. The merchandise inventory at the beginning of the year was $52,300. P. G. Ochoa, the owner, withdrew $30,500 during the year.

The Fan Shop
Work Sheet
For Year Ended December 31, 20—

Account Name	Income Statement	
	Debit	Credit
Sales		324 0 0 0 00
Sales Returns and Allowances	3 4 0 0 00	
Sales Discounts	2 7 0 7 00	
Interest Income		1 8 3 0 00
Purchases	201 4 9 0 00	
Purchases Returns and Allowances		2 8 8 0 00
Freight In	9 7 9 0 00	
Wages Expense	46 2 4 0 00	
Rent Expense	12 6 1 0 00	
Commissions Expense	8 3 1 0 00	
Supplies Expense	1 8 4 2 00	
Interest Expense	8 5 4 00	
Income Summary	52 3 0 0 00	54 5 8 0 00
Insurance Expense	1 2 4 0 00	
Depreciation Expense, Building	4 6 0 0 00	
Depreciation Expense, Equipment	2 6 0 0 00	
	347 9 8 3 00	383 2 9 0 00
Net Income	35 3 0 7 00	
	383 2 9 0 00	383 2 9 0 00

Check Figure
Cost of Goods Sold, $206,120

Required
1. Prepare an income statement.
2. Journalize the closing entries.

2,3 **LO**

PROBLEM 12-2A Here is the partial work sheet for Eckland Stereo.

Eckland Stereo
Work Sheet
For Year Ended December 31, 20—

Account Name	Balance Sheet	
	Debit	Credit
Cash	14 8 1 5 00	
Notes Receivable	7 5 0 0 00	
Accounts Receivable	30 1 7 0 00	
Merchandise Inventory	50 2 4 4 00	
Prepaid Property Taxes	2 1 1 5 00	
Prepaid Insurance	1 6 4 0 00	
Land	16 7 0 0 00	
Building	50 0 0 0 00	
Accumulated Depreciation, Building		15 9 0 0 00
Computer Equipment	6 8 9 2 00	
Accumulated Depreciation, Computer Equipment		5 6 7 4 00
Store Equipment	7 2 3 0 00	
Accumulated Depreciation, Store Equipment		4 4 2 4 00
Delivery Equipment	4 3 0 0 00	
Accumulated Depreciation, Delivery Equipment		3 4 7 0 00
Notes Payable		5 2 1 5 00
Accounts Payable		27 1 4 0 00
Mortgage Payable (current portion)		2 8 0 0 00
Mortgage Payable		65 2 0 0 00
M. J. Eckland, Capital		57 3 1 4 00
M. J. Eckland, Drawing	23 0 0 0 00	
Wages Payable		1 9 8 4 00
	214 6 0 6 00	189 1 2 1 00
Net Income		25 4 8 5 00
	214 6 0 6 00	214 6 0 6 00

Check Figure
Working capital, $69,345

Required
1. Prepare a statement of owner's equity (no additional investment).
2. Prepare a balance sheet.
3. Determine the amount of the working capital.
4. Determine the current ratio (carry to two decimal places).

4,5 **LO**

PROBLEM 12-3A The following partial work sheet covers the affairs of Masanto and Company for the year ended June 30:

Masanto and Company
Work Sheet
For Year Ended June 30, 20—

Account Name	Income Statement Debit	Income Statement Credit	Balance Sheet Debit	Balance Sheet Credit
Cash			21 0 3 4 00	
Accounts Receivable			89 0 1 6 00	
Merchandise Inventory			116 4 0 0 00	
Prepaid Insurance			3 2 1 0 00	
Delivery Equipment			12 4 0 0 00	
Accumulated Depreciation, Delivery Equipment				4 6 0 0 00
Store Equipment			30 4 0 0 00	
Accumulated Depreciation, Store Equipment				8 7 0 0 00
Accounts Payable				55 3 0 0 00
P. R. Masanto, Capital				172 7 2 0 00
P. R. Masanto, Drawing			26 0 0 0 00	
Sales		516 0 0 0 00		
Purchases	399 1 0 1 00			
Purchases Returns and Allowances		9 6 0 0 00		
Purchases Discounts		6 8 0 0 00		
Freight In	14 0 0 0 00			
Salary Expense	46 0 0 0 00			
Truck Expense	10 6 0 0 00			
Supplies Expense	2 7 0 0 00			
Miscellaneous Expense	1 4 5 9 00			
Income Summary	112 2 0 0 00	116 4 0 0 00		
Salaries Payable				1 2 4 0 00
Insurance Expense	2 8 4 0 00			
Depreciation Expense, Delivery Equipment	1 4 0 0 00			
Depreciation Expense, Store Equipment	2 6 0 0 00			
	592 9 0 0 00	648 8 0 0 00	298 4 6 0 00	242 5 6 0 00
Net Income	55 9 0 0 00			55 9 0 0 00
	648 8 0 0 00	648 8 0 0 00	298 4 6 0 00	298 4 6 0 00

Required

1. Journalize the six adjusting entries.
2. Journalize the closing entries.
3. Journalize the reversing entry.

Check Figure
Reversing entry amount, $1,240

PROBLEM 12-4A The following accounts appear in the ledger of Celso and Company as of June 30, the end of this fiscal year:

 1,2,4,5

Cash	$ 15,349
Accounts Receivable	13,810
Merchandise Inventory	50,280
Prepaid Insurance	1,385
Store Equipment	18,640
Accumulated Depreciation, Store Equipment	6,882
Accounts Payable	10,065
B. E. Celso, Capital	96,424
B. E. Celso, Drawing	30,000
Sales	208,030

(Continued)

Sales Returns and Allowances	$ 1,740
Purchases	133,050
Purchases Returns and Allowances	4,295
Purchases Discounts	3,853
Freight In	8,350
Wages Expense	35,400
Advertising Expense	7,710
Rent Expense	12,000
Store Supplies Expense	1,835

The data needed for the adjustments on June 30 are as follows:

a–b. Merchandise inventory, June 30, $54,600.
   c. Insurance expired for the year, $475.
   d. Depreciation for the year, $4,380.
   e. Accrued wages on June 30, $1,492.

Check Figure
Net income, $14,066

Required

1. Prepare a work sheet for the fiscal year ended June 30.
2. Prepare an income statement.
3. Prepare a statement of owner's equity. No additional investments were made during the year.
4. Prepare a balance sheet.
5. Journalize the adjusting entries.
6. Journalize the closing entries.
7. Journalize the reversing entry.

Problem Set B

For additional help, see the demonstration problem at the beginning of each chapter in your Working Papers.

1,4  **PROBLEM 12-1B** A partial work sheet for McKnight Music Store is presented here. The merchandise inventory at the beginning of the fiscal period was $48,473. W. J. McKnight, the owner, withdrew $40,000 during the year.

McKnight Music Store
Work Sheet
For Year Ended December 31, 20—

Account Name	Income Statement Debit	Income Statement Credit
Sales		315 4 8 3 00
Sales Returns and Allowances	4 3 4 8 00	
Sales Discounts	1 8 1 7 00	
Interest Income		9 2 5 00
Purchases	185 2 7 2 00	
Purchases Returns and Allowances		1 5 4 7 00
Freight In	9 1 7 3 00	
Wages Expense	40 6 1 5 00	
Rent Expense	10 8 4 0 00	
Commissions Expense	8 2 2 0 00	
Supplies Expense	1 8 2 6 00	
Interest Expense	1 2 5 8 00	
Income Summary	48 4 7 3 00	48 8 5 0 00
Insurance Expense	2 6 2 4 00	
Depreciation Expense, Building	4 2 2 0 00	
Depreciation Expense, Equipment	4 5 0 0 00	
	323 1 8 6 00	366 8 0 5 00
Net Income	43 6 1 9 00	
	366 8 0 5 00	366 8 0 5 00

Required

1. Prepare an income statement.
2. Journalize the closing entries.

Check Figure
Cost of Goods Sold, $192,521

2,3 LO

PROBLEM 12-2B Here is the partial work sheet for Meyer Mountain Shop.

Meyer Mountain Shop
Work Sheet
For Year Ended December 31, 20—

Account Name	Balance Sheet									
	Debit					Credit				
Cash	18	5	2	5	00					
Notes Receivable	4	5	0	0	00					
Accounts Receivable	22	6	8	0	00					
Merchandise Inventory	53	5	4	2	00					
Prepaid Property Taxes	1	8	2	0	00					
Prepaid Insurance	2	4	5	0	00					
Land	18	6	0	0	00					
Building	42	0	0	0	00					
Accumulated Depreciation, Building						22	5	0	0	00
Computer Equipment	4	4	2	4	00					
Accumulated Depreciation, Computer Equipment						2	2	5	0	00
Store Equipment	7	4	8	0	00					
Accumulated Depreciation, Store Equipment						5	0	8	5	00
Delivery Equipment	5	7	4	0	00					
Accumulated Depreciation, Delivery Equipment						3	2	2	5	00
Notes Payable						6	5	0	0	00
Accounts Payable						19	4	5	5	00
Mortgage Payable (current portion)						2	5	0	0	00
Mortgage Payable						54	6	0	0	00
M. E. Meyer, Capital						75	0	8	5	00
M. E. Meyer, Drawing	35	2	5	0	00					
Wages Payable						1	4	6	0	00
	217	0	1	1	00	192	6	6	0	00
Net Income						24	3	5	1	00
	217	0	1	1	00	217	0	1	1	00

Check Figure
Working capital, $73,602

Required

1. Prepare a statement of owner's equity (no additional investment).
2. Prepare a balance sheet.
3. Determine the amount of the working capital.
4. Determine the current ratio (carry to two decimal places).

4,5 LO

PROBLEM 12-3B The following partial work sheet covers the affairs of Ketcher and Company for the year ended June 30:

Ketcher and Company
Work Sheet
For Year Ended June 30, 20—

Account Name	Income Statement Debit	Income Statement Credit	Balance Sheet Debit	Balance Sheet Credit
Cash			37 3 0 2 00	
Accounts Receivable			97 5 5 7 00	
Merchandise Inventory			117 2 7 4 00	
Prepaid Insurance			2 4 1 0 00	
Delivery Equipment			12 7 0 0 00	
Accumulated Depreciation, Delivery Equipment				6 2 4 0 00
Store Equipment			35 9 0 0 00	
Accumulated Depreciation, Store Equipment				10 4 8 0 00
Accounts Payable				77 3 2 8 00
J. Ketcher, Capital				193 8 1 0 00
J. Ketcher, Drawing			40 3 5 0 00	
Sales		532 2 6 2 00		
Purchases	397 8 3 0 00			
Purchases Returns and Allowances		8 8 1 7 00		
Purchases Discounts		6 9 3 5 00		
Freight In	23 4 0 0 00			
Salary Expense	54 7 0 0 00			
Truck Expense	9 4 9 2 00			
Supplies Expense	2 4 1 6 00			
Miscellaneous Expense	1 8 0 0 00			
Income Summary	113 2 0 2 00	117 2 7 4 00		
Salaries Payable				1 6 4 5 00
Insurance Expense	2 9 4 0 00			
Depreciation Expense, Delivery Equipment	2 8 0 0 00			
Depreciation Expense, Store Equipment	2 7 1 8 00			
	611 2 9 8 00	665 2 8 8 00	343 4 9 3 00	289 5 0 3 00
Net Income	53 9 9 0 00			53 9 9 0 00
	665 2 8 8 00	665 2 8 8 00	343 4 9 3 00	343 4 9 3 00

Required

1. Journalize the six adjusting entries.
2. Journalize the closing entries.
3. Journalize the reversing entry.

Check Figure
Reversing entry amount, $1,645

PROBLEM 12-4B The following accounts appear in the ledger of Sheldon Company on January 31, the end of this fiscal year:

LO 1,2,4,5

Cash	$ 16,400
Accounts Receivable	15,100
Merchandise Inventory	55,500
Prepaid Insurance	3,080
Store Equipment	24,900
Accumulated Depreciation, Store Equipment	3,860
Accounts Payable	14,400
M. E. Sheldon, Capital	126,384

(Continued)

M. E. Sheldon, Drawing	$ 36,000
Sales	227,000
Sales Returns and Allowances	2,000
Purchases	172,000
Purchases Returns and Allowances	2,375
Purchases Discounts	3,567
Freight In	7,491
Wages Expense	24,800
Advertising Expense	5,912
Rent Expense	12,900
Store Supplies Expense	1,503

The data needed for adjustments on January 31 are as follows:

a–b. Merchandise inventory, January 31, $55,750.
   c. Insurance expired for the year, $1,285.
   d. Depreciation for the year, $5,482.
   e. Accrued wages on January 31, $1,503.

Check Figure
Net loss, $1,684

Required

1. Prepare a work sheet for the fiscal year ended January 31.
2. Prepare an income statement.
3. Prepare a statement of owner's equity. No additional investments were made during the year.
4. Prepare a balance sheet.
5. Journalize the adjusting entries.
6. Journalize the closing entries.
7. Journalize the reversing entry.

Comprehensive Review Problem

You are to record transactions completed by Fabulous Furnishings during the month of February of this year. Beginning balances for the accounts listed below have been provided in your Working Papers. This company is located in Dallas. To gain practice in completing the steps in the accounting cycle, assume that the fiscal period consists of one month.

CHART OF ACCOUNTS

Assets (100–199)
111 Cash
112 Petty Cash Fund
113 Accounts Receivable
114 Merchandise Inventory
118 Prepaid Insurance
122 Equipment
123 Accumulated Depreciation, Equipment

Liabilities (200–299)
221 Accounts Payable
226 Employees' Income Tax Payable
227 FICA Tax Payable
228 State Unemployment Tax Payable
229 Federal Unemployment Tax Payable
230 Salaries Payable

Owner's Equity (300–399)
311 M. L. Langdon, Capital
312 M. L. Langdon, Drawing
313 Income Summary

Revenue (400–499)
411 Sales
412 Sales Returns and Allowances

Cost of Goods Sold (500–599)
511 Purchases
512 Purchases Returns and Allowances
513 Purchases Discounts
514 Freight In

Expenses (600–699)
611 Salary Expense
612 Payroll Tax Expense
613 Rent Expense
614 Utilities Expense
616 Supplies Expense
617 Insurance Expense
618 Depreciation Expense, Equipment
619 Miscellaneous Expense

JOURNALS

Sales Journal, page 56
Purchases Journal, page 62
Cash Receipts Journal, page 69
Cash Payments Journal, page 75
General Journal, pages 89–95

ACCOUNTS RECEIVABLE

Fashion Decor
Hotel Beritz
Jason and Waldon

ACCOUNTS PAYABLE

Brandon, Inc.
Kingston Fabrics
Magnuson Textiles
Tyson Manufacturing Company

TRANSACTIONS

The following transactions were completed during February of this year.

Feb. 1 Reversed the adjusting entry for accrued salaries, $620.

1 Sold merchandise on account to Hotel Beritz, $12,520.86, invoice no. 5221.

2 Issued Ck. No. 7216, $16,593.46, to Kingston Fabrics, in payment of its invoice no. D1739 for $16,932.10 less 2 percent discount.

5 Bought merchandise on account from Magnuson Textiles, $4,874.80, invoice no. RE275, dated February 2; terms 1/10, n/30; FOB Louisville; freight prepaid and added to the invoice, $158 (total, $5,032.80).

5 Received an electric bill and paid Countywide Power, Ck. No. 7217, $358.

6 Received check from Jason and Waldon, $10,780.51, in payment of account.

7 Issued Ck. No. 7218, $9,684.18, to Magnuson Textiles, in payment of its invoice no. RE64 for $9,782 less 1 percent discount.

9 Cash sales for February 1 through February 9, $9,745.40.

12 Recorded the payroll in the payroll register for regular semimonthly salaries for period ended February 12. Salaries: R. W. Harris, $2,840; T. L. Newkirk, $2,374. Income tax withholdings are $287 for Harris and $216 for Newkirk. Assume the following tax rates and taxable earnings limits (see the payroll register in your Working Papers for beginning cumulative earnings):

- Social Security taxable earnings, $106,800, with a rate of 6.2 percent.
- Medicare taxable earnings, all earnings, with a rate of 1.45 percent.

12 Recorded the payroll entry, crediting Salaries Payable.

12 Issued Ck. No. 7219, $2,335.74, to R. W. Harris. Issued Ck. No. 7220, $1,976.39, to T. L. Newkirk. Use two lines and debit Salaries Payable. (Verify these amounts.)

12 Recorded payroll taxes. Assume the following tax rates and taxable earnings:

- Federal unemployment taxable earnings, $7,000, with a rate of 0.8 percent.
- State unemployment taxable earnings, $7,000, with a rate of 5.4 percent. *Note*: Harris's taxable earnings for unemployment amount to $1,535 and Newkirk's amount to $2,374.

12 Received a credit memo from Magnuson Textiles for defective merchandise, $692, credit memo no. 916.

14 Issued Ck. No. 7221, $2,900.80, to Mid-State Bank for monthly deposit of January employees' federal income tax withheld, $1,285, and FICA taxes, $1,615.80.

CHAPTER ASSIGNMENTS

Feb. 14   Sold merchandise on account to Jason and Waldon, $15,781.30, invoice no. 5222.

     14   Issued Ck. No. 7222, $4,298.97, to Magnuson Textiles, in payment of its invoice no. RE275 less the credit memo for defective merchandise and less the discount ($41.83). *Note*: Debit Accounts Payable, $4,340.80, and credit Purchases Discounts, $41.83. Verify these amounts: $5,032.80, less $158 freight, less $692 return, less 1 percent cash discount (cash discounts can't be taken on freight). Remember to add $158 freight back to compute the cash credit.

     18   Bought merchandise on account from Brandon, Inc., $21,375.20, invoice no. 164M, dated February 14; terms 2/10, n/30; FOB Miami; freight prepaid and added to the invoice, $1,242 (total, $22,617.20).

     18   Cash sales for February 10 through February 18, $7,889.24.

     19   Issued Ck. No. 7223 payable to Quicker Printing for invoice forms, $336 (not previously recorded). (Debit Supplies Expense.)

     19   Received check from Fashion Decor, $4,830.65, in payment of account.

     22   Issued Ck. No. 7224, $12,540, to Tyson Manufacturing Company, in payment of its invoice no. 9264D.

     22   Sold merchandise on account to Fashion Decor, $17,435.32, invoice no. 5223.

     24   Issued credit memo no. 214 to Fashion Decor, $185, for merchandise returned.

     24   Bought merchandise on account from Kingston Fabrics, $16,536.90, invoice no. D1797, dated February 22; terms 2/10, n/30; FOB Dallas.

     26   Recorded the payroll in the payroll register for regular semimonthly salaries for period ended February 26. Salaries: R. W. Harris, $2,840; T. L. Newkirk, $2,374. Income tax withholdings are $287 for Harris and $216 for Newkirk. *Note*: See the entry of February 12 for taxable earnings limits and tax rates. See the payroll register this payroll's beginning cumulative earnings.

     26   Recorded the payroll entry, crediting Salaries Payable.

     26   Issued Ck. No. 7225, $2,335.74, to R. W. Harris. Issued Ck. No. 7226, $1,976.39, to T. L. Newkirk. Use two lines and debit Salaries Payable.

     26   Ck. No. 7227 voided.

     26   Recorded payroll taxes. Assume the following tax rates and taxable earnings:
        • Federal unemployment taxable earnings, $7,000, with a rate of 0.8 percent.
        • State unemployment taxable earnings, $7,000, with a rate of 0.8 percent.
     Note: Harris's taxable earnings for unemployment are zero because earnings exceeded $7,000 in the prior pay period. Newkirk's taxable earnings for unemployment amount to $46.

     27   Issued Ck. No. 7228, $1,035, to JIT Freight Line for transportation charge on merchandise purchased from Kingston Fabrics.

     28   Issued Ck. No. 7229, $55.60, payable to Cash to reimburse the petty cash fund. Petty cash payments consist of Supplies Expense, $30.24, and Miscellaneous Expense, $25.36.

     28   Cash sales for February 19 through February 28, $8,986.60.

     28   Issued Ck. No. 7230, $2,290, to Global Rental Agency for monthly rent.

     28   M. L. Langdon (owner) withdrew $5,000 for personal use, Ck. No. 7231.

Required

1. Journalize and post the transactions completed during February using either a general journal or special journals or both. (Your instructor will assign you which one(s) to use.)

General Journal

a. Post daily all entries involving customer accounts to the accounts receivable ledger.

b. Post daily all entries involving creditor accounts to the accounts payable ledger.

c. Post daily the general journal entries to the general ledger.

Special Journals

a. Post daily the amounts in the Other Accounts columns of the special journals.

b. Post daily the general journal.

c. Post the totals of the special columns of the special journals at the end of the month.

2. Prepare a schedule of accounts receivable and a schedule of accounts payable.

3. Complete the work sheet for February.

Data for the month-end adjustments are as follows:

a–b. Merchandise inventory at February 28, $45,484.

  c. Salaries accrued at February 28, $2,084.

  d. Insurance expired during February, $210.

  e. Depreciation of equipment during February, $1,885.

4. Journalize and post the adjusting entries.

5. Prepare an income statement.

6. Prepare a statement of owner's equity. (No additional investment was made during the month.)

7. Prepare a balance sheet.

8. Journalize and post the closing entries.

9. Prepare a post-closing trial balance.

ACTIVITIES

CONSIDER AND COMMUNICATE

A music store sells new instruments. The store also sells used instruments for people who are willing to give the store part of the sales price. The sales of used instruments, called commissions, amount to about one-fourth of total sales. On the firm's classified income statement under the Revenue heading are both New Instrument Sales and Sales Commissions. Comment on this practice.

WHAT'S WRONG WITH THIS PICTURE?

What if the freight charges on a new desk for the owner were journalized and posted to the Freight In account? Would this affect the Cost of Goods Sold section? If so, how?

CRITICAL THINKING

You are an owner/bookkeeper in a country whose economy has been nearly destroyed. Goods are scarce; in fact, you have no goods to sell at the start of each day. You go out early each morning to purchase goods and haul them back to sell. At the end of the day, you have sold everything. Prepare a Cost of Goods Sold section for a day when you purchased $400 in goods. What conclusion can you draw?

A QUESTION OF ETHICS

Marty is an accountant. Sometimes printouts of financial statements have errors and are not usable. Marty doesn't like to waste anything, so he takes the unusable financial statements to his son's day care center to use for drawing paper. Explain why you think this is or is not unethical behavior.

All About You Spa

Closing Entries and Financial Statements

It is now August 31. You have journalized and posted the adjustments in the All About You Spa accounting records, and Ms. Valli wants to see financial statements for the last two months (July and August).

Directions for Closing Entries

Why is it essential that you generate and print your income statement and statement of owner's equity *before* zeroing out or closing the temporary owner's equity accounts?

In many cases (although not required for this problem), you may wish to save a data file before closing with "BC" (before closing) included in the name so that you can go back to it later and review Income Statement and Statement of Owner's Equity reports if desired. Then save the data file with "PC" (post-closing) included in the name after generating closing entries.

Generate the Balance Sheet report *after* the closing entries so that it shows the final balance of the capital account after the income statement and drawing accounts have been closed to it.

Check Figures

3. Net income, $13,756.32
3. A. Valli, Capital (end of period), $58,640.94
5. Closing Journal Entries report total, $114,131.30
6. Post-closing trial balance total, $81,259.70
7. Balance Sheet report total assets, $81,035.06

1. Open the file entitled **All_About_You_Spa_Ch12.IA7**. Enter your name when prompted and click **OK**. Select "Yes" or "No" as desired when asked if you want to open on-screen instructions and check figures. As a reminder, these instructions may be opened at any time by clicking on the **Info.** toolbar button.

2. Click on the **Save As** toolbar button. When the Save As window appears, select the folder in which you wish to save your data files (if not already selected). In the File Name box, key **All_About_You_Ch12_Your_Name.IA7** (for example, All_About_You_Spa_Ch12_John_Doe.IA7) to identify the file containing your work. Click on the **Save** button.

3. Display an income statement and a statement of owner's equity. Click on the **Reports** toolbar button, then in turn click on **Income Statement** and **Statement of Owner's Equity** to generate each of these financial statements. To print these reports, click on the **Print** button at the bottom of each report window.

4. Generate closing entries. Select **Generate Closing Journal Entries** from the **Options** menu. When the dialog box appears, click **Yes** to confirm that you wish the computer to generate the closing journal entries. The entries will display in a preview window. Click on the **Post** button to post the closing journal entries to the general journal.

5. Display the closing journal entries. Click on the **Reports** toolbar button. Click on **Journals** and **General Journal** to choose the report to display. Click on **Customize Journal Report**. In the Reference drop-down list, choose "Clo. Ent." and then click the **OK** button to display the Closing Journal Entries report. To print the report, click on the **Print** button.

6. Display a post-closing trial balance. Click on the **Reports** toolbar button. Click on **Ledger Reports** and **Trial Balance** to choose the report to display. To print the report, click on the **Print** button at the bottom of the report window.

7. Display a balance sheet. Click on the **Reports** toolbar button, then click on **Balance Sheet** to generate this financial statement. To print the report, click on the **Print** button at the bottom of the report window.

8. Click on the **Save** toolbar button to save your data file.

9. Click on the **Check** toolbar button to check your solution against the answer key.

Congratulations! You have completed your work with All About You Spa.

PART 4

Notes Payable

13

ORANGE JULIUS, Minneapolis, Minnesota

In 1926, Julius Freed opened an orange juice stand in Los Angeles. Sales were initially modest, but that changed in a couple years. In 1929, Freed's real estate broker developed a mixture that made the acidic orange juice less bothersome to his stomach. Freed's stand began serving the smoother, foamier drink—and sales skyrocketed. People began lining up at the stand and shouting, "Give me an Orange, Julius!" Thus, the Orange Julius chain was born.

Many people dream about owning their own business, like Julius Freed. However, the reason why most of them do not follow their dream is lack of funds. The Small Business Administration helps new businesses to acquire funding. Ultimately, if the applicant is qualified, she or he will have to sign a note payable—a promise to pay a specific sum, on a specific date, at a stated rate of interest. In this chapter, you will learn how to record notes payable and the related entries regarding interest.

WHY IT MATTERS

LEARNING OBJECTIVES

After you have completed this chapter, you will be able to do the following:

1 Define promissory note.

2 Calculate the interest on promissory notes.

3 Determine the due dates of promissory notes.

4 Make journal entries for (a) notes given to secure an extension of time on an open account; (b) payment of an interest-bearing note at maturity; (c) notes given in exchange for merchandise or other property purchased; (d) notes given to secure a cash loan, when the borrower receives the full face value of the note; (e) notes given to secure a cash loan, when the bank discounts the note; (f) payment of a discounted note at maturity; and (g) renewal of a note at maturity.

5 Complete a notes payable register.

6 Make journal entries for (a) adjustment for accrued interest on notes payable, (b) adjustment for Discount on Notes Payable, and (c) conversion of Discount on Notes Payable to Interest Expense.

ACCOUNTING LANGUAGE

Accrued interest on notes payable (p. 546)

Contra-liability account (p. 543)

Discount (p. 541)

Discounting a note payable (p. 541)

Duration (p. 536)

Interest (p. 535)

Maker (p. 535)

Maturity date (p. 536)

Maturity value (p. 539)

Notes payable register (p. 545)

Notice of maturity (p. 539)

Payee (p. 535)

Principal (p. 536)

Proceeds (p. 541)

Promissory note (p. 535)

Credit plays an extremely important role in the operation of most business enterprises. Credit may be extended on a charge-account basis, with payment generally due in 25 to 30 days. This type of credit involves the Accounts Payable and Accounts Receivable accounts. Credit may also be granted by giving or receiving notes for specific transactions. This sort of credit involves the Notes Payable and Notes Receivable accounts. The notes, which represent formal instruments of credit, are known as *promissory notes*. They are customarily used as evidence of credit transactions for periods longer than 30 days. For example, promissory notes may be used in sales of equipment on the installment plan and for transactions involving large amounts of money.

Promissory notes are also used to grant extensions of credit beyond the original credit terms. For example, suppose that Mory Company buys merchandise from Barnes Company with terms of 2/10, n/30. Mory Company finds that it can't pay its bill within the 30-day period. To preserve its credit standing, Mory Company offers a note. The advantages to Barnes Company are as follows: (1) Barnes now has specific evidence of the transaction, (2) the note may carry interest, and (3) Barnes can borrow from the bank by pledging the note as security for a loan.

Most companies become involved with notes at one time or another, either by issuing notes to creditors, by receiving notes from customers, or by issuing notes to banks in order to borrow money. Consequently, an accountant must be acquainted with the procedures for handling promissory notes.

PROMISSORY NOTES

A **promissory note**—usually referred to simply as a *note*—is a written promise to pay a certain sum at a fixed or determinable future time. Like a check, it must be payable to the order of a particular person or firm, known as the **payee**. It must also be signed by the person or firm making the promise, known as the **maker**. In Figure 1, Dana Manufacturing Company is the payee, and Whitewater Raft Supply is the maker.

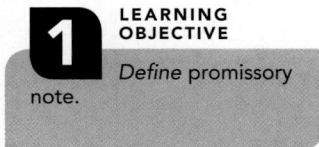

LEARNING OBJECTIVE 1

Define promissory note.

PROMISSORY NOTE

$900.00   May 12, 20--
                                                                          Seattle, WA

For value received, the undersigned, ___Whitewater Raft Supply___ ("Maker") promises to pay in lawful money of the United States of America to ___Dana Manufacturing Company___ , (the "Payee") at Seattle, Washington, or at such other place as the Holder may from time to time designate in writing, the principal sum of ___Nine Hundred and 00/100___ Dollars ($900.00), together with interest at the rate of _Six_ and 00/100 percent (_6_ %) per annum until the principal is paid in full. The principal and interest are due in _60 days_ .

The principal amount of this Promissory Note, together with any accrued interest, may be prepaid in whole or in part at any time, without penalty.

If Maker defaults in the payment of this Promissory Note, the outstanding principal balance shall bear interest at twelve percent (12%) per annum compounded annually, or the maximum rate permitted by law, whichever is less.

If suit is brought on this Promissory Note, or if it is placed in the hands of an attorney for collection after default in any payment, the undersigned promises and agrees to pay all costs of collection, including attorney's fees incurred.

Presentment, notice of dishonor, and protest are hereby waived by all makers, sureties, guarantors, and endorsers hereof. This Promissory Note shall be the joint and several obligation of all makers, sureties, guarantors and endorsers, and shall be binding upon them and their successors and assigns.

                                                                          MAKER
                                                                          D. M. Bruce

---

FIGURE 1

Promissory note

Remember

A note is a formal written promise to pay an amount of money at a definite time, as opposed to the "open account" relationship in Accounts Receivable or Accounts Payable.

CALCULATING INTEREST

Interest is a charge made for the use of money. To the maker of the note, interest is an expense. The amount of interest a maker pays is expressed as a certain percentage of the principal of the note for a period of one year (or less). The following formula is used to calculate interest:

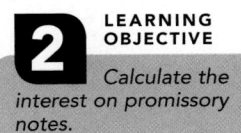

LEARNING OBJECTIVE 2

Calculate the interest on promissory notes.

| **Interest** (in dollars) | = | **Principal** of Note (in dollars) | × | **Rate** of Interest (as a percentage of the principal) | × | **Time** of Note (expressed as a year or fraction of a year) |

The liability incurred when borrowing money can be short-term or long-term in nature. Some debts last only a few days, whereas others—such as those for major construction projects— can last 30, or even 50, years.

© ANDERS ADERMARK/ISTOCKPHOTO.COM

The **principal** is the face amount of the note. The *rate of interest* is a percentage of the principal, such as 5 percent or 6 percent. Since 1 percent equals ¹⁄₁₀₀ or 0.01, then 10 percent equals ¹⁰⁄₁₀₀ or 0.10.

Time, or the length of life of the note, is usually expressed in days or months. It is the period between the note's date of issue (starting date) and its **maturity date** (the due date or interest payment date). It is stated in terms of a year or fraction of a year. Examples are

$$1 \text{ year} = 1 \qquad 6 \text{ months} = \frac{6}{12} \qquad 3 \text{ months} = \frac{3}{12}$$

$$90 \text{ days} = \frac{90}{360} \qquad 24 \text{ days} = \frac{24}{360}$$

The usual commercial practice is to use a 360-day year, making the denominator of the fraction 360. However, agencies of the federal government use the actual number of days in the year.

Example 1 $8,000, 6 percent, 1 year.

Interest = Principal × Rate × Time

Interest = $8,000 × 0.06 × 1 = $480

Example 2 $40,000, 5.5 percent, 4 months.

Interest = Principal × Rate × Time

$$\textbf{Interest} = \textbf{\$40,000} \times \textbf{0.055} \times \frac{\textbf{4}}{\textbf{12}} = \textbf{\$733.33}$$

Example 3 $80,000, 6 percent, 60 days.

Interest = Principal × Rate × Time

$$\textbf{Interest} = \textbf{\$80,000} \times \textbf{0.06} \times \frac{\textbf{60}}{\textbf{360}} = \textbf{\$800}$$

DETERMINING DUE DATES

LEARNING OBJECTIVE **3**

Determine the due dates of promissory notes.

The period of time between a promissory note's issue date and its maturity date is called the **duration** of the note. The duration of a note, as we have said, may be expressed in either days or months. If the time of the note is expressed in months, the maturity date is the corresponding day in the month after the specified number of months has elapsed. For example, a note dated March 15 with a time period of three months has a due date of June 15. In those cases in which there is no date in the month of maturity that corresponds to the issuance date, the due date becomes the last day of the month. For example, a three-month note dated March 31 would be due on June 30.

But suppose that the period of time a note has to run is expressed in days. When counting the number of days, begin with the day after the date the note was issued, since the note states "after date." The last day, however, is counted. Let's say that the due date of a promissory note is specified as 60 days after April 8. The due date is June 7.

April								May								June						
S	M	T	W	T	F	S		S	M	T	W	T	F	S		S	M	T	W	T	F	S
		1	2	3	4	5						1	2	3		1	2	3	4	5	6	7
6	7	8	9	10	11	12		4	5	6	7	8	9	10		8	9	10	11	12	13	14
13	14	15	16	17	18	19		11	12	13	14	15	16	17		15	16	17	18	19	20	21
20	21	22	23	24	25	26		18	19	20	21	22	23	24		22	23	24	25	26	27	28
27	28	29	30					25	26	27	28	29	30	31		29	30					

22 days
8th through the 30th
30 − 8 = 22 days left

+ 31 days

= 53 days have passed
60 − 53 = 7 days remaining after May 31
June 7 due date

The due date is determined by the following steps:

STEP 1. Determine the number of days remaining in the month of issue by subtracting the date of the note from the number of days in the month in which it is dated.

STEP 2. Add as many full months as possible without exceeding the number of days in the note, counting the full number of days in these months.

STEP 3. Determine the number of days remaining in the month in which the note matures by subtracting the total days counted so far from the number of days in the note, as shown here.

> **Remember**
>
> When counting the time period of a note, the date the note was issued is *not* counted, but the due date *is* counted.

April (30 − 8)	= 22 days left in April
May	= 31 days
Total days so far	= 53 days
June (60 − 53)	= 7th day of June (due date)

Now, suppose you have a 120-day note dated May 20:

May (31 − 20)	= 11 days left in May
June	= 30 days
July	= 31 days
August	= 31 days
Total days so far	= 103 days
September (120 − 103)	= 17th day of September (due date)

TRANSACTIONS INVOLVING NOTES PAYABLE

The following types of transactions involve the issuance and payment of notes payable:

1. Note given to a supplier in return for an extension of time for payment of an open account (charge account)
2. Note given in exchange for merchandise or other property purchased
3. Note given as evidence of a loan
4. Note renewed at maturity

In our examples, we assume that all the notes are due within one year; thus they are classified on the balance sheet as Current Liabilities. However, if notes are not due within one year, that portion of the note that is due within one year is a Current Liability, and the remainder is classified as a Long-Term Liability. Interest expense is classified on the income statement as Interest Expense (if significant) or Other Expense.

Note Given to Secure an Extension of Time on an Open Account

LEARNING OBJECTIVE **4a**

Make journal entries for notes given to secure an extension of time on an open account.

When a firm wishes to obtain an extension of time for the payment of an account, the firm may ask a supplier to accept a note for all or part of the amount due. For example, let's say that Whitewater Raft Supply prefers not to pay its open account with Dana Manufacturing Company when it becomes due. Dana Manufacturing Company agrees to accept a 60-day, 6 percent, $900 note from Whitewater Raft Supply in settlement of the account. The entry that caused the account to be put on Dana Manufacturing Company's books came about when Whitewater Raft Supply bought merchandise on account on April 12, with terms 2/10, n/30.

Original Purchase

In general journal form, the entry looks like this:

		GENERAL JOURNAL			PAGE _____
Date		Description	Post. Ref.	Debit	Credit
20—					
Apr.	12	Purchases		9 0 0 00	
		Accounts Payable, Dana			
		Manufacturing Company			9 0 0 00
		Terms 2/10, n/30.			

Payment by Note

On May 12, Whitewater Raft Supply records the issuance of the note in its general journal.

		GENERAL JOURNAL			PAGE _____
Date		Description	Post. Ref.	Debit	Credit
20—					
May	12	Accounts Payable, Dana			
		Manufacturing Company		9 0 0 00	
		Notes Payable			9 0 0 00
		Gave a 60-day, 6 percent			
		note, in settlement of our			
		open account.			

By T accounts, the transactions look like this:

Purchases			Accounts Payable			Notes Payable	
+	−	−	+		−	+	
Apr. 12	900		May 12	900	Apr. 12	900	May 12	900

Observe that the previous entry cancels out the Accounts Payable, Dana Manufacturing Company, account and substitutes Notes Payable. The note does not *pay* the debt, it merely changes the liability status from an account payable to a note payable. Dana Manufacturing Company prefers the note to the open account because, in the case of default and a subsequent lawsuit to collect, the possession of the note improves Dana Manufacturing Company's legal position. The note is written evidence of the debt and the amount owed. In addition, Dana Manufacturing Company is, in this case, entitled to 6 percent interest.

Payment of an Interest-Bearing Note at Maturity

LEARNING OBJECTIVE 4b *Make journal entries for payment of an interest-bearing note at maturity.*

When a note payable falls due, payment may be made directly to the holder, or it may be made to a bank with which the note was left for collection. The maker knows the identity of the original payee, of course, but he or she may not know who the holder of the note is at maturity. The payee may have transferred the note by endorsement to another party or may have left it with a bank for collection. When a note is left with a bank for collection, the bank usually mails the maker a **notice of maturity** specifying the terms, the due date of the note, and the **maturity value** (the principal of the note plus the interest). For example, Dana Manufacturing Company turned the note over to its bank, the New National Bank, for collection. Accordingly, the bank sent Whitewater Raft Supply a notice of maturity of the note.

Whitewater Raft Supply pays the note on July 11. In general journal form, the entry is as follows:

		GENERAL JOURNAL				PAGE _____
Date		Description	Post. Ref.	Debit		Credit
20—						
July	11	Notes Payable		9 0 0 00		
		Interest Expense		9 00		
		Cash				9 0 9 00
		Paid note to Dana				
		Manufacturing Company.				

> **Remember**
>
> Notes Payable is listed in the Current Liabilities section of the balance sheet (if payable in less than one year). Interest expense is listed as Interest Expense (if significant) or Other Expense on the income statement.

Because Interest = Principal × Rate × Time, we perform this calculation:

$$\text{Interest} = \$900 \times 0.06 \times \frac{60}{360} = \underline{\$9}$$

Cash				Notes Payable				Interest Expense		
	+	−			−	+			+	−
Bal.	10,000	July 11 909		July 11 900		May 12 900		July 11 9		

Note Given in Exchange for Assets Purchased

LEARNING OBJECTIVE 4c *Make journal entries for notes given in exchange for merchandise or other property purchased.*

Occasionally, when the price of an item is high or the credit period is long, a buyer gives a note instead of buying the item on account. For example, Whitewater Raft Supply issues a 90-day, 5 percent interest-bearing note for $7,000 to Wilder Equipment

Company in exchange for equipment purchased June 5 and records the transaction in the general journal as follows:

	GENERAL JOURNAL			PAGE ____	
Date	Description	Post. Ref.	Debit	Credit	
20—					
June 5	Store Equipment		7 0 0 0 00		
	Notes Payable			7 0 0 0 00	
	Acquired equipment				
	from Wilder Equipment				
	Company, 90 days, 5 percent.				

When Whitewater Raft Supply pays the note at maturity, the entry in its books is the same as the entry it makes for the payment of any interest-bearing note. The entry, in general journal form, is as follows:

	GENERAL JOURNAL			PAGE ____	
Date	Description	Post. Ref.	Debit	Credit	
20—					
Sept. 3	Notes Payable		7 0 0 0 00		
	Interest Expense		8 7 50		
	Cash			7 0 8 7 50	
	Paid note to Wilder				
	Equipment Company.				

Remember

Do not count the day the note is issued when calculating the due date of a note.

The due date for the note is determined as follows:

June (30 – 5)	= 25 days left in June
July	= 31 days
August	= 31 days
Total days so far	= 87 days
September (90 – 87)	= 3rd day of September (due date)

And because Interest = Principal × Rate × Time,

$$\text{Interest} = \$7{,}000 \times 0.05 \times \frac{90}{360} = \$87.50$$

Note Given to Secure a Cash Loan

Businesses frequently need to stock up on merchandise in large amounts in order to meet seasonal demands. Sometimes their usual receipts from customers are not enough to cover the sudden volume of purchases. During such periods, firms customarily borrow money from banks, through the medium of short-term notes, to finance their operations.

LEARNING OBJECTIVE 4d

Make journal entries for notes given to secure a cash loan, when the borrower receives the full face value of the note.

Borrowing from a Bank When Borrower Receives Full Face Value of Note

In one type of bank loan, a business firm signs an interest-bearing note and receives the full face value of the note. The borrower repays the principal plus interest. For example, on June 7, Whitewater Raft Supply borrows $8,500 from Foster National

Bank for 120 days with interest of 5.5 percent payable at maturity. The entry to record the transaction is as follows:

Date	Description	Post. Ref.	Debit	Credit
20—				
June 7	Cash		8 5 0 0 00	
	Notes Payable			8 5 0 0 00
	Gave Foster National Bank			
	a 120-day, 5.5 percent note.			

Note Paid to the Bank at Maturity

After Whitewater Raft Supply has paid the note and interest, its accountant makes the following entry on the books:

Date	Description	Post. Ref.	Debit	Credit
20—				
Oct. 5	Notes Payable		8 5 0 0 00	
	Interest Expense		1 5 5 83	
	Cash			8 6 5 5 83
	Paid note to Foster National			
	Bank.			

> **Remember**
> The debit to Notes Payable represents the face value of the note.

Interest = Principal × Rate × Time

$$\text{Interest} = \$8{,}500 \times 0.055 \times \frac{120}{360} = \$155.83$$

Borrowing from a Bank When Bank Discounts Note (Deducts Interest in Advance)

In another type of bank loan, the bank deducts the interest in advance, which is called **discounting a note payable.** For example, on June 22, Whitewater Raft Supply borrows $12,000 for 60 days from Westmore National Bank, and the bank requires Whitewater Raft Supply to sign a note. From the face value of the note, the bank deducts 5 percent interest for 60 days, so Whitewater Raft Supply actually gets only $11,900 ($12,000 − $100). This interest deducted in advance by a bank is called the **discount**. The principal of the loan left after the discount has been subtracted is called the **proceeds,** which is the amount the borrower has available to use. Since all the interest is deducted at the time the loan is made, the note must state that only the face amount is to be paid at maturity. The calculation for the discount is as follows:

> **4e LEARNING OBJECTIVE**
> *Make journal entries for notes given to secure a cash loan, when the bank discounts the note.*

Interest = Principal × Rate × Time

$$\text{Interest} = \$12{,}000 \times 0.05 \times \frac{60}{360} = \$100$$

The bank deducts the discount from the face amount of the note before making the money available to the borrower.

Principal	$12,000
− Discount	100
Proceeds	$11,900

You Make the Call

A friend of yours, Marty, is preparing to start a small business. He needs startup cash and is excited that he has been approved for a loan from one of the local banks. He has not had any experience in the area of financing. Marty tells you enthusiastically, "The bank told me it was a discounted note payable. I can't wait to spend that $25,000." How are you going to tell him that the note he signed stating that he is borrowing $25,000 at 9 percent, due in one year, may not be discounted in the way he thinks it is?

SOLUTION

Obviously, Marty has not taken an accounting class or done much research on the matter. He needs to understand that a discounted note payable means that he will not get the face value of the note, but rather will receive the face value minus the interest:

Interest = $25,000 × 0.09 × 1 = $2,250

Principal	$25,000
− Discount	2,250
Proceeds	$22,750

Therefore, Marty has $22,750, not $25,000, available to use.

Entry When Note Discounted at Bank Matures Before End of Fiscal Period

As long as a note begins and matures during the same fiscal period, the borrower may debit all the interest (or discount) to Interest Expense. Assume that also on June 7, Whitewater Raft Supply issues a discounted note payable to Westmore National Bank. The $10,000, 120-day, 6 percent note that Whitewater Raft Supply submits to the bank is dated June 7 and therefore matures October 5. Since Whitewater Raft Supply's fiscal period is from January 1 to December 31, the company can include the entire amount of interest in the Interest Expense account. Accordingly, Whitewater Raft Supply records the transaction as follows:

Remember

When a note is discounted, the proceeds received are reduced by the amount of the interest expense.

Date		Description	Post. Ref.	Debit	Credit
20—					
June	7	Cash		9 8 0 0 00	
		Interest Expense		2 0 0 00	
		Notes Payable			10 0 0 0 00
		Discounted our 120-day, non-			
		interest-bearing note at Westmore			
		National Bank, discount rate			
		6 percent.			
		($10,000 × 0.06 × 120/360)			

Note Paid to the Bank at Maturity

When the note becomes due, Whitewater Raft Supply pays the bank only the *face value of the note* and records the transaction as follows:

LEARNING OBJECTIVE 4f

Make journal entries for payment of a discounted note at maturity.

Date		Description	Post. Ref.	Debit	Credit
20—					
Oct.	5	Notes Payable		10 0 0 0 00	
		Cash			10 0 0 0 00
		Paid Westmore National			
		Bank on our note payable			
		discounted June 7.			

Entry When Note Discounted at Bank Matures After End of Fiscal Period

Instead of the entire duration of the note (such as 90 or 60 days) being included in one 12-month fiscal period, assume that the duration extends into the next fiscal period. In this case, the journal entry must include a debit to Discount on Notes Payable instead of a debit to Interest Expense. In other words, Discount on Notes Payable is substituted for Interest Expense, using the same dollar amount.

Discount on Notes Payable is a contra-liability account; it is a deduction from Notes Payable. Recall that we defined the Accumulated Depreciation account as a contra-asset account—for example, a deduction from Equipment with the plus and minus signs reversed. Similarly, Discount on Notes Payable is a contra account—a deduction from Notes Payable with the plus and minus signs reversed. In T account form, these accounts look like this:

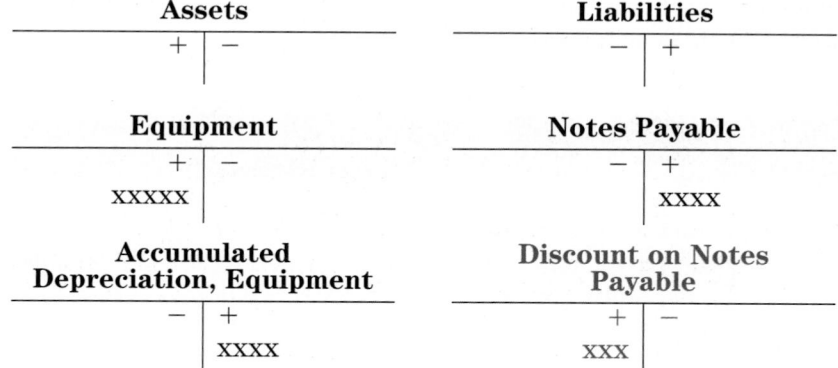

On a balance sheet, the contra account is deducted as follows:

Assets		
Plant and Equipment:		
Equipment	$xxxxx	
Less Accumulated Depreciation	xxxx	$xxxx
Liabilities		
Current Liabilities:		
Notes Payable	$ xxxx	
Less Discount on Notes Payable	xxx	$ xxx

Remember

If a note payable discounted at a bank comes due *before* the end of the fiscal period, debit Interest Expense for the amount of the discount. If the note comes due *after* the end of the fiscal period, debit Discount on Notes Payable for the amount of the discount.

At the end of the fiscal period, an adjusting entry must be made to record the accrued interest expense and the discount on notes payable for the time between the date the note is issued and the end of the fiscal period. The note is outstanding during the period. We will describe this type of adjusting entry in the section "End-of-Fiscal-Period Adjustments" later in the chapter.

Let's say that on December 1, Whitewater Raft Supply borrows $8,000 from Midland Bank for 120 days. The bank deducts 6 percent interest (in advance) for 120 days, $160, and gives Whitewater Raft Supply $7,840. Whitewater Raft Supply's fiscal period is from January 1 through December 31, so the entry in the general journal is as follows:

Date	Description	Post. Ref.	Debit	Credit
20—				
Dec. 1	Cash		7 8 4 0 00	
	Discount on Notes Payable		1 6 0 00	
	Notes Payable			8 0 0 0 00
	Discounted our 120-day,			
	non-interest-bearing note at			
	Midland Bank; discount rate			
	6 percent.			
	($8,000 × 0.06 × 120/360)			

Renewal of Note at Maturity

LEARNING OBJECTIVE 4g

Make journal entries for renewal of a note at maturity.

A maker (or borrower) unable to pay a note in full at maturity may arrange to renew all or part of the note. At this time, the company usually pays the interest on the old note. For example, assume that on June 25, Whitewater Raft Supply issues a 45-day note to Batisto, Inc., for $9,500, with interest at 5.5 percent. The original entry in general journal form is as follows:

Date	Description	Post. Ref.	Debit	Credit
20—				
June 25	Accounts Payable, Batisto, Inc.		9 5 0 0 00	
	Notes Payable			9 5 0 0 00
	Issued a 45-day, 5.5 percent			
	note.			

Renewal of Note with Payment of Interest

When a firm renews an interest-bearing note, while paying interest owed, the accountant first makes an entry for payment of the interest on the existing note up to the present date. This entry occurs on August 9, the maturity date of the note:

Date	Description	Post. Ref.	Debit	Credit
20—				
Aug. 9	Interest Expense		6 5 31	
	Cash			6 5 31
	Interest payment on note to			
	Batisto, Inc.			

Interest = Principal × Rate × Time

$$\text{Interest} = \$9{,}500 \times 0.055 \times \frac{45}{360} = \$65.31$$

The accountant then makes a separate entry for the issuance of the new note, to run for 30 days at 6 percent (the interest rate has been increased and the number of days decreased), as follows:

Date	Description	Post. Ref.	Debit	Credit
Aug. 9	Notes Payable		9 5 0 0 00	
	Notes Payable			9 5 0 0 00
	Canceled note to Batisto, Inc.,			
	by issuing a new 30-day,			
	6 percent note.			

Renewal of Note with Payment of Interest and Part Payment of Principal

What if the maker decides to pay only *part* of a note at maturity? Let's assume that, instead of taking the course of action we have just described, Whitewater Raft Supply pays $1,500 on the principal of the note that is due (the old note), and also pays the entire interest on it. In other words, the maker pays the interest up to the present date for the old note, plus $1,500 to reduce the principal from $9,500 to $8,000, and issues a *new* note for $8,000.

Date	Description	Post. Ref.	Debit	Credit
Aug. 9	Notes Payable		1 5 0 0 00	
	Interest Expense		6 5 31	
	Cash			1 5 6 5 31
	Interest and partial principal			
	payment on note to Batisto, Inc.			
9	Notes Payable		8 0 0 0 00	
	Notes Payable			8 0 0 0 00
	Canceled note to Batisto, Inc., by			
	issuing a new 30-day, 6 percent note.			

NOTES PAYABLE REGISTER

Ordinarily, small businesses issue notes to relatively few creditors. These firms can record the details of the notes on s tubs similar to check stubs, or they can just keep duplicate copies of the notes. However, if a firm issues many notes, it may be more convenient to keep a separate record listing the details of each note. This type of record is called a **notes payable register**.

An illustration of a notes payable register in abbreviated form for Whitewater Raft Supply through August 9 is shown at the top of the next page. More elaborate notes payable registers may include columns listing note numbers, addresses of payees, and similar information.

NOTES PAYABLE REGISTER

Date		Payee	Amount	Time	Rate	Interest	Due Date	Date Paid	Remarks
20—									
May	12	Dana Manufacturing Company	9 0 0 00	60 days	6%	9 00	7/11	7/11	Open account.
June	5	Wilder Equipment Company	7 0 0 0 00	90 days	5%	8 7 50	9/3	9/3	Bought equipment.
	7	Foster National Bank	8 5 0 0 00	120 days	5.5%	1 5 5 83	10/5	10/5	Loan, received full principal.
	7	Westmore National Bank	10 0 0 0 00	120 days	6%	2 0 0 00	10/5	10/5	Loan, discount $200.
	25	Batisto, Inc.	9 5 0 0 00	45 days	5.5%	6 5 31	8/9	Renewed	Open account.
Aug.	9	Batisto, Inc.	9 5 0 0 00	30 days	6%	4 7 50	9/8		Renewed June 25 note.
			OR IF PARTIAL PAYMENT						
Aug.	9	Batisto, Inc.	8 0 0 0 00	30 days	6%	4 0 00	9/8		Renewed June 25 note with partial payment of $1,500.

At the end of the fiscal period, the firm may prepare a schedule of notes payable by listing the unpaid notes that appear in the notes payable register. This schedule is similar to a schedule of accounts payable. The total of the schedule is compared with the balance of Notes Payable.

END-OF-FISCAL-PERIOD ADJUSTMENTS

When notes start in one fiscal period and mature in the next, adjusting entries must be made both for accrued interest and for discounts on notes payable. Otherwise, neither the expenses incurred by the business firm during a fiscal period nor its liabilities at the end of the fiscal period would be correctly stated.

Accrued Interest on Notes Payable

On all interest-bearing notes, interest expense *accrues*, or *accumulates*, daily. Consequently, if any notes payable are outstanding at the end of a fiscal period, the **accrued interest on notes payable** (that is, the interest due but not yet paid) should be calculated and recorded. For example, assume that a firm has two notes payable outstanding as of December 31, the end of the current fiscal period.

$12,000, 60 days, 5%, dated December 10
$7,200, 90 days, 6%, dated December 2

> **Remember**
>
> Accrual-basis accounting requires adjustment for notes spanning two or more fiscal periods so that interest expense and discount on notes payable are allocated properly to the periods affected.

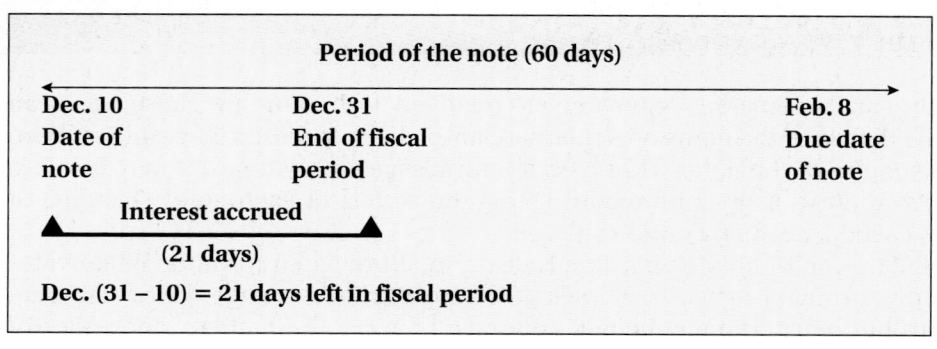

Period of the note (60 days)		
Dec. 10	Dec. 31	Feb. 8
Date of note	End of fiscal period	Due date of note

Interest accrued
(21 days)

Dec. (31 – 10) = 21 days left in fiscal period

Interest = Principal $\times$ Rate $\times$ Time

Interest = $12,000 \times 0.05 \times \dfrac{21}{360}$ = $35.00

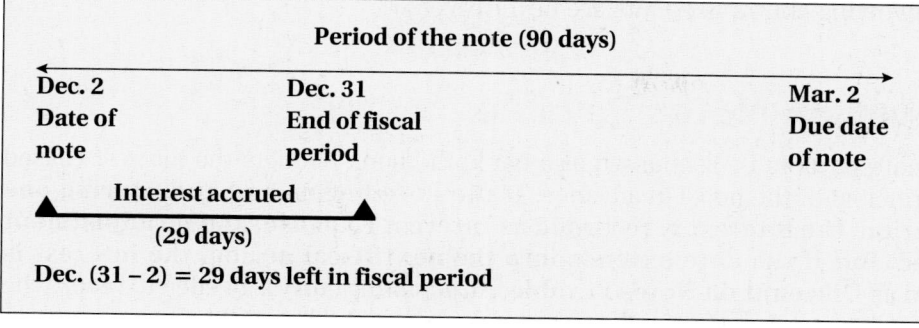

Period of the note (90 days)

Dec. 2
Date of
note

Dec. 31
End of fiscal
period

Mar. 2
Due date
of note

Interest accrued
(29 days)

Dec. (31 – 2) = 29 days left in fiscal period

Interest = Principal $\times$ Rate $\times$ Time

Interest = $7,200 \times 0.06 \times \dfrac{29}{360}$ = $34.80

Obviously, both notes extend into the next fiscal period; if they didn't, there would be no need for an adjustment. When paying interest on notes—except for notes discounted at a bank—you usually pay the principal and interest together on the day the note matures, or becomes due. But since *these* notes have not matured, the interest expense has been neither paid nor recorded. Therefore, the firm has to make an adjustment, because the accountant tries to portray the firm's expenses and liabilities for the current fiscal period as accurately as possible. In general journal form, the adjusting entry for the interest expense accrued on the two notes is as follows:

Date		Description	Post. Ref.	Debit	Credit
20—		Adjusting Entry			
Dec.	31	Interest Expense		6 9 80	
		Interest Payable			6 9 80
		($35.00 + $34.80)			

Like all other adjustments, this one is first recorded in the Adjustments columns of the work sheet. By assuming an Interest Expense balance of $925 before adjustment of Interest Expense, the T accounts are as follows:

Interest Expense			Interest Payable	
+	–		–	+
Dec. 31 Bal. 925.00				Dec. 31 Adj. 69.80
Adj. 69.80				

This situation parallels the adjustment for accrued salaries, in which the objective is to record the additional amount of salaries incurred and owed at the end of the year. In each adjusting entry, debit an expense account and credit a payable account.

Salary Expense			Salaries Payable	
+	–		–	+
Dec. 31 Adj. xxx				Dec. 31 Adj. xxx

The adjusting entry to record interest expense (not involving a discount) may also be reversed at the beginning of the year. Recall that **the rule for reversing entries is: If an adjusting entry increases an asset or liability account that does not have a previous balance, then you may reverse the adjusting entry.** Entries involving contra accounts are never reversed.

Discount on Notes Payable

When a note payable is discounted at a bank, the bank deducts the interest (based on the principal of the note) in advance. **If the note begins and ends during one fiscal period, the interest is recorded as Interest Expense, and no adjustment is needed. But if the note extends into the next fiscal period, the interest is recorded as Discount on Notes Payable.** An adjusting entry is needed to record the interest for the number of days the note was outstanding during the fiscal period.

Recall our original entry made on December 1, in which the firm discounted its $8,000, 120-day, non-interest-bearing note at the bank; discount rate 6 percent.

Date	Description	Post. Ref.	Debit	Credit
20—				
Dec. 1	Cash		7 8 4 0 00	
	Discount on Notes Payable		1 6 0 00	
	Notes Payable			8 0 0 0 00
	Discounted our 120-day,			
	non-interest-bearing note at			
	Midland Bank; discount rate			
	6 percent.			

Period of the note (120 days)

Dec. 1	Dec. 31	Mar. 31
Date of note	End of fiscal period	Due date of note

Dec. (31 − 1) = 30 days left in fiscal period

Interest = Principal × Rate × Time

$$\text{Interest} = \$8,000 \times 0.06 \times \frac{30}{360} = \underline{\$40.00}$$

FIGURE 2

Partial work sheet for Whitewater Raft Supply

Account Name	Trial Balance	
	Debit	Credit
Discount on Notes Payable	1 6 0 00	
Interest Expense	9 2 5 00	
Interest Payable		

LEARNING
OBJECTIVE 6b

Make journal
entries for adjustment
for Discount on
Notes Payable.

Since there are 30 days between December 1 and December 31, Whitewater Raft Supply's accountant has to make an adjusting entry to record the Interest Expense:

Date		Description	Post. Ref.	Debit	Credit
20—		Adjusting Entry			
Dec.	31	Interest Expense		4 0 00	
		Discount on Notes Payable			4 0 00

In T accounts, it looks this way:

Interest Expense		Discount on Notes Payable	
+	–	+	–
Dec. 31 Bal. 925.00		Dec. 1. 160.00	Dec. 31 Adj. 40.00
Adj. 40.00			

In addition to recording Interest Expense, the adjusting entry also reduces the balance of Discount on Notes Payable to its correct amount. This adjustment and the adjusting entry for accrued interest payable are shown on the partial work sheet in Figure 2. At the end of the year, the Interest Expense account is closed along with all the other expense accounts.

Two journal entries can be used to record the final payment of the discounted note to the bank. The first is like the payment of any discounted note.

		GENERAL JOURNAL			PAGE ___
Date		Description	Post. Ref.	Debit	Credit
20—					
Mar.	31	Notes Payable		8 0 0 0 00	
		Cash			8 0 0 0 00
		Paid the bank on the 120-day			
		non-interest-bearing note,			
		dated December 1 and			
		discounted at 6 percent.			

LEARNING
OBJECTIVE 6c

Make journal
entries for conversion of
Discount on Notes Payable
to Interest Expense.

The Discount on Notes Payable that was on the books has now become entirely an expense, and so it is converted into Interest Expense. Notice that the interest expense is calculated based on 90 days (January 1 through March 31), rather than 120 days. This is because 30 days of interest expense on the 120-day loan was recorded as an adjusting entry in the previous year.

Adjustments		Income Statement		Balance Sheet	
Debit	Credit	Debit	Credit	Debit	Credit
	(b) 4 0 00			1 2 0 00	
(a) 6 9 80		1 0 3 4 80			
(b) 4 0 00					
	(a) 6 9 80				6 9 80

Date	Description	Post. Ref.	Debit	Credit
Mar. 31	Interest Expense		1 2 0 00	
	Discount on Notes Payable			1 2 0 00
	To expense the discount for			
	the current year for the 120-			
	day note, dated December 1			
	and discounted at 6 percent.			
	($8,000 × 0.06 × 90/360)			

In T accounts, the entries for the interest on the discounted note payable look like this:

	Interest Expense	
	+	−
Bal.	925.00	
Dec. 31 Adj.	69.80	
Adj.	40.00	Dec. 31 Clos. 1,034.80
Mar. 31	120.00	

	Discount on Notes Payable	
	+	−
Dec. 1	160.00	Dec. 31 Adj. 40.00
Bal.	120.00	Mar. 31 120.00

CHAPTER REVIEW

Study & Practice

1 LEARNING OBJECTIVE
Define promissory note.

A **promissory note** is a written promise to pay a certain sum at a fixed or determinable future time.

2 LEARNING OBJECTIVE
Calculate the interest on promissory notes.

The formula used to calculate interest is as follows:

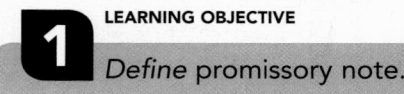

Interest = **Principal** of Note × **Rate** of Interest × **Time** of Note
(in dollars)   (in dollars)   (as a percentage   (expressed as a
                                    of the principal)   year or fraction
                                                      of a year)

PRACTICE EXERCISE 1

Compute the amount of interest on the following notes payable:

a.   A 30-day note for $1,500 at 6 percent.

b.   A 3-month note for $2,800 at 5 percent.

PRACTICE EXERCISE 1 SOLUTION

a. Interest = $1,500 \times 0.06 \times \dfrac{30}{360} = \underline{\underline{\$7.50}}$

b. Interest = $2,800 \times 0.05 \times \dfrac{3}{12} = \underline{\underline{\$35.00}}$

LEARNING OBJECTIVE

3

Determine the due dates of promissory notes.

Use the following steps to determine the due date:

STEP 1. Determine the number of days remaining in the month of issue by subtracting the date of the note from the number of days in the month in which it is dated.

STEP 2. Add as many full months as possible without exceeding the number of days in the note, counting the full number of days in these months.

STEP 3. Determine the number of days remaining in the month in which the note matures by subtracting the total days counted so far from the number of days in the note.

PRACTICE EXERCISE 2

Determine the due dates of the following notes payable:

a. A 90-day note dated April 3.
b. A 60-day note dated March 7.
c. A 120-day note dated July 12.

PRACTICE EXERCISE 2 SOLUTION

a.

April (30 – 3)	=	27 days left in April
May	=	31 days
June	=	30 days
Total days so far	=	88 days
July (90 – 88)	=	2nd day of July (due date)

b.

March (31 – 7)	=	24 days left in March
April	=	30 days
Total days so far	=	54 days
May (60 – 54)	=	6th day of May (due date)

c.

July (31 – 12)	=	19 days left in July
August	=	31 days
September	=	30 days
October	=	31 days
Total days so far	=	111 days
November (120 – 111)	=	9th day of November (due date)

4a LEARNING OBJECTIVE

Make journal entries for notes given to secure an extension of time on an open account.

When a firm wishes to obtain an extension of time for the payment of an account, the firm may ask a supplier to accept a note for all or part of the amount due. The note does not *pay* the debt, it merely changes the liability status for an account payable to a note payable.

PRACTICE EXERCISE 3a

Journalize the following transaction:

May   15   Issued a 60-day, 6 percent note for $900 payable to Travers Manufacturing Company, in place of the open account.

PRACTICE EXERCISE 3a SOLUTION

Date		Description	Post. Ref.	Debit	Credit
20—					
May	15	Accounts Payable, Travers			
		Manufacturing Company		9 0 0 00	
		Notes Payable			9 0 0 00
		Gave a 60-day, 6 percent			
		note, in settlement of our			
		open account.			

4b LEARNING OBJECTIVE

Make journal entries for payment of an interest-bearing note at maturity.

When a note payable falls due, payment may be made directly to the holder, or it may be made to a bank with which the note was left for collection.

PRACTICE EXERCISE 3b

Journalize the following transaction:

July   14   Paid at maturity the note given to Travers Manufacturing Company in Practice Exercise 3a.

PRACTICE EXERCISE 3b SOLUTION

Date		Description	Post. Ref.	Debit	Credit
20—					
July	14	Notes Payable		9 0 0 00	
		Interest Expense		9 00	
		Cash			9 0 9 00
		Paid note to Travers			
		Manufacturing Company.			
		($900 × 0.06 × 60/360)			

LEARNING OBJECTIVE

4c
Make journal entries for notes given in exchange for merchandise or other property purchased.

Occasionally, when the price of an item is high or the credit period is long, a buyer gives a note instead of buying the item on account. When the buyer pays the note at maturity, the entry in its books is the same as the entry it makes for the payment of any interest-bearing note.

PRACTICE EXERCISE 3c

Journalize the following transaction:

June 3   Issued a 90-day, 5.5 percent note for $7,000 payable to Ward Equipment Company, for equipment.

PRACTICE EXERCISE 3c SOLUTION

Date	Description	Post. Ref.	Debit	Credit
20—				
June 3	Equipment		7 0 0 0 00	
	Notes Payable			7 0 0 0 00
	Acquired equipment from			
	Ward Equipment Company,			
	90 days, 5.5 percent.			

LEARNING OBJECTIVE

4d
Make journal entries for notes given to secure a cash loan, when the borrower receives the full face value of the note.

In one type of bank loan, a business firm signs an interest-bearing note and receives the full face value of the note. The borrower repays the principal plus interest. In another type of bank loan, the bank deducts the interest in advance, which is called **discounting a note payable**. This interest deducted in advance by a bank is called the **discount**. The principal of the loan left after the discount has been subtracted is called the **proceeds**, which is the amount the borrower has available to use.

PRACTICE EXERCISE 3d

Journalize the following transaction:

June 11   Borrowed $5,000 from Fisher National Bank, giving in exchange a 120-day, 5 percent note (received full face amount).

PRACTICE EXERCISE 3d SOLUTION

Date		Description	Post. Ref.	Debit	Credit
20—					
June	11	Cash		5 0 0 0 00	
		Notes Payable			5 0 0 0 00
		Gave Fisher National Bank			
		a 120-day, 5 percent note.			

LEARNING OBJECTIVE

4e *Make journal entries for notes given to secure a cash loan, when the bank discounts the note.*

As long as a note begins and matures during the same fiscal period, the borrower may debit all the interest (or discount) to Interest Expense.

PRACTICE EXERCISE 3e

Journalize the following transaction:

June   19   Borrowed $9,000 from Western National Bank for 90 days; discount rate is 6.5 percent; issued a note for $9,000.

PRACTICE EXERCISE 3e SOLUTION

Date		Description	Post. Ref.	Debit	Credit
20—					
June	19	Cash		8 8 5 3 75	
		Interest Expense		1 4 6 25	
		Notes Payable			9 0 0 0 00
		Discounted our 90-day, note at			
		Western National Bank,			
		discount rate 6.5 percent.			
		($9,000 × 0.065 × 90/360)			

LEARNING OBJECTIVE

4f *Make journal entries for payment of a discounted note at maturity.*

When a discounted note becomes due, the borrower pays the bank only the *face value of the note*. If the entire **duration** of the note extends into the next fiscal period, the journal entry must include a debit to Discount on Notes Payable instead of a debit to Interest Expense.

PRACTICE EXERCISE 3f

Journalize the payment of the note issued in Practice Exercise 3e:

Sept.   17   Paid $9,000 to Western National Bank for 90-day note payable.

PRACTICE EXERCISE 3f SOLUTION

Date		Description	Post. Ref.	Debit	Credit
20—					
Sept.	17	Notes Payable		9 0 0 0 00	
		Cash			9 0 0 0 00
		Paid Western National			
		Bank on our note payable			
		discounted June 19.			

LEARNING OBJECTIVE

Make journal entries for renewal of a note at maturity.

For a renewal of a note payable, if interest is paid on the old note at time of renewal, first record the interest payment. Next, debit the old note to take it off the books, and credit the new note to put it on the books.

PRACTICE EXERCISE 3g

Journalize the following transaction:

Aug. 11   Canceled a 45-day note payable to Baker, Inc., for $11,500, with interest at 6 percent, by issuing a new note to run for 30 days at 6 percent. Interest of 45 days of interest was paid at time of renewal.

PRACTICE EXERCISE 3g SOLUTION

Date		Description	Post. Ref.	Debit	Credit
20—					
Aug.	11	Interest Expense		8 6 25	
		Cash			8 6 25
		Interest payment on note to			
		Baker, Inc.			
		($11,500 × 0.06 × 45/360)			
	11	Notes Payable		11 5 0 0 00	
		Notes Payable			11 5 0 0 00
		Canceled note to Baker, Inc.,			
		by issuing a new 30-day, 6 percent			
		note.			

LEARNING OBJECTIVE

Complete a notes payable register.

A **notes payable register** is an auxiliary record used for listing the details of notes issued. For each note, list the date, payee, amount, time, rate, interest, due date, date paid, and relevant remarks.

PRACTICE EXERCISE 4

Prepare a notes payable register for the transactions in Practice Exercises 3a–g.

PRACTICE EXERCISE 4 SOLUTION

NOTES PAYABLE REGISTER

Date	Payee	Amount	Time	Rate	Interest	Due Date	Date Paid	Remarks
20—								
May 15	Travers Manufacturing Company	9 0 0 00	60 days	6%	9 00	7/14	7/14	Open account.
June 3	Ward Equipment Company	7 0 0 0 00	90 days	5.5%	9 6 25	9/1	9/1	Bought equipment.
11	Fisher National Bank	5 0 0 0 00	120 days	5%	8 3 33	10/9	10/9	Loan, received full principal.
19	Western National Bank	9 0 0 0 00	90 days	6.5%	1 4 6 25	9/17	9/17	Loan, discount $146.25.
27	Baker, Inc.	11 5 0 0 00	45 days	6%	8 6 25	8/11	Renewed	Open account.
Aug. 11	Baker, Inc.	11 5 0 0 00	30 days	6%	5 7 50	9/10	9/10	Renewed June 27 note.

6a **LEARNING OBJECTIVE**

Make journal entries for adjustment for accrued interest on notes payable.

When the time period of the note spans two fiscal periods, record interest expense incurred for the number of days the note is outstanding during the fiscal period.

PRACTICE EXERCISE 5a

Assume that Joel Company has two notes payable outstanding as of December 31:

$8,000, 60 days, 6%, dated December 12
$5,500, 120 days, 7%, dated December 19

Provide the adjusting entry for the interest expense accrued on the two notes.

PRACTICE EXERCISE 5a SOLUTION

GENERAL JOURNAL   PAGE _____

Date	Description	Post. Ref.	Debit	Credit
20—	Adjusting Entry			
Dec. 31	Interest Expense		3 8 16	
	Interest Payable			3 8 16
	($25.33 + $12.83)			

Calculation of accrued interest:

$$\$8,000 \times 0.06 \times \frac{19}{360} = \$25.33$$

$$\$5,500 \times 0.07 \times \frac{12}{360} = \$12.83$$

LEARNING OBJECTIVE

6b

Make journal entries for adjustment for Discount on Notes Payable.

If a discounted note extends into the next fiscal period, the Discount on Notes Payable is adjusted to reflect the portion of the discount that has become interest expense for the current fiscal period.

PRACTICE EXERCISE 5b

Assume that on December 5, a firm discounted its $7,500, 120-day, non-interest-bearing note at the bank; discount rate 6.5 percent. Provide the year-end adjusting entry to record the Interest Expense.

PRACTICE EXERCISE 5b SOLUTION

	GENERAL JOURNAL				PAGE _____
Date	Description	Post. Ref.	Debit		Credit
20—	Adjusting Entry				
Dec. 31	Interest Expense		3 5 21		
	Discount on Notes Payable				3 5 21
	($7,500 × 0.065 × 26/360)				

LEARNING OBJECTIVE

6c

Make journal entries for conversion of Discount on Notes Payable to Interest Expense.

Upon payment of a discounted note spanning two fiscal periods, the remainder of the Discount on Notes Payable has become an expense and must be converted to Interest Expense.

PRACTICE EXERCISE 5c

Journalize the entry on the note in Practice Exercise 5b above to convert the remaining Discount on Notes Payable to Interest Expense.

PRACTICE EXERCISE 5c SOLUTION

	GENERAL JOURNAL				PAGE _____
Date	Description	Post. Ref.	Debit		Credit
20—					
Apr. 4	Interest Expense		1 2 7 29		
	Discount on Notes Payable				1 2 7 29
	($7,500 × 0.065 × 94/360)				

Interest Expense					Discount on Notes Payable			
	+		−			+		−
Dec. 31 Adj.	35.21	Dec. 31 Clos.	35.21		Dec. 1	162.50	Dec. 31 Adj.	35.21
Apr. 4	127.29				Bal.	127.29	Apr. 4	127.29

Glossary

Accrued interest on notes payable The interest that is due (not yet paid) on notes payable that are outstanding at the end of the fiscal period. *(p. 546)*

Contra-liability account A deduction from a liability, such as Discount on Notes Payable, which is a deduction from the balance of Notes Payable. *(p. 543)*

Discount Interest deducted in advance by a bank that makes a loan. *(p. 541)*

Discounting a note payable The procedure by which a bank deducts interest in advance when it loans money with a note. *(p. 541)*

Duration The period of time a note is outstanding; the length of time in days or months from a note's issue date to its maturity date. *(p. 536)*

Interest A charge made for the use of money. *(p. 535)*

Maker An individual or firm that signs a promissory note. *(p. 535)*

Maturity date The due date of a promissory note. *(p. 536)*

Maturity value The principal of the note plus interest. *(p. 539)*

Notes payable register An auxiliary record used for listing the details of notes issued. *(p. 545)*

Notice of maturity A notice specifying the terms and due date of a promissory note that has been left with a bank for collection; mailed by the bank to the maker. *(p. 539)*

Payee The party receiving payment, such as on a note receivable or an account receivable. *(p. 535)*

Principal The face amount of a note. *(p. 536)*

Proceeds The principal of a loan less the discount. *(p. 541)*

Promissory note A written promise to pay a certain sum at a fixed or determinable future time. *(p. 535)*

CHAPTER ASSIGNMENTS

Discussion Questions

1. Define *promissory note* and identify the two major parties involved.
2. Explain how to determine the maturity date of a note.
3. Describe the basic formula for the calculation of interest on a note. Explain each element.
4. Distinguish between a regular note and a discounted note.
5. Differentiate between the principal value of a note and the maturity value of a note.
6. Explain the difference when making an entry for a note discounted at a bank in which the note matures before the end of the fiscal period and one in which the note matures after the end of the fiscal period. Does either situation require an adjusting entry?
7. Briefly explain the Discount on Notes Payable account. What is its classification?
8. Why is it necessary to make an adjusting entry for accrued interest on an interest-bearing note payable? Can the entry be reversed?

Exercises

2,3 **LO**

PRACTICE EXERCISES 1,2

EXERCISE 13-1 Part A: Calculate the interest on the following notes:

Principal	Interest Rate (percent)	Number of Days
1. $14,600	5.5%	30 days
2. 11,200	6.5	60 days
3. 6,400	5	90 days
4. 9,500	6	120 days
5. 3,500	7	3 months

Part B: Determine the maturity dates on the following notes:

Date of Issue	Life of Note
1. January 18	90 days
2. February 12	6 months
3. June 21	60 days
4. September 10	4 months
5. November 17	30 days

EXERCISE 13-2 On April 3, Arlo Dade gave a 60-day, 6.5 percent note, dated April 3, to Cane Company, a creditor, in the amount of $6,500.

a. What is the due date of the note?
b. How much interest is to be paid on the note at maturity?
c. Write the entries in general journal form to record both issuance of the note by the maker and payment of the note at maturity as they would appear on Dade's books.

PRACTICE EXERCISES
1,2,3a,3b

EXERCISE 13-3 As a result of a loan from Plateau State Bank, Trent Company signed a 90-day note, dated March 12, for $12,700 that the bank discounted at 7 percent. Journalize the entries for the maker in general journal form to record the following, assuming that the note is paid in the same fiscal period:

a. Issuance of the note on March 12.
b. Payment of the note at maturity.

PRACTICE EXERCISES 3e,3f

EXERCISE 13-4 In arranging for a 90-day loan from a bank, Mandy Company has the option of either (1) giving a $50,000, 6 percent interest-bearing note, dated November 3, that will be accepted at face value; or (2) giving a $50,000 note that will be discounted at 6 percent.

a. What is the amount of interest in each case?
b. What is the amount of cash Mandy Company actually receives in each case?

PRACTICE EXERCISES
1,3d,3e

EXERCISE 13-5 Make entries in a notes payable register (page 5) to document the following events. Show the computation of the interest and due dates.

Mar. 15 Gave a 45-day, 6 percent note, dated March 15, for $3,500, to Duffy Company to apply on account.

Apr. 10 Borrowed $6,800 from Delta State Bank, giving a 90-day, 6.5 percent note, dated April 10 (received full face value).

20 Bought merchandise from Maxwell, Inc., with a $3,560, 45-day, 5.5 percent note, dated April 20.

29 Paid Duffy Company the amount owed on the note of March 15.

PRACTICE EXERCISES 1,2,4

EXERCISE 13-6 Gates Supply Company completed the following transactions. Record them in general journal form.

a. Purchased merchandise for $16,500 on November 17, giving a 30-day, 6.5 percent note, dated November 17, to Liston Company in exchange for the merchandise.
b. On December 17, Gates is unable to pay the principal of the note due but pays the interest due.

PRACTICE EXERCISES
3b,3c,3g,5a

c. On December 17, Gates renews the $16,500 note for 60 days at 7 percent, dated December 17.

d. On December 31, Gates makes the adjusting entry for accrued interest.

4a,4b,6a **LO**

PRACTICE EXERCISES
3a,3b,5a

EXERCISE 13-7 On September 10, R. Casson issued a 120-day, 6 percent note, dated September 10, to Swan Construction, a creditor, for $9,600. Write the entries in general journal form to record the following transactions. Assume that closing entries were made at the appropriate time.

a. Issuance of the note on September 10.

b. Adjusting entry for accrued interest on December 31, the end of the fiscal year.

c. Reversing entry on January 1.

d. Payment of the note plus interest on January 8.

4e,4f,6b,6c **LO**

PRACTICE EXERCISES
3e,3f,5b,5c

EXERCISE 13-8 On December 5, M. Valenty borrowed $8,500 from Costner State Bank for 45 days, with a discount rate of 7 percent. Accordingly, M. Valenty signed a note for $8,500, dated December 5. The end of M. Valenty's fiscal year is December 31. Write entries in general journal form to record the following transactions. Assume the closing entries were made at the appropriate time.

a. Issuance of the note on December 5.

b. Adjusting entry on December 31.

c. Payment of the note at maturity on January 19.

d. Conversion of the Discount on Notes Payable to Interest Expense for the current year.

Problem Set A

For additional help, see the demonstration problem at the beginning of each chapter in your Working Papers.

2,4a,4b,4d **LO**

PROBLEM 13-1A The following were among this year's transactions of Bosko Company, which uses a periodic inventory system:

Jan. 8   Bought merchandise on account from Larkin Company, $4,460; terms 3/10, n/30.

      18   Paid Larkin Company for the invoice of January 8.

Feb. 14   Bought merchandise on account from Rizor Company, $4,500; terms net 30 days.

Mar. 16   Gave a 45-day, 6 percent note, dated March 16, for $4,500 to Rizor Company to apply on account.

Apr. 30   Paid Rizor Company the amount owed on the note of March 16.

May   24   Borrowed $12,000 from Kent National Bank, giving a 90-day, 5.75 percent note, dated May 24, for that amount (received full face value).

Aug. 22   Paid Kent National Bank the amount due on the note of May 24.

Check Figure
April 30 Interest Expense debit, $33.75

Required

Record these transactions in the general journal (page 47).

PROBLEM 13-2A The following were among this year's transactions of Zamora Company, which uses a periodic inventory system:

Jan. 31   Bought merchandise on account from Menkon Company, $3,560; terms net 30 days.

Mar. 2   Gave a 60-day, 5.5 percent note, dated March 2, for $3,560 to Menkon Company to apply on account.

May 1   Paid Menkon Company the amount owed on the note of March 2.

     5   Bought merchandise on account from Barstow Company, $9,500; terms 3/10, n/30.

June 4   Gave a 45-day, 5 percent note, dated June 4, for $9,500 to Barstow Company to apply on account.

July 19   Paid Barstow Company the interest due on the note of June 4 and renewed the obligation by issuing a new 60-day, 5.5 percent note, dated July 19, for $9,500 (two entries).

Sept. 17   Paid Barstow Company the amount owed on the note of July 19.

Oct. 18   Borrowed $18,000 from Riverside Bank for 60 days; discount rate is 6.5 percent. Accordingly, signed a discounted note for $18,000, dated October 18. (Use Interest Expense because the note will mature in the present fiscal period.)

Dec. 17   Paid Riverside Bank at maturity of note.

Required
Record these transactions in the general journal (pages 36 and 37).

Check Figure
May 1 Interest
Expense debit, $32.63

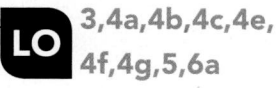

PROBLEM 13-3A The following were among the transactions of Kirsten's Craft Shop during this year. The firm, whose fiscal year ends on December 31, uses a periodic inventory system.

Jan. 25   Bought merchandise on account from Rossy Company, $3,565; terms 2/10, n/30.

Feb. 24   Gave a 30-day, 5 percent note, dated February 24, for $3,565 to Rossy Company to apply on account.

Mar. 26   Paid $2,000 as partial payment on principal as well as the full interest on the note given to Rossy Company. Issued a new 45-day, 6 percent note, dated March 26, for $1,565 (two entries).

May 10   Paid Rossy Company the amount owed on the note of March 26.

June 26   Borrowed $8,000 from Old Town Bank for 90 days; discount rate is 5.5 percent. Accordingly, signed a discounted note for $8,000 dated June 26.

Sept. 24   Paid Old Town Bank the amount owed on the note of June 26.

Oct. 28   Bought display racks for $1,235 from Carson's Fixtures. Issued a 90-day, 5.25 percent note, dated October 28.

Dec. 31   Recorded the adjusting entry for accrued interest on the note given to Carson's Fixtures.

Jan. 1   Recorded the reversing entry. (Assume closing entries were journalized and posted.)

Required
1. Record these transactions in the general journal (pages 12 and 13).
2. Immediately after each journal entry, record each note in the notes payable register (page 5). Fill in the date paid after journalizing the entry to pay the note, or fill in "renewed" if not paid.

Check Figure
Adjusting Entry, Interest
Expense debit, $11.53

4a,4b,4c,4d,4e
4g,5,6a,6b,6c **LO**

PROBLEM 13-4A The following were among the transactions of Carpenter Company during this year. The firm, whose fiscal year ends on December 31, uses a periodic inventory system.

June	12	Gave a 30-day, 5.5 percent note, dated June 12, for $60,000 to Paschal, Inc., for an addition to the building.
	15	Borrowed $28,000 from Menso Bank, signing a 3-month, 6 percent note, dated June 15, for that amount (received full face value).
July	12	Paid Paschal, Inc., the amount owed on the note of June 12.
	12	Gave a 120-day, 6.5 percent note, dated July 12, for $8,245 to Clarkson., Inc., for office equipment. The invoice was not previously recorded.
Sept.	15	Paid interest on the note issued to Menso Bank; renewed the loan by issuing a new 60-day, 6.5 percent note, dated September 15.
Nov.	9	Paid Clarkson, Inc., the amount owed on the note of July 12.
	14	Gave two notes to NadCo in settlement of its November 14 invoice for merchandise, as follows: $11,500 note for 30 days at 6 percent, dated November 14; $10,300 note for 60 days at 6 percent, dated November 14. The invoice was not previously recorded.
	14	Paid the note given to Menso Bank.
Dec.	14	Paid the amount owed on the 30-day note given to NadCo.
	15	Issued a 90-day, 6.5 percent note, dated December 15, to Hazel Company in settlement of November 15 invoice for merchandise, $16,538. The invoice was previously recorded.
	18	Borrowed $35,000 from Tragar Bank for 30 days; discount rate is 7.25 percent. Accordingly, signed a discounted note for $35,000, dated December 18. (Debit Discount on Notes Payable, since the note extends into the next fiscal period.)

Check Figure
Adjusting Entry, Interest
Payable credit, $128.46

Required
1. Record these transactions in a general journal (pages 18–21).
2. Immediately after each journal entry, record each note in the notes payable register (page 7). Fill in the date paid after journalizing the entry to pay the note, or fill in "renewed" if not paid.
3. On December 31, record the adjusting entries to adjust for accrued interest expense for the NadCo and Hazel notes, as well as the adjustment of Discount on Notes Payable for the Tragar Bank note.
4. On January 1, record the reversing entry. (Assume that closing entries have been made.)
5. On January 13, record the payment of the note to NadCo.
6. On January 17, record the payment of the note to Tragar Bank.
7. On January 17, record the entry to expense the discount on the Tragar note.
8. On March 15, record the payment of the note to Hazel Company.

Problem Set B

For additional help, see the demonstration problem at the beginning of each chapter in your Working Papers.

2,4a,4b,4d **LO**

PROBLEM 13-1B The following were among this year's transactions of Moore Appliances, which uses a periodic inventory system:

Jan.	15	Bought merchandise on account from Joyce Wholesalers, $4,560; terms 3/10, n/30.
	21	Paid Joyce Wholesalers for the invoice of January 15.
Feb.	25	Bought merchandise on account from Miguel Company, $3,745; terms net 30 days.
Mar.	27	Gave a 60-day, 6 percent note, dated March 27, for $3,745 to Miguel Company to apply on account.
May	26	Paid Miguel Company the amount owed on the note of March 27.
June	18	Borrowed $9,000 from Trident Bank, giving a 90-day, 5.5 percent note, dated June 18, for that amount (received full face value).
Sept.	16	Paid Trident Bank the amount due on the note of June 18.

Required

Record these transactions in a general journal (page 36).

Check Figure
May 26 Interest Expense debit, $37.45

 LO 4a,4b,4e,4g

 GL

PROBLEM 13-2B The following were among this year's transactions of U.S. Yarn Shop, which uses a periodic inventory system:

Jan.	25	Bought merchandise on account from Greg Morkin, $5,000; terms net 30 days.
Feb.	24	Gave a 45-day, 6 percent note, dated February 24, for $5,000 to Greg Morkin to apply on account.
Apr.	10	Paid Greg Morkin the amount owed on the note of February 24.
May	24	Bought merchandise on account from Teskey Company, $7,300; terms net 30 days.
June	23	Gave a 30-day, 5.5 percent note, dated June 23, for $7,300 to Teskey Company to apply on account.
July	23	Paid Teskey Company the interest due on the note of June 23 and renewed the obligation by issuing a new 60-day, 6 percent note, dated July 23, for $7,300 (two entries).
Sept.	21	Paid Teskey Company the amount owed on the note of July 23.
	25	Borrowed $14,000 from Vesco Bank for 90 days; discount rate is 6.5 percent. Accordingly, signed a discounted note for $14,000, dated September 25. (Use Interest Expense because the note will mature in the present fiscal period.)
Dec.	24	Paid Vesco Bank at maturity of note.

Required

Record these transactions in a general journal (pages 27 and 28).

Check Figure
April 10 Interest Expense debit, $37.50

 **LO** 3,4a,4b,4c,4e, 4f,4g,5,6a

PROBLEM 13-3B The following were among the transactions of Cliff Shop during this year. The firm, whose fiscal year ends on December 31, uses a periodic inventory system.

Jan.	11	Bought merchandise on account from Hardin Company, $4,350; terms net 30 days.
Feb.	10	Gave a 30-day, 6 percent note, dated February 10, for $4,350 to Hardin Company to apply on account.

Mar. 12   Paid $2,350 as partial payment on principal as well as the full interest on the note given to Hardin Company. Issued a new 60-day, 6.5 percent note, dated March 12, for $2,000 (two entries).

May 10   Borrowed $12,000 from Washburn Bank for 120 days; discount rate is 6 percent. Accordingly, signed a discounted note for $12,000, dated May 10.

     11   Paid Hardin Company the amount owed on the note of March 12.

Sept. 7   Paid Washburn Bank the amount owed on the note of May 10.

Nov. 17   Bought a laptop computer for $1,150 from Byte Equipment. Issued a 90-day, 6 percent note, dated November 17.

Dec. 31   Recorded the adjusting entry for accrued interest on the note given to Byte Equipment.

Jan. 1   Recorded the reversing entry. (Assume the closing entries were journalized and posted.)

Check Figure
Adjusting entry, Interest
Expense debit, $8.43

Required

1. Record these transactions in the general journal (pages 10 and 11).
2. Immediately after each journal entry, record each note in the notes payable register (page 5).
3. Fill in the date paid after journalizing the entry to pay the note, or fill in "renewed" if not paid.

4a,4b,4c,4d,4e
4g,5,6a,6b,6c

PROBLEM 13-4B The following were among the transactions of Kenton Company during this year. The firm, whose fiscal year ends on December 31, uses a periodic inventory system.

May 24   Gave a 60-day, 5.5 percent note, dated May 24, for $60,000 to Dart Builders for additional office space.

June 20   Borrowed $15,500 from Ford Bank, signing a 3-month, 6 percent note, dated June 20, for that amount (received full face value).

July 15   Gave a 120-day, 6 percent note, dated July 15, for $10,400 to Charley's Carpentry for shelving units. The invoice was not previously recorded.

     23   Paid Dart Builders the amount owed on the note of May 24.

Sept. 20   Paid interest on the note issued to Ford Bank; renewed the loan by issuing a new 60-day, 6.5 percent note, dated September 20.

Oct. 27   Gave two notes to Cory Company in settlement of its October 27 invoice for merchandise, as follows: $12,000 note for 45 days at 6 percent, dated October 27; $12,000 note for 60 days at 6.25 percent, dated October 27. The invoice was not previously recorded.

Nov. 12   Paid Charley's Carpentry the amount owed on the note of July 15.

      19   Paid the note given to Ford Bank.

Dec. 11   Paid the amount owed on the 45-day note given to Cory Company.

      15   Issued a 60-day, 6.5 percent note, dated December 15, to McNary Company in settlement of November 15 invoice for merchandise, $11,360. The invoice was previously recorded.

      18   Borrowed $25,500 from Hartman Bank for 60 days; discount rate is 6.5 percent. Accordingly, signed a discounted note for $25,500, dated December 18. (Debit Discount on Notes Payable, since the note extends into next fiscal period.)

      26   Paid the amount owed on the 60-day note given to Cory Company.

Required

1. Record these transactions in a general journal (pages 26–29).
2. Immediately after each journal entry, record each note in the notes payable register (page 7). Fill in the date paid after journalizing the entry to pay the note, or fill in "renewed" if not paid.
3. On December 31, record the adjusting entries to adjust for accrued interest expense for the McNary Company note, as well as the adjustment of Discount on Notes Payable for the Hartman Bank note.
4. On January 1, record the reversing entry. (Assume that closing entries have been made.)
5. On February 13, record the payment of the note to McNary Company.
6. On February 16, record the payment of the note to Hartman Bank.
7. On February 16, record the entry to expense the discount on the Hartman Bank note.

Check Figure
December 18 Discount on Notes Payable debit, $276.25

ACTIVITIES

CONSIDER AND COMMUNICATE

Your friend needs to buy a $1,000 component to replace some essential sound equipment. He has neither that much cash nor credit available. He has heard of promissory notes and asks for your help. Explain the concept of a promissory note, what it will mean when your friend signs it, and why the total of the payments on the note at maturity will be greater than the original $1,000.

WHAT'S WRONG WITH THIS PICTURE?

The owner of a business told her accountant that she "paid" her personal revolving charge account with a 30-day, 6.5 percent note for $10,000, signed by her business. At the end of the 30 days, the owner told her accountant that she paid off the interest due and signed another 30-day, 9 percent note. What problems, if any, do you see with this scenario?

CRITICAL THINKING

Your supervisor has asked you to audit some journal entries recorded by her client's bookkeeper. Review the following transactions. If there is an error, rejournalize the entry. If the bookkeeper's entry is correct, write OK next to the date on your paper. The fiscal period begins January 1 and ends on December 31.

Apr. 4   Borrowed $3,500 from Stanford Bank for 90 days, discount rate 6 percent. Signed a discounted note for $3,500 dated April 4.

June 30   Bought a new air conditioning system (Building), giving a 90-day, 6.5 percent note, dated June 30, to Young Company, $55,300.

July 3   Paid the $3,500 note to Stanford Bank dated April 4.

Sept. 28   Paid the entire interest due to Young Company as well as $25,300 toward the principal. Issued a new $30,000, 120-day, 6.5 percent note, dated September 28.

Nov. 20   Borrowed $5,000 from Litchfield Bank for 45 days, discount rate 5.5 percent. Signed a discounted note for $5,000 dated November 20.

Dec. 31   Journalized the adjusting entries for the outstanding notes owed to Young Company and Litchfield Bank.

GENERAL JOURNAL   **PAGE** _____

Date		Description	Post. Ref.	Debit						Credit					
20—															
Apr.	4	Cash		3	5	0	0	00							
		Interest Expense											5	2	50
		Notes Payable								3	4	4	7	50	
June	30	Building		55	3	0	0	00							
		Notes Payable								55	3	0	0	00	
July	3	Notes Payable		3	5	0	0	00							
		Discount on Notes Payable				5	2	50							
		Cash								3	5	5	2	50	
Sept.	28	Cash		25	3	0	0	00							
		Notes Payable								25	3	0	0	00	
	28	Notes Payable		30	0	0	0	00							
		Notes Payable								30	0	0	0	00	
Nov.	20	Cash		4	9	6	5	62							
		Discount on Notes Payable				3	4	38							
		Notes Payable								5	0	0	0	00	
		Adjusting Entries													
Dec.	31	Interest Expense			5	7	3	63							
		Interest Payable									5	7	3	63	
	31	Discount on Notes Payable				3	1	32							
		Interest Payable										3	1	32	

Notes Receivable

14

WHY IT MATTERS

APPLE INC., Cupertino, California

Apple Inc. is a multinational corporation that designs and manufactures consumer electronics and computer software products. Apple was established on April 1, 1976, by Steve Jobs and Steve Wozniak, and incorporated on January 3, 1977.

Since its inception, Apple has transformed itself into one of the world's most admired companies (as ranked by *Fortune* magazine) with annual sales of over $10 billion and net income of over $1 billion. Occasionally Apple might accept a promissory note, or notes receivable, from a customer for a sale of merchandise. Typically the customer would have 60 to 120 days to make payment to Apple on the amount owed plus interest. In this chapter, we will look at a number of transactions involving notes receivable.

LEARNING OBJECTIVES

After you have completed this chapter, you will be able to do the following:

1 Write the journal entries to record (a) receipt of a note from a charge customer; (b) receipt of payment of an interest-bearing note at maturity; (c) receipt of a note as a result of granting a personal loan; (d) receipt of a note in exchange for merchandise or other property; (e) renewal of a note at maturity and payment of interest; (f) renewal of a note with payment of interest and partial payment of principal;

(g) a dishonored note receivable; (h) collection of a note receivable formerly dishonored; (i) discounting an interest-bearing note receivable.

2 Complete a notes receivable register.

3 Write the journal entry to record the adjustment for accrued interest on notes receivable.

ACCOUNTING LANGUAGE

Accrued interest income on notes receivable (p. 579)

Contingent liability (p. 575)

Discount period (p. 574)

Discounting notes receivable (p. 573)

Dishonored note receivable (p. 572)

Maturity value (p. 573)

Notes receivable register (p. 578)

Business firms receive promissory notes either regularly or occasionally for a variety of reasons. Sometimes a business firm accepts a promissory note from a customer at the time of sale. Companies frequently accept promissory notes from charge account customers who request an extension of time to settle past-due accounts. In effect, they substitute notes receivable for accounts receivable. The net result is that the charge customer receives an extension of time for the payment of a debt. Notes receivable may be written for short periods of time, even days or weeks. They can also be written for very long periods of time, as when a bank receives a 30-year mortgage note. The life of a note is whatever is agreed upon by all parties.

Obviously, getting a note receivable is not as good as having cash in hand. However, it offers several advantages to the company: (1) the note represents proof of the original transaction, (2) the note may bear interest, and (3) the note may be pledged as security for a loan from a bank. Banks, in fact, loan a higher proportion of the face value on notes (Notes Receivable) than of open accounts (Accounts Receivable).

Notes receivable also come into being when a company grants loans to employees or preferred customers or suppliers. In some industries, the credit period is often longer than 30 days; here, the transactions are frequently evidenced by notes rather than by open accounts. Examples are sales of farm machinery, construction equipment, and trucks.

Now let's see how to journalize transactions involving notes receivable for Whitewater Raft Supply. The accounts involved are Notes Receivable (classified as a current asset on the balance sheet in our examples, although it could be classified as a long-term asset if the repayment period is longer than a year) and Interest Income (classified as other income on the income statement).

FYI

Banks may grant loans for 100 percent of the face value of notes but a lesser percentage of the face value of open accounts.

Remember

A note receivable on the books of the payee company is a note payable on the books of the company signing the note.

TRANSACTIONS FOR NOTES RECEIVABLE

In the examples used throughout this chapter, we will assume that all notes received are recorded in a single current asset account, Notes Receivable, and are payable at New National Bank.

Note from a Charge Customer to Extend Time on Account

On March 7, Whitewater Raft Supply sold $930 worth of merchandise to Green River Rafts, with the customary terms of 2/10, n/30, and made the original entry in its sales journal. On April 6, Green River Rafts sent Whitewater Raft Supply a note for $930, payable within 30 days, at 6 percent interest. The note, dated April 6, was in settlement of the transaction of March 7. Whitewater Raft Supply recorded this new development in its general journal as follows:

LEARNING OBJECTIVE **1a**

Write the journal entry to record receipt of a note from a charge customer.

	GENERAL JOURNAL			PAGE _____	
Date	Description	Post. Ref.	Debit	Credit	
20—					
Apr. 6	Notes Receivable		9 3 0 00		
	Accounts Receivable, Green				
	River Rafts			9 3 0 00	
	Received a 30-day, 6 percent				
	note, dated April 6, in				
	settlement of open account.				

A note receivable and an account receivable differ in the strength of legal claim they represent and in the way interest is earned—a note is more formal.

Remember

T accounts for the transactions look like this:

Accounts Receivable		Sales		Notes Receivable	
+	−	−	+	+	−
Mar. 7 930	Apr. 6 930		Mar. 7 930	Apr. 6 930	

Receipt of Payment of an Interest-Bearing Note at Maturity

On May 6, Green River Rafts paid Whitewater Raft Supply in full: principal plus interest. Whitewater Raft Supply recorded the transaction in the general journal as follows:

LEARNING OBJECTIVE **1b**

Write the journal entry to record receipt of payment of an interest-bearing note at maturity.

Date	Description	Post. Ref.	Debit	Credit	
20—					
May 6	Cash		9 3 4 65		
	Notes Receivable			9 3 0 00	
	Interest Income			4 65	
	Received full payment of				
	Green River Rafts' note.				
	($930 × 0.06 × 30/360)				

Calculations are included to show how the amounts were determined. They would not normally appear in journal entries.

Remember

Let's look at the T accounts for this entry:

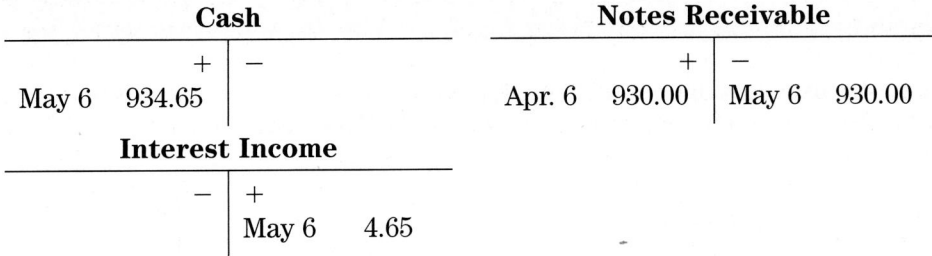

Cash			Notes Receivable		
+	−			+	−
May 6 934.65			Apr. 6 930.00		May 6 930.00

Interest Income	
−	+
	May 6 4.65

If using special journals, this transaction would be recorded directly in the cash receipts journal rather than in the general journal. But, for the sake of simplicity and clarity, we will use the general journal format to illustrate entries throughout this chapter.

Note Received as a Result of Granting a Personal Loan

LEARNING OBJECTIVE 1c
Write the journal entry to record receipt of a note as a result of granting a personal loan.

Sometimes employees, preferred customers, or suppliers may want to borrow cash from the business. When that is the case, the business often accepts a note receivable. Let's say that Grace Martin, an employee of Whitewater Raft Supply, borrows $1,000 from her employer for three months at 5 percent. Her note is dated April 8. In general journal form, the entry is as follows:

Date	Description	Post. Ref.	Debit	Credit
20—				
Apr. 8	Notes Receivable		1 0 0 0 00	
	Cash			1 0 0 0 00
	Granted a loan to Grace Martin,			
	3 months, 5 percent, dated April 8.			

When the loan reaches maturity, Martin pays the principal plus interest.

Date	Description	Post. Ref.	Debit	Credit
20—				
July 8	Cash		1 0 1 2 50	
	Notes Receivable			1 0 0 0 00
	Interest Income			1 2 50
	Received full payment of Grace			
	Martin's note, dated April 8.			
	($1,000 × 0.05 × 3/12)			

Note Received in Exchange for Merchandise or Other Property

LEARNING OBJECTIVE 1d
Write the journal entry to record receipt of a note in exchange for merchandise or other property.

Business firms that sell high-priced durable goods for which the credit period is longer than the normal 30 days may regularly accept notes from their customers.

On April 9, Whitewater Raft Supply sold merchandise to Floyd Mercantile for $1,200. Floyd Mercantile gave Whitewater Raft Supply a promissory note, promising to pay the full amount within 60 days; the note specified 5.5 percent interest. When this type of transaction occurs occasionally, the transaction is recorded in the general journal as follows:

Date		Description	Post. Ref.	Debit	Credit
20—					
Apr.	9	Notes Receivable		1 2 0 0 00	
		Sales			1 2 0 0 00
		Floyd Mercantile, 60-day,			
		5.5 percent note, dated			
		April 9.			

Renewal of Note at Maturity and Payment of Interest

If the maker of a note is unable to pay the entire principal at maturity, the company may be allowed to renew all or part of the note.

Now suppose that Floyd Mercantile is not able to pay the note at maturity and offers to pay the interest on the current note and to issue a new note, for 30 days at 6 percent. Whitewater Raft Supply makes the entries in the general journal as follows. Note that two entries are required. One entry records the interest on the old note. The second entry cancels the old note and records the new note.

LEARNING OBJECTIVE 1e

Write the journal entries to record renewal of a note at maturity and payment of interest.

Date		Description	Post. Ref.	Debit	Credit
20—					
June	8	Cash		1 1 00	
		Interest Income			1 1 00
		Received payment of			
		interest on Floyd Mercantile note,			
		dated April 9.			
		($1,200 × 0.055 × 60/360)			
	8	Notes Receivable		1 2 0 0 00	
		Notes Receivable			1 2 0 0 00
		Floyd Mercantile, renewal			
		of note, dated April 9; new			
		note is dated June 8, 30			
		days, 6 percent.			

For a renewal of a note receivable, credit the old note to take it off the books, and debit the new note to put it on the books.

Remember

When a note is renewed, it is customary for the debtor or maker to pay the interest on the old note and then issue a new note.

Renewal of Note with Payment of Interest and Partial Payment of Principal

Sometimes the maker of a note cancels the original note by paying the interest, plus part of the principal, and issuing a new note. Suppose that, as a substitute for the $1,200 note described earlier, Floyd Mercantile gives Whitewater Raft Supply $500

LEARNING OBJECTIVE 1f

Write the journal entries to record renewal of a note with payment of interest and partial payment of principal.

toward the principal and a new note for $700 in addition to the interest on the old note.

Whitewater Raft Supply records the transactions in the general journal as follows:

Date		Description	Post. Ref.	Debit				Credit			
20—											
June	8	Cash		5	1	1	00				
		Notes Receivable						5	0	0	00
		Interest Income							1	1	00
		Floyd Mercantile note, dated									
		April 9, partial payment of the									
		principal and payment of the interest.									
	8	Notes Receivable		7	0	0	00				
		Notes Receivable						7	0	0	00
		Floyd Mercantile, renewal of note,									
		dated April 9; new note is dated									
		June 8, 30 days, 6 percent.									

DISHONORED NOTES RECEIVABLE

LEARNING OBJECTIVE **1g**
Write the journal entry to record a dishonored note receivable.

When the maker of a note fails to pay the principal amount or to renew the note at maturity, the note is said to be a dishonored note receivable. The maker of the note is still obligated to pay the principal plus interest, and the creditor should take legal steps to collect the debt. However, the balance of the Notes Receivable account shows only the principal of notes that have not yet matured. A note that is past due, or dishonored, should be removed from the Notes Receivable account and added to the Accounts Receivable account; the amount listed should be the principal plus interest. In other words, once a note receivable comes due and is not collected, it is "in default." But the maker still owes the payee, so the amount owed (principal plus interest) is put back into Accounts Receivable.

For example, Whitewater Raft Supply holds a 60-day, 5 percent note for $950, dated April 20, from Hartman Guides, which fails to pay by the due date. Thus the note is dishonored at maturity. Whitewater Raft Supply then makes the following entry in its general journal to remove the dishonored note from the Notes Receivable account.

Date		Description	Post. Ref.	Debit				Credit			
20—											
June	19	Accounts Receivable, Hartman									
		Guides		9	5	7	92				
		Notes Receivable						9	5	0	00
		Interest Income								7	92
		Hartman Guides dishonored									
		its 60-day, 5 percent note for									
		$950, dated April 20.									
		($950 × 0.05 × 60/360)									

Hartman Guides owes both the principal and the interest, and the account should reflect the full amount owed. Note particularly that Whitewater Raft Supply credits the Interest Income account, even though Hartman Guides did not pay the interest. This is consistent with the accrual basis of accounting: Revenue is recorded when it is *earned*, rather than when it is received. If Hartman Guides should ever ask Whitewater Raft Supply to act as a credit reference, or if Hartman Guides ever asks for credit in the future, subsidiary records will show all past dealings, including the dishonored note.

Collection of a Note Formerly Dishonored

Now suppose that, 30 days after its note has been dishonored, Hartman Guides pays the balance of its account, plus an additional 30 days' interest at 5 percent on the amount owed. The entry in Whitewater Raft Supply's general journal is as follows:

Date		Description	Post. Ref.	Debit	Credit
20—					
July	19	Cash		9 6 1 91	
		Accounts Receivable, Hartman Guides			9 5 7 92
		Interest Income			3 99
		Hartman Guides paid the dishonored note, plus interest for 30 days at 5 percent. ($957.92 × 0.05 × 30/360)			

Whitewater Raft Supply gets its money in the long run anyway, and it can now consider the matter closed.

DISCOUNTING NOTES RECEIVABLE

Instead of keeping notes receivable until they come due, a firm can raise cash by selling its notes receivable to a bank or finance company. This type of financing is called **discounting notes receivable** because the bank deducts the interest or discount from the maturity value of the note to determine the proceeds (that is, the amount of money received by the payee). The **maturity value** is the principal (face value) of the note plus interest from the date of the note until the due date.

In the process of discounting a note receivable, the payee endorses the note (as it would a check) and delivers it to the financial institution. The financial institution gives out cash now in exchange for the right to collect the principal and interest when the note comes due. The discount rate is the annual rate (percentage of maturity value) charged by the financial institution for buying the note. The financial institution generally discounts at a higher interest rate than stated in the note because the financial institution assumes increased risk of the maker's possible default.

A Discounted Note: Example 1

Whitewater Raft Supply granted an extension on an open account by accepting a 60-day, 5 percent note for $1,800, dated April 20, from Bowers River Co. To raise cash to buy additional merchandise, Whitewater Raft Supply sold the note to New National Bank on May 5. The bank charged a discount rate of 6 percent. In handling discounted notes receivable, you should follow a definite step-by-step procedure.

Remember

Whitewater Raft Supply records Interest Income, which is consistent with the accrual basis of accounting (record income when earned and expenses when incurred).

LEARNING OBJECTIVE 1h

Write the journal entry to record collection of a note receivable formerly dishonored.

LEARNING OBJECTIVE 1i

Write the journal entry to record discounting an interest-bearing note receivable.

STEP 1. Diagram the situation. A diagram of the situation looks like this:

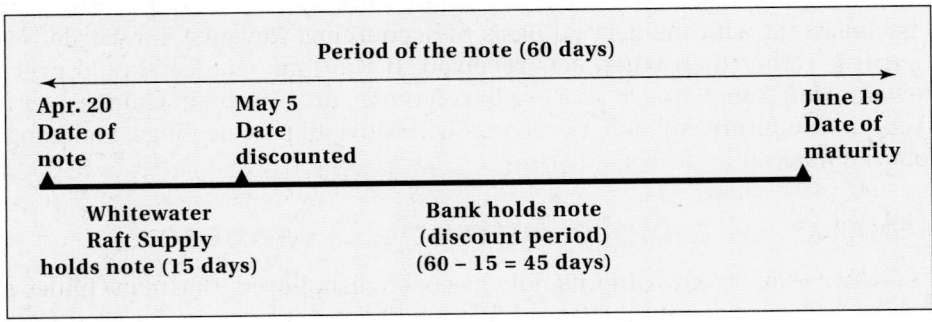

STEP 2. Determine the discount period. The **discount period** of the note consists of the interval between the date the note is given to the bank and the maturity date of the note. (In other words, the discount period is the time the note has left to run.)

April 30 − 20	=	10 days left in April
May	=	5 days in May
Days held by endorser	=	15 days

Discount period (bank holds note),
(Total days − days held by endorser)
60 days − 15 days = 45 days

STEP 3. Record the formula. Next we determine the value of the note at maturity and deduct the amount of the bank's discount from it, using the following formula:

Principal ($1,800)
+ Interest to maturity date (5%, 60 days)

Value at maturity
− Discount (6%, 45 days)

Proceeds

STEP 4. Complete the formula. After we set up the problem, we can complete the calculation:

Principal	$1,800.00
+ Interest (5%, 60 days)	15.00
Value at maturity	$1,815.00
− Discount (6%, 45 days)	13.61
Proceeds	$1,801.39

$$\text{Interest} = \text{Principal} \times \text{Rate} \times \text{Time}$$

$$\text{Interest} = \$1,800 \times 0.05 \times \frac{60}{360} = \underline{\$15.00}$$

$$\text{Discount} = \$1,815 \times 0.06 \times \frac{45}{360} = \underline{\$13.61}$$

Note that, in our calculations, we figure the discount on the value of the note at maturity ($1,815). The proceeds are the amount that Whitewater Raft Supply receives from the bank; this amount is therefore debited to Cash. *If the amount of the proceeds is greater than the amount of the principal, the difference represents Interest Income,* because Whitewater Raft Supply made money on the deal. *If the amount of the proceeds is less than the principal, on the other hand, the deficiency represents Interest Expense,* because Whitewater Raft Supply lost money in the deal.

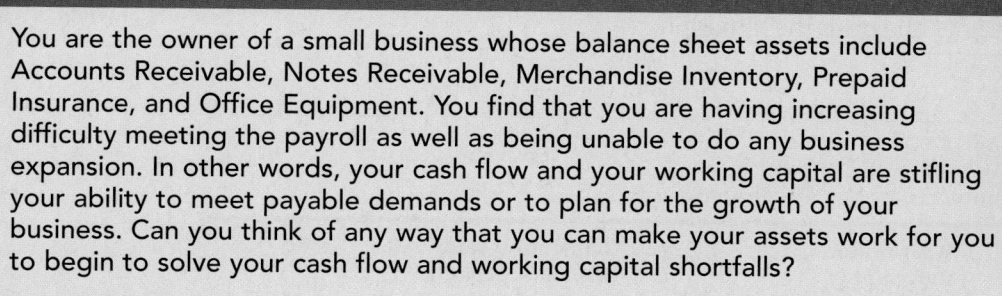

You Make the Call

You are the owner of a small business whose balance sheet assets include Accounts Receivable, Notes Receivable, Merchandise Inventory, Prepaid Insurance, and Office Equipment. You find that you are having increasing difficulty meeting the payroll as well as being unable to do any business expansion. In other words, your cash flow and your working capital are stifling your ability to meet payable demands or to plan for the growth of your business. Can you think of any way that you can make your assets work for you to begin to solve your cash flow and working capital shortfalls?

SOLUTION

Included in your current assets are notes receivable—promises to pay you money but in future payments at a particular interest rate. At this point, you may choose not to wait for those payments to be received. In fact, if they are current notes receivable, you may be able to sell all or part of them for a percentage of their future value to a bank or finance company and receive the cash immediately.

STEP 5. Record the entry. Look at the entry in Whitewater Raft Supply's general journal:

Date		Description	Post. Ref.	Debit	Credit
20—					
May	5	Cash		1 8 0 1 39	
		Notes Receivable			1 8 0 0 00
		Interest Income			1 39
		Discounted at the bank Bowers River Co.'s note, dated April 20. The bank discount rate is 6 percent.			

Contingent Liability

At the time Whitewater Raft Supply discounted Bowers River Co.'s note at the bank, Whitewater Raft Supply had to endorse the note. By this endorsement, Whitewater Raft Supply agreed to pay the note when it became due if the maker did not pay it. Therefore the endorser has a **contingent liability** for payment of the note. If the maker dishonors the note, the endorser is liable. In other words, the liability of the endorser is contingent upon the possible dishonoring of the note by the maker. It follows that, if the credit rating of the endorser of the note is good, a bank is usually willing to accept and discount a note. The endorser, by virtue of his or her endorsement, or guarantee, agrees to pay the note at maturity *if* it is not paid by the maker. The fact that the note receivable is pledged as security, along with the amount of the contingent liability, should be shown as a note to the endorser's balance sheet.

Payment of a Discounted Note by the Maker

The bank collects the principal plus the interest on a discounted note directly from the maker. When the maker pays the bank, the endorser no longer has any contingent liability; the note to the endorser's balance sheet can be eliminated when the note is paid. A journal entry is not required.

A Discounted Note: Example 2

On April 24, Whitewater Raft Supply received a 90-day, 5.5 percent, $2,500 note, dated April 24, from L. R. Ray. On May 4, Whitewater Raft Supply discounted the note at New National Bank. The discount rate charged by the bank is 6.5 percent.

STEP 1. Diagram the situation.

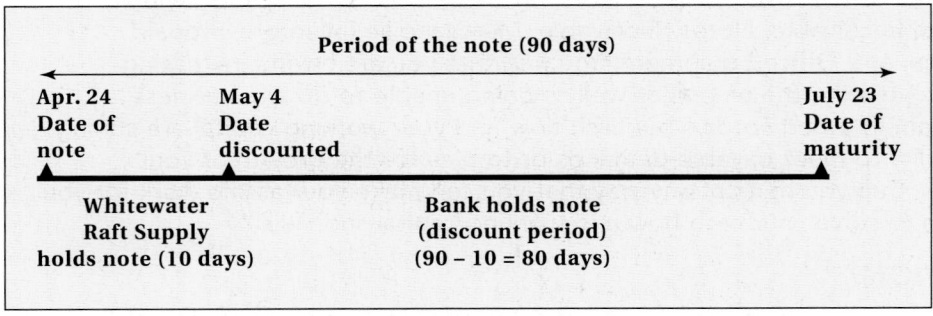

```
                    Period of the note (90 days)
◄──────────────────────────────────────────────────────────►
Apr. 24          May 4                                July 23
Date of          Date                                 Date of
note             discounted                            maturity
▲                ▲                                        ▲
└────────────────┴────────────────────────────────────────┘
   Whitewater                Bank holds note
   Raft Supply               (discount period)
holds note (10 days)         (90 − 10 = 80 days)
```

STEP 2. Determine the discount period.

April 30 − 24	=	6 days left in April
May	=	4 days in May
Days held by endorser	=	10 days

Discount period (bank holds note),
(Total days − days held by endorser)
90 days − 10 days = 80 days

STEP 3. Record the formula.

   Principal ($2,500)
+ Interest (5.5%, 90 days)

   Value at maturity
− Discount (6.5%, 80 days)

   Proceeds

STEP 4. Complete the formula.

Principal	$2,500.00	Interest = Principal × Rate × Time
+ Interest (5.5%, 90 days)	34.38	Interest = $2,500 × 0.055 × $\frac{90}{360}$ = 34.38
Value at maturity	$2,534.38	
− Discount (6.5%, 80 days)	36.61	Discount = $2,534.38 × 0.065 × $\frac{80}{360}$ = 36.61
Proceeds	$2,497.77	

STEP 5. Record the entry, recognizing that the amount of the proceeds is a debit to Cash. If the amount of the proceeds is less than the principal, debit Interest Expense for the difference.

Date	Description	Post. Ref.	Debit	Credit
20—				
May 4	Cash		2 4 9 7 77	
	Interest Expense		2 23	
	Notes Receivable			2 5 0 0 00
	Discounted at the bank L. R. Ray's			
	note, dated April 24. The bank			
	discount rate is 6.5 percent.			

Companies with seasonal peaks and lows may need to sign a promissory note for a certain period of time to increase their inventory prior to the time it will actually be sold.

© FRANCES ROBERTS/ALAMY

A Discounted Note: Example 3

On May 9, Macy and Son gave Whitewater Raft Supply a 60-day, 6 percent note for $4,500, dated May 9. On June 2, Whitewater Raft Supply discounted the note at New National Bank. The bank charges a discount rate of 6.5 percent.

STEP 1. Diagram the situation.

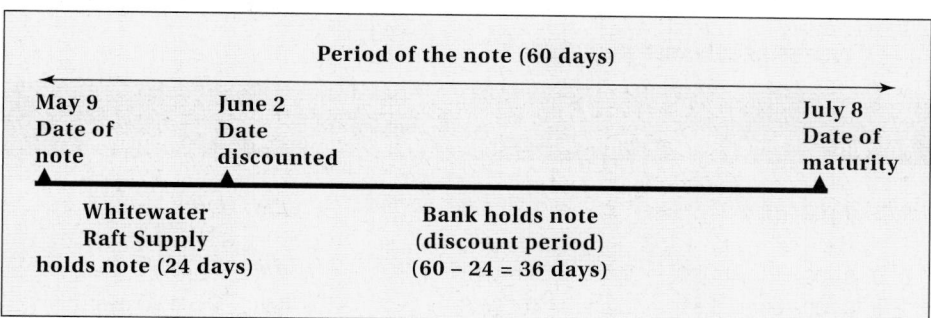

STEP 2. Determine the discount period.

May (31 – 9)	=	22 days left in May
June	=	2 days in June
Days held by endorser	=	24 days

Discount period (bank holds note),
(Total days – days held by endorser)
60 days – 24 days = 36 days

STEP 3. Record the formula.

	Principal ($4,500)
+	Interest (6%, 60 days)
	Value at maturity
–	Discount (6.5%, 36 days)
	Proceeds

Remember

If the amount of the proceeds is greater than the principal (not maturity value), interest income is earned. Conversely, if the proceeds are less than the principal, interest expense is incurred.

STEP 4. Complete the formula.

Principal	$4,500.00	Interest = Principal × Rate × Time
+ Interest (6%, 60 days)	45.00	Interest $= \$4{,}500 \times 0.06 \times \dfrac{60}{360} = \underline{\$45.00}$
Value at maturity	$4,545.00	
− Discount (6.5%, 36 days)	29.54	Discount $= \$4{,}545 \times 0.065 \times \dfrac{36}{360} = \$29.54$
Proceeds	$4,515.46	

STEP 5. Record the entry, as shown. If the amount of the proceeds is greater than the principal, credit Interest Income for the difference.

Date	Description	Post. Ref.	Debit	Credit
20—				
June 2	Cash		4 5 1 5 46	
	Notes Receivable			4 5 0 0 00
	Interest Income			1 5 46
	Discounted at bank the note			
	received from Macy and Son			
	dated May 9; discount rate,			
	6.5 percent.			

Notes Receivable Register

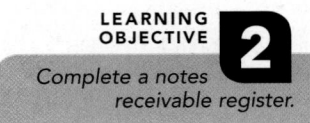

LEARNING OBJECTIVE **2**

Complete a notes receivable register.

Companies that have a significant number of notes receivable may find it worthwhile to set up a separate list to keep track of them. This list is called a **notes receivable register** (see Figure 1). Information is taken from the face of each note. Columns are included to record the specifics of each note. At the end of the fiscal period, the accountant makes a schedule of notes receivable by listing the unpaid notes that appear in the notes receivable register. Also, the total of the schedule is compared with the balance of the Notes Receivable account. The two should match.

FIGURE 1　Notes receivable ledger

NOTES RECEIVABLE REGISTER

Date	Maker	Where payable	Amount	Time	Rate	Interest	Due Date	Discounted Bank	Discounted Date	Date Paid	Remarks
20—											
Apr. 6	Green River Rafts	New Nat.	9 3 0 00	30 d	6%	4 65	5/6			5/6	Open account.
8	Grace Martin	New Nat.	1 0 0 0 00	3 m	5%	1 2 50	7/8			7/8	Employee loan.
9	Floyd Mercantile	New Nat.	1 2 0 0 00	60 d	5.5%	1 1 00	6/8			Ren.	Open account.
20	Hartman Guides	New Nat.	9 5 0 00	60 d	5%	7 92	6/19			7/19	Dishonored 6/19; note paid 7/19.
20	Bowers River Co.	New Nat.	1 8 0 0 00	60 d	5%	1 5 00	6/19	New Nat.	5/5	—	Discount. @ 6%, $1,801.39 proceeds.
24	L. R. Ray	New Nat.	2 5 0 0 00	90 d	5.5%	3 4 38	7/23	New Nat.	5/4	—	Discount. @ 6.5%, $2,497.77 proceeds.
May 9	Macy and Son	New Nat.	4 5 0 0 00	60 d	6%	4 5 00	7/8	New Nat.	6/2		Discount. @ 6.5%, $4,515.46 proceeds.
June 8	Floyd Mercantile	New Nat.	1 2 0 0 00	30 d	6%	6 00	7/8				Renewed 4/9 note.
			OR IF PARTIAL PAYMENT								
June 8	Floyd Mercantile	New Nat.	7 0 0 00	30 d	6%	3 50	7/8				Renewed 4/9 note with part. payment of $500 plus interest.

END-OF-FISCAL-PERIOD ADJUSTMENT: ACCRUED INTEREST ON NOTES RECEIVABLE

Accrued interest income on notes receivable is the interest that is due (not yet received) on notes receivable that are outstanding at the end of the fiscal period. Whenever a firm receives *or* issues an interest-bearing note, the interest accrues daily. As a result, any interest-bearing note that overlaps fiscal periods requires an adjusting entry in order for the financial statements to present a true picture of the firm's net income and financial condition.

> **3** **LEARNING OBJECTIVE**
> *Write the journal entry to record the adjustment for accrued interest on notes receivable.*

For example, let's say that a firm has two notes receivable on December 31, the end of the fiscal period:

$8,000, 90 days, 6%, dated November 28
$6,500, 60 days, 5.5%, dated December 20

We can diagram the situation as follows:

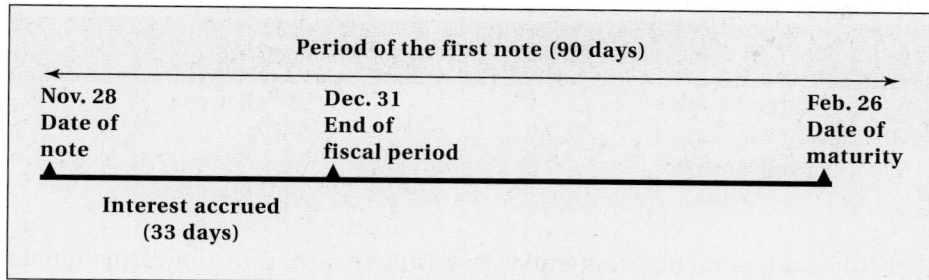

Nov. (30 − 28)	=	2 days left in November
Dec.	=	31 days in December
Total	=	33 days left in the fiscal period

Interest = Principal × Rate × Time

$$\text{Interest} = \$8,000 \times 0.06 \times \frac{33}{360} = \underline{\$44.00}$$

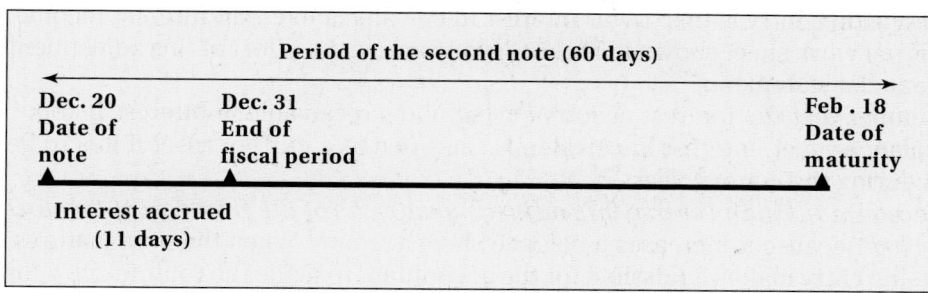

Dec. (31 − 20) = 11 days left in the fiscal period

$$\text{Interest} = \$6,500 \times 0.055 \times \frac{11}{360} = \underline{\$10.92}$$

The maker doesn't ordinarily pay the interest until the note comes due. Since these notes have not matured, the interest income has been neither paid nor recorded ($44.00 + $10.92 = $54.92).

FIGURE 2

Effect of the adjusting entry on the financial statements

Account Name	Trial Balance	
	Debit	Credit
Notes Receivable	14 5 0 0 00	
Interest Income		7 4 4 20
Interest Receivable		

Remember

When a firm has notes that extend from one fiscal period into the next, an adjusting entry is required. Since the interest is not collected until the note becomes due, it is necessary to record the interest income for each fiscal period in which interest is earned. The interest would be accrued only on the accrual basis.

In the firm's general journal, the adjusting entry for the interest income accrued on the two notes looks like this:

				GENERAL JOURNAL			PAGE ____		
Date		Description	Post. Ref.		Debit			Credit	
20—		Adjusting Entry							
Dec.	31	Interest Receivable			5 4 92				
		Interest Income						5 4 92	

Like all other adjustments, this entry was first recorded in the Adjustments columns of the work sheet. Here is a T account picture of the situation, assuming a balance in Interest Income of $744.20 before adjustment:

Interest Receivable		Interest Income	
+	−	−	+
			Dec. 31 Bal. 744.20
Dec. 31 Adj. 54.92			31 Adj. 54.92

The adjusting entry is this: Debit Interest Receivable and credit Interest Income. On the partial work sheet shown in Figure 2, you can see the effect of this adjustment on the financial statements.

Remember that the interest accompanying notes receivable is Interest Income. On the balance sheet, Interest Receivable is classified as a current asset if it is to be received during the coming year.

The accountant may reverse this adjusting entry as of the first day of the next fiscal period because it increases a balance sheet account. When the note matures, the reversing entry makes it possible for the accountant to make the routine entry for the receipt of payment of an interest-bearing note: a debit to Cash, a credit to Notes Receivable, and a credit to Interest Income. This procedure is most convenient, especially when a significant number of notes is involved.

	Adjustments		Income Statement		Balance Sheet	
	Debit	Credit	Debit	Credit	Debit	Credit
					14 5 0 0 00	
		(a) 5 4 92		7 9 9 12		
(a)	5 4 92				5 4 92	

CHAPTER REVIEW

Study & Practice

1a LEARNING OBJECTIVE
Write the journal entry to record receipt of a note from a charge customer.

To record receipt of a note from a charge customer, debit Notes Receivable for the principal of the note and credit the charge customer's Accounts Receivable account for the principal of the note.

PRACTICE EXERCISE 1a

Journalize the following transaction:

May   15   Received a note for $960 from Singer & Moore, Inc., in settlement of the sale of April 16, 30 days, 8 percent.

PRACTICE EXERCISE 1a SOLUTION

	GENERAL JOURNAL				PAGE ____

Date	Description	Post. Ref.	Debit	Credit
20—				
May 15	Notes Receivable		9 6 0 00	
	Accounts Receivable, Singer &			
	Moore, Inc.			9 6 0 00
	Received a 30-day, 8 percent			
	note, dated May 15, in			
	settlement of open account.			

1b LEARNING OBJECTIVE
Write the journal entry to record receipt of payment of an interest-bearing note at maturity.

To record receipt of payment of an interest-bearing note at maturity, credit Notes Receivable for the principal of the note, credit Interest Income for the amount of interest, and debit Cash for the principal of the note plus the amount of interest.

PRACTICE EXERCISE 1b

Journalize the following transaction:

June   14   Received payment at maturity of principal plus interest on Singer & Moore, Inc.'s note from Practice Exercise 1a.

PRACTICE EXERCISE 1b SOLUTION

	GENERAL JOURNAL			PAGE _____	
Date	Description	Post. Ref.	Debit	Credit	
20—					
June 14	Cash		9 6 6 40		
	Notes Receivable			9 6 0 00	
	Interest Income			6 40	
	Received full payment of				
	Singer & Moore, Inc.'s note.				
	($960 × 0.08 × 30/360)				

1c LEARNING OBJECTIVE

Write the journal entry to record receipt of a note as a result of granting a personal loan.

To record receipt of a note as a result of granting a personal loan, debit Notes Receivable for the principal of the note and credit Cash for the principal of the note. When the loan reaches maturity, the maker must pay the principal plus interest.

PRACTICE EXERCISE 1c

Journalize the following transaction:

Aug.   20   Granted a loan to Graham Marco, an employee, for $550 for 2 months, 6 percent, dated August 20.

PRACTICE EXERCISE 1c SOLUTION

	GENERAL JOURNAL			PAGE _____	
Date	Description	Post. Ref.	Debit	Credit	
20—					
Aug. 20	Notes Receivable		5 5 0 00		
	Cash			5 5 0 00	
	Granted a loan to Graham				
	Marco, 2 months, 6 percent,				
	dated August 20.				

1d LEARNING OBJECTIVE

Write the journal entry to record receipt of a note in exchange for merchandise or other property.

To record receipt of a note in exchange for merchandise or other property, debit Notes Receivable for the face value of the note and credit Sales for the face value of the note.

PRACTICE EXERCISE 1d

Journalize the following transaction:

Sept.   19   Received a note for $1,680 from Mitch Kane and Company for merchandise sold, 60 days, 6.5 percent, dated September 19.

PRACTICE EXERCISE 1d SOLUTION

	GENERAL JOURNAL				PAGE _____	
Date	Description	Post. Ref.	Debit		Credit	
20—						
Sept. 19	Notes Receivable		1 6 8 0	00		
	Sales				1 6 8 0	00
	Mitch Kane and Company,					
	60-day, 6.5 percent note,					
	dated September 19.					

1e   **LEARNING OBJECTIVE**

Write the journal entries to record renewal of a note at maturity and payment of interest.

If the maker of a note is unable to pay the entire principal at maturity, the company may be allowed to renew all or part of the note. When this occurs, two journal entries are required. The first entry records the interest on the old note, and the second entry cancels the old note and records the new note.

PRACTICE EXERCISE 1e

Journalize the following transactions:

Nov.   18   Received interest from Mitch Kane and Company on its note of September 19 from Practice Exercise 1d.

       18   Mitch Kane and Company renews the note by issuing a new note, 30 days, 7.5 percent, dated November 18.

PRACTICE EXERCISE 1e SOLUTION

	GENERAL JOURNAL				PAGE _____	
Date	Description	Post. Ref.	Debit		Credit	
20—						
Nov. 18	Cash		1 8	20		
	Interest Income				1 8	20
	Received payment of interest on					
	Mitch Kane and Company note,					
	dated September 19.					
	($1,680 × 0.065 × 60/360)					
18	Notes Receivable		1 6 8 0	00		
	Notes Receivable				1 6 8 0	00
	Mitch Kane and Company, renewal					
	of note, dated September 19;					
	new note is dated November 18,					
	30 days, 7.5 percent.					

LEARNING OBJECTIVE

1f
Write the journal entries to record renewal of a note with payment of interest and partial payment of principal.

Sometimes the maker of a note cancels the original note by paying the interest, plus part of the principal, and issuing a new note. When this happens, two journal entries are required. The first entry records the interest on the old note and the partial payment of principal, and the second entry cancels the old note and records the new note.

PRACTICE EXERCISE 1f

Journalize the following transaction:

Mar.   18   Received interest and $1,500 partial payment from Gil Johnson Manufacturing on its $3,500, 30-day, 6.5 percent interest note of February 16.

18   Gil Johnson Manufacturing renews the note by issuing a new note, 30 days, 8 percent, dated March 18, for $2,000.

PRACTICE EXERCISE 1f SOLUTION

			GENERAL JOURNAL				PAGE ____
	Date		Description	Post. Ref.	Debit	Credit	
20—							
Mar.	18	Cash			1 5 1 8 96		
		Notes Receivable				1 5 0 0 00	
		Interest Income				1 8 96	
		Gil Johnson Manufacturing					
		note, dated February 16, partial					
		payment of the principal					
		and payment of the interest.					
		($3,500 × 0.065 × 30/360)					
	18	Notes Receivable			2 0 0 0 00		
		Notes Receivable				2 0 0 0 00	
		Gil Johnson Manufacturing,					
		renewal of note, dated					
		February 16; new note is dated					
		March 18, 30 days, 8 percent.					

LEARNING OBJECTIVE

1g
Write the journal entry to record a dishonored note receivable.

When the maker of a note fails to pay the principal amount or to renew the note at maturity, the note is said to be a **dishonored note receivable**. The maker of the note is still obligated to pay principal plus interest. Since the balance of the Notes Receivable account shows only the principal of notes that have not yet matured, a note that is past due, or dishonored, should be removed from the Notes Receivable account and added to the Accounts Receivable account; the amount listed should be the principal plus interest.

PRACTICE EXERCISE 1g

Journalize the following transaction:

June 2   Crown Lumber Company dishonored its note of April 3 for $1,850 at 5.5 percent, for 60 days.

PRACTICE EXERCISE 1g SOLUTION

	GENERAL JOURNAL			PAGE ____
Date	**Description**	**Post. Ref.**	**Debit**	**Credit**
20—				
June 2	Accounts Receivable, Crown			
	Lumber Company		1 8 6 6 96	
	Notes Receivable			1 8 5 0 00
	Interest Income			1 6 96
	Crown Lumber Company			
	dishonored its 60-day, 5.5 percent			
	note for $1,850, dated April 3.			
	($1,850 × 0.055 × 60/360)			

1h LEARNING OBJECTIVE

Write the journal entry to record collection of a note receivable formerly dishonored.

To record collection of a note receivable formerly dishonored, credit the customer's Accounts Receivable account for the principal and interest of the note *before* it had been dishonored, credit Interest Income for the additional interest accrued on the note, and debit Cash for the amount of principal plus the additional interest accrued.

PRACTICE EXERCISE 1h

Journalize the following transaction:

July 2   Crown Lumber Company paid its dishonored note, plus additional interest for 30 days at 6.5 percent.

PRACTICE EXERCISE 1h SOLUTION

	GENERAL JOURNAL			PAGE ____
Date	**Description**	**Post. Ref.**	**Debit**	**Credit**
20—				
July 2	Cash		1 8 7 7 07	
	Accounts Receivable, Crown			
	Lumber Company			1 8 6 6 96
	Interest Income			1 0 11
	Crown Lumber Company paid			
	the dishonored note, plus interest			
	for 30 days at 6.5 percent.			
	($1,866.96 × 0.065 × 30/360)			

1i LEARNING OBJECTIVE

Write the journal entry to record discounting an interest-bearing note receivable.

Instead of keeping notes receivable until they come due, a firm can raise cash by selling its notes receivable to a bank or finance company. This type of financing is called **discounting notes receivable** because the bank deducts the interest or discount from the **maturity value** (face value) of the note to determine the proceeds.

To record discounting an interest-bearing note receivable, the proceeds are debited to Cash. The principal of the note is credited to Notes Receivable. If the amount of the proceeds is greater than the amount of the principal, the difference is credited to Interest Income. If the amount of the proceeds is less than the principal, the deficiency is debited to Interest Expense.

PRACTICE EXERCISE 1i

Journalize the following transaction:

Oct. 3   Discounted at Central Trust Bank a note received from Corson Electronics, dated September 20, $1,178, 7 percent, 60 days. The discount rate is 8 percent.

PRACTICE EXERCISE 1i SOLUTION

		GENERAL JOURNAL				PAGE

Date		Description	Post. Ref.	Debit	Credit
20—					
Oct.	3	Cash		1 1 7 9 29	
		Notes Receivable			1 1 7 8 00
		Interest Income			1 29
		Discounted at the bank			
		Corson Electronics' note, dated			
		September 20. The bank discount			
		rate is 8 percent.			

Calculation of Oct. 3 journal entry:

Principal	$1,178.00
+ Interest (7%, 60 days)	13.74
Value at maturity	$1,191.74
− Discount (8%, 47 days)	12.45
Proceeds	$1,179.29

$$\text{Interest} = \$1{,}178.00 \times 0.07 \times \frac{60}{360} = \$13.74$$

$$\text{Discount} = \$1{,}191.74 \times 0.08 \times \frac{47}{360} = \$12.45$$

2 LEARNING OBJECTIVE

Complete a notes receivable register.

A **notes receivable register** is a supplementary record in which a firm lists details of notes received. For each note, list the date, the maker, where the note is payable, the amount, the time period, the interest rate, the amount of interest, the due date, the date paid, and relevant remarks.

PRACTICE EXERCISE 2

Prepare a notes receivable ledger for the transactions in Practice Exercises 1a–i. Assume that all notes are payable at Central Trust Bank.

PRACTICE EXERCISE 2 SOLUTION

NOTES RECEIVABLE REGISTER

Date	Maker	Where Payable	Amount	Time	Rate	Interest	Due Date	Discounted Bank	Discounted Date	Date Paid	Remarks
20—											
Feb. 16	Gil Johnson	Cen. Trust	3 5 0 0 00	30 d	6.5%	1 8 96	3/18			Ren.	Open account.
Mar. 18	Gil Johnson	Cen. Trust	2 0 0 0 00	30 d	8%	1 3 33	4/17			4/17	Renewed 2/16 with part. payment note of $1,500 plus interest.
Apr. 3	Crown Lumber Company	Cen. Trust	1 8 5 0 00	60 d	5.5%	1 6 96	6/2			7/2	Dishonored 6/2; note paid 7/2.
May 15	Singer & Moore, Inc.	Cen. Trust	9 6 0 00	30 d	8%	6 40	6/14			6/14	Open account.
Aug. 20	Graham Marco	Cen. Trust	5 5 0 00	2 m	6%	5 50	10/20			10/20	Employee loan.
Sept. 19	Mitch Kane and Company	Cen. Trust	1 6 8 0 00	60 d	6.5%	1 8 20	11/18			Ren.	Open account.
20	Corson Electronics	Cen. Trust	1 1 7 8 00	60 d	7%	13 74	11/19	Cen. Trust	10/3	—	Discount. @ 8%, $1,179.29 proceeds.
Nov. 18	Mitch Kane and Company	Cen. Trust	1 6 8 0 00	30 d	7.5%	1 0 50	12/18				

3 **LEARNING OBJECTIVE**

Write the journal entry to record the adjustment for accrued interest on notes receivable.

Accrued interest income on notes receivable is the interest that is due (not yet received) on notes receivable that are outstanding at the end of the fiscal period. Whenever a firm receives or issues an interest-bearing note, the interest accrues daily. As a result, any interest-bearing note that overlaps fiscal periods requires an adjusting entry in order for the financial statements to present a true picture of the firm's net income and financial condition.

PRACTICE EXERCISE 3

Journalize the adjusting entry for the following two notes:
a. $9,000, 90 days, 8 percent, dated November 28
b. $5,200, 60 days, 7 percent, dated December 20

PRACTICE EXERCISE 3 SOLUTION

GENERAL JOURNAL   PAGE _____

Date	Description	Post. Ref.	Debit	Credit
20—	Adjusting Entry			
Dec. 31	Interest Receivable		7 7 12	
	Interest Income			7 7 12
	($66.00 + $11.12)			
	($9,000 × 0.08 × 33/360 = $66.00)			
	($5,200 × 0.07 × 11/360 = $11.12)			

Before a Test Check: Chapters 13–14

PART I: NOTES PAYABLE

A. On September 20 of this year, B. Mann issued a 120-day, 9 percent note, dated September 20, to L. Roo, a creditor, for $12,000. Answer the following questions about the note:

1. What is the due date?
2. What is the face value?
3. How much is the total interest?
4. What is the maturity value?
5. What is the amount of the adjusting entry for interest expense on December 31?

B. On October 20 of this year, D. Dagostino borrowed $8,000 from the bank, signing a 90-day, discounted 8 percent note dated October 20. Answer the following questions about the note:

1. What is the due date?
2. What is the face value?
3. How much is the total interest?
4. On October 20, the entry to record the note includes a debit to Cash. Is the other debit to Interest Expense or to Discount on Notes Payable? How much is that debit?
5. What is the amount of the proceeds?
6. What is the amount of the adjusting entry on December 31?
7. What are the debit and credit accounts in the December 31 adjusting entry?
8. On the date of payment of the note, besides debiting Notes Payable and crediting Cash for the face value of the note, what are the debit and credit accounts and amounts needed to report the entire amount of interest on the note?

PART II: NOTES RECEIVABLE

A. The Glen Company received a $9,000, 60-day, 8.5 percent note, dated December 3 of this year, as an extension of a charge account for Fryer Company. Determine the following:

1. The debit and credit accounts involved in recording the $9,000 note
2. The debit and credit accounts and amounts involved in the December 31 adjusting entry
3. The due date
4. The maturity value
5. The debit and credit accounts and amounts involved in the receipt of payment from Fryer Company, assuming a reversing entry was made on January 1

B. On April 8 of this year, Tickner Company received a 90-day, 8 percent note for $6,500, dated April 8, for merchandise sold to Ward Company. Tickner endorsed the note in favor of its bank on April 28. The bank discounted the note at 8.5 percent, paying the proceeds to Tickner Company. Determine the following:

1. Number of days Tickner Company held the note
2. Number of days in the discount period
3. Face value
4. Maturity value
5. Discount
6. Proceeds
7. Will interest income or interest expense be recorded by the payee (Tickner Company)?
8. What is the amount of interest income or interest expense recorded by the payee (Tickner Company)?

ANSWERS: PART I

A. 1. January 18 of the next year; **2.** $12,000; **3.** $360; $12,000 × 0.09 × 120/360 = $360; **4.** $12,360; $12,000 + $360 = $12,360; **5.** $306; $12,000 × 0.09 × 102/360 = $306

B. 1. January 18 of the next year; **2.** $8,000; **3.** $160; $8,000 × 0.08 × 90/360 = $160; **4.** Discount on Notes Payable, $160; **5.** $7,840; $8,000 − $160; **6.** $128; $8,000 × 0.08 × 72/360 = $128; **7.** Debit Interest Expense, credit Discount on Notes Payable; **8.** Debit Interest Expense, $32; credit Discount on Notes Payable, $32; $160 − $128 = $32

ANSWERS: PART II

A. 1. Debit Notes Receivable, $9,000; credit Accounts Receivable, Fryer Company, $9,000; **2.** Debit Interest Receivable, $59.50; credit Interest Income, $59.50; $9,000 × 0.085 × 28/360 = $59.50; **3.** February 1 of the next year; **4.** $9,127.50; $9,000 + $127.50; = $9,127.50; $9,000 × 0.085 × 60/360 = $127.50; **5.** Debit Cash, $9,127.50; credit Notes Receivable, $9,000, credit Interest Income, $127.50

B. 1. 20 days; **2.** 70 days; **3.** $6,500; **4.** $6,630; $6,500 + $130 = $6,630; $6,500 × 0.08 × 90/360 = $130; **5.** $109.58; $6,630 × 0.085 × 70/360 = $109.58; **6.** $6,520.42; $6,630 − $109.58 = $6,520.42; **7.** Interest Income; **8.** $20.42; $6,520.42; − $6,500 = $20.42

Glossary

Accrued interest income on notes receivable The interest that is due (not yet received) on notes receivable, which are outstanding at the end of the fiscal period. (p. 579)

Contingent liability A liability that is dependent upon certain conditions or events taking place—for example, if a note receivable is discounted at a bank and then the maker does not pay. The payee or endorser of the dishonored note is then liable to pay the bank. (p. 575)

Discount period The time between the date a note receivable is discounted and the date it matures. (p. 574)

Discounting notes receivable The process by which a firm may raise cash by selling a note receivable to a bank or finance company. The bank deducts the discount from the maturity value of the note to determine the proceeds (amount of money) that the firm receives. (p. 573)

Dishonored note receivable A note whose maker fails to pay the principal amount or to renew the note at maturity. (p. 572)

Maturity value The principal (face value) of a note plus interest from the date of the note until the due date. (p. 573)

Notes receivable register A supplementary record in which a firm lists details of notes received. (p. 578)

CHAPTER ASSIGNMENTS

Discussion Questions

1. When is it necessary to make an adjusting entry for accrued interest on an interest-bearing note receivable, and why? What is the adjusting entry? Can the adjusting entry be reversed?
2. From the point of view of a creditor, what are the advantages of having a note receivable over having an account receivable?
3. Describe the formula for calculating the proceeds of an interest-bearing note receivable discounted at a bank. Define the terms.
4. Explain why a business would sell its notes receivable to a bank or finance company.
5. In discounting an interest-bearing note receivable, why is the discount figured on the maturity value of the note?
6. Explain how to record a discounted note receivable.
7. Explain what *contingent liability* means in relation to the endorser of a note.
8. What is the purpose of maintaining a notes receivable register?

Exercises

1a,1b

PRACTICE EXERCISES 1a,1b

EXERCISE 14-1 On March 11, Rainz Company received a 90-day, 6 percent note for $1,500, dated March 11, from J. Rose, a charge customer, to satisfy his open account receivable.

a. What is the due date of the note?

b. How much interest is due at maturity?

Given the preceding data, write entries in general journal form on the books of Rainz Company to record the following:

c. Receipt of the note from J. Rose in settlement of his account.

d. Receipt of the principal and interest at maturity.

Given the same data, write entries in general journal form on Rose's books to record the following:

e. Issuance of the note by Rose in settlement of his account.

f. Payment of the note at maturity.

1b,1c **LO**

PRACTICE EXERCISES 1b,1c

EXERCISE 14-2 Prepare entries in general journal form to record the following:

May   5   Received a 2-month, 6 percent note from Paul Dantz for a $575 personal loan.

July   5   Received the total amount due from Dantz.

1e,1f **LO**

PRACTICE EXERCISES 1e,1f

EXERCISE 14-3 Prepare entries in general journal form to record the following:

June   4   Received payment from Paulson Company of interest on a 45-day, 6.5 percent note for $7,800, dated April 20, and renewal of the note for 60 days at 7 percent.

July   8   Received payment of interest from Nahla Company on a 60-day, 7 percent note for $8,500, dated May 9, and partial payment of $3,000 on the principal. Received a 7.5 percent, 30-day note for $5,500 dated July 8.

1d,1i **LO**

PRACTICE EXERCISES 1d,1i

EXERCISE 14-4 On May 10, Morris Company received a 90-day, 6.5 percent note for $7,500, dated May 10, for merchandise sold to Baar Company. Morris Company endorsed the note in favor of its bank on May 28. The bank discounted the note at 7 percent, paying the proceeds to Morris Company. Determine the following facts:

a. Number of days Morris Company held the note

b. Number of days in the discount period

c. Face value

d. Maturity value

e. Discount

f. Proceeds

g. Interest income or expense recorded by the payee (Morris Company)

1a,1i **LO**

PRACTICE EXERCISES 1a,1i

EXERCISE 14-5 Prepare entries in general journal form to record the following:

June   12   Sold merchandise on account to K. Perrot; terms 3/10, n/30; $1,740.

July   12   Received $740 in cash from K. Perrot and a 60-day, 7 percent note for $1,000 dated July 12.

Aug.   17   Discounted the note at the bank at 7.5 percent.

EXERCISE 14-6 The following T accounts show a series of four transactions concerning a sale of merchandise on account and subsequent payment of the amount owed. Describe what happened in each transaction.

LO 1a,1b

PRACTICE EXERCISES 1a,1b

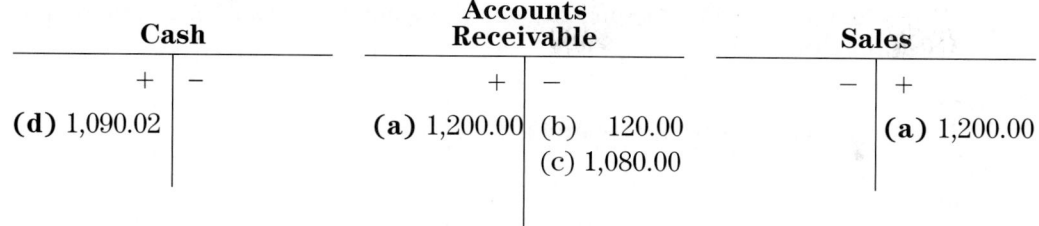

Cash		Accounts Receivable		Sales
+	−	+	−	−	+
(d) 1,090.02		**(a)** 1,200.00	**(b)** 120.00		**(a)** 1,200.00
			(c) 1,080.00		

Interest Income		Notes Receivable		Sales Returns and Allowances
−	+	+	−	+	−
	(d) 10.02	**(c)** 1,080.00	**(d)** 1,080.00	**(b)** 120.00	

EXERCISE 14-7 Prepare entries in general journal form to record the following:

LO 1g,1h

PRACTICE EXERCISES 1g,1h

Aug. 6 Ward Company failed to pay its 30-day, 6 percent note for $830, dated July 7. The note is thus dishonored at maturity.

Sept. 5 Ward Company pays the balance of its account, plus an additional 30 days' interest at 6.5 percent on the amount owed.

EXERCISE 14-8 Write entries in general journal form to record the following transactions for Ballard Company, whose fiscal year ends on December 31:

LO 1a,1b,3

PRACTICE EXERCISES 1a,1b,3

Year 1

Dec. 3 Ballard Company received from RJB Services an $8,500, 120-day, 6.5 percent note, dated December 3, as an extension of a charge account.

    31 The adjusting entry for accrued interest.

    31 The closing entry (for practice), assuming all other closing entries were made.

Year 2

Jan. 1 The reversing entry.

Apr. 2 Receipt of the principal and interest at maturity.

Problem Set A

For additional help, see the demonstration problem at the beginning of each chapter in your Working Papers.

PROBLEM 14-1A Following are selected transactions carried out by Blakely Company this year:

LO 1a,1b,1d

Jan. 12 Sold merchandise on account to G. Hardin; 3/10, n/30; $2,450.

    22 Received a check from G. Hardin for the sale of January 12.

Feb. 17 Sold merchandise on account to K. Blaine; 2/10, n/30; $3,545.

Mar. 19 Received a 30-day, 5.5 percent note, dated this day, for $3,545 from K. Blaine for the amount owed on account.

Apr.   18   Received a check from K. Blaine for the amount owed on the note of March 19.

June   1   Sold merchandise to Magovey Company for $4,550, receiving a 60-day, 5.5 percent note, dated this day. (This sale was not previously recorded.)

July   31   Received payment from Magovey Company for the amount owed on the note of June 1.

Check Figure
Interest on Blaine note, $16.25

Required

Record these transactions in the general journal (page 23).

PROBLEM 14-2A Here are some of the transactions carried out by Geary Company this year:

Jan.   7   Sold merchandise on account to Edge Imports; 2/10, n/30; $2,835.

Feb.   6   Received a 30-day, 6 percent note, dated this day, for $2,835 from Edge Imports on account.

Mar.   8   Received payment from Edge Imports for the amount owed on its note of February 6.

Apr.   25   Sold merchandise on account to Katie's Gift Shop; 2/10, n/30; $3,460.

May   25   Received a 45-day, 5.75 percent note, dated May 25, for $3,460 from Katie's Gift Shop on account.

July   9   Katie's Gift Shop paid the interest on its note of May 25 and renewed the obligation by issuing a new 60-day, 6 percent note for $3,460, dated July 9.

Sept.   7   Received a check from Katie's Gift Shop for the amount owed on its note of July 9.

        15   Sold merchandise to Reinhold, Inc., for $4,898, receiving a 30-day, 6.25 percent note, dated this day (not previously recorded).

        25   Discounted the note received from Reinhold, Inc., at All State Bank; discount rate, 7 percent.

Check Figure
Interest Income on Edge Imports note, $14.18

Required

1. Record these transactions in the general journal (pages 11 and 12).
2. Immediately after each journal entry, record each note receivable in the notes receivable register (page 7).
   a.   All notes are payable at All State Bank.
   b.   Fill in the date paid after journalizing the receipt of payment of the note, or fill in "renewed" or "discounted" when appropriate.

PROBLEM 14-3A Selected transactions of Larry's Center carried out this year are as follows:

Jan.   10   Sold merchandise on account to Oscar Stores; 3/10, n/30; $5,692.

Feb.   9   Received a 30-day, 5.75 percent note, dated February 9, for $5,692 from Oscar Stores to apply on account.

Mar.   11   Received $2,719.27 from Oscar Stores as partial payment on its note dated February 9: $2,692 as partial payment on the principal, and $27.27 interest on $5,692 for 30 days at 5.75 percent. Received a new 30-day, 6.5 percent note for $3,000, dated March 11.

Apr.   4   Sold merchandise to Fletcher Sports for $3,479, receiving a 60-day, 6 percent note, dated April 4 (not previously recorded).

        10   Received a check from Oscar Stores for the amount owed on its note of March 11.

Apr. 12   Discounted the note received from Fletcher Sports at Landon Bank; discount rate, 6.5 percent.

May 10   Sold merchandise on account to Lindstrom, Inc.; 2/10, n/30; $2,910.

June 9   Received a 45-day, 6 percent note, dated June 9, for $2,910 from Lindstrom, Inc., to apply on account.

Required

Record these transactions in the general journal (pages 17 and 18).

Check Figure
Proceeds of the Fletcher Sports note discounted on April 12, $3,480.80

 1a,1b,1c,1d,1e,1i,3

PROBLEM 14-4A Here are selected transactions of Wilbur's Food Supply carried out during the year ended December 31:

June 9   Received a 60-day, 6.75 percent note, dated June 9, for $4,245 from Mackie's Foods for merchandise. (The sale was not previously recorded.)

21   Received a 30-day, 6 percent note, dated June 21, for $3,873 from Lundgren Restaurants, a charge customer, for a sale previously recorded.

July 11   Received a 90-day, 6.5 percent note, dated July 11, for $2,110 from Angus, Inc., a charge customer, for a sale previously recorded.

21   Received a check from Lundgren Restaurants in payment of principal and interest on its note.

Aug. 8   Received payment of interest from Mackie's Foods for its note of June 9 and also a new 30-day, 7 percent note, dated August 8, for $4,245 (two entries).

20   Received a 60-day, 6.25 percent note, dated August 20, for $3,450 from C. Tinker, a charge customer, for a sale previously recorded.

Sept. 7   Mackie's Foods paid its note, dated August 8, principal plus interest.

9   Discounted the note received from C. Tinker at Handley Bank; discount rate, 6.5 percent.

Oct. 9   Received a check from Angus, Inc., in payment of principal and interest on its note.

Dec. 6   Received a 60-day, 6.5 percent note, dated December 6, for $3,210 from L. Kwan, a charge customer, for a sale previously recorded.

8   Received a 30-day, 6.5 percent note, dated December 8, for $1,780 from C. Brandmeir, an employee, for a personal loan.

Required

1. Record these transactions in the general journal (pages 47–49).
2. Show the calculation of each due date.
3. On December 31, record the adjusting entry to account for accrued interest receivable for the L. Kwan and C. Brandmeir notes, which are not due to be paid until the next fiscal period.
4. On January 1, record the reversing entry. (Assume closing entries have been made.)
5. On January 7, record the receipt of payment on the C. Brandmeir note.

Check Figure
Adjustment for interest receivable, $21.88

Problem Set B

For additional help, see the demonstration problem at the beginning of each chapter in your Working Papers.

PROBLEM 14-1B Hinkle Company carried out the following transactions this year:

Jan.	19	Sold merchandise on account to Clemons Company; 2/10, n/30; $2,744.
	29	Received a check from Clemons Company for the sale of January 19.
Feb.	23	Sold merchandise on account to Rickles Company; 3/10, n/30; $2,295.
Mar.	25	Received a 60-day, 6.5 percent note, dated this day, for $2,295 from Rickles Company for the amount owed on account.
May	24	Received a check from Rickles Company for the amount owed on the note of March 25.
June	8	Sold merchandise to Juan's Interiors for $4,533, receiving a 120-day, 6.25 percent note, dated June 8 (not previously recorded).
Oct.	6	Received payment from Juan's Interiors for the amount owed on its note of June 8.

Check Figure
Interest on Rickles Company note, $24.86

Required

Record these transactions in the general journal (page 23).

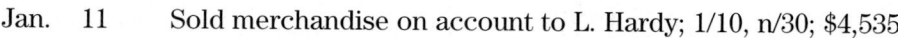

PROBLEM 14-2B Hadaka, Inc., carried out the following transactions this year:

Jan.	11	Sold merchandise on account to L. Hardy; 1/10, n/30; $4,535.
Feb.	10	Received a 30-day, 6 percent note, dated this day, for $4,535 from L. Hardy on account.
Mar.	12	Received payment from L. Hardy for the amount owed on its note of February 10.
Apr.	28	Sold merchandise on account to Ella's Gallery; 1/10, n/30; $5,800.
May	28	Received a 60-day, 6.5 percent note, dated this day, for $5,800 from Ella's Gallery on account.
July	27	Ella's Gallery paid the interest on its note of May 28 and renewed the obligation by issuing a new 60-day, 7 percent note for $5,800, dated July 27.
Sept.	25	Received a check from Ella's Gallery for the amount owed on its note of July 27.
Oct.	11	Sold merchandise to Newman, Inc., for $6,457, receiving a 30-day, 6.75 percent note, dated this day (not previously recorded).
	21	Discounted the note received from Newman, Inc., at California Bank; discount rate, 7.5 percent.

Check Figure
Interest Income on the L. Hardy note, $22.68

Required

1. Record these transactions in the general journal (pages 11 and 12).
2. Immediately after each journal entry, record each note receivable in the notes receivable register (page 7).
   a. All notes are payable at California Bank.
   b. Fill in the date paid after journalizing the receipt of payment of the note, or fill in "renewed" or "discounted" when appropriate.

PROBLEM 14-3B Here are some selected transactions carried out by Crandal's Nursery this year.

Jan.	7	Sold merchandise on account to Alaska Gardens; 2/10, n/30; $5,930.
Feb.	6	Received a 30-day, 5.5 percent note, dated February 6, for $5,930 from Alaska Gardens to apply on account.
Mar.	8	Received $2,027.18 from Alaska Gardens as payment on its note dated February 6: $2,000 as partial payment on the principal, and $27.18 as interest on $5,930 for 30 days at 5.5 percent. Received a new 30-day, 6 percent note for $3,930, dated March 8.
Apr.	7	Received a check from Alaska Gardens for the amount owed on its note of March 8.
	13	Sold merchandise to L. Fritz for $3,399, receiving a 60-day, 6.5 percent note, dated April 13 (not previously recorded).
	21	Discounted the note received from L. Fritz at Kamdon Bank; discount rate, 7 percent.
May	23	Sold merchandise on account to Hagar Company; 3/10, n/30; $1,424.
June	22	Received a 60-day, 6.5 percent note, dated June 22, for $1,424 from Hagar Company for the amount owed on account.

Required

Record these transactions in the general journal (pages 17 and 18).

Check Figure
Proceeds of the L. Fritz note discounted on April 21, $3,401.08

PROBLEM 14-4B Ebert's Printing Company completed the following transactions during the year ended December 31:

June	16	Received a 60-day, 5.5 percent note, dated June 16, for $2,160 from Carlo's Office Supply for the sale of merchandise. (The sale was not previously recorded.)
	26	Received a 30-day, 6.5 percent note, dated June 26, for $3,680 from Dillon, Inc., a charge customer, for a sale previously recorded.
July	7	Received a 90-day, 5.5 percent note, dated July 7, for $4,160 from Carter Office Supply, a charge customer, for a sale previously recorded.
	26	Received a check from Dillon, Inc., in payment of principal and interest on its note.
Aug.	15	Received payment of interest from Carlo's Office Supply for its note of June 16 and also a new 30-day, 6 percent note, dated August 15, for $2,160 (two entries).
	22	Received a 90-day, 6.5 percent note, dated August 22, for $2,745 from E. Mason and Company, a charge customer, for a sale previously recorded.
Sept.	14	Carlo's Office Supply paid its note dated August 15, principal plus interest.
	14	Discounted the note received from E. Mason and Company at Harris Bank; discount rate, 7 percent.
Oct.	5	Received a check from Carter Office Supply in payment of principal and interest on its note.
Dec.	16	Received a 60-day, 6.5 percent note, dated December 16, for $6,367 from Lambert and Roberts Company, a charge customer, for a sale previously recorded.
	19	Received a 45-day, 6.75 percent note, dated December 19, for $1,432 from B. Jenkins, an employee, for a personal loan.

Required

1. Record these transactions in the general journal (pages 47–49).
2. Show the calculation of each due date.
3. On December 31, record the adjusting entry to account for accrued interest receivable for the Lambert and Roberts Company and B. Jenkins notes, which are not due to be paid until the next fiscal period.
4. On January 1, record the reversing entry. (Assume closing entries have been made.)
5. On February 2, record the receipt of payment from B. Jenkins.

ACTIVITIES

CONSIDER AND COMMUNICATE

The term *discount* or *discounting* is used repeatedly in accounting. For example, it is common to see references to "a sales discount of 2 percent," "discounting our note at the bank," "discounting a customer's note at the bank," and "trade discount." Explain how discounting is similar in these cases and how these situations differ.

WHAT'S WRONG WITH THIS PICTURE?

You loaned $25,000 to a close friend to buy an off-road vehicle. You planned to have him sign a note receivable, with the off-road vehicle becoming collateral or security for the note in case your friend failed to pay you. However, in the excitement and rush to get the vehicle, you forgot to have your friend sign the note, and you also forgot to make the arrangements for collateral. Nothing was signed prior to your giving your friend the cash. How should this transaction have been handled? What are the possible consequences of this transaction between you and your friend?

CRITICAL THINKING

A client would like you to explain some options he has regarding discounting of a 6 percent, 60-day, $2,400 note receivable. He wants to know what he will receive in proceeds and what will be his interest income (or expense) if he discounts the note (a) after 10 days with a discount rate of 7 percent, (b) after 50 days with a 7.5 percent discount rate, or (c) after 5 days with a discount rate of 6.5 percent. Make the calculations for the client and explain the different outcomes to him.

PART 5

Uncollectible Accounts

15

NORDSTROM

NORDSTROM, Seattle, Washington

Nordstrom is an upscale department store chain founded in Seattle by John W. Nordstrom in 1901. In addition to its department stores, Nordstrom also operates its own bank called Nordstrom Bank, which offers its own line of credit cards for Nordstrom customers to use.

Credit can be a good thing when used carefully. However, during the economic slump that started in late 2008, retailers such as Nordstrom experienced a large jump in store credit card delinquencies and write-offs. In a recent SEC filing, Nordstrom reported that its bad debts expense related to its store credit card business increased 158 percent when 2009's first quarter was compared with 2008's first quarter. This economic phenomenon is also being experienced by other high-end retailers such as Neiman Marcus, Bloomingdale's, and Fifth Avenue Saks.

In this chapter, you will learn how retailers like Nordstrom manage their accounts receivable delinquencies and how these delinquent accounts affect net profit.

LEARNING OBJECTIVES

After you have completed this chapter, you will be able to do the following:

1 *Make the adjusting entry to record estimated bad debt losses by using the allowance method of recording bad debts. (a) Determine the amount of the adjusting entry by aging Accounts Receivable. (b) Determine the amount of the adjusting entry by using a percentage of Accounts Receivable. (c) Calculate the amount of the adjusting entry by using a percentage of net sales or net credit sales.*

2 *Journalize the entries to write off accounts receivable as being uncollectible, using the allowance method of accounting for bad debt losses.*

3 *Journalize entries to reinstate accounts receivable previously written off, using the allowance method.*

4 *Journalize the entries to write off accounts receivable as being uncollectible, using the specific charge-off method.*

5 *Journalize entries to reinstate accounts receivable previously written off, using the specific charge-off method.*

ACCOUNTING LANGUAGE

Aging of Accounts Receivable (p. 602)

Allowance method of accounting for bad debt losses (p. 600)

Bankruptcy (p. 613)

Book value of Accounts Receivable (p. 601)

Net expected realizable value of Accounts Receivable (p. 601)

Specific charge-off method of accounting for bad debt losses (p. 616)

Statute of limitations (p. 614)

The use of credit for both buying and selling goods and services has become standard practice for businesses of all types and levels: retailers, wholesalers, and manufacturers. You have learned to record sales of goods on account as a debit to Accounts Receivable and a credit to Sales. You have also learned to record collections on account as a debit to Cash and a credit to Accounts Receivable.

Business firms selling goods or services on credit will find that not all the accounts receivable (charge accounts) are collected in full. As a result, the unpaid accounts must eventually be written off as uncollectible or as bad debts. In other words, a firm that grants credit will not collect from everyone, and therefore the firm needs to plan for these anticipated losses. In this chapter, we discuss ways to provide for losses as well as to write off customer accounts that are no longer collectible.

TWO METHODS OF ACCOUNTING FOR UNCOLLECTIBLE ACCOUNTS

There are two methods of accounting for uncollectible accounts: the allowance method and the specific charge-off method.

The Allowance Method

The allowance method is consistent with the matching principle, in that it enables firms to match sales of one period with bad debt losses of the same period; and it is consistent with the accrual method of accounting required by generally accepted accounting principles (GAAP).

The Specific Charge-Off Method

The specific charge-off method traditionally has been used by small businesses. The specific charge-off method is the only method approved for federal income tax purposes. Many companies, especially larger firms, use the allowance method for external reporting—that is, for their own financial statements. They use the specific charge-off method for federal income tax reporting. The adjustments required on their tax returns are not entered in the companies' books.

THE CREDIT DEPARTMENT

The Credit Department has to keep a watchful eye on customers. It evaluates the debt-paying ability of prospective customers and determines the maximum amount of credit to extend to each customer. Retail stores selling to individuals rely on reports from local retail credit bureaus. When wholesalers and manufacturers grant credit to customers, they use reports from national credit-rating institutions, wholesale credit bureaus, and the financial statements of prospective customers. Firms that make many sales on credit find it worthwhile to subscribe to these credit bureaus or credit-rating agencies. These credit-reporting organizations maintain files of current financial information on charge customers, establish credit ratings for each charge customer, and conduct special investigations on request from their clients.

Incurring excessive credit losses is always unfavorable for a seller because any firm needs to be paid for its sales on account. Surprisingly, it may also be bad if a

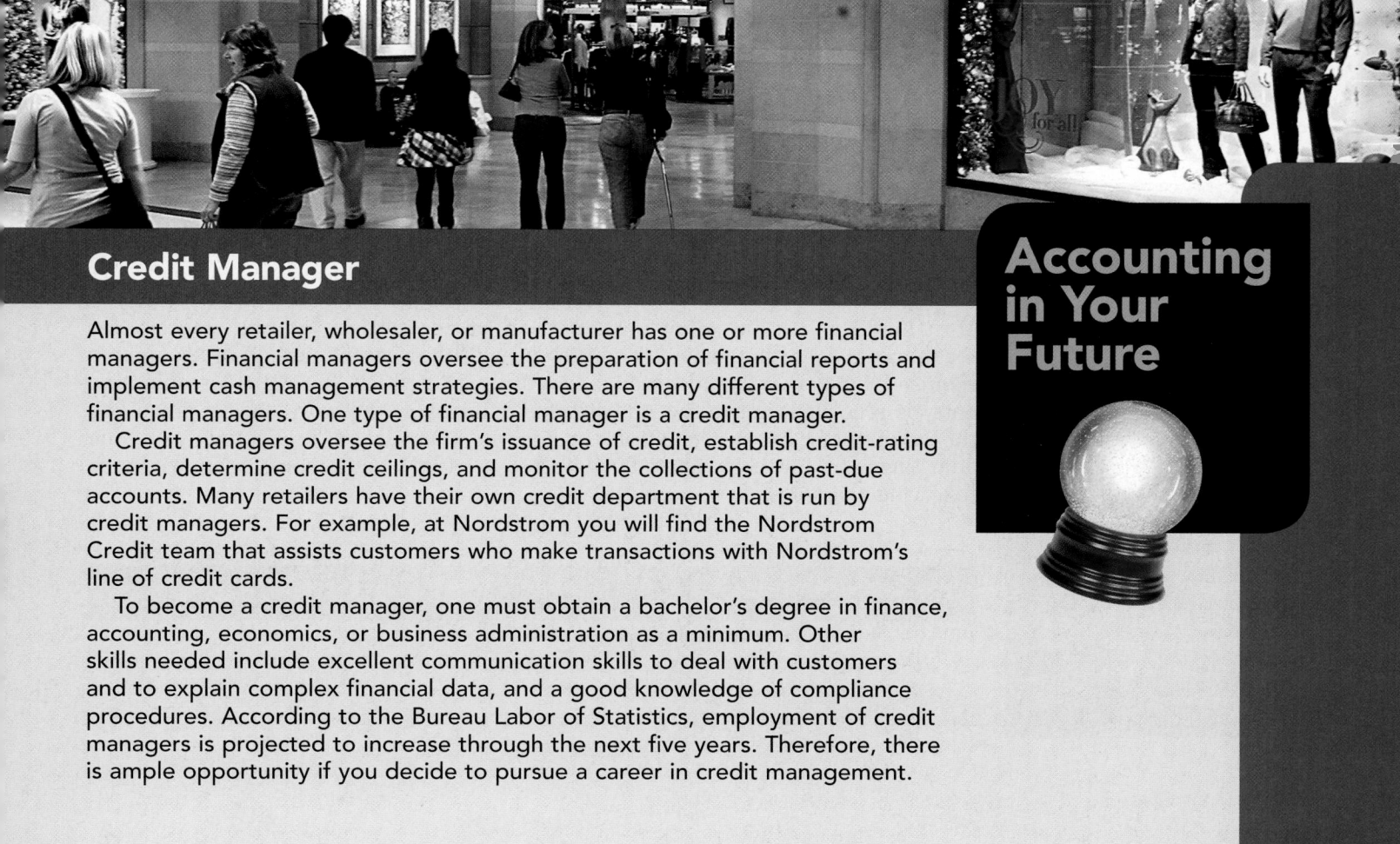

Credit Manager

Accounting in Your Future

Almost every retailer, wholesaler, or manufacturer has one or more financial managers. Financial managers oversee the preparation of financial reports and implement cash management strategies. There are many different types of financial managers. One type of financial manager is a credit manager.

Credit managers oversee the firm's issuance of credit, establish credit-rating criteria, determine credit ceilings, and monitor the collections of past-due accounts. Many retailers have their own credit department that is run by credit managers. For example, at Nordstrom you will find the Nordstrom Credit team that assists customers who make transactions with Nordstrom's line of credit cards.

To become a credit manager, one must obtain a bachelor's degree in finance, accounting, economics, or business administration as a minimum. Other skills needed include excellent communication skills to deal with customers and to explain complex financial data, and a good knowledge of compliance procedures. According to the Bureau Labor of Statistics, employment of credit managers is projected to increase through the next five years. Therefore, there is ample opportunity if you decide to pursue a career in credit management.

firm has no credit losses. Such a distinction may mean that the firm is turning down applications for credit, even though most applicants would indeed pay their bills. If credit requirements are too rigid, the firm not only loses many immediate sales but may create considerable ill will. A sound credit policy should provide for a limited amount of credit losses. It is the responsibility of the Credit Department to keep these losses within acceptable limits.

MATCHING BAD DEBT LOSSES WITH SALES

> **Remember**
>
> The matching principle attempts to match the amount of expenses incurred with the revenue earned for the same fiscal period.

A basic principle of the accrual basis of accounting is that revenue for a fiscal period be matched with the expenses incurred to earn that revenue. This matching principle is consistent with our earlier presentation of adjusting entries. For example, depreciation represents the allocation of the cost of equipment to the particular periods or years benefited. In making the adjustment, we allocate this expense to that year. Thus, we debit Depreciation Expense, Equipment, and credit Accumulated Depreciation, Equipment. Similarly, when a firm sells merchandise on account to a customer who may eventually refuse to pay the bill for the merchandise, the firm has a bad debt loss potential. The firm must try to match the loss with the revenue earned for the year in which the sale is made.

At the time of the sale, the company does not *know* that it has incurred a loss; it believes that the customer will pay the debt. If it did not, the company would not have extended credit to that customer in the first place. In other words, the firm making the credit sale has increased its revenue account, but it does not know at the time of the sale whether the money earned will be collected. As a matter of fact, the firm will not be certain of the loss until it has repeatedly failed in its attempts to collect the bill. The final recognition of the loss will probably occur many months after the sale. *In order to match the bad debt losses for the year with the sales for the same year, the firm must make an estimate of the losses as a means of providing for them in advance.* The allowance method of accounting for bad debt losses provides the means for matching bad debt losses with the applicable sales in the company's financial statements.

THE ALLOWANCE METHOD OF ACCOUNTING FOR BAD DEBTS

> **LEARNING OBJECTIVE 1**
>
> *Make the adjusting entry to record estimated bad debt losses by using the allowance method of recording bad debts.*

Most big firms use the **allowance method of accounting for bad debt losses** for financial reporting, which is consistent with the accrual method of accounting required by generally accepted accounting principles (GAAP). An adjusting entry is recorded first in the Adjustments columns of the work sheet—much like the adjustment for depreciation. In general journal and T account form, the adjusting entry for the estimated bad debt losses for Huan Company is shown in the following examples.

> **Remember**
>
> With the accrual method of accounting, revenue is recorded when it is earned rather than when it is received.

Date		Description	Post. Ref.	Debit	Credit
20—		Adjusting Entry			
Dec.	31	Bad Debts Expense		1 2 0 0 00	
		Allowance for Doubtful Accounts			1 2 0 0 00

Bad Debts Expense			Allowance for Doubtful Accounts		
+	−		−	+	
Adj.	1,200			Bal.	2,200
				Adj.	1,200
				Bal.	3,400

The purpose of the adjusting entry is to increase Bad Debts Expense by the amount of the estimated loss and to produce a collectible figure for the book value of Accounts Receivable. **Allowance for Doubtful Accounts is classified as a deduction from Accounts Receivable. As such, it is a contra account, similar to Accumulated Depreciation.** Just as the book value of Equipment equals the cost of Equipment minus Accumulated Depreciation, Equipment, the **book value of Accounts Receivable** equals Accounts Receivable minus Allowance for Doubtful Accounts. Accountants also refer to the book value of Accounts Receivable as the **net expected realizable value of Accounts Receivable**.

Because a firm cannot know with certainty which accounts won't be fully collected, it's not possible to credit Accounts Receivable directly. However, on the basis of its experience, a firm is able to estimate what this year's bad debt losses will be. The firm bases its estimate on a year's sales, but it can't say with certainty *which* specific credit sales, by customer name, will not be paid.

Prior to adjustments, the **Bad Debts Expense account has no previous balance, as the account is not used during the fiscal period**. The firm's accountant makes an adjusting entry to increase Bad Debts Expense and immediately closes the account along with all other expense accounts. Allowance for Doubtful Accounts, on the other hand, has a balance that is carried over from previous years and is not closed. Notice where these accounts appear in the partial work sheet shown in Figure 1.

Note that Accounts Receivable is recorded in the debit column, and Allowance for Doubtful Accounts is recorded in the credit column. The $1,200 adjustment is added to the previous credit balance of $2,200, resulting in $3,400 being recorded in the Balance Sheet Credit column. As you can see, Allowance for Doubtful Accounts is handled much like Accumulated Depreciation. Both are recorded as credits in the Adjustments and Balance Sheet columns of the work sheet; also, the adjustments are never reversed because both accounts have previous balances after the first year of operation.

Bad Debts Expense and Allowance for Doubtful Accounts on Financial Statements

The Bad Debts Expense account appears on the income statement as an operating expense. Some firms subdivide operating expenses into selling expenses and general expenses, in which case they list Bad Debts Expense as a general expense. *(Reason: The decision to grant credit is usually a function of the administrative rather than the sales staff.)*

Allowance for Doubtful Accounts is listed immediately below Accounts Receivable in the Current Assets section of the balance sheet, as shown in Figure 2.

The $58,600 ($62,000 − $3,400) represents the anticipated net realizable value of Accounts Receivable; this is also known as the book value of Accounts Receivable. The net realizable value is the amount of cash the seller eventually expects to collect from gross accounts receivable. Allowance for Doubtful Accounts is classified as a contra account, because it is a deduction from an asset.

Using the Allowance Method—Three Ways of Estimating the Amount of Bad Debts Expense

1. Based on the aging of Accounts Receivable
2. Based on a percentage of Accounts Receivable
3. Based on a percentage of net sales or net credit sales

FIGURE 1

Partial work sheet for Huan Company

Account Name	Trial Balance	
	Debit	Credit
Accounts Receivable	62 0 0 0 00	
Allowance for Doubtful Accounts		2 2 0 0 00
Equipment	74 0 0 0 00	
Accumulated Depreciation, Equipment		22 0 0 0 00
Bad Debts Expense		
Depreciation Expense, Equipment		

FIGURE 2

Partial balance sheet for Huan Company

Huan Company
Balance Sheet
December 31, 20—

Assets

Current Assets:		
Cash		$24,000
Notes Receivable		9,000
Accounts Receivable	$62,000	
Less Allowance for Doubtful Accounts	3,400	58,600
Merchandise Inventory		94,000
Prepaid Insurance		600
Total Current Assets		$186,200
Property and Equipment:		
Equipment	$74,000	
Less Accumulated Depreciation	28,000	$46,000

Management—on the basis of its judgment and past experience—has to make a reasonable estimate of the amount of its uncollectible accounts. It stands to reason that any such estimate is modified by business trends. In a period of prosperity and high employment, you can usually expect fewer losses from uncollectible accounts than in a period of recession.

The next question is: "For the adjusting entry, how does management estimate the dollar amount of bad debts expense?" The estimate can be made in several ways. Figure 3 illustrates the adjustment approaches to estimating the amount of bad debts expense.

Adjusting Entry Based on Aging Accounts Receivable

LEARNING OBJECTIVE 1a

Determine the amount of the adjusting entry by aging Accounts Receivable.

The most common technique for estimating the total uncollectible amount of Accounts Receivable is based on **aging of Accounts Receivable**. When a company uses the aging method, each charge customer's account "is aged" by (1) determining the age, in number of days, of each account and (2) determining the number of days the account is past due. The accounts in a company's accounts receivable ledger are listed by name and amount. Columns are set up for various age groups. As an example, we use the accounts receivable of Walen Company. The partial aging schedule is shown in Figure 4.

Huan Company
Work Sheet
For Year Ended December 31, 20—

	Adjustments		Income Statement		Balance Sheet		
	Debit	Credit	Debit	Credit	Debit	Credit	
					62 0 0 0 00		
		(e) 1 2 0 0 00				3 4 0 0 00	
					74 0 0 0 00		
		(h) 6 0 0 0 00				28 0 0 0 00	
	(e) 1 2 0 0 00		1 2 0 0 00				
	(h) 6 0 0 0 00		6 0 0 0 00				

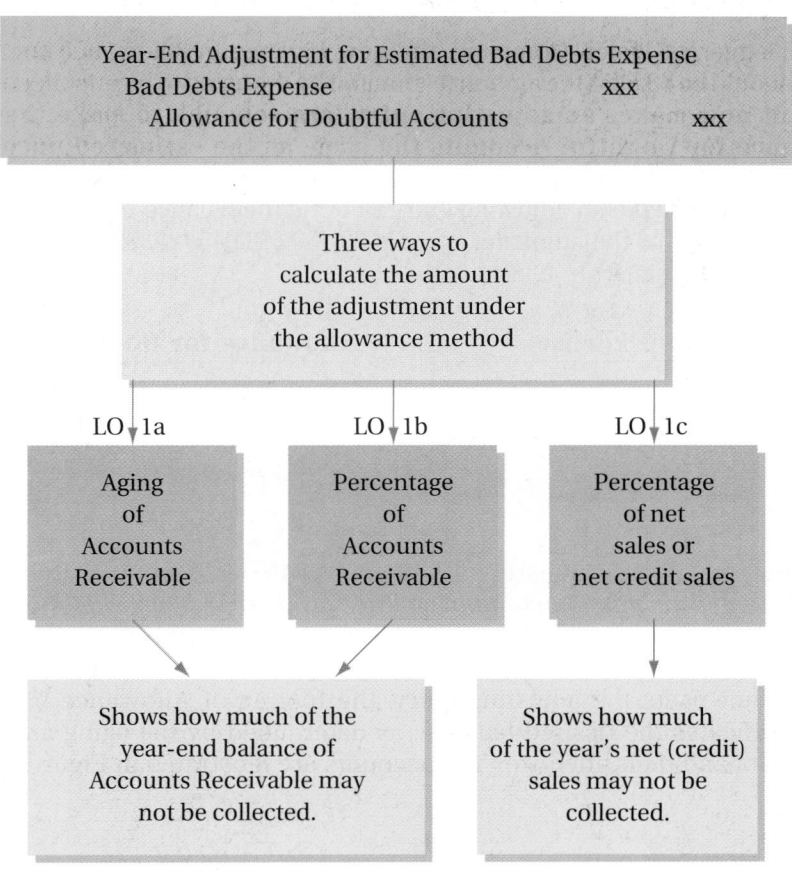

Year-End Adjustment for Estimated Bad Debts Expense
Bad Debts Expense   xxx
    Allowance for Doubtful Accounts   xxx

Three ways to
calculate the amount
of the adjustment under
the allowance method

LO 1a

Aging
of
Accounts
Receivable

LO 1b

Percentage
of
Accounts
Receivable

LO 1c

Percentage
of net
sales or
net credit sales

Shows how much of the
year-end balance of
Accounts Receivable may
not be collected.

Shows how much
of the year's net (credit)
sales may not be
collected.

FIGURE 3

Allowance method:
Three ways of estimating
the amount of bad
debts expense

FIGURE 4

Partial aging schedule

			Days Past Due					
ANALYSIS OF ACCOUNTS RECEIVABLE BY AGE								
Customer Name	Balance	Not Yet Due	1–30	31–60	61–90	91–180	181–365	Over 365
A. Allen	852.00	852.00						
B. Borne	656.00				656.00			
C. Clauson	232.90			232.90				
D. Dalton	834.00	834.00						
E. Essen	433.10			433.10				
Total	94,437.00	78,200.00	8,250.00	3,280.00	1,975.00	1,380.00	892.00	460.00

Based on its past experience, a company can estimate that a given percentage of accounts in each age group will be uncollectible. Next, the accountant multiplies the total amount for each age group by the percentage for that group. This results in the amount estimated to be uncollectible for that group. Let's continue with the Accounts Receivable of Walen Company.

Age of Accounts	Amount	Estimated Percentage Uncollectible	Allowance for Doubtful Accounts
Not due yet	$78,200	2%	$78,200 × 0.02 = $1,564
1 to 30 days	8,250	4	8,250 × 0.04 = 330
31 to 60 days	3,280	10	3,280 × 0.10 = 328
61 to 90 days	1,975	20	1,975 × 0.20 = 395
91 to 180 days	1,380	30	1,380 × 0.30 = 414
181 to 365 days	892	50	892 × 0.50 = 446
Over 365 days	460	80	460 × 0.80 = 368
Total	$94,437		$3,845

In the ledger of Walen Company, the new balance in Allowance for Doubtful Accounts should be $3,845 (the amount estimated by the aging to be uncollectible). **The accountant now makes an adjusting entry large enough to make the balance of Allowance for Doubtful Accounts the same as the estimated uncollectible amount**. Walen Company had a credit balance of $355 in Allowance for Doubtful Accounts. We now make an adjusting entry to bring the balance of the account up to $3,845. The amount of the adjusting entry is $3,490 ($3,845 – $355). This situation is illustrated by T accounts:

Bad Debts Expense		**Allowance for Doubtful Accounts**

	+	−			−	+	
Adj.	3,490					Bal.	355
						Adj.	3,490
						Bal.	3,845

To sum up: The firm estimates that $3,845 of Accounts Receivable is uncollectible. *It now has to bring the balance of Allowance for Doubtful Accounts up to the desired amount of $3,845.* Allowance for Doubtful Accounts has a present credit balance of $355, so the firm adjusts for the difference, $3,490. After the accountant posts the adjusting entry, the footing of Allowance for Doubtful Accounts indicates the desired balance, as determined by the aging analysis. The adjusting data and their effects on the accounts are illustrated in Figure 5.

FIGURE 5

Partial work sheet for Walen Company

Account Name	Trial Balance	
	Debit	Credit
Accounts Receivable	94 4 3 7 00	
Allowance for Doubtful Accounts		3 5 5 00
Bad Debts Expense		

Bad Debts Expense ($3,490) appears on the income statement in the general expense portion of Operating Expenses. Like all expenses, it is closed into Income Summary at the end of the fiscal period. For emphasis, let's repeat the placement of the accounts on the balance sheet.

Walen Company
Balance Sheet
December 31, 20—

Assets

Current Assets:

Cash		$ 9,600
Notes Receivable		4,500
Accounts Receivable	$94,437	
Less Allowance for Doubtful Accounts	3,845	90,592

FYI

Aging of Accounts Receivable is easily accomplished by computer accounting programs.

Adjusting Entry Based on Estimating Bad Debts as a Percentage of Accounts Receivable

Some firms take an average of the actual bad debt losses of previous years as a percentage of Accounts Receivable. For example, we'll use a different company, Raymond Company. The firm calculated the amount of the adjustment for uncollectible accounts as follows:

1b LEARNING OBJECTIVE

Determine the amount of the adjusting entry by using a percentage of Accounts Receivable.

End of Year	Balance of Accounts Receivable	Total Actual Losses from Accounts Receivable (Accounts Receivable Written Off)
2010	$ 45,000	$1,640
2011	57,000	1,428
2012	49,000	1,572
	$151,000	$4,640

The firm's average loss over three consecutive years is:

$$\frac{\$4,640}{\$151,000} = 0.03 = \underline{\underline{3\%}}$$

Assume that, at the end of 2013, the balance of Accounts Receivable is $60,100 and the credit balance of Allowance for Doubtful Accounts is $285. The amount of

Walen Company
Work Sheet
For Year Ended December 31, 20—

Adjustments		Income Statement		Balance Sheet	
Debit	Credit	Debit	Credit	Debit	Credit
				94 4 3 7 00	
	(a) 3 4 9 0 00				3 8 4 5 00
(a) 3 4 9 0 00		3 4 9 0 00			

Ratio Analysis

Accounts Receivable Turnover

Accounts receivable turnover is the number of times charge accounts are turned over (paid off) during a given year. A turnover implies a sale on account followed by the cash collection of the amount owed.

$$\text{Accounts Receivable Turnover} = \frac{\text{Net Sales on Account}}{\text{Average Accounts Receivable}}$$

$$\text{Average Accounts Receivable} = \frac{\text{Beginning Accounts Receivable} + \text{Ending Accounts Receivable}}{2}$$

Going back to Southern Office Furniture, let's assume the following information for 2011 and 2010.

	2011	2010
Net sales on account (from the sales journal)	$330,000	$302,000
Beginning accounts receivable (from Accounts Receivable account)	39,680	37,500
Ending accounts receivable (from Accounts Receivable account)	45,840	39,680

2011

$$\text{Average Accounts Receivable} = \frac{\$39,680 + \$45,840}{2} = \frac{\$85,520}{2} = \$42,760$$

$$\text{Account Receivable Turnover} = \frac{\$330,000}{\$42,760} = \underline{7.72} \text{ times per year}$$

2010

$$\text{Average Accounts Receivable} = \frac{\$37,500 + \$39,680}{2} = \frac{\$77,180}{2} = \$38,590$$

$$\text{Accounts Receivable Turnover} = \frac{\$302,000}{\$38,590} = \underline{7.83} \text{ times per year}$$

A lower turnover rate indicates that a firm is experiencing greater difficulty in collecting charge accounts. In addition, more investment capital is tied up in accounts receivable.

The receivable turnover deteriorated slightly from 7.83 in 2010 to 7.72 in 2011, possibly because the seller granted easier credit terms or the buyers incurred cash flow problems because of a declining economy. From the end of 2010 to the end of 2011, the receivables balance increased almost 16% from $39,680 to $45,840. However, over the same period, net sales increased only 9.3%. This trend would be of concern to management and owners.

SMALL BUSINESS SUCCESS

Collecting on Accounts Receivable

Collecting on accounts receivables is an extremely important process for any small business. Without the ability to successfully collect accounts receivables, many businesses will eventually end up without adequate cash flow and possibly even go bankrupt.

Certain steps should be taken before granting customers credit. These steps include:

- *Screening customers carefully.* This includes confirming employment and income information, running a credit check on the customer, and ensuring that the company has correct contact information for the potential credit customer.
- *Being aware of the law regarding accepting checks.* Many small businesses will no longer accept checks due to the amount of NSF checks written by customers. NSF checks are checks that are written by customers but are not honored by the bank because of insufficient funds in the customers' accounts. If the business decides to accept checks, they should take the time to be aware of the law regarding NSF checks. Each state has its own laws regarding the potential civil and criminal penalties related to NSF checks.
- *Having an established credit policy.* Establishing a credit policy before granting credit will help to ensure successful collection on accounts. A credit policy could involve such items as sending invoices out immediately after sales and

sending past-due notices when invoices are 30, 60, and/or 90 days old. Calling customers of past-due accounts to follow up on balances and charging interest on past-due accounts are also good policies.

After an account is 90 days past due, the company should make a decision about further collection procedures. The company has two choices: either hiring a collection agency or taking the customer to court.

When a business hires a collection agency, the collection agency will work to collect the past due amount. The business, typically, is not required to handle the account any further. If the collection agency is able to collect the account, it will keep a portion (possibly up to 50%) of the amount collected before turning over the remaining amount to the business.

Another option is for the business to take the customer to court. With this option, the business would be best served by hiring an attorney that could guide the business throughout the legal process.

Throughout the collection of accounts receivable, it is important that the business is aware of the Fair Debt Collection Practices Act (FDCPA) that is enforced by the Federal Trade Commission (FTC). The FDCPA protects consumers from abusive, unfair, and/or deceptive practices when dealing with debt collectors. In addition, the act requires that businesses follow certain rules when contacting the customer.

Accounts Receivable the company estimates to be uncollectible is $1,803 ($60,100 × 0.03). Since $1,803 is the desired balance, the amount of the adjustment is $1,518 ($1,803 − $285). As in the case of aging Accounts Receivable, when you figure the adjustment for bad debts as a percentage of Accounts Receivable, **you make an**

adjusting entry to bring the balance of Allowance for Doubtful Accounts up to the desired amount. Notice how the adjusting entry looks:

Bad Debts Expense			Allowance for Doubtful Accounts		
+	–		–	+	
Adj. 1,518				Bal.	285
				Adj.	1,518
				Bal.	1,803

You would then record the adjustment in the work sheet as shown in Figure 6. Let's examine a portion of the balance sheet derived from the work sheet.

Raymond Company
Balance Sheet
December 31, 2013

Assets		
Current Assets:		
Cash		$18,362
Notes Receivable		2,000
Accounts Receivable	$60,100	
Less Allowance for Doubtful Accounts	1,803	58,297

In this statement, the book value of Accounts Receivable is shown as $58,297 ($60,100 – $1,803).

Adjusting Entry Based on Estimating Bad Debts as a Percentage of Net Sales or Net Credit Sales

Some businesses prefer a simplified method for determining the amount of the adjustment for Bad Debts Expense. They multiply the current year's sales by a set percentage rate and then record the adjusting entry for that amount. We'll use a different company as an illustration, Paschal Company.

Estimate Based on Net Sales

For example, the actual losses from sales on account for Paschal Company have averaged approximately 1 percent of net sales (Sales less Sales Returns and Allowances and less Sales Discounts). The firm makes virtually all sales on credit. Based on this information, the company computes the amount of the adjustment for bad debts expense as 1 percent of net sales.

FIGURE 6

Partial work sheet for Raymond Company

Account Name	Trial Balance		
	Debit	Credit	
Cash	18 3 6 2 00		
Notes Receivable	2 0 0 0 00		
Accounts Receivable	60 1 0 0 00		
Allowance for Doubtful Accounts		2 8 5 00	
Bad Debts Expense			

The figure for net sales is shown in the following partial income statement:

Paschal Company
Income Statement
For Year Ended June 30, 20—

Revenue from Sales:			
Sales		$712,000	
Less: Sales Returns and Allowances	$29,000		
Sales Discounts	1,500	30,500	
Net Sales			$681,500

One percent of net sales is $6,815 ($681,500 × 0.01), **so the firm uses this amount directly for the adjusting entry, adding it to both accounts,** as shown in the following T accounts. In contrast to the previously illustrated aging and percentage of accounts receivable methods, **the sales methods ignore any existing balance in the allowance account to calculate Bad Debts Expense.**

Bad Debts Expense			**Allowance for Doubtful Accounts**		
+	–		–	+	
Adj.	6,815			Bal.	310
				Adj.	6,815
				Bal.	7,125

Figure 7 shows how to record the adjustment in the work sheet. A portion of the balance sheet is as follows:

Paschal Company
Balance Sheet
June 30, 20—

Assets		
Current Assets:		
Accounts Receivable	$64,500	
Less Allowance for Doubtful Accounts	7,125	57,375

> **Remember**
>
> Companies may change the percentage used for estimating bad debts based on changes in the economy. For example, a company wouldn't use the same percentage for estimating bad debts in a year when the economy was weak as they would in a year when the economy was strong.

Estimate Based on Net Credit Sales

Many companies that sell on both a cash and a credit basis compute the amount of their adjustment for bad debts on net credit sales only. As an example, we'll use

Raymond Company
Work Sheet
For Year Ended December 31, 2013

Adjustments		Income Statement		Balance Sheet	
Debit	Credit	Debit	Credit	Debit	Credit
				18 3 6 2 00	
				2 0 0 0 00	
				60 1 0 0 00	
	(e) 1 5 1 8 00				1 8 0 3 00
(e) 1 5 1 8 00		1 5 1 8 00			

Account Name	Trial Balance		
	Debit	Credit	
Accounts Receivable	64 5 0 0 00		
Allowance for Doubtful Accounts		3 1 0 00	
Sales		712 0 0 0 00	
Sales Returns and Allowances	29 0 0 0 00		
Sales Discounts	1 5 0 0 00		
Bad Debts Expense			

a different business firm, Snow Company. The business's credit sales, recorded in a sales journal, total $736,000. Sales Returns and Allowances and Sales Discounts relating to credit sales are $25,200 and $5,200, respectively. Snow Company has a credit balance in the Allowance for Doubtful Accounts of $356 and records the adjustment for bad debts at ¾ percent of net credit sales. Look at the calculation and adjustment that follow:

Credit (charge) sales		$736,000
Less: Sales Returns and Allowances	$25,200	
Sales Discounts	5,200	30,400
Net credit sales		$705,600

$ 705,600
× 0.0075
$ 5,292

By T accounts, the amount of the adjustment is added to both accounts as shown:

Bad Debts Expense		Allowance for Doubtful Accounts	
+	−	−	+
Adj. 5,292			Bal. 356
			Adj. 5,292
			Bal. 5,648

Note that a firm using this simplified method multiplies net sales or net credit sales by the given percentage in order to determine the amount of the adjustment. **The present balance of Allowance for Doubtful Accounts is not involved in determining the amount of the adjustment**. If the given percentage does not adequately provide for the firm's losses (that is, if it yields either too little or too much), the firm merely changes the percentage.

CLOSING THE BAD DEBTS EXPENSE ACCOUNT

Up to now, we have seen that the firm's accountant first records the adjusting entry for bad debts in the appropriate columns of the work sheet. The T accounts for Snow Company are repeated here.

Paschal Company
Work Sheet
For Year Ended December 30, 20—

Adjustments		Income Statement		Balance Sheet	
Debit	Credit	Debit	Credit	Debit	Credit
				64 5 0 0 00	
	(e) 6 8 1 5 00				7 1 2 5 00
			712 0 0 0 00		
		29 0 0 0 00			
		1 5 0 0 00			
(e) 6 8 1 5 00		6 8 1 5 00			

Bad Debts Expense				Allowance for Doubtful Accounts		
	+	−			−	+
Adj.	5,292				Bal.	356
					Adj.	5,292
					Bal.	5,648

Next, the accountant closes Bad Debts Expense, along with all other expenses, into the Income Summary account. **The Bad Debts Expense account is not used during the year, so the only entries in it are the adjusting entry and the closing entry**. This represents the beginning and the end of Bad Debts Expense for the fiscal period. In other words, the only entry in Bad Debts Expense is the adjusting entry, and, as we said, this account is immediately closed out. After the adjusting entry and closing entry have been posted, the accounts look like this:

Bad Debts Expense				Allowance for Doubtful Accounts		
	+	−			−	+
Adj.	5,292	Clos.	5,292		Bal.	356
					Adj.	5,292
					Bal.	5,648

Allowance for Doubtful Accounts

It is apparent that Allowance for Doubtful Accounts remains open. Rather than have the balance continually increase because of the successive adjustments on the credit side of the account, the accountant uses the debit side of the account to write off charge accounts that are considered uncollectible.

Consider Allowance for Doubtful Accounts as a reservoir: We fill it up at the end of the year through the medium of the adjusting entry by crediting the account. During the following year, we drain off the reservoir through the medium of write-offs by debiting the account. To avoid the possibility of the reservoir's "running dry," *the accountant should make the adjusting entry large enough to provide for all possible write-offs.*

> **Remember**
>
> Allowance for Doubtful Accounts increases when the adjustment is made at the end of the year (credit) and decreases as write-offs occur during the year (debits).

WRITING OFF ACCOUNTS AS UNCOLLECTIBLE

LEARNING OBJECTIVE **2**

Journalize the entries to write off accounts receivable as being uncollectible, using the allowance method of accounting for bad debt losses.

Entry to Write Off a Charge Account in Full

Suppose that, after all attempts to collect a customer's debt have failed, a firm decides that the account is definitely uncollectible. In such a case, the firm should write off the amount due. Let's use the write-off of an uncollectible customer from Paschal Company. Assume that in July the firm decides that the $891.40 account of a customer, B. Logan, is uncollectible. The accountant records the write-off by making the following entry:

			GENERAL JOURNAL				PAGE 116	
Date		Description	Post. Ref.	Debit			Credit	
20—								
July	15	Allowance for Doubtful Accounts		8 9 1 40				
		Accounts Receivable, B. Logan					8 9 1 40	
		Wrote off the account as uncollectible.						

By T accounts, the entry looks like this:

Accounts Receivable			Allowance for Doubtful Accounts		
+	−		−	+	
Bal. 64,500.00	July 15 891.40		July 15 891.40	Bal.	7,125.00
Bal. 63,608.60			(Logan's write-off)		
				Bal.	6,233.60

The accountant also posts the entry to the account of B. Logan in the accounts receivable subsidiary ledger.

NAME	B. Logan						
ADDRESS	2137 Bancroft Road						
	Boston, MA 02101						

Date		Item	Post. Ref.	Debit	Credit	Balance
20—						
June	30	Balance	✓			8 9 1 40
July	15	Written off	J116		8 9 1 40	————

Note that the entry just shown does not change the net realizable value or book value of Accounts Receivable.

Account Name	Balances Before Write-off	Balances After Write-off
Accounts Receivable	$64,500.00	$63,608.60
Less Allowance for Doubtful Accounts	7,125.00	6,233.60
Book value (net realizable value)	$57,375.00	$57,375.00

Remember

An entry to write off an account receivable does not change the book value of Accounts Receivable because Accounts Receivable and Allowance for Doubtful Accounts are reduced by the same amount.

Also note that **the entry to write off an account does not involve an expense account**. The adjusting entry, which was made on June 30, provides for the expense. The estimated expense was recorded *during the year in which the sale was made*, even though this account is written off in a later year.

Entry to Write Off a Charge Account Paid in Part

Sometimes a partial payment is involved in a write-off of an account. When this happens, it may be due to a bankruptcy settlement. The federal laws governing **bankruptcy** legally excuse a debtor from paying off certain obligations. For example, on April 21, Paschal Company received 10 cents on the dollar (10 percent) in settlement of a $683 account owed by its customer R. L. Renk, a bankrupt customer. In general journal form, the entry is as follows:

When a company does not have adequate cash to pay its bills, it may file for bankruptcy protection to reorganize or simply sell off its inventory and other assets and go out of business. If the company files for bankruptcy protection to reorganize, it may pay off only part of its debt to its creditors.

Date		Description	Post. Ref.	Debit	Credit
20—					
Apr.	21	Cash		6 8 30	
		Allowance for Doubtful Accounts		6 1 4 70	
		Accounts Receivable, R. L. Renk			6 8 3 00
		Settlement in bankruptcy, wrote off			
		account balance as uncollectible.			
		($683 × 0.10 = $68.30)			

Compound Entry to Write Off a Number of Accounts as Uncollectible

Rather than writing off each uncollectible account separately during the year, a firm may write off a number of accounts at the end of the year by using a compound entry. For example, assume that on December 31, Olney Company writes off the following accounts of charge customers as being uncollectible: M. Bell, $1,151.27;

O. Cox, $1,138.10; C. Lync, $1,112.00; and D. Ross, $1,175.00. The accountant records the write-offs by making the following entry:

Date	Description	Post. Ref.	Debit	Credit
20—				
Dec. 31	Allowance for Doubtful Accounts		4 5 7 6 37	
	Accounts Receivable, M. Bell			1 1 5 1 27
	Accounts Receivable, O. Cox			1 1 3 8 10
	Accounts Receivable, C. Lync			1 1 1 2 00
	Accounts Receivable, D. Ross			1 1 7 5 00
	Wrote off the accounts as			
	uncollectible.			

Write-Offs Seldom Agree with Previous Estimates

The total amount of Accounts Receivable written off during a given year does not ordinarily agree with the estimate of uncollectible accounts previously debited to Bad Debts Expense and credited to Allowance for Doubtful Accounts. In the usual situation, the amounts written off as uncollectible turn out to be less than the estimated amount. At the end of a given year, there is normally a credit balance in Allowance for Doubtful Accounts.

However, if the amounts written off are greater than the estimated amounts, Allowance for Doubtful Accounts temporarily has a debit balance. The debit balance is eliminated by the adjusting entry at the end of the year, which results in a credit to, or increase in, Allowance for Doubtful Accounts.

COLLECTION OF ACCOUNTS PREVIOUSLY WRITTEN OFF

LEARNING OBJECTIVE 3

Journalize entries to reinstate accounts receivable previously written off, using the allowance method.

Occasionally an account that was previously written off as uncollectible may later be recovered, either in part or in full. In such cases, the firm's accountant restores the account to the books, or reinstates it, by an entry that is the exact opposite of the write-off entry.

As an example, Parsons Company sells merchandise on account to P. Nichols for $585 on May 5, 2010. Here is the entry in general journal form:

Date	Description	Post. Ref.	Debit	Credit
2010				
May 5	Accounts Receivable, P. Nichols		5 8 5 00	
	Sales			5 8 5 00
	Sold merchandise on account,			
	2/10, n/30.			

Parsons Company makes many unsuccessful attempts to collect the Nichols debt, and the **statute of limitations** finally expires. Since the statute of limitations is set at three years in many states, let's say that Parsons Company has not been able to collect any money at all from Nichols during a three-year period and that Nichols has remained within the jurisdiction of the court. This means that the debt is outlawed by the statute of limitations. In other words, the firm cannot use the courts to force the debtor to pay up. Accordingly, three years later, on June 10, the accountant for Parsons Company writes off the account of P. Nichols as uncollectible.

Date		Description	Post. Ref.	Debit	Credit
2013					
June	10	Allowance for Doubtful Accounts		5 8 5 00	
		Accounts Receivable, P. Nichols			5 8 5 00
		Wrote off the account as			
		uncollectible.			

But on September 15, 2013, P. Nichols suddenly pays her account in full! The entry to reinstate the account is the reverse of the entry used to write off the account.

Date		Description	Post. Ref.	Debit	Credit
2013					
Sept.	15	Accounts Receivable, P. Nichols		5 8 5 00	
		Allowance for Doubtful Accounts			5 8 5 00
		Reinstated the account.			

The way is now clear to record the collection of the account.

Date		Description	Post. Ref.	Debit	Credit
	15	Cash		5 8 5 00	
		Accounts Receivable, P. Nichols			5 8 5 00
		Collected account in full.			

Now suppose instead that P. Nichols had gone into bankruptcy and settled her account with Parsons Company by paying it 5 cents on the dollar. Parsons Company would realize that there was no hope of collecting any more, so the accountant would reinstate the account only for the amount collected, like this:

Date		Description	Post. Ref.	Debit	Credit
2013					
Sept.	15	Accounts Receivable, P. Nichols		2 9 25	
		Allowance for Doubtful Accounts			2 9 25
		Settlement in bankruptcy, 5 percent			
		of $585, so reinstated the account			
		to the extent of the settlement.			
		($585 × 0.05 = $29.25)			

The subsequent entry to record the cash receipt would be as follows:

Date	Description	Post. Ref.	Debit	Credit
15	Cash		2 9 25	
	Accounts Receivable, P. Nichols			2 9 25
	Settlement in bankruptcy,			
	5 percent of $585.			

SPECIFIC CHARGE-OFF OF BAD DEBTS

The **specific charge-off method of accounting for bad debt losses** is a simpler system for writing off charge accounts determined to be uncollectible. No adjusting entry is made because there is no attempt to provide for bad debt losses in advance or to match revenue with related expenses. Instead, when a firm decides that a specific customer account is never going to be collected, the accountant makes an entry in the general journal debiting Bad Debts Expense and crediting Accounts Receivable. Thus Allowance for Doubtful Accounts does not exist in the firm's chart of accounts. Traditionally, this method has been used primarily by small companies and professional enterprises. As we stated previously, the specific charge-off method is required for federal income tax reporting, but is not allowed under GAAP. We'll use a different business as an illustration, Roly Company.

For example, on April 16, 2010, Roly Company sold merchandise on account to H. R. Mitchell for $182.10, making the following entry in the general journal:

Date		Description	Post. Ref.	Debit	Credit
2010					
Apr.	16	Accounts Receivable, H. R. Mitchell		1 8 2 10	
		Sales			1 8 2 10
		Sold merchandise on account,			
		n/30.			

Mitchell never paid his bill. Finally, three years later, on September 1, the account is written off as follows:

Date		Description	Post. Ref.	Debit	Credit
2013					
Sept.	1	Bad Debts Expense		1 8 2 10	
		Accounts Receivable, H. R. Mitchell			1 8 2 10
		Wrote off an uncollectible account.			

By T accounts, the entries look like this:

Accounts Receivable					Sales					Bad Debts Expense		
	+	−			−	+					+	−
2010		2013				2010			2013			
Apr. 16	182.10	Sept. 1	182.10			Apr. 16	182.10		Sept. 1	182.10		

You can see that revenue does not match expenses for a particular year. Roly Company counted the original sale of $182.10 in 2010, thereby overstating true revenue for that year. It counted Bad Debts Expense three years later in 2013, thereby overstating expenses for that year. Note that Roly Company did not use the account titled Allowance for Doubtful Accounts. In other words, if you wait until you consider an account to be a bad debt and then write it off, with no provision for realistically estimating the losses in advance, you are making unrealistic assumptions. On the balance sheet, Accounts Receivable is stated at the gross amount only; there is no book value or net realizable value. As a result, both assets and owners' equity are overstated.

The specific charge-off method is simple to use but can cause inaccurate matching of revenue and expenses. Nevertheless, this method is used for tax purposes by most businesses, even though they may use the allowance method for financial reporting.

To reinstate an account previously written or charged off, let's say that on May 2, 2014, H. R. Mitchell returns and pays his $182.10 bill. We show the entries in general journal form.

5 LEARNING OBJECTIVE
Journalize entries to reinstate accounts receivable previously written off, using the specific charge-off method.

Date		Description	Post. Ref.	Debit	Credit
2014					
May	2	Accounts Receivable, H. R. Mitchell		1 8 2 10	
		Bad Debts Recovered			1 8 2 10
		Reinstated the account.			
	2	Cash		1 8 2 10	
		Accounts Receivable, H. R. Mitchell			1 8 2 10
		Collected account in full.			

With T accounts, the entries look like this:

Accounts Receivable					Bad Debts Recovered					Cash		
	+	−			−	+					+	−
2014		2014				2014			2014			
May 2	182.10	May 2	182.10			May 2	182.10		May 2	182.10		

For a small company that uses the specific charge-off method alone, the account entitled Bad Debts Recovered is classified as a revenue account and would be listed in the Other Income section of the income statement. The Accounts Receivable account was placed back on the books, so that the firm would have a record of H. R. Mitchell's account. Note that this method of accounting is not consistent with the accrual method. The following chart illustrates a comparison of journal entries involved in the allowance method and the specific charge-off method.

Comparison of Two Methods of Adjustment, Write-Off, Reinstatement, and Collection		
	Allowance Method	**Specific Charge-Off Method**
Original sale	Accounts Receivable, J. Smith Sales	Accounts Receivable, J. Smith Sales
Adjustment	Bad Debts Expense Allowance for Doubtful Accounts	No entry required
Write-off	Allowance for Doubtful Accounts Accounts Receivable, J. Smith	Bad Debts Expense Accounts Receivable, J. Smith
Reinstatement	Accounts Receivable, J. Smith Allowance for Doubtful Accounts	Accounts Receivable, J. Smith Bad Debts Recovered (Other Income)
Collection	Cash Accounts Receivable, J. Smith	Cash Accounts Receivable, J. Smith

FEDERAL INCOME TAX REQUIREMENT

All firms except financial institutions are required to use the specific charge-off method for reporting on their federal income tax returns. A separate record should be maintained for reporting bad debt losses. For each account charged off, this record must contain the following:

1. A description of the debt, including the amount, and the date it became due
2. The name of the debtor
3. The efforts that have been made to collect the debt
4. Why it has been decided that the debt is worthless

CHAPTER REVIEW

Study & Practice

1   LEARNING OBJECTIVE

Make the adjusting entry to record estimated bad debt losses by using the allowance method of recording bad debts.

The adjusting entry is a debit to Bad Debts Expense and a credit to Allowance for Doubtful Accounts.

LEARNING OBJECTIVE

1a

Determine the amount of the adjusting entry by aging Accounts Receivable.

Classify each charge customer's account according to the number of days past due (30 days, 60 days, and so on). Multiply the total for each time period by a given percentage deemed to be uncollectible, and sum the totals. Assuming that Allowance for Doubtful Accounts has a credit balance, subtract the amount of the credit balance from the amount estimated to be uncollectible to get the amount of the adjusting entry.

PRACTICE EXERCISE 1a

Watts Company uses the aging method of estimating bad debts as of December 31, the end of the fiscal year. An aging schedule reveals the following:

Age of Accounts	Amount	Estimated Percentage Uncollectible	Allowance for Doubtful Accounts
Not due yet	$ 82,500	1%	$82,500 × 0.01 = $ 825.00
1 to 30 days	10,675	2	10,675 × 0.02 = 213.50
31 to 60 days	6,720	4	6,720 × 0.04 = 268.80
61 to 90 days	4,200	10	4,200 × 0.10 = 420.00
91 to 180 days	2,850	30	2,850 × 0.30 = 855.00
181 to 365 days	1,125	50	1,125 × 0.50 = 562.50
Over 365 days	840	60	840 × 0.60 = 504.00
Total	$108,910		$3,648.80

Assume that the credit balance of Allowance for Doubtful Accounts is $455. Journalize the adjusting entry for estimated credit losses on December 31.

PRACTICE EXERCISE 1a SOLUTION

Date		Description	Post. Ref.	Debit	Credit
20—		Adjusting Entry			
Dec.	31	Bad Debts Expense		3 1 9 3 80	
		Allowance for Doubtful Accounts			3 1 9 3 80
		($3,648.80 – $455)			

Bad Debts Expense		
	+	–
Adj.	3,193.80	

Allowance for Doubtful Accounts		
	–	+
	Bal.	455.00
	Adj.	3,193.80
	Bal.	3,648.80

LEARNING OBJECTIVE

1b

Determine the amount of the adjusting entry by using a percentage of Accounts Receivable.

Multiply the balance of Accounts Receivable by the given percentage. Next, assuming that Allowance for Doubtful Accounts has a credit balance, subtract the amount of the credit balance from the percentage amount to get the amount of the adjusting entry.

PRACTICE EXERCISE 1b

James Company uses the allowance method of estimating losses from bad debts. James Company considers estimated losses to be 3 percent of Accounts Receivable. On December 31, the Accounts Receivable balance was $48,230, and Allowance for Doubtful Accounts had a credit balance of $320. Journalize the adjusting entry to record the estimated bad debt losses.

PRACTICE EXERCISE 1b SOLUTION

Date		Description	Post. Ref.	Debit	Credit
20—		Adjusting Entry			
Dec.	31	Bad Debts Expense		1 1 2 6 90	
		Allowance for Doubtful Accounts			1 1 2 6 90
		[($48,230 × 0.03) − $320]			

Bad Debts Expense

	+	−
Adj.	1,126.90	

Allowance for Doubtful Accounts

	−	+	
		Bal.	320.00
		Adj.	1,126.90
		Bal.	1,446.90

1c LEARNING OBJECTIVE

Calculate the amount of the adjusting entry by using a percentage of net sales or net credit sales.

Multiply the amount of net sales or net credit sales by the given percentage and make the adjusting entry for the amount determined.

PRACTICE EXERCISE 1c

Wilkes Company uses the allowance method of estimating losses due to bad debts. A partial income statement for the company follows.

Wilkes Company
Income Statement
For Year Ended December 31, 20—

Revenue from Sales:			
Sales			$489,000
Less: Sales Returns and Allowances		$25,000	
Sales Discounts		925	25,925
Net Sales			$463,075

The company estimates that bad debt losses will be ¾ percent of net sales. Assume the Allowance for Doubtful Accounts account has a credit balance of $275. Journalize the adjusting entry to record the estimated bad debt losses.

PRACTICE EXERCISE 1c SOLUTION

Date		Description	Post. Ref.	Debit	Credit
20—		Adjusting Entry			
Dec.	31	Bad Debts Expense		3 4 7 3 06	
		Allowance for Doubtful Accounts			3 4 7 3 06
		($463,075 × 0.0075)			

Bad Debts Expense

	+	−
Adj.	3,473.06	

Allowance for Doubtful Accounts

	−	+	
		Bal.	275.00
		Adj.	3,473.06
		Bal.	3,748.06

2 LEARNING OBJECTIVE

Journalize the entries to write off accounts receivable as being uncollectible, using the allowance method of accounting for bad debt losses.

Debit Allowance for Doubtful Accounts and credit Accounts Receivable.

PRACTICE EXERCISE 2

On June 15, the account balance of H. Walker of $1,262 is written off by Story's Office Supplies. Journalize the write-off of H. Walker's account, using the allowance method.

PRACTICE EXERCISE 2 SOLUTION

GENERAL JOURNAL   PAGE 116

Date		Description	Post. Ref.	Debit	Credit
20—					
June	15	Allowance for Doubtful Accounts		1 2 6 2 00	
		Accounts Receivable, H. Walker			1 2 6 2 00
		Wrote off the account as			
		uncollectible.			

3 LEARNING OBJECTIVE

Journalize entries to reinstate accounts receivable previously written off, using the allowance method.

Debit Accounts Receivable and credit Allowance for Doubtful Accounts (the opposite of a write-off).

PRACTICE EXERCISE 3

Using the information from Practice Exercise 2, assume that on December 20, H. Walker pays his account in full. Journalize the entry to reinstate H. Walker's account and the payment of his account in full, using the allowance method.

PRACTICE EXERCISE 3 SOLUTION

Date		Description	Post. Ref.	Debit	Credit
20—					
Dec.	20	Accounts Receivable, H. Walker		1 2 6 2 00	
		Allowance for Doubtful Accounts			1 2 6 2 00
		Reinstated the account.			
	20	Cash		1 2 6 2 00	
		Accounts Receivable, H. Walker			1 2 6 2 00
		Collected account in full.			

4 **LEARNING OBJECTIVE**
Journalize the entries to write off accounts receivable as being uncollectible, using the specific charge-off method.

Debit Bad Debts Expense and credit Accounts Receivable.

PRACTICE EXERCISE 4

Using the information from Practice Exercise 2, journalize the write-off of H. Walker's account, using the specific charge-off method.

PRACTICE EXERCISE 4 SOLUTION

Date		Description	Post. Ref.	Debit	Credit
20—					
June	15	Bad Debts Expense		1 2 6 2 00	
		Accounts Receivable, H. Walker			1 2 6 2 00
		Wrote off an uncollectible			
		account.			

5 **LEARNING OBJECTIVE**
Journalize entries to reinstate accounts receivable previously written off, using the specific charge-off method.

Debit Accounts Receivable and credit Bad Debts Recovered.

PRACTICE EXERCISE 5

Using the information from Practice Exercise 2, reinstate the account of H. Walker and collect the amount due on December 20, using the specific charge-off method.

PRACTICE EXERCISE 5 SOLUTION

Date		Description	Post. Ref.	Debit	Credit
20—					
Dec.	20	Accounts Receivable, H. Walker		1 2 6 2 00	
		Bad Debts Recovered			1 2 6 2 00
		Reinstated the account.			
	20	Cash		1 2 6 2 00	
		Accounts Receivable, H. Walker			1 2 6 2 00
		Collected account in full.			

Glossary

Aging of Accounts Receivable To analyze the accounts receivable by classifying the outstanding balance of each charge customer's account according to the amount of time it has been outstanding. Multiply the total for each time period by a percentage deemed to be uncollectible and sum the totals to determine the balance of Allowance for Doubtful Accounts. (p. 602)

Allowance method of accounting for bad debt losses A method that requires an adjusting entry to debit Bad Debts Expense and to credit Allowance for Doubtful Accounts to match losses from uncollectible accounts with sales of the same period. Write-offs of uncollectible accounts are debited to Allowance for Doubtful Accounts and credited to Accounts Receivable. (p. 600)

Bankruptcy A condition governed by federal law in which a debtor is excused from certain obligations incurred. (p. 613)

Book value of Accounts Receivable The balance of Accounts Receivable after deducting the balance of Allowance for Doubtful Accounts; also called the *net expected realizable value of Accounts Receivable.*

The amount of cash expected to be collected eventually from gross receivables. (p. 601)

Net expected realizable value of Accounts Receivable The balance of Accounts Receivable after deducting the balance of Allowance for Doubtful Accounts; also called the *book value of Accounts Receivable.* The amount of cash expected to be collected eventually from gross receivables. (p. 601)

Specific charge-off method of accounting for bad debt losses A method of recognizing bad debts that requires no adjusting entry. The accountant debits Bad Debts Expense and credits Accounts Receivable. This method is required for federal income tax reporting but is not allowed under GAAP. (p. 616)

Statute of limitations Laws that limit the period of time in which legal action may be taken; with regard to bad debts, laws limiting the period of time during which the courts may force a debtor to pay a debt, usually three years for charge accounts. (p. 614)

CHAPTER ASSIGNMENTS

Discussion Questions

1. What is meant by aging of Accounts Receivable?
2. When an account is written off under the allowance method of accounting for bad debts, why doesn't the book value of Accounts Receivable decrease?
3. Explain how the book value of Accounts Receivable is calculated.
4. Describe the concept of Allowance for Doubtful Accounts, how it comes into existence, and what happens to it during the accounting period.
5. Suppose that the estimate of bad debts is based on the aging method and that Allowance for Doubtful Accounts has a debit balance. Explain how this situation is handled in terms of accounting procedure.
6. If the allowance method of accounting for bad debts is used to determine the amount of the adjusting entry, explain the difference between using a percentage of Accounts Receivable and a percentage of net sales.
7. Discuss why the allowance method of handling bad debts is considered more in accordance with GAAP than the specific charge-off method. Is it ever acceptable to use the specific charge-off method?
8. Assume that a customer's account was written off as uncollectible and is paid at a later date. What journal entries are made on the seller's books using the allowance method? What entry is made on the buyer's books?

Exercises

PRACTICE EXERCISE 1a

EXERCISE 15-1 Norris Company uses the allowance method of estimating losses from bad debts. Management analyzed its accounts receivable balances on December 31 and determined the following aged balances:

Age of Accounts	Amount	Estimated Percentage Uncollectible	Allowance for Doubtful Accounts
Not due yet	$125,000	1%	
31 to 60 days	18,000	2	
61 to 120 days	10,000	5	
121 to 365 days	2,400	30	
Over 365 days	3,800	60	
	$159,200		

Compute the estimate of the amount of uncollectible accounts. Write the adjusting entry for estimated credit losses on December 31. The credit balance of Allowance for Doubtful Accounts is $3,120.

PRACTICE EXERCISE 1b

EXERCISE 15-2 Grable Company uses the allowance method of estimating losses from bad debts. Grable Company considers estimated losses to be 3 percent of Accounts Receivable. On December 31, the Accounts Receivable balance was $63,000, and Allowance for Doubtful Accounts had a credit balance of $320. Journalize the adjusting entry to record the estimated bad debt losses.

EXERCISE 15-3 Estrella Company uses the allowance method of estimating losses due to bad debts. On December 31, before any adjustments have been recorded, the ledger contains the following balances:

PRACTICE EXERCISE 1c

Sales	$180,000
Sales Returns and Allowances	27,000

The company estimates that bad debt losses will be ¾ percent of net sales. Journalize the adjusting entry to record the estimated bad debt losses. The Allowance for Doubtful Accounts account has a credit balance of $320.

EXERCISE 15-4 Gray Company uses the allowance method of handling losses due to bad debts. Gray Company's Accounts Receivable account has a balance of $82,000. Net sales for the year total $104,000. Write the adjusting entry to record the estimated bad debt losses under each of the following conditions. Assume that Allowance for Doubtful Accounts has a credit balance of $650.

PRACTICE EXERCISES 1a,1c

a. Aging of the charge accounts in the accounts receivable ledger indicates doubtful accounts of $1,570.
b. Bad debt losses are estimated at ¾ percent of net sales.

EXERCISE 15-5 On June 1, Roy Supply's Accounts Receivable balance was $26,436. The balance of the contra account Allowance for Doubtful Accounts was $1,630 credit. On June 20, the account balance of Moore's Bakery of $570 was written off.

PRACTICE EXERCISE 2

a. Journalize the write-off of the Moore's Bakery account using the allowance method.
b. Using T accounts, determine what is now the net realizable value of Accounts Receivable. How would this be shown in the financial statements? (The period ends December 31, 20—.)

EXERCISE 15-6 Morgan's Shop had the following selected transactions this year. Assuming that Morgan's Shop uses the allowance method of accounting for bad debt losses, record the three transactions in general journal form. Allowance for Doubtful Accounts has a credit balance of $346.

PRACTICE EXERCISES 1c,2,3

a. Wrote off the account of D. Yang as uncollectible, $280.
b. Reinstated the account of R. Fedor, which had been written off during the preceding year, $65; received $65 cash in full payment.
c. Estimated bad debt losses to be 1 percent of net sales of $82,350.

EXERCISE 15-7 Using the same data as in Exercise 15-6, assume that Morgan's Shop uses the specific charge-off method of accounting for bad debt losses. Record transactions *a* and *b* in general journal form.

PRACTICE EXERCISES 4,5

EXERCISE 15-8 With reference to Exercise 15-5:

PRACTICE EXERCISES 4,5

a. Use the specific charge-off method of accounting for bad debt losses to write off the Moore's Bakery account.
b. Reinstate the Moore's Bakery account and collect the amount due.

Dec. 31 Recorded the entry to close the appropriate account to Income Summary.

Required

1. Open the following accounts, recording the credit balance of Allowance for Doubtful Accounts as of January 1 of this fiscal year:

114	Allowance for Doubtful Accounts	$5,272.36
313	Income Summary	—
642	Bad Debts Expense	—

2. Record in a general journal, pages 24 and 25, the transactions and the adjusting and closing entries. After each entry, post to the three selected ledger accounts.
3. Prepare the Current Assets section of the balance sheet. Other pertinent accounts are Cash, $14,227.12; Merchandise Inventory, $146,507.50; and Prepaid Insurance, $756.00.

Problem Set B

For additional help, see the demonstration problem at the beginning of each chapter in your Working Papers.

1a,2

PROBLEM 15-1B On December 31 of last year, the accountant for Basset Co. prepared a balance sheet that included $198,654 in Accounts Receivable and $13,528 (credit) in Allowance for Doubtful Accounts. Selected transactions that occurred during January of this year are as follows:

a. Sales of merchandise on account, $192,300.
b. Sales returns and allowances related to sales of merchandise on account, $5,619.
c. Cash payments by charge customers (no cash discounts), $157,930.26.
d. Account of Clarke Company written off as uncollectible, $1,349.34.
e. By the process of aging Accounts Receivable, on January 31 it was decided that Allowance for Doubtful Accounts should be adjusted to a balance of $23,471.10.
f. Closed the Bad Debts Expense account.

Required

1. Record the entries in a general journal, page 36. Record the letter in the Date column.
2. Record the balance in Allowance for Doubtful Accounts.
3. Post the appropriate entries to the accounts for Allowance for Doubtful Accounts and Bad Debts Expense.

1a

PROBLEM 15-2B Malcolm Company uses the aging method of estimating bad debts as of December 31, the end of the fiscal year. Terms of sales are net 30 days. While preparing the aging schedule, the accountant became very ill and was unable to finish the job. The accountant's report, as he left it, is as follows:

Customer Name	Balance	Not Yet Due	Days Past Due			
			1–30	31–60	61–90	Over 90
Balance Forward	$352,292	$192,800	$94,400	$37,452	$14,960	$12,680

EXERCISE 15-3 Estrella Company uses the allowance method of estimating losses due to bad debts. On December 31, before any adjustments have been recorded, the ledger contains the following balances:

Sales	$180,000
Sales Returns and Allowances	27,000

The company estimates that bad debt losses will be ¾ percent of net sales. Journalize the adjusting entry to record the estimated bad debt losses. The Allowance for Doubtful Accounts account has a credit balance of $320.

EXERCISE 15-4 Gray Company uses the allowance method of handling losses due to bad debts. Gray Company's Accounts Receivable account has a balance of $82,000. Net sales for the year total $104,000. Write the adjusting entry to record the estimated bad debt losses under each of the following conditions. Assume that Allowance for Doubtful Accounts has a credit balance of $650.

a. Aging of the charge accounts in the accounts receivable ledger indicates doubtful accounts of $1,570.
b. Bad debt losses are estimated at ¾ percent of net sales.

EXERCISE 15-5 On June 1, Roy Supply's Accounts Receivable balance was $26,436. The balance of the contra account Allowance for Doubtful Accounts was $1,630 credit. On June 20, the account balance of Moore's Bakery of $570 was written off.

a. Journalize the write-off of the Moore's Bakery account using the allowance method.
b. Using T accounts, determine what is now the net realizable value of Accounts Receivable. How would this be shown in the financial statements? (The period ends December 31, 20—.)

EXERCISE 15-6 Morgan's Shop had the following selected transactions this year. Assuming that Morgan's Shop uses the allowance method of accounting for bad debt losses, record the three transactions in general journal form. Allowance for Doubtful Accounts has a credit balance of $346.

a. Wrote off the account of D. Yang as uncollectible, $280.
b. Reinstated the account of R. Fedor, which had been written off during the preceding year, $65; received $65 cash in full payment.
c. Estimated bad debt losses to be 1 percent of net sales of $82,350.

EXERCISE 15-7 Using the same data as in Exercise 15-6, assume that Morgan's Shop uses the specific charge-off method of accounting for bad debt losses. Record transactions *a* and *b* in general journal form.

EXERCISE 15-8 With reference to Exercise 15-5:

a. Use the specific charge-off method of accounting for bad debt losses to write off the Moore's Bakery account.
b. Reinstate the Moore's Bakery account and collect the amount due.

Problem Set A

For additional help, see the demonstration problem at the beginning of each chapter in your Working Papers.

1a,2  LO

 GL

PROBLEM 15-1A The balance sheet prepared by D.H. Allen Co. for December 31 of last year includes $215,320 in Accounts Receivable and $13,281 (credit) in Allowance for Doubtful Accounts. The following transactions occurred during January of this year:

a. Sales of merchandise on account, $196,200.
b. Sales returns and allowances related to sales of merchandise on account, $5,359.
c. Cash payments by charge customers (no cash discounts), $192,802.
d. Account of Simons and Tyne written off as uncollectible, $1,591.
e. By the process of aging Accounts Receivable, on January 31 it was decided that Allowance for Doubtful Accounts should be adjusted to a balance of $18,258.
f. Closed the Bad Debts Expense account.

Check Figure
Bad Debts Expense debit,
$6,568

Required

1. Record the entries in a general journal, page 36. Record the letter in the Date column.
2. Record the balance in Allowance for Doubtful Accounts.
3. Post the appropriate entries to the accounts for Allowance for Doubtful Accounts and Bad Debts Expense.

1a  LO

PROBLEM 15-2A Jilson Company uses the aging method of estimating bad debts as of December 31, the end of the fiscal year. Terms of sales are net 30 days. While in the process of completing the aging schedule, the accountant became very ill and was unable to finish the job. The accountant's report, as she left it, appears as follows:

Customer Name	Balance	Not Yet Due	Days Past Due			
			1–30	31–60	61–90	Over 90
Balance Forward	$389,900	$249,200	$76,280	$38,848	$15,032	$10,540

The accountant still had to analyze the following accounts:

Account	Amount	Due Date
L. Flynn	$1,823	January 16 (next year)
B. French	3,780	November 28
C. Gilmore	6,711	November 17
L. Hemmit	9,590	January 27 (next year)
P. Lord	3,602	September 10
C. Newton	1,483	October 16

From past experience, the company has found that the following percentages for estimated uncollectible accounts produce an adequate balance for Allowance for Doubtful Accounts:

Days Past Due	Estimated Percentage Uncollectible
Not yet due	2%
1 to 30 days	4
31 to 60 days	20
61 to 90 days	30
Over 90 days	50

Prior to aging the accounts receivable, Allowance for Doubtful Accounts had a credit balance of $4,536.

Required

1. Enter the Balance Forward balances and complete the aging schedule.
2. Complete the table for estimating the allowance for doubtful accounts.
3. Record the adjusting entry in general journal form.

 LO 1c,2,3

PROBLEM 15-3A On January 1 of this year, Norm Company had a credit balance of $1,926 in Allowance for Doubtful Accounts. During the year, Norm Company completed the following selected transactions:

Feb. 11 Wrote off as uncollectible a $694 account of Nate Company, which had gone out of business, leaving no assets.

May 5 Wrote off the account of C. Teddy as uncollectible, $348.32.

19 Received $189 unexpectedly from C. Welsh, whose account had been written off two years earlier in the amount of $189. Reinstated the account and recorded the collection of $189.

Aug. 3 Collected 10 percent of the $269 owed by C. C. Mark, a bankrupt customer. Wrote off the remainder as worthless.

Sept. 24 Received $195 from C. Teddy as partial payment of the account written off on May 5. He wrote a letter stating that he expects to pay the balance soon. Accordingly, reinstated the account for the amount of the original obligation, $348.32.

Dec. 29 Journalized a compound entry to write off the following accounts as uncollectible: N. C. Agar, $372.40; R. L. Bolt, $248.72; C. Egger, $288.00.

31 Recorded the adjusting entry for estimated bad debt losses at ½ percent of net sales of $302,526.

31 Closed the Bad Debts Expense account.

Required

1. Record the opening balance in the ledger account for Allowance for Doubtful Accounts.
2. Record the entries in a general journal, pages 73 and 74.
3. Post the entries to the ledger accounts for Allowance for Doubtful Accounts and Bad Debts Expense.

 **LO** 1a,2,3

PROBLEM 15-4A The following are among the transactions completed by Warton Building Supplies this year:

Feb. 6 Wrote off as uncollectible the account of Milo, Inc., $1,251.17. The company had gone out of business, leaving no assets.

Mar. 15 Reinstated the account of L. Whinn, which had been written off in the preceding year; received $217.16 in full payment of account.

Aug. 17 Received $154 unexpectedly from C. P. Brent, whose account had been written off last year in the amount of $154. Reinstated the account and recorded the collection of $154.

Oct. 15 Reinstated the account of Dolan and Son, which had been written off two years earlier, and received $839.70 in full payment.

Dec. 29 Journalized a compound entry to write off the following accounts as uncollectible: D. C. Lake, $368.00; R. R. Mort, $752.28; N. Shell, $1,374.91; D. Trent, $1,962.15.

31 On the basis of an aged analysis of Accounts Receivable of $87,811.14, estimated that $5,772.55 will be uncollectible. Recorded the adjusting entry.

Dec. 31 Recorded the entry to close the appropriate account to Income Summary.

Required

1. Open the following accounts, recording the credit balance of Allowance for Doubtful Accounts as of January 1 of this fiscal year:

114	Allowance for Doubtful Accounts	$5,272.36
313	Income Summary	—
642	Bad Debts Expense	—

2. Record in a general journal, pages 24 and 25, the transactions and the adjusting and closing entries. After each entry, post to the three selected ledger accounts.
3. Prepare the Current Assets section of the balance sheet. Other pertinent accounts are Cash, $14,227.12; Merchandise Inventory, $146,507.50; and Prepaid Insurance, $756.00.

Problem Set B

For additional help, see the demonstration problem at the beginning of each chapter in your Working Papers.

PROBLEM 15-1B On December 31 of last year, the accountant for Basset Co. prepared a balance sheet that included $198,654 in Accounts Receivable and $13,528 (credit) in Allowance for Doubtful Accounts. Selected transactions that occurred during January of this year are as follows:

a. Sales of merchandise on account, $192,300.
b. Sales returns and allowances related to sales of merchandise on account, $5,619.
c. Cash payments by charge customers (no cash discounts), $157,930.26.
d. Account of Clarke Company written off as uncollectible, $1,349.34.
e. By the process of aging Accounts Receivable, on January 31 it was decided that Allowance for Doubtful Accounts should be adjusted to a balance of $23,471.10.
f. Closed the Bad Debts Expense account.

Required

1. Record the entries in a general journal, page 36. Record the letter in the Date column.
2. Record the balance in Allowance for Doubtful Accounts.
3. Post the appropriate entries to the accounts for Allowance for Doubtful Accounts and Bad Debts Expense.

PROBLEM 15-2B Malcolm Company uses the aging method of estimating bad debts as of December 31, the end of the fiscal year. Terms of sales are net 30 days. While preparing the aging schedule, the accountant became very ill and was unable to finish the job. The accountant's report, as he left it, is as follows:

| Customer Name | Balance | Not Yet Due | Days Past Due | | | |
			1–30	31–60	61–90	Over 90
Balance Forward	$352,292	$192,800	$94,400	$37,452	$14,960	$12,680

The accountant still had to analyze the following accounts:

Account	Amount	Due Date
P. Gandor	$3,890	January 12 (next year)
R. Nolan	3,245	December 22
L. Porges	7,948	November 2
C. Quinn	8,691	August 18
T. Regis	1,985	December 3
P. Rita	1,375	January 22 (next year)

From past experience, the company has found that the following percentages for estimated uncollectible accounts produce an adequate balance for Allowance for Doubtful Accounts:

Days Past Due	Estimated Percentage Uncollectible
Not yet due	2%
1 to 30 days	4
31 to 60 days	20
61 to 90 days	30
Over 90 days	50

Prior to aging the accounts receivable, Allowance for Doubtful Accounts had a credit balance of $7,467.

Required

1. Enter the Balance Forward balances and complete the aging schedule.
2. Complete the table for estimating the allowance for doubtful accounts.
3. Record the adjusting entry in general journal form.

Check Figure
Allowance for Doubtful Accounts credit, $24,733

 **LO** 1c,2,3

PROBLEM 15-3B On January 1 of this year, Reek's Wholesale Meats had a credit balance of $4,234 in Allowance for Doubtful Accounts. During the year, the company completed the following selected transactions:

Feb. 8 Wrote off as uncollectible a $462 account of Sager Market, which had gone out of business, leaving no assets.

May 3 Wrote off the account of Mary's Catering as uncollectible, $220.80.

17 Collected 5 percent of the $1,777 owed by Link Company, a bankrupt customer. Wrote off the remainder as worthless.

Aug. 2 Received $228.40 unexpectedly from Dayton Company, whose account had been written off two years earlier in the amount of $228.40. Reinstated the account and recorded the collection of $228.40.

Sept. 11 Received $173 from Mary's Catering as partial payment of the account written off on May 3. She wrote a letter saying that she expects to pay the balance soon. Accordingly, reinstated the account for the amount of the original obligation, $220.80.

Dec. 30 Journalized a compound entry to write off the following accounts as uncollectible: C. D. French, $326.32; Southworth Inn, $282.52; Hill's Drive-In, $566.30.

31 Recorded the adjusting entry for estimated bad debt losses at ½ percent of net sales of $584,290.

31 Closed the Bad Debts Expense account.

Required

1. Record the opening balance in the ledger account for Allowance for Doubtful Accounts.
2. Record the entries in a general journal, pages 73 and 74.
3. Post the entries to the ledger accounts for Allowance for Doubtful Accounts and Bad Debts Expense.

1a,2,3  LO

PROBLEM 15-4B The following transactions were among those completed by Childer Wholesale Jewelers this year:

Feb. 15 Wrote off as uncollectible the account of Mabes, Inc., $1,762.50. The company had gone out of business, leaving no assets.

Mar. 14 Reinstated the account of Goodwin, Inc., which had been written off in the preceding year; received $323.12 in full payment of account.

July 27 Received $214.26 unexpectedly from Clem and Son, whose account had been written off last year in the amount of $214.26. Reinstated the account and recorded the collection of $214.26.

Oct. 14 Reinstated the account of C. P. Start, which had been written off two years earlier, and received $674 in full payment.

Dec. 28 Journalized a compound entry to write off the following accounts as uncollectible: L. Brent, $365.00; C. Goody, $327.16; Eng and Bree, $716.42; Globe Jewelry, $2,379.60.

31 On the basis of an aged analysis of Accounts Receivable of $184,164.22, estimated that $5,597 will be uncollectible. Recorded the adjusting entry.

31 Recorded the entry to close the appropriate account to Income Summary.

Required

1. Open the following accounts, recording the credit balance of Allowance for Doubtful Accounts as of January 1 of this fiscal year:

114	Allowance for Doubtful Accounts	$5,112.16
313	Income Summary	—
642	Bad Debts Expense	—

2. Record in a general journal, pages 24 and 25, the transactions and the adjusting and closing entries. After each entry, post to the three selected ledger accounts.
3. Prepare the Current Assets section of the balance sheet. Other pertinent accounts are Cash, $14,421.40; Notes Receivable, $2,720.00; Merchandise Inventory, $323,213.41; and Prepaid Insurance, $720.00.

ACTIVITIES

CONSIDER AND COMMUNICATE

The owner of the business where you work is puzzled. He asks you how he can account for these delinquent accounts. You know about the allowance method and the specific charge-off method.

Explain why the allowance method of accounting for bad debts is preferable to the specific charge-off method for financial reporting.

CRITICAL THINKING

Your supervisor has asked you to do some work for her on Megan Company's accounts receivables.

Selected information from Megan Company follows.

	12/31/09	12/31/10
Net Credit Sales	$248,000	$290,000
Accounts Receivable	59,000	65,000
Allowance for Doubtful Accounts (credit balance)	700	700

For each situation, your supervisor suggests you do the following:

1. Write the correct entry for Megan Company to record either estimated Bad Debts Expense or actual Bad Debts Expense, depending upon the method used to value Accounts Receivable.
2. Determine the balance of Allowance for Doubtful Accounts at the end of December 2010.

Situation A—Megan Company ages Accounts Receivable to determine the amount of the adjustment for estimated Bad Debts Expense.

The following facts are available:

Age of Accounts	12/31/10 Balance	Estimated Percentage Uncollectible
Not due yet	$44,500	1%
1 to 30 days	12,500	3
31 to 60 days	4,300	6
61 to 90 days	2,700	12
Over 90 days	1,000	30

Situation B—Megan Company uses a percentage of Accounts Receivable to determine the amount of the adjustment for estimated Bad Debts Expense. The firm's average actual bad debt losses over the prior three consecutive years were 3 percent. The firm feels that this is a reasonable estimate of Bad Debts Expense.

A QUESTION OF ETHICS

As the company bookkeeper reviewing delinquent accounts receivable, you find that a relative of yours has not paid his account amounting to $550. You know that he has been experiencing financial difficulties, and so you set his account aside and do not include it with the other past due accounts sent to a credit collection agency. Comment on this action.

16 Ending Merchandise Inventory

WHY IT MATTERS

iROBOT, Bedford, Massachusetts

iRobot was founded in 1990 by two roboticists and their professor at the Massachusetts Institute of Technology with the vision of making practical robots a reality. That vision has been a success. In 2008, iRobot generated more than $307 million in revenue, with its award-winning Roomba floor vacuuming robot leading the charge. Roombas are powered by a rechargeable battery and have sensors that detect particularly dirty spots and prevent the robot from falling off ledges.

iRobot sells its robots and their accessories directly and through various distributors and retailers. In order to sell these products, iRobot and the stores that sell them must keep inventory on hand. These companies must also select a method of inventory valuation, which is important because the amount of ending inventory has a significant impact on a business's bottom line. In this chapter, you will learn the various methods of inventory valuation and the importance of the value of ending merchandise inventory.

LEARNING OBJECTIVES

After you have completed this chapter, you will be able to do the following:

1 Determine the overstatement or understatement of cost of goods sold, gross profit, and net income resulting from a change in the ending merchandise inventory amount.

2 Determine unit cost, the value of the ending inventory, and the cost of goods sold under the periodic inventory system by the following methods: (a) specific identification; (b) weighted-average-cost; (c) first-in, first-out; and (d) last-in, first-out.

3 Determine the unit cost, the value of ending inventory, and the cost of goods sold under the perpetual inventory system by the following methods: (a) moving-average-cost method; and (b) last-in, first-out method.

4 Complete a perpetual inventory record card.

ACCOUNTING LANGUAGE

Consistency principle *(p. 643)*

First-in, first-out (FIFO) method *(p. 641)*

Last-in, first-out (LIFO) method *(p. 642)*

Lower-of-cost-or-market (LCM) rule *(p. 644)*

Moving-average-cost method *(p. 645)*

Specific identification method *(p. 640)*

Weighted-average-cost method *(p. 641)*

One of the most important aspects of the operation of any merchandising business is the accounting for and valuation of the merchandise in stock. We define *merchandise inventory* as goods purchased by the company and held for resale to customers in the ordinary course of business. Merchandise Inventory and the related T accounts are as shown in Figure 1.

Firms take a physical inventory at the end of their fiscal periods. At this time, the most up-to-date figure is included in the Adjustments columns of the work sheet. Remember, under the periodic inventory system, Merchandise Inventory requires two adjusting entries:

a. The first entry removes or "reverses out" the value of the beginning merchandise inventory.

b. The second entry adds in the value of the ending merchandise inventory.

Assume that a firm has a beginning merchandise inventory amounting to $275,000. The cost of the ending merchandise inventory is $283,000. The adjustment is described by T accounts as follows:

Merchandise Inventory					Income Summary			
	+	−			**(a)**	275,000	**(b)**	283,000
Bal.	275,000	**(a)**	275,000					
(b)	283,000							

Merchandise inventory and
related T accounts

Assets		Revenue		Expenses	
+	−	−	+	+	−

Merchandise Inventory		Sales		Purchases	
+	−	−	+	+	−
For periodic inventory, record latest inventory in an adjusting entry at end of fiscal period.	For periodic inventory, remove beginning inventory in an adjusting entry at end of fiscal period.		Record the sale of merchandise at its selling price.	Record the purchase of merchandise at its cost.	

Sales Returns and Allowances		Purchases Returns and Allowances	
+	−	−	+
Record the return of, or allowances on, merchandise previously sold at its selling price.			Record the return of, or allowances on, merchandise previously purchased at its cost.

Remember

Contra accounts (like Sales Returns and Allowances or Purchases Discounts) have signs opposite those of the accounts to which they are related.

Sales Discounts		Purchases Discounts	
+	−	−	+
Record cash discounts taken by customers.			Record cash discounts taken when paying vendors.

Freight In	
+	−
Record freight charges on incoming merchandise shipments at cost.	

The same adjustment appears in the work sheet. In this example, the ending inventory amount of $283,000 is given. However, in a practical business situation, the cost of the ending inventory must be determined. Counting the goods on hand is a relatively easy although time-consuming procedure compared with the more difficult task of assigning a dollar amount to those goods in a time of changing prices. We talk mainly about the Merchandise Inventory account because of its relative importance. However, the same principle applies to other assets, such as raw materials for a manufacturer.

In previous chapters, we learned how to record journal entries and adjustments using either the periodic inventory system or the perpetual inventory system. Now, we will examine the valuation of inventories under both of these systems. Remember that some merchandising firms take a physical inventory of merchandise on hand and then attach a value to it. This is known as a periodic inventory system, as shown in the example involving the two adjusting entries for Merchandise Inventory. Other merchandising firms keep continuous records of inventories by recording all transactions, so that at any given time they know what they should have on hand and the current cost of each item. This is known as a perpetual inventory system.

> **Remember**
>
> The only time a value of the inventory is known is when a physical inventory is taken.

THE IMPORTANCE OF INVENTORY VALUATION

Merchandise Inventory is the only account that can appear on both major financial statements. On the balance sheet, it appears under Current Assets. On the income statement, it is listed under Cost of Goods Sold. Why is the valuation of merchandise inventory so important? In many firms, merchandise inventory is the current asset with the largest dollar amount. Likewise, as a part of Cost of Goods Sold, it materially affects the net income because the cost of goods sold is often the largest deduction from sales. As a result, inventory determination plays an important role in matching costs with revenue for a given period.

Differing costs of ending merchandise inventory have a dramatic effect on net income. We can see this in the partial income statements that follow (Figures 2 through 6).

Now assume that instead of the correct value for ending merchandise inventory of $283,000 (Figure 2), you in error record its value at $233,000, that is, it was understated (too low) by $50,000. The result would be a net income of only $222,000 (Figure 3).

From Figures 2 and 3, you can see that if the ending merchandise inventory is understated (too low) by $50,000, the net income will be understated (too low) by $50,000 because the two are directly related to each other. **The understatement of ending inventory increases the amount of Cost of Goods Sold. When Cost of Goods Sold increases, net income decreases.**

Similarly, **if the ending merchandise inventory is overstated (too high), net income will be overstated (too high; Figure 4). The overstatement of**

> **1 LEARNING OBJECTIVE**
>
> *Determine the overstatement or understatement of cost of goods sold, gross profit, and net income resulting from a change in the ending merchandise inventory amount.*

YEAR 1 — CORRECT ENDING INVENTORY STATED		
Net Sales		$903,000
Cost of Goods Sold:		
Merchandise Inventory (beginning)	$275,000	
Purchases (net)	418,000	
Cost of Goods Available for Sale	$693,000	
Less Merchandise Inventory (ending)	283,000	
Cost of Goods Sold		410,000
Gross Profit		$493,000
Operating Expenses		221,000
Net Income		$272,000

FIGURE 2

Partial income statement with correct ending inventory

FIGURE 3

Effect of understated ending inventory on net income in year 1

YEAR 1 — ENDING INVENTORY UNDERSTATED BY $50,000

Net Sales		$903,000
Cost of Goods Sold:		
Merchandise Inventory (beginning)	$275,000	
Purchases (net)	418,000	
Cost of Goods Available for Sale	$693,000	
Less Merchandise Inventory (ending)	233,000	
Cost of Goods Sold		460,000
Gross Profit		$443,000
Operating Expenses		221,000
Net Income		$222,000

Remember

The ending inventory of one year becomes the beginning inventory of the next year.

Remember

An error made in the ending inventory in one period will be carried to the next period in the beginning inventory. This is important because of the direct relationship between ending inventory and net income.

ending inventory decreases the amount of Cost of Goods Sold. When Cost of Goods Sold is decreased, net income increases.

From Figures 2 and 4 you can see that if the *ending* inventory is overstated (too high) by $50,000, net income is overstated (too high) by $50,000.

But there is something else you have to take into account. Because the *ending* inventory of one year becomes the beginning inventory of the following year, the net income of the following year is also affected, but in an opposite direction. Let's continue our examples into year 2. The understated $233,000 *ending* inventory of year 1 (Figure 3) becomes the *beginning* inventory of year 2 (Figure 5). Similarly, if the *beginning* inventory (the *ending* inventory of the prior year) is understated by $50,000, the net income will be overstated because the two are inversely related to each other. Similarly, **if the *beginning* inventory is overstated, the net income will be understated.**

Now look at Figure 6 to see what happens when the overstated $333,000 ending inventory of year 1 becomes the beginning inventory of year 2.

If the *beginning* inventory is overstated by $50,000, the net income will be understated by $50,000, because the two are inversely related to each other. And similarly, **if the *beginning* inventory is understated, the net income will be overstated**.

In other words, over a two-year period, the total net income will be correct, because the overstatement of one year cancels out the understatement of the following year, and vice versa. At the end of a two-year period, the balance sheet is

FIGURE 4

Effect of overstated ending inventory on net income in year 1

YEAR 1 — ENDING INVENTORY OVERSTATED BY $50,000

Net Sales		$903,000
Cost of Goods Sold:		
Merchandise Inventory (beginning)	$275,000	
Purchases (net)	418,000	
Cost of Goods Available for Sale	$693,000	
Less Merchandise Inventory (ending)	333,000	
Cost of Goods Sold		360,000
Gross Profit		$543,000
Operating Expenses		221,000
Net Income		$322,000

FIGURE 5

Effect of understated ending inventory in year 1 on net income in year 2

YEAR 2 — UNDERSTATED ENDING INVENTORY ($233,000) OF YEAR 1 BECOMES BEGINNING INVENTORY OF YEAR 2

Net Sales		$975,000
Cost of Goods Sold:		
Merchandise Inventory (beginning)	$233,000	
Purchases (net)	466,000	
Cost of Goods Available for Sale	$699,000	
Less Merchandise Inventory (ending)	203,000	
Cost of Goods Sold		496,000
Gross Profit		$479,000
Operating Expenses		223,000
Net Income		$256,000

FIGURE 6

Effect of overstated ending inventory in year 1 on net income in year 2

YEAR 2 — OVERSTATED ENDING INVENTORY ($333,000) OF YEAR 1 BECOMES BEGINNING INVENTORY OF YEAR 2

Net Sales		$975,000
Cost of Goods Sold:		
Merchandise Inventory (beginning)	$333,000	
Purchases (net)	466,000	
Cost of Goods Available for Sale	$799,000	
Less Merchandise Inventory (ending)	203,000	
Cost of Goods Sold		596,000
Gross Profit		$379,000
Operating Expenses		223,000
Net Income		$156,000

correct because *ending* inventory and *ending* capital are both correctly stated. We can summarize this in the following table:

Year	Ending Inventory of $233,000 ($50,000 understatement)	Ending Inventory of $333,000 ($50,000 overstatement)
	Net Income	Net Income
1	$222,000	$322,000
2	256,000	156,000
Total	$478,000	$478,000

If *ending* inventory is *understated*, net income for the period will be *understated*.

If *ending* inventory is *overstated*, net income for the period will be *overstated*.

If *beginning* inventory is *understated*, net income for the period will be *overstated*.

If *beginning* inventory is *overstated*, net income for the period will be *understated*.

Ratio Analysis

Merchandise Inventory Turnover

Merchandise inventory turnover is the number of times a firm's average inventory is sold during a given year.

$$\text{Merchandise Inventory Turnover} = \frac{\text{Cost of Goods Sold}}{\text{Average Merchandise Inventory}}$$

$$\text{Average Merchandise Inventory} = \frac{\text{Beginning Merchandise Inventory + Ending Merchandise Inventory}}{2}$$

Going back to Southern Furniture, the company used in the Ratio Analysis feature in Chapter 12 (pages 493–494), let's assume the following information for 2011 and 2010:

	2011	2010
Beginning Merchandise Inventory (from the Cost of Goods Sold section of the income statement)	$ 46,000	$ 64,000
Ending Merchandise Inventory (from the Cost of Goods Sold section of the income statement or the balance sheet)	58,000	46,000
Cost of Goods Sold (from the Cost of Goods Sold section of the income statement)	278,000	248,000

2011

$$\text{Average Merchandise Inventory} = \frac{\$46,000 + \$58,000}{2} = \frac{\$104,000}{2} = \underline{\$52,000}$$

$$\text{Merchandise Inventory Turnover} = \frac{\$278,000}{\$52,000} = \underline{5.35} \text{ times per year}$$

2010

$$\text{Average Merchandise Inventory} = \frac{\$64,000 + \$46,000}{2} = \frac{\$110,000}{2} = \underline{\$55,000}$$

$$\text{Merchandise Inventory Turnover} = \frac{\$248,000}{\$55,000} = \underline{4.51} \text{ times per year}$$

With each turnover of merchandise, the company makes a gross profit, so the higher the turnover, the better.

The inventory turnover improved from 4.51 in 2010 to 5.35 in 2011 because the inventory was lower on average in 2011 as compared to 2010.

THE NEED FOR AND THE TAKING OF INVENTORIES

Firms that want to satisfy their customers have to maintain large and varied inventories of goods. Efficient purchasing also requires that the company take advantage of quantity discounts and of special buys of seasonal or distressed merchandise.

Care should be taken to count all goods belonging to the firm. Sometimes the goods may not be physically present; this occurs while the goods are being transported. **From the seller's position, merchandise sold FOB destination should be included in the seller's inventory** because the seller is paying the freight charges. **From the buyer's position, merchandise purchased FOB shipping point should be included in the buyer's inventory** because the buyer is paying the freight charges. Title transfer or ownership of the goods depends on who has paid the freight.

© ANDERSEN ROSS/DIGITAL VISION/JUPITER IMAGES

Maintaining accurate and up-to the-minute inventory counts is critical to the success of any business, and handheld scanners make that a reality.

Inventory Control

A small business such as a bicycle shop or an antique store may keep track of its inventories manually. However, to have up-to-date counts of inventory items on hand, most firms use computers. Software programs that record transactions and produce inventory reports are readily available. These reports include a description of each item in stock, the number of units on hand, the cost of each unit, and the number of units sold, as well as the number of units to be reordered. Also, management can use inventory reports to determine and analyze buying and selling trends.

METHODS OF ASSIGNING COSTS TO ENDING INVENTORY—PERIODIC INVENTORY SYSTEM

After the items have been described and counted, the unit costs are inserted on the inventory sheet and the total costs are extended. How do you determine unit cost? You might think that this is rather elementary. Indeed, it would be *if* all the purchases of a given article had been made at the same price per unit. In that case, to determine the total unit cost, you would need only to look up one invoice, check the unit price, and then multiply it by the number of items present. But nothing is ever that simple. A firm usually buys a number of batches of a given item during the year, and the unit costs can vary. A bottle of shampoo that cost $2.70 in January might cost $2.75 in October. Which unit cost should you assign to the goods on hand?

There are four main methods of assigning costs to goods in the ending inventory: (1) specific identification; (2) weighted-average-cost; (3) first-in, first-out; and (4) last-in, first-out.

FYI

More and more companies stock fewer inventory items than in the past. Many companies use the just-in-time (JIT) method: ordering the necessary inventory just in time to deliver it to the customer. This can save time and money.

Example of Inventory Valuation

Whitewater Raft Supply keeps an inventory of Draco life vests (#931) purchased from Dana Manufacturing Company. This year, Whitewater Raft Supply sells 80 of these life vests and has 29 remaining in stock. The company started the year with 24 in stock and bought more as the year went on, as follows:

Accounting in Your Future

Inventory Control Specialist

Retailers, wholesalers, and manufacturers all have inventory, and all need some form of inventory control. Inventory control is critical because running out of inventory can shut down operations and cause a loss of revenue, while at the same time too much inventory can be very costly. Many of these businesses have an inventory control specialist employed to take charge of the control of inventory.

Inventory control specialists have numerous job duties. Some of their duties consist of classifying, labeling, and warehousing all inventory for future use; using handheld scanners to count the inventory in stock and posting the totals to inventory records, manually or by using computer software programs; assisting in the receiving and shipping department in logging all incoming inventory purchases; verifying clerical counts against the physical count of stock and adjusting errors if needed; and preparing lists and reports of depleted items, shortages, defective items, and so forth.

The majority of opportunities in inventory control require a bachelor's degree, along with solid math skills. Although the employment of inventory control specialists is not expected to have as significant a job growth as other professions, the increasing role of retail outlets and warehouses, as well as catalog, mail, telephone, and Internet shopping services, should bolster employment.

Jan. 1	Beginning inventory	24 units @ $58 each =	$1,392
Mar. 16	Purchase	30 units @ $63 each =	1,890
July 29	Purchase	35 units @ $65 each =	2,275
Nov. 18	Purchase	20 units @ $67 each =	1,340
	Total available	109 units	$6,897

Now let's compute the cost of goods sold (80 life vests) and the value of the ending inventory (29 life vests) using the four different methods.

Specific Identification Method

When a firm sells big-ticket items (cars, appliances, furniture, jewelry), the cost is low to keep track of the purchase price of each individual article and determine the exact cost of the goods sold. Such a firm uses the **specific identification method** of inventory control. Although Whitewater Raft Supply would not use specific identification for small items such as life vests, let's assume for illustrative purposes that Whitewater Raft Supply records the sale of each life vest using the specific identification method. Because life vests have imprinted manufactured date codes, Whitewater Raft Supply can identify each life vest with a specific purchase invoice listing the unit cost. When Whitewater Raft Supply takes inventory at the end of the year, it finds that there are 29 life vests left in stock; 7 of these were bought in March, 10 were bought in July, and 12 were bought in November. Costs are assigned to the ending inventory as follows:

Mar. 16	Purchase	7 units @ $63 each =	$ 441
July 29	Purchase	10 units @ $65 each =	650
Nov. 18	Purchase	12 units @ $67 each =	804
	Total	29 units	$1,895

Whitewater Raft Supply determines the cost of goods sold by subtracting the value of the ending inventory from the total cost of goods available for sale:

Total life vests available (109 units)	$6,897
Less ending inventory (29 units)	1,895
Cost of goods sold (80 units)	$5,002

Weighted-Average-Cost Method

An alternative to keeping track of the cost of each item purchased is to use the **weighted-average-cost method** to find the cost per unit of all like articles available for sale during the period. First, Whitewater Raft Supply finds the total cost of the life vests it had on hand during the year by multiplying the number of units by their respective purchase costs.

2b LEARNING OBJECTIVE

Determine unit cost, the value of the ending inventory, and the cost of goods sold under the periodic inventory system by the weighted-average-cost method.

Jan. 1	Beginning inventory	24 units @ $58 each =	$1,392
Mar. 16	Purchase	30 units @ $63 each =	1,890
July 29	Purchase	35 units @ $65 each =	2,275
Nov. 18	Purchase	20 units @ $67 each =	1,340
	Total available	109 units	$6,897

Next Whitewater Raft Supply finds the average cost per life vest.

Average Cost per Unit = Total Cost ÷ Total Units
Average Cost per Unit = $6,897 ÷ 109 units = $63.28

Value of Ending Inventory = Number of Units × Average Cost per Unit
Value of Ending Inventory = 29 × $63.28 = $1,835.12

According to this method, the beginning inventory is *weighted* (that is, multiplied by the number of units it comprises). Each purchase thereafter is weighted by the number of units involved in that purchase. In other words, the more you buy at a time, the more that purchase influences the average cost.

Total life vests available (109 units)	$6,897.00
Less ending inventory (29 units)	1,835.12
Cost of goods sold (80 units)	$5,061.88

First-In, First-Out (FIFO) Method

The **first-in, first-out (FIFO) method** is based on the flow-of-cost assumption that costs of merchandise sold should be charged against revenue in the order in which the costs were incurred. To determine the cost of goods sold, the accountant records the oldest (first) cost first, then the next-oldest cost, and so on. First-in, first-out is a logical way for a firm to rotate its stock of merchandise. Think of a grocery store selling milk. Because milk will sour, the oldest milk is moved up to the front of the shelf. As a result, the ending inventory consists of the freshest milk.

Again, let's return to Whitewater Raft Supply's life vests. To repeat, 109 life vests were available for sale during the year:

2c LEARNING OBJECTIVE

Determine unit cost, the value of the ending inventory, and the cost of goods sold under the periodic inventory system by the first-in, first-out method.

Jan.	1	Beginning inventory	24 units @ $58 each =	$1,392
Mar.	16	Purchase	30 units @ $63 each =	1,890
July	29	Purchase	35 units @ $65 each =	2,275
Nov.	18	Purchase	20 units @ $67 each =	1,340
		Total available	109 units	$6,897

Whitewater Raft Supply sold 80 units. The accountant calculates the total cost of the life vests sold on a first-in, first-out (FIFO) basis, as follows:

Jan.	1	Beginning inventory	24 units @ $58 each =	$1,392
Mar.	16	Purchase	30 units @ $63 each =	1,890
July	29	Purchase	26 units @ $65 each =	1,690
		Total	80 units	$4,972

Whitewater Raft Supply has the 29 newest or most recently purchased units on hand in the ending inventory. The accountant records the ending inventory at the most recent costs, like this:

Nov.	18	Purchase	20 units @ $67 each =	$1,340
July	29	Purchase	9 units @ $65 each =	585
		Total	29 units	$1,925

The accountant now verifies the total cost of the 80 units sold:

$$\text{Cost of Goods Sold} = \text{Total Available} - \text{Ending Inventory}$$
$$\$4,972 = \$6,897 - \$1,925$$

Last-In, First-Out (LIFO) Method

The **last-in, first-out (LIFO) method** is based on the flow-of-cost assumption that the most recently purchased articles are sold first and the articles remaining in the ending inventory are the oldest items. As an example, think of a coal yard selling coal. When the coal yard buys coal from its supplier, the new coal is added to the top of the pile. When the coal yard sells coal to its customer, coal is taken off the top of the pile. Consequently, the ending inventory consists of those first few tons at the bottom of the pile. And, unless the pile is exhausted, they will never be sold.

Meanwhile, back at Whitewater Raft Supply, the firm sold 80 units. The accountant calculates the cost of the life vests sold on a last-in, first-out (LIFO) basis:

Nov.	18	Purchase	20 units @ $67 each =	$1,340
July	29	Purchase	35 units @ $65 each =	2,275
Mar.	16	Purchase	25 units @ $63 each =	1,575
		Total	80 units	$5,190

Whitewater Raft Supply has the 29 oldest units (or the units at the bottom of the pile) on hand in the ending inventory. The accountant records the ending inventory at the earliest costs, like this:

Jan.	1	Beginning inventory	24 units @ $58 each =	$1,392
Mar.	16	Purchase	5 units @ $63 each =	315
		Total	29 units	$1,707

The accountant now verifies the total cost of the 80 units sold:

$$\text{Cost of Goods Sold} = \text{Total Available} - \text{Ending Inventory}$$
$$\$5,190 = \$6,897 - \$1,707$$

Comparison of Methods

If prices don't change very much, all inventory methods give just about the same results. However, in a dynamic market where prices are constantly rising and falling, each method may yield different amounts. Here is a comparison of the results of the sale of the life vests, using the four methods we described.

Method	Cost of Goods Sold (80 Units)	Ending Inventory (29 Units)
Specific identification	$5,002.00	$1,895.00
Weighted-average-cost	5,061.88	1,835.12
First-in, first-out	4,972.00	1,925.00
Last-in, last-out	5,190.00	1,707.00

Assume that Whitewater Raft Supply sells the 80 life vests for $110 apiece, for a total of $8,800. The four methods yield the following gross profits:

	Specific Identification	Weighted-Average-Cost	First-In, First-Out	Last-In, Last-Out
Sales	$8,800.00	$8,800.00	$8,800.00	$8,800.00
Cost of goods sold	5,002.00	5,061.88	4,972.00	5,190.00
Gross profit	$3,798.00	$3,738.12	$3,828.00	$3,610.00

> **Remember**
>
> Goods do not always move as described in the FIFO, LIFO, and weighted-average-cost methods. The goods are assumed to move as described for the purpose of costing.

The effects of the methods are as follows:

1. Specific identification matches costs exactly with revenues.
2. Weighted-average-cost is a compromise between LIFO and FIFO, both for the amount of the ending inventory and for the cost of goods sold.
3. FIFO provides the most realistic amount for ending merchandise inventory in the Current Assets section of the balance sheet. The ending inventory is valued at the most recent costs, referred to as replacement cost.
4. LIFO provides the most realistic amount for the Cost of Goods Sold section of the income statement, because the items that have been sold will have to be replaced at the most recent costs.

Tax Effect of LIFO

In a period of rising prices, LIFO yields the lowest gross profit and hence the lowest income taxes because the most recent (higher) costs are assigned to the cost of goods sold (expense). For the past 40 years, prices in most industries have just kept going up, providing a built-in income tax advantage for users of LIFO. In effect, a business using LIFO is postponing paying income taxes. Since the money is not paid to the government, the business has the use of the money. Consequently, the money saved can be used to finance the purchase of more inventory or to pay off interest-bearing debts. When prices fall, companies using LIFO are at a disadvantage from the standpoint of income taxes.

Bear in mind that the cost figure determined by the different methods may have nothing to do with the physical flow of the goods. By physical flow, we mean the order in which specific items are taken out of inventory and sold.

The **consistency principle** is a fundamental principle of accounting. We have seen that a firm can increase or decrease its gross profit, and likewise its net income and income taxes, by changing the flow-of-cost assumption from one method to another—from FIFO to LIFO, for example. Although a firm may change its method of assigning inventory costs, it may not change back and forth repeatedly. Consistency in the method of determining cost of goods sold and the related cost of the ending inventory is necessary to conform with generally accepted accounting principles. A

> **Remember**
>
> The cost figure determined by the different methods may have nothing to do with the physical flow of goods.

business must disclose any change it makes in its method of accounting for inventories for book purposes. For income tax purposes, a business must consistently use the same method of accounting for inventories. Only with IRS approval can a company change its accounting method for inventories.

LOWER-OF-COST-OR-MARKET RULE

All the methods for determining the cost of ending inventory are based on cost per unit. In our examples, prices were generally rising. However, sometimes the replacement cost of items in stock is *less* than the original market cost. The word *market* refers to the current price charged in the market. It is the price at which, *at the time of taking the inventory,* the items could be bought through the usual channels and in the usual quantities. The current prices may be quoted in catalogs or reflect contract quotations.

The **lower-of-cost-or-market (LCM) rule** says that, under certain conditions, when the replacement or market cost is lower than the original cost, the inventory should be valued at the lower cost to comply with the accounting concept of conservatism. For example, the inventory of a store includes 20 leather purses originally purchased for $24 each (total, $480). At the time the inventory is being taken, the same type of leather purse may be purchased (replaced) for $17 each (total, $340). Under the lower-of-cost-or-market rule, the inventory is valued at $340. In this example, the original cost of $24 may have been determined by the specific identification method, the weighted-average-cost method, or the FIFO method. Under the tax law, the lower-of-cost-or-market rule may not be used when the original cost is determined by the LIFO method because this method already offers tax advantages.

METHODS OF ASSIGNING COSTS TO ENDING INVENTORY—PERPETUAL INVENTORY SYSTEM

When a company uses the perpetual inventory system, the value of the ending inventory and cost of goods sold will be the same under the specific identification method and the first-in, first-out method. However, under the weighted-average-cost method and the last-in, first-out method, the value of the ending inventory and cost of goods sold will be different. We will now demonstrate how to calculate the weighted-average-cost method and last-in, first-out method for Whitewater Raft Supply assuming the perpetual inventory system.

Remember, Whitewater Raft Supply had 109 life vests available for sale during the year:

Jan.	1	Beginning inventory	24 units @ $58 each =	$1,392
Mar.	16	Purchase	30 units @ $63 each =	1,890
July	29	Purchase	35 units @ $65 each =	2,275
Nov.	18	Purchase	20 units @ $67 each =	1,340
		Total available	109 units	$6,897

Now assume that Whitewater Raft Supply sold 80 units on the following dates:

Feb.	28	15 units
Apr.	3	17 units
June	21	16 units
Dec.	2	32 units
		80 units

Moving-Average-Cost Method

When a company uses the perpetual inventory system and records inventory under the weighted-average-cost method, an average cost of inventory must be determined before each sale. This method, when completed using the perpetual inventory system, is often called the **moving-average-cost method**.

To calculate the moving average cost per unit, Whitewater Raft Supply divides the total cost *at time of sale* by the total units *at time of sale*.

LEARNING OBJECTIVE

3a

Determine unit cost, the value of the ending inventory, and the cost of goods sold under the perpetual inventory system by the moving-average-cost method.

Moving Average Cost per Unit = Total Cost *at time of sale* ÷ Total Units *at time of sale*

The accountant calculates the total cost of the life vests on a moving average basis as follows:

		Purchases	Cost of Goods Sold	Ending Inventory	Average Cost per Unit
Jan.	1			24 units @ $58.00 each = $1,392.00	Avg = $1,392 / 24 units = $58.00
Feb.	28		15 units @ $58.00 each = $ 870.00	9 units @ $58.00 each = $ 522.00	Avg = $522 / 9 units = $58.00
Mar.	16	30 units @ $63 each = $1,890		9 units @ $58.00 each = $ 522.00 30 units @ $63.00 each = 1,890.00 39 units $2,412.00	Avg = $2,412 / 39 units = $61.85
Apr.	3		17 units @ $61.85 each = $1,051.45	22 units @ $61.85 each = $1,360.70	Avg = $1,360.70 / 22 units = $61.85
June	21		16 units @ $61.85 each = $ 989.60	6 units @ $61.85 each = $ 371.10	Avg = $371.10 / 6 units = $61.85
July	29	35 units @ $65 each = $2,275		6 units @ $61.85 each = $ 371.10 35 units @ $65.00 each = 2,275.00 41 units $2,646.10	Avg = $2,646.10 / 41 units = $64.54
Nov.	18	20 units @ $67 each = $1,340		41 units @ $64.54 each = $2,646.10* 20 units @ $67.00 each = 1,340.00 61 units $3,986.10	Avg = $3,986.10 / 61 units = $65.35
Dec.	2		32 units @ $65.35 each = $2,091.20 $5,002.25	29 units @ $65.35 each = $1,895.15	

* Rounded

Notice that on the sale of April 3, the accountant uses the average cost per unit on hand ($61.85, or $2,412/39 units) when determining the cost of goods sold. Each time there is a change in inventory, the accountant must calculate a new average.

LEARNING
OBJECTIVE
3b

Determine unit cost, the value of the ending inventory, and the cost of goods sold under the perpetual inventory system by the last-in, first-out method.

Last-In, First-Out (LIFO) Method

When using the last-in, first-out (LIFO) method under the perpetual inventory system, the accountant must keep a running total of ending inventory. Each time a sale happens, the accountant looks to the previous inventory balance to determine which units are sold. Whitewater Raft Supply calculates the total cost of the life vests sold on a last-in, first-out (LIFO) basis as follows:

	Purchases	Cost of Goods Sold	Ending Inventory
Jan. 1			24 units @ $58 each = $1,392
Feb. 28		15 units @ $58 each = $ 870	9 units @ $58 each = $ 522
Mar. 16	30 units @ $63 each = $1,890		9 units @ $58 each = $ 522 30 units @ $63 each = 1,890 39 units $2,412
Apr. 3		17 units @ $63 each = $1,071	9 units @ $58 each = $ 522 13 units @ $63 each = 819 22 units $1,341
June 21		13 units @ $63 each = $ 819 3 units @ $58 each = $ 174	6 units @ $58 each = $ 348
July 29	35 units @ $65 each = $2,275		6 units @ $58 each = $ 348 35 units @ $65 each = 2,275 41 units $2,623
Nov. 18	20 units @ $67 each = $1,340		6 units @ $58 each = $ 348 35 units @ $65 each = 2,275 20 units @ $67 each = 1,340 61 units $3,963
Dec. 2		20 units @ $67 each = $1,340 12 units @ $65 each = $ 780 $5,054	6 units @ $58 each = $ 348 23 units @ $65 each = 1,495 29 units $1,843

For example, note that for the sale on April 3 of 17 life vests, the last units in (March 16 purchase) were the first units sold. This left the company with 9 units from beginning inventory and 13 units (30 – 17) from the March 16 purchase. Next, review the December 2 sale of 32 units. Twenty units were sold from the last units in (November 18 purchase) and 12 units were sold from the July 29 purchase.

Whitewater Raft Supply's accountant now verifies the total cost of the 80 life vests sold:

Cost of Goods Sold = Total Available − Ending Inventory

$5,054   = $6,897   − $1,843

Remember, that the calculation of the first-in, first-out (FIFO) method would be the same under either method. In summary, here is a comparison of the results of the sale of the life vests using the perpetual inventory system.

Method	Cost of Goods Sold (80 Units)	Ending Inventory (29 Units)
Moving-average-cost	$5,002.25	1,895.15
First-in, first-out	4,972.00	1,925.00
Last-in, last-out	5,054.00	1,843.00

Perpetual Inventory Record

When a firm uses the perpetual inventory system, Merchandise Inventory is a controlling account. The firm maintains an individual record (either manually or on the computer) for each kind of product in the subsidiary ledger, recording the number of units received as "units received" and the number of units sold as "units sold." The firm records the remaining balance after each receipt or sale. Companies may keep perpetual inventories by any of the four methods. Assume that Whitewater Raft Supply maintains a perpetual inventory of rafting paddles on a LIFO basis, as shown in Figure 7.

The ending balance of 30 units amounts to $2,223 ($648 + $1,575). Nineteen paddles were sold at $115 each, for total sales of $2,185, and gross profit is $775.

Sales	$2,185
Less Cost of Goods Sold	1,410
Gross Profit	$ 775

4 LEARNING OBJECTIVE

Complete a perpetual inventory record card.

Perpetual Inventory Records in Electronic Accounting Systems

Computers—which can retrieve an item of stored information in a fraction of a second—have enabled business firms to maintain perpetual inventories even when a wide variety of products and a large volume of transactions are involved. Think of the benefits a computer terminal would provide for a car parts store connected to its regional distribution center.

Each item of stock in the inventory is assigned a code number. Whenever the amount of an item changes, information concerning the change is fed into

FIGURE 7 Perpetual inventory record card

INVENTORY RECORD CARD

ITEM Rafting Paddles, Clayton No. 841   LOCATION Warehouse, Rafting Accessory Section

MAXIMUM 40   MINIMUM 40   METHOD LIFO

	Purchased at Cost			Sales			Cost of Goods Sold			Inventory at Cost		
Date	Units	Cost	Total	Units	Price	Total	Units	Cost	Total	Units	Cost	Total
1/2	Bal.									14	$72	$1,008
2/6				5	$115	$ 575	5	$72	$ 360	9	72	648
2/22	35	$75	$2,625							{ 9	72	648
										35	75	2,625
3/14				6	115	690	6	75	450	{ 9	72	648
										29	75	2,175
3/29				8	115	920	8	75	600	{ 9	72	648
										21	75	1,575
Total	35		$2,625	19		$2,185	19		$1,410			

the computer by an online data entry terminal. The computer performs the arithmetic operations and determines the new balance in accordance with the inventory method in use: LIFO, FIFO, or moving-average. Thus the firm can determine the current status of any given item instantaneously. Whenever desired, the computer can list the balances of all the items in the inventory, in terms of both units and dollars.

As another illustration, in many department stores the cash registers (terminals) are linked directly to a computer center. When a sale is made, the salesperson punches in the item number, the quantity, and the price of the item. In other stores, clerks use a wand or gun to scan bar codes on individual tickets. And in supermarkets across the country, cashiers pass purchased items over scanners at the checkout register. With the information about the sale stored in the computer, management may obtain inventory quantities, costs, and total sales at any time as well as the program's prompting reordering of items that have reached a critical level.

Our discussion of perpetual inventories has been geared to merchandising firms. However, manufacturing concerns use perpetual inventories almost exclusively. A lumber mill, for example, uses the balances of daily inventories as a basis for deciding which sizes of lumber to cut: 2" × 4" × 8', 1" × 3" × 6', and so on.

CHAPTER REVIEW

Study & Practice

LEARNING OBJECTIVE

1 *Determine the overstatement or understatement of cost of goods sold, gross profit, and net income resulting from a change in the ending merchandise inventory amount.*

The amounts of the beginning and ending merchandise inventories appear in the Cost of Goods Sold section of the income statement.

If the Ending Inventory Is	Net Income Will Be
Understated	Understated
Overstated	Overstated
If the Beginning Inventory Is	**Net Income Will Be**
Understated	Overstated
Overstated	Understated

PRACTICE EXERCISE 1

a. If the ending inventory for Company A is understated by $35,320, how will this impact net income and by how much?

b. If the ending inventory for Company B is overstated by $7,262, how will this impact net income and by how much?

c. If the beginning inventory of Company C is understated by $16,838, how will this impact net income and by how much?

d. If the beginning inventory of Company D is overstated by $29,310, how will this impact net income and by how much?

PRACTICE EXERCISE 1 SOLUTION

a. Net income will be understated by $35,320 because Cost of Goods Sold will be overstated.

b. Net income will be overstated by $7,262 because Cost of Goods Sold will be understated.

c. Net income will be overstated by $16,838 because Cost of Goods Sold will be understated.

d. Net income will be understated by $29,310 because Cost of Goods Sold will be overstated.

LEARNING OBJECTIVE

2a
Determine unit cost, the value of the ending inventory, and the cost of goods sold under the periodic inventory system by the specific identification method.

Used for high-value items when a firm can identify each item on hand with its respective price.

PRACTICE EXERCISE 2a

Assume that Thomas Hardware Store has a September beginning inventory of custom stone outdoor fireplaces consisting of 165 units @ $290 each, or $47,850. During the month, the following purchases were made:

Sept.	6	20 units @ $300 each =	$ 6,000
	12	17 units @ $320 each =	5,440
	15	25 units @ $330 each =	8,250
	26	12 units @ $350 each =	4,200
		74 units	$23,890

When Thomas Hardware Store takes inventory at the end of the month, it finds that there are 39 outdoor fireplaces left in stock; 10 of these were bought on September 6, 9 were bought on September 12, 18 were bought on September 15, and 2 were bought on September 26. Determine the value of the ending inventory and the cost of goods sold using the specific identification method.

PRACTICE EXERCISE 2a SOLUTION

Sept.	6	Purchase	10 units @ $300 each =	$ 3,000
	12	Purchase	9 units @ $320 each =	2,880
	15	Purchase	18 units @ $330 each =	5,940
	26	Purchase	2 units @ $350 each =	700
		Total	39 units	$12,520

Beginning inventory (165 units)	$47,850
Purchases (74 units)	23,890
Total outdoor fireplaces available (239 units)	$71,740
Less ending inventory (39 units)	12,520
Cost of goods sold (200 units)	$59,220

2b **LEARNING OBJECTIVE**

Determine unit cost, the value of the ending inventory, and the cost of goods sold under the periodic inventory system by the weighted-average-cost method.

Number of Units of Each Purchase × Unit Price = Cost of Each Purchase.
Cost of Beginning Inventory + Costs of All Purchases = Total Cost.
Total Cost ÷ Total Units = Weighted-Average Cost per Unit.

PRACTICE EXERCISE 2b

Shrout, Inc., has a February beginning inventory of model #J678 oscillating floor heaters consisting of 150 units at $79 each. Purchases and sales during February are as follows:

Feb. 3 Sold 10 units.
    10 Purchased 10 units @ $81 each.
    14 Sold 14 units.
    23 Purchased 22 units @ $83 each.
    26 Sold 17 units.

Calculate the cost of the ending inventory under the weighted-average-cost method.

PRACTICE EXERCISE 2b SOLUTION

Feb.	1	Beginning inventory	150 units @ $79 each =	$11,850
	10	Purchase	10 units @ $81 each =	810
	23	Purchase	22 units @ $83 each =	1,826
		Total available	182 units	$14,486

Average Cost per Unit = $14,486 ÷ 182 units = $79.59

Number of Units Sold = 10 + 14 + 17 = 41 units

Number of Units in Ending Inventory = 182 units − 41 units = 141 units

Value of Ending Inventory = 141 units × $79.59 = $11,222.19

2c **LEARNING OBJECTIVE**

Determine unit cost, the value of the ending inventory, and the cost of goods sold under the periodic inventory system by the first-in, first-out method.

Costs are charged against revenue in the order in which they were incurred. This method produces the most realistic amount for the Current Assets section of the balance sheet.

PRACTICE EXERCISE 2c

Refer to the information in Practice Exercise 2b. Calculate the cost of the ending inventory under the first-in, first-out method.

PRACTICE EXERCISE 2c SOLUTION

Feb.	23	Purchase	22 units @ $83 each =	$ 1,826
	10	Purchase	10 units @ $81 each =	810
	1	Beginning inventory	109 units @ $79 each =	8,611
		Ending inventory	141 units	$11,247

2d **LEARNING OBJECTIVE**
Determine unit cost, the value of the ending inventory, and the cost of goods sold under the periodic inventory system by the last-in, first-out method.

Costs that are charged against revenue are the most recent costs. This method produces the most realistic amount for the Cost of Goods Sold section of the income statement. In an era of rising prices, the LIFO method yields the lowest net income. Firms must be consistent in their use of inventory methods.

PRACTICE EXERCISE 2d

Refer to the information in Practice Exercise 2b. Calculate the cost of the ending inventory under the last-in, first-out method.

PRACTICE EXERCISE 2d SOLUTION

Feb.	1	Beginning inventory	141 units @ $79 each =	$11,139
		Ending inventory	141 units	$11,139

3a **LEARNING OBJECTIVE**
Determine unit cost, the value of the ending inventory, and the cost of goods sold under the perpetual inventory system by the moving-average-cost method.

PRACTICE EXERCISE 3a

Refer to the information in Practice Exercise 2b. Assume that Shrout, Inc., uses the perpetual inventory system. Calculate the cost of goods sold and the cost of the ending inventory under the moving-average-cost method.

PRACTICE EXERCISE 3a SOLUTION

	Purchases	Cost of Goods Sold	Ending Inventory	Average Cost per Unit
Feb. 1			150 units @ $79.00 each = $11,850.00	Avg = $11,850 / 150 units = $79.00
3		10 units @ $79.00 each = $ 790.00	140 units @ $79.00 each = $11,060.00	Avg = $11,060 / 140 units = $79.00
10	10 units @ $81 each = $ 810.00		140 units @ $79.00 each = $11,060.00 10 units @ $81.00 each = 810.00 150 units $11,870.00	Avg = $11,870 / 150 units = $79.13
14		14 units @ $79.13 each = $ 1,107.82	136 units @ $79.13 each = $10,761.68	Avg = $10,761.68 / 136 units = $79.13
23	22 units @ $83 each = $1,826.00		136 units @ $79.13 each = $10,761.68 22 units @ $83.00 each = 1,826.00 158 units $12,587.68	Avg = $12,587.68 / 158 units = $79.67
26		17 units @ $79.67 each = $1,354.39 $3,252.21	141 units @ $79.67 each = $11,233.47	

3b **LEARNING OBJECTIVE**

Determine unit cost, the value of the ending inventory, and the cost of goods sold under the perpetual inventory system by the last-in, first-out method.

PRACTICE EXERCISE 3b

Refer to the information in Practice Exercise 2b. Assume that Shrout, Inc., uses the perpetual inventory system. Calculate the cost of goods sold and the cost of the ending inventory under the last-in, first-out method.

PRACTICE EXERCISE 3b SOLUTION

	Purchases	Cost of Goods Sold	Ending Inventory
Feb. 1			150 units @ $79 each = $11,850
3		10 units @ $79 each = $ 790	140 units @ $79 each = $11,060
10	10 units @ $81 each = $ 810		140 units @ $79 each = $11,060 10 units @ $81 each = 810 150 units $11,870
14		10 units @ $81 each = $ 810 4 units @ $79 each = $ 316	136 units @ $79 each = $10,744
23	22 units @ $83 each = $1,826		136 units @ $79 each = $10,744 22 units @ $83 each = 1,826 158 units $12,570
26		17 units @ $83 each = $1,411 $3,327	136 units @ $79 each = $10,744 5 units @ $83 each = 415 141 units $11,159

LEARNING OBJECTIVE

4

Complete a perpetual inventory record card.

The perpetual inventory record card contains columns for the following information: date of purchase, number of units purchased, cost per unit purchased, total cost of purchase, number of units sold, selling price per unit of goods sold, total selling price of units sold, number of units sold, cost per unit sold, total cost of goods sold, number of units in ending inventory, cost per unit of goods in ending inventory, and total cost of goods in ending inventory.

PRACTICE EXERCISE 4

Answer the following questions about the perpetual inventory record card provided below.

a. Why were the paddles sold on March 14 removed from the $72 inventory at cost amount instead of the $75 inventory at cost amount?

b. Assume that the inventory valuation method being used was LIFO instead of FIFO. By how much would the ending inventory at cost amount differ? (Hint: Refer to the perpetual inventory record card on page 647.)

PRACTICE EXERCISE 4 SOLUTION

a. The sale was made from the $72 inventory at cost amount because the method being used is FIFO, which means that the oldest purchased inventory is the first used to fulfill a sale.

b. $2,250 (FIFO) − [$1,575 + $648 (LIFO)] = $27

INVENTORY RECORD CARD

ITEM Rafting Paddles, Clayton No. 841

LOCATION Warehouse, Rafting Accessory Section

MAXIMUM 40   **MINIMUM** 40   **METHOD** FIFO

	Purchased at Cost			Sales			Cost of Goods Sold			Inventory at Cost		
Date	Units	Cost	Total	Units	Price	Total	Units	Cost	Total	Units	Cost	Total
1/2	Bal.									14	$72	$1,008
2/6				5	$115	$ 575	5	$72	$ 360	9	72	648
2/22	35	$75	$2,625							{ 9	72	648
										35	75	2,625
3/14				6	115	690	6	72	432	{ 3	72	216
										35	75	2,625
3/29				8	115	920	3	72	216			
							5	75	375	{ 30	75	2,250
Total	35		$2,625	19		$2,185	19		$1,383			

Glossary

Consistency principle An accounting principle that requires that a particular accounting procedure, once adopted, not be changed from one fiscal period to another. *(p. 643)*

First-in, first-out (FIFO) method A procedure for assigning costs to merchandise sold based on the flow-of-cost assumption that units are sold in the order in which they were acquired. Unsold units on hand at date of inventory are assumed to be valued at the most recent costs. *(p. 641)*

Last-in, first-out (LIFO) method A procedure for assigning costs to merchandise sold based on the flow-of-cost assumption that units sold are recorded at the costs of the most recently acquired units. Unsold units on hand at date of inventory are assumed to be valued at the earliest costs. *(p. 642)*

Lower-of-cost-or-market (LCM) rule In cases where there is a difference between the original price and the market price of goods, using the lower price for determining the value of the ending inventory. The term *market price* means current replacement price. *(p. 644)*

Moving-average-cost method A modification of the weighted-average-cost method, used for computing the average cost of a perpetual inventory. The firm determines the moving-average unit price each time inventory is purchased. *(p. 645)*

Specific identification method Counting the actual cost of each individual item in the ending inventory. *(p. 640)*

Weighted-average-cost method A procedure for determining the cost of the ending inventory by multiplying the weighted-average cost per unit by the number of remaining units. *(p. 641)*

CHAPTER ASSIGNMENTS

Discussion Questions

1. Explain the consistency principle. How can the consistency principle relate to inventory costing?
2. In periods of steadily rising prices, which inventory method (weighted-average-cost, FIFO, or LIFO) will give (a) the highest net income? (b) the lowest net income?
3. If the ending merchandise inventory of Year 1 is mistakenly understated by $3,000, what is the effect on the following:
   a. Year 1's net income?
   b. Year 1's balance sheet?
   c. Year 2's net income?
4. State an advantage and a disadvantage of LIFO.
5. What is meant by the specific identification method of pricing inventory? Give an example of a situation in which this method would be suitable.
6. Because of an error, goods costing $2,700 were omitted from the ending inventory. What effect does this omission have on the company's gross profit in the current year and in the following year?
7. If there is an error that understates the ending inventory of $255,000 of year 1 by $3,500, what is the effect on net income? What will the impact be on the net income of year 2?
8. Which inventory method is the same regardless of using the perpetual or periodic inventory system? How do the other two methods differ when using the perpetual inventory system?

Exercises

EXERCISE 16-1 An abbreviated income statement for Morley Company for this fiscal year is as follows:

 **LO** 1

PRACTICE EXERCISE 1

Net Sales		$155,000
Cost of Goods Sold:		
Merchandise Inventory, January 1	$132,000	
Purchases (net)	25,000	
Cost of Goods Available for Sale	$157,000	
Less Merchandise Inventory, Dec. 31	37,000	
Cost of Goods Sold		120,000
Gross Profit		$ 35,000
Operating Expenses		18,000
Net Income		$ 17,000

An accountant discovers that the ending inventory is overstated by $5,700. What effect does this have on cost of goods sold, gross profit, and net income in this fiscal year?

EXERCISE 16-2 Condensed income statements for Saunder Company for two years are presented here.

 LO 1

PRACTICE EXERCISE 1

	2010		2009	
Net Sales		$91,000		$98,000
Cost of Goods Sold:				
Merchandise Inventory (beginning)	$12,000		$15,000	
Purchases (net)	47,000		49,000	
Cost of Goods Available for Sale	$59,000		$64,000	
Less Merchandise Inventory (ending)	14,000		12,000	
Cost of Goods Sold		45,000		52,000
Gross Profit		$46,000		$46,000
Operating Expenses		23,000		21,000
Net Income		$23,000		$25,000

After the end of 2010, it was discovered that an error had been made in 2009. Ending inventory in 2009 should have been $11,000 instead of $12,000. Determine the corrected net income for 2009 and 2010.

a. Did the error understate or overstate cost of goods sold for 2009?
b. Did the error understate or overstate net income for 2009?
c. What is the amount of total net income for the two-year period with the error ($12,000) and corrected ($11,000)?

EXERCISE 16-3 The records of Kramer Company show the following data as of January 31, the end of the fiscal year. Determine the value of the ending merchandise inventory.

 LO 1

PRACTICE EXERCISE 1

a. Cost of goods on hand, based on physical count, $203,250.
b. Cost of defective goods (to be thrown away) included in **a**, $430.
c. Cost of goods shipped out FOB destination on January 30, with an expected delivery date of approximately four days, $2,983; not included in **a**.

d. Goods purchased January 28, FOB shipping point, delivered to the transportation company on January 31, $1,259; not included in **a**.

e. Cost of goods sold to a customer on January 30, paid for in full and awaiting shipping instructions, $1,761; not included in **a**.

2b,2c,2d **LO**

PRACTICE EXERCISES
2b,2c,2d

EXERCISE 16-4 Megan's Garden Shop maintains an inventory of mower blades on a periodic basis. Purchases of the blades during the year are as shown.

Jan.   1   Inventory of 30 units @ $215 each.
Mar.   8   Purchased 20 units @ $220 each.
May   15   Purchased 15 units @ $225 each.
         30   Purchased 20 units @ $228 each.

The ending inventory, by physical count, is 52 units. Determine the value of the ending inventory and the cost of goods sold by the following methods: weighted-average-cost; first-in, first-out; and last-in, first-out. (Round all computations to two decimal places.)

2b,2c,2d **LO**

PRACTICE EXERCISES
2b,2c,2d

EXERCISE 16-5 Landor Office Supplies records inventory on a periodic basis and has a July beginning inventory of model 77 desk lamps consisting of 188 units at $84.50 each. Purchases and sales during July are as follows:

July   5   Sold 15 units.
         12   Purchased 12 units @ $86 each.
         14   Sold 18 units.
         25   Purchased 25 units @ $88 each.
         30   Sold 19 units.

Calculate the cost of the ending inventory under each of the following methods: weighted-average-cost; first-in, first-out; and last-in, first-out. (Round all computations to two decimal places.)

2b,2c,2d **LO**

PRACTICE EXERCISES
2b,2c,2d

EXERCISE 16-6 If the mower blades in Exercise 16-4 were sold during the year for $265 each, determine the gross profit using the weighted-average-cost; and first-in, first-out; and last-in, first-out methods.

3a,3b **LO**

PRACTICE EXERCISES
3a,3b

EXERCISE 16-7 Using the information in Exercise 16-5, assume that Landor Office Supplies records inventory on a perpetual basis and calculate the cost of the ending inventory under each of the following methods: moving-average-cost; and last-in, first-out. (Round all computations to two decimal places.)

4 **LO**

PRACTICE EXERCISE 4

EXERCISE 16-8 Enviro Systems keeps perpetual inventories on energy-efficient stoves, using the first-in, first-out method. Determine the cost of goods sold in each sale and the inventory balance after each sale by completing the inventory record card (omitting the sales column) for the following purchases and sales of energy-efficient stoves:

Jan.   1   Inventory of 40 units @ $415 each.
         25   Sold 14 units.
Mar.   4   Purchased 20 units @ $420 each.
         15   Sold 12 units.
June   5   Sold 12 units.
         22   Purchased 20 units @ $422 each.

Problem Set A

For additional help, see the demonstration problem at the beginning of each chapter in your Working Papers.

PROBLEM 16-1A Boloit and Company's inventory of LB163 on January 1 was 10,000 gallons, costing $0.42 per gallon (periodic inventory). In addition to this beginning inventory, purchases during the next six months were as follows:

Date			Quantity (Gallons)	Cost per Gallon	Total Cost
Jan.	1	Inventory	10,000	$0.42	$4,200
	14		11,000	0.43	4,730
Feb.	21		9,000	0.44	3,960
Mar.	7		7,000	0.445	3,115
Apr.	19		10,000	0.45	4,500
May	5		9,000	0.46	4,140
June	2		10,000	0.47	4,700
	29		6,000	0.48	2,880

The inventory on June 30 was 15,000 gallons. During this six-month period, Boloit and Company sold LB163 for $0.60 per gallon. Assume that no liquid was lost through evaporation or leakage.

Required
1. Find the cost of the ending inventory by the following methods:
   a. Weighted-average-cost (Round to three decimal places.)
   b. First-in, first-out
   c. Last-in, first-out
2. Determine the cost of goods sold according to the three methods of costing inventory.
3. Determine the amount of the gross profit according to the three methods of costing inventory.

Check Figure
Ending inventory under
FIFO, $7,110

PROBLEM 16-2A Cozler Jewelers uses the periodic inventory system. Data pertaining to the inventory on January 1, the beginning of the fiscal year, purchases during the year, and the inventory count on December 31 are as follows:

	Model		
	JG491	**CP925**	**8M21**
Inventory, Jan. 1	12 @ $433	4 @ $785	20 @ $319
First purchase	18 @ $445	8 @ $786	27 @ $321
Second purchase	24 @ $451	10 @ $787	29 @ $322
Third purchase	18 @ $451	7 @ $788	31 @ $324
Fourth purchase	14 @ $457		25 @ $327
Inventory, Dec. 31	16	8	30

Required
1. Determine the cost of the inventory on December 31 by the weighted-average-cost method. (Round to two decimal places.)
2. Determine the cost of the inventory on December 31 by the first-in, first-out method.
3. Determine the cost of the inventory on December 31 by the last-in, first-out method.

Check Figure
Weighted-average-cost ending
inventory, $23,147.68

PROBLEM 16-3A Globe Company uses the perpetual inventory system. Globe Company has beginning inventory on December 1 of 225 units at $35. Data pertaining to the purchases and sales during the month are as follows:

| Date | Purchases | | Sales | |
	Units	Cost per Unit	Units	Price per Unit
Dec. 2	30	$36.00		
10			25	$60.00
15	20	37.00		
20			60	60.00
22			75	60.00
30	45	38.00		

Check Figure

Moving-average-cost ending inventory, $5,766.05

Required

1. Determine the cost of goods sold for December and the cost of the inventory on December 31 by the moving-average-cost method. (Round to two decimal places.)

2. Determine the cost of goods sold for December and the cost of the inventory on December 31 by the last-in, first-out method.

PROBLEM 16-4A Blake Company's beginning inventory of R317 is 160 units at a cost of $45 each. Dates of purchases and sales for a three-month period are as follows:

| Date | Purchases | | Sales | |
	Units	Cost per Unit	Units	Price per Unit
Jan. 16	225	$46.00		
18			70	$54.00
29			140	55.00
Feb. 5	235	47.60		
14			135	56.00
22			195	57.00
26	225	48.20		
Mar. 4			75	58.00
11	155	48.50		
17			85	59.00
30			135	59.00

Blake Company maintains a perpetual inventory record using the first-in, first-out method. The minimum number of units allowed in inventory is 80; the maximum is 420. Data for the month of January are recorded in the Working Papers.

Check Figure

Cost of goods sold, $39,099

Required

1. Record the data for purchases and sales of item R317 and for cost of goods sold in a perpetual inventory record using the first-in, first-out method for the months of February and March.

2. Determine the total cost of goods sold during the three-month period.

3. Determine the total sales for the three-month period.

4. Determine the gross profit from sales of item R317 for the period.

Problem Set B

For additional help, see the demonstration problem at the beginning of each chapter in your Working Papers.

 **LO** 2b,2c,2d

PROBLEM 16-1B Pardee Chemical's inventory of ND301 on January 1 was 7,500 gallons, costing $0.54 per gallon (periodic inventory). In addition to this beginning inventory, purchases during the next six months were as follows:

Date		Quantity (Gallons)	Cost per Gallon	Total Cost
Jan.	1 Inventory	7,500	$0.54	$4,050
	26	9,000	0.545	4,905
Feb.	4	11,000	0.55	6,050
	21	8,000	0.55	4,400
Mar.	7	10,000	0.555	5,550
	24	9,000	0.55	4,950
Apr.	19	8,000	0.55	4,400
May	31	7,000	0.55	3,850
June	15	5,000	0.57	2,850

Pardee Chemical's inventory on June 30 was 12,000 gallons. During this six-month period, the firm sold ND301 at $0.70 per gallon. Assume that no liquid was lost through evaporation or leakage.

Required
1. Find the cost of the ending inventory by the following methods:
   a. Weighted-average-cost (Round to three decimal places.)
   b. First-in, first-out
   c. Last-in, first-out
2. Determine the cost of goods sold according to the three methods of costing inventory.
3. Determine the amount of the gross profit according to the three methods of costing inventory.

Check Figure
Ending inventory under FIFO, $6,700

LO 2b,2c,2d

PROBLEM 16-2B ManCo Stereo uses the periodic inventory system. Data for its inventories on January 1, the beginning of the fiscal year, purchases during the year, and the inventory count at December 31 are as follows:

	Model		
	JG491	CP925	8M21
Inventory, Jan. 1	5 @ $527	5 @ $589	18 @ $327
First purchase	8 @ $456	8 @ $780	22 @ $363
Second purchase	10 @ $465	7 @ $831	34 @ $380
Third purchase	9 @ $425	6 @ $633	15 @ $358
Fourth purchase	8 @ $488		
Inventory, Dec. 31	9	8	21

Required
1. Determine the cost of the inventory on December 31 by the weighted-average-cost method. (Round to two decimal places.)
2. Determine the cost of the inventory on December 31 by the first-in, first-out method.
3. Determine the cost of the inventory on December 31 by the last-in, first-out method.

Check Figure
Weighted-average-cost ending inventory, $17,572.36

3a,3b

PROBLEM 16-3B Tri Workout Clothing Store uses the perpetual inventory system. Tri Workout has beginning inventory on February 1 of 650 units at $72. Data pertaining to the purchases and sales during the month are as follows:

Date		Purchases		Sales	
		Units	Cost per Unit	Units	Price per Unit
Feb.	3	15	$75.00		
	7			85	$90.00
	12			40	90.00
	18	30	76.00		
	24			60	90.00
	28	40	77.00		

Check Figure

Last-in, first-out cost of goods sold, $13,485

Required

1. Determine the cost of goods sold for February and the cost of the inventory on February 28 by the moving-average-cost method. (Round to two decimal places.)
2. Determine the cost of goods sold for February and the cost of the inventory on February 28 by the last-in, first-out method.

4 **LO**

PROBLEM 16-4B Baylor Company's beginning inventory of D520 is 150 units at a cost of $89 each. Dates of purchases and sales for a three-month period are as follows:

Date		Purchases		Sales	
		Units	Cost per Unit	Units	Price per Unit
Jan.	16	225	$90.50		
	18			70	$105.00
	29			130	105.00
Feb.	2	170	92.00		
	11			120	107.00
	17	200	95.00		
	27			160	112.00
Mar.	9			90	112.00
	14	120	97.50		
	22			70	112.00
	29			65	112.80

Baylor Company maintains a perpetual inventory record using the first-in, first-out method. The minimum number of units allowed in inventory is 130; the maximum is 450. Data for the month of January are recorded in the Working Papers.

Check Figure

Cost of goods sold, $64,552.50

Required

1. Record the data for purchases and sales of item D520 and for cost of goods sold in a perpetual inventory record using the first-in, first-out method for the months of February and March.
2. Determine the total cost of goods sold during the three-month period.
3. Determine the total sales for the three-month period.
4. Determine the gross profit from sales of item D520 for this period.

ACTIVITIES

CONSIDER AND COMMUNICATE

A person you work for in the accounting department is confused about FIFO and LIFO as methods of charging cost of goods sold against revenue. Explain, for each method, which units are used to calculate the cost of the ending inventory and which financial statement is emphasized. Also indicate which method results in a lower net income (assuming rising cost per unit).

CRITICAL THINKING

Your supervisor has asked you to evaluate the following situation and conditions: John Joseph's Music Store has taken inventory of the flutes, saxophones, and other reed instruments, as well as miscellaneous musical items that it sells retail. As the store's accountant, you gave your assistant instructions about taking the inventory and asked that unusual items be flagged for your review. Your assistant flagged the following items that need your review to determine if the item was correctly handled on the year-end inventory:

a. Last year's Model CB-4, tenor saxophone, is included in inventory at a cost of $357. (You happen to know that this outdated model can be purchased for $150, now that the new model is out.)

b. A purchase of two alto saxophones at $350 each was sent by the supplier on 12/29, FOB destination. The shipment had not arrived and was not included in inventory.

c. A purchase of two oboes at $450 each was sent by the supplier on 12/30, FOB shipping point. The shipment had not arrived and was not included in inventory.

d. You have received a credit memo for a damaged piccolo, cost $248, from a supplier. The supplier issued the notice based on your promise to ship the damaged unit back after the end of the year. The item is still in the warehouse, and the cost of $248 is included in the inventory.

e. A customer has paid $740 in full for a custom-made Native American flute that cost $540. The customer requested that you deliver it at the end of the first week of the new year. The value of the special flute is included in the inventory, as no one remembered to put a "sold" tag on it.

f. The shop owner has taken home a one-of-a-kind tenor saxophone to use during the holidays, after which he will return the saxophone to the shop. Retail value is $2,650; cost, $2,250. This item was not counted in inventory.

g. According to the company's layaway policy, a sale is not recorded until the merchandise is paid for in full, and then delivery is made. A customer has paid 25 percent of the $960 price of a French horn. The horn is set aside because the customer has put money down on it, and the $810 cost is not included in the inventory.

Required

1. What is the correct treatment for each item? Should you include it in inventory or exclude it? Why?

2. Was the item handled correctly by your assistant? If it was not correctly handled, what must be done to correct the inventory? Should you increase inventory (if so, by what amount) or decrease inventory (if so, by what amount)?

A QUESTION OF ETHICS

A large computer retailer has taken year-end inventory and has valued 80 Microgate X computers at $1,100 each, or $88,000—the original cost of the Microgate Xs. Current technologies have allowed the supplier to reduce the cost of the Microgate X to $900 each, although the computer store has not purchased any Microgate Xs at this price. Is the owner doing anything unethical by valuing the 80 Microgate Xs at the original cost of $88,000?

Estimating the Value of Inventories

LEARNING OBJECTIVES

After you have completed this appendix, you will be able to do the following:

 1 Estimate the value of inventory by the retail method.

 2 Estimate the value of inventory by the gross-profit method.

ACCOUNTING LANGUAGE

Gross-profit method *(p. 666)*

Normal markup *(p. 662)*

Retail method *(p. 662)*

To function efficiently, management must have interim income statements and balance sheets prepared monthly. Management needs a physical inventory at the end of the year, because inventory balance figures are an integral element of financial statements. However, because it is both time-consuming and expensive to take a physical inventory, management finds it more expedient to estimate the value of the ending inventory each month and to use these estimates on the monthly financial statements. Let's take a look at the two most frequently used methods of estimating the value of inventories: the retail method and the gross-profit method.

RETAIL METHOD OF ESTIMATING THE VALUE OF INVENTORIES

LEARNING OBJECTIVE 1

Estimate the value of inventory by the retail method.

The **retail method**, widely used by retail businesses, is based on both the cost and retail value of the goods. The retailer buys merchandise at cost, then adds the normal markup and prices the goods at the retail level. The **normal markup**—which is the normal amount, or percentage, that you add to the cost of an item to arrive at its selling price—covers operating expenses and profit. If a firm uses the retail method of estimating inventories, it must record the purchases-related accounts at both cost and retail values. The firm's accountant records retail values in supplementary records; he or she also records the physical inventory taken at the end of the previous year at both cost and retail values.

Example 1

Hall & Company takes a physical inventory at the end of each year and estimates the value of the inventory at the end of each month for its monthly financial statements.

The accountant for Hall & Company needs the following information to estimate the value of the ending merchandise inventory at cost:

- Cost value and retail value of merchandise on hand at the beginning of the month. (The inventory at the beginning of a given month is the same as the inventory at the end of the preceding month.)

	At Cost	At Retail
Merchandise Inventory (beginning)	$82,400	$137,200

- Delivered cost of purchases during the month, both cost value and retail value. The retail amounts include the cost plus the company's standard markup.

	At Cost		At Retail	
Purchases		$165,490		$275,816
Less: Purchases Returns and Allowances	$4,600		$7,600	
Purchases Discounts	3,800	8,400	6,400	14,000
Net Purchases		$157,090		$261,816
Add Freight In		8,710		14,518
Delivered Cost of Purchases		$165,800		$276,334

- Net sales for the month. All sales are recorded at retail price levels, as listed on sales slips and cash register tapes.

		At Retail	
Sales			$303,300
Less: Sales Returns and Allowances		$14,000	
Sales Discounts		5,300	19,300
Net Sales			$284,000

The accountant can determine the cost value of the ending inventory by following these four steps:

STEP 1. Determine the dollar value of goods available for sale, at cost and at retail. The cost amounts are the same as the Cost of Goods Available for Sale, which is part of the Cost of Goods Sold section of the income statement.

	At Cost	At Retail
Beginning inventory	$ 82,400	$137,200
Plus delivered cost of purchases	165,800	276,334
Goods available for sale	$248,200	$413,534

STEP 2. Find the ratio of the cost value of goods available for sale to the retail value of goods available for sale.

$$\frac{\text{Cost Value of Goods Available for Sale}}{\text{Retail Value of Goods Available for Sale}} = \frac{\$248,200}{\$413,534} = 60\% \text{ (rounded)}$$

STEP 3. Determine the retail value (selling price) of ending inventory.

Retail value of goods available	$413,534
Less net sales	284,000
Retail value of ending inventory	$129,534

Think of the retail value of the ending inventory this way: If the firm had $413,534 of goods available for sale, and $284,000 was actually sold, then the amount left over should be $129,534.

STEP 4. Convert the retail value of the ending inventory into the cost value of the ending inventory by using this formula and rounding to the nearest dollar:

$$\$129,534 \times 60\% = \$129,534 \times 0.60 = \underline{\$77,720} \text{ (rounded)}$$

Therefore, on its income statement for the month, Hall & Company records the value of the ending inventory as $77,720. If the retail value is $129,534 and 40 percent of this amount represents markup, the remaining 60 percent must be the cost.

Example 2

Halpin Company has the following account balances, as shown by T accounts:

Merchandise Inventory

+	−
Bal. 210,160	

Purchases

+	−
720,327	

Sales

−	+
	985,000

Purchases Returns and Allowances

−	+
	32,716

Sales Returns and Allowances

+	−
25,000	

Purchases Discounts

−	+
	14,082

Freight In

+	−
37,911	

Retail value of beginning inventory is $296,000 (the accountant picks up this amount from a report dated the end of the preceding month).

Delivered Cost of Purchases = Purchases − Purchases Returns and
Allowances − Purchases Discounts + Freight In
= $720,327 − $32,716 − $14,082 + $37,911
= $711,440

Retail value of delivered cost of purchases is $1,001,708 (the normal markup is added to the cost amount).

Net Sales = Sales − Sales Returns and Allowances
= $985,000 − $25,000
= $960,000

Again, the information is obtained by following the four steps:

STEP 1. Determine the dollar value of goods available for sale, at cost and at retail.

	At Cost	At Retail
Beginning inventory	$210,160	$ 296,000
Plus delivered cost of purchases	711,440	1,001,708
Goods available for sale	$921,600	$1,297,708

STEP 2. Find the ratio of the cost value of goods available for sale to the retail value of goods available for sale.

$$\frac{\text{Cost Value of Goods Available for Sale}}{\text{Retail Value of Goods Available for Sale}} = \frac{\$921,600}{\$1,297,708} = \underline{\underline{71\%}} \text{ (rounded)}$$

STEP 3. Determine the retail value (selling price) of ending inventory.

Retail value of goods available	$1,297,708
Less net sales	960,000
Retail value of ending inventory	$ 337,708

STEP 4. Convert the retail value of ending inventory into the cost value of ending inventory by using this formula and rounding to the nearest dollar:

$$\$337,708 \times 71\% = \$337,708 \times 0.71 = \underline{\underline{\$239,773}} \text{ (rounded)}$$

These examples assume that the retailer maintains the normal markup. In other words, we are assuming that the composition or mix of the items in the ending inventory, in terms of the ratio of cost price to retail price, remains the same for the entire stock of goods available for sale.

Markups and Markdowns

In our examples, the retailers used normal markups, but some stores use additional markups and markdowns. Retailers impose additional markups on top of normal markups when the merchandise involved is in great demand. Because of the highly desirable nature of certain goods (such as up-to-the-minute fashion), a store may feel that it can get higher-than-normal prices for these goods. Conversely, a store uses markdowns to sell slow-moving merchandise during a clearance sale.

When a store using the retail inventory method imposes additional markups and markdowns, it must keep track of them, so that it can calculate the ratio of the cost value of goods available to the retail value of goods available. Look at the following example of how a store keeps track of markups and markdowns:

STEP 1. Determine the dollar value of goods available for sale, at cost and at retail.

	At Cost	At Retail
Beginning inventory	$ 60,000	$ 90,000
Plus delivered cost of purchases	110,000	165,000
Plus additional markups		4,000
Goods available for sale	$170,000	$259,000

STEP 2. Find the ratio of the cost value of goods available for sale to the retail value of goods available for sale.

$$\frac{\text{Cost Value of Goods Available for Sale}}{\text{Retail Value of Goods Available for Sale}} = \frac{\$170,000}{\$259,000} = \underline{\underline{66\%}} \text{ (rounded)}$$

STEP 3. Determine the retail value (selling price) of ending inventory.

Retail value of goods available	$259,000
Less net sales	200,000
Less markdowns	3,000
Retail value of ending inventory	$ 56,000

STEP 4. Convert the retail value of the ending inventory into the cost value of the ending inventory by using this formula and rounding to the nearest dollar:

$56,000 × 0.66 = $36,960

The accountant adds any additional markups in the retail column of his or her Excel spreadsheet because such markups result in an increase in the retail value of the goods available for sale. For example, let's say that the price of a popular item is $40, and a store seizes the opportunity and marks it up to $49; this is a $9 increase in the retail value of the goods available for sale. On the other hand, when a store marks down the price of an item, the accountant deducts the amount of the markdown from the retail value of the goods available for sale (step 3) to obtain the retail value of the merchandise inventory at the end of a given month. For example, say that the price tag of an item is $389, but nobody is buying, so the store marks it down to $359. This means that there has been a $30 decrease in the retail value of these goods available for sale.

END-OF-YEAR PROCEDURE

It is important to take a physical inventory at the end of the year. Physical inventories may also be taken periodically during the year to spot-check the estimated inventories. Most retail stores record items in stock on the inventory sheets at retail prices (they take the total of all the price tags). It is then necessary to convert the total of the retail values into the total of the cost values, as in step 4. For example, suppose that the total retail value of the merchandise on all the inventory sheets is $96,000, and the ratio of cost value to retail value is

$$\frac{\text{Cost Value of Goods Available}}{\text{Retail Value of Goods Available}} = 70\%$$

The cost value of the goods is $96,000 × 0.70 = $67,200. The only difference between the steps taken to prepare the end-of-the-year statement and the steps taken to prepare the interim or monthly statements is that at the end of the year there is a physical count of the merchandise, and consequently you begin with step 4.

However, to determine the magnitude of shoplifting, or to verify the accuracy of the evaluation of the physical inventory, some firms go through the full procedure of estimating the value of the inventory at the end of the year. Then they take a physical count of the goods on hand and compare this value with the value of the estimated inventory.

GROSS-PROFIT METHOD OF ESTIMATING THE VALUE OF INVENTORIES

LEARNING OBJECTIVE 2

Estimate the value of inventory by the gross-profit method.

Sometimes a firm may find that the total of the retail prices of the beginning inventory and purchases is not readily available; in such cases, the firm naturally cannot use the retail method of estimating the value of the ending inventory. The **gross-profit method** is an alternative procedure that achieves the same objective.

The key element in this method is that the percentage of gross profit earned in the prior year will remain the same for the present year.

The term *gross profit*, as used on income statements, represents net sales less cost of goods sold:

Net sales	$60,000
Less cost of goods sold	45,000
Gross profit	$15,000

You arrive at the amount for the percentage of gross profit by dividing the gross profit by the net sales:

$$\text{Percentage of Gross Profit} = \frac{\text{Gross Profit}}{\text{Net Sales}} = \frac{\$15,000}{\$60,000} = \underline{\underline{25\%}}$$

A 25 percent gross-profit rate means that there is $0.25 of gross profit for every $1 of net sales. *Gross profit* is the profit earned on the sale of merchandise *before* other expenses are deducted. You can compute the gross-profit rate or percentage by using amounts from a recent income statement, or you may compute the percentage of gross profit from income statements from past years, using averages of amounts. The variation from year to year is usually relatively minor, unless marked changes in the firm's buying and selling policies have taken place.

You need the following information for the current year:

- Sales (balance of account to date)
- Sales Returns and Allowances (balance of account to date)
- Sales Discounts (balance of account to date)
- Beginning Merchandise Inventory (ending inventory of the previous period)
- Purchases (balance of account to date)
- Purchases Returns and Allowances (balance of account to date)
- Purchases Discounts (balance of account to date)
- Freight In (balance of account to date)

Example 1

On the night of April 29, Northeast Mountain Bikes Company was destroyed by fire. However, the company's books and records of transactions were saved. For insurance purposes, the owner must estimate the value of the inventory by the gross-profit method. The owner knows that the average gross-profit percentage for the past five years is 32 percent. By journalizing and posting the transactions of the current month, the company's accounts can be brought up to date from these sources:

- Sales (from sales journal, cash receipts journal, and invoices through April 29)
- Sales Returns and Allowances (from cash receipts journal and general journal)
- Merchandise Inventory, December 31 (ending inventory of last fiscal period)
- Purchases (from purchases journal and invoices through April 29)
- Purchases Returns and Allowances (from general journal)
- Purchases Discounts (from cash payments journal)
- Freight In (from purchases journal, cash payments journal, and invoices through April 29)

The owner of Northeast Mountain Bikes Company arranges these figures in the customary income statement format, extending from Sales to Gross Profit (see Figure 1).

FIGURE 1

Partial income statement for Northeast Mountain Bikes Company (without gross profit computed)

Northeast Mountain Bikes Company
Partial Income Statement
For Period January 1 through April 29, 20—

Revenue from Sales:			
Sales			$217,000
Less: Sales Returns and Allowances			17,000
Net Sales			$200,000
Cost of Goods Sold:			
Merchandise Inventory, January 1, 20—		$ 72,000	
Purchases		$136,000	
Less: Purchases Returns and Allowances	$14,000		
Purchases Discounts	2,400	16,400	
Net Purchases		$119,600	
Add Freight In		7,400	
Delivered Cost of Purchases		127,000	
Cost of Goods Available for Sale		$199,000	
Less Merchandise Inventory, April 29, 20—		⬭	
Cost of Goods Sold			⬭
Gross Profit			$ ⬭

$$\text{Percentage of Gross Profit} = \frac{\text{Gross Profit}}{\text{Net Sales}} = \frac{\text{Gross Profit}}{\$200,000} = \underline{\underline{32\%}}$$

$$\text{Gross Profit} = 0.32 \times \$200,000 = \underline{\underline{\$64,000}}$$

Next fill in the Gross Profit blank in the income statement (see Figure 2).

FIGURE 2

Partial income statement for Northeast Mountain Bikes Company (with gross profit computed)

Northeast Mountain Bikes Company
Partial Income Statement
For Period January 1 through April 29, 20—

Revenue from Sales:			
Sales			$217,000
Less: Sales Returns and Allowances			17,000
Net Sales			$200,000
Cost of Goods Sold:			
Merchandise Inventory, January 1, 20—		$ 72,000	
Purchases		$136,000	
Less: Purchases Returns and Allowances	$14,000		
Purchases Discounts	2,400	16,400	
Net Purchases		$119,600	
Add Freight In		7,400	
Delivered Cost of Purchases		127,000	
Cost of Goods Available for Sale		$199,000	
Less Merchandise Inventory, April 29, 20—		⬭	
Cost of Goods Sold			136,000
Gross Profit			$ 64,000

To find the cost of the merchandise at the end (April 29), we work backward. The cost of goods sold is the difference between net sales and gross profit, or $136,000 ($200,000 – $64,000). The equation follows below.

$$\text{Cost of Goods Sold} = \text{Net Sales} - \text{Gross Profit}$$
$$= \$200,000 - \$64,000$$
$$= \underline{\underline{\$136,000}}$$

Now that we have filled in the amounts for Gross Profit and Cost of Goods Sold, the partial income statement (from Cost of Goods Available for Sale through Gross Profit) looks like this:

Cost of Goods Available for Sale	$199,000	
Less Merchandise Inventory, April, 29, 20—	?	
Cost of Goods Sold		136,000
Gross Profit		$ 64,000

The cost of the merchandise inventory on April 29 is the difference between the cost of the goods available for sale and the cost of goods sold, or $63,000 ($199,000 – $136,000). The equation is as follows:

$$\text{Cost of Ending Inventory} = \text{Cost of Goods Available for Sale} - \text{Cost of Goods Sold}$$
$$= \mathbf{\$199,000 - \$136,000}$$
$$= \mathbf{\$63,000}$$

Cost of Goods Available for Sale	$199,000	
Less Merchandise Inventory, April, 29, 20—	63,000	
Cost of Goods Sold		136,000
Gross Profit		$ 64,000

The income statement is a very useful device in the box of tools that you have been accumulating. That is why we suggested earlier that you memorize the form to implant it firmly in your mind; then it will always be at your fingertips when you need it to do a specific job.

Example 2

Bellows Beauty Supply has an average gross-profit rate of 34 percent. Its account balances on May 31 of this year are shown by the following T accounts and by the partial income statement in Figure 3.

Merchandise Inventory		Purchases		Sales	
+	−	+	−	−	+
Bal. 83,118		201,067			314,719

	Purchases Returns and Allowances		Sales Returns and Allowances	
	−	+	+	−
		11,228	12,491	

	Purchases Discounts		Sales Discounts	
	−	+	+	−
		3,715	6,228	

	Freight In	
	+	−
	12,834	

	FIGURE 3
Partial income statement for Bellows Beauty Supply	

Bellows Beauty Supply
Partial Income Statement
For Period January 1 through May 31, 20—

Revenue from Sales:				
Sales				$314,719
Less: Sales Returns and Allowances			$ 12,491	
Sales Discounts			6,228	18,719
Net Sales				$296,000
Cost of Goods Sold:				
Merchandise Inventory, January 1, 20—			$ 83,118	
Purchases		$201,067		
Less: Purchases Returns and Allowances	$11,228			
Purchases Discounts	3,715	14,943		
Net Purchases		$186,124		
Add Freight In		12,834		
Delivered Cost of Purchases			198,958	
Cost of Goods Available for Sale			$282,076	
Less Merchandise Inventory, May 31, 20—			86,716	
Cost of Goods Sold				195,360
Gross Profit				$100,640

$$\text{Percentage of Gross Profit} = \frac{\text{Gross Profit}}{\text{Net Sales}} = \frac{\text{Gross Profit}}{\$296,000} = \underline{\underline{34\%}}$$

$$\text{Gross Profit} = \text{Net Sales} \times 0.34 = \$296,000 \times 0.34 = \$100,640$$

$$\begin{aligned}\text{Cost of Goods Sold} &= \text{Net Sales} - \text{Gross Profit}\\ &= \$296,000 - \$100,640 = \$195,360\end{aligned}$$

The cost of goods sold is equal to net sales minus gross profit, or $195,360 ($296,000 − $100,640). The ending merchandise inventory is the cost of goods available for sale minus the cost of goods sold, or $86,716 ($282,076 − $195,360).

$$\begin{aligned}\text{Ending Inventory} &= \text{Cost of Goods Available for Sale} - \text{Cost of Goods Sold}\\ &= \$282,076 - \$195,360 = \$86,716\end{aligned}$$

Glossary

Gross-profit method An alternative procedure (vs. the retail method) to estimating the value of inventories. The key element in this method is that the percentage of gross profit earned in the prior year will remain the same for the present year. (p. 666)

Normal markup The amount or percentage that is normally added to the cost of an item to arrive at its selling price. (p. 662)

Retail method A widely used procedure for estimating the value of inventories. The key elements in this method are the cost of the goods and the retail value of the goods both being recorded. (p. 662)

Problems

PROBLEM 16A-1 You are given the following information for Walden Toys at the end of its fiscal year, October 31:

LO 1

	At Cost	At Retail
Sales		$264,789
Sales Returns and Allowances		10,659
Purchases	$152,806	254,600
Purchases Returns and Allowances	7,026	11,712
Merchandise Inventory (beginning)	59,172	98,640
Freight In	8,042	13,534

Required

1. Determine the cost of the ending merchandise inventory as of October 31, presenting details of your computations.
2. At the end of the year, Walden Toys takes a physical inventory at marked selling prices and finds that the retail stock totals $98,889. There is a possibility that the difference between the estimated ending inventory and the actual physical inventory is due to shoplifting. Convert the value of the physical inventory at retail into its value at cost, and determine the amount of the loss.

Check Figure
Amount of the loss, $1,225.80

PROBLEM 16A-2 On May 10 of this year, a fire in the night destroyed the entire stock of merchandise of Kay's Crafts. Most of the accounting records were destroyed also. However, from assorted statements and documents, the firm's accountant was able to piece together the balances of several accounts. Over the past three years, the percentage of gross profit averaged 40 percent.

LO 2

Merchandise Inventory, January 1 (beginning of fiscal year)	$128,859
Account balances, as of May 10:	
Purchases	163,970
Purchases Returns and Allowances	984
Freight In	7,906
Sales	219,540
Sales Returns and Allowances	660

Required

Determine the cost of the ending merchandise inventory as of May 10, giving details of your computations.

Check Figure
Cost of ending inventory, $168,423

PROBLEM 16A-3 On the morning of July 27, the owner of Simone's opened her store and discovered that a robbery had taken place over the weekend. A large part of the stock had been stolen. However, the following information for the period January 1 through July 27 was available. Each year during the past four years, the store had earned an average 34 percent gross profit on sales.

LO 2

Merchandise Inventory, January 1	
(beginning of fiscal year)	$190,389
Account balances, as of July 27:	
Purchases	408,692
Purchases Returns and Allowances	10,986
Purchases Discounts	8,244
Freight In	24,703
Sales	596,134
Sales Returns and Allowances	6,134

Check Figure
Cost of ending inventory,
$215,154

Required

1. Determine the cost of the ending merchandise inventory as of July 27, giving details of your computations.
2. By physical count, the cost of the remaining inventory on hand is $80,940. What is the amount of the loss to be claimed for insurance purposes?

Property and Equipment and Intangible Assets

WHY IT MATTERS

SPANGLES, Wichita, Kansas

Think about the last time you had a hamburger—maybe it was at your local fast-food restaurant. If you were lucky, maybe it was a Spangles burger. Spangles enjoys a reputation in the Wichita, Kansas, area of providing high-quality food and offering a 1/3-lb. hamburger that has been voted "Best Burger" year after year.

Spangles is known not only for its food, but also for its retro look. When you walk into a Spangles restaurant, you step back into a 1950's diner complete with neon lights, pictures of pop stars from the '50s, and a Wurlitzer jukebox.

Two brothers, Craig and Dale Steven, opened their first restaurant in 1978. Following that first restaurant, Spangles continued to grow, developing into a multistore success. Currently, Spangles operates 25 restaurants in the Wichita, Kansas, area.

Spangles' success couldn't have happened without a continuing investment in property and equipment. The property and equipment that Spangles owns, such as buildings, hamburger grills, refrigerators, neon lights, and Wurlitzer jukeboxes, create the atmosphere that continues to cause all cool people to say, "Spangles, it just tastes better!"

LEARNING OBJECTIVES

After you have completed this chapter, you will be able to do the following:

1 Identify and record the different types of property and equipment.

2 Allocate costs to Land and Buildings for a lump-sum purchase.

3 Calculate depreciation by using the (a) straight-line method, (b) double-declining-balance method, (c) units-of-production method, and (d) MACRS method.

4 Differentiate among capital expenditures, revenue expenditures, and extraordinary-repairs expenditures.

5 Prepare journal entries for (a) discarding, (b) selling, and (c) exchanging assets.

6 Understand the importance of property and equipment records.

7 Identify and record the different types of intangibles.

ACCOUNTING LANGUAGE

Accelerated depreciation (p. 680)

Accumulated Depreciation (p. 678)

Amortization (p. 698)

Book value (p. 678)

Buildings (p. 676)

Capital expenditures (p. 687)

Copyright (p. 699)

Depreciation (p. 677)

Depreciation base (p. 678)

Double-declining-balance method (p. 680)

Equipment (p. 676)

Extraordinary-repairs expenditures (p. 687)

Fixed assets (p. 674)

Franchise (p. 699)

Gain on Disposal of Property and Equipment (p. 694)

Goodwill (p. 699)

Intangible assets (p. 698)

Land (p. 675)

Land Improvements (p. 676)

Leasehold Improvements (p. 676)

Loss on Disposal of Property and Equipment (p. 691)

Modified Accelerated Cost Recovery System (MACRS) (p. 684)

Patent (p. 699)

Revenue expenditures (p. 687)

Salvage value (p. 678)

Straight-line method (p. 679)

Trademark (p. 699)

Units-of-production method (p. 682)

Useful life (p. 679)

Take a moment to think about all of the different assets that a fast-food restaurant might have. Your list might include such items as building, stove, oven, tables, chairs, and art deco. When businesses purchase assets, these assets are often referred to as **fixed assets**. Fixed assets are different than merchandise, which is bought for resale. Items most frequently classified as fixed assets (or property and equipment) are equipment, furniture, machinery, tools, buildings, land improvements, and land.

INITIAL COSTS OF PROPERTY AND EQUIPMENT

The original cost of property and equipment includes all normal expenditures necessary to acquire, install, and prepare the property and equipment for its intended use. For example, imagine that a fast-food restaurant, Ham's Burgers, purchases a new refrigerator. The cost of the refrigerator includes not only the invoice price (less any discount for paying cash) but also sales tax, freight charges, insurance costs while it is being transported, and costs of dealer preparation. If Ham's Burgers pays for the refrigerator in cash, the accountant for Ham's Burgers would record the following journal entry:

1 **LEARNING OBJECTIVE**

Identify and record the different types of property and equipment.

Date		Description	Post. Ref.	Debit	Credit
Year 1					
Jan.	2	Equipment		3 8 2 9 00	
		Cash			3 8 2 9 00
		Purchased refrigerator.			

If Ham's Burgers were to buy instead a second-hand refrigerator that needs repair before it can be used, the cost of the repairs would be debited to the appropriate asset account, in this case, Equipment.

The accountant should debit only normal and necessary costs to the asset accounts. This rules out expenditures that result from carelessness, vandalism, and other abnormal causes. For example, suppose that while installing the refrigerator an employee accidentally dropped the refrigerator, making a dent. The cost of the repair is not part of the cost of the refrigerator; that cost is debited to an expense account, such as Repair Expense. The cost is charged as an expense and not as an asset because the repair does not *add* to the value or usefulness of the asset—it simply restores its usefulness.

> **Remember**
>
> Normal costs of acquiring the asset, such as its transportation and installation, are debited to the asset account. Other expenditures, from abnormal causes, are debited to an expense account.

DIFFERENT TYPES OF FIXED ASSETS

Businesses such as Ham's Burgers have many different types of fixed assets. Fixed assets are usually broken out into five different categories: land, land improvements, buildings, leasehold improvements, and equipment. Fixed assets are reported at cost on the balance sheet.

Land

Land is the property that is used in the operations of a business. The cost of the land includes the amount paid for the land plus incidental charges connected with the purchase, such as real estate agents' commissions paid by the buyer, escrow and legal fees, delinquent taxes paid by the buyer, plus any costs of surveying, clearing, draining, or grading the land. In addition, the municipality or county—either at the time of purchase or later—may assess the buyer special taxes for such items as the installation of paved streets, curbs, sidewalks, and sewers. The buyer debits these assessments to the Land account, since the items are considered as permanent as the land. If a business entity buys land for a building site and the land happens to have old buildings standing on it, the firm debits the cost of the structures (as well as the costs of demolishing them) to the Land account.

Land Improvements

When a company purchases land, additional costs usually happen to improve the land. An accountant uses the asset account **Land Improvements** to record these improvements. Land improvements (1) have a determinable or finite useful life or (2) are not directly associated with a building. Land improvements are recorded separately from the land. Examples of land improvements include driveways, parking lots, landscaping, fences, and outdoor lighting systems.

Buildings

Buildings is an asset account that include such items as warehouses, offices, and retail stores. If a building is constructed, the cost of a building includes not only labor and materials, but also architectural and engineering fees, insurance premiums during construction, interest on construction loans during the period of construction, and all other necessary and normal expenditures incurred to prepare the asset for its intended use. The cost of the building can be further broken down into components. The costs that are unrelated to the operation and maintenance of the building can be depreciated over a shorter life. Examples include carpet, cabinets, and decorative elements.

Leasehold Improvements

Improvements that are made to rental property are recorded as leasehold improvements. **Leasehold Improvements** is an asset account used to record improvements to rented property that are made or paid by the lessee (renter or tenant) but become the property of the lessor (owner or landlord) at the end of the lease term. An example would include remodeling an office suite to fit the business needs of the lessee.

Equipment

Equipment is a fixed asset account that includes furniture, vehicles, computers, office equipment, and manufacturing machinery. The cost of equipment would include not only the purchase price but also such items as sales taxes, freight, installation, and assembly.

Remember

If land and building are bought as one property, the land and building must be separated for accounting purposes. Two accounts will be recorded: Land and Buildings.

LUMP-SUM PURCHASE—ALLOCATING COSTS OF LAND AND BUILDINGS

LEARNING OBJECTIVE **2**

Allocate costs to Land and Buildings for a lump-sum purchase.

Business has been great for Ham's Burgers! They are planning on expanding to a new location and have located a piece of property that includes land and a building. In other words, Ham's Burgers pays one price and will purchase two fixed assets—building and land. So, the question is: How should the price be allocated among the two elements?

When there is no qualified appraisal available, you accept the ratio established by the county or municipal tax assessor. For example, suppose that Ham's Burgers buys some real property, including land and a building, for $1,600,000. The assessor valued this property for tax purposes at $1,300,000: $700,000 for the land and $600,000 for the building.

Allocation of the purchase price involves the following steps:

STEP 1. Determine the asset percentages based on the assessed value.

$$\frac{\text{Assessed Value of Land}}{\text{Total Assessed Value}} = \frac{\$700,000}{\$1,300,000} = 53.8\% \text{ (rounded)}$$

$$\frac{\text{Assessed Value of Land Building}}{\text{Total Assessed Value}} = \frac{\$600,000}{\$1,300,000} = 46.2\% \text{ (rounded)}$$

STEP 2. Determine the purchase price allocated to each asset by multiplying the purchase price by the asset percentages.

Purchase price × **STEP 1** = $1,600,000 × 53.8% = $860,800
Purchase price × **STEP 1** = $1,600,000 × 46.2% = $739,200

STEP 3. Record the journal entry for the purchase.

Date		Description	Post. Ref.	Debit	Credit
Year 1					
Jan.	13	Land		860 8 0 0 00	
		Buildings		739 2 0 0 00	
		Cash			1,600 0 0 0 00

For recordkeeping purposes, you separate the land and building because of the different useful lives involved.

THE NATURE AND RECORDING OF DEPRECIATION

When accountants use the term **depreciation**, they mean the process of allocating the cost of an asset to an expense over its useful life. Depreciation represents a systematic procedure for spreading the cost of fixed assets (other than land) over the fiscal periods in which the company receives services from the assets. Accountants record depreciation on long-lived assets such as land improvements, building, and equipment, but *never* on land. Depreciation is recorded as an operating expense on the income statement.

Remember the refrigerator that Ham's Burgers bought? When the accountant recorded the cost of the refrigerator, it was recorded as a fixed asset. This is because the refrigerator will be used over several fiscal periods. In accordance with the matching principle, Ham's Burgers will spread the cost of the refrigerator out over several periods so that the company properly matches the expense with the revenues it helps generate (see Figure 1).

> **Remember**
>
> Land *is not* depreciated because its useful life never ends!

Cost = $3,829
Useful Life = 5 years

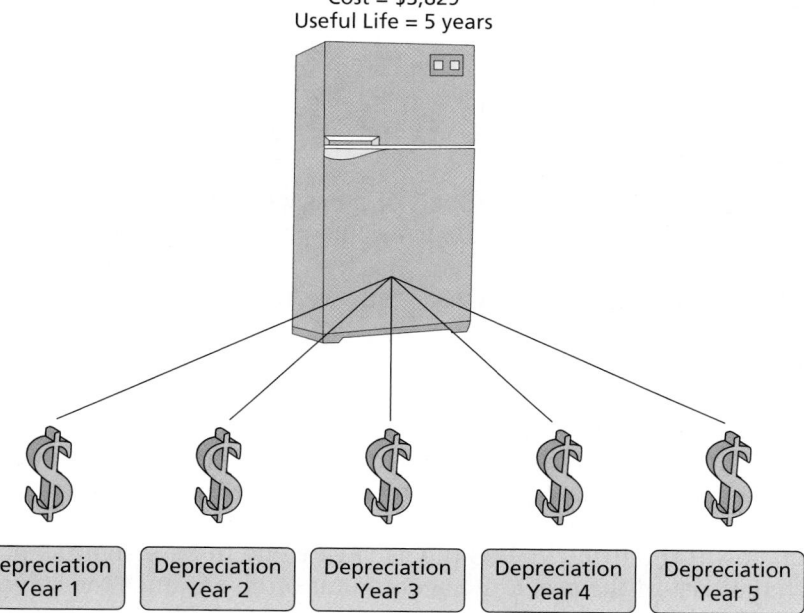

| Depreciation Year 1 | Depreciation Year 2 | Depreciation Year 3 | Depreciation Year 4 | Depreciation Year 5 |

FIGURE 1

Cost spread out over useful life

Assume that depreciation for the refrigerator will be $765.80. Ham's Burgers will record an adjusting entry for depreciation of the refrigerator as follows:

Date		Description	Post. Ref.	Debit	Credit
Year 1					
Dec.	31	Depreciation Expense, Equipment		7 6 5 80	
		Accumulated Depreciation,			
		Equipment			7 6 5 80

Accumulated Depreciation is contra-asset, or a deduction from the related asset account. Accumulated Depreciation accumulates the depreciation for the asset. After Year 1, the Accumulated Depreciation, Equipment account will have $765.80 and after Year 2, $1,531.60 ($765.80 × 2).

Fixed assets are reported on the balance sheet at their **book value** (sometimes called *carrying value*). Book value is equal to the cost of the asset minus the accumulated depreciation. At the end of Year 2, the refrigerator would be reported on the balance sheet as follows:

Property and Equipment:		
Equipment	$ 3,829.00	
Less: Accumulated Depreciation	(1,531.60)	$2,297.40

You can record depreciation as an adjusting entry at the end of each month or postpone recording it until the end of the fiscal year, except when there is a change in the assets, such as a sale or a trade-in. In that case, first record depreciation of the asset from the beginning of the fiscal year until the date of the change, and *then* make any other accounting entries to record the sale or trade-in.

Determining the Amount of Depreciation

To determine the amount of depreciation of a fixed asset, you will need to know three things:

1. Depreciation base
2. Useful life
3. Method of depreciation

Depreciation Base

The **depreciation base** is the full depreciation of an asset. The depreciation base equals the total cost of an asset minus its salvage value or trade-in value.

Depreciation Base = Total Cost of an Asset – Salvage Value or Trade-in Value

The cost of the asset should include all costs associated with getting the asset ready to use. **Salvage value** (or trade-in value) is the expected value of the asset at disposal. When a business entity first puts an asset into service, it is hard to predict the amount of the salvage or trade-in value, especially when such a trade-in will not take place for many years. Many firms make estimates of salvage value based on their own experience or on data supplied by trade associations or government agencies. If the firm expects the salvage value to be insignificant in comparison with the cost of the asset, the accountant often assumes the salvage value to be zero. Some accountants refer to salvage or trade-in value as *residual value.*

Useful Life

For accounting purposes, the **useful life** of an asset is the expected use of the asset, in keeping with the company's replacement policy. The length of an asset's useful life is affected not only by the amount of physical wear and tear to which it is subjected, but also by technological change and innovation. An average car, for example, may have a useful life of five years. However, a car rental company may replace its cars every year in order to offer customers the latest models. A company operating a fleet of cars for its sales force may replace the cars every three years.

CALCULATING DEPRECIATION

The objective of recording depreciation is to systematically allocate the cost of a long-lived asset over the asset's useful life. However, a firm need not use the same method of depreciation for all its assets.

The most common methods of computing depreciation are the

- straight-line method,
- double-declining-balance method, and
- units-of-production method.

For each separate asset, a company should use the same method of depreciation for each year, to follow the principle of consistency. Since depreciation is an expense, its amount will be subtracted from total revenue to arrive at net income. If the depreciation method is changed from year to year, it becomes impossible to compare the firm's performance from one year to the next.

Straight-Line Method

A business that uses the **straight-line method** calculates an equal amount of depreciation expense for each year of service anticipated. Figure 2 shows the straight-line depreciation for a new fryer. The accountant computes the annual depreciation by dividing the depreciation base (cost minus salvage value, if any) by the number of years of useful life predicted for the asset.

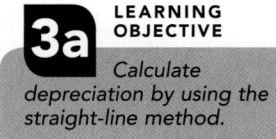

LEARNING OBJECTIVE
3a
Calculate depreciation by using the straight-line method.

$$\text{Depreciation per Year} = \frac{\text{Cost} - \text{Salvage Value}}{\text{Useful Life (in years)}}$$

The percentage rate of depreciation per year is determined by dividing the number of years of useful life into 1. For example, assuming that an asset has an estimated useful life of five years, the percentage rate of depreciation per year would be:

$$\frac{1}{5 \text{ years}} = 0.20 \times 100\% = 20\%$$

The depreciation can be applied against the depreciation base (cost less salvage value) to determine the depreciation.

Now let's look at an example.

FIGURE 2

Straight-line depreciation
for fryer

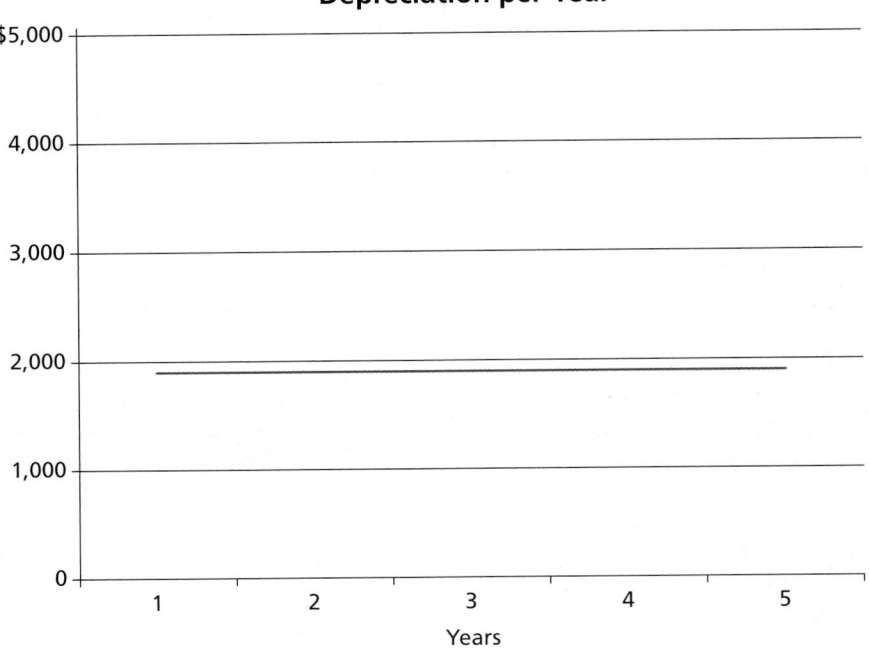

FIGURE 2

Straight-line depreciation for fryer

**Straight-Line Method
Depreciation per Year**

Example.   Ham's Burgers purchases a new 65-lb. capacity fryer costing $10,500 and having a useful life of five years. The estimated salvage (or trade-in) value at the end of five years is $1,000.

$$\text{Depreciation per Year} = \frac{\$10,500 - \$1,000}{5 \text{ years}} = \frac{\$9,500}{5 \text{ years}} = \$1,900$$

- OR -

$$\text{Depreciation Rate per Year} = \frac{1}{5} = 0.20 \times 100\% = 20\%$$

$$\text{Depreciation per Year} = (\$10,500 - \$1,000) \times 20\% = \$1,900$$

Double-Declining-Balance Method

LEARNING OBJECTIVE 3b

Calculate depreciation by using the double-declining-balance method.

The **double-declining-balance method** is an accelerated method of depreciation that allows larger amounts of depreciation to be taken in the early years of an asset's life. In **accelerated depreciation**, depreciation is sped up. Larger amounts of depreciation are taken during the early life of an asset, and smaller amounts are taken during the later years of an asset's life. Some accountants reason that the amount charged to depreciation should be higher during an asset's early years, when it is more productive and efficient, to offset the higher repair and maintenance expenses of the asset's later years. The total annual expense then tends to be equalized over the entire life of the asset. Figure 3 on page 682 shows the double-declining-balance depreciation for a new fryer.

For an asset that has a life of three years or more, this method allows a firm to calculate depreciation by multiplying the book value (cost less accumulated depreciation) at the beginning of the year by twice the straight-line rate. **Salvage value or trade-in value is not used in determining depreciation by the double-declining-balance method until the end of the depreciation schedule.** As with other methods, an asset may not be depreciated below its salvage value.

To compute depreciation by the double-declining-balance method, follow these steps:

STEP 1. Calculate the straight-line depreciation rate.

$$\text{Straight-Line Depreciation Rate} = \frac{1}{\text{Useful Life}}$$

STEP 2. Multiply the straight-line rate by 2.

$$\textbf{STEP 1} \times 2$$

STEP 3. Multiply the book value of the asset at the beginning of the year by double the straight-line rate.

Depreciation Expense per Year = Book Value at Beginning of Year × **STEP 2**

STEP 4. Do not depreciate below salvage value. The amount of depreciation can only reduce book value to salvage value.

During the first year, the book value of an asset is the same as its cost, because no depreciation has been taken. So for the first year only, multiply the cost by twice the straight-line rate.

Example.   Ham's Burgers purchases a new 65-lb. capacity fryer costing $10,500 and having a useful life of five years. The estimated salvage (or trade-in) value at the end of five years is $1,000.

STEP 1. Compute the straight-line depreciation rate.

$$\text{Straight-Line Depreciation Rate} = \frac{1}{5} = 0.20$$

STEP 2. Multiply the straight-line rate by 2.

$$0.20 \times 2 = 0.40$$

STEP 3. Depreciation Expense per Year = Book Value at Beginning of Year × 0.40.

Year	Beginning Book Value	Straight-Line Rate	Double-Declining-Balance Rate	Double-Declining-Balance Rate Computation of Depreciation Expense	Ending Book Value
1	$10,500	$\frac{1}{5} = 0.20$	0.40	$10,500 × 0.40 = $4,200	$10,500 – $4,200 = $6,300
2	6,300	$\frac{1}{5} = 0.20$	0.40	6,300 × 0.40 = 2,520	6,300 – 2,520 = 3,780
3	3,780	$\frac{1}{5} = 0.20$	0.40	3,780 × 0.40 = 1,512	3,780 – 1,512 = 2,268
4	2,268	$\frac{1}{5} = 0.20$	0.40	2,268 × 0.40 = 907*	2,268 – 907 = 1,361
5	1,361	–	–	$1,361 – $1,000 = 361	1,361 – 361 = 1,000
Total				$9,500	

* rounded

STEP 4. Notice that in year 5 the depreciation expense is limited because ending book value cannot go below the salvage (or trade-in) value.

   Observe carefully that the salvage (or trade-in) value is not used until the fifth year. When you use the double-declining-balance method and there is a salvage value involved, the book value gradually declines until it reaches the amount of the salvage value. *An asset must not be depreciated beyond its salvage (or trade-in) value.* For example, consider the fryer. During the fifth year, the normal depreciation would be 40 percent of the book value at the beginning of

> **Remember**
>
> Under the double-declining-balance method, the ending book value cannot go below the salvage value. The depreciation expense may be limited in the last year.

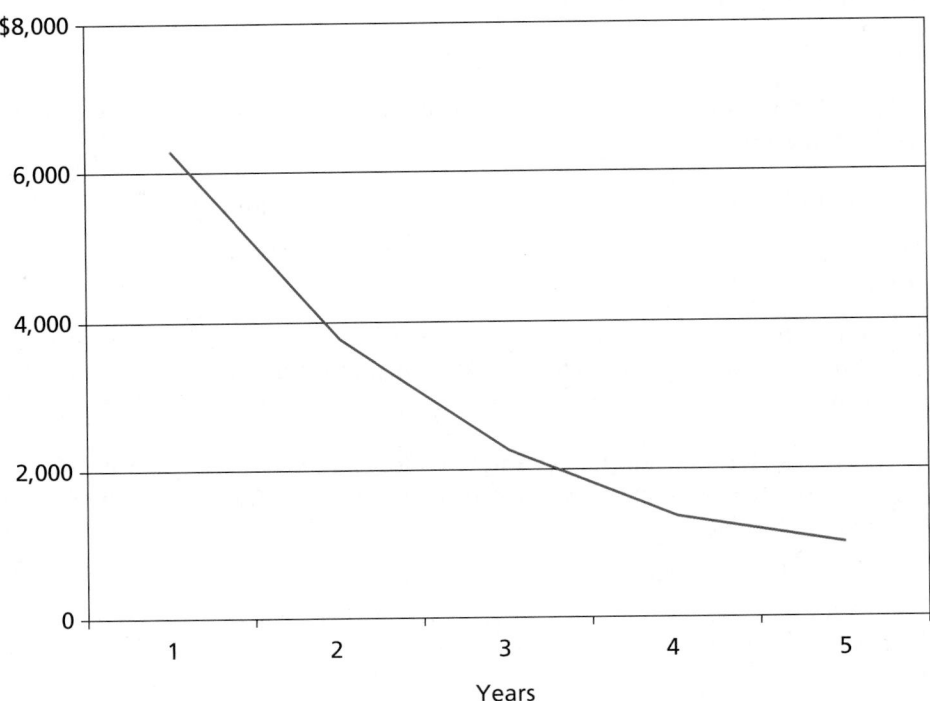

FIGURE 3
Double-declining-balance
depreciation for fryer

the year. Normally, depreciation for the year and the ending book value would be calculated as:

$$\text{Depreciation Expense} = \$1,361 \times 40\% = \underline{\underline{\$544}} \text{ (rounded)}$$

$$\text{Book Value at End of Year} = \$1,361 - \$544 = \underline{\underline{\$817}}$$

Notice that if you calculate depreciation in this manner, the book value of the fryer ($817) dips below the established salvage (or trade-in) value ($1,000). The maximum amount of depreciation that can be taken is $9,500 ($10,500 cost – $1,000 salvage value). Therefore, the depreciation expense can only be recorded as $361 ($1,361 – $1,000).

Units-of-Production Method

LEARNING
OBJECTIVE **3c**

*Calculate
depreciation by using the
units-of-production
method.*

The **units-of-production method** allocates an asset's cost based on its usage or productivity within the period. Usage or productivity within a period could be such items as miles driven, units produced, or number of hours used.

To compute depreciation by the units-of-production method, follow these steps:

STEP 1. Calculate the depreciation per unit.

$$\text{Depreciation per Unit} = \frac{\text{Cost} - \text{Salvage Value}}{\text{Estimated Life in Units of Production}}$$

STEP 2. Multiply the depreciation per unit by the number of units produced.

$$\text{Depreciation Expense per Year} = \textbf{STEP 1} \times \text{Number of Units Produced}$$

Example.   A salesperson's car costs $24,000 and has a useful life of 60,000 miles. The estimated salvage (or trade-in) value at the end of 60,000 miles is $7,200. The car is driven 18,500 miles this year and 20,000 miles next year.

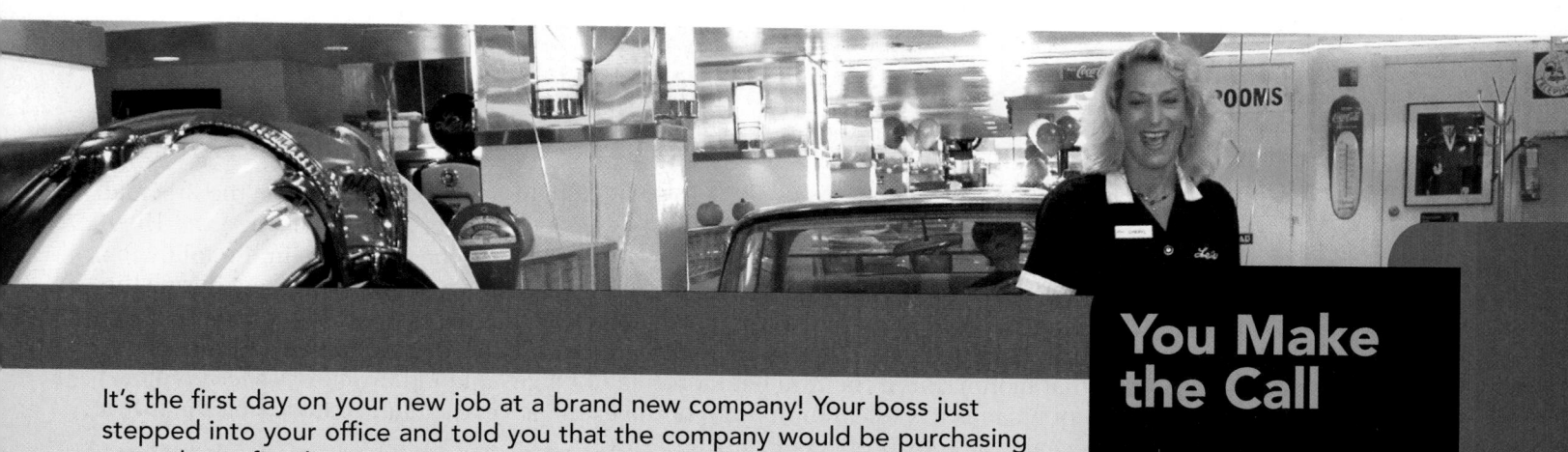

You Make the Call

It's the first day on your new job at a brand new company! Your boss just stepped into your office and told you that the company would be purchasing several new fixed assets over the next couple of weeks. She mentioned that she understands there are several different methods used to calculate depreciation such as straight-line, double-declining-balance, and units-of-production, but she is unsure of how the different methods affect the income of a company. She is also wondering about repairs and maintenance on the fixed assets and their effect on selecting a depreciation method. What if the assets are expected to have increasing repairs and maintenance—would there be a good method to use for these assets?

You are eager to impress your new boss with your knowledge of depreciation. How would you answer her?

SOLUTION

The choice of depreciation methods does have an impact on income and assets of the business. The straight-line method allocates an even amount of depreciation each year over the useful life of the asset; therefore, the impact on income will be stable. On the other hand, an accelerated depreciation method, such as double-declining-balance, records a larger amount of depreciation at the beginning of the asset's useful life and less later on. Income will be smaller in the beginning of the asset's life and will grow as the asset is further depreciated, because there will be a greater depreciation expense to deduct from revenue.

Repairs and maintenance of the new fixed assets should also be considered when selecting a depreciation method. If the company expects the repairs and maintenance to be the same over the life of the asset, the company should choose the straight-line method. However, if the company expects that the fixed assets will need an increasing amount of repairs as the asset ages, the company would be best to choose an accelerated depreciation method, such as the double-declining-balance method.

STEP 1.

$$\text{Depreciation per Mile} = \frac{\$24,000 - \$7,200}{60,000 \text{ miles}} = \frac{\$16,800}{60,000 \text{ miles}} = \$0.28 \text{ per mile}$$

STEP 2.

Year 1: Depreciation for 18,500 miles = 18,500 miles × $0.28 per mile = $5,180

Year 2: Depreciation for 20,000 miles = 20,000 miles × $0.28 per mile = $5,600

> **Remember**
>
> Once you have computed the depreciation per unit (mile, hour, etc.), you must then multiply the unit amount by the number of units produced for the year.

DEPRECIATION FOR PERIODS OF LESS THAN A YEAR

Businesses do not buy nor sell or discard all their depreciable assets on the first and last days of their fiscal period. They buy and sell assets throughout the year. How, then, do they calculate depreciation? As you look at the examples in the following table, remember that when a business entity acquires a depreciable asset during the year, the accountant usually figures depreciation to the nearest whole month. If the firm held the asset for *less* than half a given month, the accountant doesn't count that month. But if the firm held it for half of a given month or more, the accountant counts it as a whole month. Both of the examples in the table assume that the firm's fiscal year ends on December 31.

Date Acquired	Cost	Salvage Value	Method	Useful Life	Depreciation for First Year
May 12	$8,000	$1,000	Straight-line	5 years	$\dfrac{\$8,000 - \$1,000}{5 \text{ years}} = \$1,400$ per year $\$1,400 \times \dfrac{8}{12} = \$933.33$ for 8 months
October 19	$6,000	$ 200	Double-declining-balance	8 years	$\$6,000 \times 0.25 = \$1,500$ for first year $\$1,500 \times \dfrac{2}{12} = \$250$ for 2 months

Remember

When you calculate depreciation for less than a year, it's easy to incorrectly assume the number of months. Make sure to count the number of months. October 1, the tenth month, through the end of the year, the twelfth month, *is three months, not two.*

The depreciation expense for asset that was acquired on May 12 was computed from May 1, counting the entire month because the firm held the asset for half of the month or more. However, the depreciation expense for the asset acquired on October 19 was computed from November 1, not including the month of October because the firm held the asset for less than half of the month. Since the asset was held for less than half of the month of October, the accountant doesn't count that month.

Software programs, such as QuickBooks or Peachtree, are readily available to calculate and keep track of depreciation by the various methods.

DEPRECIATION FOR FEDERAL INCOME TAX

LEARNING OBJECTIVE 3d

Calculate depreciation by using the MACRS method.

Business firms are entitled to deduct depreciation on their income tax returns. However, the amount recorded on a company's income statement (involving the use of the straight-line method, double-declining-balance method, or units-of-production method) may differ from the amount recorded on the company's income tax return.

Modified Accelerated Cost Recovery System

For property acquired after 1986, a schedule of depreciation called the **Modified Accelerated Cost Recovery System (MACRS)** has been established. Under MACRS, assets are divided into classes. Here are the property classes as defined:

FYI

MACRS is generally not acceptable for financial reporting under GAAP. However, MACRS is often used by small businesses if its use doesn't result in a material difference from book depreciation.

Property Class	Description
3-year property	Certain horses and tractor units for use over the road
5-year property	Autos, light and heavy duty general purpose trucks, computers, and office equipment (copiers, etc.); also, furniture, appliances, window treatments, and carpeting used in residential rental buildings
7-year property	Office furniture and fixtures and any property that does not have a class life and that is not, by law, in any other class
10-year property	Vessels, barges, tugs, and similar water transportation equipment
15-year property	Wharves, roads, fences, and any municipal wastewater treatment plant
20-year property	Certain farm buildings and municipal sewers
27.5-year residential rental property	Rental houses and apartments
39-year real property	Office buildings, store buildings, and warehouses

Following are the approved schedules of percentage of cost allocated (written off or depreciated) each year for three-year, five-year, and seven-year property. These schedules are based on the half-year convention (where only half the depreciation is taken in the first and final years of service).

Year	Three-Year	Five-Year	Seven-Year
1	33.33	20.00	14.29
2	44.45	32.00	24.49
3	14.81	19.20	17.49
4	7.41	11.52	12.49
5	100.00	11.52	8.93
6		5.76	8.92
7		100.00	8.93
8			4.46
			100.00

FYI

Depreciation for five-year property is recorded over six fiscal years because under IRS guidelines, only a half-year's depreciation is taken during the first and final years of service.

Note: If more than 40 percent of the new property is placed in service during the fourth quarter of the year (October, November, and December), then a quarterly schedule must be used, known as the mid-quarter convention. The mid-quarter convention rate schedules, similar to the rate schedule shown previously, are published by the IRS.

For residential and nonresidential real property, the property is considered placed in service during the middle of the month (called the mid-month convention).

To determine the depreciation for the year for income tax purposes, follow these steps:

STEP 1. Determine into which of the eight classes the asset falls.

STEP 2. Consult the schedule to determine the percentage figure for each year.

STEP 3. Multiply the cost of the asset by the percentage figure.

Depreciation Expense = Cost × **STEP 2**

Example. Ham's Burgers purchases a new fixture (classified as seven-year property) having a cost of $300.

STEP 1. Determine into which of the eight classes the asset falls: *seven-year property*

STEP 2. Consult the schedule to determine the percentage figure for each year: *14.29%* for first year

STEP 3. Multiply the cost of the asset by the percentage figure.

Depreciation Expense for Year 1 = $300 × 0.1429 = $42.87

From time to time, Congress changes the allowable depreciation in order to stimulate business investment in equipment. The IRS makes it possible for small businesses to deduct the full cost of machines, computers, furniture, and the like in the year placed in service (called the Section 179 deduction). Presently, the limit is $250,000 (indexed for inflation), but it may be changed.

The IRS has issued various publications on depreciation, including Publication 946, How to Depreciate Property. These publications are updated frequently and are available at the Internal Revenue Service's Web site (www.irs.gov).

Tax Depreciation

SMALL BUSINESS SUCCESS

In this chapter, you learned the MACRS method of computing depreciation for tax purposes. Tax depreciation can be complicated, and if you are not familiar with the rules, it is often best handled by consulting an accountant that is well-versed in current tax laws.

In addition to the MACRS method of depreciation, occasionally the Treasury Department will allow additional depreciation to be taken on certain qualifying assets. This is often called "bonus depreciation." Although bonus depreciation is an extremely complicated area of tax depreciation, let's review a very basic example so that we understand the general law.

Portland Rail Company purchased a 7-year asset for $12,000 on February 1, 2011. Portland Rail Company is electing to take bonus depreciation on the asset. Portland Rail Company will be allowed a total depreciation on the asset of $6,857.40.

Bonus depreciation (50%)	$12,000 × 0.50 = $6,000
MACRS depreciation	($12,000 − $6,000) × 0.1429 = $857.40
Total depreciation	$6,000 + $857.40 = $6,857.40

Notice that the taxpayer is allowed to deduct 50% of the cost of the asset immediately and also is allowed a deduction for the applicable cost percentage (0.1429) on the remaining basis ($6,000).

At this time, it's not important that you completely understand the calculation; however, you should have an understanding that tax depreciation rules occasionally change, allowing for more depreciation than just MACRS. This is an excellent example of why it is important for accountants to continue to remain current with recent legislation and tax laws.

Within the past several years, "bonus depreciation" has been offered to taxpayers several times. The current bonus depreciation rules are set to expire at the end of 2009. At the time of this book's publication, the bonus depreciation rules had not been extended.

If you take a tax class at your college, you will have the opportunity to learn more about tax depreciation and other aspects of taxes. This type of course is highly recommended for all accounting majors and also for small business owners.

CAPITAL AND REVENUE EXPENDITURES

The term *expenditure* refers to spending, either by paying cash now or by promising to pay in the future for services received or assets purchased. After paying the initial price for an asset, you often have to pay out more, either to maintain the asset's operating efficiency or to increase its capacity. So there are two classifications of expenditures: capital and revenue.

Capital expenditures include the initial costs debited to property and equipment; they also include any costs of enlarging or increasing the capacity of assets. Capital expenditures benefit more than one accounting period. Examples are expenditures for buying a building, enlarging it, putting in air conditioning, and replacing a stairway with an elevator. All these expenditures result in debits to an asset account. For example, suppose that Ham's Burgers spends $20,000 to modify an existing fast-food restaurant by enlarging it. The expenditure would be recorded as follows:

LEARNING OBJECTIVE 4

Differentiate among capital expenditures, revenue expenditures, and extraordinary-repairs expenditures.

Date	Description	Post. Ref.	Debit	Credit
	Buildings		20 0 0 0 00	
	Cash			20 0 0 0 00
	Enlargement of restaurant.			

Revenue expenditures include the costs of maintaining the operation of an asset, such as the expense of making normal repairs. Examples are expenditures for painting, plumbing repairs, property taxes, and so on. These expenditures provide benefit only during the current accounting period and are recorded as debits to expense accounts. For example, assume that Ham's Burgers spent $350 repairing the plumbing in an existing fast-food restaurant. This expenditure would be recorded as follows:

Date	Description	Post. Ref.	Debit	Credit
	Equipment Repairs Expense		3 5 0 00	
	Cash			3 5 0 00
	Repairs to plumbing.			

EXTRAORDINARY-REPAIRS EXPENDITURES

Extraordinary-repairs expenditures refer to a major overhaul or reconditioning that either extends the useful life of an asset beyond its original estimated life or increases its estimated trade-in value. An accountant usually records expenditures for extraordinary repairs as a debit to the asset account and a credit to Cash or Accounts Payable.

For example, on January 3, Year 1, Ham's Burgers bought a used truck for $18,000. The truck's estimated useful life is four years and its trade-in value is $5,600; straight-line annual depreciation expense is $3,100. On January 5, Year 4, Ham's Burgers puts in a new engine and has other major repairs done, for which it spends $3,480 in cash. The entry in general journal form is as follows:

Date		Description	Post. Ref.	Debit	Credit
Year 4					
Jan.	5	Truck		3 4 8 0 00	
		Cash			3 4 8 0 00
		New engine installed in			
		company truck.			

This extraordinary repair extends the life of the truck from the present one additional year to three additional years. Here are the balances, together with the $3,480 payment, as shown by T accounts:

Truck		Accumulated Depreciation, Truck	
+	−	−	+
Jan. 3, Year 1 18,000			Dec. 31, Year 1 3,100
Jan. 5, Year 4 3,480			Dec. 31, Year 2 3,100
			Dec. 31, Year 3 3,100

The truck's book value before the extraordinary repair was $8,700 ($18,000 − $9,300). The book value of the truck after the extraordinary repair is $12,180 ($18,000 + $3,480 − $9,300). We can see the increase in the Truck account in the balance sheet as follows:

Property and Equipment:		
Truck	$21,480	
Less: Accumulated Depreciation	(9,300)	$12,180

When it comes to recording the remaining depreciation on the truck, the accountant now has a new cost base, which he or she uses to determine the new depreciation base. Assume that the trade-in value is still $5,600.

New book value ($21,480 − $9,300)	$12,180
Less trade-in value	5,600
New depreciation base	$ 6,580

Depreciation expense = $6,580 ÷ 3 years = $2,193 (rounded)

The adjusting entry for depreciation of the truck at the end of Year 4 is as follows:

Date		Description	Post. Ref.	Debit	Credit
Year 4		Adjusting Entry			
Dec.	31	Depreciation Expense, Truck		2 1 9 3 00	
		Accumulated Depreciation, Truck			2 1 9 3 00

Assuming that no additional expenditures are made for extraordinary repairs, the adjusting entries for the remaining two years (Years 5 and 6) will be $2,193 (rounded) for Year 5 and $2,194 (remaining depreciable value) for Year 6.

DISPOSITION OF PROPERTY AND EQUIPMENT

Sooner or later a business entity disposes of its long-lived assets by (1) discarding or retiring them, (2) selling them, or (3) trading them in for other assets.

Follow these steps to record an asset that has been discarded or sold:

STEP 1. Record the entry to depreciate the asset up to date, if applicable.

STEP 2. Calculate the book value.

$$\text{Book Value} = \text{Cost} - \text{Accumulated Depreciation}$$

STEP 3. Determine the gain or loss.

$$\text{Gain} = \text{Amount Received Greater than Book Value}$$

$$\text{Loss} = \text{Amount Received Less than Book Value}$$

STEP 4. Record the entry to discard or sell the asset. Debit cash for the amount received, if any; debit Accumulated Depreciation; credit the asset; and if applicable, debit Loss on Disposal of Property and Equipment, or credit Gain on Disposal of Property and Equipment.

Let's look at some examples. (If using special journals, entries involving Cash would be recorded in the cash journals; however, for our purposes, we present all the following entries in general journal form.)

> **Remember**
>
> If the assets are not fully depreciated when disposing, the accountant must first make an entry to bring the depreciation up to date.

Discarding or Retiring Property and Equipment

When a company decides to discard or retire an asset, the company must record a journal entry to remove the asset and the associated accumulated depreciation. Assets can be discarded or retired when they have been either fully or partially depreciated. Let's look at the discarding of a fully depreciated asset first.

Discarding of Fully Depreciated Assets

A display case that originally cost $1,760, with a zero salvage value, and that has been fully depreciated is given away as junk on July 10. The present status of the accounts is as follows:

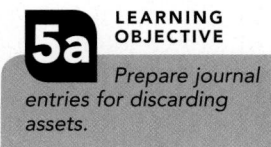

LEARNING OBJECTIVE 5a

Prepare journal entries for discarding assets.

Store Equipment		Accumulated Depreciation, Store Equipment	
+	−	−	+
Bal. 1,760		Bal. 1,760	

STEP 1. No entry is required because the asset is fully depreciated. Although fully depreciated assets are retained on the books as long as they remain in use, the firm may not take any additional depreciation on them.

STEP 2. Once an asset is fully depreciated, the asset's book value remains at its estimated salvage value unless an extraordinary repair is made or the company disposes of the asset.

$$\text{Book Value} = \$1,760 - \$1,760 = \$0$$

STEP 3. If an asset is fully depreciated and the company does not receive any cash for discarding the asset, there is no gain or loss recognized.

STEP 4. The journal entry to record the disposal of the display case looks like this:

Date		Description	Post. Ref.	Debit	Credit
July	10	Accumulated Depreciation,			
		Store Equipment		1 7 6 0 00	
		Store Equipment			1 7 6 0 00
		Discarded a fully depreciated			
		display case.			

Discarding an Asset Not Fully Depreciated

On August 12, Ham's Burgers discards a printer that originally cost $1,720. No salvage value is recognized. Accumulated Depreciation up to the end of the previous year is $1,032. Depreciation for the current year through August 12 is $352. The present balances of the accounts are as follows:

Office Equipment

+	−
Bal. 1,720	

Accumulated Depreciation, Office Equipment

−	+
	Bal. 1,032

STEP 1. Record the entry to depreciate the printer up to date.

Date		Description	Post. Ref.	Debit	Credit
Aug.	12	Depreciation Expense, Office			
		Equipment		3 5 2 00	
		Accumulated Depreciation,			
		Office Equipment			3 5 2 00
		Depreciation on printer			
		for the partial year.			

The T accounts look like this:

Depreciation Expense, Office Equipment

+	−
352	

Accumulated Depreciation, Office Equipment

−	+
	Bal. 1,032
	352
	1,384

STEP 2. Calculate the book value.

$$\text{Book Value} = \$1,720 - \$1,384 = \$336$$

STEP 3. Determine the gain or loss.

Because the firm realized nothing from the disposal of the asset, the loss is for the same amount as the book value.

$$\text{Loss} = \$0 - \$336 = \$(336)$$

Remember

A gain occurs when the amount received for an asset is greater than the book value. A loss occurs when the amount received is less than the book value. To calculate the book value, the depreciation must be brought up to date before a sale, disposal, or trade-in.

STEP 4. The journal entry to record the disposal of the printer is as follows:

Date		Description	Post. Ref.	Debit	Credit
Aug.	12	Accumulated Depreciation,			
		Office Equipment		1 3 8 4 00	
		Loss on Disposal of Property			
		and Equipment		3 3 6 00	
		Office Equipment			1 7 2 0 00
		Discarded a printer.			

The T accounts after recording the journal entries look like this:

Accumulated Depreciation, Office Equipment		Loss on Disposal of Property and Equipment		Office Equipment	
−	+	+	−	+	−
1,384	Bal. 1,032	336		Bal. 1,720	1,720
	352				
	1,384				

Loss on Disposal of Property and Equipment is an expense account that appears under Other Expenses on the income statement and is used when a firm sells or trades in an asset and receives an amount less than the book value of the asset.

> **Remember**
>
> Gains or losses from disposal of assets are reported in either the Other Revenue or the Other Expenses section of the income statement. The gain or loss is not considered to be part of the income or sales account because it is not part of the essential activities of the company.

Selling of Property and Equipment

Many times instead of simply discarding a long-lived asset, a business will choose instead to sell the asset.

> **5b LEARNING OBJECTIVE**
> *Prepare journal entries for selling assets.*

Sale of an Asset at a Loss

Suppose that Ham's Burgers sells a kitchen range for $150. This kitchen range originally cost $2,100; accumulated depreciation up to the end of the previous year (December 31) was $1,680. Yearly depreciation is $210. The kitchen range is sold on August 21.

The present balances of the accounts are as follows:

Equipment		Accumulated Depreciation, Equipment	
+	−	−	+
Bal. 2,100			Bal. 1,680

STEP 1. Record the entry to depreciate the kitchen range up to date.

Date		Description	Post. Ref.	Debit	Credit
Aug.	21	Depreciation Expense,			
		Equipment		1 4 0 00	
		Accumulated Depreciation,			
		Equipment			1 4 0 00
		Depreciation on kitchen range for			
		8 months ($210 × 8/12).			

By T accounts, the situation looks like this:

Depreciation Expense, Equipment			Accumulated Depreciation, Equipment		
+	−			−	+
140			Bal.		1,680
					140
					1,820

STEP 2. Calculate the book value.

$$\text{Book Value} = \$2,100 - \$1,820 = \$280$$

STEP 3. Determine the gain or loss.

Note that the book value of the kitchen range is $280. When Ham's Burgers sells it for $150, the loss is $130 because the amount received for the kitchen range is $130 less than its book value.

$$\text{Loss} = \$150 - \$280 = \$(130)$$

STEP 4. The entry, in general journal form, to record the sale of the kitchen range is as follows:

Date		Description	Post. Ref.	Debit	Credit
Aug.	21	Cash		1 5 0 00	
		Accumulated Depreciation,			
		Equipment		1 8 2 0 00	
		Loss on Disposal of Property			
		and Equipment		1 3 0 00	
		Equipment			2 1 0 0 00
		Sold kitchen range for $150			
		having an original cost of			
		$2,100 and accumulated			
		depreciation of $1,820.			

For purposes of illustration, let's record this entry in the T accounts as follows:

Cash			Accumulated Depreciation, Equipment		
+	−			−	+
150				1,820	Bal. 1,680
					140
					1,820

Loss on Disposal of Property and Equipment			Equipment		
+	−			+	−
130			Bal. 2,100		2,100

Sale of an Asset at a Gain

Suppose that Ham's Burgers sells a dishwasher for $400. Ham's Burgers had originally paid $4,400; accumulated depreciation to the end of the previous year, December 31, was $3,960. Yearly depreciation is $360. The dishwasher is sold on October 18. The present balances of the accounts are as follows:

Equipment				Accumulated Depreciation, Equipment		
	+	–			–	+
Bal.	4,400				Bal.	3,960

STEP 1. Record the entry to depreciate the dishwasher up to date.

Date		Description	Post. Ref.	Debit	Credit
Oct.	18	Depreciation Expense,			
		Equipment		3 0 0 00	
		Accumulated Depreciation,			
		Equipment			3 0 0 00
		Depreciation on dishwasher			
		for 10 months ($360 × 10/12).			

> **Remember**
> The calculations shown in the explanation are for illustration and would not normally appear in practice.

By T accounts, the situation looks like this:

Depreciation Expense, Equipment				Accumulated Depreciation, Equipment		
	+	–			–	+
	300				Bal.	3,960
						300
						4,260

STEP 2. Calculate the book value.

$$\text{Book Value} = \$4,400 - \$4,260 = \$140$$

STEP 3. Determine the gain or loss.

Note that the book value of the dishwasher is $140. When Ham's Burgers sells it for $400, the gain is $260 because the amount received for the dishwasher is $260 more than its book value.

$$\text{Gain} = \$400 - \$140 = \$260$$

STEP 4. The entry, in general journal form, to record the sale of the dishwasher is as follows:

Date		Description	Post. Ref.	Debit	Credit
Oct.	18	Cash		4 0 0 00	
		Accumulated Depreciation,			
		Equipment		4 2 6 0 00	
		Equipment			4 4 0 0 00
		Gain on Disposal of Property			
		and Equipment			2 6 0 00
		Sold a dishwasher for $400			
		having an original cost of			
		$4,400 and accumulated			
		depreciation of $4,260.			

The T accounts look like this:

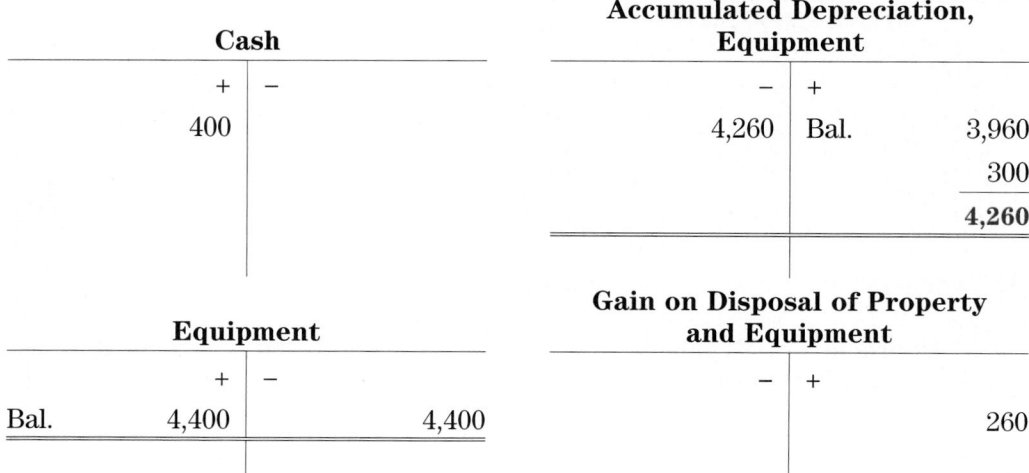

The revenue account **Gain on Disposal of Property and Equipment** appears under Other Income on the income statement and is used when a firm sells or trades in an asset and receives an amount greater than the book value for that asset.

Exchange of Long-Lived Assets for Other Similar Assets

LEARNING OBJECTIVE 5c

Prepare journal entries for exchanging assets.

Often a business trades in one asset for another, using the old asset as partial payment for the new one. The trade-in allowance may differ from the book value of the asset. If the trade-in allowance is greater than the book value, the firm has a gain; if the trade-in allowance is less than the book value, it has a loss. In most cases, if there is a gain or loss, the business will record it. There a few exceptions to this general rule. You will learn these exceptions when you take Intermediate Accounting. For now, we will assume that the business will always record the gain or loss.

Gain = Market Value (or Trade-in Allowance) Greater than Book Value

Loss = Market Value (or Trade-in Allowance) Less than Book Value

Gains and losses are recorded for GAAP (generally accepted accounting principles) purposes; however, federal income tax laws state that when assets held for productive use are exchanged for similar assets (called a like-kind or Section 1031 exchange), *no gain or loss is recognized.* In effect, the gain or loss is absorbed into the recorded cost of the new asset.

Exchange When Trade-in Value Is Greater than Book Value

Ham's Burgers bought a copier for $2,600. After some years, Ham's Burgers decides to trade it in on a new model. The old copier has accumulated depreciation of $2,480 *on the date of the trade-in*, leaving a book value of $120 ($2,600 – $2,480). The new copier has a list price of $3,350; however, the salesperson gives Ham's Burgers a trade-in allowance of $310 on the old copier, and Ham's Burgers pays the difference in cash. The present status of the accounts is as follows:

Office Equipment				Accumulated Depreciation, Office Equipment		
	+	–			–	+
Bal.	2,600				Bal.	2,480

Assuming that this transaction has "commercial substance," the accountant will record gain of $190 ($310 – $120).

The Ham's Burgers' accountant records the transaction by the following steps:

STEP 1. Debit Office Equipment (new) for its list price, $3,350.

STEP 2. Close or clear the Accumulated Depreciation account of the old office equipment: debit Accumulated Depreciation, Office Equipment, $2,480.

STEP 3. Calculate the gain and then credit Gain on Disposal of Property and Equipment.

$$\text{Gain} = \$310 – \$120 = \$190$$

STEP 4. Credit Cash, $3,040 (quoted price of the new copier, $3,350, minus the $310 trade-in allowance on the old copier).

STEP 5. Close or clear the account of the old copier: credit Office Equipment (old), $2,600.

Here is the entry in general journal form with the steps labeled:

Date	Description	Post. Ref.	Debit	Credit
	(1) Office Equipment (new)		3 3 5 0 00	
	(2) Accumulated Depreciation,			
	Office Equipment		2 4 8 0 00	
	(3) Gain on Disposal of Property			
	and Equipment			1 9 0 00
	(4) Cash			3 0 4 0 00
	(5) Office Equipment (old)			2 6 0 0 00
	Bought a new copier having			
	a list price of $3,350.			
	Received a trade-in allowance			
	of $310 on old copier, which			
	had an original cost of $2,600			
	and accumulated depreciation			
	of $2,480.			

Exchange When Trade-in Value Is Less than Book Value

Suppose Ham's Burgers bought a delivery truck for $30,400. Four years later, the truck has accumulated depreciation of $26,200 (book value = $30,400 – $26,200 = $4,200).

Ham's Burgers buys a new truck, with a list price of $35,400, trading in the old one, for which Ham's Burgers is allowed only $2,800, and paying the difference in cash. Assume that the depreciation for the year is already up to date and that this transaction has "commercial substance." The present status of the accounts is as follows:

	Truck			Accumulated Depreciation, Truck		
	+	−			−	+
Bal.	30,400				Bal.	26,200

Since this exchange is considered to have "commercial substance," Ham's Burgers is required to record the loss of $1,400 ($2,800 trade-in value − $4,200 book value).

The Ham's Burgers' accountant records the transaction by the following steps:

STEP 1. Debit Truck (new) for its list price, $35,400.

STEP 2. Close or clear the Accumulated Depreciation account of the old truck: debit Accumulated Depreciation, Truck, $26,200.

STEP 3. Calculate the loss and then debit Loss on Disposal of Property and Equipment.

$$\text{Loss} = \$2,800 - \$4,200 = \$(1,400)$$

STEP 4. Credit Cash, $32,600 (quoted price of the new truck, $35,400, minus the $2,800 trade-in allowance on the old truck).

STEP 5. Close or clear the account of the old truck: credit Truck (old), $30,400.

The entry in general journal form is as follows:

For income tax purposes, gain or loss is not recognized when assets held for productive use are exchanged for similar assets—the gain or loss is absorbed into the recorded cost of the new asset.

Date	Description	Post. Ref.	Debit	Credit
	(1) Truck (new)		35 4 0 0 00	
	(2) Accumulated Depreciation, Truck		26 2 0 0 00	
	(3) Loss on Disposal of Property and			
	Equipment		1 4 0 0 00	
	(4) Cash			32 6 0 0 00
	(5) Truck (old)			30 4 0 0 00
	Bought a new truck having			
	a list price of $35,400.			
	Received a trade-in allowance of			
	$2,800 on old truck, which had			
	an original cost of $30,400 and			
	accumulated depreciation of			
	$26,200.			

PROPERTY AND EQUIPMENT RECORDS

Depreciation, which is regarded as an expense, vitally affects the net income of any business. Because net income is affected, the amount of income taxes owed is likewise affected; not only Depreciation Expense, but also Gain (or Loss) on Disposal of Property and Equipment, affects net income. For income tax purposes, the business must be able to justify the amount of depreciation taken, as well as the gain or loss on disposal of assets.

We have discussed Property and Equipment as a category on a classified balance sheet. Following is an illustration of the Property and Equipment section of a balance sheet:

Property and Equipment:

Land		$ 95,000
Land Improvements	$ 3,000	
Less: Accumulated Depreciation	(2,300)	
Total Land Improvements		700
Buildings	$ 60,000	
Less: Accumulated Depreciation	(28,000)	
Total Buildings		32,000
Office Equipment	$ 6,000	
Less: Accumulated Depreciation	(4,500)	
Total Office Equipment		1,500
Store Equipment	$ 18,000	
Less: Accumulated Depreciation	(14,000)	
Total Store Equipment		4,000
Delivery Equipment	$ 20,000	
Less: Accumulated Depreciation	(12,000)	
Total Delivery Equipment		8,000
Total Property and Equipment		$141,200

Subsidiary ledgers can be used when recording property and equipment. For example, the Store Equipment account represents a functional group; it includes all types of equipment used in the operation of a store. Examples of store equipment are display cases, cash registers, counters, and storage shelves.

When using subsidiary ledgers, Store Equipment is a controlling account; the property and equipment ledger is a subsidiary ledger. This relationship is like that of Accounts Receivable, which is a controlling account, and the accounts receivable ledger, which is a subsidiary ledger with an account for each individual charge customer. Figure 4 shows a record card in a firm's property and equipment ledger. Posting to the subsidiary ledger will also be noted by a check mark in the journal's Post. Ref. column when the asset accounts and the related accumulated depreciation accounts are debited or credited.

FIGURE 4

Property and equipment record

PROPERTY AND EQUIPMENT RECORD

ITEM **Cash Register**	ACCOUNT NO. **128-1**
SERIAL NO. **ND37-4163**	MAKER **Security, Inc.**
FROM WHOM PURCHASED **Tran Equipment Company**	ESTIMATED
ESTIMATED LIFE **5 years**	SALVAGE VALUE **$300**
DEPRECIATION / DEPRECIATION / DEPRECIATION	RATE OF
METHOD **Straight-line** / PER YEAR **$900** / PER MONTH **$75**	DEPRECIATION **20%**

DATE	EXPLANATION	ASSET			ACCUMULATED DEPRECIATION			BOOK VALUE
		DEBIT	CREDIT	BALANCE	DEBIT	CREDIT	BALANCE	
7/3/Yr. 1		4,800		4,800				4,800
12/31/Yr. 1						450	450	4,350
12/31/Yr. 2						900	1,350	3,450
12/31/Yr. 3						900	2,250	2,550

Accounting software programs can also be used to record information about property and equipment. The detail that can be provided from an accounting software program concerning fixed assets enables the accountant to easily view information about the company's fixed assets. The amount of depreciation and accumulated depreciation for each asset can be easily determined. Property and equipment records are also valuable when a business has to submit insurance claims in the event of insured losses. An example of a depreciation record in QuickBooks for the cash register asset follows.

Store Equipment		
Cash Register		
Accumulated Depreciation		
12/31/2007	−450.00	−450.00
12/31/2008	−900.00	−1,350.00
12/31/2009	−900.00	−2,250.00
Total Accumulated Depreciation	−2,250.00	−2,250.00

INTANGIBLE ASSETS

Another type of long-lived assets is **intangible assets**. Intangible assets are assets that are purchased for use in the business and have a useful life longer than one year *but have no physical substance*. Examples of intangible assets include patents, trademarks, copyrights, franchises, and goodwill. Purchased intangible assets are recorded at their original cost plus all other costs necessary to get the asset ready for use. Intangible assets are recorded on the balance sheet in the long-term asset category.

Suppose that on January 2, Ham's Burgers purchases a patent costing $20,000 with a useful life of 10 years. If Ham's Burgers pays for the patent in cash, the accountant for Ham's Burgers would record the following journal entry:

Date		Description	Post. Ref.	Debit	Credit
Jan.	2	Patent		20 0 0 0 00	
		Cash			20 0 0 0 00
		Purchase of patent.			

Remember that the allocation of the cost of property and equipment is called depreciation. For intangible assets, we will allocate the cost in a similar manner—except that it is called **amortization**. Amortization is the process of allocating the cost of an intangible to an expense over its legal life or useful life (whichever is shorter). Amortization expense is recorded on the income statement.

Ham's Burgers' accountant would record amortization on the patent as follows:

Date		Description	Post. Ref.	Debit	Credit
Dec.	31	Amortization Expense		2 0 0 0 00	
		Patent			2 0 0 0 00
		Amortization of patent			
		($20,000/10).			

Notice that most businesses, when recording amortization expense, credit the intangible asset directly rather than crediting accumulated amortization.

Let's take a look at several different types of intangibles.

Patent

A **patent** is an exclusive right to sell or produce an invention. A patent has a legal life of 20 years; however, the estimated useful life is often less. A patent will be amortized over the shorter of its legal life or estimated useful life.

Copyright

A **copyright** is the exclusive right of protection granted to creators of artistic works, such as a song, painting, book, or photograph. Copyrights have a legal life of the artist's life plus 70 years.

Trademark

A **trademark** represents a word, slogan, or symbol that identifies a company or product. We are all familiar with trademarks—probably one of the most recognized is the McDonald's golden arches. Trademarks can be registered for 10 years and can be renewed for another 10 years indefinitely. A trademark *is not* amortized because the asset's useful life is indefinite; however, it is reviewed every year for impairment. Impairment, which happens when the future benefits are less than book value, is a topic that you will discuss in Intermediate Accounting.

Franchises

A **franchise** is an exclusive right to use a company's name and to sell its products. The last time you went to a fast-food restaurant, you probably were at a franchise. Franchises are amortized over the life of the franchise agreement.

Goodwill

Goodwill is recorded on the balance sheet when a business purchases another business. Goodwill is calculated as:

$$\text{Goodwill} = \text{Purchase Price} - \text{Fair Value of Net Assets Acquired}$$

Goodwill represents the value of the business over its identified assets. Some reasons for goodwill could be reputation, business location, or exceptional employees. Goodwill *is not* amortized because it is considered to have an indefinite useful life. Because goodwill is not amortized it must be valued for impairment every year. Valuing goodwill for impairment is a topic that you will discuss in Intermediate Accounting.

CHAPTER REVIEW

Study & Practice

1 LEARNING OBJECTIVE

Identify and record the different types of property and equipment.

There are five main types of property and equipment: **land**, **land improvements**, **buildings**, **leasehold improvements**, and **equipment**. All costs necessary to acquire, install, and prepare the property and equipment for its intended use are recorded as debits to the appropriate asset account.

PRACTICE EXERCISE 1

Happy Crepes purchases an industrial oven for $6,000. In addition to the cost of the oven, Happy Crepes pays for the following: freight, $500; sales tax, $375; installation, $200; testing, $50; and repairs for carelessness, $75. What is the initial cost of the industrial oven? How are the repairs recorded and why?

PRACTICE EXERCISE 1 SOLUTION

$$\text{Initial cost} = \$6,000 + \$500 + \$375 + \$200 + \$50 = \$7,125$$

The repairs are recorded a debit to an expense account, Repairs Expense, because the repairs do not add value or usefulness of the oven.

2 LEARNING OBJECTIVE

Allocate costs to Land and Buildings for a lump-sum purchase.

Lump-sum purchases involve paying one purchase price for several different assets. Each asset must be recorded separately using the following steps:

STEP 1. Determine the asset percentages based on the assessed value.

STEP 2. Determine the purchase price allocated to each asset by multiplying the purchase price by the asset percentages.

STEP 3. Record the journal entry for the purchase.

PRACTICE EXERCISE 2

Red Line Burgers purchases land and a building for a combined price of $2,000,000. The assessor valued this property for tax purposes at $1,800,000: $1,400,000 for the land and $400,000 for the building. Record the journal entry for the purchase.

PRACTICE EXERCISE 2 SOLUTION

STEP 1.

$$\frac{\text{Assessed Value of Land}}{\text{Total Assessed Value}} = \frac{\$1,400,000}{\$1,800,000} = 77.8\% \text{ (rounded)}$$

$$\frac{\text{Assessed Value of Building}}{\text{Total Assessed Value}} = \frac{\$400,000}{\$1,800,000} = 22.2\% \text{ (rounded)}$$

STEP 2.

$$\text{Land} = \$2,000,000 \times 77.8\% = \$1,556,000$$

$$\text{Building} = \$2,000,000 \times 22.2\% = \$444,000$$

STEP 3.

Date	Description	Post. Ref.	Debit	Credit
	Land		1,556 0 0 0 00	
	Buildings		444 0 0 0 00	
	Cash			2,000 0 0 0 00
	Purchased land and			
	building for cash.			

3 **LEARNING OBJECTIVE**

Calculate depreciation by using the (a) straight-line method, (b) double-declining-balance method, (c) units-of-production method, and (d) MACRS method.

$$\text{Straight-Line Method} = \frac{\text{Cost} - \text{Salvage Value}}{\text{Useful Life}}$$

Double-Declining-Balance Method
= Book Value at Beginning of Year × Twice Straight-Line Rate

Units-of-Production Method

$$= \frac{\text{Cost} - \text{Salvage Value}}{\text{Estimated Life in Units of Production}} \times \text{Number of Units Produced}$$

$$\text{MACRS Method} = \text{Cost} \times \text{Percentage Figure}$$

PRACTICE EXERCISE 3

At the beginning of the fiscal year, Chicky Chicken bought a new fryer for $8,000, with an estimated salvage (or trade-in) value of $1,000 and an estimated useful life of five years. Determine the amount of depreciation for the first and second years for the following methods: straight-line, double-declining-balance, units-of-production (useful life is 12,000 hours; Year 1 use is 2,500 hours; Year 2 use, 1,400 hours), and MACRS (assume five-year class).

PRACTICE EXERCISE 3 SOLUTION

Straight-Line Depreciation

Year 1: $\dfrac{\$8,000 - \$1,000}{5 \text{ years}} = \dfrac{\$7,000}{5 \text{ years}} = \$1,400$

Year 2: $\dfrac{\$8,000 - \$1,000}{5 \text{ years}} = \dfrac{\$7,000}{5 \text{ years}} = \$1,400$

Double-Declining-Balance Depreciation

Year 1:

STEP 1. Straight-Line Depreciation Rate $= \dfrac{1}{5} = 20\%$

STEP 2. $2 \times 20\% = 40\%$

STEP 3. $\$8,000 \times 40\% = \$3,200$

Year 2:

STEP 1. Straight-Line Depreciation Rate $= \dfrac{1}{5} = 20\%$

STEP 2. $2 \times 20\% = 40\%$

STEP 3. $(\$8,000 - \$3,200) \times 40\% = \$1,920$

Units-of-Production Depreciation

Year 1:

STEP 1. $\dfrac{\$8,000 - \$1,000}{12,000 \text{ hours}} = \$0.58$ per hour (rounded)

STEP 2. $2,500 \times \$0.58 = \$1,450$

Year 2:

STEP 1. $\dfrac{\$8,000 - \$1,000}{12,000 \text{ hours}} = \$0.58$ per hour (rounded)

STEP 2. $1,400 \times \$0.58 = \$812$

MACRS Depreciation

Year 1: $\$8,000 \times 20\% = \$1,600$

Year 2: $\$8,000 \times 32\% = \$2,560$

LEARNING OBJECTIVE

4 *Differentiate among capital expenditures, revenue expenditures, and extraordinary-repairs expenditures.*

Capital expenditures include the initial costs to purchase property and equipment and also any costs of enlarging or increasing the capacity of assets. Capital expenditures are recorded as debits to an asset account. **Revenue expenditures** include the costs of maintaining the operations of an asset and are recorded as debits to expense accounts. **Extraordinary-repairs expenditures** are treated as capital expenditures.

PRACTICE EXERCISE 4

Beagles Bagels just bought a machine for $3,000, with an estimated life of six years and an estimated salvage value of $500. On January 5, Beagles Bagels incurred $300 for inspection and lubrication of the machine. On November 30, Beagles Bagels paid $800 to replace the engine. Beagles estimates that this repair will extend the life of the machine. Record the journal entries for January 5 and November 30.

PRACTICE EXERCISE 4 SOLUTION

Date		Description	Post. Ref.	Debit	Credit
Jan.	5	Machine Maintenance Expense		3 0 0 00	
		Cash			3 0 0 00
		Inspection and lubrication of machine.			
Nov.	30	Machine		8 0 0 00	
		Cash			8 0 0 00
		Major overhaul and replacement of			
		engine.			

LEARNING OBJECTIVE

5 *Prepare journal entries for (a) discarding, (b) selling, and (c) exchanging assets.*

When a firm changes its Property and Equipment accounts as a result of selling, exchanging, or discarding its assets, the accountant must close or clear the asset accounts along with their respective Accumulated Depreciation accounts. Follow these steps to record an asset that has been discarded or sold:

STEP 1. Record the entry to depreciate the asset up to date, if applicable.

STEP 2. Calculate the book value.

$$\text{Book Value} = \text{Cost} - \text{Accumulated Depreciation}$$

STEP 3. Determine the gain or loss.

$$\text{Gain} = \text{Amount Received Greater than Book Value}$$

$$\text{Loss} = \text{Amount Received Less than Book Value}$$

STEP 4. Record the entry to discard or sell the asset. Debit cash for the amount received, if any; debit Accumulated Depreciation; credit the asset; and if applicable, debit Loss on Disposal of Property and Equipment or credit Gain on Disposal of Property and Equipment.

When a firm trades in one asset for a similar asset, if the exchange has "commercial substance" the business is required to record a gain or loss on the exchange. The entry must include the following steps:

STEP 1. Debit the account of the new asset for its list price.

STEP 2. Close or clear the Accumulated Depreciation account of the old asset by debiting it.

STEP 3. Calculate the gain or loss and then debit Loss on Disposal of Property and Equipment or credit Gain on Disposal of Property and Equipment.

$$\text{Gain} = \text{Market Value (Trade-in Allowance) Greater than Book Value}$$

$$\text{Loss} = \text{Market Value (Trade-in Allowance) Less than Book Value}$$

STEP 4. Credit Cash for the quoted price of the new asset minus the trade-in allowance.

STEP 5. Close or clear the account of the old asset by crediting it.

PRACTICE EXERCISE 5

On June 25, Pound Company discarded office equipment with no salvage value. The following details are taken from the property and equipment record: cost, $800; accumulated depreciation as of the previous December 31, $620; monthly depreciation, $14. Journalize entries to record the depreciation of the office equipment to date and to record the disposal of the office equipment.

PRACTICE EXERCISE 5 SOLUTION

STEP 1. Record the entry to depreciate the office equipment up to date.

Date		Description	Post. Ref.	Debit	Credit
June	25	Depreciation Expense, Office Equipment		8 4 00	
		Accumulated Depreciation, Office Equipment			8 4 00
		Depreciation on office equipment for the partial year ($14 × 6 months).			

STEP 2. Calculate the book value.

$$\text{Book Value} = \$800 - \$704 = \$96$$

STEP 3. Determine the gain or loss.

$$\text{Loss} = \$0 - \$96 = \$(96)$$

STEP 4. The journal entry to record the disposal of the office equipment is as follows:

Date		Description	Post. Ref.	Debit	Credit
June	25	Accumulated Depreciation,			
		Office Equipment		7 0 4 00	
		Loss on Disposal of Property			
		and Equipment		9 6 00	
		Office Equipment			8 0 0 00
		Discarded office equipment.			

LEARNING OBJECTIVE

Understand the importance of property and equipment records.

When using subsidiary ledgers, property and equipment records should consist of a controlling account and a subsidiary ledger. Many software programs such as QuickBooks or Peachtree provide detail concerning fixed assets. For income tax purposes, this detail is a must.

LEARNING OBJECTIVE

Identify and record the different types of intangibles.

Intangible assets are assets that are purchased for use in the business and have a useful life longer than one year *but have no physical substance.* Some examples of intangibles are **patents**, **copyrights**, **trademarks**, **franchises**, and **goodwill**. Intangible assets with a definite useful life are amortized. **Amortization** is the process of allocating the cost of an intangible to an expense over its legal life or useful life (whichever is shorter). Intangible assets that have an indefinite life, such as goodwill and trademarks, are not amortized.

PRACTICE EXERCISE 6

On January 2, Stan's Burgers purchased a patent for $18,000 with a legal life of 20 years and a remaining useful life of 10 years. Journalize entries to record the purchase of the patent and the adjusting entry for amortization.

PRACTICE EXERCISE 6 SOLUTION

Date		Description	Post. Ref.	Debit	Credit
Jan.	2	Patent		18 0 0 0 0	
		Cash			18 0 0 0 00
		Purchase of patent.			
Dec.	31	Amortization Expense		1 8 0 0 00	
		Patent			1 8 0 0 00
		Amortization of patent			
		($18,000/10).			

Before a Test Check: Chapters 15–17

PART I: TRUE/FALSE QUESTIONS

For each of the following statements, circle T if the statement is true and F if the statement is false.

T F **1.** The Allowance for Doubtful Accounts account is a current liability.

T F **2.** Under the allowance method of handling bad debt losses, accounts considered uncollectible are written off by debiting Allowance for Doubtful Accounts.

T F **3.** There is an adjusting entry required when the specific charge-off method is used to handle bad debt losses.

T F **4.** FIFO will result in the lowest net income during periods of rising prices.

T F **5.** An account called Cost of Goods Sold is included in the general ledger when the perpetual inventory system is used.

T F **6.** The income statement and the balance sheet both include the balance of the ending merchandise inventory for the same fiscal period (using the periodic inventory system).

T F **7.** When an extraordinary repair on an asset is made, the cost should be credited to the asset account.

T F **8.** When a business sells equipment for an amount greater than its book value, a loss is recorded.

T F **9.** Depreciation amounts are estimates of the loss of value of an asset over a period of time.

T F **10.** The FIFO inventory valuation method assumes that the items on hand are the most recent ones purchased.

PART II: COMPLETION

Complete each of the following statements by writing the appropriate word(s) in the space provided.

1. The balance of Accounts Receivable after one has deducted the balance of Allowance for Doubtful Accounts is called the _____.

2. A method of accounting for bad debt losses that requires a debit to Bad Debts Expense and a credit to Accounts Receivable is called the _____ method.

3. A federal law excusing a debtor from certain obligations incurred is called _____.

4. A process of assigning costs to goods sold based on the flow-of-cost assumption that units sold are recorded at the costs of the most recently acquired goods is called _____.

5. A method of inventory valuation requiring that the actual cost of each individual item in the ending inventory be used is called the _____ method.

6. The inventory system in which a running balance is kept of the inventory on hand and the current cost of each item is called the _____ system.

7. Expenditures for improvements that are not as permanent as the land or not directly associated with a building are debited to the _____ account.

8. The type of depreciation method that allows recording of larger amounts of depreciation in the early years of an asset's use is called a(n) _____ method.

9. The costs of normal day-to-day expenses associated with an asset are called _____.

10. The inventory system that requires a physical count and then attaches a value to that count is called the _____ inventory system.

PART III: MATCHING

For each numbered item, choose the matching term and write the identifying letter in the answer column.

_____ 1. The systematic expensing of the cost of equipment over its useful life.

_____ 2. Cost of major overhaul of an asset.

_____ 3. Cost less salvage (or trade-in) value.

_____ 4. Federal law excusing a debtor from certain obligations incurred.

_____ 5. Analysis of the composition of outstanding accounts receivable.

_____ 6. Cost less accumulated depreciation.

_____ 7. Balance of Accounts Receivable minus Allowance for Doubtful Accounts.

_____ 8. Method of inventory valuation ideal for high-priced units.

_____ 9. Method of inventory valuation that yields the most realistic value of the asset.

_____ 10. Method of inventory valuation that yields the lowest net income during a period of rising prices.

A. Perpetual system
B. Book value
C. Net realizable value
D. Periodic system
E. Depreciation
F. Aging
G. Capital expenditure
H. Revenue expenditure
I. Depreciation base
J. Specific identification
K. FIFO
L. LIFO
M. Weighted average
N. Bankruptcy
O. Extraordinary-repairs expenditure

ANSWERS: PART I

1. F; **2.** T; **3.** F; **4.** F; **5.** T; **6.** T; **7.** F; **8.** F; **9.** F; **10.** T

ANSWERS: PART II

1. book value or net realizable value; **2.** specific charge-off; **3.** bankruptcy; **4.** LIFO; **5.** specific identification; **6.** perpetual inventory; **7.** Land Improvements; **8.** accelerated; **9.** revenue expenditures; **10.** periodic

ANSWERS: PART III

1. E; **2.** O; **3.** I; **4.** N; **5.** F; **6.** B; **7.** C; **8.** J; **9.** K; **10.** L

Glossary

Accelerated depreciation Depreciation methods in which relatively larger amounts of depreciation are recorded during the early years of an asset's use and decreasing amounts in later years. *(p. 680)*

Accumulated Depreciation A contra-asset account that accumulates the depreciation for an asset. *(p. 678)*

Amortization The process of allocating the cost of an intangible to an expense over its useful life. *(p. 698)*

Book value Cost of the asset minus the accumulated depreciation. Sometimes called carrying value. *(p. 678)*

Buildings An asset account that includes warehouses, offices, and retail stores. *(p. 676)*

Capital expenditures Costs incurred for the purchase of property and equipment, as well as the cost of increasing the capacity or quality of assets; the firm receives services or benefits from this property and equipment for more than one accounting period. *(p. 687)*

Copyright The exclusive right of protection granted to creators of artistic works, such as a song, painting, book, or photograph. *(p. 699)*

Depreciation The process of allocating the cost of an asset to an expense over its useful life. *(p. 677)*

Depreciation base Total cost of an asset less its salvage or trade-in value. *(p. 678)*

Double-declining-balance method An accelerated method of depreciation; book value at the beginning of the year multiplied by twice the straight-line rate. *(p. 680)*

Equipment An asset account that includes furniture, vehicles, computers, office equipment, and manufacturing machinery. *(p. 676)*

Extraordinary-repairs expenditures Costs incurred for major overhauls or reconditioning of assets; repairs that either significantly prolong the life of the asset or increase its estimated salvage value. *(p. 687)*

Fixed assets Assets that are purchased for use in the business and have a useful life longer than one year. *(p. 674)*

Franchise An exclusive right to use a company's name and to sell its products. *(p. 699)*

Gain on Disposal of Property and Equipment The account in which a gain is recorded when a firm sells or trades in an asset and receives an amount in excess of the book value for that asset; it appears under Other Income on the income statement. *(p. 694)*

Goodwill Represents the value of the business over its identified assets. *(p. 699)*

Intangible assets Assets that are purchased for use in the business and have a useful life longer than one year but have no physical substance. *(p. 698)*

Land An asset account that includes property that is used in the operations of a business. *(p. 675)*

Land Improvements An asset account covering expenditures for improvements that are (1) not as permanent as the land or (2) not directly associated with a building. These include driveways, parking lots, landscaping, fences, and outdoor lighting systems. *(p. 676)*

Leasehold Improvements An asset account used to record improvements to rented property that are made or paid by the lessee (renter or tenant) but become the property of the lessor (owner or landlord) at the end of the lease term. An example would include remodeling an office suite to fit the business needs of the lessee. *(p. 676)*

Loss on Disposal of Property and Equipment The account in which a loss is recorded when a firm sells or trades in an asset and receives an amount less than the book value for that asset; it appears under Other Expenses on the income statement. *(p. 691)*

Modified Accelerated Cost Recovery System (MACRS) An accelerated method of depreciation that is used to determine allowable depreciation for federal income tax returns based on property acquired after 1986; assets are divided into eight classes. *(p. 684)*

Patent Exclusive right to sell or produce an invention. *(p. 699)*

Revenue expenditures Costs incurred to maintain the operation of assets, such as normal repair expenses and fuel expenses. *(p. 687)*

Salvage value The expected value of the asset at disposable; sometimes called trade-in value or residual value. *(p. 678)*

Straight-line method A method of depreciation that assigns equal amounts of depreciation to each year of the asset's depreciable life. (Cost minus salvage value divided by useful life [in years].) *(p. 679)*

Trademark Represents a word, slogan, or symbol that identifies a company or product. *(p. 699)*

Units-of-production method A method of depreciation that allocates an asset's costs based on its usage or productivity within the period. (Cost minus salvage value divided by estimated life in units of production multiplied by the number of units produced.) *(p. 682)*

Useful life The length of time an asset is expected to be used. *(p. 679)*

CHAPTER REVIEW

CHAPTER ASSIGNMENTS

Discussion Questions

1. What costs should be included in the purchase of property and equipment? Give examples of possible expenditures that should be included in determining the total cost of an asset, such as a machine.
2. Identify the five different types of property and equipment and give an example of each.
3. Define depreciation and discuss the most common methods of computing depreciation.
4. Explain how an asset's estimated salvage (or trade-in) value is treated in computing depreciation under the double-declining-balance method and the straight-line method.
5. Explain how MACRS differs from other methods of depreciation.
6. Differentiate between capital expenditures and revenue expenditures. Give two examples of each type of expenditure for a truck.
7. Distinguish between expenditures for ordinary repairs and extraordinary-repairs expenditures.
8. What is meant by disposition of an asset? List the situations involving disposition of assets.
9. Explain the two entries usually involved in the disposition of an asset.
10. What is an intangible asset? Identify the different types of intangible assets including if the intangible asset is amortized.

Exercises

PRACTICE EXERCISE 1

EXERCISE 17-1 Leslie Manufacturing Company purchased land adjacent to its factory for the installation of a holding area for equipment. Expenditures by the company were as follows: purchase price, $173,000; paving, $5,300; title search and other fees, $760; grading, $3,000; demolition of a shack on the property, $4,600; lighting, $8,200; signs, $2,850; broker's fees, $10,240; landscaping, $10,600. Determine the amount that should be debited to the Land account and record the journal entry assuming that Leslie purchases the land with cash.

PRACTICE EXERCISE 2

EXERCISE 17-2 Portillo Plumbing purchases land and building for a combined price of $400,000. The assessor valued this property for tax purposes at $360,000: $135,000 for the land and $225,000 for the building. Record the journal entry for the purchase.

PRACTICE EXERCISE 3

EXERCISE 17-3 At the beginning of the fiscal year, Denny Services bought a new copier for $6,500, with an estimated salvage (or trade-in) value of $500 and an estimated useful life of five years. Determine the amount of the depreciation for the first and second years by the following methods:

a. Straight-line
b. Double-declining-balance
c. Units-of-production (Useful life is 8,400 hours. Year 1 use is 1,050 hours; Year 2 use, 500 hours. Compute depreciation per hour, then depreciation for Year 1 and Year 2.)
d. MACRS (Assume the asset was purchased after 1986 and is 5-year property. Calculate the depreciation for income tax reporting.)

Round annual depreciation to whole dollars.

EXERCISE 17-4 Connelly Company just bought a machine for $8,000, with an estimated life of five years and an estimated salvage value of $2,200; straight-line depreciation expense is $1,160. Record journal entries for the following transactions:

PRACTICE EXERCISE 4

Jan. 12 Issued Ck. No. 5221 for $250 for inspection and lubrication of the machine.

Oct. 15 Issued Ck. No. 5562 for $1,970 to replace the motor and rollers. Connelly Company estimates that this repair will extend the life of the machine about two years.

EXERCISE 17-5 On April 28, Whitmire Exercise Mart discarded exercise equipment that cost $7,300. The Accumulated Depreciation account shows depreciation of $7,300 as of the previous December 31. Make the entry in general journal form to record the disposal of the asset.

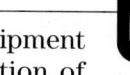

PRACTICE EXERCISE 5

EXERCISE 17-6 On February 28, Reyes Company discarded office equipment with no salvage value. The following details are taken from the property and equipment record: cost, $2,000; accumulated depreciation as of the previous December 31, $1,820; monthly depreciation, $14. Journalize entries to record the depreciation of the office equipment to date and to record the disposal of the office equipment.

PRACTICE EXERCISE 5

EXERCISE 17-7 On June 20, JAX Communications sold editing equipment that cost $3,800 for $1,550. Accumulated depreciation up to the end of the previous year was $2,350. Monthly depreciation is $32. Make the necessary general journal entries.

PRACTICE EXERCISE 5

EXERCISE 17-8 On June 25, Wynn Assemblers trades in a machine for a new one priced at $8,460, receiving a trade-in allowance of $1,500 on the old machine. Wynn Assemblers makes a down payment of $1,200 in cash and issues a 60-day, 9 percent note for the remainder. The property and equipment record shows the following: cost (of old machine), $6,000; accumulated depreciation as of last December 31, $4,800; monthly depreciation, $100. Assuming this exchange has commercial substance, make entries in general journal form to record the depreciation of the old machine to date and to record the trade-in and purchase of the new machine.

PRACTICE EXERCISE 5

EXERCISE 17-9 On September 27, Nichols Florists traded in its old delivery van for a new one, which cost $15,000. Nichols got a trade-in allowance of $500 on the old van and paid the difference in cash. The property and equipment record shows the following: cost (of old van), $12,000; accumulated depreciation as of last December 31, $9,500; monthly depreciation, $200. Assuming this exchange has commercial substance, make entries in general journal form to record the depreciation of the old van to date and to record the trade-in and purchase of the new van.

PRACTICE EXERCISE 5

EXERCISE 17-10 Fusion Advertising purchased a patent on January 2 for $25,000. The patent has a useful life of 5 years and a legal life of 20 years. Record the journal entry for the purchase of patent and the adjusting entry at December 31 to recognize amortization.

PRACTICE EXERCISE 6

CHAPTER ASSIGNMENTS

Problem Set A

For additional help, see the demonstration problem at the beginning of each chapter in your Working Papers.

Check Figure
Double-declining-balance method, book value at end of Year 4, $3,629

PROBLEM 17-1A At the beginning of a fiscal year, Flowers Company buys a truck for $28,000. The machine's estimated life is five years, and its estimated salvage value is $3,000.

Required
Using the following four methods, determine the annual depreciation of the truck for each of the estimated five years of life, the accumulated depreciation at the end of each year, and the book value of the truck at the end of each year. Round annual depreciation to whole dollars.

a. Straight-line method
b. Double-declining-balance method
c. Units-of-production method (Useful life is 100,000 miles. Year 1 use is 10,000 miles; Year 2 use, 20,000 miles; Year 3 use, 40,000 miles; Year 4 use, 18,000 miles; and Year 5 use, 12,000 miles.) Round depreciation per unit to two decimal places.
d. MACRS method (Assume the asset was purchased after 1986 and is 5-year property.)

PROBLEM 17-2A During a three-year period, Abrams Electric completed the following transactions related to its service truck:

Year 1

Jan.   4   Bought a used service truck for cash, $18,600.

Nov. 21   Paid garage for maintenance repairs to the truck, $146.

Dec. 31   Recorded the adjusting entry for depreciation for the fiscal year. The estimated life of the truck is four years, and it has an estimated salvage value of $3,800. Abrams uses the straight-line method of depreciation.

      31   Closed the expense accounts to the Income Summary account.

Year 2

Apr.   2   Paid garage for tune-up of truck, $86.

May 24   Bought tires for the truck, $335.

Dec. 31   Recorded the adjusting entry for depreciation for the fiscal year.

      31   Closed the expense accounts to the Income Summary account.

Year 3

June   6   Paid garage for maintenance repairs to truck, $362.

      27   Traded in the used truck for a new truck that cost $22,800, receiving a trade-in allowance of $7,500 and paying the difference in cash. Recorded the entry to depreciate the truck up to the present date. Made the entry to record the exchange, assuming the exchange has commercial substance.

Dec. 31   Recorded the adjusting entry for depreciation of the new truck for the fiscal year. The estimated life of the truck is six years, and it has an estimated trade-in value of $2,600. Abrams Electric uses the straight-line method of depreciation.

      31   Closed the expense accounts to the Income Summary account.

Required

1. Record the transactions in general journal form, pages 97 and 98.
2. After journalizing each entry, post to the following ledger accounts: Truck, No. 131; Accumulated Depreciation, Truck, No. 132; Truck Repair Expense, No. 519; Depreciation Expense, Truck, No. 523; and Loss on Disposal of Property and Equipment, No. 640.

Check Figure
Year 2, adjustment amount, $3,700

PROBLEM 17–3A During a three-year period, Craig Excavation completed the following transactions pertaining to its front-end loader:

 **LO** 3,4,5

Year 1

June 30 Bought a front-end loader, $39,500, paying $15,500 in cash and issuing a series of four notes for $6,000 each to come due at six- month intervals. Payments are to include principal plus 9 percent interest on all outstanding notes.

July 1 Paid transportation charges for the loader, $550.

Dec. 31 Paid the principal, $6,000, on the first note, plus interest of $1,080 on $24,000 on all the notes.

31 Made the adjusting entry to record depreciation on the loader for the fiscal year. The estimated life of the loader is four years; it has a salvage value of $3,000. Craig's accountant uses the double-declining-balance method.

31 Closed the expense accounts to the Income Summary account.

Year 2

Mar. 14 Paid for normal mechanical repairs to the front-end loader, $1,835.

June 30 Paid the principal, $6,000, on the second note, plus interest of $810 on $18,000 on the remaining notes.

Dec. 31 Paid the principal, $6,000, on the third note, plus interest of $540 on $12,000 on the remaining notes.

31 Recorded the adjusting entry for depreciation for the fiscal year.

31 Closed the expense accounts to the Income Summary account.

Year 3

Apr. 21 Paid for normal mechanical repairs to the front-end loader, $750.

June 30 Paid the principal, $6,000, plus interest of $270 on $6,000 on the fourth note.

Sept. 27 Craig Excavation decided to get rid of its loader and use the services of an equipment rental firm in the future. Sold the loader for $6,200 cash. Made the entry to depreciate the loader to date ($5,632.03). Made the entry to account for the sale of the loader.

Dec. 31 Closed the expense accounts to the Income Summary account.

Required

1. Record the transactions in general journal form, pages 192–194.
2. After making each journal entry, post to the following ledger accounts: Equipment, No. 141; Accumulated Depreciation, Equipment, No. 142; Equipment Maintenance Expense, No. 529; Depreciation Expense, Equipment, No. 533; Interest Expense, No. 541; and Loss on Disposal of Property and Equipment, No. 542.

Check Figure
Year 3, Income Summary debit, $9,838.75

PROBLEM 17–4A The general ledger of Bray Personnel Service includes controlling accounts for Office Equipment, No. 123, and Accumulated Depreciation, Office Equipment, No. 124. Bray's accountant also records the details of each item of office equipment in a subsidiary ledger. During a three-year period, the following transactions affecting office equipment took place:

 **LO** 3,5,6

Year 1

Jan.   5   Bought the following from Just-In-Time, Inc., for cash:

Filing cabinet, $240, account no. 123-1, expected life five years, salvage value zero.

Executive desk, $960, account no. 123-2, expected life six years, salvage value zero.

Executive chair, $360, account no. 123-3, expected life three years, salvage value zero.

(The above assets will be depreciated using the straight-line method.)

7   Paid Clements and Johnson $1,280 for a custom-made counter, account no. 123-4, expected life 10 years, salvage value zero; depreciation by straight-line method.

Dec. 31   Made the adjusting entry to record depreciation of office equipment for the fiscal year (total depreciation, $456; verify this figure).

31   Closed the Depreciation Expense, Office Equipment account into the Income Summary account.

Year 2

June 29   Bought a carpet from Poet Floor Coverings on account, $1,280, account no. 123-5, estimated life eight years, salvage value zero; depreciation by double-declining-balance method.

Dec. 31   Recorded the adjusting entry for depreciation of office equipment for the fiscal year (depreciation for six months on the carpet; total depreciation, $616; verify this figure).

31   Closed the Depreciation Expense, Office Equipment account into the Income Summary account.

Year 3

June 30   Traded in the executive chair for a new one from Gomez and Sheamer, account no. 123-6. The new chair cost $520, has an estimated life of eight years, and has a zero salvage value; depreciation using the straight-line method. Bray Personnel Service received a trade-in allowance of $50 on the old chair and paid the balance in cash. Recorded the entry to depreciate the old chair to date. Made the entry to record the exchange of assets, assuming the exchange has commercial value.

Dec. 31   Made the adjusting entry to record depreciation of office equipment for the fiscal year (depreciation for six months on the chair; total depreciation, $648.50; verify this figure).

31   Closed the Depreciation Expense, Office Equipment and Loss on Disposal of Property and Equipment accounts into the Income Summary account.

Check Figure
Year 3, Income Summary debit, $718.50

Required

1. Record the transactions in general journal form, pages 136 and 137.
2. With the purchase of each new asset, open an account in the subsidiary ledger.
3. After each entry, post to the two controlling accounts and to the subsidiary ledger.
4. Make a list of the balances in the subsidiary ledger accounts at the end of Year 3 and compare the totals with the balances of the two controlling accounts.

Problem Set B

For additional help, see the demonstration problem at the beginning of each chapter in your Working Papers.

PROBLEM 17–1B At the beginning of a fiscal year, Reaves Company buys a machine for $42,000. The machine has an estimated life of five years and an estimated salvage value of $4,000.

Required
Using the following four methods, determine the annual depreciation of the machine for each of the estimated five years of its life, the accumulated depreciation at the end of each year, and the book value of the machine at the end of each year. Round annual depreciation to whole dollars.

Check Figure
Double-declining-balance method, book value at end of Year 4, $5,443

a. Straight-line method
b. Double-declining-balance method
c. Units-of-production method (Useful life is 380,000 units. Year 1 use is 60,000 units; Year 2 use, 80,000 units; Year 3 use, 100,000 units; Year 4 use, 88,000 units; and Year 5 use, 52,000 units.)
d. MACRS method (Assume the asset was purchased after 1986 and is 7-year property.)

PROBLEM 17–2B During a three-year period, 5TH Street Motel completed the following transactions pertaining to its pickup truck:

Year 1

Jan. 11 Bought a used pickup truck for cash, $8,800.

Nov. 16 Paid garage for maintenance repairs to pickup truck, $273.

Dec. 31 Recorded the adjusting entry for depreciation for the fiscal year, using the straight-line method of depreciation. The estimated life of the pickup truck is four years, and it has an estimated trade-in value of $2,200.

31 Closed the expense accounts to the Income Summary account.

Year 2

Mar. 4 Paid garage for tune-up and minor repairs, $88.

May 27 Bought a tire for the truck, $105.

Dec. 31 Recorded the adjusting entry for depreciation for the fiscal year.

31 Closed the expense accounts to the Income Summary account.

Year 3

Feb. 13 Paid garage for maintenance repairs to pickup truck, $436.

June 22 Traded in the pickup truck for another pickup truck priced at $9,460, receiving a trade-in allowance of $1,040 and paying the difference in cash. Recorded the entry to depreciate the old truck to date. Made the entry to record the exchange, assuming the exchange has commercial substance.

Dec. 31 Recorded the adjusting entry for depreciation of the new pickup truck for the fiscal year, using the straight-line method of depreciation. The estimated life of the new truck is six years, and it has an estimated trade-in value of $2,500.

31 Closed the expense accounts to the Income Summary account.

Required
1. Record the transactions in general journal form, pages 97 and 98.
2. After journalizing each entry, post to the following ledger accounts: Truck, No. 131; Accumulated Depreciation, Truck, No. 132; Truck Repair Expense, No. 519; Depreciation Expense, Truck, No. 523; and Loss on Disposal of Property and Equipment, No. 640.

Check Figure
Year 2, adjustment amount, $1,650

PROBLEM 17–3B During a three-year period, Youngblood Construction Company completed the following transactions connected with its bulldozer:

Year 1

June 30 Bought a bulldozer, $120,400, paying $40,400 in cash and issuing a series of four notes for $20,000 each to come due at six-month intervals. Payments are to include principal plus 9 percent interest on all outstanding notes.

July 2 Paid transportation charges for the bulldozer, $3,600.

Dec. 31 Paid the principal, $20,000, on the first note, plus interest of $3,600 on $80,000 on all the notes.

31 Made the adjusting entry to record depreciation on the bulldozer for the fiscal year, using the double-declining-balance method ($24,800; verify this figure). The estimated life of the bulldozer is five years, and it has an estimated salvage value of $11,600.

31 Closed the expense accounts to the Income Summary account.

Year 2

Apr. 24 Paid for maintenance repairs to the bulldozer, $5,936.

June 30 Paid the principal, $20,000, on the second note, plus interest of $2,700 on $60,000 on the remaining notes.

Dec. 31 Paid the principal, $20,000, on the third note, plus interest of $1,800 on $40,000 on the remaining notes.

31 Recorded the adjusting entry for depreciation for the fiscal year.

31 Closed the expense accounts to the Income Summary account.

Year 3

May 19 Paid for maintenance repairs to the bulldozer, $2,185.

June 30 Paid the principal, $20,000, plus interest of $900 on $20,000, on the fourth note.

Sept. 29 Youngblood Construction decided to get rid of its bulldozer and use the services of an equipment rental firm in the future. Sold the bulldozer for $24,000 cash. Made the entry to depreciate the bulldozer to date. Made the entry to account for the sale of the bulldozer.

Dec. 31 Closed the expense accounts to the Income Summary account.

Check Figure
Year 3, Income Summary debit, $38,605

Required

1. Record the transactions in general journal form, pages 192–194.
2. After making each journal entry, post to the following ledger accounts: Equipment, No. 141; Accumulated Depreciation, Equipment, No. 142; Equipment Maintenance Expense, No. 529; Depreciation Expense, Equipment, No. 533; Interest Expense, No. 541; and Loss on Disposal of Property and Equipment, No. 542.

3,5,6 **LO**

PROBLEM 17–4B The general ledger of Rafferty Insurance Agency includes controlling accounts for Office Equipment, No. 123, and Accumulated Depreciation, Office Equipment, No. 124. Rafferty's accountant also records the details of each item of office equipment in a subsidiary ledger. The following transactions affecting office equipment occurred during a three-year period:

Year 1

Jan. 4 Bought the following from Poland Office Supplies for cash:

Executive desk, $1,028, account no. 123-1, estimated life eight years, salvage value zero.

Executive chair, $375, account no. 123-2, estimated life three years, salvage value zero.

Filing cabinet, metal, $300, account no. 123-3, estimated life five years, salvage value zero.

(The above assets will be depreciated using the straight-line method.)

Jan.   9 Paid French Cabinet Shop $2,080 for a custom-made counter, account no. 123-4, estimated life ten years, salvage value zero; depreciation by straight-line method.

Dec. 31 Made the adjusting entry to record depreciation of office equipment for the fiscal year (total depreciation, $521.50; verify this figure).

      31 Closed the Depreciation Expense, Office Equipment account into the Income Summary account.

Year 2

June 27 Bought a rug from Italy Furniture on account, $1,720, account no. 123-5, estimated life eight years, salvage value zero; depreciation by double-declining-balance method.

Dec. 31 Recorded the adjusting entry for depreciation of office equipment for the fiscal year (depreciation for six months on the rug; total depreciation, $736.50; verify this figure).

      31 Closed the Depreciation Expense, Office Equipment account into the Income Summary account.

Year 3

June 23 Traded in the executive desk for a new one, which cost $1,330, from Persia, Inc., account no. 123-6, receiving a trade-in allowance of $580 on the old desk and paying the balance in cash. Expected life of the new desk is eight years, with a zero salvage value; depreciated using straight-line method. Made the entry to depreciate the old desk to date. Made the entry to record the exchange of assets, assuming the exchange has commercial substance.

Dec. 31 Made the adjusting entry to record depreciation of office equipment for the fiscal year (depreciation for six months on the desk; total depreciation, $852.38; verify this figure).

      31 Closed the Depreciation Expense, Office Equipment and Loss on Disposal of Property andEquipment accounts into the Income Summary account.

Required

1. Record the transactions in general journal form, pages 136 and 137.
2. With the purchase of each new asset, open an account in the subsidiary ledger.
3. After each entry, post to the two controlling accounts and to the subsidiary ledger.
4. Make a list of the balances in the subsidiary ledger accounts at the end of Year 3 and compare the totals with the balances of the two controlling accounts.

Check Figure
Year 3, Income Summary debit, $1,043.38

ACTIVITIES

INTERNET LINKS TO ACCOUNTING

Now that you understand how a company accounts for property and equipment, let's see review Ford Motor Company's long-term assets. Go to http://www.ford.com/about-ford/investor-relations and click on Company Reports to access the 2008 Annual Report.

1. What are the property and equipment (P&E) categories that Ford Motor Company reported on its 2008 balance sheet? (See also note 12 in the notes to the financial statements.)
2. As of December 31, 2008, what was the total amount that the company had invested in property and equipment before accumulated depreciation was deducted?

3. What depreciation method(s) does Ford use? What are the estimated useful lives used for the buildings and land improvements and for the machinery and equipment?

CONSIDER AND COMMUNICATE

Kason Miller owns a small catering service. The company owns a delivery van as well as ovens and large cooking containers. He is confused about the different traditional depreciation methods he may use for financial reporting. Explain briefly to him the features and consequences of using each method.

WHAT'S WRONG WITH THIS PICTURE?

Your employer, who is ordering equipment for a new office, has signed the purchase orders for new equipment without looking at them carefully. As you complete an invoice for items for the employee lunchroom, you are tempted to change the order from one microwave to two microwaves and quietly take the second one home to compensate yourself for all the hard work you have done on your own time to get the new office ready. You are a trusted employee, and you are sure that if your employer found out what you had done there would be no real repercussions. What if you go ahead with this idea? How could it be discovered? Assume that you are the one who would accept shipment when the microwaves are delivered.

CRITICAL THINKING

Robin's Cycle Shop owns various depreciable assets, which were purchased beginning in 2004. The only record you can find on December 31, 2009 (prior to any depreciation adjustments for 2009) is the general ledger account for Equipment, which has a balance of $50,500, and the general ledger account for Accumulated Depreciation, Equipment, which has a balance of $29,690, plus the following information. You will need to prepare supporting schedules by asset classification and expense for each prior year before you can calculate the 2009 depreciation.

Depreciable Assets					
Asset	Bought	Method	Life	Cost	Salvage Value
Van #1	1/1/2004	DDB	5 yrs.	$13,000	$1,000
Office Desks	7/1/2004	SL	5 yrs.	2,500	500
Van #2	7/1/2006	DDB	5 yrs.	20,000	2,000
Trailer	9/1/2008	DDB	5 yrs.	12,000	1,500
Computer	12/1/2008	SL	5 yrs.	3,000	0

Total Depreciation	
2004	$ 5,400
2005	3,520
2006	6,272
2007	7,923
2008	6,575
	$29,690

Required
1. Classify assets by type: Delivery Equipment or Office Equipment.
2. Recompute depreciation for 2004, 2005, 2006, 2007, and 2008. Round each year's depreciation expense to whole dollars.
3. Compute depreciation for 2009.

PART 6

Partnerships

18

MAXWELL LOCKE & RITTER, Austin, Texas

Most sole proprietorships eventually recognize that by combining talent with other individuals in the same industry, their businesses can grow. Many accounting firms start this way—which is exactly what happened with Maxwell Locke & Ritter LLP. LLP stands for "limited liability partnership;" and, is a partnership that provides liability protection for the partners. In 1991 Earl Maxwell, Tom Locke, and Mark Ritter established the Maxwell Locke & Ritter partnership in an effort to combine talent, knowledge, and clients. The founding partners believe that their practice should focus on three things: their clients, their people, and their community.

In this chapter we will learn the advantages and disadvantages of partnerships and also identify the different types of partnerships. We will also learn the journal entries for formation of a partnership, division of partnership income or loss, withdrawal of a partner, and liquidation of the partnership.

WHY IT MATTERS

LEARNING OBJECTIVES

After you have completed this chapter, you will be able to do the following:

1 (a) Define the various kinds of partnerships and list the main advantages and disadvantages of a partnership, and (b) journalize initial investments of a partnership.

capital investments, and (c) salary and interest allowances.

4 Prepare a statement of partners' equity.

2 Provide for the division of net income or loss of a partnership on the basis of (a) fractional shares, (b) ratio of capital investments, and (c) salary and interest allowances.

5 Journalize entries involving the sale of a partnership interest or withdrawal of a partner.

3 Journalize the closing entries for a partnership on the basis of (a) fractional shares, (b) ratio of

6 Journalize entries pertaining to the liquidation of a partnership involving the immediate sale of the assets for cash.

ACCOUNTING LANGUAGE

Co-ownership *(p. 719)*

Dissolution *(p. 736)*

Distributive share *(p. 725)*

General partnership (GP) *(p. 718)*

Limited liability partnership (LLP) *(p. 719)*

Limited partnership (LP) *(p. 719)*

Liquidation *(p. 740)*

Mutual agency *(p. 719)*

Partnership *(p. 718)*

Partnership agreement *(p. 720)*

Realization *(p. 740)*

Up until now, we have been dealing entirely with sole proprietorships. In this chapter, we turn our attention to partnerships. According to The Uniform Partnership Act, a **partnership** is "an association of two or more persons who carry on, as co-owners, a business for profit." In professions and firms that stress personal service, partnerships are widely used. Each professional practitioner can maintain his or her own clientele, yet share with colleagues the expenses of operating an office or clinic. Partnerships are also popular in manufacturing and trade because they afford a means of combining the capital and abilities of two or more persons.

TYPES OF PARTNERSHIPS

LEARNING OBJECTIVE 1a

Define the various kinds of partnerships and list the main advantages and disadvantages of a partnership.

There are three types of partnerships: general, limited, and limited liability partnerships.

General Partnership (GP)

A **general partnership (GP)** is an association of two or more people or firms to carry on, as co-owners, a business for profit. The partners are called *general partners*, and each partner is personally liable for all of the debts the partnership incurs during his or her association with the firm. Because of the unlimited liability of the general partners, firms today are usually not set up as general partnerships.

Limited Partnership (LP)

A **limited partnership (LP)** is an organization with two or more people or firms with at least one general partner and one limited partner. The general partner (with unlimited liability) may have little or no investment, organizes the partnership, manages day-to-day operations, and controls the operation of the partnership. The *limited partner* or partners have the largest share of invested capital, are not involved in the day-to-day operations, and usually cannot lose more than their capital contribution. Limited partnerships used to be the preferred entity as vehicles for raising capital. They have generally been replaced by limited liability corporations (LLCs) or corporations, which are discussed in Chapter 19.

Limited Liability Partnership (LLP)

A **limited liability partnership (LLP)** is an organization similar to a limited partnership except that all partners may take an active role in the business of the partnership with only their invested capital at risk. Many law and accounting firms are now operated as LLPs.

CHARACTERISTICS OF A PARTNERSHIP

General, limited, and limited liability partnerships all share the following characteristics.

Co-ownership of Partnership Property

All partners are co-owners of the assets of the partnership. For example, Duncan and James formed a 50-50 partnership to run an accounting practice. The partnership owns two buildings of equal value. According to the **co-ownership** concept, each partner owns half of each building, as well as half of the other assets of the firm.

Limited Life

A partnership may be ended by the death or withdrawal of any partner. Other factors that may bring about the end of a partnership include the bankruptcy or incapacity of a partner, the expiration of the period of time specified in the partnership agreement, or the completion of the project for which the partnership was formed.

Mutual Agency

The **mutual agency** concept allows each partner to enter into binding contracts in the name of the firm for the purchase or sale of goods or services within the normal scope of the firm's business and based upon the provisions of the partnership agreement.

> **Remember**
>
> Just because a partnership ends does not necessarily mean that the business ends. It can continue under a new written partnership agreement or as another type of entity.

Taxation

Federal income taxes are not levied against a partnership as an entity, although a partnership must file an information return (Form 1065) containing an income statement, balance sheet, and report of the distributive shares of income (the shares of the year's net income allocated to each partner). A partner has to file an individual income tax return and has to pay taxes on his or her share of the net income, whether or not this share is actually taken out of the business.

Unlimited Liability

General partners of a partnership are personally liable for all debts that are incurred by the partnership. For example, suppose that the partnership Duncan & James (both general partners) owes $50,000 to a creditor. The creditor could take the personal assets of either Duncan or James in order to satisfy the $50,000 debt.

Figure 1 lists the advantages and disadvantages of partnerships.

FIGURE 1 Advantages and disadvantages of partnerships

Advantages of a Partnership	Disadvantages of a Partnership
Able to pool abilities and capital of two or more persons	General partners have unlimited liability
Easy to form	Limited life
Legal restrictions are minimal—must have legal purpose but no limitations on type of activities	Mutual agency: The actions of one partner are binding on the other partners, unless limited by the partnership agreement
Nontaxable (pass-through) entity	Hard to transfer interest to another individual or entity as all partners must agree
	Potential strain on personal relationships

PARTNERSHIP AGREEMENTS

Although a general partnership may be formed on the basis of an oral understanding, a limited partnership and a limited liability partnership must be based upon a written contract, called a **partnership agreement**. The following provisions are usually included:

- Effective date of the agreement
- Names and addresses of the partners
- Name, location, and nature of the business
- Type of partnership
- Management structure
- Duration of the agreement
- Investment of each partner
- Procedure for sharing profits and losses
- Withdrawals to be allowed each partner
- Procedure for a partner's exit from the business
- Provision for division of assets upon liquidation

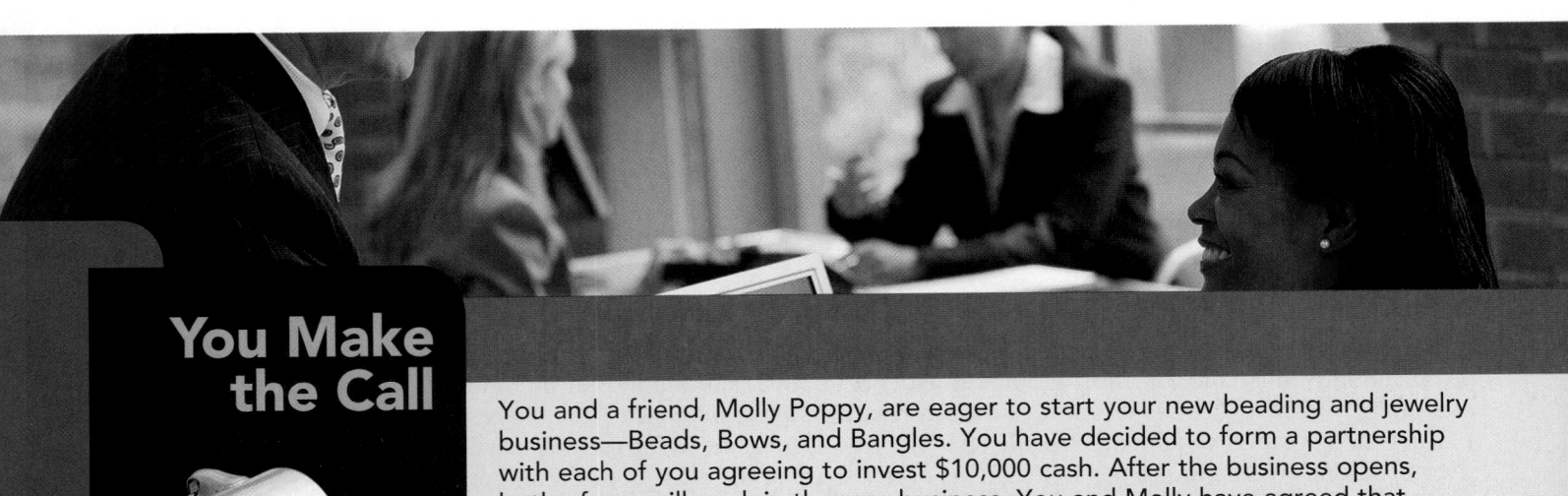

You Make the Call

You and a friend, Molly Poppy, are eager to start your new beading and jewelry business—Beads, Bows, and Bangles. You have decided to form a partnership with each of you agreeing to invest $10,000 cash. After the business opens, both of you will work in the new business. You and Molly have agreed that all income and losses will be divided equally between the partners. Since you are taking this accounting class, you have told Molly that you would be able to create a partnership agreement for your lawyer to review. What items should you ensure that your partnership agreement have? Why is a partnership agreement so important?

made. Assume that the present appraised value of Duncan's equipment is $9,000. Therefore, the accountant records Duncan's investment as follows:

Date	Description	Post. Ref.	Debit	Credit
Feb. 2	Cash		183 3 0 0 00	
	Accounts Receivable		17 6 0 0 00	
	Equipment		9 0 0 0 00	
	Allowance for Doubtful Accounts			5 0 0 00
	Accounts Payable			8 4 0 0 00
	Notes Payable			1 6 0 0 00
	R. P. Duncan, Capital			199 4 0 0 00
	To record the original			
	investment of R. P. Duncan.			

The accountant debits Accounts Receivable for the face amount of the accounts taken over by the new partnership and credits Allowance for Doubtful Accounts for the amount estimated to be uncollectible, which in this case is $500. Any definitely uncollectible customer accounts are excluded from those being taken over by the new business (in this case, the $400 in uncollectible accounts is subtracted from the $18,000 in Accounts Receivable).

The accountant debits the new firm's Equipment accounts for the present appraised values. The accumulated depreciation is not recorded because the appraised value of the equipment represents the new book value for the partnership.

> **Remember**
> An original investment by a partner may include liabilities as well as assets.

Additional Investments

Now let's say that eight months have gone by, and the new partnership needs more cash. On October 1, each partner invests an additional $7,000. The entry is as follows:

GENERAL JOURNAL				PAGE 28
Date	Description	Post. Ref.	Debit	Credit
20—				
Oct. 1	Cash		14 0 0 0 00	
	S. A. James, Capital			7 0 0 0 00
	R. P. Duncan, Capital			7 0 0 0 00
	To record additional			
	investments.			

> **FYI**
> Additional investments appear in the same place on the statement of partners' equity as on the statement of owner's equity.

At the end of the year, before the books are closed, the Capital accounts of the partners appear as follows:

GENERAL LEDGER

ACCOUNT R. P. Duncan, Capital   ACCOUNT NO. 301

Date	Item	Post. Ref.	Debit	Credit	Balance Debit	Balance Credit
20—						
Feb. 2		J1		199 4 0 0 00		199 4 0 0 00
Oct. 1		J28		7 0 0 0 00		206 4 0 0 00

			Post.			Balance	
ACCOUNT S. A. James, Capital						**ACCOUNT NO. 303**	
Date	Item	Post. Ref.	Debit	Credit	Debit	Credit	
20—							
Feb. 2		J1		190 0 0 0 00		190 0 0 0 00	
Oct. 1		J28		7 0 0 0 00		197 0 0 0 00	

Drawing Accounts

Drawing accounts of partners serve the same purpose as the Drawing account of the owner of a sole proprietorship. Debits to the Drawing accounts originate through transactions such as those listed here and illustrated in Figure 2.

- Withdrawal of cash by R. P. Duncan, $4,620, March 17.
- Withdrawal of cash by S. A. James, $3,742, May 4.

FIGURE 2

Debits to Drawing accounts of partners

Date	Description	Post. Ref.	Debit	Credit
20—				
Mar. 17	R. P. Duncan, Drawing		4 6 2 0 00	
	Cash			4 6 2 0 00
	To record a cash withdrawal.			
May 4	S. A. James, Drawing		3 7 4 2 00	
	Cash			3 7 4 2 00
	To record a cash withdrawal.			

DIVISION OF NET INCOME OR NET LOSS

Recall that the closing entries for a *sole proprietorship* require the following steps:

STEP 1. Close the revenue accounts into the Income Summary account.

STEP 2. Close the expense accounts into the Income Summary account (the expense accounts do not include any payments to the owner).

STEP 3. Close the Income Summary account into the Capital account by the amount of the net income or loss.

STEP 4. Close the Drawing account into the Capital account.

The only differences between closing entries for a partnership and those for a sole proprietorship occur in steps 3 and 4. Instead of a single Capital account and a single Drawing account, in a partnership each partner has a separate Capital and Drawing account. Therefore, there will be as many capital and drawing accounts as there are partners. Income Summary is closed into the Capital accounts by the amount of the net income or loss to be distributed to each partner, and the Drawing accounts are closed into the respective Capital accounts.

Closing entries for a *partnership* require the following steps:

STEP 1. Close the revenue accounts into the Income Summary account.

STEP 2. Close the expense accounts into the Income Summary account (the expense accounts do not include any payments to the owner).

STEP 3. Close the Income Summary account into each partner's Capital account by each partner's share of the net income or loss.

STEP 4. Close each partner's Drawing account into the respective Capital account.

Let's look at step 3. The partnership agreement should specify the arrangement for the division of net income or net loss. However, if the partnership agreement fails to do this, from a legal standpoint, the partners should share any net income or loss equally. This is true regardless of differences in amounts invested, in special skills provided, or in time devoted to the business. The share of net income (or net loss) allocated to each partner is known as his or her **distributive share**.

Partners may use any one of a number of alternative methods of sharing partnership earnings, or they may use a combination of methods. The variety of methods reflects the different values of the services or investments contributed by individual partners. We discuss four methods for sharing earnings:

1. Division of income based on fractional shares
2. Division of income based on the ratio of capital investments
3. Division of income based on salary allowances
4. Division of income based on interest allowances

Let's look at two examples of each method for the partnership of Durr & Jacob LLP.

	Example 1 Information	Example 2 Information
Net Income (Loss)	$248,000	$ (4,000)
D. R. Durr, Capital	300,000	300,000
D. R. Durr, Drawing	120,000	120,000
N. A. Jacob, Capital	75,000	75,000
N. A. Jacob, Drawing	20,000	20,000

The balances of the Capital accounts represent the partners' individual investments at the beginning of the year. The balances of the Drawing accounts represent the total personal withdrawals during the year. For the example 1 information, these are shown by T accounts as follows:

D. R. Durr, Capital			N. A. Jacob, Capital	
−	+		−	+
	Bal. 300,000			Bal. 75,000

D. R. Durr, Drawing			N. A. Jacob, Drawing	
+	−		+	−
Bal. 120,000			Bal. 20,000	

Division of Income Based on Fractional Shares

The simplest way to divide net income or loss is to allot each partner a stated fraction of the total. You can establish the size of the fraction by taking into consideration (1) the amount of each partner's investment and (2) the value of the services rendered by each partner. Assume that the partnership agreement stipulates that profits and losses are to be divided this way: three-fourths to Durr and one-fourth to Jacob.

When partners share net income on a fractional basis, this basis is often expressed as a ratio. We can express Durr's three-fourths and Jacob's one-fourth as a $3:1$ (3-to-1) ratio.

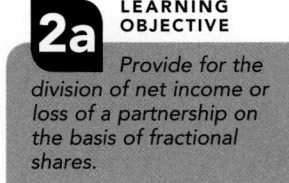

LEARNING OBJECTIVE 2a

Provide for the division of net income or loss of a partnership on the basis of fractional shares.

Closing entries for a partnership are similar to those of a sole proprietorship. The partnership agreement should detail the percentages of net income or net loss to attribute to each partner. In the case of Russ & Daughters, it would appear that there are at least three partners. They may divide the income based on fractional shares, the ratio of capital investments, salary allowances, or interest allowances.

When you list the division of net income as a ratio and want to turn the ratio into a fraction, do it this way: First add the figures; then use the total as the denominator of the fraction.

3 : 1 $\qquad$ (3 + 1 = 4) $\qquad$ $\frac{3}{4}$ and $\frac{1}{4}$

or (in the case of three partners):

5 : 3 : 1 $\qquad$ (5 + 3 + 1 = 9) $\qquad$ $\frac{5}{9}$ and $\frac{3}{9}$ and $\frac{1}{9}$

or (in the case of four partners):

3 : 2 : 1 : 1 $\qquad$ (3 + 2 + 1 + 1 = 7) $\qquad$ $\frac{3}{7}$ and $\frac{2}{7}$ and $\frac{1}{7}$ and $\frac{1}{7}$

The accountant may present a report of the division of net income as a separate statement or record it on the income statement, immediately below Net Income.

Net Income of $248,000

The division of net income is calculated as:

D. R. Durr = $248,000 \times \frac{3}{4}$ = \$186,000

N. A. Jacob = $248,000 \times \frac{1}{4}$ = \$62,000

The accountant would record the division of net income on the income statement as:

Durr & Jacob LLP
Partial Income Statement
For Year Ended December 31, 20—

Revenue from Sales:

	D. R. Durr	N. A. Jacob	Total
Net Income			$248,000
Division of Net Income:	D. R. Durr	N. A. Jacob	Total
Fractional Share	$186,000	$62,000	$248,000

Financial statements for a partnership are basically the same as those of other business entities except for one main difference—the section showing the division of net income.

The division of net income is recorded as a closing entry in step 3 of the closing procedure, whether or not the partner has withdrawn his or her share of income. The entry is as follows:

LEARNING OBJECTIVE

3a *Journalize the closing entries for a partnership on the basis of fractional shares.*

Date		Description	Post. Ref.	Debit	Credit
20—		Closing Entry			
Dec.	31	Income Summary		248 0 0 0 00	
		D. R. Durr, Capital			186 0 0 0 00
		N. A. Jacob, Capital			62 0 0 0 00

The entries for step 4, closing the Drawing accounts into the Capital accounts, are as follows:

Date		Description	Post. Ref.	Debit	Credit
20—		Closing Entries			
Dec.	31	D. R. Durr, Capital		120 0 0 0 00	
		D. R. Durr, Drawing			120 0 0 0 00
	31	N. A. Jacob, Capital		20 0 0 0 00	
		N. A. Jacob, Drawing			20 0 0 0 00

Now let's see what these entries look like in T accounts, with steps 3 and 4 labeled:

Income Summary

(3) Closing 248,000	Bal. 248,000

D. R. Durr, Capital

−	+
(4) 120,000	Bal. 300,000
	(3) 186,000

N. A. Jacob, Capital

−	+
(4) 20,000	Bal. 75,000
	(3) 62,000

D. R. Durr, Drawing

+	−
Bal. 120,000	(4) Closing 120,000

N. A. Jacob, Drawing

+	−
Bal. 20,000	(4) Closing 20,000

Net Loss of $4,000

The division of net loss is calculated as:

$$\text{D. R. Durr} = \$(4,000) \times \frac{3}{4} = \$(3,000)$$

$$\text{N. A. Jacob} = \$(4,000) \times \frac{1}{4} = \$(1,000)$$

The lower portion of the income statement reflects the net loss. (The parentheses around the totals indicate that the figures are negative numbers.)

Revenue from Sales:			
Net Loss			$(4,000)
Division of Net Loss:	D. R. Durr	N. A. Jacob	Total
Fractional Share	$(3,000)	$(1,000)	$(4,000)

The closing entries and posting to the ledger accounts are shown below and in the T accounts that follow:

Date		Description	Post. Ref.	Debit	Credit
20—		Closing Entries			
Dec.	31	D. R. Durr, Capital		3 0 0 0 00	
		N. A. Jacob, Capital		1 0 0 0 00	
		Income Summary			4 0 0 0 00
	31	D. R. Durr, Capital		120 0 0 0 00	
		D. R. Durr, Drawing			120 0 0 0 00
	31	N. A. Jacob, Capital		20 0 0 0 00	
		N. A. Jacob, Drawing			20 0 0 0 00

Income Summary

Bal.	4,000	(3) Closing 4,000

D. R. Durr, Capital

−	+
(3) 3,000	Bal. 300,000
(4) 120,000	

N. A. Jacob, Capital

−	+
(3) 1,000	Bal. 75,000
(4) 20,000	

D. R. Durr, Drawing

+	−
Bal. 120,000	(4) Closing 120,000

N. A. Jacob, Drawing

+	−
Bal. 20,000	(4) Closing 20,000

Senior Manager—Public Accounting

Accounting in Your Future

Brian Fleming, CPA and Senior Manager for Deloitte Tax LLP, currently works in the Washington National Tax Office of Deloitte Tax LLP in Washington, D.C. He works in the Federal Tax Accounting (Periods and Methods) group that deals with the timing of income and deduction for federal income tax purposes. He has had the opportunity while working for this partnership to work for partners of Deloitte Tax LLP who were former Treasury or IRS officials as they consult with Deloitte offices around the world on federal income tax issues.

Brian believes that there are three keys to a successful career in accounting:

1. *Exhibit a positive attitude and strong work ethic.* Your willingness to accept new projects, adapt to change, volunteer for responsibilities, teach others, and stay focused and positive under pressure will be just as important in your career as your ability to deal effectively with the technical issues before you.
2. *Communicate well and often.* Although accounting can be considered a "numbers" field, good oral and written communication skills are imperative for success in this career.
3. *Be a problem solver.* Accounting requires strong analytical skills. When you identify a problem, don't just raise the issue for others to solve—formulate options and recommendations for your supervisor to consider in making his or her decision.

Brian states that public accounting firms or partnerships, such as Deloitte Tax LLP, offer a wealth of opportunities to gain a wide array of experience in a short amount of time. These partnerships sponsor formal training and continuing education programs and offer a clear path for promotions and career advancement. Most public accounting firms, such as Deloitte Tax LLP, require that an employee has earned a minimum of a bachelor's degree in accounting and has also met the requirements to become a certified public accountant (CPA).

Division of Income Based on Ratio of Capital Investments

2b LEARNING OBJECTIVE

Provide for the division of net income or loss of a partnership on the basis of ratio of capital investments.

Allocating earnings to partners on the basis of the amounts of their investment often works well for enterprises whose earnings are closely related to the amount of money invested, such as real estate ventures, cattle feeding operations, and the like. Suppose that the partners of Durr & Jacob LLP have agreed to share earnings or losses according to the ratio of their investments at the beginning of the year.

Remember that Durr had $300,000 and Jacob had $75,000 in their Capital accounts. You can calculate their respective shares as follows:

Durr	$300,000	Durr's share $= \dfrac{\$300,000}{\$375,000} = 0.80$ or 80%
Jacob	75,000		
Total	$375,000	Jacob's share $= \dfrac{\$75,000}{\$375,000} = 0.20$ or 20%

Net Income of $248,000

When the partnership has a net income of $248,000, the accountant determines the distribution like this:

Durr's share of earnings	$248,000 \times 0.80 = \underline{\$198,400}$
Jacob's share of earnings	$248,000 \times 0.20 = \underline{\$\ 49,600}$

The section of the income statement showing the division of net income looks like this:

Revenue from Sales:			
Net Income			$248,000
Division of Net Income:	D. R. Durr	N. A. Jacob	Total
Capital Investment Ratio	$198,400	$49,600	$248,000

LEARNING OBJECTIVE 3b
Journalize the closing entries for a partnership on the basis of ratio of capital investments.

The accompanying closing entries are as follows:

Date		Description	Post. Ref.	Debit	Credit
20—		Closing Entries			
Dec.	31	Income Summary		248 0 0 0 00	
		D. R. Durr, Capital			198 4 0 0 00
		N. A. Jacob, Capital			49 6 0 0 00
	31	D. R. Durr, Capital		120 0 0 0 00	
		D. R. Durr, Drawing			120 0 0 0 00
	31	N. A. Jacob, Capital		20 0 0 0 00	
		N. A. Jacob, Drawing			20 0 0 0 00

Net Loss of $4,000

When the partnership has a net loss of $4,000, the accountant calculates the sharing of the loss as follows:

Durr's share of the loss	$(4,000) \times 0.80 = \$(3,200)$
Jacob's share of the loss	$(4,000) \times 0.20 = \underline{\$\ \ (800)}$

The section of the income statement showing the division of net loss and the accompanying closing entries look like this:

Revenue from Sales:

	D. R. Durr	N. A. Jacob	Total
Net Loss			$(4,000)
Division of Net Loss:	D. R. Durr	N. A. Jacob	Total
Capital Investment Ratio	$(3,200)	$(800)	$(4,000)

Date	Description	Post. Ref.	Debit	Credit
20—	Closing Entries			
Dec. 31	D. R. Durr, Capital		3 2 0 0 00	
	N. A. Jacob, Capital		8 0 0 00	
	Income Summary			4 0 0 0 00
31	D. R. Durr, Capital		120 0 0 0 00	
	D. R. Durr, Drawing			120 0 0 0 00
31	N. A. Jacob, Capital		20 0 0 0 00	
	N. A. Jacob, Drawing			20 0 0 0 00

> **Remember**
> Closing the Drawing accounts into the Capital accounts is the same, regardless of whether a business produces a net income or a net loss.

Note that the entries for step 4—closing the Drawing accounts into the Capital accounts—are always the same, regardless of whether the firm finishes the year with a net income or a net loss.

Division of Income Based on Salary Allowances

Salary allowances are purely allocations of net income. They are used as a means of recognizing and rewarding differences in ability and in the amount of time devoted to the business. **Salary allowances are different from payments to the partners, which are recorded in the Drawing accounts.** They are also different from payments to employees, which are recorded as Salary Expense or Wages Expense. For income tax purposes they are called guaranteed payments. The payments are determined without regard to the income of the partnership.

2c LEARNING OBJECTIVE
Provide for the division of net income or loss of a partnership on the basis of salary and interest allowances.

Suppose that Durr's and Jacob's partnership agreement provides for yearly salaries of $60,000 and $40,000, respectively, with the remainder of the net income to be divided equally. (It would also be possible to divide the remainder on the basis of the ratio of investments or any other ratio agreed to by the partners.)

Net Income of $248,000

When there is a net income of $248,000, the Division of Net Income section of the income statement is as follows:

Revenue from Sales:

	D. R. Durr	N. A. Jacob	Total
Net Income			$248,000
Division of Net Income:	D. R. Durr	N. A. Jacob	Total
Salary Allowances	$ 60,000	$ 40,000	$100,000
Excess of Income over Allowances Allocated Equally	74,000	74,000	148,000
Net Income	$134,000	$114,000	$248,000

> **Remember**
> If the partnership agreement does not stipulate the allocation of the net income or loss after allowances, it is assumed to be divided equally.

The accountant determines the allocation of the remainder as follows:

Net income	$248,000
Less amount allocated as salaries ($60,000 + $40,000)	(100,000)
Remainder	$148,000

$$\text{Remainder} \div 2 = \frac{\$148,000}{2} = \$74,000$$

LEARNING OBJECTIVE 3c

Journalize the closing entries for a partnership on the basis of salary and interest allowances.

Now look at the closing entries:

Date		Description	Post. Ref.	Debit	Credit
20—		Closing Entries			
Dec.	31	Income Summary		248 0 0 0 00	
		D. R. Durr, Capital			134 0 0 0 00
		N. A. Jacob, Capital			114 0 0 0 00
	31	D. R. Durr, Capital		120 0 0 0 00	
		D. R. Durr, Drawing			120 0 0 0 00
	31	N. A. Jacob, Capital		20 0 0 0 00	
		N. A. Jacob, Drawing			20 0 0 0 00

Net Loss of $4,000

When salary allowances are stipulated in the partnership agreement, they must be allocated (not necessarily paid) regardless of whether there is enough net income to cover them.

The accountant determines the remainder as follows:

Net income	$ (4,000)
Less amount allocated as salaries ($60,000 + $40,000)	(100,000)
Remainder	$(104,000)

$$\text{Remainder} \div 2 = \frac{\$(104,000)}{2} = \$(52,000)$$

The income statement and the closing entries appear as follows:

Remember

Salary allowances are included in the Division of Net Income or Loss section of the income statement.

Revenue from Sales:			
Net Loss			$ (4,000)
Division of Net Loss:	D. R. Durr	N. A. Jacob	Total
Salary Allowances	$ 60,000	$ 40,000	$100,000
Excess of Allowances over			
Income Allocated Equally	(52,000)	(52,000)	(104,000)
Net Income (Loss)	$ 8,000	$(12,000)	$ (4,000)

Date		Description	Post. Ref.	Debit	Credit
20—		Closing Entries			
Dec.	31	N. A. Jacob, Capital		12 0 0 0 00	
		Income Summary			4 0 0 0 00
		D. R. Durr, Capital			8 0 0 0 00
	31	D. R. Durr, Capital		120 0 0 0 00	
		D. R. Durr, Drawing			120 0 0 0 00
	31	N. A. Jacob, Capital		20 0 0 0 00	
		N. A. Jacob, Drawing			20 0 0 0 00

After posting, the partners' equity accounts look like this:

Income Summary

Bal.	4,000	(3) Closing	4,000

D. R. Durr, Capital

−		+	
(4)	120,000	Bal.	300,000
		(3)	8,000

N. A. Jacob, Capital

−		+	
(3)	12,000	Bal.	75,000
(4)	20,000		

D. R. Durr, Drawing

+		−	
Bal.	120,000	(4) Closing	120,000

N. A. Jacob, Drawing

+		−	
Bal.	20,000	(4) Closing	20,000

As a result of the $4,000 net loss for the year and the activity in the Drawing accounts, Durr's Capital account decreased by $112,000 (credit $8,000 and debit $120,000), and Jacob's Capital account decreased by $32,000 (debit $12,000 and debit $20,000).

Division of Income Based on Interest Allowances

Sometimes a partnership agreement stipulates an allowance for interest on the partners' capital investments. This clause acts as an incentive for partners not only to leave their investments in the business, but even to increase them. For example, suppose that the partners at Durr & Jacob LLP are allowed, in addition to their salary allowances of $60,000 and $40,000, 6 percent interest on their Capital balances at the beginning of the fiscal year; the remainder is to be divided equally. Interest allowances, like salary allowances, are just allocations of net income.

> **Remember**
>
> Interest allowances are frequently used to reward the investment of partners, particularly when the investments are not equal.

Interest allowance for Durr $300,000 × 0.06 = $18,000

Interest allowance for Jacob $75,000 × 0.06 = $ 4,500

Net Income of $248,000

The section of the income statement relating to the division of a $248,000 net income appears as follows:

Revenue from Sales:

	D. R. Durr	N. A. Jacob	Total
Net Income			$248,000
Division of Net Income:	D. R. Durr	N. A. Jacob	Total
Salary Allowances	$ 60,000	$ 40,000	$100,000
Interest Allowances	18,000	4,500	22,500
Excess of Income over			
Allowances Allocated Equally	62,750	62,750	125,500
Net Income	$140,750	$107,250	$248,000

The accountant calculates the remainder in the following way:

Net income		$248,000
Less:		
Amount allocated as salaries		
($60,000 + $40,000)	$(100,000)	
Amount allocated as interest		
($18,000 + $4,500)	(22,500)	(122,500)
Remainder		$125,500

$$\text{Remainder} \div 2 = \frac{\$125,500}{2} = \underline{\$62,750}$$

And the closing entries look like the following:

Date		Description	Post. Ref.	Debit	Credit
20—		Closing Entries			
Dec.	31	Income Summary		248 0 0 0 00	
		D. R. Durr, Capital			140 7 5 0 00
		N. A. Jacob, Capital			107 2 5 0 00
	31	D. R. Durr, Capital		120 0 0 0 00	
		D. R. Durr, Drawing			120 0 0 0 00
	31	N. A. Jacob, Capital		20 0 0 0 00	
		N. A. Jacob, Drawing			20 0 0 0 00

Net Loss of $4,000

The accountant handles interest allowances the same way as salary allowances: Both must be allocated, whether or not there is enough net income to cover them. The section of the income statement relating to the division of a $4,000 net loss appears as follows:

Revenue from Sales:

	D. R. Durr	N. A. Jacob	Total
Net Loss			$ (4,000)
Division of Net Loss:	D. R. Durr	N. A. Jacob	Total
Salary Allowances	$ 60,000	$ 40,000	$ 100,000
Interest Allowances	18,000	4,500	22,500
Excess of Allowances over			
Income Allocated Equally	(63,250)	(63,250)	(126,500)
Net Income (Loss)	$ 14,750	$(18,750)	$ (4,000)

The accountant computes the remainder as follows:

Net loss		$ (4,000)
Less:		
Amount allocated as salaries ($60,000 + $40,000)	$(100,000)	
Amount allocated as interest ($18,000 + $4,500)	(22,500)	(122,500)
Remainder		$(126,500)

$$\text{Remainder} \div 2 = \frac{\$(126,500)}{2} = \$(63,250)$$

And the closing entries look like those below.

Date		Description	Post. Ref.	Debit	Credit
20—		Closing Entries			
Dec.	31	N. A. Jacob, Capital		18 7 5 0 00	
		Income Summary			4 0 0 0 00
		D. R. Durr, Capital			14 7 5 0 00
	31	D. R. Durr, Capital		120 0 0 0 00	
		D. R. Durr, Drawing			120 0 0 0 00
	31	N. A. Jacob, Capital		20 0 0 0 00	
		N. A. Jacob, Drawing			20 0 0 0 00

After posting, the partners' equity accounts look like this:

Income Summary

Bal.	4,000	(3) Closing	4,000

D. R. Durr, Capital

	−	+	
(4)	120,000	Bal.	300,000
		(3)	14,750

N. A. Jacob, Capital

	−	+	
(3)	18,750	Bal.	75,000
(4)	20,000		

D. R. Durr, Drawing

	+	−	
Bal.	120,000	(4) Closing	120,000

N. A. Jacob, Drawing

	+	−	
Bal.	20,000	(4) Closing	20,000

> **Remember**
>
> The Income Summary account is closed into the partners' Capital accounts by the amount of each partner's distributive share of net income or loss.

FINANCIAL STATEMENTS FOR A PARTNERSHIP

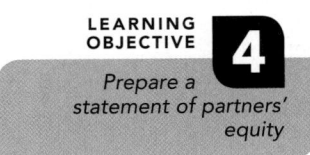

LEARNING OBJECTIVE 4

Prepare a statement of partners' equity

Changes in the balances of the partners' Capital accounts are recorded in the statement of partners' equity, which is just like a statement of owner's equity for a sole proprietorship, except that there is a separate column for each partner. The following statement of partners' equity presents the division of income based on the fractional shares method.

Durr & Jacob LLP Statement of Partners' Equity For Year Ended December 31, 20—			
	D. R. Durr	N. A. Jacob	Total
Capital, January 1, 20—	$300,000	$ 75,000	$375,000
Net Income for the Year	186,000	62,000	248,000
Total	$486,000	$137,000	$623,000
Less Withdrawals for the Year	120,000	20,000	140,000
Capital, December 31, 20—	$366,000	$117,000	$483,000

Remember

A partner is taxed on the net income share, not on what the partner withdraws.

When a partner makes an additional permanent investment after the beginning of the fiscal period, the accountant records this amount right below the beginning balance of the Capital accounts.

Partners have to pay federal income taxes on the basis of each partner's distributive share (share of net income) in the business. For example, D. R. Durr's taxable income is $186,000, even though he withdrew only $120,000. He lists $186,000 on his personal income tax return. The Internal Revenue Code requires that details of the distributive share of each partner must be recorded on a U.S. Partnership Return of Income (Form 1065).

DISSOLUTION OF A PARTNERSHIP

One disadvantage of a partnership is its limited life. Any change in the partnership association formally ends the partnership. When a partnership dissolves, the main visible result is a change in the names listed in the partnership agreement and a change in the division of net income; usually the routine transactions of the business continue. For example, suppose that a partnership originally consists of partners Allen, Bronson, and Callahan. Then Callahan withdraws his or her investment from the firm, and a new partnership emerges: partners Allen and Bronson. During the transition, business is continued. In other words, in a **dissolution**, the original partnership is dissolved by either the sale of one partner's interest in the firm to a new partner or the withdrawal of a partner. The firm continues to operate as before.

Sale of a Partnership Interest

LEARNING OBJECTIVE 5

Journalize entries involving the sale of a partnership interest or withdrawal of a partner.

When a partner retires, that partner may sell his or her interest to a person outside the firm who is acceptable to the remaining partners. Let's say that, at the end of a given year, N. A. Jacob has a Capital balance of $163,520 and decides to sell his interest to K. R. Gott for $182,000. The accountant makes the following entry to account for the transfer of ownership:

Date	Description	Post. Ref.	Debit	Credit
20—				
Dec. 31	N. A. Jacob, Capital		163 5 2 0 00	
	K. R. Gott, Capital			163 5 2 0 00
	To transfer Jacob's equity			
	in the partnership to Gott.			

The difference between $182,000 and $163,520 represents a personal profit to Jacob, not to the partnership. The new partner, buyer K. R. Gott, paid the $182,000 directly to the old partner, seller N. A. Jacob, without affecting the partnership accounting records. *There has been no change in the partnership's assets or liabilities; consequently, there is no change in the total partners' equity.* However, if the firm is to continue, Durr (the other original partner) must be willing to accept Gott as a new partner.

Withdrawal of a Partner

The partnership agreement should outline a set procedure to follow if one of the partners withdraws. Such a procedure usually entails an examination of the books and a revaluation of the partnership's assets and liabilities to reflect current market values.

Partner Withdraws Book Value of His or Her Equity After Revaluation

Suppose that J. W. Navarro is retiring from the partnership of Turner, Navarro, and Teague LP. The partnership agreement stipulates that net income and net loss shall be shared on an equal basis; it also provides for an examination of the financial statements and revaluation of assets in the event that a partner retires. Figure 3 shows the firm's balance sheet immediately prior to the review and revaluation.

> **Remember**
>
> A loss or gain on revaluation is shared according to the ratio agreed upon in the partnership agreement.

FIGURE 3

Balance sheet for Turner, Navarro, and Teague LP

Turner, Navarro, and Teague LP Balance Sheet September 30, 20—			
Assets			
Current Assets			
Cash		$168,000	
Accounts Receivable	$68,000		
Less Allowance for Doubtful Accounts	4,500	63,500	
Merchandise Inventory		217,500	
Total Current Assets			$449,000
Property and Equipment:			
Equipment		$200,000	
Less Accumulated Depreciation		61,000	139,000
Total Assets			$588,000
Liabilities			
Accounts Payable			$ 12,500
Partners' Equity			
R. L. Turner, Capital		$260,000	
J. W. Navarro, Capital		96,000	
P. R. Teague, Capital		219,500	
Total Partners' Equity			575,500
Total Liabilities and Partners' Equity			$588,000

At this point, an accountant (usually someone from an outside firm) examines the books and the firm's assets are appraised. This review and appraisal indicate that Merchandise Inventory is undervalued by $9,600, that Allowance for Doubtful Accounts should be increased by $300, and that Equipment is overvalued by $2,100. The accountant allocates the net difference between debits and credits to the partners' Capital accounts, according to their basis for sharing profits and losses.

Date		Description	Post. Ref.	Debit	Credit
20—					
Sept.	30	Merchandise Inventory		9 6 0 0 00	
		Allowance for Doubtful Accounts			3 0 0 00
		Equipment			2 1 0 0 00
		R. L. Turner, Capital			2 4 0 0 00
		J. W. Navarro, Capital			2 4 0 0 00
		P. R. Teague, Capital			2 4 0 0 00
		To record the revaluation of			
		the assets; net increase in			
		partners' equity is $7,200.			

After the entry has been posted, the partners' equity accounts look like this:

R. L. Turner, Capital		
−	+	
	Bal.	260,000
	Sept. 30	2,400
		262,400

J. W. Navarro, Capital		
−	+	
	Bal.	96,000
	Sept. 30	2,400
		98,400

P. R. Teague, Capital		
−	+	
	Bal.	219,500
	Sept. 30	2,400
		221,900

After the accountant has recorded the revaluation of the firm's assets, J. W. Navarro withdraws cash from the partnership equal to her equity, which leads to the following entry:

Date		Description	Post. Ref.	Debit	Credit
Sept.	30	J. W. Navarro, Capital		98 4 0 0 00	
		Cash			98 4 0 0 00
		To record the withdrawal of			
		J. W. Navarro.			

Partner Withdraws More than Book Value of His or Her Equity

Sometimes a partner withdraws more cash than the amount of his or her Capital account. There are two possible reasons for this.

1. The business is prosperous and shows excellent potential for growth.
2. The remaining partners are so anxious for the partner to retire that they are willing to buy out the partner.

When Navarro announced that she was going to retire, for example, Turner and Teague agreed to pay her $99,400 for her interest in the partnership. Because the balance of her Capital account after the revaluation is $98,400, the excess of $1,000 ($99,400 − $98,400) must be deducted from the Capital accounts of the remaining partners, in accordance with their basis for sharing profits and losses. The general journal entry appears as follows:

Date		Description	Post. Ref.	Debit	Credit
20—					
Sept.	30	J. W. Navarro, Capital		98 4 0 0 00	
		R. L. Turner, Capital		5 0 0 00	
		P. R. Teague, Capital		5 0 0 00	
		Cash			99 4 0 0 00
		To record the withdrawal of			
		J. W. Navarro.			

Partner Withdraws Less than Book Value of His or Her Equity

Sometimes a partner may be so anxious to retire that he or she is willing to take less than the current value of his or her equity just to get out of the partnership or out of the business. In the firm of Turner, Navarro, and Teague, let's say that Navarro is willing to withdraw if she gets just $94,200 cash out of it. Because the balance of her Capital account after the revaluation is $98,400, the difference ($4,200) represents a bonus to the remaining partners. The entry to record this situation is as follows:

Date		Description	Post. Ref.	Debit	Credit
20—					
Sept.	30	J. W. Navarro, Capital		98 4 0 0 00	
		R. L. Turner, Capital			2 1 0 0 00
		P. R. Teague, Capital			2 1 0 0 00
		Cash			94 2 0 0 00
		To record the withdrawal of			
		J. W. Navarro.			

Death of a Partner

The death of a partner automatically ends the partnership, and the partner's estate is entitled to receive the amount of his or her equity. The death of a partner makes it necessary to close the books immediately so that the accountant can determine the firm's net income for the current fiscal period. Partnership agreements usually provide for an examination and revaluation of the assets at this time. After the accountant has determined the current value of the deceased partner's Capital account, the remaining partners and the executor of the deceased partner's estate must agree on the method of payment. The journal entries are similar to those made for the withdrawal of a partner. To be certain that there is enough cash to meet such a demand, partners and partnerships often carry life insurance policies.

> **Remember**
>
> The death of a partner automatically ends a partnership. The books must be closed to determine the net income or net loss.

LIQUIDATION OF A PARTNERSHIP

A **liquidation** means an end, not only of the partnership, but of the business itself. This final winding-up process involves selling assets, paying off liabilities, and distributing the remaining cash to the partners. The closing entries are journalized and posted prior to the liquidation.

The accountant journalizes the entries for each step of the liquidation process as follows:

STEP 1. Sale of the assets, using the Loss or Gain from Realization account. The accountant debits this account for losses and credits it for gains. In this respect the account is comparable to the Cash Short and Over account. The word **realization** refers to the sale of the assets for cash.

STEP 2. Allocation of the loss or gain. The accountant closes the Loss or Gain from Realization account into the partners' Capital accounts according to the profit and loss ratio. It must be closed as a separate account because it came into being after the regular closing entries had been recorded.

STEP 3. Payment of the liabilities. The firm makes final settlement with all creditors.

STEP 4. Distribution of the remaining cash to the partners, in accordance with the balances of their Capital accounts.

Occasionally it takes a long time to convert merchandise inventory and other assets into cash; on the other hand, things can move quickly. It is impossible to predict how long liquidation operations may take. In the process, several things may happen. We will discuss two possibilities here.

Our first example concerns the partnership of Ramirez, Sheon, and Tom LLP. The partners share profits and losses as follows: Ramirez one-half; Sheon one-fourth; Tom one-fourth. Let's look at an abbreviated balance sheet for this firm (Figure 4).

Remember

Upon liquidation,
creditors are first in
line, before partners'
interests.

Assets Are Sold at a Profit

Assume that the firm sells its merchandise inventory for $46,000 and the other assets for $70,000. Figure 5 shows the journal entries to cover this transaction. (Amounts in parentheses are purely explanatory.)

FIGURE 4

Balance sheet for Ramirez,
Sheon, and Tom LLP

Ramirez, Sheon, and Tom LLP Balance Sheet June 30, 20—		
Assets		
Cash	$70,000	
Merchandise Inventory	40,000	
Other Assets	60,000	
Total Assets		$170,000
Liabilities		
Accounts Payable		$ 15,000
Partners' Equity		
G. P. Ramirez, Capital	$59,000	
C. L. Sheon, Capital	55,000	
R. H. Tom, Capital	41,000	155,000
Total Liabilities and Partners' Equity		$170,000

FIGURE 5

Journal entries—assets sold at profit

Date	Description	Post. Ref.	Debit	Credit
20—				
June 30	Cash ($46,000 + $70,000)		116 0 0 0 00	
(1)	Merchandise Inventory			40 0 0 0 00
	Other Assets			60 0 0 0 00
	Loss or Gain from Realization			16 0 0 0 00
	Sold the assets at a gain.			
(2) 30	Loss or Gain from Realization		16 0 0 0 00	
	G. P. Ramirez, Capital (½)			8 0 0 0 00
	C. L. Sheon, Capital (¼)			4 0 0 0 00
	R. H. Tom, Capital (¼)			4 0 0 0 00
	To allocate the net gain to the			
	partners' Capital accounts			
	according to the profit and			
	loss ratio.			
(3) 30	Accounts Payable		15 0 0 0 00	
	Cash			15 0 0 0 00
	To pay the claims of creditors.			
(4) 30	G. P. Ramirez, Capital ($59,000 + $8,000)		67 0 0 0 00	
	C. L. Sheon, Capital ($55,000 + $4,000)		59 0 0 0 00	
	R. H. Tom, Capital ($41,000 + $4,000)		45 0 0 0 00	
	Cash			171 0 0 0 00
	To distribute the remaining			
	cash to the partners			
	according to their account			
	balances.			

The T accounts for the Cash and Capital accounts look like this:

Cash				
	+		−	
Bal.	70,000	(3)		15,000
(1)	116,000	(4)		171,000

C. L. Sheon, Capital				
	−		+	
(4)	59,000	Bal.		55,000
		(2)		4,000

G. P. Ramirez, Capital				
	−		+	
(4)	67,000	Bal.		59,000
		(2)		8,000

R. H. Tom, Capital				
	−		+	
(4)	45,000	Bal.		41,000
		(2)		4,000

The balance of Cash before the final distribution to the partners should equal the total of the balances of their Capital accounts.

Remember

Assets Are Sold at a Loss: Partners' Capital Accounts Sufficient to Absorb Loss

Now suppose that the partnership of Ramirez, Sheon, and Tom LLP sells its merchandise inventory for only $36,000 and its other assets for $52,000. The journal entries would look like those in Figure 6.

FIGURE 6

FIGURE 6

Journal entries—assets sold at loss

Date		Description	Post. Ref.	Debit	Credit
20—					
June	30	Cash ($36,000 + $52,000)		88 0 0 0 00	
(1)		Loss or Gain from Realization		12 0 0 0 00	
		Merchandise Inventory			40 0 0 0 00
		Other Assets			60 0 0 0 00
		Sold the assets at a loss.			
(2)	30	G. P. Ramirez, Capital (½)		6 0 0 0 00	
		C. L. Sheon, Capital (¼)		3 0 0 0 00	
		R. H. Tom, Capital (¼)		3 0 0 0 00	
		Loss or Gain from Realization			12 0 0 0 00
		To allocate the net loss to the			
		partners' Capital accounts			
		according to the profit and			
		loss ratio.			
(3)	30	Accounts Payable		15 0 0 0 00	
		Cash			15 0 0 0 00
		To pay the claims of creditors.			
(4)	30	G. P. Ramirez, Capital ($59,000 – $6,000)		53 0 0 0 00	
		C. L. Sheon, Capital ($55,000 – $3,000)		52 0 0 0 00	
		R. H. Tom, Capital ($41,000 – $3,000)		38 0 0 0 00	
		Cash			143 0 0 0 00
		To distribute the remaining			
		cash to the partners			
		according to their account			
		balances.			

Remember

As the last step in the liquidation process, cash remaining is distributed to the partners according to their Capital account balances.

The T accounts for the Cash and Capital accounts look like this:

Cash

	+	−	
Bal.	70,000	(3)	15,000
(1)	88,000	(4)	143,000

C. L. Sheon, Capital

	−	+	
(2)	3,000	Bal.	55,000
(4)	52,000		

G. P. Ramirez, Capital

	−	+	
(2)	6,000	Bal.	59,000
(4)	53,000		

R. H. Tom, Capital

	−	+	
(2)	3,000	Bal.	41,000
(4)	38,000		

CHAPTER REVIEW

Study & Practice

1 **LEARNING OBJECTIVE**

(a) Define the various kinds of partnerships and list the main advantages and disadvantages of a partnership, and (b) journalize initial investments of a partnership.

There are three types of **partnerships**:

1. **General partnership (GP)**—association of two or more people or firms to carry on, as co-owners, a business for profit.
2. **Limited partnership (LP)**—organization with two or more people or firms with at least one general partner and one limited partner.
3. **Limited liability partnership (LLP)**—organization similar to a limited partnership except that all partners may take an active role in the business of the partnership with only their invested capital at risk.

Advantages:

- Combining of people's abilities and investments to carry on a business
- Ease of formation
- Legal restrictions are minimal
- Nontaxable entity

Disadvantages:

- Unlimited liability of a general partner
- Limited life
- **Mutual agency**
- Hard to transfer interest
- Strain on personal relationships

The accountant makes a separate journal entry for the investment of each partner. The investments may include cash and other assets, along with any related liabilities.

PRACTICE EXERCISE 1

Cecilia Lovick and Sam Ammons decide to form a partnership on July 10 for the operation of a law firm. Cecilia is contributing the assets and liabilities of her current practice. The balances are as follow: Cash $28,000; Equipment $15,000; Accumulated Depreciation $9,500; Accounts Payable $10,200; and Notes Payable $18,000. The appraised value of the equipment is $12,000. Sam is contributing cash of $15,000. Record the general journal entry to record Cecilia's and Sam's investment in the partnership.

PRACTICE EXERCISE 1 SOLUTION

		GENERAL JOURNAL			PAGE 1

Date		Description	Post. Ref.	Debit	Credit
20—					
July	10	Cash		28 0 0 0 00	
		Equipment		12 0 0 0 00	
		Accounts Payable			10 2 0 0 00
		Notes Payable			18 0 0 0 00
		Cecilia Lovick, Capital			11 8 0 0 00
		To record the original			
		investment of Cecilia Lovick.			
	10	Cash		15 0 0 0 00	
		Sam Ammons, Capital			15 0 0 0 00
		To record the original			
		investment of Sam Ammons.			

2 LEARNING OBJECTIVE

Provide for the division of net income or loss of a partnership on the basis of (a) fractional shares, (b) ratio of capital investments, and (c) salary and interest allowances.

The division of net income or loss may be reported as a separate statement or shown at the bottom of the income statement below Net Income. There are generally three ways to calculate the division of net income or loss:

a. Division by fractional shares:

Net Income or Loss × Each Partner's Fraction

b. Ratio of capital investments:

$$\text{Net Income or Loss} \times \frac{\text{Partner's Beginning Capital}}{\text{Total Partners' Capital Balances}}$$

c. Division on the basis of salary and interest allowances:

1. Net Income or Loss − Salary or Interest Allowances
2. Divide the remainder by specified shares (usually equal)

PRACTICE EXERCISE 2

Aiden Martz and Hannah Johnasen currently operate the Rainy Day Books partnership. Rainy Day Books has a net income for the year of $480,000. The partnership agreement stipulates that profits and losses are to be divided three-fourths to Aiden Martz and one-fourth to Hannah Johnasen. Martz's Capital account before division of income is $200,000, and Johnasen's Capital is $100,000. Martz's Drawing account is $80,000, and Johnasen's Drawing account is $60,000. Calculate the division of income based on (a) fractional shares and (b) ratio of capital investments.

PRACTICE EXERCISE 2 SOLUTION

a. Fractional shares:

	A. Martz	H. Johnasen	Total
Net Income			$480,000
Division of Net Income:			
Capital Investment Ratio	$360,000	$120,000	$480,000

A. Martz = $480,000 \times \dfrac{3}{4} = \$360,000$

H. Johnasen = $480,000 \times \dfrac{1}{4} = \$120,000$

b. Ratio of capital investments:

	A. Martz	H. Johnasen	
Net Income			$480,000
Division of Net Income:	A. Martz	H. Johnasen	Total
Capital Investment Ratio	$320,000	$160,000	$480,000

A. Martz = $480,000 \times \dfrac{\$200,000}{\$300,000} = \$320,000$

H. Johnasen = $480,000 \times \dfrac{\$100,000}{\$300,000} = \$160,000$

3 LEARNING OBJECTIVE
Journalize the closing entries for a partnership on the basis of (a) fractional shares, (b) ratio of capital investments, and (c) salary and interest allowances.

STEP 1. Close the revenue accounts into the Income Summary account.

STEP 2. Close the expense accounts into the Income Summary account (the expense accounts do not include any payments to the owner).

STEP 3. Close the Income Summary account into each partner's Capital account by each partner's share of the net income or loss.

STEP 4. Close each partner's Drawing account into the respective Capital account.

PRACTICE EXERCISE 3

Using Practice Exercise 2, journalize step 3 and step 4 of the closing entries for (a) fractional shares for the year ended December 31.

PRACTICE EXERCISE 3 SOLUTION

Date		Description	Post. Ref.	Debit	Credit
20—		Closing Entries			
Dec.	31	Income Summary		480 0 0 0 00	
		A. Martz, Capital			360 0 0 0 00
		H. Johnasen, Capital			120 0 0 0 00
	31	A. Martz, Capital		80 0 0 0 00	
		A. Martz, Drawing			80 0 0 0 00
	31	H. Johnasen, Capital		60 0 0 0 00	
		H. Johnasen, Drawing			60 0 0 0 00

4 LEARNING OBJECTIVE
Prepare a statement of partners' equity.

The format of a statement of partners' equity is the same as that for a statement of owner's equity. One column per partner is used to record each partner's beginning capital, additional investment, share of net income, withdrawals, and ending capital. A Total column is used to record the combined total for each line.

PRACTICE EXERCISE 4

Using Practice Exercise 2, prepare a statement of partners' equity for (a) fractional shares for the year ended December 31.

PRACTICE EXERCISE 4 SOLUTION

Martz & Johnasen
Statement of Partners' Equity
For Year Ended December 31, 20—

	A. Martz	H. Johnasen	Total
Capital, January 1, 20—	$200,000	$100,000	$300,000
Net Income for the Year	360,000	120,000	480,000
Total	$560,000	$220,000	$780,000
Less Withdrawals for the Year	80,000	60,000	140,000
Capital, December 31, 20—	$480,000	$160,000	$640,000

5 **LEARNING OBJECTIVE**

Journalize entries involving the sale of a partnership interest or withdrawal of a partner.

Any change in the composition of partners results in a **dissolution** of the partnership. For the sale of a partnership interest, debit the Capital account of the old partner and credit the Capital account of the new partner. When a partner withdraws, there is a revaluation of the assets. Next, an entry is made debiting the partner's Capital account and crediting Cash.

PRACTICE EXERCISE 5

Jackson Khan has a Capital balance of $182,530 and decides to sell his interest in the partnership to Ella Cavazos for $190,000. Journalize the entry to account for the transfer of ownership on December 31.

PRACTICE EXERCISE 5 SOLUTION

Date		Description	Post. Ref.	Debit	Credit
20—					
Dec.	31	J. Khan, Capital		182 5 3 0 00	
		E. Cavazos, Capital			182 5 3 0 00
		To transfer Khan's equity			
		in the partnership to Cavazos.			

The difference between $190,000 and $182,530 represents a personal profit to Khan, not to the partnership.

6 **LEARNING OBJECTIVE**

Journalize entries pertaining to the liquidation of a partnership involving the immediate sale of the assets for cash.

A **liquidation** requires four steps.

STEP 1. Sale of the assets, using the Loss or Gain from Realization account. The accountant debits this account for losses and credits it for gains.

STEP 2. Allocation of the loss or gain. The accountant closes the Loss or Gain from Realization account into the partners' Capital accounts according to the profit and loss ratio.

STEP 3. Payment of the liabilities. The firm makes final settlement with all creditors.

STEP 4. Distribution of the remaining cash to the partners, in accordance with the balances of their Capital accounts.

PRACTICE EXERCISE 6

Assume that Williamson and Burnet LLP liquidates its partnership. Tom Williamson and Lonnie Burnet share in profits and losses equally. Before liquidation the partnership balance sheet is as follows:

Williamson and Burnet LLP
Balance Sheet
December 31, 20—

Assets		
Cash	$20,000	
Merchandise Inventory	5,000	
Other Assets	10,000	
Total Assets		$35,000
Liabilities		
Accounts Payable		$ 7,000
Partners' Equity		
T. Williamson, Capital	$14,000	
L. Burnet, Capital	14,000	28,000
Total Liabilities and Partners' Equity		$35,000

Assume that the partnership sells its merchandise inventory for $8,000 and the other assets for $18,000. Journalize the entries to cover this transaction.

PRACTICE EXERCISE 6 SOLUTION

Date	Description	Post. Ref.	Debit	Credit
20—				
Dec. 31	Cash ($8,000 + $18,000)		26 0 0 0 00	
	Merchandise Inventory			5 0 0 0 00
	Other Assets			10 0 0 0 00
	Loss or Gain from Realization			11 0 0 0 00
	Sold the assets at a gain.			
31	Loss or Gain from Realization		11 0 0 0 00	
	T. Williamson, Capital			5 5 0 0 00
	L. Burnet, Capital			5 5 0 0 00
	To allocate the net gain to the			
	partners' Capital accounts			
	according to the profit and			
	loss ratio.			
31	Accounts Payable		7 0 0 0 00	
	Cash			7 0 0 0 00
	To pay the claims of creditors.			
31	T. Williamson, Capital ($14,000 + $5,500)		19 5 0 0 00	
	L. Burnet, Capital ($14,000 + $5,500)		19 5 0 0 00	
	Cash			39 0 0 0 00
	To distribute the remaining			
	cash to the partners according			
	to their account balances.			

Glossary

Co-ownership A situation in which each party owns a fractional share of all the assets. *(p. 719)*

Dissolution The ending of a partnership because of a change in personnel and the forming of a new partnership. The transition results primarily in changes to the Capital accounts, with routine business being carried on as usual. *(p. 736)*

Distributive share The share of the net income (or net loss) allocated to each partner. *(p. 725)*

General partnership (GP) An association of two or more persons to carry on, as co-owners, a business for profit. The partners are general partners who actively and publicly participate in the transactions of the firm and have unlimited liability. *(p. 718)*

Limited liability partnership (LLP) An organization similar to a limited partnership except that all partners may take an active role in the business of the partnership with only their invested capital at risk. *(p. 719)*

Limited partnership (LP) A partnership with at least one general partner and one limited partner. The general partner normally manages the partnership and the limited partner or partners have the largest share of invested capital and usually cannot lose more than their capital contribution. *(p. 719)*

Liquidation The ending of a partnership, involving the sale of the assets, payment of the liabilities, and distribution of the remaining cash to the partners. *(p. 740)*

Mutual agency The ability of each partner to act as an agent of the firm, thereby committing the entire firm to a binding contract. *(p. 719)*

Partnership An association of two or more persons who carry on, as co-owners, a business for profit. *(p. 718)*

Partnership agreement A written contract that details the provisions of a partnership. *(p. 720)*

Realization Conversion into cash, as happens in the case of the sale of assets. *(p. 740)*

CHAPTER ASSIGNMENTS

Discussion Questions

1. List the main advantages and disadvantages of a partnership.
2. List six provisions that should be included in a partnership agreement.
3. What do accountants mean by co-ownership of partnership property?
4. Are partnerships required to pay federal income taxes? Why or why not?
5. Explain why a partner's distributive share in the division of partnership income does not involve cash.
6. Holliman and Jarman are in the process of forming a partnership. Holliman wishes to invest the assets and liabilities of his business, Holliman's Upholstery. Is it possible to simply list these assets and liabilities at the same amounts on the new partnership books? Explain your answer.
7. How does the dissolution of a partnership differ from a liquidation?
8. What four steps are followed in a liquidation?

Exercises

1b

PRACTICE EXERCISE 1

EXERCISE 18-1 J.A. Horne, as his original investment in the firm of Horne and Kingsbury, contributes equipment that had been recorded in the books of his own business as costing $120,000, with accumulated depreciation of $92,000. The partners agree on a valuation of $70,000. They also agree to accept Horne's accounts receivable of $66,000, collectible to the extent of 85 percent. Give the journal entry to record Horne's investment in the partnership of Horne and Kingsbury on July 15.

EXERCISE 18-2 L. Rodman, H. Saddler, and T. Schenk agreed to share earnings or losses according to the ratio of their investments at the beginning of the year ($30,000, $25,000, and $45,000, respectively). Calculate the partner shares under the following conditions: (a) $27,000 net income; (b) $24,000 net loss.

PRACTICE EXERCISE 2

EXERCISE 18-3 The partnership agreement of Sigmon and Willie provides for salary allowances of $78,000 per year for Sigmon and $66,000 per year for Willie. They share the remaining balance of net income on the basis of three-fifths for Sigmon and two-fifths for Willie. The net income amounts to $146,000. Calculate the total share for each partner.

PRACTICE EXERCISE 2

EXERCISE 18-4 Beaudry and Clemente share profits and losses on a fractional-share basis with two-fifths for Beaudry and three-fifths for Clemente. This year the firm has a net income of $65,000. The beginning Capital balances for the year were $90,000 for Beaudry and $130,000 for Clemente. The balances of the Drawing accounts are $30,000 for Beaudry and $24,000 for Clemente. Journalize the entries to close Income Summary and the partners' Drawing accounts on December 31.

PRACTICE EXERCISES 2,3

EXERCISE 18-5 The partners J. W. Deboer and R. S. Sonnier have agreed to salary allowances of $80,000 and $92,000, respectively. In addition, they are allowed 9 percent interest on their Capital balances at the beginning of the year. The remainder is to be divided equally. Deboer's Capital balance was $110,000, and Sonnier's Capital balance was $120,000. Complete the section of the income statement related to the division of a $202,000 net income.

PRACTICE EXERCISE 2

EXERCISE 18-6 Soper is retiring from the partnership of Strader, Blanks, and Soper. The profit and loss ratio is 2 : 2 : 1, respectively. After the accountant has posted the revaluation and closing entries, the credit balances in the Capital accounts are Strader, $53,000; Blanks, $43,000; and Soper, $21,000. Journalize the entries to record the retirement of Soper under each of the following unrelated assumptions:

a. Soper retires, taking $21,000 of partnership cash for her equity.
b. Soper retires, taking $27,000 of partnership cash for her equity.

PRACTICE EXERCISE 5

EXERCISE 18-7 Friday is the senior member of the partnership of Friday, Horning, and Jerome. When Friday dies, the firm's accountant revalues the assets. The following assets are to be increased in value by these amounts: Merchandise Inventory, $28,000; Building, $56,000. The value of the asset, Equipment, is to be decreased by $9,000. Assuming that the partnership profit and loss ratio is 2 : 2 : 1, respectively, write the journal entry to show the revaluation of the assets on June 5 prior to dissolution of the firm.

EXERCISE 18-8 Stricklan and Carper are partners who share profits and losses equally. The credit balances of their Capital accounts before liquidation are $70,000 and $90,000, respectively. When they liquidate their partnership, they sell the noncash assets and pay all the partnership's liabilities, leaving a balance of $110,000 in cash. (a) What is the amount of loss or gain on realization? (b) How much cash should be distributed to each partner?

PRACTICE EXERCISE 6

Problem Set A

For additional help, see the demonstration problem at the beginning of each chapter in your Working Papers.

2,3

PROBLEM 18-1A The partnership of R. S. Johnson, B. J. Williams, and F. A. Brown has a net income of $240,000 for the current year. The balances in the partners' Capital accounts at the beginning of the year were $64,000, $68,000, and $75,000, respectively. At the end of the year, the balances of the Drawing accounts are $26,000, $29,300, and $27,000, respectively. The partnership agreement stipulates salary allowances as follows: Johnson, $68,300; Williams, $63,000; Brown, $76,000. The partnership agreement also allows interest of 10 percent on the balances of the partners' Capital accounts at the beginning of the year. The remainder of the net income, after salary and interest allowances, is divided equally.

Check Figure
Total Interest Allowances,
$20,700

Required
1. Prepare the section of the income statement for the current year that deals with division of net income.
2. Prepare the entries to close the firm's Income Summary and Drawing accounts on December 31.
3. Assuming a net income of $210,000, prepare the section of the income statement that deals with division of net income.

2,5

PROBLEM 18-2A R. C. Jones and S. K. Miller are forming a partnership for a beauty salon and plan to work full time in the salon. Jones will make an initial investment of $45,000 and Miller, $35,000. They are considering the following plans for the division of net income:

a. Division in the same ratio as the balances of their Capital accounts.
b. Interest of 10 percent on the balances of their Capital accounts at the beginning of the year and the remainder of the net income to be divided equally.
c. Salary allowances of $42,500 to Jones and $33,500 to Miller, based on the value of their services, interest of 10 percent on the balances of their Capital accounts at the beginning of the year, and the remainder of the net income to be divided equally.

Check Figure
With net income of $120,000,
S. K. Miller (b) interest allowance,
$3,500

Required
1. Using the form in the Working Papers, record the distributive shares of net income for each of the partners, assuming (a) a net income of $120,000 (calculate ratio to 4 decimal places) and (b) a net income of $74,000.
2. Which plan is the fairest? Give reasons for your opinion.
3. Assume that three years later, on December 31, 20—, Jones' Capital balance is $68,000. With the approval of Miller, Jones sells her interest to two new partners, J. K. Gonzalez for $38,000 and F. R. Harris for $30,000. Journalize the entry to account for the transfer of ownership.
4. (a) Assume that S. K. Miller, the remaining original partner, decides to withdraw from the partnership two years after Jones's sale of her partnership interest. The partnership agreement stipulates that net income and net loss be shared on a 2 : 1 : 1 ratio (Miller, Gonzalez, and Harris, respectively) and that an examination and revaluation of assets will take place upon retirement of a partner.

   The revaluation shows that Merchandise Inventory is undervalued by $20,000, that Equipment is overvalued by $4,800, and that Allowance for Doubtful Accounts should be increased by $1,500. As of December 31, journalize the allocation of the net difference between debits and credits to the partners' Capital accounts, according to the 2 : 1 : 1 ratio.

(b) Assume S. K. Miller's Capital balance is $72,150 before the revaluation. Journalize on December 31, 20—, the withdrawal of Miller assuming he withdraws cash.

PROBLEM 18-3A The following are the adjusted account balances of Davis and Rodriguez LLP as of December 31, the end of the current fiscal year.

Accounts Payable	$ 67,782
Accounts Receivable	54,507
Accumulated Depreciation, Equipment	46,287
Allowance for Doubtful Accounts	1,879
Cash	73,231
C. E. Davis, Capital	61,200
C. E. Davis, Drawing	32,640
Equipment	75,315
Freight In	22,488
General Expenses (control)	14,939
Interest Expense	3,500
Merchandise Inventory, December 31	132,042
Notes Payable	29,900
Prepaid Insurance	735
Purchases	540,716
Purchases Discounts	4,305
Purchases Returns and Allowances	25,960
S. A. Rodriguez, Capital	49,960
S. A. Rodriguez, Drawing	24,480
Sales	775,500
Sales Returns and Allowances	37,575
Selling Expenses (control)	38,588

There were no changes in the partners' Capital accounts during the year. The merchandise inventory at the beginning of the year was $144,059. The partnership agreement provides for salary allowances of $63,000 for Davis and $59,000 for Rodriguez. It also stipulates an interest allowance of 10 percent on invested capital at the beginning of the year, with the remainder of the net income to be divided equally.

Required

1. Prepare an income statement for the year.
2. Prepare a statement of partners' equity for the year.
3. Prepare a classified balance sheet for the partnership at the end of the year.

Check Figure
Net Income, $135,942

PROBLEM 18-4A The partnership of Wilson, Martinez, and Anderson is to be liquidated as of June 30 of this year. The partners share profits and losses in the ratio of 2 : 2 : 1, respectively. The firm's post-closing trial balance looks like this:

Wilson, Martinez, and Anderson Post-Closing Trial Balance June 30, 20—		
Account Name	Debit	Credit
Cash	41,917	
Merchandise Inventory	61,230	
Other Assets	47,268	
Accounts Payable		13,135
G. T. Wilson, Capital		56,160
R. F. Martinez, Capital		43,680
M. K. Anderson, Capital		37,440
	150,415	150,415

The firm's realization and liquidation transactions are as follows:

June 30   The merchandise inventory sold for $58,280; the other assets sold for $55,090.

30   The accountant allocated the loss or gain from realization to the partners' Capital accounts according to the profit and loss ratio.

30   The firm paid its creditors in full.

30   The firm distributed the remaining cash to the partners in accordance with the balances in their Capital accounts.

Check Figure
Gain from realization, $4,872

Required
1. Record the balances in the selected ledger accounts.
2. Record the liquidating transactions in general journal form.
3. Post the entries to the ledger accounts.

Problem Set B

For additional help, see the demonstration problem at the beginning of each chapter in your Working Papers.

2,3 **LO**

PROBLEM 18-1B The partnership of A. C. Taylor, R. M. Thomas, and D. T. Hernandez has a net income of $175,300 for this year. The balances in the partners' Capital accounts at the beginning of the year were $46,000, $51,500, and $58,000, respectively. At the end of the year, the balances of the Drawing accounts are $25,000, $29,200, and $24,250, respectively. The partnership agreement stipulates salary allowances as follows: Taylor, $44,500; Thomas, $47,500; Hernandez, $48,400. It also allows 10 percent interest on the balances of the partners' Capital accounts at the beginning of the year. The remainder of the net income, after salary and interest allowances, is divided equally.

Check Figure
Assuming a net income of $109,000, A. C. Taylor, Net Income, $33,450

Required
1. Prepare the section of the income statement for the current year that deals with the division of net income.
2. Prepare entries to close the firm's Income Summary and Drawing accounts on December 31.
3. Assuming a net income of $109,000, prepare the section of the income statement that deals with division of net income.

2,5 **LO**

PROBLEM 18-2B X. R. Lopez and L. O. Moore, interior designers, are forming a partnership. Both plan to work in the firm on a full-time basis. Lopez's initial investment is $20,000; Moore's investment, $30,000. They are considering the following plans for the division of net income:

a. Division in the same ratio as the balances of their Capital accounts.
b. Interest of 10 percent on the balances of their Capital accounts at the beginning of the year and the remainder of the net income to be divided equally.
c. Salary allowances of $54,000 to Lopez and $57,000 to Moore, based on the value of their services, interest of 9 percent on the balances of their Capital accounts at the beginning of the year, and the remainder of the net income to be divided equally.

Required

1. Using the form provided in the Working Papers, record the distribution of net income for each of the partners, assuming (a) a net income of $117,000 and (b) a net income of $104,000.
2. Which plan is the fairest? Give reasons for your opinion.
3. Assume that three years later, on December 31, 20—, Lopez's Capital balance is $47,000. With the approval of Moore, Lopez sells his interest to two new partners, E. S. Clark for $23,000 and P. S. Lewis for $24,000. Journalize the entry to account for the transfer of ownership.
4. (a) Assume that L. O. Moore, the remaining original partner, decides to withdraw from the partnership two years after Lopez's sale of his partnership share. The partnership agreement stipulates that net income and net loss be shared on a 2 : 1 : 1 ratio (Moore, Clark, and Lewis, respectively) and that an examination and revaluation of assets will take place upon retirement of a partner.

   The revaluation shows that Merchandise Inventory is undervalued by $9,000, that Equipment is overvalued by $2,100, and that Allowance for Doubtful Accounts should be increased by $600. As of December 31, journalize the allocation of the net difference between debits and credits to the partners' Capital accounts, according to the 2 : 1 : 1 ratio.

   (b) Assume L. O. Moore Capital balance is $65,000 before the revaluation. Journalize on December 31, 20—, the withdrawal of Moore assuming he withdraws cash.

Check Figure
X. R. Lopez's share of $117,000 net income, Plan C, $56,550

PROBLEM 18-3B The following are the adjusted account balances of Martin and Jackson LLP of December 31, the end of the fiscal year:

 LO 2,4

Accounts Payable	$ 69,812
Accounts Receivable	60,143
Accumulated Depreciation, Equipment	47,756
Allowance for Doubtful Accounts	2,192
Cash	64,617
Equipment	80,710
Freight In	27,380
General Expenses (control)	14,495
Interest Expense	2,000
J. V. Martin, Capital	65,280
J. V. Martin, Drawing	30,192
Merchandise Inventory, December 31	128,760
Notes Payable	16,320
Prepaid Insurance	704
Purchases	522,043

Purchases Discounts	$ 4,516
Purchases Returns and Allowances	26,204
Sales	761,332
Sales Returns and Allowances	36,590
S. C. Jackson, Capital	53,040
S. C. Jackson, Drawing	29,376
Selling Expenses (control)	36,273

The merchandise inventory at the beginning of the year was $141,929, and there were no changes in the partners' Capital accounts during the year. The partnership agreement provides for salary allowances of $61,900 for Martin and $59,350 for Jackson. The agreement also stipulates an interest allowance of 10 percent on invested capital at the beginning of the year. The remainder of the net income is to be divided equally.

Check Figure
Total assets, $284,986

Required

1. Prepare an income statement for the year.
2. Prepare a statement of partners' equity for the year.
3. Prepare a classified balance sheet for the partnership at the end of the year.

 6 **LO**

PROBLEM 18-4B The partnership of Thompson, White, and Lee is to be liquidated as of October 31 of this year. The partners share profits and losses in the ratio of 2: 2: 1, respectively. The firm's post-closing trial balance looks like this:

Thompson, White, and Lee Post-Closing Trial Balance October 31, 20—		
Account Name	**Debit**	**Credit**
Cash	37,774	
Merchandise Inventory	67,912	
Other Assets	48,945	
Accounts Payable		15,877
B. T. Thompson, Capital		54,388
F. K. White, Capital		43,814
Y. C. Lee, Capital		40,552
	154,631	154,631

The firm's realization and liquidation transactions are as follows:

Oct. 31 The merchandise inventory sold for $66,520; the other assets sold for $45,720.

31 The accountant allocated the loss or gain from realization to the partners' Capital accounts according to the profit and loss ratio.

31 The firm paid its creditors in full.

31 The firm distributed the remaining cash to the partners in accordance with the balances in their Capital accounts.

Check Figure
Loss from realization, $4,617

Required

1. Record the balances in the selected ledger accounts.
2. Record the liquidating transactions in general journal form.
3. Post the entries to the ledger accounts.

ACTIVITIES

INTERNET LINKS TO ACCOUNTING

The Nolo Web site (www.nolo.com) has been in existence since 1971 and provides legal information for consumers and small businesses. Using the Nolo Web site, perform a search on how to Create a Partnership Agreement. In the Search box, type in "partnership agreement" and below the box select "Search Entire Site." Then, click Search. Choose "Creating a Partnership Agreement."
1. How can a partnership agreement help a business?
2. What major areas should be covered by a partnership agreement?
3. Which state does not have its own laws governing partnerships?

CONSIDER AND COMMUNICATE

A friend of yours is looking for a partner to begin a children's-wear boutique. She has fashion merchandising and sales education and experience, as well as cash and a good credit rating. She is enthusiastic and anxious to begin the new business. You have cash, a desire to own a business, and sales experience, and you feel you could get along well with this potential partner. Why would you hesitate? What should you discuss with your friend about partnerships?

CRITICAL THINKING

The following information concerns the partnership of Smith and Garcia LLP.

The partnership agreement provides for salary allowances of $91,900 for Smith and $89,350 for Garcia. The agreement also stipulates interest of 10 percent on invested capital at the beginning of the year (Smith, $95,280; Garcia, $53,040). There were no changes in the partners' Capital accounts during the year. The remainder of the net income is to be divided equally. Using this information, fill in the missing numbers in the partial income statement from Net Income through Division of Net Income for Smith and Garcia LLP and in the statement of partners' equity.

Smith and Garcia LLP
Partial Income Statement
For Year Ended December 31, 20—

	J. V. Smith	S. C. Garcia	Total
Net Income			$205,302
Division of Net Income:	J. V. Smith	S. C. Garcia	Total
Salary Allowances	$	$	$
Interest Allowances			
Excess of Income over			
Allowances Allocated Equally			9,220
Net Income	$106,038	$99,264	$205,302

Smith and Garcia LLP
Statement of Partners' Equity
For Year Ended December 31, 20—

	J. V. Smith	S. C. Garcia	Total
Capital, January 1, 20—	$	$	$
Net Income for the Year			205,302
Total	$	$	$353,622
Less Withdrawals for the Year	90,192	89,376	
Capital, December 31, 20—	$	$	$

A QUESTION OF ETHICS

Mary and James are partners. Mary wanted to purchase a newer model computer. James said it was too expensive and had capabilities that they did not need. While James was on vacation, Mary bought the computer anyway. She believed that if James saw how much quicker the newer computer would be, he would be convinced of its benefits. Did Mary act appropriately under the rules of a partnership? Is what Mary did ethical?

Corporate Organization and Capital Stock

CARNIVAL CORPORATION, Miami, Florida (USA) and London, England (UK)

Carnival Cruise Lines represents the classic "American dream" of growing a small company into a world-recognized business. What began as a single, secondhand ship and a one-way trip from Miami to San Juan has grown into the "The World's Most Popular Cruise Line."

Carnival Cruise Lines was formed in 1972 by Ted Arison. The business started out as a small-time operation but continued to grow into the most sailed and profitable cruise line. In 1987, the business decided to become a corporation. Today, Carnival Corporation is the world's first global cruise operator, operating with 12 brands including Carnival, Princess Cruises, and Holland America Line.

The decision to become a corporation allowed for a large amount of money to come into the business, enabling Carnival to expand further through acquisition (or purchases) of other businesses. In this chapter, you will learn about corporations, how to record transactions for stock, and how to prepare corporate balance sheets.

LEARNING OBJECTIVES

After you have completed this chapter, you will be able to do the following:

1 *Define corporation.*

2 *Name advantages and disadvantages of the corporate form of business.*

3 *Describe the formation of a corporation.*

4 *Journalize entries for the issuance of par-value stock.*

5 *Journalize entries for the issuance of no-par value stock.*

6 *Journalize entries for the sale of stock on the subscription basis.*

7 *Prepare a classified balance sheet for a corporation, including Subscriptions Receivable, Paid-in Capital, and Retained Earnings accounts.*

ACCOUNTING LANGUAGE

Articles of incorporation (p. 761)
Authorized capital (p. 761)
Capital stock (p. 761)
Capital stock subscription (p. 773)
Charter (p. 759)
Closely held corporation (p. 762)
Common stock (p. 766)
Corporation (p. 759)
Cumulative preferred stock (p. 767)
Deficit (p. 776)
Discount (p. 770)
Dividends (p. 763)
Double taxation (p. 760)
Issued stock (p. 765)
Legal capital (p. 772)
Limited liability company (LLC) (p. 760)
No-par value stock (p. 765)
Noncumulative preferred stock (p. 767)

Nonparticipating preferred stock (p. 767)
Outstanding stock (p. 765)
Paid-in Capital (p. 771)
Paid-in Capital in Excess of Par Value (p. 770)
Par-value stock (p. 765)
Participating preferred stock (p. 767)
Preemptive right (p. 763)
Preferred stock (p. 766)
Premium (p. 769)
Publicly traded corporation (p. 762)
Retained Earnings (p. 765)
S corporation (p. 760)
Stated value (p. 772)
Stock certificates (p. 762)
Stockholders' equity (p. 764)
Stockholders' ledger (p. 768)
Surplus (p. 776)
Treasury stock (p. 765)

Remember

Sole proprietorships and partnerships are generally limited to the wealth of their few owners.

Business organizations are usually classified as sole proprietorships, partnerships, or corporations. Corporations are fewest in number, but they account for more business transactions than the other two types of organizations combined. Frequently, as we learned in the Why It Matters introduction, a firm that begins as a sole proprietorship or a partnership needs more investment capital as it grows and prospers. To raise additional investment capital, the firm incorporates. Other businesses are organized as corporations from the outset. Because of the predominance of corporations, everyone entering the business world should be familiar with the corporate form of organization and its financial structure. In this chapter we will explore this form of business entity—the corporation.

DEFINITION OF A CORPORATION

In 1818, Chief Justice John Marshall defined a **corporation** as "an artificial being, invisible, intangible, and existing only in contemplation of the law." A corporation does indeed act as an artificial legal being, deriving its existence from its **charter**, or written permit. In every respect it is a separate legal entity, having a continuous existence apart from that of its owners, the stockholders. As an entity, a corporation may own property, enter into contracts, sue in the courts, be sued, and so forth.

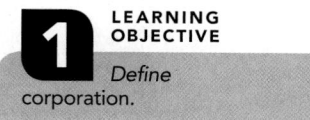

1 LEARNING OBJECTIVE
Define corporation.

ADVANTAGES AND DISADVANTAGES OF THE CORPORATE FORM

As with all business entity forms, there are advantages and disadvantages of the corporate form of business, as shown in Figure 1 and discussed next.

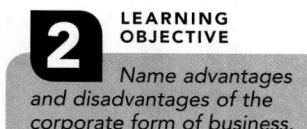

2 LEARNING OBJECTIVE
Name advantages and disadvantages of the corporate form of business.

Advantages of the Corporate Form

The corporate form has a number of advantages.

1. **Limited liability.** As a separate legal entity, a corporation is responsible for its own debts. All that a stockholder can lose is the amount of his or her investment.

2. **Ease of raising capital.** A corporation can accumulate more investment capital than a sole proprietorship or partnership because a corporation can sell stock and issue corporate debt (bonds). Some corporations have more than 1 million stockholders.

3. **Ease of transferring ownership rights.** Ownership rights in a corporation are represented by shares of stock, which can readily be transferred from one person to another without the permission of other stockholders, unless restricted by a shareholders' agreement.

4. **Continuous existence.** The length of life of a corporation is stipulated in its charter; when the charter expires, it may be renewed. The death, incapacity, or withdrawal of an owner does not affect the life of a corporation.

5. **No mutual agency.** Stockholders who are not officers do not have the power to bind the corporation to contracts. Since owners do not participate in management, the corporation is free to employ the managerial talent it believes can best accomplish its objectives.

> **Remember**
> The owners of sole proprietorships and general partnerships are personally liable for the entire debt of the business.

Advantages of a Corporation		Disadvantages of a Corporation	
Limited liability			
		Additional taxation	**TAX + TAX**
Ease of raising capital		Government regulation	
Ease of transferring ownership rights		Lack of control by owners	
Continuous existence			
No mutual agency			

FIGURE 1

Advantages and disadvantages of corporations

Corporations pay taxes on profits and distribute dividends.

Shareholders receive dividends and pay taxes on dividends.

Disadvantages of the Corporate Form

The corporate form also has a number of disadvantages.

1. **Additional taxation.** In addition to the usual property and payroll taxes, corporations must pay income taxes. Since corporations are separate legal entities, they pay federal and state income taxes in their own names. Part of the corporation's net income goes to the stockholders in the form of dividends; this money is personal income to the stockholders, and consequently the stockholders have to pay personal income taxes on it, currently taxed at a lower favorable tax rate of 15 percent. This tax at the corporate and stockholder level is known as **double taxation**. It represents the corporate form's greatest disadvantage. The corporation may also have to pay charter fees to the state in return for the issuance of a charter.

2. **Government regulation.** Since states create corporations by granting charters, states can exercise closer control and supervision over corporations than over sole proprietorships and partnerships. Corporations whose stock is traded on a stock exchange (publicly traded), such as the New York Stock Exchange (NYSE), are subject to extensive government regulations from the Securities and Exchange Commission (SEC) and others.

3. **Lack of control by owners.** The corporate ownership is separated from the control of operations. A minority shareholder (anyone who owns less than 50 percent of the company) has very limited, if any, say in how the corporation is managed.

S CORPORATIONS AND LIMITED LIABILITY COMPANIES

There are two important exceptions to the double taxation of corporations: S corporations and limited liability companies (LLCs).

An **S corporation** is a corporation that elects with the IRS to be treated as a pass-through entity for tax purposes. The income, gains, losses, and deductions are passed through in proportion to one's share of ownership in the S corporation; therefore, an S corporation does not pay tax at the entity level. Instead, the shareholders pay the tax on any profits. An S corporation can have no more than 100 shareholders, and there are other restrictions on who can own the stock (for example, no nonresident alien shareholders are allowed).

A **limited liability company (LLC)** can elect to be treated as a partnership for income tax purposes (a pass-through entity) and retain the corporate advantage of limited liability. The operating flexibility of the LLC, in combination with the freedom from corporate-level taxation, has made the LLC a very popular form of doing business for closely held and family-owned businesses.

FORMATION OF A CORPORATION

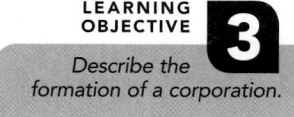

LEARNING OBJECTIVE 3

Describe the formation of a corporation.

To organize a corporation, a person or persons must submit an application for a charter, which is a written permit for a corporation to exist. The charter is issued by the appropriate official (secretary of state or attorney general) of the state in which the company is to be incorporated. The corporation files a document called the **articles of incorporation**. Application requirements vary depending on the state in which the company incorporates. They generally include at least the following points of information:

- Name and legal address of the corporation
- Nature of the business to be conducted
- Amount and description of the capital stock to be issued
- Name and addresses of the first governing body of the corporation (directors and management team)

The articles of incorporation must be accompanied by a charter fee, which may be based on the dollar amount of maximum stock investment, or **authorized capital**.

When state officials approve the articles of incorporation, these articles become the charter or governing instrument of the corporation. Shortly after receiving the charter, the promoters or the sole promoter holds an initial meeting to elect an acting board of directors and formulate bylaws. The charter and the bylaws provide the basic rules for conducting the corporation's affairs. Next, the directors meet to appoint officers to serve as active managers of the business. Then the corporation issues **capital stock**, or shares of ownership, to buyers of stock. The shares of stock are in the form of certificates. Since stockholders have come into existence at this point, they now elect a permanent board of directors.

The size of the corporation may vary in terms of number of stockholders and amount of investment. A corporation may be small, with only a few owners and a minimum investment of $1,000, or it may be giant, with more than a million owners

> **Remember**
>
> One of the advantages of a corporation is the ability to raise capital through the sale of stock.

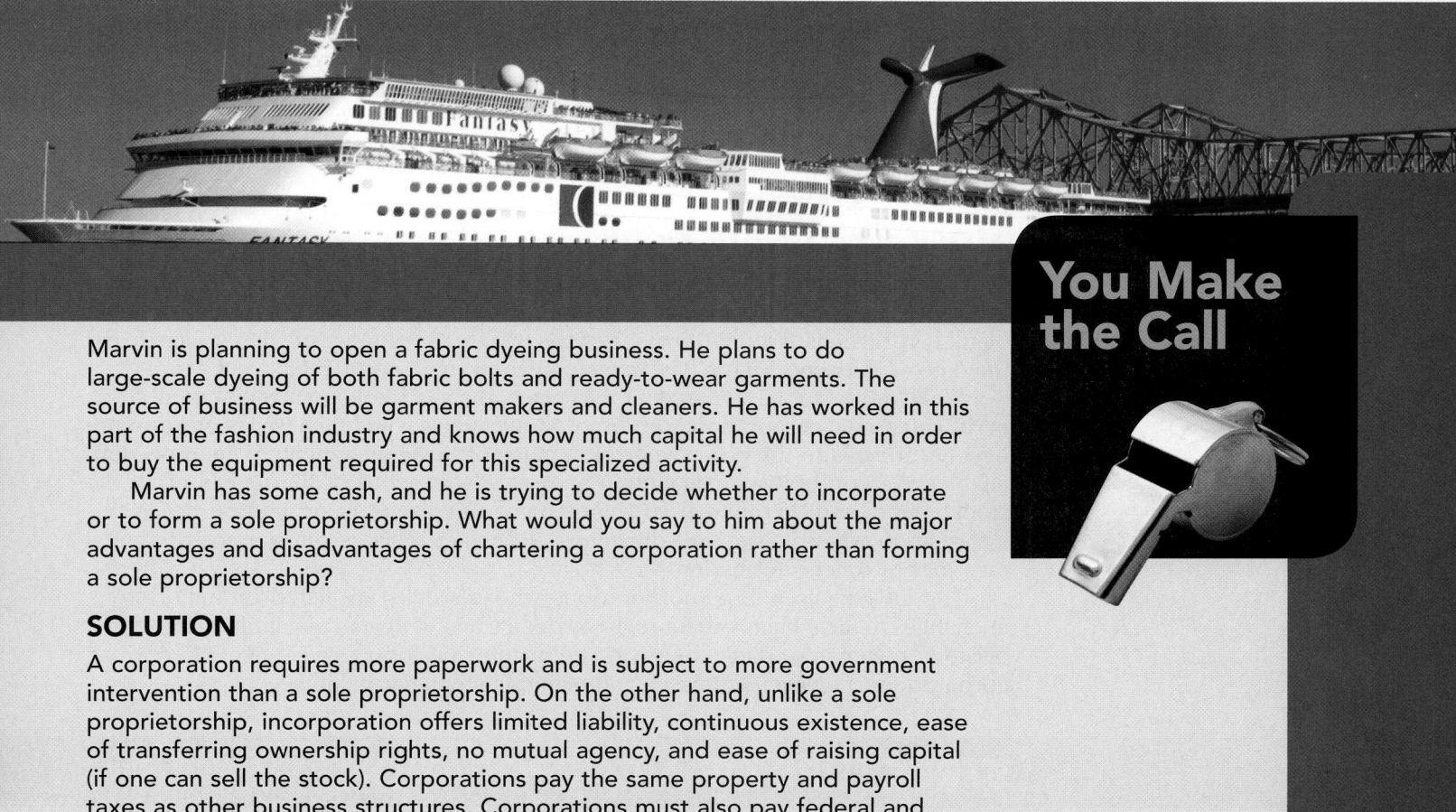

You Make the Call

Marvin is planning to open a fabric dyeing business. He plans to do large-scale dyeing of both fabric bolts and ready-to-wear garments. The source of business will be garment makers and cleaners. He has worked in this part of the fashion industry and knows how much capital he will need in order to buy the equipment required for this specialized activity.

Marvin has some cash, and he is trying to decide whether to incorporate or to form a sole proprietorship. What would you say to him about the major advantages and disadvantages of chartering a corporation rather than forming a sole proprietorship?

SOLUTION

A corporation requires more paperwork and is subject to more government intervention than a sole proprietorship. On the other hand, unlike a sole proprietorship, incorporation offers limited liability, continuous existence, ease of transferring ownership rights, no mutual agency, and ease of raising capital (if one can sell the stock). Corporations pay the same property and payroll taxes as other business structures. Corporations must also pay federal and state income taxes. In addition, stockholders must pay personal income taxes on dividends; thus, the complaint about corporate double taxation.

and an investment amounting to more than $1 billion. In a small corporation, the stockholders may also be the directors and officers. A corporation whose ownership is confined to a small group of stockholders is called a **closely held corporation**. A corporation whose ownership is widely distributed through a stock exchange or through over-the-counter markets to a large number of stockholders is called a **publicly traded corporation**.

Organization Costs

Let's suppose that a new corporation is being formed and the organizers call in an accountant to set up the books. The accountant would record the following entry for the costs of organizing the corporation as they are incurred—such as fees paid to the state, attorneys' fees, promotional costs, travel outlays, and costs of printing.

		GENERAL JOURNAL			PAGE 1	
Date		Description	Post. Ref.	Debit	Credit	
20—						
Aug.	1	Organization Expense		28 0 0 0 00		
		Cash or Accounts Payable			28 0 0 0 00	
		To record organizational				
		expenses incurred.				

Organization Expense will appear on the income statement as an operating expense. Even though the organization costs benefit a corporation for many years, it is nearly impossible to match the benefits to the costs over the years of existence of the corporation. Therefore, corporations now expense the organization costs to Organization Expense rather than the prior method of amortizing the costs over a minimum of five years through a series of adjusting entries. For income tax purposes, organization costs up to $5,000 can be immediately expensed. Any remaining amount must be amortized over 180 months.

Stock Certificate Book

One necessary element of organization costs is the printing of **stock certificates**. The stock certificate provides evidence of ownership in the corporation. On each blank certificate is written the name of the owner, the number of shares issued, and the date of issuance. Figure 2 is an example of a stock certificate.

When a transfer of ownership takes place, the stockholder surrenders the stock certificate to the corporation; the corporation cancels it and then issues one or more new certificates to the new owner(s) in place of these documents. This procedure enables the corporation to maintain an up-to-date record of the names of all the stockholders and the number of shares owned by each. A corporation needs this information when it pays out dividends and when it sends out notices of annual meetings or other information.

The law requires large corporations whose stocks are listed on major stock exchanges to have independent registrars and transfer agents maintain their records of stock ownership. Banks and trust companies perform this service. Many small corporations, however, still issue and maintain stock certificates.

STRUCTURE OF A CORPORATION

The stockholders own the corporation; they delegate authority to the board of directors, which manages the corporation's affairs. The board of directors, in turn, delegates authority to the management team, which is responsible for the

FIGURE 2

Stock certificate

day-to-day operations of the business. The officers themselves may also be members of the board of directors. Figure 3 shows a typical organization chart for a corporation.

Dividends are the share of the corporation's earnings distributed to stockholders that can be paid in cash or with additional shares of stock. The sources of dividends are the current year's net income and the retained earnings of prior years.

Suppose the corporation issues some new stock. Each original stockholder then may have the right to subscribe to additional shares in proportion to her or his present holding. This feature is known as the **preemptive right**. For example,

> **FYI**
>
> Generally, the board of directors are also stockholders, although this is not always true.

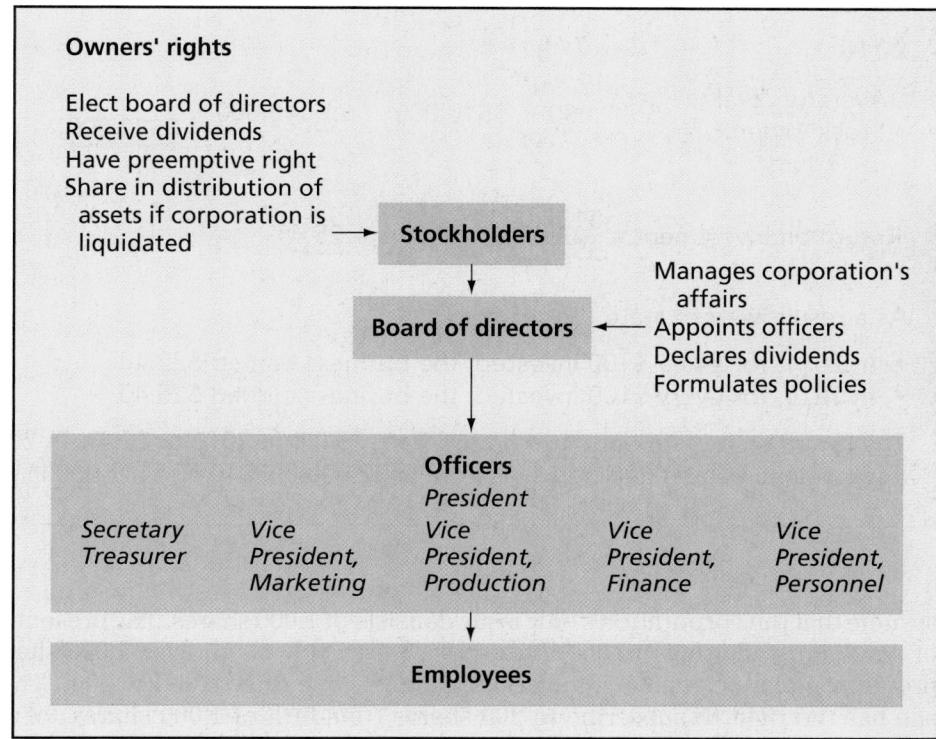

FIGURE 3

Organization chart for a corporation

> **Remember**
>
> The stockholders are the owners of the corporation through their ownership of stock.

Ratio Analysis

Return on Investment (Yield)

Return on investment represents the earning power of the owner's investment in the business.

$$\frac{\text{Return on}}{\text{Investment}} = \frac{\text{Net Income for the Year}}{\text{Average Total Stockholders' Equity}}$$

$$\frac{\text{Average Total}}{\text{Stockholders'}}_{\text{Equity}} = \frac{\text{Beginning Stockholders' Equity} + \text{Ending Stockholders' Equity}}{2}$$

Winter Ski Corporation reports on its balance sheet and income statement the following information for 2011 and 2010:

	2011	2010
Beginning balance of Stockholders' Equity	$530,000	$510,000
Ending balance of Stockholders' Equity	515,000	530,000
Net income	117,000	132,000

2011

$$\frac{\text{Average Total}}{\text{Stockholders'}}_{\text{Equity}} = \frac{\$515,000 + \$530,000}{2} = \frac{\$1,045,000}{2} = \underline{\$522,500}$$

$$\text{Return on Investment} = \frac{\$117,000}{\$522,500} = 0.224 = \underline{22.4\%}$$

2010

$$\frac{\text{Average Total}}{\text{Stockholders'}}_{\text{Equity}} = \frac{\$530,000 + \$510,000}{2} = \frac{\$1,040,000}{2} = \underline{\$520,000}$$

$$\text{Return on Investment} = \frac{\$132,000}{\$520,000} = 0.254 = \underline{25.4\%}$$

As a result, we can state the following:

- In 2011, for every $100 invested, the business earned $22.40.
- In 2010, for every $100 invested, the business earned $25.40.

The return on investment deteriorated from 25.4% in 2010 to 22.4% in 2011 because net income declined 11% from $132,000 in 2010 to $117,000 in 2011.

assume that the corporation's new issue consists of 1,000 shares. The present amount of stock outstanding is 10,000 shares, of which Ruth Allen owns 2,000 shares. Her proportion of stock held to stock outstanding is one-fifth (2,000/10,000). Therefore, she has the right to subscribe to 200 shares (one-fifth of 1,000 shares) of the new issue.

STOCKHOLDERS' EQUITY

The owners' equity in a corporation is called **stockholders' equity**, or *capital*. Just as in sole proprietorships and partnerships, the equity of the owners represents the excess of assets over liabilities. Of the five major classifications of accounts, the main difference for a corporation occurs in the stockholders' equity classification, where capital stock accounts replace owners' Capital accounts. The **Retained Earnings** account is used to record earnings reinvested into the business. Figure 4 compare accounts for a sole proprietorship with those for a corporation.

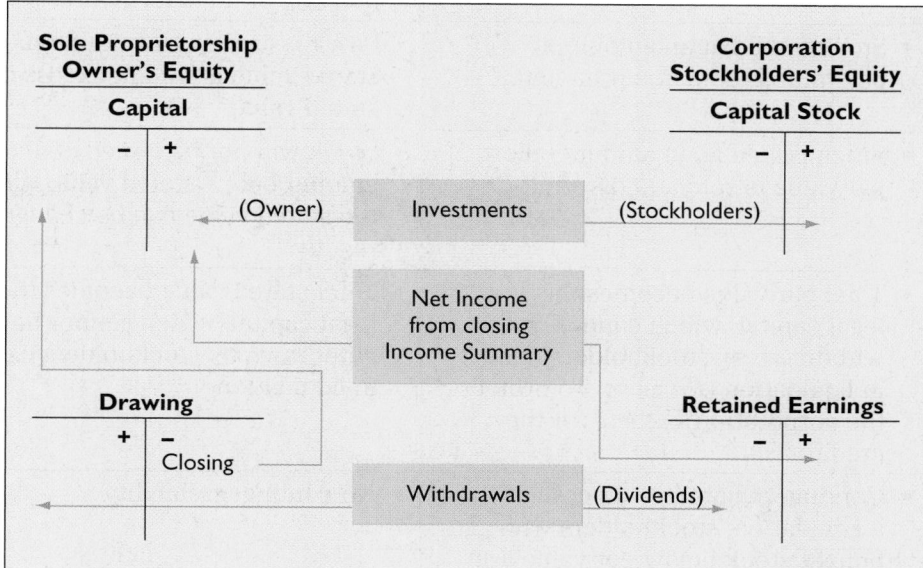

FIGURE 4

Comparison of accounts—sole proprietorship versus corporation

CAPITAL STOCK

Capital stock refers to shares of ownership in a corporation. Authorized capital stock is the maximum number of shares designated in the charter. **Issued stock** refers to the shares apportioned out to the stockholders. Stock that is actually in the hands of stockholders is called **outstanding stock**. Occasionally, a corporation may buy back its own stock or receive it as a donation; consequently, the number of shares that have been issued may differ from the number outstanding. Such reacquired stock is generally known as **treasury stock**.

A corporation may acquire treasury stock to:

1. Reissue shares to officers and employees under bonus and stock compensation plans
2. Rid the company of disgruntled investors
3. Increase trading of the company's stock in the securities market in the hopes of enhancing its market value

Classes of Capital Stock

To appeal to as many investors as possible, a corporation may issue more than one kind of stock. **The two main types of stock are *common* and *preferred*.** Each type may have a variety of characteristics. Some may be **par-value stock** (a value is printed on the stock certificate), and some may be **no-par value stock** (no value is printed on the stock certificate). We will refer to these types of stock frequently. Following is a brief comparison of par-value and no-par value stock:

Par-Value Stock	No-Par Value Stock
• Has a par value (in dollars) printed on the face of the stock certificates	• Has no dollar value printed on the face of the stock certificates
• Has the par value listed in the corporation's charter	• Has no dollar value per share of stock listed in the corporation's charter
• The par value is used to record the shares of stock issued	• The stated value is used to record the shares of stock issued
• Par value can be changed only by amending the corporation's charter	• Stated value is an arbitrary amount and can be changed during a meeting of the board of directors
• Stock issued at an amount above par value is sold at a premium	• Stock issued at an amount above stated value is sold in excess of stated value
• Stock issued at an amount below par value is sold at a discount	• Stock will not be issued at an amount below stated value, since the stated value can be changed readily
• Total par value becomes the legal capital, which cannot be withdrawn by stockholders except in liquidation (*Purpose:* To protect the corporation's assets for the creditors)	• Total stated value becomes the legal capital, which cannot be withdrawn by stockholders except in liquidation
• Contingent liability—in case of a liquidation, stockholders who bought stock below par value are liable for the corporation's debts to the extent of the discount	• No contingent liability

Common Stock

When a corporation issues only one type of stock, it is called **common stock** and may be either par-value or no-par value stock. Common stocks are shares that may yield dividends, but only after owners of preferred stock have been paid. Holders of common stock have the rights listed in Figure 3, with voting privileges of one vote for each share of stock.

Preferred Stock

Preferred stock, which is generally par-value stock, has two preferences. (1) A preference as to dividends: corporations pay dividends on preferred stock (if dividends are declared at all) before they pay dividends on common stock. They pay dividends on preferred stock at a uniform rate—a disadvantage if a corporation is very successful because the preferred shareholder is limited to the stated rate of dividends. The dividend on preferred stock consists of a percentage of the par value of the stock. (2) If the corporation is liquidated, holders of preferred stock are paid off before holders of common stock. In most circumstances, however, holders of preferred stock do not have voting privileges. There are several specific types of preferred stock.

Remember

Since preferred stock can be cumulative or noncumulative, participating or nonparticipating, there are four possible combinations.

Cumulative and Noncumulative Preferred Stock

Suppose that a corporation has a bad year and finds that it is not able to pay the dividend on its preferred stock. In this case, the dividend is said to be *passed*. Dividends on **cumulative preferred stock** may accrue to stockholders. The corporation has to pay these dividends in full before it can pay any dividends to common stockholders. However, for stockholders who own **noncumulative preferred stock**, dividends do not accumulate. In other words, if the corporation passes dividends, they are gone forever. Since preferred stockholders naturally want a regular dividend, most preferred stock is cumulative.

Participating and Nonparticipating Preferred Stock

The dividend on preferred stock consists of an established percentage of the par value of that stock. Some preferred stock, however, provides for the possibility of dividends in excess of this established amount; this kind of preferred stock is called **participating preferred stock**. Holders of participating preferred stock first get the regular dividend that is due them. Then the corporation allocates a stipulated amount to holders of its common stock. And *then* the stockholders who own participating preferred stock are allowed to participate or share in the extra earnings if they are distributed as cash dividends. The dividends of **nonparticipating preferred stock**, on the other hand, are limited to the regular rate. Most preferred stock is nonparticipating.

© PAUL SAKUMA/AP PHOTO

All corporations begin life by applying for a charter or permit. Whether the corporation is small, medium, or large, its articles of incorporation must include information about the nature of the business and a description of the capital stock structure. Many corporations start small and grow over time, which allows them to raise additional capital and grow even larger.

ISSUING STOCK

Stock is issued when the buyer has paid for it in full or when the corporation has received noncash assets in exchange for its stock. A corporation may issue par-value stock at an amount equal to, above, or below its par value.

Issuing Stock at Par for Cash

When stock is issued, there is a separate ledger account for each class of stock. The accountant records investments of cash as debits to Cash and credits to the Stock accounts for the total amount of the par value. Remember that par value is the face value printed on each stock certificate. This designation of par value is a convenient means of dividing the corporation's capital into units, with the ownership of each unit known.

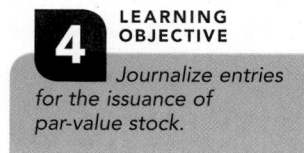

4 LEARNING OBJECTIVE

Journalize entries for the issuance of par-value stock.

For example, Tico Cruise Corporation is organized on July 16 with authorized capital of 4,000 shares of $100-par preferred 8 percent stock and 20,000 shares of $50-par common stock. On August 1, Tico Cruise Corporation issues for cash 2,000 shares of preferred 8 percent stock at par and 10,000 shares of common stock at par. In general journal form, the entry looks like this:

					GENERAL JOURNAL										PAGE	1	
Date		Description				Post. Ref.		Debit					Credit				
20—																	
Aug.	1	Cash					700	0	0	0	00						
		Preferred 8 Percent Stock										200	0	0	0	00	
		Common Stock										500	0	0	0	00	
		Issued 2,000 shares of															
		preferred 8 percent stock at															
		par and 10,000 shares of															
		common stock at par.															

In terms of T accounts, the situation looks like this:

Cash			Preferred 8 Percent Stock	
+	−		−	+
Aug. 1 700,000				Aug. 1 200,000
				(2,000 shares × $100 each)

			Common Stock	
			−	+
				Aug. 1 500,000
				(10,000 shares × $50 each)

The capital stock accounts (Preferred 8 Percent Stock and Common Stock) are controlling accounts. The subsidiary ledger is known as the **stockholders' ledger**. The stockholders' ledger may consist of the stock certificate book or a supplementary record showing the name and address of each stockholder and the number of shares owned.

Issuing Stock at Par for Assets and Organization Expense

Corporations often accept assets other than cash in exchange for their stock. Suppose that also on August 1, Tico Cruise Corporation received equipment (fair market value, $11,000), a building (fair market value, $140,000), and land (fair market value, $120,000) in exchange for 5,420 shares of common stock. Tico Cruise Corporation would record the transaction as shown in the following journal entry.

Date		Description	Post. Ref.	Debit	Credit
20—					
Aug.	1	Equipment		11 0 0 0 00	
		Building		140 0 0 0 00	
		Land		120 0 0 0 00	
		Common Stock			271 0 0 0 00
		Exchanged 5,420 shares of			
		common stock for equipment,			
		building, and land.			

When a corporation accepts an asset other than cash, the accountant records the asset at its fair market value. The goal of the accountant is to have a realistic base on which to calculate future depreciation.

Suppose that a corporation gives shares of its stock to its organizers in exchange for their services in setting up the corporation. Assume that on August 1, Tico Cruise Corporation issues 100 shares of common stock to its organizers when the current market price of the stock was $50. The accountant handles it this way:

Date		Description	Post. Ref.	Debit	Credit
20—					
Aug.	1	Organization Expense		5 0 0 0 00	
		Common Stock			5 0 0 0 00
		Issued 100 shares of common			
		stock to the promoters in			
		exchange for their services in			
		organizing the corporation.			

If the fair market value of the asset or service is not determinable, as in the case of organization expense, then the current market price of the stock on the date the asset or service is acquired is used.

Issuing Stock at a Premium

A newly organized corporation, such as Tico Cruise Corporation, generally issues its stock at par. However, after the business has been operating for some time, the directors may realize that they need additional investment capital. Perhaps the business has been so successful that they want to expand it. Or perhaps they need to cover losses suffered during the early years of the business. So the directors decide to issue some new stock. The present market price of the original stock affects the price they can secure for the new shares. The market price of the stock of a corporation is usually influenced by the following factors:

1. The earnings record, financial condition, and dividend record of the corporation
2. The potential for growth in earnings of the corporation
3. The supply of and demand for money for investment purposes in the money market as a whole
4. General business conditions and prospects for the future

When a corporation issues stock at a price above par value, the stock is said to be issued at a **premium**. The premium is the amount by which the issuing price of the new stock exceeds the par value. The premium may exist because the corporation has performed successfully in the past and has good prospects for growth in earnings in the future. Conversely, when a corporation sells its stock at a price below par value, the stock is said to be issued at a **discount.** The discount is the amount by which the issuing price of the new stock falls below the par value. This discount may exist because the corporation incurred losses during its early period, or perhaps its prospects for the future are not too promising.

Premium on Stock

When a corporation issues stock at a price *above* its par value, the accountant debits Cash or other noncash assets for the amount received, credits the stock account for the par value, and credits a premium account, called **Paid-in Capital in Excess of Par Value,** for the difference between the amount received and the par value. Suppose Tico Cruise Corporation issues 900 shares of $100-par cumulative preferred 8 percent stock at $103 on November 1. In general journal form, the entry looks like this:

Date		Description	Post. Ref.	Debit	Credit
20—					
Nov.	1	Cash		92 7 0 0 00	
		Preferred 8 Percent Stock			90 0 0 0 00
		Paid-in Capital in Excess of			
		Par Value			2 7 0 0 00
		Issued 900 shares at $103			
		per share.			

In terms of T accounts, the entry looks like this:

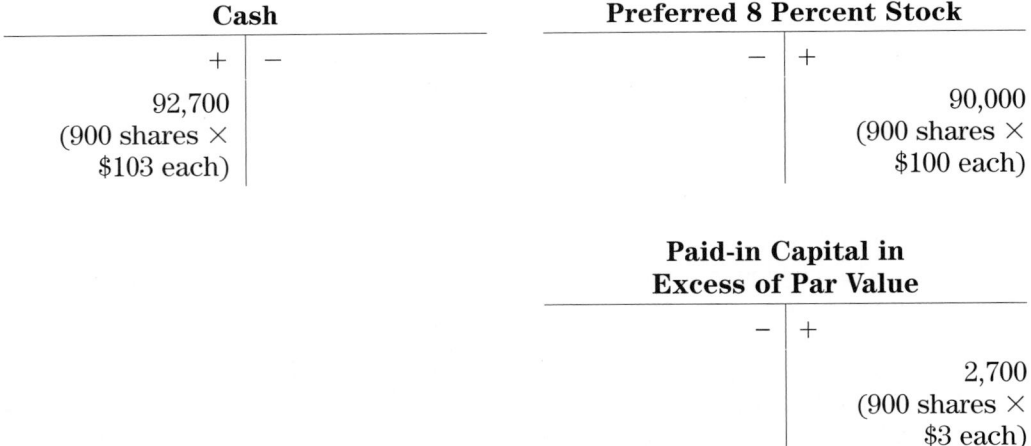

Cash

+	−
92,700 (900 shares × $103 each)	

Preferred 8 Percent Stock

−	+
	90,000 (900 shares × $100 each)

Paid-in Capital in Excess of Par Value

−	+
	2,700 (900 shares × $3 each)

In the case of par-value stock, the stock account contains only the total par value of the stock. The Paid-in Capital in Excess of Par Value account is treated as an addition to stockholders' equity. Why would buyers be willing to pay a premium for Tico Cruise Corporation's 8 percent preferred stock? The 8 percent rate may be higher than the current market rate for this type of stock. For example, other companies in comparable financial condition may be paying only 6 percent dividends on their stock.

Let's review the placement of the major accounts presented thus far in the fundamental accounting equation:

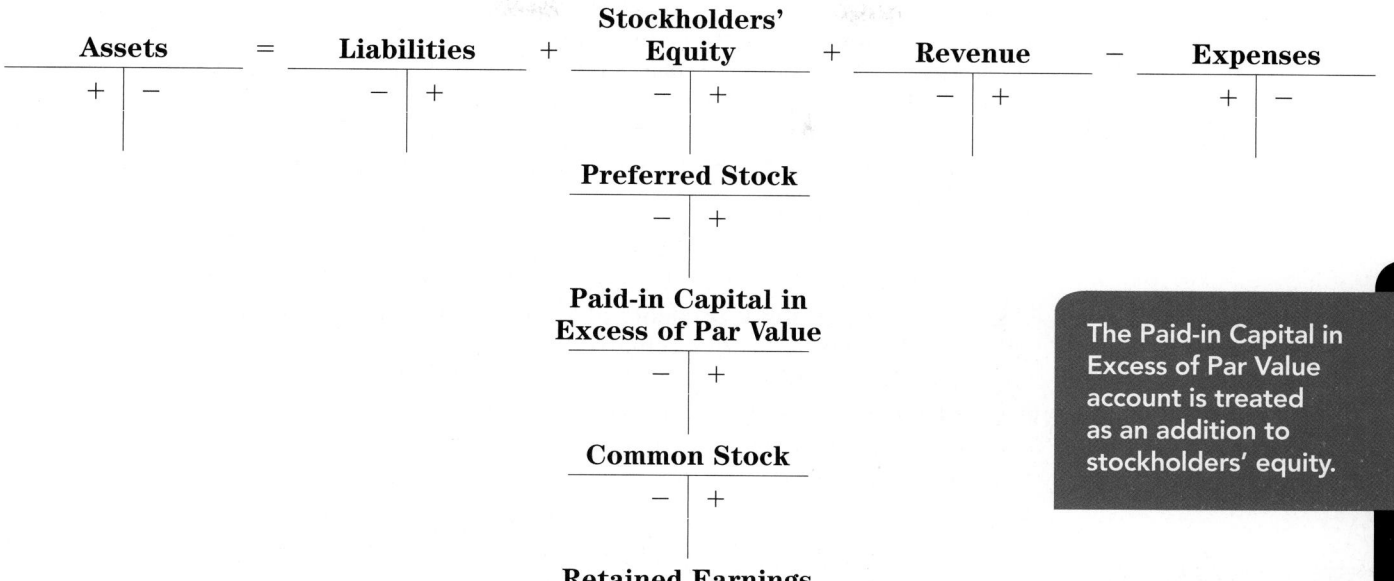

Assets	=	Liabilities	+	Stockholders' Equity	+	Revenue	−	Expenses
+ | −		− | +		− | +		− | +		+ | −

Preferred Stock

− \| +

Paid-in Capital in Excess of Par Value

− \| +

> The Paid-in Capital in Excess of Par Value account is treated as an addition to stockholders' equity.
>
> **Remember**

Common Stock

− \| +

Retained Earnings

− \| +

The Stockholders' Equity section of the balance sheet of Tico Cruise Corporation—showing the stock and premium accounts—looks like this:

Stockholders' Equity		
Paid-in Capital:		
Preferred 8 Percent Stock, cumulative, $100 par (4,000 shares authorized, 2,900 shares issued)	$290,000	
Paid-in Capital in Excess of Par Value	2,700	$ 292,700
Common Stock, $50 par (20,000 shares authorized, 15,520 shares issued)		776,000
Total Paid-in Capital		$1,068,700
Retained Earnings		45,000
Total Stockholders' Equity		$1,113,700

Notice that the listing of the stock states the par value, the number of shares authorized, and the number of shares issued. The record also describes preferred stock as cumulative. If the preferred stock is noncumulative or nonparticipating, as in this case, the record does not mention it. Preferred stock is assumed to be noncumulative and nonparticipating unless otherwise stated.

> **FYI**
>
> A corporation can also issue preferred stock at a discount or common stock at a premium or discount.

Stockholders' Equity is divided into two major sections: **Paid-in Capital** and Retained Earnings. Paid-in or contributed capital includes the investments made by all the types of shareholders owning common and preferred stock in the corporation.

For the Retained Earnings account, note that the amount is not necessarily in the form of cash. Retained earnings represents accumulated net income (not necessarily cash) kept in the company and not paid to stockholders in the form of dividends.

No-Par Value Stock

Preferred stock generally has a par value. However, common stock may or may not have a par value. If it does not have a par value, it is referred to as *no-par value stock*. Corporations in all fifty states can issue no-par value stock, and some states only have no-par value stock. The main advantages claimed for no-par value stock are as follows:

1. Since it does not have a par value, no-par value stock has no fixed price. This allows for greater flexibility for the corporation issuing the stock.
2. No-par value stock prevents any misconception on the part of inexperienced stockholders as to the value of the stock. In the case of par stock, investors might believe that the stock is worth the amount printed on the face of the stock certificate. Actually, the market value of the stock may differ markedly from the par value, as a result of ups and downs in the corporation's past earnings and future prospects.

Stated Value and No-Par Value Stock

Remember

Most states allow corporations to issue no-par, stated value stock. The stated value of the outstanding shares then becomes the legal capital of the corporation.

When all of a company's stock is of the par-value type, the par value of the shares represents the company's **legal capital**, which stockholders cannot withdraw. This law protects creditors. When various state legislatures passed laws permitting corporations to issue no-par value stock, they tried to continue to protect creditors by stipulating that all or part of the amount the corporation receives for its no-par value shares be exempt from withdrawal by stockholders. This amount is known as the stock's **stated value**. The minimum stated value per share of no-par value stock varies from state to state. In some states, the board of directors of the corporation, if it wishes, may choose a stated value for the company's no-par value stock that is higher than the minimum required by the state law.

Established Amount of Stated Value

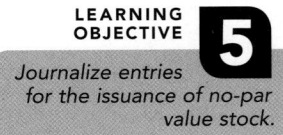

LEARNING OBJECTIVE 5

Journalize entries for the issuance of no-par value stock.

Travel and Adventure Corporation is located in a state that allows the board of directors of a corporation to designate a stated value for its stock. Accordingly, the board of directors of Travel and Adventure Corporation chooses a stated value of $55 per share for its common stock. On June 20, Travel and Adventure Corporation issues 1,400 shares at $66 per share, receiving cash. The accountant uses the account Paid-in Capital in Excess of Stated Value to record the amount received over and above the stated value.

The accountant's entry, in general journal form, is as follows:

Date		Description	Post. Ref.	Debit	Credit
20—					
June	20	Cash		92 4 0 0 00	
		Common Stock			77 0 0 0 00
		Paid-in Capital in Excess of			
		Stated Value			15 4 0 0 00
		Issued 1,400 shares at $66			
		per share.			

Next, on September 10, Travel and Adventure Corporation issues an additional 1,000 shares at $60 per share, receiving cash. The entry in general journal form is as follows:

Date		Description	Post. Ref.	Debit	Credit
20—					
Sept.	10	Cash		60 0 0 0 00	
		Common Stock			55 0 0 0 00
		Paid-in Capital in Excess of			
		Stated Value			5 0 0 0 00
		Issued 1,000 shares at $60			
		per share.			

In terms of T accounts, the entries look like this:

Cash

	+	−
June 20	92,400	
Sept. 10	60,000	

Common Stock

	−	+
		June 20 77,000 (stated value)
		Sept. 10 55,000 (stated value)

Paid-in Capital in Excess of Stated Value

	−	+
		June 20 15,400 (excess)
		Sept. 10 5,000 (excess)

Subscriptions and Stock Issuance

We have been talking about corporations that issue stock for which investors pay in full, either by giving cash or by giving noncash assets or organizational services. However, a corporation often sells its stock directly to investors on a subscription contract (installment) basis. This type of sale is recorded as a **capital stock subscription**. This means that the investor enters into a contract with the corporation, promising to pay at a later date for a specified number of shares at an agreed-upon price. The corporation agrees to issue the shares when the investor has paid for them in full.

The accountant records the amount of the subscription, which is an asset, in the Subscriptions Receivable account and credits the par or stated value of the stock to Stock Subscribed, a stockholders' equity account. The accountant then records the difference between the subscription price and the par value under Paid-in Capital in Excess of Par Value. In the case of no-par value stock, the difference between the subscription price and the stated value is recorded under Paid-in Capital in Excess of Stated Value.

As the investor sends in payments, the accountant records them as debits to Cash and credits to Subscriptions Receivable. When the investor finishes paying for all the shares, the accountant records the issuance of the stock as a debit to Stock Subscribed and a credit to Common Stock or Preferred Stock. When investors want subscriptions to both common and preferred stock, the accountant uses separate accounts for each. We can best describe the procedure with an example.

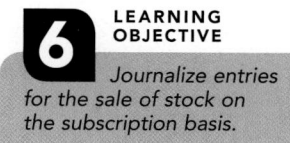

6 LEARNING OBJECTIVE
Journalize entries for the sale of stock on the subscription basis.

FYI

You can buy and sell stock of publicly traded companies through a large selection of brokers and brokerage firms in person, by phone, or on the Internet. Most charge for buying and selling stock.

Subscription Transactions: Par-Value Stock

Alaskan Eco-Adventures, Inc., a newly organized company, has the following transactions involving its own stock:

June 15 Received subscriptions to 6,000 shares of common stock ($100 par value) from various subscribers at $104 per share, with a down payment of 40 percent of the subscription price.

July   1 Received 30 percent of the subscription price from all subscribers (6,000 shares).

      15 Received 30 percent of the subscription price from subscribers to 500 shares, and issued 500 shares.

The general journal is shown in Figure 5. The items in parentheses are explanations; they would not actually appear in the journal.

This illustrates that Common Stock Subscribed represents the total par value of the shares subscribed. **It also illustrates the fact that a firm does not issue stock until the investor has paid for it in full.** Since only 500 shares were paid for in full, the firm issued only 500 shares.

Common Stock Subscribed represents the total par value or stated value of the shares subscribed. It is a temporary account to handle subscribed shares that have not yet been paid for in full. When the investors finish paying for the shares, the accountant records the issuance of stock by debiting the Common Stock Subscribed account and crediting the Common Stock account.

Remember

For the sale of common stock on a subscription basis, use Common Stock Subscribed. Do not issue the stock until it is paid for in full.

FIGURE 5

Journal entries for subscription transactions—par-value stock

GENERAL JOURNAL   PAGE 1

Date		Description	Post. Ref.	Debit	Credit
20—					
June	15	Subscriptions Receivable,			
		Common Stock (6,000 shares ×			
		$104 per share)		624 0 0 0 00	
		Common Stock Subscribed			
		(6,000 shares × $100 per share)	316		600 0 0 0 00
		Paid-in Capital in Excess of			
		Par Value (6,000 shares ×			
		$4 per share)			24 0 0 0 00
		Received subscriptions to			
		6,000 shares at $104 per			
		share.			
	15	Cash (6,000 shares × $104 per			
		share × 0.40)		249 6 0 0 00	
		Subscriptions Receivable,			
		Common Stock			249 6 0 0 00
		Received 40 percent of the			
		subscription of June 15 on			
		6,000 shares.			
July	1	Cash (6,000 shares × $104 per			
		share × 0.30)		187 2 0 0 00	
		Subscriptions Receivable,			
		Common Stock			187 2 0 0 00
		Received 30 percent of the			
		subscription of June 15 on			
		6,000 shares.			

GENERAL JOURNAL PAGE 1

Date		Description	Post. Ref.	Debit	Credit
July	15	Cash (500 shares × $104 per			
		share × 0.30)		15 6 0 0 00	
		Subscriptions Receivable,			
		Common Stock			15 6 0 0 00
		Received 30 percent, the			
		final installment of the			
		subscription of June 15, on			
		500 shares.			
	15	Common Stock Subscribed	316	50 0 0 0 00	
		Common Stock (500 shares ×			
		$100 per share)	314		50 0 0 0 00
		Issued 500 shares.			

Stock may be paid for in installments, but it is not issued until it is paid for in full. This requires two entries—one to record the final receipt of payment and one to issue the stock.

Remember

In the ledger accounts for stock issued and subscribed, always list the number of shares in the Item column. Here is an example for Common Stock and Common Stock Subscribed:

Stock accounts are always credited at par value or stated value when stock is issued.

Remember

ACCOUNT Common Stock ACCOUNT NO. 314

Date		Item	Post. Ref.	Debit	Credit	Balance Debit	Balance Credit
20—							
July	15	500 shares	J1		50 0 0 0 00		50 0 0 0 00

ACCOUNT Common Stock Subscribed ACCOUNT NO. 316

Date		Item	Post. Ref.	Debit	Credit	Balance Debit	Balance Credit
20—							
June	15	6,000 sh.	J1		600 0 0 0 00		600 0 0 0 00
July	15	(500 sh.)	J1	50 0 0 0 00			550 0 0 0 00

The "Item" column in a handwritten ledger page or another notation space in a computerized general ledger package should be used to show the number of shares subscribed and shares issued.

Remember

Controlling Accounts and Subsidiary Ledgers

Investors may finish paying for subscriptions at different times, and the firm issues stock when the individual subscriber has paid in full. Therefore, the firm's accountant has to maintain an account for each individual subscriber.

As a result, the books exhibit the following relationships between controlling accounts and subsidiary ledgers:

Controlling Account	Subsidiary Ledger
Subscriptions Receivable, Preferred 9 Percent Stock	Preferred 9 percent stock subscribers' ledger
Subscriptions Receivable, Common Stock	Common stock subscribers' ledger

These records are similar to the Accounts Receivable controlling account and the accounts receivable ledger.

The firm's accountant also has to keep an accurate record of the number of shares owned by each stockholder. Consequently, each stock account is a controlling account:

Controlling Account	Subsidiary Ledger
Preferred 9 Percent Stock	Preferred 9 percent stockholders' ledger
Common Stock	Common stockholders' ledger

As we have said, a small corporation may use its stock certificate book as a subsidiary ledger. Naturally, the accountant must see to it that the information is complete, so that the company can declare and pay dividends correctly. Cash dividends are paid on outstanding stock only.

ILLUSTRATION OF A CORPORATE BALANCE SHEET

LEARNING OBJECTIVE 7

Prepare a classified balance sheet for a corporation, including Subscriptions Receivable, Paid-in Capital, and Retained Earnings accounts.

To reinforce your understanding of the accounts introduced in this chapter, examine the balance sheet shown in Figure 6 to see where each account is placed. Because this balance sheet covers so many of the concepts just discussed, you will probably want to refer back to it in the future. Notice that Retained Earnings is added separately to Total Paid-in Capital. In this case, the Retained Earnings account has a $170,000 credit balance. **This credit balance represents a surplus, and it is the normal balance. However, if a company had big losses, its Retained Earnings account could have a debit balance, which is called a deficit**. On a balance sheet, a Retained Earnings account with a debit balance is subtracted from Total Paid-in Capital.

NEW ACCOUNTS AND THE FUNDAMENTAL ACCOUNTING EQUATION

The placement and use of the accounts we have introduced in this chapter with respect to the fundamental accounting equation are shown in Figure 7 on page 778.

FIGURE 6

Balance sheet—Caitlin, Inc.

Caitlin, Inc.
Balance Sheet
June 30, 20—

Assets

Current Assets:			
Cash		$ 27,000	
Notes Receivable		50,000	
Accounts Receivable	$419,000		
Less Allowance for Doubtful Accounts	12,000	407,000	
Subscriptions Receivable, Preferred			
9 Percent Stock		14,000	
Subscriptions Receivable, Common Stock		30,000	
Merchandise Inventory		279,000	
Prepaid Insurance		3,500	
Total Current Assets			$810,500
Investments:			
Friedman Equipment Company 8 Percent			
Bonds			16,000
Property and Equipment:			
Store Equipment	$ 82,000		
Less Accumulated Depreciation	19,000	$ 63,000	
Delivery Equipment	$ 60,000		
Less Accumulated Depreciation	40,000	20,000	
Total Property and Equipment			83,000
Intangible Assets:			
Patents			8,000
Total Assets			$917,500

Liabilities

Current Liabilities:			
Accounts Payable		$281,500	
Notes Payable		20,000	
Salaries Payable		3,000	
Interest Payable		1,000	
Total Liabilities			$305,500

Stockholders' Equity

Paid-in Capital:			
Preferred 7 Percent Stock, $50 par			
(2,000 shares authorized and issued)		$100,000	
Preferred 9 Percent Stock, $50 par			
(4,000 shares authorized,			
1,500 shares issued)	$ 75,000		
Preferred 9 Percent Stock Subscribed			
(500 shares)	25,000		
Paid-in Capital in Excess of Par Value	2,000	102,000	
Common Stock, no-par, stated value			
$10 per share (20,000 shares			
authorized, 14,000 shares issued)	$140,000		
Common Stock Subscribed (2,000 shares)	20,000		
Paid-in Capital in Excess of Stated Value	80,000	240,000	
Total Paid-in Capital		$442,000	
Retained Earnings		170,000	
Total Stockholders' Equity			612,000
Total Liabilities and Stockholders' Equity			$917,500

FIGURE 7 Accounts related to capital stock

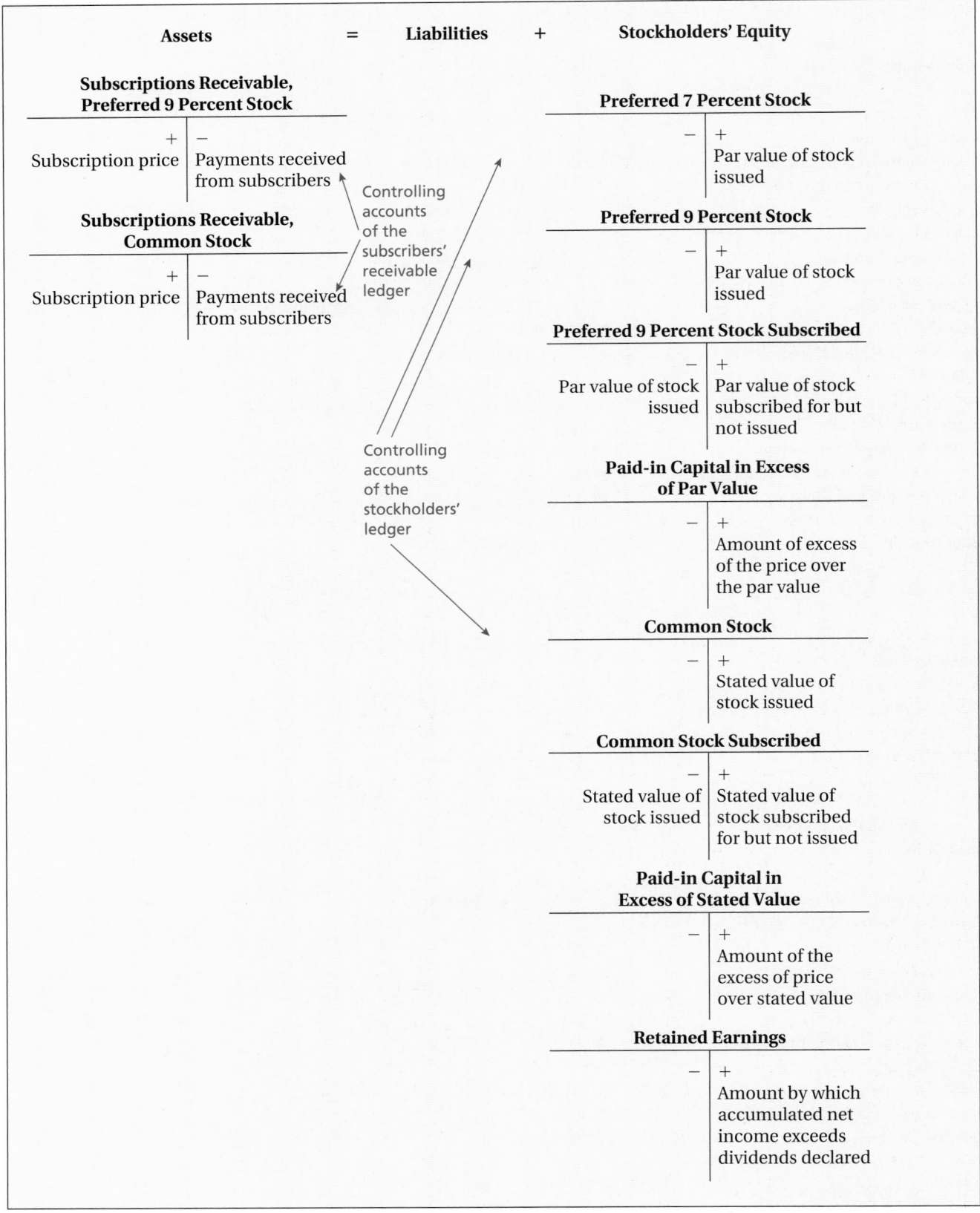

Manager of Tour Directors

Monica Hoffman has a dream job. She's the manager of tour directors for a cruise line. Monica is responsible not only for ensuring that all guest experiences are high quality, but also for hiring, training, and working directly with all tour directors. She also helps determine the itineraries and tours that are offered on their many cruises. Monica is required to stay current on the scientific, political, environmental, and global factors surrounding the countries that directly impact the itineraries and tours.

It sounds like Monica doesn't need to know accounting, right? Monica, however, says that she relies heavily on the accounting knowledge that she learned in college. Monica reviews daily her division performance reports, including the sales revenues that her team creates through offering optional tours. She is also responsible for creating annual budgets for her department and tracking expenses through monthly financial reports. Monica also ensures that the system and processes for ordering, purchasing, tracking, and accounting for land tour supplies are in place and maintained.

While Monica doesn't have an undergraduate degree in accounting, she did take several accounting classes in college. She says these classes have given her the organizational skills, knowledge, and experience in tracking details needed for projecting budgets and managing her department's financial responsibilities.

CHAPTER REVIEW

Study & Practice

1 **LEARNING OBJECTIVE**
Define corporation.

A **corporation** is defined as "an artificial being, invisible, intangible, and existing only in contemplation of the law."

2 **LEARNING OBJECTIVE**
Name advantages and disadvantages of the corporate form of business.

A corporation has the following advantages over a sole proprietorship or a general partnership: limited liability, ease of raising capital, ease of transferring ownership rights, continuous existence, and no mutual agency. Three disadvantages of a corporation are additional taxation, government regulation, and lack of control by owners.

3 *Describe the formation of a corporation.*

To form a corporation, a person or persons must file **articles of incorporation** with the state. The corporation may be small (**closely held**) or large (**publicly traded**). Stock may be sold to raise capital. **Dividends** (an amount per share owned) may be paid to stockholders. The **Capital Stock** accounts in a corporation replace owner's capital accounts in sole proprietorships.

LEARNING OBJECTIVE

4 *Journalize entries for the issuance of par-value stock.*

The entry for the issuance of **par-value stock** for cash is a debit to Cash and credits to the Stock accounts. When stock is exchanged for assets other than cash, those asset accounts are debited. When stock is issued for more than its par value, the accountant must credit a Premium account. For stock issued at a discount, a Discount account is debited.

PRACTICE EXERCISE 1

On April 1, Mesa Rose Airlines Corporation issued 10,000 shares of preferred 6 percent stock, $8 par value, at $10. Journalize the transaction.

PRACTICE EXERCISE 1 SOLUTION

Date		Description	Post. Ref.	Debit	Credit
20—					
Apr.	1	Cash (10,000 shares x $10 per share)		100 0 0 0 00	
		Preferred 6 Percent Stock			
		(10,000 shares x $8 per share)			80 0 0 0 00
		Paid-in Capital in Excess of			
		Par Value [10,000 shares x			
		($10 per share − $8 per share)]			20 0 0 0 00
		Issued 10,000 shares at $10			
		per share.			

LEARNING OBJECTIVE

5 *Journalize entries for the issuance of no-par value stock.*

The entry for the issuance of **no-par value stock** for cash is a debit to Cash and credit to the Stock account. When the stock is issued for more than its stated value, the accountant must credit a Premium account.

PRACTICE EXERCISE 2

On May 15, Rainforest Zip-Line Corporation issued 2,200 shares of common stock, no par value, stated value $45, at $50 per share, receiving cash. Journalize the transaction.

PRACTICE EXERCISE 2 SOLUTION

Date	Description	Post. Ref.	Debit	Credit
20—				
May 15	Cash (2,200 shares x $50 per share)		110 0 0 0 00	
	Common Stock (2,200 shares x			
	$45 per share)			99 0 0 0 00
	Paid-in Capital in Excess of			
	Stated Value [2,200 shares x			
	($50 per share − $45 per share)]			11 0 0 0 00
	Issued 2,200 shares at $50			
	per share.			

6 LEARNING OBJECTIVE

Journalize entries for the sale of stock on the subscription basis.

The entry for the sale of stock on a subscription (installment) basis is a debit to a Subscriptions Receivable account (a current asset) and a credit to a Stock Subscribed account (a **Paid-in Capital** account). When the subscription is paid in full and the stock is issued, the entry is a debit to a Stock Subscribed account and a credit to a Stock account.

PRACTICE EXERCISE 3

Dusty Derek Jeep Tours, Inc., has authorized capital consisting of 10,000 shares of cumulative preferred 8 percent stock, $80 par value, and 20,000 shares of common stock, $20 par value. Record the following transactions in general journal form:

Feb. 1 Received subscriptions to 4,000 shares of preferred 8 percent stock at $82 per share, with a down payment of 40 percent of the subscription price.

Mar. 1 Received 50 percent of the subscription price from all subscribers.

Apr. 1 Received 10 percent of the subscription price from all subscribers and issued the stock certificates.

PRACTICE EXERCISE 3 SOLUTION

Date	Description	Post. Ref.	Debit	Credit
20—				
Feb. 1	Subscriptions Receivable,			
	Preferred 8 Percent Stock (4,000			
	shares × $82 per share)		328 0 0 0 00	
	Preferred 8 Percent Stock			
	Subscribed (4,000 shares ×			
	$80 per share)			320 0 0 0 00
	Paid-in Capital in Excess of			
	Par Value (4,000 shares ×			
	$2 per share)			8 0 0 0 00
	Received subscriptions to			
	4,000 shares at $82 per share.			

(Continued)

Date	Description	Post. Ref.	Debit	Credit
Feb. 1	Cash (4,000 shares × $82 per share × 0.40)		131 2 0 0 00	
	Subscriptions Receivable, Preferred 8 Percent Stock			131 2 0 0 00
	Received 40 percent of the subscription of Feb. 1 on 4,000 shares.			
Mar. 1	Cash (4,000 shares × $82 per share × 0.50)		164 0 0 0 00	
	Subscriptions Receivable, Preferred 8 Percent Stock			164 0 0 0 00
	Received 50 percent of the subscription of Feb. 1 on 4,000 shares.			
Apr. 1	Cash (4,000 shares × $82 per share × 0.10)		32 8 0 0 00	
	Subscriptions Receivable, Preferred 8 Percent Stock			32 8 0 0 00
	Received 10 percent, the final installment of the subscription of Feb. 1, on 4,000 shares.			
1	Preferred 8 Percent Stock Subscribed		320 0 0 0 00	
	Preferred 8 Percent Stock (4,000 shares × $80 per share)			320 0 0 0 00
	Issued 4,000 shares.			

LEARNING OBJECTIVE 7

Prepare a classified balance sheet for a corporation, including Subscriptions Receivable, Paid-in Capital, and Retained Earnings accounts.

The accounts shown in Figure 7 are used to prepare a classified balance sheet. A classified balance sheet is presented in Figure 6.

PRACTICE EXERCISE 4

Rosetta's Helicopter Tours, Inc., has a charter authorizing it to issue 5,000 shares of $25 par-value preferred 6 percent stock and 15,000 shares of no-par value common stock (stated value $15). The following account balances are from the Balance Sheet columns of the work sheet:

Retained Earnings	$ 91,200
Common Stock Subscribed (2,000 shares)	30,000
Common Stock	105,000
Preferred 6 Percent Stock	85,000
Paid-in Capital in Excess of Stated Value	22,700

Prepare the Stockholders' Equity section of the balance sheet.

PRACTICE EXERCISE 4 SOLUTION

Stockholders' Equity			
Paid-in Capital:			
Preferred 6 Percent Stock, $25 par			
(5,000 shares authorized, 3,400 shares issued)		$ 85,000	
Common Stock, no-par, stated value $15 per share			
(15,000 shares authorized, 7,000 shares issued)	$105,000		
Common Stock Subscribed (2,000 shares)	30,000		
Paid-in Capital in Excess of Stated Value	22,700	157,700	
Total Paid-in Capital		$242,700	
Retained Earnings		91,200	
Total Stockholders' Equity			$333,900

Glossary

Articles of incorporation Application for a charter. (p. 761)

Authorized capital The maximum number of shares that may be issued for each class of stock (common and preferred). (p. 761)

Capital stock General term referring to shares of ownership in a corporation. (p. 761)

Capital stock subscription Purchase of stock on contract or installment basis. (p. 773)

Charter Written permit, issued by a state government, for a corporation to exist; state-approved articles of incorporation. (p. 759)

Closely held corporation A corporation having a relatively small group of owners. (p. 762)

Common stock Stock whose owners are paid dividends only after owners of preferred stock have been paid (residual share); holders of common stock have voting privileges. (p. 766)

Corporation "An artificial being, invisible, intangible, and existing only in contemplation of the law." As such, it is a separate legal entity. (p. 759)

Cumulative preferred stock Preferred stock whose holders must be paid accumulated dividends or dividends passed (dividends that the firm has failed to pay in prior years) before any dividends can be paid to holders of common stock. (p. 767)

Deficit A debit or negative balance in the Retained Earnings account. (p. 776)

Discount The amount by which the issuing price of the new stock falls below the par value. (p. 770)

Dividends Distributions of earnings of a corporation, in the form of either cash or additional shares of stock. (p. 763)

Double taxation Taxation of corporate income at two separate points. First, the net income of the corporation is taxed because the corporation is a separate entity. When the net income is distributed as dividends to stockholders, it becomes part of the personal income of the individual stockholder and is taxed a second time. (p. 760)

Issued stock Stock issued by a corporation. (p. 765)

Legal capital Minimum capital stock investment that a corporation must maintain; capital that is not subject to withdrawal by stockholders; usually equal to par or stated value. (p. 772)

Limited liability company (LLC) An entity that can elect to be treated as a partnership for tax purposes and a corporation for legal purposes (limited liability); a very popular form of ownership for closely held and family-owned businesses. (p. 760)

No-par value stock Stock that has no value printed on the stock certificates. (p. 765)

Noncumulative preferred stock Preferred stock in which dividends passed do not accumulate; once they are passed, they are gone forever. (p. 767)

Nonparticipating preferred stock Stock in which the dividends are limited to the regular rate. (p. 767)

Outstanding stock Stock actually in the possession of stockholders (issued stock less the number of shares reacquired by the company). (p. 765)

Paid-in Capital A caption on the balance sheet listed immediately under Stockholders' Equity. The Paid-in Capital section includes the Stock accounts and their related Premium or Discount accounts. (p. 771)

Paid-in Capital in Excess of Par Value The account name for amounts by which the issuing price of a stock exceeds the par value. (p. 770)

Par-value stock Stock for which a uniform face value, indicating the amount per share to be entered in the Capital Stock account, is printed on the stock certificates. (p. 765)

Participating preferred stock Preferred stock whose holders share in any extra dividends distributed by the corporation after the regular dividend has been paid to holders of preferred stock and a stipulated dividend has been paid to holders of common stock. (p. 767)

Preemptive right A stockholder's right to maintain the same proportionate ownership in a corporation in the future as she or he does originally, through the privilege of subscribing to a new issue of stock in the same proportion as her or his present ownership. (p. 763)

Preferred stock Stock whose holders are paid dividends at a uniform rate before any dividends are paid to holders of common stock. The holder of preferred stock also has preference in the distribution of assets in the event of a liquidation. (p. 766)

Premium The amount by which the issuing price of a stock exceeds the par value. (p. 769)

Publicly traded corporation A corporation having a large group of owners with shares traded on a stock exchange or in over-the-counter markets. (p. 762)

Retained Earnings A stockholders' equity account representing capital generated by the corporation's earnings that remain in the firm; the amount by which net income exceeds dividends paid over the life of the corporation. (p. 765)

S corporation A corporation that elects with the IRS to be treated as a pass-through entity for income tax purposes. There are restrictions on the number (currently there can be no more than 100 shareholders) and type of shareholders an S corporation may have. An S corporation enjoys the absence of double taxation while having limited liability. (p. 760)

Stated value The amount per share of no-par value stock that is recorded in the corporation's stock accounts; an amount designated by law as not subject to withdrawal by stockholders. (p. 772)

Stock certificates Documents giving evidence of ownership in shares of stock; issued only when the stockholder has paid for the shares in full. (p. 762)

Stockholders' equity The owners' equity in a corporation. Also referred to as *capital*. (p. 764)

Stockholders' ledger A record showing the name and address of each stockholder and the number of shares owned. (p. 768)

Surplus A credit or positive balance in the Retained Earnings account. (p. 776)

Treasury stock A corporation's own stock, which it has issued and which was at one time outstanding, that the firm reacquires. (p. 765)

CHAPTER ASSIGNMENTS

Discussion Questions

1. If a corporation sells its stock at a premium, is the amount of the premium recorded as revenue to the firm?
2. Explain the difference between capital stock and retained earnings.
3. Identify the main advantages and disadvantages of the corporate form of business organization as compared to sole proprietorship and general partnership forms. In your opinion, which is the greatest advantage and which is the greatest disadvantage?
4. What is the purpose of Common Stock Subscribed, and what happens to the account?
5. In what respect is a corporation a separate legal entity?
6. List the advantages preferred stockholders have over common stockholders. What are the disadvantages?
7. In regard to stock, what is the difference between par value and stated value?
8. Classify each of the following accounts as asset, liability, stockholders' equity, revenue, or expense, and indicate the normal balance of each account:
   a. Common Stock
   b. Common Stock Subscribed
   c. Subscriptions Receivable, Common Stock
   d. Retained Earnings
   e. Preferred 8 Percent Stock
   f. Organization Expense
   g. Paid-in Capital in Excess of Par Value

Exercises

EXERCISE 19–1 Describe the transactions recorded in the following accounts of Perez Company:

 **LO** 3,4

PRACTICE EXERCISE 1

Cash			
(1)	320,000	(2)	2,500

Common Stock			
		(1)	320,000
		(2)	1,500

Organization Expense	
(2)	4,000

EXERCISE 19–2 Hall Corporation is authorized to issue 60,000 shares of $65 par-value common stock. Record the following transactions in general journal form:

 **LO** 4

PRACTICE EXERCISE 1

Feb. 10 Sold 10,500 shares of common stock at $66 per share; received cash.

27 Issued 3,000 shares of common stock in exchange for land with a fair market value of $92,000 and a building with a fair market value of $108,750.

Mar. 3 Sold 4,800 shares of common stock at $66.50 per share; received cash.

EXERCISE 19–3 On July 2, Young Corporation issued for cash 18,000 shares of no-par value common stock (with a stated value of $14 per share) at $18. On July 17, it issued for cash 1,000 shares of $80-par preferred 10 percent stock at $82.

 **LO** 4,5

PRACTICE EXERCISES 1,2

a. Write the entries in general journal form for July 2 and July 17.
b. What is the total amount invested by all stockholders as of July 17?

EXERCISE 19–4 Allen Corporation was organized on April 8 of this year. The corporation was authorized to issue 900 shares of cumulative preferred 9 percent stock, $100 par value, and 9,000 shares of common stock, $35 par value. Record in general journal form the following transactions, completed during the firm's first year of operations:

 **LO** 4

PRACTICE EXERCISE 1

Apr. 8 Sold 3,200 shares of common stock at par for cash.

8 Issued 90 shares of common stock to an attorney in return for legal services pertaining to incorporation. The stock is selling at par.

May 7 Sold 500 shares of preferred stock at $109; received cash.

Aug. 12 Issued 3,000 shares of common stock in exchange for land with a fair market value of $105,000.

EXERCISE 19–5 Sanchez Tours, Inc., is authorized to issue 260,000 shares of no-par value common stock, $8 stated value. Record the following transactions in general journal form:

 **LO** 5

PRACTICE EXERCISE 2

May 23 Sold 10,000 shares of common stock at $11 per share for cash.

June 19 Sold 15,000 shares of common stock at $10 per share for cash.

PRACTICE EXERCISE 3

EXERCISE 19–6 Wright Bakery has authorized capital consisting of 25,000 shares of cumulative preferred 9 percent stock, $100 par value, and 25,000 shares of common stock, $30 par value. Record the following transactions in general journal form:

a. Received subscriptions to 12,000 shares of common stock at $33 per share, with a down payment of 50 percent of the subscription price.
b. Received 30 percent of the subscription price from all subscribers.
c. Received 20 percent of the subscription price from all subscribers and issued the stock certificates.

PRACTICE EXERCISES 2,3

EXERCISE 19–7 Describe the transactions recorded in the following ledger accounts of King Corporation:

	Cash		
	+	–	
(a)	25,000		
(c)	34,500		
(d)	25,500		

	Common Stock		
	–	+	
		(a)	22,000
		(e)	45,000

	Subscriptions Receivable, Common Stock		
	+	–	
(b)	60,000	(c)	34,500
		(d)	25,500

	Common Stock Subscribed		
	–	+	
(e)	45,000	(b)	45,000

	Paid-in Capital in Excess of Stated Value		
	–	+	
		(a)	3,000
		(b)	15,000

PRACTICE EXERCISE 4

EXERCISE 19–8 Scott's Deli, Inc., has a charter authorizing it to issue 3,000 shares of $50 par-value preferred 8 percent stock and 12,000 shares of no-par value common stock (stated value $30). The following account balances are from the Balance Sheet columns of the work sheet:

Retained Earnings (debit balance)	$ 86,700
Common Stock Subscribed (2,500 shares)	75,000
Common Stock	150,000
Preferred 8 Percent Stock	60,000
Paid-in Capital in Excess of Stated Value	37,500

Prepare the Stockholders' Equity section of the balance sheet.

Problem Set A

For additional help, see the demonstration problem at the beginning of each chapter in your Working Papers.

PROBLEM 19–1A Three people—Baker, Adams, and Nelson—organized Dog-Eared Book Shoppe, Inc. The charter of this corporation authorizes capital consisting of the following:

a. 2,600 shares of preferred 9 percent stock, $50 par value
b. 25,000 shares of common stock, $15 par value

During its first year of operations, Dog-Eared Book Shoppe, Inc., completed the following transactions that affected stockholders' equity:

June 1 Issued to Baker 4,000 shares of common stock, at par, for cash.

2 Bought equipment from Adams for $45,000. Adams accepted 3,000 shares of common stock in exchange for the equipment.

2 Bought land and a building from Nelson. The fair market value of the land was $20,000 and of the building, $60,000. There is an outstanding mortgage on the property of $46,250, held by Western Savings Bank. The corporation assumed responsibility for paying the mortgage. Nelson accepted 2,250 shares of common stock at par for her equity.

5 Paid an attorney $4,800 for reimbursement of state fees and for performing services related to incorporation.

7 Issued 150 shares of common stock to Baker for organizational services. The stock is selling at par.

July 7 Issued 675 shares of preferred 9 percent stock at $53 per share to investors for cash.

Aug. 3 Issued 425 shares of preferred 9 percent stock at $54 per share to investors for cash.

Required
1. Record the transactions in general journal form on page 1.
2. Post the entries to the following accounts: Preferred 9 Percent Stock, Paid-in Capital in Excess of Par Value, and Common Stock.
3. Prepare the Stockholders' Equity section of the balance sheet as of December 31, the end of the first year of operations. Net income for the year was $56,000, and no dividends were declared during the year. As a result, Retained Earnings has a credit balance of $56,000.

Check Figure
August 3, Credit to Preferred 9 Percent Stock, $21,250

PROBLEM 19–2A Green Caterers, Inc., was organized on May 4 of this year and has a charter that stipulates the following authorized capital:

a. 15,000 shares of preferred 9 percent stock, $15 par value
b. 65,000 shares of common stock, $5 par value

Green Caterers, Inc., completed the following transactions during its first year of operations:

May 8 Received subscriptions to 24,000 shares of common stock at $25 per share; collected 65 percent of the subscription price.

June 7 Subscribers to 24,000 shares of common stock paid an additional 20 percent of the subscription price.

July 6 Subscribers to 24,000 shares of common stock paid an additional 15 percent of the subscription price. Green Caterers, Inc., issued the 24,000 shares of stock.

Required
Record the transactions in general journal form.

Check Figure
June 7, Debit to Cash, $120,000

4,5,6

GL

PROBLEM 19–3A Clean Today, Inc., was organized on October 1 of this year, with a charter providing for authorized capital as follows:

a. 8,000 shares of preferred 7 percent stock, $50 par value
b. 100,000 shares of no-par value common stock, $10 stated value

During the first year of operations, Clean Today, Inc., completed the following transactions:

Oct. 1   Received subscriptions to 12,200 shares of common stock at $12 per share, collecting 30 percent of the subscription price.

3   Bought equipment from Carter, one of the promoters, for $65,000. In return for the equipment, Carter accepted 5,000 shares of common stock.

12   Subscribers to 12,200 shares of common stock paid an additional 30 percent of the subscription price.

14   Issued 500 shares of common stock to Carter at $10.75 per share in return for promotional services valued at $5,375.

25   Paid an attorney $4,865 for reimbursement of state fees and for performing services needed for incorporating the firm.

29   Subscribers to 12,200 shares of common stock paid the remaining 40 percent of the subscription price; Clean Today, Inc., then issued the stock.

Nov. 4   Received subscriptions to 8,000 shares of common stock at $16 per share, collecting 55 percent of the subscription price.

30   Subscribers to 8,000 shares of common stock paid the remaining 45 percent of the subscription price; Clean Today, Inc., then issued the stock.

Check Figure
Nov. 4, Debit to
Cash, $70,400

Required

Record the transactions in general journal form.

7 LO

PROBLEM 19–4A Monte Vista Landscape Company, Inc., has authorized capital of 3,500 shares of preferred 9 percent stock, $100 par value, and 35,000 shares of no-par value common stock, stated value $20. The following account balances are taken from the Balance Sheet columns of the work sheet for the fiscal year ended December 31 of this year. The accounts are listed in alphabetical order.

Accounts Payable	$589,723
Accounts Receivable	718,347
Accumulated Depreciation, Building	82,314
Accumulated Depreciation, Equipment	133,814
Allowance for Doubtful Accounts	22,705
Building	403,920
Cash	91,657
Common Stock	367,200
Common Stock Subscribed	91,800
Equipment	295,137
Land	104,040
Merchandise Inventory	491,314
Mortgage Payable (long-term liability)	140,760
Notes Payable	55,692
Paid-in Capital in Excess of Par Value	6,120
Paid-in Capital in Excess of Stated Value	114,750
Patents	21,787

Preferred 9 Percent Stock	$253,900
Preferred 9 Percent Stock Subscribed	52,000
Retained Earnings (credit balance)	284,580
Subscriptions Receivable, Common Stock	49,572
Subscriptions Receivable, Preferred 9 Percent Stock	19,584

Required

Check Figure
Total Liabilities and Stockholders' Equity, $1,956,525

1. Determine the number of shares of preferred 9 percent stock subscribed and issued.
2. Determine the number of shares of common stock subscribed and issued.
3. Prepare a classified balance sheet.

Problem Set B

For additional help, see the demonstration problem at the beginning of each chapter in your Working Papers.

PROBLEM 19–1B Three people—Hill, Ramirez, and Campbell—organized A1 Rentals, Inc., with a charter providing for the following authorized capital:

 LO 4,7

a. 10,000 shares of preferred 9 percent stock, $40 par value
b. 65,000 shares of common stock, $8 par value

During its first year of operations, A1 Rentals, Inc., completed the following transactions that affected stockholders' equity:

July	5	Issued to Hill 4,500 shares of common stock, at par, for cash.
	6	Paid an attorney $4,250 for performing services related to incorporation as well as for reimbursement of state fees.
	6	Bought equipment from Campbell for $27,880. Campbell accepted 3,485 shares of common stock in exchange for the equipment.
	6	Bought land and a building from Ramirez. The fair market value of the land was $148,000 and of the building, $62,600. There is an outstanding mortgage on the property of $166,200, held by Apple Savings Bank. The corporation assumed responsibility for paying the mortgage. Ramirez accepted 5,550 shares of common stock at par for his equity.
	8	Issued 400 shares of common stock to Hill for organizational services. The stock is selling at par.
Aug.	5	Issued 475 shares of preferred 9 percent stock at $54 per share to investors for cash.
	31	Issued 600 shares of preferred 9 percent stock at $53 per share to investors for cash.

Required

Check Figure
Total Stockholders' Equity, $221,025

1. Record the transactions in general journal form on page 1.
2. Post the entries to the following accounts: Preferred 9 Percent Stock, Paid-in Capital in Excess of Par Value, and Common Stock.
3. Prepare the Stockholders' Equity section of the balance sheet as of December 31, the end of the first year of operations. Net income for the year was $52,095, and no dividends were declared during the year. As a result, Retained Earnings has a credit balance of $52,095.

4,6 LO

PROBLEM 19–2B Horse Productions, Inc., was organized on June 4 of this year and has a charter that stipulates the following authorized capital:

a. 10,000 shares of preferred 9 percent stock, $60 par value
b. 35,000 shares of common stock, $22 par value

During the first year of its operations, Horse Productions, Inc., completed the following transactions:

June 15 Received subscriptions to 8,000 shares of common stock at $22 per share; collected 60 percent of the subscription price.

Aug. 15 Subscribers to 8,000 shares of common stock paid an additional 25 percent of the subscription price.

Sept. 17 Subscribers to 8,000 shares of common stock paid an additional 15 percent of the subscription price. Horse Productions, Inc., issued the 8,000 shares of stock.

Check Figure
Aug. 15, Debit to
Cash, $44,000

Required
Record the transactions in general journal form.

4,5,6 LO

PROBLEM 19–3B Roberts Corporation was organized on April 1 of this year, with a charter providing for the following authorized capital:

a. 4,000 shares of preferred 10 percent stock, $50 par value
b. 25,000 shares of no-par value common stock, $25 stated value

During the first year of operations, Roberts Corporation completed the following transactions:

Apr. 2 Bought land from Roberts for $142,900. Roberts accepted 5,400 shares of common stock for the land.

4 Received subscriptions to 3,500 shares of common stock at $28 per share, collecting 45 percent of the subscription price.

6 Issued 150 shares of common stock to Roberts at $26 per share in return for organizational services.

10 Subscribers to 3,500 shares of common stock paid an additional 35 percent of the subscription price.

13 Paid an attorney $2,840 for performing services and for reimbursement of state fees needed for incorporating the firm.

14 Received subscriptions to 950 shares of preferred 10 percent stock at $52 per share, collecting 20 percent of the subscription price.

21 Subscribers to 3,500 shares of common stock paid the remaining 20 percent of the subscription price; Roberts Corporation then issued the stock.

May 9 Received subscriptions to 4,000 shares of common stock at $28 per share, collecting 60 percent of the subscription price.

17 Subscribers to 950 shares of preferred 10 percent stock paid an additional 50 percent of the subscription price.

23 Sold 350 shares of preferred 10 percent stock at $52 per share for cash.

Check Figure
May 23, Debit to
Cash, $18,200

Required
Record the transactions in general journal form.

PROBLEM 19–4B Mitchell Farms, Inc., has authorized capital of 10,000 shares of preferred 5 percent stock, $50 par value, and 50,000 shares of common stock, par value $5. The following account balances are taken from the Balance Sheet columns of the work sheet for the fiscal year ended December 31 of this year. The accounts are listed in alphabetical order.

Accounts Payable	$ 82,786
Accounts Receivable	212,554
Accumulated Depreciation, Building	62,024
Accumulated Depreciation, Equipment	94,966
Allowance for Doubtful Accounts	11,117
Building	261,120
Cash	163,304
Common Stock	144,800
Common Stock Subscribed	20,800
Equipment	107,680
Land	81,200
Merchandise Inventory	98,554
Mortgage Payable (long-term liability)	85,680
Notes Payable	33,456
Paid-in Capital in Excess of Par Value, Preferred Stock	3,672
Paid-in Capital in Excess of Par Value, Common Stock	51,400
Patents	13,097
Preferred 5 Percent Stock	183,200
Preferred 5 Percent Stock Subscribed	20,400
Retained Earnings (credit balance)	171,360
Subscriptions Receivable, Common Stock	17,748
Subscriptions Receivable, Preferred 5 Percent Stock	10,404

Required

1. Determine the number of shares of preferred 5 percent stock subscribed and issued.
2. Determine the number of shares of common stock subscribed and issued.
3. Prepare a classified balance sheet.

Check Figure

Total Liabilities and Stockholders' Equity, $797,554

ACTIVITIES

INTERNET LINKS TO ACCOUNTING

Now that you have learned about the issuance of stock, let's take a look at the General Electric Company. You should be able to use what you have learned and the information provided in a company's annual report to find the answers to certain questions regarding the company's capital stock. Look at GE's 2008 Annual Report (or 10-K) by going to **www.ge.com/ar2008/index.html.** Click on Downloads and then on Audited Financial Statements. The statement of financial position (balance sheet) information is on page 52.

1. What are the dollar amount of common stock and the number of common shares outstanding as reported on the statement of financial position as of December 31, 2008? (*Hint:* Look at the statement of financial position.)
2. Does GE report any treasury stock? If so, what is the value of treasury stock as of December 31, 2008?
3. What is the value of GE's Retained Earnings as of December 31, 2008?

CONSIDER AND COMMUNICATE

Shirley, a friend of yours, is trying to understand the difference between common stock and preferred stock. Write a short memo to Shirley answering her questions. Make sure to review the privileges and rights that each shareholder has.

WHAT'S WRONG WITH THIS PICTURE?

After having been a partner in a partnership for five years, you decided to leave the partnership and form a corporation. After completing the necessary organization steps and forming a board of directors, you sold stock to raise the necessary capital. You have retained control of 51 percent of the stock. One day, one of your former partners (who owns 20 percent of the stock in your corporation) sends you a bill for $10,000 for an advertising campaign. He hired the public relations company to increase the visibility of the corporation in which he is a stockholder. Are you going to pay the $10,000 bill your former partner incurred? Why or why not?

CRITICAL THINKING

You asked your new assistant, Jeffrey, to prepare the Stockholders' Equity section of the balance sheet. Following is a copy of the result. You know that the Total Liabilities amount is correct and that Total Stockholder's Equity should be $1,170,350. Check your assistant's work and comment on its accuracy and logic. Prepare a corrected Stockholders' Equity section.

Total Liabilities			$ 786,175
Stockholders' Equity			
Paid-in Capital:			
Preferred 9 Percent Stock, $100 par (3,500 shares authorized, 2,539 shares issued)	$ 603,900		
Preferred 9 Percent Stock Subscribed (520 shares)	52,000		
Paid-in Capital in Excess of Par Value	6,120	$ 662,020	
Common Stock, no-par, stated value $20 per share (35,000 shares authorized, 18,360 shares issued)	$1,067,200		
Common Stock Subscribed (4,590 shares)	91,800		
Paid-in Capital in Excess of Stated Value	114,750	1,273,750	
Total Paid-in Capital		$1,935,770	
Retained Earnings		284,580	
Total Stockholders' Equity			1,651,190
Total Liabilities and Stockholders' Equity			$2,437,365

Corporate Taxes, Retained Earnings, and Dividends

SPRINKLES CUPCAKES, Beverly Hills, California

Sprinkles Cupcakes, Inc., opened its doors in April 2005 in Beverly Hills, California. The corporation was co-founded by husband-and-wife team Charles and Candace Nelson. Using high-quality ingredients, such as pure Madagascar Bourbon vanilla, fresh bananas and carrots, rich chocolate sprinkles from France, and Belgian chocolate, Sprinkles Cupcakes has strived to create the very best cupcake. Each cupcake is priced at $3.25, and the Beverly Hills location has sold up to 3,000 cupcakes in a day.

What Sprinkles Cupcakes is doing must be working! It has been featured on numerous television shows, including The *Oprah Winfrey Show* and *Good Morning America*, and has expanded to six nationwide locations.

Sprinkles Cupcakes is working hard to become a great American brand. Charles and Candace Nelson have a 20-year business plan that addresses some of the items we will be discussing in this chapter, such as corporate income taxes, retained earnings, and payment of dividends.

LEARNING OBJECTIVES

After you have completed this chapter, you will be able to do the following:

1 Calculate corporate income tax.

2 Journalize entries for corporate income taxes.

3 Journalize closing entries for a corporation.

4 Journalize entries for the appropriation of Retained Earnings.

5 Journalize entries for the declaration and payment of cash dividends.

6 Calculate dividends on cumulative preferred stock.

7 Journalize entries for the declaration and issuance of stock dividends.

8 Complete a corporate statement of retained earnings and a balance sheet, including the following types of accounts: Appropriated Retained Earnings, Stock Dividend Distributable, Dividends Payable, and Income Tax Payable.

9 Describe guidelines for accounting reports.

ACCOUNTING LANGUAGE

Appropriation of Retained Earnings (p. 799)

Cash dividend (p. 801)

Conservatism (p. 809)

Date of declaration (p. 802)

Date of payment (p. 802)

Date of record (p. 802)

Dividends in arrears (p. 803)

Estimated tax payments (p. 795)

Full disclosure (p. 809)

Materiality (p. 809)

Minute book (p. 807)

Stock dividend (p. 804)

Stock split (p. 806)

Unappropriated Retained Earnings (p. 801)

In the previous chapter, you learned the definition of a corporation and various journal entries for the issuance of corporate stock. In this chapter, we now turn our attention to the year-to-year entries for taxes, dividends, and retained earnings.

PROCEDURE FOR RECORDING AND PAYING INCOME TAXES

Corporate net income is determined very much like that of sole proprietorships and partnerships.

$$\text{Revenue} - \text{Expenses} = \text{Net Income}$$

You can compare most of the revenue and expense accounts of a corporation to those of sole proprietorships and partnerships and they would be very similar. The net income of a sole proprietorship and the distributive shares of net income of a partnership are taxable as part of each owner's personal income. Since the corporation is a separate legal entity, however, it must pay income taxes in its own name. Corporations are subject to federal income taxes, and many states and cities also impose an income tax on them. We will talk about only the income tax levied by the federal government, but the same basic principles apply to state and city income taxes, if applicable.

Corporate Income Tax Rates

Corporations are subject to a graduated-rate structure (the higher the income, the higher the tax rate), as demonstrated in Figure 1.

1 LEARNING OBJECTIVE

Calculate corporate income tax.

Taxable Income		The Tax Is:	
Over:	But not over:		Of the amount over:
$ 0	$ 50,000	15%	$ 0
50,000	75,000	$ 7,500 + 25%	50,000
75,000	100,000	13,750 + 34%	75,000
100,000	335,000	22,250 + 39%	100,000
335,000	10,000,000	113,900 + 34%	335,000
10,000,000	15,000,000	3,400,000 + 35%	10,000,000
15,000,000	18,333,333	5,150,000 + 38%	15,000,000
18,333,333	….	35%	0

FIGURE 1

Corporate tax rates

Following are three examples.

Example 1: Taxable Income of $79,000
$13,750 + [0.34 × ($79,000 − $75,000)] $ 15,110

Example 2: Taxable Income of $200,000
$22,250 + [0.39 × ($200,000 − $100,000)] $ 61,250

Example 3: Taxable Income of $10,800,000
$3,400,000 + [0.35 × ($10,800,000 − $10,000,000)] $3,680,000

Personal service corporations, such as attorneys, accountants, doctors, and consultants, are taxed at a flat rate of 35 percent. This is one reason why a professional group may be structured as a limited liability partnership or an S corporation rather than as a corporation.

Income Tax Entries for a Corporation

2 LEARNING OBJECTIVE

Journalize entries for corporate income taxes.

Most corporations are required to estimate in advance the amount of their federal income taxes for the upcoming fiscal year. The corporation then pays the estimated amount in four quarterly installments during the year, called **estimated tax payments**.

Let's assume that Red Velvet Cupcakes, Inc., estimates that its federal income tax for the forthcoming fiscal year will be $30,830. The firm's accountant records four quarterly payments as:

Date		Description	Post. Ref.	Debit	Credit
Year 1					
Apr.	15	Income Tax Expense		7 7 0 7 50	
		Cash			7 7 0 7 50
		Paid first quarterly			
		installment of estimated			
		federal income tax for the			
		year (one-fourth of $30,830).			

The Income Tax Expense account is handled like any other expense account, except that the accountant usually makes a separate entry closing Income Tax Expense into Income Summary.

At the end of the fiscal year, after the corporation determines the exact amount of its income, it calculates how much income tax it owes.

Assume that Red Velvet Cupcakes, Inc., overpaid its federal income taxes by $5,450, or the amount of income tax the corporation has paid in advance exceeds its tax liability for the year. The accountant records the following entry:

Date		Description	Post. Ref.	Debit	Credit
Year 1					
Dec.	31	Prepaid Income Tax		5 4 5 0 00	
		Income Tax Expense			5 4 5 0 00
		Overpayment of federal			
		income tax for the year.			

Usually, however, the amount of income tax paid in advance is less than the amount of the tax liability. Assume instead that Red Velvet Cupcakes's accountant determines that the taxable income of the corporation for the year was $128,000 (revenues of $996,000 and expenses of $868,000). The accountant determines that the corporation now owes $33,170 in income taxes and has underpaid its income tax liability by $2,340 ($33,170 − $30,830). In this case, the accountant would record the following adjusting entry:

Date		Description	Post. Ref.	Debit	Credit
Year 1					
Dec.	31	Income Tax Expense		2 3 4 0 00	
		Income Tax Payable			2 3 4 0 00
		Remaining federal income			
		tax due for the year.			

The corporation is required to make full payment of its final tax with its income tax return, which would be recorded as:

Date		Description	Post. Ref.	Debit	Credit
Year 2					
Mar.	15	Income Tax Payable		2 3 4 0 00	
		Cash			2 3 4 0 00
		Paid tax liability for previous			
		year.			

FYI

The tax return is due two-and-one-half months after the close of the fiscal year. For corporations whose year-end is December 31, the tax return is due on March 15.

Notice that the corporation paid a total tax of $33,170.

First quarterly installment of estimated federal income tax	$ 7,707.50
Second quarterly installment of estimated federal income tax	7,707.50
Third quarterly installment of estimated federal income tax	7,707.50
Fourth quarterly installment of estimated federal income tax	7,707.50
Additional tax owed	2,340.00
Total tax	$33,170.00

Income Statement Net Income Versus Taxable Income

In our example, we assumed that the accountant for Red Velvet Cupcakes, Inc., determined the income tax for the year by multiplying the corporation's income before income taxes for the year (as shown on the income statement) by the tax rate. The accountant maintained that the corporation's income before income tax was its taxable income. In real life, things aren't quite that simple. The net income shown on the income statement may differ considerably from the income reported for tax purposes. Here are some of the reasons why:

1. The depreciation method used for income statement purposes may differ from the method used for tax purposes. For example, the firm might use the straight-line method of depreciation for its income statement, but for tax purposes the business must use such IRS-prescribed methods as MACRS.

2. Some items listed on the income statement, such as interest on state and municipal bonds, are not taxable. Some expenses listed on the income statement, such as 50 percent of meals and entertainment expenses, club dues, penalties, and political contributions, are not deductible for tax purposes.

3. A corporation may capitalize certain types of expenditures as assets on its financial statements, and these same expenditures may be listed on the tax return as expenses. For example, a company would include prepaid advertising on its balance sheet as an asset, whereas it may be able to deduct it as an expense on its tax return.

Financial Statements

After the corporation has completed any adjusting entries for the year, the accountant can now prepare the financial statements. The financial statements for a corporation are similar to those of a sole proprietorship. The main financial statements for a corporation and their order of presentation are as follows:

1. Income statement
2. Statement of retained earnings (counterpart in most respects to the statement of owner's equity)
3. Balance sheet

CLOSING ENTRIES FOR A CORPORATION

At the end of the corporation's fiscal year and after the financial statements have been prepared, the accountant will record the closing entries. Remember that Red Velvet Cupcakes, Inc., had revenues of $996,000 and expenses of $868,000. In this example, to save time, "Revenues" represents all temporary-equity accounts having a credit balance and "Expenses" represents all temporary-equity accounts having a debit balance. The accountant will record the closing entries as follows:

3 LEARNING OBJECTIVE

Journalize closing entries for a corporation.

Date		Description	Post. Ref.	Debit	Credit
Year 1		Closing Entries			
Dec.	31	Revenues		996 0 0 0 00	
		Income Summary			996 0 0 0 00
	31	Income Summary		868 0 0 0 00	
		Expenses			868 0 0 0 00

(continued)

Dec.	31	Income Summary	33	1	7	0	00					
		Income Tax Expense						33	1	7	0	00
	31	Income Summary	94	8	3	0	00					
		Retained Earnings						94	8	3	0	00

Let's summarize the steps for journalizing the closing entries of a corporation:

STEP 1. Close revenue accounts into Income Summary.

STEP 2. Close expense accounts into Income Summary.

STEP 3. Close Income Tax Expense into Income Summary by the amount of the actual income tax for the year.

STEP 4. Close Income Summary into Retained Earnings by the amount of the net income (Revenues – Expenses – Income Tax Expense).

The Retained Earnings account is classified as a stockholders' equity account. It is a permanent or real account, as opposed to a temporary-equity or nominal account. After the accountant has finished posting to the Retained Earnings account, the account balance represents accumulated earnings if it is a credit balance. If the Retained Earnings account has a debit balance, it represents a deficit. In T account form, the entries for the year are as follows:

Cash

+	−	
	Apr. 15	7,707.50
	June 15	7,707.50
	Sept. 15	7,707.50
	Dec. 15	7,707.50

Income Tax Expense

	+		−	
Apr. 15	7,707.50	Dec. 31 Clos.	33,170.00
June 15	7,707.50		
Sept. 15	7,707.50		
Dec. 15	7,707.50		
Dec. 31 Adj.	2,340.00		

Revenues

−		+	
Dec. 31 Clos.	996,000	Bal.	996,000

Expenses

	+	−	
Bal.	868,000	Dec. 31 Clos.	868,000

Income Tax Payable

−	+	
	Dec. 31 Adj.	2,340.00

Income Summary

Dec. 31 (Exp.)	868,000	Dec. 31 (Rev.)	996,000
Dec. 31 (Inc. Tax)	33,170		
Dec. 31 Clos.	94,830		

Retained Earnings

−	+	
	Dec. 31	94,830

One disadvantage of the regular corporate form is double taxation. Not only do the owners and employees pay income taxes based on their income, but the corporation itself has to pay taxes on its income as though it were a person. And like a person, the percentage of taxes is based on how much income it earns. If the corporation is a limited liability corporation or an S corporation, there is no double taxation. The taxable income passes through to the shareholders or members, so there is only one level of taxation.

Although income taxes are considered a necessary expense of conducting business, most companies show income tax expense as a separate line item on the financial statements. It is common practice to make a separate entry to close Income Tax Expense into Income Summary rather than including the amount for income tax with the total amounts for all the other expenses. This procedure makes the amount of taxable income more evident from a quick analysis of Income Summary. Notice in the Income Summary T account that the balance of the account prior to transferring the Income Tax Expense balance is $128,000 ($996,000 − $868,000), the taxable income. If the amount of income tax were closed into Income Summary with all the other expenses, the amount of taxable income would not be as obvious.

> **Remember**
>
> When recording closing entries for corporations, it is common practice to make a separate entry for income tax expense.

REASONS FOR APPROPRIATING RETAINED EARNINGS

Since a corporation declares dividends out of its Retained Earnings, the *amount* of dividends is necessarily limited by the amount of Retained Earnings. However, rather than using the entire balance of Retained Earnings for cash or stock dividends, the board of directors may wish to earmark part of Retained Earnings for some specific purpose.

Such a restriction constitutes an **appropriation of Retained Earnings**. Let's say that the directors decide to provide for future expansion. The board passes a resolution, which is recorded in the minutes of a meeting, restricting or appropriating a certain amount of Retained Earnings for future expansion.

For example, Red Velvet Cupcakes, Inc., plans to erect a new store building. To finance the project, it decides to restrict Retained Earnings for a total amount of

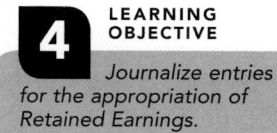

4 **LEARNING OBJECTIVE**

Journalize entries for the appropriation of Retained Earnings.

$300,000 at the rate of $50,000 per year for six years. On February 5, the board of directors approves the appropriation of Retained Earnings and records the approval in the minutes of the meeting. The minutes of the meeting are the source document for the accounting entry. The accountant makes the first entry on the day of approval, February 5, and then makes any subsequent entries to appropriate Retained Earnings at the end of each year, after the closing entries.

Date		Description	Post. Ref.	Debit	Credit
Year 2					
Feb.	5	Retained Earnings		50 0 0 0 00	
		Retained Earnings Appropriated			
		for Building			50 0 0 0 00
		To appropriate Retained			
		Earnings, as ordered by the			
		board of directors in the			
		meeting of February 5.			

This appropriation of Retained Earnings does *not* represent a separate cash fund of $50,000. Consider cash dividends for a moment. If we think of the Retained Earnings account as a reservoir from which cash dividends are declared, then this reservoir has been reduced by $50,000. **If the corporation does not declare and pay out these dividends, then the firm is preserving its net assets (*assets minus liabilities*), particularly cash.** Of course, the $50,000 would not necessarily be in the form of cash. Perhaps the company can earn a higher return by putting the money into merchandise inventory or paying off its debts.

At the end of the six-year period, although the corporation does *not* have an actual $300,000 fund of cash, there is an additional $300,000 accumulated in net assets. The corporation can now formulate plans to convert the $300,000 increase in net assets into cash in order to put a down payment on the building.

When the objective—buying or erecting the building—has been accomplished, the corporation no longer needs to restrict Retained Earnings. The accountant may then reverse the six previous entries as follows:

Date		Description	Post. Ref.	Debit	Credit
Year 7					
Mar.	18	Retained Earnings Appropriated			
		for Building		300 0 0 0 00	
		Retained Earnings			300 0 0 0 00
		To return to Retained Earnings the			
		balance in the Retained Earnings			
		Appropriated for Building account, as			
		ordered by the board of directors			
		in the meeting of March 18.			

Other examples of appropriated Retained Earnings accounts include:

- Retained Earnings Appropriated for Plant Expansion (no specific objective stated)
- Retained Earnings Appropriated for Bonded Indebtedness (an obligation imposed by contract)
- Retained Earnings Appropriated for Self-Insurance (workers' compensation or medical insurance for employees)
- Retained Earnings Appropriated for Inventory Losses (in the event of a price drop)
- Retained Earnings Appropriated for Contingencies (in the event of a "rainy day")

Each appropriated Retained Earnings is labeled "Retained Earnings Appropriated for _____." Therefore, the account Retained Earnings represents **unappropriated Retained Earnings**. Later in the chapter, we'll show the placement of these accounts as they appear in the statement of retained earnings.

DECLARATION AND PAYMENT OF A DIVIDEND

A dividend is a distribution—of cash or other assets or shares of stock—that a corporation makes to its stockholders. Dividends are allocated to persons who own stock according to the number of shares they own and according to whether the stock is preferred or common. We discuss two types of dividends: cash dividends and stock dividends. Both cash dividends and stock dividends reduce Retained Earnings.

Cash Dividends

A **cash dividend** is the most common form of dividend. It ordinarily represents a share of the current earnings paid to stockholders as a reward for their investment. The board of directors declares dividends, generally paying up to a certain percentage of the firm's net income. The cash dividend is expressed as a specific amount per share—for example, $1.12 per share. A stockholder who owns 100 shares is thus entitled to $112.

5 LEARNING OBJECTIVE

Journalize entries for the declaration and issuance of cash dividends.

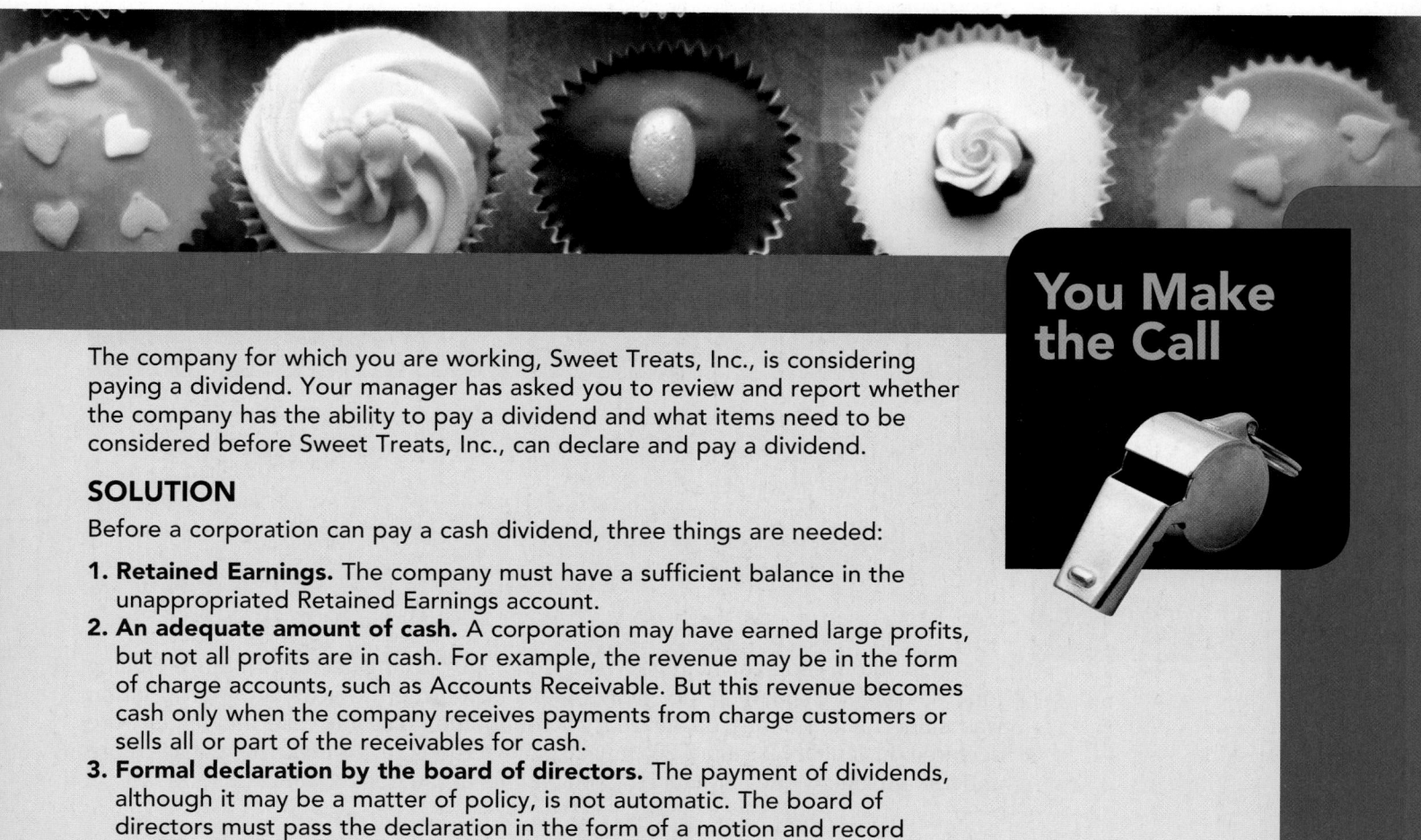

You Make the Call

The company for which you are working, Sweet Treats, Inc., is considering paying a dividend. Your manager has asked you to review and report whether the company has the ability to pay a dividend and what items need to be considered before Sweet Treats, Inc., can declare and pay a dividend.

SOLUTION

Before a corporation can pay a cash dividend, three things are needed:

1. **Retained Earnings.** The company must have a sufficient balance in the unappropriated Retained Earnings account.
2. **An adequate amount of cash.** A corporation may have earned large profits, but not all profits are in cash. For example, the revenue may be in the form of charge accounts, such as Accounts Receivable. But this revenue becomes cash only when the company receives payments from charge customers or sells all or part of the receivables for cash.
3. **Formal declaration by the board of directors.** The payment of dividends, although it may be a matter of policy, is not automatic. The board of directors must pass the declaration in the form of a motion and record it in the minutes—the source document for the accounting entry.

Dividend Dates

Three significant dates are involved in the declaration and payment of a dividend:

1. **Date of declaration** The date on which the board of directors votes to declare dividends. The entry recorded as of this date debits Retained Earnings and credits Dividends Payable. (Dividends Payable is classified as a current liability.)

2. **Date of record** The date as of which the ownership of shares is set. This date determines a person's eligibility for dividends and ordinarily is about three weeks after the date of declaration. No accounting entry is made; a memo entry is made in the minutes or sometimes in the general journal.

3. **Date of payment** The date on which payment is made; on this date, the accountant debits the amount to Dividends Payable and credits it to Cash.

For example, on January 20, the board of directors of Red Velvet Cupcakes, Inc., declares a quarterly cash dividend of $0.91 per share on 5,000 shares, or $4,550 (5,000 shares × $0.91 = $4,550) to stockholders of record as of February 11, payable on February 20. The entries are as follows:

Date		Description	Post. Ref.	Debit	Credit
Year 2					
Jan.	20	Retained Earnings		4 5 5 0 00	
		Dividends Payable			4 5 5 0 00
		To record the declaration of			
		a quarterly cash dividend			
		on common stock at the rate			
		of $0.91 per share to			
		stockholders of record as			
		of February 11, payable on			
		February 20, as ordered by			
		the board of directors in			
		the meeting of January 20.			

Date		Description	Post. Ref.	Debit	Credit
Year 2					
Feb.	20	Dividends Payable		4 5 5 0 00	
		Cash			4 5 5 0 00
		Payment of quarterly dividend			
		declared on January 20 to			
		stockholders of record as			
		of February 11.			

Let's take a moment to review the Retained Earnings account before closing for Red Velvet Cupcakes, Inc. Remember that during the year, an appropriation was made for a building on February 5. In addition, regular cash dividends were declared on January 20, April 20, July 20, and October 20. To make the entries more understandable, we have included explanations in the Item column:

ACCOUNT Retained Earnings   **ACCOUNT NO. 316**

Date		Item	Post. Ref.	Debit	Credit	Balance Debit	Balance Credit
Year 1							
Dec.	31	Net income			94 8 3 0 00		94 8 3 0 00
Year 2							
Jan.	20	Cash dividend		4 5 5 0 00			90 2 8 0 00
Feb.	5	Appropriation		50 0 0 0 00			40 2 8 0 00
Apr.	20	Cash dividend		4 5 5 0 00			35 7 3 0 00
July	20	Cash dividend		4 5 5 0 00			31 1 8 0 00
Oct.	20	Cash dividend		4 5 5 0 00			26 6 3 0 00

Notice that both the cash dividends and the appropriation reduce Retained Earnings. The ending balance of $26,630 in the Retained Earnings account will appear in the Trial Balance columns of a work sheet (if used) and on the statement of retained earnings for the year ended December 31, Year 2.

Cash Dividends on Cumulative Preferred Stock

In Chapter 19, you learned that preferred stock can be either cumulative preferred stock or noncumulative preferred stock. Remember, cumulative preferred stock accrues dividends, and in noncumulative preferred stock, dividends do not accumulate. In other words, if the corporation does not pay a dividend, cumulative preferred stockholders have a dividend preference and are entitled to receive any dividends not paid in the past and the current dividend amount due before the corporation can pay any dividends to common stockholders. Any dividends not paid in the past are called **dividends in arrears**. Dividends in arrears are not reported on any financial statement and do not represent liabilities. This is because dividends are not recorded as liabilities until the board of directors declares the dividends.

Let's look at an example. Suppose that Red Velvet Cupcakes, Inc., has outstanding 10,000 shares of $30 par, 8 percent cumulative preferred stock and 80,000 shares of $15 par value common stock. The corporation declares and pays dividends, as presented in Figure 2. Preferred stockholders, if paid, will receive dividends equal to $24,000 (10,000 shares × $30 par value × 0.08)

Information about each year is summarized below:

YEAR 1: The preferred stockholders were paid the full $24,000 dividend amount, while the common stockholders received the remaining dividend amount, $6,000 ($30,000 − $24,000).

YEAR 2: Since Red Velvet Cupcakes, Inc., did not pay any dividends, none of the stockholders received a dividend payment. As a result, there are dividends in arrears equal to $24,000 due to preferred stockholders the next time a dividend payment is made.

YEAR 3: Preferred stockholders received dividends in arrears of $24,000 plus the current dividend payment of $24,000, totaling $48,000. Notice that preferred

6 LEARNING OBJECTIVE

Calculate dividends on cumulative preferred stock.

		Dividends Paid		
Year	Dividends Declared	Preferred Stockholders	Common Stockholders	Dividends in Arrears
1	$ 30,000	$24,000	$ 6,000	$ 0
2	0	0	0	24,000
3	50,000	48,000	2,000	0
4	100,000	24,000	76,000	0

FIGURE 2

Declaration and payment of dividends—Red Velvet Cupcakes, Inc.

stockholders are paid out all current dividends and dividends in arrears before common stockholders receive any remaining amount. Common stockholders receive the remainder of the dividend, $2,000 ($50,000 – $48,000).

YEAR 4: Common stockholders receive the benefit of the large dividend payment this year. Preferred stockholders are paid their dividend amount of $24,000, while common stockholders receive the remainder, $76,000 ($100,000 – $24,000).

Stock Dividends

A **stock dividend** is a distribution, on a pro rata (proportional) basis, of additional shares of a company's stock to the stockholders. In other words, the dividend consists of shares of stock rather than cash. You could describe it as a dividend payable in stock. Generally, stock dividends consist of common stock distributed to holders of common stock. Stock dividends are usually issued by corporations that retain cash in order to finance future expansion.

Suppose that the board of directors of Mom's Bakery, Inc., declared a 10 percent stock dividend on October 11 of Year 3 to stockholders of record as of November 1, distributable on November 16. The ledger account for Common Stock on October 11 looks like this in T account form:

Common Stock

−	+
	Bal. 200,000
	$40 par value
	per share
	(5,000 shares)

Number of shares in the stock dividend:
10 percent of 5,000 shares = 500 shares

The current market value of the shares is $47 per share (par value $40). The entries, in general journal form, to record the stock dividend are as follows:

Date		Description	Post. Ref.	Debit	Credit
Year 3					
Oct.	11	Retained Earnings (500 shares ×			
		$47 each)		23 5 0 0 00	
		Stock Dividend Distributable			
		(500 shares × $40 each)			20 0 0 0 00
		Paid-in Capital in Excess of Par Value			3 5 0 0 00
		To record the declaration of			
		a 10 percent stock dividend			
		to stockholders of record			
		as of November 1, distributable			
		on November 16, as ordered			
		by the board of directors in			
		the meeting of October 11.			
Nov.	16	Stock Dividend Distributable		20 0 0 0 00	
		Common Stock			20 0 0 0 00
		Issuance of a stock dividend			
		(500 shares), declared on			
		October 11 to stockholders			
		of record as of November 1.			

Stock Dividend Distributable is a stockholders' equity account representing the total par value of the shares of stock to be issued. If the account is on the books at the time of the preparation of a balance sheet, the accountant lists it in the Paid-in Capital section, just below Common Stock.

As demonstrated in Figure 3, a stock dividend—unlike a cash dividend—does *not* result in a reduction of assets. It transfers amounts among the stockholders' equity accounts. The stock dividend increases the Capital Stock accounts and decreases the Retained Earnings account without making any change in the total stockholders' equity.

The stock dividend has no effect on the proportionate share of ownership held by an individual stockholder. For example, Scott James owns 500 shares of Mom's Bakery, Inc.'s stock, which represents a one-tenth share in the corporation, since the total number of shares issued was 5,000. The corporation declares a 10 percent stock dividend. As his part of this dividend, James receives 50 shares (10 percent of 500 shares). His total stock now amounts to 550 shares; the corporation's total issued stock is now at 5,500 shares. Consequently, Scott James still has a one-tenth share in the ownership (550 shares ÷ 5,500 shares).

For accounting purposes, corporations make a distinction between a stock dividend of less than 20–25 percent, called a small stock dividend, and a stock dividend of 20–25 percent or more (large stock dividend). The preceding example represented a small stock dividend (10 percent), in which the accountant debited Retained Earnings for the fair market value of the shares issued. If the stock dividend had been a large stock dividend, the accountant would have debited Retained Earnings for the par or stated value of the shares to be issued instead of for the fair market value.

Stock Dividend:

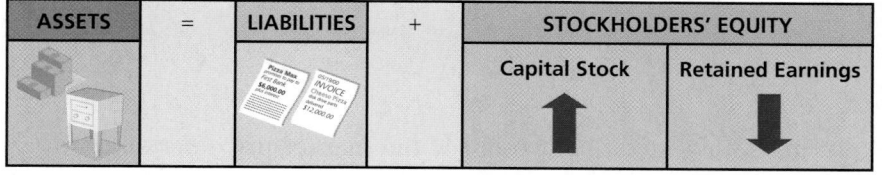

Cash Dividend:

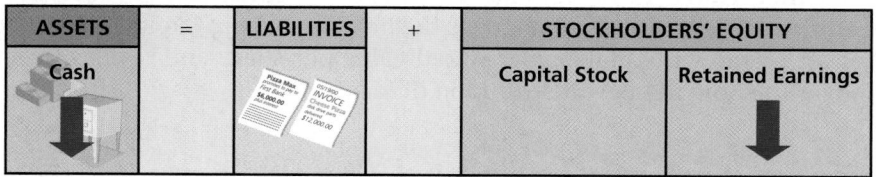

FIGURE 3

Stock dividend versus cash dividend

Reasons for Issuing Stock Dividends

Since a stockholder's proportionate share of equity in a company does not change when the company issues a stock dividend, why does a corporation bother with stock dividends? Here are a few reasons:

1. Stock dividends appease stockholders by giving them additional shares of stock. The corporation can conserve its cash, and the stockholders feel partially rewarded. They didn't get cash, but at least they got something.

2. Stock dividends tend to increase the marketability of the company's stock by increasing the number of shares outstanding and thereby decreasing the market price per share. Stock with a lower price per share is more easily sold to the public.

3. Stock dividends enable stockholders to postpone any income tax liability until they sell the shares. Stock dividends are not considered to be income to the recipients. Therefore, the recipients do not have to pay any income tax upon the receipt of stock dividends.

STOCK SPLIT

When there is a **stock split**, a corporation splits or subdivides its stock, on the basis of its par or stated value, and issues a proportionate number of additional shares. For example, a corporation with 10,000 shares of $50 par-value stock outstanding may reduce the par value to $25 and increase the number of shares to 20,000 through a 2-for-1 stock split. If you own 200 shares before the split, you will own 400 shares after it. The company may call in all the old shares and issue certificates for new ones (either in paper or electronic form) on a 2-for-1 basis, or it may issue an additional share for each old share. At the date of declaration of a stock split, the accountant does not record a journal entry, but would record a memorandum notation in the general journal as follows:

FYI

Accountants record stock splits with a memorandum entry.

Date		Description	Post. Ref.	Debit	Credit
20—					
Oct.	15	The board of directors have this day			
		ordered a 2-for-1 stock split, increasing			
		the outstanding shares from 10,000 to			
		20,000 and reducing the par value from			
		$50 to $25.			

This 2-for-1 stock split reduces the market price per share by approximately half, thereby increasing the stock's salability. Since each share now costs less, more investors are able to afford the stock.

Since there is no change in Retained Earnings, a journal entry is not required. The accountant changes the headings of the Capital Stock accounts in the ledger to show the new par or stated value per share and revises the stockholders' ledger to show the new distribution of shares.

Effect of Dividends and Stock Splits on Assets and Stockholders' Equity

Remember

A stock split does not change Retained Earnings because total paid-in capital remains the same after a split.

We have learned about several different types of dividends and stock transactions in this chapter. Let's take a moment to summarize the effect on the Assets and Stockholders' Equity sections of the balance sheet for each type of transaction.

Transaction	Assets	Paid-in Capital	Retained Earnings
Cash dividend	Decreases Cash when paid	No effect	Decreases when declared
Small stock dividend (less than 20%–25%)	No effect	Increases when declared	Decreases when declared
Stock split	No effect	No effect	No effect

Minute Book

The **minute book** is an important source document for any accounting entries involving the declaration of dividends and the appropriation of Retained Earnings. The minute book is just like the minute book of a club: It is an electronic narrative of all actions taken at official meetings of the board of directors. A corporation's minute book may also contain details relating to purchasing property and equipment, obtaining bank loans, establishing officers' compensation, and so on.

STATEMENT OF RETAINED EARNINGS AND BALANCE SHEET FOR A CORPORATION

We have discussed a number of possible situations that would affect the status of retained earnings within a given period of time. These changes are reported on a separate financial statement called a *statement of retained earnings*. Generally, this statement lists only those items that represent significant changes. For example, the statement of retained earnings for Basset Hound Bagels, Inc., (Figure 4) lists specific appropriations for property expansion and possible price declines. The statement of retained earnings for a corporation may be compared, in some respects, to a statement of owner's equity for a sole proprietorship or partnership, with the ending balances appearing in the stockholders' or owners' equity section of a balance sheet.

To better visualize the relationship of the statement of retained earnings to the balance sheet, Figure 5 presents the balance sheet for Basset Hound Bagels, Inc. The accountant may use the account Paid-in Capital from Donation to record a situation in which the corporation receives a material gift. For example, the city of Ainley gave Basset Hound Bagels, Inc., an acre of land valued at $11,650 as an incentive to locate a manufacturing plant there. The accountant for Basset Hound Bagels, Inc., debited Land and credited Paid-in Capital from Donation for $11,650 each at that time.

8 LEARNING OBJECTIVE

Complete a corporate statement of retained earnings and a balance sheet, including the following types of accounts: Appropriated Retained Earnings, Stock Dividend Distributable, Dividends Payable, and Income Tax Payable.

Basset Hound Bagels, Inc.
Statement of Retained Earnings
For Year Ended December 31, 20—

Unappropriated Retained Earnings:			
Unappropriated Retained Earnings, Jan. 1, 20—	$112,700		
Net Income for the Year	73,000	$185,700	
Less: Cash Dividends Declared	$ 20,000		
Stock Dividends Declared	39,500		
Transfer to Appropriation for Property			
Expansion (see below)	4,000		
Transfer to Appropriation for Possible			
Price Declines (see below)	3,000	66,500	
Unappropriated Retained Earnings, Dec. 31, 20—			$119,200
Appropriated Retained Earnings:			
Appropriated for Property Expansion, Jan. 1, 20—	$ 16,000		
Add Appropriation for the Year (see above)	4,000		
Appropriated for Property Expansion, Dec. 31, 20—		$ 20,000	
Appropriated for Possible Price Declines, Jan. 1, 20—	$ 15,000		
Add Appropriation for the Year (see above)	3,000		
Appropriated for Possible Price Declines, Dec. 31, 20—		18,000	
Retained Earnings Appropriated, Dec. 31, 20—			38,000
Total Retained Earnings, Dec. 31, 20—			$157,200

FIGURE 4

Statement of retained earnings—Basset Hound Bagels, Inc.

Remember

The ending balances of unappropriated Retained Earnings and each appropriation account will appear in the Stockholders' Equity section of the corporation's balance sheet.

FIGURE 5

Balance sheet—Basset
Hound Bagels, Inc.

Basset Hound Bagels, Inc.
Balance Sheet
December 31, 20—

Assets

Current Assets:			
Cash		$ 11,170	
Accounts Receivable	$163,390		
Less Allowance for Doubtful Accounts	4,290	159,100	
Merchandise Inventory		320,220	
Total Current Assets			$490,490
Property and Equipment:			
Land		$ 40,000	
Building	$160,000		
Less Accumulated Depreciation	78,000	82,000	
Equipment	$ 80,760		
Less Accumulated Depreciation	26,750	54,010	
Total Property and Equipment			176,010
Intangible Assets:			
Copyrights		$ 7,200	
Patents		7,000	
Total Intangible Assets			14,200
Total Assets			$680,700

Liabilities

Current Liabilities:			
Accounts Payable	$ 85,690		
Notes Payable	16,000		
Income Tax Payable	9,200		
Dividends Payable	4,000		
Interest Payable	960		
Total Current Liabilities		$115,850	
Long-Term Liabilities:			
Mortgage Payable (due July 1, 20—)		54,000	
Total Liabilities			$169,850

Stockholders' Equity

Paid-in Capital:			
Preferred 7 Percent Stock, $25 par (4,600 shares authorized and issued)		$115,000	
Common Stock, no par, stated value $10 per share (20,000 shares authorized, 16,000 shares issued)	$160,000		
Stock Dividend Distributable (3,950 shares)	39,500		
Common Stock Subscribed (500 shares)	5,000		
Paid-in Capital in Excess of Stated Value	22,500	227,000	
Paid-in Capital from Donation		11,650	
Total Paid-in Capital		$353,650	
Retained Earnings:			
Unappropriated Retained Earnings	$119,200		
Appropriated:			
$20,000 for Property Expansion			
$18,000 for Possible Price Declines			
Total Appropriated Retained Earnings	38,000		
Total Retained Earnings		157,200	
Total Stockholders' Equity			510,850
Total Liabilities and Stockholders' Equity			$680,700

GUIDELINES FOR ACCOUNTING REPORTS

We have called accounting the "language of business." This language is used in accounting reports or statements. Accountants want to make sure that their reports are clear and consistent. To make their reports consistent, accountants follow certain guidelines. Three of these fundamental guidelines are full disclosure, materiality, and conservatism.

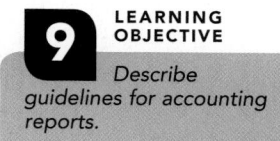

LEARNING OBJECTIVE 9
Describe guidelines for accounting reports.

Full Disclosure

To disclose means "to uncover or make known." The guideline of **full disclosure** requires that anyone preparing a financial statement include enough information so that the statement is complete. Leaving relevant information out of a report or including half-truths is not acceptable. Information included in the report must not lead the reader to wrong conclusions.

Example: At the end of its report, a business includes a note about a lawsuit in which it is involved. The note also states that the case has not been settled and that no financial claim has yet been made against the company. This note prepares the readers to expect a possible financial claim that the company may have to pay. The report would not meet the requirement of full disclosure if it failed to mention the lawsuit and the possible claim.

Materiality

If something is "material," it is important and carries weight. The guideline of **materiality** states that relatively important data are included in financial reports. Important data are material; unimportant data are immaterial. Accounting staffs deal with many different kinds of financial transactions involving small dollar amounts. These transactions may have very little effect on the results shown in financial statements and would not be likely to influence decisions made by users of the financial statements.

Example: In an annual report of a business reporting a profit of $14 million a year, the understatement of profit by $2,000 may be immaterial. The same understatement of profit for a business reporting profit of $122,000 would be material.

Conservatism

To be conservative means to take the safe route. When faced with a decision about which accounting procedures to apply, accountants generally follow the "safer" principle. According to the guideline of **conservatism**, they use the alternative that is the least likely to result in an overstatement of income or asset value.

Example: An accountant is estimating an amount of money to be received in the future. The accountant must choose between $12,000 and $22,000. Conservatism requires the accountant to choose the smaller amount.

CHAPTER REVIEW

Study & Practice

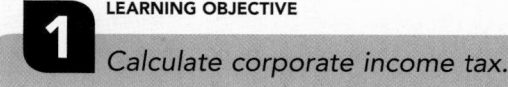

LEARNING OBJECTIVE 1
Calculate corporate income tax.

Corporations are subject to a graduated-rate structure (the higher the income, the higher the tax rate). To calculate corporate income tax, use Figure 1 located on page 795.

PRACTICE EXERCISE 1

Calculate the corporate income tax on taxable income of $875,000.

PRACTICE EXERCISE 1 SOLUTION

Using Figure 1 on page 795, the corporate income tax is calculated as:

$$\$113,900 + [0.34 \times (\$875,000 - \$335,000)] = \underline{\$297,500}$$

2 LEARNING OBJECTIVE

Journalize entries for corporate income taxes.

A corporation has to estimate the federal income tax that it will have to pay for the forthcoming year. The amount of the estimate is to be paid in four quarterly installments. The entry when each installment is paid is a debit to Income Tax Expense and a credit to Cash. At the end of the year, when the exact amount of taxable income is known, an adjusting entry is made for the amount either underpaid or overpaid. If the tax is underpaid, the entry is a debit to Income Tax Expense and a credit to Income Tax Payable. The liability must be paid within two-and-one-half months. If the tax is overpaid, the entry is a debit to Prepaid Income Tax and a credit to Income Tax Expense.

PRACTICE EXERCISE 2

Apple Dumpling, Inc., made four quarterly estimated income tax payments of $25,000 during the current year. At the end of the year, the corporation's tax liability is $110,000. Record the journal entry for the first quarterly estimated tax payment and also the entry to adjust the Income Tax Expense account at year-end.

PRACTICE EXERCISE 2 SOLUTION

Entry to record the first quarterly estimated tax payment:

Date		Description	Post. Ref.	Debit	Credit
20—					
Apr.	15	Income Tax Expense		25 0 0 0 00	
		Cash			25 0 0 0 00
		Paid first quarterly installment of			
		estimated federal income tax for			
		the year.			

Entry to adjust the income tax expense account at year-end:

Date		Description	Post. Ref.	Debit	Credit
20—					
Dec.	31	Income Tax Expense		10 0 0 0 00	
		Income Tax Payable			10 0 0 0 00
		Remaining federal income tax			
		due for the year.			

LEARNING OBJECTIVE

3

Journalize closing entries for a corporation.

The steps in the closing process for a corporation are as follows:

STEP 1. Close revenue accounts into Income Summary.

STEP 2. Close expense accounts into Income Summary.

STEP 3. Close Income Tax Expense into Income Summary by the amount of the actual income tax for the year.

STEP 4. Close Income Summary into Retained Earnings by the amount of the net income (Revenues – Expenses – Income Tax Expense).

PRACTICE EXERCISE 3

Summarized below are the revenue, expense, and income tax items related to Lemon's Baked Goods, Inc. Provide the closing entries for Lemon's Baked Goods, Inc.

Total Revenues	$135,000
Total Expenses	60,000
Income Tax Expense	13,750

PRACTICE EXERCISE 3 SOLUTION

Date		Description	Post. Ref.	Debit	Credit
		Closing Entries			
Dec.	31	Revenues		135 0 0 0 00	
		Income Summary			135 0 0 0 00
	31	Income Summary		60 0 0 0 00	
		Expenses			60 0 0 0 00
	31	Income Summary		13 7 5 0 00	
		Income Tax Expense			13 7 5 0 00
	31	Income Summary		61 2 5 0 00	
		Retained Earnings			61 2 5 0 00

LEARNING OBJECTIVE

4

Journalize entries for the appropriation of Retained Earnings.

An **appropriation of Retained Earnings** is a restriction of a portion of the Retained Earnings account, making the amount unavailable for dividends. The entry in each case is a debit to Retained Earnings and a credit to Retained Earnings Appropriated for _____ (some specific purpose). The Retained Earnings account by itself is unappropriated.

PRACTICE EXERCISE 4

On February 5, Early Morning Coffee Corporation's board of directors approved plans to build a new manufacturing plant. To finance the project, it decides to restrict Retained Earnings for a total amount of $1,225,000 at the rate of $122,500 per year for 10 years. Record the entry to appropriate Retained Earnings on February 5.

PRACTICE EXERCISE 4 SOLUTION

Date		Description	Post. Ref.	Debit	Credit
Year 1					
Feb.	5	Retained Earnings		122 5 0 0 00	
		Retained Earnings Appropriated			
		for Building			122 5 0 0 00
		To appropriate Retained			
		Earnings, as ordered by the			
		board of directors in the			
		meeting of February 5.			

5 LEARNING OBJECTIVE

Journalize entries for the declaration and payment of cash dividends.

The entry for the declaration of a cash dividend is a debit to Retained Earnings and a credit to Dividends Payable. The entry for the payment of a cash dividend is a debit to Dividends Payable and a credit to Cash.

PRACTICE EXERCISE 5

In-Flight Meal and Beverage Corporation declared cash dividends of $62,750 on July 15 for stockholders of record as of August 1, payable on August 15. Record the entries (if any) for the declaration of dividends, record date, and payment of dividends.

PRACTICE EXERCISE 5 SOLUTION

Entry to record the date of declaration:

Date		Description	Post. Ref.	Debit	Credit
20—					
July	15	Retained Earnings		62 7 5 0 00	
		Dividends Payable			62 7 5 0 00
		To record the declaration of cash			
		dividends of $62,750 to stockholders			
		of record as of August 1, payable			
		on August 15, as ordered by the			
		board of directors in the meeting			
		of July 15.			

Entry to record the date of record:
No accounting entry is needed; a memo entry is made in the minutes or sometimes in the general journal.

Entry to record the date of payment:

Date	Description	Post. Ref.	Debit	Credit
20—				
Aug. 15	Dividends Payable		62 7 5 0 00	
	Cash			62 7 5 0 00
	Payment of cash dividends			
	declared on July 15 to			
	stockholders of record as			
	of August 1.			

LEARNING OBJECTIVE

6

Calculate dividends on cumulative preferred stock.

Stockholders of cumulative preferred stock have a dividend preference and are entitled to receive **dividends in arrears** and current dividends payable before any common stockholders. Dividends in arrears represent the amount of dividends not paid in previous years to preferred stockholders.

PRACTICE EXERCISE 6

Caboose Deli Corporation has outstanding 8,000 shares of $25 par, 6 percent cumulative preferred stock and 60,000 shares of $10 par value common stock. The corporation declares and pays dividends as follows: Year 1, $14,000; Year 2, $3,000; Year 3, $30,000. Determine the dividends paid to preferred and common stockholders.

PRACTICE EXERCISE 6 SOLUTION

If dividends are paid, preferred stockholders will receive $12,000 (8,000 × $25 × 0.06).

Year	Dividends Declared	Dividends Paid		Dividends in Arrears
		Preferred Stockholders	Common Stockholders	
1	$14,000	$12,000	$2,000	$ 0
2	3,000	3,000	0	9,000
3	30,000	21,000	9,000	0

YEAR 1: Preferred stockholders receive $12,000, and common stockholders receive the remainder, $2,000 ($14,000 – $12,000).

YEAR 2: Preferred stockholders receive the entire dividend of $3,000 and have $9,000 of dividends in arrears ($12,000 – $3,000).

YEAR 3: Preferred stockholders receive $9,000 of dividends in arrears plus the current dividend payable of $12,000 for a total of $21,000. Common stockholders receive the remainder of $9,000 ($30,000 – $21,000).

LEARNING OBJECTIVE

7

Journalize entries for the declaration and issuance of stock dividends.

The entry for the declaration of a small **stock dividend** is a debit to Retained Earnings for the amount of the number of shares multiplied by the market value per share, a credit to Stock Dividend Distributable for the amount of the number of shares multiplied by the par or stated value per share, and a credit to Paid-in Capital in Excess of Par (or Stated) Value. The entry for the issuance of stock is a debit to Stock Dividend Distributable and a credit to Common Stock.

PRACTICE EXERCISE 7

The board of directors of Claudia's Homemade Tortilla Factory, Inc., declared an 8 percent stock dividend on May 13 of Year 3 to common stockholders of record as of June 1, distributable on June 15. According to the Stockholders' Equity section of the balance sheet, Claudia's Homemade Tortilla Factory, Inc., has 60,000 shares of common stock outstanding, $4 par value. The current market value of the shares is $18 per share. Prepare the journal entries for the declaration and issuance of the stock dividend.

PRACTICE EXERCISE 7 SOLUTION

Claudia's Homemade Tortilla Factory, Inc., will issue 4,800 shares (8 percent of 60,000 shares).

Entry to record the declaration of stock dividend:

Date		Description	Post. Ref.	Debit	Credit
Year 3					
May	13	Retained Earnings (4,800 shares × $18 each)		86 4 0 0 00	
		Stock Dividend Distributable (4,800 shares × $4 each)			19 2 0 0 00
		Paid-in Capital in Excess of Par Value			67 2 0 0 00
		To record the declaration of an 8 percent stock dividend to stockholders of record as of June 1, distributable on June 15, as ordered by the board of directors in the meeting of May 13.			

Entry to record the issuance of stock dividend:

Date		Description	Post. Ref.	Debit	Credit
Year 3					
June	15	Stock Dividend Distributable		19 2 0 0 00	
		Common Stock			19 2 0 0 00
		Issuance of a stock dividend (4,800 shares), declared on May 13 to stockholders of record as of June 1.			

8 LEARNING OBJECTIVE

Complete a corporate statement of retained earnings and a balance sheet, including the following types of accounts: Appropriated Retained Earnings, Stock Dividend Distributable, Dividends Payable, and Income Tax Payable.

A statement of retained earnings consists of two sections: **Unappropriated Retained Earnings** and Appropriated Retained Earnings. Unappropriated Retained Earnings reflects the increases and decreases in the Retained Earnings account, consisting of net income, dividends, and transfers to Appropriated Retained Earnings accounts. The Appropriated Retained Earnings section consists of a listing of each Appropriated Retained Earnings account, including additions or deductions affecting each account.

On a corporate balance sheet, Stock Dividend Distributable is listed under Paid-in Capital. Dividends Payable and Income Tax Payable are listed under Current Liabilities.

PRACTICE EXERCISE 8

Prepare the Stockholders' Equity section of the balance sheet from the following account balances:

Retained Earnings	$230,000
Common Stock, $5 par (50,000 shares authorized, 20,000 shares issued)	100,000
Preferred 8 Percent Stock, $20 par (8,000 shares authorized, 1,000 shares issued)	20,000
Paid-in Capital in Excess of Par Value—Common	140,000
Preferred 8 Percent Stock Subscribed (600 shares)	12,000

PRACTICE EXERCISE 8 SOLUTION

Stockholders' Equity			
Paid-in Capital:			
Preferred 8 Percent Stock, $20 par (8,000 shares authorized, 1,000 shares issued)	$ 20,000		
Preferred 8 Percent Stock Subscribed (600 shares)	12,000	$ 32,000	
Common Stock, $5 par (50,000 shares authorized, (20,000 shares issued)	$100,000		
Paid-in Capital in Excess of Par Value	140,000	240,000	
Total Paid-in Capital		$272,000	
Retained Earnings		230,000	
Total Stockholders' Equity			$502,000

9 LEARNING OBJECTIVE

Describe guidelines for accounting reports.

Three of the guidelines used to make accounting reports consistent are:
1. **Full disclosure**—Requires that financial statements and their accompanying notes contain all information that would influence a user's understanding of a firm's financial position.
2. **Materiality**—Refers to the inclusion in financial statements of important items that significantly affect a firm's financial position.
3. **Conservatism**—Means that, when accountants are faced with major uncertainties as to which alternative accounting procedure to apply, they should choose the procedure that is least likely to overstate a firm's revenues and assets or understate its expenses and liabilities.

Glossary

Appropriation of Retained Earnings Designation of a portion of Retained Earnings for a specific purpose; the amount appropriated may not be used for cash or stock dividends. *(p. 799)*

Cash dividend Distribution of a corporation's earnings to stockholders in the form of cash. *(p. 801)*

Conservatism An accounting rule that means that, when accountants are faced with major uncertainties as to which alternative accounting procedure to apply, they should choose the procedure that is least likely to overstate a firm's revenues and assets or understate its expenses and liabilities. *(p. 809)*

Date of declaration The date on which the board of directors votes to declare dividends. *(p. 802)*

Date of payment The date on which dividends are paid. *(p. 802)*

Date of record The date as of which the ownership of shares is set, determining a person's eligibility for dividends. *(p. 802)*

Dividends in arrears Any dividends not paid in the past to cumulative preferred stockholders. *(p. 803)*

Estimated tax payments Payments that are made by a corporation on estimated federal income taxes for the forthcoming year; typically made quarterly. *(p. 795)*

Full disclosure An accounting rule requiring that financial statements and their accompanying notes contain all information that would influence a user's understanding of a firm's financial position. *(p. 809)*

Materiality An accounting rule that refers to the inclusion in financial statements of important items that significantly affect a firm's financial position. *(p. 809)*

Minute book A written narrative of all actions taken at official meetings of the board of directors; source document for dividend accounting entries. *(p. 807)*

Stock dividend Distribution of a corporation's Retained Earnings to stockholders in the form of shares of the corporation's own stock. *(p. 804)*

Stock split A deliberate reduction of the par value or stated value of a corporation's stock and the issuing of a proportionate number of additional shares. *(p. 806)*

Unappropriated Retained Earnings The portion of Retained Earnings available for distribution as dividends to the stockholders. *(p. 801)*

CHAPTER ASSIGNMENTS

Discussion Questions

1. How does a corporation account for federal income taxes? What are the related journal entries?
2. Name and explain the three dates that are involved in processing a cash dividend.
3. What effect does a cash dividend have on stockholders' equity? What effect does a stock dividend have?
4. Describe the difference between a small stock dividend and a stock split.
5. Classify each of the following accounts as asset, liability, stockholders' equity, revenue, or expense, and indicate the normal balance of each account:
   a. Paid-in Capital in Excess of Par Value
   b. Preferred 7 Percent Stock
   c. Stock Dividend Distributable
   d. Appropriated Retained Earnings
   e. Paid-in Capital from Donation
   f. Retained Earnings
   g. Common Stock Subscribed
   h. Subscriptions Receivable, Common Stock
   i. Common Stock
6. Explain why an appropriation of Retained Earnings is not the same thing as setting aside cash. How does a corporation dispose of a Retained Earnings Appropriated account, such as Retained Earnings Appropriated for Building?
7. How do the closing entries for a corporation differ from the closing entries for a sole proprietorship?
8. What are some possible reasons why a corporation's net income shown on its income statement may differ from the amount of its taxable income?

Exercises

EXERCISE 20-1 Using the tables presented in Figure 1 on page 795, compute Phillips Corporation's first-year total tax on a taxable income of $235,000.

PRACTICE EXERCISE 1

EXERCISE 20-2 Evans, Inc., estimates that its federal income tax for the forthcoming fiscal year will be $115,000.

PRACTICE EXERCISE 2

a. Record the first journal entry for the four quarterly payments.
b. Assume that Evans, Inc., underpaid its tax liability by $7,830. Record the adjusting journal entry required at December 31 and the entry when the amount due is paid on March 15.

EXERCISE 20-3 Summarized below are the revenue, expense, and income tax items related to Turner Nurses-Aide, Inc. Provide the closing entries for Turner Nurses-Aide, Inc.

PRACTICE EXERCISE 3

Total Revenues	$287,500
Total Expenses	132,890
Income Tax Expense	43,548

EXERCISE 20-4 Describe the entries recorded by letters in the following T accounts.

PRACTICE EXERCISES 2,3

Income Tax Expense		Cash		Revenues		Retained Earnings
+	−	+	−	−	+	− +
(a)	(e)		(a)	(c)		(f)
(b)						

Income Summary		Income Tax Payable		Expenses
		−	+	+ −
(d)	(c)		(b)	(d)
(e)				
(f)				

EXERCISE 20-5 On January 3, the board of directors of Torres Company, Inc., voted to appropriate $90,000 of the corporation's unappropriated Retained Earnings to Retained Earnings Appropriated for Property Expansion. This is the fourth such appropriation; it gives a balance of $298,000 in Retained Earnings Appropriated for Property Expansion. On September 1, the corporation buys a warehouse for $320,000 (building, $190,000; land, $130,000), paying $135,000 down and financing the remainder on a mortgage note. The board of directors at the September 1 meeting orders the corporation to release on September 2 the $298,000 of the Retained Earnings Appropriated for Property Expansion. Write the entries to record the following:

PRACTICE EXERCISE 4

a. The appropriation of Retained Earnings on January 3.
b. The purchase of the building and land on September 1.
c. The release of $298,000 of the Retained Earnings Appropriated for Property Expansion on September 2.

PRACTICE EXERCISE 5

EXERCISE 20-6 The dates connected with a cash dividend of $115,000 on a corporation's common stock are April 12, April 29, and May 8. Present the entries in general journal form pertaining to the declaration and payment of the dividend.

PRACTICE EXERCISE 6

EXERCISE 20-7 Parker Flowers in Bloom Corporation has outstanding 24,500 shares of $10 par, 4 percent cumulative preferred stock and 78,500 shares of $2 par value common stock. The corporation declares and pays dividends as follows: Year 1: $8,000; Year 2: $0; Year 3: $30,000. Determine the dividends paid to preferred and common stockholders.

PRACTICE EXERCISE 7

EXERCISE 20-8 On December 31, the Stockholders' Equity section of Collins Auto Body Repair, Inc.'s balance sheet is as follows:

Stockholders' Equity		
Paid-in Capital:		
Common Stock, no par, stated value $20 per share		
(30,000 shares authorized, 18,000 shares issued)	$360,000	
Paid-in Capital in Excess of Stated Value	54,000	
Total Paid-in Capital		$414,000
Retained Earnings:		
Unappropriated Retained Earnings	$205,020	
Appropriated for Contingencies	91,800	
Total Retained Earnings		296,820
Total Stockholders' Equity		$710,820

On March 6 of the following year, when the stock was selling at $38 per share, the board of directors declared a 20 percent stock dividend, distributable on March 28 to stockholders of record on March 22. Give the entries to record the declaration and distribution of the stock dividend, assuming that it is a small stock dividend.

PRACTICE EXERCISE 8

EXERCISE 20-9 A corporation's balance sheet includes the following:

Preferred 9 Percent Stock, $100 par	$205,800
Preferred 9 Percent Stock Subscribed	115,900
Common Stock, no-par, stated value $10 per share	299,500
Paid-in Capital in Excess of Stated Value	131,200
Retained Earnings (credit balance)	154,250

a. How much of the corporation's capital is the result of the preferred 9 percent stock?
b. How much of the corporation's capital is the result of the common stock?
c. What is the total stockholders' equity?

EXERCISE 20-10 Indicate the effect, if any, of each of the following transactions on total Retained Earnings of Little Red Caboose, Inc.:

a. Paid accounts payable.
b. Wrote off Accounts Receivable against Allowance for Doubtful Accounts.
c. Bought equipment on account, $58,000.

d. The board of directors declared a 20 percent stock dividend to be issued 30 days from the present date.

e. The board of directors voted to appropriate $98,000 for future expansion.

f. Issued 2,500 shares of $25 par-value common stock, receiving $34 per share.

g. Issued the stock dividend declared in transaction d.

EXERCISE 20-11 Prepare the Stockholders' Equity section of the balance sheet from the following account balances:

Retained Earnings	$143,000
Common Stock, $40 par (30,000 shares authorized, 10,000 shares issued)	400,000
Preferred 10 Percent Stock, $50 par (2,000 shares authorized, 500 shares issued)	25,000
Paid-in Capital in Excess of Par Value (for Common Stock)	40,000
Preferred 10 Percent Stock Subscribed (400 shares)	20,000

PRACTICE EXERCISE 8

Problem Set A

For additional help, see the demonstration problem at the beginning of each chapter in your Working Papers.

PROBLEM 20-1A Some of the transactions of Miss Ellie's Sweet Tea Distributor, Inc., during this fiscal year are as follows:

LO 2,4,5,7

Mar. 15   Paid balance due on previous year's federal income tax, $8,450.

Apr. 15   Paid $28,640 for the first quarterly installment of estimated federal income tax for this year.

June 15   Paid $28,640 for the second quarterly installment of estimated federal income tax for this year.

July 12   Declared a cash dividend of $40,836 ($4.98 per share on 8,200 shares of common stock, $50 par) to stockholders of record as of July 22, payable on August 7.

Aug. 7   Paid the cash dividend.

Sept. 15   Paid $28,640 for the third quarterly installment of estimated federal income tax for this year.

18   Declared a 10 percent stock dividend on common stock outstanding to stockholders of record as of September 28, distributable on October 6. Current market value of stock: $64 per share (8,200 shares outstanding before stock dividend).

Oct. 6   Issued stock comprising the stock dividend.

Nov. 14   Declared a cash dividend of $40,590 ($4.50 per share on 9,020 shares of common stock) to stockholders of record as of November 30, payable on December 8.

Dec. 8   Paid the cash dividend.

15   Paid $28,640 for the fourth quarterly installment of estimated federal income tax for this year.

31   The board of directors authorized the appropriation of Retained Earnings for contingencies, $24,688.

31   Recorded $7,042 additional federal income tax allocable to taxable income for the year in an adjusting entry.

Required
Record these transactions in general journal form.

Check Figure
Nov. 14, Retained Earnings
Debit, $40,590

PROBLEM 20-2A The trial balance for David's Fly Fishing Tackle, Inc., dated December 31 of this year, follows. To reduce the number of accounts in the trial balance, Selling Expenses (control) is used in place of all selling expenses. Likewise, General Expenses (control) is used in place of all general expenses.

David's Fly Fishing Tackle, Inc. Trial Balance December 31, 20—		
Account Name	**Debit**	**Credit**
Cash	40,142	
Notes Receivable	30,000	
Accounts Receivable	276,355	
Allowance for Doubtful Accounts		5,490
Merchandise Inventory	571,423	
Prepaid Insurance	2,644	
Equipment	173,623	
Accumulated Depreciation—Equipment		32,834
Patents	19,584	
Accounts Payable		149,224
Preferred 9 Percent Stock ($100 par)		153,000
Preferred 9 Percent Stock Subscribed		30,600
Paid-in Capital in Excess of Par Value		6,732
Common Stock ($20 stated value)		306,000
Paid-in Capital in Excess of Stated Value		36,720
Retained Earnings		159,120
Sales		3,605,900
Purchases	2,630,152	
Purchases Discounts		15,920
Freight In	109,587	
Selling Expenses (control)	405,848	
General Expenses (control)	114,444	
Income Tax Expense	131,224	
Interest Income		3,486
	4,505,026	4,505,026

Additional information is as follows:
a. The charter states that authorized preferred 9 percent stock amounts to 2,000 shares and authorized common stock amounts to 20,000 shares.
b. Merchandise Inventory, December 31 (ending inventory) is $592,100.
c. No dividends were declared and paid during the year.

Check Figure
Total Stockholders' Equity,
$991,894

Required
1. Prepare an income statement for the year ended December 31, 20—.
2. Prepare a statement of retained earnings for the year ended December 31, 20—.
3. Prepare a classified balance sheet.

PROBLEM 20-3A The account balances taken from the general ledger for River Falls Beverages, Inc., are as follows:

Accounts Payable	$285,940
Accounts Receivable	386,660
Accumulated Depreciation—Building	72,700
Accumulated Depreciation—Equipment	76,100
Allowance for Doubtful Accounts	14,137
Building	270,865

Cash	$ 48,890
Common Stock, $15 stated value	322,500
Dividends Payable	14,680
Equipment	142,500
Income Tax Payable	44,680
Land	38,000
Merchandise Inventory	727,882
Mortgage Payable (due in 8 years)	124,500
Notes Receivable	37,000
Paid-in Capital from Donation	36,000
Paid-in Capital in Excess of Par Value	5,000
Paid-in Capital in Excess of Stated Value	55,640
Patents	18,400
Preferred 8 Percent Stock, $100 par value	250,000
Preferred 8 Percent Stock Subscribed (700 shares)	70,000
Prepaid Insurance	2,630
Retained Earnings	235,300
Retained Earnings Appropriated for Inventory Losses	13,800
Retained Earnings Appropriated for Property Expansion	23,500
Stock Dividend Distributable (1,890 shares)	28,350

Additional information is as follows:
a. Preferred 8 percent stock: 3,000 shares authorized, 2,500 shares issued
b. Common stock: 30,000 shares authorized, 21,500 shares issued

Required
Prepare a classified balance sheet dated December 31.

Check Figure
Total Liabilities and Stockholders' Equity, $1,509,890

 **LO** 3,4,5,7,8

PROBLEM 20-4A The Stockholders' Equity section of the balance sheet for Aardvark Archery Bows and Arrows, Inc., as of January 1 is as follows:

Stockholders' Equity			
Paid-in Capital:			
Preferred 9.5 Percent Stock, $100 par (4,000 shares authorized, 2,300 shares issued)	$230,000		
Paid-in Capital in Excess of Par Value	9,200	$239,200	
Common Stock, no par, stated value $20 per share			
(23,000 shares authorized, 19,000 shares issued)	$380,000		
Paid-in Capital in Excess of Stated Value	152,000	532,000	
Total Paid-in Capital		$771,200	
Retained Earnings:			
Unappropriated Retained Earnings	$195,075		
Appropriated for Expansion	41,310		
Total Retained Earnings		236,385	
Total Stockholders' Equity			$1,007,585

Some of the transactions that took place during the year are as follows:

Feb. 24   Declared the regular semiannual $4.75 per share dividend on the preferred stock and a $1.50 per share dividend on the common stock to stockholders of record as of March 15, payable on March 23.

Mar. 23   Paid cash dividends declared on February 24.

23   27   Received subscriptions to 1,200 shares of common stock at $31 per share, collecting 60 percent of the subscription price.

Apr. 19   Subscribers to 1,200 shares of common stock paid the remaining 40 percent of the subscription price; Aardvark Archery Bows and Arrows, Inc., then issued the 1,200 shares.

Aug. 24   Declared the regular semiannual $4.75 per share dividend on the preferred stock and $1.30 per share dividend on the common stock to stockholders of record as of September 15, payable on September 23.

Sept. 23   Paid cash dividends declared on August 24.

Dec. 20   Declared a 10 percent stock dividend on common stock outstanding to stockholders of record as of January 15, distributable on January 23. Current market value of the stock is $32 per share.

31   Increased the appropriation for expansion by $30,000.

31   After the accountant has closed all revenue, expense, and Income Tax Expense accounts, the Income Summary account has a credit balance of $165,500. Closed the Income Summary account.

Check Figure
Total Stockholders' Equity,
$1,133,675

Required

1. Enter in the ledger accounts the balances appearing in the Stockholders' Equity section of the balance sheet as of January 1. In the Item column of the stock accounts, record the word *Balance* on the first line and the number of shares on the second line.

2. Journalize entries in general journal form on pages 54 and 55 to record the transactions that occurred during the year, and post to the stockholders' equity accounts.

3. Prepare the Stockholders' Equity section of the balance sheet as of December 31.

Problem Set B

For additional help, see the demonstration problem at the beginning of each chapter in your Working Papers.

2,4,5,7 **LO**

PROBLEM 20-1B Some of the transactions of Pampered Queen Bath Products, Inc., during this fiscal year are as follows:

Mar. 15   Paid balance due on previous year's federal income tax, $7,230.

Apr. 15   Paid $83,760 for the first quarterly installment of estimated federal income tax for this year.

June 15   Paid $83,760 for the second quarterly installment of estimated federal income tax for this year.

July 16   Declared a cash dividend of $76,800 ($6.40 per share on 12,000 shares of common stock, $65 par) to stockholders of record as of July 31, payable on August 10.

Aug. 10   Paid the cash dividend.

Sept. 15   Declared a 10 percent stock dividend on common stock outstanding to stockholders of record as of September 30, distributable on October 9. Current market value of stock: $99 per share (12,000 shares outstanding before stock dividend).

Sept. 15   Paid $83,760 for the third quarterly installment of estimated federal income tax for this year.

Oct. 9   Issued stock comprising the stock dividend.

Nov. 17   Declared a cash dividend of $84,480 ($6.40 per share on 13,200 shares of common stock) to stockholders of record as of November 30, payable on December 9.

Dec. 9   Paid the cash dividend.

Dec. 15   Paid $83,760 for the fourth quarterly installment of estimated federal income tax for this year.

31   The board of directors authorized the appropriation of Retained Earnings for property expansion, $53,750.

31   Recorded $2,850 additional federal income tax allocable to taxable income for the year in an adjusting entry.

Required

Record these transactions in general journal form.

Check Figure
Nov. 17, Retained Earnings
Debit, $84,480

PROBLEM 20-2B The trial balance for Fancy Petals Florist, Inc., dated May 31 of this year, follows. To reduce the number of accounts in the trial balance, Selling Expenses (control) is used in place of all selling expenses. Likewise, General Expenses (control) is used in place of all general expenses.

Fancy Petals Florist, Inc. Trial Balance May 31, 20—		
Account Name	Debit	Credit
Cash	93,542	
Accounts Receivable	303,268	
Allowance for Doubtful Accounts		5,710
Merchandise Inventory	580,390	
Store Supplies	1,928	
Store Equipment	220,400	
Accumulated Depreciation—Store Equipment		35,557
Patents	16,585	
Notes Payable		32,000
Accounts Payable		154,782
Preferred 8 Percent Stock ($100 par)		120,000
Paid-in Capital in Excess of Par Value		6,000
Common Stock ($20 stated value)		330,000
Common Stock Subscribed		90,000
Paid-in Capital in Excess of Stated Value		42,000
Retained Earnings		157,896
Sales		3,121,638
Purchases	2,146,267	
Purchases Discounts		16,279
Freight In	84,780	
Selling Expenses (control)	410,970	
General Expenses (control)	117,094	
Interest Expense	4,712	
Income Tax Expense	131,926	
	4,111,862	4,111,862

Additional information is as follows:

a. The charter states that authorized preferred 8 percent stock amounts to 1,400 shares and authorized common stock amounts to 20,000 shares.

b. Merchandise Inventory, May 31 (ending inventory), $594,313.

c. No dividends were declared and paid during the year.

Required

1. Prepare an income statement for the year ended May 31, 20—.

2. Prepare a statement of retained earnings for the year ended May 31, 20—.

3. Prepare a classified balance sheet.

Check Figure
Total Stockholders' Equity,
$1,051,874

8 LO

PROBLEM 20-3B The account balances taken from the general ledger for Edwards, Inc., are as follows:

Accounts Payable	$ 345,046
Accounts Receivable	497,036
Accumulated Depreciation—Building	190,945
Accumulated Depreciation—Equipment	104,650
Allowance for Doubtful Accounts	17,260
Building	367,000
Cash	63,545
Common Stock, $15 stated value	550,800
Dividends Payable	25,092
Equipment	223,075
Income Tax Payable	63,036
Land	76,500
Merchandise Inventory	1,048,080
Mortgage Payable (due in 7 years)	149,000
Notes Receivable	38,560
Paid-in Capital from Donation	22,000
Paid-in Capital in Excess of Par Value	6,120
Paid-in Capital in Excess of Stated Value	110,160
Patents	25,000
Preferred 8 Percent Stock, $100 par value	232,000
Preferred 8 Percent Stock Subscribed (735 shares)	73,500
Prepaid Insurance	2,938
Retained Earnings	326,500
Retained Earnings Appropriated for Inventory Losses	25,700
Retained Earnings Appropriated for Property Expansion	49,000
Stock Dividend Distributable (3,395 shares)	50,925

Additional information is as follows:
a. Preferred 8 percent stock: 3,000 shares authorized, 2,320 shares issued
b. Common stock: 40,000 shares authorized, 36,720 shares issued

Check Figure
Total Paid-in Capital, $1,045,505

Required
Prepare a classified balance sheet dated December 31.

3,4,5,7,8 LO

PROBLEM 20-4B The Stockholders' Equity section of the balance sheet for Choo's Video, Inc., as of January 1 is as follows:

Stockholders' Equity		
Paid-in Capital:		
Preferred 9 Percent Stock, $100 par (8,000 shares authorized, 6,900 shares issued)	$ 690,000	
Paid-in Capital in Excess of Par Value	27,600	$ 717,600
Common Stock, no par, stated value $20 per share (90,000 shares authorized, 55,080 shares issued)	$1,101,600	
Paid-in Capital in Excess of Stated Value	330,480	1,432,080
Total Paid-in Capital		$2,149,680
Retained Earnings:		
Unappropriated Retained Earnings	$ 642,600	
Appropriated for Contingencies	129,400	
Total Retained Earnings		772,000
Total Stockholders' Equity		$2,921,680

Some of the transactions that took place during the year are as follows:

May 10   Declared the regular semiannual $4.50 per share dividend on the preferred stock and a $1.40 per share dividend on the common stock to stockholders of record as of June 1, payable on June 10.

June 2   Received subscriptions to 11,000 shares of common stock at $27 per share, collecting 60 percent of the subscription price.

10   Paid cash dividends declared on May 10.

26   Subscribers to 11,000 shares of common stock paid the remaining 40 percent of the subscription price; Choo's Video, Inc., then issued the 11,000 shares.

Nov. 10   Declared the regular semiannual $4.50 per share dividend on the preferred stock and $1.60 per share dividend on the common stock to stockholders of record as of December 1, payable on December 10.

Dec. 10   Paid cash dividends declared on November 10.

27   Declared a 5 percent stock dividend on common stock outstanding to stockholders of record as of January 14, distributable on January 30. Current market value of the stock is $27 per share.

31   Increased the appropriation for contingencies by $53,000.

31   After the accountant has closed all revenue, expense, and Income Tax Expense accounts, the Income Summary account has a credit balance of $340,000. Closed the Income Summary account.

Required

1. Enter in the ledger accounts the balances appearing in the Stockholders' Equity section of the balance sheet as of January 1. In the Item column of the stock accounts, record the word *Balance* on the first line and the number of shares on the second line.

2. Journalize entries in general journal form on pages 54 and 55 to record the transactions that occurred during the year, and post to the stockholders' equity accounts.

3. Prepare the Stockholders' Equity section of the balance sheet as of December 31.

Check Figure
Total Stockholders' Equity,
$3,313,740

ACTIVITIES

INTERNET LINKS TO ACCOUNTING

In this chapter, you learned about income tax expense and cash dividends. You should be able to use what you have learned to determine the amount of cash used for payment of income tax expense and cash dividends paid during the year. Let's take a look at Kraft Foods Inc. The Kraft Foods Inc. 2008 Annual Report (or 10-K) is located at www.kraftfoodscompany.com/Investor/sec-filings-annual-report/annual_reports.htm. Click on "View the most recent edition of our annual report."

1. For the year ended 2008, how much was reported in net revenues on Kraft Foods Inc.'s consolidated statement of earnings?

2. What was the company's current provision for income tax expense for 2008? (*Hint:* Look at Kraft Foods Inc.'s consolidated statement of earnings.)

3. How much did the company pay in cash for income tax expenses during 2008? (*Hint:* Look near the end of the consolidated statement of cash flows.)

4. What is one reason that a company's income tax expense and the amount it paid in cash for income taxes might differ? From what you have learned in this chapter, you should be able to come up with one explanation.

5. How much cash, if any, did Kraft Foods Inc. pay in dividends during 2008? (*Hint:* Look in the consolidated statement of cash flows.)

WHAT'S WRONG WITH THIS PICTURE?

Suppose that a stockholder who received notice of a 2-for-1 stock split told you that he had just doubled his money. Is the stockholder correct? If not, what has actually happened?

CRITICAL THINKING

You have just received the following note dated November 30 from one of your corporation's stockholders:

> *"Help! Please explain why I haven't received my dividend check. I own 100 shares that I bought at $30 and they are now selling for $35. I read in the annual report that the board of directors declared a 10 percent stock dividend, but I haven't received a dime yet. What is going on? Where is my dividend check? I was a stockholder of record on the declaration date of the dividend."*

Assume that he was a stockholder of record for both of the following dividends. The following selected journal entries may help you answer his questions.

	GENERAL JOURNAL				PAGE 78
Date	Description	Post. Ref.	Debit	Credit	
20—					
Sept. 15	Retained Earnings		98 0 0 0 00		
	Stock Dividend Distributable			65 0 0 0 00	
	Paid-in Capital in Excess of				
	Par Value			33 0 0 0 00	
	To record the declaration of				
	a 10 percent stock dividend				
	to stockholders of record as				
	of September 30,				
	distributable on October 9.				
Oct. 9	Stock Dividend Distributable		65 0 0 0 00		
	Common Stock			65 0 0 0 00	
	Issuance of a stock dividend				
	declared on September 15 to				
	stockholders of record as of				
	September 30.				
Nov. 17	Retained Earnings		74 8 0 0 00		
	Dividends Payable			74 8 0 0 00	
	To record the declaration of				
	a cash dividend of $6.80				
	per share to stockholders of				
	record as of November 30,				
	payable on December 9.				
Dec. 9	Dividends Payable		74 8 0 0 00		
	Cash			74 8 0 0 00	
	Payment of cash dividend				
	declared on November 17.				

A QUESTION OF ETHICS

Your friend has been telling you that she knows someone in a publicly traded corporation who gives her information that lets her know when to buy and sell stock in that corporation. Consequently, your friend has made quite a bit of money. She has offered to share these inside tips with you for a small percentage of any gain you may make as a result. Her offer is very tempting to you. Are these friendly tips ethical?

Corporate Bonds

PULTE HOMES, INC., Bloomfield Hills, Michigan

Pulte Homes, Inc., specializes in offering communities and home styles for buyers at every point on the home ownership spectrum, from first homes to urban developments to lifestyle communities for active adults. William Pulte, the founder of Pulte Homes, Inc., built his first home in 1950, and the corporation built its first subdivision in 1961 in Detroit. Since then, the company has built more than 500,000 homes. In April 2009, Pulte Homes, Inc., announced its intention of purchasing rival homebuilder Centex. With the merger with Centex finalized in late 2009, Pulte Homes is now the largest U.S. homebuilder.

The growth that Pulte Homes, Inc., has undergone since its start in 1950 requires a large amount of cash flow. One way for a corporation to obtain cash is by issuing bonds. Bonds payable, such as the ones issued by Pulte Homes, Inc., are debts of the corporation that require repayment. In this chapter we will learn about the various types of bonds, why a corporation might issue bonds, and how the issuing and repayment of bonds are recorded by the corporation.

WHY IT MATTERS

LEARNING OBJECTIVES

After you have completed this chapter, you will be able to do the following:

1 Journalize transactions involving the issuance of bonds at a premium or discount and the interest payment on bonds.

2 Journalize adjusting entries for amortization of bond premiums and discounts and for accrued interest payable.

3 Journalize entries pertaining to the establishment of a bond sinking fund, the receipt of income from sinking fund investments, and the eventual payment of the principal of the bonds.

4 Journalize transactions involving the redemption of bonds.

ACCOUNTING LANGUAGE

Amortization (p. 836)
Bond (p. 830)
Bond issue (p. 830)
Callable bonds (p. 846)
Contra-liability account (p. 841)
Discount (p. 841)
Face value (p. 830)
Indenture (p. 846)

Leverage (p. 832)
Maturity date (p. 830)
Premium (p. 835)
Redeem (p. 846)
Secured bonds (p. 831)
Serial bonds (p. 831)
Sinking fund (p. 843)
Term bonds (p. 831)
Unsecured bonds (p. 831)

In our discussions of corporations, we have assumed that the company got the money it needed for building and expansion by selling stock and from retaining earnings. There is another possibility: A corporation can borrow money for a long period (5 to 100 years) by issuing bonds. A **bond** is a long-term obligation that provides capital. For all practical purposes, a bond is a long-term promissory note. Bonds are recorded as Bonds Payable on the balance sheet of a corporation in the Long-Term Liabilities section. A **bond issue** refers to the total number of bonds that a corporation issues at the same time. Bonds are issued in denominations of $1,000 or $5,000 each, with $1,000 being more common. All bond payables have a **face value**, or the value that the corporation will pay at maturity. The end of the life of a bond is called the **maturity date** and is the day the corporation agrees to pay the bondholders. You can get a better picture of bonds by comparing them with capital stock.

Remember

A bondholder is a creditor of a corporation; a stockholder is an owner.

Bonds	Capital Stock
Bondholders are creditors; they receive interest and are eventually repaid the principal.	Stockholders are owners; they receive dividends.
Bonds Payable is classified as a long-term liability account.	Capital stock is subdivided into Common Stock and Preferred Stock accounts, which are stockholders' equity accounts.
Interest paid on bonds is an expense that must be paid year after year. Otherwise, bondholders may initiate bankruptcy proceedings against the debtor corporation.	Dividends are not expenses; they are distributions of net income.
Interest expense is deducted to arrive at net income.	Dividends are not deducted to arrive at net income. They are deducted from Retained Earnings.

CLASSIFICATION OF BONDS

Just as car manufacturers offer different models with various combinations of accessories, corporations have created a wide variety of bonds, each with a slightly different combination of characteristics, to appeal to different investors.

Bondholders may hold the bonds themselves, or the bonds may be held in the bondholders' brokerage accounts. Bond investments are also made through mutual funds. For example, the Vanguard High-Yield Corporate Fund invests in approximately 300 different corporate bonds. Bonds are rated by financial services companies such as Moody's or Standard & Poor's. These companies rate bonds based on their risk, with low-risk bonds having a Triple A (AAA) rating and high-risk bonds having a rating of C or D.

Bonds Classified as to Time of Payment

- **Term bonds** All term bonds of a particular issue have the same term, or time period to maturity. Thus, the entire issue of bonds comes due at the same time. For example, $1,000,000 worth of 10-year bonds issued January 1, 2010, all mature on January 1, 2020.

- **Serial bonds** Serial bonds of a particular issue have a series of maturity dates. For example, $1,000,000 worth of bonds issued March 1, 2010, may mature as follows:

$100,000 on March 1, 2015
$100,000 on March 1, 2016
$100,000 on March 1, 2017
$100,000 on March 1, 2018
$100,000 on March 1, 2019
$100,000 on March 1, 2020
$100,000 on March 1, 2021
$100,000 on March 1, 2022
$100,000 on March 1, 2023
$100,000 on March 1, 2024

Bonds Classified as to Security

- **Secured bonds** When bonds are secured, they are covered or collateralized by mortgages on real estate or by titles to personal property. In case the corporation defaults in its payment of principal or interest, the bondholders, acting through a trustee, may take over the pledged assets.

- **Unsecured bonds** Unsecured bonds, also called *debenture bonds*, are backed only by the corporation's credit standing, or good name. Such bonds usually succeed only when issued by financially strong firms.

FYI

Secured bonds may be called mortgage bonds or equipment trust certificate bonds.

A bond can have characteristics of both classifications. For example, if a corporation issues 20-year mortgage bonds, the bonds are term bonds and secured bonds.

WHY A CORPORATION ISSUES BONDS

A corporation that needs money on a long-term basis has the choice of raising the necessary funds by issuing (1) common stock, (2) preferred stock, or (3) bonds.

Each choice has advantages and disadvantages. Since the holders of common stock control the corporation through their voting power, they choose the means of financing. Corporate boards of directors calculate the pros and cons of bonds as follows.

Advantages of Issuing Bonds

1. The bond-issuing corporation has the prospect of earning a greater return on the money it raises than it has to pay out in interest. This is known as **leverage**. For example, if a firm can borrow money at an interest rate of 8 percent and use this cash in the business to earn a net income of 15 percent (after taxes), then the additional earnings of 7 percent (15 percent − 8 percent) are available to pay dividends to the holders of common stock or reinvest in the company. Thus, debt is used as a *lever* to raise the owners' rate of return.
2. Interest payments are tax-deductible expenses.
3. Bondholders cannot vote; therefore, the existing common stockholders retain control of the company's affairs.

Disadvantages of Issuing Bonds

1. Bondholders are creditors of the corporation, so interest payments must be made to bondholders each year. In contrast, a corporation pays dividends to stockholders only when it has enough money to do so and when the board of directors declares a dividend.
2. The corporation must eventually pay back the principal of the bonds it issues, but it does not have to repay the money it receives from issuing stock.

When a corporation is trying to decide whether to issue additional stock or to issue bonds, an important factor is estimated future earnings and the probable stability of these earnings. The advantages and disadvantages of issuing bonds become apparent in the following example.

Midwest Development Corp., which has 160,000 shares of $50-par common stock outstanding ($8,000,000), wishes to raise an additional $4,000,000 for expansion. Midwest Development Corp. is considering three alternatives for raising the money:

- **Plan 1** Issue an additional $4,000,000 of common stock, thereby increasing the total stock outstanding from 160,000 to 240,000 shares.
- **Plan 2** Issue $4,000,000 of 8 percent cumulative preferred stock.
- **Plan 3** Issue $4,000,000 of 7 percent bonds.

Figure 1 shows how Midwest Development Corp. comes out if it has a yearly income from operations of (1) $1,680,000 and (2) $300,000. (We assume that the combined federal and state income taxes amount to 40 percent.)

You can see that plan 3 offers the greatest advantage to the original holders of common stock, provided that the company's earnings are large enough to pay the bondholders and still leave a sizable share for the holders of common stock. When the company has a *low* level of earnings, plan 1 is most advantageous to the holders of common stock because there are no prior claims of bondholders or preferred stockholders. The firm can use a combination of the three, but this entails larger financing costs.

Remember

You may hear of corporations "selling" bonds; however, bonds are liabilities. The issuing corporation is borrowing money from the bondholder.

FIGURE 1	Midwest Development Corp.—Comparison of plans for raising money

	Income from Operations $1,680,000			Income from Operations $300,000		
	Plan 1 Issue Common Stock	Plan 2 Issue Preferred Stock	Plan 3 Issue Bonds	Plan 1 Issue Common Stock	Plan 2 Issue Preferred Stock	Plan 3 Issue Bonds
Common stock now outstanding (160,000 shares)	$ 8,000,000	$ 8,000,000	$ 8,000,000	$ 8,000,000	$ 8,000,000	$ 8,000,000
Additional common stock, $50 par (80,000 shares)	4,000,000			4,000,000		
Preferred stock, 8% cumulative		4,000,000			4,000,000	
Bonds, 7%			4,000,000			4,000,000
Total capitalization	$12,000,000	$12,000,000	$12,000,000	$12,000,000	$12,000,000	$12,000,000
Income from operations (before income taxes)	$ 1,680,000	$ 1,680,000	$ 1,680,000	$ 300,000	$ 300,000	$ 300,000
Deduct bond interest expense	0	0	280,000	0	0	280,000
Income before income taxes	$ 1,680,000	$ 1,680,000	$ 1,400,000	$ 300,000	$ 300,000	$ 20,000
Deduct federal and state income taxes (40%)	672,000	672,000	560,000	120,000	120,000	8,000
Net income	$ 1,008,000	$ 1,008,000	$ 840,000	$ 180,000	$ 180,000	$ 12,000
Deduct preferred dividends		320,000			320,000	
Earnings (loss) available to common shareholders	$ 1,008,000	$ 688,000	$ 840,000	$ 180,000	$ (140,000)	$ 12,000
Earnings (loss) available to common shareholders	$ 1,008,000	$ 688,000	$ 840,000	$ 180,000	$ (140,000)	$ 12,000
Common shares outstanding	240,000	160,000	160,000	240,000	160,000	160,000
Earnings (loss) per share of common stock	$4.20	$4.30	$5.25	$0.75	$(0.875)	$0.075

You Make the Call

Your friend, Maleeha Gorman, is thinking about investing in the corporate bond market. You have told her that you studied bonds in accounting class and would be able to help her understand the different types of bonds available. How would you advise Maleeha about getting started investing in bonds?

SOLUTION

Investing in bonds can often provide a higher yield than investing in other types of investments. However, that higher yield often comes with some risk. Many corporate bonds are not secured by collateral. Therefore, if the corporation that is issuing the bond goes bankrupt, the chance of the investor recovering his or her investment is slim.

Before investing in bonds, your friend Maleeha should review the credit rating associated with each bond. All bonds have credit ratings that are published by financial services companies such as Moody's (www.moodys.com) and Standard & Poor's (www.standardandpoors.com). A bond with a Triple A (AAA) rating has the highest credit rating and very low risk. Bonds that are rated as C or D are often considered junk bonds and have very high risk.

Another option for investing in bonds is for Maleeha to invest in municipal bonds. Municipal bonds, often called munis, are issued by government entities such as school districts and are generally lower risk than corporate bonds. Most munis are exempt from federal income taxes and from state and local taxes, especially in the state of issue.

ACCOUNTING FOR THE ISSUANCE OF BONDS

LEARNING OBJECTIVE 1

Journalize transactions involving the issuance of bonds at a premium or discount and the interest payment on bonds.

Remember

Bonds Payable is a long-term liability. Its normal balance is a credit.

When a corporation issues bonds at face value, it records the transaction as a debit to Cash and a credit to Bonds Payable. Bonds Payable is a long-term liability account. For example, on January 1, Sean Construction Corporation issues $500,000 of 6 percent, 5-year bonds at face value, with interest payable semiannually, on June 30 and December 31. Sean Construction Corporation's entry to record the sale of the bonds, in general journal form, is as follows:

Date	Description	Post. Ref.	Debit	Credit
20—				
Jan. 1	Cash		500 0 0 0 00	
	Bonds Payable			500 0 0 0 00
	Sold 5-year, 6 percent bonds,			
	dated January 1, at face value.			

If there is more than one bond issue, the company keeps a separate account for each issue. The listing on the balance sheet should identify the issue by stipulating its interest rate and due date.

Throughout the life of the bond, the corporation is required to pay interest. A 5-year semiannual bond, such as the one in our example, would require 10 interest payments (5 years at 2 times per year). The interest payment is calculated as:

$$\text{Face Value} \times \text{Interest Rate} \times \text{Time Period}$$

The interest for the Sean Construction Corporation bond would be $15,000 ($500,000 $\times 0.06 \times {}^{6}/_{12}$). At the end of the life of the bond, the corporation is then required to pay the bondholders the face value of the bond, or $500,000. The following diagram depicts the bond issued by Sean Construction Corporation.

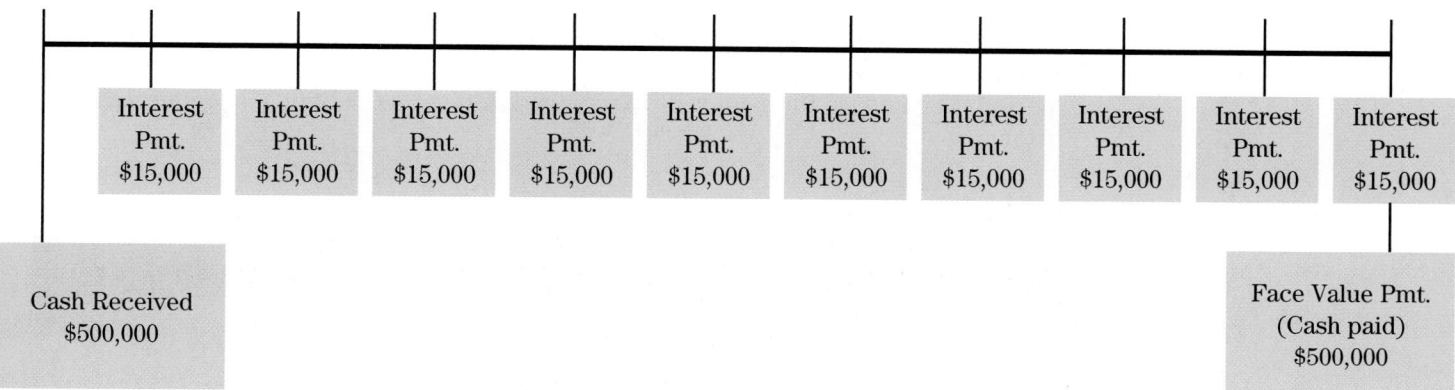

Bonds Sold at a Premium

The corporation may receive a price for its bonds that is above or below their face value, depending on the rate of interest offered and the general credit standing of the company. If a corporation offers a rate of interest that is higher than the market rate for similar securities, investors may be willing to pay a **premium** for the bonds.

For example, on January 1, Sean Construction Corporation issues $750,000 of 9 percent, 10-year bonds at 103, with interest payable semiannually, on June 30 and December 31. The term "103" refers to the price of the bonds; it is a percentage of the face value of the bonds, with the percent symbol omitted. This is how the securities exchanges record bond prices. In this example, $750,000 of bonds at 103 means 103 percent of $750,000 ($750,000 $\times$ 1.03 = $772,500). Sean Construction Corporation's entry to record the sale of the bonds, in general journal form, is as follows:

Date		Description	Post. Ref.	Debit	Credit
20—					
Jan.	1	Cash		772 5 0 0 00	
		Bonds Payable			750 0 0 0 00
		Premium on Bonds Payable			22 5 0 0 00
		Sold 10-year, 9 percent			
		bonds, dated January 1, at 103.			

Premium on Bonds Payable represents the amount received over and above the face value of the bonds. The accountant lists Premium on Bonds Payable right below the bond account in the Long-Term Liabilities section of the balance sheet. To illustrate the placement of Bonds Payable and Premium on Bonds Payable, a partial balance sheet on January 1 is shown here.

Sean Construction Corporation
Balance Sheet
January 1, 20—

Long-Term Liabilities:		
9 Percent Bonds Payable, due January 1, 20—	$750,000	
Plus Premium on Bonds Payable	22,500	$772,500

The corporation will write off or amortize Premium on Bonds Payable over the remaining life of the bond issue through an adjusting entry at the end of the fiscal period. The entries for each year to pay the interest on the bonds, in general journal form, are

Date	Description	Post. Ref.	Debit	Credit
20—				
June 30	Interest Expense		33 7 5 0 00	
	Cash			33 7 5 0 00
	Semiannual interest			
	payment on bonds, face			
	value of $750,000, 9 percent.			
	($750,000 × 0.09 × $^{6}/_{12}$)			

Date	Description	Post. Ref.	Debit	Credit
20—				
Dec. 31	Interest Expense		33 7 5 0 00	
	Cash			33 7 5 0 00
	Semiannual interest			
	payment on bonds, face			
	value of $750,000, 9 percent.			
	($750,000 × 0.09 × $^{6}/_{12}$)			

Adjusting Entry for Bonds Sold at a Premium

As previously stated, the Premium on Bonds Payable account is written off, or *amortized*, over the life of the bond. What is **amortization**? Amortization represents the write-off of the premium account and is calculated as:

Premium on Bonds Payable ÷ Bond Life

The amortization for Sean Construction Corporation would be $2,250 ($22,500 ÷ 10 years).

A company records bond amortization by debiting the Premium on Bonds Payable account and using Interest Expense as the offsetting credit. The entry appears as an adjusting entry at the end of the fiscal period. It is first recorded in the Adjustments columns of the work sheet, like any other adjusting entry. The entry to amortize or write off one year of the $22,500 premium on the 10-year bonds issued by Sean Construction Corporation is as follows:

Date		Description	Post. Ref.	Debit	Credit
20—		Adjusting Entries			
Dec.	31	Premium on Bonds Payable		2 2 5 0 00	
		Interest Expense			2 2 5 0 00
		($22,500 ÷ 10 years)			

By T accounts, the entries for the year look like this:

Cash					Bonds Payable			
	+	−				−	+	
Jan. 1	772,500	June 30	33,750				Jan.1	750,000
		Dec. 31	33,750					

Interest Expense					Premium on Bonds Payable			
	+	−				−	+	
June 30	33,750	Dec. 31 Adj.	2,250	Dec. 31 Adj.	2,250		Jan.1	22,500
Dec. 31	33,750	Clos.	65,250					

The adjusting entry reduces the balance of the Interest Expense account from $67,500 ($33,750 + $33,750) to $65,250 ($67,500 − $2,250). The accountant then closes Interest Expense into Income Summary in the amount of $65,250. The adjusting entry also has the effect of reducing the Premium on Bonds Payable account at the rate of $2,250 per year until it reaches zero, when the bonds come due.

> **Remember**
> A premium reduces a corporation's total interest expense over the life of the bond.

In this illustration, we showed the amortization of the bond premium calculated by the straight-line method on an annual basis, which will also be used in the problems. This is like calculating depreciation by the straight-line method. (One can also record the amortization of the bond premium, just as one can record depreciation, on a monthly or semiannual basis.) Many corporations, however, amortize premiums on bonds using the effective interest rate method, which is covered in more advanced accounting courses.

Returning to our illustration, after the accountant records the adjusting entry, the balance of Interest Expense is $65,250. This amount represents the annual interest expense on the books. Here is another way of looking at it:

Cash to Be Paid

Face value of the bonds	$750,000	
Interest (20 payments of $33,750 each)	675,000	$1,425,000

Less Cash Received

Face value of the bonds	$750,000	
Plus premium on the bonds	22,500	772,500

Excess of Cash to Be Paid over Cash Received

(Interest expense for 10 years) $ 652,500

$$\text{Interest Expense per Year} = \frac{\$652,500}{10 \text{ years}} = \$65,250$$

Example: Bonds Sold at a Premium, with Interest Payment Dates That Do Not Coincide with the End of the Fiscal Year

On March 1, George's Electronics issues $6,000,000 worth of 20-year, 9 percent bonds, at 104, dated March 1, with interest payable semiannually, on September 1 and March 1. The corporation's fiscal year ends on December 31. A diagram of the dates looks like this:

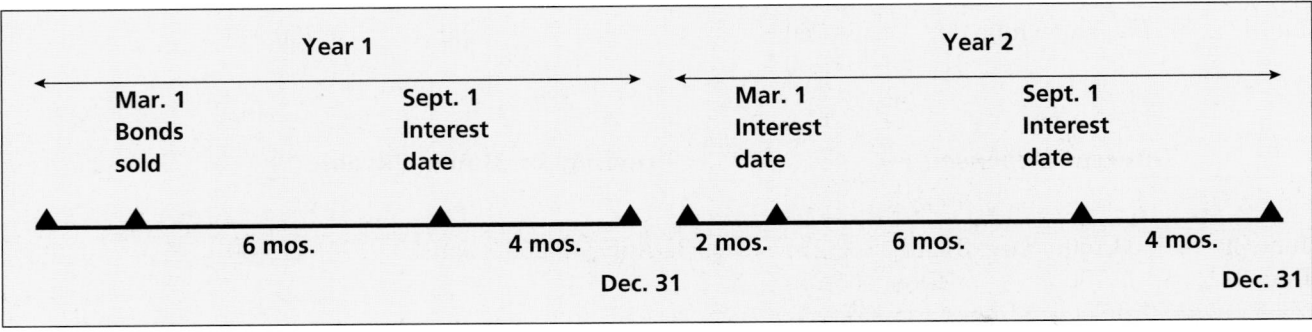

Since the date on which the interest has to be paid does not coincide with the end of the fiscal year, George's Electronics has to make an adjusting entry for the accrued interest for the period from September 1 to December 31. The entries for the first year, in general journal form, are as follows:

Date		Description	Post. Ref.	Debit	Credit
Year 1					
Mar.	1	Cash ($6,000,000 × 1.04)		6,240 0 0 0 00	
		Bonds Payable			6,000 0 0 0 00
		Premium on Bonds Payable			240 0 0 0 00
		Sold 20-year, 9 percent			
		bonds, dated March 1, at 104.			

Date		Description	Post. Ref.	Debit	Credit
Year 1					
Sept.	1	Interest Expense		270 0 0 0 00	
		Cash			270 0 0 0 00
		Semiannual interest on			
		bonds, face value of			
		$6,000,000, 9 percent.			
		($6,000,000 × 0.09 × $^{6}/_{12}$)			

Date		Description	Post. Ref.	Debit	Credit
Year 1		Adjusting Entries			
Dec.	31	Premium on Bonds Payable		10 0 0 0 00	
		Interest Expense			10 0 0 0 00
		($240,000 × $^{10 months}/_{240 months}$)			
	31	Interest Expense		180 0 0 0 00	
		Interest Payable			180 0 0 0 00
		($6,000,000 × 0.09 × $^{4}/_{12}$)			
		Closing Entry			
	31	Income Summary		440 0 0 0 00	
		Interest Expense			440 0 0 0 00

The amortization of the premium on December 31 is for only part of a year. The next year, amortization will be for a full year. The adjusting entry for accrued interest on a bond is like the one for accrued interest on an interest-bearing note payable. In T account form, the first-year entries look like this:

Cash

	+		−	
Year 1		Year 1		
Mar. 1	6,240,000	Sept. 1	270,000	

Bonds Payable

	−		+	
		Year 1		
		Mar. 1	6,000,000	

Interest Expense

	+		−	
Year 1		Year 1		
Sept. 1	270,000	Dec. 31 Adj.	10,000	
Dec. 31 Adj.	180,000	31 Clos.	440,000	

Premium on Bonds Payable

	−		+	
Year 1		Year 1		
Dec. 31 Adj.	10,000	Mar. 1	240,000	

Income Summary

Year 1		Year 1		
(Int. Exp.)	440,000	Clos.	xxxx	

Interest Payable

	−		+	
		Year 1		
		Dec. 31 Adj.	180,000	

Because the adjusting entry for accrued interest opened a new balance sheet account, Interest Payable, George's Electronics' accountant should make a reversing entry as of the first day of the next fiscal year. The reversing entry enables the accountant to follow the regular routine for the payment of six months' interest on March 1 without having to split up the interest for the period between September 1 of one year and March 1 of the following year.

Date		Description	Post. Ref.	Debit	Credit
Year 2		Reversing Entry			
Jan.	1	Interest Payable		180 0 0 0 00	
		Interest Expense			180 0 0 0 00

The entries for the rest of the second year are

Date		Description	Post. Ref.	Debit	Credit
Year 2					
Mar.	1	Interest Expense		270 0 0 0 00	
		Cash			270 0 0 0 00
		Semiannual interest on			
		bonds, face value of			
		$6,000,000, 9 percent.			
		($6,000,000 × 0.09 × $^6/_{12}$)			

Date		Description	Post. Ref.	Debit	Credit
Year 2					
Sept.	1	Interest Expense		270 0 0 0 00	
		Cash			270 0 0 0 00
		Semiannual interest on			
		bonds, face value of			
		$6,000,000, 9 percent.			
		($6,000,000 × 0.09 × $^6/_{12}$)			

Date		Description	Post. Ref.	Debit	Credit
Year 2		Adjusting Entries			
Dec.	31	Premium on Bonds Payable		12 0 0 0 00	
		Interest Expense			12 0 0 0 00
		($240,000 × $^{12\ months}/_{240\ months}$)			
	31	Interest Expense		180 0 0 0 00	
		Interest Payable			180 0 0 0 00
		($6,000,000 × 0.09 × $^4/_{12}$)			
		Closing Entry			
	31	Income Summary		528 0 0 0 00	
		Interest Expense			528 0 0 0 00

Here are the relevant T accounts from the previous year posted to date:

Cash

	+		−	
Year 1		Year 1		
Mar. 1	6,240,000	Sept. 1	270,000	
		Year 2		
		Mar. 1	270,000	
		Sept. 1	270,000	

Interest Expense

	+		−	
Year 1		Year 1		
Sept. 1	270,000	Dec. 31 Adj.	10,000	
Dec. 31 Adj.	180,000	31 Clos.	440,000	
Year 2		Year 2		
Mar. 1	270,000	Jan. 1 Rev.	180,000	
Sept. 1	270,000	Dec. 31 Adj.	12,000	
Dec. 31 Adj.	180,000	31 Clos.	528,000	

Income Summary

Year 1		Year 1		
(Int. Exp.)	440,000	Clos.		xxxx
Year 2		Year 2		
(Int. Exp.)	528,000	Clos.		xxxx

Bonds Payable

	−		+	
		Year 1		
		Mar. 1	6,000,000	

Premium on Bonds Payable

		−	+	
Year 1			Year 1	
Dec. 31 Adj.	10,000		Mar. 1	240,000
Year 2				
Dec. 31 Adj.	12,000			

Interest Payable

		−	+	
			Year 1	
			Dec. 31 Adj.	180,000
Year 2			Year 2	
Jan. 1 Rev.	180,000		Dec. 31 Adj.	180,000

Bonds Sold at a Discount

A corporation can also issue bonds that will pay a rate of interest that is less than the prevailing market rate of interest for comparable bonds. If this happens, the corporation is said to sell its bonds at less than face value—or at a **discount**.

To demonstrate this, assume that on January 1, Stewart, Inc., issues 6 percent, 20-year bonds with a face value of $700,000, at 96, with interest to be paid semiannually, on June 30 and December 31. Stewart, Inc., will record the following journal entry:

Date		Description	Post. Ref.	Debit	Credit
20—					
Jan.	1	Cash ($700,000 × 0.96)		672 0 0 0 00	
		Discount on Bonds Payable		28 0 0 0 00	
		Bonds Payable			700 0 0 0 00
		Sold 20-year, 6 percent			
		bonds, dated January 1, at 96.			

> **Remember**
>
> Contra accounts have their signs reversed. Since the signs for Bonds Payable are debit minus and credit plus, the signs for Discount on Bonds Payable are the opposite.

The Discount on Bonds Payable account is a **contra-liability account**; it is listed on a classified balance sheet as a deduction from Bonds Payable. A partial balance sheet on January 1 is as follows:

	Stewart, Inc.		
	Balance Sheet		
	January 1, 20—		

Long-Term Liabilities:		
6 Percent Bonds Payable, due January 1, 20—	$700,000	
Less Discount on Bonds Payable	28,000	$672,000

The journal entries for the payment of interest semiannually, each year are as follows:

Date		Description	Post. Ref.	Debit	Credit
20—					
June	30	Interest Expense		21 0 0 0 00	
		Cash			21 0 0 0 00
		Semiannual interest on bonds, face			
		value of $700,000, 6 percent.			
		($700,000 × 0.06 × $^6/_{12}$)			

Date		Description	Post. Ref.	Debit	Credit
20—					
Dec.	31	Interest Expense		21 0 0 0 00	
		Cash			21 0 0 0 00
		Semiannual interest on bonds, face			
		value of $700,000, 6 percent.			
		($700,000 × 0.06 × $^6/_{12}$)			

Adjusting Entry for Bonds Sold at a Discount

The corporation amortizes the Discount on Bonds Payable account, as it does the Premium on Bonds Payable account, over the life of the bond issue. The amortization of the Discount on Bonds Payable account is calculated as:

$$\text{Discount on Bonds Payable} \div \text{Bond Life}$$

The write-off consists of an adjusting entry at the end of the fiscal period. Again, the accountant uses Interest Expense as the offsetting account in the adjusting entry. The adjusting entry to amortize one year of the $28,000 discount on the 20-year bonds issued by Stewart, Inc., is as follows:

Date		Description	Post. Ref.	Debit	Credit
20—		Adjusting Entry			
Dec.	31	Interest Expense		1 4 0 0 00	
		Discount on Bonds Payable			1 4 0 0 00
		($28,000 ÷ 20 years)			

By T accounts, the entries for the year look like this:

Cash					Bonds Payable			
+		**−**				**−**	**+**	
Jan. 1	672,000	June 30	21,000				Jan. 1	700,000
		Dec. 31	21,000					

Interest Expense					Discount on Bonds Payable			
+		**−**				**+**	**−**	
June 30	21,000	Dec. 31 Clos.	43,400	Jan. 1	28,000		Dec. 31 Adj.	1,400
Dec. 31	21,000							
31 Adj.	1,400							

The adjusting entry increases the balance of Interest Expense from $42,000 ($21,000 + $21,000) to $43,400 ($42,000 + $1,400). The accountant then closes Interest Expense into Income Summary in the amount of $43,400. The adjusting entry also has the effect of reducing the Discount on Bonds Payable account at the rate of $1,400 per year until it reaches zero, when the bonds come due.

Here is another way of looking at the interest expense for a bond issued at a discount:

> **Remember**
>
> A discount increases a corporation's total interest expense over the life of the bonds.

Cash to Be Paid

Face value of the bonds	$700,000	
Interest (40 payments of $21,000 each)	840,000	$1,540,000

Less Cash Received

Face value of the bonds	$700,000	
Less discount on the bonds	28,000	672,000

Excess of Cash to Be Paid over Cash Received

(Interest expense for 20 years)		$ 868,000

$$\text{Interest Expense per Year} = \frac{\$868,000}{20 \text{ years}} = \$ 43,400$$

BOND SINKING FUND

To provide greater security for bondholders, the bond agreement may specify that the issuing corporation make annual deposits of cash into a special fund—called a **sinking fund**—to be used to pay off the bond issue when it comes due. The company keeps the sinking fund separate from its other assets and puts the cash deposited in the sinking fund to work by investing it in income-producing securities. When the bonds mature, the total of the annual deposits plus the earnings on the investments should add up to approximately the face value of the bonds. The sinking fund may be controlled by either the corporation or a trustee—usually a bank.

When the corporation deposits cash in its sinking fund, it records the transaction as a debit to Sinking Fund Cash and a credit to Cash. When the corporation or the trustee invests the sinking fund cash, the transaction is recorded as a debit to Sinking Fund Investments and a credit to Sinking Fund Cash. **Both Sinking Fund Cash and Sinking Fund Investments are classified as investment accounts**.

3 LEARNING OBJECTIVE

Journalize entries pertaining to the establishment of a bond sinking fund, the receipt of income from sinking fund investments, and the eventual payment of the principal of the bonds.

Accounting in Your Future

Remember

There are two bond sinking fund asset accounts—the cash fund and the investment fund.

These accounts are classified as long-term assets because their use is restricted to paying off the bond issue—long-term liabilities. When the corporation receives interest or dividend income on the investments, it debits Sinking Fund Cash and credits Sinking Fund Income. Sinking Fund Income is classified as an Other Income account on the income statement.

For example, Flores Development issues $800,000 worth of 10-year bonds dated January 1, with the provision that at the end of each of the 10 years, it will make an equal deposit into a sinking fund. Flores Development, which manages its own sinking fund, intends to invest this money in securities that will yield approximately 6 percent per year. Let's assume that, according to compound interest tables, an annual deposit of $60,693 will accumulate to approximately $800,000 in 10 years, given the 6 percent annual interest rate.

The following are a few of the many routine transactions that affect the sinking fund during the 10-year period:

- **Annual deposits of cash in bond sinking fund**

Date	Description	Post. Ref.	Debit	Credit
	Sinking Fund Cash		60 6 9 3 00	
	Cash			60 6 9 3 00
	Annual deposit in bond			
	sinking fund, according to			
	bond agreement.			

Like a large corporation, the government may want to sell bonds, often called municipal bonds, to raise additional money for projects. The government may, at the same time, set up a bond sinking fund to provide reassurance to bondholders that the bonds will be paid when due. A sinking fund is similar to putting money aside for a specific future purchase.

- **Purchase of investments** Time of purchase and amount invested may vary.

Date	Description	Post. Ref.	Debit	Credit
	Sinking Fund Investments		59 7 3 0 00	
	Sinking Fund Cash			59 7 3 0 00
	Bought $60,000 of			
	Consolidated Steel 7			
	percent bonds at 99½, plus			
	$30 brokerage commission.			
	($60,000 × 0.995 = $59,700;			
	$59,700 + $30 = $59,730)			

- **Receipt of income from investments** Interest and dividends at different times during the year.

Date	Description	Post. Ref.	Debit	Credit
	Sinking Fund Cash		6 5 7 0 00	
	Sinking Fund Income			6 5 7 0 00
	Received interest and dividends			
	on sinking fund investments.			

- **Sale of investments** Investments may be sold and the proceeds reinvested. Assume Flores Development sold investments with a basis of $147,200 for $148,960, recognizing a gain of $1,760.

Date	Description	Post. Ref.	Debit	Credit
	Sinking Fund Cash		148 9 6 0 00	
	Sinking Fund Investments			147 2 0 0 00
	Gain on Sale of Sinking Fund			
	Investments			1 7 6 0 00
	Sold sinking fund investments,			
	yielding a gain of $1,760.			

- **Payment of bonds** Cash available consists of the sinking fund after the sale of the investments plus the last annual deposit, which should bring the sinking fund up to approximately $800,000.

Date	Description	Post. Ref.	Debit	Credit
	Bonds Payable		800 0 0 0 00	
	Sinking Fund Cash			800 0 0 0 00
	Paid bond obligation with			
	sinking fund cash.			

REDEMPTION OF BONDS

LEARNING OBJECTIVE 4

Journalize transactions involving the redemption of bonds.

To protect itself against a decline in market interest rates, a corporation may issue **callable bonds**. Callable bonds give the corporation the right—as stipulated in the bond **indenture**, or agreement—to **redeem** or buy back the bonds at a specified figure—the *call price*—that is ordinarily higher than the face value.

Morris, Inc., issues $2,000,000 worth of 9 percent, 20-year callable bonds, with a call price of 104. Later, interest rates in general fall. Under the new market conditions, Morris, Inc., could sell $2,000,000 worth of bonds at face value, with an interest rate of 6 percent. It would benefit Morris, Inc., to buy back the bonds, even though it would have to pay $2,080,000 for them ($2,000,000 × 1.04), then turn around and issue new bonds at 6 percent. The annual savings in interest would amount to $60,000 (3 percent of $2,000,000). Even if a corporation's bonds are not callable, it may still buy its own bonds on the open market, if it can find any for sale.

When a corporation redeems its bonds at a price that is less than their book value, it realizes a gain. Conversely, if it redeems its bonds at a price that is more than their book value, it incurs a loss. The book value is the sum of the Bonds Payable account and the Premium on Bonds Payable account (or the Bonds Payable account less the Discount on Bonds Payable account).

For example, Seneri, Inc., a different corporation, has $500,000 worth of callable bonds outstanding on December 31, with a call price of 105; there is an unamortized discount of $2,000. Seneri, Inc., pays the interest to date on December 31 and exercises its option of calling in or redeeming the bonds on the same date, December 31. The entry is shown below in general journal form. The loss represents the difference between the book value and the price paid (also determined by the difference between debits and credits).

Date		Description	Post. Ref.	Debit	Credit
20—					
Dec.	31	Bonds Payable		500 0 0 0 00	
		Loss on Redemption of Bonds		27 0 0 0 00	
		Cash ($500,000 × 1.05)			525 0 0 0 00
		Discount on Bonds Payable			2 0 0 0 00
		To record redemption of			
		bonds at 105.			

Recall that, even if a corporation's bonds are not callable, the firm can buy back the bonds—all of them, or as many as it can find on the open market. For example, Vince Fabrics, another corporation, has $1,000,000 worth of 7 percent bonds outstanding, on which there is an unamortized premium of $30,000. On July 15, Vince Fabrics buys $100,000 of bonds (one-tenth of the original issue) in the open market at 97, plus 15 days' accrued interest. The entry, in general journal form, is as follows:

Date		Description	Post. Ref.	Debit	Credit
20—					
July	15	Bonds Payable		100 0 0 0 00	
		Premium on Bonds Payable			
		($30,000 × $\frac{1}{10}$)		3 0 0 0 00	
		Interest Expense			
		($100,000 × 0.07 × $\frac{15}{360}$·)		2 9 1 67	
		Cash [($100,000 × 0.97) + $291.67]			97 2 9 1 67
		Gain on Redemption of Bonds			6 0 0 0 00
		To record redemption of bonds			
		at 97, plus accrued interest.			

*We will use the commercial practice of 360 days, as we used when calculating interest on notes receivables and notes payables, instead of 365 days.

Redemption in effect cancels all or a portion of the Bonds Payable account, as well as the accompanying premium or discount. **We list Gain (or Loss) on Redemption of Bonds on the income statement under the heading Other Income (or Other Expense).**

BALANCE SHEET

The balance sheet of Hank Jones Electronics, Inc., shown in Figure 2 on the next page, shows how to place the accounts introduced in this chapter.

FIGURE 2

Balance sheet for Hank Jones Electronics, Inc.

Hank Jones Electronics, Inc.
Balance Sheet
December 31, 20—

Assets

Current Assets:			
Cash		$ 14,000	
Notes Receivable		30,000	
Accounts Receivable	$220,000		
Less Allowance for Doubtful Accounts	4,000	216,000	
Merchandise Inventory		647,000	
Total Current Assets			$ 907,000
Investments:			
Sinking Fund Cash		$ 5,000	
Sinking Fund Investments		84,000	
Total Investments			89,000
Property and Equipment:			
Land		$ 70,000	
Building	$180,000		
Less Accumulated Depreciation	45,000	135,000	
Equipment	$222,000		
Less Accumulated Depreciation	32,000	190,000	
Total Property and Equipment			395,000
Intangible Assets:			
Goodwill		$ 20,000	
Patents		8,000	
Total Intangible Assets			28,000
Total Assets			$1,419,000

Liabilities

Current Liabilities:			
Accounts Payable		$ 70,000	
Income Tax Payable		8,000	
Dividends Payable		12,000	
Total Current Liabilities			$ 90,000
Long-Term Liabilities:			
6 Percent Bonds Payable, due			
December 31, 20—	$100,000		
Less Discount on Bonds Payable	3,000	$ 97,000	
8 Percent Bonds Payable, due			
March 31, 20—	$200,000		
Plus Premium on Bonds Payable	2,000	202,000	
Total Long-Term Liabilities			299,000
Total Liabilities			$ 389,000

Stockholders' Equity

Paid-in Capital:			
Common Stock, $10 Par (100,000 shares			
authorized, 40,000 shares issued)	$400,000		
Paid-in Capital in Excess of Par Value	220,000		
Total Paid-in Capital		$620,000	
Retained Earnings:			
Unappropriated Retained Earnings	$310,000		
Appropriated for Property Expansion	100,000		
Total Retained Earnings		410,000	
Total Stockholders' Equity			1,030,000
Total Liabilities and Stockholders' Equity			$1,419,000

CHAPTER REVIEW

Study & Practice

1 **LEARNING OBJECTIVE**
Journalize transactions involving the issuance of bonds at a premium or discount and the interest payment on bonds.

A **bond** is sold at a **premium** when the stated rate of interest is higher than the market rate of interest. The entry for selling a bond at a premium is a debit to Cash, a credit to Bonds Payable, and a credit to Premium on Bonds Payable. A bond is sold at a **discount** when the stated rate of interest is less than the market rate of interest. The entry for selling a bond at a discount is a debit to Cash, a debit to Discount on Bonds Payable, and a credit to Bonds Payable. Interest payments are typically recorded semiannually. The entry to record interest paid involves a debit to Interest Expense and a credit to Cash.

PRACTICE EXERCISE 1

On January 1, Jalle, Inc., issued $600,000 of 15-year, 6 percent bonds at 102, with interest payable seminannually. Journalize the entry for issuance of the bond on January 1 and the entry to record the first interest payment on June 30.

PRACTICE EXERCISE 1 SOLUTION

Date		Description	Post. Ref.	Debit	Credit
Year 1					
Jan.	1	Cash ($600,000 × 1.02)		612 0 0 0 00	
		Bonds Payable			600 0 0 0 00
		Premium on Bonds Payable			12 0 0 0 00
		Sold 15-year, 6 percent bonds,			
		dated January 1, at 102.			
June	30	Interest Expense		18 0 0 0 00	
		Cash			18 0 0 0 00
		Semiannual interest			
		payment on bonds, face value			
		of $600,000, 6 percent.			
		($600,000 × 0.06 × $^{6}/_{12}$)			

2 **LEARNING OBJECTIVE**
Journalize adjusting entries for amortization of bond premiums and discounts and for accrued interest payable.

Premiums and discounts are written off, or amortized, over the remaining life of the bond from the time of the sale. The entry to record the **amortization**, or write off, of a premium is a debit to Premium on Bonds Payable and a credit to Interest Expense. The entry to record the amortization, or write off, of a discount is a debit to Interest Expense and a credit to Discount on Bonds Payable. Accrued interest represents the amount of interest incurred between the last interest payment date and the end of the fiscal period. The entry to record accrued interest is a debit to Interest Expense and a credit to Interest Payable.

PRACTICE EXERCISE 2

Record the adjusting entry for amortization of the bond premium for the bond issued by Jalle, Inc., in Practice Exercise 1.

PRACTICE EXERCISE 2 SOLUTION

Date			Description	Post. Ref.	Debit	Credit
20—			Adjusting Entry			
Dec.	31		Premium on Bonds Payable		8 0 0 00	
			Interest Expense			8 0 0 00
			($12,000 ÷ 15 years)			

3 LEARNING OBJECTIVE

Journalize entries pertaining to the establishment of a bond sinking fund, the receipt of income from sinking fund investments, and the eventual payment of the principal of the bonds.

The entry to establish a bond **sinking fund** is a debit to Sinking Fund Cash and a credit to Cash. The entry for the receipt of income from sinking fund investments is a debit to Sinking Fund Cash and a credit to Sinking Fund Income. The entry for the payment of the principal of the bonds is a debit to Bonds Payable and a credit to Sinking Fund Cash.

PRACTICE EXERCISE 3

Stanley Construction Corporation issued $600,000 worth of 20-year bonds dated January 1, with the provision that at the end of each of the 20 years, it will make an equal deposit into a sinking fund. Stanley intends to invest this money in securities that will yield approximately 4 percent per year. Assume that an annual deposit of $20,150 will accumulate to approximately $600,000 in 20 years, given the 4 percent annual interest rate. Stanley also bought $20,000 of 7 percent bonds at 98, plus a $15 brokerage commission, from Soo Cycles. Record the following journal entries:

a. The annual deposits of cash in the bond sinking fund.
b. The purchase of investments from Soo Cycles.

PRACTICE EXERCISE 3 SOLUTION

Date		Description	Post. Ref.	Debit	Credit
	a.	Sinking Fund Cash		20 1 5 0 00	
		Cash			20 1 5 0 00
		Annual deposit in bond sinking fund,			
		according to bond agreement.			
	b.	Sinking Fund Investments		19 6 1 5 00	
		Sinking Fund Cash			19 6 1 5 00
		Bought $20,000 of Soo Cycles			
		7 percent bonds at 98, plus $15			
		brokerage commission.			
		($20,000 × 0.98 = $19,600;			
		$19,600 + $15 = $19,615)			

LEARNING OBJECTIVE

4

Journalize transactions involving the redemption of bonds.

Assuming interest is paid up to date, the entry for the redemption of bonds is a debit to Bonds Payable, either a debit to Premium on Bonds Payable or a credit to Discount on Bonds Payable, either a debit to Loss on Redemption of Bonds or a credit to Gain on Redemption of Bonds, and a credit to Cash. If there is accrued interest on the bonds, the entry would also include a debit to Interest Expense.

PRACTICE EXERCISE 4

Bilbao Corporation has the following account balances: Bonds Payable, $800,000; Discount on Bonds Payable, $20,000. As a step in redeeming the bond issue, Bilbao Corporation buys $80,000 worth of its bonds (one-tenth of the original issue) on the open market at 96. Give the entry to record the redemption.

PRACTICE EXERCISE 4 SOLUTION

Date	Description	Post. Ref.	Debit	Credit
	Bonds Payable		80 0 0 0 00	
	Cash ($80,000 × 0.96)			76 8 0 0 00
	Discount on Bonds Payable			
	($20,000 × $^1/_{10}$)			2 0 0 0 00
	Gain on Redemption of Bond			1 2 0 0 00
	To record redemption of			
	bonds at 96.			

Before a Test Check: Chapters 18–21

PART I: TRUE/FALSE QUESTIONS

T   F   **1.** A salary allowance represents a withdrawal by a partner for personal use when allocating partnership net income to partners.

T   F   **2.** Mutual agency means that each partner can enter into contracts in the name of the firm.

T   F   **3.** The primary difference between accounting for a sole proprietorship and accounting for a partnership is in the owners' equity accounts.

T   F   **4.** Stockholders' equity in a corporation can also be referred to as capital.

T   F   **5.** The Organization Expense account for a corporation is classified as an expense account.

T   F   **6.** Double taxation means that corporate income is taxed first at the corporate level and then again as dividends to stockholders.

T   F   **7.** The issuance of a stock dividend results in a decrease in the assets of a corporation.

T   F   **8.** When retained earnings are appropriated for property expansion, cash is set aside to pay for the expansion.

T   F   **9.** Dividends are declared only by a vote of the board of directors that is recorded in the minute book.

T   F   **10.** The limit of liability is the same for partners in a general partnership as for stockholders in a corporation.

T F **11.** A premium on bonds payable is amortized over the period from the date of issue until the maturity date.

T F **12.** Discount on Bonds Payable is classified as a contra-liability account.

PART II: COMPLETION

1. _____ occurs when a partnership ends, the assets are sold, creditors are paid, and the remaining cash is distributed among the partners.

2. The ability of each partner to act as an agent of the firm, thereby committing the entire firm to a binding contract, is called _____.

3. A corporation's stock that is in the hands of its stockholders is called _____.

4. The owners of a corporation are referred to as _____.

5. A distribution of earnings of a corporation in the form of cash is called a(n) _____.

6. A distribution of a corporation's retained earnings to stockholders in the form of shares of corporate stock is called a(n) _____.

7. A restriction of a portion of retained earnings designated for a specific purpose is called a(n) _____.

8. The systematic writing off of a bond premium or discount over the remaining life of the bond is called _____.

9. The _____ is the excess of the price received over the face value of a bond.

10. An account such as Discount on Bonds Payable, which represents a deduction from a liability, is called a(n) _____ account.

PART III: APPLICATION

A. Partnerships

Calculations Involving Division of Net Income

Leonard and Reeves are partners in the Cruise Line Shop LLC. Balances in the Capital accounts of Leonard and Reeves at the beginning of the year are $90,000 and $70,000, respectively. The net income of the firm for the year is $80,000. Calculate each partner's share of net income under the specified conditions. The first answer is given as an example.

0. Equally.
1. Ratio of 3:1.
2. In the ratio of the balances of their Capital accounts at the beginning of the year.
3. Salary allowances of $30,000 to Leonard and $35,000 to Reeves; the remainder divided equally.
4. Interest allowances of 9 percent on the balances of their Capital accounts at the beginning of the year; the remainder divided equally.
5. Salary allowances of $25,000 to Leonard and $30,000 to Reeves and interest allowances of 10 percent on the balances of their Capital accounts at the beginning of the year; the remainder divided equally.

	Leonard's Share	Reeve's Share
0.	$40,000	$40,000
1.		
2.		
3.		
4.		
5.		

B. Corporations

Stockholders' Equity

The charter of the Zimmerman Corporation authorized the issuance of 20,000 shares of cumulative preferred 8 percent stock, $50 par, and 160,000 shares of common stock, $10 par. At the end of this year, the balances of the stockholders' equity accounts are as follows:

Common Stock	$750,000
Paid-in Capital from Donation	6,500
Preferred 8 Percent Stock	240,000
Preferred 8 Percent Stock Subscribed	30,000
Retained Earnings (credit balance)	240,000

Prepare the Stockholders' Equity section of the balance sheet, including descriptive details of stock accounts, for the end of this year.

ANSWERS: PART I

1. F;   **2.** T;   **3.** T;   **4.** T;   **5.** T;   **6.** T;   **7.** F;   **8.** F;   **9.** T;   **10.** F;   **11.** T;   **12.** T

ANSWERS: PART II

1. Liquidation;   **2.** mutual agency;   **3.** outstanding stock;   **4.** stockholders;
5. cash dividend;   **6.** stock dividend;   **7.** appropriation of retained earnings;
8. amortization;   **9.** premium;   **10.** contra-liability

ANSWERS: PART III

A. Partnerships

	Leonard's Share	Reeves' Share
0.	$40,000	$40,000
1.	60,000	20,000
2.	45,000	35,000
3.	37,500	42,500
4.	40,900	39,100
5.	38,500	41,500

Calculations:
1. Leonard: $80,000 × (3/4) = $60,000; Reeve: $80,000 × (1/4) = $20,000
2. Leonard: $80,000 × ($90,000 / $160,000) = $45,000; Reeve: $80,000 × ($70,000/$160,000)
= $35,000
3. $80,000 − ($30,000 + $35,000) = $15,000; $15,000 / 2 = $7,500
Leonard: $30,000 + $7,500 = $37,500; Reeve: $35,000 + $7,500 = $42,500
4. $90,000 × 0.09 = $8,100; $70,000 × 0.09 = $6,300
$80,000 − ($8,100 + $6,300) = $65,600; $65,600 / 2 = $32,800
Leonard: $32,800 + $8,100 = $40,900; Reeve: $32,800 + $6,300 = $39,100
5. $90,000 × 0.10 = $9,000; $70,000 × 0.10 = $7,000
$80,000 − ($25,000 + $30,000 + $9,000 + $7,000) = $9,000; $9,000 / 2 = $4,500
Leonard: $25,000 + $9,000 + $4,500 = $38,500; Reeve: $30,000 + $7,000 +
$4,500 = $41,500

B. Corporations

Stockholders' Equity			
Paid-in Capital:			
Preferred 8 Percent Stock, $50-Par, Cumulative			
(20,000 shares authorized, 4,800 shares issued)	$240,000		
Preferred 8 Percent Stock Subscribed (600 shares)	30,000	$ 270,000	
Common Stock, $10 Par (160,000 shares			
authorized, 75,000 shares issued)		750,000	
Paid-in Capital from Donation		6,500	
Total Paid-in Capital		$1,026,500	
Retained Earnings		240,000	
Total Stockholders' Equity			$1,266,500

Glossary

Amortization The systematic writing off of costs, discounts, or premiums over a period of years. (p. 836)

Bond A long-term obligation that provides capital. (p. 830)

Bond issue The total number of bonds that a corporation issues at one time, in denominations of $1,000 or $5,000 each. (p. 830)

Callable bonds Bonds that give the corporation the right to redeem or buy back the bonds, prior to the date of maturity, at a specified figure, known as the *call price*. (p. 846)

Contra-liability account A deduction from a liability, such as Discount on Bonds Payable, which is a deduction from the balance of Bonds Payable. (p. 841)

Discount The amount by which the issue price is less than the face value of a bond. (p. 841)

Face value The value that a corporation will pay at a bond's maturity. (p. 830)

Indenture A bond agreement, or contract, between the corporation and its bondholders. (p. 846)

Leverage The use of debt as a lever to raise the owners' rate of return by earning income on borrowed money at a higher rate than that paid to borrow the money (as, for example, borrowing money at 8 percent and using it to earn a 15 percent rate of return). (p. 832)

Maturity date The end of the life of a bond; the day the issuer agrees to pay the bondholders. (p. 830)

Premium The excess of the price received over the face value of a bond. (p. 835)

Redeem Buy back or repurchase bonds from bondholders. (p. 846)

Secured bonds Bonds that are covered or backed by mortgages on real estate or by titles to personal property that may be claimed by the bondholders in the event that the issuing corporation defaults on its payment of principal or interest. (p. 831)

Serial bonds Bonds of a particular issue that have a series of maturity dates. (p. 831)

Sinking fund A special fund of cash accumulated over the life of a bond issue to enable the issuing corporation to pay off the bonds when they mature (come due). The fund is kept separate from other assets, and the cash is invested in income-producing securities. (p. 843)

Term bonds Bonds of a particular issue that all have the same maturity date. (p. 831)

Unsecured bonds Bonds backed only by the credit standing (good name) of the issuing corporation; also called *debenture bonds*. (p. 831)

CHAPTER ASSIGNMENTS

Discussion Questions

1. What is a bond discount, and how is it reported on a balance sheet?
2. What are two definite obligations a corporation incurs when it issues bonds?
3. Distinguish between the following: secured bonds and unsecured bonds; term bonds and serial bonds.
4. What is meant by amortization? What accounts are debited and credited in the amortization of a bond premium?
5. If the market rate of interest is lower than the rate of interest stated in the bond agreement, will the bonds be sold at a premium or a discount? Why?

6. What is a bond sinking fund? What is the title of the account involved, and how is it classified on a balance sheet?

7. What do accountants mean by the redemption of callable bonds? What is involved in the journal entry?

8. Why would a corporation want to exercise the callable provision of a bond when it could wait longer to pay off the debt?

Exercises

EXERCISE 21–1 Journalize the following transactions for Nguyen Corporation:

PRACTICE EXERCISE 1

July 1   Issued $600,000 worth of 8 percent, 20-year bonds at 102.

Oct. 1   Issued $500,000 worth of 9 percent, 10-year bonds at 103.

EXERCISE 21–2 Journalize the adjusting entry on December 31, the company's year end, to amortize the premium resulting from the issuance on January 1 of $400,000 worth of 10-year bonds at 104.

PRACTICE EXERCISE 2

EXERCISE 21–3 On January 1, Murphy, Inc., issues 7 percent, 20-year bonds with a face value of $650,000 at 96. Interest is payable on June 30 and December 31. Journalize the following entries:

PRACTICE EXERCISES 1,2

a. Issuance of the bonds

b. Payment of semiannual interest on June 30 and December 31

c. Adjusting entry to amortize the discount on December 31, the company's year end

---

EXERCISE 21–4 Rivera, Inc., issued $800,000 of 30-year, 9 percent bonds, dated March 1. Interest is payable on March 1 and September 1. The fiscal year extends from January 1 through December 31. Journalize entries for the following:

PRACTICE EXERCISES 1,2

Sept. 1   Payment of semiannual interest

Dec. 31   Adjustment for accrued interest expense

EXERCISE 21–5 On April 1, Cook Corporation issues $1,000,000 of 10-year, 9 percent bonds at 98, dated April 1, with interest payable semiannually on October 1 and April 1. The corporation's fiscal year ends on December 31. Journalize the issuance of the bonds, the payment of the semiannual interest on October 1, and the adjusting entries to amortize the Discount on Bonds Payable and record the accrued interest as of December 31.

PRACTICE EXERCISES 1,2

EXERCISE 21–6 Describe the entries in the following T accounts:

PRACTICE EXERCISES 1,2

Cash				Bonds Payable			Interest Expense		
+	−			−	+		+	−	
(1) 1,040,000	**(2)** 80,000				**(1)** 1,000,000	**(2)** 80,000	**(4)** 2,000
						(3) 20,000	**(5)** 98,000
							(6) 20,000

Premium on Bonds Payable		Income Summary	
−	+	(5) 98,000	
(4) 2,000	(1) 40,000		

Interest Payable	
−	+
(6) 20,000	(3) 20,000

PRACTICE EXERCISE 3

EXERCISE 21–7 Morgan, Inc., has outstanding $650,000 of 10-year sinking fund bonds. At the end of the ninth year after it had issued the bonds, the balance of Morgan Inc.'s Sinking Fund Investments account is $598,600. List the entries to record the following transactions.

a. The sale of the investments for $611,000
b. The final deposit in the sinking fund, bringing the balance of the account up to $650,000
c. The payment of the bonds

PRACTICE EXERCISE 4

EXERCISE 21–8 Peterson Corporation has the following account balances: Bonds Payable, $1,300,000; Premium on Bonds Payable, $40,000. As a step in redeeming the bond issue, Peterson Corporation buys $130,000 worth of its bonds (one-tenth of the original issue) on the open market at 97. Give the entry to record the redemption.

Problem Set A

For additional help, see the demonstration problem at the beginning of each chapter in your Working Papers.

1,2 LO

PROBLEM 21–1A During two consecutive years, Cooper Company, Inc., completed the following transactions:

Year 1

Jan.   2   Issued $1,000,000 face value, 30-year, 8 percent bonds, dated January 1 of this year, at 97. Interest is payable semiannually on June 30 and December 31.

June   30   Paid semiannual interest on the bonds.

Dec.   31   Paid semiannual interest on the bonds.

       31   Recorded an adjusting entry for amortization of discount on bonds.

       31   Closed the Interest Expense account.

Year 2

June   30   Paid semiannual interest on the bonds.

Dec.   31   Paid semiannual interest on the bonds.

       31   Recorded an adjusting entry for amortization of discount on bonds.

       31   Closed the Interest Expense account.

Check Figure
Adjustment, Year 1, Discount on Bonds Payable, $1,000 Credit

Required
Record the transactions in general journal form.

PROBLEM 21–2A Reed Hotel, Inc., completed the following selected transactions:  **LO** 1,2

Year 1

Apr. 1   Issued $1,200,000 worth of 30-year, 9 percent bonds, dated April 1 of this year, at 103. Interest is payable semiannually on October 1 and April 1.

Oct. 1   Paid semiannual interest on the bonds.

Dec. 31   Recorded an adjusting entry for amortization of premium on bonds.

      31   Recorded an adjusting entry for accrued interest payable.

      31   Closed the Interest Expense account.

Year 2

Jan. 1   Reversed the adjusting entry for accrued interest payable.

Apr. 1   Paid semiannual interest on the bonds.

Oct. 1   Paid semiannual interest on the bonds.

Dec. 31   Made an adjusting entry to record amortization of premium on bonds.

      31   Made an adjusting entry to record accrued interest payable.

      31   Closed the Interest Expense account.

Required

1. Record the transactions in general journal form using pages 98 and 99 of the general journal.
2. Post entries to the Interest Expense account, No. 581. Label the adjusting, closing, and reversing entries.

Check Figure
Adjustment, Year 2, Premium on Bonds Payable, $1,200 Debit

PROBLEM 21–3A During two consecutive years, Schwartz Freight Line Corporation completed the following transactions relating to its $15,000,000 issue of 25-year, 7 percent bonds, dated May 1 of the first year. Interest is payable on May 1 and November 1. The corporation's fiscal year extends from January 1 through December 31.   **LO** 1,2,3

Year 1

May 1   Sold the bond issue at $97^3/4$.

Nov. 1   Paid semiannual interest on the bonds.

Dec. 31   Deposited $216,560 in a bond sinking fund.

     31   Made an adjusting entry to record amortization of bond discount.

     31   Made an adjusting entry to record accrued interest payable.

     31   Closed the Interest Expense account.

Year 2

Jan. 1   Reversed the adjustment for accrued interest payable.

      9   Bought various securities with sinking fund cash; cost, $216,560.

May 1   Paid semiannual interest on the bonds.

Nov. 1   Paid semiannual interest on the bonds.

Dec. 31   Recorded the receipt of $16,245 of income derived from sinking fund investments, depositing the cash in the sinking fund.

Dec. 31   Deposited $322,500 in the bond sinking fund.

    31   Made an adjusting entry to record amortization of bond discount.

    31   Made an adjusting entry to record accrued interest payable.

    31   Closed the Sinking Fund Income account.

    31   Closed the Interest Expense account.

Check Figure
Year 2, Ending balance of
Discount on Bonds Payable,
$315,000 Debit

Required

1. Record the transactions in general journal form using pages 217 and 218 of the general journal.
2. Post entries to the Discount on Bonds Payable account, No. 242, and the Interest Expense account, No. 581. Label the adjusting, closing, and reversing entries.

1,2,3  **LO**

PROBLEM 21–4A On May 1, Steele Recreation Corporation issued $4,500,000 worth of 10-year, 8 percent bonds, dated May 1, with interest payable on May 1 and November 1. The corporation's fiscal year is the calendar year. The following transactions pertain to the bond issue for the first two years:

Year 1

May   1   Sold the bond issue at 102.

Nov. 1   Paid semiannual interest on the bonds.

Dec. 31   Deposited $80,250 in a bond sinking fund.

    31   Recorded an adjusting entry for amortization of bond premium.

    31   Recorded an adjusting entry for accrued interest payable.

    31   Closed the Interest Expense account.

Year 2

Jan.   1   Reversed the adjusting entry for accrued interest payable.

   12   Bought various securities with sinking fund cash; cost, $80,250.

May   1   Paid semiannual interest on the bonds.

July   1   Recorded the receipt of $2,907 of income derived from sinking fund investments, depositing the cash in the sinking fund.

    2   Bought various securities with sinking fund cash; cost, $2,907.

Nov. 1   Paid semiannual interest on the bonds.

Dec. 31   Recorded the receipt of $3,249 of income derived from sinking fund investments, depositing the cash in the sinking fund.

    31   Deposited $101,500 in the bond sinking fund.

    31   Recorded an adjusting entry for amortization of bond premium.

    31   Recorded an adjusting entry for accrued interest payable.

    31   Closed the Sinking Fund Income account.

    31   Closed the Interest Expense account.

Check Figure
Adjustment, Year 2, Interest
Payable, $60,000 Credit

Required

1. Record the transactions in general journal form using pages 252–254 of the general journal.
2. Post entries to the Premium on Bonds Payable account, No. 243, and the Interest Expense account, No. 581. Label the appropriate entries in the ledger accounts as adjusting, closing, or reversing.

Problem Set B

For additional help, see the demonstration problem at the beginning of each chapter in your Working Papers.

PROBLEM 21–1B During two consecutive years, Benson Corporation completed the following transactions:

Year 1

Jan.	2	Issued $3,400,000 face value, 10-year, 8 percent bonds, dated January 1 of this year, at 106. Interest is payable semiannually on June 30 and December 31.
June	30	Paid semiannual interest on the bonds.
Dec.	31	Paid semiannual interest on the bonds.
	31	Recorded an adjusting entry for amortization of premium on bonds.
	31	Closed the Interest Expense account.

Year 2

June	30	Paid semiannual interest on the bonds.
Dec.	31	Paid semiannual interest on the bonds.
	31	Recorded an adjusting entry for amortization of premium on bonds.
	31	Closed the Interest Expense account.

Required
Record the transactions in general journal form.

Check Figure
Year 2, June 30 Interest Expense
Debit, $136,000

PROBLEM 21–2B Neal Bakers, Inc., completed the following selected transactions:

Year 1

Mar.	1	Issued $840,000 worth of 20-year, 8 percent bonds, dated March 1 of this year, at 103. Interest is payable semiannually on September 1 and March 1.
Sept.	1	Paid semiannual interest on the bonds.
Dec.	31	Recorded an adjusting entry for amortization of premium on bonds.
	31	Recorded an adjusting entry for accrued interest payable.
	31	Closed the Interest Expense account.

Year 2

Jan.	1	Reversed the adjusting entry for accrued interest payable.
Mar.	1	Paid semiannual interest on the bonds.
Sept.	1	Paid semiannual interest on the bonds.
Dec.	31	Made an adjusting entry to record amortization of premium on bonds.
	31	Made an adjusting entry to record accrued interest payable.
	31	Closed the Sinking Fund Income account.
	31	Closed the Interest Expense account.

Required
1. Record the transactions in general journal form using pages 172 and 173 of the general journal.
2. Post entries to the Interest Expense account, No. 581. Label the adjusting, closing, and reversing entries.

Check Figure
Year 2, December 31 Closing
Entry, Income Summary
Debit, $65,940

1,2,3 LO

PROBLEM 21–3B During two consecutive years, Horton Medical Clinic completed the following transactions relating to its $6,750,000 issue of 30-year, 7 percent bonds, dated April 1 of the first year. Interest is payable April 1 and October 1. The corporation's fiscal year extends from January 1 through December 31.

Year 1

Apr.   1   Sold the bond issue at 98.

Oct.   1   Paid semiannual interest on the bonds.

Dec.   31   Deposited $59,625 in a bond sinking fund.

        31   Made an adjusting entry to record amortization of bond discount.

        31   Made an adjusting entry to record accrued interest payable.

        31   Closed the Interest Expense account.

Year 2

Jan.   1   Reversed the adjusting entry for accrued interest payable.

        4   Bought various securities with sinking fund cash; cost, $59,625.

Apr.   1   Paid semiannual interest on the bonds.

Oct.   1   Paid semiannual interest on the bonds.

Dec.   31   Recorded the receipt of $4,629 of income derived from sinking fund investments, depositing the cash in the sinking fund.

        31   Deposited $82,950 in the bond sinking fund.

        31   Made an adjusting entry to record amortization of bond discount.

        31   Made an adjusting entry to record accrued interest payable.

        31   Closed the Sinking Fund Income account.

        31   Closed the Interest Expense account.

Check Figure

Year 2, Ending balance of Discount on Bonds Payable, $127,125 Debit

Required

1. Record the transactions in general journal form using pages 140 and 141 of the general journal.
2. Post entries to the Discount on Bonds Payable account, No. 242, and the Interest Expense account, No. 581. Label the adjusting, closing, and reversing entries.

1,2,3 LO

PROBLEM 21–4B On June 1, Dominguez Design Products, Inc., whose fiscal year is the calendar year, issued $14,400,000 worth of 20-year, 8 percent bonds, dated June 1, with interest payable on June 1 and December 1. The following transactions pertain to the bond issue for the first two years:

Year 1

June   1   Sold the bond issue at 101.

Dec.   1   Paid semiannual interest on the bonds.

        31   Deposited $284,400 in a bond sinking fund.

        31   Recorded an adjusting entry for amortization of bond premium.

        31   Recorded an adjusting entry for accrued interest payable.

        31   Closed the Interest Expense account.

Year 2

Jan.	1	Reversed the adjusting entry for accrued interest payable.
	9	Bought various securities with sinking fund cash; cost, $284,400.
June	1	Paid semiannual interest on the bonds.
July	1	Recorded the receipt of $9,737 of income derived from sinking fund investments, depositing the cash in the sinking fund.
	8	Bought various securities with sinking fund cash; cost, $9,737.
Dec.	1	Paid semiannual interest on the bonds.
	31	Recorded the receipt of $19,190 of income derived from sinking fund investments, depositing the cash in the sinking fund.
	31	Deposited $402,000 in the bond sinking fund.
	31	Recorded an adjusting entry for amortization of bond premium.
	31	Recorded an adjusting entry for accrued interest payable.
	31	Closed the Sinking Fund Income account.
	31	Closed the Interest Expense account.

Required

1. Record the transactions in general journal form using pages 325–327 of the general journal.
2. Post entries to the Premium on Bonds Payable account, No. 243, and the Interest Expense account, No. 581. Label the appropriate entries in the ledger accounts as adjusting, closing, or reversing.

Check Figure
Year 2, Ending balance of Premium on Bonds Payable, $132,600 Credit

ACTIVITIES

INTERNET LINKS TO ACCOUNTING

Learning about bonds may seem overwhelming at first. Let's review the Investinginbonds.com Web site (www.investinginbonds.com) and look at some examples. Click on See Corporate Market At-A-Glance on the homepage. Then, under Show Me Corporate Price Data, click on Most active bonds during the last trading day to find information on corporate bond issues. Hopefully, after working through the following problems, understanding bonds might not seem quite so complicated!

1. Can you tell from the information provided whether the bonds are selling at a premium or a discount? If yes, how can you tell?

Assume the following fictional bond is listed at Investinginbonds.com and that interest is paid semiannually:

Trade Date	Company	CUSIP	Coupon	Maturity	Price	Yield	Volume
12/31/2010	XL Corporation	1123XL3	6.200	12/31/2020	101.772	5.443	1K

- CUSIP is a unique number used to identify a specific bond. The acronym stands for the "Committee on Uniform Security Identification Procedures."
- Coupon is the rate of interest payable annually.
- Yield is the annual return you earn on the bond, based on the price you paid and the interest payment you receive.
- Volume is the amount in millions of dollars of a given wholesale transaction. Since "K" represents 1,000, the 1K size means $1 million $\times$ 1,000 = $1,000,000,000, or $1 billion.

2. What is the journal entry to record the issue of this bond on December 31, 2010?
3. What is XL Corporation's journal entry to record the first semiannual interest payment on June 30, 2011?
4. What is XL Corporation's adjusting journal entry to record amortization of the bond premium on December 31, 2011? (Use the straight-line method.)
5. How do semiannual interest payments and amortization of the bond premium affect the Interest Expense account? (*Hint:* Look at the journal entries you prepared above.)

CONSIDER AND COMMUNICATE

A fellow student states that bond premium and bond discount are the same, because (a) they are reduced by amortization; (b) both occur because the cash received differs from the face value of the bond; and (c) both affect interest expense. Respond to the accuracy of this statement.

PART 7

The Statement of Cash Flows—Indirect Method

22

WHY IT MATTERS

LIL' PALS PET PHOTOGRAPHY, Memphis, Tennessee

Lil' Pals Pet Photography is a mobile photography studio specializing in taking beautiful pictures of very special family members—customers' pets. The mobile studio comes to the customers' homes or local vet clinic, pet store, groomer, or grocery store. Pictures are taken on site in the mobile studio using the latest in modern digital photography technology. Customers are able to review their pictures and place their order immediately after the photo shoot. Pictures are then picked up in a few days at the host location.

We have learned that the owners of Lil' Pals Pet Photography can review their income statement to determine their net profit for the year, but how do the owners know the sources and uses of cash? How do they know how much cash was received from customers or the amount of cash spent on operating expenses such as gas and photography supplies? In this chapter, we will learn about the statement of cash flows, which details the sources and uses of cash.

LEARNING OBJECTIVES

After you have completed this chapter, you will be able to do the following:

1   Describe the statement of cash flows, and define cash and cash equivalents.

2   State the purpose of the statement of cash flows.

3   State the uses of the statement of cash flows by management, investors, and creditors.

4   Identify cash inflows and outflows as operating, investing, or financing activities.

5   Prepare the Operating Activities section of the statement of cash flows using the indirect method.

6   Prepare the Investing Activities and Financing Activities sections of the statement of cash flows.

7   Prepare a schedule of noncash investing and financing transactions.

8   Be able to interpret the statement of cash flows and understand the benefits to users.

ACCOUNTING LANGUAGE

Cash equivalents *(p. 865)*

Direct method *(p. 867)*

Financing activities *(p. 866)*

Indirect method *(p. 867)*

Investing activities *(p. 866)*

Operating activities *(p. 865)*

Statement of cash flows *(p. 864)*

Certainly the financial statements presented in earlier chapters are important. Each statement serves a specific purpose. The income statement shows the results of operations. The statement of retained earnings (or statement of owner's equity) shows additional investments by owners and payments to owners. The balance sheet portrays a company's financial condition. However, there are important questions that these statements do not answer. For example, what new assets did the firm invest in (buy) during the year? If liabilities increased during the year, where were the proceeds spent? Or, if liabilities decreased, how were they reduced? Did a corporation's operations for the year generate enough cash to pay dividends or allow for owner withdrawals? If a corporation issued common stock during the year, where were the proceeds spent?

You may wonder why these questions can't be answered by the financial statements that you have already learned about. When the income statement is prepared on the accrual basis, it does not show the amounts of cash either generated or paid. The amounts of cash involved in changes in the balances of assets and liabilities during the year are not shown on the balance sheet. The statement of retained earnings shows only transactions that affect equity accounts. The statement of cash flows was developed to explain the reasons for the inflows and outflows of cash.

A BROAD LOOK AT THE STATEMENT OF CASH FLOWS

LEARNING OBJECTIVE 1

Describe the statement of cash flows, and define cash and cash equivalents.

Definition

The **statement of cash flows** is a financial statement that explains in detail how the balance of cash and cash equivalents has changed between the beginning and the end of a fiscal period. The Financial Accounting Standards Board requires a statement of cash flows as part of a full set of financial statements.

On the statement of cash flows, cash is defined to include both cash as you think of it and cash equivalents. **Cash equivalents** are short-term, highly liquid investments, including money market accounts, U.S. Treasury bills, and commercial paper, that mature within 90 days from the date acquired. Money market accounts are interest-bearing accounts available at banks and other financial institutions. U.S. Treasury bills may be considered short-term government bonds. Commercial paper is another corporation's short-term, interest-bearing notes.

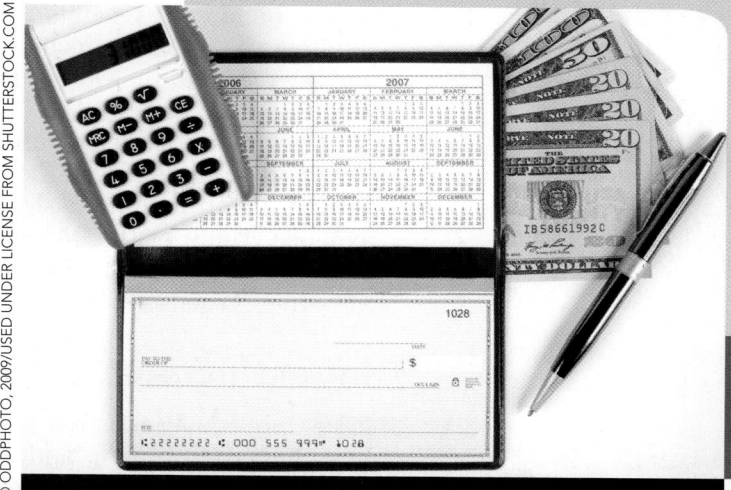

© ODDPHOTO, 2009/USED UNDER LICENSE FROM SHUTTERSTOCK.COM

Cash, checking accounts, and savings accounts, as well as money market funds, U.S. Treasury bills, and commercial paper with a 90-day or less maturity, are all considered cash and cash equivalents.

Purpose

The main purpose of the statement of cash flows is to provide a summary of information concerning a company's cash receipts and payments during a fiscal period. A secondary purpose is to provide information about a firm's operating, investing, and financing activities during a fiscal period. The statement of cash flows also serves to reconcile the beginning and ending cash balance for the period.

2 **LEARNING OBJECTIVE** *State the purpose of the statement of cash flows.*

Uses of the Statement of Cash Flows

Management's Use of the Statement of Cash Flows

Management uses the statement of cash flows to determine the liquidity of the business, to determine dividend policy, and to evaluate possible investments and means of financing. Management asks the following questions:

3 **LEARNING OBJECTIVE** *State the uses of the statement of cash flows by management, investors, and creditors.*

Liquidity Is enough cash being generated to enable the company to pay its bills?

Dividend policy Is enough cash being generated to enable the corporation to establish a regular cash dividend policy?

Investment and financing If the firm borrows to buy an asset, is enough cash being generated to make the payments?

Investors' and Creditors' Use of the Statement of Cash Flows

Investors (stockholders) are interested in a corporation's ability to pay dividends and increase the value of the company. Creditors are concerned with a company's ability to pay its liabilities. Both investors and creditors are interested in the firm's ability to generate future cash flows as well as its need for additional financing.

CLASSIFICATIONS OF CASH FLOWS

The statement of cash flows classifies cash receipts and payments into three categories: operating activities, investing activities, and financing activities.

4 **LEARNING OBJECTIVE** *Identify cash inflows and outflows as operating, investing, or financing activities.*

Operating Activities

Operating activities is the first category on the statement of cash flows, and this category lists and classifies cash inflows and outflows from a variety of sources. *Cash inflows* include cash receipts from customers for the sale of merchandise and services and cash receipts in the form of interest and dividend income. Think of the items listed on an income statement; include the Revenue from Sales section, and then refer to the Other Income section to include interest income and dividend income.

Cash outflows include cash payments for merchandise purchases and operating expenses, such as Wages Expense and Rent Expense. Cash outflows for operating activities also include cash payments in the form of interest and income taxes expense. Think of the items listed on an income statement; include merchandise purchases and the Operating Expenses (Selling and General) section, then refer to the Other Expenses section to include interest expense.

Investing Activities

Investing activities is the second category listed on the statement of cash flows. It includes (1) buying and selling property and equipment (long-term assets); (2) acquiring and selling investments other than cash equivalents; and (3) making and collecting loans. *Cash inflows* include the cash received from selling property and equipment, from selling investments, and from collecting loans. *Cash outflows* include cash paid to purchase property and equipment, cash invested in another corporation's stocks or bonds, and cash loaned to borrowers.

Financing Activities

Financing activities, the last category on the statement of cash flows, include cash transactions that involve borrowing from or repaying creditors, as well as additional cash investments from owners and transactions that reduce owners' investments. *Cash inflows* include proceeds received from short- or long-term borrowing (issuing notes or bonds) and those from issuing stock for cash. *Cash outflows* include repayments of loans (notes and bonds) and payments to owners, including personal withdrawals and cash dividends.

Operating Activities	
Cash Inflows (Receipts):	*Cash Outflows (Payments):*
• From customers for the sales of merchandise and services • For interest income • For dividend income	• For merchandise purchases • For operating expenses • For interest expense • For income tax expense
Investing Activities	
Cash Inflows (Receipts):	*Cash Outflows (Payments):*
• From the sale of property and equipment • From the sale of investments or bonds in another corporation • From the collection of loan principal from borrowers	• To purchase property and equipment • To purchase investments or bonds in another corporation • For loans made to borrowers
Financing Activities	
Cash Inflows (Receipts):	*Cash Outflows (Payments):*
• From short- or long-term borrowings • From issuance of stock	• For repayments of loans • For payments to owners (drawings or dividends)

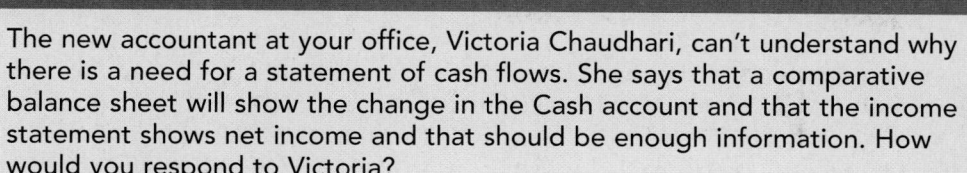

You Make the Call

The new accountant at your office, Victoria Chaudhari, can't understand why there is a need for a statement of cash flows. She says that a comparative balance sheet will show the change in the Cash account and that the income statement shows net income and that should be enough information. How would you respond to Victoria?

SOLUTION

The statement of cash flows explains in detail how the balance of cash and cash equivalents has changed between the beginning and the end of a fiscal period. It shows the sources and uses of cash. The Financial Accounting Standards Board requires a statement of cash flows as part of a full set of financial statements.

A secondary purpose of the statement of cash flows is to provide information about a firm's operating, investing, and financing activities during a fiscal period so that a firm may better plan for future cash needs.

FORM OF THE STATEMENT OF CASH FLOWS

As you have learned in this chapter, the statement of cash flows is divided into three categories: operating activities, followed by investing activities, followed by financing activities. Within each activity, cash inflows and outflows are shown separately. For example, suppose that a company sells its used equipment for $5,000 in cash. Next, the company buys new equipment for $30,000, paying cash. Under investing activities, the sale of equipment, $5,000, is listed as an inflow of cash. The purchase of equipment, $30,000, is listed as an outflow of cash.

The statement of cash flows may be presented using one of two methods: the direct method or the indirect method. The **direct method** primarily involves converting each amount recorded on the income statement from the accrual basis to the cash basis. The direct method shows the specific sources and uses of cash, such as cash received from customers or cash paid for inventory, during a fiscal period. If a company chooses to present the statement of cash flows using the direct method, it must also present the statement of cash flows using the indirect method in a note to the financial statements.

The **indirect method** involves adjusting net income to determine cash flows from operating activities. This method is the more popular method when preparing the statement of cash flows generally because it is easier and less costly to prepare.

Each method changes how the Operating Activities section of the statement of cash flows is presented. The Investing Activities and Financing Activities sections remain the same regardless of which method is used, as does the net increase or decrease in cash.

We will present the statement of cash flows using the indirect method in this chapter. First, we present an example of a complete statement of cash flows in

FIGURE 1

Statement of cash flows for
Anderson Corporation

Anderson Corporation
Statement of Cash Flows
For Year Ended December 31, 2011

Cash Flows from (used by) Operating Activities:		
Net Loss		$(10,000)
Add (Deduct) Items to Convert Net Loss		
from Accrual Basis to Cash Basis:		
Depreciation Expense, Equipment	$18,000	
Gain on Disposal of Property and Equipment	(4,500)	
Decrease in Accounts Receivable (net)	13,400	
Increase in Merchandise Inventory	(26,000)	
Increase in Prepaid Insurance	(100)	
Decrease in Accounts Payable	(15,200)	
Decrease in Wages Payable	(200)	
Increase in Property Tax Payable	150	
Increase in Interest Payable	650	(13,800)
Net Cash Flows used by Operating Activities		$(23,800)
Cash Flows from (used by) Investing Activities:		
Sale of Equipment	$16,075	
Net Cash Flows from Investing Activities		16,075
Cash Flows from (used by) Financing Activities:		
Issuance of Note	$25,000	
Issuance of Common Stock	12,250	
Payment of Dividends	(15,050)	
Net Cash Flows from Financing Activities		22,200
Net Increase (Decrease) in Cash		$ 14,475
Cash, January 1, 2011		38,400
Cash, December 31, 2011		$ 52,875

Figure 1 so you can see the entire picture. Then we provide two companies as illustrations—a one-owner business and a corporation.

A statement of cash flows using the direct method is illustrated in the appendix following this chapter.

DEVELOPING THE STATEMENT OF CASH FLOWS

Remember

> The three categories of cash flows relate to the three sections of the statement of cash flows: operating, investing, and financing activities.

To prepare the statement of cash flows, we need the company's income statement and statement of retained earnings or statement of owner's equity (depending on the type of company) for the present fiscal period, and its balance sheets at the beginning and end of the fiscal period.

Preparing the statement of cash flows involves four steps:

STEP 1. Determine the change in cash.

STEP 2. Determine the net cash flows from operating activities.

STEP 3. Determine the net cash flows from investing activities.

STEP 4. Determine the net cash flows from financing activities.

Illustration 1

Our first illustration is for Jenny's Paintings, a one-owner merchandising business operating on the accrual basis. The financial statements for Jenny's Paintings are presented here.

Jenny's Paintings
Income Statement
For Year Ended December 31, 2011

Net Sales		$800,000
Cost of Goods Sold:		
Merchandise Inventory, January 1, 2011	$126,000	
Delivered Cost of Purchases	514,000	
Cost of Goods Available for Sale	$640,000	
Less Merchandise Inventory, December 31, 2011	130,000	
Cost of Goods Sold		510,000
Gross Profit		$290,000
Operating Expenses:		
Salary Expense	$100,000	
Rent Expense	20,000	
Depreciation Expense, Equipment	22,000	
Supplies Expense	1,600	
Insurance Expense	400	
Total Operating Expenses		144,000
Net Income		$146,000

Jenny's Paintings
Statement of Owner's Equity
For Year Ended December 31, 2011

J. K. Kim, Capital, January 1, 2011		$233,200
Investments during the Year	$ 0	
Net Income	146,000	
Subtotal	$146,000	
Less Withdrawals	150,000	
Decrease in Capital		(4,000)
J. K. Kim, Capital, December 31, 2011		$229,200

Jenny's Paintings
Comparative Balance Sheet
December 31, 2011 and December 31, 2010

	2011	2010	Increase or (Decrease)
Assets			
Cash	$ 31,400	$ 35,000	$ (3,600)
Accounts Receivable (net)	45,600	33,000	12,600
Merchandise Inventory	130,000	126,000	4,000
Prepaid Insurance	2,300	1,400	900
Equipment	136,600	136,600	0
Less Accumulated Depreciation	(62,000)	(40,000)	(22,000)
Total Assets	$283,900	$292,000	$ (8,100)
Liabilities			
Accounts Payable	$ 51,500	$ 56,000	$ (4,500)
Salaries Payable	3,200	2,800	400
Total Liabilities	$ 54,700	$ 58,800	$ (4,100)
Owner's Equity			
J. K. Kim, Capital	229,200	233,200	(4,000)
Total Liabilities and Owner's Equity	$283,900	$292,000	$ (8,100)

Step 1: Determine the Change in Cash

Jenny's Paintings had a $3,600 ($31,400 – $35,000) decrease in cash for the year. This information is found on the comparative balance sheet. This change in cash will be verified on the statement of cash flows at the bottom of the statement as shown below.

Jenny's Paintings
Statement of Cash Flows
For Year Ended December 31, 2011

Net Increase (Decrease) in Cash	$(3,600)
Cash, January 1, 2011	35,000
Cash, December 31, 2011	$31,400

Step 2: Determine the Net Cash Flows from Operating Activities

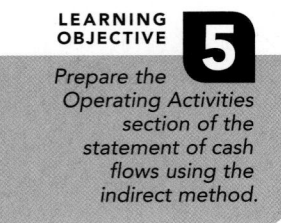

LEARNING OBJECTIVE 5

Prepare the Operating Activities section of the statement of cash flows using the indirect method.

Convert Net Income to Cash Flows from Operations. The purpose of the statement of cash flows is to show how an increase or decrease in cash came about. In essence, the company's income statement must be converted to a cash basis. In the Operating Activities section of the statement of cash flows, the indirect method lists only the adjustments necessary to convert net income to cash flows from operations as determined by changes in balance sheet accounts (assets, liabilities, and capital). This is required because under the accrual system, income is counted when it is earned, not when cash is received. The same holds true for expenses. Expenses are deducted when incurred, not when cash is paid. To convert from the accrual to the cash basis, we must add to or deduct from net income to get to the correct amount for cash.

A discussion on how to convert an income statement from the accrual basis to the amount of cash actually received or paid out follows.

Step 2a: Identify Net Income (Loss)

The net income for Jenny's Paintings is $146,000 as found on the income statement. This amount is listed first in the Operating Activities section of the statement of cash flows.

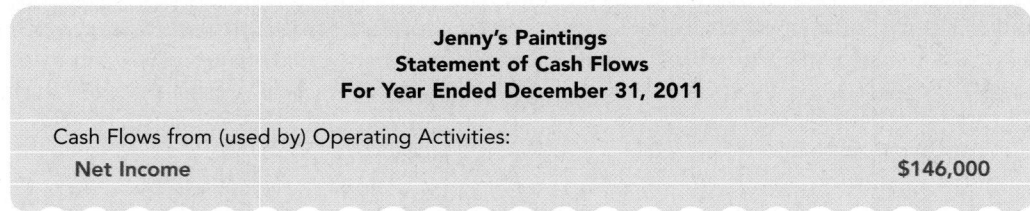

Jenny's Paintings
Statement of Cash Flows
For Year Ended December 31, 2011

Cash Flows from (used by) Operating Activities:	
Net Income	$146,000

Step 2b: Add (Deduct) Noncash Operating Income and Expense Items

Next, we will add or subtract noncash operating income and expense items. Remember, when preparing the Operating Activities section, we want to convert net income (which includes cash and noncash items) to a cash-only basis. Some common noncash operating income and expense items are Depreciation Expense, Amortization Expense, and Gain (or Loss) on Disposal of Property and Equipment.

Depreciation Expense. Jenny's Paintings had $22,000 recorded as Depreciation Expense, Equipment on the income statement for the current year. Depreciation

Expense decreases net income but represents a noncash expense. Since this non-cash amount was deducted from net income, we will need to add it back in order to convert net income to a cash-only basis.

Jenny's Paintings
Statement of Cash Flows
For Year Ended December 31, 2011

Cash Flows from (used by) Operating Activities:	
Net Income	$146,000
Add (Deduct) Items to Convert Net Income	
from Accrual Basis to Cash Basis:	
Depreciation Expense, Equipment	$22,000

Since there are no other noncash operating income and expense items listed on the income statement, we will then add or deduct changes in current assets (other than cash) and current liabilities.

Step 2c: Add (Deduct) Changes in Current Assets (Other than Cash) and Current Liabilities

To convert net income from an accrual basis to a cash basis, we will adjust net income for the changes in current assets (other than Cash) and current liabilities that are found on the balance sheet. Let's look at the first current asset—Accounts Receivable.

Increase in Accounts Receivable. The Accounts Receivable account increased by $12,600 ($45,600 – $33,000). An increase in accounts receivable corresponds with an increase in sales. The following summary journal entry explains the effect of accounts receivable and sales:

GENERAL JOURNAL　　　　　　　　　　　　　**PAGE** _____

Date	Description	Post. Ref.	Debit	Credit
	Cash		787 4 0 0 00	
	Accounts Receivable		12 6 0 0 00	
	Sales			800 0 0 0 00

The sales of $800,000 (found on the income statement) is recorded as a credit and the change in accounts receivable is recorded as a debit. The difference of $787,400 represents the cash received from sales. Notice that not all of the sales recorded on the income statement were received in cash. The $12,600 relates to sales from customers made on account.

The $12,600 increase in accounts receivable, representing noncash sales, will need to be subtracted from net income to determine operating cash flows.

Jenny's Paintings
Statement of Cash Flows
For Year Ended December 31, 2011

Cash Flows from (used by) Operating Activities:	
Net Income	$146,000
Add (Deduct) Items to Convert Net Income	
from Accrual Basis to Cash Basis:	
Depreciation Expense, Equipment	$ 22,000
Increase in Accounts Receivable (net)	(12,600)

If Accounts Receivable had *increased* between the beginning and the end of the fiscal period, cash receipts from customers would be *less* than the revenue listed on the income statement and would need to be subtracted from net income. If Accounts Receivable had *decreased* between the beginning and the end of the fiscal period, cash receipts from customers would be *more* than the revenue listed on the income statement and would need to be added to net income.

Increase in Merchandise Inventory. In order to analyze the Merchandise Inventory account, it will help if we review all of the T accounts related to cost of goods—Cash, Merchandise Inventory, Accounts Payable, and Cost of Goods Sold.

Cash				Merchandise Inventory				
+	−			+		−		
	(c)	518,500	Jan. 1	126,000	(a)		510,000	
			(b)	514,000				
			Dec. 31	130,000				

Accounts Payable				Cost of Goods Sold		
−	+			+	−	
	Jan. 1	56,000				
(c) 518,500	(b)	514,000	(a)	510,000		
	Dec. 31	51,500				

Transaction (a) represents the cost of goods sold that is reported on the income statement, $510,000. Notice that this represents both cash and noncash purchases. Transaction (b) represents the purchases of inventory for the year, $514,000, while transaction (c) represents the cash payments for inventory for the year, $518,500.

		GENERAL JOURNAL			PAGE _____
Date		Description	Post. Ref.	Debit	Credit
2011					
	(a)	Cost of Goods Sold		510 0 0 0 00	
		Merchandise Inventory			510 0 0 0 00
		To record cost of goods sold			
		as shown on the income			
		statement.			
	(b)	Merchandise Inventory		514 0 0 0 00	
		Accounts Payable			514 0 0 0 00
		To record purchase of			
		inventory.			
	(c)	Accounts Payable		518 5 0 0 00	
		Cash			518 5 0 0 00
		To record payment of cash for			
		inventory.			

The cash payments for inventory sold during the year are $8,500 ($518,500 − $510,000) higher than what is represented as Cost of Goods Sold on the income statement. This difference is comprised of two parts: the change in inventory,

$4,000 ($130,000 – $126,000), and the change in accounts payable, $(4,500) ($51,500 – $56,000).

The increase in inventory of $4,000 will need to be subtracted from net income to eliminate the noncash portion of cost of goods sold.

Jenny's Paintings
Statement of Cash Flows
For Year Ended December 31, 2011

Cash Flows from (used by) Operating Activities:		
Net Income		$146,000
Add (Deduct) Items to Convert Net Income		
from Accrual Basis to Cash Basis:		
Depreciation Expense, Equipment	$ 22,000	
Increase in Accounts Receivable (net)	(12,600)	
Increase in Merchandise Inventory	(4,000)	

Increase in Prepaid Insurance.

The Prepaid Insurance account for Jenny's Paintings increased by $900 during the year. This means that $900 more in cash than the $400 listed as Insurance Expense on the income statement was paid out. A summary journal entry would look like this:

GENERAL JOURNAL **PAGE** ____

Date	Description	Post. Ref.	Debit	Credit
	Prepaid Insurance		9 0 0 00	
	Cash			9 0 0 00

Notice that the Cash account decreased but there was no impact on the Insurance Expense account included in net income. Therefore, the $900 increase will need to be subtracted from net income to reflect the additional decrease in the Cash account.

Jenny's Paintings
Statement of Cash Flows
For Year Ended December 31, 2011

Cash Flows from (used by) Operating Activities:		
Net Income		$146,000
Add (Deduct) Items to Convert Net Income		
from Accrual Basis to Cash Basis:		
Depreciation Expense, Equipment	$ 22,000	
Increase in Accounts Receivable (net)	(12,600)	
Increase in Merchandise Inventory	(4,000)	
Increase in Prepaid Insurance	(900)	

If a prepaid expense (like Prepaid Rent or Prepaid Insurance) had *increased* between the beginning and the end of the fiscal period, cash payments for the item(s) would have been *more* than the amount listed as expense (Rent Expense or Insurance Expense) and would need to be subtracted from net income. If a prepaid expense (like Prepaid Rent or Prepaid Insurance) had *decreased* between the beginning and the end of the fiscal period, cash payments for the item(s) would have been *less* than the amount listed as expense (Rent Expense or Insurance Expense) and would need to be added to net income.

Decrease in Accounts Payable.

Jenny's Paintings' Accounts Payable account decreased by $4,500. This decrease was reviewed in the T accounts and journal entries shown when we discussed the Merchandise Inventory account on pages 872–873. The reduction in the Accounts Payable account means that the company paid cash of $4,500 to suppliers that was not reflected in the cost of goods sold shown on the income statement. This additional cash outflow of $4,500 needs to be subtracted from net income to reflect operating activities on a cash basis.

Jenny's Paintings
Statement of Cash Flows
For Year Ended December 31, 2011

Cash Flows from (used by) Operating Activities:		
Net Income		$146,000
Add (Deduct) Items to Convert Net Income		
from Accrual Basis to Cash Basis:		
Depreciation Expense, Equipment	$ 22,000	
Increase in Accounts Receivable (net)	(12,600)	
Increase in Merchandise Inventory	(4,000)	
Increase in Prepaid Insurance	(900)	
Decrease in Accounts Payable	(4,500)	

Increase in Salaries Payable.

The Salaries Payable account increased by $400 during the year. As depicted in the following summary journal entry, Jenny's Paintings' Salary Expense account included $400 of noncash expense.

GENERAL JOURNAL				PAGE _____	
Date	Description	Post. Ref.	Debit	Credit	
	Salaries Expense		4 0 0 00		
	Salaries Payable			4 0 0 00	

The company would add the increase in Salary Expense of $400 to net income to adjust for the noncash expense.

Jenny's Paintings
Statement of Cash Flows
For Year Ended December 31, 2011

Cash Flows from (used by) Operating Activities:		
Net Income		$146,000
Add (Deduct) Items to Convert Net Income		
from Accrual Basis to Cash Basis:		
Depreciation Expense, Equipment	$ 22,000	
Increase in Accounts Receivable (net)	(12,600)	
Increase in Merchandise Inventory	(4,000)	
Increase in Prepaid Insurance	(900)	
Decrease in Accounts Payable	(4,500)	
Increase in Salaries Payable	400	400

Now that we have made adjustments for all noncash operating income and expense items and changes in current assets (other than Cash) and current liabilities, we can compute the net cash flows from operating activities. The net cash flows from operating activities is calculated by adding or subtracting the changes to net income. Therefore, net cash flows from operating activities for Jenny's Paintings is $146,400.

Jenny's Paintings
Statement of Cash Flows
For Year Ended December 31, 2011

Cash Flows from (used by) Operating Activities:		
Net Income		$ 146,000
Add (Deduct) Items to Convert Net Income		
from Accrual Basis to Cash Basis:		
Depreciation Expense, Equipment	$ 22,000	
Increase in Accounts Receivable (net)	(12,600)	
Increase in Merchandise Inventory	(4,000)	
Increase in Prepaid Insurance	(900)	
Decrease in Accounts Payable	(4,500)	
Increase in Salaries Payable	400	400
Net Cash Flows from Operating Activities		$146,400

There is an easy way to remember how to prepare the Operating Activities section using the indirect method. Figure 2 illustrates the adjustments that we just made. Take some time to review this figure. It will help you out when preparing the Operating Activities section of the statement of cash flows.

Step 3: Determine the Net Cash Flows from Investing Activities

Investing activities are concerned with changes in property and equipment (long-term assets). There were no changes in the Equipment account balance between the beginning and end of the fiscal period. However, the Accumulated Depreciation account balance increased from $40,000 to $62,000. This $22,000 change is accounted for by recording $22,000 as Depreciation Expense, Equipment on the income statement. This amount is not paid to anyone and thus represents a noncash item.

LEARNING OBJECTIVE

6

Prepare the Investing Activities and Financing Activities sections of the statement of cash flows.

Noncash Operating Income and Expense Items	
Depreciation Expense Amortization Expense	**+**
Gain on Disposal of Property and Equipment*	**—**
Loss on Disposal of Property and Equipment*	**+**

*Will be discussed later in the chapter.

Changes in Current Assets (Other than Cash) and Current Liabilities	
Increase in Current Assets	**—**
Decrease in Current Assets	**+**
Increase in Current Liabilities	**+**
Decrease in Current Liabilities	**—**

FIGURE 2

Items to convert net income from accrual basis to cash basis

The change in depreciation expense is added to net income in the operating activities section as demonstrated above. Since there are no other changes in long-term assets, we can say that there have been no cash transactions involving investing activities.

Step 4: Determine the Net Cash Flows from Financing Activities

Record Cash Payments of Drawings.   Financing activities include additions to or reductions in owner's equity. On the statement of owner's equity, we note $150,000 in personal withdrawals, which we assume are in the form of cash. The withdrawals result in a decrease in cash. We can easily check our assumption that the withdrawals involved cash by reviewing the transactions affecting the J. K. Kim, Drawing, account. We record $150,000 as an outflow of cash in the Financing Activities section.

Jenny's Paintings Statement of Cash Flows For Year Ended December 31, 2011		
Cash Flows from (used by) Financing Activities:		
Payment of Personal Withdrawals	$(150,000)	
Net Cash Flows used by Financing Activities		$(150,000)

Putting these cash conversions all together, we have the complete statement of cash flows for Jenny's Paintings.

Jenny's Paintings Statement of Cash Flows For Year Ended December 31, 2011		
Cash Flows from (used by) Operating Activities:		
Net Income		$146,000
Add (Deduct) Items to Convert Net Income		
from Accrual Basis to Cash Basis:		
Depreciation Expense, Equipment	$ 22,000	
Increase in Accounts Receivable (net)	(12,600)	
Increase in Merchandise Inventory	(4,000)	
Increase in Prepaid Insurance	(900)	
Decrease in Accounts Payable	(4,500)	
Increase in Salaries Payable	400	400
Net Cash Flows from Operating Activities		$146,400
Cash Flows from (used by) Financing Activities:		
Payment of Personal Withdrawals	$(150,000)	
Net Cash Flows used by Financing Activities		(150,000)
Net Increase (Decrease) in Cash		$ (3,600)
Cash, January 1, 2011		35,000
Cash, December 31, 2011		$ 31,400

Illustration 2

Our next example shows how to prepare the statement of cash flows for a corporation. Bryan Corporation is a merchandising business operating on an accrual basis. This example will be worked in a very similar manner to the previous illustration. We will use the same steps that we learned for Jenny's Paintings. In this example, you will also learn how to handle sale of equipment, issuance on note payable, and issuance of stock. Following are the financial statements for Bryan Corporation.

Bryan Corporation
Income Statement
For Year Ended December 31, 2011

Revenue from Sales:		
Sales	$615,000	
Less Sales Returns and Allowances	6,000	
Net Sales		$609,000
Cost of Goods Sold:		
Merchandise Inventory, January 1, 2011	$224,000	
Purchases	$426,000	
Less Purchases Returns and Allowances	3,000	
Net Purchases	$423,000	
Add Freight In	47,000	
Delivered Cost of Purchases	470,000	
Cost of Goods Available for Sale	$694,000	
Less Merchandise Inventory, December 31, 2011	260,000	
Cost of Goods Sold		434,000
Gross Profit		$175,000
Operating Expenses:		
Wages Expense	$116,400	
Rent Expense	30,000	
Depreciation Expense, Equipment	24,000	
Supplies Expense	3,000	
Property Tax Expense	2,000	
Insurance Expense	1,500	
Total Operating Expenses		176,900
Income from Operations		$ (1,900)
Other Income:		
Gain on Disposal of Property and Equipment	$ 5,000	
Other Expenses:		
Interest Expense	600	4,400
Net Income		$ 2,500

Bryan Corporation
Statement of Retained Earnings
For Year Ended December 31, 2011

Retained Earnings, January 1, 2011		$ 94,600
Net Income for the Year	$ 2,500	
Less Cash Dividends Declared	16,000	
Decrease in Retained Earnings		(13,500)
Retained Earnings, December 31, 2011		$ 81,100

Bryan Corporation Comparative Balance Sheet December 31, 2011 and December 31, 2010			
	2011	**2010**	**Increase or (Decrease)**
Assets			
Cash	$ 47,800	$ 33,400	$ 14,400
Accounts Receivable (net)	66,400	69,000	(2,600)
Merchandise Inventory	260,000	224,000	36,000
Prepaid Rent	3,000	3,000	0
Prepaid Insurance	2,000	900	1,100
Equipment	114,000	143,000	(29,000)
Less Accumulated Depreciation	(47,000)	(35,000)	(12,000)
Total Assets	$446,200	$438,300	$ 7,900
Liabilities			
Accounts Payable	$ 28,600	$ 39,700	$(11,100)
Notes Payable	24,000	0	24,000
Wages Payable	2,100	2,400	(300)
Dividends Payable	2,000	3,000	(1,000)
Property Tax Payable	1,300	1,100	200
Interest Payable	600	0	600
Total Liabilities	$ 58,600	$ 46,200	$ 12,400
Stockholders' Equity			
Common Stock	$306,500	$297,500	$ 9,000
Retained Earnings	81,100	94,600	(13,500)
Total Stockholders' Equity	$387,600	$392,100	$ (4,500)
Total Liabilities and Stockholders' Equity	$446,200	$438,300	$ 7,900

Step 1: Determine the Change in Cash

Bryan Corporation had a $14,400 ($47,800 – $33,400) increase in cash for the year. This information is found on the comparative balance sheet. This change in cash will be verified on the statement of cash flows at the bottom of the statement as follows.

Bryan Corporation Statement of Cash Flows For Year Ended December 31, 2011	
Net Increase (Decrease) in Cash	$14,400
Cash, January 1, 2011	33,400
Cash, December 31, 2011	$47,800

Step 2: Determine the Net Cash Flows from Operating Activities

As we learned earlier when completing Jenny's Paintings' statement of cash flows, in order to prepare the Operating Activities section we must convert net income to cash flows from operations as determined by the changes in balance sheet accounts. Let's follow the same steps as we did with Jenny's Paintings.

Step 2a: Identify Net Income (Loss)

Bryan Corporation had net income of $2,500 during the year. This is listed first in the Operating Activities section of the statement of cash flows.

Bryan Corporation
Statement of Cash Flows
For Year Ended December 31, 2011

Cash Flows from (used by) Operating Activities:	
Net Income	$2,500

Step 2b: Add (Deduct) Noncash Operating Income and Expense Items

Depreciation Expense.   Depreciation Expense is treated as an addition to cash flows. Remember, Depreciation Expense is a noncash expense that we subtracted in determining net income, so this noncash expense will need to be added back to determine net income on a cash basis. Bryan Corporation had $24,000 recorded as Depreciation Expense on the income statement for the current year; therefore an adjustment of $24,000 will be added to net income.

Bryan Corporation
Statement of Cash Flows
For Year Ended December 31, 2011

Cash Flows from (used by) Operating Activities:		
Net Income		$2,500
Add (Deduct) Items to Convert Net Income		
from Accrual Basis to Cash Basis:		
Depreciation Expense, Equipment	$24,000	

Gain (or Loss) on Disposal of Property and Equipment.   Gain (or Loss) on Disposal of Property and Equipment is a noncash net income item. If you remember the general entry associated with gains or losses, the gain or loss amount is not usually the amount of cash received. Furthermore, although the cash received when disposing of property and equipment is reported on the statement of cash flows, the cash received is reported in the Investing Activities section, not the Operating Activities section. Because of these two reasons, an adjustment must be made to net income for a gain or loss on disposal of property and equipment.

In reviewing Bryan Corporation's income statement, we notice a gain on disposal of property and equipment of $5,000. This gain is treated as a deduction from cash flows and will be subtracted from net income. The gain of $5,000 is a noncash income item that was added in determining net income, therefore this noncash income will need to be subtracted to report net income on a cash-only basis.

Bryan Corporation
Statement of Cash Flows
For Year Ended December 31, 2011

Cash Flows from (used by) Operating Activities:		
Net Income		$2,500
Add (Deduct) Items to Convert Net Income		
from Accrual Basis to Cash Basis:		
Depreciation Expense, Equipment	$24,000	
Gain on Disposal of Property and Equipment	(5,000)	

Loss on Disposal of Property and Equipment is treated in the opposite manner. A loss is an addition to cash flows and is added to net income in the Operating Activities section of the statement of cash flows.

Step 2c: Add (Deduct) Changes in Current Assets (Other than Cash) and Current Liabilities

As mentioned in Illustration 1, to convert net income from an accrual basis to a cash basis, we will adjust net income for the changes in current assets (other than Cash) and current liabilities that are found on the balance sheet. Since many of the current assets and current liabilities that we discussed with Jenny's Paintings' statement of cash flows are also listed on Bryan Corporation's balance sheet, this should be a good review of what you have learned thus far.

Decrease in Accounts Receivable.   In Illustration 1, the Accounts Receivable account for Jenny's Paintings increased by $12,600; however, Bryan Corporation experienced a decrease of $2,600 ($66,400 – $69,000) in its Accounts Receivable account. When Accounts Receivable decreases, this means that less was recorded as revenue than was received in cash. Therefore, the $2,600 decrease in Accounts Receivable will need to be added to net income to determine operating cash flows.

Bryan Corporation Statement of Cash Flows For Year Ended December 31, 2011	
Cash Flows from (used by) Operating Activities:	
Net Income	$2,500
Add (Deduct) Items to Convert Net Income	
from Accrual Basis to Cash Basis:	
Depreciation Expense, Equipment	$ 24,000
Gain on Disposal of Property and Equipment	(5,000)
Decrease in Accounts Receivable (net)	2,600

Increase in Merchandise Inventory.   As we did with Jenny's Paintings earlier, it helps if we review all of the T accounts related to cost of goods.

Cash			
+	−		
	(c)		481,100

Merchandise Inventory				
	+	−		
Jan. 1	224,000	(a)		434,000
(b)	470,000			
Dec. 31	260,000			

Accounts Payable			
−	+		
	Jan. 1		39,700
(c) 481,100	(b)		470,000
	Dec. 31		28,600

Cost of Goods Sold			
+	−		
(a)	434,000		

Transaction (a) represents the cost of goods sold (both cash and noncash purchases) that is reported on the income statement, $434,000. Transaction (b) represents the purchases of inventory for the year, $470,000. Transaction (c) represents the cash payments for inventory for the year, $481,100. The cash payments for inventory sold during the year are $47,100 ($481,100 – $434,000) higher than what is represented as Cost of Goods Sold on the income statement. As explained earlier, this difference is comprised of two parts: the change in inventory, $36,000 ($260,000 – $224,000), and the change in accounts payable, $11,100 ($39,700 – $28,600).

When inventory increases, more goods were purchased than were actually sold. Therefore, the increase in inventory of $36,000 will need to be subtracted from net income to eliminate the noncash portion of cost of goods sold.

Bryan Corporation
Statement of Cash Flows
For Year Ended December 31, 2011

Cash Flows from (used by) Operating Activities:		
Net Income		$2,500
Add (Deduct) Items to Convert Net Income		
from Accrual Basis to Cash Basis:		
Depreciation Expense, Equipment	$ 24,000	
Gain on Disposal of Property and Equipment	(5,000)	
Decrease in Accounts Receivable (net)	2,600	
Increase in Merchandise Inventory	(36,000)	

Increase in Prepaid Insurance. If a prepaid expense increases, cash payments for the item(s) are more than the amount listed as expense and will need to be subtracted from net income. If a prepaid expense decreases, cash payments for the item(s) are less than the amount listed as expense and will need to be added to net income. Since Bryan Corporation's Prepaid Insurance account increased by $1,100 during the year, net income will need to be reduced by that amount.

Bryan Corporation
Statement of Cash Flows
For Year Ended December 31, 2011

Cash Flows from (used by) Operating Activities:		
Net Income		$2,500
Add (Deduct) Items to Convert Net Income		
from Accrual Basis to Cash Basis:		
Depreciation Expense, Equipment	$ 24,000	
Gain on Disposal of Property and Equipment	(5,000)	
Decrease in Accounts Receivable (net)	2,600	
Increase in Merchandise Inventory	(36,000)	
Increase in Prepaid Insurance	(1,100)	

Decrease in Accounts Payable. Bryan Corporation's Accounts Payable account decreased by $11,100. This decrease was reviewed in the T accounts and accompanying explanation for the Merchandise Inventory account on pages 880–881. The decrease in the Accounts Payable account means that the company paid cash of $11,100 to suppliers that was not reflected in the Cost of Goods Sold shown on the income statement. Therefore, the $11,100 should be subtracted from net income.

Bryan Corporation
Statement of Cash Flows
For Year Ended December 31, 2011

Cash Flows from (used by) Operating Activities:		
Net Income		$2,500
Add (Deduct) Items to Convert Net Income		
from Accrual Basis to Cash Basis:		
Depreciation Expense, Equipment	$ 24,000	
Gain on Disposal of Property and Equipment	(5,000)	
Decrease in Accounts Receivable (net)	2,600	
Increase in Merchandise Inventory	(36,000)	
Increase in Prepaid Insurance	(1,100)	
Decrease in Accounts Payable	(11,100)	

Decrease in Wages Payable. Bryan Corporation's Wages Payable account decreased by $300 during the year. When accrued liabilities (like Wages Payable) decrease, more wages were paid than were actually recorded in net income, so we decrease net income. In Bryan Corporation's case, net income is reduced by $300.

Bryan Corporation
Statement of Cash Flows
For Year Ended December 31, 2011

Cash Flows from (used by) Operating Activities:		
Net Income		$2,500
Add (Deduct) Items to Convert Net Income		
from Accrual Basis to Cash Basis:		
Depreciation Expense, Equipment	$ 24,000	
Gain on Disposal of Property and Equipment	(5,000)	
Decrease in Accounts Receivable (net)	2,600	
Increase in Merchandise Inventory	(36,000)	
Increase in Prepaid Insurance	(1,100)	
Decrease in Accounts Payable	(11,100)	
Decrease in Wages Payable	(300)	

Increase in Property Tax Payable and Interest Payable. The entries for Property Tax Payable and Interest Payable are the same as the previous entry for Wages Payable. However, in this case, we are dealing with an increase in accrued liabilities rather than a decrease. Bryan Corporation's Property Tax Payable account increased by $200 during the year, while its Interest Payable account increased by $600. When accrued liabilities (like Property Tax Payable and Interest Payable) increase, less property taxes and interest was paid for than actually used or expired, so we increase net income. In Bryan Corporation's case, net income is increased by $200 and $600, respectively.

Bryan Corporation
Statement of Cash Flows
For Year Ended December 31, 2011

Cash Flows from (used by) Operating Activities:		
Net Income		$2,500
Add (Deduct) Items to Convert Net Income		
from Accrual Basis to Cash Basis:		
Depreciation Expense, Equipment	$ 24,000	
Gain on Disposal of Property and Equipment	(5,000)	
Decrease in Accounts Receivable (net)	2,600	
Increase in Merchandise Inventory	(36,000)	
Increase in Prepaid Insurance	(1,100)	
Decrease in Accounts Payable	(11,100)	
Decrease in Wages Payable	(300)	
Increase in Property Tax Payable	**200**	
Increase in Interest Payable	**600**	

Following is the completed Cash Flows from Operating Activities section. The net cash flows *used* by operating activities is $23,600. We report net cash flows *used* because this is an outflow of cash (or negative amount).

Bryan Corporation
Statement of Cash Flows
For Year Ended December 31, 2011

Cash Flows from (used by) Operating Activities:		
Net Income		$2,500
Add (Deduct) Items to Convert Net Income		
from Accrual Basis to Cash Basis:		
Depreciation Expense, Equipment	$ 24,000	
Gain on Disposal of Property and Equipment	(5,000)	
Decrease in Accounts Receivable (net)	2,600	
Increase in Merchandise Inventory	(36,000)	
Increase in Prepaid Insurance	(1,100)	
Decrease in Accounts Payable	(11,100)	
Decrease in Wages Payable	(300)	
Increase in Property Tax Payable	200	
Increase in Interest Payable	600	(26,100)
Net Cash Flows used by Operating Activities		**$(23,600)**

Notice that we did not record an adjustment for the change in notes payable and dividends payable. This is because notes and dividends are reported in the Financing Activities section of the statement of cash flows rather than the Operating Activities section.

Step 3: Determine the Net Cash Flows from Investing Activities

Record Cash Receipts from the Sale of Equipment. Investing activities include changes in property and equipment (long-term assets). During 2011, Equipment decreased from $143,000 to $114,000. On the income statement, a Gain on Disposal of Property and Equipment of $5,000 is listed in the Other Income section. In addition, the Accumulated Depreciation account increased only $12,000 even though there was $24,000 reported in the Depreciation Expense account on the income statement. Examine the general ledger accounts and journals to reconstruct the transactions. Reviewing the ledger accounts shows the following information in T-account form:

Cash			Equipment		
+	−		+	−	
(a) 22,000			Jan. 1 143,000	(a)	29,000
			Dec. 31 114,000		

Accumulated Depreciation, Equipment			Depreciation Expense, Equipment		
−	+		+	−	
	Jan. 1 35,000	(b)	24,000		
(a) 12,000	(b) 24,000				
	Dec. 31 47,000				

Gain on Disposal of Property and Equipment	
−	+
	(a) 5,000

The following entries are found in the general journal:

		GENERAL JOURNAL			PAGE _____

Date	Description	Post. Ref.	Debit	Credit
2011				
(a)	Cash		22 0 0 0 00	
	Accumulated Depreciation,			
	Equipment		12 0 0 0 00	
	Equipment			29 0 0 0 00
	Gain on Disposal of Property			
	and Equipment			5 0 0 0 00
	To record the sale of			
	equipment.			
(b)	Depreciation Expense, Equipment		24 0 0 0 00	
	Accumulated Depreciation,			
	Equipment			24 0 0 0 00
	To record the depreciation			
	of equipment.			

By reconstructing the entries, we spot the debit to Cash of $22,000. We list sale of equipment, $22,000, as a positive cash flow under Investing Activities. Notice that we do not record any adjustment in this section for the depreciation. This is because the adjustment for Depreciation Expense was already made in the Operating Activities section.

Bryan Corporation
Statement of Cash Flows
For Year Ended December 31, 2011

Cash Flows from (used by) Investing Activities:		
Sale of Equipment	$22,000	
Net Cash Flows from Investing Activities		22,000

Step 4: Determine the Net Cash Flows from Financing Activities

Convert Notes Payable to Cash Receipts from the Issuance of a Note. During 2011, Notes Payable increased from $0 to $24,000. We must examine the general ledger account and journals to reconstruct the transaction(s). The following entry is found in the general journal:

	GENERAL JOURNAL			PAGE ____

Date	Description	Post. Ref.	Debit	Credit
2011				
Oct. 2	Cash		24 0 0 0 00	
	Notes Payable			24 0 0 0 00
	Borrowed from County Bank.			
	Issued 120-day, 10 percent			
	note dated October 2.			

We list the issuance of the note for $24,000 as a positive cash flow under Financing Activities.

Bryan Corporation
Statement of Cash Flows
For Year Ended December 31, 2011

Cash Flows from (used by) Financing Activities:	
Issuance of Note	$24,000

Convert Common Stock to Cash Receipts from the Issuance of Common Stock. During 2011, Common Stock increased from $297,500 to $306,500. Examine the general ledger account and journals to reconstruct the transaction(s). The following entry is found in the general journal:

	GENERAL JOURNAL			PAGE ____

Date	Description	Post. Ref.	Debit	Credit
2011				
June 16	Cash		9 0 0 0 00	
	Common Stock			9 0 0 0 00
	To record the sale of 900			
	shares of $10 par			
	common stock at par value.			

We list the sale of common stock as a positive cash flow under Financing Activities.

Bryan Corporation
Statement of Cash Flows
For Year Ended December 31, 2011

Cash Flows from (used by) Financing Activities:	
Issuance of Note	$ 24,000
Issuance of Common Stock	9,000

Convert Dividends to Cash Payments of Dividends.   On the statement of retained earnings, we note $16,000 listed as cash dividends. During 2011, Dividends Payable decreased from $3,000 to $2,000. Evidently, $1,000 more was paid in cash than is recorded as cash dividends. The calculation looks like this:

	Cash Dividends Declared	$16,000
+	Beginning Dividends Payable	3,000
=	Total	$19,000
−	Ending Dividends Payable	2,000
=	Cash Payments of Dividends	$17,000

Bryan Corporation
Statement of Cash Flows
For Year Ended December 31, 2011

Cash Flows from (used by) Financing Activities:		
Issuance of Note	$ 24,000	
Issuance of Common Stock	9,000	
Payment of Dividends	(17,000)	
Net Cash Flows from Financing Activities		16,000

Let's put all these conversions together in the correct format to make up the statement of cash flows for Bryan Corporation shown in Figure 3.

SCHEDULE OF NONCASH INVESTING AND FINANCING TRANSACTIONS

LEARNING OBJECTIVE 7

Prepare a schedule of noncash investing and financing transactions.

A company occasionally engages in significant transactions that do not affect cash directly. For example, a corporation may issue a long-term mortgage for the purchase of land and building. Or it may issue common stock for the land and building. These transactions represent important investing and financing activities, but they would not show up on a statement of cash flows because they do not involve either cash receipts or cash payments. However, since these transactions will affect future cash flows, the Financial Accounting Standards Board has determined that they should be presented in a separate schedule at the bottom of the statement of cash flows. An example of such a schedule is shown here.

Schedule of Noncash Investing and Financing Transactions	
Issue of Mortgage Payable for Building	$900,000

In this way, readers of the statement of cash flows will have a complete picture of a company's investing and financing activities.

FIGURE 3

Completed statement of cash flows for Bryan Corporation

Bryan Corporation
Statement of Cash Flows
For Year Ended December 31, 2011

Cash Flows from (used by) Operating Activities:		
Net Income		$ 2,500
Add (Deduct) Items to Convert Net Income		
from Accrual Basis to Cash Basis:		
Depreciation Expense, Equipment	$ 24,000	
Gain on Disposal of Property and Equipment	(5,000)	
Decrease in Accounts Receivable (net)	2,600	
Increase in Merchandise Inventory	(36,000)	
Increase in Prepaid Insurance	(1,100)	
Decrease in Accounts Payable	(11,100)	
Decrease in Wages Payable	(300)	
Increase in Property Tax Payable	200	
Increase in Interest Payable	600	(26,100)
Net Cash Flows used by Operating Activities		$(23,600)
Cash Flows from (used by) Investing Activities:		
Sale of Equipment	$ 22,000	
Net Cash Flows from Investing Activities		22,000
Cash Flows from (used by) Financing Activities:		
Issuance of Note	$ 24,000	
Issuance of Common Stock	9,000	
Payment of Dividends	(17,000)	
Net Cash Flows from Financing Activities		16,000
Net Increase (Decrease) in Cash		$ 14,400
Cash, January 1, 2011		33,400
Cash, December 31, 2011		$ 47,800

INTERPRETING THE STATEMENT OF CASH FLOWS

Interpretation of the statement of cash flows begins with the net cash flows from operating activities. Is the net cash flow a positive amount, and how does it compare with net income on the income statement? It is useful to note the net cash flows from operating activities to see if the company is covering its cash outflows for dividends listed in the Financing Activities section. It is also useful to examine the Investing and Financing Activities sections to determine if the company is expanding and how the expansion is being financed. If the expansion is being financed primarily by long-term debt, we can be certain that, unless the expansion produces more cash revenue or a reduction in cash expenses, cash flows from operating activities will decline in the future as interest payments are made.

Anyone who uses financial statements can gather a great deal of information from the statement of cash flows. Let's take a closer look at Bryan Corporation's statement of cash flows to see what we can find out.

Benefits to Users

Managers, investors, and creditors all use the statement of cash flows to judge how a company is doing. What kinds of conclusions could they draw about Bryan Corporation from studying its financial statements?

8 LEARNING OBJECTIVE

Be able to interpret the statement of cash flows and understand the benefits to users.

The statement of cash flows shows *why* cash has changed, whereas a comparative balance sheet shows only by how much cash has changed.

Remember

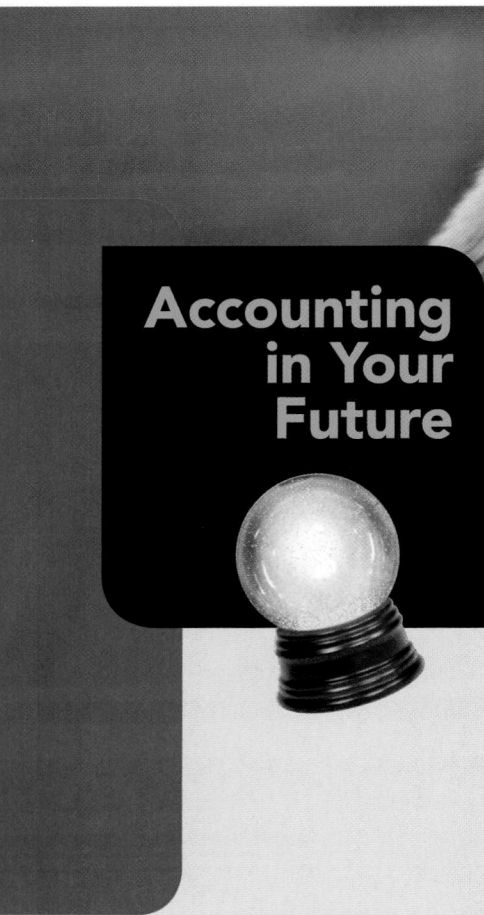

Accounting in Your Future

Photographer

When you think about users of financial statements, you don't often think about photographers. However, Bill Woodhull, a photographer from Austin, Texas, states that "any businessperson needs to understand the monetary system and how it works." Bill uses financial statements in order to make management decisions that will help his photography business grow. As a photographer, he relies on the income statement to help determine pricing of products and also to keep expenses under control and on budget.

Another financial statement that he often reviews is the statement of cash flows. The statement of cash flows allows Bill to track the cash of his business. As a business owner, Bill likes to know the inflows of cash such as from customer sales and the outflows of cash such as expenses and owner drawings. The statement of cash flows also provides Bill with powerful insight into the liquidity of his company. Bill can easily tell if he is generating enough cash to pay his suppliers or if he is able to pay wages to a new photography assistant.

The statement of cash flows, along with all other financial statements, are useful tools to more than just accountants. It is important that all business owners are familiar with these tools.

Remember

Working Capital = Current Assets – Current Liabilities

Current Ratio = Current Assets ÷ Current Liabilities

Return on Stockholders' Equity = Net Income Available to Common Stock/ [(Beg. Common Stockholders' Equity + End. Common Stockholders' Equity)/2]

Bryan Corporation should review carefully the statement of cash flows to determine its financial position. The $14,400 increase in cash is higher than the $2,500 net income. This in itself would not be overly concerning, however, users of the statement of cash flows are also interested in the company's ability to generate enough cash to pay its bills and pay dividends.

Let's look first at the operating activities section. The negative $23,600 Net Cash Flows used by Operating Activities is bad news indeed. Bryan Corporation should take a look at the following items when reviewing the operating activities section:

- How do the cash receipts from customers compare to the cash payments made for operating activities?

- How does the issuance of the note payable ($24,000) affect cash flows? Is the interest payment excessive?

- Is the merchandise inventory salable? If so, can it be worked down to generate more cash?

In reviewing the investing activities section, Bryan Corporation should consider the $22,000 generated from the sale of equipment. Will the equipment have to be replaced? If so, how will it be financed?

Although the company had a comfortable beginning credit balance of $94,600 in Retained Earnings ($97,100 after closing the net income into Retained Earnings), the declaration and payment of cash dividends might not have been the best decision.

Since the corporation had very little net income, the corporation actually had to borrow funds to pay its dividends. Would Bryan Corporation have been better off by not actually paying the dividend?

By using additional analytical tools, some interesting facts are discovered. Bryan Corporation's working capital is $320,600 ($379,200 − $58,600); its current ratio is 6.47:1 ($379,200 ÷ $58,600); and its quick ratio is 1.95:1 ($114,200 ÷ $58,600). However, the firm is still not generating enough cash to pay its bills. Incidentally, the return on stockholders' equity $2,500/[($306,500 + $297,500)/2)] = 0.008 is very low.

CHAPTER REVIEW

Study & Practice

1 LEARNING OBJECTIVE

Describe the statement of cash flows, and define cash *and* cash equivalents.

The **statement of cash flows** explains the changes in cash and cash equivalents between the beginning and the end of a fiscal period. **Cash equivalents** are short-term (mature 90 days or less from the date acquired) investments in money market accounts, U.S. Treasury bills, and commercial paper. Commercial paper consists of promissory notes issued by corporations.

2 LEARNING OBJECTIVE

State the purpose of the statement of cash flows.

The statement of cash flows provides a summary of information concerning a company's cash receipts and payments during a fiscal period. A secondary purpose is to provide information about a firm's operating, investing, and financing activities during a fiscal period. The statement of cash flows also serves to reconcile the beginning and ending cash balance for the period.

3 LEARNING OBJECTIVE

State the uses of the statement of cash flows by management, investors, and creditors.

The statement of cash flows is useful to management, and also to investors and creditors, in assessing or evaluating the liquidity of a business, including the ability of the business to generate future cash flows and to pay its debts and dividends.

4 **LEARNING OBJECTIVE**

Identify cash inflows and outflows as operating, investing, or financing activities.

Cash flows are classified as operating activities, investing activities, or financing activities. **Operating activities** include the cash effects of transactions that enter into the determination of net income. **Investing activities** include cash flows involving the making and collecting of loans, the buying and selling of investments, and the buying and selling of property and equipment. **Financing activities** include cash flows involving the selling or retiring of bonds, the issuing or paying of notes, the issuing of stock or investment by the owner, and payments of personal withdrawals or dividends.

PRACTICE EXERCISE 1

W. Chan, Inc., had the following transactions during the year. Classify each transaction as (O) an operating activity, (I) an investing activity, (F) a financing activity, or (X) a noncash transaction. Also note each transaction as a plus (+) for an inflow of cash, a minus (–) for an outflow of cash, or zero (0) if the transaction is neither an inflow nor an outflow.

1. Paid a $15,000 dividend to common stockholders.
2. Loaned $20,000 to a customer and accepted a note receivable.
3. Sold equipment for $15,000.
4. Paid $13,000 for salaries.
5. Received cash from customers of $60,000.
6. Purchased equipment in exchange for a note payable.
7. Paid $1,500 for income taxes.

PRACTICE EXERCISE 1 SOLUTION

1. Paid a $15,000 dividend to common stockholders: (F, –)
2. Loaned $20,000 to a customer and accepted a note receivable: (I, –)
3. Sold equipment for $15,000: (I, +)
4. Paid $13,000 for salaries: (O, –)
5. Received cash from customers of $60,000: (O, +)
6. Purchased equipment in exchange for a note payable: (X, 0)
7. Paid $1,500 for income taxes: (O, –)

5 **LEARNING OBJECTIVE**

Prepare the Operating Activities section of the statement of cash flows using the indirect method.

Preparing the Operating Activities section of the statement of cash flows involves converting a company's net income from an accrual to a cash basis. To convert a company's net income to a cash basis, we start with net income from the income statement and then make adjustments for noncash operating income and expense items and changes in current assets (other than Cash) and current liabilities.

PRACTICE EXERCISE 2

Hi-Country Quilts reports net income of $65,000 for the year ended December 31, 2011. The income statement also reveals Depreciation Expense, Equipment of $10,000 and a Loss on Disposal of Property and Equipment of $800. The comparative balance sheet reveals that Accounts Receivable, net decreased by $2,000; Prepaid Rent increased by $1,000; Accounts Payable increased by $1,300; and Salaries Payable decreased by $200. Prepare the Operating Activities section of the statement of cash flows for Hi-Country Quilts.

PRACTICE EXERCISE 2 SOLUTION

Hi-Country Quilts
Statement of Cash Flows
For Year Ended December 31, 2011

Cash Flows from (used by) Operating Activities:		
Net Income		$65,000
Add (Deduct) Items to Convert Net Income		
from Accrual Basis to Cash Basis:		
Depreciation Expense, Equipment	$10,000	
Loss on Disposal of Property and Equipment	800	
Decrease in Accounts Receivable (net)	2,000	
Increase in Prepaid Rent	(1,000)	
Increase in Accounts Payable	1,300	
Decrease in Salaries Payable	(200)	12,900
Net Cash Flows from Operating Activities		$77,900

6 LEARNING OBJECTIVE

Prepare the Investing Activities and Financing Activities sections of the statement of cash flows.

The Investing Activities section of the statement of cash flows is concerned with changes in property and equipment (long-term assets). The Financing Activities section includes additions to or reductions in owner's or stockholders' equity.

PRACTICE EXERCISE 3

Refer to the information presented in Practice Exercise 2. In addition, Hi-Country Quilts sold equipment for $1,000 and issued a note for $5,800. The owner, Shawna Smith, withdrew $18,000 for personal use. Prepare the Investing Activities and Financing Activities sections of the statement of cash flows for Hi-Country Quilts.

PRACTICE EXERCISE 3 SOLUTION

Hi-Country Quilts
Statement of Cash Flows
For Year Ended December 31, 2011

Cash Flows from (used by) Investing Activities:		
Sale of Equipment	$ 1,000	
Net Cash Flows from Investing Activities		1,000
Cash Flows from (used by) Financing Activities:		
Issuance of Note	$ 5,800	
Payment of Personal Withdrawals	(18,000)	
Net Cash Flows used by Financing Activities		(12,200)

LEARNING OBJECTIVE

7 *Prepare a schedule of noncash investing and financing transactions.*

A company is required to prepare a schedule of noncash investing and financing transactions for transactions that represent important investing and financing activities but do not include cash receipts or payments. This schedule is presented at the bottom of the statement of cash flows.

PRACTICE EXERCISE 4

Sunset Corporation purchased land for $200,000 by issuing a 20-year note payable. Prepare a schedule of noncash investing and financing transactions for Sunset Corporation.

PRACTICE EXERCISE 4 SOLUTION

Schedule of Noncash Investing and Financing Transactions	
Issue of Note Payable for Land	$200,000

LEARNING OBJECTIVE

8 *Be able to interpret the statement of cash flows and understand the benefits to users.*

The statement of cash flows is useful in determining why cash has changed and the sources and uses of cash. Managers, investors, and creditors all use the statement of cash flows to judge how a company is doing.

Glossary

Cash equivalents Items included in the broad definition of cash. Included are short-term, highly liquid investments, such as money market accounts, U.S. Treasury bills, and commercial paper, having maturities with a maximum of 90 days from the date acquired. (p. 865)

Direct method A method used to prepare the Operating Activities section of the statement of cash flows that primarily involves converting each amount recorded on the income statement from the accrual basis to the cash basis to show such items as cash receipts from customers and cash payments for purchases and operating expenses. (p. 867)

Financing activities A category on the statement of cash flows (involving inflows and outflows) that includes borrowing money or repaying loans and additional cash investments or reductions of owners' investments through cash dividends or personal withdrawals. (p. 866)

Indirect method A method used to prepare the Operating Activities section of the statement of cash flows that involves making adjustments to net income for noncash operating income and expense items and changes in current assets (other than Cash) and current liabilities. (p. 867)

Investing activities A category on the statement of cash flows (involving inflows and outflows) that includes the buying and selling of property and equipment, the acquiring and selling of investments other than cash equivalents, and the making and collecting of loans. (p. 866)

Operating activities A category on the statement of cash flows (involving inflows and outflows) that includes cash receipts from customers for the sale of merchandise and services, cash receipts from interest and dividends, cash payments for merchandise purchases, cash payments for operating expenses, cash payments for interest, and cash payments for income taxes. (p. 865)

Statement of cash flows A financial statement that explains in detail how the balance of cash and cash equivalents has changed between the beginning and the end of a fiscal period. A schedule on the statement presents important noncash investing and financing activities that occurred during the same period. (p. 864)

CHAPTER ASSIGNMENTS

Discussion Questions

1. What are the three categories listed on the statement of cash flows? Give two examples of each category.

2. What is included in *cash* as the term is used on a statement of cash flows?

3. What are the purposes of the statement of cash flows?

4. What are the effects of the following items on cash flows from operating activities?
   a. an increase in Accounts Receivable, $15,000
   b. an increase in Interest Payable, $400
   c. Depreciation Expense, Equipment, $92,000

5. In which of the three categories listed on a statement of cash flows would each of the following appear? Also, state for each item whether it represents a cash inflow or outflow.
   a. Cash purchase of land
   b. Cash payment of wages
   c. Cash payment of dividends
   d. Cash sale of investments
   e. Cash proceeds from issuing stock
   f. Cash payment of interest

6. Laura Company sold equipment at a gain of $1,000. The equipment cost $47,000 and had accumulated depreciation of $40,000. Describe how this event is handled in the statement of cash flows.

7. As a means of gaining a greater return on its cash balance, Bucek Company transferred $20,000 from its checking account to a money market account, purchased an $11,000 three-month U.S. Treasury bill, and bought $13,000 of another company's stock. How will each of these transactions affect the statement of cash flows?

8. Lee, Inc., has a net loss of $110,000 for the fiscal year but a positive cash flow of $10,000. What are some conditions that might have caused this situation?

Exercises

EXERCISE 22-1 C. Gharpurey, Inc., had the following transactions during the year. Classify each transaction as (O) an operating activity, (I) an investing activity, (F) a financing activity, or (X) a noncash transaction. Also note each transaction as a plus (+) for an inflow of cash, a minus (–) for an outflow of cash, or zero (0) if the transaction is neither an inflow nor an outflow.

LO 4

PRACTICE EXERCISE 1

1. Paid $4,500 interest.
2. Repaid the principal of a mortgage of $42,000.
3. Paid $5,000 for rent.
4. Paid $6,800 for computer equipment.
5. Sold equipment for $7,000.
6. Extended a customer's note of $1,600.
7. Purchased a bond for $10,000.
8. Paid $4,000 of federal income taxes.
9. Received cash from customers of $73,000.

EXERCISE 22-2 Identify if the following would be added (+) or subtracted (–) from net income in determining net cash flows from operating activities using the indirect method.

LO 5

PRACTICE EXERCISE 2

1. Increase in Merchandise Inventory
2. Depreciation Expense
3. Decrease in Prepaid Insurance

4. Decrease in Accounts Payable
5. Increase in Salaries Payable
6. Gain on Disposal of Property and Equipment
7. Increase in Accounts Receivable (net)
8. Loss on Disposal of Property and Equipment

5 LO

PRACTICE EXERCISE 2

EXERCISE 22-3 Red Cab Company reports net income of $32,000 for the year ended December 31, 2011. The income statement also reveals Depreciation Expense, Equipment of $6,500 and a Gain on Disposal of Property and Equipment of $1,200. The comparative balance sheet reveals that Accounts Receivable, net decreased by $1,300; Prepaid Insurance decreased by $800; Accounts Payable increased by $1,800; and Rent Payable decreased by $750. Prepare the Operating Activities section of the statement of cash flows for Red Cab Company using the indirect method.

5 LO

PRACTICE EXERCISE 2

EXERCISE 22-4 FGH Corporation reported net income of $135,000 for 2011. Depreciation Expense, Equipment of $13,000 was included on the income statement. The December 31 balances of current assets and current liabilities follow.

Accounts	2011	2010
Accounts Receivable (net)	$ 87,500	$ 98,000
Merchandise Inventory	105,000	137,000
Prepaid Insurance	15,400	13,200
Accounts Payable	67,300	69,000
Salaries Payable	15,300	12,800

Prepare the Operating Activities section of the statement of cash flows for FGH Corporation using the indirect method.

5,6 LO

PRACTICE EXERCISES 2,3

EXERCISE 22-5 The T accounts for Equipment; Accumulated Depreciation, Equipment; and Loss on Disposal of Property and Equipment for Zhang Company at the end of 2010 follow.

Equipment				**Accumulated Depreciation, Equipment**			
	+	−			−	+	
Beg. Bal.	75,600	Disposal	16,200	Disposal	8,100	Beg. Bal.	55,800
Purchases	24,300					Adjusting	12,600
End. Bal.	83,700					End. Bal.	60,300

Loss on Disposal of Property and Equipment

	+	−
Disposal	5,400	

New equipment was bought for cash, and the used equipment was sold for cash. Compute the amounts to be included on the statement of cash flows, and indicate where these amounts should be shown.

6 LO

PRACTICE EXERCISE 3

EXERCISE 22-6 The T accounts for Dividends Payable; Common Stock; Paid-in Capital in Excess of Par Value; and Retained Earnings for Mariano Corporation at the end of 2010 follow.

Dividends Payable		
−	+	
	Beg. Bal.	15,000
5,000		
	End. Bal.	10,000

Common Stock		
−	+	
	Beg. Bal.	70,350
		10,125
	End. Bal.	80,475

Paid-in Capital in Excess of Par Value		
−	+	
	Beg. Bal.	50,187
		23,162
	End. Bal.	73,349

Retained Earnings			
−		+	
Dividend	30,000	Beg. Bal.	157,496
		Net Income	92,438
		End. Bal.	219,934

Compute the amounts to be included on the statement of cash flows, and indicate where these amounts should be shown.

EXERCISE 22-7 Tripp Triathlon Training Camp reported net income of $46,153 for 2011. The December 31 balances of select accounts follow.

LO 6

PRACTICE EXERCISE 3

Accounts	2011	2010
Land	$33,450	—
Equipment	24,440	$32,690
Accumulated Depreciation, Equipment	14,275	12,240
Notes Payable	7,690	13,690
N. R. Tripp, Capital	66,894	95,741

The following additional information was taken from Tripp Triathlon Training Camps' records:

a. Depreciation Expense for the year was $5,785.
b. Land was acquired with cash.
c. Tripp sold equipment for $10,000, realizing a gain of $5,500.
d. A partial payment on the non-interest-bearing note payable was made.
e. N. R. Tripp withdrew $75,000.

Prepare the Investing and Financing Activities sections of the statement of cash flows for Tripp Triathlon Training Camp.

EXERCISE 22-8 Boston Shipping Corporation issued 30,000 shares of common stock, $5 par value in exchange for equipment with a fair market value of $187,250. Prepare a schedule of noncash investing and financing transactions for Boston Shipping Corporation.

LO 7

PRACTICE EXERCISE 4

Problem Set A

For additional help, see the demonstration problem at the beginning of each chapter in your Working Papers.

PROBLEM 22-1A The financial statements of Perkins Realty follow.

 LO 5,6

Perkins Realty
Income Statement
For Year Ended December 31, 2011

Revenue:		
Income from Services		$96,107
Expenses:		
Commissions Expense	$27,864	
Advertising Expense	7,560	
Repairs Expense	1,688	
Rent Expense	4,860	
Telephone Expense	1,242	
Depreciation Expense, Automobile	3,078	
Depreciation Expense, Office Equipment	1,647	
Insurance Expense	554	
Utilities Expense	2,201	
Total Expenses		50,694
Net Income		$45,413

Perkins Realty
Statement of Owner's Equity
For Year Ended December 31, 2011

F. N. Perkins, Capital, January 1, 2011		$30,915
Investments during the Year	$ 0	
Net Income	45,413	
Subtotal	$45,413	
Less Withdrawals	40,500	
Increase in Capital		4,913
F. N. Perkins, Capital, December 31, 2011		$35,828

Perkins Realty
Comparative Balance Sheet
December 31, 2011 and December 31, 2010

	2011	2010	Increase or (Decrease)
Assets			
Cash	$22,896	$13,892	$9,004
Prepaid Rent	1,215	405	810
Prepaid Insurance	837	1,013	(176)
Automobile	15,390	15,390	0
Less Accumulated Depreciation	(6,156)	(3,078)	(3,078)
Office Equipment	8,235	8,235	0
Less Accumulated Depreciation	(6,589)	(4,942)	(1,647)
Total Assets	$35,828	$30,915	$4,913
Owner's Equity			
F. N. Perkins, Capital	$35,828	$30,915	$4,913
Total Liabilities and Owner's Equity	$35,828	$30,915	$4,913

Check Figure
Net Cash Flows from Operating
Activities, $49,504

Required

Prepare a statement of cash flows for the year 2011, using the indirect method of presenting cash flows from operating activities.

5,6  **LO**

PROBLEM 22-2A Leon Van and Storage's financial statements for the current year follow.

Leon Van and Storage
Income Statement
For Year Ended December 31, 2011

Revenue:		
Revenue from Moving Services	$149,760	
Revenue from Storage Rentals	87,264	
Total Revenue		$237,024
Expenses:		
Wages Expense	$140,520	
Truck Repair Expense	5,568	
Gas and Oil Expense	4,356	
Insurance Expense	3,420	
Supplies Expense	1,488	
Depreciation Expense, Building	11,544	
Depreciation Expense, Trucks	22,560	
Interest Expense	12,120	
Total Expenses		201,576
Net Income		$ 35,448

Leon Van and Storage
Statement of Owner's Equity
For Year Ended December 31, 2011

G. A. Leon, Capital, January 1, 2011		$273,648
Investments during the Year	$ 0	
Net Income	35,448	
Subtotal	$35,448	
Less Withdrawals	32,400	
Increase in Capital		3,048
G. A. Leon, Capital, December 31, 2011		$276,696

Leon Van and Storage
Comparative Balance Sheet
December 31, 2011 and December 31, 2010

	2011	2010	Increase or (Decrease)
Assets			
Cash	$ 44,160	$ 12,732	$ 31,428
Prepaid Insurance	4,572	1,488	3,084
Land	38,640	38,640	0
Building	376,800	376,800	0
Less Accumulated Depreciation	(130,560)	(119,016)	(11,544)
Trucks	112,800	112,800	0
Less Accumulated Depreciation	(45,120)	(22,560)	(22,560)
Total Assets	$401,292	$400,884	$ 408
Liabilities			
Mortgage Payable	$124,596	$127,236	$ (2,640)
Owner's Equity			
G. A. Leon, Capital	276,696	273,648	3,048
Total Liabilities and Owner's Equity	$401,292	$400,884	$ 408

Required

Prepare a statement of cash flows for the year 2011, using the indirect method of presenting cash flows from operating activities.

Check Figure

Net Cash Flows used by Financing Activities, $(35,040)

PROBLEM 22-3A The financial statements for Salinas Marine Sales follow.

 LO 5,6

Salinas Marine Sales
Income Statement
For Year Ended December 31, 2011

Revenue from Sales:		
Net Sales		$891,120
Cost of Goods Sold:		
Merchandise Inventory, January 1, 2011	$160,404	
Delivered Cost of Purchases	654,336	
Cost of Goods Available for Sale	$814,740	
Less Merchandise Inventory, December 31, 2011	165,300	
Cost of Goods Sold		649,440
Gross Profit		$241,680
Operating Expenses:		
Salary Expense	$131,856	
Rent Expense	28,800	
Depreciation Expense, Equipment	35,520	
Supplies Expense	3,300	
Insurance Expense	1,440	
Total Operating Expenses		200,916
Net Income		$40,764

Salinas Marine Sales
Statement of Owner's Equity
For Year Ended December 31, 2011

W. A. Salinas, Capital, January 1, 2011		$296,604
Investments during the Year	$ 0	
Net Income	40,764	
Subtotal	$40,764	
Less Withdrawals	48,000	
Decrease in Capital		(7,236)
W. A. Salinas, Capital, December 31, 2011		$289,368

Salinas Marine Sales
Comparative Balance Sheet
December 31, 2011 and December 31, 2010

	2011	2010	Increase or (Decrease)
Assets			
Cash	$ 45,168	$ 46,092	$ (924)
Accounts Receivable (net)	61,356	50,592	10,764
Merchandise Inventory	165,300	160,404	4,896
Prepaid Insurance	2,604	1,824	780
Equipment	185,880	185,880	0
Less Accumulated Depreciation	(142,080)	(106,560)	(35,520)
Total Assets	$318,228	$338,232	$(20,004)
Liabilities			
Accounts Payable	$ 24,672	$ 38,340	$(13,668)
Salaries Payable	4,188	3,288	900
Total Liabilities	$ 28,860	$ 41,628	$(12,768)
Owner's Equity			
W. A. Salinas, Capital	289,368	296,604	(7,236)
Total Liabilities and Owner's Equity	$318,228	$338,232	$(20,004)

Required

Prepare a statement of cash flows for the year 2011, using the indirect method of presenting cash flows from operating activities.

Check Figure
Net Cash Flows from Operating Activities, $47,076

PROBLEM 22-4A The financial statements for Wilkerson Corporation follow.

Additional information contained in the records revealed that equipment, having a cost of $37,600 and accumulated depreciation of $28,480, was sold for $14,400 cash. Also, 3,760 shares of common stock having a par value of $10 per share were sold for $43,200 cash.

 5,6

Wilkerson Corporation
Income Statement
For Year Ended December 31, 2011

Revenue from Sales:		
Sales	$709,512	
Less Sales Returns and Allowances	8,624	
Net Sales		$700,888
Cost of Goods Sold:		
Merchandise Inventory, January 1, 2011	$282,096	
Delivered Cost of Purchases	504,608	
Cost of Goods Available for Sale	$786,704	
Less Merchandise Inventory, December 31, 2011	304,072	
Cost of Goods Sold		482,632
Gross Profit		$218,256
Operating Expenses:		
Salary Expense	$ 81,992	
Rent Expense	14,400	
Advertising Expense	5,120	
Depreciation Expense, Equipment	17,728	
Insurance Expense	2,168	
Miscellaneous Expense	736	
Total Operating Expenses		122,144
Income from Operations		$ 96,112
Other Income:		
Interest Income	$ 376	
Gain on Disposal of Property and Equipment	5,280	
Total Other Income	$ 5,656	
Other Expenses:		
Interest Expense	256	5,400
Income Before Income Taxes		$101,512
Income Tax Expense		30,936
Net Income		$ 70,576

Wilkerson Corporation
Statement of Retained Earnings
For Year Ended December 31, 2011

Retained Earnings, January 1, 2011		$ 82,792
Net Income	$70,576	
Less: Cash Dividends Declared	42,400	
Increase in Retained Earnings		28,176
Retained Earnings, December 31, 2011		$110,968

Wilkerson Corporation
Comparative Balance Sheet
December 31, 2011 and December 31, 2010

	2011	2010	Increase or (Decrease)
Assets			
Cash	$ 19,840	$ 5,392	$ 14,448
Notes Receivable	0	2,296	(2,296)
Accounts Receivable (net)	109,936	50,888	59,048
Merchandise Inventory	304,072	282,096	21,976
Prepaid Advertising	992	768	224
Prepaid Insurance	344	168	176
Equipment	176,296	213,896	(37,600)
Less Accumulated Depreciation	(62,024)	(72,776)	10,752
Total Assets	$549,456	$482,728	$ 66,728
Liabilities			
Notes Payable	$ 2,080	$ 7,360	$ (5,280)
Accounts Payable	65,584	63,456	2,128
Salaries Payable	1,760	2,320	(560)
Income Tax Payable	3,864	4,208	(344)
Dividends Payable	3,160	3,576	(416)
Interest Payable	32	208	(176)
Total Liabilities	$ 76,480	$ 81,128	$ (4,648)
Stockholders' Equity			
Common Stock	$343,608	$306,008	$ 37,600
Paid-in Capital in Excess of Par Value	18,400	12,800	5,600
Retained Earnings	110,968	82,792	28,176
Total Stockholders' Equity	$472,976	$401,600	$ 71,376
Total Liabilities and Stockholders' Equity	$549,456	$482,728	$ 66,728

Check Figure

Net Cash Flows from Investing Activities, $16,696

Required

Prepare a statement of cash flows for the year 2011, using the indirect method of presenting cash flows from operating activities.

Problem Set B

For additional help, see the demonstration problem at the beginning of each chapter in your Working Papers.

5,6 **LO**   **PROBLEM 22-1B** The financial statements of Compton and Company follow.

Compton and Company
Income Statement
For Year Ended December 31, 2011

Revenue:		
Income from Services		$82,707
Expenses:		
Wages Expense	$38,233	
Rent Expense	780	
Advertising Expense	546	
Utilities Expense	993	
Depreciation Expense, Equipment	10,673	
Supplies Expense	611	
Insurance Expense	312	
Miscellaneous Expense	419	
Total Expenses		52,567
Net Income		$30,140

Compton and Company
Statement of Owner's Equity
For Year Ended December 31, 2011

K. A. Compton, Capital, January 1, 2011		$84,523
Investments during the Year	$ 0	
Net Income	30,140	
Subtotal	$30,140	
Less Withdrawals	46,800	
Decrease in Capital		(16,660)
K. A. Compton, Capital, December 31, 2011		$67,863

Compton and Company
Comparative Balance Sheet
December 31, 2011 and December 31, 2010

	2011	2010	Increase or (Decrease)
Assets			
Cash	$ 8,835	$ 14,972	$ (6,137)
Prepaid Insurance	827	677	150
Equipment	90,220	90,220	0
Less Accumulated Depreciation	(32,019)	(21,346)	(10,673)
Total Assets	$ 67,863	$ 84,523	$(16,660)
Owner's Equity			
K. A. Compton, Capital	$ 67,863	$ 84,523	$(16,660)
Total Liabilities and Owner's Equity	$ 67,863	$ 84,523	$(16,660)

Required

Prepare a statement of cash flows for the year 2011, using the indirect method of presenting cash flows from operating activities.

Check Figure
Net Cash Flows used by
Financing Activities, $(46,800)

PROBLEM 22-2B Trim Cuts Barbershop uses the cash basis. The financial statements for Trim Cuts Barbershop follow.

LO 5,6

Trim Cuts Barbershop
Income Statement
For Year Ended December 31, 2011

Revenue:		
Income from Services		$111,274
Expenses:		
Salary Expense	$62,150	
Rent Expense	11,400	
Supplies Expense	2,081	
Insurance Expense	437	
Utilities Expense	1,596	
Depreciation Expense, Equipment	1,824	
Depreciation Expense, Furniture	789	
Interest Expense	352	
Miscellaneous Expense	105	
Total Expenses		80,734
Net Income		$ 30,540

Trim Cuts Barbershop
Statement of Owner's Equity
For Year Ended December 31, 2011

C. L. Herron, Capital, January 1, 2011		$20,064
Investments during the Year	$ 0	
Net Income	30,540	
Subtotal	$30,540	
Less Withdrawals	35,340	
Decrease in Capital		(4,800)
C. L. Herron, Capital, December 31, 2011		$15,264

Trim Cuts Barbershop
Comparative Balance Sheet
December 31, 2011 and December 31, 2010

	2011	2010	Increase or (Decrease)
Assets			
Cash	$ 9,195	$13,082	$(3,887)
Prepaid Insurance	1,425	1,055	370
Equipment	9,120	9,120	0
Less Accumulated Depreciation	(5,471)	(3,647)	(1,824)
Furniture	5,548	5,548	0
Less Accumulated Depreciation	(2,368)	(1,579)	(789)
Total Assets	$17,449	$23,579	$(6,130)
Liabilities			
Notes Payable	$ 2,185	$ 3,515	$(1,330)
Owner's Equity			
C. L. Herron, Capital	15,264	20,064	(4,800)
Total Liabilities and Owner's Equity	$17,449	$23,579	$(6,130)

Check Figure

Net Cash Flows from Operating Activities, $32,783

Required

Prepare a statement of cash flows for the year 2011, using the indirect method of presenting cash flows from operating activities.

PROBLEM 22-3B The financial statements for Nobleman Fine Clothes follow.

 LO 5,6

Nobleman Fine Clothes
Income Statement
For Year Ended December 31, 2011

Revenue from Sales:		
Net Sales		$769,140
Cost of Goods Sold:		
Merchandise Inventory, January 1, 2011	$146,313	
Delivered Cost of Purchases	552,708	
Cost of Goods Available for Sale	$699,021	
Less Merchandise Inventory, December 31, 2011	110,385	
Cost of Goods Sold		588,636
Gross Profit		$180,504
Operating Expenses:		
Salary Expense	$124,155	
Rent Expense	24,300	
Depreciation Expense, Equipment	28,026	
Supplies Expense	2,889	
Insurance Expense	1,350	
Miscellaneous Expense	648	
Total Operating Expenses		181,368
Net Loss		$ (864)

Nobleman Fine Clothes
Statement of Owner's Equity
For Year Ended December 31, 2011

B. T. Nobleman, Capital, January 1, 2011		$262,926
Investments during the Year	$ 0	
Subtotal	$ 0	
Less: Net Loss	864	
Withdrawals	13,500	
Decrease in Capital		(14,364)
B. T. Nobleman, Capital, December 31, 2011		$248,562

Nobleman Fine Clothes
Comparative Balance Sheet
December 31, 2011 and December 31, 2010

	2011	2010	Increase or (Decrease)
Assets			
Cash	$ 39,393	$ 28,404	$ 10,989
Accounts Receivable (net)	56,556	43,011	13,545
Merchandise Inventory	110,385	146,313	(35,928)
Prepaid Insurance	2,799	1,341	1,458
Equipment	164,034	164,034	0
Less Accumulated Depreciation	(84,078)	(56,052)	(28,026)
Total Assets	$289,089	$327,051	$(37,962)
Liabilities			
Accounts Payable	$ 37,872	$ 61,101	$(23,229)
Salaries Payable	2,655	3,024	(369)
Total Liabilities	$ 40,527	$ 64,125	$(23,598)
Owner's Equity			
B. T. Nobleman, Capital	248,562	262,926	(14,364)
Total Liabilities and Owner's Equity	$289,089	$327,051	$(37,962)

Check Figure
Net Cash Flows from Operating
Activities, $24,489

Required

Prepare a statement of cash flows for the year 2011, using the indirect method of presenting cash flows from operating activities.

5,6 **LO**

PROBLEM 22-4B Kline Corporation's financial statements follow.

Additional information contained in the records revealed that equipment, having a cost of $52,500 and accumulated depreciation of $44,700, was sold for $14,342 cash. Also, 5,250 shares of common stock having a par value of $10 per share were sold for $63,000.

Kline Corporation
Income Statement
For Year Ended December 31, 2011

Revenue from Sales:		
Sales	$1,043,973	
Less Sales Returns and Allowances	12,726	
Net Sales		$1,031,247
Cost of Goods Sold:		
Merchandise Inventory, January 1, 2011	$ 416,535	
Delivered Cost of Purchases	738,255	
Cost of Goods Available for Sale	$1,154,790	
Less Merchandise Inventory, December 31, 2011	442,523	
Cost of Goods Sold		712,267
Gross Profit		$ 318,980
Operating Expenses:		
Wages Expense	$ 132,720	
Rent Expense	21,000	
Depreciation Expense, Equipment	25,800	
Supplies Expense	3,098	
Insurance Expense	1,260	
Total Operating Expenses		183,878
Income from Operations		$ 135,102
Other Income:		
Gain on Disposal of Property and		
Equipment	$ 6,542	
Other Expenses:		
Interest Expense	830	5,712
Income Before Income Taxes		$ 140,814
Income Tax Expense		47,367
Net Income		$ 93,447

Kline Corporation
Statement of Retained Earnings
For Year Ended December 31, 2011

Retained Earnings, January 1, 2011		$122,105
Net Income	$93,447	
Less Cash Dividends Declared and Paid	63,000	
Increase in Retained Earnings		30,447
Retained Earnings, December 31, 2011		$152,552

Kline Corporation
Comparative Balance Sheet
December 31, 2011 and December 31, 2010

	2011	2010	Increase or (Decrease)
Assets			
Cash	$ 40,265	$ 11,498	$ 28,767
Accounts Receivable (net)	104,622	77,396	27,226
Merchandise Inventory	442,523	416,535	25,988
Prepaid Rent	6,300	6,300	0
Prepaid Insurance	1,386	1,355	31
Equipment	263,529	316,029	(52,500)
Less Accumulated Depreciation	(93,135)	(112,035)	18,900
Total Assets	$765,490	$ 717,078	$ 48,412
Liabilities			
Notes Payable	$ 10,920	$ 25,410	$(14,490)
Accounts Payable	33,306	62,622	(29,316)
Wages Payable	1,092	2,090	(998)
Income Tax Payable	11,844	10,983	861
Dividends Payable	12,600	12,600	0
Interest Payable	126	1,218	(1,092)
Total Liabilities	$ 69,888	$ 114,923	$(45,035)
Stockholders' Equity			
Common Stock	$532,550	$ 480,050	$ 52,500
Paid-in Capital in Excess of Par Value	10,500	0	10,500
Retained Earnings	152,552	122,105	30,447
Total Stockholders' Equity	$695,602	$ 602,155	$ 93,447
Total Liabilities and Stockholders' Equity	$765,490	$ 717,078	$ 48,412

Required
Prepare a statement of cash flows for the year 2011, using the indirect method of presenting cash flows from operating activities.

Check Figure
Net Cash Flows from Investing Activities, $14,342

ACTIVITIES

INTERNET LINKS TO ACCOUNTING

Now that you have a better understanding of the statement of cash flows and how it is prepared using the indirect method, let's take a look at the 2008 financial information for Skechers USA, Inc. Go to Skechers' corporate information page at www.skx.com. Scroll to the bottom of the page and, under the Investor Relations heading, click SEC Filings. In the SEC Filing Keyword Search box, type 10-K and then press the Search button. In the list of forms, select the 10-K that was filed on 03/02/09. Click on Entire Document, the first link that appears in the list. The statement of cash flows is on page 44 of the 10-K report.

1. Does Skechers use the direct or indirect method for its statement of cash flows? How can you tell?

2. What were Skechers' net income (net earnings) amounts reported for 2008 and 2007?

3. What were Skechers' net cash flows from operating activities, investing activities, and financing activities for 2008 and 2007? What are the main reasons for any significant differences in those three categories between the two years?

4. Did Skechers' statement of cash flows disclose any noncash investing and financing activities? If so, what was disclosed?

CONSIDER AND COMMUNICATE

Your manager feels strongly that all he needs from the accountant are the income statement, statement of owner's equity, and balance sheet. He does not want to pay the additional fees for preparation of a statement of cash flows. Explain to your manager why this additional statement is important.

CRITICAL THINKING

Following is a partially completed statement of cash flows for Culwell Company. Selected line descriptions and amounts have been left out because the accounting intern was not sure what to do. Fill in the missing items.

Culwell Company
Statement of Cash Flows
For Year Ended June 30, 2011

Cash Flows from (used by) ___a___ Activities:		
___b___		c
Add (Deduct) Items to Convert Net Income		
from Accrual Basis to Cash Basis:		
Depreciation Expense, Building	$ 23,200	
Depreciation Expense, Equipment	d	
___e___ in Accounts Receivable (net)	(18,043)	
Increase in Merchandise Inventory	(5,200)	
___f___ in Prepaid Insurance	350	
Decrease in Accounts Payable	(14,340)	
___g___ in Salaries Payable	432	
___h___ in Income Tax Payable	(432)	
Increase in Interest Payable	250	(6,483)
Net Cash Flows from ___i___ Activities		$443,517
Cash Flows from (used by) ___j___ Activities:		
___k___ from Notes Receivable	$ 97,820	
Net Cash Flows from ___l___ Activities		m
Cash Flows from (used by) ___n___ Activities:		
___o___ of Note	$ (6,400)	
Issuance of Common Stock	p	
Payment of Dividends	(13,594)	
Net Cash Flows used by Financing Activities		(15,174)
Net Increase (Decrease) in Cash		q
Cash, ___r___		47,840
Cash, ___s___		t

Statement of Cash Flows—Direct Method

LEARNING OBJECTIVES

After you have completed this chapter, you will be able to do the following:

 1   *Prepare the operating activities section of the statement of cash flows using the direct method.*

The purpose of the statement of cash flows is to convert an income statement for a business from an accrual basis to a cash basis. Two methods are available. Under the indirect method, which was presented in Chapter 22, net income is adjusted from an accrual basis to a cash basis. The indirect method lists only the adjustments necessary to convert net income to cash flows from operations as determined by changes in balance sheet accounts (assets, liabilities, and capital). The direct method, on the other hand, adjusts *each item* in a firm's income statement from the accrual basis to the cash basis.

Both methods are presently in use. **Remember that under both methods, the amount of increase or decrease in cash over the period should be the same.**

GUIDELINES FOR CONVERSION

Each method uses the same three classifications: operating activities, investing activities, and financing activities. Remember that only the Operating Activities section is different when presenting the indirect or direct method. Therefore, in this section, we will only explain the Operating Activities section using the direct method.

Illustration

We will return to an example that was presented in Chapter 22 (Illustration 1, Jenny's Paintings). First, we present the financial statements for Jenny's Paintings.

Jenny's Paintings
Income Statement
For Year Ended December 31, 2011

Net Sales		$800,000
Cost of Goods Sold:		
Merchandise Inventory, January 1, 2011	$126,000	
Delivered Cost of Purchases	514,000	
Cost of Goods Available for Sale	$640,000	
Less Merchandise Inventory, December 31, 2011	130,000	
Cost of Goods Sold		510,000
Gross Profit		$290,000
Operating Expenses:		
Salary Expense	$100,000	
Rent Expense	20,000	
Depreciation Expense, Equipment	22,000	
Supplies Expense	1,600	
Insurance Expense	400	
Total Operating Expenses		144,000
Net Income		$146,000

Jenny's Paintings
Statement of Owner's Equity
For Year Ended December 31, 2011

J. K. Kim, Capital, January 1, 2011		$233,200
Investments during the Year	$ 0	
Net Income	146,000	
Subtotal	$146,000	
Less Withdrawals	150,000	
Decrease in Capital		(4,000)
J. K. Kim, Capital, December 31, 2011		$229,200

Jenny's Paintings
Comparative Balance Sheet
December 31, 2011 and December 31, 2010

	2011	2010	Increase or (Decrease)
Assets			
Cash	$ 31,400	$ 35,000	$ (3,600)
Accounts Receivable (net)	45,600	33,000	12,600
Merchandise Inventory	130,000	126,000	4,000
Prepaid Insurance	2,300	1,400	900
Equipment	136,600	136,600	0
Less Accumulated Depreciation	(62,000)	(40,000)	(22,000)
Total Assets	$283,900	$292,000	$ (8,100)
Liabilities			
Accounts Payable	$ 51,500	$ 56,000	$ (4,500)
Salaries Payable	3,200	2,800	400
Total Liabilities	$ 54,700	$ 58,800	$ (4,100)
Owner's Equity			
J. K. Kim, Capital	229,200	233,200	(4,000)
Total Liabilities and Owner's Equity	$283,900	$292,000	$ (8,100)

Cash Flows from Operating Activities

In determining cash flows from operating activities using the direct method, we will review each item on the income statement individually. Let's start with Net Sales.

Convert Net Sales to Cash Receipts from Customers. Net Sales is in the form of cash and customer charge accounts. During 2011, Accounts Receivable, net increased from $33,000 to $45,600. Evidently, $12,600 more was recorded in the customer charge accounts than was collected in cash. The amount of cash received from customers is calculated like this:

	Net Sales	$800,000
+	Beginning Accounts Receivable	33,000
=	Total	$833,000
−	Ending Accounts Receivable	45,600
=	Cash Receipts from Customers	$787,400

Jenny's Paintings
Statement of Cash Flows
For Year Ended December 31, 2011

Cash Flows from (used by) Operating Activities:

Cash Receipts from Customers	$787,400

Convert Delivered Cost of Purchases to Cash Payments for Merchandise Purchases. During 2011, Accounts Payable decreased from $56,000 to $51,500. Evidently, $4,500 more was paid in cash than was recorded as amounts owed to creditors. Starting with the $514,000 listed as Delivered Cost of Purchases on the income statement, we'll say that we paid the beginning Accounts Payable ($56,000) and did not pay the ending Accounts Payable ($51,500). The amount of cash paid to creditors is calculated in the following manner:

	Delivered Cost of Purchases	$514,000
+	Beginning Accounts Payable	56,000
=	Total	$570,000
−	Ending Accounts Payable	51,500
=	Cash Payments for Merchandise Purchases	$518,500

Here's another way to analyze the situation. Assume the company pays its beginning balance of Accounts Payable first. Next, of the $514,000 listed on the income statement as Delivered Cost of Purchases, all but $51,500 (the ending balance of Accounts Payable) was paid out. The calculation looks like this:

	Beginning Accounts Payable	$ 56,000	or		Beginning Accounts Payable	$ 56,000
+	Delivered Cost of Purchases	514,000		+	Delivered Cost of Purchases Paid in Cash ($514,000 − $51,500)	462,500
=	Total	$570,000		=	Cash Payments for Merchandise Purchases	$518,500
−	Ending Accounts Payable	51,500				
=	Cash Payments for Merchandise Purchases	$518,500				

Jenny's Paintings
Statement of Cash Flows
For Year Ended December 31, 2011

Cash Flows from (used by) Operating Activities:		
Cash Receipts from Customers		$787,400
Cash Payments for:		
Merchandise Purchases	$(518,500)	

Operating Expenses

In this section of the statement of cash flows, each expense is listed in the same order as it appears on the income statement.

Convert Salary Expense to Cash Payments to Employees. On the income statement, Salary Expense is $100,000. On the comparative balance sheet, Salaries Payable increased from $2,800 to $3,200. Evidently, $400 less than the $100,000 listed on the income statement was paid out in cash to employees. The calculation looks like this:

	Salary Expense	$100,000
+	Beginning Salaries Payable	2,800
=	Total	$102,800
−	Ending Salaries Payable	3,200
=	Cash Payments to Employees	$ 99,600

Convert Rent Expense to Cash Payments for Rent. Since there is no amount listed on the balance sheet as Prepaid Rent or Rent Payable, we can conclude that the $20,000 listed on the income statement was indeed paid in cash.

Convert Depreciation Expense, Equipment to Cash Payments for Depreciation. Because the amount listed as Depreciation Expense, Equipment is not paid to anyone, no cash is involved. Depreciation expense is a noncash expense—ignore it.

Convert Supplies Expense to Cash Payments for Supplies. Since there is no amount included in Accounts Payable for supplies, we can conclude that the $1,600 listed as Supplies Expense on the income statement was indeed paid in cash.

Convert Insurance Expense to Cash Payments for Insurance. During 2011, Prepaid Insurance increased from $1,400 to $2,300. Evidently, Jenny's Paintings bought more insurance than was used up (expired) during the year. So $900 more in cash than the $400 listed as Insurance Expense on the income statement was paid out. The calculation looks like this:

	Insurance Expense	$ 400
+	Ending Prepaid Insurance	2,300
=	Total	$2,700
−	Beginning Prepaid Insurance	1,400
=	Cash Payments for Insurance	$1,300

Jenny's Paintings
Statement of Cash Flows
For Year Ended December 31, 2011

Cash Flows from (used by) Operating Activities:			
Cash Receipts from Customers			$ 787,400
Cash Payments for:			
Merchandise Purchases		$(518,500)	
Operating Expenses:			
Employees	$(99,600)		
Rent	(20,000)		
Supplies	(1,600)		
Insurance	(1,300)		
Total Operating Expenses		(122,500)	
Total Cash Payments			(641,000)
Net Cash Flows from Operating Activities			$ 146,400
Cash Flows from (used by) Financing Activities:			
Payment of Personal Withdrawals		$(150,000)	
Net Cash Flows used by Financing Activities			(150,000)
Net Increase (Decrease) in Cash			$ (3,600)
Cash, January 1, 2011			35,000
Cash, December 31, 2011			$ 31,400

Although we do not discuss it here, notice that the cash flows used by financing activities are reported exactly the same as under the indirect method. The Investing Activities section would also be reported exactly the same, if presented. The only change to the statement of cash flows when using the direct method is in the cash flows from Operating Activities section.

Problems

PROBLEM 22A-1 The financial statements for Cochran Company follow.

LO 1

Cochran Company
Income Statement
For Year Ended December 31, 2011

Revenue:		
Net Sales		$740,000
Cost of Goods Sold:		
Merchandise Inventory, January 1, 2011	$103,000	
Delivered Cost of Purchases	390,790	
Cost of Goods Available for Sale	$493,790	
Less Merchandise Inventory, December 31, 2011	137,000	
Cost of Goods Sold		356,790
Gross Profit		$383,210
Operating Expenses:		
Salary Expense	$104,000	
Rent Expense	18,000	
Advertising Expense	12,000	
Supplies Expense	845	
Depreciation Expense, Equipment	12,000	
Utilities Expense	1,790	
Insurance Expense	2,400	
Miscellaneous Expense	360	
Total Operating Expenses		151,395
Net Income		$231,815

Cochran Company
Statement of Owner's Equity
For Year Ended December 31, 2011

S. C. Cochran, Capital, January 1, 2011		$220,300
Investments during the Year	$ 0	
Net Income	231,815	
Subtotal	$231,815	
Less Withdrawals	54,000	
Increase in Capital		177,815
S. C. Cochran, Capital, December 31, 2011		$398,115

Cochran Company
Comparative Balance Sheet
December 31, 2011 and December 31, 2010

	2011	2010	Increase or (Decrease)
Assets			
Cash	$181,675	$ 42,500	$139,175
Accounts Receivable (net)	41,000	32,000	9,000
Merchandise Inventory	137,000	103,000	34,000
Prepaid Insurance	3,540	2,560	980
Equipment:	128,000	128,000	0
Less Accumulated Depreciation	(34,000)	(22,000)	(12,000)
Total Assets	$457,215	$286,060	$171,155
Liabilities			
Accounts Payable	$ 56,000	$ 62,860	$ (6,860)
Salaries Payable	3,100	2,900	200
Total Liabilities	$ 59,100	$ 65,760	$ (6,660)
Owner's Equity			
S. C. Cochran, Capital	398,115	220,300	177,815
Total Liabilities and Owner's Equity	$457,215	$286,060	$171,155

Check Figure
Net Cash Flows from Operating
Activities, $193,175

Required

Using the statements of Cochran Company, construct a statement of cash flows, using the direct method, for the year ended December 31, 2011.

1 **LO**

PROBLEM 22A-2 The financial statements for Toobin Company follow.

Toobin Company
Income Statement
For Year Ended December 31, 2011

Revenue from Sales:		
Net Sales		$630,000
Cost of Goods Sold:		
Merchandise Inventory, January 1, 2011	$110,000	
Delivered Cost of Purchases	360,000	
Cost of Goods Available for Sale	$470,000	
Less Merchandise Inventory, December 31, 2011	135,000	
Cost of Goods Sold		335,000
Gross Profit		$295,000
Operating Expenses:		
Salary Expense	$110,000	
Rent Expense	20,000	
Advertising Expense	14,000	
Supplies Expense	790	
Depreciation Expense, Equipment	12,000	
Utilities Expense	1,870	
Insurance Expense	2,600	
Miscellaneous Expense	510	
Total Operating Expenses		161,770
Net Income		$133,230

Toobin Company
Statement of Owner's Equity
For Year Ended December 31, 2011

J. Toobin, Capital, January 1, 2011		$218,000
Investments during the Year	$ 0	
Net Income	133,230	
Subtotal	$133,230	
Less Withdrawals	20,000	
Increase in Capital		113,230
J. Toobin, Capital, December 31, 2011		$331,230

Toobin Company
Comparative Balance Sheet
December 31, 2011 and December 31, 2010

	2011	2010	Increase or (Decrease)
Assets			
Cash	$129,450	$ 44,340	$ 85,110
Accounts Receivable (net)	35,000	20,000	15,000
Merchandise Inventory	135,000	110,000	25,000
Prepaid Insurance	2,540	2,560	(20)
Equipment	132,000	132,000	0
Less Accumulated Depreciation	(45,000)	(33,000)	(12,000)
Total Assets	$388,990	$275,900	$113,090
Liabilities			
Accounts Payable	$ 54,660	$ 55,000	$ (340)
Salaries Payable	3,100	2,900	200
Total Liabilities	$ 57,760	$ 57,900	$ (140)
Owner's Equity			
J. Toobin, Capital	331,230	218,000	113,230
Total Liabilities and Owner's Equity	$388,990	$275,900	$113,090

Check Figure
Net Cash Flows from Operating
Activities, $105,110

Required

Using the statements of Toobin Company, construct a statement of cash flows, using the direct method, for the year ended December 31, 2011.

Comparative Financial Statements

WHY IT MATTERS

VBT, Bristol, Vermont

Vermont Bicycle Touring, now known as VBT, was founded in 1971 when a college professor with a passion for bicycling took a group of six people on a weekend ride through Woodstock, Vermont.

Today, VBT offers 28 unique bicycling vacations throughout Europe, North America, Asia, and South America. VBT provides "custom VBT bicycles, breathtaking bike routes, expert Trip leaders, outstanding hotels, fun discovery excursions, and full van support."

VBT was ranked one of the "Best Bicycling Outfitters on Earth" in the 2009 survey of the world's top adventure travel outfitters by *National Geographic Adventure* magazine. VBT also ranks well in terms of service and customer satisfaction. But how does VBT know how it compares financially to other outfitting companies? Or how well the company did this year as compared to last year?

In this chapter, you will learn the tools that businesses, investors, and owners use to interpret a company's financial condition and results of operations.

LEARNING OBJECTIVES

After you have completed this chapter, you will be able to do the following:

1 Prepare a comparative income statement and balance sheet involving horizontal analysis.

2 Prepare a comparative income statement and balance sheet involving vertical analysis.

3 Express income statement data in trend percentages.

4 Compute (a) working capital, (b) current ratio, (c) quick ratio,

(d) accounts receivable turnover, (e) merchandise inventory turnover, (f) ratio of stockholders' equity to liabilities, and (g) ratio of property and equipment to long-term liabilities.

5 Calculate (a) equity per share, (b) rate of return on common stockholders' equity, (c) earnings per share of common stock, and (d) price-earnings ratio.

ACCOUNTING LANGUAGE

Accounts receivable turnover (p. 930)

Base year (p. 917)

Common-size statement (p. 926)

Current ratio (p. 928)

Earnings per share (p. 934)

Horizontal analysis (p. 917)

Liquidate (p. 933)

Merchandise inventory turnover (p. 930)

Price-earnings ratio (p. 934)

Profitability (p. 916)

Quick assets (p. 928)

Quick ratio (p. 928)

Solvency (p. 916)

Trend percentages (p. 925)

Vertical analysis (p. 921)

Working capital (p. 928)

Accounting is the process of analyzing, classifying, recording, summarizing, and *interpreting* business transactions. We are now ready to interpret the information. How do you draw conclusions from financial data that have been summarized in financial statements?

The financial condition of a company and the results of operations of business enterprises are of interest not only to owners, employers, and managers, but also to creditors and to prospective owners and creditors. Everybody is interested in two aspects of an enterprise:

1. Its **solvency**, or its ability to pay its debts

2. Its **profitability**, or its ability to earn a reasonable profit on the owners' investment

This chapter explains the techniques used to determine solvency and profitability.

TYPES OF COMPARISON

To interpret a set of facts, you have to have similar data with which to compare it. In other words, a given set of facts by itself is not significant. If you are told that a certain corporation earned a net income of $156,000 during the past year, this figure by itself is not meaningful. Does this net income indicate a successful year or a poor year? Does it compare favorably or unfavorably with other years? Does it represent a reasonable return on sales and investment? How does it compare with the net income of other firms in the same industry?

A company's financial statements are meaningful only if you analyze them on a comparative basis. There are three useful bases for making such a comparison:

1. Statements of the same company for the current year and one or more prior years
2. Financial data for other companies in the same industry
3. Previously established financial standards or objectives

COMPARATIVE STATEMENTS

One technique for analyzing and interpreting financial data is the preparation of comparative statements. Two types of analysis—horizontal and vertical—are commonly used.

Horizontal Analysis

Income Statement

Horizontal analysis is the comparison of the same item in a company's financial statements for two or more periods. Let's look at the comparative income statement (Figure 1) for Dynamo Bike Shop, Inc., for 2011 and 2010.

Note that for each item on the income statement, the accountant expressed the difference—that is, the increase or decrease in 2011 over 2010—first in dollars and then in percentages. Look at the increase in Sales for example. Subtract Sales in 2010 from Sales in 2011.

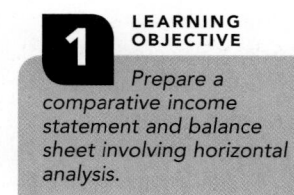
LEARNING OBJECTIVE

1

Prepare a comparative income statement and balance sheet involving horizontal analysis.

$982,100	Sales for 2011
−861,700	Sales for 2010
$120,400	Increase of 2011 over 2010

To calculate the *percentage* increase in Sales in 2011 over 2010, divide the dollar increase by the amount of Sales during the base year. (*Note:* The expression **base year** means the year you are using as a basis for comparison, which is the earlier year.) Then round the answer to three decimal places and multiply by 100 to change the decimal to a percentage.

$$\frac{\$120,400}{\$861,700} = 0.140 \text{ (rounded)} \times 100 = \underline{\underline{14.0\%}}$$

Now look at the change in Sales Returns and Allowances:

$12,500	Sales Returns and Allowances for 2011
−13,100	Sales Returns and Allowances for 2010
$ (600)	Decrease of 2011 over 2010

The percentage rate of decrease is

$$\frac{\$(600)}{\$13,100} = (0.046) \text{ (rounded)} \times 100 = \underline{\underline{(4.6)\%}}$$

Accountants and investors appraising an income statement often use the percentage change in net sales as a basis for comparison. In other words, they compare all other percentage changes with the percentage change in net sales to determine reasonably whether the other percentage changes are out of line. If net sales

> The percentage of increase or (decrease) is calculated by dividing the dollar amount of increase or (decrease) by the base year amount, rounding the answer to three decimal places, and multiplying by 100.

Remember

FIGURE 1 Comparative income statement for Dynamo Bike Shop, Inc. (horizontal analysis)

Dynamo Bike Shop, Inc.
Comparative Income Statement
For Years Ended December 31, 2011 and December 31, 2010

	2011	2010	Increase or (Decrease) Amount	Percent
Revenue from Sales:				
Sales	$ 982,100	$861,700	$120,400	14.0%
Less Sales Returns and Allowances	12,500	13,100	(600)	(4.6)%
Net Sales	$ 969,600	$848,600	$121,000	14.3%
Cost of Goods Sold:				
Merchandise Inventory, January 1	$ 206,500	$138,700	$ 67,800	48.9%
Delivered Cost of Purchases	804,800	636,600	168,200	26.4%
Cost of Goods Available for Sale	$1,011,300	$775,300	$236,000	30.4%
Less Merchandise Inventory, December 31	348,400	206,500	141,900	68.7%
Cost of Goods Sold	$ 662,900	$568,800	$ 94,100	16.5%
Gross Profit	$ 306,700	$279,800	$ 26,900	9.6%
Operating Expenses:				
Selling Expenses:				
Sales Salary Expense	$ 114,650	$102,400	$ 12,250	12.0%
Delivery Expense	12,950	13,700	(750)	(5.5)%
Advertising Expense	7,900	6,900	1,000	14.5%
Depreciation Expense, Equipment	6,800	6,600	200	3.0%
Store Supplies Expense	450	600	(150)	(25.0)%
Total Selling Expenses	$ 142,750	$130,200	$ 12,550	9.6%
General Expenses:				
Office Salary Expense	$ 33,440	$ 27,680	$ 5,760	20.8%
Depreciation Expense, Building	14,200	14,200	0	0.0%
Bad Debts Expense	6,200	5,400	800	14.8%
Property Taxes Expense	6,100	5,200	900	17.3%
Insurance Expense	1,100	1,000	100	10.0%
Miscellaneous General Expense	680	720	(40)	(5.6)%
Total General Expenses	$ 61,720	$ 54,200	$ 7,520	13.9%
Total Operating Expenses	$ 204,470	$184,400	$ 20,070	10.9%
Income from Operations	$ 102,230	$ 95,400	$ 6,830	7.2%
Other Expenses:				
Interest Expense	7,920	7,860	60	0.8%
Income Before Income Taxes	$ 94,310	$ 87,540	$ 6,770	7.7%
Income Tax Expense	18,420	18,010	410	2.3%
Net Income	$ 75,890	$ 69,530	$ 6,360	9.1%

increased approximately 14 percent from 2010 to 2011, other percentage changes should also amount to approximately 14 percent. If they vary considerably from 14 percent, they may be out of line, and you should investigate to find the reasons for the difference. Let's look at the main items on the income statement.

Item	Percentage Change
Net Sales	14.3%
Cost of Goods Sold	16.5
Gross Profit	9.6
Total Operating Expenses	10.9
Net Income	9.1

Horizontal analysis of an income statement lets management see the percentage of increase and decrease for each component of the income statement.

You can see that the percentage changes in Gross Profit, Total Operating Expenses, and Net Income are considerably less than the percentage change in Net Sales. Since Gross Profit is determined by subtracting Cost of Goods Sold from Net Sales, you should investigate the entire Cost of Goods Sold section of the income statement. The percentage changes in items in the Cost of Goods Sold section are:

Item	Percentage Change
Merchandise Inventory, January 1	48.9%
Delivered Cost of Purchases	26.4
Merchandise Inventory, December 31	68.7

The merchandise inventory of January 1 was a carryover from the previous year, but why the large increase in Delivered Cost of Purchases? And look at the large increase in Merchandise Inventory at the end of the year. Buying all those goods required a large cash investment, which either increased debt and related interest expense or decreased investments and related interest income. In addition, carrying the larger inventory increased handling and storage expense plus the risk of an inventory write-off due to obsolescence. Also, with such a large increase in Merchandise Inventory, we would expect a larger increase in sales. Is the increase in sales large enough?

Incidentally, a percentage change can be calculated only when a positive amount is reported in the base year. For example, let's say a company had a net loss of $3,500 in Year 1 (base year) and a net income of $2,000 in Year 2. Because the $3,500 is not a positive amount, it is not possible to state the amount of the change as a percentage.

Balance Sheet

Now look at the balance sheet in Figure 2, which shows the comparison between 2011 and 2010. Again you see why changes are expressed in both dollars and percentages. Items showing either a large dollar change or a large percentage change really stand out.

FIGURE 2   Comparative balance sheet for Dynamo Bike Shop, Inc. (horizontal analysis)

Dynamo Bike Shop, Inc.
Comparative Balance Sheet
December 31, 2011 and December 31, 2010

			Increase or (Decrease)	
	2011	2010	Amount	Percent
Assets				
Current Assets:				
Cash	$ 21,800	$ 38,700	$ (16,900)	(43.7)%
Accounts Receivable	79,700	81,400	(1,700)	(2.1)%
Less Allowance for Doubtful Accounts	(3,300)	(2,600)	(700)	26.9%
Merchandise Inventory	348,400	206,500	141,900	68.7%
Prepaid Insurance	2,000	2,100	(100)	(4.8)%
Total Current Assets	$448,600	$326,100	$122,500	37.6%
Investments:				
Sinking Fund Cash	$ 4,100	$ 5,800	$ (1,700)	(29.3)%
Sinking Fund Investments	61,700	59,400	2,300	3.9%
Total Investments	$ 65,800	$ 65,200	$ 600	0.9%
Property and Equipment:				
Land	$ 40,000	$ 40,000	$ 0	0.0%
Building	160,000	160,000	0	0.0%
Less Accumulated Depreciation	(56,800)	(42,600)	(14,200)	33.3%
Equipment	88,600	86,000	2,600	3.0%
Less Accumulated Depreciation	(41,000)	(34,200)	(6,800)	19.9%
Total Property and Equipment	$190,800	$209,200	$ (18,400)	(8.8)%
Intangible Assets:				
Patents	$ 3,000	$ 4,000	$ (1,000)	(25.0)%
Total Assets	$708,200	$604,500	$103,700	17.2%
Liabilities				
Current Liabilities:				
Accounts Payable	$ 70,100	$ 29,000	$ 41,100	141.7%
Income Tax Payable	12,800	5,600	7,200	128.6%
Dividends Payable	12,000	4,000	8,000	200.0%
Salaries Payable	5,700	4,000	1,700	42.5%
Total Current Liabilities	$100,600	$ 42,600	$ 58,000	136.2%
Long-Term Liabilities:				
Bonds Payable, 6%, due December 31, 2018	$100,000	$100,000	$ 0	0.0%
Less Discount on Bonds Payable	(2,200)	(2,400)	200	(8.3)%
Total Long-Term Liabilities	$ 97,800	$ 97,600	$ 200	0.2%
Total Liabilities	$198,400	$140,200	$ 58,200	41.5%
Stockholders' Equity				
Paid-in Capital:				
Common Stock, $100 par (4,000 shares authorized, 3,000 shares issued)	$300,000	$300,000	$ 0	0.0%
Paid-in Capital in Excess of Par Value	86,000	86,000	0	0.0%
Total Paid-in Capital	$386,000	$386,000	$ 0	0.0%
Retained Earnings:				
Unappropriated	$103,800	$ 66,300	$ 37,500	56.6%
Appropriated for Property Expansion	20,000	12,000	8,000	66.7%
Total Retained Earnings	$123,800	$ 78,300	$ 45,500	58.1%
Total Stockholders' Equity	$509,800	$464,300	$ 45,500	9.8%
Total Liabilities and Stockholders' Equity	$708,200	$604,500	$103,700	17.2%

The following items are based on data from the comparative balance sheet:

Item	Increase or (Decrease) Amount	Increase or (Decrease) Percentage
Cash	$ (16,900)	(43.7)%
Merchandise Inventory	141,900	68.7
Accounts Payable	41,100	141.7

Recall that the comparative income statement already exposed the increase in the Merchandise Inventory account. You should also consider the effects of changes in the balances of other related accounts. The fact that Cash is down by 43.7 percent while Accounts Payable is up by 141.7 percent may indicate a pending financial crisis. To pay its bills, the firm may be forced to liquidate that large stock of goods by selling it at cost, or even less. The other current liabilities also show significant unfavorable increases. Note the 128.6 percent increase in Income Tax Payable, the 200 percent increase in Dividends Payable, and the 42.5 percent increase in Salaries Payable. One point in the company's favor, though, is the decrease in Accounts Receivable. The increase in Allowance for Doubtful Accounts, although a relatively small amount, could be considered unreasonable when expressed as a percentage (on the other hand, the increase may involve just one account).

Vertical Analysis

Income Statement

Another tool accountants can use to analyze financial statements is **vertical analysis**. Using this method, you can see in a single statement the relationship of each part to the whole. For an income statement, *the whole is net sales*. Although each percentage applies to a single item only, you can quickly see the relative importance of each item on the statement. Let's look first at the comparative income statement (Figure 3 on page 922) and then at the comparative balance sheet (Figure 4 on page 923) for Dynamo Bike Shop, Inc.—this time, arranged for vertical analysis.

When you arrange an income statement for vertical analysis, you express each item as a *percentage of net sales*. In other words, you divide each item by net sales. Following is an illustration:

2 LEARNING OBJECTIVE
Prepare a comparative income statement and balance sheet involving vertical analysis.

$$\text{Gross Profit \%} = \text{Gross Profit} \div \text{Net Sales}$$

$$\text{Gross Profit \% (2011)} = \frac{\$306,700}{\$969,600} = 0.3163 = \underline{\underline{31.6\%}}$$

$$\text{Gross Profit \% (2010)} = \frac{\$279,800}{\$848,600} = 0.3297 = \underline{\underline{33.0\%}}$$

$$\text{Income from Operations \%} = \text{Income from Operations} \div \text{Net Sales}$$

$$\text{Income from Operations \% (2011)} = \frac{\$102,230}{\$969,600} = 0.1054 = \underline{\underline{10.5\%}}$$

$$\text{Income from Operations \% (2010)} = \frac{\$95,400}{\$848,600} = 0.1124 = \underline{\underline{11.2\%}}$$

$$\text{Net Income \%} = \text{Net Income} \div \text{Net Sales}$$

$$\text{Net Income \% (2011)} = \frac{\$75,890}{\$969,600} = 0.0783 = \underline{\underline{7.8\%}}$$

$$\text{Net Income \% (2010)} = \frac{\$69,530}{\$848,600} = 0.0819 = \underline{\underline{8.2\%}}$$

FIGURE 3　Comparative income statement for Dynamo Bike Shop, Inc. (vertical analysis)

Dynamo Bike Shop, Inc.
Comparative Income Statement
For Years Ended December 31, 2011 and December 31, 2010

	2011		2010	
	Amount	Percent*	Amount	Percent*
Revenue from Sales:				
Sales	$ 9,821	101.3%	$861,700	101.5%
Less Sales Returns and Allowances	12,500	1.3	13,100	1.5
Net Sales	$ 969,600	100.0%	$848,600	100.0%
Cost of Goods Sold:				
Merchandise Inventory, January 1	$ 206,500	21.3%	$138,700	16.3%
Delivered Cost of Purchases	804,800	83.0	636,600	75.0
Cost of Goods Available for Sale	$1,011,300	104.3%	$775,300	91.4%
Less Merchandise Inventory, December 31	348,400	35.9	206,500	24.3
Cost of Goods Sold	$ 662,900	68.4%	$568,800	67.0%
Gross Profit	$ 306,700	31.6%	$279,800	33.0%
Operating Expenses:				
Selling Expenses:				
Sales Salary Expense	$ 114,650	11.8%	$102,400	12.1%
Delivery Expense	12,950	1.3	13,700	1.6
Advertising Expense	7,900	0.8	6,900	0.8
Depreciation Expense, Equipment	6,800	0.7	6,600	0.8
Store Supplies Expense	450	0.0	600	0.1
Total Selling Expenses	$ 142,750	14.7%	$130,200	15.3%
General Expenses:				
Office Salary Expense	$ 33,440	3.4%	$ 27,680	3.3%
Depreciation Expense, Building	14,200	1.5	14,200	1.7
Bad Debts Expense	6,200	0.6	5,400	0.6
Property Taxes Expense	6,100	0.6	5,200	0.6
Insurance Expense	1,100	0.1	1,000	0.1
Miscellaneous General Expense	680	0.1	720	0.1
Total General Expenses	$ 61,720	6.4%	$ 54,200	6.4%
Total Operating Expenses	$ 204,470	21.1%	$184,400	21.7%
Income from Operations	$ 102,230	10.5%	$ 95,400	11.2%
Other Expenses:				
Interest Expense	7,920	0.8	7,860	0.9
Income Before Income Taxes	$ 94,310	9.7%	$ 87,540	10.3%
Income Tax Expense	18,420	1.9	18,010	2.1
Net Income	$ 75,890	7.8%	$ 69,530	8.2%

*There may be slight differences in the tenth's place due to the rounding methods of various calculators and computers. For the same reason, percentages may not add up to exactly 100 percent.

You could also interpret the percentages as shown here:

2011

- For every $100 in net sales, gross profit was $31.60.
- For every $100 in net sales, income from operations was $10.50.
- For every $100 in net sales, net income was $7.80.

2010

- For every $100 in net sales, gross profit was $33.00.
- For every $100 in net sales, income from operations was $11.20.
- For every $100 in net sales, net income was $8.20.

| FIGURE 4 | Comparative balance sheet for Dynamo Bike Shop, Inc. (vertical analysis) |

Dynamo Bike Shop, Inc.
Comparative Balance Sheet
December 31, 2011 and December 31, 2010

	2011		2010	
	Amount	Percent*	Amount	Percent*
Assets				
Current Assets:				
Cash	$ 21,800	3.1%	$ 38,700	6.4%
Accounts Receivable	79,700	11.3	81,400	13.5
Less Allowance for Doubtful Accounts	(3,300)	(0.5)	(2,600)	(0.4)
Merchandise Inventory	348,400	49.2	206,500	34.2
Prepaid Insurance	2,000	0.3	2,100	0.3
Total Current Assets	$448,600	63.3%	$326,100	53.9%
Investments:				
Sinking Fund Cash	$ 4,100	0.6%	$ 5,800	1.0%
Sinking Fund Investments	61,700	8.7	59,400	9.8
Total Investments	$ 65,800	9.3%	$ 65,200	10.8%
Property and Equipment:				
Land	$ 40,000	5.6%	$ 40,000	6.6%
Building	160,000	22.6	160,000	26.5
Less Accumulated Depreciation	(56,800)	(8.0)	(42,600)	(7.0)
Equipment	88,600	12.5	86,000	14.2
Less Accumulated Depreciation	(41,000)	(5.8)	(34,200)	(5.7)
Total Property and Equipment	$190,800	26.9%	$209,200	34.6%
Intangible Assets:				
Patents	$ 3,000	0.4%	$ 4,000	0.7%
Total Assets	$708,200	100.0%	$604,500	100.0%
Liabilities				
Current Liabilities:				
Accounts Payable	$ 70,100	9.9%	$ 29,000	4.8%
Income Tax Payable	12,800	1.8	5,600	0.9
Dividends Payable	12,000	1.7	4,000	0.7
Salaries Payable	5,700	0.8	4,000	0.7
Total Current Liabilities	$100,600	14.2%	$ 42,600	7.0%
Long-Term Liabilities:				
Bonds Payable, 6%, due December 31, 2018	$100,000	14.1%	$100,000	16.5%
Less Discount on Bonds Payable	(2,200)	(0.3)	(2,400)	(0.4)
Total Long-Term Liabilities	$ 97,800	13.8%	$ 97,600	16.1%
Total Liabilities	$198,400	28.0%	$140,200	23.2%
Stockholders' Equity				
Paid-in Capital:				
Common Stock, $100 par (4,000 shares authorized,				
3,000 shares issued)	$300,000	42.4%	$300,000	49.6%
Paid-in Capital in Excess of Par Value	86,000	12.1	86,000	14.2
Total Paid-in Capital	$386,000	54.5%	$386,000	63.9%
Retained Earnings:				
Unappropriated	$103,800	14.7%	$ 66,300	11.0%
Appropriated for Property Expansion	20,000	2.8	12,000	2.0
Total Retained Earnings	$123,800	17.5%	$ 78,300	13.0%
Total Stockholders' Equity	$509,800	72.0%	$464,300	76.8%
Total Liabilities and Stockholders' Equity	$708,200	100.0%	$604,500	100.0%

*Percentages may not add up exactly due to rounding.

Again we see the relative importance in 2011 of Delivered Cost of Purchases (83.0 percent of Net Sales) and ending Merchandise Inventory (35.9 percent of Net Sales). In the area of Selling Expenses, the percentage of Sales Salary Expense declined slightly from that of 2010. Advertising Expense as a percentage of Net Sales remained the same. (Is that necessarily a good sign?)

Balance Sheet

When you perform a vertical analysis of a comparative balance sheet, you express the figure for each item as a *percentage of total assets*, or as a percentage of the total of liabilities and stockholders' equity, which is the same figure. (See Figure 4.) For example, suppose you want to find the percentage of total assets represented by Cash, Accounts Receivable, and Merchandise Inventory. (In referring to Accounts Receivable, we mean net Accounts Receivable [Accounts Receivable less Allowance for Doubtful Accounts].)

$$\text{Cash \%} = \text{Cash} \div \text{Total Assets}$$

$$\text{Cash \% (2011)} = \frac{\$21,800}{\$708,200} = 0.0308 = \underline{\underline{3.1\%}}$$

$$\text{Cash \% (2010)} = \frac{\$38,700}{\$604,500} = 0.0640 = \underline{\underline{6.4\%}}$$

$$\text{Accounts Receivable, net \%} = \text{Net Accounts Receivable} \div \text{Total Assets}$$

$$\text{Accounts Receivable, net \% (2011)} = \frac{\$79,700 - \$3,300}{\$708,200} = 0.1079 = \underline{\underline{10.8\%}}$$

$$\text{Accounts Receivable, net \% (2010)} = \frac{\$81,400 - \$2,600}{\$604,500} = 0.1304 = \underline{\underline{13.0\%}}$$

$$\text{Merchandise Inventory \%} = \text{Merchandise Inventory} \div \text{Total Assets}$$

$$\text{Merchadise Inventory \% (2011)} = \frac{\$348,400}{\$708,200} = 0.4920 = \underline{\underline{49.2\%}}$$

$$\text{Merchandise Inventory \% (2010)} = \frac{\$206,500}{\$604,500} = 0.3416 = \underline{\underline{34.2\%}}$$

One could also interpret the above percentages as follows:

2011

- Of every $100 in total assets, $3.10 was in cash.
- Of every $100 in total assets, $10.80 was net accounts receivable.
- Of every $100 in total assets, $49.20 was merchandise inventory.

2010

- Of every $100 in total assets, $6.40 was in cash.
- Of every $100 in total assets, $13.00 was net accounts receivable.
- Of every $100 in total assets, $34.20 was merchandise inventory.

These percentages accentuate Dynamo Bike Shop's poor status with respect to Cash and Merchandise Inventory, as well as its favorable status with respect to Accounts Receivable. Also striking a warning note is that the percentage of Accounts Payable more than doubled during 2011.

Our illustrations show full income statements and balance sheets. But sometimes accountants prepare financial statements in condensed form and put the details in supporting schedules. In this case, the figures are taken from the supporting schedules, and the percentages are calculated in the same way. Since the percentages are rounded, the Percent column may not always add to exactly 100 in vertical

FYI

On an income statement arranged for vertical analysis, each dollar amount is expressed as a percentage of net sales. On a balance sheet arranged for vertical analysis, each dollar amount is expressed as a percentage of total assets or total liabilities and stockholders' equity.

Financial Analyst

Amid Guthikonda uses the financial tools you learned in this chapter every day. He works as a financial analyst for a large mutual fund company. As a financial analyst he is responsible for gathering financial information, analyzing the information using tools such as horizontal and vertical analysis, and then making recommendations. Amid's job involves reading financial statements to determine a company's value and project its future earnings.

Amid has a strong background in problem-solving, analytical, and math skills thanks to the courses that he took at the local university while working on his Bachelor's degree in Accounting. He is currently studying to become a Chartered Financial Analyst (CFA). To qualify for this designation, Amid must pass a three-part exam that covers such subjects as securities analysis, accounting, economics, asset valuation, and portfolio management.

Amid states that to become a financial analyst you will need to "study hard in school" and "take as many classes as you can in the areas of accounting, finance, economics, business, mathematics, and law." As a financial analyst, you will have the opportunity to use the tools you have learned to provide guidance to businesses in making investment decisions.

analysis. (The Percent column is never added in horizontal analysis because it does not involve a common base.)

A spreadsheet tool such as Microsoft Excel is often useful when calculating horizontal and vertical analysis. Most accounting software programs such as Peachtree and QuickBooks can be imported into Excel so that the financial statements can be easily analyzed.

TREND PERCENTAGES

When analyzing financial statements, you may also use percentages to determine trends, or general directions that become evident only when you make a comparison covering a period of years. **Trend percentages** is a form of horizontal analysis. The percentages are calculated by dividing a specific item on an income statement by the corresponding item on the base year income statement. Here is the way to calculate the percentages:

3 LEARNING OBJECTIVE

Express income statement data in trend percentages.

1. Select a representative year as the base year.

2. Label the base year 100 percent.

3. Express all other years as percentages of the base year.

Let's say that you have been able to pull the following figures from the income statements for Dynamo Bike Shop, Inc., for 2007 through 2011.

Item	Year				
	2007	2008	2009	2010	2011
Net Sales	$714,200	$782,380	$806,400	$848,600	$969,600
Cost of Goods Sold	466,150	519,180	540,300	568,800	662,900
Gross Profit	248,050	263,200	266,100	279,800	306,700

You establish 2007 as the base year and calculate the trend percentages for Net Sales by dividing the Net Sales for each year by the Net Sales for 2007.

For 2008: $\dfrac{\$782,380}{\$714,200} = 1.095 \times 100 = \underline{\underline{109.5\%}}$

For 2009: $\dfrac{\$806,400}{\$714,200} = 1.129 \times 100 = \underline{\underline{112.9\%}}$

For 2010: $\dfrac{\$848,600}{\$714,200} = 1.188 \times 100 = \underline{\underline{118.8\%}}$

For 2011: $\dfrac{\$969,600}{\$714,200} = 1.358 \times 100 = \underline{\underline{135.8\%}}$

You determine trend percentages for Cost of Goods Sold and Gross Profit the same way. Here are the results, with the percentages rounded as before.

Item	Year				
	2007	2008	2009	2010	2011
Net Sales	100.0%	109.5%	112.9%	118.8%	135.8%
Cost of Goods Sold	100.0	111.4	115.9	122.0	142.2
Gross Profit	100.0	106.1	107.3	112.8	123.6

Observe that, over the five-year period, the trend of Net Sales is upward. However, Cost of Goods Sold is going up at a more rapid rate. In other words, over the five years, Cost of Goods Sold increased faster than Net Sales, resulting in smaller increases in Gross Profit. This is fine if the company's plan is to achieve a greater volume of sales accompanied by more moderate profits. But if this shrinking Gross Profit is *not* consistent with company policy, then it may be a sign that the company is not passing along its increased costs to its customers.

INDUSTRY COMPARISONS

Vertical analysis, using percentage figures, is very useful when you wish to compare the figures for one company with the average figures for the given industry. The format of the financial statement defines it as a **common-size statement**. You express all items as percentages of a common base. Common-size statements can be used to compare one company with another as well as with industry averages. For the income statement, the common base is again net sales. Net sales is set at 100 percent, and all other items are expressed as a percentage of net sales. Trade and marketing associations often gather information and publish common-size statements.

You Make the Call

The following data were analyzed by the new accounting assistant:

Gross sales	$102,000
Sales returns and allowances	4,804
Sales discounts	1,040
Cost of goods sold	54,540
Operating expenses	36,890

The accounting assistant concluded the gross profit percentage for the year is 40.8 percent and the income from operations percentage for the year is 4.6 percent.

You are suspicious of the percentages she has reported. Check the numbers. If there are errors, do you have any suggestions for the next step?

SOLUTION

The accounting assistant did make errors in the calculations. The gross profit percentage for the year should be 43.3 percent instead of 40.8 percent. The discrepancy occurred because the assistant divided gross profit by gross sales instead of net sales.

$$\text{Gross Profit \%} = \frac{(\$102,000 - \$4,804 - \$1,040) - \$54,540}{\$102,000 - \$4,804 - \$1,040} = 0.4328 = \underline{\underline{43.3\%}}$$

The income from operations percentage for the year should be 4.9 percent instead of 4.6 percent. The error occurred because the assistant divided income from operations by gross sales instead of net sales.

$$\text{Income from Operations \%} = \frac{(\$102,000 - \$4,804 - \$1,040) - \$54,540 - \$36,890}{(\$102,000 - \$4,804 - \$1,040)} = 0.0491 = \underline{\underline{4.9\%}}$$

The assistant needs to be informed of the errors, be given the correct formulas to use, and be reminded of the importance of calculating data correctly.

ANALYSIS BY CREDITORS AND MANAGEMENT

Because management is vitally interested in increasing the company's solvency and profitability, managers are concerned with all types of analytical tools and techniques. Because creditors want assurance of being repaid, they are concerned first with the company's solvency and second with its profitability.

Current means within one year or the operating cycle, whichever is longer.

How Do Short-Term Creditors and Management Analyze an Enterprise?

Bankers and other short-term creditors are primarily interested in the *current* position of a given firm: Does the firm have enough money coming in to meet its current operating needs and to pay its current debts promptly? Let's use as an example some calculations derived from the comparative financial statements of Dynamo Bike Shop, Inc., for 2011 and 2010.

Working Capital

LEARNING OBJECTIVE 4a

Compute working capital.

Working capital is the excess of current assets over current liabilities. One determines the working capital for Dynamo Bike Shop, Inc., as shown in the following equations:

Working capital equals current assets minus current liabilities.

$$\text{Working Capital} = \text{Current Assets} - \text{Current Liabilities}$$

$$\text{Working Capital (2011)} = \$448,600 - \$100,600 = \underline{\underline{\$348,000}}$$

$$\text{Working Capital (2010)} = \$326,100 - \$42,600 = \underline{\underline{\$283,500}}$$

Dynamo Bike Shop has $348,000 of capital available to work with during 2011 compared with $283,500 of capital available to work with during 2010.

Current Ratio

LEARNING OBJECTIVE 4b

Compute current ratio.

The relationship of a company's current assets to its current liabilities is its **current ratio**. You arrive at this figure by dividing current assets by current liabilities.

To compute the current ratio, divide current assets by current liabilities.

$$\text{Current Ratio} = \frac{\text{Current Assets}}{\text{Current Liabilities}}$$

$$\text{Current Ratio (2011)} = \frac{\$448,600}{\$100,600} = \underline{\underline{4.46}}$$

$$\text{Current Ratio (2010)} = \frac{\$326,100}{\$42,600} = \underline{\underline{7.65}}$$

A firm's current ratio reveals its current debt-paying ability. Dynamo Bike Shop's current ratio of 4.46 in 2011 indicates that there is $4.46 of cash coming in within a year from now for every dollar Dynamo Bike Shop has to pay out within a year. But the firm was better off in 2010, because in that year, it had $7.65 coming in within a year for every dollar to be paid out within the year.

From the point of view of bankers and other creditors, the adequacy of a company's current ratio depends on what type of business the firm is in. A favorable ratio for a merchandising business is generally 2—higher if the type of merchandise the firm sells is subject to abrupt changes in design or technology that create higher risk. But a public utility, which has no inventories other than supplies, is considered solvent even if its current ratio is less than 1. But notice that a current ratio of 4.46 for Dynamo Bike Shop only indicates that current assets (not cash inflows) at one point in time (year-end date, for example) exceed current liabilities (not cash outflows).

Quick Ratio

LEARNING OBJECTIVE 4c

Compute quick ratio.

The relationship of a company's current assets that can be quickly converted into cash to its current liabilities is known as its **quick ratio** or *acid-test ratio*. **Quick assets** are Cash, current Notes Receivable, net Accounts Receivable (that is, Accounts Receivable less Allowance for Doubtful Accounts), Interest Receivable, and Marketable Securities. They do not include inventories and prepaid expenses because these are less easily converted into cash than are other current assets. Determine the quick ratio by dividing quick assets by current liabilities.

$$\text{Quick Ratio} = \frac{\text{Quick Assets}}{\text{Current Liabilities}}$$

$$\text{Quick Ratio (2011)} = \frac{\$21,800 + (\$79,700 - \$3,300)}{\$100,600} = \frac{\$98,200}{\$100,600} = \underline{\underline{0.98}}$$

$$\text{Quick Ratio (2010)} = \frac{\$38,700 + (\$81,400 - \$2,600)}{\$42,600} = \frac{\$117,500}{\$42,600} = \underline{\underline{2.76}}$$

Dynamo Bike Shop's quick ratio of 0.98 in 2011 indicates that there are 98 cents in cash coming in quickly—without involving the liquidation of inventory—for every dollar it has to pay out on a given date. For 2010, there was $2.76 that the firm could realize quickly for every dollar it had to pay out on a given date.

A quick ratio of 1 is normally considered satisfactory. However, the quick ratio for Dynamo Bike Shop exposes a precarious short-term financial position. Consider this quick ratio in conjunction with the company's working capital and its current ratio. Although working capital and current ratio are two indicators of a firm's ability to meet its current obligations, they don't reveal the *composition of its current assets*—a very important factor.

Relationship of Each Current Asset to Total Current Assets

Suppose that you are asked to find out the proportionate position of each item in the list of current assets of Dynamo Bike Shop. Your first step is to compile a schedule of each current asset as it relates to total current assets, as shown in the following illustration:

| | December 31, 2011 | | December 31, 2010 | |
	Amount	Percent	Amount	Percent
Assets				
Current Assets:				
Cash	$ 21,800	4.9%	$ 38,700	11.9%
Accounts Receivable (net)	76,400	17.0	78,800	24.2
Merchandise Inventory	348,400	77.7	206,500	63.3
Prepaid Insurance	2,000	0.4	2,100	0.6
Total Current Assets	$448,600	100.0%	$326,100	100.0%

As an example, cash as a percentage of total current assets is calculated like this:

$$\frac{\$21,800}{\$448,600} = 0.0486 = \underline{\underline{4.9\%}}$$

We have already commented on the large increase in the proportion of merchandise inventory (it was 63.3 percent of current assets in 2010 but amounts to 77.7 percent of current assets in 2011). This change, coupled with the decline in the cash position (11.9 percent of current assets for 2010; only 4.9 percent of current assets for 2011), reinforces the message we got from the decline in the quick ratio: The firm may have a hard time paying its current debts.

Accounts Receivable Turnover

Since money tied up in accounts receivable does not yield any revenue, a firm tries to collect accounts receivable promptly and to keep them at a minimum. It can use the cash it gets from collection of accounts receivable to reduce bank loans or to

LEARNING OBJECTIVE

4d

Compute accounts receivable turnover.

take advantage of cash discounts. This action reduces the amount of interest it has to pay and the cost of the merchandise it buys. It also reduces the risk of loss from bad debts.

Accounts receivable turnover is the number of times charge accounts are turned over (or paid off) per year. A turnover implies a sale on account followed by payment of the debt in cash. Compute this by *dividing net sales on account by average net accounts receivable*. If possible, use the average of the monthly balances of Accounts Receivable because this allows for seasonal fluctuations. If you don't have figures for monthly balances, use the average of the balances at the beginning and the end of the year. Here is how accounts receivable turnover looks for Dynamo Bike Shop. (You have to take the beginning balance of net Accounts Receivable for 2010, which was $61,460, from the 2009 balance sheet. Net sales on account (charge sales, not cash sales), taken from the sales journal, were $773,020 for 2011 and $678,880 for 2010.)

$$\text{Accounts Receivable Turnover} = \frac{\text{Net Sales on Account}}{\text{Average Accounts Receivable (Net)}}$$

$$\text{Average Accounts Receivable} = \frac{\text{Beginning Accounts Receivable (Net)} + \text{Ending Accounts Receivable (Net)}}{2}$$

$$\text{Accounts Receivable Turnover (2011)} = \frac{\$773,020}{\left(\dfrac{\$78,800 + \$76,400}{2}\right)} = \frac{\$773,020}{\$77,600} = \underline{\underline{9.96}} \text{ times per year}$$

$$\text{Accounts Receivable Turnover (2010)} = \frac{\$678,880}{\left(\dfrac{\$61,460 + \$78,800}{2}\right)} = \frac{\$678,800}{\$70,130} = \underline{\underline{9.68}} \text{ times per year}$$

You can use the accounts receivable turnover to determine the number of days that the receivables were on the books. Calculate this by dividing 365 days by the turnover figure:

$$\text{Year (2011)} = \frac{365 \text{ days}}{9.96 \text{ times per year}} = 36.65 \text{ or } \underline{\underline{37}} \text{ days}$$

$$\text{Year (2010)} = \frac{365 \text{ days}}{9.68 \text{ times per year}} = 37.71 \text{ or } \underline{\underline{38}} \text{ days}$$

It took an average of one day less to collect accounts receivable in 2011 than it did in 2010. This reduction represents a slight improvement in collections for Dynamo Bike Shop. Since the company's credit terms are net 30 days, 37 or 38 days is reasonable.

Merchandise Inventory Turnover

LEARNING OBJECTIVE 4e
Compute merchandise inventory turnover.

Merchandise inventory turnover is the number of times a company's average inventory is sold during a given year. Calculate this by *dividing Cost of Goods Sold by average Merchandise Inventory*. Here is the calculation for Dynamo Bike shop (beginning Merchandise Inventory for 2010, taken from the 2009 balance sheet, was $138,700):

$$\text{Merchandise Inventory Turnover} = \frac{\text{Cost of Goods Sold}}{\text{Average Merchandise Inventory}}$$

$$\text{Average Merchandise Inventory} = \frac{\text{Beginning Merchandise Inventory} + \text{Ending Merchandise Inventory}}{2}$$

$$\text{Merchandise Inventory Turnover (2011)} = \frac{\$662,900}{\left(\dfrac{\$206,500 + \$348,400}{2}\right)} = \frac{\$662,900}{\$277,450} = \underline{\underline{2.39}} \text{ times per year}$$

$$\text{Merchandise Inventory Turnover (2010)} = \frac{\$568,800}{\left(\dfrac{\$138,700 + \$206,500}{2}\right)} = \frac{\$568,800}{\$172,600} = \underline{\underline{3.30}} \text{ times per year}$$

If possible, you should use the average of the monthly balances of Merchandise Inventory (add them and divide by 12). The figure for merchandise inventory turnover varies depending on the type of product involved. You can compare the figure for merchandise inventory turnover for one company with figures for the rest of the industry as a test of merchandising efficiency. Each turnover yields a gross profit or markup to the company. Note that there has been a serious decline in the rate of merchandise inventory turnover for Dynamo Bike Shop. This is something to investigate further with management and monitor for future corrective action.

You may also use the figure for merchandise inventory turnover to determine the number of days that the merchandise was kept in stock. Calculate this the same way you calculate the number of days that the receivables were collectible: divide 365 days by the turnover figure.

$$\text{Year (2011)} = \frac{365 \text{ days}}{2.39 \text{ times per year}} = 152.72 \text{ or } \underline{\underline{153}} \text{ days}$$

$$\text{Year (2010)} = \frac{365 \text{ days}}{3.30 \text{ times per year}} = 110.61 \text{ or } \underline{\underline{111}} \text{ days}$$

Note that Dynamo Bike Shop's merchandise remained in stock 42 days longer in 2011 than it did in 2010. This fact surely calls for an investigation of the company's sales and purchasing practices.

In addition to yielding a higher gross profit, rapid merchandise inventory turnover has other advantages. The money invested in the inventory is tied up for a shorter period of time; storage costs are lower; there is less risk of spoilage (if the merchandise is perishable); there is less risk of change in demand (if the merchandise is affected by changes in style or in business conditions).

How Do Long-Term Creditors and Management Analyze an Enterprise?

Long-term creditors include secured creditors (such as banks) and bondholders. Whenever specific property has been pledged, secured creditors have first claim on the property in the event that the company cannot keep up its payments. Even in the case of debentures (unsecured bonds), the bondholders have a prior claim to the general assets of the company, a claim that takes precedence over that of the stockholders. Management is concerned with taking care of the company's present obligations, as well as preserving its credit standing, and hence its ability to borrow in the future.

Two ratios that are particularly useful from the standpoint of long-term creditors are the ratio of stockholders' equity to liabilities and the ratio of property and equipment to long-term liabilities.

Ratio of Stockholders' Equity to Liabilities

The ratio of stockholders' equity to liabilities is the ratio of the stockholders' investment to the creditors' claims.

In calculating any ratio, we mean the ratio *of* one thing *to* something else. When we write the ratio as a fraction, we put the *of* part in the numerator and the *to* part in the denominator. Look at this calculation for Dynamo Bike Shop:

4f LEARNING OBJECTIVE

Compute ratio of stockholders' equity to liabilities.

$$\text{Ratio of Stockholders' Equity to Liabilities} = \frac{\text{Stockholders' Equity}}{\text{Liabilities}}$$

$$\text{Ratio of Stockholders' Equity to Liabilities (2011)} = \frac{\$509,800}{\$198,400} = \underline{\underline{2.57}}$$

$$\text{Ratio of Stockholders' Equity to Liabilities (2010)} = \frac{\$464,300}{\$140,200} = \underline{\underline{3.31}}$$

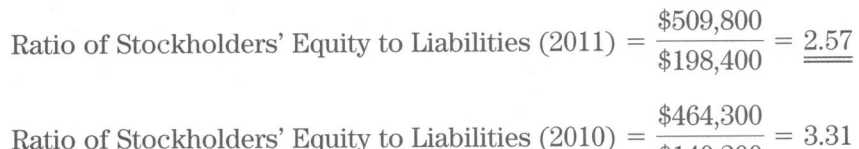

Remember

To find the ratio of ... to ..., divide the "of ..." amount by the "to ..." amount.

In 2011 for every $2.57 of stockholders' investment, the creditors have loaned $1. Dynamo Bike Shop's ratio of stockholders' equity to liabilities shows a decline since 2010, from 3.31 to 2.57. Creditors like to see a high proportion of stockholders' equity because stockholders' equity, or owners' equity, acts as a buffer in case the company has to absorb losses. Also, owners often prefer a high proportion of equity to liabilities.

Ratio of Property and Equipment to Long-Term Liabilities

LEARNING OBJECTIVE 4g

Compute ratio of property and equipment to long-term liabilities.

There is another factor that provides a margin of safety to mortgage holders and bondholders—the ratio of the value of a firm's total property and equipment to its long-term liabilities. This ratio also indicates the potential ability of the enterprise to borrow more money on a long-term basis. Let's look at the calculation for Dynamo Bike Shop.

$$\text{Ratio of Property and Equipment to Long-Term Liabilities} = \frac{\text{Property and Equipment}}{\text{Long-Term Liabilities}}$$

$$\text{Ratio of Property and Equipment to Long-Term Liabilities (2011)} = \frac{\$190,800}{\$97,800} = \underline{\underline{1.95}}$$

$$\text{Ratio of Property and Equipment to Long-Term Liabilities (2010)} = \frac{\$209,200}{\$97,600} = \underline{\underline{2.14}}$$

In 2010, there was $2.14 book value of property and equipment for every dollar of long-term liabilities. In 2011, there is $1.95 book value of property and equipment for every dollar of long-term liabilities. This ratio, too, has deteriorated.

As we have seen, a firm's creditors and managers may use any of eight devices to determine the financial position of a firm:

- Working capital
- Current ratio
- Quick ratio
- Relationship of each current asset to total current assets
- Accounts receivable turnover
- Merchandise inventory turnover
- Ratio of stockholders' equity to liabilities
- Ratio of property and equipment to long-term liabilities

ANALYSIS BY OWNERS AND MANAGEMENT

In addition to being concerned about the solvency and profitability of a company, owners and managers are vitally interested in the value of and return on investment in the company. In many cases, the owners are the managers. In other situations, managers are employed by the owners. What diagnostic tools do owners and managers use to determine the financial health of their company?

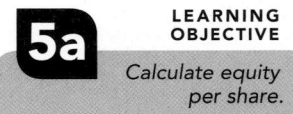

5a   LEARNING OBJECTIVE

Calculate equity per share.

Equity per Share

When you examine the annual report of a corporation, you encounter the term *book value per share*, also referred to as *equity per share*. If a corporation has only one class of common stock outstanding, equity per share is determined by dividing the total stockholders' equity by the number of shares of stock issued and outstanding. Here are the calculations for Dynamo Bike Shop.

$$\text{Equity per Share} = \frac{\text{Total Stockholders' Equity Available to a Class of Stock}}{\text{Number of Shares Issued and Outstanding}}$$

$$\text{Equity per Share (2011)} = \frac{\$509,800}{3,000 \text{ shares}} = \underline{\underline{\$169.93}} \text{ per share}$$

$$\text{Equity per Share (2010)} = \frac{\$464,300}{3,000 \text{ shares}} = \underline{\underline{\$154.77}} \text{ per share}$$

When there are shares of preferred stock outstanding, you must deduct the liquidation value of the preferred stockholders' equity, including any dividends in arrears on cumulative preferred stock, to arrive at the stockholders' equity available to holders of common stock.

The term *equity per share* does *not* mean the cash value or market value of a share; it means the amount that would be distributed per share of stock on a book basis *if* the corporation were to **liquidate** (wind up its affairs by paying off its creditors and selling its assets for cash) without incurring any expenses, gains, or losses in selling its assets and paying its liabilities. The equity per share increases as a firm retains net income. This concept of equity per share is important in contracts involving the sale of stock. For example, a large stockholder might obtain an option to buy the shares of small stockholders at the value of the equity per share as of a certain future date.

Rate of Return on Common Stockholders' Equity

A corporation exists first and foremost to earn a net income for its stockholders. Therefore, the rate of return on the common stockholders' equity is important as a means of measuring how good or bad the investment is. This rate is calculated by dividing the net income available to holders of common stock by the *average value* of their equity. Here is the calculation for Dynamo Bike Shop (beginning common stockholders' equity for 2010 was $422,100):

Rate of Return on Common Stockholders' Equity

$$= \frac{\text{Net Income Available to Common Stock}}{\text{Average Common Stockholders' Equity}}$$

Average Common Stockholders' Equity

$$= \frac{\text{Beginning Common Stockholders' Equity} + \text{Ending Common Stockholders' Equity}}{2}$$

Rate of Return on Common Stockholders' Equity (2011)

$$= \frac{\$75,890}{\left(\dfrac{\$464,300 + \$509,800}{2}\right)} = \frac{\$75,890}{\$487,050} = 0.1558 = \underline{\underline{15.6\%}}$$

Rate of Return on Common Stockholders' Equity (2010)

$$= \frac{\$69,530}{\left(\dfrac{\$422,100 + \$464,300}{2}\right)} = \frac{\$69,530}{\$443,200} = 0.1569 = \underline{\underline{15.7\%}}$$

The rate of return on common stockholders' equity declined 0.1 percent.

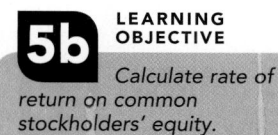

LEARNING OBJECTIVE
5b
Calculate rate of return on common stockholders' equity.

Earnings per Share of Common Stock

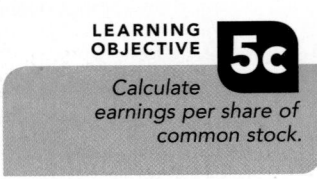

LEARNING OBJECTIVE 5c

Calculate earnings per share of common stock.

You often see **earnings per share** of stock listed in the financial columns of newspapers or on Internet investment sites. If a corporation has no preferred stock outstanding, compute the earnings per share of common stock by dividing net income by the average number of shares of common stock outstanding during the year. When there is preferred stock, you must first deduct any dividends on preferred stock to arrive at the amount available to common stock. Here is the calculation of earnings per share of common stock for Dynamo Bike Shop:

$$\text{Earnings per Share of Common Stock} = \frac{\text{Net Income Available to Common Stock}}{\text{Average Number of Shares of Common Stock Outstanding}}$$

$$\text{Earnings per Share of Common Stock (2011)} = \frac{\$75,890}{3,000 \text{ shares}} = \$25.30 \text{ per share}$$

$$\text{Earnings per Share of Common Stock (2010)} = \frac{\$69,530}{3,000 \text{ shares}} = \$23.18 \text{ per share}$$

Any big change during the year in the *number* of shares outstanding naturally has a significant impact on the amount of earnings per share. That's why a company must disclose (or show) the average number of shares outstanding and disclose any information relating to stock dividends and stock splits. If the company has stock options or stock awards outstanding, the earnings per share must also be computed taking into account the additional shares of stock that could potentially be outstanding. This calculation is called *diluted earnings per share*. Diluted earnings per share is discussed in intermediate accounting.

Price-Earnings Ratio

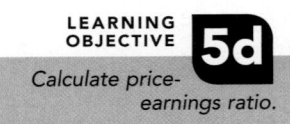

LEARNING OBJECTIVE 5d

Calculate price-earnings ratio.

The **price-earnings ratio** is a measure commonly used to determine whether the market price of a corporation's stock is reasonable. You calculate the price-earnings ratio of a company's stock by dividing the market price per share by the annual earnings per share. Suppose that the market price of a share of common stock of Dynamo Bike Shop at the end of 2011 is $57.51, and that at the end of 2010 it was $69.72. Here is how you calculate the price-earnings ratio:

$$\text{Price-Earnings Ratio} = \frac{\text{Market Price per Share}}{\text{Earnings per Share}}$$

$$\text{Price-Earnings Ratio (2011)} = \frac{\$57.51}{\$25.30} = 2.27$$

$$\text{Price-Earnings Ratio (2010)} = \frac{\$69.72}{\$23.18} = 3.01$$

What constitutes a reasonable price-earnings ratio varies from one industry to another and with the state of the economy. From 1920 to the mid-1990s, the year-end price-earnings ratio was mostly between 10:1 and 20:1, except for a select number of years. Since then, the ratio has fluctuated to a high of 46.50:1 in 2001 due to the recession to a more sustainable region of 17.40:1 in 2006 due to higher earnings growth.

You may also use the price-earnings ratio in this manner: If the acceptable price-earnings ratio for a given stock is 16:1 and the earnings per share equal $2.50, it follows that the maximum reasonable price you ought to pay for the stock is $40 (that is, $2.50 × 16). But what if the stock is selling for only $20? You may well consider it to be undervalued.

Summary of Analytical Tools and Techniques

Figure 5 shows a summary of the analytical tools that are used by owners, creditors, and management to analyze solvency, profitability, and return on investment. Remember, these tools are only useful when you use them on a comparative basis such as from one year to another or from one company to another.

Summary of analytical tools **FIGURE 5**

Analytical Tools	Formula	What It Tells You
Solvency and Profitability Tools:		
Working Capital	Current Assets – Current Liabilities	The company's ability to meet current operating needs and pay current debts
Current Ratio	$\dfrac{\text{Current Assets}}{\text{Current Liabilities}}$	The company's current debt-paying ability
Quick Ratio	$\dfrac{\text{Quick Assets}}{\text{Current Liabilities}}$	The company's current debt-paying ability out of quick assets only
Accounts Receivable Turnover	$\dfrac{\text{Net Sales on Account}}{\text{Average Account Receivable (Net)}}$	The company's ability to collect receivables
Merchandise Inventory Turnover	$\dfrac{\text{Cost of Goods Sold}}{\text{Average Merchandise Inventory}}$	The number of times a company's average inventory is sold during a given year
Ratio of Stockholders' Equity to Liabilities	$\dfrac{\text{Stockholders' Equity}}{\text{Liabilities}}$	The company's margin of safety to mortgage holders and bondholders
Ratio of Property and Equipment to Long-Term Liabilities	$\dfrac{\text{Property and Equipment}}{\text{Long-Term Liabilities}}$	The company's margin of safety to long-term creditors and the company's potential ability to borrow more money on a long-term basis
Return on Investment:		
Equity per Share	$\dfrac{\text{Total Stockholders' Equity Available to a Class of Stock}}{\text{Number of Shares Issued and Outstanding}}$	The amount that would be distributed per share if the corporation were to liquidate and sell the assets for their book value
Rate of Return on Common Stockholders' Equity	$\dfrac{\text{Net Income Available to Common Stock}}{\text{Average Common Stockholders' Equity}}$	The profitability of the investment
Earnings per Share	$\dfrac{\text{Net Income Available to Common Stock}}{\text{Average Number of Shares of Common Stock Outstanding}}$	The profitability of the investment
Price-Earnings Ratio	$\dfrac{\text{Market Price per Share}}{\text{Earnings per Share}}$	To determine if the market price of a corporation's stock is reasonable and to indicate future earnings prospects

CHAPTER REVIEW

Study & Practice

1 LEARNING OBJECTIVE

Prepare a comparative income statement and balance sheet involving horizontal analysis.

Horizontal analysis involves the comparison of the same item on an income statement or balance sheet for two or more periods. First, determine the difference between the two periods. Next, express the difference as a percentage of the **base year** or period (usually the earliest period).

PRACTICE EXERCISE 1

Calculate the amount and percentage of increase or decrease for the following items (horizontal analysis). Round to three decimal places.

Item	2011	2010
Cash	$ 70,803	$ 74,126
Notes Receivable	56,580	38,460
Equipment (net)	166,000	161,500
Retained Earnings	115,310	139,500

PRACTICE EXERCISE 1 SOLUTION

Item	Increase or (Decrease) Amount	Increase or (Decrease) Percentage
Cash	$ (3,323)	(4.5)%
Notes Receivable	18,120	47.1
Equipment (net)	4,500	2.8
Retained Earnings	(24,190)	(17.3)

2 LEARNING OBJECTIVE

Prepare a comparative income statement and balance sheet involving vertical analysis.

In **vertical analysis**, each item in a financial statement is expressed as a percentage of a base amount. For an income statement, the base amount is net sales. For a balance sheet, the base amount is total assets or total liabilities and stockholders' equity.

PRACTICE EXERCISE 2

Using the following revenue and expense data, prepare a comparative income statement, expressing each item for both 2011 and 2010 as a percentage of net sales (vertical analysis). Round to three decimal places.

Item	2011	2010
Sales (net)	$445,000	$410,000
Cost of Goods Sold	260,000	248,115
Selling Expenses	20,300	14,000
General Expenses	11,240	10,270
Income Tax Expense	28,230	22,680

PRACTICE EXERCISE 2 SOLUTION

	2011		2010	
	Amount	Percent*	Amount	Percent*
Net Sales	$445,000	100.0%	$410,000	100.0%
Cost of Goods Sold	260,000	58.4	248,115	60.5
Gross Profit	$185,000	41.6%	$161,885	39.5%
Operating Expenses:				
Total Selling Expenses	$ 20,300	4.6%	$ 14,000	3.4%
Total General Expenses	11,240	2.5	10,270	2.5
Total Operating Expenses	$ 31,540	7.1%	$ 24,270	5.9%
Income Before Income Taxes	$153,460	34.5%	$137,615	33.6%
Income Tax Expense	28,230	6.3	22,680	5.5
Net Income	$125,230	28.1%	$114,935	28.0%

*There may be slight differences in the tenth's place due to the rounding methods of various calculators and computers. For the same reason, percentages may not add up to exactly 100 percent.

3 LEARNING OBJECTIVE

Express income statement data in trend percentages.

Income statement data shown in **trend percentages** involve a comparison of the same item over a number of periods. One period or year (usually the earliest) is designated as the base period and the amount for this period is set at 100 percent. Each amount in later years is expressed as a percentage of the amount for the base period.

PRACTICE EXERCISE 3

Calculate trend percentages for the following items. Use 2008 as the base year. Round to three decimal places.

Item	Year			
	2008	2009	2010	2011
Net Sales	$487,000	$435,000	$402,000	$405,000
Cost of Goods Sold	130,000	125,000	132,000	144,000
Merchandise Inventory	45,000	44,000	33,000	31,000

PRACTICE EXERCISE 3 SOLUTION

Item	Year			
	2008	2009	2010	2011
Net Sales	100.0%	89.3%	82.5%	83.2%
Cost of Goods Sold	100.0	96.2	101.5	110.8
Merchandise Inventory	100.0	97.8	73.3	68.9

4 LEARNING OBJECTIVE

Compute (a) working capital, (b) current ratio, (c) quick ratio, (d) accounts receivable turnover, (e) merchandise inventory turnover, (f) ratio of stockholders' equity to liabilities, and (g) ratio of property and equipment to long-term liabilities.

Short-term creditors and management use the following techniques:

Working Capital = Current Assets – Current Liabilities

$$\text{Current Ratio} = \frac{\text{Current Assets}}{\text{Current Liabilities}}$$

$$\text{Quick Ratio} = \frac{\text{Quick Assets}}{\text{Current Liabilities}}$$

$$\text{Accounts Receivable Turnover} = \frac{\text{Net Sales on Account}}{\text{Average Accounts Receivable (Net)}}$$

$$\text{Merchandise Inventory Turnover} = \frac{\text{Cost of Goods Sold}}{\text{Average Merchandise Inventory}}$$

Long-term creditors and management use the following ratios:

$$\text{Ratio of Stockholders' Equity to Liabilities} = \frac{\text{Stockholders' Equity}}{\text{Liabilities}}$$

$$\text{Ratio of Property and Equipment to Long-Term Liabilities} = \frac{\text{Property and Equipment}}{\text{Long-Term Liabilities}}$$

PRACTICE EXERCISE 4a–c

The following items are taken from the balance sheet of Sea Trout Company:

Cash	$180,000
Accounts Receivable (net)	438,000
Merchandise Inventory	143,000
Prepaid Expenses	9,150
Accounts Payable	84,500
Notes Payable (current)	34,300
Salaries Payable	4,500

Use the information above to answer Practice Exercises 4a–c.

PRACTICE EXERCISE 4a

Compute the working capital for Sea Trout Company.

PRACTICE EXERCISE 4a SOLUTION

Working Capital = ($180,000 + $438,000 + $143,000 + $9,150) − ($84,500 + $34,300 + $4,500)
= $770,150 − $123,300 = $646,850

PRACTICE EXERCISE 4b

Compute the current ratio for Sea Trout Company. Round to two decimal places.

PRACTICE EXERCISE 4b SOLUTION

$$\text{Current Ratio} = \frac{\$770,150}{\$123,300} = 6.25$$

PRACTICE EXERCISE 4c

Compute the quick ratio for Sea Trout Company. Round to two decimal places.

PRACTICE EXERCISE 4c SOLUTION

$$\text{Quick Ratio} = \frac{(\$180,000 + \$438,000)}{\$123,300} = 5.01$$

PRACTICE EXERCISE 4d–g

The following selected items are taken from the financial statements of Strunk, Inc. Assume that Strunk, Inc.'s liabilities consist only of Accounts Payable and Long-Term Liabilities and that all sales are made on account. Common stock is the only stock issued by Strunk.

Item	2011	2010
Accounts Receivable (net)	$ 509,000	$ 487,000
Merchandise Inventory	442,000	418,000
Property and Equipment	2,375,000	2,017,000
Accounts Payable	21,500	18,225
Long-Term Liabilities	974,500	956,775
Stockholders' Equity	4,000,000	3,820,000
Sales (net)	1,963,000	1,927,000
Cost of Goods Sold	1,413,000	1,431,000
Gross Profit	550,000	496,000
Net Income	192,000	175,000

Use the information above to answer Practice Exercises 4d–g.

PRACTICE EXERCISE 4d

Compute the accounts receivable turnover for Strunk, Inc. for 2011. Round to two decimal places.

PRACTICE EXERCISE 4d SOLUTION

$$\text{Accounts Receivable Turnover} = \frac{\$1,963,000}{\left(\frac{\$487,000 + \$509,000}{2}\right)} = \frac{\$1,963,000}{\$498,000} = \underline{\underline{3.94}} \text{ times per year}$$

PRACTICE EXERCISE 4e

Compute the merchandise inventory turnover for Strunk, Inc. for 2011. Round to two decimal places.

PRACTICE EXERCISE 4e SOLUTION

$$\text{Merchandise Inventory Turnover} = \frac{\$1,413,000}{\left(\frac{\$418,000 + \$442,000}{2}\right)} = \frac{\$1,413,000}{\$430,000} = \underline{\underline{3.29}} \text{ times per year}$$

PRACTICE EXERCISE 4f

Compute the ratio of stockholders' equity to liabilities for Strunk, Inc. for 2011. Round to two decimal places.

PRACTICE EXERCISE 4f SOLUTION

$$\text{Ratio of Stockholders' Equity to Liabilities} = \frac{\$4,000,000}{\$21,500 + \$974,500} = \frac{\$4,000,000}{\$996,000} = \underline{\underline{4.02}}$$

PRACTICE EXERCISE 4g

Compute the ratio of property and equipment to long-term liabilities for Strunk, Inc. for 2011. Round to two decimal places.

PRACTICE EXERCISE 4g SOLUTION

Ratio of Property and Equipment to Long-Term Liabilities $= \dfrac{\$2,375,000}{\$974,500} = \underline{\underline{2.44}}$

5 LEARNING OBJECTIVE

Calculate (a) equity per share, (b) rate of return on common stockholders' equity, (c) earnings per share of common stock, and (d) price-earnings ratio.

Owners and managers use the following measures:

Equity per Share $= \dfrac{\text{Total Stockholders' Equity Available to a Class of Stock}}{\text{Number of Shares Issued and Outstanding}}$

Rate of Return on Common Stockholders' Equity $= \dfrac{\text{Net Income Available to Common Stock}}{\text{Average Common Stockholders' Equity}}$

Earnings per Share of Common Stock $= \dfrac{\text{Net Income Available to Common Stock}}{\text{Average Number of Shares of Common Stock Outstanding}}$

Price-Earnings Ratio $= \dfrac{\text{Market Price per Share}}{\text{Earnings per Share}}$

PRACTICE EXERCISE 5a–d

The Stockholders' Equity section of the balance sheet of Aransas Corporation is as follows:

Stockholders' Equity		
Paid-in Capital:		
Common Stock, $2 par (100,000 shares authorized, 40,000 shares issued and outstanding)	$ 80,000	
Paid-in Capital in Excess of Par Value	30,000	
Total Paid-in Capital	$110,000	
Retained Earnings	70,000	
Total Stockholders' Equity		$180,000

Net income for the year is $62,000. Stockholders' equity was $109,000 at the beginning of the year. The present market price of the stock is $22 per share.

Use the information above to answer Practice Exercises 5a–d.

PRACTICE EXERCISE 5a

Compute the equity per share for Aransas Corporation. Round to two decimal places.

PRACTICE EXERCISE 5a SOLUTION

Equity per Share $= \dfrac{\$180,000}{40,000 \text{ shares}} = \underline{\underline{\$4.50}}$ per share

PRACTICE EXERCISE 5b

Compute the rate of return on common stockholders' equity for Aransas Corporation. Round to two decimal places.

PRACTICE EXERCISE 5b SOLUTION

Rate of Return on Common Stockholders' Equity $= \dfrac{\$62,000}{\left(\dfrac{\$109,000 + \$180,000}{2}\right)} = \dfrac{\$62,000}{\$144,500} = 0.4291 = \underline{\underline{42.91\%}}$

PRACTICE EXERCISE 5c

Compute the earnings per share of common stock for Aransas Corporation. Round to two decimal places.

PRACTICE EXERCISE 5c SOLUTION

Earnings per Share of Common Stock $= \dfrac{\$62,000}{40,000 \text{ shares}} = \underline{\underline{\$1.55}}$ per share

PRACTICE EXERCISE 5d

Compute the price-earnings ratio for Aransas Corporation. Round to two decimal places.

PRACTICE EXERCISE 5d SOLUTION

Price-Earnings Ratio $= \dfrac{\$22.00}{\$1.55} = \underline{\underline{14.19}}$

Glossary

Accounts receivable turnover The number of times charge accounts are paid off per year; a turnover is a sale on account and subsequent repayment. (p. 930)

Base year The year used as a basis for comparison. (p. 917)

Common-size statement A financial statement using vertical analysis with all items expressed as percentages; allows comparison of one company with another as well as with industry averages. (p. 926)

Current ratio Current assets divided by current liabilities. (p. 928)

Earnings per share The proportionate amount of a company's net earnings for each outstanding share of common stock. (p. 934)

Horizontal analysis Comparing the same item in the financial statements of an enterprise for two or more periods. (p. 917)

Liquidate To wind up the affairs of a business by paying off the creditors and selling the assets for cash. (p. 933)

Merchandise inventory turnover The number of times a company's average inventory is sold during a given year. (p. 930)

Price-earnings ratio A common measure for deciding whether a stock's market price is reasonable; calculated by dividing the market price per share by the annual earnings per share. (p. 934)

Profitability An enterprise's ability to earn a reasonable profit on the owners' investment. (p. 916)

Quick assets Cash, current Notes Receivable, net Accounts Receivable, Interest Receivable, and Marketable Securities. (p. 928)

Quick ratio Quick assets divided by current liabilities. Also called *acid-test ratio*. (p. 928)

Solvency An enterprise's ability to pay its debts. (p. 916)

Trend percentages Percentages calculated by dividing a specific item on an income statement by the corresponding item on the base year income statement. (p. 925)

Vertical analysis Portraying items in financial statements as percentages (or proportional parts) of a given item on the same financial statement. (p. 921)

Working capital The excess of current assets over current liabilities. (p. 928)

CHAPTER ASSIGNMENTS

Discussion Questions

1. A company has a net income percentage of 10 percent. What does this mean?
2. What does an increase in the accounts receivable turnover indicate as far as a company is concerned?
3. What is the difference between a firm's solvency and its profitability?
4. How does a company's current ratio differ from its quick ratio?
5. Why is a high merchandise inventory turnover more desirable than a low turnover?
6. Describe the difference between horizontal analysis and vertical analysis with regard to comparative balance sheets.
7. Which of the following types of business firms would you expect to have a high merchandise inventory turnover?

    a. Furniture store
    b. Women's clothing boutique
    c. Jeweler
    d. Gift shop
    e. Grocery
    f. Florist

8. Why are creditors interested in the ratio of stockholders' equity to liabilities? Is it more desirable to have a high ratio or a low ratio?

Exercises

EXERCISE 23-1 Calculate the amount and percentage of increase or decrease for the following items (horizontal analysis). Round to three decimal places.

PRACTICE EXERCISE 1

Item	2011	2010
Cash	$ 53,400	$ 60,000
Notes Receivable	32,000	25,000
Equipment (net)	160,500	162,500
Retained Earnings	100,200	105,000

EXERCISE 23-2 Using the following revenue and expense data, prepare a comparative income statement, expressing each item for both 2011 and 2010 as a percentage of net sales (vertical analysis). Round to three decimal places.

PRACTICE EXERCISE 2

Item	2011	2010
Sales (net)	$903,000	$650,000
Cost of Goods Sold	501,000	468,145
Selling Expenses	90,500	38,000
General Expenses	21,850	26,500
Income Tax Expense	48,125	44,340

EXERCISE 23-3 Calculate trend percentages for the following items. Use 2008 as the base year. Round to three decimal places.

PRACTICE EXERCISE 3

	Year			
Item	2008	2009	2010	2011
Net Sales	$688,000	$665,000	$632,000	$605,000
Cost of Goods Sold	370,000	365,000	392,000	362,000
Merchandise Inventory	75,000	72,000	65,000	62,000

LO 4a,4b,4c

EXERCISE 23-4 The following items are from the balance sheets of J. J. Jackson Company as of December 31, 2011 and 2010.

PRACTICE EXERCISES
4a,4b,4c

	2011	2010
Current Assets:		
Cash	$198,000	$189,000
Notes Receivable	15,000	14,000
Accounts Receivable (net)	87,000	78,000
Merchandise Inventory	273,000	236,000
Total Current Assets	$573,000	$517,000
Current Liabilities	$228,000	$182,000

Calculate the following for each year (round to two decimals):

a. Working capital
b. Current ratio
c. Quick ratio

LO 4a,4b,4c

EXERCISE 23-5 The following items are taken from the balance sheet of Minshew Company:

PRACTICE EXERCISES
4a,4b,4c

Cash	$126,000
Accounts Receivable (net)	378,000
Merchandise Inventory	123,000
Prepaid Expenses	3,850
Accounts Payable	175,700
Notes Payable (current)	18,500
Salaries Payable	3,800

Compute the following:

a. Working capital
b. Current ratio
c. Quick ratio

LO 2,4d,4e

EXERCISE 23-6 The following data are taken from the financial statements of Perrotta Company. For 2011, calculate the gross profit percentage, the accounts receivable turnover, and the merchandise inventory turnover. Round to two decimal places.

PRACTICE EXERCISES
2,4d,4e

CHAPTER ASSIGNMENTS

Item	2011	2010
Sales on account (net)	$625,000	$700,000
Cost of Goods Sold	416,000	520,000
Merchandise Inventory (at end of year)	138,400	130,500
Accounts Receivable (net) (at end of year)	100,600	103,500

4d,4e,4g,5b **LO**

PRACTICE EXERCISES
4d,4e,4g,5b

EXERCISE 23-7 The following items are taken from the financial statements of Tyler Company. All sales are made on account. Common stock is the only stock issued by Tyler Company.

Item	2011	2010
Accounts Receivable (net)	$ 421,000	$ 392,000
Merchandise Inventory	312,000	285,000
Property and Equipment	2,504,000	2,200,000
Long-Term Liabilities	1,012,000	1,000,000
Stockholders' Equity	3,985,000	3,645,000
Sales (net)	1,852,000	1,688,000
Gross Profit	563,000	515,000
Net Income	197,000	185,000

Compute the following for 2011:

a. Accounts receivable turnover
b. Merchandise inventory turnover
c. Ratio of property and equipment to long-term liabilities
d. Rate of return on common stockholders' equity

5a,5b,5c,5d **LO**

PRACTICE EXERCISES
5a,5b,5c,5d

EXERCISE 23-8 The Stockholders' Equity section of the balance sheet of Jordan Corporation is as follows:

Stockholders' Equity		
Paid-in Capital:		
Common Stock, $5 par (100,000 shares		
authorized, 80,000 shares issued		
and outstanding)	$ 400,000	
Paid-in Capital in Excess of Par Value	140,000	
Total Paid-in Capital	$ 540,000	
Retained Earnings	290,000	
Total Stockholders' Equity		$830,000

Net income for the year is $123,000. Stockholders' equity was $879,000 at the beginning of the year. The present market price of the stock is $44 per share. Determine the following, rounding to two decimal places:

a. Equity per share
b. Rate of return on common stockholders' equity.
c. Earnings per share
d. Price-earnings ratio

Problem Set A

For additional help, see the demonstration problem at the beginning of each chapter in your Working Papers.

PROBLEM 23-1A During 2011, Ortiz's Jewelry Store, Inc., put on a sales promotion campaign that cost $9,672 more than it usually spent on advertising. Following is a condensed partial comparative income statement for the fiscal years ended December 31, 2011, and December 31, 2010.

Ortiz's Jewelry Store, Inc. Comparative Income Statement For Years Ended December 31, 2011 and December 31, 2010		
	2011	2010
Revenue from Sales:		
Sales	$376,760	$276,000
Less Sales Returns and Allowances	46,000	20,000
Net Sales	$330,760	$256,000
Cost of Goods Sold	205,140	156,000
Gross Profit	$125,620	$100,000
Operating Expenses:		
Selling Expenses	$ 66,925	$ 55,300
General Expenses	19,104	14,310
Total Operating Expenses	$ 86,029	$ 69,610
Income from Operations	$ 39,591	$ 30,390
Other Expenses	397	305
Income Before Income Taxes	$ 39,194	$ 30,085
Income Tax Expense	7,000	6,000
Net Income	$ 32,194	$ 24,085

Required
1. Using horizontal analysis, prepare a comparative income statement for the two-year period. Round percentages to three decimal places.
2. Comment on the percentages of increase or decrease.

Check Figure
Increase in Income Before Income Taxes, 30.3 percent

PROBLEM 23-2A Use the comparative income statement for Ortiz's Jewelry Store, Inc., presented in Problem 23–1A.

Required
1. Using vertical analysis, prepare a comparative income statement for the two-year period. Round percentages to three decimal places.
2. Comment on the percentage figures.

Check Figure
2010 percentage of Income Before Income Taxes to Net Sales, 11.8 percent

PROBLEM 23-3A The condensed comparative income statement of McCourt Manufacturing Corporation follows.

McCourt Manufacturing Corporation Comparative Income Statement For Years Ended December 31, 2009, 2010, 2011 (in thousands)			
	2009	2010	2011
Sales (net)	$15,000	$16,350	$17,101
Cost of Goods Sold	10,600	11,769	12,040
Gross Profit	$ 4,400	$ 4,581	$ 5,061
Operating Expenses:			
Selling Expenses	$ 2,142	$ 2,288	$ 2,437
General Expenses	1,390	1,392	1,397
Total Operating Expenses	$ 3,532	$ 3,680	$ 3,834
Income Before Income Taxes	$ 868	$ 901	$ 1,227
Income Tax Expense	295	306	417
Net Income	$ 573	$ 595	$ 810

Check Figure

2011 percentage of Net Income, 141.4 percent

Required

1. Express the income statement data in trend percentages. Round to the nearest tenth of a percent (three decimal places).
2. Comment on any significant relationships revealed by the percentages.

4a,4b,4c,4e, 5b,5c,5d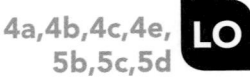

PROBLEM 23-4A Following are the year-end financial statements of Steve's Music Store.

Steve's Music Store Income Statement For Year Ended December 31, 2010		
Revenue from Sales:		
Sales		$567,000
Cost of Goods Sold:		
Merchandise Inventory, January 1, 2010	$ 84,000	
Delivered Cost of Purchases	353,200	
Cost of Goods Available for Sale	$437,200	
Less Merchandise Inventory, December 31, 2010	93,030	
Cost of Goods Sold		344,170
Gross Profit		$222,830
Operating Expenses:		
Selling Expenses (control)	$118,125	
General Expenses (control)	58,065	
Total Operating Expenses		176,190
Income from Operations		$ 46,640
Other Expenses:		
Interest Expense		7,200
Income Before Income Taxes		$ 39,440
Income Tax Expense		8,700
Net Income		$ 30,740

Steve's Music Store
Balance Sheet
December 31, 2010

Assets

Current Assets:

Cash	$ 23,430	
Notes Receivable	6,600	
Accounts Receivable (net)	85,470	
Merchandise Inventory	93,030	
Prepaid Expenses	1,980	
Total Current Assets		$210,510
Property and Equipment:		
Store Equipment (net)	$ 50,985	
Office Equipment (net)	15,510	
Delivery Equipment (net)	82,005	
Total Property and Equipment		148,500
Total Assets		$359,010

Liabilities

Current Liabilities:

Notes Payable	$ 3,960	
Accounts Payable	59,000	
Total Current Liabilities		$ 62,960
Long-Term Liabilities:		
Mortgage Payable (due June 30, 2015)		89,810
Total Liabilities		$152,770

Stockholders' Equity

Common Stock, $7 par (20,000 shares authorized and issued)	$140,000	
Retained Earnings	66,240	
Total Stockholders' Equity		206,240
Total Liabilities and Stockholders' Equity		$359,010

The current market price of common stock is $29.50 per share. At the beginning of the year, stockholders' equity was $192,000.

Required

Determine the following, showing the figures you used in your calculations (round to two decimal places):

Check Figure
Price-earnings ratio, 19.16

1. Working capital
2. Current ratio
3. Quick ratio
4. Merchandise inventory turnover
5. Number of days merchandise inventory kept in stock
6. Rate of return on common stockholders' equity
7. Earnings per share of common stock
8. Price-earnings ratio

Problem Set B

For additional help, see the demonstration problem at the beginning of each chapter in your Working Papers.

PROBLEM 23-1B During 2011, Bryant Design, Inc., put on a sales promotion campaign that cost $4,831 more than it usually spent for advertising. The condensed partial comparative income statement for the fiscal years ended December 31, 2011, and December 31, 2010, follows.

Bryant Design, Inc. Comparative Income Statement For Years Ended December 31, 2011 and December 31, 2010		
	2011	2010
Revenue from Sales:		
Sales	$ 320,500	$258,468
Less Sales Returns and Allowances	26,190	19,400
Net Sales	$ 294,310	$239,068
Cost of Goods Sold	167,105	139,254
Gross Profit	$127,205	$ 99,814
Operating Expenses:		
Selling Expenses	$ 57,891	$ 49,060
General Expenses	17,006	15,321
Total Operating Expenses	$ 74,897	$ 64,381
Income from Operations	$ 52,308	$ 35,433
Other Expenses	707	595
Income Before Income Taxes	$ 51,601	$ 34,838
Income Tax Expense	10,630	7,177
Net Income	$ 40,971	$ 27,661

Check Figure

Increase in Income Before
Income Taxes, 48.1 percent

Required

1. Using horizontal analysis, prepare a comparative income statement for the two-year period. Round percentages to three decimal places.
2. Comment on the percentages of increase or decrease.

 2 LO

PROBLEM 23-2B Use the comparative income statement for Bryant Design, Inc., presented in Problem 23–1B.

Check Figure

2009 percentage of
Income Before Income
Taxes to Net Sales, 14.6 percent

Required

1. Using vertical analysis, prepare a comparative income statement for the two-year period. Round percentages to three decimal places.
2. Comment on the percentage figures.

 3 LO

PROBLEM 23-3B Following is the condensed comparative income statement of Patrick Electric Corporation:

Patrick Electric Corporation Comparative Income Statement For Years Ended December 31, 2009, 2010, 2011 (in thousands)			
	2009	2010	2011
Sales (net)	$9,900	$10,175	$11,301
Cost of Goods Sold	5,700	5,861	6,791
Gross Profit	$4,200	$ 4,314	$ 4,510
Operating Expenses:			
Selling Expenses	$1,235	$ 1,249	$ 1,263
General Expenses	690	802	817
Total Operating Expenses	$1,925	$ 2,051	$ 2,080
Income Before Income Taxes	$2,275	$ 2,263	$ 2,430
Income Tax Expense	400	462	486
Net Income	$1,875	$ 1,801	$ 1,944

Check Figure

2011 percentage of
Net Income, 103.7 percent

Required

1. Express the income statement data in trend percentages. Round to the nearest tenth of a percent (three decimal places).
2. Comment on any significant relationships revealed by the percentages.

PROBLEM 23-4B Following are the year-end financial statements of Swick Corporation.

LO 4a,4b,4c, 4e,5b,5c,5d

Swick Corporation
Income Statement
For Year Ended December 31, 2010

Revenue from Sales:		
Sales		$536,000
Cost of Goods Sold:		
Merchandise Inventory, January 1, 2010	$102,000	
Delivered Cost of Purchases	314,000	
Cost of Goods Available for Sale	$416,000	
Less Merchandise Inventory, December 31, 2010	109,000	
Cost of Goods Sold		307,000
Gross Profit		$229,000
Operating Expenses:		
Selling Expenses (control)	$105,100	
General Expenses (control)	62,700	
Total Operating Expenses		167,800
Income from Operations		$ 61,200
Other Expenses:		
Interest Expense		5,740
Income Before Income Taxes		$ 55,460
Income Tax Expense		10,000
Net Income		$ 45,460

Swick Corporation
Balance Sheet
December 31, 2010

Assets		
Current Assets:		
Cash	$ 25,525	
Notes Receivable	5,400	
Accounts Receivable (net)	75,500	
Merchandise Inventory	109,000	
Prepaid Expenses	1,890	
Total Current Assets		$217,315
Property and Equipment:		
Store Equipment (net)	$ 42,120	
Office Equipment (net)	12,290	
Delivery Equipment (net)	69,400	
Total Property and Equipment		123,810
Total Assets		$341,125

Liabilities		
Current Liabilities:		
Notes Payable	$10,700	
Accounts Payable	32,025	
Total Current Liabilities		$ 42,725
Long-Term Liabilities:		
Mortgage Payable (due June 30, 2013)		92,400
Total Liabilities		$135,125

Stockholders' Equity		
Common Stock, $15 par (10,000 shares authorized and issued)	$150,000	
Retained Earnings	56,000	
Total Stockholders' Equity		206,000
Total Liabilities and Stockholders' Equity		$341,125

The current market price of common stock is $43 per share. At the beginning of the year, stockholders' equity was $174,000.

Check Figure
Price-earnings ratio, 9.45

Required

Determine the following, showing the figures you used in your calculations (round to two decimal places):

1. Working capital
2. Current ratio
3. Quick ratio
4. Merchandise inventory turnover
5. Number of days merchandise inventory kept in stock
6. Rate of return on common stockholders' equity
7. Earnings per share of common stock
8. Price-earnings ratio

ACTIVITIES

INTERNET LINKS TO ACCOUNTING

American Eagle Outfitters, Inc. specializes in high-quality, trendy clothing geared toward 15- to 25-year-olds. American Eagle Outfitters has over 1,100 mall-based stores nationwide and also sells a large amount of clothing online and through its *AE Magazine*. Let's take a look at American Eagle Outfitters, Inc.'s 2008 annual report and see how American Eagle Outfitters' financial statements look. Then we will compare those results with another company in the same industry, Abercrombie & Fitch, Inc. To view American Eagle Outfitters' 2008 annual report, visit http://phx.corporate-ir.net/phoenix.zhtml?c=81256&p=irol-homeprofile. Under the Investor Information section, click on Historical Annual Reports and you should find the 2008 Annual Report listed. Open the Annual Report and scroll down until you reach the consolidated statements of income on page 37 of the Annual Report. Using the consolidated statement of income, answer the following questions:

1. Does American Eagle Outfitters, Inc. present its comparative financial statements horizontally or vertically in its Annual Report?
2. What was American Eagle Outfitters' net income for each of the three years ended January 31, 2009, February 2, 2008, and February 3, 2007? What does that information tell you about how American Eagle Outfitters did over those three years?
3. Abercrombie & Fitch Co. reported net income of $272,255,000, $475,697,000, and $422,186,000 for the years ended January 31, 2009, February 2, 2008, and February 3, 2007, respectively. Compare these two companies by using the net income (loss) data for the three years. What trends do you see? Which company would you consider the better investment based on the information provided? Explain your reasoning.
4. We have compared two similar-size closing retailers. Would it be reasonable to compare American Eagle Outfitters, Inc. to a much smaller or larger clothing store? Why or why not?

WHAT'S WRONG WITH THIS PICTURE?

What if you see that purchases discounts for this year are 5 percent lower than for last year? Who would you talk to about it? What is happening? How has it affected your "bottom line"?

A QUESTION OF ETHICS

A manager of a company is evaluated on the gross profit percentage of his department. To boost sales, in spite of potential higher uncollectible accounts expense and company policy, he unduly extends more credit. Comment on this tactic.

Manufacturing Accounting

TESLA MOTORS INC., San Carlos, California

Tesla Motors Inc. is a Silicon Valley–based company that engineers and manufactures electric cars. The Tesla Roadster, the company's first vehicle, can travel 244 miles on a single charge of its lithium-ion battery pack and can accelerate from 0 to 60 mph in 3.7 seconds. The Roadster starts at a steep price of $109,000. However, many customers feel that the benefits of an electric car—decreased dependence on foreign oil, zero emissions, and a cost of less than two cents per mile driven—far outweigh the cost.

In addition to the Roadster, Tesla is currently working on manufacturing a more budget-friendly electric car, the Model S. With production scheduled to begin in late 2011, the Model S has an anticipated base price of $49,900 and will have a range of up to 300 miles.

In this chapter, we will learn about accounting for manufacturing companies such as Tesla Motors and how their accounting procedures differ from service and merchandising companies.

WHY IT MATTERS

LEARNING OBJECTIVES

After you have completed this chapter, you will be able to do the following:

1 Prepare a statement of cost of goods manufactured.

2 Complete a work sheet for a manufacturing enterprise and journalize the adjusting and closing entries.

3 Define a job-order cost accounting system and make the related entries.

4 Define a process cost accounting system and make the related entries.

ACCOUNTING LANGUAGE

Direct labor *(p. 954)*

Finished Goods Inventory *(p. 956)*

Indirect labor *(p. 955)*

Indirect materials *(p. 955)*

Job-order cost accounting system *(p. 963)*

Manufacturing overhead *(p. 955)*

Manufacturing Summary *(p. 957)*

Process cost accounting system *(p. 965)*

Raw materials *(p. 954)*

Raw Materials Inventory *(p. 955)*

Work-in-Process Inventory *(p. 956)*

In this chapter, we will discuss another type of business operation: manufacturing. The accounting principles we have already discussed pertain to manufacturing concerns, but manufacturers also have special procedures to account for manufacturing costs. We will describe how manufacturers determine the total cost of goods manufactured during each accounting period. To acquaint you with the end results, early in the chapter we present a statement of cost of goods manufactured. This statement will enable you to understand the function of the work sheet and its relationship to the financial statements. This chapter is only an introduction to accounting for manufacturing operations. As you continue your accounting education, you will have the opportunity to deal with more advanced systems and procedures.

COMPARISON OF INCOME STATEMENTS AND BALANCE SHEETS FOR MERCHANDISING AND MANUFACTURING ENTERPRISES

Manufacturing and merchandising companies have the same type of revenue accounts. However, a merchant buys goods in a finished condition and later sells them at a higher price in the same condition. A manufacturer, on the other hand, buys raw materials, transforms them into finished goods, and later sells the finished goods.

Income Statement

To compare the two types of companies, study the income statements for a merchandising firm and for a manufacturing firm shown in Figure 1.

A Merchandising Company, Inc.
Income Statement
For Year Ended December 31, 20—

Sales (net)		$2,500,000
Cost of Goods Sold:		
Merchandise Inventory, January 1, 20—	$ 390,000	
Delivered Cost of Purchases	1,200,000	
Cost of Goods Available for Sale	$1,590,000	
Less Merchandise Inventory, December 31, 20—	250,000	
Cost of Goods Sold		1,340,000
Gross Profit		$1,160,000
Operating Expenses:		
Selling Expenses (control)	$ 300,000	
General Expenses (control)	132,000	
Total Operating Expenses		432,000
Income from Operations		$ 728,000
Other Expenses:		
Interest Expense		18,000
Income Before Income Taxes		$ 710,000
Income Tax Expense		241,400
Net Income		$ 468,600

Bergman Manufacturing Company, Inc.
Income Statement
For Year Ended December 31, 20—

Sales (net)		$2,500,000
Cost of Goods Sold:		
Finished Goods Inventory, January 1, 20—	$ 390,000	
Cost of Goods Manufactured	1,200,000	
Cost of Goods Available for Sale	$1,590,000	
Less Finished Goods Inventory, December 31, 20—	250,000	
Cost of Goods Sold		1,340,000
Gross Profit		$1,160,000
Operating Expenses:		
Selling Expenses (control)	$ 300,000	
General Expenses (control)	132,000	
Total Operating Expenses		432,000
Income from Operations		$ 728,000
Other Expenses:		
Interest Expense		18,000
Income Before Income Taxes		$ 710,000
Income Tax Expense		241,400
Net Income		$ 468,600

FIGURE 1

Comparison of income statements for a merchandising and manufacturing firm

Merchandising Firm	Manufacturing Firm
Beginning Merchandise Inventory Plus Delivered Cost of Purchases	Beginning Finished Goods Inventory Plus Cost of Goods Manufactured
Cost of Goods Available for Sale Less Ending Merchandise Inventory	Cost of Goods Available for Sale Less Ending Finished Goods Inventory
Cost of Goods Sold	Cost of Goods Sold

Cost of Goods Manufactured for a manufacturer is the equivalent of Delivered Cost of Purchases for a merchandiser.

FYI

The main difference between accounting for a merchandising business and for a manufacturing business is in determining the cost of goods sold.

Statement of Cost of Goods Manufactured

LEARNING OBJECTIVE **1**

Prepare a statement of cost of goods manufactured.

As an illustration, we'll use the statement of cost of goods manufactured for Bergman Manufacturing Company, Inc., shown in Figure 2. **Because Cost of Goods Manufactured is included on the income statement, the accountant naturally prepares the statement of cost of goods manufactured first.** Notice that we have provided the income statement for Bergman Manufacturing Company, Inc., in Figure 1.

Elements of Manufacturing Costs

No matter what type of product a manufacturer produces, the three elements that make up the cost of the goods manufactured are *raw materials used*, *direct labor*, and *manufacturing overhead*.

Raw Materials Used　　Raw materials are the materials that enter directly into—and become a part of—the finished product. The delivered cost of these materials is Cost of Raw Materials Used. For example, if you are manufacturing tables, you need wood, glue, hardware, finishing materials, etc. Raw materials are also called *direct materials*.

Direct Labor　　Direct labor consists of the wages paid to factory employees who work—with machines or hand tools—directly on the materials to convert them into finished products. The manufacturer debits the Direct Labor account for the gross wages of those who work directly on the raw materials. The cost of direct labor varies directly with the level of production.

FIGURE 2

Statement of cost of goods manufactured for Bergman Manufacturing Company, Inc.

Bergman Manufacturing Company, Inc. Statement of Cost of Goods Manufactured For Year Ended December 31, 20—			
Work-in-Process Inventory, January 1, 20—			$ 140,000
Raw Materials:			
Raw Materials Inventory, January 1, 20—	$ 90,000		
Raw Materials Purchases (net)	230,000		
Cost of Raw Materials Available for Use	$320,000		
Less Raw Materials Inventory, December 31, 20—	100,000		
Cost of Raw Materials Used		$220,000	
Direct Labor		565,000	
Manufacturing Overhead:			
Indirect Labor	$106,000		
Supervisory Salaries	110,000		
Heat, Light, and Power	42,000		
Depreciation Expense, Factory Equipment	46,000		
Depreciation Expense, Factory Building	25,000		
Repairs and Maintenance	24,000		
Factory Insurance Expired	22,000		
Factory Supplies Used	14,000		
Miscellaneous Factory Costs	16,000		
Total Manufacturing Overhead		405,000	
Total Manufacturing Costs			1,190,000
Total Cost of Work-in-Process During Period			$1,330,000
Less Work-in-Process Inventory, December 31, 20—			130,000
Cost of Goods Manufactured			$1,200,000

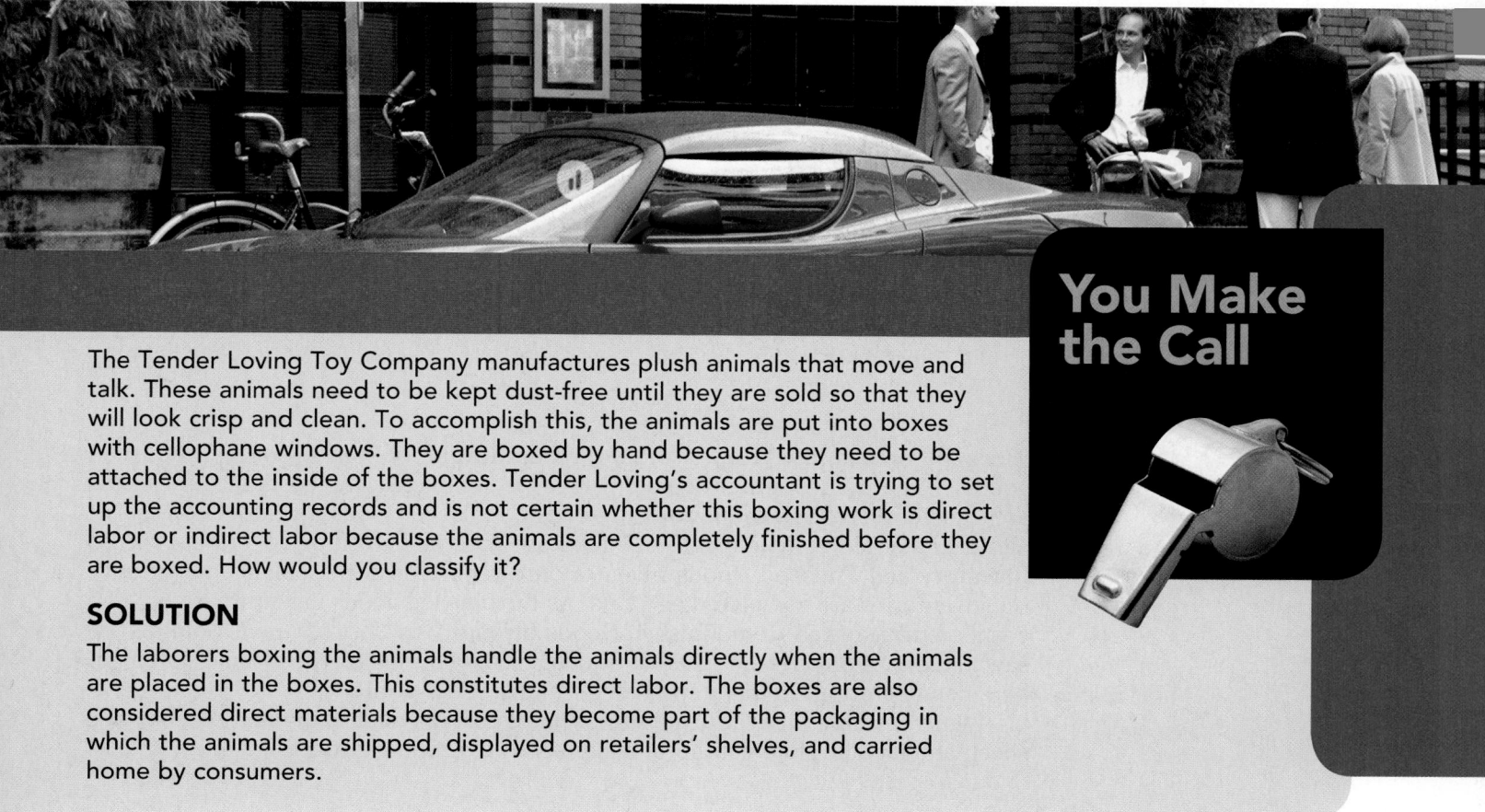

You Make the Call

The Tender Loving Toy Company manufactures plush animals that move and talk. These animals need to be kept dust-free until they are sold so that they will look crisp and clean. To accomplish this, the animals are put into boxes with cellophane windows. They are boxed by hand because they need to be attached to the inside of the boxes. Tender Loving's accountant is trying to set up the accounting records and is not certain whether this boxing work is direct labor or indirect labor because the animals are completely finished before they are boxed. How would you classify it?

SOLUTION

The laborers boxing the animals handle the animals directly when the animals are placed in the boxes. This constitutes direct labor. The boxes are also considered direct materials because they become part of the packaging in which the animals are shipped, displayed on retailers' shelves, and carried home by consumers.

Manufacturing Overhead **Manufacturing overhead** consists of manufacturing costs (other than raw materials used and direct labor) that cannot be traced directly to products being manufactured. A manufacturer uses Manufacturing Overhead as a control account. The specific titles of accounts in the manufacturing overhead subsidiary ledger vary from company to company. In Figure 2, the accounts in the manufacturing overhead ledger are Indirect Labor; Supervisory Salaries; Heat, Light, and Power; Depreciation Expense, Factory Equipment; Depreciation Expense, Factory Building; Repairs and Maintenance; Factory Insurance Expired; Factory Supplies Used; and Miscellaneous Factory Costs.

> **Remember**
>
> The cost of manufacturing any product consists of direct (raw) materials, direct labor, and manufacturing overhead.

   Indirect labor is the wages paid to those people who keep the plant in operation, rather than directly working on production. Examples are operations personnel, maintenance workers, and timekeepers.

   The balance of Factory Supplies Used reveals the cost of materials used to keep the plant in operation (oil, grease, and so on). These items are also called **indirect materials**.

   Other items that may be included in Manufacturing Overhead are taxes on factory building and equipment, taxes on raw materials and work-in-process inventories, patents written off, and small tools written off.

Balance Sheet

The balance sheet of a manufacturing firm will be very similar to that of a merchandising company. However, instead of one inventory account—Merchandising Inventory—there will be three inventory accounts listed on the balance sheet: Finished Goods Inventory, Work-in-Process Inventory, and Raw Materials Inventory. Shown in Figure 3 is the Current Assets section of the balance sheet for Bergman Manufacturing Company, Inc.

   Raw Materials Inventory consists of the direct materials not yet used. When raw materials, direct labor, and manufacturing overhead are used, this creates

FIGURE 3

Balance sheet for Bergman Manufacturing Company, Inc.

Bergman Manufacturing Company, Inc.
Balance Sheet
December 31, 20—

Current Assets:		
Cash		$124,000
Accounts Receivable	$180,000	
Less Allowance for Doubtful Accounts	6,000	174,000
Raw Materials Inventory		100,000
Work-in-Process Inventory		130,000
Finished Goods Inventory		250,000
Prepaid Insurance		3,000
Total Current Assets		$781,000

Work-in-Process Inventory. Work-in-Process Inventory consists of all unfinished goods. When the work-in-process inventory is completed, the costs of these items are transferred to **Finished Goods Inventory**. Finished Goods Inventory consists of all items that are complete but not sold. Raw Materials Inventory, Work-in-Process Inventory and Finished Goods Inventory are reported on the balance sheet until the inventories are completed and sold. As the finished goods inventory is sold, the costs are transferred from Finished Goods Inventory to Cost of Goods Sold. As we saw in Figure 1 on page 953, Cost of Goods Sold is reported on the income statement of a manufacturing company when determining gross profit.

Figure 4 summarizes how the statement of cost of goods manufactured, balance sheet, and income statement for a manufacturing firm tie in together.

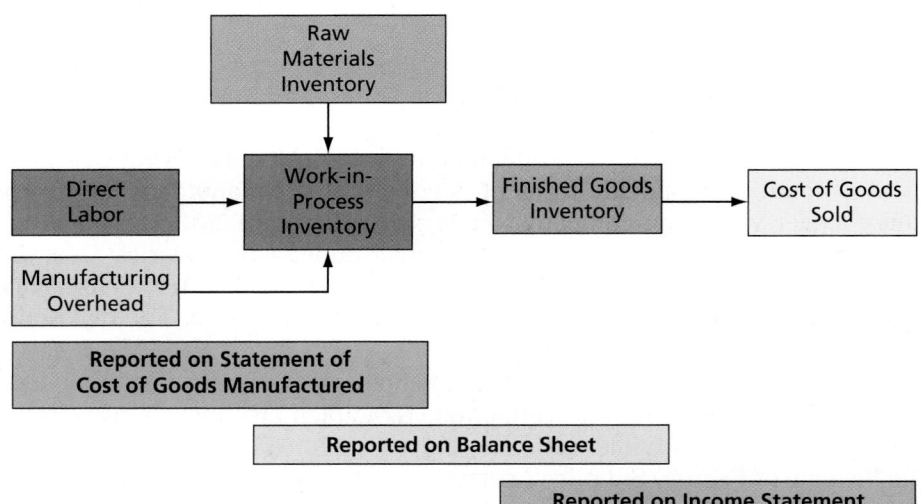

WORK SHEET FOR A MANUFACTURING FIRM

LEARNING OBJECTIVE 2

Complete a work sheet for a manufacturing enterprise and journalize the adjusting and closing entries.

Let's examine the work sheet for Bergman Manufacturing Company, Inc., shown in Figure 5 (pages 958–959). Notice that a manufacturer's work sheet must include two extra Debit and Credit columns headed Statement of Cost of Goods Manufactured. Notice also that all accounts in the Trial Balance columns representing manufacturing costs have debit balances, just as expense accounts have debit balances. Next, look at the adjusting entries for inventories. (We are assuming that Bergman Manufacturing Company, Inc., uses a periodic inventory system.) A manufacturer, like a merchandiser, takes two steps to adjust inventory: The accountant (1) takes off (or closes off) the beginning inventory and (2) adds on the ending inventory. However, in manufacturing accounting, remember that three inventories are involved: Raw Materials, Work-in-Process, and Finished Goods.

Adjusting Entries

Since Raw Materials Inventory and Work-in-Process Inventory appear in the statement of cost of goods manufactured, the accountant adjusts them using the **Manufacturing Summary** account, an account similar to Income Summary used to make adjustments to Raw Materials and Work-in-Process Inventory accounts and to close out all other manufacturing accounts. Since Finished Goods Inventory appears on the income statement, the accountant adjusts it using the Income Summary account. Finished Goods Inventory for a manufacturing firm is equivalent to Merchandise Inventory for a merchandising firm.

> The raw materials inventory and the work-in-process inventory are adjusted using the Manufacturing Summary account.
>
> **Remember**

Data for the adjustments are as follows:

a.–b. Raw materials inventory at December 31, $100,000

c.–d. Work-in-process inventory at December 31, $130,000

e.–f. Finished goods inventory at December 31, $250,000

In T account form, the adjusting entries for the inventory accounts are:

Raw Materials Inventory			
+		−	
Bal.	90,000	(a)	90,000
(b)	100,000		

Work-in-Process Inventory			
+		−	
Bal.	140,000	(c)	140,000
(d)	130,000		

Manufacturing Summary			
(a)	90,000	(b)	100,000
(c)	140,000	(d)	130,000

Finished Goods Inventory			
+		−	
Bal.	390,000	(e)	390,000
(f)	250,000		

Income Summary			
(e)	390,000	(f)	250,000

g. Depreciation of factory building, $25,000

h. Depreciation of factory equipment, $46,000

i. Expired factory insurance, $22,000 (assuming the unexpired portion had already been calculated)

j. Depreciation of office equipment, $5,000

k. Estimated uncollectible accounts, $6,000 (determined by an aging analysis)

l. Income tax, $241,400 (based on a taxable income before income taxes of $710,000; the accountant determined this by completing the Income Statement columns of the work sheet without including income tax expense)

> The adjustments, other than those for the inventory accounts, are like the ones we have already seen.
>
> **FYI**

Notice how the figures in the Adjustments columns are transferred to the remaining columns of the work sheet. Just as the accountant transfers the figures on the Income Summary line into the Income Statement columns as separate figures, he or she also transfers the four figures on the Manufacturing Summary lines into the Statement of Cost of Goods Manufactured columns as separate figures, like this:

> Cost of Goods Manufactured is the equivalent of Delivered Cost of Purchases for a merchandising firm.
>
> **Remember**

Account Name	Adjustments		Statement of Cost of Goods Manufactured		Income Statement	
	Debit	Credit	Debit	Credit	Debit	Credit
Manufacturing Summary	(a) 90 0 0 0 00	(b)100 0 0 0 00	90 0 0 0 00	100 0 0 0 00		
	(c) 140 0 0 0 00	(d)130 0 0 0 00	140 0 0 0 00	130 0 0 0 00		
Income Summary	(e)390 0 0 0 00	(f) 250 0 0 0 00			390 0 0 0 00	250 0 0 0 00

FIGURE 5   Work sheet for Bergman Manufacturing Company, Inc.

Account Name	Trial Balance Debit	Trial Balance Credit	Adjustments Debit	Adjustments Credit
Cash	124 0 0 0 00			
Notes Receivable	50 0 0 0 00			
Accounts Receivable	180 0 0 0 00			
Allowance for Doubtful Accounts		2 5 0 0 00		(k) 3 5 0 0 00
Raw Materials Inventory	90 0 0 0 00		(b) 100 0 0 0 00	(a) 90 0 0 0 00
Work-in-Process Inventory	140 0 0 0 00		(d) 130 0 0 0 00	(c) 140 0 0 0 00
Finished Goods Inventory	390 0 0 0 00		(f) 250 0 0 0 00	(e) 390 0 0 0 00
Prepaid Insurance	25 0 0 0 00			(i) 22 0 0 0 00
Land	316 0 0 0 00			
Factory Building	700 0 0 0 00			
Accumulated Deprec., Factory Building		250 0 0 0 00		(g) 25 0 0 0 00
Factory Equipment	360 0 0 0 00			
Accumulated Deprec., Factory Equipment		218 0 0 0 00		(h) 46 0 0 0 00
Office Equipment	62 0 0 0 00			
Accumulated Deprec., Office Equipment		40 0 0 0 00		(j) 5 0 0 0 00
Notes Payable		40 0 0 0 00		
Accounts Payable		55 5 5 0 00		
Dividends Payable		12 0 0 0 00		
Bonds Payable		280 0 0 0 00		
Common Stock		310 0 0 0 00		
Paid-in Capital in Excess of Par Value		100 0 0 0 00		
Retained Earnings		314 9 0 0 00		
Sales (net)		2,500 0 0 0 00		
Raw Materials Purchases	230 0 0 0 00			
Direct Labor	565 0 0 0 00			
Indirect Labor	106 0 0 0 00			
Supervisory Salaries	110 0 0 0 00			
Heat, Light, and Power	42 0 0 0 00			
Repairs and Maintenance	24 0 0 0 00			
Factory Supplies Used	14 0 0 0 00			
Miscellaneous Factory Costs	16 0 0 0 00			
Selling Expenses (control)	300 0 0 0 00			
General Expenses (control)	123 5 0 0 00		(j) 5 0 0 0 00 (k) 3 5 0 0 00	
Interest Expense	18 0 0 0 00			
Income Tax Expense	137 4 5 0 00		(l) 103 9 5 0 00	
	4,122 9 5 0 00	4,122 9 5 0 00		
Manufacturing Summary			(a) 90 0 0 0 00 (c) 140 0 0 0 00	(b) 100 0 0 0 00 (d) 130 0 0 0 00
Income Summary			(e) 390 0 0 0 00	(f) 250 0 0 0 00
Depreciation Expense, Factory Building			(g) 25 0 0 0 00	
Depreciation Expense, Factory Equipment			(h) 46 0 0 0 00	
Factory Insurance Expired			(i) 22 0 0 0 00	
Income Tax Payable				(l) 103 9 5 0 00
			1,305 4 5 0 00	1,305 4 5 0 00
Cost of Goods Manufactured				
Net Income				

Bergman Manufacturing Company, Inc.
Work Sheet
For Year Ended December 31, 20—

| Statement of Cost of Goods Manufactured | | Income Statement | | Balance Sheet | |
Debit	Credit	Debit	Credit	Debit	Credit
				124 0 0 0 00	
				50 0 0 0 00	
				180 0 0 0 00	
					6 0 0 0 00
				100 0 0 0 00	
				130 0 0 0 00	
				250 0 0 0 00	
				3 0 0 0 00	
				316 0 0 0 00	
				700 0 0 0 00	
					275 0 0 0 00
				360 0 0 0 00	
					264 0 0 0 00
				62 0 0 0 00	
					45 0 0 0 00
					40 0 0 0 00
					55 5 5 0 00
					12 0 0 0 00
					280 0 0 0 00
					310 0 0 0 00
					100 0 0 0 00
					314 9 0 0 00
			2,500 0 0 0 00		
230 0 0 0 00					
565 0 0 0 00					
106 0 0 0 00					
110 0 0 0 00					
42 0 0 0 00					
24 0 0 0 00					
14 0 0 0 00					
16 0 0 0 00					
		300 0 0 0 00			
		132 0 0 0 00			
		18 0 0 0 00			
		241 4 0 0 00			
90 0 0 0 00	100 0 0 0 00				
140 0 0 0 00	130 0 0 0 00				
		390 0 0 0 00	250 0 0 0 00		
25 0 0 0 00					
46 0 0 0 00					
22 0 0 0 00					
					103 9 5 0 00
1,430 0 0 0 00	230 0 0 0 00				
	1,200 0 0 0 00	1,200 0 0 0 00			
1,430 0 0 0 00	1,430 0 0 0 00	2,281 4 0 0 00	2,750 0 0 0 00	2,275 0 0 0 00	1,806 4 0 0 00
		468 6 0 0 00			468 6 0 0 00
		2,750 0 0 0 00	2,750 0 0 0 00	2,275 0 0 0 00	2,275 0 0 0 00

On the work sheet, the accountant transfers the cost of goods manufactured ($1,200,000, the difference between the debit and credit totals in the Statement of Cost of Goods Manufactured columns) to the Income Statement Debit column as shown in the following section of Bergman Manufacturing Company, Inc.'s, work sheet.

| Account Name | Statement of Cost of Goods Manufactured | | Income Statement | |
	Debit	Credit	Debit	Credit
	1,430 0 0 0 00	230 0 0 0 00		
Cost of Goods Manufactured		1,200 0 0 0 00	1,200 0 0 0 00	
	1,430 0 0 0 00	1,430 0 0 0 00	2,281 4 0 0 00	2,750 0 0 0 00
Net Income			468 6 0 0 00	
			2,750 0 0 0 00	2,750 0 0 0 00

The adjusting entries are provided in summary for Bergman Manufacturing Company in Figure 6 (page 961).

Closing Entries

Here are the steps to take in making the closing entries for a manufacturer:

STEP 1. Close the costs that appear on the statement of cost of goods manufactured into the Manufacturing Summary account.

STEP 2. Close the Manufacturing Summary account into the Income Summary account (by the amount of the cost of goods manufactured).

STEP 3. Close the revenue accounts into the Income Summary account.

STEP 4. Close the expense accounts into the Income Summary account.

STEP 5. Close the Income Tax Expense account into the Income Summary account.

STEP 6. Close the Income Summary account into the Retained Earnings account (by the amount of the net income).

Following are T accounts for Manufacturing Summary and Income Summary, labeled so that you can easily identify the manufacturing accounts recorded. The closing entries are also shown in Figure 6.

> **Remember**
>
> Manufacturing Summary is closed into Income Summary by the amount of the Cost of Goods Manufactured.

Manufacturing Summary

Raw Materials Inventory, Jan. 1	90,000	Raw Materials Inventory, Dec. 31	100,000
Work-in-Process Inventory, Jan. 1	140,000	Work-in-Process Inventory, Dec. 31	130,000
Raw Materials Purchases	230,000	Closing	1,200,000
Direct Labor	565,000	(To Income Summary)	
Indirect Labor	106,000		
Supervisory Salaries	110,000		
Heat, Light, and Power	42,000		
Repairs and Maintenance	24,000		
Factory Supplies Used	14,000		
Miscellaneous Factory Costs	16,000		
Depr. Expense, Factory Building	25,000		
Depr. Expense, Factory Equipment	46,000		
Factory Insurance Expired	22,000		
	1,430,000		**1,430,000**

Income Summary

Finished Goods Inventory, Jan. 1	390,000	Finished Goods Inventory, Dec. 31	250,000
Closing (From Manufacturing Summary)	1,200,000	Closing (Sales)	2,500,000
Closing (Expenses)	450,000		
Closing (Income Tax Expense)	241,400		
Closing (To Retained Earnings)	468,600		
	2,750,000		**2,750,000**

GENERAL JOURNAL   PAGE _____

Date		Description	Post. Ref.	Debit	Credit
20—		Adjusting Entries			
Dec.	31	Manufacturing Summary		90 0 0 0 00	
		Raw Materials Inventory			90 0 0 0 00
	31	Raw Materials Inventory		100 0 0 0 00	
		Manufacturing Summary			100 0 0 0 00
	31	Manufacturing Summary		140 0 0 0 00	
		Work-in-Process Inventory			140 0 0 0 00
	31	Work-in-Process Inventory		130 0 0 0 00	
		Manufacturing Summary			130 0 0 0 00
	31	Income Summary		390 0 0 0 00	
		Finished Goods Inventory			390 0 0 0 00
	31	Finished Goods Inventory		250 0 0 0 00	
		Income Summary			250 0 0 0 00
	31	Depreciation Expense, Factory Building		25 0 0 0 00	
		Accumulated Depreciation, Factory Building			25 0 0 0 00
	31	Depreciation Expense, Factory Equipment		46 0 0 0 00	
		Accumulated Depreciation, Factory Equipment			46 0 0 0 00
	31	Factory Insurance Expired		22 0 0 0 00	
		Prepaid Insurance			22 0 0 0 00
	31	General Expenses (control)		5 0 0 0 00	
		Accumulated Depreciation, Office Equipment			5 0 0 0 00
	31	General Expenses (control)		3 5 0 0 00	
		Allowance for Doubtful Accounts			3 5 0 0 00
	31	Income Tax Expense		103 9 5 0 00	
		Income Tax Payable			103 9 5 0 00

FIGURE 6

Adjusting and closing entries for Bergman Manufacturing Company, Inc.

(continued)

FIGURE 6
(concluded)

	GENERAL JOURNAL			PAGE _____

Date	Description	Post. Ref.	Debit	Credit
20—	Closing Entries			
Dec. 31	Manufacturing Summary		1,200 0 0 0 00*	
	Raw Materials Purchases			230 0 0 0 00
	Direct Labor			565 0 0 0 00
	Indirect Labor			106 0 0 0 00
	Supervisory Salaries			110 0 0 0 00
	Heat, Light, and Power			42 0 0 0 00
	Repairs and Maintenance			24 0 0 0 00
	Factory Supplies Used			14 0 0 0 00
	Miscellaneous Factory Costs			16 0 0 0 00
	Depreciation Expense, Factory Building			25 0 0 0 00
	Depreciation Expense, Factory Equipment			46 0 0 0 00
	Factory Insurance Expired			22 0 0 0 00
31	Income Summary		1,200 0 0 0 00	
	Manufacturing Summary			1,200 0 0 0 00*
31	Sales (net)		2,500 0 0 0 00	
	Income Summary			2,500 0 0 0 00
31	Income Summary		450 0 0 0 00	
	Selling Expenses (control)			300 0 0 0 00
	General Expenses (control)			132 0 0 0 00
	Interest Expense			18 0 0 0 00
31	Income Summary		241 4 0 0 00	
	Income Tax Expense			241 4 0 0 00
31	Income Summary		468 6 0 0 00	
	Retained Earnings			468 6 0 0 00

* Note: The December 31 closing entry credit to Manufacturing Summary is equal to Cost of Goods Manufactured (as shown on the work sheet). It is solely a coincidence that the December 31 debit entry to close the costs that appear on the statement of cost of goods manufactured is equal to the December 31 credit entry.

DETERMINING THE VALUE OF ENDING INVENTORIES

A manufacturer has to record the costs of the ending inventories for (1) raw materials, (2) work-in-process, and (3) finished goods. The manufacturer first lists these costs in the Adjustments columns of the work sheet and then carries the figures forward into the financial statement columns. Consider raw materials inventory and work-in-process inventory separately, because each poses a slightly different set of problems.

Raw Materials Inventory

The items that make up the raw materials inventory are in the same form they were in when the manufacturer bought them; nothing has been done to them yet. So the accountant first determines the quantities on hand and the unit costs and then figures the value of the inventory. The value of the ending inventory may be calculated by either FIFO, LIFO, or weighted-average-cost method. You may also use the lower-of-cost-or-market rule. These alternatives involve periodic and perpetual inventory systems.

A manufacturer may choose to use a *perpetual inventory system*, which provides a continuous or running balance of the firm's inventory. When a firm that uses a perpetual inventory system buys raw materials, it immediately debits Raw Materials Inventory for the cost of these materials. When the materials are put into production, the manufacturer credits Raw Materials Inventory for the cost of the materials used and debits Work-in-Process Inventory. The same debiting and crediting process goes on in the Work-in-Process Inventory and the Finished Goods Inventory accounts as the materials go through the manufacturing process. If a company keeps a perpetual inventory, it verifies the balance of the account periodically by physically counting the goods on hand. Any discrepancy that exists can be handled by an adjusting entry either debiting or crediting the Inventory account and either debiting or crediting the Cost of Goods Sold account.

Work-in-Process Inventory

How do you calculate the cost of the work-in-process inventory? We have seen that the cost of manufacturing any product consists of (1) *raw materials used*, (2) *direct labor expended*, and (3) *manufacturing overhead*. Therefore, the manufacturer keeps a record of the amount and cost of raw materials placed in production. The manufacturer also records the cost of direct labor expended on the ending work-in-process inventory.

The third item, manufacturing overhead, consists of a group of accounts such as Heat, Light, and Power; Repairs and Maintenance; and Miscellaneous Factory Costs; to name a few. The manufacturer cannot calculate the *exact* cost of manufacturing overhead included in the ending work-in-process inventory and must therefore estimate this cost. One way the firm does this is by using a percentage of the direct labor cost involved in the ending inventory. The reasoning here is that since manufacturing overhead is closely related to the level of production, and since the level of production varies directly with the amount of direct labor, the cost of manufacturing overhead should be regarded as a percentage of direct labor. For example, Heat, Light, and Power are part of manufacturing overhead and vary directly with the level of production.

You may determine the percentage for manufacturing overhead from the most recent statement of cost of goods manufactured. The manufacturing overhead rate for Bergman Manufacturing Company, Inc., is as follows:

$$\text{Manufacturing Overhead Rate} = \frac{\text{Manufacturing Overhead}}{\text{Direct Labor}} = \frac{\$405,000}{\$565,000} = 0.72 = \underline{\underline{72\%}} \text{ (rounded)}$$

In heavily computerized factories, machine time used or some other appropriate measure may be more accurate than direct labor in apportioning manufacturing overhead.

COST ACCOUNTING SYSTEMS FOR MANUFACTURING OPERATIONS

There are two principal cost accounting systems: (1) the job-order cost accounting system and (2) the process cost accounting system.

Job-Order Cost Accounting System

In a **job-order cost accounting system**, materials, labor, and overhead costs are accumulated *by the job or batch* on a job-order cost sheet as the batch is transferred through the various production departments. The job order may originate from a

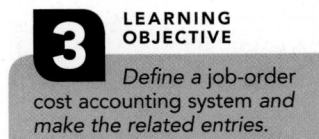

3 LEARNING OBJECTIVE
Define a job-order cost accounting system and make the related entries.

customer's request or be initiated by the company itself to increase its inventory of finished products. After the job is completed and included in the finished goods inventory, the cost per unit can be calculated by dividing the total costs of materials, labor, and overhead accumulated from each department by the total units completed in the job or batch. For each job order, there is a definite beginning and, when the objective has been achieved, a definite ending.

For example, one of the products made by Robles Manufacturing Company is bicycle pumps. The company has an order for 5,000 pumps. Robles Manufacturing sets up a subsidiary Work-in-Process Inventory account in the work-in-process subsidiary ledger and titles it Work in Process—Job Order 72. Work-in-Process Inventory is a control account, and the subsidiary ledger contains an account for each job order number. Following are typical entries pertaining to Job Order 72. These entries relate to a perpetual inventory system.

a. Purchased raw materials, $100,000, paying cash. (For simplicity, assume that all payments are made in cash.)

	GENERAL JOURNAL			PAGE _____
Date	Description	Post. Ref.	Debit	Credit
	Raw Materials Inventory		100 0 0 0 00	
	Cash			100 0 0 0 00

b. Placed $80,000 of raw materials into production.

Date	Description	Post. Ref.	Debit	Credit
	Work-in-Process Inventory		80 0 0 0 00	
	Raw Materials Inventory			80 0 0 0 00

c. Issued checks for direct labor, $40,000.

Date	Description	Post. Ref.	Debit	Credit
	Work-in-Process Inventory		40 0 0 0 00	
	Cash			40 0 0 0 00

d. Applied manufacturing overhead at the rate of 70 percent of direct labor.

Date	Description	Post. Ref.	Debit	Credit
	Work-in-Process Inventory		28 0 0 0 00	
	Manufacturing Overhead			28 0 0 0 00
	($40,000 x 0.70)			

e. Transferred completed production to Finished Goods Inventory.

Date	Description	Post. Ref.	Debit	Credit
	Finished Goods Inventory		148 0 0 0 00	
	Work-in-Process Inventory			148 0 0 0 00
	($80,000 + $40,000 + $28,000)			

To carry on its production, Robles Manufacturing must keep a variety of raw materials. Consequently, Raw Materials Inventory (sometimes called Materials) is a control account, and the materials ledger contains a separate account for each type of material. As mentioned before, since Robles Manufacturing may be working on a number of job orders at the same time, Work-in-Process Inventory is also a control account. Finally, Finished Goods Inventory is a control account, and the finished goods ledger contains a separate account for bicycle pumps as well as a separate account for each other product manufactured.

The entries involving the inventories in T account form are as follows:

General Ledger

Raw Materials Inventory		Work-in-Process Inventory		Finished Goods Inventory		Manufacturing Overhead		Cash	
Bal. xxx	(b) 80,000	Bal. xxx	(e) 148,000	Bal. xxx		Bal. xxx	(d) 28,000	Bal. xxx	(a) 100,000
(a) 100,000		(b) 80,000		(e) 148,000					(c) 40,000
		(c) 40,000							
		(d) 28,000							

Materials Ledger			Work-in-Process Ledger			Finished Goods Ledger	
Material A			**Job Order 72**			**Product No. 1**	
Bal. xx	(b) 60,000		Bal. xx	(e) 148,000		Bal. xx	
(a) 100,000			(b) 80,000			(e) 148,000	
			(c) 40,000				
Material B			(d) 28,000			**Product No. 2**	
Bal. xx	(b) 10,000		**Job Order 73**			Bal. xx	
Material C			Bal. xx			**Product No. 3**	
Bal. xx	(b) 10,000		**Job Order 74**			Bal. xx	
			Bal. xx				

Since the Manufacturing Overhead account is a control account, it will be debited when actual expenses are paid. Note that a variety of materials are used for Job Order 72. Note the output of Job Order 72 is Product No. 1.

Process Cost Accounting System

A **process cost accounting system** is used by manufacturers of homogeneous units (items that are exactly the same and are not distinguishable from one another) in a continuous production process. For example, the production of cement or flour is the result of a continuous process. Also, in the case of cement, one 90-pound bag of cement is the same as another 90-pound bag of cement.

Production of such goods is continuous and is completed in stages, with one department completing one stage and another department completing the next stage.

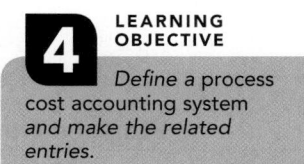

LEARNING OBJECTIVE

4

Define a process cost accounting system and make the related entries.

Companies whose product is homogeneous, such as this wheat processing plant, use a process cost accounting system. In this plant, one bag of grain is indistinguishable from the next.

Each department accumulates the costs of materials, labor, and overhead. As a result, in a process cost accounting system, costs are accumulated by department, in contrast to the job-order cost system, where costs are accumulated by the job or batch. The cost per unit of output in a process cost accounting system is calculated by dividing each department's costs of materials, labor, and overhead by the equivalent units of output processed in each department. The calculations of equivalent units and equivalent unit costs are complex calculations covered in a more advanced managerial or cost accounting text.

There is a Work-in-Process Inventory account for each department that is debited for the costs of materials, labor, and overhead used by that department. In the continuous process, the production of the first department is passed on to the second department. For example, assume that the production of rolled roofing takes place in two departments. The journal entry to record the transfer of $20,000 worth of inventory from the Work-in-Process Inventory—Department 1 to Work-in-Process Inventory—Department 2 would be recorded as follows:

FYI

Other industries using process cost accounting systems are producers of paper, aluminum, and soft drinks.

GENERAL JOURNAL   PAGE _____

Date	Description	Post. Ref.	Debit	Credit
	Work-in-Process Inventory—			
	Department 2		20 0 0 0 00	
	Work-in-Process Inventory—			
	Department 1			20 0 0 0 00

Notice that the first department's total cost is debited to the second department's Work-in-Process Inventory account. The flow of production from Department 1 to Department 2 and ending up in Finished Goods Inventory is illustrated in T accounts using symbolic amounts. Note that additional raw materials have been added in Department 2.

Work-in-Process Inventory—Department 1

Raw Materials	10,000	To Department 2	20,000
Direct Labor	5,000		
Manufacturing Overhead	5,000		

Work-in-Process Inventory—Department 2

From		To Finished	
Department 1	20,000	Goods	27,000
Raw Materials	1,000		
Direct Labor	2,000		
Manufacturing Overhead	4,000		

Finished Goods Inventory

From Department 227,000	

CHAPTER REVIEW

Study & Practice

LEARNING OBJECTIVE

1 *Prepare a statement of cost of goods manufactured.*

The statement of cost of goods manufactured includes the beginning work-in-process inventory, plus the cost of **raw materials** used, plus **direct labor**, plus **manufacturing overhead**, less the ending work-in-process inventory.

PRACTICE EXERCISE 1

Prepare a statement of cost of goods manufactured for Jackson Manufacturing Company, using any of the following balances that you need:

Raw Materials Purchases (net)	$521,000
Raw Materials Inventory, January 31	63,000
Raw Materials Inventory, January 1	22,350
Work-in-Process Inventory, January 1	267,500
Work-in-Process Inventory, January 31	189,000
Finished Goods Inventory, January 31	234,000
Direct Labor	789,000
Manufacturing Overhead	454,000
Finished Goods Inventory, January 1	223,000

PRACTICE EXERCISE 1 SOLUTION

Jackson Manufacturing Company
Statement of Cost of Goods Manufactured
For Month Ended January 31, 20—

Work-in-Process Inventory, January 1, 20—			$ 267,500
Raw Materials:			
Raw Materials Inventory, January 1, 20—	$ 22,350		
Raw Materials Purchases (net)	521,000		
Cost of Raw Materials Available for Use	$543,350		
Less Raw Materials Inventory, January 31, 20—	63,000		
Cost of Raw Materials Used		$480,350	
Direct Labor		789,000	
Manufacturing Overhead		454,000	
Total Manufacturing Costs			1,723,350
Total Cost of Work-in-Process During Period			$1,990,850
Less Work-in-Process Inventory, January 31, 20—			189,000
Cost of Goods Manufactured			$1,801,850

LEARNING OBJECTIVE

2

Complete a work sheet for a manufacturing enterprise and journalize the adjusting and closing entries.

A work sheet for a manufacturing company contains an extra pair of columns entitled "Statement of Cost of Goods Manufactured." Manufacturing costs—Raw Materials Purchases, Direct Labor, and Manufacturing Overhead account balances— are recorded in the Debit column. Debit amounts recorded in the **Manufacturing Summary** account (representing the beginning balances of **Raw Materials Inventory** and **Work-in-Process Inventory**) are listed in the Statement of Cost of Goods Manufactured Debit column. Credit amounts recorded in the Manufacturing Summary account (representing the ending balances of Raw Materials Inventory and Work-in-Process Inventory) are listed in the Statement of Cost of Goods Manufactured Credit column. The difference between the Statement of Cost of Goods Manufactured Debit and Credit columns is the amount of the cost of goods manufactured, and this amount is recorded as a credit to balance off the columns. The amount of the cost of goods manufactured is also recorded in the Income Statement Debit column.

PRACTICE EXERCISE 2

From the following information, journalize the closing entries for Pope Manufacturing Company.

Account Name	Statement of Cost of Goods Manufactured		Income Statement	
	Debit	Credit	Debit	Credit
Sales				140 0 0 0 00
Raw Materials Purchases	42 0 0 0 00			
Direct Labor	48 0 0 0 00			
Indirect Labor	1 0 0 0 00			
Heat, Light, and Power	4 0 0 00			
Miscellaneous Factory Costs	6 0 0 00			
Selling Expenses (control)			12 0 0 0 00	
General Expenses (control)			11 0 0 0 00	
Income Tax Expense			11 2 6 0 00	
Manufacturing Summary	6 0 0 0 00	9 0 0 0 00		
	16 2 0 0 00	38 0 0 0 00		
Income Summary			10 0 0 0 00	14 0 0 0 00
	114 2 0 0 00	47 0 0 0 00		
Cost of Goods Manufactured		67 2 0 0 00	67 2 0 0 00	
	114 2 0 0 00	114 2 0 0 00	111 4 6 0 00	154 0 0 0 00
Net Income			42 5 4 0 00	
			154 0 0 0 00	154 0 0 0 00

PRACTICE EXERCISE 2 SOLUTION

		GENERAL JOURNAL	PAGE _____		
Date		Description	Post. Ref.	Debit	Credit
20—		Closing Entries			
Dec.	31	Manufacturing Summary		92 0 0 0 00	
		Raw Materials Purchases			42 0 0 0 00
		Direct Labor			48 0 0 0 00
		Indirect Labor			1 0 0 0 00
		Heat, Light, and Power			4 0 0 00
		Misc. Factory Costs			6 0 0 00
	31	Income Summary		67 2 0 0 00	
		Manufacturing Summary			67 2 0 0 00
	31	Sales (net)		140 0 0 0 00	
		Income Summary			140 0 0 0 00
	31	Income Summary		23 0 0 0 00	
		Selling Expenses (control)			12 0 0 0 00
		General Expenses (control)			11 0 0 0 00
	31	Income Summary		11 2 6 0 00	
		Income Tax Expense			11 2 6 0 00
		($18,500 x 0.80)			
	31	Income Summary		42 5 4 0 00	
		Retained Earnings			42 5 4 0 00

LEARNING OBJECTIVE

Define a job-order cost accounting system and make the related entries.

A **job-order cost accounting system** is used by manufacturers producing distinct products in jobs or batches of a specified number of units. Each batch of units is given a job-order number. The costs of production (raw materials, direct labor, and manufacturing overhead) are debited to the account for that job-order number in the work-in-process inventory subsidiary ledger. When the job is completed, the **Finished Goods Inventory** account is debited and the Work-in-Process Inventory account is credited.

PRACTICE EXERCISE 3

South Beach Manufacturing Company manufactures plastic figurines and uses a job-order cost accounting system. Record the journal entries for the following transactions. (Assume that South Beach uses a perpetual inventory system.)

a. Purchased raw materials, $40,000, paying cash.
b. Placed $25,000 of raw materials into production.
c. Issued checks for direct labor, $18,500.
d. Applied manufacturing overhead at the rate of 80 percent of direct labor.
e. Transferred completed production to Finished Goods Inventory.

PRACTICE EXERCISE 3 SOLUTION

		GENERAL JOURNAL								PAGE _____				
Date		Description	Post. Ref.	Debit						Credit				
	a.	Raw Materials Inventory		40	0	0	0	00						
		Cash								40	0	0	0	00
	b.	Work-in-Process Inventory		25	0	0	0	00						
		Raw Materials Inventory								25	0	0	0	00
	c.	Work-in-Process Inventory		18	5	0	0	00						
		Cash								18	5	0	0	00
	d.	Work-in-Process Inventory		14	8	0	0	00						
		Manufacturing Overhead								14	8	0	0	00
		($18,000 × 0.80)												
	e.	Finished Goods Inventory		58	3	0	0	00						
		Work-in-Process Inventory								58	3	0	0	00
		($25,000 + $18,500 + $14,800)												

4 LEARNING OBJECTIVE

Define a process cost accounting system and make the related entries.

A **process cost accounting system** is used by manufacturers whose production involves a continuous process. The output consists of homogeneous units. The production flows from one department to another department. A Work-in-Process Inventory account is set up for each department to record the costs of production. The entry to record the passing on of production from one department to another is a debit to the second department's Work-in-Process Inventory account and a credit to the first department's Work-in-Process Inventory account. Upon completion of the last stage of production, the entry is a debit to Finished Goods Inventory and a credit to the last department's Work-in-Process Inventory account.

PRACTICE EXERCISE 4

X-Factor Manufacturing Company produces steel. The company uses a process cost accounting system. Assume that production of the steel is completed in two departments—Department A and Department B. Record the transaction to transfer inventory worth $134,250 from Department A to Department B.

PRACTICE EXERCISE 4 SOLUTION

Date	Description	Post. Ref.	Debit					Credit				
	Work-in-Process Inventory—											
	Department B		134	2	5	0	00					
	Work-in-Process Inventory—											
	Department A							134	2	5	0	00

Before a Test Check: Chapters 22–24

PART I: TRUE/FALSE

T F **1.** A company acquired a long-lived asset by issuing $480,000 par-value common stock. This event is listed under Financing Activities in a statement of cash flows.

T F **2.** It is possible for a business to have a net loss and still have a positive cash flow.

T F **3.** Money market accounts are listed as a part of cash on a statement of cash flows.

T F **4.** Cash payments to owners would be listed under Operating Activities in a statement of cash flows.

T F **5.** Generally, the lower the current ratio, the lower the risk to creditors.

T F **6.** Presenting each asset as a percentage of total assets is an example of horizontal analysis.

T F **7.** When vertical analysis is applied to the income statement, net sales is used as the base.

T F **8.** A company's solvency is its ability to pay its debt.

T F **9.** In manufacturing accounting, two inventories are involved: Raw Materials Inventory and Finished Goods Inventory.

T F **10.** The statement of costs of goods manufactured supports the income statement by providing the figure for cost of goods sold.

T F **11.** The Manufacturing Summary account is closed by an entry debiting the Income Summary account and crediting the Manufacturing Summary account.

T F **12.** Supervisory salaries are part of manufacturing overhead.

PART II: COMPLETION

1. The _____ method involves adjusting net income to determine cash flows from operating activities.

2. When preparing the Operating Activities section of the statement of cash flows using the indirect method, Gain on Disposal of Property and Equipment is _____ to (from) Net Income.

3. When preparing the Operating Activities section of the statement of cash flows using the indirect method, a decrease in the Accounts Payable account is _____ to (from) Net Income.

4. Merchandise Inventory Turnover = $\dfrac{\rule{3cm}{0.4pt}}{\text{Average Merchandise Inventory}}$.

5. Quick Ratio = $\dfrac{\rule{2cm}{0.4pt}}{\text{Current Liabilities}}$.

6. Accounts Receivable Turnover = $\dfrac{\rule{3cm}{0.4pt}}{\text{Average Accounts Receivable}}$.

7. Working Capital = _____ – Current Liabilities.

8. In a _____ cost accounting system, raw materials, direct labor, and manufacturing overhead costs are accumulated by the job.

9. _____ consists of all manufacturing costs that cannot be traced directly to products being manufactured.

10. Raw materials and work-in-process inventories are adjusted using the _____ account.

PART III: APPLICATION

A. Statement of Cash Flows

1. Shakespeare Corporation reported net income $60,000 for 2011. Depreciation Expense of $10,000 was included on the income statement. The December 31 balances of current assets and current liabilities follow:

	2011	2010
Accounts Receivable	$23,500	$22,000
Merchandise Inventory	15,000	25,000
Prepaid Insurance	5,400	6,200
Accounts Payable	7,300	9,000
Salaries Payable	5,300	2,800

Prepare the Operating Activities section of the statement of cash flows for Shakespeare Corporation.

2. Porter Corporation reported net income of $215,784 for 2011. The December 31 balances of select accounts follow.

	2011	2010
Land	$157,450	—
Equipment	78,220	$80,690
Accumulated Depreciation, Equipment	26,135	22,140
Notes Payable	12,690	19,690
Retained Earnings	78,420	105,200

The following additional information was taken from Porter Corporation's records:

a. Depreciation Expense for the year was $4,745.
b. Land was acquired with cash.
c. Porter sold equipment for $1,000, realizing a loss of $720.
d. A partial payment on the non-interest-bearing note payable was made.
e. Payment of dividends made for $242,564.

Prepare the Investing and Financing Activities sections of the statement of cash flows for Porter Corporation.

B. Financial Statement Analysis

1. Compute the current ratio if current assets are $210,000 and current liabilities are $202,000.
2. Compute working capital if total liabilities equal $400,000, long-term liabilities are $200,000, and current assets are $500,000.

C. Manufacturing Accounting

From the following balances, determine the cost of goods manufactured:

Cost of Goods Sold	$191,000
Finished Goods Inventory, January 1	459,745
Finished Goods Inventory, December 31	620,000

ANSWERS: PART I

1. F; **2.** T; **3.** T; **4.** F; **5.** F; **6.** F; **7.** T; **8.** T; **9.** F; **10.** F; **11.** T;
12. T

ANSWERS: PART II

1. indirect; **2.** subtracted; **3.** subtracted; **4.** Cost of Goods Sold; **5.** Quick Assets; **6.** Net Sales on Account; **7.** Current Assets; **8.** job-order; **9.** Manufacturing overhead; **10.** Manufacturing Summary

ANSWERS: PART III

A. 1.

Shakespeare Corporation Statement of Cash Flows For Year Ended December 31, 2011		
Cash Flows from (used by) Operating Activities:		
Net Income		$60,000
Add (Deduct) Items to Convert Net Income		
from Accrual Basis to Cash Basis:		
Depreciation Expense	$10,000	
Increase in Accounts Receivable	(1,500)	
Decrease in Merchandise Inventory	10,000	
Decrease in Prepaid Insurance	800	
Decrease in Accounts Payable	(1,700)	
Increase in Salaries Payable	2,500	20,100
Net Cash Flows from Operating Activities		$80,100

2.

Porter Corporation Statement of Cash Flows For Year Ended December 31, 2011		
Cash Flows from (used by) Investing Activities:		
Purchase of Land	$ (157,450)	
Sale of Equipment	1,000	
Net Cash Flows used by Investing Activities		$(156,450)
Cash Flows from (used by) Financing Activities:		
Payment on Note	$ (7,000)	
Payment of Dividends	(242,564)	
Net Cash Flows used by Financing Activities		$(249,564)

B. 1. 1.04 ($210,000 / $202,000); **2.** $300,000 [$500,000 − ($400,000 − $200,000)]
C. $351,255 ($191,000 + $620,000 − $459,745)

Glossary

Direct labor Wages paid to factory employees who work—with machines or hand tools—directly on raw materials to convert them into finished products. (p. 954)

Finished Goods Inventory All items that are complete but not sold. (p. 956)

Indirect labor The cost of work performed by workers who keep the plant in operation—such as operations personnel, factory maintenance workers, and timekeepers—rather than by workers who are directly occupied with production; considered part of manufacturing overhead. (p. 955)

Indirect materials Factory supplies, such as oil, grease, and cleaning fluids, used to keep the plant in operation; considered part of manufacturing overhead. (p. 955)

Job-order cost accounting system A product costing system used by companies making products in batches. Raw materials, direct labor, and manufacturing overhead costs are assigned to specific job orders. (p. 963)

Manufacturing overhead All manufacturing costs that cannot be traced directly to products being manufactured. Examples: heat, light, and power; repairs and maintenance; indirect labor; indirect materials. (p. 955)

Manufacturing Summary An account used to make adjustments to Raw Materials Inventory and

Work-in-Process Inventory accounts and to close all other manufacturing accounts. *(p. 957)*

Process cost accounting system A product costing system used by companies that maintain a continuous production flow. Manufacturing costs are assigned to departments that complete successive stages of production. *(p. 965)*

Raw materials The materials (also called *direct materials*) that enter directly into and become a part of the finished product. *(p. 954)*

Raw Materials Inventory Direct materials not yet used. *(p. 955)*

Work-in-Process Inventory All unfinished goods. *(p. 956)*

CHAPTER ASSIGNMENTS

Discussion Questions

1. In manufacturing operations, how do direct materials differ from indirect materials?
2. Which inventory accounts appear on a company's statement of cost of goods manufactured, and which appear on its income statement?
3. Compare the Manufacturing Summary account with the Income Summary account.
4. Why is cost of goods manufactured entered in the Statement of Cost of Goods Manufactured Credit and the Income Statement Debit columns on a work sheet?
5. Compare cost of goods manufactured for a manufacturing business with cost of goods sold for a merchandising business.
6. List six examples of manufacturing overhead accounts.
7. Is it possible for paint to be considered an indirect material for one company and a direct material for another company?
8. Does the Manufacturing Summary account have a balance during the fiscal period? Explain your answer.

Exercises

EXERCISE 24-1 From the following balances, determine the cost of goods manufactured:

PRACTICE EXERCISE 1

Cost of Goods Sold	$3,540,000
Finished Goods Inventory, March 1	850,000
Finished Goods Inventory, March 31	682,000

EXERCISE 24-2 Prepare a statement of cost of goods manufactured for Tina's Tiny Toys Manufacturing Company, using any of the following balances that you need:

PRACTICE EXERCISE 1

Raw Materials Purchases	$632,000
Raw Materials Inventory, June 30	74,000
Raw Materials Inventory, June 1	43,000
Work-in-Process Inventory, June 1	230,000
Work-in-Process Inventory, June 30	302,000
Finished Goods Inventory, June 30	122,000
Direct Labor	901,000
Manufacturing Overhead	676,000
Finished Goods Inventory, June 1	134,000

EXERCISE 24-3 Following are the Statement of Cost of Goods Manufactured columns and the Income Statement columns of the work sheet for Ranell Manufacturing Company for the year ended December 31. Ranell Manufacturing Company's beginning inventory of raw materials is $8,000; its beginning inventory of work-in-process is $38,400. Prepare a statement of cost of goods manufactured.

PRACTICE EXERCISE 1

Account Name	Statement of Cost of Goods Manufactured		Income Statement	
	Debit	Credit	Debit	Credit
Sales				360 0 0 0 00
Raw Materials Purchases	64 0 0 0 00			
Direct Labor	160 0 0 0 00			
Indirect Labor	3 2 0 0 00			
Heat, Light, and Power	1 6 0 0 00			
Miscellaneous Factory Costs	8 0 0 00			
Selling Expenses (control)			34 0 0 0 00	
General Expenses (control)			14 0 0 0 00	
Income Tax Expense			22 4 8 0 00	
Manufacturing Summary	8 0 0 0 00	12 0 0 0 00		
	38 4 0 0 00	40 0 0 0 00		
Income Summary			32 0 0 0 00	36 0 0 0 00
	276 0 0 0 00	52 0 0 0 00		
Cost of Goods Manufactured		224 0 0 0 00	224 0 0 0 00	
	276 0 0 0 00	276 0 0 0 00	326 4 8 0 00	396 0 0 0 00
Net Income			69 5 2 0 00	
			396 0 0 0 00	396 0 0 0 00

EXERCISE 24-4 From the information in Exercise 24-3, journalize the closing entries for Ranell Manufacturing Company.

LO 2

PRACTICE EXERCISE 2

EXERCISE 24-5 From the following balances, determine the cost of the raw materials used:

LO 1

PRACTICE EXERCISE 1

Raw Materials Purchases	$1,621,000
Raw Materials Inventory, August 31	479,000
Raw Materials Inventory, August 1	356,000

EXERCISE 24-6 From the following balances, calculate the total manufacturing costs, which contain the following three elements:

LO 2

PRACTICE EXERCISE 2

Raw Materials Used	$341,000
Direct Labor	274,000
Manufacturing Overhead (60% of direct labor cost)	

EXERCISE 24-7 Henry Corporation manufactures electric staplers and uses a job-order cost accounting system. Record the journal entries for the following transactions. (Assume that Henry uses a perpetual inventory system.)

LO 3

PRACTICE EXERCISE 3

a. Purchased raw materials, $132,000, paying cash.
b. Placed $67,000 of raw materials into production.
c. Issued checks for direct labor, $58,250.

d. Applied manufacturing overhead at the rate of 65 percent of direct labor.
e. Transferred completed production to Finished Goods Inventory.

EXERCISE 24-8 Quick Dry Paint Manufacturing Company produces household paint.
The company uses a process cost accounting system. Assume that production of the
paint is completed in two departments—the Mixing Department and the Canning
Department. Record the transaction to transfer inventory worth $267,450 from the
Mixing Department to the Canning Department.

PRACTICE EXERCISE 4

Problem Set A

For additional help, see the demonstration problem at the beginning of each chapter
in your Working Papers.

PROBLEM 24-1A Following is the statement of cost of goods manufactured for
Vermont Manufacturing Company.

Vermont Manufacturing Company Statement of Cost of Goods Manufactured For Year Ended December 31, 20—			
Work-in-Process Inventory, January 1, 20—			$ 228,000
Raw Materials:			
Raw Materials Inventory, January 1, 20—	$ 575,000		
Raw Materials Purchases (net)	741,000		
Cost of Raw Materials Available for Use	$1,316,000		
Less Raw Materials Inventory, December 31, 20—	503,500		
Cost of Raw Materials Used		$ 812,500	
Direct Labor		1,140,000	
Manufacturing Overhead:			
Indirect Labor	$ 209,000		
Supervisory Salaries	180,500		
Depreciation Expense, Factory Equipment	123,500		
Heat, Light, and Power	36,100		
Depreciation Expense, Factory Building	35,720		
Repairs and Maintenance	26,980		
Factory Supplies Used	22,800		
Factory Insurance Expired	16,720		
Property Tax on Factory Building	13,680		
Miscellaneous Factory Costs	12,160		
Total Manufacturing Overhead		677,160	
Total Manufacturing Costs			2,629,660
Total Cost of Work-in-Process During Period			$2,857,660
Less Work-in-Process Inventory, December 31, 20—			494,000
Cost of Goods Manufactured			$2,363,660

Check Figure
Amount to close Manufacturing
Summary into Income Summary,
$2,363,660

Required

1. Journalize, using page 116 of the general journal, the adjusting entries for Raw
    Materials Inventory and Work-in-Process Inventory.
2. Journalize the closing entries for manufacturing costs.
3. Post the entries to the Manufacturing Summary account, No. 511.
4. Journalize and post the entry to close the Manufacturing Summary account.

PROBLEM 24-2A Following is the trial balance of Rashid Products Company, Inc., as of December 31 of this year.

 LO 1,2

Rashid Products Company, Inc. Trial Balance December 31, 20—		
Account Name	Debit	Credit
Cash	4,620	
Accounts Receivable	39,380	
Allowance for Doubtful Accounts		1,595
Raw Materials Inventory	49,500	
Work-in-Process Inventory	78,430	
Finished Goods Inventory	75,020	
Prepaid Factory Insurance	1,980	
Machinery	145,700	
Accumulated Depreciation, Machinery		46,200
Accounts Payable		32,230
Common Stock		110,000
Paid-in Capital in Excess of Stated Value		22,000
Retained Earnings		77,000
Sales		702,625
Raw Materials Purchases	77,000	
Direct Labor	180,670	
Indirect Labor	87,890	
Heat, Light, and Power	17,600	
Machinery Repairs	9,900	
Selling Expenses (control)	153,945	
General Expenses (control)	66,055	
Income Tax Expense	3,960	
	991,650	991,650

You are given the following information for the adjustments:

a.–f. Year-end inventories: raw materials, $46,300; work-in-process, $68,740; finished goods, $75,175.

g. Allowance for Doubtful Accounts to be increased by $890 [debit General Expenses (control)].

h. Estimated depreciation of factory machinery, $11,625.

i. A study of the company's insurance policies shows that $1,430 of factory insurance expired during the year.

j. Accrued direct labor, $350; accrued indirect labor, $180; accrued sales commissions, $190 (credit Wages and Commissions Payable).

k. Additional income tax, $1,429.

Required
1. Prepare a work sheet.
2. Prepare a statement of cost of goods manufactured.
3. Prepare an income statement.

Check Figure
Net Income, $76,776

1,2  **LO**

PROBLEM 24-3A Following are the columns reflecting the statement of cost of goods manufactured and the income statement from the work sheet of Southeast Container Company, Inc., as of December 31, the end of the fiscal year. Beginning inventory of raw materials is $131,328; beginning inventory of work in process is $236,360.

Account Name	Statement of Cost of Goods Manufactured		Income Statement	
	Debit	Credit	Debit	Credit
Sales				2,849 9 2 4 00
Sales Returns and Allowances			23 5 6 0 00	
Sales Discounts			22 4 2 0 00	
Selling Expenses (control)			341 0 3 1 00	
General Expenses (control)			138 4 3 4 00	
Raw Materials Purchases	730 5 5 0 00			
Direct Labor	917 5 1 0 00			
Indirect Labor	210 1 7 8 00			
Heat, Light, and Power	51 2 6 2 00			
Factory Supervision	51 2 0 5 00			
Rent, Factory	30 4 0 0 00			
Machinery Repairs	30 2 1 0 00			
Depreciation Expense, Machinery	30 0 9 6 00			
Factory Supplies Used	11 7 8 0 00			
Factory Insurance Expired	7 2 2 0 00			
Small Tools Expense	2 3 9 4 00			
Miscellaneous Factory Costs	1 2 9 2 00			
Loss on Disposal of Equipment			16 3 4 0 00	
Interest Expense			12 9 2 0 00	
Income Tax Expense			81 7 0 0 00	
Manufacturing Summary	131 3 2 8 00	136 0 4 0 00		
	236 3 6 0 00	240 3 3 1 00		
Income Summary			344 6 6 0 00	354 7 6 8 00
	2,441 7 8 5 00	376 3 7 1 00		
Cost of Goods Manufactured		2,065 4 1 4 00	2,065 4 1 4 00	
	2,441 7 8 5 00	2,441 7 8 5 00	3,046 4 7 9 00	3,204 6 9 2 00
Net Income			158 2 1 3 00	
			3,204 6 9 2 00	3,204 6 9 2 00

Check Figure

Income from Operations, $269,173

Required

1. Prepare a statement of cost of goods manufactured.
2. Prepare an income statement.
3. Journalize the adjusting entries for the inventories.
4. Journalize the closing entries.

PROBLEM 24-4A Following are the adjusting and closing entries that appear on the books of Shark Tool Company at the end of the fiscal year, May 31.

LO 1

Date		Description	Post. Ref.	Debit	Credit
20—		**Adjusting Entries**			
May	31	Manufacturing Summary		62 0 5 0 00	
		Raw Materials Inventory			62 0 5 0 00
	31	Raw Materials Inventory		67 0 9 4 00	
		Manufacturing Summary			67 0 9 4 00
	31	Manufacturing Summary		44 6 5 4 00	
		Work-in-Process Inventory			44 6 5 4 00
	31	Work-in-Process Inventory		63 8 5 2 00	
		Manufacturing Summary			63 8 5 2 00
		Closing Entries			
	31	Purchases Discounts		2 3 0 4 00	
		Manufacturing Summary			2 3 0 4 00
	31	Manufacturing Summary		572 7 1 8 00	
		Raw Materials Purchases			142 0 2 0 00
		Direct Labor			293 3 6 4 00
		Indirect Labor			29 2 4 4 00
		Supervision			41 6 8 8 00
		Depreciation of Machinery			30 0 0 0 00
		Depreciation of Factory Building			12 0 0 0 00
		Heat, Light, and Power			8 5 2 0 00
		Repairs and Maintenance			7 6 7 4 00
		Property Tax, Machinery			1 1 1 0 00
		Property Tax, Factory Building			1 3 2 0 00
		Factory Supplies Used			4 1 2 2 00
		Factory Insurance Expired			1 0 8 0 00
		Miscellaneous Factory Costs			5 7 6 00
	31	Income Summary		546 1 7 2 00	
		Manufacturing Summary			546 1 7 2 00

Required

Prepare a statement of cost of goods manufactured for the year.

Check Figure
Cost of Goods
Manufactured, $546,172

Problem Set B

For additional help, see the demonstration problem at the beginning of each chapter in your Working Papers.

2  **PROBLEM 24-1B** Following is the statement of cost of goods manufactured for Boulder Manufacturing Company.

Boulder Manufacturing Company Statement of Cost of Goods Manufactured For Year Ended June 30, 20—			
Work-in-Process Inventory, July 1, 20—			$ 77,000
Raw Materials:			
Raw Materials Inventory, July 1, 20—	$152,600		
Raw Materials Purchases (net)	217,250		
Cost of Raw Materials Available for Use	$369,850		
Less Raw Materials Inventory, June 30, 20—	143,000		
Cost of Raw Materials Used		$226,850	
Direct Labor		320,100	
Manufacturing Overhead:			
Indirect Labor	$ 59,620		
Supervisory Salaries	41,855		
Depreciation Expense, Factory Equipment	54,400		
Depreciation Expense, Factory Building	11,990		
Heat, Light, and Power	10,230		
Repairs and Maintenance	7,920		
Factory Supplies Used	7,645		
Factory Insurance Expired	3,780		
Property Tax on Factory Building	4,125		
Miscellaneous Factory Costs	3,905		
Total Manufacturing Overhead		205,470	
Total Manufacturing Costs			752,420
Total Cost of Work-in-Process During Period			$829,420
Less Work-in-Process Inventory, June 30, 20—			96,250
Cost of Goods Manufactured			$733,170

Check Figure

Amount to close Manufacturing
Summary into Income
Summary, $733,170

Required

1. Journalize, using page 116 of the general journal, the adjusting entries for Raw Materials Inventory and Work-in-Process Inventory.
2. Journalize the closing entries for manufacturing costs.
3. Post the entries to the Manufacturing Summary account, No. 511.
4. Journalize and post the entry to close the Manufacturing Summary account.

PROBLEM 24-2B Following is the trial balance of Stopa Manufacturing Corporation as of December 31 of this year.

 LO 1,2

Stopa Manufacturing Corporation Trial Balance December 31, 20—		
Account Name	Debit	Credit
Cash	3,045	
Accounts Receivable	24,290	
Allowance for Doubtful Accounts		945
Raw Materials Inventory	32,060	
Work-in-Process Inventory	49,735	
Finished Goods Inventory	48,440	
Prepaid Factory Insurance	1,470	
Machinery	111,950	
Accumulated Depreciation, Machinery		30,240
Accounts Payable		19,215
Common Stock		70,000
Paid-in Capital in Excess of Stated Value		17,500
Retained Earnings		45,784
Sales		451,990
Raw Materials Purchases	48,965	
Direct Labor	97,448	
Indirect Labor	56,511	
Heat, Light, and Power	11,340	
Machinery Repairs	6,860	
Selling Expenses (control)	99,197	
General Expenses (control)	41,563	
Income Tax Expense	2,800	
	635,674	635,674

You are given the following information for the adjustments:

a.–f. Year-end inventories: raw materials, $28,750; work-in-process, $45,830; finished goods, $48,118.

g. Estimated depreciation of factory machinery, $7,980.

h. A study of the company's insurance policies shows that $1,085 of factory insurance expired during the year.

i. Allowance for Doubtful Accounts to be increased by $543 [debit General Expenses (control)].

j. Accrued direct labor, $252; accrued indirect labor, $84; accrued sales commissions, $98 (credit Wages and Commissions Payable).

k. Additional income tax, $800.

Required

1. Prepare a work sheet.

2. Prepare a statement of cost of goods manufactured.

3. Prepare an income statement.

Check Figure
Cost of Goods
Manufactured, $237,740

1,2

PROBLEM 24-3B Following are the columns reflecting the statement of cost of goods manufactured and the income statement from the work sheet of Lambert Motor Corporation as of December 31, the end of the fiscal year. Beginning inventory of raw materials is $85,752; beginning inventory of work in process is $152,040.

Account Name	Statement of Cost of Goods Manufactured Debit	Statement of Cost of Goods Manufactured Credit	Income Statement Debit	Income Statement Credit
Sales				1,809 8 8 8 00
Sales Returns and Allowances			15 1 2 0 00	
Sales Discounts			14 4 0 0 00	
Selling Expenses (control)			224 3 4 0 00	
General Expenses (control)			88 3 3 2 00	
Raw Materials Purchases	458 4 0 0 00			
Direct Labor	584 2 8 0 00			
Indirect Labor	133 0 0 8 00			
Heat, Light, and Power	33 1 4 4 00			
Factory Supervision	32 3 1 6 00			
Rent, Factory	21 6 0 0 00			
Machinery Repairs	21 5 0 4 00			
Depreciation Expense, Machinery	20 8 5 6 00			
Factory Supplies Used	5 8 8 0 00			
Factory Insurance Expired	4 3 2 0 00			
Small Tools Expense	1 4 8 8 00			
Miscellaneous Factory Costs	7 8 0 00			
Loss on Disposal of Equipment			9 6 0 0 00	
Interest Expense			9 1 2 0 00	
Income Tax Expense			49 8 0 0 00	
Manufacturing Summary	85 7 5 2 00	88 5 8 4 00		
	152 0 4 0 00	159 4 0 8 00		
Income Summary			221 5 2 0 00	231 3 6 0 00
	1,555 3 6 8 00	247 9 9 2 00		
Cost of Goods Manufactured		1,307 3 7 6 00	1,307 3 7 6 00	
	1,555 3 6 8 00	1,555 3 6 8 00	1,939 6 0 8 00	2,041 2 4 8 00
Net Income			101 6 4 0 00	
			2,041 2 4 8 00	2,041 2 4 8 00

Check Figure
Gross Profit, $482,832

Required

1. Prepare a statement of cost of goods manufactured.
2. Prepare an income statement.
3. Journalize the adjusting entries for the inventories.
4. Journalize the closing entries.

PROBLEM 24-4B Following are the adjusting and closing entries that appear on the books of Hoffman Belt Company at the end of the fiscal year, December 31.

Date		Description	Post. Ref.	Debit	Credit
20—		Adjusting Entries			
Dec.	31	Manufacturing Summary		121 6 4 7 00	
		Raw Materials Inventory			121 6 4 7 00
	31	Raw Materials Inventory		119 6 8 0 00	
		Manufacturing Summary			119 6 8 0 00
	31	Manufacturing Summary		154 1 0 2 00	
		Work-in-Process Inventory			154 1 0 2 00
	31	Work-in-Process Inventory		158 5 2 4 00	
		Manufacturing Summary			158 5 2 4 00
		Closing Entries			
	31	Purchases Discounts		2 6 3 1 00	
		Manufacturing Summary			2 6 3 1 00
	31	Manufacturing Summary		874 3 5 7 00	
		Raw Materials Purchases			280 4 5 6 00
		Direct Labor			373 4 0 6 00
		Indirect Labor			42 3 2 8 00
		Supervision			64 5 0 4 00
		Depreciation of Machinery			46 2 0 0 00
		Depreciation of Factory Building			26 4 0 0 00
		Heat, Light, and Power			14 1 0 2 00
		Repairs and Maintenance			10 6 4 8 00
		Property Tax, Machinery			1 3 9 7 00
		Property Tax, Factory Building			2 0 2 4 00
		Factory Supplies Used			10 4 1 7 00
		Factory Insurance Expired			1 3 2 0 00
		Miscellaneous Factory Costs			1 1 5 5 00
	31	Income Summary		869 2 7 1 00	
		Manufacturing Summary			869 2 7 1 00

Required

Prepare a statement of cost of goods manufactured for the year.

Check Figure

Cost of Goods Manufactured, $869,271

ACTIVITIES

INTERNET LINKS TO ACCOUNTING

You should now have an understanding of the materials, labor, and overhead costs involved in manufacturing a product and how these costs are determined. Let's review Harley-Davidson, Inc., a popular manufacturer of motorcycles, and examine the company's financial statements, which can be found at http://investor.harley-davidson.com. Click on SEC Filings, click on Annual in the "View:" drop-down menu and 2009 in the "Year:" drop-down menu, and select the 10-K annual report filed February 17, 2009.

1. What was the company's net income for the year ended December 31, 2008?
2. Can you tell what Harley-Davidson's cost of goods sold was for 2008 by looking at its income statement?
3. What was the value of ending inventory as of December 31, 2008?
4. Is Harley-Davidson, Inc., a manufacturing firm or a merchandising firm? (*Hint:* Review Note 2 in the Notes to Consolidated Financial Statements.)
5. Now that you have learned about job-order and process cost accounting systems, which system do you think Harley-Davidson uses for its motorcycles?

CRITICAL THINKING

Following is a statement of cost of goods manufactured for Pratas Manufacturing, Inc. Since the records that support this statement were destroyed by water damage caused by a collapsed roof, fill in the missing amounts.

Pratas Manufacturing, Inc.
Statement of Cost of Goods Manufactured
For Year Ended December 31, 20—

Work-in-Process Inventory, January 1, 20—			$
Raw Materials:			
Raw Materials Inventory, January 1, 20—	$135,000		
Raw Materials Purchases (net)			
Cost of Raw Materials Available for Use	$399,500		
Less Raw Materials Inventory, December 31, 20—			
Cost of Raw Materials Used		$253,000	
Direct Labor		553,700	
Manufacturing Overhead:			
Indirect Labor	$		
Supervisory Salaries	112,000		
Heat, Light, and Power	45,300		
Depreciation Expense, Factory Building	27,400		
Depreciation Expense, Factory Equipment	30,700		
Repairs and Maintenance	18,430		
Factory Supplies Used	11,200		
Factory Insurance Expired	24,800		
Miscellaneous Factory Costs	12,520		
Total Manufacturing Overhead		414,350	
Total Manufacturing Costs			
Total Cost of Work-in-Process During Period			$1,364,050
Less Work-in-Process Inventory, December 31, 20—			
Cost of Goods Manufactured			$1,239,050

Departmental Accounting

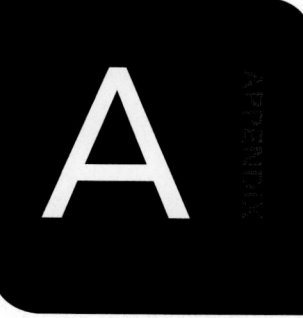

LEARNING OBJECTIVES

After you have completed this appendix, you will be able to do the following:

1 Compile a departmental income statement.

2 Understand departmental margin.

ACCOUNTING LANGUAGE

Apportionment of expenses (p. A-3)

Departmental margin (p. A-5)

Direct expenses (p. A-5)

Indirect expenses (p. A-6)

A company that carries on several different business activities should be divided into a number of subdivisions or departments. This enables the company's management to delegate authority to departmental managers, who are responsible for their respective departments, and to measure the profitability of each department. It is the element of profitability that we discuss in this appendix. The companies shown in this appendix are corporations. If your instructor covered only Chapters 1–12, some of the accounts, terms, and financial statements might look new to you. You should, however, be able to obtain a general sense of how a departmental income statement is compiled.

GROSS PROFIT BY DEPARTMENTS

A department's gross profit depends on its sales volume and its markup on the goods sold:

$$\text{Net Sales} - \text{Cost of Goods Sold} = \text{Gross Profit}$$

To determine the gross profit of a given department, you need a separate set of figures for the department for each element entering into the gross profit. There are two ways to obtain these figures:

1. Keep separate general ledger accounts for each item affecting gross profit, such as a Sales account for each department, a Sales Returns and Allowances account for each department, and so on. Then record the balances of these accounts on the income statement, OR

2. Keep only one general ledger account for each item affecting gross profit, and apportion the balance to the various departments. For example, maintain one Sales account and one Sales Returns and Allowances account for the company, and in addition keep a breakdown of sales and sales returns for each department. Then record the figures for each department on the income statement.

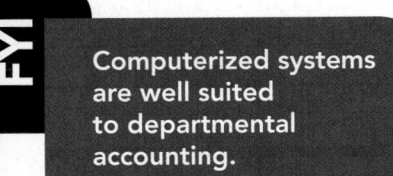

Keeping Separate Accounts by Department

Keeping separate accounts by department yields the most accurate accounting data. You need separate accounts for each department for Sales, Sales Returns and Allowances, Sales Discounts, Purchases, Purchases Returns and Allowances, Purchases Discounts, Freight In, and Merchandise Inventory. For example, Boag Hardware has five departments and uses five Sales accounts, five Sales Returns and Allowances accounts, five Sales Discounts accounts, five Merchandise Inventory accounts, and so forth. The accountant posts each total to a separate account, as indicated by the ledger account numbers.

Maintaining One General Ledger Account

When a company keeps only one general ledger account for each item involved in gross profit, the accountant has to distribute the total amount among the various departments at the end of the accounting period. To do so, the accountant has to accumulate departmental information on supplementary records. Sales, sales returns, purchases, purchases returns and allowances, purchases discounts, and so forth are recorded in a journal and are also recorded on a departmental analysis sheet. At the end of the accounting period, these analysis sheets give departmental breakdowns for each item.

Preparing a Departmental Income Statement

LEARNING OBJECTIVE 1

Compile a departmental income statement.

Joyce & Co., Inc., has two departments, A and B, and keeps separate accounts for each. The company keeps separate accounts for each item that enters into gross profit and apportions the operating expenses between Gross Profit and Income from Operations to Department A or Department B on a logical basis.

An outline of this process is as follows:

From Sales Through Income from Operations

Departmentalized

Revenue from Sales
Less Cost of Goods Sold   } Separate departmental accounts or supplementary analysis sheets

Gross Profit
Less Selling Expenses
Less General Expenses   } Account balances are apportioned

Income from Operations

Nondepartmentalized

Add Other Income
Less Other Expenses

Income Before Income Taxes
Less Income Tax Expense

Net Income

Joyce & Co., Inc.'s, income statement for the fiscal year ended December 31 appears in Figure 1 on pages A-4–A-5.

Gross Profit

Since each department keeps separate accounts for gross profit items, such as sales and cost of goods sold, these items are reported separately on the income statements.

Apportionment of Operating Expenses

Joyce & Co., Inc., combines operating expenses such as Advertising Expense and Utilities Expense. Therefore, each department must assume its share of overhead expenses. **Apportionment of expenses** is a crucial element of departmental accounting. It consists of allocating operating expenses among operating departments. You can readily identify some operating expenses as belonging to a given department. For example, if a salesperson makes sales in one department only, the accountant assigns that salesperson's salary or commission directly to that department. However, other operating expenses, such as Utilities Expense, cannot be restricted to one department and must be divided on some equitable basis. Let's look at the operating expenses of Joyce & Co. and see how they are apportioned.

Sales Salary Expense

Joyce & Co. allocates the salespersons' salaries to Department A or Department B according to the payroll register, which lists each employee by department. Department A's share is $88,625; Department B's is $52,200.

Advertising Expense

Joyce & Co. advertises only on the radio and allocates the cost of radio advertising to the two departments according to the amount of air time each department uses. In a year, Joyce & Co. buys 1,250 minutes of radio time, divided according to departments as shown here:

Advertising for Dept. A: 675 minutes or $\dfrac{675}{1,250} = \underline{\underline{54\%}}$

Advertising for Dept. B: 575 minutes or $\dfrac{575}{1,250} = \underline{\underline{46\%}}$

Dept. A's share of cost of radio advertising: 54% of $17,600 = \underline{\underline{\$9,504}}$

Dept. B's share of cost of radio advertising: 46% of $17,600 = \underline{\underline{\$8,096}}$

Depreciation Expense, Store Equipment

Joyce & Co. keeps a property and equipment ledger that notes the department in which each piece of equipment is located. The total year's depreciation of the equipment used in Department A is $1,840; the total year's depreciation of the equipment used in Department B is $1,460.

Rent Expense and Utilities Expense

Joyce & Co. rents 40,000 square feet of floor space and allocates the expenses of rent and utilities on the basis of floor space occupied by each department, as follows. (Yearly expense for rent is $16,400; yearly expense for utilities is $4,840.)

Dept. A occupies 25,000 square feet or $\dfrac{25,000}{40,000} = \underline{\underline{62.5\%}}$

Dept. B occupies 15,000 square feet or $\dfrac{15,000}{40,000} = \underline{\underline{37.5\%}}$

> **Remember**
> To apportion or to allocate means to divide up.

FIGURE 1

Income statement for
Joyce & Co., Inc.

Joyce & Co., Inc.
Income Statement
For Year Ended December 31, 20—

		Department A	
Revenue from Sales:		$560,000	
Sales		14,200	
Less: Sales Returns and Allowances			$545,800
Net Sales			
Cost of Goods Sold:			
Merchandise Inventory, Jan. 1, 20—		$ 96,400	
Purchases	$312,115		
Less: Purchases Returns and Allowances	9,580		
Purchases Discounts	5,740		
Net Purchases	$296,795		
Add Freight In	13,005		
Delivered Cost of Purchases		309,800	
Cost of Goods Available for Sale		$406,200	
Less Merchandise Inventory, Dec. 31, 20—		110,000	
Cost of Goods Sold			296,200
Gross Profit			$249,600
Operating Expenses:			
Selling Expenses:			
Sales Salary Expense	$ 88,625		
Advertising Expense	9,504		
Depreciation Expense, Store Equipment	1,840		
Total Selling Expenses		$ 99,969	
General Expenses:			
Rent Expense	$ 10,250		
Utilities Expense	3,025		
Total General Expenses		13,275	
Total Operating Expenses			113,244
Income from Operations			$136,356
Other Income:			
Interest Income			
Other Expenses:			
Interest Expense			
Income Before Income Taxes			
Income Tax Expense			
Net Income			

Dept. A's share of rent: 62.5% of $16,400 = $10,250

Dept. B's share of rent: 37.5% of $16,400 = $6,150

Dept. A's share of utilities: 62.5% of $4,840 = $3,025

Dept. B's share of utilities: 37.5% of $4,840 = $1,815

Nonapportioned Expenses

Other Income and Expense Items, such as Interest Income, Interest Expense, and Income Tax Expense, are not apportioned among the departments. Instead, these items are only included in total on the income statement.

Department B			Total	
	$240,000		$800,000	
	5,800		20,000	
		$234,200		$780,000
	$ 82,740		$179,140	
$161,175			$473,290	
4,756			14,336	
3,274			9,014	
$153,145			$449,940	
6,715			19,720	
	159,860		469,660	
	$242,600		$648,800	
	90,000		200,000	
		152,600		448,800
		$ 81,600		$331,200
	$ 52,200		$140,825	
	8,096		17,600	
	1,460		3,300	
	$ 61,756		$161,725	
	$ 6,150		$ 16,400	
	1,815		4,840	
	7,965		21,240	
		69,721		182,965
		$ 11,879		$148,235
			$ 3,624	
			2,400	1,224
				$149,459
				24,278
				$125,181

DEPARTMENTAL MARGIN

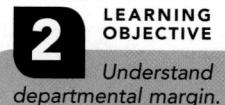

2 LEARNING OBJECTIVE
Understand departmental margin.

Departmental margin is a measurement of the contribution that a given department makes to the income of the firm—gross profit of a department minus the department's direct expenses. When a company breaks down its expense figures on a departmental-margin basis, its income statement indicates the contribution each department makes toward the overhead expenses incurred on behalf of the business as a whole. You can divide operating expenses into two classes: (1) **direct expenses**, which are incurred for the sole benefit of a given department and are under the control of the department head but not necessarily under the department being considered; and

(2) **indirect expenses**, which are incurred as overhead expenses of the entire business and thus are not under the control of one department head. For example, Sales Salary Expense is a direct expense because it is incurred purely for the benefit of one department. Officers' Salary Expense, on the other hand, is an overhead expense incurred for the business as a whole; it is not directly chargeable to one department.

Some operating expenses may be partially direct and partially indirect. For example, suppose that Rivera Company has five departments. Rivera Company's Advertising Expense consisted partially of billboard advertising, which stresses the name and location of the company, and partially of newspaper and radio advertising, which directly benefits separate departments of the company. So the part of the advertising budget that went to billboard advertising is an indirect expense, and the part that went to newspaper and radio advertising is a direct expense. When you classify an expense as direct or indirect, use this rule of thumb to identify direct expenses: **The expense would not have been incurred if the department were not in existence.** The expense must be directly related to the department.

Here is an outline of an income statement that emphasizes departmental margin:

From Sales Through Departmental Margin

Revenue from Sales	Based on separate departmental
Less Cost of Goods Sold	accounts or supplementary
	analysis sheets
Gross Profit	Expenses that are directly
Less Direct Departmental Expenses	related to the department
Departmental Margin	
Less Indirect Expenses	
Income from Operations	
Add Other Income	
Less Other Expenses	
Income Before Income Taxes	
Less Income Tax Expense	
Net Income	

The Meaning of Departmental Margin

Departmental margin is the most realistic portrayal of the profitability of a department. **If the company closes the department, the company's income before income taxes will decrease or increase by the amount of the departmental margin.** For example, assume that Rivera Company's income from operations for last year was $120,000, which is about the same as it has been for the past four years. Rivera's partial income statement, in which all operating expenses are apportioned to the various departments, shows that Department E has a loss from operations of $9,000. In an abbreviated departmental-margin format, the results of the fiscal year are shown in the following table:

Item	Department E (only)	Departments A to D (only)	Total, Departments A to E	Total, Departments A to D (with E eliminated)
Sales	$120,000	$1,480,000	$1,600,000	$1,480,000
Cost of Goods Sold	72,000	880,000	952,000	880,000
Gross Profit	$ 48,000	$ 600,000	$ 648,000	$ 600,000
Direct Departmental Expenses	32,000	336,000	368,000	336,000
Departmental Margin	$ 16,000	$ 264,000	$ 280,000	$ 264,000
Indirect Expenses	25,000	135,000	160,000	160,000
Income (Loss) from Operations	$ (9,000)	$ 129,000	$ 120,000	$ 104,000

Now suppose that Rivera Company eliminates Department E. Because Department E's departmental margin amounts to $16,000, the Income from Operations of the entire firm will decrease by $16,000 ($120,000 − $104,000 = $16,000). Another factor Rivera Company has to consider is possible "spillover sales" of Department E; that is, customers of Department E may buy things in other departments. Also, any change in income will cause a change in the amount of income taxes paid by Rivera Company. However, to simplify our analysis, we have omitted income taxes from our discussion.

The Usefulness of Departmental Margin

Income statements that show departmental margin are extremely useful when it comes to controlling a company's direct expenses, because the company can hold the head of a given department accountable for expenses directly chargeable to that department. If a department head reduces direct expenses, this action will have a favorable effect on the departmental margin.

A company that manufactures a number of different products can also use the concept of departmental margin to determine the profitability of a particular product. This is clearly one of the most important uses of departmental margin.

Management can use an income statement showing departmental margin as a tool for making future plans and analyzing future operations. Sometimes such an income statement may even lead to the elimination of a department, as we saw with Rivera Company.

> **Remember**
>
> Direct expenses are those incurred for the sole benefit of a department. If the department did not exist, the expense would not have been incurred.

Glossary

Apportionment of expenses Allocating operating expenses among operating departments. (p. A-3)

Departmental margin The contribution that a given department makes to the income of the firm—gross profit of a department minus the department's direct expenses. (p. A-5)

Direct expenses Expenses that benefit only one department and are controlled by the head of the department. (p. A-5)

Indirect expenses Overhead expenses that benefit several departments or the business as a whole and are not under the control of any one department head. (p. A-6)

Problems

PROBLEM A-1 Bay Book and Software has two sales departments: Book and Software. After recording and posting all adjustments, including the adjustments for merchandise inventory, the accountant prepared the adjusted trial balance (shown on the next page) at the end of the fiscal year.

Merchandise inventories at the beginning of the year were as follows: Book Department, $53,410; Software Department, $23,839. The bases (and sources of figures) for apportioning expenses to the two departments are as follows (rounded to the nearest dollar):

- Sales Salary Expense (payroll register): Book Department, $45,559; Software Department, $35,629

- Advertising Expense (newspaper column inches): Book Department, 550 inches; Software Department, 450 inches

- Depreciation Expense, Store Equipment (property and equipment ledger): Book Department, $7,851; Software Department, $2,682

Bay Book and Software
Adjusted Trial Balance
December 31, 20—

Account Name	Debit	Credit
Cash	31,924	
Accounts Receivable	34,880	
Allowance for Doubtful Accounts		1,893
Merchandise Inventory, Book Department	53,557	
Merchandise Inventory, Software Department	24,987	
Store Supplies	532	
Store Equipment	42,332	
Accumulated Depreciation, Store Equipment		32,619
Accounts Payable		32,280
Sales Tax Payable		895
Income Tax Payable		1,166
Common Stock		74,630
Retained Earnings		18,300
Income Summary	53,410	53,557
	23,839	24,987
Sales, Book Department		317,400
Sales, Software Department		136,000
Sales Returns and Allowances, Book Department	8,161	
Sales Returns and Allowances, Software Department	551	
Purchases, Book Department	199,895	
Purchases, Software Department	96,273	
Purchases Returns and Allowances, Book Department		2,817
Purchases Returns and Allowances, Software Department		864
Purchases Discounts, Book Department		3,923
Purchases Discounts, Software Department		2,853
Freight In, Book Department	7,250	
Freight In, Software Department	2,875	
Sales Salary Expense	81,188	
Advertising Expense	10,670	
Depreciation Expense, Store Equipment	10,533	
Store Supplies Expense	404	
Miscellaneous Selling Expense	350	
Rent Expense	6,400	
Utilities Expense	2,960	
Bad Debts Expense	1,470	
Miscellaneous General Expense	520	
Interest Expense	1,208	
Income Tax Expense	8,015	
	704,184	704,184

- Store Supplies Expense (requisitions): Book Department, $205; Software Department, $199

- Miscellaneous Selling Expense (volume of gross sales): Book Department, $240; Software Department, $110

- Rent Expense and Utilities Expense (floor space): Book Department, 9,000 square feet; Software Department, 7,000 square feet

- Bad Debts Expense (volume of gross sales): Book Department, $1,029; Software Department, $441

- Miscellaneous General Expense (volume of gross sales): Book Department, $364; Software Department, $156

Required

Prepare an income statement by department to show income from operations, as well as a nondepartmentalized income statement (using the Total columns) to show net income for the entire company.

Check Figure
Net Income, $26,429

PROBLEM A-2 La Hacienda, Inc., has two departments: Furniture and Lighting. La Hacienda's accountant prepares an adjusted trial balance (shown below) at the end of the fiscal year.

La Hacienda, Inc. Adjusted Trial Balance January 31, 20—		
Account Name	Debit	Credit
Cash	5,666	
Accounts Receivable	68,890	
Allowance for Doubtful Accounts		2,620
Merchandise Inventory, Furniture Department	84,142	
Merchandise Inventory, Lighting Department	41,138	
Store Supplies	762	
Store Equipment	50,682	
Accumulated Depreciation, Store Equipment		41,810
Accounts Payable		38,680
Sales Tax Payable		1,284
Income Tax Payable		1,733
Common Stock		69,444
Retained Earnings		41,875
Income Summary	83,850	84,142
	42,630	41,138
Sales, Furniture Department		409,800
Sales, Lighting Department		273,200
Sales Returns and Allowances, Furniture Department	11,685	
Sales Returns and Allowances, Lighting Department	1,716	
Purchases, Furniture Department	251,847	
Purchases, Lighting Department	165,242	
Purchases Returns and Allowances, Furniture Department		4,618
Purchases Returns and Allowances, Lighting Department		1,792
Purchases Discounts, Furniture Department		5,496
Purchases Discounts, Lighting Department		2,964
Freight In, Furniture Department	13,255	
Freight In, Lighting Department	6,885	
Sales Salary Expense	123,220	
Advertising Expense	14,000	
Depreciation Expense, Store Equipment	13,436	
Store Supplies Expense	742	
Miscellaneous Selling Expense	680	
Rent Expense	8,000	
Utilities Expense	4,100	
Bad Debts Expense	1,800	
Miscellaneous General Expense	820	
Interest Expense	2,800	
Income Tax Expense	22,608	
	1,020,596	1,020,596

The trial balance is prepared after all adjustments, including the adjustments for merchandise inventory, have been recorded and posted.

Merchandise inventories at the beginning of the year were as follows: Furniture Department, $83,850; Lighting Department, $42,630. The bases (and sources of figures) for apportioning expenses to the two departments are as follows (rounded to the nearest dollar):

- Sales Salary Expense (payroll register): Furniture Department, $74,800; Lighting Department, $48,420
- Advertising Expense (newspaper column inches): Furniture Department, 600 inches; Lighting Department, 400 inches
- Depreciation Expense, Store Equipment (property and equipment ledger): Furniture Department, $9,616; Lighting Department, $3,820
- Store Supplies Expense (requisitions): Furniture Department, $418; Lighting Department, $324
- Miscellaneous Selling Expense (volume of gross sales): Furniture Department, $408; Lighting Department, $272
- Rent Expense and Utilities Expense (floor space): Furniture Department, 2,500 square feet; Lighting Department, 1,500 square feet
- Bad Debts Expense (volume of gross sales): Furniture Department, $1,080; Lighting Department, $720
- Miscellaneous General Expense (volume of gross sales): Furniture Department, $492; Lighting Department, $328

Check Figure
Net Income, $53,834

Required

Prepare an income statement by department to show income from operations, as well as a nondepartmentalized income statement (using the Total columns) to show net income for the entire company.

2  **PROBLEM A-3** Moon, Inc., is considering eliminating its Drapery Department. Management does not believe that the indirect expenses and the level of operations in the other departments will be affected if the Drapery Department closes. Information from Moon's income statement for the fiscal year ended December 31, which is considered a typical year, is as follows:

	Drapery Department	All Other Departments	Total of All Departments (including Drapery)
Sales	$75,000	$563,000	$638,000
Cost of Goods Sold	49,000	395,000	444,000
Gross Profit	26,000	$168,000	$194,000
Operating Expenses	32,000	112,000	144,000
Income (Loss) from Operations	$(6,000)	$ 56,000	$ 50,000

Moon considers that $19,000 of the operating expenses of the Drapery Department are direct expenses.

Check Figure
Gross Profit, $26,000

Required

Calculate the departmental margin of the Drapery Department.

Index

Steps in the Closing Process

STEP 1. Close the revenue account(s) into Income Summary.

STEP 2. Close the expense accounts into Income Summary.

STEP 3. Close the Income Summary account into the Capital account, transferring the net income or net loss to the Capital account.

STEP 4. Close the Drawing account into the Capital account.

The Accounting Cycle

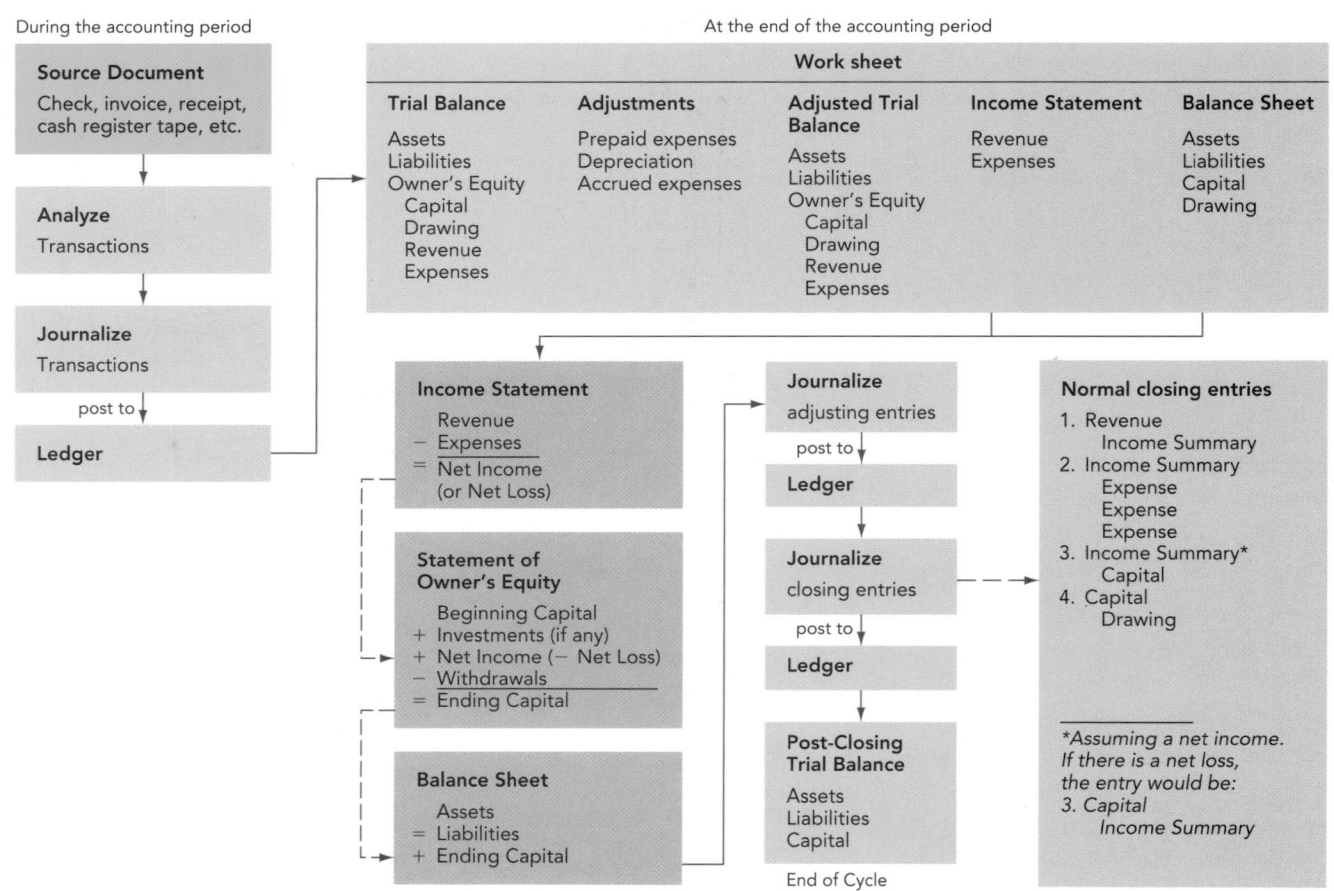

During the accounting period

Source Document
Check, invoice, receipt, cash register tape, etc.

Analyze
Transactions

Journalize
Transactions

post to

Ledger

At the end of the accounting period

Work sheet

Trial Balance
Assets
Liabilities
Owner's Equity
 Capital
 Drawing
 Revenue
 Expenses

Adjustments
Prepaid expenses
Depreciation
Accrued expenses

Adjusted Trial Balance
Assets
Liabilities
Owner's Equity
 Capital
 Drawing
 Revenue
 Expenses

Income Statement
Revenue
Expenses

Balance Sheet
Assets
Liabilities
Capital
Drawing

Income Statement
 Revenue
− Expenses
= Net Income
 (or Net Loss)

Statement of Owner's Equity
 Beginning Capital
+ Investments (if any)
+ Net Income (− Net Loss)
− Withdrawals
= Ending Capital

Balance Sheet
 Assets
= Liabilities
+ Ending Capital

Journalize
adjusting entries

post to

Ledger

Journalize
closing entries

post to

Ledger

Post-Closing Trial Balance
Assets
Liabilities
Capital

End of Cycle

Normal closing entries
1. Revenue
  Income Summary
2. Income Summary
  Expense
  Expense
  Expense
3. Income Summary*
  Capital
4. Capital
  Drawing

―――――
*Assuming a net income.
If there is a net loss,
the entry would be:
3. Capital
  Income Summary